SECOND EDITION

M O D E R N

COBOL

PROGRAMMING

SECOND EDITION

M O D E R N

COBOL

PROGRAMMING

WILSON PRICE & JACK OLSON

Mitchell McGRAW-HILL

New York St. Louis San Francisco Auckland Bogotá Caracas Hamburg
Lisbon London Madrid Mexico Milan Montreal New Delhi Paris
San Juan São Paulo Singapore Sydney Tokyo Toronto Watsonville

Mitchell **McGraw-Hill**
55 Penny Lane
Watsonville, CA 95076

Modern COBOL Programming, Second Edition

3 4 5 6 7 8 9 0 VNH VNH 9 0 9 8 7 6 5 4

ISBN 0-07-051044-X

Sponsoring editors: Raleigh S. Wilson and Steve Mitchell
Production supervisor: Pat Moran
Production services: BMR, Corte Madera, CA
     Copy edit: Karen Richardson
     Cover design: Mike Yazzolino
     Interior design: Hugh Anderson, Archetype, Inc.
     Interior design consultant: Mike Yazzolino
     Page makeup: Archetype, Inc.
     Production coordinator: Nancy Taylor Mason
     Technical illustrations: Archetype, Inc.
Printer: Von Hoffmann Press, Inc.

Library of Congress Catalog Card No.90-083375

To our patient wives
Jean and Irene
who become more special
with each passing year.

CONTENTS

CONTENTS

CHAPTER 15

Sorting in COBOL   407

CHAPTER 16

Manipulation of Character String Data   437

CHAPTER 17

Program Management   467

APPENDICES

PREFACE

Goals of the Second Edition

In the Preface of the first edition of *Modern COBOL Programming,* we made the following observation:

> Historically, during the 1970s, important programming techniques (program modularization and structured methods) developed by computer scientists found their way into the business data processing environment and COBOL programming. Even though 1974 COBOL was not completely compatible with this theory, it was possible to adapt the theory to the limitations of COBOL. The effect was *very* significant in improved program quality and programmer productivity. The 1985 COBOL Standard represents another important step forward in that it includes features specifically oriented to take advantage of modern programming techniques and theory. The result is that the "kludges" previously used to achieve good structure are no longer necessary. Program code more readily follows from the program design, resulting in programs that are easier to understand, write, and maintain.

The basic philosophy of the first edition was to teach good, solid structured programming techniques utilizing COBOL-85 to the fullest. Since its publication, we have had extensive feedback from numerous satisfied colleagues (and some not-so-satisfied) with constructive comments. Often the observation has been of the nature: "The way you handled topic X was great, *but* if you had ...." The four years since we completed the first edition has given us plenty of time to think about all those topic X's. Our three primary objectives for this revision were

1. To expand the focus on problem solving using numerous example programs, each with complete documentation based on structured techniques.

2. To exploit to the fullest the flexibility that the RM/COBOL-85 compiler provides students when using the personal computer for compiling and running their programs.

3. To include (for optional use) a COBOL work environment from which all functions of entering, editing, compiling, running, and debugging a program are accomplished under a single, unified control system.

4. To expand the book to provide complete COBOL coverage for a full year of COBOL. To this end, heavy emphasis is placed on all types of file processing activities.

It is difficult to compare this book to any of the commonly used textbooks because its focus is oriented around the convenience and power of using a personal computer for COBOL (while maintaining mainframe language capabilities). Until now, the teaching strategy for COBOL has, to an extent, been dictated by the nature of the environment in which the course is being taught: batch processing. In general, the beginning COBOL student must learn much more about COBOL before he or she can write a simple program than, for example, the beginning BASIC or Pascal student.

However, with the availability of ANSI Standard COBOL on today's powerful personal computers, that constraint no longer exists. With the interactive nature of the personal computer, it is possible to use the successful language subset approach in giving the student a small, simple programming assignment using a minimum of COBOL features. Then learning can progress quickly to a variety of topics that include random access to data files as well as the traditional batch processing concepts.

Chapter by Chapter Synopsis

The best way to tell you what the book is all about is through the following set of chapter abstracts.

1 The chapter opens with a brief introductory description of the nature of COBOL. The basic steps of the programming cycle are described. At this point, the student is given a simple interactive program that he or she can compile and then run to gain a feel for these two activities. The sample program is included on the Program/Data disk that accompanies the book so that the student does not need to enter it into the computer.

2 This chapter describes a basic subset of COBOL by examining the program of Chapter 1 and the statements of which it is comprised: ACCEPT, DISPLAY, ADD, PERFORM (in-line version that is a feature of 1985 COBOL), and STOP RUN. In addition, the WORKING STORAGE SECTION of the DATA DIVISION is described. The example used is a simple program to add two numbers, display the result, and give the user the option to repeat the sequence or terminate. At the end of this chapter, the student can write programs. Note that there are no files to open and close, no input/output records to worry about, no file descriptions, and so on.

3 Basic programming standards regarding program modularization and structure to be used throughout the book are explicitly defined in this chapter.

4 The student is first introduced to the nature of files: sequential and random. The best way to remove the mystery of a data file is for the student to create one. Through the interactive nature of the personal computer, the student can write simple programs to create a data file and enter records into it through the keyboard.

5 After creating a file, the student learns how to access data from it. This includes the screen display of a sequential file's contents and of selected records from an indexed file. The student also learns how to print a listing of the records in a file.

6 Editing of data for improved appearance of output is described in this chapter.

7 Where the basic forms of COBOL's arithmetic verbs were introduced in Chapter 2, this chapter covers all aspects of arithmetic operations including the COMPUTE verb.

8 By now the student can begin to write some substantial programs. To this end a complete set of standards for structured program design is introduced. The basic form of the IF statement (and its corresponding COBOL-85 END-IF) is introduced at this point to provide more versatility in the nature of the programming problems the student can handle.

9 With the basics mastered, the focus turns to the quality appearance of printed output. Topics in this chapter include printing headings, computing report totals, and principles of page control.

10 One common form of output is hard copy; the other common form is soft copy. This chapter focuses on designing good, functional screen layouts for both input and output of data (from random file access). The X/OPEN Standard SCREEN SECTION is used.

11 The student has already used basic forms of the IF statement. This chapter covers conditional operations in detail. Topics include compound conditionals, the EVALUATE (case structure) statement, and condition names.

12 The important topic of data validation is covered in this chapter via two extensive examples. The first involves traditional batch validation of records in a file. The second is interactive in nature and involves validating data as it is being entered into a file from the keyboard.

13 This chapter covers traditional group totals via two examples: the first a single-level group total application and the second a two-level application.

14 Subscripting and table processing (single- and multiple-level) are covered in this chapter via realistic examples.

15 Sorting, covered in this chapter, include examples of a simple sort and of using input and output procedures with the sort. The flexibility provided by COBOL-85 in defining input and output procedures is reflected in the examples.

16 The manipulation of character string data in COBOL is clumsy and is consequently downplayed in many books. This chapter is devoted exclusively to this topic. It is culminated with an example of converting a delimited file to a fixed format COBOL file format.

17 COBOL-85 is rich with capabilities (extended beyond those of COBOL-74) for using subprograms and achieving program module functional and data independence. This chapter describes calling a separately compiled program together with parameter passing. It also includes an extensive example of combining several related programs as nested programs under a menu access program.

18 This chapter begins advanced file processing topics. Its topics include relative files, changing and deleting records in a file, dynamic file access, alternate keys for indexed files, and exception handling during I-O operations.

19 The focus of this chapter is on batch processing using extensive example programs: conventional sequential master-transaction processing, batch updating an indexed file, and batch maintenance of an indexed file.

20 Corresponding to Chapter 19 this chapter focuses on interactive file activities using two example programs: transaction processing and file maintenance.

21 The culmination of file processing is an extensive order entry/invoice preparation case study. This application brings together a wide variety of principles from previous chapters. It includes a menu control system that provides access to the two relatively independent components of the system: order entry and invoice preparation.

Features

Complete and Self-Contained

Perhaps the most significant feature of this book is that it is complete and self-contained. It includes a wide variety of example programs, exercises, and programming assignments. In addition, the diskettes accompanying the book contain a high-quality COBOL compiler and data sets for all programming assignments. Features of the compiler are described later in this preface.

COBOL-85 Standard

When we discuss this book with our editors and sales representatives, they commonly refer to our work as oriented around "microcomputer COBOL." To that we say "NO!" This book is based on COBOL-85—the same COBOL-85 implemented on mainframes (or any other computer). We take full advantage of scope terminators (END-IF, END-PERFORM, and so on) to use a level of structured design that was not possible with previous versions of COBOL.

Capitalizes on the Versatility of the Personal Computer

The book's principal personal computer aspect is that it takes full advantage of the PC's capability to provide a more interesting and challenging learning situation for the student. In the batch environment of the mainframe, the student's interaction with the computer is minimal—dictated by the nature of the batch environment and by the standards of the particular installation. In the interactive environment of the personal computer, the student is in control. The student can create and delete his or her own data files, write interactive programs, and obtain almost instant turn-around when compiling and debugging.

Emphasizes File Processing Throughout

Because each student is operating with his or her own set of data files and in somewhat of a private environment, data file operations have almost limitless possibilities. For instance, in Chapter 4, the student studies two interactive programs that allow a user to create a data file and enter data into it. The first program adds records to a sequential file; with only minor changes, it is modified to one that adds records to an indexed file. In Chapter 5, the student learns how to access data from the files just created. The example programs illustrate printing a report of data stored in the file and displaying the contents on the screen of a desired record (random access of an indexed file).

Uses the X/OPEN Standard Screen Section

Unfortunately, the COBOL-85 Standard does not include screen handling capabilities. However, another standard is in use, one defined by a consortium of European computer manufacturers (called X/OPEN) as part of their effort to create portability guides. Among other things, this standard defines a SCREEN SECTION for the DATA DIVISION that allows the programmer to remove formatting data for screen I-O from the PROCEDURE DIVISION and place it in the DATA DIVISION where it belongs. RM/COBOL-85 Release 5.0 (included with this book) features a SCREEN SECTION that conforms to the X/OPEN standard.

Includes 40 Complete Example Programs

Students can learn COBOL syntax by studying syntax examples; they learn how to design good structured programs by studying good structured examples. To that end, 40 complete example programs and variations are included.

Comprehensive Program Design Documentation

Each new example program includes a full definition of the program requirements, plus comprehensive program documentation including a structure chart, a flowchart, and a pseudocode solution. The same degree of documentation is used throughout; standardization is emphasized.

Extensive End-of-Chapter Materials

Each chapter includes a variety of end-of-chapter materials. Where appropriate, the chapter summary includes:

- A general summary describing the primary topics of the chapter.
- A summary of COBOL language elements, including the general syntax format of each COBOL form presented in the chapter.
- Programming conventions established in the chapter.
- A description of error prevention/detection topics relative to the chapter.

Questions and exercises are grouped according to the following types:

- Key terminology introduced in the chapter.
- General questions covering the topics of the chapter.
- Questions relating specifically to example programs described in the chapter.
- Writing program statements that test the student's ability to apply the COBOL syntax learned in the chapter.

Numerous Programming Assignments

Each chapter includes several programming assignments that relate directly to the topics covered in the chapter. Beginning with Chapter 4, each assignment includes a standardized description of the problem, its input and output requirements, and processing requirements. This is the same format used in defining example programs within the chapter.

RM/COSTAR

The software package accompanying this book includes a control system called RM/COSTAR (identified as RM/CO*). RM/CO* is described by Ryan McFarland as "... an interactive, menu-driven environment, within which you can write, edit, compile, run and debug RM/COBOL-85 programs." It is the type of environment that is sometimes referred to as "a programmer's workbench," as opposed to a "normal" or "typical" programming environment. Typical of the conveniences provided through RM/CO* is the way in which the programmer can correct compiler-detected errors. That is, the programmer brings up (on the screen) the post-compile listing, complete with error identifications and descriptions. Then he or she makes corrections by editing the *post-compile listing*. When the correction process is completed, the changes are automatically transferred to the original source program.

However, if you have your own editor for entering and editing programs and your own set of operational procedures, you may use them instead of RM/CO* with no conflicts when using the book. Placement of the detailed description of RM/CO* in Appendix C ensures this.

A Truly Instructional Package

Extensive Teaching Ancillaries

The second edition is more than simply a textbook; it is a teaching package designed to provide broad support. The package consists of

- A comprehensive Instructor's Guide that includes chapter outlines with teaching suggestions and answers to end-of-chapter questions and exercises.
- A solutions manual with a program solution, together with the program output for each programming assignment in the text. A separate section includes listings of all data files included with the text for these assignments.
- A set of transparency masters.
- A solutions disk that contains a programmed solution for each programming assignment in the book.
- Needed Ryan-McFarland manuals.

Diskettes that Accompany the Text

The text is available with software that allows students to complete their assignments on personal computers.

Data for Programming Assignments and Example Programs

A separate Program/Data disk includes data files for every programming assignment in the book. Each file includes a quantity and variety of records sufficient to test all aspects of the student's programs and to yield meaningful reports. This disk also contains the solution for every one of the 40 example programs described in the text.

The Ryan-McFarland Compiler and Runtime System

The compiler and runtime system combination included on the diskettes accompanying this book are a special instructional version of the highly successful Ryan-McFarland RM/COBOL-85, Version 5.0. The instructional version has surprisingly few limitations (over the commercial version) and is completely adequate for almost all assignments and projects that would be assigned in a COBOL course. It includes the following features:

1. COBOL programs of up to 1,000 lines of source code can be compiled.
2. File types supported include sequential, line sequential, relative, and indexed.
3. File size limitation for indexed files is 100 records; for all others, it is 1,000 records.
4. Records in the FILE SECTION can be up to 132 bytes in length.
5. Up to four file definitions may be used in any program.
6. Indexed files may include one or two keys.
7. The CALL statement can be implemented to one level. That is, a program can call another, but the called program may not call a third program.

This is indeed a powerful system for the student.

Ryan-McFarland RM/CO*

The diskettes distributed with the text also include a copy of RM/CO*, the Ryan-McFarland program manager that coordinates all activities of using and managing COBOL programs. It also includes an editor that the student can use for entering and editing programs.

For the instructor, the text and the ancillary materials represent a complete, comprehensive teaching package. For the student, the textbook together with data/software diskettes represent a complete and economical student package. This is the right way to provide for a COBOL course.

Acknowledgments

This book is obviously not the product of our minds alone. We have gained and learned from many others: students, colleagues, and fellow authors. We would like to express our special appreciation to the many individuals who believed in this project and made valuable contributions. At Business Media Resources, Raleigh Wilson provided the resources when needed and Jane Granoff provided overall project coordination. We cannot say enough about the help Karen Richardson has been; she has gone far beyond her normal copy editing duties in ensuring correctness. Nancy Taylor Mason coordinated typesetting and getting the work completed on time. Getting down to nuts and bolts, Hugh Anderson, Richard Stum, Kirk Wettlaufer, Renee Schreiner, Michael Williams and Doris Anderson of Archetype, Incorporated of Denver, Colorado did a fine job of typesetting in a remarkably short time. To all of the contributors, we offer a special "thank you."

Wilson Price
Jack Olson

1

Getting Started

Outline

- **The Nature of COBOL**
  The Acronym *COBOL*
  The COBOL Program

- **Principles of Programming**
  The Programming Process
  A Programming Problem Definition
  The Concept of Language Translation

- **Compiling and Running Programs With RM/CO***
  What is RM/CO*
  The Overall Sequence

- **Details of RM/CO* Actions**
  RM/CO* Screens
  Compiling the Program
  Running the Program
  Ending an RM/CO* Session

- **Compiling and Running Programs Without RM/CO***
  Compiling the Program
  Running the Program

Chapter Objectives

The purpose of this chapter is to provide you with some background to the COBOL language and introduce you to the software provided with this book. You will learn about the following topics:

■ The nature of the COBOL language; the meaning of the acronym *COBOL*

■ The programming process, which consists of the following five distinct steps to solving a problem:
1. Map out the solution to the problem
2. Write the program
3. Enter the program into the computer
4. Compile the program (convert the program to a form understood by the computer)
5. Run the program (to obtain results)

■ The principle of language translation (compiling): converting a program from a "human-readable" form to a "machine-readable" form

■ Using the Ryan-McFarland RM/CO* system (if you elect to use it in this book)

■ Compiling a program

■ Running a program

The Nature of COBOL

The Acronym COBOL

To begin your study of COBOL, you should know what COBOL is, what the word *COBOL* means, where COBOL came from, and why it was developed. The word *COBOL* is an acronym for the phrase *COmmon Business-Oriented Language*. Each of these words has significance.

Common. At the time that COBOL was created (1959), most programming languages were machine-specific. This means that each language applied to a particular model of computer, and any given model of computer could not recognize any language other than its own. Thus, a program written for one model of computer could not be run on any other model of computer because the other model would not be able to interpret the language. One of the goals of COBOL was to create a *common* language that could be used with any model of computer.

Business-Oriented. Also, at that time, computer applications were considered to be either business applications or scientific applications. Scientific applications involved multitudinous complex calculations with very large or very small numbers that did not need to be totally accurate. Input and output requirements were minimal. Business applications, on the other hand, involved a great deal of input and output, required extensive output formatting capabilities to produce printed output which met business standards, did not do as much calculating as scientific applications, worked with relatively small numbers (for many scientific applications, even the size of the national debt is a relatively small number), and demanded accuracy to the penny. FORTRAN (FORmula TRANslation) was already being developed for the scientific community; the business community needed a programming language that was *oriented* toward *business* needs.

Language. The term *programming language* was used previously without being defined. Essentially, a programming language is a language for communicating commands to a computer. It has two aspects:

■ A set of rules, called syntax rules, specifying a grammar for the language

■ A facility for translating statements written in the programming language (which is understandable by people, but not by computers) into machine language (which is understood by computers, but not by most people)

To summarize, COBOL is a language designed for telling any type of computer how to do business applications. A set of COBOL statements that causes the computer to perform a specific task is a *COBOL program*.

The COBOL Program

A COBOL program, like a program in any other programming language, must perform two essential tasks:

■ Define the data to be processed

■ Define the procedures (actions) required to process the data and produce the desired results

Since a computer processes data in its internal memory, defining the data really consists of reserving a unique portion of memory for each item of data to be processed, giving that portion a unique name (the data-name) that will be used to refer to that data item throughout the program, and describing the characteristics of that data item (type, number of characters, and so on). While COBOL uses the term *data item* to refer to each of these reserved portions of memory, most other programming languages refer to them as *variables,* since their contents will vary during the execution of the program.

Processing data, usually from a data file, involves three types of activities:

■ **Input:** Copying data from outside the internal memory into specific data items

■ **Processing:** Manipulating the contents of data items by calculating, and rearranging to place the desired results in other data items

■ **Output:** Copying the data items containing the desired results to an output device (screen, printer, and so on)

The statements that accomplish processing are called *imperative statements;* they command the computer to do operations either unconditionally or based on a test. Statements that perform operations on a conditional basis are called *conditional statements.*

Principles of Programming

The Programming Process

The focus in this book is learning to program with the COBOL programming language as a tool. What does the overall process of programming a problem solution involve? It may consist of the following five steps:

1. **Task:** Map out the solution to the problem.

   Activity: Study the problem and determine what must be done. Define the procedures in ordinary English or with techniques described in the following chapters.

   End Result: A full understanding of what is to be done and how to do it.

2. **Task:** Write the program.

   Activity: The task of writing the program is called *coding;* it involves converting the English interpretation of the problem into instructions that tell the computer what to do to solve the problem. Note that when working with a language such as COBOL, this action is independent of the computer.

   End Result: A set of instructions (a program) telling the computer how to perform the steps to solve the problem. In COBOL, these instructions are called *COBOL statements* or simply *statements.* Thus, a COBOL program is made up of individual statements.

3. **Task:** Enter the program into the computer.

   Activity: At this point, the programmer must use an editor program (or a word processor) that allows text to be entered into a file from the keyboard. Appendix C describes how to use the editor included with the Ryan-McFarland COSTAR system stored on one of the diskettes included with this book. It is designed specifically for entering and editing COBOL programs. Under control of the editor, the programmer keys in the COBOL program and saves it for later use. During this time, the computer is *not* performing the operations specified in the program (that is, the program is not being run). The system is merely accepting your program. When the program entry has been completed, the program must be saved to disk storage.

End Result: The program (of statements) now resides in the memory of the computer and, by direction of the programmer, on disk storage.

4. **Task:** Compile the program.

   Activity: The programmer directs the system to convert the program from its English-like COBOL form to the equivalent binary code required by the computer. This is called *compiling* the program; it is described in more detail later in this chapter.

   End Result: A binary coded form of the program that is ready to run.

5. **Task:** Run the program.

   Activity: The programmer directs the system to run the program that has been entered and compiled. The computer carries out the action requested by each program statement and produces the results that the program is designed to yield.

   End Result: Usually computed results displayed on the screen or printed on a printer.

You should study these steps carefully because these principles will be referenced when describing how to use the COBOL system on the computer.

A Programming Problem Definition

For your first exposure to using COBOL, you will work with a program to perform the following simple task:

> Allow a user to enter two numbers of three or fewer digits, then calculate and print the sum of the numbers. Upon completing the operation, the program asks the user whether to repeat the operation or to end processing.

In this chapter, you will use a very simple prewritten program that is stored on one of the book's accompanying diskettes under the name ADDER.CBL. You will not be concerned about details of the COBOL language; only with how to handle the program itself.

A simple COBOL program to perform these functions is shown in Figure 1-1. You can see that it reads somewhat like ordinary English. Because the example definition hints at its purpose, you might be able to guess what many of the statements mean. However, ignore details of the language for now. Your first task is to understand how you will arrive at a program such as this and what you will do with it once it is written.

The Concept of Language Translation

You do not need a vast background in COBOL to guess what each statement of the program in Figure 1-1 does. The semi-English nature of COBOL is very important; the language was designed for people, not for computers. The processor of the computer cannot understand such descriptions. In fact, every instruction to the computer must be in a special binary coded form—a complicated form that would leave most of us mortals breathless. The key to wide use of the computer revolves around the use of people-oriented languages such as COBOL. But the key to using such languages itself revolves around special prewritten programs that convert from programs in COBOL into equivalent *machine language* programs in binary code. This program translation phase is done on the computer by a special *language translator* program. For languages such as COBOL, these translators are called *compilers,* and the translating operation is termed *compiling.* The preceding description of the overall programming process covered this in Step 4.

Then, under the control of the compiler, the computer will translate the entire program into machine language. During this compiling, none of the instructions is being carried out; they are merely being translated. In essence, the language processor program is treating the COBOL program, usually referred to as the *source program,* as data and is producing as output a machine language program, usually referred to as the *object program.*

The first COBOL compiler available for the IBM PC was introduced by IBM shortly after the PC itself was introduced. Since that time, a number of software companies have brought out their own compilers, many of them faster and more powerful than IBM's. The compiler included with this book is written and marketed by the Ryan-McFarland

Corporation; it is called RM/COBOL-85. All procedures for compiling and running programs that are described in this book relate specifically to RM/COBOL-85.

Compiling and Running Programs with RM/CO*

What is RM/CO*

If you intend to use RM/CO*, you should step through the following process to become familiar with the actions of compiling and running such a program.

RM/CO* (pronounced *Are-Emm-CoStar*) is described by Ryan-McFarland as:

> "... an interactive, menu-driven environment, within which you can write, edit, compile, run and debug RM/COBOL-85 programs."

It is the type of environment that is sometimes referred to as "a programmer's workbench," as opposed to a "normal" or "typical" programming environment. Let's take a moment to consider the typical programming environment, how RM/CO* differs from it, and the advantages that RM/CO* offers.

From the earlier five-step description of the programming process, you should recognize the following activities of the COBOL programmer when running a program.

Action: Use a text editor or word processor to create the COBOL source program.

Output: The source program is stored on disk as a file.

Action: Use a compiler that translates the source program into an object program.

Output: The compiled program is stored on disk as a file and, optionally, a *post-compile listing* of the program—together with the identification of any errors—is stored on disk as another file.

Figure 1-1

The ADDER COBOL Program

```
IDENTIFICATION DIVISION.
PROGRAM-ID. ADDER.

DATA DIVISION.
WORKING-STORAGE SECTION.
01  WORK-FIELDS.
        10  FIRST-NUM      PICTURE 999.
        10  SECOND-NUM     PICTURE 999.
        10  TOTAL          PICTURE 9999.
        10  CONTIN         PICTURE 9 VALUE 1.

PROCEDURE DIVISION.

ADDING-PROGRAM.
    DISPLAY " "    ERASE
    DISPLAY "Program to add pairs of numbers"

    PERFORM UNTIL CONTIN = 0
      DISPLAY " "
      DISPLAY "Please enter the first number"
      ACCEPT FIRST-NUM
      DISPLAY "Please enter the second number"
      ACCEPT SECOND-NUM
      MOVE FIRST-NUM TO TOTAL
      ADD SECOND-NUM TO TOTAL
      DISPLAY "The sum is ", TOTAL
      DISPLAY " "
      DISPLAY "Enter 1 to repeat, 0 to end"
      ACCEPT CONTIN
    END-PERFORM

    DISPLAY "Processing complete"
    STOP RUN.
```

Action: Run (execute) the program.

Output: Processed results are displayed on the screen, sent to the printer, or alternately stored on disk as a file. Usually, the data for the run is obtained from a data file stored on disk.

Notice two things about these activities:

1. You must take three separate, individual actions. To invoke each of the actions, you type a multi-letter name, along with any command-line arguments which are required.

2. You must deal with numerous interrelated files stored on disk.

In most programming environments, the multiple pieces of software are independent of one another, as illustrated in Figure 1-2, yet you must work with them in tandem. For instance, the editor and compiler are each completely self-contained and therefore have no communication with each other. The post-compile listing of the compiler includes diagnostic messages indicating syntax errors in the source program. To correct these errors, you must either print the listing or display it with a text editor, make notes as to the corrections to be made, make those corrections in the source file, and recompile the program. This process is repeated until no more errors exist.

Only then can you run the program. If the output goes to disk, you must either print the output or examine it on the screen using the text editor. If you detect errors in the results, you must make notes regarding corrections to be made, get back into the editor, make the corrections, and compile again.

With RM/CO*, the same steps are required, but their execution and the multitude of files are coordinated under the RM/CO* umbrella as illustrated in Figure 1-3. You are probably familiar with software that uses a *menu,* a list of options from which you select one to designate the action you wish to take. Since RM/CO* is *menu-driven,* you can enter the editor, compile a program, or run a program with a one- or two-key sequence. It is easy to move back and forth between activities and files in a coordinated fashion during the programming process.

Another useful function of RM/CO* is the management of files. The system allows you to set up projects for grouping your various applications. When you enter a project, RM/CO* gives you access to only those files you have assigned to that project.

In this chapter, you will learn the basics of compiling and running a program (using ADDER). Appendix C describes the details of using RM/CO*. Before attempting to run RM/CO* as described in the following sections, you should have prepared your disk environment as described in Appendix B. If not, then do so before proceeding.

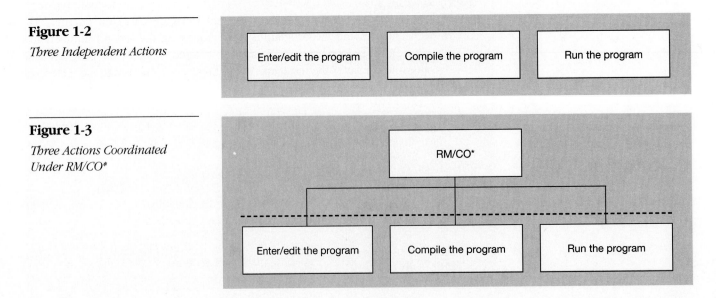

Figure 1-2

Three Independent Actions

| Enter/edit the program | Compile the program | Run the program |

Figure 1-3

*Three Actions Coordinated Under RM/CO**

RM/CO*

| Enter/edit the program | Compile the program | Run the program |

The Overall Sequence

Before running RM/CO*, you must insert the diskette(s) in the appropriate drive(s) and/or be in the proper subdirectory. This depends upon the configuration of your computer and the way you set it up. For this, refer to Appendix B.

You can run RM/CO* by typing, from the DOS prompt, the following and striking the Enter key.

```
RMCOSTAR
```

The following is the sequence of keystroke commands that you must give to the computer to compile and run the ADDER program that is available from the distribution disk accompanying this book. You can step through this sequence and observe your screen displays, or you can work through it using the directions in the sections that follow and comparing your screen displays to those shown in the accompanying figures. As you go through this, keep in mind that to select a menu option, you need only enter the first letter of the option. For instance, to compile strike the letter *C*—do *not* strike the Enter key after the letter *C*. In some cases, there will be a message telling you which key to strike to continue.

RM/CO* actions:

1. Start RM/CO* by typing

   ```
   RMCOSTAR
   ```

   and striking *Enter* from the DOS prompt (if you have not already done so).
2. When the RM/CO* screen comes up, strike the Enter key.
3. Strike the letter *E* (the Enter option)—do not strike *Enter*.

To compile:

4. Strike the letter *C* (the Compile option)—do not strike *Enter*.
5. Strike the letter *O* (the One file option)—do not strike *Enter*.
6. Strike the Escape (Esc) key—do not strike *Enter*.

To run:

7. Strike the letter *R* (the Run option)—do not strike *Enter*.
8. Strike the letter *R* (the Run option) a second time—do not strike *Enter*.
9. Strike the letter *E, then* strike *Enter*.
10. Control will be given to the ADDER program, which will display the screen shown in Figure 1-4. Figure 1-4(a) shows the computer waiting for the first number to be entered. Since the program is designed to handle numbers of up to three digits, a one-, two- or three-digit number may be entered. In Figure 1-4(b), the number 253 has been entered, and the program is now requesting the second number. In Figure 1-4(c), the second value of 75 has been entered, whereby the program has calculated and displayed the result and is awaiting a decision to continue. Entering a value of 1 will cause this process to be repeated; entering a value of 0 will cause the program to terminate.
11. After program execution has been terminated by entering a value of 0, strike any key on the keyboard to continue.

To quit RM/CO*:

12. Strike the Escape (Esc) key as directed—do not strike *Enter*.
13. Strike the letter *Q* (the Quit option)—do not strike *Enter*.
14. Strike the letter *Q* (the Quit option) again—do not strike *Enter*.

This should return you to DOS. If you had trouble with this sequence or wish to go through it with some explanation, step through the actions as you read the following.

Details of RM/CO* Actions

RM/CO* Screens

The opening RM/CO* screen is shown in Figure 1-5. If you have done your setup as described in the appendix, your screen will be the same, except that the directory identified at the top of the screen will be different. As you will learn when you study the details of RM/CO* (Appendix C), this screen lists the projects that you have created. In this case, there is only one: the EXAMPLES project under which the demonstration ADDER program is stored.

The instruction at the bottom of the screen is "Press any key for Menu." Strike the Enter key and the lower portion of the screen will be replaced by the three-option menu shown in Figure 1-6. To select a menu option, you need only enter the first letter of the option. Strike the letter *E* to enter a project—do *not* strike the Enter key after the letter *E*. RM/CO* will switch you into the ADDER project (the only project, at this point) and display a list of files currently stored under this project. Your screen should appear as shown in Figure 1-7. The only file in this project is the ADDER program, which was entered specifically when the distribution diskettes were set up. At the bottom of the screen, you see 11 options. For now, you will be using only two of them: Compile and Run.

Figure 1-4

Screen Dialogues

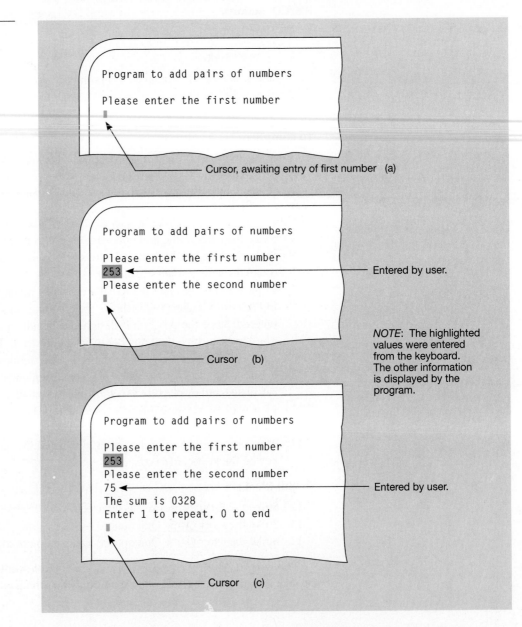

```
Program to add pairs of numbers

Please enter the first number
▮
```
———— Cursor, awaiting entry of first number (a)

```
Program to add pairs of numbers

Please enter the first number
253  ◄————  Entered by user.
Please enter the second number
▮
```
———— Cursor   (b)

NOTE: The highlighted values were entered from the keyboard. The other information is displayed by the program.

```
Program to add pairs of numbers

Please enter the first number
253
Please enter the second number
75  ◄————  Entered by user.
The sum is 0328
Enter 1 to repeat, 0 to end
▮
```
———— Cursor   (c)

Figure 1-5

The RM/CO Introduction Screen*

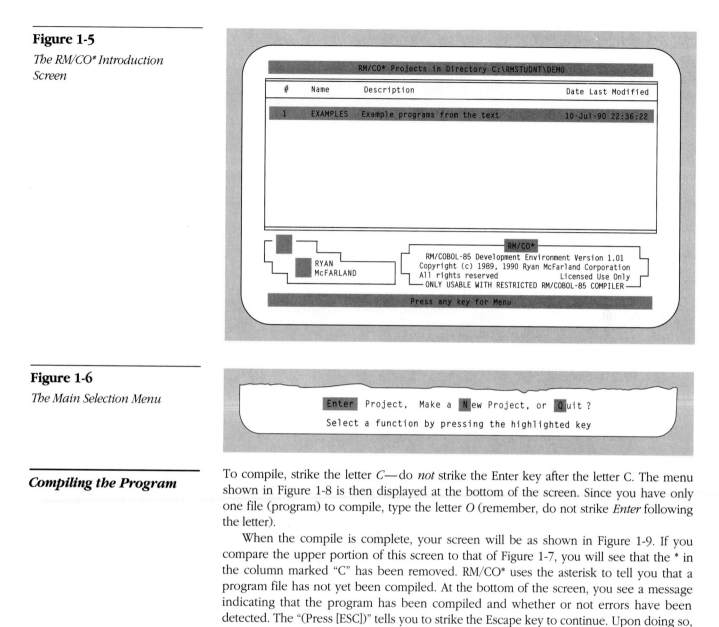

Figure 1-6

The Main Selection Menu

Compiling the Program

To compile, strike the letter *C*—do *not* strike the Enter key after the letter C. The menu shown in Figure 1-8 is then displayed at the bottom of the screen. Since you have only one file (program) to compile, type the letter *O* (remember, do not strike *Enter* following the letter).

When the compile is complete, your screen will be as shown in Figure 1-9. If you compare the upper portion of this screen to that of Figure 1-7, you will see that the * in the column marked "C" has been removed. RM/CO* uses the asterisk to tell you that a program file has not yet been compiled. At the bottom of the screen, you see a message indicating that the program has been compiled and whether or not errors have been detected. The "(Press [ESC])" tells you to strike the Escape key to continue. Upon doing so, the lower portion of the screen will be replaced with the menu in Figure 1-7.

Running the Program

To run the program from this menu, strike the letter *R* (do not strike *Enter*). Your resulting screen will be as shown in Figure 1-10 (see page 12). Strike the letter *R* once again for the Run option and your screen will display part of the program shown in Figure 1-11.

One feature of the RM/COBOL-85 system's educational version is that a special debugger is automatically active when you run a program. Although you will have little need for it with the simple programs of the first few chapters, it is quite useful for detecting errors in large, complex programs. At the bottom of the screen in Figure 1-11, the prompt

```
ST 14 ADDER C?
```

is a debugger prompt telling you that it is waiting at line (statement) 14 of the program—this is the paragraph-name ADDING-PROGRAM. To begin the run, type in the letter *E* (for Exit the debugger) *and* strike the Enter key.

Figure 1-7

Project Display and Menu

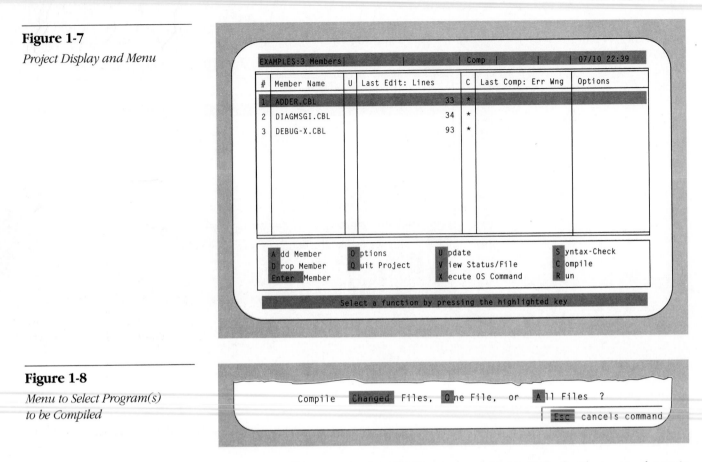

Figure 1-8

*Menu to Select Program(s)
to be Compiled*

Control will be given to the ADDER program, which will display the screen shown in Figure 1-4(a). Here the computer is waiting for the first number to be entered. Since the program is designed to handle numbers of up to three digits, a one-, two- or three-digit number may be entered. In Figure 1-4(b), the number 253 has been entered, and the program is now requesting the second number. In Figure 1-4(c), the second value of 75 has been entered, whereby the program has calculated and displayed the result and is awaiting a decision to continue. Entering a value of 1 will cause this process to be repeated; entering a value of 0 will cause the program to terminate.

When the program is terminated, control is returned to RM-CO* and the last line on the screen will be:

```
Run Complete: Press [Esc] for Menu, [F10] to see final program output
```

Strike the Escape key to return to the menu of Figure 1-7.

After completing the run, the compiled version of the program will remain on disk. If you want to run the program again, you need *not* repeat the compiling process. Once the program is compiled, it can be run as many times as desired. The only reason to recompile a program is if changes have been made to the CBL version.

Ending an RM/CO* Session

To complete this work session, you must "back out" of RM/CO*. From the menu of Figure 1-7, strike the letter *Q* to quit the project and return to the menu of Figure 1-6. Strike the letter *Q* once again to quit RM/CO*. Control of the computer will be returned to DOS.

Compiling and Running Programs Without RM/CO*

Compiling the Program

If you do not intend to use RM/CO*, you should step through the following process to become familiar with the actions of compiling and running a program. If you will be running RM/CO*, you should read these instructions because they will give you an idea of what takes place under the control of RM/CO*.

Before running the RM compiler, you must insert the diskette(s) in the appropriate drive(s) and/or be in the proper subdirectory. This depends upon the configuration of your computer and the way you set it up. If you are using a computer without a hard disk (with two floppy disk drives), you would carry out the following sequence of steps from the DOS A> prompt:

1. Insert the RM/COBOL system disk into drive B.
2. Insert the program work disk (that you created following the instructions of Appendix B) into drive A.
3. Enter the following PATH command (needed so that DOS will be able to find the RMCOBOL compiler); strike the Enter key after typing the command:

        PATH B:\

Once this is done, you can run the compiler by typing, from the A> prompt, the RM/COBOL-85 compile command of Figure 1-12. The compiler, named RMCOBOL, is activated when you type in its name. After spacing once or twice, enter the program name without the extension. The compiler expects the program to have an extension of CBL, so it is not necessary to include it in this command. Following the program name, enter the letter *L*; this causes the compiler to produce a post-compile listing of the program—complete with error messages regarding any errors detected during the compiling process.

When the compiling operation is complete, the following two additional files will be on the disk in drive A:

ADDER.COB	The compiled version of the program ADDER.CBL
ADDER.LST	The post-compile listing of the program ADDER.CBL (You will learn more about this in Chapter 2.)

Note that the names of these two files are identical to those of the COBOL program; the difference is that they have different extensions.

Since this program has been previously tested and is free of errors, the message after compiling will indicate 0 errors. The program is now ready to run.

Figure 1-9

Compilation Complete

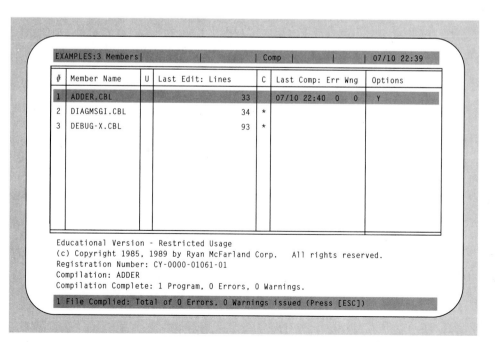

Running the Program

The last step is to run the error-free program that has just been compiled. The RMCOBOL compiler program is one of two components of the RM/COBOL-85 system. The second is the program RUNCOBOL, a program that controls the running of any RM compiled program. (RUNCOBOL is called a *run-time system.*) One feature of the RM/COBOL-85 runtime system's educational version is that a special debugger is automatically active. Although you will have little need for it with the simple programs of the first few chapters, it is quite useful for detecting errors in large, complex programs. Upon entering the RUNCOBOL command shown in Figure 1-13(a), the debugger responds as shown in Figure 1-13(b), and awaits your response. To run the program, simply type in the letter *E* (for exit the debugger and run the program) and strike the Enter key.

Figure 1-10

The Run Selection

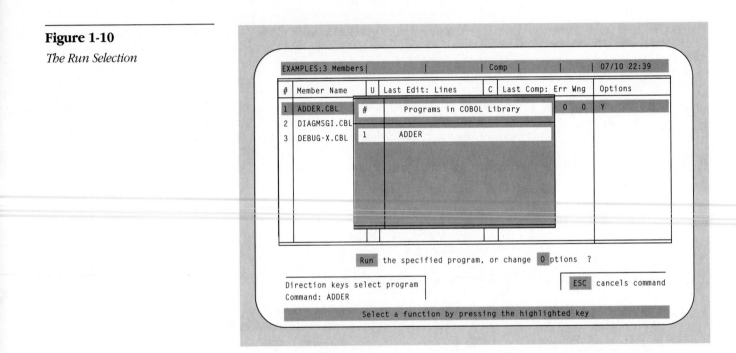

Figure 1-11

Debugger Control Awaiting User Response

Figure 1-12

Compiling an RM/COBOL Program

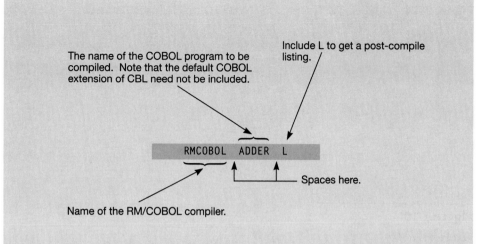

Figure 1-13

Running an RM/COBOL Program

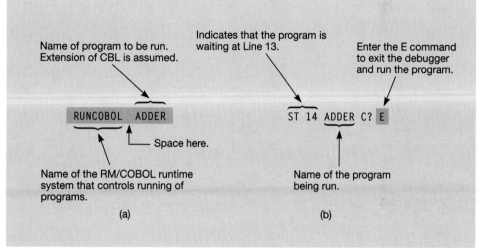

If everything has been done properly, the program will run, and the screen will appear as shown in Figure 1-14(a). Here the computer is waiting for the first number to be entered. Since the program is designed to handle numbers of up to three digits, a one, two- or three-digit number may be entered. In Figure 1-14(b), the number 253 has been entered, and the program is now requesting the second number. In Figure 1-14(c), the second value of 75 has been entered, whereby the program has calculated and displayed the result and is awaiting a decision to continue. Entering a value of 1 will cause this process to be repeated; entering a value of 0 will cause the program to terminate.

After completing the run, the compiled version of the program (named ADDER.COB) will remain on disk. If you want to run the program again, you need *not* repeat the compiling process. Once the program is compiled, it can be run as many times as desired. The only reason to recompile a program is if changes have been made to the CBL version.

Figure 1-14

Screen Dialogues

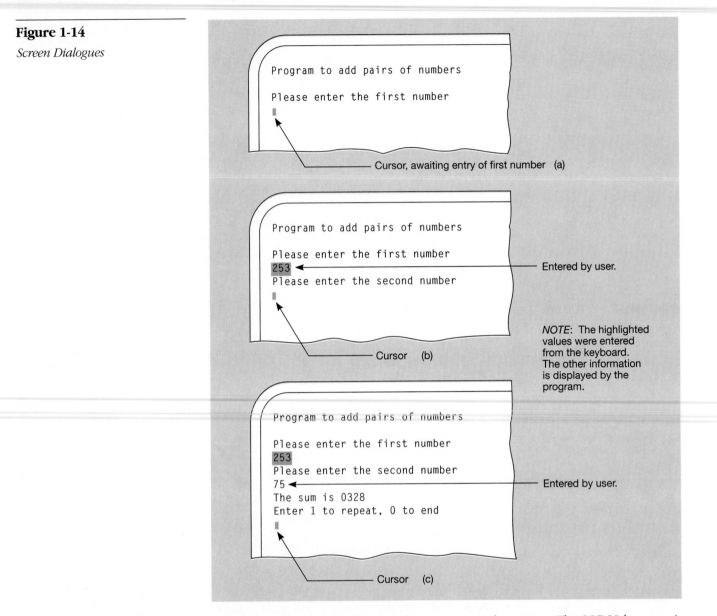

Program to add pairs of numbers

Please enter the first number

———— Cursor, awaiting entry of first number (a)

Program to add pairs of numbers

Please enter the first number
253 ————— Entered by user.
Please enter the second number

NOTE: The highlighted
values were entered
from the keyboard.
The other information
is displayed by the
program.

———— Cursor (b)

Program to add pairs of numbers

Please enter the first number
253
Please enter the second number
75 ————— Entered by user.
The sum is 0328
Enter 1 to repeat, 0 to end

———— Cursor (c)

Chapter Summary

COBOL is an acronym for COmmon Business-Oriented Language. The COBOL language is designed specifically for the heavy input/output and report generation needs of business data processing.

Each COBOL program must perform two essential tasks:

■ Define the data to be processed

■ Define the procedures (actions) required to process the data and produce the desired results

Processing data, usually from a data file, involves three types of activities:

■ **Input:** Copying data from outside the internal memory into specific data items

■ **Processing:** Manipulating the contents of data items by calculating, and rearranging to place the desired results in other data items

■ **Output:** Copying the data items containing the desired results to an output device (screen, printer, and so on)

The programming process is much more than simply writing the COBOL program. The steps to solving a problem are

1. Map out the solution to the problem
2. Write the program
3. Enter the program into the computer
4. Compile the program
5. Run the program

RM/CO* is a menu-driven software system under which you can operate in the COBOL environment. It provides for program entry and editing, compiling, and running. It also includes provisions for the convenient management of the many files with which you will be working.

If you elect not to use RM/CO*, you will need a text editor for entering your COBOL programs. You will compile a program with the RMCOBOL command and run a program with the RUNCOBOL command.

Questions and Exercises

Key Terminology

Give a brief description of each of the following terms that were introduced in this chapter.

COBOL	language translator program	processing
coding	machine language	programming language
conditional statement	menu	RM/CO*
imperative statement	object program	source program
input	output	syntax rules

General Questions

1. What does the acronym *COBOL* mean?
2. A programming language has two general aspects. What are they?
3. Define the two essential elements of a computer program written in a language such as COBOL.
4. What is the difference between an imperative statement and a conditional statement?
5. The overall task of programming a problem solution consists of the following five steps. However, they are not in the order in which they should be carried out. Place them in their proper order.
   Compile the program
   Map out the solution
   Enter the program into the computer
   Run the program
   Write the program
6. Why is it necessary to compile a COBOL program?

Programming Assignment

1-1 Compile and Run the Program ADDER

Compile and run the program ADDER and enter several sets of values. As you enter data, you will find that if you enter a three-digit number, the computer automatically accepts it and goes on to the next step. However, if you enter a number of one or two digits, it will be necessary to strike the Enter key in order to go on. This is due to the way in which the program variables have been defined. You will learn more about this in the next chapter.

2

BASIC PRINCIPLES OF COBOL

Chapter Objectives

The ADDER program of Chapter 1 served as a convenient device to learn how to compile and run a COBOL program. In this chapter, you will use the ADDER program to learn the basic elements of the COBOL language, which will allow you to write your own programs. You will learn about the following topics:

■ The division/section/paragraph/entry structure of COBOL

■ Three of the four divisions of a COBOL program: Identification, Data, and Procedure

■ How data areas for use in a program are defined in the DATA DIVISION of the program

■ The PROCEDURE DIVISION, in which directions are given to carry out the desired operations

■ The following PROCEDURE DIVISION statements, which form the basis for the ADDER program:

  ▪ ACCEPT for entering data into the computer
  ▪ DISPLAY for displaying results on the computer screen
  ▪ ADD (and other arithmetic statements) for performing arithmetic
  ▪ PERFORM for causing repeated execution of a sequence of statements
  ▪ STOP RUN for terminating execution of a program

■ Programming errors and using the compiler to help detect them

The Nature of COBOL Programs

Introduction

Now that you have had the opportunity to enter the ADDER program and run it, let's learn about COBOL principles so that you can write other programs. Each COBOL program may consist of up to four components called *divisions*, three of which are shown in the program of Figure 2-1 (from Chapter 1). Each of the COBOL divisions (parts) is clearly identified by the *division header*, which is shaded in Figure 2-1. You can see that the division header consists of the name followed by a space and the word DIVISION. Usually, the divisions of COBOL programs are further broken down. Although a detailed description of this concept will be presented later, some of the principles are important to you now. The general structure of COBOL is

> Division
>> Section
>>> Paragraph
>>> Entry

That is, a division may be broken down into sections, a section into paragraphs, and a paragraph into entries. Divisions will not always have all of these components, however.

The IDENTIFICATION DIVISION

The IDENTIFICATION DIVISION from Figure 2-1 consists of the two lines shown in Figure 2-2. The only required entry in this division is the PROGRAM-ID. The program identification (program name) chosen for this program is ADDER. You may use any name for a program, subject to the limitations for programmer-selected names as described later in this chapter. All programs in this book use the same name for both the DOS file name of the program and the COBOL program name.

You may optionally include five other paragraph entries in this division: AUTHOR, INSTALLATION, DATE-WRITTEN, DATE-COMPILED, and SECURITY. Following each of these paragraph names, you may insert descriptive comments appropriate to the entry and program. These comments are provided purely for documentation; they are ignored by the COBOL system, but are printed with the program listing when the program is compiled. However, since they are scheduled for deletion from the next COBOL standard, they are not used in this text.

The DATA DIVISION

One of the actions of the compiler is to reserve memory areas for all data that you will be using in a program. In any COBOL program, you must describe all the characteristics of any data that you want processed. This is necessary so that the compiler can set aside the correct amount of memory for each unit of data required by the program. The definition of the data needs is done in the DATA DIVISION of the program. The DATA DIVISION consists of two sections: the WORKING-STORAGE SECTION, which you will study in this chapter, and the FILE SECTION, which you will study in Chapter 4.

Each entry of the DATA DIVISION in Figure 2-1 defines one *data item* (unit of data) that will be used in the program. If you have taken another programming course, you know a data item by the name *variable*. Algebra uses a variable as an entity that can be assigned any of a range of values. Remember, data item and variable mean the same thing: a unit of data. In COBOL literature, you will also see the word *data-name*; this refers to the name used for a given data item. In Chapter 4, you will encounter the word *field*; it is used to refer to a data item that makes up part of a record. Technically, the data items of the ADDER program are fields comprising the record WORK-FIELDS.

Figure 2-1

Divisions in a COBOL Program

```
IDENTIFICATION DIVISION.
PROGRAM-ID. ADDER.

DATA DIVISION.
WORKING-STORAGE SECTION.
01  WORK-FIELDS.
    10  FIRST-NUM       PICTURE 999.
    10  SECOND-NUM      PICTURE 999.
    10  TOTAL           PICTURE 9999.
    10  CONTIN          PICTURE 9 VALUE 1.

PROCEDURE DIVISION.

ADDING-PROGRAM.
    DISPLAY " "    ERASE
    DISPLAY "Program to add pairs of numbers"

    PERFORM UNTIL CONTIN = 0
      DISPLAY " "
      DISPLAY "Please enter the first number"
      ACCEPT FIRST-NUM
      DISPLAY "Please enter the second number"
      ACCEPT SECOND-NUM
      MOVE FIRST-NUM TO TOTAL
      ADD SECOND-NUM TO TOTAL
      DISPLAY "The sum is ", TOTAL
      DISPLAY " "
      DISPLAY "Enter 1 to repeat, 0 to end"
      ACCEPT CONTIN
    END-PERFORM

    DISPLAY "Processing complete"
    STOP RUN.
```

Figure 2-2

IDENTIFICATION DIVISION Structure

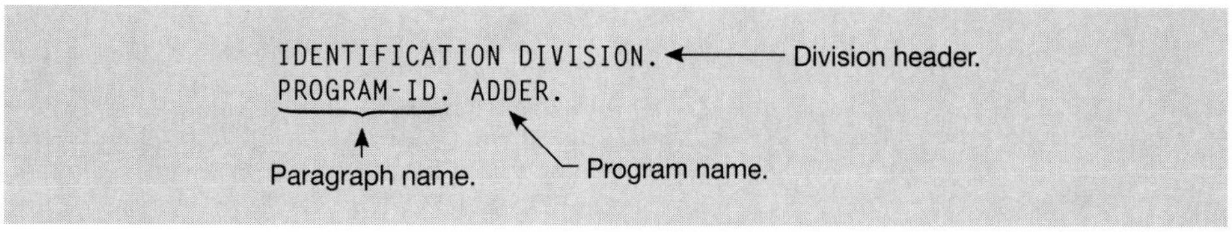

```
IDENTIFICATION DIVISION. ◄——— Division header.
PROGRAM-ID. ADDER.
```
Paragraph name.   Program name.

Figure 2-3

A Data Definition Entry from the DATA DIVISION

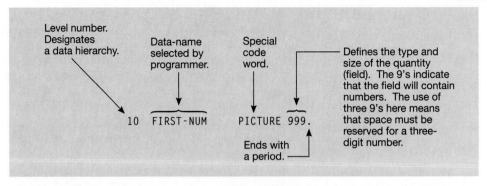

The nature of these data definition entries is illustrated in Figure 2-3 for the data item FIRST-NUM. Here you see that the definition entry consists of the following three parts:

1. A level number. In the interest of simplicity, example programs in this chapter all use the number 10. In the next chapter, you will learn how these level numbers are used to define a hierarchy of data.

2. The data-name that is selected by you, the programmer.

3. A PICTURE clause that defines the size and type of data.

In the DATA DIVISION of Figure 2-1, you see the following data items defined:

Field	Size
FIRST-NUM	3 digits
SECOND-NUM	3 digits
TOTAL	4 digits
CONTIN	1 digit

When writing the ADDER program, the program authors arbitrarily decided to allow the entry of numbers up to three digits in length. Hence, two of the PICTURE clauses in the DATA DIVISION use 999. However, when two three-digit numbers are added together, the resulting sum can consist of one more digit. For instance, adding 155 to 987 produces a sum of 1142. To accommodate this in the program, the field TOTAL is defined as four digits in length (with 9999).

Although the compiler reserves memory for data items defined in the DATA DIVISION, most compilers do *not* automatically put any data values into them when the program is loaded. For such compilers, when this program is first loaded into memory, FIRST-NUM, SECOND-NUM, and WORK will contain whatever was left from the previous program.* However, this is not the case with the field CONTIN because its definition includes a VALUE clause, as illustrated in Figure 2-4. Here the PICTURE clause is followed by a VALUE clause, which causes an initial value to be placed in memory when the program is first loaded. The need for doing this in the program ADDER will become apparent when you study the PROCEDURE DIVISION of this program.

For the sake of abbreviation, COBOL allows the use of the shortened reserved word PIC in place of PICTURE. Hence, the following two forms are equivalent:

```
10 FIRST-NUM PICTURE 999
10 FIRST-NUM PIC 999.
```

Most examples in this book use the shorter PIC.

---

* Unlike many compilers, the RM/COBOL compiler initializes to spaces all areas of the DATA DIVISION not defined using VALUE clauses. However, it is considered poor practice to operate on this assumption. All areas should explicitly be initialized with VALUE clauses or somewhere in the PROCEDURE DIVISION.

Words and Names in COBOL

The choice of words used in the program ADDER goes a long way in making the program easy to follow. For instance, it is rather apparent that SECOND-NUM refers to the second number and TOTAL to the sum of the two numbers. Furthermore, a COBOL statement such as

```
ADD SECOND-NUM TO TOTAL
```

does not require a COBOL expert to understand it. When preparing a program, you must take great care in your choice of words, since what is acceptable in English may not be acceptable in COBOL. In general, words used in COBOL can be grouped into two broad categories: *reserved words* and *programmer-selected names*.

Reserved Words

When field names are defined in the DATA DIVISION, the size and type of each field is indicated by the word PICTURE. This special word was included in COBOL by its designers to mean that the nature of a field is being defined. Special words such as PICTURE are commonly referred to as *reserved words*; COBOL contains 359 such words. (A list of reserved words may be found in Appendix E.) Simply stated, a reserved word is a word that has a special meaning to the COBOL system and must be used only in the proper context. The following are a few selected examples of reserved words:

> COBOL
> DATA
> END-OF-PAGE
> PICTURE
> ZERO

The following minor variations are not reserved words, however:

> COBOLX
> DATA-IN
> END-OFPAGE
> DATA-PICTURE
> ZEROW

Programmer-Selected Names

From the preceding, you see that the COBOL programmer must name fields. *Programmer-selected names* that you will study in this chapter fall into two categories: data-names and paragraph names. The choice of names is strictly up to you, the programmer (within certain limitations). Names should be selected that are meaningful to you and thus serve as good documentation; however, they *can* simply be a meaningless collection of letters. Each name in the example program was selected because it served to remind the program author what was being represented. For instance, using the word TOTAL quite clearly implies that this field will contain some kind of total value. Think of the confusion that could result if the names selected were those defined in Figure 2-5. The COBOL system

Figure 2-4

Assigning a Starting Value

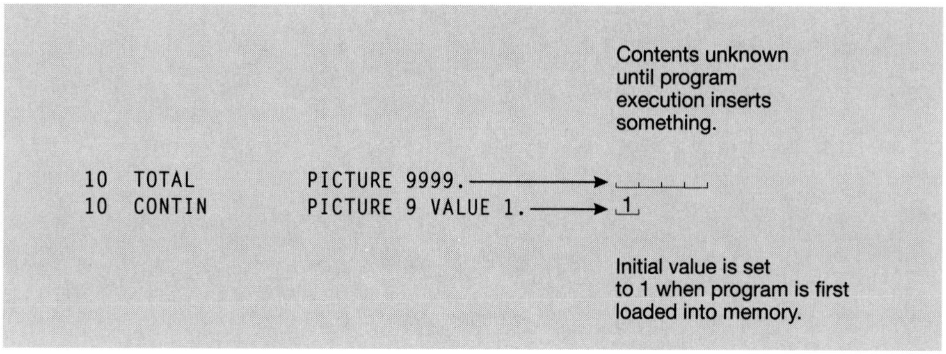

```
10   TOTAL        PICTURE 9999.  ———→  ⌞_⌟_⌟_⌟
10   CONTIN       PICTURE 9 VALUE 1.  ———→  ⌞1⌟
```

Contents unknown until program execution inserts something.

Initial value is set to 1 when program is first loaded into memory.

certainly would not care, but it would be extremely confusing to the programmer or anyone who attempted to study or modify the program. So as a general rule, you should select names that are meaningful in the context in which they are used. However, programmer-selected names must conform to the following rules:

1. Names may contain letters (A-Z), digits (0-9), or hyphens (-). No other characters, *including a blank space*, are allowed.

2. A name may be from 1 to 30 characters long.

3. The hyphen cannot be used as the first or last character in the name.

4. Each name must include at least one letter.

5. A programmer-selected name must not be a COBOL reserved word. Appendix E contains a list of all the reserved words.

The following are some examples of valid and invalid data-names:

Valid Names

OKAY
X-REPORT
WORK-FIELD
157INVOICE
A-941138
Q

Invalid Names	**Reason**
REPORT	Reserved word
5973-82	At least one letter required
GROSS PAY	Should not be a blank between GROSS and PAY
INVOICE-	Must not end with a hyphen
TAX-%	Special characters (%) not allowed

Literals in COBOL

Computer memory reserved by programmer-selected names is used in the program to hold data that can come from three different sources: from input, from elsewhere in the program, and from calculations. These names represent quantities that might change from one step in the program to the next. In addition, programs include quantities that do not change. For instance, assume that a user has made two consecutive inquiries to the computer for information. The response to these two inquiries might be as shown in Figures 2-6(a) and (b). Note that the descriptive part is the same for both, but the stock code is different. Information that is included in a program and remains fixed is commonly called *literal* data. As you will learn in the sections that follow, both the ACCEPT and DISPLAY statements of this program include literals. Technically speaking, the quantity 1 included in the VALUE portion of the definition of CONTIN (see Figure 2-4) is called a literal.

Figure 2-5

A Poor Choice of Data-Names

```
DATA DIVISION.
WORKING-STORAGE SECTION.
01  WORK-FIELDS.
    10  EMPLOYEE     PICTURE 999.
    10  TOTAL        PICTURE 999.
    10  THIRD-NUM    PICTURE 9999.
    10  FIRST-NUM    PICTURE 9 VALUE 1.
    .
    .
    .
    ADD TOTAL TO THIRD-NUM
```

Figure 2-6

Changing and Fixed Information

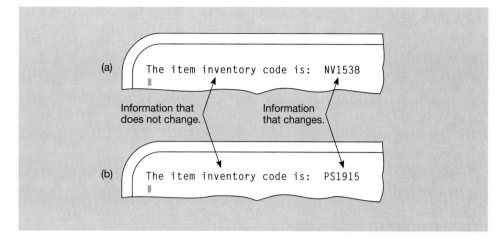

(a)   The item inventory code is: NV1538

Information that does not change.   Information that changes.

(b)   The item inventory code is: PS1915

The PROCEDURE DIVISION

COBOL Action Statements

As you learned, the IDENTIFICATION DIVISION and the DATA DIVISION provide the computer with information necessary to do the job. The PROCEDURE DIVISION contains the detailed instructions describing *actions* to be performed in carrying out the job. In general, this division consists of *paragraphs* of *statements* describing actions to be carried out. The PROCEDURE DIVISION of the ADDER program (repeated in Figure 2-7) consists of a single paragraph named ADDING-PROGRAM. Each *statement* in the paragraph tells the computer to perform an action. Note that the word *statement is* used in this book to describe entries in the PROCEDURE DIVISION; it is *not* used to describe entries in the other divisions.

Let's focus our attention on these statements and their characteristics. Notice the following for each statement in Figure 2-7:

1. Each statement starts with a verb—an action word—a word that says "Do something!" Statements in the PROCEDURE DIVISION are sometimes called *commands*, because they command the computer to do something.

2. Each statement includes data-names that have been defined previously in the DATA DIVISION. They are *not* names that are made up in the PROCEDURE DIVISION.

3. Each statement begins on a new line. This is not a COBOL requirement, but it will be used as a standard in this book.

Now consider the following statement from Figure 2-7:

        ADD SECOND-NUM TO TOTAL

What does that statement really say? It says:

> ADD the contents of the field defined by the programmer as SECOND-NUM to the contents of the field that has been defined as TOTAL.

Similarly, the statement

        ACCEPT FIRST-NUM

of Figure 2-7 directs the computer to accept a value from the keyboard and to store it in the memory area reserved for FIRST-NUM.

The Nature of Statements

A logical question at this point is, "How much latitude does the programmer have in forming statements in the PROCEDURE DIVISION?" For instance, is

```
DISPLAY THE VALUE OF FIRST-NUM
  or SHOW FIRST-NUM
```

just as valid as DISPLAY FIRST-NUM? The answer is *no!* Each COBOL statement must be structured in a predefined way. Let's consider each type of statement used in the PROCEDURE DIVISION of Figure 2-7.

Input and Output Operations

The ACCEPT Statement

The ACCEPT statement provides for the input of data from the keyboard of the computer. Its basic form is

ACCEPT data-name

This tells the computer to accept data from the keyboard and place it in the field called data-name. For instance, the program ADDER includes the following three ACCEPT statements:

```
ACCEPT FIRST-NUM
ACCEPT SECOND-NUM
ACCEPT CONTIN
```

As each statement is executed, the computer halts and awaits an entry from the keyboard. When the number is keyed in and the Enter key is pressed, the value is entered into the named field. (You have probably noticed that the computer automatically accepts the data without waiting for the Enter key if the number you enter is the maximum length of the field.) The sequence of executing these statements in the program for the first time and the effect on the corresponding memory locations are shown in Figure 2-8. This form of the ACCEPT statement is used for low-volume input. As you will learn in Chapter 10, RM/COBOL also provides a more versatile form of the ACCEPT statement for use with interactive data entry.

Figure 2-7

The PROCEDURE DIVISION from the ADDER program

```
PROCEDURE DIVISION.

ADDING-PROGRAM.
    DISPLAY " "    ERASE
    DISPLAY "Program to add pairs of numbers"

    PERFORM UNTIL CONTIN = 0
       DISPLAY " "
       DISPLAY "Please enter the first number"
       ACCEPT FIRST-NUM
       DISPLAY "Please enter the second number"
       ACCEPT SECOND-NUM
       MOVE FIRST-NUM TO TOTAL
       ADD SECOND-NUM TO TOTAL
       DISPLAY "The sum is ", TOTAL
       DISPLAY " "
       DISPLAY "Enter 1 to repeat, 0 to end"
       ACCEPT CONTIN
    END-PERFORM

    DISPLAY "Processing complete"
    STOP RUN.
```

Figure 2-8

Effect on Memory Areas of Program Execution

After execution of:	User enters:	Memory contents:		
		FIRST-NUM	SECOND-NUM	CONTIN
Initial values		?	?	1
ACCEPT FIRST-NUM	165	165	?	1
ACCEPT SECOND-NUM	50	165	50	1
ACCEPT CONTIN	0	165	50	0

The DISPLAY Statement

The DISPLAY statement provides for the output of messages and/or data to the screen in much the same way that the ACCEPT provides for input from the keyboard. Its basic format

DISPLAY output-item-1, output-item-2, and so on

essentially says, "Display the listed items one after the other on the screen." Two different forms of this statement from the ADDER program are described in Figure 2-9. In the first, the "output-item" is a message enclosed in quotes. As described earlier, a quoted item such as this is commonly called a *literal* or, more specifically, a *character literal*. It is displayed (or otherwise processed) exactly as quoted. The COBOL system does not look to see what makes up the *literal*. Note that the literal in Figure 2-9 includes the word *first*, a COBOL reserved word. This will not be treated in any special way because it is included within the quotes as part of the literal.

The second example in Figure 2-9 includes two items in the list to be displayed. The first item is a literal similar to that of the first DISPLAY. The second item is a data-name. Upon execution of this statement, the value currently stored in the memory area for TOTAL will be obtained and printed. It is important to understand that the computer will not print the word TOTAL itself.

Most COBOL statements offer a variety of allowable forms and options. For instance, with the DISPLAY statement, it is possible to display

- A single literal
- Several literals
- The value of a single program data item
- The values of several program data items
- A combination of literals and program data item values

To clearly define the many options available with various COBOL forms, a standard representation is used in COBOL. The full set of definitions is described in Chapter 3; now, however, you will only need the two forms illustrated by the following general form of the DISPLAY:

DISPLAY $\left\{ \begin{matrix} \text{data-name-1} \\ \text{literal-1} \end{matrix} \right\}$ ...

One entry above the other enclosed within braces means that one or the other must be selected. This representation allows either of the following forms:

```
DISPLAY "The sum is"
DISPLAY TOTAL
```

The series of dots (called an ellipsis), indicates that the preceding description, in this case the *data-name-1/literal-1* option, can be repeated as many times as desired. This permits the second form in Figure 2-9.

This simple form of the DISPLAY is convenient for you to get started. You will see later that RM/COBOL-85 also provides a more powerful form of the DISPLAY for use with interactive data entry.

Using Quotes for Literals

The COBOL-85 Standard requires that character literals be defined by enclosing them in quotes. However, programming situations arise in which one or more quotes must be included in a literal. The COBOL Standard method for handling this can be clumsy sometimes. Therefore, most versions of COBOL, including RM/COBOL-85, allow either the conventional quote or the single quote to identify a literal. Hence, the following are equivalent:

```
DISPLAY "The sum is ", TOTAL
DISPLAY 'The sum is ', TOTAL
```

Note that the single quote is on the same key as the double quote. The standard PC keyboard includes another character that has the appearance of an open single quote. *It is another character.* If you use the single quote, be certain to use the key containing the double quote. With the exception of one program in a later chapter, all examples in this book conform to the COBOL standard of a double quote.

Data Manipulation Operations

Consider the two-step action of adding two numbers together with a pocket calculator:

1. Enter the first number into the calculator accumulator unit.
2. Add the second number to the number currently displayed in the accumulator unit. The resulting sum replaces the first number previously stored in the accumulator unit.

The action of the ADDER program is very similar:

1. Move the first number into a work area of memory.
2. Add the second number to the number stored in the work area of memory.

Figure 2-9

Features of the DISPLAY Statement

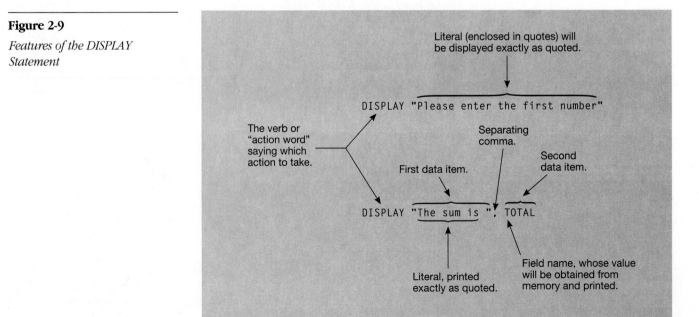

Figure 2-10

Memory Contents with Execution of the MOVE Statement

```
MOVE FIRST-NUM TO TOTAL

                                        FIRST-NUM      TOTAL      From previous
                                                                  operation.
    Memory contents:   Before execution    1 3 7       1 4 6 9

                       After execution      1 3 7       0 1 3 7
                                                              Contents of
                                                              this field
                                                              duplicated into
                                                              this field.
```

This involves the two COBOL statements MOVE and ADD. The following describes them briefly and will be adequate for programs in this and the next chapter. You will learn much more about the MOVE in Chapter 5 and the ADD in Chapter 7.

The MOVE Statement

The MOVE statement used in the ADDER program

```
MOVE FIRST-NUM TO TOTAL
```

copies the value in FIRST-NUM (which is three digits in length) to the data item TOTAL (which is four digits in length).

Copying data from one field in memory to another with the MOVE statement is a common activity in most programs. (For the beginning programmer, the choice of the word *MOVE* is unfortunate. It really should be called the *copy* statement because it *duplicates* the original field.) Basically, the preceding statement says:

Copy (*MOVE*) the contents of the field defined in the program as FIRST-NUM in the DATA DIVISION *TO* the field that has been defined as TOTAL in the DATA DIVISION.

To illustrate how this works, consider the example in Figure 2-10 of what might be in memory before and after execution of a MOVE statement. Notice that:

1. The contents of the "source" field FIRST-NUM (the data that is copied) are unchanged.

2. The original contents of the "destination" field TOTAL have been lost and replaced by the value in the source field.

3. The source field is three positions in width and the destination field is four. The numeric value of the field being copied is preserved by changing the leftmost digit of the receiving field to 0.

You also can move a fixed value into a field. For instance, if you want to place a value of 25 into TOTAL, you could do it with the following MOVE statement:

```
MOVE 25 TO TOTAL
```

The value 25 will not be interpreted by COBOL as a field name because it does not include a letter. Technically, the number 25 is called a *numeric literal.* You will see literals in a variety of applications in later programming examples.

In computing, the term *operand* is commonly encountered. An operand is any item of data that is referenced by an instruction (in COBOL, a statement). As you see, the MOVE statement includes two operands: the source data item and the destination data item. You will encounter the word *operand* in this book.

The ADD Statement

Adding the two quantities in the ADDER program is done by the statement

```
ADD SECOND-NUM TO TOTAL
```

This statement does exactly what the English interpretation suggests: it adds the value in FIRST-NUM to the value in TOTAL (with the result replacing the original value in TOTAL). It is important to understand that the value in SECOND-NUM will not be changed by the addition (similar to the MOVE in this respect). This is illustrated in Figure 2-11.

As with the MOVE, the first field of the ADD can be a literal. For instance, if you needed to add the fixed value 137 to the value in TOTAL, you would use:

```
ADD 137 TO TOTAL
```

Other Arithmetic Operations

Equivalent versions of the SUBTRACT, MULTIPLY, and DIVIDE statements are identical in form to the ADD. Each of these three statement forms is illustrated in the examples of Figure 2-12. For these examples, assume that each is independent of the other and that the values in the fields shown were placed in the fields by previous statements. Following are points that you should notice about these examples:

1. Similar to the ADD, they each operate so that the quantity in the first operand is unchanged and the quantity in the second operand is replaced by the result.

2. Consistent with the nature of the arithmetic operation, different keywords relate the two operands:

    FROM is used with the SUBTRACT statement
    BY is used with the MULTIPLY statement
    INTO is used with the DIVIDE statement

3. In all of these versions of the arithmetic statements, the first operand can be either a literal or a field defined in the DATA DIVISION. However, since the second operand is the one into which the result is placed, it must be a data item defined in the DATA DIVISION.

The following are some problems that can occur with these forms as used here (you will learn how to handle them in later chapters):

1. Data will be lost if the destination field (the second operand) is not large enough to hold the result. For instance, in the first MULTIPLY example, if the value in QUANTITY is 40000, the result 120000 will be too large for the field.

2. No provisions have been made for negative quantities. For instance, if SHIPPED is larger than TOTAL (in the first example) the minus sign of the result will be discarded.

3. No provisions have been made for fractional quantities. In the last example, 20 divided into 815 yields 40.75. However, since AMOUNT includes no decimal point specification, the quantity .75 is discarded.

Other Statements

The STOP RUN Statement

The last line of the program in Figure 2-1 is simply STOP RUN. The action of this statement is exactly what you might expect. Execution is terminated, and control is returned to the computer operating system.

Figure 2-11

Memory Contents with Execution of the ADD Statement

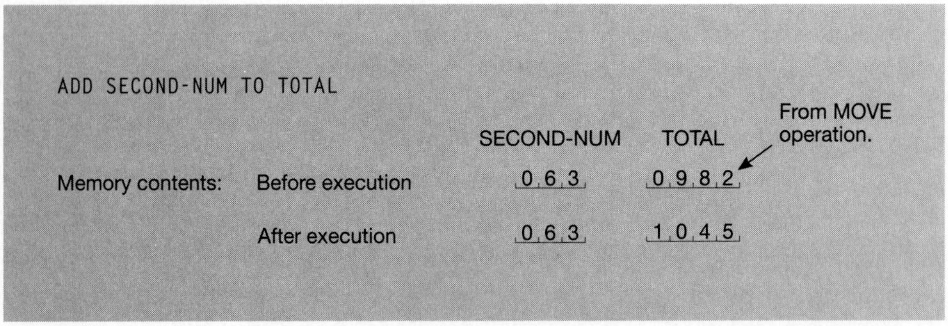

```
ADD SECOND-NUM TO TOTAL
                                                           From MOVE
                                     SECOND-NUM   TOTAL    operation.
   Memory contents:   Before execution    0 6 3      0 9 8 2
                      After execution      0 6 3      1 0 4 5
```

Figure 2-12

Arithmetic Statements

```
01  WORK-FIELDS.
    10  SHIPPED   PIC 9999.
    10  TOTAL     PIC 9999.
    10  CEILING   PIC 999.
    10  FACTOR    PIC 9.
    10  QUANTITY  PIC 99999.
    10  SPLIT     PIC 99.
    10  AMOUNT    PIC 999.
    .
    .
    .
```

Memory contents:

		SHIPPED	TOTAL
SUBTRACT SHIPPED FROM TOTAL	Before execution	0 1 0 1	0 8 1 3
	After execution	0 1 0 1	0 7 1 2

		LITERAL	CEILING
SUBTRACT 10 FROM CEILING	Before execution	1 0	1 3 0
	After execution	1 0	1 2 0

		FACTOR	QUANTITY
MULTIPLY FACTOR BY QUANTITY	Before execution	3	1 2 5 2 0
	After execution	3	3 7 5 6 0

		LITERAL	QUANTITY
MULTIPLY 2 BY QUANTITY	Before execution	2	0 8 1 3 1
	After execution	2	1 6 2 6 2

		SPLIT	AMOUNT
DIVIDE SPLIT INTO AMOUNT	Before execution	0 5	0 8 1 5
	After execution	0 5	0 1 6 3

		LITERAL	AMOUNT
DIVIDE 20 INTO AMOUNT	Before execution	2 0	0 8 1 5
	After execution	2 0	0 0 4 0

The PERFORM UNTIL Statement

When a program is executed, processing goes from one statement to the next *unless the program directs otherwise.* Thus, to cause the computer to repeat a sequence of statements, you must include appropriate statements in the program. From your experience running the ADDER program, you know that once begun, the program gives you the capability to process as many pairs of numbers as you desire. That is, execution is as illustrated in Figure 2-13.

1. The first two statements of the program are executed in sequence.

2. Upon encountering the PERFORM UNTIL, the sequence accept-calculate-display is repeated until the variable CONTIN contains a value of 0.

3. When execution finally "breaks out" of the repetitious loop, the last two statements of the program are executed in sequence.

The PERFORM UNTIL statement and the corresponding END-PERFORM control repeated execution of a statement sequence. They define a *block* of statements whose execution is controlled by the PERFORM UNTIL, as illustrated in Figure 2-14. Because of its English-like syntax, you might guess what it will do. Let's assume that you will run this program, enter two sets of values, and then quit. The sequence of execution would be as follows (remember that the initial value stored in the data item CONTIN is 1 because of the VALUE clause in its definition—see the last line of the DATA DIVISION):

1. The PERFORM checks the value stored in CONTIN; since it is equal to 1, the condition

   ```
   CONTIN = 0
   ```

   is not true, so control is allowed to continue to the DISPLAY statement on the next line.

2. From there, execution progresses from statement to statement. You enter your two numbers, get the result, and enter a value of 1 in response to the statement

   ```
   ACCEPT CONTIN
   ```

3. Upon detecting the END-PERFORM, the system automatically returns control to the PERFORM statement. Since the value in CONTIN is still 1, control again progresses to the DISPLAY statement on the next line.

4. This time, after entering your two numbers, you enter 0 for CONTIN.

5. When control is returned to the PERFORM, the test condition

   ```
   CONTIN = 0
   ```

is true. Since the statement requires that execution be repeated *until* the condition is true, the block following the PERFORM UNTIL will no longer be executed and control will be passed to the statement following the END-PERFORM. In this case, it is the DISPLAY that gives a terminating message. From there, the STOP RUN is executed, which terminates the program.

This form of the PERFORM, called the *in-line PERFORM*, is new to the 1985 COBOL Standard.

Figure 2-13

Statement Execution Sequence of the ADDER Program

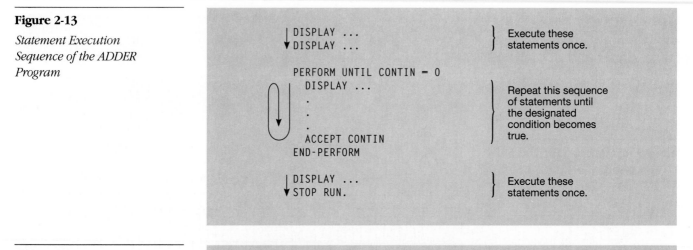

Figure 2-14

The PERFORM Statement

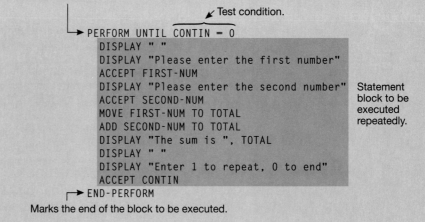

COBOL PROGRAM SHEET

System | Punching Instructions | Shoot of
Program | Graphic | Card Form # * | Identification 73 80
Programmer | Date | Punch

SEQUENCE (Page) (Serial) CONT. A B
1 3 4 6 7 8 12 16 20 24 28 32 36 40 44 48 52 56 60 64 68 72

```
IDENTIFICATION DIVISION.
PROGRAM-ID. ADDER.

DATA DIVISION.
WORKING-STORAGE SECTION.
01  WORK-FIELDS.
    10  FIRST-NUM          PICTURE 999.
    10  SECOND-NUM         PICTURE 999.
    10  TOTAL              PICTURE 9999.
    10  CONTIN             PICTURE 9 VALUE 1.

PROCEDURE DIVISION.

ADDING-PROGRAM.
    DISPLAY " "  ERASE
    DISPLAY "Program to add pairs of numbers"

    PERFORM UNTIL CONTIN = 0
        DISPLAY " "
        DISPLAY "Please enter the first number"

        ACCEPT FIRST-NUM
        DISPLAY "Please enter at the second number"
        ACCEPT SECOND-NUM
        MOVE FIRST-NUM TO TOTAL
        ADD SECOND-NUM TO TOTAL
        DISPLAY "The sum is ", TOTAL
        DISPLAY " "
        DISPLAY "Enter 1 to repeat, 0 to end"
        ACCEPT CONTIN
    END-PERFORM

    DISPLAY "Processing complete"
    STOP RUN.
```

Figure 2-15

The COBOL Coding Form

The Concept of the Sentence

From the preceding sections, you have learned that the period is used to terminate a variety of components in the IDENTIFICATION and DATA DIVISIONs. However, they have been used sparingly in the PROCEDURE DIVISION. Although each statement has been written on a separate line, only the last statement in the program is terminated by a period. Technically, any statement can be terminated by a period. In fact, a statement terminated by a period is called a *sentence*. Thus,

```
ADD 1 TO A-COUNT
```

is a statement, whereas

```
ADD 1 TO A-COUNT.
```

is a sentence. (You are accustomed to this term from using it in English.) In fact, the similarity to English is taken one step further with the ability to treat two or more statements as a single compound statement or sentence, as follows:

```
ADD 1 TO A-COUNT
ACCEPT IN-NAME
ACCEPT SAVE-AGE.
```

This sentence (which is ended only by the period) consists of three independent statements. The use (and nonuse) of periods in the PROCEDURE DIVISION of earlier versions of COBOL was very critical. The features of COBOL-85 significantly diminish the need for the sentence structure. In fact, in some cases the period can interfere with the desirable block structure that is convenient to programming techniques you will be using. In this book, the following convention for using the period in the PROCEDURE DIVISION will be used:

1. A period will follow each paragraph name; this is required by COBOL.
2. Within a paragraph, the period will not be used.
3. Each paragraph will be terminated by a period; this is required by COBOL.

The COBOL Coding Form (and Other Details)

The Coding Form

When COBOL was first devised, most programs were punched into 80-column cards and read into the computer by special card readers. As a result, the capacity of the card was a determining factor in defining how a COBOL source program should be punched into the cards. Although cards are rarely used for inputting programs on mainframe computers and were never used with the personal computer, the effects of card capacity do remain. For example, a PROCEDURE DIVISION statement cannot begin on the source line before position (column) 12. In general, it is necessary to be careful to enter the program with the exact number of spaces indicated. For convenience, program statements are commonly written on special COBOL coding forms that are marked with the exact format required by a COBOL program. As a convenient reference, the ADDER program is shown in Figure 2-15 as it would be written on one of these forms. Referring to Figure 2-1, you can see that each line from the coding form becomes one line in the program. When programs are keyed from the coding sheets, it is sometimes easy to confuse certain letters and digits (the letter *I* and the digit *1*, for instance). To avoid confusion, the following conventions of Figure 2-16 are used in the program of Figure 2-15.

Figure 2-16

Some Simple Conventions

Letter	Digit
I	*1*
O	*Ø*
Z	*2*

The COBOL coding form of Figure 2-15 was designed for COBOL programs that were punched into tabulating cards. Thus, the form is divided into four major fields:

Usage	Columns
Sequence	1-6
Indicator area	7
COBOL statements	8-72
Identification	73-80

The sequence field was especially important when programs were punched into cards because it ensured that the cards were in the correct order. The identification field provided a place for identifying the particular application. For instance, ADDER might be recorded in these columns. Generally, these two fields are for programmer documentation and are not required by the compiler. They are not usually used with PC versions of COBOL.

The indicator area, column 7, serves several purposes. If it contains an asterisk, the entire line can be used for descriptive comments and is ignored by the COBOL system. However, it will be printed as part of the program and thus serves as documentation. Other uses of this field are described in later chapters.

Columns 8-72 are used for the COBOL statements that you have been studying. Of great importance are column 8, (marked *A*) and column 12 (marked *B*). The *A* marks the first position of *Area A* of the COBOL form, which consists of columns 8-11. Similarly, the *B* marks the first position of *Area B*, which includes columns 12-72. These positions are significant because certain COBOL entries must begin in Area A, and others must begin in Area B. Most entries that must begin in Area A will extend into Area B; this is completely acceptable. The entries of Figure 2-17 illustrate this. Note that the paragraph name begins in Area A, and the DISPLAY statement begins in Area B.

Area A and Area B Entries

As you learned, each COBOL program may contain four divisions; each division may be divided into sections. For instance, the DATA DIVISION in Figure 2-1 includes the WORKING-STORAGE SECTION. Paragraph names described for use in the PROCEDURE DIVISION subdivide this portion of the program into paragraphs. So, in general, we have division names (for instance, DATA DIVISION), section names (for instance, WORKING-STORAGE SECTION) and paragraph names (selected by the programmer in the PROCEDURE DIVISION). These names and the 01 indicating a record name in the DATA DIVISION must all be coded beginning in Area A. All other entries must begin in Area B.

Figure 2-17

Using Area A and Area B

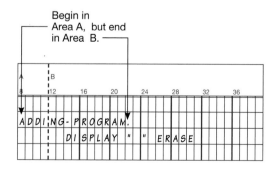

Formatting and the Use of Punctuation

The basic philosophy of COBOL is to make it as similar to ordinary English as possible. You have seen that each statement in the PROCEDURE DIVISION consists of a verb and a noun. Most of the rules for writing statements correspond to those that you might use when typing:

1. Words, whether COBOL reserved or programmer selected, must be separated by at least one space.

2. All division, section, and paragraph names must be followed by a period. The period may be followed by a space, but not preceded by a space.

3. Within the PROCEDURE DIVISION, the period will only be used following the paragraph name and following the last statement in the paragraph.

4. The comma and semicolon may be used within COBOL statements to clarify the meaning, but they are ignored by the compiler; that is, they serve merely as documentation. Generally, the style conventions that are used in this book minimize the value of the comma and semicolon. If used, they must be followed by a space or a new line, but not preceded by a space.

Indention Standards in the PROCEDURE DIVISION

In the PROCEDURE DIVISION, the paragraph name *must* begin in Area A and statements *must* be in Area B. This is the only restriction that COBOL places on you. Although a paragraph name may begin in any of the four Area A columns, the standard in this book is to always begin them in column 8. Regarding the statements making up the paragraph, indention within Area B is used to provide good documentation. For example, consider the indention of statements making up the PERFORM loop, repeated here as Figure 2-18(a). Two-position indention of the statements making up the loop clearly indicates where the loop begins and ends. By contrast, the version in Figure 2-18(b) requires that you inspect each line of code to find the END-IF. COBOL indention is commonly based on four columns. However, you will see some programs in this book that use two columns in the PROCEDURE DIVISION because they have many levels of indention.

Uppercase and Lowercase in Programs

One other point about entering the source program relates to case. Here again, the influence of the punched card is evident. That is, card punches—as well as most of the commonly used printers—were capable of printing only uppercase letters. Therefore, virtually all COBOL programs are entered in uppercase—even messages displayed on the screen are in uppercase. With the versatility of modern computers, this limitation no longer exists. COBOL-85 makes no distinction between uppercase and lowercase letters in the source program, so programs can use either. Thus, the following three forms of the PERFORM statement would all be treated identically:

```
PERFORM UNTIL CONTIN = 0
Perform Until Contin = 0
perform until contin = 0
```

Figure 2-18

Indention for Documentation Value

```
DISPLAY " "  ERASE                             DISPLAY " "  ERASE
DISPLAY "Program to add pairs of numbers"      DISPLAY "Program to add pairs of numbers"
PERFORM UNTIL CONTIN = 0                        PERFORM UNTIL CONTIN = 0
  DISPLAY " "                                   DISPLAY " "
  DISPLAY "Please enter the first number"       DISPLAY "Please enter the first number"
  ACCEPT FIRST-NUM                              ACCEPT FIRST-NUM
  DISPLAY "Please enter the second number"      DISPLAY "Please enter the second number"
  ACCEPT SECOND-NUM                             ACCEPT SECOND-NUM
  MOVE FIRST-NUM TO TOTAL                       MOVE FIRST-NUM TO TOTAL
  ADD SECOND-NUM TO TOTAL                       ADD SECOND-NUM TO TOTAL
  DISPLAY "The sum is ", TOTAL                  DISPLAY "The sum is ", TOTAL
  DISPLAY " "                                   DISPLAY " "
  DISPLAY "Enter 1 to repeat, 0 to end"         DISPLAY "Enter 1 to repeat, 0 to end"
  ACCEPT CONTIN                                 ACCEPT CONTIN
END-PERFORM                                     END-PERFORM
DISPLAY "Processing complete"                   DISPLAY "Processing complete"
STOP RUN.                                       STOP RUN.
              (a)                                             (b)
        Good indention.                                 No indention.
```

All program statements in this book use uppercase. However, messages displayed on the screen—as well as data stored in files—are in uppercase *or* lowercase, whichever is appropriate.

Errors and Error Detection

Types of Errors

One important feature of a compiler is its ability to detect certain types of errors. Unfortunately, these errors fall only in the "use of language" area and do not provide a thinking capability for the programmer.

To illustrate, assume that you use a Chinese gardener who speaks no English. You write the weekly gardening instructions in English, and a neighbor translates them into Chinese for the gardener. For the gardener's next visit, you wish to have a particular tree trimmed so you record the instruction, "Trim the tree." Seeing this statement, the translator would recognize that the required tree is not specified and would so indicate on the instruction before returning it to you for correction. Thus, the translator has detected an error and has aided you; the type of error is very important. Here, it is simply a statement that is not completely descriptive of the function to be performed. The translator realized that all of these details must be provided and was capable of detecting such an omission quickly and easily.

Now consider two variations of a different type of error. Assume that you had inadvertently stated "cut down" instead of "trim," and the statement was, "Cut down the third tree from the left." To the translator, this is a clearly defined valid task to be translated into Chinese. Receiving this instruction, the gardener would perform the task and continue on to the next chore, assuming that you knew what you were doing. On the other hand, if it were illegal to cut these trees without a special permit from the city, the gardener, after seeing this instruction, would indicate that an error had been made and would not carry out the instruction. These examples illustrate three basic types of errors commonly encountered in programming:

1. Failure to follow the rules for writing a COBOL program, thereby producing a statement that the compiler will reject.

2. Writing a statement that tells the computer to do an action that it cannot do (even though the statement itself is valid). For instance, assume that a program divides the quantity TOTAL by DATA-COUNT and that the value in DATA-COUNT is 0. Division by 0 is not possible so, even though the statement itself is a valid COBOL statement, its execution under this condition produces an error condition.

3. Making an obvious programming blunder, also called a *logic error*, in which the wrong operation is performed. For example, writing the ADD statement of the ADDER program as the following:

```
SUBTRACT SECOND-NUM FROM TOTAL
```

Compiler-Detected Errors

At the end of Chapter 1, you learned that the compiler produces a *post-compile listing* with the lines numbered for convenient reference. What you did not see was the nature of compiler-detected errors, since the program used had been tested before being loaded onto the disk. Careful program checking before compiling a program is often enough to catch most errors. Remaining errors are found by the compiler. To illustrate this, let's assume that the program of Figure 2-1 contains two errors:

1. The hyphen in WORKING-STORAGE has been omitted.

2. The ACCEPT relating to continuing has been entered as

```
ACCEPT CONT  instead of
```

```
ACCEPT CONTIN
```

The RM/COBOL-85 post-compile listing of Figure 2-19 includes the program, together with appropriate compiler *diagnostic* messages. These messages convey two basic pieces of information to you: the suspected location of the error and the type of error. For instance, following line 5, notice an error message indicating a "DATA DIVISION SYNTAX" error. The dollar sign ($) indicates the word at which the "trouble" starts. The second error (line 29) is identified even more clearly. That is, the $ is positioned at the beginning of the name CONT and the message is "IDENTIFIER UNDEFINED." Remember, all names must be defined in the DATA DIVISION, and this one was not.

In both error examples, the next statement is followed by a compiler message that indicates the position at which the "scan was resumed." This simply means that the position flagged by the $ sign above this announcement is the position at which the compiler could make sense of the program in order to resume the compile process. Some types of errors cause the compiler a great deal of confusion, and additional lines are inadvertently treated as erroneous.

The diagnostic lines include a diagnostic code relating to the type of message. For example, this listing includes the following diagnostic codes:

Diagnostic Following Line	Diagnostic Code
5	E 138
6	I 5
29	E 263
30	I 5

In general, these codes are grouped into three broad categories:

1. *I,* indicating an informational message. The example you see in Figure 2-19 simply tells you where the compiler has resumed the compiling process. These messages do not affect the compiling process.

2. *W,* indicating a warning that the compiler has detected something that was incorrect and has taken action to correct it. Warnings do not interrupt the compiling process, nor do they prevent the program from being executed. However, the programmer should correct the code that caused the warning.

3. *E,* indicating that an error has been detected that could not be corrected by the compiler. Errors do not interrupt the compiling process (except for the statements involved in the error), nor do they prevent the program from being executed. However, it is usually unwise to execute a program with errors because the compiled version of the program will be invalid. All errors should first be corrected before running the program.

Often the brief message included on the diagnostic line is enough to identify the problem for you. However, in some cases a more extensive description is needed. This is the purpose of the diagnostic code number (for instance, 138 following line 5). Appendix G lists diagnostic messages with a more extensive description of each error.

Although the diagnostic message usually tells you where the error is located, this does not always happen. For instance, assume that the data definition statement for CONTIN (in the DATA DIVISION) were entered incorrectly as

```
10 CONT PIC 9 VALUE 1.
```

This is a valid statement and would give no error at all. However, you would find *three* errors in the program because of this error. That is, for both the PERFORM and ACCEPT statements, the name CONTIN would be flagged as being undefined (refer to the post-compile listing segments of Figure 2-20). Thus, *your* error is at one point, but the compiler sees the error as being elsewhere. Note that still another error is introduced. That is, the

Figure 2-19

A Post-Compile Listing with Errors

```
LINE   DEBUG    PG/LN   A...B.......2.........3.........4.........5.........6.........7..ID

  1                      IDENTIFICATION DIVISION.
  2                      PROGRAM-ID. DIAGMSG1.
  3
  4                      DATA DIVISION.
  5                      WORKING STORAGE SECTION.
                           $
*****  1) E 138: DATA DIVISION SYNTAX (SCAN SUPPRESSED)*E*E*E*E*E*E*E*E*E*E*E*E*E*E*E*E
  6                      01  WORK-FIELDS.
                           $
*****  1) I   5: SCAN RESUME *I*I*I*I*I*I*I*I*I*I*I*I*I*I*I*I*I*I*I*I*I*I*I*I*I*I*I*I*I
*****LAST DIAGNOSTIC AT LINE:     5

  7                          10  FIRST-NUM    PICTURE 999.
  8                          10  SECOND-NUM   PICTURE 999.
  9                          10  TOTAL        PICTURE 9999.
 10                          10  CONTIN       PICTURE 9 VALUE 1.
 11
 12                      PROCEDURE DIVISION.
 13
 14    000002            ADDING-PROGRAM.
 15    000005                DISPLAY " "    ERASE
 16    000012                DISPLAY "Program to add pairs of numbers"
 17
 18    000018                PERFORM UNTIL CONTIN = 0
 19                              DISPLAY " "
 20                              DISPLAY "Please enter the first number"
 21                              ACCEPT FIRST-NUM
 22                              DISPLAY "Please enter the second number"
 23                              ACCEPT SECOND-NUM
 24                              MOVE FIRST-NUM TO TOTAL
 25                              ADD SECOND-NUM TO TOTAL
 26                              DISPLAY "The sum is ", TOTAL
 27                              DISPLAY " "
 28                              DISPLAY "Enter 1 to repeat, 0 to end"
 29                              ACCEPT CONT.
                                        $
*****  1) E 263: IDENTIFIER UNDEFINED (SCAN SUPPRESSED)*E*E*E*E*E*E*E*E*E*E*E*E*E*E*E*E
*****LAST DIAGNOSTIC AT LINE:     6

 30                              END-PERFORM
                                   $
*****  1) I   5: SCAN RESUME *I*I*I*I*I*I*I*I*I*I*I*I*I*I*I*I*I*I*I*I*I*I*I*I*I*I*I*I*I
*****LAST DIAGNOSTIC AT LINE:    29

 31
 32    000096                DISPLAY "Processing complete"
 33    000103                STOP RUN.


  2 ERRORS        0 WARNINGS    FOR PROGRAM DIAGMSG1

LAST DIAGNOSTIC AT LINE:   30
```

Callouts in figure:
- This is the beginning of trouble.
- Statement in error.
- Diagnostic codes.
- The compiler "gave up" on the preceding statement and resumed here.
- This identifier has not been defined in the DATA DIVISION.

undefined data-name used in the PERFORM causes that statement to be discarded. Hence, the END-PERFORM is left dangling with no corresponding PERFORM. Making a single correction in the DATA DIVISION (changing CONT to CONTIN) will clear up all three errors.

Such situations are not uncommon. Sometimes it takes a little detective work to find the error. However, the indicated position of the message is the first place to start.

Errors of Logic

Errors of logic are those that you make in analyzing the problem. You have already seen a very simple example in which the two numbers of ADDER were subtracted rather than added. In large programs, these errors become even more significant (and often more subtle). For instance, in a payroll program, the programmer might misinterpret the way in which Social Security withholdings are calculated and do it all wrong. Or, in another instance, the test condition for repeated execution of a PERFORM might be incorrect. In general, if a problem and its solution have been carefully checked at each step along the way, then most errors will be eliminated before the first run.

Unfortunately, the checking effort is not always thorough, and subsequently the program functions improperly. In general, logic errors tend to be very frustrating, partially because there is no single, simple means for detecting them. Very often when a beginning programmer completes a program and obtains results, there is a great sigh of relief that the program works. However, simply because something comes from the computer does not mean that it is correct. For instance, if the ADDER program contained a SUBTRACT statement rather than an ADD, the dialogue might be as shown in Figure 2-21. Needless to say, you might be somewhat embarrassed if you wrote this program for your supervisor and failed to test it. *It is critical to use test data to check every aspect of a program.* For this program, it would be necessary to use test data for checking the following:

1. Values for the two numbers to be entered in order to make certain the arithmetic is performed properly

2. A value of 1 in response to the prompt about repeating the sequence to ensure that the program does indeed repeat

3. A value of 0 in response to the prompt about repeating the sequence to ensure that the program does indeed terminate

In a later chapter, you will learn about the powerful abilities of COBOL that allow you to make decisions. Then programming really gets tough for the careless. With complex programs, you must prepare test data that tests all of the program's possibilities. When things do not go right, you will need to step through the program and carry out each of the operations as the computer would and then check the results. There is no substitute for thorough testing.

Chapter Summary

General

A COBOL program is composed of four divisions. Three divisions are described in this chapter:

IDENTIFICATION DIVISION. Defines the program ID.

DATA DIVISION. Defines names and sizes of all data values to be used in the PROCEDURE DIVISION.

PROCEDURE DIVISION. Consists of statements describing the operations to be carried out when the program is run.

Within the PROCEDURE DIVISION, statements are made up of reserved words and data-names defined in the DATA DIVISION. Each statement in this division describes an action to be taken.

Programmer-selected names must conform to the following rules:

1. Names may contain letters (A-Z), digits (0-9), or hyphens (-). No other characters, *including a blank space*, are allowed.

2. A name may be from 1 to 30 characters long.

3. The hyphen cannot be used as the first or last character in the name.

4. Each name must include at least one letter.

5. A programmer-selected name must not be a COBOL reserved word.

Figure 2-20

An Error "Here" That Gives an Error Message "There"

```
    LINE   DEBUG    PG/LN  A...B......2.........3.........4.........5.........6.........7..ID
      1                    IDENTIFICATION DIVISION.
      2                    PROGRAM-ID. DIAGMSG2.
      3
      4                    DATA DIVISION.
      5                    WORKING-STORAGE SECTION.
      6                    01  WORK-FIELDS.
      7                        10  FIRST-NUM     PICTURE 999.
      8                        10  SECOND-NUM    PICTURE 999.
      9                        10  TOTAL         PICTURE 9999.
     10                        10  CONT          PICTURE 9 VALUE 1.
     11
     12                    PROCEDURE DIVISION.
     13
     14    000002         ADDING-PROGRAM.
     15    000005             DISPLAY " "    ERASE
     16    000012             DISPLAY "Program to add pairs of numbers"
     17
     18    000018             PERFORM UNTIL CONTIN = 0
                                                 $
   *****   1) E 263: IDENTIFIER UNDEFINED (SCAN SUPPRESSED)*E*E*E*E*E*E*E*E*E*E*E*E*E*E*E*E

     19    000021                 DISPLAY " "
                                          $
   *****   1) I   5: SCAN RESUME *I*I*I*I*I*I*I*I*I*I*I*I*I*I*I*I*I*I*I*I*I*I*I*I*I*I*I*I*I*I
   *****LAST DIAGNOSTIC AT LINE:   18

     20    000027                 DISPLAY "Please enter the first number"
     21    000033                 ACCEPT FIRST-NUM
     22    000039                 DISPLAY "Please enter the second number"
     23    000045                 ACCEPT SECOND-NUM
     24    000051                 MOVE FIRST-NUM TO TOTAL
     25    000056                 ADD SECOND-NUM TO TOTAL
     26    000062                 DISPLAY "The sum is ", TOTAL
     27    000073                 DISPLAY " "
     28    000079                 DISPLAY "Enter 1 to repeat, 0 to end"
     29    000085                 ACCEPT CONTIN
                                         $
   *****   1) E 263: IDENTIFIER UNDEFINED (SCAN SUPPRESSED)*E*E*E*E*E*E*E*E*E*E*E*E*E*E*E*E
   *****LAST DIAGNOSTIC AT LINE:   19

     30                         END-PERFORM
                                       $
   *****   1) I   5: SCAN RESUME *I*I*I*I*I*I*I*I*I*I*I*I*I*I*I*I*I*I*I*I*I*I*I*I*I*I*I*I*I*I
   *****   1) E 469: SCOPE TERMINATOR MISMATCH (SCAN SUPPRESSED) *E*E*E*E*E*E*E*E*E*E*E*E*E
   *****LAST DIAGNOSTIC AT LINE:   29

     31
     32    000088                 DISPLAY "Processing complete"
                                          $
   *****   1) I   5: SCAN RESUME *I*I*I*I*I*I*I*I*I*I*I*I*I*I*I*I*I*I*I*I*I*I*I*I*I*I*I*I*I*I
   *****LAST DIAGNOSTIC AT LINE:   30

     33    000095                 STOP RUN.


      3 ERRORS      0 WARNINGS     FOR PROGRAM DIAGMSG2

   LAST DIAGNOSTIC AT LINE:   32
```

No error here. → (pointing to line 10)

CONTIN is not defined, so this entire statement is discarded. (pointing to line 18 PERFORM UNTIL CONTIN = 0)

CONTIN not defined. (pointing to line 29 ACCEPT CONTIN)

The PERFORM was discarded because of an error. Hence, the END-PERFORM has no corresponding PERFORM. (pointing to line 30 END-PERFORM)

Figure 2-21

A Distressing Screen Display

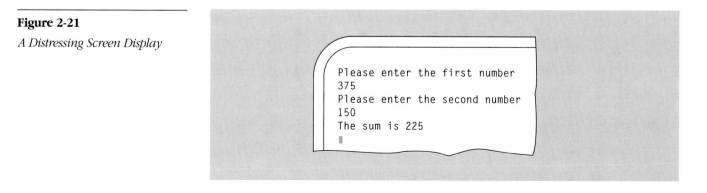

```
Please enter the first number
375
Please enter the second number
150
The sum is 225
```

The COBOL statement line includes two elements: Area A (columns 8-11) and Area B (columns 12-72). The following COBOL entries must begin in Area A; all others studied in this chapter must begin in Area B:

division headers	paragraph names
section names	01 record identifier

COBOL Language Elements

The COBOL statements you have studied in this chapter are

ACCEPT	Allows entry of data into a program through the keyboard
DISPLAY	Displays program literal data on the screen
ADD	Adds one number to another
SUBTRACT	Subtracts one number from another
MULTIPLY	Multiplies one number by another
DIVIDE	Divides one number into another
PERFORM	Provides for the repetitious execution of a sequence of statements
STOP RUN	Terminates execution of a program

Other language elements you have studied in this chapter are

PICTURE clause	Defines the size and type of a data item
VALUE clause	Assigns an initial value to a data item

Programming Conventions

When writing out programs, distinguish between the letters I, O, and Z and the digits 1, 0, and 2.

Select data-names that are meaningful in context. For instance, ACCOUNT-BALANCE would be better documentation than BAL for the balance in a customer account. Of course, always work within the COBOL rules for programmer-selected names.

Use the comma and semicolon sparingly (if at all). They are not necessary in a source program.

Indent Area B entries whenever a line is subordinate to the preceding line. For instance, indent all statements between a PERFORM and the corresponding END-PERFORM. Common COBOL practice is to use a four-space indent. Because COBOL/85 has far more extensive provisions for block structures, you may wish to use a two-space indention in the PROCEDURE DIVISION. Many examples in this book use two spaces.

Error Prevention/Detection

Program errors may be put in two broad categories: compiler-detected and logic. A compiler error results when a statement does not follow the rules of COBOL when preparing the program. A logic error is one in which the programmer simply directs the computer to do the wrong thing; for instance, to add instead of subtract. Logic errors are detected only by carefully checking the results of one or more program runs.

Questions and Exercises

Key Terminology

Give a brief description of each of the following terms that were introduced in this chapter.

Area A	field	reserved word
Area B	indicator area	runtime error
character literal	in-line PERFORM	section
coding form	literal	sentence
data item	logic error	single quote
data-name	numeric literal	statement
diagnostic message	operand	syntax error
division	paragraph	value clause
division header	picture	variable
double quote	post-compile listing	
entry	programmer-selected name	

General Questions

1. What are the three divisions of a COBOL program that you studied in this chapter? How is a division further broken down?

2. Identify each of the following as a reserved word, a valid data-name, or an invalid data-name. If invalid, give the reason.
   a. HOLD
   b. LIMIATX
   c. 123456
   d. RECORD-FIELD
   e. MAXIMUM DIFFERENCE
   f. REPORT#7
   g. LINE
   h. 5457-A-122

3. Considering the definition for the ACCEPT statement in this chapter, will the statement

   ```
   ACCEPT FIRST-NUM, SECOND-NUM
   ```

   accomplish the same thing as the following pair of statements?

   ```
   ACCEPT FIRST-NUM
   ACCEPT SECOND-NUM
   ```

   Explain your answer.

4. Designate whether each of the following begins in Area A or Area B.
   a. ADD WORK-IN, WORK-SAVE GIVING WORK-TOTAL
   b. WORKING-STORAGE SECTION.
   c. 01 entry
   d. Paragraph name
   e. PROCEDURE DIVISION.
   f. 10 entry

5. How is the indicator area on the coding sheet used?

6. What can be safely assumed about the contents of uninitialized data fields?

7. Why is it important to select meaningful data-names for fields?

8. What is an ellipsis and how is it used?

9. List the rules that will be followed in this textbook for using the period in the PROCEDURE DIVISION.

10. In compiler diagnostic messages, what is the difference between a Warning and an Error?

1. What would occur in the ADDER program if the programmer accidentally set the initial value of CONTIN to 0 in the VALUE clause?

2. What would occur in the ADDER program if the programmer accidentally left out the VALUE clause?

3. What would occur in the ADDER program if the person running the program responded to the message, "Enter 1 to repeat, 0 to end," by entering a 3?

4. What would occur in the ADDER program if the programmer omitted the line containing the END-PERFORM?

5. Assume that the MOVE statement of the ADDER program said:

   ```
   MOVE SECOND-NUM TO TOTAL
   ```

   a. What compiler diagnostic message (if any) would occur?
   b. What run-time diagnostic message (if any) would occur?
   c. If the numbers 67 and 3 were entered, what sum would print?

1. Write a DATA DIVISION that includes the following data items; select appropriate data-names:

Data	Length	
Credit limit	4	initial value must be 1500
Charge amount	3	
Monthly deductions	3	
Number of dependents	2	
Maximum transactions	2	initial value must be 25

2. Write one or more DISPLAY statements to do the following:
   a. Print the message

      ```
      SUCCESS IS GREAT
      ```

   b. Print the message

      ```
      The value of Limit is
      ```

      followed by the value stored in the variable LIMIT.

   c. Print the value stored in LIMIT followed by a message, for instance:

      ```
      155 is the value stored in Limit.
      ```

3. Write statements to perform the following:
   a. Add the contents of NUMBER and WORK and put the total in RESULT.
   b. Subtract 100 from the contents of CHARGES.
   c. Multiply the contents of CHECK by TOT and put the result in AMNT.
   d. Increase the value in COUNTER by 1.

4. Write a series of PROCEDURE DIVISION statements to display the numbers from 1 to 10 using a PERFORM UNTIL by displaying the value of the variable COUNTER. Assume that COUNTER has been defined in the DATA DIVISION with an initial value of 1. *Hint:* If, within a loop, you add 1 to a data item, the value of that data item will increase by 1 with each execution of the loop.

5. Identical to number 4, except assume that COUNTER has been given an initial value of zero.

Programming Assignments

2-1 Expand the ADDER Program to Calculate the Difference

Expand the ADDER program to calculate the difference—as well as the sum—of the two numbers entered from the keyboard. Calculate the difference by subtracting the second number from the first number. Test your program with several pairs of numbers to make certain that it works properly. (Note that the difference does not appear as a negative number when the second number is larger than the first. This problem will be addressed in Chapter 5.)

2-2 Expand the ADDER Program to Calculate the Product

Expand the ADDER program to calculate the product—as well as the sum—of the two numbers entered from the keyboard. Test your program with several pairs of numbers, including pairs of large numbers such as 800 and 900, to make certain that it works properly.

2-3 Expand the ADDER Program to Calculate the Quotient

Expand the ADDER program to calculate the quotient—as well as the sum—of the two numbers entered from the keyboard. Calculate the quotient by dividing the first number into the second number. Test your program with several pairs of numbers to make certain that it works properly. (Note that COBOL does not do "calculator arithmetic"; that is, it does not automatically calculate a quotient with a decimal portion. This problem will be addressed in Chapter 5.)

2-4 Write a program that will:

Accept three numbers from the keyboard.
Display their sum.
Repeat these operations until requested to quit.

2-5 Write a program that will:

Accept three numbers from the keyboard.
Calculate the sum of the first two numbers.
Subtract the third number from the sum of the first two.
Display the result.
Repeat these operations until requested to quit.

2-6 Write a program that will:

Accept three numbers from the keyboard.
Calculate the sum of the first two numbers
Multiply the sum by the third number.
Display the result.
Repeat these operations until requested to quit.

2-7 Write a program that will:

Accept three numbers from the keyboard.
Calculate the sum of the first two numbers.
Divide the third number into the sum.
Display the result.
Repeat these operations until requested to quit.

2-8 Calculate Squares of Numbers

This assignment involves a bit more creativity in applying your knowledge from this chapter. The program is to calculate a table of the squares of numbers and display it on the screen. A typical screen display would be as follows:

```
1       01
2       04
3       09
4       16
5       25
```

Here the calculation starts with 1 and proceeds through 5. Note that each number in the second column is simply the square of the number in the first column. The program is to accept the final value from the keyboard and then proceed to calculate and print. (In the foregoing table, the user entered a value 5, and the program would progress from 1 to 5.)

3

SOME BASIC STANDARDS

Outline

- **Program Modularization**
  The Modular Concept
  The Controlling Module
  Implementing Modular Programming Using the PERFORM

- **Representing Program Structure and Logic**
  Program Structure—Hierarchy Charts
  Program Logic—Flowcharts
  Program Logic—Pseudocode
  Numbering Program Modules

- **Scope Terminators in COBOL-85**

- **Standard Format of COBOL Statement General Form**

Chapter Objectives

The purpose of Chapter 2 was to provide enough basic elements of COBOL for you to "get off the ground" by writing some very short, simple programs. Not very much planning is involved with these; you can leap right in and prepare the final program. However, you will soon be working with programs that are long, complex, and involve many different parts. Using a standardized approach will be critical to successfully running them. The purpose of this chapter is to introduce you to some elementary programming style standards. From this chapter, you will learn about the following topics:

- Modularization, whereby a program is broken down into semi-independent segments, each with a defined purpose

- The out-of-line PERFORM statement, allowing you to direct the computer to execute a sequence of statements (a program module) that is physically located elsewhere in the program

- The hierarchy chart, a device for graphically illustrating the structure of a program and the interrelationships among program modules

- The flowchart, a device for graphically illustrating the logic of a program (the sequence in which program modules are executed)

- A module numbering convention that allows for consistent physical placement of modules within a program

- A standardized general form that is used to illustrate the format of COBOL statements

Program Modularization

The Modular Concept

The single program that you have studied thus far is relatively simple and fairly easy to visualize. However, most real-life programs are large, complex, and require many conditional operations; thus, they are very difficult to visualize. The programmer who begins writing code without first carefully analyzing all aspects of the problem will become hopelessly bogged down. Good programmers have long recognized the value of breaking a program into a series of semi-independent components or *modules*. Few programmers can grasp simultaneously all of the intricacies and interrelationships of a large, complex computer program. However, most can deal very competently with a small program or a large program that is broken down into small segments, each of which can be tackled individually. This approach is an essential element of modern programming methods.

To illustrate the technique of modularizing, let's reconsider the ADDER program from Chapter 2. Inspecting the PROCEDURE DIVISION in Figure 3-1, notice that the overall operation can be broken down into three distinct parts, each with a different *function*. The function of the first *module* is to provide general one-time descriptive information to the user. The function of the third module is to terminate operation of the program. The function of the second module, which is repeatedly executed, is to perform the job in which you are interested. As you can see from this example, the second module comprises most of the program. However, the relative sizes of the modules is not important; the important feature is that the program has been broken down into components based on the functions performed. Furthermore, these functions are relatively independent of one another. Now, if this program were much larger and more complex, the entire program might simply be too large and cumbersome to handle. However, by breaking it into three smaller modules, each functionally independent of the other, you could more easily handle each module without confusing details from the others. For a small application on which a single programmer is working, each module could be programmed independently of the others. For a very large system in which many programmers are working, each module might be assigned to a different team of programmers.

Figure 3-1

Program Modules

```
DISPLAY " "    ERASE
DISPLAY "Program to add pairs of numbers"

PERFORM UNTIL CONTIN = 0
  DISPLAY " "
  DISPLAY "Please enter the first number"
  ACCEPT FIRST-NUM
  DISPLAY "Please enter the second number"
  ACCEPT SECOND-NUM
  MOVE FIRST-NUM TO TOTAL
  ADD SECOND-NUM TO TOTAL
  DISPLAY "The sum is ", TOTAL
  DISPLAY " "
  DISPLAY "Enter 1 to repeat, 0 to end"
  ACCEPT CONTIN
END-PERFORM

DISPLAY "Processing complete"
STOP RUN.
```

Figure 3-2

A Block Representation of the Modules of a Program

Announce module	Process module	Terminate module

The Controlling Module

One way of representing the modular structure of a task is by its blocks, as shown in Figure 3-2. Each of these tasks is at the same level; that is, one does not control the other. Now, if a program is written as three independent modules, how are these components put together? One way is to "throw" all of the code together as in Figure 3-1. This might be adequate for the initial design and programming, but it is sorely lacking in the "easily modified" category of a good program. It is far better to use features of the language that allow you to maintain the modular independence of these components. One conceptual way of doing this is to include a controlling module in the program that oversees the actions of the component modules. The sequence of the controlling module's actions are

1.   "Perform" the operations of the Announce module

2.   "Perform" the operations of the Process module

3.   "Perform" the operations of the Terminate module

The relationship between the controlling module and the *subordinate* modules is shown in Figure 3-3.

Figure 3-3

The Concept of a Controlling Module

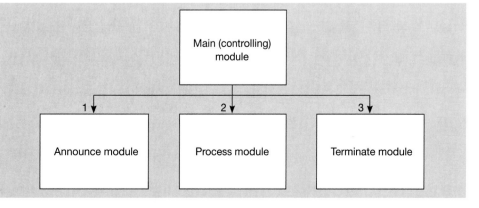

Implementing Modular Programming Using the PERFORM

The question now is, "How do you implement the structure illustrated by the chart of Figure 3-3?" The first step is to define clearly each of the three operational modules shown in Figure 3-1 as a separate paragraph. Then use the following special form of the PERFORM statement:

PERFORM paragraph-name

To illustrate, the PROCEDURE DIVISION of this program has been expanded in Figure 3-4. Note that each of the modules, including the controlling module, is identified as a separate paragraph. This makes possible the use of the alternative form of the PERFORM. The way this version of the PERFORM works is illustrated in Figure 3-5. Note that execution of the PERFORM causes program control to jump elsewhere in the program. When execution of the designated paragraph is complete, control is returned to that portion of the main program from which it left. This version of the PERFORM is commonly referred to as an *out-of-line* PERFORM because the section of code to be performed does not physically follow the PERFORM statement itself. This should be contrasted to the *in-line* form of Chapter 2 in which the code to be repeated immediately follows the PERFORM statement and is terminated by the END-PERFORM. The out-of-line version of this statement provides you with the essential element to use the modularizing techniques so important to good programming practice. Both versions of this statement are valuable in COBOL programming. The in-line PERFORM is new to the COBOL-85 Standard.

Repeated execution of a paragraph is achieved through use of virtually the same form of the PERFORM used in Chapter 2:

PERFORM PROCESS-MODULE UNTIL CONTIN = 0

Here the specified module will be repeatedly executed until the stated condition becomes true. Then, as with the in-line version, execution will continue to the next statement.

Figure 3-4

A Fully Modularized Program

```
PROCEDURE DIVISION.

MAIN-MODULE.
    PERFORM ANNOUNCE-MODULE
    PERFORM PROCESS-MODULE UNTIL CONTIN = 0
    PERFORM TERMINATE-MODULE
    STOP RUN.

ANNOUNCE-MODULE.
    DISPLAY " "   ERASE
    DISPLAY "Program to add pairs of numbers"

PROCESS-MODULE.
    DISPLAY " "
    DISPLAY "Please enter the first number"
    ACCEPT FIRST-NUM
    DISPLAY "Please enter the second number"
    ACCEPT SECOND-NUM
    MOVE FIRST-NUM TO TOTAL
    ADD SECOND-NUM TO TOTAL
    DISPLAY "The sum is ", TOTAL
    DISPLAY " "
    DISPLAY "Enter 1 to repeat, 0 to end"
    ACCEPT CONTIN

TERMINATE-MODULE.
    DISPLAY "Processing complete".
```

Figure 3-5

Execution of the Out-of-Line PERFORM

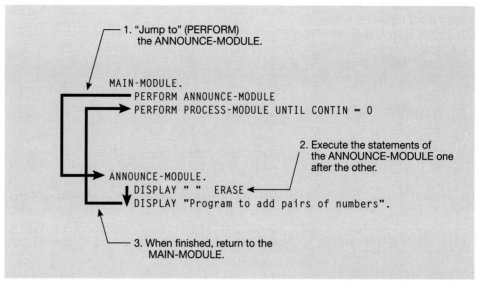

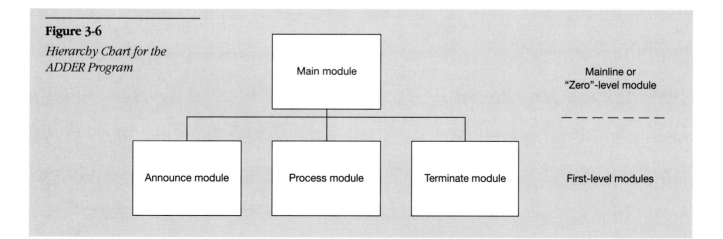

Representing Program Structure and Logic

Program Structure— Hierarchy Charts

The block representation of Figure 3-3 shows the relationship among the four elements of the program and displays their *hierarchy*. That is, three modules are subordinate to a controlling module. In a large, complex program, knowing the hierarchical relationship among elements of the program is so valuable that this block representation has been formalized. The form shown in Figure 3-6 is called a *hierarchy chart* (it is also called a *structure chart*). Here you see two module *levels*. The mainline or program controlling module is commonly referred to as the *zero-level module*. Modules that are subordinate to it are called *first-level modules*. In this case, there are three; most programs you encounter in this book will be designed around three first-level modules. Modules below the first level are termed second level, and so on. It is at the second level that you will begin to see numerous modules in a program structure. Any module that is not further broken down (it appears at the bottom of the chain) will be called a *primitive module*. Hence, in the simple hierarchy chart of Figure 3-6, all three of the first-level modules are primitive modules.

As you will learn in later chapters, a critical element in designing a program is repetitively breaking down large modules to smaller modules. The final result is a set of modules—each of which performs a single basic task and is relatively independent of the others.

Figure 3-6

Hierarchy Chart for the ADDER Program

Program Logic—Flowcharts

A hierarchy chart such as that in Figure 3-6 displays what is to be done and the interrelationship among elements. However, it does not give you an indication of *how* it is to be done. That is, no clue is given regarding the sequence in which the various modules are to be executed—it does not show the program *logic*. Obviously, the fact that the Process Module is executed repeatedly, whereas the Announce and Terminate Modules are executed only once, is a critical feature of this program.

Another commonly used programmer tool is the *flowchart*—a graphical representation of program logic. The program logic of the ADDER program is displayed by the flowchart of Figure 3-7. Here the flow of action is illustrated by arrows. You can see that different symbols are used to display different actions. For example, in (a) the diamond symbol represents a point at which the flow may go in either of two directions. An alternate to this form is shown in (b), where the predefined box is split into an upper half and a lower half. The UNTIL condition defining the condition of repetition (corresponding to the PERFORM-UNTIL statement) is entered above the broken line. The module to be performed is entered below the broken line. To clearly identify the actions, each box is appropriately labelled. As you will see in the next chapter, details of each module will be represented by a separate flowchart.

Program Logic—Pseudocode

Another useful tool for illustrating program logic is *pseudocode*. A pseudocode solution to a programming problem is an English-like description of the program actions. Figure 3-8 is a pseudocode solution for the ADDER program. One advantage of pseudocode over a flowchart is that it is easy to prepare and modify using a word processor. Also, its form is more similar to the actual program's, and some COBOL structures are more accurately illustrated using pseudocode instead of a flowchart. However, in some instances, logic can be better illustrated with a flowchart.

Example programs and programming assignments for the next two chapters will all exhibit the structure and logic illustrated by Figures 3-6, 3-7, and 3-8.

Figure 3-7

Flowchart for the ADDER Program

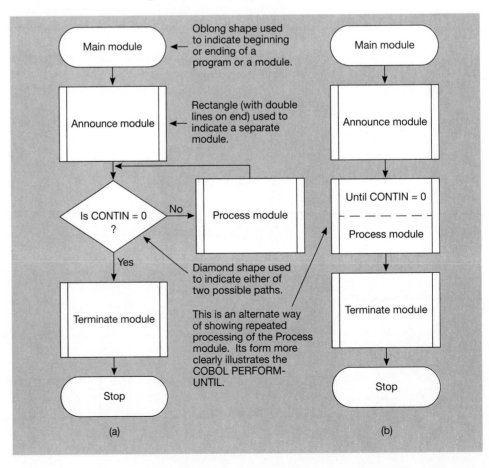

Figure 3-8

Pseudocode for the ADDER Program

```
Main-module
   Perform Announce-module
   Perform Process-module
      until user does not want to continue
   Perform Terminate-module
   Stop.

Announce-module
   Clear screen and display message

Process-module
   Accept two numbers
   Calculate sum
   Display the sum
   Query user about continuing

Terminate-module
   Display termination message
```

Numbering Program Modules

With only three second-level modules in the ADDER program, you can easily see the entire structure and all components of the program at a glance. However, as programs become larger, the number of modules increases. Correspondingly, the source program itself can be many pages in length. Under these circumstances, finding a desired module in a lengthy listing can be difficult unless some type of module identification standard is set up. For this, most COBOL installations use module (paragraph) names that consist of a number and a descriptive name. For instance, in Figure 3-6, the module name 110-Process-Input-Fields might be used instead of Process module. Notice that this module name consists of a number followed by words describing the function of the module.

For consistency within an installation, number ranges are assigned for each general category of activity. For example, a company might require that all error recovery routines be numbered in the 900-949 range. With modules physically located in the source program in numeric order, a particular module will be relatively easy to locate.

The number ranges that you will encounter in the next few chapters' examples are as follows. You will see this numbering convention expanded considerably in Chapter 8.

Number Prefix	Module Activity
000	Main controlling module
100-199	First-level modules
	Initialize actions
	Process
	Finalize actions

Using these standards, the PROCEDURE DIVISION of the ADDER program takes the form of Figure 3-9.

Scope Terminators in COBOL-85

One of the 1985 Standard's significant additions to COBOL involves the ability to define blocks of statements that can be treated as a group (this is aside from the normal paragraph grouping). The in-line PERFORM of Figure 3-10 (the main portion of the ADDER program) illustrates this. You know that the end of this loop is indicated by the END-PERFORM; that is, the END-PERFORM serves as the PERFORM *terminator*. Many other COBOL statements include equivalent terminators to indicate the range or *scope* of statements involved in the action. In general, these are called *scope terminators*. They provide very powerful capabilities for implementing structured techniques in COBOL programs.

Figure 3-9

Module Numbering

```
PROCEDURE DIVISION.

000-ADD-NUMBER-PAIRS.
    PERFORM 100-ANNOUNCE-PROGRAM
    PERFORM 110-PROCESS-USER-ENTRIES UNTIL CONTIN = 0
    PERFORM 120-ANNOUNCE-TERMINATION
    STOP RUN.

100-ANNOUNCE-PROGRAM.
    DISPLAY " "    ERASE
    DISPLAY "Program to add pairs of numbers"

110-PROCESS-USER-ENTRIES.
    DISPLAY " "
    DISPLAY "Please enter the first number"
    ACCEPT FIRST-NUM
    DISPLAY "Please enter the second number"
    ACCEPT SECOND-NUM
    MOVE FIRST-NUM TO TOTAL
    ADD SECOND-NUM TO TOTAL
    DISPLAY "The sum is ", TOTAL
    DISPLAY " "
    DISPLAY "Enter 1 to repeat, 0 to end"
    ACCEPT CONTIN

120-ANNOUNCE-TERMINATION.
    DISPLAY "Processing complete".
```

Figure 3-10

The Concept of Scope

```
PERFORM UNTIL CONTIN = 0
    .
    .
    .
    DISPLAY "Enter 1 to repeat, 0 to end"
    ACCEPT CONTIN
END-PERFORM
```

Standard Format of COBOL Statement General Form

As your study of COBOL progresses, statement forms that you will be using become more complicated and involve a variety of options. Chapter 2 introduced the standard form for representing COBOL statements. The following definitions define the complete set of standards. Within this book, all statement definitions will be correct and completely consistent with standard COBOL usage. However, in the interest of simplicity, many of the formats will illustrate only the basic forms that you will require at the time, rather than all of the options available.

1. Reserved words required in the statement are printed in capital letters and underscored:

    OPEN

2. Reserved words not required in the statement are printed in capital letters but *not* underscored; for instance, in the following clause, GREATER is required, but IS and THAN are optional:

    IS GREATER THAN

3. Names to be supplied by the programmer are indicated in lowercase by the words *data-name* or *paragraph-name* (in Chapter 4, *record-name* and *file-name* are used). The word *identifier* will be used to include the data-name; for example:

   <u>ACCEPT</u> identifier

4. When two or more data-names or identifiers are required in a statement, they will be called *identifier-1, identifier-2,* and so on:

   <u>DIVIDE</u> identifier-1 <u>BY</u> identifier-2

5. When one of two or more choices is required, the choices will be enclosed within braces, one above the other. For instance, the following means that either data-name or literal may be used:

$$\underline{\text{DISPLAY}} \begin{Bmatrix} \text{identifier} \\ \text{literal} \end{Bmatrix}$$

6. Brackets are used to enclose an optional part of a statement. For instance,

   <u>WRITE</u> record-name [<u>FROM</u> data-name]

   can also be used in the following form:

   <u>WRITE</u> record-name

7. Sometimes an optional part of a statement is selected from two or more choices. The choices are placed one above the other within braces. For instance, either HIGH or LOW may be selected or they may both be omitted.

$$\underline{\text{DISPLAY}} \begin{Bmatrix} \text{identifier} \\ \text{literal} \end{Bmatrix} \begin{bmatrix} [\underline{\text{HIGH}}] \\ [\underline{\text{LOW}}] \end{bmatrix}$$

8. Whenever an element may be used one or more times, an ellipsis is used and the optional portion is enclosed within braces, as illustrated by the following example:

$$\underline{\text{DISPLAY}} \begin{Bmatrix} \text{identifier-1} \\ \text{literal-1} \end{Bmatrix} \ldots$$

9. In certain general forms, the term *imperative statement* is encountered. For instance, a simple form of the IF statement is

   <u>IF</u> condition-test
   imperative-statement

Essentially, an imperative statement is any statement, conditional or unconditional, that can be used in the PROCEDURE DIVISION. Furthermore, in the general formats, imperative statement is interpreted to mean one *or more* statements.

However, some exceptions exist: those otherwise unconditional statement formats that allow additional actions to be taken depending on a designated condition. For instance, one form of the ADD statement allows you to add two numbers together with no further action—the action is unconditional. Another format of the ADD specifies an action to be taken *if* the resulting sum is too large for the allocated data area—a conditional action. Technically, the latter is not considered to be an imperative statement.

If you find this confusing at the moment, do not worry because the meaning will become clear as you progress. For now, simply remember where this definition is located (the end of Chapter 3) so that you can refer back later.

Chapter Summary

The purpose of this chapter has been to define some basic ground rules that you can use for preparing programs.

General

Modularization of a program is the breaking down of the program into individual units, each performing a single function.

The out-of-line PERFORM statement gives you the ability to implement modularized programs. Subordinate modules of a program are executed from a controlling module by the PERFORM.

The hierarchy (structure) chart is a graphical means for illustrating the structure of a program and interrelationships between modules.

A flowchart is a graphical means for illustrating the logic of the program. It identifies the sequence in which program modules are executed.

COBOL Statements

Standard format of COBOL general forms:

1. Required reserved words in uppercase and underscored
2. Optional reserved words in uppercase and *not* underscored
3. Programmer-supplied data-names (identifiers) in lowercase
4. Two or more identifiers use *identifier-1, identifier-2,* and so on
5. Two or more required choices enclosed in braces
6. Optional element enclosed in square brackets
7. Two or more optional choices enclosed in brackets
8. Element enclosed in braces followed by ellipsis can be repeated

PERFORM (out-of-line) Provides for the execution of a separate module located out-of-line

PERFORM-UNTIL (out-of-line) Provides for the execution of a separate module located out-of-line until a specified condition becomes true

Programming Conventions

Break program tasks into separate modules, each with a specified single task.

Select paragraph names that describe the function of the module. Number the paragraph names as follows:

Number Prefix	Module Activity
000	Main controlling module
100-199	First-level modules
	Initialize actions
	Process
	Finalize actions

Questions and Exercises

Give a brief description of each of the following terms that were introduced in this chapter.

Key Terminology

controlling module	modularization	scope terminator
flowchart	module	structure chart
hierarchy chart	out-of-line	
in-line	primitive module	

General Questions

1. What is one advantage of using modularization in a large program?
2. What is the difference between a flowchart and a structure chart?
3. When is it necessary to use an END-PERFORM?
4. The following is a limited version of the ADD statement format. Identify the meaning of each component and corresponding symbols with regard to its general form meaning (for example, ADD is a required reserved word):

$$\text{ADD} \left\{ \begin{array}{l} \text{identifier-1} \\ \text{literal-1} \end{array} \right\} \cdots \underline{\text{TO}} \text{ identifier-2 } [\underline{\text{ROUNDED}}][\text{ON } \underline{\text{SIZE}} \ \underline{\text{ERROR}} \text{ statement}]$$

Questions Relating to the Example Program

1. What would occur in the program of Figure 3-9 if the programmer accidentally left out the first PERFORM?

   PERFORM 100-ANNOUNCE-PROGRAM

2. What would occur in the program of Figure 3-9 if the programmer accidentally wrote the first PERFORM as follows?

   PERFORM 100-ANNOUNCE-PROGRAM UNTIL CONTIN = 0

3. While writing a program similar to ADDER, a programmer became confused with the module-numbering convention and mixed up the numbering, as shown in Figure 3-11. Would the program execute properly? Explain why or why not.

Figure 3-11

Confused Module Numbering

```
PROCEDURE DIVISION.

000-ADD-NUMBER-PAIRS.
    PERFORM 100-ANNOUNCE-PROGRAM
    PERFORM 120-PROCESS-USER-ENTRIES UNTIL CONTIN = 0
    PERFORM 110-ANNOUNCE-TERMINATION
    STOP RUN.

100-ANNOUNCE-PROGRAM.
    DISPLAY " "   ERASE
    DISPLAY "Program to add pairs of numbers"

110-ANNOUNCE-TERMINATION.
    DISPLAY "Processing complete".

120-PROCESS-USER-ENTRIES.
    DISPLAY " "
    DISPLAY "Please enter the first number"
    ACCEPT FIRST-NUM
    DISPLAY "Please enter the second number"
    ACCEPT SECOND-NUM
    MOVE FIRST-NUM TO TOTAL
    ADD SECOND-NUM TO TOTAL
    DISPLAY "The sum is ", TOTAL
    DISPLAY " "
    DISPLAY "Enter 1 to repeat, 0 to end"
    ACCEPT CONTIN
```

Writing Program Statements

1. In Chapter 2, "Writing Program Statements," Exercise 4 involves writing an in-line PERFORM to calculate and display the digits from 1 to 10 using the variable COUNTER that has been given an initial value of 1. Write a program segment to do this using an out-of-line PERFORM.

2. In Chapter 2, "Writing Program Statements," Exercise 5 is identical to Exercise 4, except that COUNTER contains an initial value of zero. Write a program segment here that uses an out-of-line PERFORM to calculate and display the same digits when COUNTER begins at zero.

4

CREATING DATA FILES

Outline

- **Data Storage Principles**
  Files, Records, and Fields
  Data Class
  Field Length

- **File Access and Organization**
  Sequential Access
  Random Access
  File Organization

- **Creating a Sequential Disk File**
  Example Definition—Example 4-1
  About Field Characteristics
  Program Structure and Logic—Example 4-1
  A Data Entry Program—Example 4-1

- **The ENVIRONMENT DIVISION**
  CONFIGURATION SECTION of the ENVIRONMENT DIVISION
  INPUT-OUTPUT SECTION of the ENVIRONMENT DIVISION

- **The DATA DIVISION—FILE SECTION**
  The File Description (FD)
  Data Hierarchy and Level Numbers
  The Input Record Description—Example 4-1

- **The PROCEDURE DIVISION of Example 4-1**
  Providing the User with an Option
  Preparing Data Files for Use
  Accepting the Input Data
  The WRITE Statement
  Closing Files
  Interaction with the Computer
  More About Program Logic—Example 4-1

- **Creating an Indexed Disk File**
  Example Definition—Example 4-2
  Changes to the Sequential File Creation Program
  The SELECT Statement
  The INVALID KEY Clause in the WRITE Statement
  User-Entered File Name

Chapter Objectives

As stated in Chapter 1, COBOL is "a language of business programming." Furthermore, processing data files is the cornerstone of the language. Therefore, it is appropriate to continue your study of COBOL with a typical business data processing application that involves creating data files. The focus of this chapter is on creating disk files. You will learn about the following topics:

■ The classification of data as either numeric or alphanumeric

■ The distinction between file organization (the way in which records are stored in a file) and file access (the way in which records are read from a file)

■ Characteristics of sequential and random processing of records in a file

■ Creating a sequential file

■ The ENVIRONMENT DIVISION, which defines the aspects of the program that depend on the characteristics of a specific computer. Includes the SELECT clause, which specifies the nature of a file to be processed and its directory name.

■ The FILE SECTION in the DATA DIVISION, in which the nature of the file and its detailed record format are defined

■ Defining a record and its component fields

■ Creating an indexed file

■ The following PROCEDURE DIVISION statements:
OPEN to make a file ready for use
CLOSE to terminate the use of a file
WRITE to output to a printer (or a file)

Data Storage Principles

Files, Records, and Fields

To illustrate the basic concepts of file processing, let's consider the needs of a typical business. A young programmer has decided to expand her horizons and get into the business of selling computer software by mail order. She forms her own company and names it UNISOFT, Incorporated. With her previous business background, she immediately recognizes the importance of maintaining records. So she creates a file of 3 by 5" cards with one card for each piece of software that she stocks. Figure 4-1 shows a typical card with the following information on it:

■ Stock number

■ Name of software package

■ Vendor (software company that produces the software)

■ Number of software copies currently in stock

■ Reorder level

This illustrates some basic data processing concepts. Notice that there are several items of information for each software package. Furthermore, all of the information for one software package is recorded on one card. The collection of all of the cards represents a complete inventory of all stock handled by the entrepreneur.

Figure 4-1

A Simple Card File

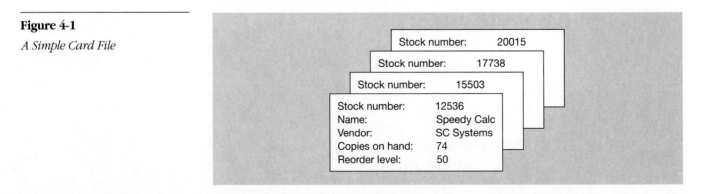

In data processing terms, each card represents a *data record*. Each record is made up of a collection of *data fields:* stock number field, name field, and so on. Finally, the collection of all of the cards is called a *file*. Thus, we have the following set of terms that are used throughout this book:

Field   A basic unit of information such as name, address, stock number, or quantity

Record   A group of related fields treated as a unit

File   The organized collection of all the records of a given type

In Chapter 2, you learned that each data item (field) to be used in a program must be defined in the DATA DIVISION. The defining entry includes two information items (in addition to the field's name): data class and field length.

Data Class

Data class refers to the type of data that is to be stored in a field. The two primary COBOL data classes used in this book are numeric and alphanumeric.

Numeric. Fields defined as numeric can contain only the digits 0 through 9 and, optionally, a sign of - or +. If a field is to be used in arithmetic operations, then it *must* be defined as numeric. You saw in the ADDER program that the data items (for instance, FIRST-NUMBER) were defined with 9 in the PICTURE clauses. The PICTURE character 9 is used to define a field as numeric.

Alphanumeric. Referring to Figure 4-1's record, you see that the Name and Vendor fields contain letters. In general, such fields can also include digits (for instance, one of the software entries shown later is "Ferrari 4-5-6 Financial Acctg.") and special characters such as the hyphen or the period. Basically, alphanumeric fields can contain any characters that can be entered through the keyboard.

COBOL also provides for the alphabetic data class, which restricts the data entered to the letters and the space character. Relatively few applications require a distinction between alphabetic and alphanumeric fields.

Referring to Figure 4-1, notice the first field: Stock number. Should this be treated as a numeric or an alphanumeric field? If all stock numbers are indeed comprised of digits, then it could be defined as a numeric field. If, on the other hand, some stock numbers have a letter suffix (for example, 1554F), then it must be defined as alphanumeric. In most cases, this book defines such "numbers" (those that would be meaningless from an arithmetic point-of-view) as alphanumeric.

Field Length

In the ADDER program, the two input fields (FIRST-NUM and SECOND-NUM) are defined as three positions in length. The field TOTAL (into which the sum was placed) was correspondingly defined as four positions in length to accommodate the maximum-sized result. In COBOL, you must tell the computer how much memory to reserve for every field to be used with a program. For data read from a file, it is critical that each field size specified in the program corresponds to the size of the fields when the file was first created. Most assignments in this book use existing files; your programs will need to conform to the definitions of the file. (Record formats are included in Appendix A.)

File Access and Organization

Broadly speaking, two different ways in which data records in a file are accessed (information is obtained from this file) are sequentially and randomly. To illustrate these methods, let's return to the example of Figure 4-1 and some of the processing activities that must be performed at UNISOFT.

Sequential Access

Periodically, the owner of UNISOFT goes through the entire file from beginning to end (inspecting each record) and generates a report listing all items for which the Copies-on-hand field has fallen below the Reorder-level value; a typical report is shown in Figure 4-2. This activity involves the following actions:

> Repeat the following until there are no more records:
> > Obtain the *next* record
> > Enter a line on the output report if item under-stocked

The most significant element of this processing activity is that records are accessed one after the other as each is encountered in the file. That is, after processing one record, she must get the "next record" in the file—the records are accessed and processed in *sequence*. In data processing terminology, this is called *sequential access* because records are accessed and processed in the sequence in which they are available from the file. Sequential access is illustrated in Figure 4-3.

Notice in the report that the records are listed in order by the Stock-number field. For most sequential processing, records of the file have been placed in some sequence that will be meaningful to the application and/or the report being generated. The record order is often the result of sorting the records for the particular report. (Chapter 15 describes sorting in COBOL.)

Random Access

In contrast to sequential access, in which the next record to be accessed is the next sequential record in the file, other processing needs require that a particular record be made available. For instance, when a customer purchases a software item, the business owner must reduce the Copies-on-hand field for the corresponding record accordingly. This processing activity involves the following actions:

> Identify the record to be processed
> Access the *selected* record from the file
> Update the Copies-on-hand field

This type of activity is called *random access* because records are accessed and processed in random order without regard to their physical positioning in the file.

Figure 4-2

A Report Generated by Sequential Processing

Figure 4-3

Sequential Accessing of Records from a File

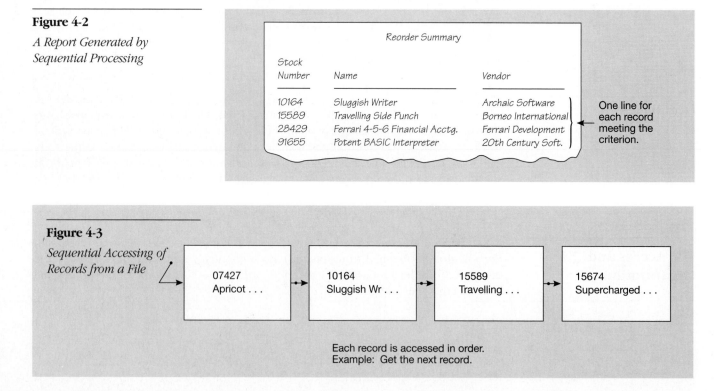

Now the question is "How does she find the selected record?" In this application, two ways are possible. She can search the file from beginning to end (sequential access) looking for the desired number. Or she can make use of the fact that the records are in order by stock number. Then she can flip to the approximate portion of the card file where she would expect to find the desired record. From there, she could move forward or backward in the file, depending upon what she found. (This is similar to using a telephone directory.)

The "key" to accessing this file's data in this way is the stock number field. The ability to access the file randomly revolves around the notion that the record contains a field that uniquely identifies each record of the file. That is, no two records will have the same value for the stock number field. This field is called the *key field*. Random access is illustrated in Figure 4-4.

Summarizing, we work with two *file access* methods (methods for accessing data from files):

Sequential access, in which the next record to be read from the file is the next one available. In programming, it is similar to saying "Give me the next record from the file."

Random access, in which the next record to be read from the file is whatever record is required for the particular application. In programming, it is similar to saying "Give me the record with the following key field value from the file."

File Organization

The simplest way of arranging or organizing records in a file is *sequential organization*. A sequentially organized file contains the data records in a continuous string of data. It includes no information about the file, individual records in the file, or where a given record is located in the file. So that file accessing software will know when it has reached

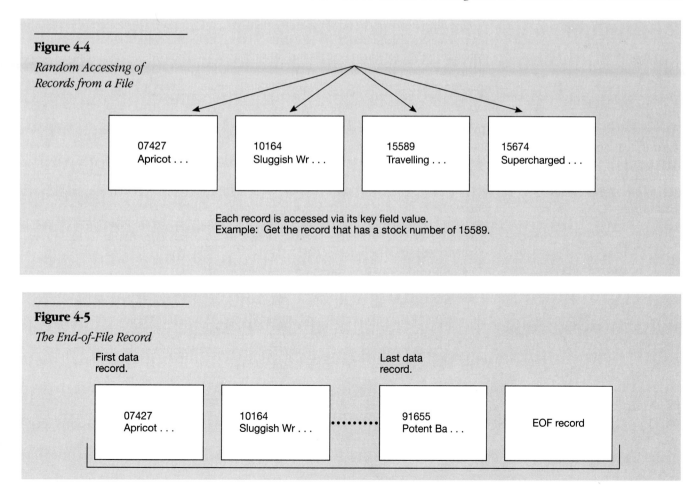

Figure 4-4

Random Accessing of Records from a File

| 07427 Apricot . . . | 10164 Sluggish Wr . . . | 15589 Travelling . . . | 15674 Supercharged . . . |

Each record is accessed via its key field value.
Example: Get the record that has a stock number of 15589.

Figure 4-5

The End-of-File Record

First data record.   Last data record.

| 07427 Apricot . . . | 10164 Sluggish Wr . . . | 91655 Potent Ba . . . | EOF record |

Figure 4-6

Random Accessing of Records from a File Using an Index

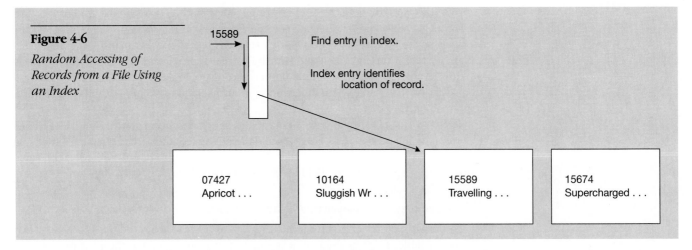

the end of a file, sequential files contain a special end-of-file record that is inserted by the file processing software when the file is created. This is illustrated in Figure 4-5. As you will learn in this chapter, COBOL allows you to test for this record during sequential access.

A sequentially organized file allows for only sequential access. If you require random access capabilities, then another file organization must be used: one that includes information about the records in the file. Several file organization methods provide random accessing capabilities. The most commonly used one is the *indexed file organization*. With the indexed organization, the file management software maintains an index based on the key field. The index is much like the index of the book: it consists of a list of key fields with identifying data regarding the exact location of that record on the computer storage medium. To access a desired record with indexed organization, the programmer need only specify the key field value of the record desired; then the file management software finds the entry in the index, locates the desired record, and makes it available to the program. Use of an index is illustrated in Figure 4-6.

In this chapter, you will see examples of both sequential access and random access using an index. In Chapters 18-20, you will study random access in more detail.

Creating a Sequential Disk File

Example Definition—Example 4-1

To take some of the mystery out of data files and where they originate, let's consider how the software file of Figure 4-1 would be created on disk. You are already familiar with the concept of creating a COBOL program and storing it onto a disk. Recall from Chapter 2 that each COBOL entry is entered according to a predefined format (for instance, certain entries must begin in the Area A of the line). Furthermore, each is entered as a separate line (record). If a data file is to be computerized, then it must be set up for the computer in much the same way. That is, each field of a record must be preassigned to a specific part of the record. With this in mind, let's assist our business friend in setting up a computerized software inventory file.

Example 4-1 Create a Sequential Inventory File
Problem Description
The owner of UNISOFT has decided to use a computer for the storage and processing of inventory and other business data. This will involve designing and creating files for data storage, and entering the data into the files. It will also require designing and programming computers to process the data. This example involves the creation of the inventory file.

Output Requirements
Name of file to be created: SOFTWARE.DL

Record specifications:

Field	Field Length	Data Type
Stock number	5	Alphanumeric
Software name	30	Alphanumeric
Vendor name	20	Alphanumeric
Copies on hand	3	Numeric
Reorder level	3	Numeric
Total record length	61	

Input Description
  Keyboard data entry

Processing Requirements
  Create a file with the format described in "Output Requirements." The data entry program must allow for keyboard data entry record-by-record. It must include the capability for the operator to terminate execution of the program when data entry is complete.

About Field Characteristics

In this problem definition, the size and class of each field is explicitly stated. If you needed to create this file and were not given that information, then before proceeding, you would need to analyze the data with which you would be working. For each field, you would need to decide how much space to reserve. For some of them, the space required is very definite; a Social Security number is such an example (9 digits). For many other fields, it is somewhat arbitrary; the Vendor name field is a good example. The following are typical names that might be encountered:

SC Systems	10-position name
Central View Software	21-position name
Frost-Free Computer Applications	32-position name

This is a substantial range. If a length is selected to accommodate the longest name, then a large amount of file storage area could be wasted, especially if most names are relatively short. If the chosen field length is very short, then resulting name abbreviations might be nearly unintelligible; for instance, a 10-position abbreviation for the above Frost-Free might be *Fr Fr Comp*.

In this example application, a length of 30 was selected—this is a commonly used field length for company names and street addresses. However, notice that the Frost-Free name is longer than the allocated 30 positions. Thus, it will have to be abbreviated to be entered, for instance:

```
Frost-Free Computer Appl.
```

Another point to notice relates to the Stock-*number* field: even though a number, it is defined as alphanumeric. Usually, the only time you define a field as numeric is when it is to be used as a number for an arithmetic or numeric editing operation. Hence, a Discount rate field or a Number of dependents field would certainly be defined as numeric, but an Employee-number field or a Social-Security-number field would be defined as alphanumeric.

Program Structure and Logic—Example 4-1

In basic structure, this data entry program is identical to the ADDER program. That is, it will consist of a controlling module with the following three subordinate modules:

■ An announcement/initialize module

■ A processing module that is repeatedly executed

■ A finalizing module

The structure chart and the flowchart are shown in Figure 4-7.

A Data Entry Program— Example 4-1

The current task is the program that will allow the card information (Figure 4-1) to be entered from the keyboard and stored as a disk file. The program to do this in Figure 4-8 includes the following new concepts:

1. The ENVIRONMENT DIVISION, which defines the aspects of the program that depend on the characteristics of a specific computer

2. A FILE SECTION in the DATA DIVISION, in which the record format is defined

3. Statements in the PROCEDURE DIVISION to use the file

4. Additional options to be used with the SELECT entry

As with all example programs, a copy of SFCREATE is stored on the diskette included with this book. Be aware that if you run this program, it will create a new copy of the data file SOFTWARE.DL, which is also stored on the diskette. Hence, with programs that create files, always be certain that you copy the program to another diskette (or to a hard drive) so that you will not destroy the data files on the original diskette. In general, you should always copy from the distribution diskette—save it as your master diskette.

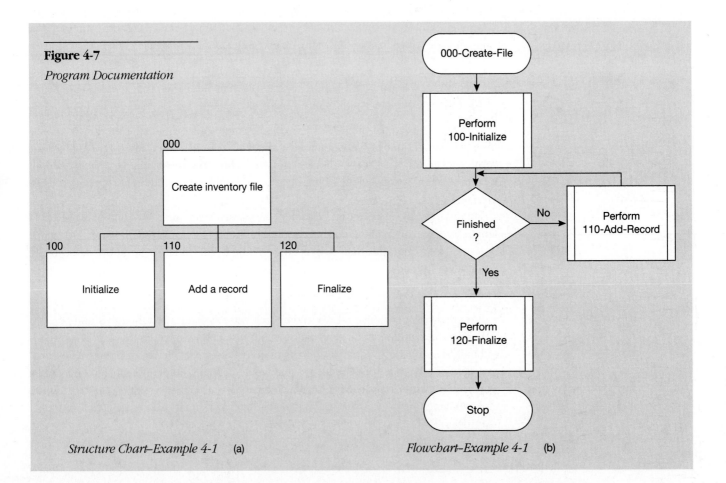

Figure 4-7

Program Documentation

Structure Chart–Example 4-1   (a)

Flowchart–Example 4-1   (b)

Figure 4-8

Program to Build a
Sequential Data File—
Example 4-1

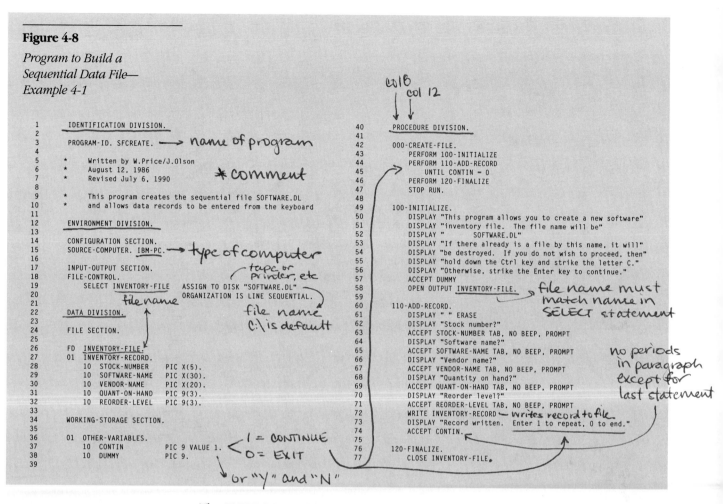

```
1        IDENTIFICATION DIVISION.
2
3        PROGRAM-ID. SFCREATE.            →  name of program
4
5        *    Written by W.Price/J.Olson
6        *    August 12, 1986                * comment
7        *    Revised July 6, 1990
8
9        *    This program creates the sequential file SOFTWARE.DL
10       *    and allows data records to be entered from the keyboard
11
12       ENVIRONMENT DIVISION.
13
14       CONFIGURATION SECTION.
15       SOURCE-COMPUTER. IBM-PC.  →  type of computer
16                                            tape or
17       INPUT-OUTPUT SECTION.                printer, etc
18       FILE-CONTROL.
19           SELECT INVENTORY-FILE   ASSIGN TO DISK "SOFTWARE.DL"
20                                    ORGANIZATION IS LINE SEQUENTIAL.
21               file name                  file name
22       DATA DIVISION.                     C:\ is default
23
24       FILE SECTION.
25
26       FD  INVENTORY-FILE.
27       01  INVENTORY-RECORD.
28           10   STOCK-NUMBER    PIC X(5).
29           10   SOFTWARE-NAME   PIC X(30).
30           10   VENDOR-NAME     PIC X(20).
31           10   QUANT-ON-HAND   PIC 9(3).
32           10   REORDER-LEVEL   PIC 9(3).
33
34       WORKING-STORAGE SECTION.
35
36       01  OTHER-VARIABLES.
37           10   CONTIN    PIC 9 VALUE 1.  < 1 = CONTINUE
38           10   DUMMY     PIC 9.          < 0 = EXIT
39
                                            ↓ or "Y" and "N"
```

```
                                    col 6
                                    │  col 12
                                    ↓  ↓
40       PROCEDURE DIVISION.
41
42       000-CREATE-FILE.
43           PERFORM 100-INITIALIZE
44           PERFORM 110-ADD-RECORD
45               UNTIL CONTIN = 0
46           PERFORM 120-FINALIZE
47           STOP RUN.
48
49       100-INITIALIZE.
50           DISPLAY "This program allows you to create a new software"
51           DISPLAY "inventory file.  The file name will be"
52           DISPLAY "        SOFTWARE.DL"
53           DISPLAY "If there already is a file by this name, it will"
54           DISPLAY "be destroyed.  If you do not wish to proceed, then"
55           DISPLAY "hold down the Ctrl key and strike the letter C."
56           DISPLAY "Otherwise, strike the Enter key to continue."
57           ACCEPT DUMMY
58           OPEN OUTPUT INVENTORY-FILE.    → file name must
59                                             match name in
60       110-ADD-RECORD.                      SELECT statement
61           DISPLAY " " ERASE
62           DISPLAY "Stock number?"
63           ACCEPT STOCK-NUMBER TAB, NO BEEP, PROMPT
64           DISPLAY "Software name?"
65           ACCEPT SOFTWARE-NAME TAB, NO BEEP, PROMPT
66           DISPLAY "Vendor name?"                          no periods
67           ACCEPT VENDOR-NAME TAB, NO BEEP, PROMPT          in paragraph
68           DISPLAY "Quantity on hand?"                      except for
69           ACCEPT QUANT-ON-HAND TAB, NO BEEP, PROMPT        last statement
70           DISPLAY "Reorder level?"
71           ACCEPT REORDER-LEVEL TAB, NO BEEP, PROMPT
72           WRITE INVENTORY-RECORD  → writes record to file
73           DISPLAY "Record written.  Enter 1 to repeat, 0 to end."
74           ACCEPT CONTIN.
75
76       120-FINALIZE.
77           CLOSE INVENTORY-FILE.
```

The ENVIRONMENT DIVISION

CONFIGURATION SECTION of the ENVIRONMENT DIVISION

The ENVIRONMENT DIVISION is the part of the COBOL program used to describe particular characteristics of the computer on which the program is to be run. It was not used in the ADDER program of Chapters 1 and 2 because it was not needed. However, it is required in any program that uses files. As you see by referring to the program of Figure 4-8, this division consists of two sections. The first is the optional CONFIGURATION SECTION:

```
ENVIRONMENT DIVISION.
CONFIGURATION SECTION.
SOURCE-COMPUTER. IBM-PC.
```

The single entry (paragraph) you see here specifies the computer on which the program will be compiled: the IBM Personal Computer in this case. An OBJECT-COMPUTER paragraph can be included if the program on which the computer is to be compiled is different than that upon which it will be executed. However, such a distinction is not necessary with RM/COBOL because of the way in which the overall system is designed.

INPUT-OUTPUT SECTION of the ENVIRONMENT DIVISION

Following the SOURCE-COMPUTER paragraph in Figure 4-8 is the INPUT-OUTPUT SECTION (see Figure 4-9), which is required to inform the system that this program uses one or more files. This section consists of a FILE-CONTROL paragraph, which contains one file-control entry for each file used in the program.

Each file-control entry is made up of a number of clauses that provide the program with information about the file: its name, the type of device on which the file is located, the actual device or file name to be used, and so on. The SELECT clause defines the internal file name (INVENTORY-FILE) that will be used throughout the program to refer to this file. The ASSIGN clause specifies both the type of device (DISK) on which the file is located and the external file name (SOFTWARE.DL) by which this file will be known to DOS. Other clauses that are part of the file-control entry will be introduced throughout the text as they are needed.

You should pay particular attention to two points in the descriptions of Figure 4-9. First, note that the internal and external file names are completely different. This is not surprising when you consider that the internal file name follows the rules of COBOL and the external file name follows the rules of DOS. It is important to remember that these names are *not* interchangeable.

Second, this entry is so long that it must be entered on two lines. The compiler only sees the end of the entry when it encounters a period. In general, long COBOL entries may extend over two or more lines. Notice that this SELECT entry can include several clauses: the SELECT, ASSIGN and ORGANIZATION clauses (technically, the quoted file name also is a separate clause). The standard practice in this book will be to place each clause of a multi-clause entry on a separate line, thereby making the entry easier to read. In that respect, you might use either of the following forms of this file-control entry:

```
SELECT INVENTORY-FILE
   ASSIGN TO DISK "SOFTWARE.DL"
   ORGANIZATION IS LINE SEQUENTIAL.
```

```
SELECT INVENTORY-FILE
   ASSIGN TO DISK
   "SOFTWARE.DL"
   ORGANIZATION IS LINE SEQUENTIAL.
```

The name used within the program for the file is INVENTORY-FILE, as defined in this entry; it is essentially a name that is "internal" to the program. The file reference SOFTWARE.DL identifies the DOS location and name of the file; it is "external" to the program. The ASSIGN TO DISK clause makes the association between the internal name and the external name. Whenever you refer to the INVENTORY-FILE within the program, the COBOL system effectively looks at the SELECT, retrieves the external name, and uses it to communicate with DOS for the input or output operations.

Figure 4-9

Features of the INPUT-OUTPUT SECTION

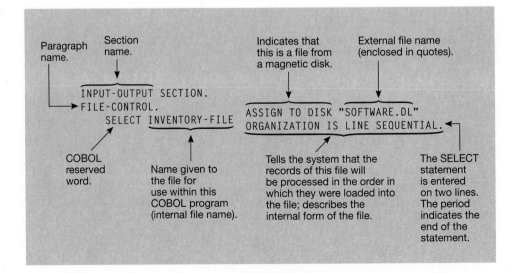

The clause LINE SEQUENTIAL specifies that the file be of a particular type. RM/COBOL-85 provides for two forms of sequential files: BINARY SEQUENTIAL and LINE SEQUENTIAL. Both types are sequential in nature and provide for sequential processing, as described earlier in this chapter. They are identical with respect to the way in which they are handled within the COBOL program. The only difference between the two is the internal coding used by the file processing software to separate one record from the other within the file, a detail with which the COBOL programmer need not be concerned. The value of a file created as LINE SEQUENTIAL is that it will have the same characteristics as a file created with an ordinary line editor. The value of using this form in a textbook is that the files can be displayed line by line on the screen using the DOS TYPE command or printed using the DOS PRINT command. A file created as BINARY SEQUENTIAL does not have this capability. For convenience, LINE SEQUENTIAL is used for all sequential files in this book. LINE SEQUENTIAL is not part of the 1985 COBOL standard, but is a feature commonly found in PC implementations of COBOL (including RM/COBOL).

In the SELECT clause, you see that the name SOFTWARE.DL was selected for the name to be used for this file. The word SOFTWARE was chosen because it is descriptive. The first letter of the extension D was selected to mean *D*ata, indicating a data file. The second letter of the extension L was selected to mean *L*ine sequential, its file type. As a standard in this book, with only a few exceptions, all line sequential files will use the extension DL.

The DATA DIVISION— FILE SECTION

In any COBOL program, you must describe in great detail all of the characteristics of any data set that you want processed. In doing so, you must give a COBOL name to each data set (data file), each broad unit of information (the data record itself), and each field of each record. Furthermore, you must define in detail all the record positions allocated to each field. This is done in the FILE SECTION of the DATA DIVISION.

The File Description (FD)

Referring to the program of Figure 4-8, you see a file description (FD) entry defining the file that you wish to create. Each file used in a program must be defined with its own file description. Later in this chapter, you will study programs that involve two files and, hence, two file descriptions. This FD, illustrated in Figure 4-10, includes the letters FD in Area A followed by the name to be used within the program for the file (INVENTORY-FILE). Note that this is the name used in the SELECT clause of the ENVIRONMENT DIVISION.*

Figure 4-10

Features of the FD

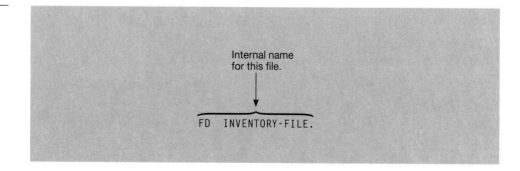

*If you look at programs written for compilers prior to COBOL-85, you will see another clause: LABEL RECORDS ARE STANDARD. This relates to the early days of computing when a variety of methods were used for including data about the file in a label record at the beginning of the file. Because of current standardization, this clause is no longer required.

Data Hierarchy and Level Numbers

The DATA DIVISION of the ADDER program contained the WORKING-STORAGE SECTION, in which work fields were defined under the 01 entry. Data definition in the FILE SECTION is similar in that you are dealing with records that are comprised of fields. In some cases, a given field can be broken down into component parts or "subfields." For instance, consider a record that includes a person's name broken down to last, first, and middle initial, and his or her birthdate broken down to the three two-position fields of month, day, and year. These could be defined as shown in Figure 4-11.

In programming, the terms *data levels* or *data hierarchy* are commonly used. In COBOL, the hierarchy of different levels of quantities is indicated by *level numbers*. The level number 01 is always used to identify a record name, and numbers 02 through 49 are used to identify fields or subfields within the record. In Figure 4-11, the indention clearly indicates the hierarchy of this data; the choice of level numbers indicates the same to COBOL. The record name PERSON-RECORD is identified by the level number 01 and the fields that make up this record by the level number 10. Those fields that consist of component parts are broken down by the level number 20. The convention used in this book is

01	Record level number (required by COBOL)
10	First level for field definition
20	Second level (definition of subfields)
30, 40	Third and fourth levels

In other words, the field level numbers will be incremented by 10. This way, a glance at the first digit tells you the level. It is rare that an application requires more than three sublevels of field breakdown. In such a case, you might want to use increments of 5 rather than 10.

A schematic representation of the record in Figure 4-11 is shown in Figure 4-12.

In COBOL, data elements are commonly referred to as items; more specifically, they can be classified as either *group items* or *elementary items*. A group item is one that is subdivided into smaller items; an elementary item is one that is not further subdivided. Therefore, the record PERSON-RECORD and the fields FULL-NAME and BIRTHDATE are group items. In this example, all of the fields with 20-level numbers (LAST-NAME and so on), and the field STATE-OF-BIRTH are elementary items. (The diagram of Figure 4-12 illustrates this concept.)

By the rules of COBOL, only elementary items may have PICTUREs. You see this in the record description of Figure 4-11. Here the record name (PERSON-RECORD) and the group items (FULL-NAME and BIRTHDATE) do not have PICTUREs associated with them, but the elementary items do.

Figure 4-11

A Record Consisting of Fields and Subfields

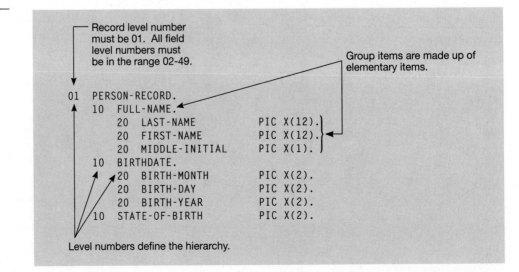

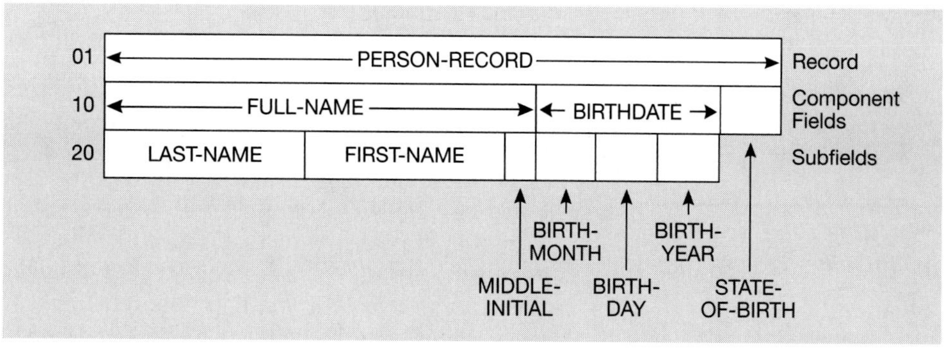

Figure 4-12

Schematic Representation of a Record Consisting of Fields and Subfields

The Input Record Description—Example 4-1

Let's compare the record description from the definition of SOFTWARE-INFO in the DATA DIVISION of Figure 4-8 to the input record format described in the problem definition.

Field	Field Length	COBOL Record Description		Positions
Stock number	5	STOCK-NUMBER	PIC X(5)	1–5
Software name	30	SOFTWARE-NAME	PIC X(30)	6–35
Vendor name	20	VENDOR-NAME	PIC X(20)	36–55
Copies on hand	3	QUANT-ON-HAND	PIC 9(3)	56–58
Reorder level	3	REORDER-LEVEL	PIC 9(3)	59–61

The correspondence of names is readily apparent; for instance, STOCK-NUMBER corresponds to stock number, SOFTWARE-NAME corresponds to the software name, and so on. In other words, each field name is defined—together with a PICTURE indicating the field width—in much the same way as in the WORKING-STORAGE SECTION. You should note two items:

1. Numeric fields are defined with 9's, alphanumeric fields are defined with X's.
2. The field length can be defined with either of the following:

    An X followed by the field length, enclosed in parentheses; for example, the 20-position VENDOR field is indicated by X(20).

    A series of X's equal in number to the field length; for example, the 5-position field STOCK-NUMBER could have been indicated by XXXXX.

As a standard in this book, data items that comprise an input or output record will be defined with the field length enclosed in parentheses. This will simplify the task of adding up the individual field lengths to check the record length. However, as you will see with certain fields (particularly those to be edited), the parentheses form is not always the most convenient.

The PROCEDURE DIVISION of Example 4-1

The overall sequence of events for this program is similar to that of the ADDER program; as would be expected, the detail is different. The following are the actions you will be seeing in this example PROCEDURE DIVISION:

    Initialize module
        Announce the program
        Give user the option to terminate
        Create the new file (it will be empty)

    Process module—repeat until the user wishes to terminate
        Accept input fields from keyboard
        Write the record to the file
        Query the user about continuing

Finalize module
"Close" the newly created file (this will cause the EOF record to be written to the file)

Let's see how these actions are implemented in the PROCEDURE DIVISION.

Providing the User with an Option

Because this program will destroy an existing file (if one exists), the user is warned and told how to abort the program. That is, from the 100-Initialize module, the announcement screen will appear as shown in Figure 4-13. As directed, holding down the Ctrl key and striking the letter *C*—commonly referred to as "Ctrl-C"—will immediately terminate processing and return control to the operating system. (Holding down the Ctrl key and striking the Break key will also terminate processing.) Notice that execution is temporarily halted by the statement:

```
ACCEPT DUMMY
```

Since the ACCEPT requires that a field name be included, the field DUMMY was defined simply for this purpose. Because the field is numeric, striking the Enter key without entering a digit will cause a value of 0 to be placed in DUMMY. However, this makes no difference because DUMMY is not used further.

Actually, terminating a program in this way is not very elegant. It would be better to ask the user if he or she wishes to continue. If the answer is No, then the remainder of the statements could be skipped and execution terminated at the STOP RUN under program control. However, this requires use of the IF statement and some additional logic, a topic covered later in this book.

Preparing Data Files for Use

From Chapter 2, you learned that it is simple to put data into the computer from the keyboard and display results on the screen. As you have learned, the Example 4-1 program defines the record area in memory that will correspond to the form that the data takes on disk. However, any COBOL program that reads or writes disk files must first get the files ready before any reading or writing can take place. This includes telling the computer whether data will be written to a file (output file), as in this example, or read from the file (input file)—as well as performing other "housekeeping" operations. The OPEN statement from line 58 of Figure 4-8 (which is repeated here) performs these functions:

```
OPEN OUTPUT INVENTORY-FILE
```

Figure 4-13

The Announcement Screen Display

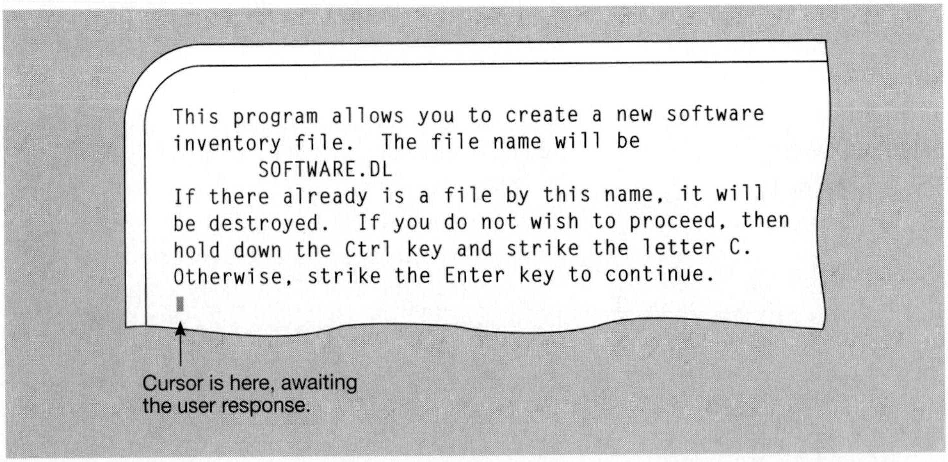

```
This program allows you to create a new software
inventory file.  The file name will be
         SOFTWARE.DL
If there already is a file by this name, it will
be destroyed.  If you do not wish to proceed, then
hold down the Ctrl key and strike the letter C.
Otherwise, strike the Enter key to continue.
```

Cursor is here, awaiting the user response.

Note that the word OPEN is followed by the word OUTPUT, indicating that the file will be used for output. (The next example program includes both input and output files.) Note that the file name used in the OPEN is the internal file name defined in the DATA DIVISION.

The general form of the OPEN for output statement is

OPEN OUTPUT {file-name-1} ...

From this form, you can see that one or more files can be opened for output with a single OPEN statement.

In this book, each file will be opened with a separate OPEN statement. The reason is that if the first file name of a multiple file name list is incorrect (generates an error), the compiler will not check the remaining file names in the list.

Accepting the Input Data

In lines 61 through 71, respective fields of the record are accepted from the keyboard. For instance, at line 63 the stock number is accepted into the field STOCK-NUMBER by the statement:

```
ACCEPT STOCK-NUMBER TAB, NO BEEP, PROMPT
```

You can see that the value from the keyboard is entered directly into the field defined as part of the output record INVENTORY-RECORD. After a value for the last field has been accepted (REORDER-LEVEL), the record can be saved (written) to disk.

The WRITE Statement

To write a record, you simply type WRITE and name the output record; for instance, line 72 of Figure 4-8 is

```
WRITE INVENTORY-RECORD
```

This causes the computer to copy the entire record (as defined in the DATA DIVISION) to disk. Each time the WRITE is executed, a newly written record will immediately follow the last one written.

The general form of the WRITE is

WRITE record-name

It is important to remember that the WRITE statement refers to the record name, not to the file name.

Closing Files

Before terminating processing, you must tell the computer that you are finished with each file that has been opened. This is done with the CLOSE statement in line 77 of Figure 4-8, which is repeated here.

```
CLOSE INVENTORY-FILE
```

When opening files, you must tell the computer whether they are input or output. When closing files, you simply name the files; you do *not* indicate input or output.

The general form of the CLOSE is

CLOSE {file-name-1} ...

Before terminating a program that processes files, the program should close each file that was opened. If this is not done with a file that is being created, then data loss is possible. In any case, it is simply good practice to "clean up" before terminating.

**Interaction with the
Computer**

The first statement of the 110-module is:

DISPLAY " " ERASE

When the ERASE clause is included with an DISPLAY, the entire screen is first erased (cleared), the cursor is positioned at the upper left corner of the screen, and then the specified output is displayed.

The simple program of Chapter 2 used the most basic version of the ACCEPT statement. Three items relating to the way in which the ACCEPT works in this example require further discussion:

1. When asked for your entries, you do not know how long they can be unless this information is included in the descriptive prompt. If the field to be entered is long (such as a software description), then it is difficult to know when the maximum size is about to be reached.

2. If the entry fills all of the positions allocated for the field, the computer accepts the entry without your striking the Enter key. Thus, you do not have the opportunity to check what has been keyed in.

3. The computer beeps with the execution of each ACCEPT; this can be distracting, especially in a room full of people.

The ACCEPT has a variety of options that allow you to control actions such as these; three of them are employed in the program of Figure 4-8. They are illustrated in Figure 4-14. As you see, the additional phrases to control these actions immediately follow the name of the data item.

TAB Forces the computer to await striking of the Return key before progressing, whether the field has been filled or not.

NO BEEP Does exactly as the words say; it restrains the computer from sounding the buzzer when the ACCEPT is executed.

PROMPT Causes a string of underscores (unless another character is explicitly designated) to be displayed on the screen in the positions from which data is to be accepted. For instance, if the software name is to be accepted, then 30 underscores will be displayed—as illustrated in Figure 4-15.

Numerous other options, as well as many other screen capabilities, are described in Chapter 10, "Improving Soft Copy Output and Keyboard Input."

**More About Program
Logic–Example 4-1**

In Figure 4-7, the overall program logic is illustrated by the flowchart. Although this shows the logical relationship between modules, it does not tell you what actions are carried out by each of the modules. Several methods can do this, two of which are detailed flowcharts and pseudocode. Although an in-depth discussion of using these tools in program design is deferred until later chapters, you should become familiar with their rudimentary forms now.

Figure 4-14

*Using Control Clauses in the
ACCEPT Statement*

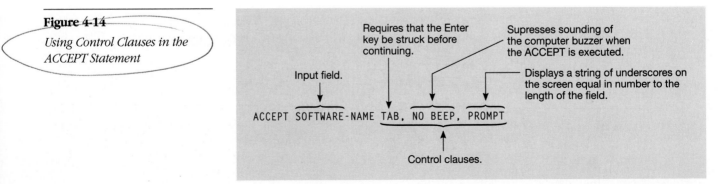

Figure 4-15

*Sample Screen
Display–Example 4-1*

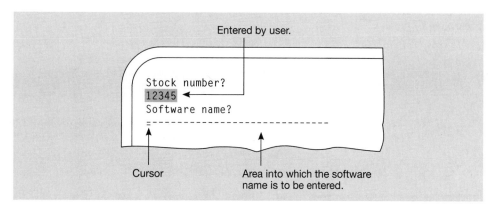

A complete set of flowcharts for this program is shown in Figure 4-16. (Appropriate descriptions of the symbol shape conventions are included.) You can see that the first level depicts the logic of the main module and the second level shows the actions carried out by each of the modules. The equivalent pseudocode solution is shown in Figure 4-17.

Notice that for both the flowchart and pseudocode solutions, line-by-line detail of the program is *not* shown. Instead, groups of actions to be taken are specified. For instance, in the 110-Add-Record module, the action "Accept input fields" is done in the program by a series of 11 statements. In Chapter 8, you will learn more about using structure charts, flowcharts, and pseudocode as tools in planning and designing a program.

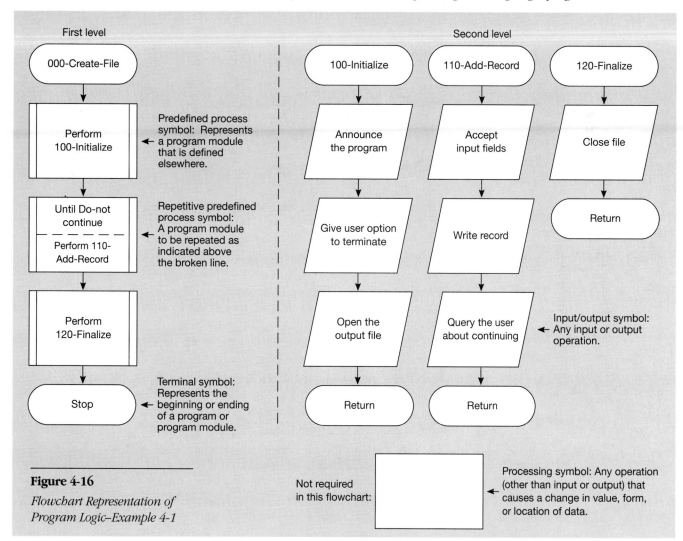

Figure 4-16

*Flowchart Representation of
Program Logic–Example 4-1*

Figure 4-17

*Pseudocode Solution—
Example 4-1.*

```
100-Initialize module
    Announce the program
    Give user the option to terminate
    Open the new file (it will be empty)
110-Add-Record module--repeat until the user wishes to terminate
    Accept input fields from keyboard
    Write the record to the file
    Query the user about continuing
120-Finalize module
    Close the newly created file
```

Creating an Indexed Disk File

As you can see, creating a sequential file by entering data through the keyboard is a relatively easy task. On the other hand, what if you needed to create an indexed file instead? Actually, changes to the program to create a sequential file would be relatively minor. Let's begin with the example definition.

Example Definition— Example 4-2

Example 4-2 Create an Indexed Inventory File

Problem Description

The software file of Example 4-2 is to be used for random processing with the Stock-number field as the key field. Hence, the file must be created as an indexed file.

Output Requirements

Name of file to be created: To be selected when the program is run. Record specifications: Same as those for Example 4-1.

Input Description

Keyboard data entry

Processing Requirements

Create an indexed file with the Stock-number field as the key field. The name to be used for the file is to be entered from the keyboard when the program is run. The data entry program must allow for keyboard data entry record-by-record. It must include the capability for the operator to terminate execution of the program when data entry is complete.

Changes to the Sequential File Creation Program

A major consideration in converting the sequential file creation program to generate an indexed file relates to the key field values. Recall from the earlier discussion of indexed files that the index is based on the key field. In turn, the key field is the field that uniquely identifies records; thus, no two records can have the same key field value. This consideration is reflected in the following changes to the original program:

1. Since COBOL will not allow you to write a record to a file with a key field value the same as another record already in the file, the program must include provisions for this possibility. This is accomplished in the WRITE statement.

2. The SELECT clause, which designates the type of file organization, must be modified to reflect the fact that the file to be created will be indexed.

3. Since the processing requirements of the problem definition specify that the name of the file be entered from the keyboard when the program is run, this must be incorporated into the program.

4. The announcement screen must be modified appropriately.

You should note that only the first two of the preceding changes are necessary to convert the program to one for creating an indexed file.

The complete program is shown in Figure 4-18. Let's consider the differences between this program, IFCREATE (Indexed File Create), and SFCREATE.

Figure 4-18

*Program to Build an
Indexed Data File—
Example 4-2*

```
1          IDENTIFICATION DIVISION.
2
3          PROGRAM-ID. IFCREATE.
4
5      *       Written by W.Price/J.Olson
6      *       July 8, 1990
7
8      *       This program creates an indexed software inventory file
9      *       and allows data records to be entered from the keyboard
10
11         ENVIRONMENT DIVISION.
12
13         CONFIGURATION SECTION.
14         SOURCE-COMPUTER. IBM-PC.
15
16         INPUT-OUTPUT SECTION.
17         FILE-CONTROL.
18             SELECT INVENTORY-FILE    ASSIGN TO DISK NEW-FILE
19                                      ORGANIZATION IS INDEXED
20                                      ACCESS IS RANDOM
21                                      RECORD KEY IS STOCK-NUMBER.
22
23         DATA DIVISION.
24
25         FILE SECTION.
26
27     FD  INVENTORY-FILE.
28     01  INVENTORY-RECORD.
29         10  STOCK-NUMBER     PIC X(5).
30         10  SOFTWARE-NAME    PIC X(30).
31         10  VENDOR-NAME      PIC X(20).
32         10  QUANT-ON-HAND    PIC 9(3).
33         10  REORDER-LEVEL    PIC 9(3).
34
35         WORKING-STORAGE SECTION.
36
37     01  OTHER-VARIABLES.
38         10  CONTIN     PIC 9 VALUE 1.
39         10  DUMMY      PIC 9.
40         10  NEW-FILE   PIC X(12).
41
42         PROCEDURE DIVISION.
43
44         000-CREATE-FILE.
45             PERFORM 100-INITIALIZE
46             PERFORM 110-ADD-RECORD
47                 UNTIL CONTIN = 0
48             PERFORM 120-FINALIZE
49             STOP RUN.
50
51         100-INITIALIZE.
52             DISPLAY " " ERASE
53             DISPLAY "This program allows you to create a new"
54             DISPLAY "software inventory file with an index"
55             DISPLAY "based on the Stock-number field."
56             DISPLAY "You will be allowed to use any file name that"
57             DISPLAY 'you desire.  However, if there is already one'
58             DISPLAY "with the name you select, it will be destroyed."
59             DISPLAY "If you do not wish to proceed, then hold"
60             DISPLAY "down the Ctrl key and strike the letter C."
61             DISPLAY "Otherwise, strike the Enter key to continue."
62             ACCEPT DUMMY
63             DISPLAY "Enter the name and extension of the new file."
64             ACCEPT NEW-FILE    TAB, NO BEEP, PROMPT
65             OPEN OUTPUT INVENTORY-FILE.
66
67         110-ADD-RECORD.
68             DISPLAY " " ERASE
69             DISPLAY "Stock number?"
70             ACCEPT STOCK-NUMBER TAB, NO BEEP, PROMPT
71             DISPLAY "Software name?"
72             ACCEPT SOFTWARE-NAME TAB, NO BEEP, PROMPT
73             DISPLAY "Vendor name?"
74             ACCEPT VENDOR-NAME TAB, NO BEEP, PROMPT
75             DISPLAY "Quantity on hand?"
76             ACCEPT QUANT-ON-HAND TAB, NO BEEP, PROMPT
77             DISPLAY "Reorder level?"
78             ACCEPT REORDER-LEVEL TAB, NO BEEP, PROMPT
79             WRITE INVENTORY-RECORD
80                 INVALID KEY
81                    DISPLAY "Stock number already in file."
82                    DISPLAY "Record not written."
83                 NOT INVALID KEY
84                    DISPLAY "Record written."
85             END-WRITE
86             DISPLAY "Enter 1 to repeat, 0 to end."
87             ACCEPT CONTIN.
88
89         120-FINALIZE.
90             CLOSE INVENTORY-FILE.
```

The SELECT Statement

For the moment, ignore the ASSIGN clause in the SELECT; the other three

```
ORGANIZATION IS INDEXED
ACCESS IS RANDOM
RECORD KEY IS STOCK-NUMBER
```

define the type of file. The two vital pieces of information that COBOL needs to create this indexed file is that 1) its organization is indexed and 2) that the key field is STOCK-NUMBER. As you can imagine, this field must be one of the fields in the record definition.

The third piece of information—that the access is to be random—is not essential to creating the file. If the access is random, then file records can be entered in any order. If access is sequential, then records *must* be entered in sequence by the STOCK-NUMBER field (the record key).

The INVALID KEY Clause in the WRITE Statement

Any inventory item that is about to be written to the file has two possibilities:

A record with that key field in the file already exists—this data will *not* be written.

A record with that key field in the file does *not* exist—this data will be written.

Figure 4-19

*The WRITE Statement and
INVALID-KEY Clause—
Example 4-2*

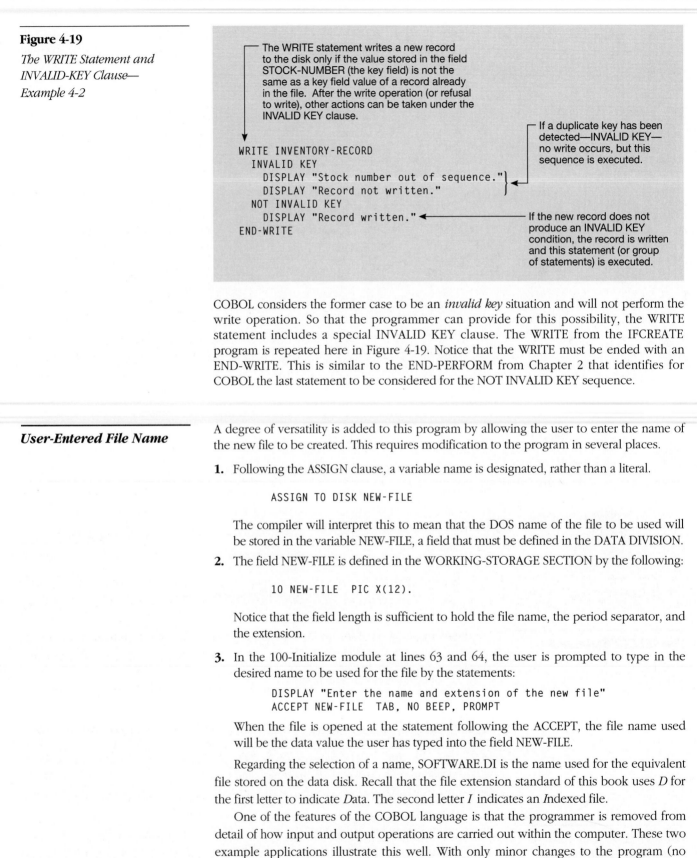

COBOL considers the former case to be an *invalid key* situation and will not perform the write operation. So that the programmer can provide for this possibility, the WRITE statement includes a special INVALID KEY clause. The WRITE from the IFCREATE program is repeated here in Figure 4-19. Notice that the WRITE must be ended with an END-WRITE. This is similar to the END-PERFORM from Chapter 2 that identifies for COBOL the last statement to be considered for the NOT INVALID KEY sequence.

User-Entered File Name

A degree of versatility is added to this program by allowing the user to enter the name of the new file to be created. This requires modification to the program in several places.

1. Following the ASSIGN clause, a variable name is designated, rather than a literal.

   ```
   ASSIGN TO DISK NEW-FILE
   ```

   The compiler will interpret this to mean that the DOS name of the file to be used will be stored in the variable NEW-FILE, a field that must be defined in the DATA DIVISION.

2. The field NEW-FILE is defined in the WORKING-STORAGE SECTION by the following:

   ```
   10 NEW-FILE  PIC X(12).
   ```

   Notice that the field length is sufficient to hold the file name, the period separator, and the extension.

3. In the 100-Initialize module at lines 63 and 64, the user is prompted to type in the desired name to be used for the file by the statements:

   ```
   DISPLAY "Enter the name and extension of the new file"
   ACCEPT NEW-FILE  TAB, NO BEEP, PROMPT
   ```

   When the file is opened at the statement following the ACCEPT, the file name used will be the data value the user has typed into the field NEW-FILE.

Regarding the selection of a name, SOFTWARE.DI is the name used for the equivalent file stored on the data disk. Recall that the file extension standard of this book uses *D* for the first letter to indicate *D*ata. The second letter *I* indicates an *I*ndexed file.

One of the features of the COBOL language is that the programmer is removed from detail of how input and output operations are carried out within the computer. These two example applications illustrate this well. With only minor changes to the program (no change to program logic except for handling duplicate key values), a file with an entirely different organization and accessing capabilities is created. In the next chapter, you will learn how to extract data from these two files.

Chapter Summary
General

You now have the capability to process data stored in disk files. A data file that is totally independent of the program is made available to the program by specifying its nature and name in the SELECT clause of the ENVIRONMENT DIVISION. This, in turn, is linked to the corresponding record defined in the DATA DIVISION.

COBOL Language Elements

The COBOL statements you have studied in this chapter are

OPEN   Identifies a file as either input or output and makes it available for within the program.

OPEN OUTPUT {file-name-1} ...

CLOSE   Terminates the use of a file within a program.

CLOSE {file-name-1} ...

WRITE   Writes a record to the specified file from the record area defined by the FD for that file. The WRITE statement must specify the record name (01) defined under the FD. The INVALID KEY clause may be used to detect a duplicate key value if the file organization is INDEXED.

WRITE record-name

The following clauses can be used with the ACCEPT statement:

NO BEEP   Suppresses the bell when a field is full

PROMPT   Displays underscore characters defining the size of the field to be entered

TAB   Requires that the Enter key be struck before accepting a data entry

Programming Conventions

For all field length definitions within input or output records, use parentheses for field length (for instance, use X(5) rather than XXXXX). This makes it easier to add up individual values to check the record length.

When defining a record in the DATA DIVISION, use a level number of 01 for the record (required by COBOL). Use 10 for the first-level fields, 20 for the second level fields, and so on.

To provide a uniform appearance to programs, use the following line spacing standards:

1. Precede and follow each division header and section header with a blank line

2. Precede FD entries, 01 record descriptions in the WORKING-STORAGE SECTION, and paragraph names with a blank line

3. In the PROCEDURE DIVISION, separate lines of code with a blank line if it improves the documentation

For file names, make selections that describe the data in the file. For the file extension, use D (for *D*ata) as the first letter and L (for *L*ine sequential) or I (for *I*ndexed) as the second letter.

Questions and Exercises

Key Terminology

Give a brief description of each of the following terms that were introduced in this chapter.

access method	file access methods	numeric
alphanumeric	file organization	random access
data class	group item	record
elementary item	indexed file organization	sequential file
external file name	internal file name	organization
FD	key field	sequential access
field	level numbers	
file	line sequential	

General Questions

1. In which division is the SELECT clause found? What is its function?
2. What is the purpose of the OPEN statement?
3. What determines whether a "number field" (stock number, employee number, and so on) should be defined as numeric or alphanumeric?
4. Describe the procedure you would follow if you were required to use sequential access to look up the word *xerophilous* in the dictionary.
5. Should the procedure in Question 4 have specified continuing to search once the desired word was found? Why or why not?

Questions Relating to the Example Programs

1. After scanning through the SFCREATE program, a programmer decides that the field DUMMY is not really required because the field CONTIN can be used in its place. The ACCEPT of line 57 is thus changed to

   ```
   ACCEPT CONTIN
   ```

   Explain what will happen in this case.
2. In both the SFCREATE and IFCREATE programs, the OPEN statement is the last statement in the 100-Initialize module. What do you think would happen if this were made the first statement of the module in both programs?
3. A programmer decided to create an indexed software file using the Vendor-name field as the key field, thereby including the following clause in the SELECT statement of the IFCREATE program. What is wrong with this idea?
4. Assume that the field CONTIN is accidentally given a value of 0 instead of 1 in the program SFCREATE. Would a file be created? Explain your answer.
5. What is the purpose of the NOT INVALID KEY clause in IFCREATE? Would the program function correctly without it?

Writing Program Statements

1. The file STUDENT.DL contains the following information:

Field	Length	Data Type
Student name	23	Alphanumeric
Student phone number	10	Alphanumeric
Tuition amount due	4	Numeric
Major field	12	Alphanumeric
Dormitory name	20	Alphanumeric
Dormitory room number	3	Numeric

   Write the following for this file:
   a. The complete SELECT statement
   b. The complete File Description entry
   c. The complete record description (the record and all fields)

2. Assume that student name is comprised of last name (15) and first name (8). Also, assume that student phone number consists of area code, exchange, and number. Revise your record description in Exercise 1c to describe these subfields.

3. The records in the STUDENT.DL file are to be entered from the keyboard and stored on a sequential disk file. The program is to consist of a controlling module with three subordinate modules.
   a. Write a program segment for the controlling module.
   b. Write a program segment for the announcement/initialize module.
   c. Write a program segment for the processing module that is repeatedly executed in order to enter each record.
   d. Write a program segment for the finalizing module.

4. In Exercises 1, 2, and 3, you have written the major portion of a program. In order to compile the program to create the STUDENT.DL file, there are still some missing statements. Which program statements need to be added?

Programming Assignments

4-1 Creating a Line Sequential Class Enrollment File

Information on class sizes and enrollments is vital to colleges and universities. This information is often maintained in a disk file which can be readily accessed for listings, inquiries, and so on. A disk file of this nature must be created by a program that accepts data for each class from the keyboard and writes that data as a record into the disk file. For this programming assignment, you will create a Line Sequential disk file of class information.

Output Rquirements:
   File name: ENROLL.DL
   Record description (one record for each class):

Record Positions	Field Description
1–3	Actual enrollment
5–26	Course name
28–41	Instructor name
44–46	Course number
47–48	Section number
51–53	Maximum permissible enrollment
54–56	Minimum permissible enrollment
57–60	Class Code (unique for each class)

Input Data:

Actual Enroll	Course Name	Instructor Name	Course Number	Sec Num	Max Enr	Min Enr	Class Code
30	Physical Anthropology	Smith, J.	001	01	75	30	0062
7	Field Work in Anthro.	Bartles, J.	028	01	12	5	0137
52	Accounting Principles	Walters, K.	001	01	50	20	0295
17	Accounting Principles	Boscom, L.	001	02	50	20	0296
20	Financial Accounting I	Krantz, R.	002	03	50	20	0517
20	Financial Accounting I	Robert, P.	002	02	50	20	0516
19	Financial Accounting I	Krantz, R.	002	03	50	20	0517
27	Advanced Financial Acc	Krebbs, R.	003	01	35	20	0683
19	Principles of Auditing	Prior, I.	017	01	30	15	0719
57	Introduct to Computers	Atweiler, B.	001	01	80	35	1010
33	Introduct to Computers	Atweiler, B.	001	02	80	35	1011
86	Introduct to Computers	Nightstalker,P	001	01	80	35	1012
45	COBOL I	Fredrickson,O.	004	01	45	25	1103
25	COBOL I	Parkinson, A.	004	02	45	25	1104
23	COBOL II	Swenson, J.	005	01	40	20	1217
15	Business Appl w/COBOL	Johnson, S.	006	01	15	10	1225
45	Beginning Pascal	Orwell, G.	015	01	50	30	1237
32	Beginning Pascal	Parkinson, A.	015	02	50	30	1238
38	Adv Pascal Programming	Orwell, G.	016	01	40	20	1245
31	Programming in C	Orwell, G.	019	01	40	25	1301
25	Ada for Software Engr.	Swenson, J.	025	01	30	15	1399

Processing Requirements:

Create a Line Sequential file by accepting the previous data from the keyboard and writing one record for each class, using the format defined under "Output requirements."

4-2 Creating an Indexed Class Enrollment File

Same as Programming Assignment 4-1, except that the file to be created is to be an Indexed file rather than a Line Sequential file.

Output Requirements:

File name: ENROLL.DI

Record description: Same as Programming Assignment 4-1.

Input Data:

Same as Programming Assignment 4-1.

Processing Requirements:

Create an Indexed file by accepting the previous data from the keyboard and writing one record for each class, using the format defined under "Output requirements." Specify sequential access. Choose an appropriate field for the record key.

4-3 Creating a Line Sequential Recordings File

In order to function efficiently, a business must keep an accurate record of sales and inventory data so that it can quickly determine which items sell well, make a profit, are available for sale, and so on. For this programming assignment, you are to create a Line Sequential disk file of inventory data for the owner of a music store that sells "oldies-but-goodies" cassette tapes and CDs.

Output Rquirements:

File name: RECORDS.DL

Record description (one record for each inventory item):

Record Positions	Field Description
1–25	Title of tape
26–50	Artist or group
51–56	Medium (CASSET or CD)
57–60	Number on hand at beginning of month
61–64	Number sold this month
65–68	Number received this month
69–72	Number currently on order
73–76	Number currently on hand
77–80	Reorder quantity
81–90	Inventory control number ("bar code")

Input Data:

Title of Tape	Artist or Group	Medium	Beg. On Hand	Number Sold	Number Recvd	On Order	Curr. On Hand	Reorder Quant	Bar Code
Chronicle	Creedence Clearwater Rev.	CASSET	157	203	200	0	154	200	7084925083
The B-52's	The B-52's	CASSET	110	124	100	0	114	150	7094983470
The B-52's	The B-52's	CD	61	98	100	0	137	100	7084936022
Who's Greatest Hits	The Who	CASSET	122	202	200	0	120	150	7084903793
Who's Greatest Hits	The Who	CD	12	211	300	0	101	150	7064525054
Fly Like an Eagle	Steve Miller	CD	57	184	250	250	66	250	7064524064
20 Greatest Hits	The Beatles	CASSET	184	165	0	200	19	200	7084599963
Living Color	Vivid	CASSET	130	120	0	150	10	150	7084576983
Living Color	Vivid	CD	13	79	100	0	166	100	7094458890
Pyromania	Def Leppard	CASSET	171	155	0	150	16	150	7104084179
Blackout	Scorpions	CD	201	127	0	150	74	150	7104020384
Sports	Huey Lewis and the News	CASSET	10	210	200	200	10	200	7104026911
Sports	Huey Lewis and the News	CD	191	101	100	150	1	150	7103997505
Nuclear Furniture	Jefferson Starship	CASSET	130	121	0	150	9	150	7103897670

Processing Requirements:

Create a Line Sequential file by accepting the previous data from the keyboard and writing one record for each inventory item, using the format defined under "Output requirements."

4-4 Creating an Indexed Recordings File

Same as Programming Assignment 4-3, except that the file to be created is to be an Indexed file rather than a Line Sequential file.

Output Rquirements:

File name: RECORDS.DI

Record description: Same as Programming Assignment 4-3.

Input Description:

Same as Programming Assignment 4-3.

Processing Requirements:

Create an Indexed file by accepting the previous data from the keyboard and writing one record for each inventory item, using the format defined under "Output requirements." Specify sequential access. Choose an appropriate field for the record key.

4-5 Creating a Line Sequential Air Traffic File

A large metropolitan airport desires to have traffic statistics to evaluate the adequacy of existing airport facilities and to make future expansion projections. To implement this project, a file of data on airport usage must be created. For this programming assignment, you will create a line sequential disk file that contains one record for each flight into or out of the airport on the preceding day.

Output Requirements:

File name: AIRPORT.DL

Record description (one record for each flight):

Record Positions	Field Description
1–6	Date of flight
7–10	Arrival/departure time
11–23	Origin/destination
24–26	Direction (IN or OUT)
27–30	Flight number
31–34	Airplane type
35–42	Airline
44–46	Runway used
49–52	Flight plan ID
54–60	Pilot's last name
61–63	Total number of seats on airplane
64–66	Actual number of passengers on flight
67–68	Number of crew members
69–73	Baggage weight (kg)
74–79	Meteorological data

Input Data:

Date	Origin/ Time	Destination	Dir.	Flt. Num.	Type	Airline	Run- way	Flt. Plan	Pilot	Seats	Num. Pass	Num. Crew	Baggage Weight	Met. Data
910823	0710	Los Angeles	OUT	15	DC10	United	32L	U305	Strahan	380	375	9	8,250	70849C
910823	0715	Philadelphia	OUT	3	747	TWA	8L	T342	Johnson	452	447	12	9,834	70849C
910823	0723	Orange County	OUT	137A	DC10	Western	16R	W395	Jones	380	380	9	8,360	70949C
910823	0738	New York	IN	2	747	American	15R	A402	Smith	452	450	12	10,037	70849C
910823	0740	Los Angeles	OUT	244	DC10	METRO	32R	W405	Green	380	375	9	8,250	70849C
910823	0810	Boston	OUT	3	747	American	18R	A407	Brown	452	420	12	9,240	70645C
910823	0815	Chicago	IN	18	DC8	United	6R	U416	Stuart	176	176	7	3,999	70645C
910823	0825	Paris/Frankft	OUT	48A	747	Lufthans	11L	I419	Adams	452	430	12	9,769	70845C
910823	0833	Tokyo/Hng Kng	IN	247R	747	JAL	27	I422	Glover	452	422	12	9,588	70845C
910823	0842	Fresno	OUT	3A	F3A	Pacific	11	P425	Jackson	45	37	3	841	70944C
910823	0900	Orange County	IN	522	DC8	Air Cal	16R	C433	Banks	176	97	7	2,203	71040L
910823	0910	New York	OUT	21	747	METRO	15R	U444	Mehan	452	452	12	10,269	71040L
910823	0922	Atlanta	OUT	23	DC10	United	6L	U445	O'Riley	380	307	9	6,975	71040L
910823	0930	San Francisco	IN	258	DC8	Western	17L	W451	Bailey	176	175	7	3,976	71039L
910823	0947	Anchorage	OUT	53	737	Alaskan	21	I472	Thurstn	103	97	6	2,203	71038L
910823	1003	Salt Lake Cty	OUT	31	DC10	United	9L	U495	Walsh	380	322	9	7,315	71038L
910823	1114	Los Angeles	OUT	537	DC8	Air Cal	32L	C513	Moeckel	176	169	7	3,839	71025R
910823	1125	Chicago	OUT	35	DC8	United	6L	U514	Runde	176	163	7	3,703	70925R
910823	1155	Boston	IN	4	737	American	15L	A519	Kingstn	103	98	6	2,226	70925R
910823	1203	New York	OUT	7	727	TWA	15R	T523	Morgan	131	129	6	2,930	70922R
910823	1217	New York	IN	6	747	METRO	15R	A600	Fleming	452	420	12	9,542	70822R
910823	1230	New Orleans	OUT	47	DC10	METRO	34R	U602	Thompsn	380	380	9	8,640	70822R
910823	1300	Philadelphia	IN	14	727	TWA	8L	T604	Lew	131	116	6	2,635	70823R
910823	1345	Dall/Ft Worth	OUT	374B	DC10	Western	22L	W607	Rickovr	380	301	9	6,839	70825R

Processing Requirements:

Create a Line Sequential file by accepting the previous data from the keyboard and writing one record for each flight, using the format defined under "Output requirements."

4-6 Creating an Indexed Air Traffic File

Same as Programming Assignment 4-5, except that the file to be created is to be an Indexed file rather than a Line Sequential file.

Output Requirements:
>   File name: AIRPORT.DI
>   Record description: Same as Programming Assignment 4-5.

Input Description:
>   Same as Programming Assignment 4-5.

Processing Requirements:
>   Create an Indexed file by accepting the previous data from the keyboard and writing one record for each flight, using the format defined under "Output requirements." Specify sequential access. Choose an appropriate field for the record key.

4-7 Creating a Line Sequential Soft Drinks File

Programming Assignment 4-3 described the data requirements of a music store. This assignment describes a different business and a different set of requirements. The subject of this assignment is a soft-drink bottler who wishes to have a file that reflects sales activity for each customer. For this programming assignment, you will create a Line Sequential disk file of sales data for each customer of the soft-drink bottler.

Output Requirements:
>   File name: DRINKS.DL
>   Record description (one record per customer):

Record Positions	Field Description
1–25	Customer name
26–30	Customer account number
31–33	Number of cases of cola sold
34–36	Number of cases of orange drink sold
37–39	Number of cases of root beer sold

Input Data:

Customer Name	Acct. Number	Number of Cases Sold: Cola	Diet	Energy Supplement
Abner's Grocery	00167	15	22	5
Bill's Cash & Carry	00195	53	51	47
Bob & Barry's Deli	00238	5	2	17
C. W. Freeman & Co.	00416	37	39	41
Dalton Brothers	00683	172	167	175
Enormous Supermarket	00777	560	545	637
Ernie's Corner Store	00832	5	1	3
Fresh 'n' Sweet Market	01695	22	21	19
George's Grocery	01937	33	32	31
Hopdale & Winyard, Inc.	02235	387	395	403
Independent Grocers, Inc.	02592	500	500	500
John's Gourmet Foods	03268	2	3	3
Kelly's Bar & Grill	03369	20	21	22
Larry's Midtown Grocery	04951	52	53	49
Morton & Morton	05000	103	102	104
Nellie's Place	06384	14	17	20
Oesler and Frankl	07300	45	40	35
Paul's Place	08311	50	4	2
Queens Grocery	10132	50	50	50
Raul & Renee Inc.	11324	25	26	28

Processing Requirements:

Create a Line Sequential file by accepting the previous data from the keyboard and writing one record for each customer, using the format defined under "Output requirements."

4-8 Creating an Indexed Soft Drinks File

Same as Programming Assignment 4-7, except that the file to be created is to be an Indexed file rather than a Line Sequential file.

Output Requirements:

File name: DRINKS.DI

Record description: Same as Programming Assignment 4-7.

Input Description:

Same as Programming Assignment 4-7.

Processing Requirements:

Create an Indexed file by accepting the previous data from the keyboard and writing one record for each customer, using the format defined under "Output requirements." Specify sequential access. Choose an appropriate field for the record key.

5

ACCESSING DATA FROM FILES

Chapter Objectives

In Chapter 4 you learned how to create data files. Therefore, it is appropriate to continue your study of COBOL with typical business data processing applications that involve accessing and processing data from files. From this chapter, you will learn about the following topics:

■ Detecting when the end of the file has been reached in sequential processing of a file

■ Accessing records sequentially from a sequential file for screen display

■ Accessing records randomly from an indexed file for screen display

■ Accessing records sequentially from a sequential file to create a printed report

■ Initializing an output line

The following COBOL language elements are described in this chapter:

■ READ to read a record from a file

■ MOVE to move information from one place in memory to another

■ AFTER ADVANCING clause in the WRITE to control line spacing

Displaying Records From a Sequential File

Example Definition— Example 5-1

The following example is somewhat contrived, but it introduces basic principles of reading data from a file. Its simplicity should make your first exposure to accessing data from a file easier. You will encounter more realistic—and more difficult—examples later.

Example 5-1 Displaying Records from a Sequential Inventory File

Problem Description

The owner of UNISOFT would like to inspect the quantity on hand value for records in the software file. Output is to be to the screen.

Output Requirements

Fields to be displayed:
Stock number
Software name
Copies on hand

Input Description

Input file name: SOFTWARE.DL

Record format:

Field	Positions	Field Length	Data Type
Stock number	1–5	5	Alphanumeric
Software name	6–35	30	Alphanumeric
Vendor name	36–55	20	Alphanumeric
Copies on hand	56–58	3	Numeric
Reorder quantity	59–61	3	Numeric

Processing Requirements

For each record, display the designated fields on the screen. The user must have the option of either terminating processing or continuing to the next record after each record is displayed. Processing must be terminated when the end of the input data file is encountered.

Detecting When the End of the Data in a File Has Been Reached

The program structure for this example is identical to Chapter 4's example programs. However, there is an important difference in the logic in that records will be read from the file and displayed until no more remain. Remember that repetition of the 110-ADD-RECORD modules of both example programs in Chapter 4 was done by asking the user if another data set was to be entered after writing the preceding record. The operations of the main module were

Perform Initialize module.
Perform Add Records module until a 0 is entered for continue.
Perform Termination module.

The repeated performing of the Add Records module involved the following overall steps:

Repeat the following sequence until a 0 is entered for continue:
Accept the next set of fields.
Write the record.
Accept the continue code.

By contrast, Example 5-1's input record will be read from a data file, placed in memory (essentially the opposite of writing), and processed. This continues until there are no more records. (For the moment, let's ignore the fact that the user must be provided with the option of terminating after any record.) Thus, the process routine will involve the following steps:

Repeat the following sequence until no more records:
Read the next record.
Display the fields.

The question now is, "How does the program know when it has run out of records?" The answer is that it detects the end-of-file (EOF) record at the end of the data file. (The EOF record is described in Chapter 4 and illustrated by Figure 4-5.)

Fortunately, COBOL includes a special capability for detecting this record. Unfortunately, that feature is not too compatible with the foregoing processing approach and modern programming techniques. This problem is illustrated in the flowchart segment of Figure 5-1. It clearly shows that the EOF record will be treated as a data record if the read-process logic is used.

However, the following approach will produce the correct overall result without attempting to process the EOF record as a data record:

Read the first record.
Repeat the following sequence until no more records:
Display the fields.
Read the next record; if no more, then "say so".

The logic of this approach is illustrated in the flowchart of Figure 5-2. Here you see that the test is always made immediately *after* reading a record and *before* processing it. Although this approach might appear to make a very simple operation clumsy, it is quite convenient when implemented in a program. This technique will be employed in the program for Example 5-1 and in most others that follow.

Figure 5-1

*Conventional
Read-Process Logic*

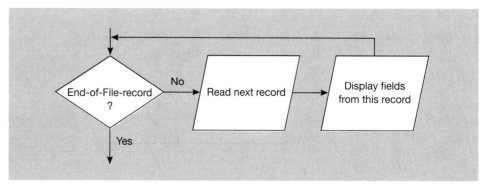

Figure 5-2

Initial Read Followed by
Process-Read Loop

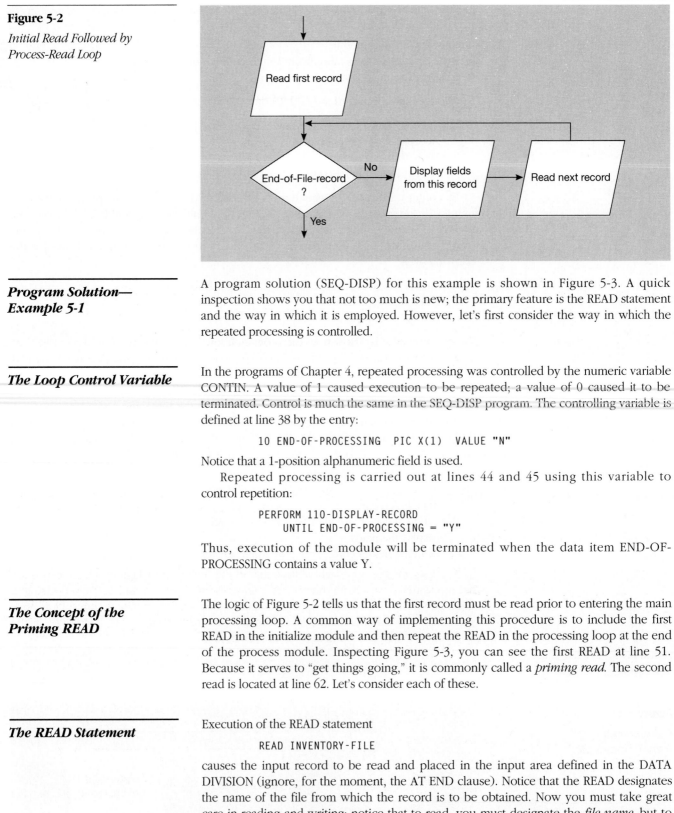

Program Solution—
Example 5-1

A program solution (SEQ-DISP) for this example is shown in Figure 5-3. A quick inspection shows you that not too much is new; the primary feature is the READ statement and the way in which it is employed. However, let's first consider the way in which the repeated processing is controlled.

The Loop Control Variable

In the programs of Chapter 4, repeated processing was controlled by the numeric variable CONTIN. A value of 1 caused execution to be repeated; a value of 0 caused it to be terminated. Control is much the same in the SEQ-DISP program. The controlling variable is defined at line 38 by the entry:

```
10 END-OF-PROCESSING  PIC X(1)  VALUE "N"
```

Notice that a 1-position alphanumeric field is used.

Repeated processing is carried out at lines 44 and 45 using this variable to control repetition:

```
PERFORM 110-DISPLAY-RECORD
    UNTIL END-OF-PROCESSING = "Y"
```

Thus, execution of the module will be terminated when the data item END-OF-PROCESSING contains a value Y.

The Concept of the
Priming READ

The logic of Figure 5-2 tells us that the first record must be read prior to entering the main processing loop. A common way of implementing this procedure is to include the first READ in the initialize module and then repeat the READ in the processing loop at the end of the process module. Inspecting Figure 5-3, you can see the first READ at line 51. Because it serves to "get things going," it is commonly called a *priming read*. The second read is located at line 62. Let's consider each of these.

The READ Statement

Execution of the READ statement

```
READ INVENTORY-FILE
```

causes the input record to be read and placed in the input area defined in the DATA DIVISION (ignore, for the moment, the AT END clause). Notice that the READ designates the name of the file from which the record is to be obtained. Now you must take great care in reading and writing; notice that to read, you must designate the *file name*, but to write, you designate the *record name*. Here is the reason: When you read a record, you *do not necessarily* know what kind of a record you are getting, so you in essence say, "Give me the next record from that file." When you write a record, however, you know exactly what kind of a record you are writing, so you specify the record name. This will become more apparent when you do more sophisticated output in later chapters.

```
 1        IDENTIFICATION DIVISION.                                39
 2                                                                40        PROCEDURE DIVISION.
 3        PROGRAM-ID.    SEQ-DISP.                                41
 4                                                                42        000-DISPLAY-INVENTORY-RECORD.
 5     *       Written by W.Price                                 43            PERFORM 100-INITIALIZE
 6     *       July 11, 1990                                      44            PERFORM 110-DISPLAY-RECORD
 7                                                                45                UNTIL END-OF-PROCESSING = "Y"
 8     *       This program displays records from the sequential  46            PERFORM 120-FINALIZE
 9     *       inventory file.  Following each record display, the 47           STOP RUN.
10     *       user is given the option to display the next record 48
11     *       or to terminate processing.                        49        100-INITIALIZE.
12                                                                 50            OPEN INPUT INVENTORY-FILE
13        ENVIRONMENT DIVISION.                                   51            READ INVENTORY-FILE
14                                                                 52                AT END
15        CONFIGURATION SECTION.                                  53                    MOVE "Y" TO END-OF-PROCESSING
16        SOURCE-COMPUTER.   IBM-PC.                              54            END-READ.
17                                                                 55
18        INPUT-OUTPUT SECTION.                                   56        110-DISPLAY-RECORD.
19        FILE-CONTROL.                                           57            DISPLAY " " ERASE
20            SELECT INVENTORY-FILE ASSIGN TO DISK "SOFTWARE.DL"  58            DISPLAY "Stock Number:      " IR-STOCK-NUMBER
21                            ORGANIZATION IS LINE SEQUENTIAL.    59            DISPLAY "Product Name:      " IR-SOFTWARE-NAME
22                                                                 60            DISPLAY "Quantity on hand: " IR-QUANT-ON-HAND
23        DATA DIVISION.                                          61            DISPLAY " "
24                                                                 62            READ INVENTORY-FILE
25        FILE SECTION.                                           63                AT END
26                                                                 64                DISPLAY "Last record. Strike Enter to terminate."
27        FD  INVENTORY-FILE.                                     65                ACCEPT END-OF-PROCESSING   PROMPT, NO BEEP
28        01  INVENTORY-RECORD.                                   66                MOVE "Y" TO END-OF-PROCESSING
29            10   IR-STOCK-NUMBER     PIC X(5).                  67                NOT AT END
30            10   IR-SOFTWARE-NAME    PIC X(30).                 68                DISPLAY "Do you want to terminate processing?"
31            10   IR-VENDOR-NAME      PIC X(20).                 69                DISPLAY "<Type an upper-case Y or N> "
32            10   IR-QUANT-ON-HAND    PIC 9(3).                  70                ACCEPT END-OF-PROCESSING   PROMPT, NO BEEP
33            10   IR-REORDER-LEVEL    PIC 9(3).                  71            END-READ.
34                                                                 72
35        WORKING-STORAGE SECTION.                                73        120-FINALIZE.
36                                                                 74            CLOSE INVENTORY-FILE.
37        01  PROGRAMMED-SWITCHES.
38            10   END-OF-PROCESSING   PIC X(1)  VALUE "N".
```

Figure 5-3

Program Solution—
Example 5-1

Now let's consider the AT END portion of the READ statement. In COBOL, whenever a READ is executed, the computer performs a special check for the EOF record. Upon detecting it, the computer can take special action. This is illustrated in Figure 5-4 by the READ from Figure 5-3.

The READ operation involves the following:

1. If the record read is a data record, the action is as if the MOVE statement did not exist.

2. If the record read is an EOF record, then nothing is placed in the input record area. Instead, the statement following the AT END is executed, and execution continues to the next statement. In this case, the value "Y" is moved into the variable END-OF-PROCESSING. You will learn more about the MOVE statement later in this chapter.

Figure 5-4

The READ/AT END

```
READ INVENTORY-FILE                              If the EOF record has
  AT END                                         been read (AT END),
      MOVE "Y" TO END-OF-PROCESSING   ◄━━━       then this statement
END-READ.                                        is to be executed.
                                                 Otherwise, it is to be
                                                 ignored.
```

The logic of this action is illustrated in Figure 5-5. Notice that the flowchart symbol used is six-sided. This symbol represents an action taken at one point in a program (line 66 of Figure 5-3, where "Y" is moved to END-OF-PROCESSING) that will modify the path of the program at some later point (the repeated processing at lines 44 and 45). Any data item that controls processing in this way (such as END-OF-PROCESSING) is called a *programmed switch*.

Alternative Actions Following the READ

Remember that in the problem definition, the user must be able to terminate processing after each record is displayed. One way of handling this is to include the NOT AT END option in the READ statement as shown in Figure 5-6 (see lines 62-71 of the program). Here you see that an EOF being read (AT END condition) triggers the MOVE in the same way as the simpler form of Figure 5-4. However, if a data record is read, the NOT AT END sequence is executed and the user is queried. Hence, as stipulated in the processing requirements, execution is terminated either by running out of records or at user request. Logic of this form of the READ is illustrated in Figure 5-7.

You should notice that this form of the READ is identical in structure to the WRITE/INVALID KEY/NOT INVALID KEY statement used in the IFCREATE program of Chapter 4.

The extent to which we will now consider the general form of the sequential READ statement is as follows:

```
READ file-name
  [AT END
    COBOL-statement ...]
  [NOT AT END
    COBOL-statement ...]
  [END-READ]
```

Data-Naming Convention

In Chapter 2, you learned that data-names should be selected so that they describe the data; for instance, for the stock number field, use STOCK-NUMBER rather than cryptic codes such as ST-NO or ST-NUM. This practice is simply good documentation that makes the program easier to understand and maintain. The last example of this chapter uses both

Figure 5-5

Logic of the READ/AT END

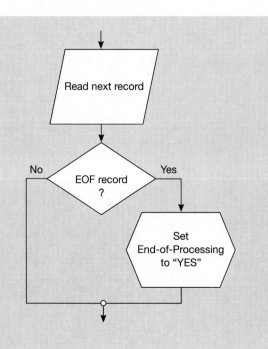

Figure 5-6

*The READ/AT END/
NOT AT END*

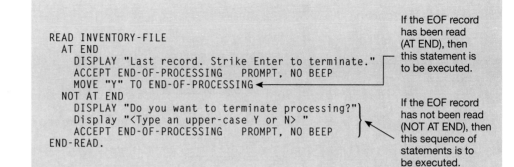

```
READ INVENTORY-FILE
  AT END
    DISPLAY "Last record. Strike Enter to terminate."
    ACCEPT END-OF-PROCESSING    PROMPT, NO BEEP
    MOVE "Y" TO END-OF-PROCESSING
  NOT AT END
    DISPLAY "Do you want to terminate processing?"
    Display "<Type an upper-case Y or N> "
    ACCEPT END-OF-PROCESSING    PROMPT, NO BEEP
END-READ.
```

If the EOF record has been read (AT END), then this statement is to be executed.

If the EOF record has not been read (NOT AT END), then this sequence of statements is to be executed.

Figure 5-7

*Logic of the READ/AT
END/NOT AT END*

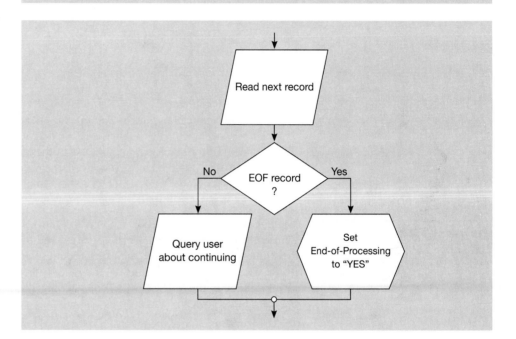

input and output files and, consequently, includes both an input and an output record in the DATA DIVISION. In order to avoid confusion among data-names, a naming convention will be used; it has been incorporated into the SEQ-DISP program and is illustrated by the following excerpt from the DATA DIVISION:

```
FD  INVENTORY-FILE.
01  INVENTORY-RECORD.
    10  IR-STOCK-NUMBER      PIC X(5).
    10  IR-SOFTWARE-NAME     PIC X(30).
    10  IR-VENDOR-NAME       PIC X(20).
    10  IR-QUANT-ON-HAND     PIC 9(3).
    10  IR-REORDER-QUANT     PIC 9(3).
```

The following naming convention is used:

1. The FD entry (file name) and the 01 entry (record name) use the same name suffixed by -FILE and -RECORD, respectively.

2. Each data-name within the record includes a two-letter prefix that is derived from the record name. In this program, IR (for INVENTORY-RECORD) was selected. It could as well have been IN—anything that easily identifies the record containing the field.

Displaying Records From an Indexed File

Example Definition—
Example 5-2

Example 5-1's program serves as a good introduction to accessing data from a file, but it has limited value in a work environment. A more useful tool would be a program that displays a record selected by the user.

Example 5-2 Displaying Records from an Indexed Inventory File

Problem Description

Before placing an order for software, many customers ask if it is in stock. Hence, the person working with the customer must have quick access to individual records in the file. That is, for a selected record, the user would like the program to display its data.

Output Requirements

Fields to be displayed:
Stock number
Software name
Copies on hand

Input Description

Input file name: SOFTWARE.DI
Record format: See Example 5-1

Processing Requirements

This program allows the user to enter the stock number of a selected software item in the inventory. The required data for that item is to be displayed on the screen. If no record for that stock number exists, then an appropriate error message must be displayed. After the data is displayed, the user must be given the option of entering the stock number for another record or terminating processing.

Program Solution—
Example 5-2

Actually, the program solution in Figure 5-8 does not include many features that are different from preceding example programs. The primary difference is the way in which the READ statement functions with indexed files when access is random. The key field—IR-STOCK-NUMBER in this case—is the clue to the way it works. Recall that the record key is defined in the SELECT statement (see line 23); it is how records are accessed from the file. The sequence of actions is as follows:

1. The stock number of the record to be accessed must be placed in the record key field.

2. The statement

```
READ INVENTORY-FILE
```

will cause the record to be read from disk and stored in the input record area for the file.

3. If the record is not found, the INVALID KEY clause is executed; in this case, an error message is displayed.

4. Optionally, a NOT INVALID KEY clause (meaning that the record has been found and read) can be included. In this case, data for the requested record is displayed.

In addition to these features of the READ statement, there are two other notable points regarding this program:

1. The processing loop is controlled by the value in the Stock-number field IR-STOCK-NUMBER. The user may enter the stock number of a desired record or enter a value of 00000 to terminate execution.

2. The user is requested in the 100-INITIALIZE module to enter the stock number for the first time (lines 50 and 51). Subsequently, the request is made at the end of the 110-DISPLAY-RECORD module (lines 68-70). The request at lines 50 and 51 therefore represent a "priming ACCEPT."

Figure 5-8

*Program Solution—
Example 5-2*

```
 1      IDENTIFICATION DIVISION.
 2
 3      PROGRAM-ID.    RAN-DISP.
 4
 5      *     Written by J.Olson
 6      *     July 6, 1990
 7
 8      *     This program displays records from the inventory
 9      *     file as requested by the user. User entry is the
10      *     stock number value of the record desired. Processing
11      *     is terminated by entry of a stock number value 00000.
12
13      ENVIRONMENT DIVISION.
14
15      CONFIGURATION SECTION.
16      SOURCE-COMPUTER.   IBM-PC.
17
18      INPUT-OUTPUT SECTION.
19      FILE-CONTROL.
20          SELECT INVENTORY-FILE   ASSIGN TO DISK "SOFTWARE.DI"
21                                  ORGANIZATION IS INDEXED
22                                  ACCESS IS RANDOM
23                                  RECORD KEY IS IR-STOCK-NUMBER.
24
25      DATA DIVISION.
26
27      FILE SECTION.
28
29      FD  INVENTORY-FILE.
30      01  INVENTORY-RECORD.
31          10  IR-STOCK-NUMBER    PIC X(5).
32          10  IR-SOFTWARE-NAME   PIC X(30).
33          10  IR-VENDOR-NAME     PIC X(20).
34          10  IR-QUANT-ON-HAND   PIC 9(3).
35          10  IR-REORDER-LEVEL   PIC 9(3).
36
37      PROCEDURE DIVISION.
38
39      000-DISPLAY-INVENTORY-RECORDS.
40          PERFORM 100-INITIALIZE
41          PERFORM 110-DISPLAY-RECORD
42              UNTIL IR-STOCK-NUMBER = "00000"
43          PERFORM 120-FINALIZE
44          STOP RUN.
45
46      100-INITIALIZE.
47          OPEN INPUT INVENTORY-FILE
48          MOVE "00000" TO IR-STOCK-NUMBER
49          DISPLAY " " ERASE
50          DISPLAY "Enter the desired stock number"
51          ACCEPT IR-STOCK-NUMBER   TAB, PROMPT, NO BEEP
52          DISPLAY " ".
53
54      110-DISPLAY-RECORD.
55          READ INVENTORY-FILE
56            INVALID KEY
57              DISPLAY "There is no record in the file for ",
58                     IR-STOCK-NUMBER
59            NOT INVALID KEY
60              DISPLAY " " ERASE
61              DISPLAY "Stock Number:     " IR-STOCK-NUMBER
62              DISPLAY "Product Name:     " IR-SOFTWARE-NAME
63              DISPLAY "Quantity on hand: " IR-QUANT-ON-HAND
64          END-READ
65
66          DISPLAY " "
67          DISPLAY " "
68          DISPLAY "To continue, enter the desired stock number."
69          DISPLAY "To exit, enter all zeroes."
70          ACCEPT IR-STOCK-NUMBER   TAB, PROMPT, NO BEEP
71          DISPLAY " ".
72
73      120-FINALIZE.
74          CLOSE INVENTORY-FILE.
```

Generating a Formatted Printing Listing

*Example Definition—
Example 5-3*

If you wanted a hard copy of the SOFTWARE.DL file that was generated by running the Example 4-1 program, you could simply use the DOS PRINT command. This is called a *file dump;* a sample is shown in Figure 5-9. Note that everything is run together, as defined by the record description of the DATA DIVISION. Reading this is probably clumsy to you because the fields are not separated; the last two numeric fields are especially inconvenient. However, the computer has no problem interpreting this because it extracts fields according to the details of the record description. To supplement the inventory system, let's consider another program for giving you a report with the fields spaced out.

Example 5-3 Print a Listing of the Inventory File

Problem Description

In any business environment, a variety of reports are created from data stored in files. Perhaps the most basic report is a file listing—a report that includes one line with all the data from each record of the file.

Output Requirements

A printed report, one line per record, with the fields arranged on the output line (the line is to be *formatted*), as follows:

Field	Print Positions
Stock number	5–9
Vendor name	13–32
Software name	35–64
Reorder level	67–69
Copies on hand	73–75

A printer spacing chart is an alternate form for expressing the report format. The following is its corresponding print chart:

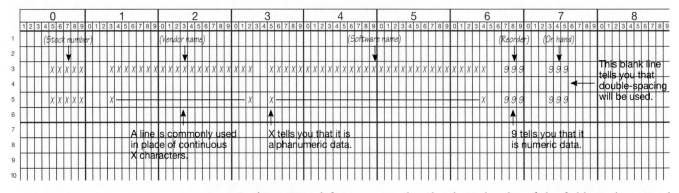

In this output definition, note that the desired order of the fields in the printed listing is not the same as that of the input record.

Input Description

Input file name: SOFTWARE.DL

Record format: See Example 5-1

Processing Requirements

Read and print, in accordance with the printer spacing chart, the contents of each record in the input file. Note in the print chart that the output is to be double-spaced (a blank line between printed lines). Terminate execution of the program when the end-of-file record is encountered.

Figure 5-9

File Dump—SOFTWARE.DL

```
07427Apricot-tree General Ledger    Apricot Software       065065
10164Sluggish Writer                Archaic Software       093100
15589Travelling Side Punch          Borneo International 180200
15674Supercharged Turbo COBOL       Borneo International 120100
28429Ferrari 4-5-6 Financial Acctg. Ferrari Development   144150
28558Orchestra II                   Ferrari Development   102100
32506Bottom View                    Galactic Bus. Mach.   105100
37188UnderWord, Rev 128             International  Soft   090075
37281UnderCalc, Rev 256             International  Soft   080075
37384UnderFile, Rev 64              International  Soft   095075
45191Word Comet 7                   Micro Am              104100
49165Sentence                       Microhard             143125
53351QBase 7000                     MicroPerimeter, Inc. 176150
60544Nobodies Disk Utilities        Nobodies, Unlimited 133100
91655Potent BASIC Interpreter       20th Century Soft.    097100
```

Problem Characteristics

Whenever a data record is read into the computer's memory, it is read exactly as recorded in the input record. Thus, a 61-position record from SOFTWARE.DL is read into 61 consecutive positions within the computer's memory. For your program to have access to individual fields, you must set up an input record definition that corresponds exactly to the record description of the program that created the file (SFCREATE). Similarly, it is necessary to set up a second record definition corresponding to the printed line that is desired. That is, the record description in the program defines the record area in memory. Then the processing becomes

1. Read a record into the input record area

2. Move each field from the input record area to the printer output record area

3. Print the information now in the printer output record area

Figure 5-10

The Read-Move-Print Sequence

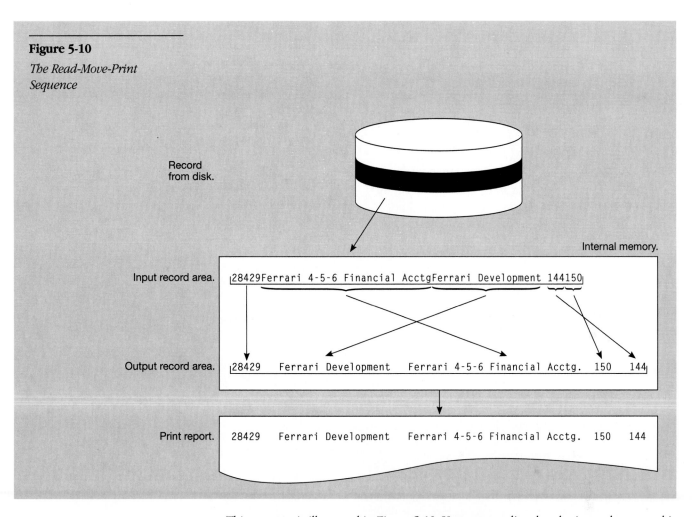

This concept is illustrated in Figure 5-10. You must realize that the input data record is read into memory in the exact format that it is stored on disk. The fields in the input record area are then moved to the output record area: a second memory area that has been set up to correspond exactly to the desired format of the printed line. Printing then consists of duplicating the output record area onto the printed page. The emphasis in the remainder of this chapter will be on defining the output record area and moving the data from the input record area to the output record area.

Flowchart and Pseudocode Solutions— Example 5-3

A full set of flowcharts for this solution is shown in Figure 5-11; a pseudocode solution is shown in Figure 5-12. The logic of this solution is especially significant because it is the basic logic of the example programs for the next two chapters.

Program Solution— Example 5-3

A program to carry out these functions is included in Figure 5-13. Topics to be discussed about this program are

1. The SELECT statement and how to handle printer output
2. Setting up the printer output record
3. Distinguishing between input and output fields
4. Data movement
5. Initializing the output line

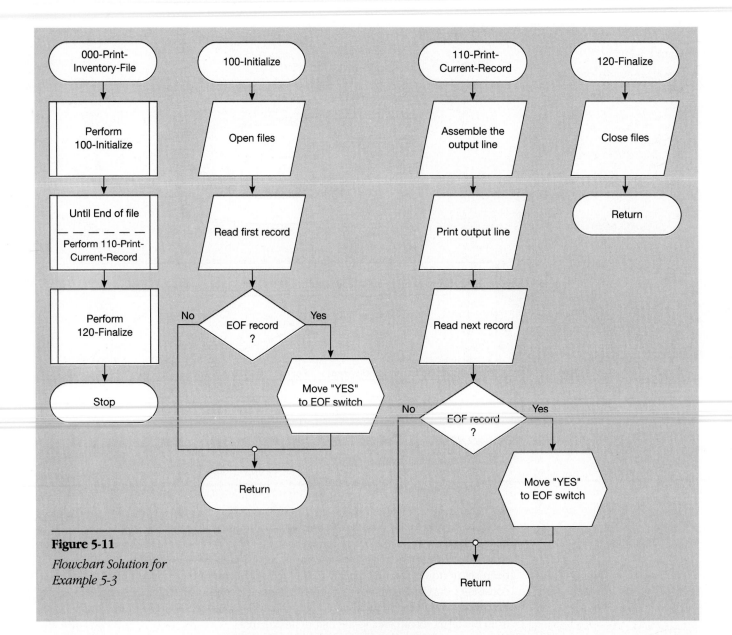

Figure 5-11

Flowchart Solution for Example 5-3

Figure 5-12

Pseudocode Solution for Example 5-3

```
100-Initialize module
    Open data files
    Read first data record
      if EOF move "Y" to EOF switch
110-Print-Current-Record module--repeat until EOF detected
    Assemble output record
    Print output record
    Read next record
      if EOF move "Y" to EOF switch
120-Finalize module
    Close data files
```

Figure 5-13

Program Solution—
Example 5-3

```
1        IDENTIFICATION DIVISION.
2
3        PROGRAM-ID. SEQ-LIST.
4
5     *     Written by W.Price/J.Olson
6     *     August 12, 1986
7     *     Revised July 6, 1990
8
9     *     This program generates a sequential listing of
10    *     the data stored in the file SOFTWARE.DL.
11    *     There is one output line for each record in the file.
12
13       ENVIRONMENT DIVISION.
14
15       CONFIGURATION SECTION.
16       SOURCE-COMPUTER. IBM-PC.
17
18       INPUT-OUTPUT SECTION.
19       FILE-CONTROL.
20          SELECT INVENTORY-FILE    ASSIGN TO DISK "SOFTWARE.DL"
21                                   ORGANIZATION IS LINE SEQUENTIAL.
22          SELECT REPORT-FILE       ASSIGN TO PRINTER "PRN-FILE".
23
24       DATA DIVISION.
25
26       FILE SECTION.
27
28       FD  INVENTORY-FILE.
29       01  INVENTORY-RECORD.
30           10  IR-STOCK-NUMBER     PIC X(5).
31           10  IR-SOFTWARE-NAME    PIC X(30).
32           10  IR-VENDOR-NAME      PIC X(20).
33           10  IR-QUANT-ON-HAND    PIC 9(3).
34           10  IR-REORDER-LEVEL    PIC 9(3).
35
36       FD  REPORT-FILE.
37       01  REPORT-LINE.
38           10  RL-STOCK-NUMBER     PIC X(5).
39           10  FILLER              PIC X(3).
40           10  RL-VENDOR-NAME      PIC X(20).
41           10  FILLER              PIC X(2).
42           10  RL-SOFTWARE-NAME    PIC X(30).
43           10  FILLER              PIC X(2).
44           10  RL-REORDER-LEVEL    PIC 9(3).
45           10  FILLER              PIC X(3).
46           10  RL-QUANT-ON-HAND    PIC 9(3).
47
48       WORKING-STORAGE SECTION.
49
50       01  PROGRAMMED-SWITCHES.
51           10  END-OF-FILE         PIC X(1)  VALUE "N".
52
53       PROCEDURE DIVISION.
54
55       000-PRINT-INVENTORY-FILE.
56           PERFORM 100-INITIALIZE
57           PERFORM 110-PRINT-CURRENT-RECORD
58               UNTIL END-OF-FILE = "Y"
59           PERFORM 120-FINALIZE
60           STOP RUN.
61
62       100-INITIALIZE.
63           OPEN INPUT INVENTORY-FILE
64           OPEN OUTPUT REPORT-FILE
65           READ INVENTORY-FILE
66               AT END MOVE "Y" TO END-OF-FILE
67           END-READ.
68
69       110-PRINT-CURRENT-RECORD.
70           MOVE SPACES TO REPORT-LINE
71           MOVE IR-STOCK-NUMBER TO RL-STOCK-NUMBER
72           MOVE IR-SOFTWARE-NAME TO RL-SOFTWARE-NAME
73           MOVE IR-VENDOR-NAME TO RL-VENDOR-NAME
74           MOVE IR-QUANT-ON-HAND TO RL-QUANT-ON-HAND
75           MOVE IR-REORDER-LEVEL TO RL-REORDER-LEVEL
76           WRITE REPORT-LINE AFTER ADVANCING 2 LINES
77           READ INVENTORY-FILE
78               AT END MOVE "Y" TO END-OF-FILE
79           END-READ.
80
81       120-FINALIZE.
82           CLOSE INVENTORY-FILE
83               REPORT-FILE.
```

The ENVIRONMENT and DATA DIVISIONs— Example 5-3

The Printer SELECT Clause

To a programmer, the word *file* generally refers to a collection of records on magnetic disk or tape. However, in COBOL the word has a broader meaning; for instance, record output to a printer is classified as a file. Hence, you must include entries in both the ENVIRONMENT and DATA DIVISIONs in order to work with a printer *file*. Actually, two approaches can be taken with regard to printer output. One is to send printed output directly to the printer, a practical approach when using a personal computer to which a printer is directly attached. The other (and more commonly used) is to send printed output to a file from which it can be printed later. This is desirable in a variety of situations. All examples in this book will direct the printer output to a file because of the versatility provided through DOS (described in the next section) and through RM/CO*.

Referring to the second SELECT of the program in Figure 5-13 (line 22), you see the following:

```
SELECT REPORT-FILE ASSIGN TO PRINTER "PRN-FILE".
```

Here the internal name REPORT-FILE is assigned to the PRINTER device (as opposed to DISK for INVENTORY-FILE in the first SELECT). The inclusion of the file name PRN-FILE tells the compiler that the printer output is to be written to the file PRN-FILE (which will be newly created). By its very nature, a printer file is sequential (records are printed one after the other), so the ORGANIZATION clause is not used.

If you desire to send the output directly to a printer, then you could use the code name PRN—a special name by which the printer is known to DOS. The SELECT statement would take the following form:

```
SELECT REPORT-FILE  ASSIGN TO PRINTER "PRN".
```

Writing Printer Output to a File

During program testing, it is sometimes convenient to have the output displayed on the screen rather than printed. There are two ways of doing this: one is to make appropriate changes in the program, and the other is to take advantage of special DOS features. The former is clumsy because each time a change is made to a program, it must be recompiled. Assume that you include the following SELECT in our program:

```
SELECT REPORT-FILE  ASSIGN TO PRINTER "PRN-FILE".
```

This will cause your output to be sent to the disk file PRN-FILE, rather than to the printer (not exactly the result you desire).

However, displaying the output on the screen or directing it to a printer is a simple matter. If you are using RM/CO*, then you should read the appropriate section of Appendix C. Virtually all of the functions that you might wish to perform in conjunction with your files can be done under the umbrella of RM/CO*. If you are not using RM/CO*, you must use the techniques described in the following section.

Redirecting Printer Output for Nonusers of RM/CO*

Fortunately, DOS allows you to redirect output by using a special command called SET. With this, you can effectively tell DOS to "send the output originally intended for the file PRN-FILE to the printer instead." The form of the command to do this is

```
SET PRN-FILE=PRN
```

Notice that the name of the file is on the left of the equals sign, and the output device is on the right. Note also that *this is a DOS command and must be entered prior to running the program.* However, you should recognize that the redirection remains in effect until changed.

On the other hand, you might want to redirect your output to the screen during the program testing phase. To do this, you need only enter the following SET command:

```
SET PRN-FILE=CON
```

The abbreviation CON means "console."

The final bit of versatility to this method is that by disabling the SET, the program will send the printed output to the named disk file (PRN-FILE in this case). This is done by the following form of the SET:

```
SET PRN-FILE=
```

At any time, you can issue a SET command and change the redirection; however, it must be done from the DOS prompt. If you are working in RM/CO*, you can easily switch temporarily to DOS.

All programs in this book illustrate sending output to the file PRN-FILE. This is especially desirable if the computer on which you are working does not have a printer and you must take the disk to another machine for the printout. Needless to say, any file name can be used.

The Output Record Description

Let's compare the record description for REPORT-LINE of Figure 5-13 to the printer record format described in the example definition.

Field	Print Positions	Field Length	COBOL Record Description	
Unused	1–4	4	FILLER	PIC X(4).
Stock number	5–9	5	RL-STOCK-NUMBER	PIC X(5).
Unused	10–12	3	FILLER	PIC X(3).
Vendor name	13–32	20	RL-VENDOR-NAME	PIC X(20).
Unused	33–34	2	FILLER	PIC X(2).
Software name	35–64	30	RL-SOFTWARE-NAME	PIC X(30).
Unused	65–66	2	FILLER	PIC X(2).
Reorder level	67–69	3	RL-REORDER-LEVEL	PIC 9(3).
Unused	70–72	3	FILLER	PIC X(3).
Copies on hand	73–75	3	RL-QUANT-ON-HAND	PIC 9(3).

Overall, you can see that the output record description entries are similar to those for the input record (remember, it is the same record that was used in Examples 5-1 and 5-2). However, in contrast to the input record in which there was no space between fields, the output record includes space between each of the output fields; these must be accounted for in the record description. As you see, this is done by including a "dummy" field with the name FILLER. FILLER is a COBOL reserved word that is included in the language just for this purpose. In COBOL-85, the word FILLER can be omitted and only the PIC entered. Programs in chapters that follow take advantage of the 1985 Standard and do not include this word. However, if you feel that it makes the definition clearer (or if you want your programs to be compatible with COBOL-74), then you should include the word FILLER.

Results to be printed must be arranged in the output record definition in memory exactly corresponding to the desired output format. Each data-name specifying an output field and each FILLER must include a PICTURE that corresponds to the output format description.

The maximum record length you should use for printed output depends upon your printer. A standard in the data processing industry is 132 print positions. Most inexpensive printers for personal computers print 80 positions at 10-character-per-inch (cpi). However, they have features that allow the user to switch over to more compact printing, thereby allowing more print positions on the 8-inch line.

Distinction between Input and Output Fields

Now that you are dealing with two files and hence two record definitions, you must be careful to remember that these memory areas are different. That is, the input record INVENTORY-RECORD will occupy one portion of memory and the output record REPORT-LINE another portion. This is illustrated in Figure 5-10. Therefore, it is important that you give different names to the corresponding fields in each of the records. For instance, assume that you defined the two records as shown in the record description segment of Figure 5-14. How would the computer handle the following statement?

```
SUBTRACT 15 FROM IR-QUANTITY-ON-HAND
```

The answer is that you have an error; the computer would not know whether to use the value of IR-QUANTITY-ON-HAND from INVENTORY-RECORD or from REPORT-LINE. The solution to this dilemma is to make the names slightly different. In this case, you should use the prefix letters for the output line RL rather than IR. This gives you a helpful mnemonic device that tells you at a glance of the PROCEDURE DIVISION whether a field is part of the input or the output record. For instance, IR-SOFTWARE-NAME (IR for *Inventory Record*) and RL-SOFTWARE-NAME (RL for *Record Line*) clearly refer to the same entity, the software name. However, the two-letter abbreviation indicates which record is used. (Another way of avoiding the "same name" problem is called *qualification of data-names*, but it is not used in this book's examples.)

Figure 5-14

*Duplicate Names in
Record Descriptions*

```
01   INVENTORY-RECORD.
     .
     .
     .
     10   IR-QUANTITY-ON-HAND        PIC 9(3).
     .
     .
     .
01   INVENTORY-REPORT-LINE.
     .
     .
     .
     10   IR-QUANTITY-ON-HAND        PIC 9(3).
```

For items not related to input or output records that are defined in the WORKING-STORAGE SECTION, a prefix is not needed. The absence of a prefix tells you that they are general WORKING-STORAGE items. On the other hand, as you will learn in a later chapter, it is convenient to define output records in the WORKING-STORAGE SECTION. These will be prefixed with two-letter abbreviations.

Features of the PROCEDURE DIVISION— Example 5-3

The OPEN Statement

This program uses two files, so both of them must be opened (see lines 63 and 64). Note that one of them is opened for input and the other for output, representing the operations that will be carried out with them. The general forms of the OPEN are

OPEN INPUT {file-name-1}...

OPEN OUTPUT {file-name-1}...

OPEN INPUT {file-name-1}... OUTPUT {file-name-2}...

The third form might seem more efficient, since the word OPEN is written only once. That is, both files could be opened with the single OPEN, as follows:

```
OPEN INPUT INVENTORY-FILE
     OUTPUT REPORT-FILE
```

However, if file-name-1 is written incorrectly, the compiler will ignore the remainder of the OPEN statement, thereby failing to check file-name-2 for validity. To provide maximum error checking, example programs in this book use an individual OPEN for each file.

The WRITE/AFTER ADVANCING Statement

The WRITE statement is used to send a record to an output device. That device can be a disk—as in Chapter 4—or a printer, as in this example. For the printer, the output will be one printed line for each execution of the WRITE statement. However, when used with a printer file, the WRITE has provisions for positioning the paper before (or after) printing. The AFTER ADVANCING clause is used in the SEQ-LIST program (line 76 is repeated here):

```
WRITE REPORT-LINE AFTER ADVANCING 2 LINES
```

This results in double-spaced output (a blank line between each printed line). If the AFTER ADVANCING clause is not included, single-spacing results. You can use any positive integer for the number of lines to be advanced. You will learn more about this clause in Chapter 7.

The MOVE Statement

The MOVE statement was introduced in Chapter 2 as the statement that is used to copy data from one field in memory to another. For instance, the statement

```
MOVE "Y" TO WS-END-OF-FILE
```

copies the letter Y into the data item WS-END-OF-FILE. Similarly, the statement

```
MOVE IR-VENDOR-NAME TO RL-VENDOR-NAME
```

copies the contents of the data item IR-VENDOR-NAME into the data item RL-VENDOR-NAME.

In the next several chapters, you will encounter the extent of this statement's general form:

$$\underline{\text{MOVE}} \left\{ \begin{array}{l} \text{data-name-1} \\ \text{literal} \end{array} \right\} \underline{\text{TO}} \text{ data-name-2}$$

To illustrate how this works, consider the example in Figure 5-15 of what might be in memory before and after execution of a MOVE statement. Here you should notice that

1. The contents of the "transmitting" field are unchanged, but the original contents of the "receiving" field have been destroyed.

2. The "transmitting" field consists of 20 characters: the name occupies 16 positions, followed by 4 trailing spaces. All 20 characters are moved to the receiving field.

Figure 5-15

Execution of the MOVE Statement

Memory contents before execution of MOVE:

A p r i c o t S o f t w a r e		B o r n e o I n t e r n a t i o n a l
IR-VENDOR-NAME		RL-VENDOR-NAME

```
MOVE IR-VENDOR-NAME TO RL-VENDOR-NAME
```

Memory contents after execution of MOVE:

A p r i c o t S o f t w a r e		A p r i c o t S o f t w a r e
IR-VENDOR-NAME		RL-VENDOR-NAME

Initializing the Output Line

Preceding portions of this chapter described how record descriptions in the DATA DIVISION cause areas that correspond exactly to the respective record descriptions to be set up within memory. It is of utmost importance to recognize that the areas are only reserved and that the COBOL standard states that the contents are undefined. Hence, these areas must be assumed to contain whatever was left over from the previous program—commonly referred to as "garbage." (This is not true of RM/COBOL-85, which initializes these areas to spaces. However, it is considered poor practice to make assumptions regarding initial values that have not explicitly been defined by the program.)

Reading a data record under control of the program or moving data from one part of memory to another causes information to be placed into the record areas. For instance, the entire 61 positions of garbage in the input area are replaced by the first data record brought in by the READ statement. Similarly, garbage in each of the output fields is replaced by fields moved from the input record. However, areas of the output record defined by FILLER will not be affected by MOVE statements that act on individual fields. To avoid a problem here, the output record is cleared to spaces by the first statement of the 110-PRINT-NEXT-RECORD module:

```
MOVE SPACES TO OUTPUT-LINE
```

The word SPACES (or SPACE) is a COBOL reserved word called a *figurative constant*. It is a special code to the COBOL system, indicating that one or more spaces (blanks) are to be provided. In this case, the entire output record area is cleared to blanks.

COBOL also permits you to create your own figurative constants with the "ALL literal" option. For example, if a line of dashes (hyphens) is to be printed, it can be created by the following statement:

```
MOVE ALL "-" TO OUTPUT-LINE
```

The statement

```
MOVE ALL "* - " TO OUTPUT-LINE
```

creates an output line that looks like this:

```
* - * - * - * - * - * - * - * - * - * -
```

As you can see from these examples, the "MOVE ALL literal" statement copies the literal to the receiving field and replicates (repeats) it throughout the field.

Note that the word ALL is required to replicate the literal throughout the receiving field. The statement

```
MOVE "-" TO OUTPUT-LINE
```

will move one dash to the left-hand position of OUTPUT-LINE and fill the remainder of OUTPUT-LINE with spaces.

If the thought crosses your mind to use the VALUE clause to define the initial contents of the FILLER areas to spaces, forget it. The VALUE clause can only be used in the WORKING-STORAGE SECTION.

Other Features of the MOVE Statement

Normally, when you move data from one place in memory to another, you think of the receiving field as being the same length as the transmitting field. However, this need not be the case; for instance, consider the example of Figure 5-16. The transmitting field, defined by a nonnumeric literal, is 7 positions long, whereas the receiving field is 10. Here EXAMPLE will be moved to the first seven positions, and the last three positions will be filled with spaces.

In general, results of a MOVE such as this depend upon whether the referenced data fields are elementary-items or group-items and numeric or nonnumeric. The rules governing movement of data are as follows:

Numeric Data—Whole Numbers (PIC 9)

1. If the receiving field is longer than the transmitting field, excess positions to the left are filled with zeros.

2. If the receiving field is shorter than the transmitting field, transmission is terminated when the receiving field is full, and excess characters to the left in the transmitting field are not moved.

Figure 5-16

Padding with Spaces

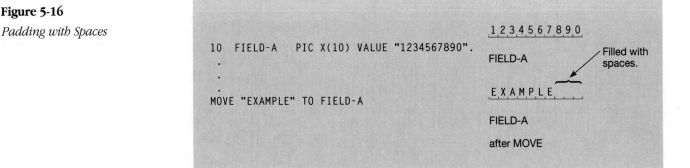

Nonnumeric Data (PIC X or Group Item)

1. Data from the transmitting field is moved *left-justified* to the receiving field (that is, it is positioned to the left within the field).

2. If the receiving field is longer than the transmitting field, excess positions to the right are filled with spaces.

3. If the receiving field is shorter than the transmitting field, movement of data is terminated when the receiving field is full; excess characters to the right in the transmitting field are not moved.

Although all of the examples in preceding chapters have involved moving in which both fields were either alphanumeric or numeric, the MOVE statement is not so restricted. For example, an integer numeric field can be moved to an alphanumeric field. You will learn more about movement of numeric data in later chapters.

Processing an Indexed File Sequentially

In this chapter, you have studied three example programs:

Example 5-1 SEQ-DISP (sequential display)

Example 5-2 RAN-DISP (random display)

Example 5-3 SEQ-LIST (sequential list)

The programs SEQ-DISP and SEQ-LIST both access the sequential file SOFTWARE.DL by accessing records sequentially (the only way possible for a sequentially organized file). On the other hand, RAN-DISP accesses the indexed file SOFTWARE.DI randomly, an action made possible by the indexed organization.

However, you should not get the idea that an indexed file can be accessed only randomly because an indexed file can be accessed *either* randomly *or* sequentially. In fact, if you wanted a detailed listing of the indexed file SOFTWARE.DI, the only changes to the SEQ-LIST program would be in the SELECT clause. That is, you would replace

```
SELECT INVENTORY-FILE    ASSIGN TO DISK "SOFTWARE.DL"
                         ORGANIZATION IS LINE SEQUENTIAL.
                         RECORD KEY IS IR-STOCK-NUMBER.
```

with

```
SELECT INVENTORY-FILE    ASSIGN TO DISK "SOFTWARE.DI"
                         ORGANIZATION IS INDEXED
                         ACCESS IS SEQUENTIAL
                         RECORD KEY IS IR-STOCK-NUMBER.
```

Notice that the organization remains INDEXED (a characteristic of SOFTWARE.DI), but the access to it is now SEQUENTIAL. *No other change would be required to access the program.* The READ statement would retain the AT END phrase because the file is being accessed sequentially and not by selected key entries. The order of the records in the printed listing would be in ascending order by the key field, regardless of the order in which the records were originally entered into the file.

Chapter Summary

General

You now have the capability to process data stored in disk files. A data file that is totally independent of the program is made available to the program by specifying its nature and name in the SELECT of the ENVIRONMENT DIVISION file-control entry. This, in turn, is linked to the corresponding record defined in the DATA DIVISION.

COBOL Language Elements

The COBOL statements that you studied in this chapter are

OPEN   Makes a file ready for use if OUTPUT creates a new file.

OPEN INPUT {file-name-1}...

OPEN OUTPUT {file-name-1}...

OPEN INPUT {file-name-1}...OUTPUT {file-name-2}...

READ Reads a record from the specified file into the record area defined by the FD for that file. The READ statement must specify the file name of the file from which data is to be read. If ACCESS IS SEQUENTIAL, then the record that is read will be the next record in the file. If ACCESS IS RANDOM, the record that is read will be the record with the key specified by the contents of the RECORD KEY field.

```
READ file-name
    [AT END
       COBOL-statement ...]
    [NOT AT END
       COBOL-statement ...]
    [END-READ]
```

WRITE Writes a record to the specified file from the record area defined by the FD for that file. Output may be to the printer or to a disk file. The WRITE statement must specify the record name (01) defined under the FD. When writing to a PRINTER device, the AFTER ADVANCING clause is used to specify line spacing.

$$\text{WRITE record-name } \underline{\text{AFTER}} \text{ ADVANCING integer} \begin{bmatrix} \text{LINE} \\ \text{LINES} \end{bmatrix}$$

MOVE Copies information from one area of memory to another. It can operate on either alphanumeric or numeric data. Transmitting and receiving fields can have different lengths. MOVE is also used to copy figurative constants (such as SPACES) and literals (such as "Y" or "CURRENT MONTH") to receiving fields. The word ALL preceding the literal causes the literal to be replicated throughout the receiving field.

$$\underline{\text{MOVE}} \begin{Bmatrix} \text{data-name-1} \\ \text{literal} \end{Bmatrix} \underline{\text{TO}} \text{ data-name-2}$$

Another language element that you have studied in this chapter is the following:

File control entry defines a file by naming it and listing its characteristics (device type, external file name, organization, and access method). One entry is required for each file.

Printer Spacing Charts

A printer spacing chart is used to define printed output by specifying the size and type of fields to be printed and the amount of space between each field.

Programming Conventions

File/record names: A file and its associated record will have the same name, suffixed by -FILE and -RECORD, respectively. The only exception is the PRINTER file, in which case the record name can have the suffix -LINE instead of -RECORD.

Field names: Field names within a record will be prefixed by a two-letter abbreviation indicating the record of which it is a member. For example:

```
FD  STUDENT-MASTER-FILE.
01  STUDENT-MASTER-RECORD.
    10  SM-STUDENT-NAME          PIC X(30).
```

Other data-names: For fields defined in WORKING-STORAGE SECTION other than those defined as part of an input or output record, you may omit two-letter prefixes. If you feel it makes your program clearer, use WS- or another meaningful abbreviation.

Indention of clauses: A single-line clause (such as AT END or AFTER ADVANCING) will be placed on a separate line and indented four spaces. When a clause contains more than one statement, or when multiple clauses (such as INVALID KEY and NOT INVALID KEY) are used, the clause names will be placed on separate lines and indented two spaces, and the statements within the clause will be indented an additional two spaces.

Error Prevention/ Detection

Since it is completely acceptable to move the contents of a field to a larger or smaller field, no diagnostic message is generated if the field sizes in a MOVE statement are different. It is the programmer's responsibility to check the program and the output to ensure that undesired truncation has not occurred.

Questions and Exercises

Give a brief description of each of the following terms that were introduced or expanded upon in this chapter.

Key Terminology

at end	hard copy	programmed switch
end-of-file record	invalid key	record key
figurative constant	left-justified	soft copy
file dump	priming read	
formatted	printer spacing chart	

General Questions

1. In which paragraph of which section of which division is the SELECT clause found? What is its function?

2. What is the function of the OPEN statement?

3. When reading and writing files, the programmer must tell the computer to read or write which of the following: the file name or the record name?

4. In studying the MOVE statement, a student encounters a problem. The student considers two 10-position fields, IR-VEHICLE and PL-VEHICLE, with contents as shown in the "before" of Figure 5-17. Upon executing the statement

        MOVE IR-VEHICLE TO PL-VEHICLE

   the student maintains that the word TOYOTA, which contains only six letters, will leave the last three letters of CHEVROLET undisturbed, with the result shown in the "after" part of Figure 5-17. Comment on this.

Figure 5-17

Before	T O Y O T A		C H E V R O L E T
	IR-VEHICLE		PL-VEHICLE

MOVE IR-VEHICLE TO PL-VEHICLE

After	T O Y O T A		T O Y O T A L E T
	IR-VEHICLE		PL-VEHICLE

Questions Relating to the Example Programs

1. A data set used in the program of Figure 5-13 contains 20 data records. What will occur when the READ statement is executed the twenty-first time? Or *will* it be executed 21 times?

2. What would occur in the program flowcharted in Figure 5-11 if the data file contained only an EOF record (no data records at all)?

3. In the SEQ-LIST program (Figure 5-13), the output line (REPORT-LINE) is initialized to spaces during the execution of the 110 module. Why not initialize the line with the VALUE SPACES clause for each FILLER? For instance, why not make Line 39 as follows?

```
10  FILLER          PIC X(3)     VALUE SPACES.
```

Writing Program Statements

1. The file STUDENT.DL is a sequential file that contains information about students at a college. Each record contains the following information about one student:

Field	Width	Data Type
Student name	23	Alphanumeric
Student phone number	10	Alphanumeric
Tuition amount due	4	Numeric
Major field	12	Alphanumeric
Dormitory name	20	Alphanumeric
Dormitory room number	3	Numeric
Student record number	6	Alphanumeric

Write the following for this file:
   a. The complete file control entry
   b. The complete file description entry
   c. The complete record description (the record and all fields)

2. Assume that the file STUDENT.DL described in Question 1 has been converted to an indexed file named STUDENT.DI. This file is based on the unique Student record number, and it is going to be used as an "inquiry file" to supply information about the student whose record number is entered.

Write the following for this file:
   a. The complete file control entry
   b. All changes that would have to be made in the answers to Questions 1b and 1c

3. The file EMP-DATA.DL is a sequential file that contains information about the employees of a company. Each record contains the following information about one employee:

Field	Record Position
Employee name	2–23
Social Security Number	24–32
Occupation code	44–45
Gender	51
Year of first employment	52–53
Record code	55

Write the following for this file:
   a. The complete file control entry
   b. The complete file description entry
   c. The complete record description (the record and all fields)

4. Assume that the file EMP-DATA.DL described in Question 3 has been converted to an indexed file named EMP-DATA.DI. This file is based on the unique Social Security Number, and it is going to be used as an "inquiry file" to supply information about the employee whose Social Security Number is entered.

Write the following for this file:
   a. The complete file control entry
   b. All changes that would have to be made in the answers to Questions 3b and 3c

Programming Assignments

Programming assignments in this and following chapters use data files. For the record description of all files used in Assignments 1-6, you must use Appendix A.

5-1 Class Enrollment Report

As discussed in Assignment 4-1, information on class sizes and enrollments is vital to colleges and universities. Administrators continually monitor this information to insure that instructional resources are being utilized as fully as possible. One common vehicle for presenting this information is the computer-generated listing. Printed output of this nature is often referred to as *hard copy,* because it is "hard enough" to pick up and carry around.

Output Requirements:

A printed report with the following output and format:

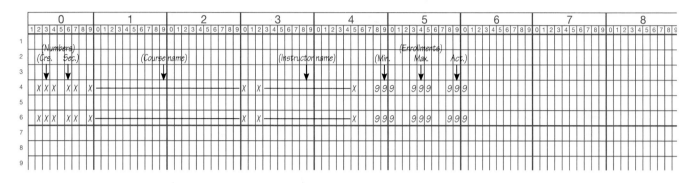

Input Description:

File name: ENROLL01.DL or ENROLL01.DI

Record description: Refer to Appendix A.

Processing Requirements:

Print one double-spaced line for each record in the file, as specified by the printer spacing chart.

5-2 Class Enrollment File Inquiry

Printed listings such as the one described in Assignment 5-1 are not ideal for several reasons. They are bulky and there are usually not enough copies for everyone. In many cases, an administrator will be interested only in data on one specific class, and it is time-consuming to have to paw through the entire listing looking for that one class. However, the most significant problem is that the listing is obsolete as soon as it is printed, because it does not reflect the changes that have been made to the file since the listing was printed.

To counter these objections, *inquiry programs* are often written. These programs permit the user to access only the desired records and to display the contents of those records on the screen *(soft copy)* rather than on the printer *(hard copy).* Assignment 5-2 consists of writing an inquiry program.

Output Requirements:

The following fields are to be displayed on the screen, each preceded by its description:

Course number

Section number

Course name

Actual enrollment

Input Description:

File name: ENROLL01.DI

Record description: Refer to Appendix A

Processing Requirements:

Request a class code from the keyboard. Then, as long as the class code is not equal to zero:

a. Read the record for that class code from the file

b. Display the output data specified above

c. Request another class code (or zero) from the keyboard

5-3 Inventory Report

The value of any given form of information display is relative to how appropriate it is. As was mentioned in Assignment 5-2, a file listing is inappropriate if current information is desired. On the other hand, if the file status at a given time is desired, the printed listing is an effective tool.

This type of output is particularly appropriate in business because business is usually conducted in specific time periods (weeks, months, quarters, fiscal years, and so on) and reports are often needed to show the business's status at the end of a specific time period. For example, the owner of a music store might wish to have a listing at the end of each month showing sales and inventory data on all tapes carried by the store.

Output Requirements:

A printed report with the following output and format:

Input Description:

File name: RECORD 01.DL or RECORD 01.DI

Record description: Refer to Appendix A

Processing Requirements:

Print one single-spaced line for each record in the file, as specified by the printer spacing chart.

5-4 Inventory File Inquiry

The output for Assignment 5-3 provides hard-copy data on an entire file at a given point in time. In this assignment, soft-copy output is required showing current values for selected records.

Output Requirements:

The following fields are to be displayed on the screen, each preceded by its description.

Title of tape

Medium

Number currently on hand

Number currently on order

Input Description:

File name: RECORD.DI

Record description: Refer to Appendix A

Processing Requirements:
>Request an Inventory Control Number (ICN) from the keyboard. Then, as long as the ICN is not equal to zero:
>a. Read the record for that ICN from the file
>b. Display the output data specified previously
>c. Request another ICN (or zero) from the keyboard

5-5 Airport Traffic Report

As discussed in Assignment 4-5, a large metropolitan airport desires to have traffic statistics to evaluate the adequacy of existing airport facilities and to make future expansion projections. The airport manager wishes to receive, each morning, a listing that shows certain selected data for each flight using the airport the preceding day.

Output Requirements:
>A printed report with the following output and format:

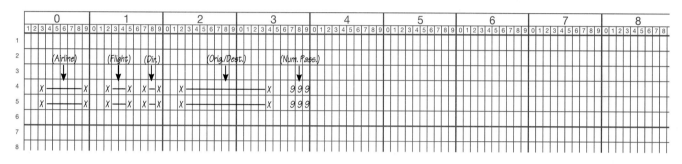

Input Description:
>File name: AIRPORT1.DL or AIRPORT1.DI
>Record description: Refer to Appendix A

Processing Requirements:
>Print one single-spaced line for each record in the file, as specified by the printer spacing chart.

5-6 Airport Traffic File Inquiry

The airport manager described in Assignment 5-5 also wishes to be able to "inquire on" the file of flight data for the previous day. (The term *inquire on* refers to the ability to access one specific record in the file and display data from that record.) In this assignment, you are to assume that the file of flight data is an indexed file and that the record key for each record is the flight number, which is unique.

Output Requirements:
>The following fields are to be displayed on the screen, each preceded by its description.
>>Airline
>>Flight number
>>Direction of flight (IN or OUT)
>>Point of origin or destination
>>Number of passengers

Input Description:
>File name: AIRPORT1.DI
>Record description: Refer to Appendix A

Processing Requirements:
>Request a flight number from the keyboard. Then, as long as the flight number is not equal to zero:
>a. Read the record for that flight from the file
>b. Display the output data specified previously
>c. Request another flight number (or zero) from the keyboard

5-7 Daily Soft Drink Report

In business, printed listings of a file's data are often used to provide management with a "picture" of the data at a given point in time. The subject of this assignment is the soft-drink bottler from Assignment 4-7. Now he wishes to have, each morning, a listing of the sales from the previous day. The bottler feels that by perusing this listing, he can remain in touch with what is happening in the business, noting fluctuations and trends in customer and product activity.

Output Requirements:
A printed report with the following output and format.

Input Description:
File name: DRINKS01.DL or DRINKS01.DI
Record description: Refer to Appendix A

Processing Requirements:
Print one double-spaced line for each record in the file, as specified by the printer spacing chart.

5-8 Soft Drinks File Inquiry

Another vital activity in business is handling customer complaints. When a customer telephones to say that the previous day's delivery was missing or incorrect, the soft-drink bottler described in Assignment 5-7 needs to be able to determine immediately just what was delivered to that customer on the previous day. While this data could be obtained from the listing produced in Assignment 5-7, it might also be desirable to obtain the data on the screen by accessing the file randomly and showing the data for the customer in question.

Output Requirements:
The following fields are to be displayed on the screen, each preceded by its description:
Customer account number
Customer name
Number of cases of cola sold
Number of cases of orange drink sold
Number of cases of root beer sold

Input Description:
File name: DRINKS01.DI
Record description: Refer to Appendix A

Processing Requirements:
Request a customer number from the keyboard. Then, as long as the customer number is not equal to zero:
a. Read the record for that customer from the file
b. Display the output data specified above
c. Request another customer number (or zero) from the keyboard

6

EDITING OPERATIONS

Chapter Objectives

The primary focus of this chapter is working with numeric data: data that includes a sign (negative) and a decimal point. Although data editing (improving the appearance for output) relates primarily to numeric data, a limited amount of alphanumeric editing is described. You will learn about the following topics:

- Using the V character in an input PICTURE to define the positioning of an understood decimal point
- Handling decimal point positioning when performing arithmetic operations
- Using the S character in a PICTURE to identify that the field can contain a negative quantity
- Storing the sign within a data field in memory
- Replacing leading zeros by spaces for printed output (zero suppression)
- Inserting dollar signs and asterisks in numeric fields for printed output
- Inserting a period in a numeric output field
- Inserting commas as appropriate in a numeric output field
- Editing alphanumeric fields for printed output
- Using the five data types: numeric, alphabetic, alphanumeric, numeric edited, and alphanumeric edited

Expanded Report Requirements

Editing of numeric data is an important element in generating easy-to-read reports. The following example illustrates basic editing.

Example 6-1 Displaying Records from a Sequential Inventory File

Example Definition—
Example 6-1

Problem Description

Now that the programs providing basic access to data in the software file are operational, the management of UNISOFT wishes to forge ahead. They need to continue providing the variety of reports and inquiry capabilities necessary to successfully running a small business. One of these reporting needs is a listing of inventory items, including the price and inventory value. Since pricing data is not included in the original software file, additional fields in the software record are needed.

Output Requirements
Print chart:

Sample output:
Sample output is shown in Figure 6-1.

Figure 6-1

Retail Value Report

07427	Apricot Software	Apricot-tree General Ledger	65	349.95	22,746.75
10164	Archaic Software	Sluggish Writer	93	49.95	4,645.35
15589	Borneo International	Travelling Side Punch	180	29.95	5,391.00
15674	Borneo International	Supercharged Turbo COBOL	120	599.00	71,880.00
28429	Ferrari Development	Ferrari 4-5-6 Financial Acctg.	144	495.00	71,280.00
28558	Ferrari Development	Orchestra II	102	649.00	66,198.00
32506	Galactic Bus. Mach.	Bottom View	105	99.95	10,494.75
37188	International Soft	UnderWord, Rev 128	90	37.50	3,375.00
37281	International Soft	UnderCalc, Rev 256	80	37.50	3,000.00
37384	International Soft	UnderFile, Rev 64	95	37.50	3,562.50
45191	Micro Am	Word Comet 7	104	399.00	41,496.00
49165	Microhard	Sentence	143	349.95	50,042.85
53351	MicroPerimeter, Inc.	QBase 7000	176	695.00	122,320.00
60544	Nobodies, Unlimited	Nobodies Disk Utilities	33	49.50	6,583.50
91655	20th Century Soft.	Potent BASIC Interpreter	97	9.50	921.50

Input Description

Input file name: SOFTWAR2.DL

Record format:

Field	Positions	Format
Stock number	1-5	
Software name	6-35	
Vendor name	36-55	
Copies on hand	56-58	*nnn*
Price	62-66	*nnn*$_\wedge$*nn**

(**Note:* The form *nnn*$_\wedge$*nn* indicates a five-digit field with an assumed decimal point between the third and fourth digits. For instance, the quantity stored as 59595 would actually represent 595.95.)

Processing Requirements

For each record, print the information shown on the print chart; output must be single-spaced. Compute the retail value for each software product in stock as:

Retail value = Copies on hand x Price

Program Solution—
Example 6-1

The program of Figure 6-2 is little different than the corresponding SEQ-LIST program in Chapter 5. Significant differences are highlighted here.

The input description of the example definition, the output requirements of this example (print chart and sample program output), and the program itself illustrate the following new concepts:

Figure 6-2

Program Solution—Example 6-1

```
 1     IDENTIFICATION DIVISION.
 2
 3     PROGRAM-ID. RET-VAL1.
 4
 5     *   Written by W.Price
 6     *   July 14, 1990
 7
 8     *   This program generates a retail value report from
 9     *   the file SOFTWAR2.DL.  For each record in the file
10     *   there is one output line that includes the retail
11     *   value (price times quantity on hand) for that item.
12
13     ENVIRONMENT DIVISION.
14
15     CONFIGURATION SECTION.
16     SOURCE-COMPUTER. IBM-PC.
17
18     INPUT-OUTPUT SECTION.
19     FILE-CONTROL.
20       SELECT INVENTORY-FILE  ASSIGN TO DISK "SOFTWAR2.DL"
21                              ORGANIZATION IS LINE SEQUENTIAL
22       SELECT REPORT-FILE   ASSIGN TO PRINTER "PRN-FILE".
23
24     DATA DIVISION.
25
26     FILE SECTION.
27
28     FD  INVENTORY-FILE.
29     01  INVENTORY-RECORD.        → INVENTORY RECORD
30         10  IR-STOCK-NUMBER    PIC X(5).
31         10  IR-SOFTWARE-NAME   PIC X(30).
32         10  IR-VENDOR-NAME     PIC X(20).
33         10  IR-QUANT-ON-HAND   PIC 9(3).
34         10                     PIC X(3).
35         10  IR-PRICE           PIC 9(3)V9(2).
36
37     FD  REPORT-FILE.
38     01  REPORT-LINE.        → REPORT LINE
39         10  RL-STOCK-NUMBER   PIC X(5).
40         10                    PIC X(2).
41         10  RL-VENDOR-NAME    PIC X(20).
42         10                    PIC X(2).
43         10  RL-SOFTWARE-NAME  PIC X(30).
44         10                    PIC X(3).
45         10  RL-QUANT-ON-HAND  PIC ZZ9.
46         10                    PIC X(2).
47         10  RL-PRICE          PIC ZZZ.99.
48         10                    PIC X(2).
49         10  RL-RETAIL-VALUE   PIC ZZZ,ZZZ.99.
```

```
50
51     WORKING-STORAGE SECTION.
52
53     01  PROGRAMMED-SWITCHES.
54         10  END-OF-FILE        PIC X  VALUE "N".
55
56       01  ARITHMETIC-WORK-AREAS.
57         10  RETAIL-VALUE       PIC 9(6)V9(2).
58
59     PROCEDURE DIVISION.
60
61     000-PRINT-INVENTORY-FILE.
62         PERFORM 100-INITIALIZE
63         PERFORM 110-PRINT-NEXT-RECORD
64             UNTIL END-OF-FILE = "Y"
65         PERFORM 120-FINALIZE
66         STOP RUN.
67
68     100-INITIALIZE.
69         OPEN INPUT INVENTORY-FILE
70         OPEN OUTPUT REPORT-FILE
71         READ INVENTORY-FILE
72             AT END MOVE "Y" TO END-OF-FILE
73         END-READ.
74
75     110-PRINT-NEXT-RECORD.  (MAIN)
76
77     *  Calculate retail value
78         MOVE IR-PRICE TO RETAIL-VALUE
79         MULTIPLY IR-QUANT-ON-HAND BY RETAIL-VALUE
80
81     *  Assemble and write output line
82         MOVE SPACES TO REPORT-LINE  — like CLS
83         MOVE IR-STOCK-NUMBER TO RL-STOCK-NUMBER
84         MOVE IR-SOFTWARE-NAME TO RL-SOFTWARE-NAME
85         MOVE IR-VENDOR-NAME TO RL-VENDOR-NAME
86         MOVE IR-QUANT-ON-HAND TO RL-QUANT-ON-HAND
87         MOVE IR-PRICE TO RL-PRICE
88         MOVE RETAIL-VALUE TO RL-RETAIL-VALUE
89         WRITE REPORT-LINE AFTER ADVANCING 2 LINES
90
91     *  Read next input record
92         READ INVENTORY-FILE
93             AT END MOVE "Y" TO END-OF-FILE
94         END-READ.
95
96     120-FINALIZE.
97         CLOSE INVENTORY-FILE
98               REPORT-FILE.
```

1. In the input record, the Price field is a dollar-cent amount requiring a decimal point; a means is required for specifying that decimal point.

2. A work field must be defined (for the retail value computation) that also includes a decimal point.

3. Referring to the print chart and sample program output, leading zeros are eliminated; for instance, 093 is printed as 93.

4. A decimal point is printed for quantities that include a decimal point; for instance, 495.00 and 49.95.

5. A comma is included for large numbers; for instance, 71,280.00 includes a comma, but 921.50 does not.

6. The input record contains a field that is not required by the application under consideration. This field must be defined, but it does not need to be named. A FILLER in an input record usually indicates the presence of one or more fields that are not used in the program.

First, let's consider how the decimal point is handled in COBOL.

Numeric Data with a Decimal Point

Decimal Point Positioning on Input

One of the important features of modern programming languages is the automatic handling of decimal points. When monetary amounts (or any other quantities involving a decimal point) are recorded in a record of a data file, the decimal point itself is usually not recorded. Thus, the quantity $13.85 would normally be recorded in four adjacent positions as 1385. Needless to say, the program must give some indication regarding actual placement of the point. COBOL does this by means of the PICTURE that defines the input field. For instance, in the record description, notice that the Price field is defined as having a format of *nnn*ₐ*nn*. That is, it consists of three digits, an implied decimal point, and two digits.

In a COBOL program's DATA DIVISION, it would be defined by the statement shown in Figure 6-3. Here, the price field is defined as a five-digit field (indicated by five 9's) with an assumed decimal point between the third and fourth digits (as indicated by the V). Because the PICTURE in the COBOL program occupies six positions (five 9's and the letter V), do not assume that the input record must allocate six positions for the field—the decimal point is assumed, not recorded. Thus, if a record read contains the quantity 19995 for this field, it will be read into IR-PRICE as a five-digit number, but will be interpreted by the computer as 199.95 (as defined by the PICTURE).

Other examples are as follows:

PICTURE	Recorded in the Record	Interpreted as
PIC 99V99	0008	00.08
PIC V999	315	.315
PIC 9(5)V99	1234567	12345.67
PIC 9(4)V9(3)	1234567	1234.567

Basic Arithmetic with Data Containing Decimal Points

Example 6-1 requires that for each record (software item), the Quantity-on-hand field be multiplied by the Price field to obtain the Retail-value quantity. Therefore, the program needs to include a work field large enough to hold the product. You can readily determine this by inspecting the component fields:

```
10 IR-QUANT-ON-HAND  PIC 9(3).
10 IR-PRICE          PIC 999V99.
```

Both of these fields include three digits to the left of the decimal point; thus, the product can be up to six digits to the left. A reasonable multiplication work area for this operation would be

```
10 RETAIL-VALUE PIC 9(6)V9(2)
```

Figure 6-3

The V PICTURE Element Indicating an Assumed Decimal Point

```
10   IR-PRICE   PIC 999V99.
```

Three digits preceding the understood decimal point.   The letter V indicates an understood decimal point.   Two digits following the understood decimal point.

If you check the print chart in the example definition, you will see that provisions have been made in the report for a number of this size. (As you will learn later in this chapter, the letter *Z* in the print chart designates a position for a digit.)

Once fields and their decimal point placements are appropriately defined in the DATA DIVISION, you can proceed to arithmetic operations in the PROCEDURE DIVISION in exactly the same way as with whole numbers. That is, all decimal positioning and alignment are handled automatically by COBOL. The two-statement sequence to carry out the desired multiplication is

```
MOVE IR-PRICE TO RETAIL-VALUE
MULTIPLY IR-QUANT-ON-HAND BY RETAIL-VALUE
```

As you will learn later in this chapter, all arithmetic operations include provisions for automatic decimal point alignment. However, other clauses can be used to accommodate those situations in which the receiving field is too small for the arithmetic result.

Negative Numbers in COBOL

Telling COBOL That a Quantity Can be Negative

If when running the ADDER program to add two numbers, you entered a negative value for either of the two numbers, you must have received a surprise. For instance, adding 20 and -15 should yield 5, but the result from the program would be 35. The reason for this is that COBOL discards all signs unless the PICTURE definition explicitly includes a sign indication. Although the RET-VAL program does not use negative numbers, other examples do.

To illustrate sign indication, consider a charge account application in which one of the steps in determining the new monthly balance is to subtract the payments from the current balance. Appropriate DATA DIVISION entries and the SUBTRACT statement are shown in Figure 6-4(a). Typical values (before and after subtraction) are illustrated in memory in Figure 6-4(b). (Notice that a small wedge indicates the position of the assumed decimal point.) In the first example, the value in IR-PAYMENTS is less than the amount in BALANCE. Hence, the result after execution is the correct value 785.28. However, in the second example, the value in IR-PAYMENTS is the larger of the two. Upon execution of the subtract operation, COBOL produces a value of -214.72. However, because the PICTURE for BALANCE does not explicitly say that this field is to retain a sign on its contents, the sign is discarded—with the result shown in the example.

In an application such as this, you must precede the PICTURE definition with a letter *S*, indicating that the sign should be retained. Then the DATA DIVISION entry becomes either of the following:

```
10 BALANCE      PIC S9999V99.
10 BALANCE      PIC S9(4)V9(2).
```

The single letter *S* preceding the numeric descriptors is sufficient to cause the system to retain any sign that results from the computation.

Storage of the Sign by the Computer

You know from earlier descriptions that the compiler reserves one byte in memory for each 9 or X in the PICTURE. You also know that the V (indicating an assumed decimal point) does not cause any memory to be reserved. For instance, the following PICTURE causes four bytes to be reserved for the field PL-NUMBER-FIELD:

```
10 PL-NUMBER-FIELD      PIC 99V99.
```

Figure 6-4

A Subtraction Operation That Can Produce a Negative Result

```
10   IR-PAYMENTS      PIC 9999V99.
.
.
.
10   BALANCE          PIC 9999V99.
.
.
.
SUBTRACT IR-PAYMENTS FROM BALANCE
```
(a)

	IR-PAYMENTS	BALANCE
Before execution	0 5 0 0 0 0	1 2 8 5 2 8
After execution	0 5 0 0 0 0	0 7 8 5 2 8
Before execution	1 5 0 0 0 0	1 2 8 5 2 8
After execution	1 5 0 0 0 0	0 2 1 4 7 2

The result is positive (214.72); it should be negative (-214.72).

(b)

Interestingly, the S sign code also does not cause any memory to be reserved for the sign if you do not explicitly tell the compiler to do so. For instance, the field PL-SIGNED-FIELD

```
10 PL-SIGNED-FIELD PIC S99V99.
```

will use only four bytes. If this is the case, then how is it possible to store four digits *and* the sign in only four positions? The technique used dates back to the early days of punched card processing, when numerous methods were used to maximize the amount of data that could be stored in an 80-column punched card. One of the methods was to record (punch) the sign in the same card column as the last digit of the numeric field. This practice has carried over to computers and is still used today.

As a rule, you can use COBOL with almost no knowledge of what is occurring within the computer. However, with signed numbers, you need to know the two ways in which the sign can be carried. The default is an *embedded sign* in which the sign is encoded in the last digit of field. (The COBOL standard allows either the first or the last position to be used—the last is most common.) Figure 6-5 illustrates the embedded sign concept.

Figure 6-5

Sign Embedded in the Last Digit

```
10 SAMPLE-FIELD   PIC S9(6).
```

Embedded negative sign	1 2 8 5 2 -8	is -128528
Embedded positive sign	1 2 8 5 2 +8	is +128528
No sign	1 2 8 5 2 8	is 128528

Field is six positions in length. The sign is embedded in the last digit.

Encoding in this way actually changes the last digit of a number to a letter (not illustrated by Figure 6-5). Fortunately, COBOL handles this automatically.

The second way in which the sign is stored is in a separate position. Thus, for instance, a six-digit number would require seven bytes: six for digits and one for the sign. The separate sign, which is designated by the SIGN clause, can be located either at the beginning or end of the field. These two cases are illustrated in Figure 6-6. Needless to say, the SIGN clause is meaningful only with numeric fields that include an S in their PICTURE. When used with a group item, this clause applies to all signed numeric fields in that group item.

Although one method might be slightly more efficient than another for a given computer, your program will function correctly regardless of the sign convention you use in the WORKING-STORAGE SECTION. However, in a record description for an input file, you must be certain that your sign designation corresponds to the way in which the data is stored. Ryan-McFarland stresses using a separate sign character to maximize data transportability. In most IBM mainframe environments, you will find that the default of an embedded sign on the rightmost digit is used; the SIGN clause is used infrequently.

Basic Editing Operations

Although assumed decimal positioning, nonsignificant zeros, and embedded signs might be adequate for internal storage of data, they are insufficient for printed or displayed output. For instance, the first line of Figure 6-7 shows typical data as it is stored in memory. Obviously, output such as this is difficult to interpret quickly. On the other hand, the second line, which is the result of editing, is much easier to read and understand. The first item is clearly a date and the second a Social Security number. Monetary amounts are indicated by a dollar sign (and a decimal point), and the minus sign in the last field is indicated by the letters CR (meaning CREDIT) following the number, a common business method for identifying a negative quantity.

Figure 6-6

Separate Sign Character

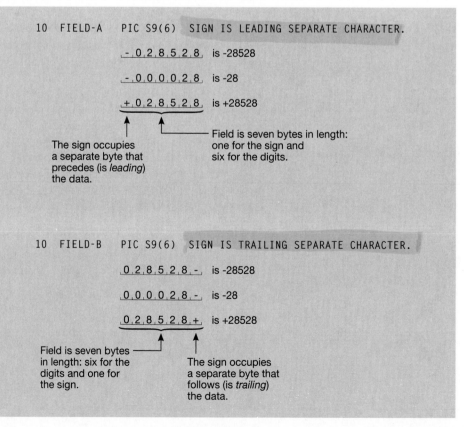

Figure 6-7

The Effect of Editing on Output

						Embedded minus. ↓
013191	495138762	01156273	095	109846	013117	06042̄
1/31/91	495-13-8762	$11,562.73	9.5%	$1,098.46	$131.17	$60.42 CR

The process of transforming data from its internal memory form to a more readable form is called *editing*. The RET-VAL1 program (Figure 6-2) includes editing of numeric fields for the output report. To see how editing works, refer to Figure 6-8; it shows one of the output lines from the report of Figure 6-1 and relevant statements from the RET-VAL1 program. Here you can see the two basic elements of editing data:

- a PICTURE that defines the format of the edit field
- a MOVE statement that moves the data into that edit field

In other words, editing occurs when data is moved (MOVE statement) to a data item defined with a PICTURE that contains edit codes. In this example, RL-PRICE is a *numeric-edited item* because the PICTURE ZZZ.99 contains the Z and period codes. The PICTURE definition string of characters comprising an edited data item can be up to 30 characters in length. The characters must be formed according to very specific and detailed rules governing exactly which characters may be used, the sequences and combinations in which they may appear, and the functions that they perform.

There are two broad categories of editing operations: suppression with replacement and insertion. *Suppression with replacement* editing is the replacing of leading zeros with another character (spaces or asterisks). *Insertion* editing is, as the name suggests, inserting punctuation or sign characters into the field. The RET-VAL1 program uses both suppression with replacement and insertion.

Figure 6-8

Editing the Price Field from the RET-VAL1 Program

Typical output line from the RET-VAL1 program:

```
91655  20th Century Soft.    Potent BASIC Interpreter        97    9.50       921.50
```

Relevant statements from the RET-VAL1 program:

```
10  IR-PRICE        PIC 9(3)V9(2).           0 0 9 5 0
.
.
.
10  RL-PRICE        PIC ZZZ.99.                9 . 5 0
.
.
.
MOVE IR-PRICE TO RL-PRICE
```

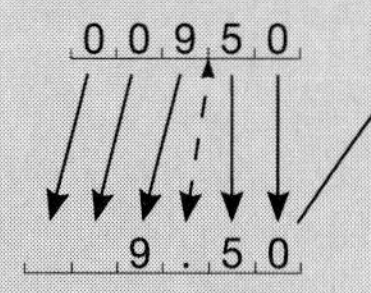

When data in IR-PRICE is moved to RL-PRICE (a numeric-edited item), the leading zeros are replaced by spaces and the decimal point is inserted.

Figure 6-9

Zero Suppression with Blank Replacement

```
    PIC 9999      PIC ZZZZ      PIC ZZZ9

      1234          1234          1234
      0123           123           123
      0001             1             1
      0000                           0
       ↑             ↑             ↑
   In Memory      Printed       Printed


   PIC 999V99     PIC ZZZ.ZZ    PIC ZZZ.99    PIC ZZ9.99

     12345         123.45        123.45        123.45
     00123           1.23          1.23          1.23
     00010            .10           .10          0.10
     00007            .07           .07          0.07
     00000                          .00          0.00
       ↑             ↑             ↑             ↑
   In Memory      Printed       Printed       Printed
```

Zero Suppression with Blank Replacement

Zero suppression with blank replacement is further illustrated by the examples of Figure 6-9. Notice that there must be as many Z and 9 characters in the edited data item as there are digits (9's) in the numeric field from which the data is moved. Also, notice that you must use the 9 character at the point where you want the suppression operation turned off. With whole number fields, it is common to include a single right most 9 so that a 0 will be printed for a zero number (for instance, use ZZZ9). If the data item includes a decimal point, the 9 character is commonly used following the decimal point (for instance, ZZZ.99). However, suppression will not proceed to the right of the decimal point for a nonzero number (see the fourth line of the second group in Figure 6-9). As is the case in these examples, all Z edit characters must be to the left of the 9 characters. For example, ZZ9.9Z is not permitted. Also, data symbols cannot be mixed to the right of the decimal point; for instance, ZZZ.Z9 is not valid.

Zero Suppression with Asterisk Replacement

In some situations, it is desirable to replace leading spaces with asterisk characters rather than with spaces. For instance, a printed amount

    $ 125.36

could be changed fraudulently to:

    $34,125.36

One way of preventing this is by *zero suppression with asterisk replacement,* in which the leading zeros are replaced with asterisk characters, yielding

    $***125.36

The edit PICTURE for asterisk replacement is identical to that for blank replacement, except that the * is used in place of the Z. For example:

ZZZ.99	causes zero replacement
***.99	causes asterisk replacement

Categorizing the Numeric-Editing Symbols

COBOL beginners are often overwhelmed by the wide variety of editing symbols available and the ways in which they function. Before proceeding to the insertion symbols, let's look at one way in which PICTURE symbols may be classified.

Each character in the character string of the PICTURE clause specifies the type of information to be contained in that position of the data item. There are three basic types of information: data, punctuation, and sign.

A *data position* in an editing PICTURE contains data. In other words, each PICTURE character that specifies a data position is replaced by one data character from the sending field. The numeric characters that specify a data position are

> 9, Z, and *
> - (minus) and $ under some conditions

There must be one data position for each digit in the field being moved (the source field). Figure 6-10 illustrates the Z and * characters functioning as data positions.

Figure 6-10

Data Position Characters

Five numeric data positions.

Five 9 symbols.	Three * symbols and two 9 symbols.	Two Z symbols and three 9 symbols.
999.99	***.99	ZZ9.99

Each data position (9, Z, or *) will be replaced with a digit from the transmitting field (or a blank or an * for leading zeros).

A *punctuation position* contains punctuation. Such positions in the edited field are in addition to the data positions. The characters that specify punctuation are

> , (comma), . (period), $, B, and / (slash)

For instance, a 6-digit field defined by

```
PIC 9999V99
```

could be edited by the edited item:

```
PIC Z,ZZZ.99
```

This PICTURE consists of eight positions: six are data (Z and 9) and two are punctuation: (, and .).

A *sign position* contains an indication of the sign of the data item. The characters that specify a sign position are

> +, -, CR (CREDIT), and DB (DEBIT).

Like punctuation positions, sign positions in an edited field are in addition to the data positions. For instance, a field defined by

```
PIC S999V99
```

could be edited by the edited item

```
PIC ZZZ.99CR
```

The input field consists of five digits. (It also includes a sign which could be embedded or separate character—it makes no difference.) The edit field correspondingly includes five data positions. It also includes two positions for sign: the letters *CR*. Including the period punctuation position, this edit PICTURE is eight positions—five data, one punctuation, and two sign. If the source field is negative, the letters *CR* are printed to indicate this; if positive, the *CR* is replaced with spaces.

Insertion

The Comma Editing Symbol

A guideline that you can use in defining an edit PICTURE is that you must define the editing string of characters so that they correspond to the way in which you want the output to appear. For instance, in the RET-VAL1 program, the retail value is to be printed with a decimal point and a comma (if the amount exceeds 999.99). The following is typical output:

```
125,301.80
  3,450.25
    595.50
```

The edit PICTURE consists of two punctuation symbols and eight data symbols, as follows:

```
PIC ZZZ,ZZZ.99
```

You can see that the comma is positioned at the point desired for printing. Although positioning the comma every three digits is common practice, it could be positioned anywhere. With zero suppression specified, the comma is also suppressed if no digits are printed to the left of it.

The Dollar Sign Editing Symbol

In printed output, dollar and cent amounts are commonly preceded by a dollar sign. For instance, a dollar sign could be included in the preceding example; the following is the PICTURE definition and corresponding sample output:

```
PIC $ZZZ,ZZZ.99
$125,301.80
$  3,450.25
$    595.50
```

Alternately, the asterisk suppression symbol can be used to protect against fraud.

```
PIC $ZZZ,ZZZ.99
$125,301.80
$**3,450.25
$****595.50
```

Another technique used with the dollar sign is to cause it to float—that is, be positioned to the immediate left of the first nonzero digit. This is illustrated by the following examples:

```
PIC $$$$,$$$.99
$125,301.80
  $3,450.25
    $595.50
```

Note that the first dollar sign is treated as an insertion symbol (it is a punctuation position) and the other six are data positions. Thus, the number of data positions is eight: six dollar signs and two 9 characters. Beginners frequently forget the "extra" dollar sign that functions as the insertion character.

Signs

If a field contains a sign, then the corresponding edit field should include provisions for printing a sign indication. One way to do this is to use a minus sign in the edit PICTURE in exactly the same way that the dollar sign is used in the preceding example. To illustrate, assume that a field is defined with

```
PIC S9999V99
```

An edit PICTURE that could be used and typical corresponding output are

```
PIC -ZZZ,ZZZ.99
```

Negative numbers in the source field

```
-125,301.80
-  3,450.25
-    595.50
```

Positive numbers in the source field

```
125,301.80
  3,450.25
    595.50
```

Notice that if the number is positive, the sign is replaced with a blank.

If you want the minus sign to float, the corresponding form is identical to that of the floating dollar sign. For example:

```
PIC ----,---.99
    -125,301.80
      -3,450.25
        -595.50
```

As with the floating dollar sign, one minus sign serves as the insertion symbol. In this case, six minus signs, together with the two 9 symbols, define the eight data positions of the field.

COBOL also allows you to position the sign character (a minus, the letters *CR*, or the letters *DB*) to the right of the field, as is shown by the following examples:

```
PIC ZZZ,ZZZ.99-
```

Negative numbers in the source field

```
125,301.80-
  3,450.25-
    595.50-
```

Positive numbers in the source field

```
125,301.80
  3,450.25
    595.50
```

```
PIC ZZZ,ZZZ.99CR
```

Negative numbers in the source field

```
125,301.80CR
  3,450.25CR
    595.50CR
```

Positive numbers in the source field

```
125,301.80
  3,450.25
    595.50
```

Editing Alphanumeric Fields

When discussing editing, we commonly think of numeric fields. However, a limited amount of insertion editing is possible with alphanumeric fields. There are three alphanumeric editing symbols:

B, 0 (zero), and / (slash)

Their uses are illustrated in the examples of Figure 6-11.

Figure 6-11

Examples of Alphanumeric Editing

If This Data:	Is Moved to This PICTURE:	The Result will be:
920714	99/99/99	92/07/14
920714	XX/XX/XX	92/07/14
123456789	X(3)BX(2)BX(4)	123 45 6789
PRICE&OLSON	X(5)BXBX(5)	PRICE & OLSON
1	X0	10
385	9(3)0(6)	385000000
111	0X0BX0X	010 101
111	/B9B9B9B/	/ 1 1 1 /
407PRG	X(3)BBX(3)	407 PRG
R30945F	XB9(5)/X	R 30945/F

Symbols That Can Appear in a PICTURE Clause

Data Position Symbols

You have now seen a plethora of symbols that can be used in forming a PICTURE symbol; the following is a summary of them.

Data position symbols reserve a position in the edit PICTURE for data from the source field. The characters that specify a data position are X, A, 9, Z, and *; in some conditions, the - (minus) and $ also represent data positions.

- **X** specifies that the position is to contain one alphanumeric data character. An alphanumeric data character is any character in the computer's character set.

- **A** specifies that the position is to contain one alphabetic data character. The alphabetic characters are the letters *A* through *Z*, *a* through *z*, and the space. The A descriptor is used primarily for documentation. It offers little advantage over the X descriptor because the system makes no check to assure that nonalphabetic information is contained in an alphabetic field.

- **9** specifies that the position is to contain one numeric data character. The numeric characters are the digits 0 through 9.

- **Z** specifies that the position is to contain one significant numeric data character. If the data character is not significant, the Z is replaced by a space. This is called zero suppression.

- ***** specifies that the position is to contain one significant numeric data character. If the data character is not significant, the * character remains in that position of the field. It is used to fill in the insignificant (blank) positions of a monetary amount.

- **-** Each minus after the first minus specifies that the position is to contain one significant numeric data character. If the data character is not significant, the - is replaced by a space. If the quantity is negative, a - will be positioned as described under the following descriptions of punctuation.

- **$** Each $ after the first $ specifies that the position is to contain one significant numeric data character. If the data character is not significant, the $ is replaced by a space. A $ will be positioned as described under the following descriptions of punctuation.

Punctuation Position Symbols

A punctuation position contains punctuation that will be inserted into the field. The characters that specify punctuation are decimal point, comma, $, B, 0, and / (slash).

- **.** (decimal point) remains undisturbed if it is significant. If it is not significant, it is replaced by a space. It is considered significant if it is followed by 9's in the PICTURE or if the data item is not equal to zero. In addition to being a punctuation character, it specifies the location of the decimal point in the receiving item.

- **,** remains undisturbed if it is significant (the edited field includes one or more nonzero digits to the left of the comma). Each comma that is not significant is replaced by a space.

- **$** remains undisturbed during the editing process if only one $ is included. If two or more are included, then zero suppression results and the $ is positioned to the immediate left of the first significant digit.

- **B** is always replaced by a space. It is used to insert blank spaces whenever desired in the edit field.

- **0** (zero) remains undisturbed during the editing process.

- **/** remains undisturbed during the editing process.

Sign Position Symbols

Sign position symbols indicate the sign of the data item. The characters that specify a sign position are +, -, CR, and DB.

- **+** will remain undisturbed if the data item is not negative. If the data item is negative, the + will be replaced by -.

- **-** (a single minus) will remain undisturbed only if the data item is negative. For a nonnegative data item, the minus is replaced by a space. If two or more minuses are included, then zero suppression occurs and the minus is positioned to the immediate left of the first significant digit.

- **CR** and **DB** will remain undisturbed only if the data item is negative. For a nonnegative data item, these characters are replaced by spaces.

Other PICTURE Symbols

In addition to the preceding symbols, the following characters may appear in a PICTURE:

- **S** specifies that the sign of the item is to be retained. If the S is not present, the value in the field will be unsigned and therefore positive. The S is intended for use with a numeric field and may *not* be used in an edited PICTURE.

- **V** indicates the position of the understood decimal point. In effect, it says, "This number does not contain an actual decimal point, but if it did, this is where it would be."

- **P** is called a *scaling character*. Each P specifies that the decimal point is to be moved one position before the data item is used in a calculation. Examples in this book do not use a scaling factor.

More Editing Examples

A variety of editing examples is included in Figure 6-12; these illustrate a wide range of commonly used editing techniques. Inspecting the examples, you see that the simple COBOL action of moving data to an edit field results in a lot of detailed work. It is sobering to realize that if the MOVE statement did not do this, the programmer desiring editing would have to write detailed instructions specifying each action to be carried out in the editing process.

Common Editing Problems

You should remember two important points about floating symbols. First, the PICTURE must contain one floating symbol for each data character to be inserted, plus one floating symbol for the symbol itself. For example, the PICTURE

        $,$$$.99

is not valid for a six-character data field because it contains only four $ symbols and two 9's to accommodate six data characters and a $. For a six-character field with a floating $, the PICTURE would have to be

        $$,$$$.99

The second point is that only one type of floating character can be used in a PICTURE; it is not permissible to mix floating characters. (For the purposes of this rule, floating characters are defined as $, Z, *, + and -.) The * can be used only for check protection; it cannot be used to print an identifying * to the right of a total.

The examples of Figure 6-13(a) illustrate the violation of some of these editing rules. The examples of Figure 6-13(b), although they may appear at first glance to be invalid, are actually valid edit PICTUREs.

Figure 6-12

Examples of Editing

Source Field		Destination Field	
PICTURE	**Data**	**PICTURE**	**Edited Result**
9(4)V99	001003	9,999.99	0,010.03
9(4)V99	000007	9,999.99	0,000.07
9(4)V99	000000	9,999.99	0,000.00
9(4)V99	001003	$9,999.99	$0,010.03
9(4)V99	000007	$9,999.99	$0,000.07
9(4)V99	000000	$9,999.99	$0,000.00
9(4)V99	001003	$Z,ZZZ.99	$ 10.03
9(4)V99	000007	$Z,ZZZ.99	$ .07
9(4)V99	000000	$Z,ZZZ.99	$ .00
9(4)V99	001003	$Z,ZZZ.ZZ	$ 10.03
9(4)V99	000007	$Z,ZZZ.ZZ	$ .07
9(4)V99	000000	$Z,ZZZ.ZZ	
9(4)V99	001003	$$,$$$.99	$ 10.03
9(4)V99	000007	$$,$$$.99	$ .07
9(4)V99	000000	$$,$$$.99	$ .00
9(4)V99	001003	$$,$$$.$$	$ 10.03
9(4)V99	000007	$$,$$$.$$	$ .07
9(4)V99	000000	$$,$$$.$$	
9(4)V99	001003	**,***.99	****10.03
9(4)V99	000007	**,***.99	******.07
9(4)V99	000000	**,***.99	******.00
9(4)V99	001003	**,***.**	****10.03
9(4)V99	000007	**,***.**	******.07
9(4)V99	000000	**,***.**	******.**
9(4)V99	001003	$*,***.99	$***10.03
9(4)V99	000007	$*,***.99	$*****.07
9(4)V99	000000	$*,***.99	$*****.00
9(4)V99	001003	$*,***.**	$***10.03
9(4)V99	000007	$*,***.**	$*****.07
9(4)V99	000000	$*,***.**	******.**

Examples of Editing: Zero Suppression   (a)

Source Field PICTURE	Destination Field PICTURE	Edited Result	
		If Data = +00010001	**If Data = -001001**
S9(4)V99	++,+++.99	+10.01	-10.01
S9(4)V99	--,---.99	10.01	-10.01
S9(4)V99	Z,ZZZ.99CR	10.01	10.01CR
S9(4)V99	Z,ZZZ.99BBCR	10.01	10.01 CR
S9(4)V99	Z,ZZZ.99DB	10.01	10.01DB
S9(4)V99	Z,ZZZ.99+	10.01+	10.01-
S9(4)V99	Z,ZZZ.99-	10.01	10.01-
S9(4)V99	Z,ZZZ.99	10.01	10.01
S9(4)V99	-$Z,ZZZ.99	$ 10.01	-$ 10.01
S9(4)V99	-$$,$$$.99	$10.01	- $10.01

Examples of Editing: Signed Numbers   (b)

Figure 6-13

Additional Examples

Erroneous PICTURE	Nature of Error
`$$$,ZZZ.99`	Mixed floating symbols are not permitted.
`,ZZZ.99`	Same as above.
`***,ZZZ.99`	Same as above.
`$$$,***.99`	Same as above.
`ZZZ,Z9Z.99`	Z must not appear to the right of 9.
`ZZZ,ZZZ.Z9`	Mixed characters to right of decimal point are not permitted.
`Z.-99`	Fixed sign must be leftmost or rightmost character.
`$-ZZ,ZZZ.99`	Same as above.
`----,--$.99`	$ cannot follow floating sign.
`XX-XX-XX`	- cannot be used for punctuation.
`XX:XX`	: cannot be used for punctuation.

Common Editing Errors   (a)

```
-ZZ9
ZZ9-
.99
-.99
.999,999
$---,---9
-$ZZ,ZZZ.99
```

Valid Edit Forms   (b)

More About Data and Data Handling

Data Types

It should now be apparent that the data items fall into five categories: alphanumeric, alphabetic, numeric, alphanumeric edited, and numeric edited. These categories are used by the COBOL compiler to determine the validity of the instructions in the PROCEDURE DIVISION. (For example, it would obviously be invalid to move alphabetic data to a numeric field or to use any type of data other than numeric data in an arithmetic operation. However, COBOL does not check the actual data to see that it conforms to the PICTURE; this is the programmer's responsibility.) COBOL uses the following rules in determining the data category of an item:

■ **Alphabetic:** The PICTURE is composed of the A descriptor (or the A and the B). An alphabetic data item should contain only the uppercase letters *A* through *Z*, the lowercase letters *a* through *z* and the space.

■ **Numeric:** The PICTURE is composed of the 9 descriptor. It may also contain one V, one S, and/or any number of P descriptors. A numeric data item should contain only the digits 0 through 9 and a sign.

■ **Alphanumeric:** The PICTURE is composed of the X descriptor. An alphanumeric data item may contain any character. Any PICTURE containing one or more of the descriptors A and 9, X and 9, or X and A is considered alphanumeric.

■ **Alphanumeric Edited:** The PICTURE is composed of the descriptors X and B, 0, or /.

■ **Numeric Edited:** The presence of any of the following descriptors designates a data item as numeric edited:

```
$ Z , . * + - CR DB
```

In addition, the PICTURE for a numeric-edited item may contain any of the following characters:

```
9 0 B P V /
```

Data Movement

Chapter 5 includes a brief summary of rules governing moving data when both the sending and receiving fields are either numeric or alphanumeric. In this chapter, you have learned how to edit by moving numeric data to numeric-edited data items and alphanumeric data to alphanumeric-edited data items. With the preceding summary of five data types with which you can work, the logical question is: What are the restrictions on data movement if the sending data is a different data type than the receiving data item? For instance, is it possible to move from a numeric data item to an alphanumeric data item. The answer is summarized in the table of Figure 6-14. The representation AN/AN means that an alphanumeric to alphanumeric move occurs; N/N means that a numeric to numeric move occurs. Any combination of sending and receiving data items marked "Illegal" represent an invalid combination for the MOVE and will be flagged by the compiler.

Arithmetic Operations and Edited Fields

In the RET-VAL1 program, the Price is multiplied by the Quantity-on-hand to obtain the Retail-value. Relevant statements for this action are repeated here in Figure 6-15. Notice that a separate work area for the arithmetic operation is set up in the WORKING-STORAGE SECTION (it is RETAIL-VALUE). After the computation, the result is moved from the work area into the numeric-edited data item RL-RETAIL-VALUE.

Sending Field	Receiving Field				
	Alphanumeric	Alphanumeric Edited	Numeric	Numeric Edited	Group
Alphanumeric	Left justification Receiving field shorter: truncation Receiving field longer: padding with spaces	Same as AN/AN also Editing is performed	Illegal	Illegal	Same as AN/AN
Alphanumeric edited	Same as AN/AN in COBOL-74. De-editing occurs in COBOL-85.	Same as AN/AN also Editing is performed	Illegal	Illegal	Same as AN/AN
Numeric *Integer* *Noninteger*	Same as AN/AN Illegal	Same as AN/AN also Editing is performed Illegal	Decimal point alignment Receiving field shorter: truncation Receiving field longer: padding with zeros	Same as N/N also Editing is performed	Same as AN/AN
Numeric edited	Same as AN/AN	Same as AN/AN also Editing is performed	Illegal in COBOL-74 De-editing occurs in COBOL-85	Illegal	Same as AN/AN
Group	Same as AN/AN	Same as AN/AN (No editing is performed)	Illegal	Illegal	Same as AN/AN

Figure 6-14

MOVE Statement Summary

AN/AN=Alphanumeric to alphanumeric
N/N=Numeric to numeric

In case the idea has occurred to you of eliminating the work field and performing the arithmetic using the edited field, forget it. Only numeric items can be involved in arithmetic operations; *numeric-edited items cannot be.* Thus, for instance, the sequence

```
MOVE IR-PRICE TO RL-RETAIL-VALUE
MULTIPLY IR-QUANT-ON-HAND BY RL-RETAIL-VALUE
```

is not valid because one of the operands in the MULTIPLY (RL-RETAIL-VALUE) is not a numeric item. However, you will learn about an alternative in Chapter 7.

Figure 6-15

Using a Work Area for a Computation

```
        From the input record.
        10   IR-QUANT-ON-HAND      PIC 9(3).
        .
        .
        .
        10   IR-PRICE              PIC 9(3)V9(2).
        .
        .
        .
        From the output record.
        10   RL-RETAIL-VALUE       PIC ZZZ,ZZZ.99.
        .
        .
        .
        From WORKING-STORAGE.
        10   RETAIL-VALUE          PIC 9(6)V99.
        .
        .
        .
        From the PROCEDURE DIVISION.
        MOVE IR-PRICE TO RETAIL-VALUE
        MULTIPLY IR-QUANT-ON-HAND BY RETAIL-VALUE
```

Chapter Summary

General

Always include the sign character S in a field that might contain a negative number; otherwise, the sign will be discarded during program execution.

The V does *not* cause a memory position to be reserved for a data item because the decimal position is understood by the COBOL system. For instance, the PICTURE 999V99 will require 5 memory positions.

In contrast to the V, the decimal point (period) in a picture does require a position in the output line. For instance, 999.99 will require 6 positions.

The sign is stored with a data value in memory in either of two ways: imbedded in the data field and in a separate character. Embedded is the default. This is only important if you are processing a data file in which the sign is stored in a separate character.

There are two basic elements of editing data:

- A PICTURE that defines the format of the edit field
- A MOVE statement that moves the data into that edit field

Editing occurs when data is moved to a data item defined with a PICTURE that contains edit codes.

There are two broad categories of editing operations: suppression with replacement and insertion. *Suppression with replacement* editing is the replacing of leading zeros with another character (space or asterisk). *Insertion* editing is inserting punctuation or sign characters into the field.

A sign can be positioned to the right or to the left of a data field for editing. The letters *CR* or *DB* can alternately be used to the right of a field for negative sign indication.

Limited editing can be done on alphanumeric fields. The three alphanumeric-editing symbols are B, 0 (zero), and / (slash).

COBOL supports five data types:

- numeric
- alphabetic
- alphanumeric
- numeric edited
- alphanumeric edited

Programming Conventions

In preceding chapters, the length of PICTURE character string has been designated by using parentheses. For example, PIC X(5) is preferable to PIC XXXXX. Do not use this method for edit field descriptions. For instance, use ZZZ,ZZZ.99 rather than Z(3),Z(3).9(2). The latter tends to be too confusing. Repeating the elements as in the former produces a form that is similar to the way the finished output will appear. Use the same form on the printed spacing chart.

Error Prevention/ Detection

If numeric output is incorrect, it could be a result of failing to include the sign character S in a field involved in an arithmetic operation. Be especially alert with arithmetic work areas in the WORKING-STORAGE SECTION.

Count *all* characters in the edit PICTURE when setting up the output line. Remember, the understood decimal point in memory requires a position when printed on the output line in an edit PICTURE including a decimal point.

The floating fill characters $ and * require an extra position in the output PICTURE. For instance, the PICTURE $$$$.99 can handle a number up to 999.99 (it will be printed as $999.99).

Do not mix floating symbols ($, Z, *, +, and -) in an edit picture.

Do not use numeric-edited items as operands involved in arithmetic operations because this is not valid.

Questions and Exercises

Give a brief description of each of the following terms that were introduced in this chapter.

Key Terminology

alphabetic PICTURE	numeric-edited PICTURE
alphanumeric-edited PICTURE	numeric PICTURE
alphanumeric PICTURE	punctuation position
edit	sign position
edited item	suppression
embedded sign	suppression with replacement
float	zero suppression
insertion editing	zero suppression with asterisk replacement

General Questions

1. What is wrong with the following field definition?

   ```
   10 CHECK-FIELD PIC 99V99V99.
   ```

2. What are the two general methods by which the sign of a numeric field is stored in memory?

3. In a program that performed a series of calculations, the programmer discovered that some results of extensive calculations came out positive when they should have been negative. This happened even though the input fields included the S character for sign and the output edit descriptions also included appropriate sign indication. Describe a likely reason for these erroneous results.

4. A dollar and cent field to be edited will always be less than 1,000. What is wrong with the PICTURE $$$.99 for this field?

5. What are the different ways that a negative amount can be indicated on an output line?

6. The following appeared in a program. What is wrong with it?

```
10 FIELD-A PIC 9(3).9(2).
10 FIELD-B PIC 9(3).9(2).
          .
          .
          .
10 RL-TOTAL PIC 999.99-.
          .
          .
          .
MOVE FIELD-A TO RL-TOTAL
ADD FIELD-B TO RL-TOTAL
```

Questions Relating to the Example Programs

1. What changes would be necessary to the RET-VAL1 program (Figure 6-2) if the Quantity-on-hand field could be either positive or negative?

2. What do you think could happen if the work area RETAIL-VALUE of the RET-VAL1. program were defined as follows?

```
10 RETAIL-VALUE PIC S9(4)V9(2).
```

Writing Program Statements

1. The following are data PICTUREs and corresponding data field values. How will each field be interpreted by a program?

PICTURE	Recorded in the Record
99V9	125
V999	014
9999V9	28001
9(4)V99	987654
9(4)V9(3)	9876543

2. Write an input record description for the following EXAMPLE-RECORD:

Field	Field Positions	Format
Employee number	1–5	
Name	6–27	
Hours worked	31–33	$nn_\wedge n$
Pay rate	34–37	$nn_\wedge nn$
Bonus increment	38–40	$_\wedge nnn$
Accumulated vacation	41–42	nn

3. For each case given, write the edited result (the contents of the destination field) after the data in the source field has been moved to it.

Source Field PICTURE	Source Field Contents	Destination Field PICTURE
a. S9(4)V99	013487	$Z,ZZZ.99BCR
b. S9(4)V99	-600000	$Z,ZZZ.99BCR
c. S9(4)V99	-001372	$Z,ZZZ.99
d. S9(4)V99	-001372	$B9,999.99+

4. Write the PICTURE that specifies the required editing for each situation given. In each one, the PICTURE of the source field is given first, followed by the editing specifications for the destination field.

a. S9(6)V99; zero suppression, fixed $, credit symbol "-" following number.

b. Same as (a). In addition, specify one blank space between the $ and the beginning of the data, and two blank spaces between the end of the data and the -.

c. S9(6)V99; floating $, credit symbol CR.

d. 9(4); print as dollars and cents, with fixed dollar sign and check-protection asterisks.

e. S9(5); zero suppression; precede the most significant digit with a "-" if the data is negative and a space if the data is positive.

f. S9(5); the amount represents thousands of dollars; print as whole dollars (no decimal point). Suppress insignificant zeros. Precede the most significant digit with a - if the number is negative and a + if the number is positive.

5. Using the EXAMPLE-RECORD in Exercise 2, write an output record description to include appropriate editing for the numeric fields.

a. Are dollar signs and leading zero suppression applicable to any of the numeric fields?

b. Do any of the numeric fields need to be signed?

6. For each case given, write the edited result (the contents of the destination field) after the data in the source field has been moved to it.

Source Field PICTURE	Source Field Contents	Destination Field PICTURE
a. S9(5)V99	-0150915	$ZZ,ZZZ.99CR
b. S9(4)V99	005000	$Z,ZZZ.99-
c. S9(6)V99	00233642	$***,***.99-
d. S9(5)	-00015	- - - - - -
e. S9(6)V99	00006001	$$$$,$$$.99-
f. S9(5)	20000	+++,+++

7. The following edit PICTUREs are incorrect. Rewrite them so that they are correctly stated.

a. --,--$.99

b. $$,***.99

c. ZZ,Z9Z.99

d. ZZ,ZZZ.Z9

e. ZZZ.-99

f. XX:XX:XX

Programming Assignments

Programming assignments in this and following chapters use data files. For the record description of all files used in the assignments, you must use Appendix A.

6-1 Airport Traffic Listing

The manager of the Anacin airport has a favorite project to study airline traffic into and out of the airport. In order to see if her ideas have any potential, she needs a printed listing of selected fields from an airport file.

Output Requirements:
A printed report with the following output and format.

Field	Beginning Column	Output Format
Flight ID	1	Insert hyphen between positions 1 and 2 *x-xxxx*
Date of flight	9	Insert slashes: *mm/dd/yy*
Arrival/departure time	19	Insert colon: *hh:mm*
Total seats on airplane	26	Suppress leading zeros
Number of passengers on flight	31	Suppress leading zeros
Number of crew members	36	Suppress leading zeros
Generalized performance score	41	Use floating minus sign, insert comma and decimal point

You must prepare a printer spacing chart from the above table.

Input Description:
File name: AIRPORT1.DL
Record description: See Appendix A

Processing Requirements:
For each record in the file:
1. Edit each field as designated in the preceding Output Format description.
2. Print one double-spaced line for each record in the file.

6-2 Employee Earnings Report

The Donut Manufacturing Company maintains an employee payroll file that includes, for each employee, total earnings, taxes withheld, and Social Security (FICA) withheld since the beginning of the year. These are called year-to-date (YTD) values. To start each payroll period, the payroll clerk needs a detail report of these year-to-date figures.

Output Requirements:
A printed report with the following output and format.

Field	Beginning Column	Output Format
Social Security number	1	Insert hyphens; for instance: 123-45-6789
Employee name	13	
Monthly gross pay	38	Insert decimal point and commas and zero suppress
Year-to-date earnings	47	Same actions as Gross pay
Year-to-date income tax withholding	60	Same actions as Gross pay
Year-to-date FICA withholding	71	Same actions as Gross pay

You must prepare a printer spacing chart from the above table.

Input Description:
    File name: EMPLOYEE.DL
    Record description: See Appendix A

Processing Requirements:
    For each record in the file:
    1. Edit each field as designated in the preceding Output Format description.
    2. Print one double-spaced line for each record in the file.

6-3 List of Students

A local college maintains a student master file for each student enrolled at the college. The student record includes data regarding credit units that the student has completed and grade points. The registrar would like a printed scholarship list of students.

Output Requirements:
    A printed report with the following output and format.

Field	Beginning Column	Output Format
Social Security number	1	Insert hyphens; for instance: 123-45-6789
Student last name	11	
Student first name	23	
Cumulative units	36	Insert a decimal point, suppress leading zeros
Cumulative points	42	Same as cumulative points
Cumulative GPA	48	Insert a decimal point, suppress leading zeros
GPA last semester	53	Same as cumulative GPA

You must prepare a printer spacing chart from the above table.

Input Description:
    File name: STUDENTS.DL
    Record description: See Appendix A

Processing Requirements:
    For each record in the file:

    1. Calculate the cumulative GPA as:

$$= \frac{\text{Cumulative points}}{\text{Cumulative units}}$$

    2. Edit each field as designated in the preceding Output Format description.
    3. Print one double-spaced line for each record in the file.

6-4 Enrollment Report

During the registration process at most institutions, the administration carefully monitors enrollment in order to modify class offerings to accommodate course demand. One useful way of reporting is to compare actual enrollment to minimum acceptable enrollment by class.

Output Requirements:

A printed report with the following output and format.

Field	Beginning Column	Output Format
Class code	1	
Course name	6	*print full field with 1 blank btwn each field*
Course number	23	
Section number	27	
Instructor name	30	
Minimum permissible enrollment	45	Zero suppress **Z**
Actual enrollment	50	Zero suppress
Enrollment as percentage of minimum	55	Format: *nnn.n* Insert decimal point zero suppress

You must prepare a printer spacing chart from the above table.

Input Description:

File name: ENROLL01.DL

Record description: See Appendix A

Processing Requirements:

For each record in the file:

1. Calculate the enrollment as percentage of minimum

$$= \frac{\text{minimum permissible enrollment}}{\text{actual enrollment}} \times 100$$

2. Print one double-spaced line for each record in the file, as specified by the above table.

print FullField
with 1 blank
btwn each field

7

ARITHMETIC OPERATIONS

Chapter Objectives

You have had a brief introduction to the basic forms of the four COBOL arithmetic statements: ADD, SUBTRACT, MULTIPLY, and DIVIDE. In addition to these forms, several others fulfill a variety of calculational needs. This chapter describes in detail the calculational capabilities of COBOL. You will learn about the following topics:

■ The GIVING form of arithmetic statements, whereby values of the operands involved in the arithmetic operation are unchanged—with the result stored in another data item

■ Rounding off the result of a calculation

■ Handling data overflow in which the destination data item is not large enough to hold the calculated result (the SIZE ERROR clause)

■ The general forms of the ADD, SUBTRACT, MULTIPLY, and DIVIDE statements

■ The COMPUTE statement, which allows arithmetic operations to be designated in an algebra expression form

The GIVING Option in Arithmetic Operations

How the GIVING Works

In Chapter 2, you used the simplest forms of the COBOL computational capabilities. That is, in an arithmetic operation between two quantities, the result replaced one of the quantities. For example, in the statement

```
ADD FIELD-A TO FIELD-B
```

the quantity in FIELD-A is added to the quantity in FIELD-B. FIELD-A is unchanged, but the sum replaces the original quantity in FIELD-B.

Another form of the arithmetic statements leaves the contents of both component fields unchanged and places the result in a third field. The following is an example of the ADD:

```
ADD FIELD-A TO FIELD-B GIVING FIELD-C
```

The sequence of events when COBOL carries out this operation is illustrated in Figure 7-1. The steps are as follows:

1. A temporary work area is set up to hold the result of the arithmetic operation.

2. The operation is carried out; the result is in the temporary work area.

3. The contents of the temporary work area are moved to the field designated by the GIVING.

In the sections that follow, you will learn about the multiple options for each of the arithmetic statements.

Figure 7-1

Action of the ADD/GIVING Statement

	ADD FIELD-A TO FIELD-B GIVING FIELD-C			
Memory	FIELD-A	FIELD-B	Temporary work area	FIELD-C
Initial contents.	1 5 3 6 2	9 8 7 1 5		?
Create temporary work area.	1 5 3 6 2	9 8 7 1 5		?
Move FIELD-B contents to work area.	1 5 3 6 2	9 8 7 1 5	0 9 8 7 1 5	?
Add FIELD-A contents to work area.	1 5 3 6 2	9 8 7 1 5	1 1 4 0 7 7	?
Move contents of work area to FIELD-C.	1 5 3 6 2	9 8 7 1 5		1 1 4 0 7 7

Using Numeric-Edited Data Items in a GIVING Clause

You know that the fields involved in arithmetic operations must be numeric; numeric-edited data items are not allowed. However, referring to the preceding description of the ADD/GIVING example, you can see that the GIVING field (FIELD-C in this case) is *not* involved in arithmetic. COBOL sets up a temporary work area for the calculation, then *moves* the value to the GIVING field. Hence, the field following the GIVEN clause can be a *numeric-edited data item.* This is true of all the arithmetic operations.

Insufficient Positions for a Result Field

An arithmetic result may "overflow" the result field in two possible ways. COBOL provides means for handling both of them.

Losing Digits to the Right of the Decimal Point

One of the *overflow* possibilities occurs when the destination field does not have sufficient positions to handle the arithmetic result. For instance, in Figure 7-2, notice the FIELD-C is defined with only one digit to the right of the decimal, whereas FIELD-A and FIELD-B both have two. In this case, the 8 is discarded or *truncated.* This action is done automatically and without warning.

The standard arithmetic rule used in most applications for handling situations such as illustrated by Figure 7-2 is to *round off.* With this rule, if the leftmost digit to be discarded is 5 or greater, then the number is rounded up; otherwise, it is truncated. The following examples illustrate rounding off to one decimal place.

779.60 rounds to 779.6
779.64 rounds to 779.6
779.65 rounds to 779.7
779.69 rounds to 779.7

To implement rounding, you need only include the ROUNDED clause in the arithmetic statement.

```
ADD FIELD-A TO FIELD-B
  GIVING C ROUNDED
```

Figure 7-2

Truncation in an Arithmetic Operation

```
10  FIELD-A     PIC 999V99.
10  FIELD-B     PIC 999V99.
10  FIELD-C     PIC 999V9.

ADD FIELD-A TO FIELD-B
    GIVING FIELD-C
```

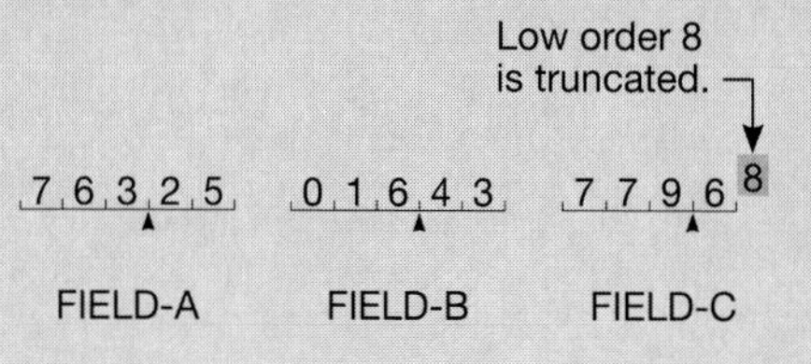

Losing Significant Digits

The second—and more serious—of the two overflow possibilities occurs when there are insufficient positions to the left to hold the result. A very simple case is shown in Figure 7-3, in which the QUANT-ON-HAND field is not large enough to hold the result when IR-RECEIVED is added to it. Relating this back to the software inventory application, this is especially serious because the computer data will show only 386 units on hand, when in reality there are 1386.

Detection of Arithmetic Overflow

Obviously, overflow can be avoided by making arithmetic fields large enough to hold any value resulting from a given operation. However, performing some actions—such as accumulating an unusual data set—might cause unexpectedly large results, producing an overflow.

Figure 7-3

*Losing a Significant Digit—
Arithmetic Overflow*

```
10  IR-RECEIVED      PIC 999.
.
.
.
10  QUANT-ON-HAND    PIC 999.
.
.
.
ADD IR-RECEIVED TO QUANT-ON-HAND
```

	IR-RECEIVED	QUANT-ON-HAND
Before	5 0 0	8 8 6
After	5 0 0	¹3 8 6

High-order 1 is
truncated (discarded).

To safeguard against the resulting loss of data, COBOL includes provisions to assist you in dealing with this "size error" problem. You can specify, by the SIZE ERROR clause, the action to be taken when the result of an arithmetic operation is numerically too large to fit into the receiving field. This applies *only* to left truncation that is overflow (not to right truncation). Inclusion of the size error capability and its effect on the nature of the arithmetic operation are illustrated in Figure 7-4. When the SIZE ERROR clause is specified, COBOL executes the arithmetic operation in its work area. If ROUNDING has been specified, it rounds the result. Then it checks to see if the result field is large enough to contain the result.

■ If the result is large enough, the result is moved to the result field and the program continues.

■ If the result field is not large enough, the program executes the statement(s) following the words SIZE ERROR. When this occurs, the contents of the result field are not altered.

Figure 7-4

*Effect of the
ON SIZE ERROR*

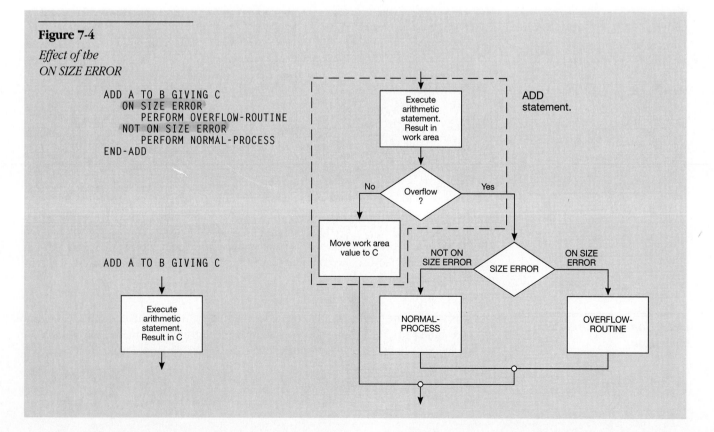

The SIZE ERROR clause can be included following any arithmetic statement; its format for the ADD is

```
ADD ...
    [ON SIZE ERROR
        imperative-statement-1]
    [NOT ON SIZE ERROR
        imperative-statement-2]
    [END-ADD]
```

The SIZE ERROR also detects division by zero with the DIVIDE statement.

If the SIZE ERROR clause is not specified and a size error occurs, no indication is given. The result is moved to the result field with truncation and the program continues to the next statement.

If a size error occurs, the statements to be executed depend entirely on program requirements. Perhaps all that might be needed is to output a message; perhaps the program should perform a routine that will attempt to correct the situation; perhaps the program should stop. Some examples of typical SIZE ERROR clause coding are given in Figure 7-5.

Complete Forms of the Arithmetic Statements

The ADD Statement

There are two formats of the ADD statement. The one you have been using since Chapter 2 has the following general format:

$$\underline{\text{ADD}} \begin{Bmatrix} \text{identifier-1} \\ \text{literal-1} \end{Bmatrix} \text{...} \quad \underline{\text{TO}} \{\text{identifier-2 [ROUNDED]}\}\text{...}$$

```
    [ON SIZE ERROR
        imperative-statement-1]
    [NOT ON SIZE ERROR
        imperative-statement-2]
    [END-ADD]
```

As you recall from Chapter 2, the quantities being added can be either data fields in memory or actual fixed numeric values (numeric literals). This is indicated by the two items, one over the other, enclosed in braces.

Notice that the general form includes the ellipsis on the first operand. This tells you that there can be one *or more* quantities preceding the TO. For example:

```
ADD FIELD-A FIELD-B FIELD-C 25 TO FIELD-D
```

Figure 7-5

Examples of the ON SIZE ERROR Clause

```
MULTIPLY QUANT BY PRICE GIVING PRICE-EXT
   ON SIZE ERROR
      PERFORM SIZE-ERROR--RTN
   END-MULTIPLY

DIVIDE TOTAL BY COUNTER GIVING AVERAGE
   ON SIZE ERROR
      DISPLAY "Value of COUNTER is zero when attempting"
      DISPLAY "to calculate average--terminating."
      CLOSE ...
      STOP RUN
   END-DIVIDE

ADD A, B, C, D, E GIVING HOLD
   ON SIZE ERROR
      MOVE CUSTOMER-NUM-IN TO CUSTOMER-NUM-ERR
      WRITE ERROR-RECORD
   NOT ON SIZE ERROR
      WRITE PRINT-RECORD
   END-ADD
```

Here the contents of FIELD-A, FIELD-B, and FIELD-C and the fixed value 25 will be added to the value stored in SUM-FIELD. The result will replace the original contents of SUM-FIELD. If you find this string of fields confusing, you can use commas to separate, as follows:

```
ADD FIELD-A, FIELD-B, FIELD-C, 25 TO FIELD-D
```

Some programmers feel that the documentation value is enhanced by using multiple program lines, as follows:

```
ADD FIELD-A
    FIELD-B
    FIELD-C
    25   TO FIELD-D
```

The ellipsis on the second operand of the general format (following the TO) tell you that this field can be repeated also. For instance, if you needed to add 12.5 to each of three fields, the statement could take the following form:

```
ADD 12.5 TO FIELD-A, FIELD-B, FIELD-C
```

This is equivalent to three independent ADD statements:

```
ADD 12.5 TO FIELD-A
ADD 12.5 TO FIELD-B
ADD 12.5 TO FIELD-C
```

The second of the ADD statement formats includes the GIVING; its general format is

$$
\underline{\text{ADD}} \left\{ \begin{array}{l} \text{identifier-1} \\ \text{literal-1} \end{array} \right\} \dots \quad \underline{\text{TO}} \left\{ \begin{array}{l} \text{identifier-2} \\ \text{literal-2} \end{array} \right\}
$$

```
GIVING {identifier-3 [ROUNDED]}...
[ON SIZE ERROR
    imperative-statement-1]
[NOT ON SIZE ERROR
    imperative-statement-2]
[END-ADD]
```

Notice that the TO is optional in this format. Thus, the following examples are equivalent:

```
ADD FIELD-A FIELD-B FIELD-C 25 FIELD-D
    GIVING SUM-FIELD

ADD FIELD-A FIELD-B FIELD-C 25 TO FIELD-D
    GIVING SUM-FIELD
```

In this case, the TO tends to be misleading because the form can be interpreted to suggest that the field following the TO (FIELD-D in this case) is treated differently than the others. It is not.

If you need to have the resulting sum stored in two or more fields, you can include each of them following the GIVING. For instance:

```
ADD FIELD-A FIELD-B FIELD-C 25 FIELD-D
    GIVING SUM-FIELD HOLD-FIELD

ADD FIELD-A
    FIELD-B
    FIELD-C
    25
    FIELD-D
  GIVING
    SUM-FIELD
    HOLD-FIELD
```

Here the resulting sum will be moved to both SUM-FIELD and HOLD-FIELD.

The SUBTRACT Statement

As with the ADD, there are two forms of the SUBTRACT. The general format of the first form is

$$\underline{\text{SUBTRACT}} \begin{Bmatrix} \text{identifier-1} \\ \text{literal-1} \end{Bmatrix} \cdots \quad \underline{\text{FROM}} \; \{\text{identifier-2 } [\underline{\text{ROUNDED}}]\} \cdots$$

```
[ON SIZE ERROR
    imperative-statement-1]
[NOT ON SIZE ERROR
    imperative-statement-2]
[END-SUBTRACT]
```

The following is an example of the SUBTRACT:

```
SUBTRACT PAYMENTS ALLOWANCE OTHER-CREDITS FROM BALANCE
```

Alternative ways of writing this are

```
SUBTRACT PAYMENTS, ALLOWANCE, OTHER-CREDITS FROM BALANCE

SUBTRACT PAYMENTS
     ALLOWANCE
     OTHER-CREDITS  FROM BALANCE
```

The action of this statement will be to subtract the values in the three fields PAYMENTS, ALLOWANCE, and OTHER-CREDITS from the quantity in BALANCE. The result will replace the original contents of BALANCE.

The second format of the SUBTRACT uses the GIVING; its partial general format is

$$\underline{\text{SUBTRACT}} \begin{Bmatrix} \text{identifier-1} \\ \text{literal-1} \end{Bmatrix} \cdots \quad \underline{\text{FROM}} \begin{Bmatrix} \text{identifier-2} \\ \text{literal-2} \end{Bmatrix}$$

```
GIVING {identifier-3 [ROUNDED]}...
[ON SIZE ERROR
    imperative-statement-1]
[NOT ON SIZE ERROR
    imperative-statement-2]
[END-SUBTRACT]
```

This is best illustrated with an example (the following two forms are equivalent):

```
SUBTRACT PAYMENTS ALLOWANCE OTHER-CREDITS FROM OLD-BALANCE
     GIVING NEW-BALANCE

SUBTRACT PAYMENTS
     ALLOWANCE
     OTHER-CREDITS  FROM OLD-BALANCE
                    GIVING NEW-BALANCE
```

Here the values in PAYMENTS, ALLOWANCE, and OTHER-CREDITS are subtracted from the quantity in OLD-BALANCE. OLD-BALANCE is unchanged; the result is placed in NEW-BALANCE.

Notice that in contrast to the ADD in which TO is optional, the FROM is required in this format of the SUBTRACT.

The MULTIPLY Statement

The MULTIPLY statement is slightly different than the ADD and SUBTRACT statements regarding the way in which operand repetition is done. The general form of the first format is

$$\text{\underline{MULTIPLY}} \begin{Bmatrix} \text{identifier-1} \\ \text{literal-1} \end{Bmatrix} \text{\underline{BY}} \{\text{identifier-2 [\underline{ROUNDED}]}\} \ldots$$

```
[ON SIZE ERROR
   imperative-statement-1]
[NOT ON SIZE ERROR
   imperative-statement-2]
[END-MULTIPLY]
```

This form allows you to multiply several quantities by a single quantity. For instance, the statement

```
MULTIPLY FACTOR BY FIELD-A, FIELD-B, FIELD-C
```

causes the values in FIELD-A, FIELD-B, and FIELD-C to be multiplied (independent of one another) by the value in FACTOR. This is equivalent to the following three statements:

```
MULTIPLY FACTOR BY FIELD-A
MULTIPLY FACTOR BY FIELD-B
MULTIPLY FACTOR BY FIELD-C
```

The second format of the MULTIPLY includes the GIVING; its general format is as follows:

$$\text{MULTIPLY} \begin{Bmatrix} \text{identifier-1} \\ \text{literal-1} \end{Bmatrix} \text{\underline{BY}} \begin{Bmatrix} \text{identifier-2} \\ \text{literal-2} \end{Bmatrix}$$

```
GIVING {identifier-3 [ROUNDED]}...
[ON SIZE ERROR
   imperative-statement-1]
[NOT ON SIZE ERROR
   imperative-statement-2]
[END-MULTIPLY]
```

When doing multiplication operations with quantities that have decimal points, you will commonly use the ROUNDED clause. For instance, assume that the software company has a discount rate in the input record with the following definition:

```
10 IR-DISCOUNT-RATE  PIC V999.
```

For each sale, you need to calculate the discount (in dollars and cents) as the discount rate times the price. If DISCOUNTED-PRICE is defined with PIC 999V99, the multiplication would be done with the statement shown in Figure 7-6. Sample memory contents illustrate how this works.

In this general format of the MULTIPLY, you can see that only identifier-3 has ellipsis; thus, you can multiply two quantities and have the result duplicated to one or more fields.

Figure 7-6

Rounding the Result of a Multiplication

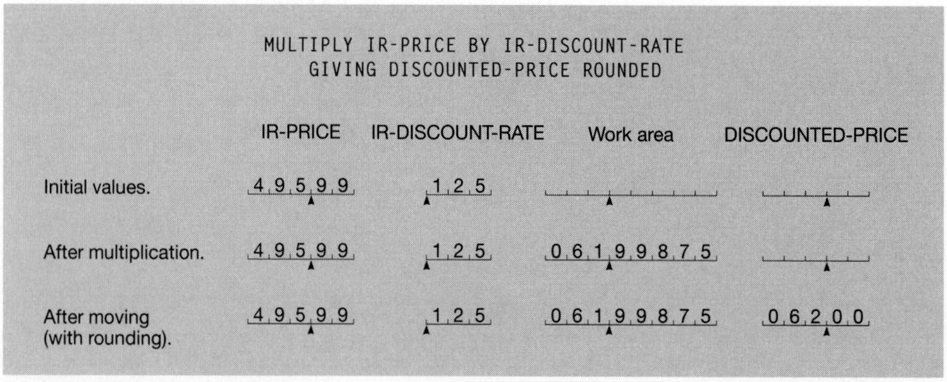

```
        MULTIPLY IR-PRICE BY IR-DISCOUNT-RATE
              GIVING DISCOUNTED-PRICE ROUNDED
```

	IR-PRICE	IR-DISCOUNT-RATE	Work area	DISCOUNTED-PRICE
Initial values.	4,9,5,9,9	1,2,5		
After multiplication.	4,9,5,9,9	1,2,5	0,6,1,9,9,8,7,5	
After moving (with rounding).	4,9,5,9,9	1,2,5	0,6,1,9,9,8,7,5	0,6,2,0,0

The DIVIDE/INTO Statement

The DIVIDE statement can be used with the INTO (introduced in Chapter 2) or the BY; in all, it has five formats.

The first two formats are identical to the two MULTIPLY formats; the general forms are

DIVIDE $\begin{Bmatrix} \text{identifier-1} \\ \text{literal-1} \end{Bmatrix}$ INTO {identifier-2 [ROUNDED]} ...

    [ON SIZE ERROR

       imperative-statement-1]

    [NOT ON SIZE ERROR

       imperative-statement-2]

    [END-DIVIDE]

DIVIDE $\begin{Bmatrix} \text{identifier-1} \\ \text{literal-1} \end{Bmatrix}$ INTO $\begin{Bmatrix} \text{identifier-2} \\ \text{literal-2} \end{Bmatrix}$

    GIVING {identifier-3 [ROUNDED]}...

    [ON SIZE ERROR

       imperative-statement-1]

    [NOT ON SIZE ERROR

       imperative-statement-2]

    [END-DIVIDE]

These statements function as you would expect; for instance, consider the statements

```
DIVIDE 12 INTO FIELD-B
DIVIDE WS-COUNT INTO TOTAL-SALES GIVING AVERAGE-SALES
```

In the first statement, 12 is divided into the contents of FIELD-B with the quotient being stored in FIELD-B. In the second statement, WS-COUNT is divided into TOTAL-SALES and the result is stored in AVERAGE-SALES.

In a division operation, a remainder often is left. For instance, with whole numbers, if you divide 25 by 7, the quotient is 3 and the remainder is 4. Some applications require the remainder. For instance, assume that you are working on an inventory application in which the quantity on hand for the item is measured in ounces (rather than the number of units). One of the requirements of the application is that the weight for all items in the inventory be summed and printed at the end of the report. (You will learn how to do this in the next chapter.) Although weights of individual items are measured in ounces, the total is to be printed in pounds and ounces. As an example, consider the total weight of 877 ounces.

$$\frac{877}{16} = 54 \text{ with a remainder of } 13$$

The quotient 54 is the number of pounds and the remainder 13 is the number of remaining ounces. The next form of the DIVIDE (actually the fourth format in the COBOL standard) gives you the capability to obtain both of these.

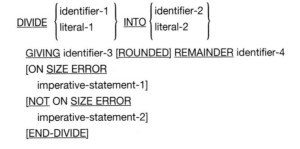

DIVIDE $\begin{Bmatrix} \text{identifier-1} \\ \text{literal-1} \end{Bmatrix}$ INTO $\begin{Bmatrix} \text{identifier-2} \\ \text{literal-2} \end{Bmatrix}$

    GIVING identifier-3 [ROUNDED] REMAINDER identifier-4

    [ON SIZE ERROR

       imperative-statement-1]

    [NOT ON SIZE ERROR

       imperative-statement-2]

    [END-DIVIDE]

The preceding pound/ounce calculation is shown in Figure 7-7.

The DIVIDE/BY Statement

The two forms of the DIVIDE/BY statement are basically the same as those of the DIVIDE/INTO statement, except that the two operands are effectively reversed.

$$\underline{\text{DIVIDE}} \left\{ \begin{matrix} \text{identifier-1} \\ \text{literal-1} \end{matrix} \right\} \underline{\text{BY}} \left\{ \begin{matrix} \text{identifier-2} \\ \text{literal-2} \end{matrix} \right\}$$

$\underline{\text{GIVING}}$ {identifier-3 [$\underline{\text{ROUNDED}}$]}...

[ON $\underline{\text{SIZE ERROR}}$

imperative-statement-1]

[$\underline{\text{NOT}}$ ON $\underline{\text{SIZE ERROR}}$

imperative-statement-2]

[$\underline{\text{END-DIVIDE}}$]

$$\underline{\text{DIVIDE}} \left\{ \begin{matrix} \text{identifier-1} \\ \text{literal-1} \end{matrix} \right\} \underline{\text{BY}} \left\{ \begin{matrix} \text{identifier-2} \\ \text{literal-2} \end{matrix} \right\}$$

$\underline{\text{GIVING}}$ identifier-3 [$\underline{\text{ROUNDED}}$] $\underline{\text{REMAINDER}}$ identifier-4

[ON $\underline{\text{SIZE ERROR}}$

imperative-statement-1]

[$\underline{\text{NOT}}$ ON $\underline{\text{SIZE ERROR}}$

imperative-statement-2]

[$\underline{\text{END-DIVIDE}}$]

The division of Figure 7-7 could be done with the DIVIDE/BY statement, as follows:

```
DIVIDE TOTAL-OUNCES BY 16
    GIVING POUNDS
        REMAINDER OUNCES
```

Whether you use the INTO or BY form is a matter of personal choice; sometimes one yields better documentation than the other.

Figure 7-7

Capturing the Remainder of a Division

```
10   TOTAL-OUNCES    PIC 9(4).
10   POUNDS          PIC 9(3).
10   OUNCES          PIC 9(2).
     .
     .
     .
DIVIDE 16 INTO TOTAL-OUNCES
    GIVING POUNDS
        REMAINDER OUNCES
```

	TOTAL-OUNCES	POUNDS	OUNCES
Initial values.	1 6	0 8 7 7	?	?
After division.	1 6	0 8 7 7	0 5 4	1 3
			↑	↑
			Quotient	Remainder

The COMPUTE Statement

Complex Computations

The arithmetic operations discussed so far have been simple ones with relatively few operands. In some cases, business computations are not so simple. The desired result sometimes must be obtained through a series of calculations determined by a mathematical formula such as

Accumulation of simple interest	$A = P(1 + rt)$
Accumulation of compound interest	$A = P(1 + i)^t$
Proceeds from discounted note	$P = S \dfrac{Sdt}{360}$
Annual percentage rate	$r = \dfrac{2mi}{P(n + 1)}$
Annual depreciation (straight line method)	$D = \dfrac{C - S}{y}$
Annual depreciation (sum of years digits method)	$D = \dfrac{C - S}{n(n + 1)/2}$

All but one could be calculated by using conventional arithmetic commands that you have already studied, but the coding would be cumbersome. For example, the following sequence calculates annual percentage rate:

```
MULTIPLY 2 BY M GIVING WORK1
MULTIPLY I BY WORK1
ADD N, 1 GIVING WORK2
MULTIPLY P BY WORK2
DIVIDE WORK2 INTO WORK1 GIVING R
```

Performing the exponentiation required by the second formula could be done, but it would require program logic and a knowledge of mathematics; it would be especially clumsy if the exponent were not a whole number. As a solution to these problems, the COBOL language includes the COMPUTE statement, which allows you to express a series of calculations in a form very similar to the equivalent mathematical formula. The basic format of the COMPUTE is

```
COMPUTE {identifier-1 [ROUNDED]}...= arithmetic-expression
    [ON SIZE ERROR
        imperative-statement-1]
    [NOT ON SIZE ERROR
        imperative-statement-2]
    [END-COMPUTE]
```

Here identifier-1 is an item with a numeric or numeric-edited PICTURE. Arithmetic expression is described next.

Evaluation of Arithmetic Expressions

The term *expression* carries much the same meaning in COBOL as in algebra—that is, any collection of constants (numeric literals) and variables (identifiers) related by arithmetic operators. For the construction of arithmetic expressions, COBOL includes five arithmetic operators:

Operation	Operator	Corresponds to COBOL Verb
Addition	+	ADD
Subtraction	-	SUBTRACT
Multiplication	*	MULTIPLY
Division	/	DIVIDE
Exponentiation (raising to a power)	**	No corresponding verb

Note that the four basic operations use the same symbols as ordinary arithmetic, with the exception that * (asterisk) is used to denote multiplication.

As an illustration of how the typical COMPUTE appears, the quantity

$$a = b - 25 + c$$

can be calculated as shown in Figure 7-8. Parentheses can be used to indicate grouping of terms in much the same way as in algebra. For example, computation of simple interest by the formula

$$A = P(1 + rt)$$

would be coded as shown in Figure 7-9.

One item of which you should be aware is that implied multiplication does not exist with the COMPUTE statement. That is, the form rt in algebra means r times t. If the equivalent—RT—is written in COBOL, the compiler will interpret RT as a data-name defined somewhere in the DATA DIVISION. Furthermore, unlike algebra, parentheses can never be used to imply multiplication. The algebraic form

$$P(1 + rt)$$

in COBOL becomes

$$P * (1 + R * T)$$

Figure 7-8

The COMPUTE Statement

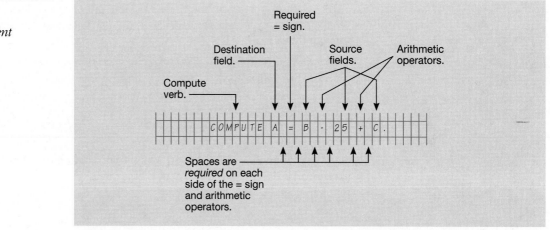

Figure 7-9

Using Parentheses in the COMPUTE

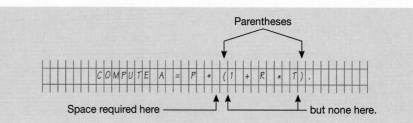

Another important point relates to the sequence in which the operations are performed. Specifically, if R = 0.06 and T = 10, which of the following two methods should be used in evaluating within the parentheses?

$$(1 + 0.06) \times 10 \qquad\qquad \text{or} \quad 1 + (0.06 \times 10)$$
$$(1.06) \times 10 \qquad\qquad\qquad\qquad 1 + (0.6)$$
$$10.6 \qquad\qquad\qquad\qquad\qquad 1.6$$

Note that the addition is done first in the form on the left, but in that on the right, the multiplication is done first. Due to the nature of the computation (simple interest), we know that the form on the right is correct. But how does the computer know which sequence to use? The answer is that it employs a set of *hierarchy rules* that are virtually identical to those of ordinary arithmetic:

1. Expressions in parentheses are calculated according to the remainder of the rules in hierarchy, starting with the innermost set of parentheses and working out.

2. The expression is scanned from left to right. As each exponentiation is encountered, it is carried out.

3. The expression is again scanned from left to right. As each multiplication or division is encountered, it is carried out.

4. The expression is again scanned from left to right. As each addition or subtraction is encountered, it is carried out.

Given these hierarchy rules, COBOL evaluates the simple interest form correctly because the multiplication operation will be performed before the addition. Most aspects of this hierarchy are illustrated by the statement in Figure 7-10. To carry out the evaluation in this sequence of operations, assume that each field contains the quantity indicated.

Figure 7-10

Hierarchy of Operations

```
COMPUTE R = A + B * C / D - E + (F * (G - H)) - I ** J
```

```
A  +  B  *   C   / D  -  E  +  (F  *  (G   -   H))  -  I  **  J
37 +  3  *  125  / 5  - 25  +  (7  *  (50  -  46))  -  2  **  3
37 +  3  *  125  / 5  - 25  +  (7  *   4)  -  2  **  3
37 +  3  *  125  / 5  - 25  +  28  -  2  **  3
37 +  3  *  125  / 5  - 25  +  28  -  8
37 +  375  / 5  - 25  +  28  -  8
37 +  75  - 25  +  28  -  8
112  - 25  +  28  -  8
87  +  28  -  8
115  -  8
107        Final result moved to R.
```

Rounding, Size Errors, and Intermediate Results

The requirements for rounding and the possibility of a size error do not disappear simply because the COMPUTE statement is used. Rounding may still be required and a size error may still occur; you see in the general format of the COMPUTE statement that it includes provisions for both.

Figure 7-10 shows that COBOL, in carrying out the computations required by the COMPUTE statement, generates intermediate results, which it retains in compiler-generated work areas. Only when the final result has been obtained in the work area is it moved to the data-name field. You should be aware that rounding is not done for the intermediate results. If specified, it is done *only* when the final result is moved to the destination field.

Chapter Summary

General

The GIVING form of the arithmetic statement moves the calculated result to a separate data item not associated with the calculations themselves. The data items involved in the calculation are not changed.

The GIVING data item of an arithmetic statement can be numeric edited because it is not involved in the calculation.

When the destination data item of an arithmetic statement has insufficient positions to the right of the decimal position, excess digits to the right are discarded, resulting in truncation. Using the ROUNDED clause causes the number to be rounded off.

When the destination data item of an arithmetic statement has insufficient positions to the left of the decimal position, excess digits to the left are discarded. This is called an overflow condition and will be undetected unless the ON SIZE ERROR clause is included in the statement.

The COMPUTE statement allows the use of algebra-like formulas in defining a series of calculations to be carried out.

COBOL Language Elements

The COBOL statements you have studied in this chapter are

ADD   Adds two or more numeric operands together. The sum can replace the value of one (or more) of the operands or can be moved to a separate operand or operands, depending upon the format of the ADD.

Format 1

$$\underline{\text{ADD}} \begin{Bmatrix} \text{identifier-1} \\ \text{literal-1} \end{Bmatrix} \dots \quad \underline{\text{TO}} \ \{\text{identifier-2} \ [\underline{\text{ROUNDED}}]\}\dots$$

[ON SIZE ERROR
   imperative-statement-1]
[NOT ON SIZE ERROR
   imperative-statement-2]
[END-ADD]

Format 2

$$\underline{\text{ADD}} \begin{Bmatrix} \text{identifier-1} \\ \text{literal-1} \end{Bmatrix} \dots \quad \underline{\text{TO}} \begin{Bmatrix} \text{identifier-2} \\ \text{literal-2} \end{Bmatrix}$$

GIVING {identifier-3 [ROUNDED]}...
[ON SIZE ERROR
   imperative-statement-1]
[NOT ON SIZE ERROR
   imperative-statement-2]
[END-ADD]

SUBTRACT   Subtracts one, or the sum of two or more, numeric data items, and sets the values of one or more data items equal to the result.

Format 1

$$\underline{\text{SUBTRACT}} \begin{Bmatrix} \text{identifier-1} \\ \text{literal-1} \end{Bmatrix} \dots \quad \underline{\text{FROM}} \ \{\text{identifier-2} \ [\underline{\text{ROUNDED}}]\}\dots$$

[ON SIZE ERROR
   imperative-statement-1]
[NOT ON SIZE ERROR
   imperative-statement-2]
[END-SUBTRACT]

Format 2

$$\text{SUBTRACT} \begin{Bmatrix} \text{identifier-1} \\ \text{literal-1} \end{Bmatrix} ... \quad \underline{\text{FROM}} \begin{Bmatrix} \text{identifier-2} \\ \text{literal-2} \end{Bmatrix}$$

GIVING {identifier-3 [ROUNDED]}...

[ON SIZE ERROR

    imperative-statement-1]

[NOT ON SIZE ERROR

    imperative-statement-2]

[END-SUBTRACT]

MULTIPLY   Multiplies numeric data items and sets the value of designated data items equal to the product.

Format 1

$$\underline{\text{MULTIPLY}} \begin{Bmatrix} \text{identifier-1} \\ \text{literal-1} \end{Bmatrix} \underline{\text{BY}} \{\text{identifiter-2 [ROUNDED]}\}...$$

[ON SIZE ERROR

    imperative-statement-1]

[NOT ON SIZE ERROR

    imperative-statement-2]

[END-MULTIPLY]

Format 2

$$\underline{\text{MULTIPLY}} \begin{Bmatrix} \text{identifier-1} \\ \text{literal-1} \end{Bmatrix} \underline{\text{BY}} \begin{Bmatrix} \text{identifier-2} \\ \text{literal-2} \end{Bmatrix}$$

GIVING {identifier-3 [ROUNDED]}...

[ON SIZE ERROR

    imperative-statement-1]

[NOT ON SIZE ERROR

    imperative-statement-2]

[END-MULTIPLY]

DIVIDE   Divides one numeric data item into others and set the values of designated data items equal to the quotient and, optionally, the remainder.

Format 1

$$\underline{\text{DIVIDE}} \begin{Bmatrix} \text{identifier-1} \\ \text{literal-1} \end{Bmatrix} \underline{\text{INTO}} \ \{\text{identifier-2 [ROUNDED]}\}...$$

[ON SIZE ERROR

    imperative-statement-1]

[NOT ON SIZE ERROR

    imperative-statement-2]

[END-DIVIDE]

Format 2

$$\underline{\text{DIVIDE}} \begin{Bmatrix} \text{identifier-1} \\ \text{literal-1} \end{Bmatrix} \underline{\text{INTO}} \begin{Bmatrix} \text{identifier-2} \\ \text{literal-2} \end{Bmatrix}$$

GIVING {identifier-3 [ROUNDED]}...

[ON SIZE ERROR

    imperative-statement-1]

[NOT ON SIZE ERROR

    imperative-statement-2]

[END-DIVIDE]

Format 3

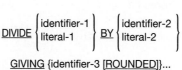

DIVIDE { identifier-1 / literal-1 } BY { identifier-2 / literal-2 }

GIVING {identifier-3 [ROUNDED]}...
[ON SIZE ERROR
    imperative-statement-1]
[NOT ON SIZE ERROR
    imperative-statement-2]
[END-DIVIDE]

Format 4

DIVIDE { identifier-1 / literal-1 } INTO { identifier-2 / literal-2 }

GIVING identifier-3 [ROUNDED] REMAINDER identifier-4
[ON SIZE ERROR
    imperative-statement-1]
[NOT ON SIZE ERROR
    imperative-statement-2]
[END-DIVIDE]

Format 5

DIVIDE { identifier-1 / literal-1 } BY { identifier-2 / literal-2 }

GIVING identifier-3 [ROUNDED] REMAINDER identifier-4
[ON SIZE ERROR
    imperative-statement-1]
[NOT ON SIZE ERROR
    imperative-statement-2]
[END-DIVIDE]

COMPUTE   Performs calculations by direction of an arithmetic expression.

COMPUTE {identifier-1 [ROUNDED]}...= arithmetic-expression
[ON SIZE ERROR
    imperative-statement-1]
[NOT ON SIZE ERROR
    imperative-statement-2]
[END-COMPUTE]

Programming Conventions

Use the COMPUTE statement whenever the sequence of calculations is defined by any but the simplest formula. Breaking a formula down into a series of basic operations is painstaking and can be error prone.

Use the GIVING form of the arithmetic statements if (1) you do not want to change the value of any operand involved in the operation, or (2) the destination data item is numeric edited.

The many formats of the DIVIDE statement can be confusing. In choosing between the INTO and BY formats, select the one that best documents the application itself. If you need to retain the REMAINDER, then use either format 4 or format 5.

Error Prevention/ Detection

The careful selection of PICTURE clauses will usually avoid the problems of truncation and size errors. You must continually be aware of field sizes, especially for intermediate work areas defined in the WORKING-STORAGE SECTION.

Whenever there is any doubt about the ability of a data item used as an accumulator to hold a calculational result, use the SIZE ERROR clause in the arithmetic statement.

When using arithmetic statements without the GIVING clause, make certain that the destination data item is large enough to hold the calculated result. This is especially significant when multiplying and dividing.

Questions and Exercises

Key Terminology

Give a brief description of each of the following terms that were introduced in this chapter.

overflow
round off
truncate

General Questions

1. For each value of A + B given, identify which will produce a size error as a result of executing the following statement. Assume that C has a PIC of 9(4)V99.

        ADD A, B GIVING C

   a. A + B = 1342.647   c. A + B = 583.2
   b. A + B = 15762.49253   d. A + B = 23682

2. In the addition operations (A + B) of the preceding exercise, will use of the ROUNDED clause have any effect on the overflow conditions?

3. A student observes, "The ROUNDED option should be used whenever an arithmetic operation involves decimal positions. When multiplying Quantity Sold (PIC 999) by Unit Price (PIC 999V99) to obtain Total Price (PIC 9(6)V99), the result will be more accurate if ROUNDED is specified." Comment on this.

4. Since the GIVING clause can be used in any arithmetic operation, should it be used all the time?

5. Is there any clause that can be used in conjunction with the arithmetic operations in order to obtain an answer as a numeric-edited field?

6. What is the difference between using the statement DIVIDE FIELD-A INTO FIELD-B as opposed to the statement DIVIDE FIELD-B BY FIELD-A?

7. A student asks, "Why should I bother using the COMPUTE statement when I can ADD, SUBTRACT, MULTIPLY, or DIVIDE just fine?" How would you answer this question?

8. When the COMPUTE statement is used in a program for a complex arithmetic operation, how does the computer know which sequence to follow?

Writing Program Statements

1. Write an arithmetic expression for each of the following:
   a. R times the difference between P and Q.
   b. P minus the product of Q and R.

   c. $\dfrac{2mi}{P(n + 1)}$.

2. Write the COBOL arithmetic statements to do the arithmetic expressions from Exercise 1a and b. Do not use the COMPUTE statement. Put your answer in a field called ANS.

3. Write a COMPUTE statement to accomplish the arithmetic expression in Exercise 1c. Put your answer in a field called ANS.

4. Write COBOL statements to do the following arithmetic operations:
   a. Add five fields (A, B, C, D, and E) together and put the answer in a field called TOTL.
   b. Subtract DEPT-SALES from TOTAL-SALES, but do not destroy the contents of either field.
   c. Multiply RATE times HOURS and put the answer in WKLY-PAY.

5. Using the DIVIDE statement, write solutions for the following arithmetic operations:
    a. How do you compute the ratio of DEPT-SALES to TOTAL-SALES?
    b. How can you figure out an AVG-GRADE from a field called TOTAL-STUDENTS and a field called TOTAL-EXAM-SCORES?
    c. Can you determine a person's RATE if you have a field called WKLY-PAY and another one called HOURS?

6. Given the following definitions for X and Y and answers for the field Z, write COBOL statements to ADD, SUBTRACT, MULTIPLY, and DIVIDE that correspond.

    X PIC S99   VALUE -10.

    Y PIC S9(3)   VALUE 200.

    X PIC S9(5).

    Answers for Z
    a. 00190
    b. 00210
    c. -02000
    d. -00020

7. Using the fields X and Y and their values from Exercise 6, you need to write a COMPUTE statement that creates an answer of 105 for the field Z. This time, a numeric literal of 2 should be used.

Programming Assignments

7-1 Soft Drink Sales Analysis Report

The manager of a soft drinks distributorship decides to analyze sales of each customer. Not only does he want to know the total sales for each type of beverage for each customer, but he is also interested in actual sales as compared to target sales.

Output Requirements:

A printed report with the following output and format.

Field	Beginning Column	Output Format
Customer name	1	
Customer telephone number	27	Insert appropriate punctuation; for instance: (208)555-1212
Monthly sales (number of cases)		
Cola drinks	41	Zero suppress
Percent of Cola target	45	Format is: *nnn.n* Insert a decimal point and zero suppress
Diet drinks	51	Zero suppress
Percent of Diet target	55	Same as Percent Cola
Energy Supplement drinks	61	Zero suppress
Percent of Energy target	65	Same as Percent Cola
Total monthly sales (dollars)	72	Format is: *nn,nnn.nn* Insert decimal point and comma and zero suppress

You must prepare a printer spacing chart from the above table.

Input Description:
　File name: DRINKS01.DL
　Record description: See Appendix A

Processing Requirements:
　For each record in the file:

1. For each drink, calculate the percent of target as:

$$= \frac{\text{Monthly sales for drink}}{\text{Monthly target sales for drink}} \times 100$$

   The percent must include three digits to the left of the decimal and one to the right; for instance, 125.6.

2. Round off each percentage calculation.

3. Calculate the Total monthly sales (dollars) for the three drinks. Be certain to make your result field large enough to hold the maximum possible value.

4. Edit each field as designated in the preceding Output Format description.

5. Print one double-spaced line for each record in the file.

7-2 Investment Calculations

The formula for computing how much money to invest to get a specified amount in the future is

$$M = \frac{D}{(1 + i)^n}$$

where

　D is the amount of money desired in the future
　i is the interest rate per compounding period
　n is the number of compounding interest periods at rate i
　M is the amount of money that must be invested

An investor would like a program that would allow her to experiment from her keyboard to study the effect of changing the different variables.

Output Requirements:
　After the input, clear the screen and display the following (include an appropriate screen description for each field).

Field	Output Format
D	Insert comma
	Use floating dollar sign
I (Annual interest rate)	
Y (Number of years)	
M	Same as D

Input Description:
　The user must enter the following from the keyboard.

Field	Permissible Values
D	Maximum allowable value is 99,999
I (Annual interest rate)	Range will be 4.0% to 20.0%
Y (Number of years)	Range will be 1 to 25
Number of compounding periods per year	Range will be 1 to 365

Processing Requirements:

1. Allow for repeated processing so that a user may enter two or more sets of data. Provide for terminating execution when the user is finished.

2. Calculate the interest rate i using the following formula:

$$i = \frac{I}{100 \times \text{number of compounding periods per year}}$$

3. Calculate the number of interest periods n using the following formula:
$n = Y \times$ number of compounding periods per year

8

STRUCTURED PROGRAM DESIGN AND CONDITIONAL OPERATIONS

Outline

- **Introducing Structured Design and Structured Programming**
  Defining a "Good" Program
  About Problem Solving
  The Meaning of the Word *Structured* in Programming

- **Further Modularization of the RET-VAL1 Program**
  Three Functions of the Process Module
  A Subjective Decision in Modularizing
  Placement of Input and Output Statements
  Module Numbering

- **Structured Programming**
  Introduction
  The Sequence Structure
  The Looping Structure
  The Selection Structure
  The Case Structure

- **Two Program Logic Tools**
  Flowcharts to Illustrate Program Logic
  Pseudocode

- **COBOL Conditional Capabilities**
  The If-Else
  Relational Operators and Expressions
  The IF Statement

Chapter Objectives

In preceding chapters, you have used standards and techniques for designing and writing good programs. This chapter goes one step further and formalizes the overall procedure. From this chapter, you will learn about the following topics:

■ The principle of top-down design (structured design), a means by which a problem is solved by successively breaking it down to smaller, more manageable components

■ The structure (hierarchy) chart as a tool to illustrate the relationship of multiple modules of a program to one another

■ A full expansion of the module numbering standards first introduced in Chapter 3

■ Structured programming as a set of methods and techniques used in producing "good" programs

■ The four structures of structured programming theory:
   Sequence—consecutive actions executed unconditionally
   Looping—repeated execution of a sequence
   Selection—execution of either of two alternatives, depending on the result of a test
   Case—execution of one of multiple alternatives, depending on the result of a test (an expansion of the selection)

■ The flowchart as a tool to develop and display the logic of a program

■ Pseudocode as a tool to develop and display the logic of a program

■ The IF statement for implementing the selection structure in COBOL

■ Relational operators and expressions that form the basis for conditional testing

Introducing Structured Design and Structured Programming

Defining a "Good" Program

This chapter is devoted to setting some ground rules for writing good programs. The first point to consider is what is meant by a "good" program. To an extent, this depends upon your point of view. If you are a beginning student attempting to get your first program working, then a good program is one that compiles without error and gives the correct results. If, for example, you erroneously add 1 instead of 2 in a particular statement, then the results will be incorrect, and the program is not "good." It makes no difference whether your error is typographical or the result of misunderstanding the problem statement from the instructor. If the program will not perform as required, then it is incorrect. Thus, the first measure of a good program (and the most essential) is that it be *correct*.

Giving the correct results is hardly the only criterion for a good program. Other factors are involved, many revolving around the environment in which program is used and the high cost of preparing it. As a rule, a programmer does not function in an isolated environment. Indeed, most large programs involve teams of individuals working together. Furthermore, a large portion of the average COBOL programmer's time is spent modifying existing programs. The environment in which the program is to be used partially determines the relative importance of the "good" criterion factors and whether or not a program is "good."

If a program were to be written, placed in service, and never seen again, then it probably would not matter how clumsy it was to read. However, the realities of programming simply do not work that way. A good program must be *readable* and *understandable*. This need is obvious if several people are working on a single program or different parts of a large program. Comprehensible coding is essential for maintaining the program because someone other than the original author may need to modify it at a later date.

To this end, the program should also be designed so that it is *easily modified*. This relates to changing operations performed by the program, *not* to correcting a program that is in error. In any business environment, procedures and needs of the organization are constantly changing. Government regulations change, organizations expand into new activities, competition forces more efficient operation, newer computer hardware make possible operations that were previously impractical, and so on. The business environment is constantly changing, and programs must be modified to reflect this change. A good program is designed so that it can be easily changed to reflect the changing needs of the organization.

In the early days of computing, a very important feature of a good program was *program efficiency:* it had to execute quickly and occupy as little memory as possible. For instance, an inquiry program that requires 5 minutes to find a customer's bank balance when the customer is waiting at the teller's window is not a very good program. Nor would anyone be happy with a program that requires 720K of memory when only 580K is available. As the speed and capacities of modern computers have rapidly increased and cost has decreased, program efficiency has become much less of a factor. However, it is still a good idea to use easily implemented procedures that appreciably improve program efficiency. In some instances, this can be especially important when running large, demanding jobs on a personal computer.

In the early days of computing, a lot of "lone rangers" wrote programs. The standards for writing good programs were few and far between. There were nearly as many approaches to programming as there were programmers—intuition and finger-crossing were prevalent. However, during the 1970s, the work of computer scientists began to have a profound effect on programming techniques as common-sense theories became usable tools for the everyday programmer.

From this book, you will not simply learn COBOL, but you will learn how to design and write programs in COBOL using good programming techniques.

About Problem Solving

A student must focus on two different topics when taking a first programming course:

- The *syntax* of the programming language. These are the rules for preparing the program code; for instance, how you set up the DATA DIVISION, the forms of the PERFORM statement, and so on. This has been your primary focus for the first several chapters.

- Designing program solutions to problems. This is largely independent of the programming language to be used for implementing the solution.

Chapter 2 introduced you to some of the basic tools for designing and writing good programs. You learned about such topics as modularizing a solution and using a structure chart to display the structure, and representing program logic through flowcharts and pseudocode. Although some repetition is involved, let's quickly review some basics.

Given a particular task to program, you can consider the overall job to consist of two broad parts:

1. You must determine *what* is to be done. In doing so, you must break the job down into modules, each performing a single, relatively independent function. The structure chart (or hierarchy chart) is a graphical means of showing relationships between elements; it gives an indication of the *physical structure* of the solution.

2. You must determine *how* to do the task. This does *not* mean to "write the program." It involves defining the sequence in which tasks are carried out—the *logical structure* of the solution. Flowcharts and pseudocode are tools that you use in this stage.

Programs that you have studied and programming assignments at the end of chapters all have the same physical structure as the ADDER program as restructured in Chapter 3. Also, even though some of the detailed logical structure has varied slightly from one program to the next, overall logical structure has been the same as that of ADDER. Hence, you have been able to focus your entire attention on the syntax of COBOL and using it in writing your programs. However, beginning in the next chapter, structure will become increasingly complex—with the result that a systematic approach to problem solving will become critical.

The Meaning of the Word Structured in Programming

The word *structured* is *the* word in modern programming practice. However, it is often used in different ways. For instance, you will hear people talk about *structured design*. This is most commonly associated with the action of breaking a program down into independent modules. In general usage, you can think of it as equivalent to *top-down design*. Recall that top-down design is the action of breaking a task into smaller subtasks and those tasks into still smaller subtasks until each is of a manageable size and performs a single function. For convenient reference, let's call any module that is not broken down further a *primitive module*.

On the other hand, you will encounter the phrase *structured program*. A structured program is one composed of only certain logical structures (sequence, selection, and looping described later in this chapter). The word *structured* has quite different meanings in these two usages. But usually, the two are very similar.

Further Modularization of the RET-VAL1 Program

Three Functions of the Process Module

For your first look beyond the basic structure of ADDER, let's inspect the PROCEDURE DIVISION of the RET-VAL1 program more closely—see Figure 8-1. In doing so, you will be "looking backwards"; that is, you will be determining a more detailed physical structure

```
PROCEDURE DIVISION.

000-PRINT-INVENTORY-FILE.
    PERFORM 100-INITIALIZE
    PERFORM 110-PRINT-NEXT-RECORD
        UNTIL END-OF-FILE = "Y"
    PERFORM 120-FINALIZE
    STOP RUN.

100-INITIALIZE.
    OPEN INPUT INVENTORY-FILE
    OPEN OUTPUT REPORT-FILE
    READ INVENTORY-FILE
        AT END MOVE "Y" TO END-OF-FILE
    END-READ.

110-PRINT-NEXT-RECORD.

* Calculate retail value.
    MOVE IR-PRICE TO RETAIL-VALUE
    MULTIPLY IR-QUANT-ON-HAND BY RETAIL-VALUE

* Assemble and write output line.
    MOVE SPACES TO REPORT-LINE
    MOVE IR-STOCK-NUMBER TO RL-STOCK-NUMBER
    MOVE IR-SOFTWARE-NAME TO RL-SOFTWARE-NAME
    MOVE IR-VENDOR-NAME TO RL-VENDOR-NAME
    MOVE IR-QUANT-ON-HAND TO RL-QUANT-ON-HAND
    MOVE IR-PRICE TO RL-PRICE
    MOVE RETAIL-VALUE TO RL-RETAIL-VALUE
    WRITE REPORT-LINE AFTER ADVANCING 2 LINES

* Read next input record.
    READ INVENTORY-FILE
        AT END MOVE "Y" TO END-OF-FILE
    END-READ.

120-FINALIZE.
    CLOSE INVENTORY-FILE
        REPORT-FILE.
```

Figure 8-1

PROCEDURE DIVISION from the RET-VAL1 Program

by looking at the program. The 110 module, the first-level process module, actually involves three basic activities:

- Calculating the retail value
- Assembling and writing the output line
- Reading the next record

Hence, you could argue that the 110 module is not a primitive module and should be broken down further. You should also notice that the action of reading a record is done in two different modules: the READ for the first record in the 100 module and the READ for subsequent records in the 110 module.

This further modularization of the program produces the structure chart shown in Figure 8-2. Now there is a distinct second level of modules. Notice that the 800-READ module is subordinate to two modules (100 and 110)—consistent with the fact that records are read from both of the modules. This is encoded into the structure chart block by the shaded upper-right corner. (For the moment, ignore the choice of module numbers; module numbering will be described soon.)

This structure is implemented in the program of Figure 8-3; notice the following points about it:

- The physical layout of the modules clearly corresponds to the zero and first levels of the structure chart. You see the overall structure in these first four modules. If you are interested in detail, you can inspect the modules that follow.

- The 800-READ module is performed from both the 100-INITIALIZE and the 110-PRINT modules. Thus, the READ statement itself need not be repeated at two different places in the program.

A Subjective Decision in Modularizing

When the objective is to simplify the programming activity and make the program easier to understand and follow, you might argue that to break out the calculation into a separate module (300) is really not necessary. After all, it is only a two-statement sequence and the activity is straightforward. Perhaps those two statements should be left in the 110 module. If such a fine distinction is made in a large program, you might end up with so many short modules that their sheer numbers would make program logic clumsy to follow. With this in mind, leaving them as part of the 110 module would probably be a good idea.

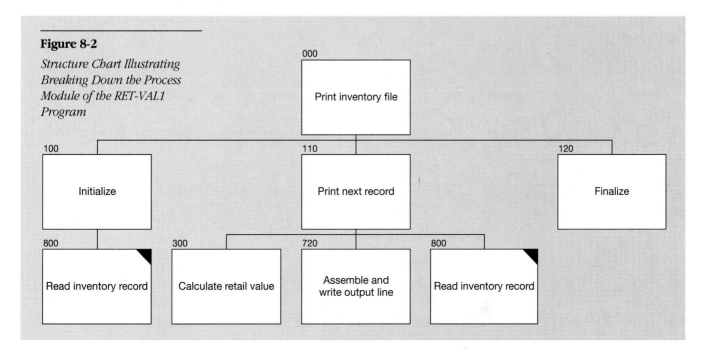

Figure 8-2

Structure Chart Illustrating Breaking Down the Process Module of the RET-VAL1 Program

Figure 8-3

*Additional Modules in the
RET-VAL1 Program*

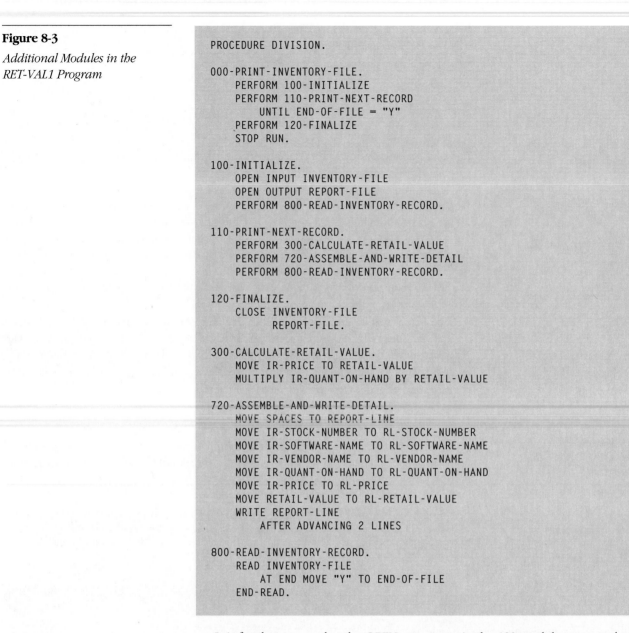

```
PROCEDURE DIVISION.

000-PRINT-INVENTORY-FILE.
    PERFORM 100-INITIALIZE
    PERFORM 110-PRINT-NEXT-RECORD
        UNTIL END-OF-FILE = "Y"
    PERFORM 120-FINALIZE
    STOP RUN.

100-INITIALIZE.
    OPEN INPUT INVENTORY-FILE
    OPEN OUTPUT REPORT-FILE
    PERFORM 800-READ-INVENTORY-RECORD.

110-PRINT-NEXT-RECORD.
    PERFORM 300-CALCULATE-RETAIL-VALUE
    PERFORM 720-ASSEMBLE-AND-WRITE-DETAIL
    PERFORM 800-READ-INVENTORY-RECORD.

120-FINALIZE.
    CLOSE INVENTORY-FILE
          REPORT-FILE.

300-CALCULATE-RETAIL-VALUE.
    MOVE IR-PRICE TO RETAIL-VALUE
    MULTIPLY IR-QUANT-ON-HAND BY RETAIL-VALUE

720-ASSEMBLE-AND-WRITE-DETAIL.
    MOVE SPACES TO REPORT-LINE
    MOVE IR-STOCK-NUMBER TO RL-STOCK-NUMBER
    MOVE IR-SOFTWARE-NAME TO RL-SOFTWARE-NAME
    MOVE IR-VENDOR-NAME TO RL-VENDOR-NAME
    MOVE IR-QUANT-ON-HAND TO RL-QUANT-ON-HAND
    MOVE IR-PRICE TO RL-PRICE
    MOVE RETAIL-VALUE TO RL-RETAIL-VALUE
    WRITE REPORT-LINE
        AFTER ADVANCING 2 LINES

800-READ-INVENTORY-RECORD.
    READ INVENTORY-FILE
        AT END MOVE "Y" TO END-OF-FILE
    END-READ.
```

It is for that reason that the OPEN statements in the 100 module are not placed in a separate open module. You should be aware that some programmers do prefer a separate module for these statements. The value of doing so is a matter of opinion.

Remember, the ultimate purpose of modularization is to simplify your program. Avoid slavishly following a set of standards when doing so detracts from the overall quality of the program.

**Placement of Input and
Output Statements**

In the RET-VAL1 program, the input file is read from two different places in the program. Although this program has only one place where writing occurs, most COBOL programs have several. Practice has shown that program design, implementation, and debugging are often simplified if all reading of a given file is done from a single statement and all writing to a given file is done by a single statement. The program of Figure 8-3 achieves this for the READ because the READ statement is placed in a separate module from which it is performed. Even though there is only one WRITE in this program, the practice of isolating both the input and output activities yields the final form of the structure chart in Figure 8-4 and the program in Figure 8-5 (see page 164). Notice that the calculation has been returned to the 110 module.

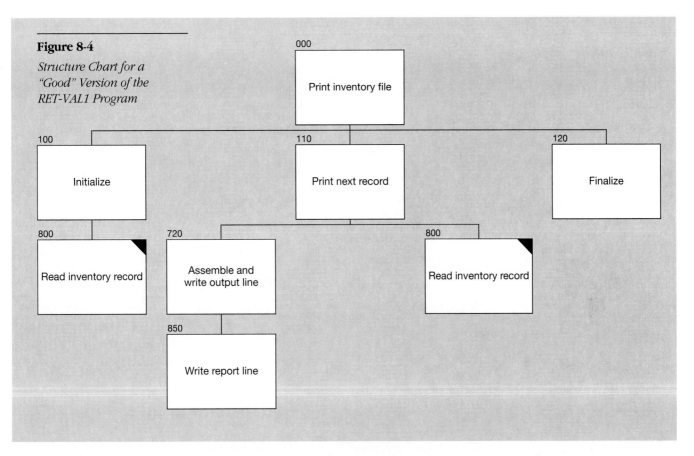

Figure 8-4

Structure Chart for a "Good" Version of the RET-VAL1 Program

Module Numbering

In Chapter 3, you were introduced to predetermined numbering ranges for program modules. Such standardization is important in an environment that includes many programs and/or more than one person programming since it achieves a commonality from one program to another. The complete set of module numbers used as the standard for this book are tabulated in Figure 8-6 (see page 165).

These number assignments have been made to provide a rigorous framework that yields a useful commonality between programs, yet is relatively simple to use and remember. Any module-numbering/naming convention that is too complex or difficult to remember and use will cause you a lot of unnecessary confusion.

Structured Programming

Introduction

Once a problem has been broken down into basic components, or individual modules, then the programming may begin. The first step is to define the *program logic*; that is, after the *what* has been defined, the *how* must be determined.

Structured programming can be considered a set of methods and techniques to be used in producing "good" programs. In general, structured techniques are applicable to virtually all languages. Unfortunately, COBOL was not designed with structured methods in mind. However, significant additions were made to COBOL with the 1985 Standard to make it more compatible with structured methods. Thus, in using structured methods, you should be realistic and keep in mind that the COBOL language does have some shortcomings in this area.

One of the important features of a computer's machine language is the inclusion of an instruction to break the sequence of proceeding from one instruction to the next and allow the program to jump elsewhere. For example, the PERFORM statement of COBOL requires that execution jump to another paragraph. At a machine language level, this is done with a special instruction to "jump" to another instruction. This type of need was

Figure 8-5

A "Good" Structured Program—RET-VAL1

```
PROCEDURE DIVISION.

000-PRINT-INVENTORY-FILE.
    PERFORM 100-INITIALIZE
    PERFORM 110-PRINT-NEXT-RECORD
        UNTIL END-OF-FILE = "Y"
    PERFORM 120-FINALIZE
    STOP RUN.

100-INITIALIZE.
    OPEN INPUT INVENTORY-FILE
    OPEN OUTPUT REPORT-FILE
    PERFORM 800-READ-INVENTORY-RECORD.

110-PRINT-NEXT-RECORD.


*   Calculate retail value.
    MOVE IR-PRICE TO RETAIL-VALUE
    MULTIPLY IR-QUANT-ON-HAND BY RETAIL-VALUE

    PERFORM 720-ASSEMBLE-AND-WRITE-DETAIL
    PERFORM 800-READ-INVENTORY-RECORD.

120-FINALIZE.
    CLOSE INVENTORY-FILE
         REPORT-FILE.

720-ASSEMBLE-AND-WRITE-DETAIL.
    MOVE SPACES TO REPORT-LINE
    MOVE IR-STOCK-NUMBER TO RL-STOCK-NUMBER
    MOVE IR-SOFTWARE-NAME TO RL-SOFTWARE-NAME
    MOVE IR-VENDOR-NAME TO RL-VENDOR-NAME
    MOVE IR-QUANT-ON-HAND TO RL-QUANT-ON-HAND
    MOVE IR-PRICE TO RL-PRICE
    MOVE RETAIL-VALUE TO RL-RETAIL-VALUE
    PERFORM 850-WRITE-REPORT-LINE.

800-READ-INVENTORY-RECORD.
    READ INVENTORY-FILE
        AT END MOVE "Y" TO END-OF-FILE
    END-READ.

850-WRITE-REPORT-LINE.
    WRITE REPORT-LINE
        AFTER ADVANCING 2 LINES.
```

reflected in the early high-level languages such as FORTRAN, BASIC, and COBOL in the form of a GO TO statement. (The GO TO still exists in the current COBOL language, but with proper design, it is seldom needed when programming.) The GO TO functions somewhat like the PERFORM, except that no return is associated with it. In general, it gives the programmer the ability to cause execution to jump from one place to another in a program.

In 1968, Professor Edsger Dijkstra of the Netherlands authored a paper entitled "GO TO Statement Considered Harmful." In his paper, he expressed the observation that the fewer GO TO operations in a program, the better the quality of the program. Generally, programs that were organized to minimize use of the GO TO were easier to write, debug, and modify. Basically, he stated that the more jumping around a program does, the more potential there is for trouble. Careful study and analysis of any problem to be programmed will usually lead to a better designed program in which the various components have a clear, logical relationship.

Figure 8-6

Module-Numbering Convention

Number Prefix	Module Activity
000	Main controlling module
100–199	First-level modules:
	initialize
	process
	finalize
200–299	General initialization activities in which the initialize module must be broken into submodules
300–699	General processing activities
700–799	Preparation of output:
700–719	for headings
720–739	for detail lines
740–789	for intermediate total lines
780–799	for final total lines
800–899	Input and output:
800–849	input (for instance, READ)
850–899	output (for instance, WRITE)
900–999	Exception processing

This is also the essence of techniques stressed in this book. Too often, a programmer will rush to the detailed coding process without really knowing how to solve the problem. Programming languages that include a GO TO statement provide such a programmer with a crutch to patch up sloppy work resulting from poor planning. Unfortunately, the resulting program almost always ends up being difficult to debug and maintain.

The basis for structured programming was set forth in a paper presented in 1966 by two computer scientists, Bohm and Jacopini. In their paper, they proved mathematically that any computer program can be represented in a chart form using the three basic structured flowchart forms shown in Figure 8-7.

The Sequence Structure

The *sequence* structure represents the progression from one component of a program to the next. For instance, the statements to set up the output line from RET-VAL1, repeated here as Figure 8-8, provide a good example. As you know, execution of these statements progresses from one to the next.

The Looping Structure

The *looping* structure provides the ability to execute a sequence of operations repeatedly until a given condition occurs (or as long as a specified condition exists). You are familiar with this structure, which was used in two forms of the PERFORM statement. The comparable examples shown in Figure 8-9 are taken from different versions of the ADDER program.

Figure 8-7

The Basic Constructs of Structured Programming

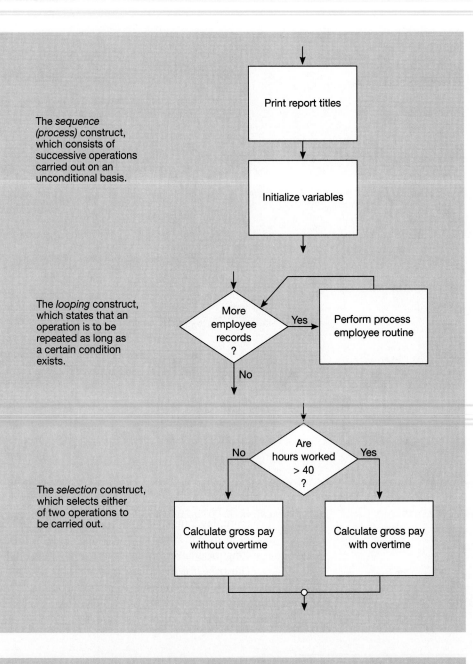

The *sequence (process)* construct, which consists of successive operations carried out on an unconditional basis.

The *looping* construct, which states that an operation is to be repeated as long as a certain condition exists.

The *selection* construct, which selects either of two operations to be carried out.

Figure 8-8

Sequentially Executed Statements

Sequence structure: statements executed one after the other.

```
720-ASSEMBLE-AND-WRITE-DETAIL.
    MOVE SPACES TO REPORT-LINE
    MOVE IR-STOCK-NUMBER TO RL-STOCK-NUMBER
    MOVE IR-SOFTWARE-NAME TO RL-SOFTWARE-NAME
    MOVE IR-VENDOR-NAME TO RL-VENDOR-NAME
    MOVE IR-QUANT-ON-HAND TO RL-QUANT-ON-HAND
    MOVE IR-PRICE TO RL-PRICE
    MOVE RETAIL-VALUE TO RL-RETAIL-VALUE
    PERFORM 850-WRITE-REPORT-LINE.
```

Figure 8-9

Examples of Looping from the ADDER Program

```
        PERFORM UNTIL CONTIN = 0
            .
            .  (Statements to be executed)
            .
        END-PERFORM

        PERFORM 110-PROCESS-USER-ENTRIES UNTIL CONTIN = 0
            .
            .
            .
        110-PROCESS-USER-ENTRIES.
            .
            .  (Statements to be executed)
            .
```

Recall from Chapter 3 that the first of the PERFORM formats in Figure 8-9 is called an in-line PERFORM because the statements forming the loop physically follow the PERFORM statement. The second format is an out-of-line PERFORM because the statements comprising the loop are physically removed from the PERFORM statement itself.

The logic of both these forms is that of the looping construction as shown in Figure 8-10. Note that the structure itself does not dictate whether the operations to be carried out are in-line or out-of-line. It simply indicates that certain actions are to be repeated until a particular condition becomes true. Also note that if the condition is initially true, the operations will not be carried out at all. This form of the loop is called a *pre-test loop* because the test is made prior to executing the statements comprising the loop.

A *post-test loop* is one in which the test is made after the loop statements have been executed, as illustrated in Figure 8-11. With a post-test, the loop statements are always executed at least one time. The default for the PERFORM is pre-test, but the TEST clause can be used to force a post-test. For instance, in the following PERFORM, the test is made after the 300 module is executed.

```
        PERFORM 300-SAMPLE-ROUTINE
            WITH TEST AFTER
            UNTIL CHECK-VALUE = 100
```

In most cases, the default pre-test is the one to use. Occasionally, however, needs of the program dictate using the post-test.

Figure 8-10

The Looping Structure—Pre-test

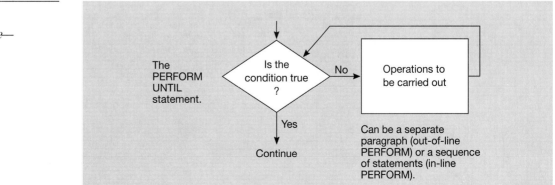

Figure 8-11

*The Looping Structure—
Post-test*

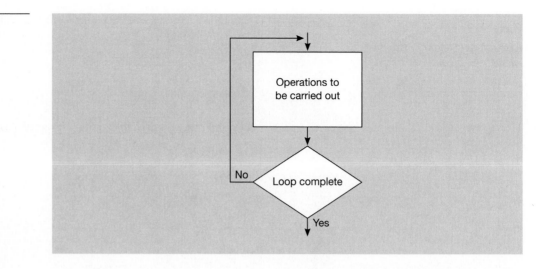

The Selection Structure

The *selection structure* represents decision-making ability, a feature that you have not yet used (it is covered later in this chapter). To illustrate selection, consider the following example:

Example 8-1

A record-of-the-month club gives members bonus points for each record purchased. If the member purchases the monthly feature, five bonus points are awarded; otherwise, only three bonus points are awarded.

This can be reworded in pseudocode form as follows:

```
If monthly feature purchased
   then award five points
   else award three points.
```

This structure is commonly referred to as the IF-THEN-ELSE structure; its structured form is shown in Figure 8-12.

In programming, you frequently will encounter situations in which a single action is to be taken if a condition is true. If it is not true, there is no alternative action. A slight variation of Example 8-1 illustrates this case.

Example 8-2

After a time, the management of the record club concludes that the bonus point program is much too generous and changes it. A member is to receive three bonus points only with the purchase of the monthly feature.

Figure 8-12

*The Selection Structure—
Example 8-1*

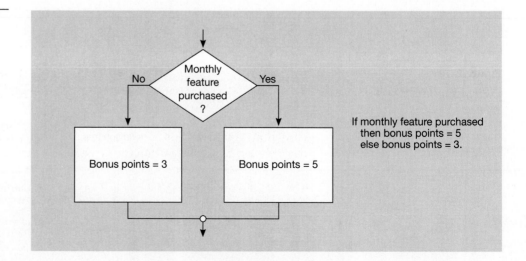

Actually, this is a special case of the selection structure and is illustrated in Figure 8-13. In COBOL, selection is implemented with the IF statement, as described later in this chapter. You will use it in Chapter 9's programs.

Figure 8-13

Special Case of Selection Structure—Example 8-2

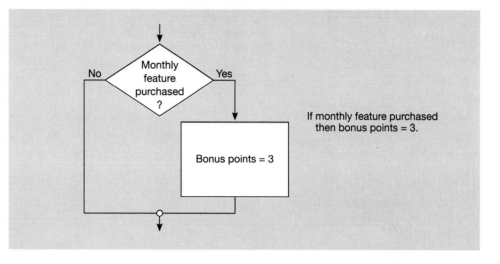

The Case Structure

Although the preceding three structures form the basis for structured programming, one additional structure is commonly implemented in most programming languages. The *case structure* is effectively a repeated application of the selection in which one of any number of actions can be taken as a result of a test. This is best illustrated by another variation of Example 8-1.

Example 8-3

The record club gives members bonus points for feature records purchased as follows:

1	3 bonus points
2	5 bonus points
3	6 bonus points
4 or more	8 bonus points

Figure 8-14 shows the case structure. One of the features of COBOL-85 is the powerful EVALUATE statement, which implements the case structure. You will learn to use the EVALUATE in Chapter 11.

As indicated, the case structure is simply a repeated application of the selection structure. For instance, prior to COBOL-85, the needs of Example 8-3 would have been handled with repeated selection structures (IF statements), as illustrated by the flowchart segment of Figure 8-15.

Two Program Logic Tools

Flowcharts to Illustrate Program Logic

As you know, structure charts illustrate what is to be done and the relationships between various components of the program, but they do not convey the logic of the solution. In Chapter 3, you were introduced to two tools for this purpose: the flowchart and pseudocode. Each of these two methods has its strong and weak points; each has its proponents and opponents. In some instances, a pseudocode solution serves very well; in other instances, a flowchart can clearly illustrate otherwise complex logic. An approach that works well for one person might be inadequate for another. The objective is to achieve good, structured programs. To do this, you might prefer one method or the other or a combination of both. Both forms are used for program development in this book.

All flowcharts in this book are built from the three basic structures of structured programming—sequence, selection, and looping—and the supplemental case structure. The original ADDER program from Chapter 2 is flowcharted in Figure 8-16 to illustrate basic principles. Here you see an identification of the standard flowchart symbols that will be used throughout this book.

This flowchart does not illustrate, however, the modularized nature of the program (which is implemented by using the PERFORM statement). The flowcharting standard for a sequence of operations that is "defined elsewhere" is a rectangle with extra vertical lines,

Figure 8-14

The Case Structure—Example 8-2

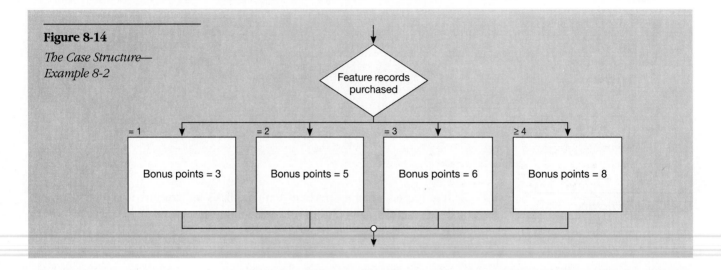

Figure 8-15

Simulating the Case Structure with a Series of Selections

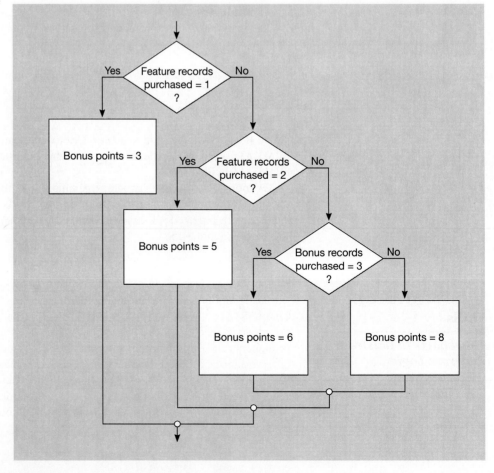

Figure 8-16

A Flowchart Representation of the ADDER Program

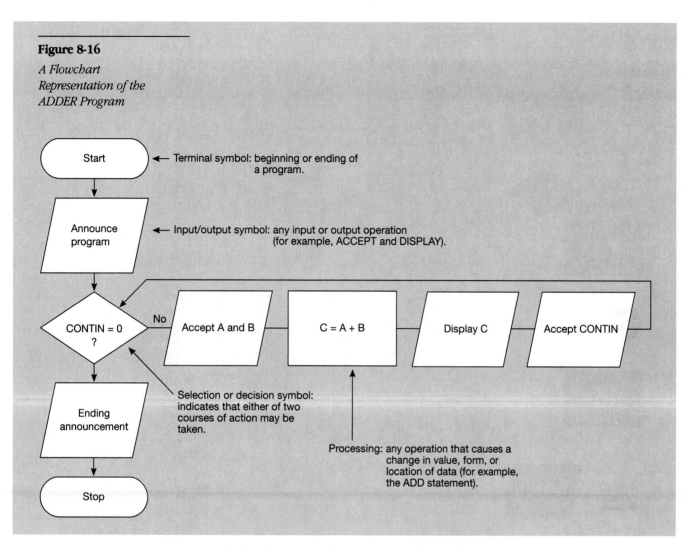

as illustrated in Figure 8-17. Here the description in the predefined process symbol is simply the name of the routine ("Process Data" in this case) where the actions are carried out. Details of the actions are contained in a separate flowchart module, as shown to the right of Figure 8-17. Note that the terminal symbol at the top of this flowchart contains the module name (the name referenced in the predefined process block) that refers to the module. Flowcharts in this book use the actual paragraph name, thereby linking the flowchart directly to the corresponding COBOL program.

Pseudocode

One way to gain an insight into the confusing logic of a large program is to illustrate various actions with structured flowcharts described in the preceding section. Another useful tool is called *pseudocode*. Instead of using flowchart blocks to represent programming logic steps, pseudocode uses statements that are a cross between actual language statements and ordinary English. Through a stepwise refinement that is very similar to the stepwise top-down modular refinement, lines of pseudocode can be expanded into the actual program itself.

For example, let's consider how a pseudocode solution to the Process-user-entries module of the modularized ADDER program might have been handled. The first step is

```
Process-user-entries Module.
   Process a pair of numbers.
```

Figure 8-17

The Predefined Process Flowchart Symbol

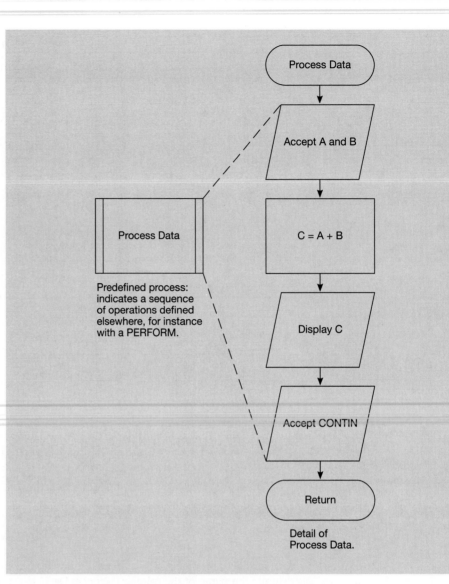

The next step in this solution would be to expand the detail.

```
Process-user-entries Module.
    Accept two numbers
    Calculate sum
    Display result
    Query about continuing.
```

As we see, the nature of the program is beginning to take form; the next refinement step is

```
110-PROCESS-USER-ENTRIES.
    DISPLAY prompts
    ACCEPT FIRST-NUM and SECOND-NUM
    MOVE FIRST-NUM TO TOTAL
    ADD SECOND-NUM TO TOTAL
    DISPLAY TOTAL
    Query about continuing.
```

Note that at this point, the pseudocode is a cross between an English description of the actions to take place and the COBOL program. The next step is to convert the remaining descriptions into COBOL statements.

One of the advantages of pseudocode is that it can be prepared with a word processing program and be included as part of the program documentation. For instance, the second pseudocode step provides good documentation of the general operations performed by this module.

COBOL Conditional Capabilities

The If-Else

The remaining topic in this chapter is the conditional capabilities provided by the IF statement in COBOL. Actually, you have already used conditional operations. For instance:

Perform a routine
   until a designated condition occurs.

From an indexed file, Read a specified record
   INVALID KEY (*if* there is no such record)
      take an action
   NOT INVALID KEY (*else* if the record exists)
      take another action

The above description of the indexed file read is much like the form of the COBOL IF statement. That is:

```
If a condition is true
    take an action
else
        take another action
```

Notice that the test consists of two broad elements: the condition test that is determined to be true or false, and the actions to be taken depending upon the test condition. Let's consider the test first condition.

Relational Operators and Expressions

You have used one form of the condition test in the PERFORM/UNTIL that repeatedly executes your processing modules. For example, your file processing programs have used a statement such as:

```
PERFORM 200-PRINT-NEXT-RECORD
    UNTIL END-OF-FILE = "Y"
```

In this statement, the condition test is

```
END-OF-FILE = "Y"
```

Note that as a condition form, it does not say that END-OF-FILE is *equal to* Y. Basically, it *asks* if the value stored in END-OF-FILE is equal to the literal Y. As such, it is called a *relational expression* and can have a value of true or false. That is, if the value stored in END-OF-FILE is Y, the condition is true; if anything else, the condition is false.

The relational expression consists of three basic parts, as illustrated in Figure 8-18.

Figure 8-18

The Relational Expression

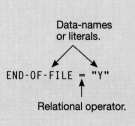

The general form of the relational test is

$$\left\{\begin{array}{l} \text{identifier-1} \\ \text{literal-1} \\ \text{arithmetic-expr-1} \end{array}\right\} \text{relational operator} \left\{\begin{array}{l} \text{identifier-2} \\ \text{literal-1} \\ \text{arithmetic-expr-1} \end{array}\right\}$$

The relational operator may be any of the following:

```
IS GREATER THAN
IS LESS THAN
IS EQUAL TO
```

The following are examples of relational tests that may be used in an IF statement:

```
BALANCE IS GREATER THAN MAX-BAL
VACATION-DAYS IS LESS THAN 90
SS-NUMBER IS EQUAL TO SS-NUMBER-HOLD
GENDER IS EQUAL TO "F"
```

The words IS and THAN of the relational operators are not underscored and thus are optional. Hence, the preceding four examples could be written as follows:

```
BALANCE GREATER MAX-BAL
VACATION-DAYS LESS 90
SS-NUMBER EQUAL SS-NUMBER-HOLD
GENDER EQUAL "F"
```

COBOL also allows you to use the common mathematical operators <, =, and > in relational tests.

Symbol	COBOL Operator
<	IS LESS THAN
=	IS EQUAL TO
>	IS GREATER THAN

Using these symbols, you can write the preceding examples as follows:

```
BALANCE > MAX-BAL
VACATION-DAYS < 90
SS-NUMBER = SS-NUMBER-HOLD
GENDER = "F"
```

In some instances, a *negation* of a test is convenient to use. For instance, what if the required test on the field HOURS-WORKED were that it be less than or equal to 40? Then we could write the test, using the operator NOT, as

```
HOURS-WORKED IS NOT GREATER THAN 40
```

In general, each of the relational operators can be expanded to include the negation, or NOT, operator as follows:

```
IS [NOT] GREATER THAN
IS [NOT] LESS THAN
IS [NOT] EQUAL TO
```

The negation can also be used in conjunction with the previous mathematical operators, as illustrated by the following examples:

```
BALANCE NOT > MAX-BAL
VACATION-DAYS NOT < 90
SS-NUMBER NOT = SS-NUMBER-HOLD
```

The IF Statement

The IF statement gives you the capability of executing the selection structure. As an illustration, consider the next example.

Example 8-4

In one portion of a payroll processing program, the application requires that the seniority field in the input record be tested and that the action to be taken is

If greater than 20
> Set AMOUNT-OUT equal to the value in AMOUNT.
> Write the EMPLOYEE record.
> Increase the value of S-COUNT by 1.

If not greater than 20
> Set AMOUNT-OUT equal to the value in LOW-AMOUNT.
> Increase the value of L-COUNT by 1.

A flowchart representation of this need is shown in Figure 8-19(a); the corresponding IF statement to perform these operations is shown in Figure 8-19(b).

The partial general form, reflected in the example of Figure 8-19, is as follows:

```
IF condition
   imperative-statement-1
[ELSE
   imperative-statement-2]
END-IF
```

The statement functions exactly as the English suggests. If the condition is true, the first statement(s) is/are executed; if false, the second statement(s) is/are executed. In both instances, execution then continues to the statement following the END-IF.

Figure 8-19

An Example of the IF/ELSE/END-IF

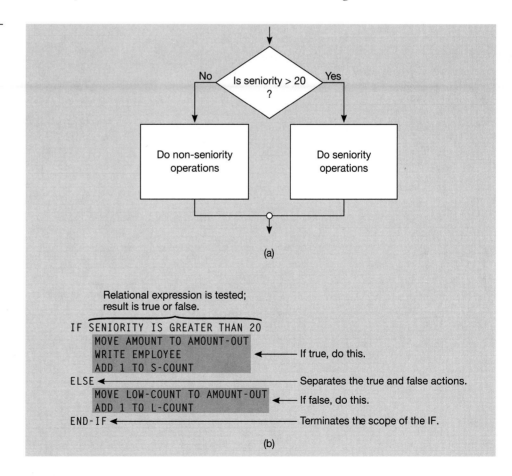

In Example 8-4, if the actions to be taken had been separate modules, then PERFORM statements would have been used; that is, the IF would take the form

```
IF SENIORITY IS GREATER THAN 20
    PERFORM 300-SENIORITY-PROCESSING
ELSE
    PERFORM 310-NON-SENIORITY-PROCESSING
END-IF
```

Referring back to the general form, notice that the ELSE clause is optional. This gives the ability to either perform an action or skip it, as illustrated by the flowchart of Figure 8-20(a). Referring to Example 8-4, if the requirement were to do seniority operations when the condition is true but take no seniority actions if false, the IF statement would be as shown in Figure 8-20(b).

Now the question that should come to mind is, "What kind of statements can be included as part of a block?" The answer is "virtually any." Remember from Chapter 3 that the term *imperative statement* means almost any statement (or collection of statements) that can appear in the PROCEDURE DIVISION, including conditional statements such as the IF/END-IF. The exceptions are those otherwise unconditional statement forms that include conditional options. For example, the READ with the AT END option or the ADD with the ON OVERFLOW option are not considered imperative statements as defined by the statement general format. Then by the preceding definitions, a conditionally executed block may itself include another IF/END-IF, and so on. In other words, the logic of an IF/END-IF can be very complex. Prior to introduction of the END-IF scope terminator in COBOL-85, there were severe restrictions on the use of IF statements within other IF statements. You will see examples of the versatility of the IF/END-IF in Chapter 11.

Figure 8-20

An Example of the IF/END-IF

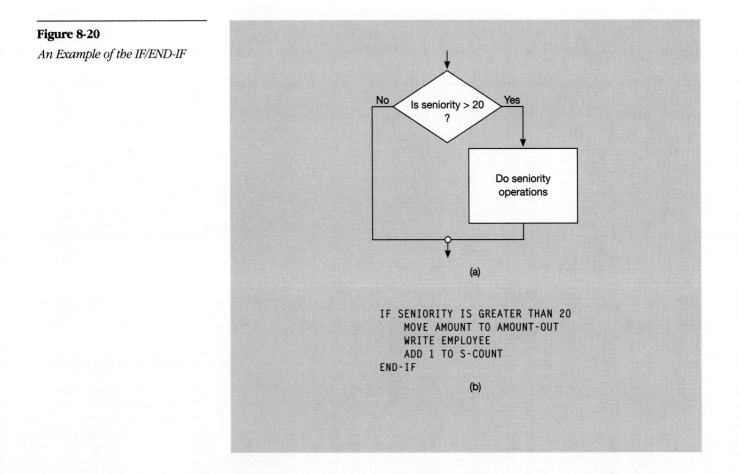

Chapter Summary

General

A "good" program: produces the correct results, is readable and understandable, and is easily modified.

The overall task of programming consists of two broad parts: determining *what* is to be done—identifying the physical structure; and determining *how* to do it—identifying the logical structure.

Structured design (top-down design) is the process of successively breaking a task into subtasks until each is of manageable size.

The four structures of structured programming theory are

Sequence—consecutive actions executed unconditionally

Looping—repeated execution of a sequence

Selection—execution of any either of two alternatives, depending on the result of a test

Case—execution of one of multiple alternatives, depending on the result of a test (an expansion of the selection)

A flowchart displays the logic of a program solution. The flowchart symbols used in this book are

Processing	Any operation (other than input or output) that causes a change in value, form, or location of data.	
Input/output	Any input or output operation.	
Decision	Indicates that either of two actions may be taken.	
Path Modification	An action that will cause a change in the sequence of operations at a later point in the program.	
Terminal	The beginning or ending of a program or module.	
Predefined Process	A program module that is defined elsewhere.	
Repetitive Predefined Process	A program module defined elsewhere that is to be repeatedly executed. The repetition condition is entered above the dotted line. (For post-test—WITH TEST AFTER—the repetition condition is entered below the dotted line.)	

Pseudocode is a programming tool for designing the logic of a program solution. The actions of each module are described in ordinary English, then refined to a program solution form.

COBOL Language Elements

The COBOL statement you have studied in this chapter is

IF   Provides the selection capability whereby either of two actions can be taken as the result of a condition test.

IF condition
   {imperative-statement-1}...
[ELSE
   {imperative-statement-2}...]
END-IF

The other language element you have studied in this chapter is
Relational expression—Used as the test condition in an IF statement.

$$\begin{Bmatrix} \text{identifier-1} \\ \text{literal-1} \\ \text{arithmetic-expr-1} \end{Bmatrix} \text{relational operator} \begin{Bmatrix} \text{identifier-2} \\ \text{literal-1} \\ \text{arithmetic-expr-1} \end{Bmatrix}$$

Programming Conventions

Within a program, each file to be read will have a READ statement in a separate module that is executed from wherever a read operation is required for that file.

Similarly, there will be a single WRITE statement for each output file (except for some applications, two WRITE statements will be required, as described in Chapter 9).

The following module-numbering convention is used in this book:

Number Prefix	Module Activity
000	Main controlling module

100–199	First-level modules:
	    initialize
	    process
	    finalize

200–299	General initialization activities in which
	    the initialize module must be broken into
	        submodules.

300–699	General processing activities
700–799	Preparation of output:
700–719	for headings
720–739	for detail lines
740–789	for intermediate total lines
780–799	for final total lines
800–899	Input and output:
800–849	input (for instance, READ)
850–899	output (for instance, WRITE)
900–999	Exception processing

Questions and Exercises

Key Terminology

Give a brief description of each of the following terms that were introduced in this chapter.

case structure	physical structure	relational expression
flowchart	post-test loop	selection structure
imperative statement	pre-test loop	sequence structure
logical structure	primitive module	structured design
looping structure	program logic	structured program
negation	pseudocode	syntax

General Questions

1. What are the four structures of structured programming?

2. Why is the case structure deemed not essential to structured programming theory?

3. The relational test can involve identifiers or literals. Would it be practical to compare two literals? Explain.

4. What are program module numbers? Do they serve any useful purpose?

5. Three "tools" are discussed in this and earlier chapters in conjunction with structured program development. What are they?

6. What are the three relational operators that can be used when writing relational expressions?

7. What is structured design or "top-down" design?

Writing Program Statements

1. Write relational tests for each of the following:
   a. New balance exceeds credit limit
   b. Record type is not zero
   c. Union dues are less than or equal to maximum dues
   d. Number of dependents is four or more
   e. Inventory code is F8117G

2. Write COBOL statements to perform each of the following operations, using the basic IF form described in the preceding pages:
   a. If CHECK-VALUE is 9, then display the message "Check value point".
   b. If GPA is equal to or exceeds 3.2, then increase CREDIT-POINTS by 1.
   c. Calculate COMMISSION given SALES, QUOTA, LOW-RATE, and HIGH-RATE as follows:

      if SALES exceed QUOTA
      COMMISSION = 1.2 x SALES x HIGH-RATE
      if SALES does not exceed QUOTA
      COMMISSION = 1.2 x SALES x LOW-RATE

      In both cases, add COMMISSION to TOTAL-AMOUNT and continue processing.

3. Write relational tests for each of the following.
   a. Cost is less than selling price.
   b. Department code is 50AP-52X.
   c. Inventory on hand is less than or equal to order amount.
   d. Available credit is not greater than credit limit.
   e. GPA is 3.5 or better.

4. Write COBOL statements to complete each of the following operations, using the basic IF form described in the preceding pages.
   a. If INV-ON-HAND greater than ORDER-AMT, then display the message "Overstocked Item".
   b. Compute GROSS-MARGIN equal TOTAL-SALES minus TOTAL-COSTS for all departments except "TOYS-30F". Add GROSS-MARGIN to TOTAL-GM only when it is computed.
   c. When union dues are equal to or greater than maximum dues, display "Dues Paid". Otherwise, deduct $5 from NET-PAY and add $5 to union dues.

Programming Assignments

Programming assignments in this and following chapters use data files. For the record description of all files used in the assignments you must use Appendix A.

8-1 Courses Below Minimum Enrollment

The college administration officials of Programming Assignment 6-4 have determined that they need a list of courses falling below a percentage of the minimum enrollment.

Output Requirements:

A printed report with the following output and format (note that this is the same as the output of Figure 6-4).

Field	Beginning Column	Output Format
Class code	1	
Course name	6	
Course number	23	
Section number	27	
Instructor name	30	
Minimum permissible enrollment	45	Zero suppress
Actual enrollment	50	Zero suppress
Enrollment as percentage of minimum	55	Format: *nnn.n* Insert decimal point zero suppress

Prepare a printer spacing chart.

Input Description:

File name: ENROLL01.DL
Record description: See Appendix A
Keyboard input: Cutoff percentage
(refer to Processing Requirements)

Processing Requirements:

1. Accept from the keyboard a value for the Cutoff percentage. The range can be from 25 to 100 percent.
2. Convert the Cutoff percentage to a fractional value by dividing it by 100.

For each record in the file:

3. Calculate the Enrollment cutoff as
   Cutoff percentage x Minimum permissible enrollment
4. If the Actual enrollment is less than the Enrollment cutoff, print the record as described in Programming Assignment 6-4.

Program run: Make a program run using a Cutoff percentage of 80%.

8-2 Student Scholarship Summary

The registrar of Programming Assignment 6-3 would like the program modified to print a list of students with a value for GPA greater than 2.5. Furthermore, he wants some additional information printed.

Output Requirements:

A printed report with the following output and format.

Field	Beginning Column	Output Format
Social Security number	1	Insert hyphens; for instance: 123-45-6789
Student last name	11	
Student first name	23	
Class standing	36	Print the word FRESHMAN, SOPHOMORE, JUNIOR, SENIOR, or GRADUATE
Cumulative units	43	Insert a decimal point, suppress leading zeros
Cumulative points	52	Same as cumulative points
Cumulative GPA	58	Insert a decimal point, suppress leading zeros
GPA last semester	63	Same as cumulative GPA

Prepare a printer spacing chart.

Input Description:

File name: STUDENTS.DL

Record description: See Appendix A

Processing Requirements:

For each record in the file:

1. Calculate the Cumulative GPA as

$$= \frac{\text{Cumulative points}}{\text{Cumulative units}}$$

2. If the Cumulative GPA is less than 2.5, skip this record; otherwise, continue to the next step.

3. Edit each field as designated in the preceding Output Format description.

4. In place of the Class-standing code, print the appropriate word as follows:

    1 FRESHMAN
    2 SOPHOMORE
    3 JUNIOR
    4 SENIOR
    5 GRADUATE

5. Print one double-spaced line for each record that qualifies.

9

PREPARATION OF REPORTS

Outline

■ **Report Headings—Example 9-1**
  Example Definition—Example 9-1
  Sample Output—Example 9-1
  Program Solution—Example 9-1

■ **Variable Line Spacing**
  Using Records from the WORKING-STORAGE SECTION
  Printing Using Multiple Output Record Formats
  Defining Headings in the WORKING-STORAGE SECTION
  Defining the Detail Line in the WORKING-STORAGE SECTION
  The WRITE-FROM Option

■ **Obtaining the Date from the System**

■ **Report Totals**
  Example Definition—Example 9-2
  Sample Output—Example 9-2
  Accumulators
  Program Solution—Example 9-2
  The INITIALIZE Statement

■ **Principles of Page Control**
  Page Layout Design
  The WRITE Statement

■ **A Page Control Example**
  Example Definition—Example 9-3
  Sample Output—Example 9-3
  Program Solution—Example 9-3

■ **Program Control of the Printer**

Chapter Objectives

In the preceding chapters, the focus has been on learning the basics of COBOL and simply "getting things to work right." Until now, good printed output was correct output. One of the important focuses of COBOL is preparing printed output in usable, easy-to-read copy—that is, *report generation*. The purpose of this chapter is to develop techniques for preparing good reports. This chapter includes three variations of the RET-VAL1 program; from them, you will learn about the following topics:

The RET-VAL2 program—Example 9-1:

■ Designing and printing descriptive headings

■ Defining multiple output areas and defining records in the WORKING-STORAGE SECTION, and writing from these areas

■ Using a variable quantity to control line spacing

The RET-VAL3 program—Example 9-2:

■ Using accumulators to total the values of one or more selected fields of a record and printing totals that summarize the data of the report

■ Using the INITIALIZE statement, which allows you to give an initial value to one or more data items

■ Using the VALUE clause at a group level

The RET-VAL4 program—Example 9-3:

■ Controlling the printing of a long report from page to page (page control)

■ Numbering pages

■ Printing descriptive headings at the top of each new page

■ Advancing the printer to the top of each new page

Report Headings— Example 9-1

Example Definition— Example 9-1

When discussing programs to produce printed output, little attention has been given to "frills" such as descriptive headings to identify the information being printed. For example, consider the computer output in Figure 9-1(a). It is certainly not obvious what these numbers mean. However, if the report is printed with appropriate headings, as shown in Figure 9-1(b), the printed page is self descriptive. The first example program of this chapter demonstrates how to produce output like this.

Example 9-1 Preparing a Report With Page and Column Headings

Problem Description

The retail value report program (RET-VAL1 from Chapter 6) must be expanded to include headings. Descriptive information desired is: a general report title, the date the report is prepared, and a set of column headings identifying each column of output on the printed report.

Output Requirements

The output requirements of this report include the detailed record-by-record output of RET-VAL1, together with descriptive headings. The format is shown in the printer spacing chart of Figure 9-2.

Input Description

Input file name: SOFTWAR2.DL

Figure 9-1

Sample Reports

```
            07427   Apricot-tree General Ledger      65   349.95
            10164   Sluggish Writer                  93    49.95
            15589   Travelling Side Punch           180    29.95
            15674   Supercharged Turbo COBOL        120   599.00
            28429   Ferrari 4-5-6 Financial Acctg.  144   495.00
            28558   Orchestra II                    102   649.00


                    A Simple Report      (a)


            SOFTWARE INVENTORY/PRICE SUMMARY    7/19/91

         Stock                             Total
         Number  Description               Units  Price

            07427   Apricot-tree General Ledger      65   349.95
            10164   Sluggish Writer                  93    49.95
            15589   Travelling Side Punch           180    29.95
            15674   Supercharged Turbo COBOL        120   599.00
            28429   Ferrari 4-5-6 Financial Acctg.  144   495.00
            28558   Orchestra II                    102   649.00


                A Report with Descriptive Headings      (b)
```

Record Format:

Field	Positions	Data Type	Format
Stock number	1–5	Alphanumeric	
Software name	6–35	Alphanumeric	
Vendor name	36–55	Alphanumeric	
Copies on hand	56–58	Numeric	*nnn*
Not used*	59–61		
Price	62–66		*nnn*∧*nn*

Note: The data in these columns is not used in this application, but the positions must be accounted for in the record description.

Processing Requirements

Obtain the current date from the system. Then print the headings at the top of the page and data lines, one line per data record, as shown in the printer spacing chart.

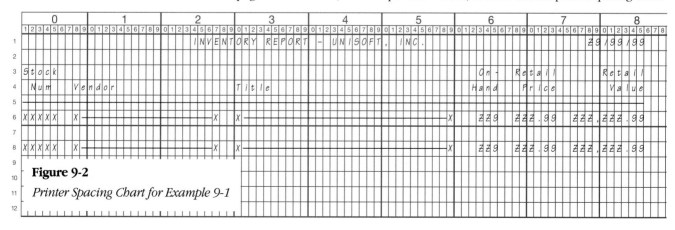

Figure 9-2

Printer Spacing Chart for Example 9-1

Sample Output— Example 9-1

A sample report for this example is shown in Figure 9-3. You can see its two types of output: descriptive heading lines and lines containing data from the input file. *Heading lines* are printed lines that describe the data that is printed. The first line is a general *report description* line and identifies the report; it also includes the date the report was run.

```
              INVENTORY REPORT - UNISOFT, INC.                    7/13/91

Stock                                              On-   Retail      Retail
Num    Vendor              Title                    Hand  Price       Value
-------------------------------------------------------------------------------
07427  Apricot Software    Apricot-tree General Ledger   65  349.95   22,746.75

10164  Archaic Software    Sluggish Writer           93   49.95    4,645.35

15589  Borneo International Travelling Side Punch    180   29.95    5,391.00

15674  Borneo International Supercharged Turbo COBOL 120  599.00   71,880.00

28429  Ferrari Development  Ferrari 4-5-6 Financial Acctg.  144  495.00  71,280.00

28558  Ferrari Development  Orchestra II             102  649.00   66,198.00

32506  Galactic Bus. Mach.  Bottom View             105   99.95   10,494.75

37188  International Soft   UnderWord, Rev 128        90   37.50    3,375.00

37281  International Soft   UnderCalc, Rev 256        80   37.50    3,000.00

37384  International Soft   UnderFile, Rev 64         95   37.50    3,562.50

45191  Micro Am            Word Comet 7             104  399.00   41,496.00

49165  Microhard           Sentence                 143  349.95   50,042.85

53351  MicroPerimeter, Inc. QBase 7000              176  695.00  122,320.00

60544  Nobodies, Unlimited Nobodies Disk Utilities  133   49.50    6,583.50

91655  20th Century Soft.  Potent BASIC Interpreter  97    9.50      921.50
```

Figure 9-3

*A Sample Report—
Example 9-1*

**Program Solution—
Example 9-1**

Reports commonly contain two or three such description lines and include a page number for multiple page reports.

The printed output from the input file in this report consists of one line for each input record; these are called *detail lines*. In general, a detail line in a report is a line derived from data in a single record.

You will encounter one other type of output line in most reports: summary lines. A *summary line* is one that includes output created from two or more records from the input file. Typically, these contain totals for numeric fields in the input record. For instance, a summary line for an inventory report might include the total inventory value. You will learn about calculating totals and printing summary lines in Example 9-2.

A complete solution to the example is shown in Figures 9-4 through 9-7 (pages 187 through 190). If you compare the structure chart of Figure 9-4 to that of Figure 8-4, you will see that they are similar with the exception of added modules for (1) obtaining the run date and (2) printing the headings.

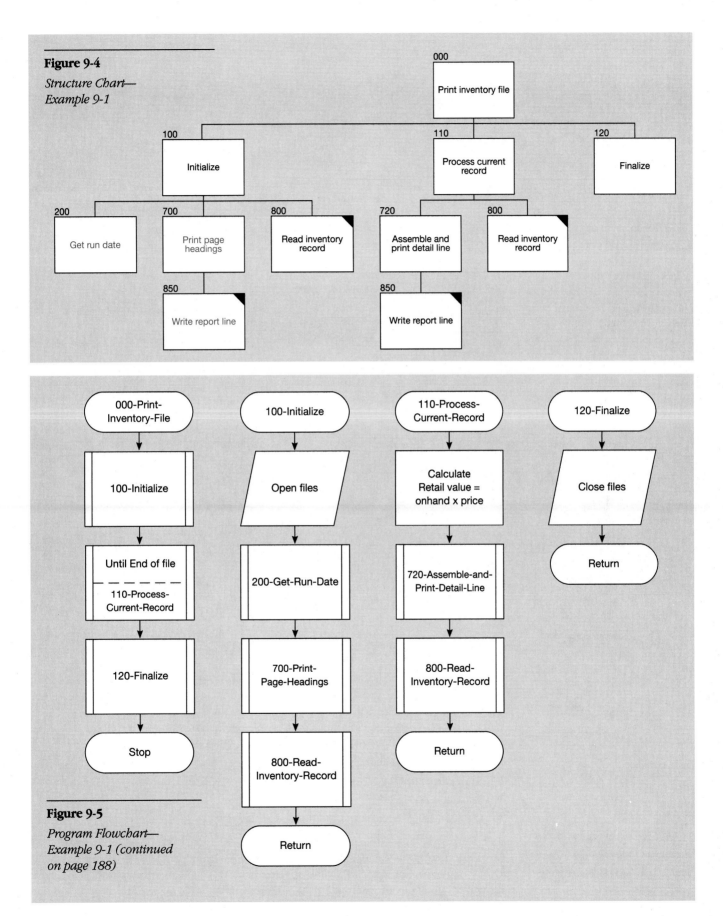

Figure 9-4

Structure Chart—Example 9-1

Figure 9-5

Program Flowchart—Example 9-1 (continued on page 188)
(continued on page 188)

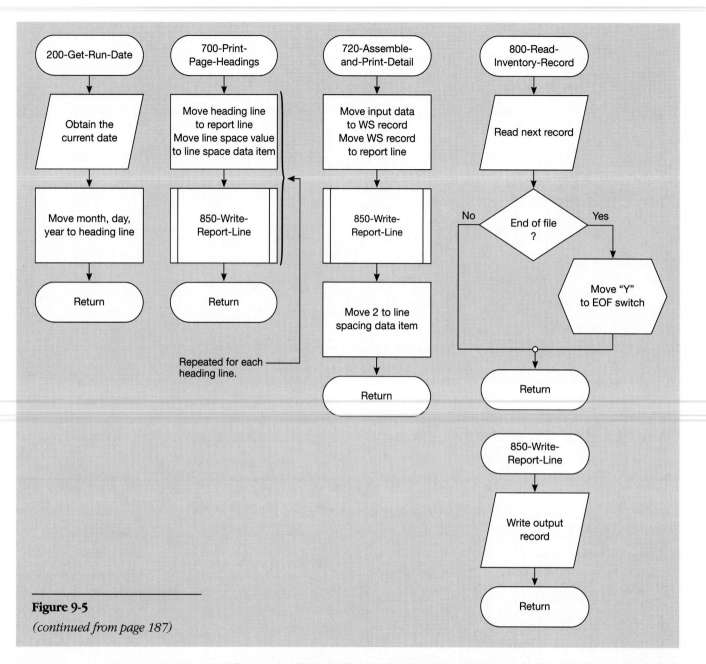

Figure 9-5
(continued from page 187)

The program logic is illustrated by the flowchart of Figure 9-5 and the pseudocode of Figure 9-6. Here you can see that the logic of the 200-Get-Run-Date and the 700-Print-Page-Headings modules is a simple sequence of actions.

The program structure and logic are clearly evident in the program of Figure 9-7. From this program, you will learn the following new COBOL concepts:

■ Controlling line spacing (variable line spacing)
■ Setting up output records in the WORKING-STORAGE SECTION
■ Printing report headings
■ Obtaining the current date from the operating system

Variable Line Spacing

In all the preceding examples and programming assignments, printed output has been either single- or double-spaced: line spacing has been the same throughout the report. However, the needs of Example 9-1 are different. That is, if you refer to the printer chart

Figure 9-6

*Program Pseudocode—
Example 9-1*

```
100-Initialize module
     Open data files
     Perform 200-Get-Run-Date module
     Perform 700-Print-Page-Headings module
     Perform 800-Read-Inventory-Record module

110-Process-Current-Record module
     Calculate Retail-value equals
          Quantity-on-hand times Price
     Perform 720-Assemble-and-Print-Detail module
     Perform 800-Read-Inventory-Record module

120-Finalize
     Close files

200-Get-Run-Date
     Obtain the current date
     Move month, day, and year to heading line

700-Print-Page-Headings (do the following for each heading line)
     Move heading to report output line
     Move line spacing value to line spacing data item
     Perform 850-Write-Report-Line module

720-Assemble-and-Print-Detail
     Move input data to output detail record
     Move output detail record to report output line
     Perform 850-Write-Report-Line module
     Move 2 to line spacing data item

800-Read-Inventory-Record
     Read next record
          if EOF move "Y" to EOF switch

850-Write-Report-Line
     Print the output record
```

of Figure 9-2 and the sample output of Figure 9-3, you will see the following spacing:

■ No blank line preceding the main heading line
■ One blank line preceding the first column heading line
■ No blank lines preceding the second column heading line
■ No blank lines preceding the row of hyphens
■ No blank lines preceding the first detail line
■ One blank line each detail line after the first

As you progress, you will see that the specifications for the vertical spacing of the printed output become very detailed. Experienced systems analysts soon learn what is required to produce printed output that is both attractive and easy to read. As a result, such specifications are commonly encountered by the working programmer.

The clumsy part of this output is that the first detail line will be printed by a statement such as:

```
WRITE REPORT-LINE
    AFTER ADVANCING 1 LINE
```

However, the corresponding WRITE for all other detail lines will take the form:

```
WRITE REPORT-LINE
    AFTER ADVANCING 2 LINES
```

The simplest way of handling this situation (and those that are even more complex) is to use a data item in place of the numeric literal specifying the number of lines to be

```
  1         IDENTIFICATION DIVISION.                                   75      01  COLUMN-HEADING-2.
  2                                                                    76          10                      PIC X(7)    VALUE " Num".
  3         PROGRAM-ID. RET-VAL2.                                      77          10                      PIC X(22)   VALUE "Vendor".
  4                                                                    78          10                      PIC X(32)   VALUE "Title".
  5     *   Written by W.Price / Modified by J. Olson                  79          10                      PIC X(7)    VALUE "Hand".
  6     *   July 14, 1990      / July 25, 1990                         80          10                      PIC X(10)   VALUE "Price".
  7                                                                    81          10                      PIC X(7)    VALUE "Value".
  8     *   This program is RET-VAL1, modified to print heading lines. 82
  9                                                                    83      01  DETAIL-LINE                          VALUE SPACES.
 10     *   This program generates a retail value report from         84          10  RL-STOCK-NUMBER     PIC X(5).
 11     *   the file SOFTWAR2.DL.  For each record in the file         85          10                      PIC X(2).
 12     *   there is one output line that includes the retail         86          10  RL-VENDOR-NAME      PIC X(20).
 13     *   value (price times quantity on hand) for that item.       87          10                      PIC X(2).
 14                                                                    88          10  RL-SOFTWARE-NAME    PIC X(30).
 15         ENVIRONMENT DIVISION.                                      89          10                      PIC X(3).
 16                                                                    90          10  RL-QUANT-ON-HAND    PIC ZZ9.
 17         CONFIGURATION SECTION.                                     91          10                      PIC X(2).
 18         SOURCE-COMPUTER. IBM-PC.                                   92          10  RL-PRICE            PIC ZZZ.99.
 19                                                                    93          10                      PIC X(2).
 20         INPUT-OUTPUT SECTION.                                      94          10  RL-RETAIL-VALUE     PIC ZZZ,ZZZ.99.
 21         FILE-CONTROL.                                              95
 22             SELECT INVENTORY-FILE  ASSIGN TO DISK "SOFTWAR2.DL"    96      PROCEDURE DIVISION.
 23                                    ORGANIZATION IS LINE SEQUENTIAL.97
 24             SELECT REPORT-FILE     ASSIGN TO PRINTER "PRN-FILE".   98      000-PRINT-INVENTORY-FILE.
 25                                                                    99          PERFORM 100-INITIALIZE
 26         DATA DIVISION.                                             100         PERFORM 110-PROCESS-CURRENT-RECORD
 27                                                                    101             UNTIL END-OF-FILE = "Y"
 28         FILE SECTION.                                              102         PERFORM 120-FINALIZE
 29                                                                    103         STOP RUN.
 30         FD  INVENTORY-FILE.                                        104
 31         01  INVENTORY-RECORD.                                      105     100-INITIALIZE.
 32             10  IR-STOCK-NUMBER    PIC X(5).                       106         OPEN INPUT INVENTORY-FILE
 33             10  IR-SOFTWARE-NAME   PIC X(30).                      107         OPEN OUTPUT REPORT-FILE
 34             10  IR-VENDOR-NAME     PIC X(20).                      108         PERFORM 200-GET-RUN-DATE
 35             10  IR-QUANT-ON-HAND   PIC 9(3).                       109         PERFORM 700-PRINT-PAGE-HEADINGS
 36             10                     PIC X(3).                       110         PERFORM 800-READ-INVENTORY-RECORD.
 37             10  IR-PRICE           PIC 9(3)V9(2).                  111
 38                                                                    112     110-PROCESS-CURRENT-RECORD.
 39         FD  REPORT-FILE.                                           113
 40         01  REPORT-LINE            PIC X(85).                      114     *   Calculate retail value
 41                                                                    115         MOVE IR-PRICE TO RETAIL-VALUE
 42         WORKING-STORAGE SECTION.                                   116         MULTIPLY IR-QUANT-ON-HAND BY RETAIL-VALUE
 43                                                                    117
 44         01  PROGRAMMED-SWITCHES.                                   118         PERFORM 720-ASSEMBLE-AND-PRINT-DETAIL
 45             10  END-OF-FILE        PIC X      VALUE "N".           119         PERFORM 800-READ-INVENTORY-RECORD.
 46                                                                    120
 47         01  ARITHMETIC-WORK-AREAS.                                 121     120-FINALIZE.
 48             10  RETAIL-VALUE       PIC 9(6)V9(2).                  122         CLOSE INVENTORY-FILE
 49                                                                    123               REPORT-FILE.
 50         01  PRINT-CONTROL-VARIABLES.                               124
 51             10  LINE-SPACING       PIC 9.                          125     200-GET-RUN-DATE.
 52                                                                    126         ACCEPT RUN-DATE FROM DATE
 53         01  RUN-DATE.                                              127         MOVE RUN-MONTH TO PH-MONTH
 54             10  RUN-YEAR           PIC 99.                         128         MOVE RUN-DAY   TO PH-DAY
 55             10  RUN-MONTH          PIC 99.                         129         MOVE RUN-YEAR  TO PH-YEAR.
 56             10  RUN-DAY            PIC 99.                         130
 57                                                                    131     700-PRINT-PAGE-HEADINGS.
 58         01  PAGE-HEADING-LINE.                                     132         MOVE PAGE-HEADING-LINE TO REPORT-LINE
 59             10                     PIC X(23)   VALUE SPACES.       133         MOVE ZERO TO LINE-SPACING
 60             10                     PIC X(32)   VALUE               134         PERFORM 850-WRITE-REPORT-LINE
 61                     "INVENTORY REPORT - UNISOFT, INC.".            135         MOVE COLUMN-HEADING-1 TO REPORT-LINE
 62             10                     PIC X(22)   VALUE SPACES.       136         MOVE 2 TO LINE-SPACING
 63             10  PH-MONTH           PIC Z9.                         137         PERFORM 850-WRITE-REPORT-LINE
 64             10                     PIC X       VALUE "/".          138         MOVE COLUMN-HEADING-2 TO REPORT-LINE
 65             10  PH-DAY             PIC 99.                         139         MOVE 1 TO LINE-SPACING
 66             10                     PIC X       VALUE "/".          140         PERFORM 850-WRITE-REPORT-LINE
 67             10  PH-YEAR            PIC 99.                         141         MOVE ALL "-" TO REPORT-LINE
 68                                                                    142         PERFORM 850-WRITE-REPORT-LINE.
 69         01  COLUMN-HEADING-1.                                      143
 70             10                     PIC X(62)   VALUE "Stock".      144     720-ASSEMBLE-AND-PRINT-DETAIL.
 71             10                     PIC X(5)    VALUE "On-".        145         MOVE IR-STOCK-NUMBER TO RL-STOCK-NUMBER
 72             10                     PIC X(11)   VALUE "Retail".     146         MOVE IR-SOFTWARE-NAME TO RL-SOFTWARE-NAME
 73             10                     PIC X(7)    VALUE "Retail".     147         MOVE IR-VENDOR-NAME TO RL-VENDOR-NAME
 74                                                                    148         MOVE IR-QUANT-ON-HAND TO RL-QUANT-ON-HAND
                                                                       149         MOVE IR-PRICE TO RL-PRICE
                                                                       150         MOVE RETAIL-VALUE TO RL-RETAIL-VALUE
                                                                       151         MOVE DETAIL-LINE TO REPORT-LINE
                                                                       152         PERFORM 850-WRITE-REPORT-LINE
                                                                       153         MOVE 2 TO LINE-SPACING.
                                                                       154
                                                                       155     800-READ-INVENTORY-RECORD.
                                                                       156         READ INVENTORY-FILE
                                                                       157             AT END MOVE "Y" TO END-OF-FILE
                                                                       158         END-READ.
                                                                       159
                                                                       160     850-WRITE-REPORT-LINE.
                                                                       161         WRITE REPORT-LINE
                                                                       162             AFTER ADVANCING LINE-SPACING LINES.
```

Figure 9-7

The RET-VAL2 Program—
Example 9-1

advanced. That is:

```
WRITE REPORT-LINE
      AFTER ADVANCING LINE-SPACING LINES
```

Here the data item LINE-SPACING is defined in the WORKING-STORAGE SECTION as a one digit field, as follows:

```
10 LINE-SPACING  PIC 9.
```

Then prior to executing the WRITE, you would move the appropriate value into LINE-SPACING, as follows:

```
MOVE 1 TO LINE-SPACING   (for single-spacing with the WRITE)
MOVE 2 TO LINE-SPACING   (for double-spacing with the WRITE)
```

This technique is called *variable line spacing.*

Appropriate code from the RET-VAL2 program that uses variable line spacing is shown in Figure 9-8. For the sake of discussion, the MOVE statements that change the value in LINE-SPACING (the data item used in the AFTER ADVANCING clause of the WRITE) are highlighted and the PERFORM statements are numbered. Let's consider the action that occurs for the first heading line. Prior to printing the first heading line, a value of 0 is moved into the data item LINE-SPACING by the statement (shaded in Figure 9-8):

```
MOVE ZERO TO LINE-SPACING
```

In the case of the first heading line, it is assumed that the paper has been positioned in the printer at the point where the first heading line is to be printed. Thus, there is no need to advance the page prior to printing. (Note that ZERO is one of the figurative constants available in COBOL. Either ZERO or ZEROS can be used to indicate a numeric value of 0.)

Referring to the numbers to the left of each PERFORM in Figure 9-8, line spacing control during execution of this program is summarized by the following:

Figure 9-8

*Variable Line Spacing—
Example 9-1*

```
700-PRINT-PAGE-HEADINGS.
    MOVE PAGE-HEADING-LINE TO REPORT-LINE
    MOVE ZERO TO LINE-SPACING        ← LINE-SPACING will contain a value
  ① PERFORM 850-WRITE-REPORT-LINE       of 0 when the WRITE is performed from here.
    MOVE COLUMN-HEADING-1 TO REPORT-LINE
    MOVE 1 TO LINE-SPACING
  ② PERFORM 850-WRITE-REPORT-LINE   ← LINE-SPACING will contain a value
    MOVE COLUMN-HEADING-2 TO REPORT-LINE    of 2 when the WRITE is performed from here.
    MOVE 2 TO LINE-SPACING
  ③ PERFORM 850-WRITE-REPORT-LINE   ←
    MOVE ALL "-" TO REPORT-LINE          LINE-SPACING will contain a value of 1 when
  ④ PERFORM 850-WRITE-REPORT-LINE.  ←  the WRITE is performed from both of these.

720-ASSEMBLE-AND-PRINT-DETAIL.
    .
    .
    .
  ⑤ PERFORM 850-WRITE-REPORT-LINE   ← The first time this PERFORM is executed,
    MOVE 2 TO LINE-SPACING.            LINE-SPACING contains 1 (remaining from
                                       printing the column headings).  Thereafter,
                                       it contains 2 from this MOVE.
```

These statements change the line spacing value.

PERFORM	LINE-SPACING Value	Result
1	0	The first heading line is printed without paper movement.
2	2	The paper is advanced two lines before printing; thus, one blank line precedes the first column heading line.
3	1	Normal single-spacing results; therefore, no blank line precedes the second column heading line.
4	1 (no change)	Normal-single spacing for the row of hyphens.
5 (first time)	1 (no change)	Normal single-spacing for the first detail line.
5 (subsequent)	2	The paper is advanced two lines before printing; thus, one blank line precedes each detail line.

Using Records from the WORKING–STORAGE SECTION

Printing Using Multiple Output Record Formats

In all of the earlier programs, both the input and output record formats are described in respective FDs of the FILE SECTION. As you know, the output record describes the exact form of the printed line. Each printing operation involves the WRITE statement, such as:

```
WRITE REPORT-LINE ...
```

This causes the computer to print the data exactly as defined in the record description for REPORT-LINE in the DATA DIVISION. However, the program of Example 9-1 involves printing descriptive heading lines, as well as detail lines containing data from the input records. In Figure 9-9 (the first few lines from the printed report of Figure 9-3), you can see that there will be five different format descriptions to print these lines: four for the headings and one for the detail line.

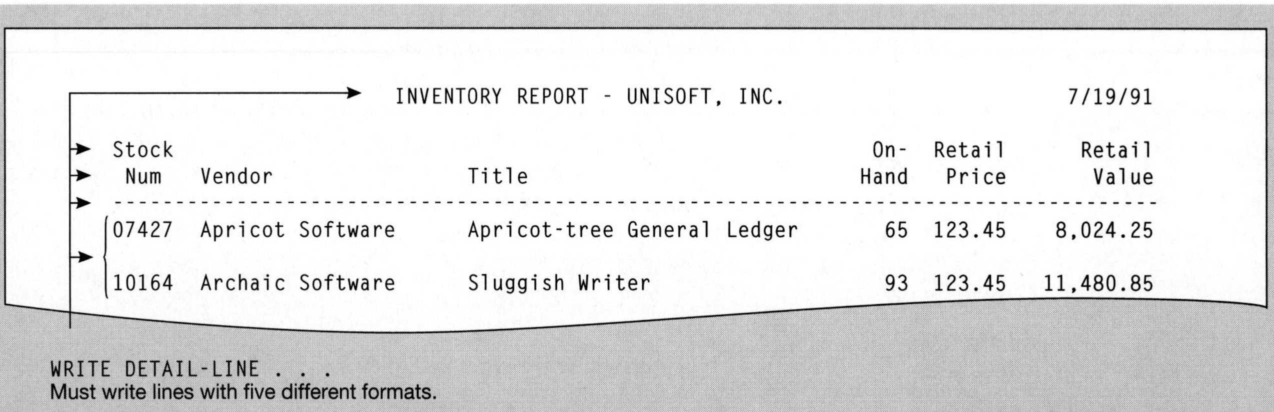

```
            INVENTORY REPORT - UNISOFT, INC.                7/19/91

Stock                                          On-  Retail    Retail
Num   Vendor           Title                   Hand  Price     Value
--------------------------------------------------------------------
07427 Apricot Software  Apricot-tree General Ledger   65 123.45   8,024.25

10164 Archaic Software  Sluggish Writer               93 123.45  11,480.85
```

```
WRITE DETAIL-LINE . . .
```
Must write lines with five different formats.

Figure 9-9

Printing Lines with Different Formats

One way of doing this is to define the output record (in the FD) as a single field (elementary item) large enough to contain the longest line being printed. In the program of Figure 9-7, you see this is the FD entry:

```
FD REPORT-FILE.
01 REPORT-LINE      PIC X(85).
```

Then two or more additional areas are defined in the WORKING-STORAGE SECTION that correspond exactly to the required output formats.

Also in Figure 9-7, you can see that the heading lines and the detail line are defined by the following records:

PAGE-HEADING-LINE
COLUMN-HEADING-1
COLUMN-HEADING-2
DETAIL-LINE

The overall function of writing a line then involves:

1. Moving the record to be printed from the WORKING-STORAGE SECTION to the output record defined by the FD

2. Moving the line spacing value to the line spacing data item

3. Performing the module to write the line

For example, the statements to write the first column heading line are

```
MOVE COLUMN-HEADING-1 TO REPORT-LINE
MOVE 2 TO LINE-SPACING
PERFORM 850-WRITE-REPORT-LINE
```

Next, let's consider how headings are defined in the WORKING-STORAGE SECTION.

Defining Headings in the WORKING-STORAGE SECTION

To illustrate, consider the first column heading line, which is defined in the WORKING-STORAGE SECTION by the following:

```
01 COLUMN-HEADING-1.
    10              PIC X(62)   VALUE "Stock".
    10              PIC X(5)    VALUE "On-".
    10              PIC X(11)   VALUE "Retail".
    10              PIC X(7)    VALUE "Retail".
```

Because the record is defined in the WORKING-STORAGE SECTION, the VALUE clause can be used (remember, the VALUE clause cannot be used in the FILE SECTION, except for condition names). Notice that in setting up this line, the counts for the FILLER values have been selected to produce the desired spacing. (Remember that COBOL-85 allows you to omit the reserved word FILLER.) For instance, the first FILLER is 62 positions. The literal "Stock" will be positioned to the left of this 62 position area and the remaining positions filled with spaces. Thus, the next literal (On-) will be positioned beginning column 63—this is as required by the printer spacing chart (see Figure 9-2).

Here notice that each column heading is defined as a separate FILLER. This is convenient and simplifies changing the spacing between one or more of the columns. However, the last three column headings could have been defined with a single entry, as follows:

```
01 COLUMN-HEADING-1.
    10              PIC X(62)   VALUE "Stock".
    10              PIC X(23)
                    VALUE "On-  Retail Inventory".
```

Alternately, the entire heading could be defined with a single literal. However, because of its length, you would need to continue the literal over two lines, as shown in Figure 9-10. Here the literal starts with the opening quote (preceding the word *Stock*), continues to the last statement position (column 72), and begins on the next line, following another open quote. The continuation line is indicated by a hyphen in column 7. Notice that there is no closing quote on the line to be continued. Defining column headings in this way tends to be clumsy and error prone. Continuation lines for literals are not used in this book's examples.

Figure 9-10

Continuation of a Literal

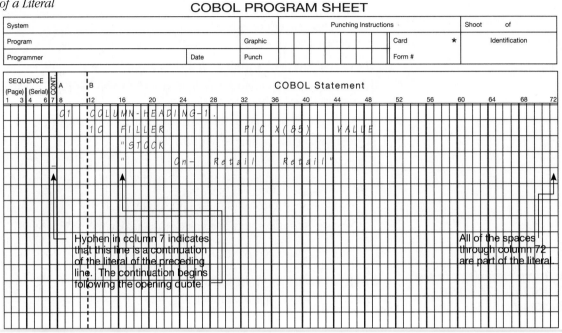

COBOL PROGRAM SHEET

Defining the Detail Line in the WORKING-STORAGE SECTION

The following are the first few lines of the detail line record from the RET-VAL2 program of Figure 9-7:

```
01  DETAIL-LINE              VALUE SPACES.
    10  RL-STOCK-NUMBER      PIC X(5).
    10                       PIC X(2).
    10  RL-VENDOR-NAME       PIC X(20).
```

Notice that this differs from a corresponding definition you would use in the FD because the VALUE clause is used to initialize the entire group item (DETAIL-LINE) to spaces. This is necessary to ensure that each of the FILLER areas contains spaces and not garbage as is normal for fields defined in the WORKING-STORAGE SECTION. (*Note:* The RM/COBOL-85 compiler initializes all such work areas to spaces even though the 1985 Standard does not require initialization.)

Until now, all data movement has involved moving from one elementary item to another. In this example, a group item consisting of several fields is moved to an elementary item. This is quite valid: you can refer to any individual elementary item when moving or to the composite group item. In this case, DETAIL-LINE is treated by the MOVE statement as one large block of information being moved to REPORT-LINE.

The WRITE-FROM Option

In using output record definitions in the WORKING-STORAGE SECTION, you must first move the record to the output record of the FD and then write. For instance:

```
MOVE PAGE-HEADING-LINE TO
WRITE REPORT-LINE
```

However, these two statements (MOVE and WRITE) can be replaced by the following WRITE-FROM statement:

```
WRITE REPORT-LINE FROM PAGE-HEADING-LINE.
```

This programmer convenience factor allows the programmer to combine the move and write operations.

Note that this only saves you writing the MOVE statement; you must still define the output line in the FD and the various print records in the WORKING-STORAGE SECTION.

Because this method is not compatible with the single-write module concept introduced in Chapter 8, the WRITE-FROM is not used in this book.

Obtaining the Date from the System

Virtually all computers have an internal clock for maintaining the time and date. This information is available to the COBOL program via a form of the ACCEPT statement. The particular form that you see in the RET-VAL2 program (Figure 9-7, lines 53–56 and 126) is

```
01 RUN-DATE.
   10 RUN-YEAR          PIC 99.
   10 RUN-MONTH         PIC 99.
   10 RUN-DAY           PIC 99.
         .
         .
         .
      ACCEPT RUN-DATE FROM DATE
```

The identifier RUN-DATE must be a six-position field to hold the date; it is returned to the program in a *yymmdd* (year/month/day) form. You see this breakdown in the definition of RUN-DATE. After the date is accessed, its three components are moved to the WORKING-STORAGE SECTION record definition by the MOVE statements (lines 127–129):

```
MOVE RUN-MONTH  TO  PH-MONTH
MOVE RUN-DAY    TO  PH-DAY
MOVE RUN-YEAR   TO  PH-YEAR.
```

As you can see by the following general form, this version of the ACCEPT can also return the day and time:

$$\underline{\text{ACCEPT}} \text{ identifier } \underline{\text{FROM}} \left\{ \begin{array}{l} \underline{\text{DATE}} \\ \underline{\text{DAY}} \\ \underline{\text{TIME}} \end{array} \right\}$$

The reserved word DAY causes the date to be copied into the field specified as *identifier*; the format is the Julian date (*yyddd*) in which *ddd* is the day of the year. For instance, February 4, 1991, would be returned as the five-digit value 91035. The reserved word TIME causes the time to be returned based on a 24-hour clock with two digits for the hour, two for the minute, two for the seconds, and two for hundredths of a second. For instance, a time of 1:29 and 25.38 seconds would be returned as the eight-digit 13292538.

Report Totals

Example Definition— Example 9-2

The second example program of this chapter demonstrates calculating totals based on data fields in a file.

Example 9-2 Preparing a Report With Report Totals

Problem Description

The retail value report program RET-VAL2 must be expanded to include a total line at the end of the report. This line is to include a count of the number of records processed and the total retail value of all items in the inventory.

Output Requirements

The output requirements of this report are identical to those of RET-VAL2, except that a summary line is required that includes the total number of records processed and the total retail value. The format is shown in the printer spacing chart of Figure 9-11.

Input Description

Input file name: SOFTWAR2.DL (same as the RET-VAL2 program)
Record format: See Example 9-1

Processing Requirements

General processing requirements for this example are the same as those for Example 9-1, except that totals must be accumulated. As each detail record is read, it must be counted. Each retail value figure (calculated as the Price times the Quantity-on-hand) must be added to an accumulator that totals the retail value.

Figure 9-11

Printer Spacing Chart for Example 9-2

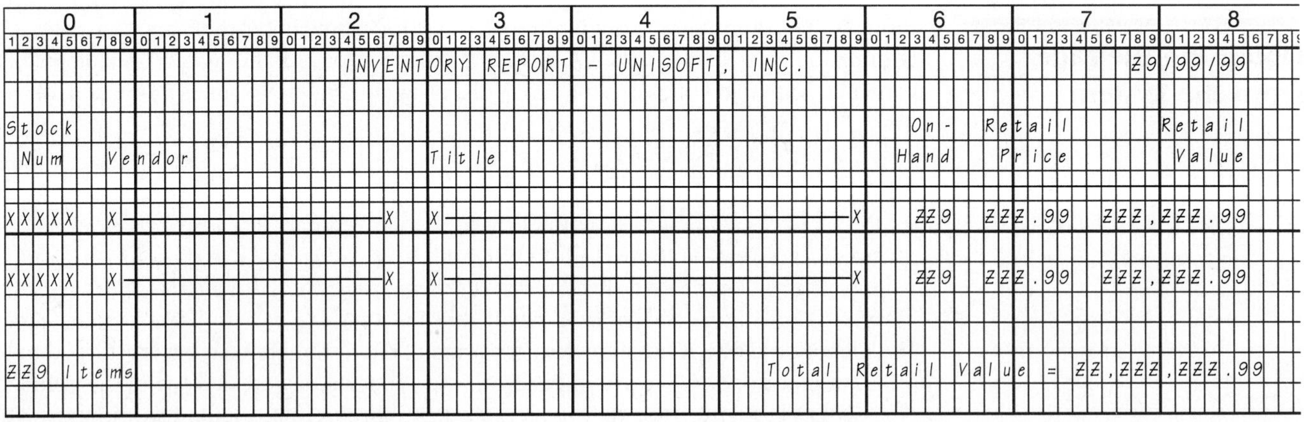

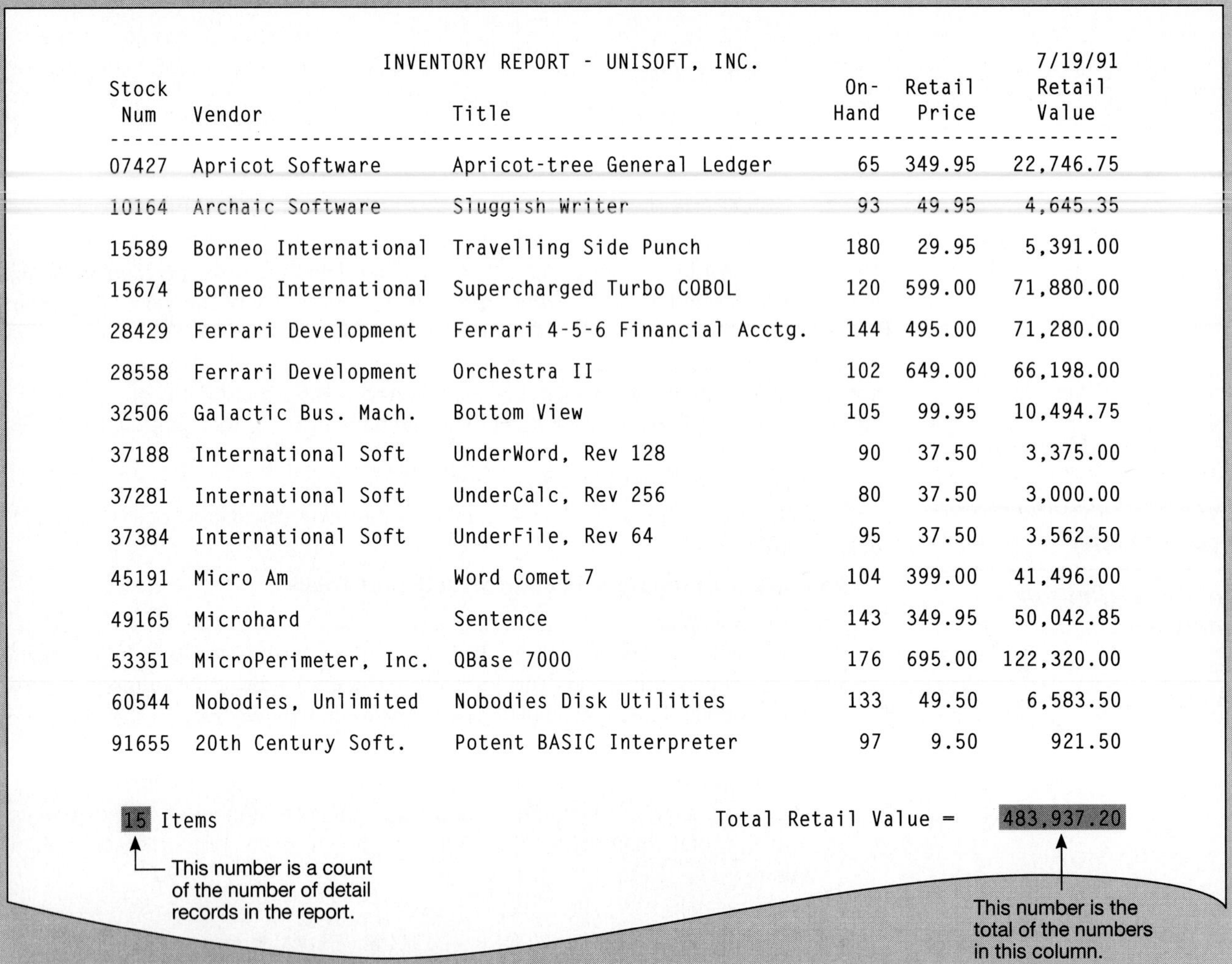

Figure 9-12

Sample Output—Example 9-2

```
                    INVENTORY REPORT - UNISOFT, INC.               7/19/91
   Stock                                              On-   Retail   Retail
   Num    Vendor               Title                  Hand  Price    Value
   -------------------------------------------------------------------------
   07427  Apricot Software     Apricot-tree General Ledger    65  349.95   22,746.75
   10164  Archaic Software     Sluggish Writer                93   49.95    4,645.35
   15589  Borneo International  Travelling Side Punch         180   29.95    5,391.00
   15674  Borneo International  Supercharged Turbo COBOL      120  599.00   71,880.00
   28429  Ferrari Development   Ferrari 4-5-6 Financial Acctg. 144 495.00   71,280.00
   28558  Ferrari Development   Orchestra II                  102  649.00   66,198.00
   32506  Galactic Bus. Mach.  Bottom View                   105   99.95   10,494.75
   37188  International Soft    UnderWord, Rev 128             90   37.50    3,375.00
   37281  International Soft    UnderCalc, Rev 256             80   37.50    3,000.00
   37384  International Soft    UnderFile, Rev 64              95   37.50    3,562.50
   45191  Micro Am             Word Comet 7                  104  399.00   41,496.00
   49165  Microhard            Sentence                      143  349.95   50,042.85
   53351  MicroPerimeter, Inc. QBase 7000                    176  695.00  122,320.00
   60544  Nobodies, Unlimited  Nobodies Disk Utilities       133   49.50    6,583.50
   91655  20th Century Soft.   Potent BASIC Interpreter       97    9.50      921.50

   15 Items                               Total Retail Value =   483,937.20
```

└── This number is a count
of the number of detail
records in the report.

This number is the
total of the numbers
in this column.

**Sample Output—
Example 9-2**

A sample report for this example is shown in Figure 9-12. In addition to the headings, you can see that it contains a summary line with the number of detail lines (records) in this report and the total retail value.

Accumulators

A person preparing the report of Figure 9-12 manually would probably obtain the summary data by first typing all of the detail lines and then going back and adding up all of the typed figures to get the necessary totals. Such a procedure would be impractical for the computer. Instead, the program must accumulate its summary totals from each detail record as that detail record is processed. When the last record is processed, the summary total calculations will be complete. Then final output of the summary line requires only that the summary totals be assembled and printed. This can be accomplished by defining a data field in the WORKING-STORAGE SECTION for each summary total required and adding the values for each detail record to these data fields as they are calculated. Data fields used in this way are called *accumulators* because they are used to accumulate totals. To use a data field as an accumulator, you must:

1. Define the accumulator in the WORKING-STORAGE SECTION. It must have a numeric PICTURE, and it must be large enough to contain the largest value that might be accumulated.

2. Initialize the accumulator. To accumulate a true total, the accumulator must start out with an initial value of zero. This is usually accomplished by including the VALUE ZERO clause in the accumulator definition. However, it is also possible, and sometimes necessary, to initialize the accumulator by moving zeroes to it in the PROCEDURE DIVISION.

3. Add the necessary value to the value already in the accumulators, as each record is processed.

4. Print the contents of the accumulator by moving them to an output field. To make theprinted data more readable, you normally define the output field as a numeric-edited item.

This notion of accumulating is illustrated by the sample sequence of Figure 9-13, in which the calculated values for retail value of the first two records are 8,024.25 and 11,480.85.

Figure 9-13

*The Principle of
Accumulating*

```
RETAIL-VALUE  PIC 9(6)V9(2).
    .
    .
    .
TOTAL-VALUE  PIC 9(8)V9(2).
```

	RETAIL-VALUE	TOTAL-VALUE (Before)	TOTAL-VALUE (After)
Initialization `MOVE ZERO TO TOTAL-VALUE`		?	0
First execution of accumulation `ADD RETAIL-VALUE TO TOTAL-VALUE`	8024.25	0	8024.25
Second execution of accumulation `ADD RETAIL-VALUE TO TOTAL-VALUE`	11480.85	8024.25	19505.10

Program Solution— Example 9-2

A complete solution to Example 9-2 is shown in Figures 9-14 through 9-17. Since this example is an expansion of Example 9-1, its structure and logic are simple extensions of Example 9-1. All modifications and additions to Example 9-1 are highlighted.

The structure chart of Figure 9-14 differs from that of Figure 9-4 only by the addition of two highlighted modules to handle the total line.

As described in the preceding discussion of accumulators, the program logic must reflect: initialization of the accumulators, accumulating, and printing the summary line. These elements are highlighted in the flowchart of Figure 9-15 and the pseudocode of Figure 9-16.

The program structure and logic are clearly evident in the program of Figure 9-17 (see page 202). You can see that the additions are relatively minor. From the preceding discussion of accumulators, these additions should be relatively clear to you. Within the processing loop, totals are accumulated. After detecting the EOF record, the summary line is processed from the 120-FINALIZE module by executing the 730-ASSEMBLE-AND-PRINT-TOTAL module.

The INITIALIZE Statement

The two accumulators of this program defined by

```
01  ACCUMULATORS.
    10 TOTAL-VALUE   \PIC 9(8)V9(2).
    10 RECORD-COUNT PIC 9(3).
```

must be set to zero as part of the initialization procedure. This can be done with the following MOVE statements:

```
MOVE ZERO TO TOTAL-VALUE
MOVE ZERO TO RECORD-COUNT
```

You can take advantage of the MOVE capability that allows you to move a value to one or more destination data items by using the following form:

```
MOVE ZERO TO TOTAL-VALUE, RECORD-COUNT
```

An alternate approach (used in the RET-VAL3 program) is to initialize using the INITIALIZE statement, as follows:

```
INITIALIZE ACCUMULATORS
```

Figure 9-14

Structure Chart— Example 9-2

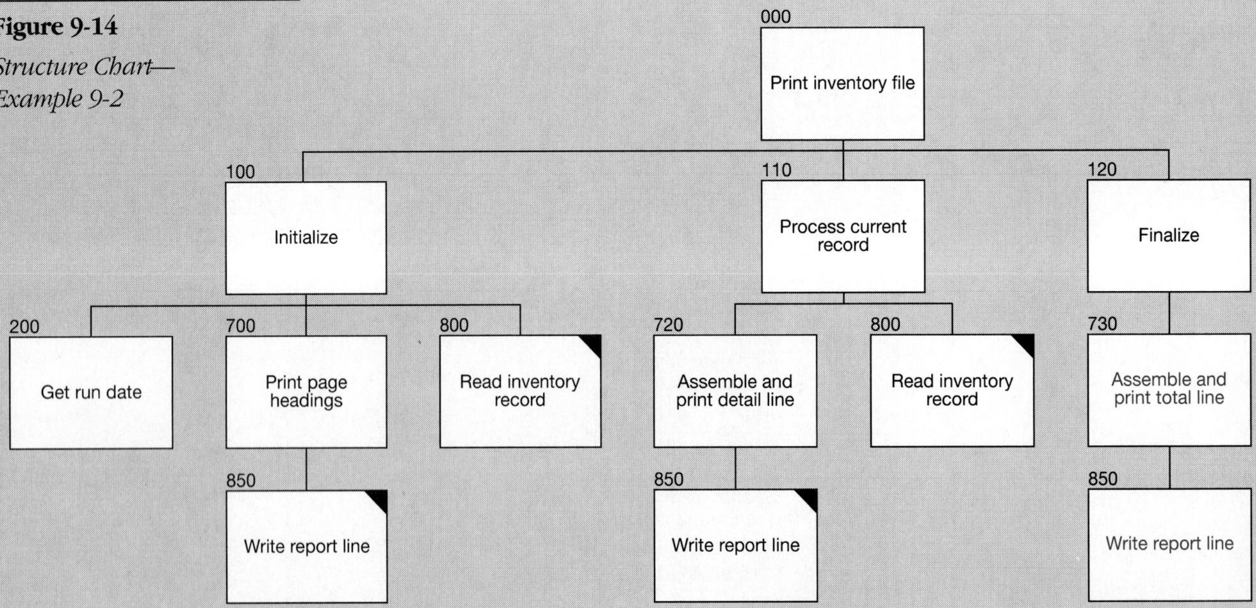

Notice that the data item ACCUMULATORS is the group item under which the elementary data items TOTAL-VALUE and RECORD-COUNT are defined. The advantages of this statement are that:

■   It can designate one or more group items to be initialized and thereby initialize each elementary item comprising the group item(s).

■   A group item can consist of both numeric and alphanumeric elementary items. Numeric items are initialized to zero and alphanumeric items initialized to spaces.

Principles of Page Control

Page Layout Design

The one deficiency of the RET-VAL3 program is that a report generated from a large data file will require more than one page. The resulting output will print to the bottom of the page and continue across the perforation. When the pages are separated at the perforations, the user will have a real mess. That is, only the first page will have report headings. Furthermore, it will be difficult to know the page order once the pages are separated.

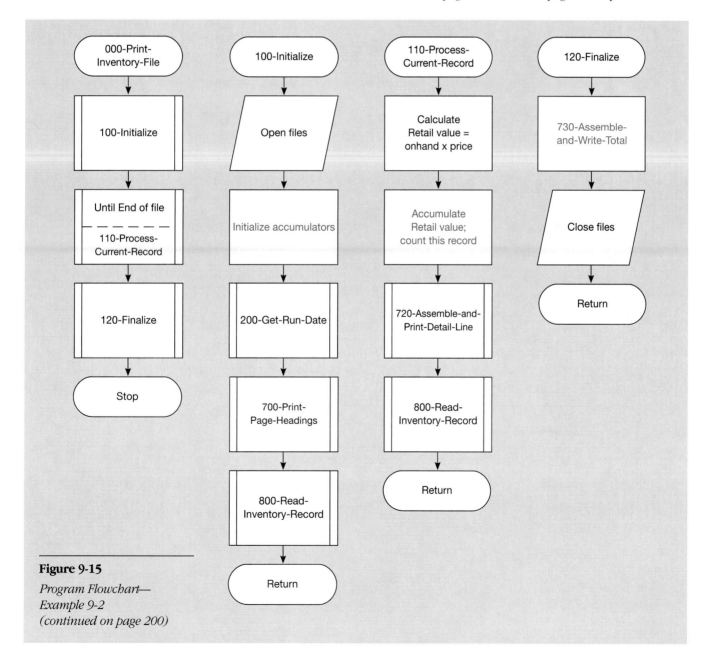

Figure 9-15

Program Flowchart—
Example 9-2
(continued on page 200)

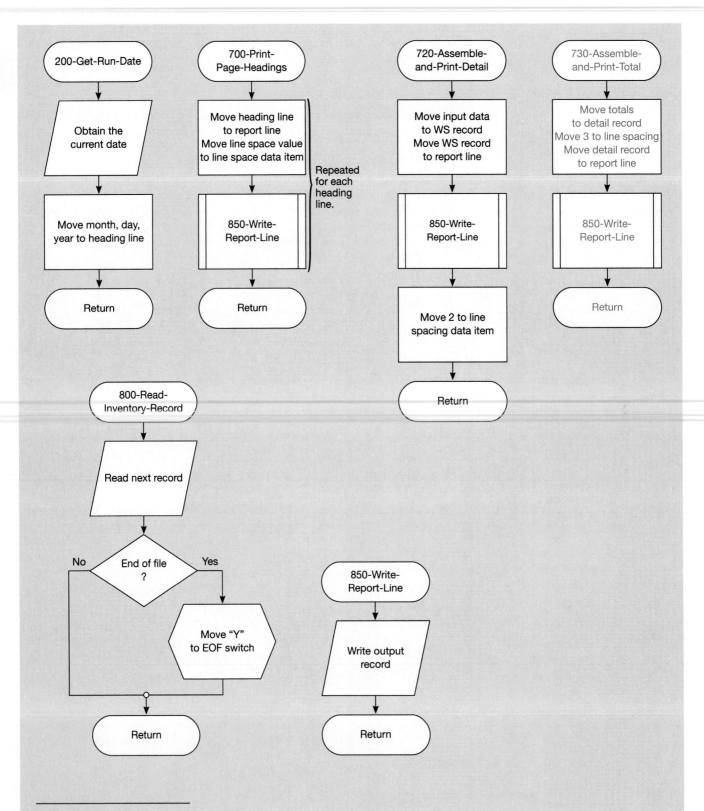

Figure 9-15

(continued from page 199)

Figure 9-16

Program Pseudocode—
Example 9-2

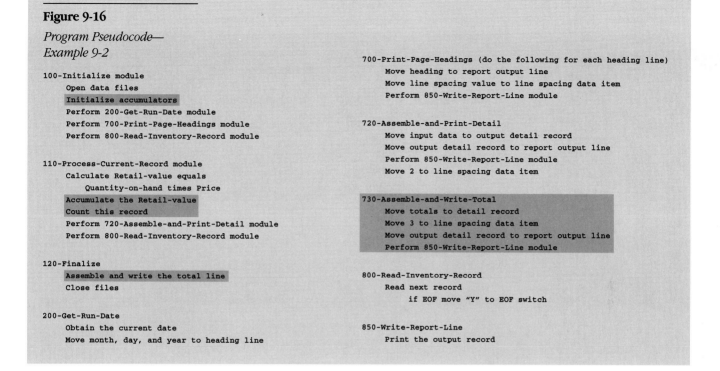

```
100-Initialize module
      Open data files
      Initialize accumulators
      Perform 200-Get-Run-Date module
      Perform 700-Print-Page-Headings module
      Perform 800-Read-Inventory-Record module

110-Process-Current-Record module
      Calculate Retail-value equals
          Quantity-on-hand times Price
      Accumulate the Retail-value
      Count this record
      Perform 720-Assemble-and-Print-Detail module
      Perform 800-Read-Inventory-Record module

120-Finalize
      Assemble and write the total line
      Close files

200-Get-Run-Date
      Obtain the current date
      Move month, day, and year to heading line
```

```
700-Print-Page-Headings (do the following for each heading line)
      Move heading to report output line
      Move line spacing value to line spacing data item
      Perform 850-Write-Report-Line module

720-Assemble-and-Print-Detail
      Move input data to output detail record
      Move output detail record to report output line
      Perform 850-Write-Report-Line module
      Move 2 to line spacing data item

730-Assemble-and-Write-Total
      Move totals to detail record
      Move 3 to line spacing data item
      Move output detail record to report output line
      Perform 850-Write-Report-Line module

800-Read-Inventory-Record
      Read next record
          if EOF move "Y" to EOF switch

850-Write-Report-Line
      Print the output record
```

This introduces the topic of *page control*, the controlling of printed output to conform to the boundaries of the page on which it is printed. You have already observed the painstaking detail that goes into planning the report form that culminates in the printer spacing chart. The final element of this planning is the effective use of the page. For page layout, the page is commonly considered in three parts:

Top margin	The area between the top of the page and the first printed line. No printing is in the top margin. When a report is run, the top margin is usually determined by inserting the paper in the printer at the desired position of the first line of the page (usually a report heading line).
Body	The portion of the page on which printing occurs.
Bottom margin	The area at the bottom of the page following the last printed line. No printing is allowed in this area, except for total lines. That is, if the last detail line is printed on the last line of the body, it is considered better to print the total line in the bottom margin, rather than by itself on the next page.

Instead of measuring in terms of inches (as the typewriter does), page planning is commonly done in terms of lines on the page, in which the standard line spacing is 6 lines per inch (commonly abbreviated 6 LPI). Hence, if you are using an 11-inch form, there are 66 lines per page. If you desired top and bottom margins of 1 inch (6 lines), the body of your report would consist of

66 - 6 - 6 = 54 lines

Then your program would need appropriate control to progress to a new page after 54 lines have been printed on the current page. Example 9-3 will show you how this is done.

Figure 9-17

The RET-VAL3 Program—
Example 9-2

```
1       IDENTIFICATION DIVISION.
2
3       PROGRAM-ID. RET-VAL3.
4
5   *   Written by W.Price / Modified by J. Olson
6   *   July 14, 1990      / July 25, 1990
7
8   *   This program is RET-VAL2, modified to print a total line.
9
10  *   This program generates a retail value report from
11  *   the file SOFTWAR2.DL. For each record in the file
12  *   there is one output line that includes the retail
13  *   value (price times quantity on hand) for that item.
14
15      ENVIRONMENT DIVISION.
16
17      CONFIGURATION SECTION.
18      SOURCE-COMPUTER. IBM-PC.
19
20      INPUT-OUTPUT SECTION.
21      FILE-CONTROL.
22          SELECT INVENTORY-FILE   ASSIGN TO DISK "SOFTWAR2.DL"
23                                  ORGANIZATION IS LINE SEQUENTIAL.
24          SELECT REPORT-FILE      ASSIGN TO PRINTER "PRN-FILE".
25
26      DATA DIVISION.
27
28      FILE SECTION.
29
30      FD  INVENTORY-FILE.
31      01  INVENTORY-RECORD.
32          10  IR-STOCK-NUMBER     PIC X(5).
33          10  IR-SOFTWARE-NAME    PIC X(30).
34          10  IR-VENDOR-NAME      PIC X(20).
35          10  IR-QUANT-ON-HAND    PIC 9(3).
36          10                      PIC X(3).
37          10  IR-PRICE            PIC 9(3)V9(2).
38
39      FD  REPORT-FILE.
40      01  REPORT-LINE             PIC X(85).
41
42      WORKING-STORAGE SECTION.
43
44      01  PROGRAMMED-SWITCHES.
45          10  END-OF-FILE         PIC X       VALUE "N".
46
47      01  ARITHMETIC-WORK-AREAS.
48          10  RETAIL-VALUE        PIC 9(6)V9(2).
49
50      01  ACCUMULATORS.
51          10  TOTAL-VALUE         PIC 9(8)V9(2).
52          10  RECORD-COUNT        PIC 9(3).
53
54      01  PRINT-CONTROL-VARIABLES.
55          10  LINE-SPACING        PIC 9.
56
57      01  RUN-DATE.
58          10  RUN-YEAR            PIC 99.
59          10  RUN-MONTH           PIC 99.
60          10  RUN-DAY             PIC 99.
61
62      01  PAGE-HEADING-LINE.
63          10                      PIC X(23)   VALUE SPACES.
64          10                      PIC X(32)   VALUE
65                                  "INVENTORY REPORT - UNISOFT, INC.".
66          10                      PIC X(22)   VALUE SPACES.
67          10  PH-MONTH            PIC Z9.
68          10                      PIC X       VALUE "/".
69          10  PH-DAY              PIC 99.
70          10                      PIC X       VALUE "/".
71          10  PH-YEAR             PIC 99.
72
73      01  COLUMN-HEADING-1.
74          10                      PIC X(62)   VALUE "Stock".
75          10                      PIC X(5)    VALUE "On-".
76          10                      PIC X(11)   VALUE "Retail".
77          10                      PIC X(7)    VALUE "Retail".
78
79      01  COLUMN-HEADING-2.
80          10                      PIC X(7)    VALUE " Num".
81          10                      PIC X(22)   VALUE "Vendor".
82          10                      PIC X(32)   VALUE "Title".
83          10                      PIC X(7)    VALUE "Hand".
84          10                      PIC X(10)   VALUE "Price".
85          10                      PIC X(7)    VALUE "Value".
86
87      01  DETAIL-LINE                         VALUE SPACES.
88          10  RL-STOCK-NUMBER     PIC X(5).
89          10                      PIC X(2).
90          10  RL-VENDOR-NAME      PIC X(20).
91          10                      PIC X(2).
92          10  RL-SOFTWARE-NAME    PIC X(30).
93          10                      PIC X(3).
94          10  RL-QUANT-ON-HAND    PIC ZZ9.
95          10                      PIC X(2).
96          10  RL-PRICE            PIC ZZZ.99.
97          10                      PIC X(2).
98          10  RL-RETAIL-VALUE     PIC ZZZ,ZZZ.99.
99
100     01  TOTAL-LINE.
101         10  TL-RECORD-COUNT     PIC ZZ9.
102         10                      PIC X(48)   VALUE " Items".
103         10                      PIC X(21)   VALUE
104                                 "Total Retail Value = ".
105         10  TL-TOTAL-VALUE      PIC ZZ,ZZZ,ZZZ.99.
106
107     PROCEDURE DIVISION.
108
109     000-PRINT-INVENTORY-FILE.
110         PERFORM 100-INITIALIZE
111         PERFORM 110-PROCESS-CURRENT-RECORD
112             UNTIL END-OF-FILE = "Y"
113         PERFORM 120-FINALIZE
114         STOP RUN.
115
116     100-INITIALIZE.
117         OPEN INPUT INVENTORY-FILE
118         OPEN OUTPUT REPORT-FILE
119         INITIALIZE ACCUMULATORS
120         PERFORM 200-GET-RUN-DATE
121         PERFORM 700-PRINT-PAGE-HEADINGS
122         PERFORM 800-READ-INVENTORY-RECORD.
123
124     110-PROCESS-CURRENT-RECORD.
125
126     * Calculate retail value
127         MOVE IR-PRICE TO RETAIL-VALUE
128         MULTIPLY IR-QUANT-ON-HAND BY RETAIL-VALUE
129
130     * Increment accumulators
131         ADD RETAIL-VALUE TO TOTAL-VALUE
132         ADD 1 TO RECORD-COUNT
133
134         PERFORM 720-ASSEMBLE-AND-PRINT-DETAIL
135         PERFORM 800-READ-INVENTORY-RECORD.
136
137     120-FINALIZE.
138         PERFORM 730-ASSEMBLE-AND-PRINT-TOTAL
139         CLOSE INVENTORY-FILE
140             REPORT-FILE.
141
142     200-GET-RUN-DATE.
143         ACCEPT RUN-DATE FROM DATE
144         MOVE RUN-MONTH TO PH-MONTH
145         MOVE RUN-DAY   TO PH-DAY
146         MOVE RUN-YEAR  TO PH-YEAR.
147
148     700-PRINT-PAGE-HEADINGS.
149         MOVE PAGE-HEADING-LINE TO REPORT-LINE
150         MOVE ZERO TO LINE-SPACING
151         PERFORM 850-WRITE-REPORT-LINE
152         MOVE COLUMN-HEADING-1 TO REPORT-LINE
153         MOVE 2 TO LINE-SPACING
154         PERFORM 850-WRITE-REPORT-LINE
155         MOVE COLUMN-HEADING-2 TO REPORT-LINE
156         MOVE 1 TO LINE-SPACING
157         PERFORM 850-WRITE-REPORT-LINE
158         MOVE ALL "-" TO REPORT-LINE
159         PERFORM 850-WRITE-REPORT-LINE.
160
161     720-ASSEMBLE-AND-PRINT-DETAIL.
162         MOVE IR-STOCK-NUMBER TO RL-STOCK-NUMBER
163         MOVE IR-SOFTWARE-NAME TO RL-SOFTWARE-NAME
164         MOVE IR-VENDOR-NAME TO RL-VENDOR-NAME
165         MOVE IR-QUANT-ON-HAND TO RL-QUANT-ON-HAND
166         MOVE IR-PRICE TO RL-PRICE
167         MOVE RETAIL-VALUE TO RL-RETAIL-VALUE
168         MOVE DETAIL-LINE TO REPORT-LINE
169         PERFORM 850-WRITE-REPORT-LINE
170         MOVE 2 TO LINE-SPACING.
171
172     730-ASSEMBLE-AND-PRINT-TOTAL.
173         MOVE RECORD-COUNT TO TL-RECORD-COUNT
174         MOVE TOTAL-VALUE TO TL-TOTAL-VALUE
175         MOVE 3 TO LINE-SPACING
176         MOVE TOTAL-LINE TO REPORT-LINE
177         PERFORM 850-WRITE-REPORT-LINE.
178
179     800-READ-INVENTORY-RECORD.
180         READ INVENTORY-FILE
181             AT END MOVE "Y" TO END-OF-FILE
182         END-READ.
183
184     850-WRITE-REPORT-LINE.
185         WRITE REPORT-LINE
186             AFTER ADVANCING LINE-SPACING LINES.
```

The WRITE Statement

You have used the WRITE statement with the AFTER ADVANCING clause in any of your programs requiring output that is not single-spaced. For instance, to get double-spaced output, your WRITE statement would be

```
WRITE REPORT-LINE AFTER ADVANCING 2 LINES
```

Example 9-1 took this one step further by using a data item instead of a numeric literal; this provides the capability for variable line spacing. For Example 9-3, it will be necessary to advance the paper to the top of the next page. One way of doing this is to set the value in the line-spacing data item to a value that will skip sufficient lines to achieve the proper positioning. For instance, if the body of the report is 54 lines, the two margins account for 12 lines. After printing the last line of the body, a value of 12 could be moved into the line-spacing data item before printing the first line of the heading.

However, COBOL includes a special facility for advancing to the top of the next page without using a line counter. For instance, the following sequence will print the first heading at the top of the next page—regardless of where the paper is currently positioned in the printer.

```
MOVE PAGE-HEADING-LINE TO REPORT-LINE
WRITE REPORT-LINE
      AFTER ADVANCING PAGE
```

This causes a special code to be transmitted to the printer which, through its internal design, causes it to move the paper up to the next page before printing.

You can see that the WRITE statement has broader capabilities than those you have used previously. Although all examples in this book use AFTER ADVANCING, COBOL also provides the BEFORE ADVANCING option. That is, the printer can either be directed to advance the paper, then print—or print and then advance the paper. The extent of the general WRITE form that you will see in this book is

The words *ADVANCING* and *LINES* are optional and may be omitted; their sole purpose is for documentation. The following are some important things to keep in mind when using the ADVANCING option in a program:

1. The value of *integer* must be zero or positive (negative values are not allowed). The use of the integer 0 specifies printing without spacing (overprinting).

2. The ADVANCING option is required only when something other than ordinary single-spacing is required. A WRITE statement without the ADVANCING option is interpreted as WRITE...AFTER ADVANCING 1 LINE.

3. It is possible to use BEFORE ADVANCING with some WRITE statements and AFTER ADVANCING with other WRITE statements in the same program. However, it is not advisable to do so. The reason is that a mixture of the two can easily produce unexpected spacing and/or overprinting (the printing of one line directly on top of the preceding line). As a general rule, only the AFTER option should be used in the ADVANCING clause.

A Page Control Example

Example Definition— Example 9-3

The third example program of this chapter demonstrates the basic principles of page control.

Example 9-3 Page Control

Problem Description

The retail value report program RET-VAL3 must be expanded to include page control. After each page is filled, the program must progress to the top of the next page, print the heading lines, then resume printing detail lines.

Output Requirements

The output requirements of this report are identical to those of RET-VAL3, except that each page must include a page number and heading lines. The format is shown in the printer spacing chart of Figure 9-18.

Input Description

Input file name: SOFTWAR3.DL

Record format: Same as that of SOFTWAR2.DL, Example 9-1

Note: The only difference between this file and that used in the previous examples is that it contains more records in order to illustrate progression from page to page.

Processing Requirements

General processing requirements for this example are the same as those for Example 9-2, except for page control. Page control will require

1. A counter that is incremented by the amount in the Line-spacing data item with each line printed
2. Testing of the line counter to determine if the page is full
3. For a new page condition, moving the paper to a new page, printing the headings, and continuing with detail line output
4. A page counter that is incremented by 1 with each new page and printed with the heading

except that totals must be accumulated. As each detail record is read, it must be counted. Each retail value figure (calculated as the Price times the Quantity-on-hand) must be added to an accumulator that totals the retail value.

Sample Output—Example 9-3

A portion of the first page and the last page of the report for this example are shown in Figure 9-19. You can see that each page includes the heading lines and that the first heading line also includes the page number. Naturally, the report totals are printed only on the last page.

Figure 9-18

Printer Spacing Chart for Example 9-3

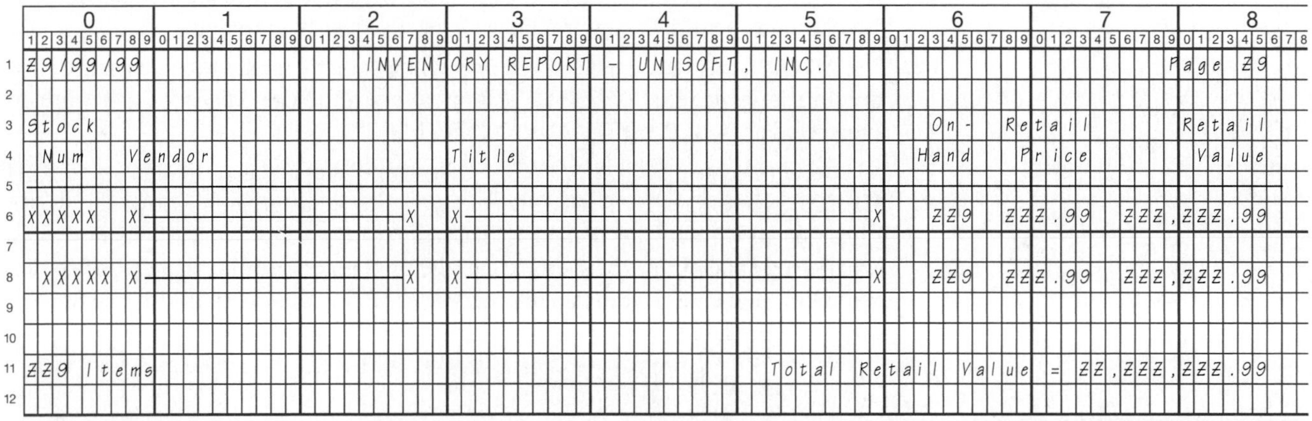

Program Solution—Example 9-3

A complete solution to the Example 9-3 is shown in Figures 9-20 through 9-23. Since this example is an expansion of Example 9-2, its structure and logic are simple extensions of Example 9-2. All modifications and additions to Example 9-2 are highlighted.

The structure chart of Figure 9-20 (see page 206) differs from that of Figure 9-14 because the page headings must now be printed from within the process loop (when the page fills), as well as during the initialization. Furthermore, a characteristic of COBOL—coupled with the programming standards used in this book—requires that a separate write module be used in order to position the paper at the top of the page.

```
7/22/91                    INVENTORY REPORT - UNISOFT, INC.              Page  1

Stock                                              On-    Retail      Retail
  Num    Vendor            Title                    Hand   Price       Value
_____

07410  Apricot Software  Apricot-tree Accounts Payable    27   349.95    9,448.65

07414  Apricot Software  Apricot-tree Accts. Receivable   18   349.95    6,299.10

07427  Apricot Software  Apricot-tree General Ledger      65   349.95   22,746.75

07432  Apricot Software  Apricot-tree Hourly Payroll      35   349.95   12,248.25

07436  Apricot Software   Apricot-tree Inventory Control  25   349.95    8,748.75
```

```
7/22/91                    INVENTORY REPORT - UNISOFT, INC.              Page  3

Stock                                              On-    Retail      Retail
  Num    Vendor            Title                    Hand   Price       Value
_____

91655  20th Century Soft.  Potent BASIC Interpreter      97     9.50      921.50

91659  20th Century Soft.  Potent Interpretive COBOL    143   349.99   50,048.57

91663  20th Century Soft.  Potent Interpretive Fortran  159   349.99   55,648.41

91667  20th Century Soft.  Potent Interpretive RPG      102   349.99   35,698.98


  54 Items                              Total Retail Value =  1,320,351.11
```

Figure 9-19

Sample Output—Example 9-3

As described in the processing requirements, the program logic must reflect both progressing to a new page when the current page is full and page counting. The flowchart elements of Figure 9-21 are only those modules that require changes from the program of Example 9-2. The highlighted elements identify the necessary additions to the program. The corresponding pseudocode is shown in Figure 9-22 (see page 208).

The program structure and logic are clearly evident in the highlighted portions of the program in Figure 9-23 (see page 209). Let's consider each of these additions.

700-PRINT-PAGE-HEADINGS. This module is executed from the 100 module, line 127 (to print headings on the first page), and from the 720 module, line 171 (to print headings on subsequent pages). Actions in this module are

1. Increasing the page number data item by 1; its value is initially 0 from the VALUE clause (see line 59). Hence, for the first page, its value will be 1.

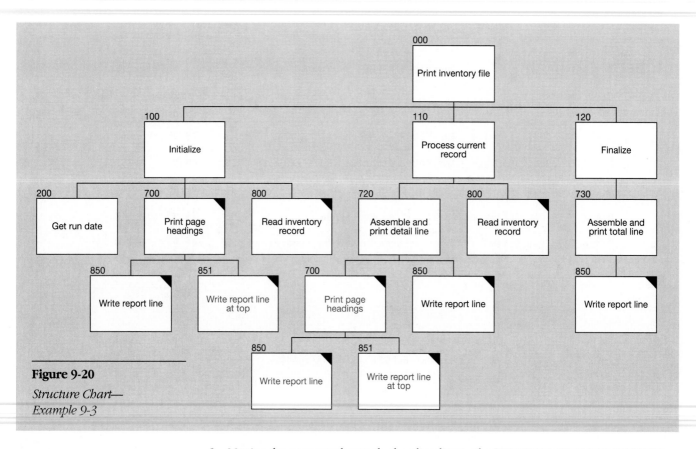

Figure 9-20

Structure Chart—
Example 9-3

2. Moving the page number to the heading line in the WORKING-STORAGE SECTION.

3. Moving the heading line to the printer output area.

4. Performing the 851 module that uses the WRITE/AFTER PAGE.

The remainder of this module is identical to that of Example 9-2.

720-ASSEMBLE-AND-PRINT-DETAIL. Before the detail line is printed, a test must be made to ensure that there is sufficient space for the line without spilling over into the bottom margin. LINES-USED-ON-PAGE contains a count of the number of lines already used. LINE-SPACING contains a count of the number of lines that will be required by this print operation. If the sum of these exceeds the maximum allowable lines on the page, then the paper should be positioned to the top of a new page and the headings printed before printing the detail line. This is accomplished by the following statements (lines 169–172):

```
IF LINES-USED-ON-PAGE + LINE-SPACING
    IS GREATER THAN LINES-DESIRED-ON-PAGE
        PERFORM 700-PRINT-PAGE-HEADINGS
END-IF
```

850-WRITE-REPORT-LINE. After each line is printed, the number of lines used must be added to the line counter. Conveniently, the number of lines used during any write operation is contained in the data item LINE-SPACING. Hence, the needed tallying is done with the following statement:

```
ADD LINE-SPACING TO LINES-USED-ON-PAGE.
```

851-WRITE-REPORT-LINE-AT-TOP. This is the new module required to achieve progression to the top of the new page. After executing the write operation, the line counter is initialized to 1 (the first heading line has been printed) by the following statement:

```
MOVE 1 TO LINES-USED-ON-PAGE.
```

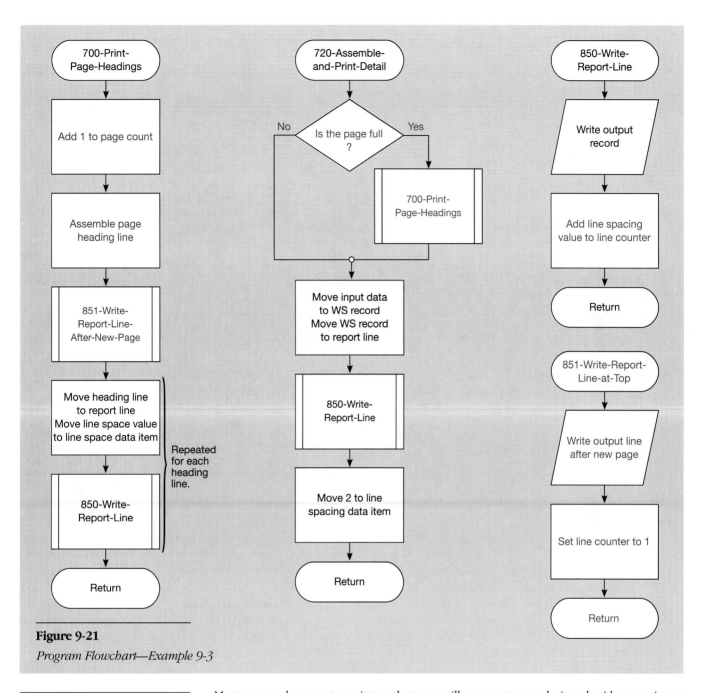

Figure 9-21

Program Flowchart—Example 9-3

Program Control of the Printer

Most personal computer printers that you will encounter are designed with a maximum print width of 8 1/2 inches, corresponding to the standard typewriter paper size. Using standard printing of 10 characters per inch and 1/2 inch margins on the left and right, the maximum width line you can print is 75 characters. As you will see in chapters that follow, a 75 position line is not adequate for many reports.

However, almost all printers used with personal computers provide for control of the size of printed characters. Compressed printing is the most common type of size control. With compressed printing, each character is made narrower and more are printed per inch, typically 17. At 17 characters per inch, your 7.5 inch print line can accommodate approximately 127 characters.

Some printers provide for control of printing characteristics via switches or control buttons on the front of the computer. If your printer has these controls, then you need not be too concerned about the remainder of this section.

Figure 9-22

Program Pseudocode—
Example 9-3

```
100-Initialize module
    Open data files
    Initialize accumulators
    Perform 200-Get-Run-Date module
    Perform 700-Print-Page-Headings module
    Perform 800-Read-Inventory-Record module

110-Process-Current-Record module
    Calculate Retail-value equals
        Quantity-on-hand times Price
    Accumulate the Retail-value
    Count this record
    Perform 720-Assemble-and-Print-Detail module
    Perform 800-Read-Inventory-Record module

120-Finalize
    Assemble and write the total line
    Close files

200-Get-Run-Date
    Obtain the current date
    Move month, day, and year to heading line
```

```
700-Print-Page-Headings
    Increment the page number
    Move heading (with page number)
        to report output line
    Perform 851-Write-Report-Line-at-Top module
    (Repeat the following for each remaining heading line)
    Move heading to report output line
    Move line spacing value to line spacing data item
    Perform 850-Write-Report-Line module

720-Assemble-and-Print-Detail
    If page full
        Perform 700-Print-Page-Headings
    Move input data to output detail record
    Move output detail record to report output line
    Perform 850-Write-Report-Line module
    Move 2 to line spacing data item

730-Assemble-and-Write-Total
    Move totals to detail record
    Move 3 to line spacing data item
    Move output detail record to report output line
    Perform 850-Write-Report-Line module

800-Read-Inventory-Record
    Read next record
        if EOF move "Y" to EOF switch

850-Write-Report-Line
    Print the output record
    Add Line-spacing value to Lines-used

851-Write-Report-Line-at-Top
    Print the output record after advancing page
    Set the value of Lines-used to 1
```

Whether or not a given printer with controllable printing can be set manually, it can be set with special binary codes sent by the computer. For instance, if the binary equivalent of the decimal number 15 is sent to a printer, the printer circuitry of most printers will switch over to compressed printing. Similarly, the code 18 will reset the printer to conventional 10 characters per inch.

How do you implement this in your programming? The answer is that if you require compressed printing for a report, then your program should send the compressed printing code to the printer in the initialize module. Once your program is completed, it is a good idea to return the printer to standard 10 character per inch printing—done in the finalize module. Figure 9-24 includes appropriate segments from the RET-VAL4 program showing how to achieve the desired printer control. Significant items about this example are

■ The binary codes are defined under a special record in the WORKING-STORAGE SECTION, which includes the clause USAGE IS BINARY. As a result, all data items defined under this record will be allocated two memory bytes and data stored will be encoded in binary number form.

■ Two data items are defined: one with the code for compressed printing and the other for standard printing. Note that almost all printers use these codes—you may wish to check your printer to ensure that it does.

■ In the 100 module, the SET-COMPRESSED data item is moved to the printer output area, 0 is moved to LINE-SPACING, and the 850 module (write the line) is performed. With 0 line spacing, the paper will not be moved upon execution of the WRITE.

Figure 9-23

The RET-VAL4 Program—Example 9-3

```
1      IDENTIFICATION DIVISION.
2
3      PROGRAM-ID. RET-VAL4.
4
5    *     Written by W.Price / Modified by J. Olson
6    *     July 14, 1990      / July 25, 1990
7
8    *     This program is RET-VAL3, modified for page control.
9    *     A different data file is used to provide enough records.
10
11   *     This program generates a retail value report from
12   *     the file SOFTWAR3.DL. For each record in the file
13   *     there is one output line that includes the retail
14   *     value (price times quantity on hand) for that item.
15
16     ENVIRONMENT DIVISION.
17
18     CONFIGURATION SECTION.
19     SOURCE-COMPUTER. IBM-PC.
20
21     INPUT-OUTPUT SECTION.
22     FILE-CONTROL.
23         SELECT INVENTORY-FILE    ASSIGN TO DISK "SOFTWAR3.DL"
24                                  ORGANIZATION IS LINE SEQUENTIAL.
25         SELECT REPORT-FILE       ASSIGN TO PRINTER "PRN-FILE".
26
27     DATA DIVISION.
28
29     FILE SECTION.
30
31     FD  INVENTORY-FILE.
32     01  INVENTORY-RECORD.
33         10  IR-STOCK-NUMBER      PIC X(5).
34         10  IR-SOFTWARE-NAME     PIC X(30).
35         10  IR-VENDOR-NAME       PIC X(20).
36         10  IR-QUANT-ON-HAND     PIC 9(3).
37         10                       PIC X(3).
38         10  IR-PRICE             PIC 9(3)V9(2).
39
40     FD  REPORT-FILE.
41     01  REPORT-LINE              PIC X(85).
42
43     WORKING-STORAGE SECTION.
44
45     01  PROGRAMMED-SWITCHES.
46         10  END-OF-FILE          PIC X       VALUE "N".
47
48     01  ARITHMETIC-WORK-AREAS.
49         10  RETAIL-VALUE         PIC 9(6)V9(2).
50
51     01  ACCUMULATORS.
52         10  TOTAL-VALUE          PIC 9(8)V9(2).
53         10  RECORD-COUNT         PIC 9(3).
54
55     01  PRINT-CONTROL-VARIABLES.
56         10  LINE-SPACING         PIC 9.
57         10  LINES-DESIRED-ON-PAGE  PIC 99    VALUE 54.
58         10  LINES-USED-ON-PAGE   PIC 99.
59         10  PAGE-NUMBER          PIC 99      VALUE ZERO.
60
61     01  RUN-DATE.
62         10  RUN-YEAR             PIC 99.
63         10  RUN-MONTH            PIC 99.
64         10  RUN-DAY              PIC 99.
65
66     01  PAGE-HEADING-LINE.
67         10  PH-MONTH             PIC Z9.
68         10                       PIC X       VALUE "/".
69         10  PH-DAY               PIC 99.
70         10                       PIC X       VALUE "/".
71         10  PH-YEAR              PIC 99.
72         10                       PIC X(15)   VALUE SPACES.
73         10                       PIC X(32)   VALUE
74              "INVENTORY REPORT - UNISOFT, INC.".
75         10                       PIC X(23)   VALUE SPACES.
76         10                       PIC X(5)    VALUE "Page ".
77         10  PH-PAGE-NUMBER       PIC Z9.
78
79     01  COLUMN-HEADING-1.
80         10                       PIC X(62)   VALUE "Stock".
81         10                       PIC X(5)    VALUE "On-".
82         10                       PIC X(11)   VALUE "Retail".
83         10                       PIC X(7)    VALUE "Retail".
84
85     01  COLUMN-HEADING-2.
86         10                       PIC X(7)    VALUE " Num".
87         10                       PIC X(22)   VALUE "Vendor".
88         10                       PIC X(32)   VALUE "Title".
89         10                       PIC X(7)    VALUE "Hand".
90         10                       PIC X(10)   VALUE "Price".
91         10                       PIC X(7)    VALUE "Value".
92
93     01  DETAIL-LINE                          VALUE SPACES.
94         10  RL-STOCK-NUMBER      PIC X(5).
95         10                       PIC X(2).
96         10  RL-VENDOR-NAME       PIC X(20).
97         10                       PIC X(2).
98         10  RL-SOFTWARE-NAME     PIC X(30).
99         10                       PIC X(3).
100        10  RL-QUANT-ON-HAND     PIC ZZ9.
101        10                       PIC X(2).
102        10  RL-PRICE             PIC ZZZ.99.
103        10                       PIC X(2).
```

```
104        10  RL-RETAIL-VALUE      PIC ZZZ,ZZZ.99.
105
106    01  TOTAL-LINE.
107        10  TL-RECORD-COUNT      PIC ZZ9.
108        10                       PIC X(48)   VALUE " Items".
109        10                       PIC X(21)   VALUE
110             "Total Retail Value = ".
111        10  TL-TOTAL-VALUE       PIC ZZ,ZZZ,ZZZ.99.
112
113    PROCEDURE DIVISION.
114
115    000-PRINT-INVENTORY-FILE.
116        PERFORM 100-INITIALIZE
117        PERFORM 110-PROCESS-CURRENT-RECORD
118            UNTIL END-OF-FILE = "Y"
119        PERFORM 120-FINALIZE
120        STOP RUN.
121
122    100-INITIALIZE.
123        OPEN INPUT INVENTORY-FILE
124        OPEN OUTPUT REPORT-FILE
125        INITIALIZE ACCUMULATORS
126        PERFORM 200-GET-RUN-DATE
127        PERFORM 700-PRINT-PAGE-HEADINGS
128        PERFORM 800-READ-INVENTORY-RECORD.
129
130    110-PROCESS-CURRENT-RECORD.
131
132  * Calculate retail value
133        MOVE IR-PRICE TO RETAIL-VALUE
134        MULTIPLY IR-QUANT-ON-HAND BY RETAIL-VALUE
135
136  * Increment accumulators
137        ADD RETAIL-VALUE TO TOTAL-VALUE
138        ADD 1 TO RECORD-COUNT
139
140        PERFORM 720-ASSEMBLE-AND-PRINT-DETAIL
141        PERFORM 800-READ-INVENTORY-RECORD.
142
143    120-FINALIZE.
144        PERFORM 730-ASSEMBLE-AND-PRINT-TOTAL
145        CLOSE INVENTORY-FILE
146              REPORT-FILE.
147
148    200-GET-RUN-DATE.
149        ACCEPT RUN-DATE FROM DATE
150        MOVE RUN-MONTH TO PH-MONTH
151        MOVE RUN-DAY   TO PH-DAY
152        MOVE RUN-YEAR  TO PH-YEAR.
153
154    700-PRINT-PAGE-HEADINGS.
155        ADD 1 TO PAGE-NUMBER
156        MOVE PAGE-NUMBER TO PH-PAGE-NUMBER
157        MOVE PAGE-HEADING-LINE TO REPORT-LINE
158        PERFORM 851-WRITE-REPORT-LINE-AT-TOP
159        MOVE COLUMN-HEADING-1 TO REPORT-LINE
160        MOVE 2 TO LINE-SPACING
161        PERFORM 850-WRITE-REPORT-LINE
162        MOVE COLUMN-HEADING-2 TO REPORT-LINE
163        MOVE 1 TO LINE-SPACING
164        PERFORM 850-WRITE-REPORT-LINE
165        MOVE ALL "-" TO REPORT-LINE
166        PERFORM 850-WRITE-REPORT-LINE.
167
168    720-ASSEMBLE-AND-PRINT-DETAIL.
169        IF LINES-USED-ON-PAGE + LINE-SPACING
170            IS GREATER THAN LINES-DESIRED-ON-PAGE
171                PERFORM 700-PRINT-PAGE-HEADINGS
172        END-IF
173        MOVE IR-STOCK-NUMBER TO RL-STOCK-NUMBER
174        MOVE IR-SOFTWARE-NAME TO RL-SOFTWARE-NAME
175        MOVE IR-VENDOR-NAME TO RL-VENDOR-NAME
176        MOVE IR-QUANT-ON-HAND TO RL-QUANT-ON-HAND
177        MOVE IR-PRICE TO RL-PRICE
178        MOVE RETAIL-VALUE TO RL-RETAIL-VALUE
179        MOVE DETAIL-LINE TO REPORT-LINE
180        PERFORM 850-WRITE-REPORT-LINE
181        MOVE 2 TO LINE-SPACING.
182
183    730-ASSEMBLE-AND-PRINT-TOTAL.
184        MOVE RECORD-COUNT TO TL-RECORD-COUNT
185        MOVE TOTAL-VALUE TO TL-TOTAL-VALUE
186        MOVE 3 TO LINE-SPACING
187        MOVE TOTAL-LINE TO REPORT-LINE
188        PERFORM 850-WRITE-REPORT-LINE.
189
190    800-READ-INVENTORY-RECORD.
191        READ INVENTORY-FILE
192            AT END MOVE "Y" TO END-OF-FILE
193        END-READ.
194
195    850-WRITE-REPORT-LINE.
196        WRITE REPORT-LINE
197            AFTER ADVANCING LINE-SPACING LINES
198        ADD LINE-SPACING TO LINES-USED-ON-PAGE.
199
200    851-WRITE-REPORT-LINE-AT-TOP.
201        WRITE REPORT-LINE
202            AFTER ADVANCING PAGE
203        MOVE 1 TO LINES-USED-ON-PAGE.
```

Figure 9-24

Controlling Printer Character Width

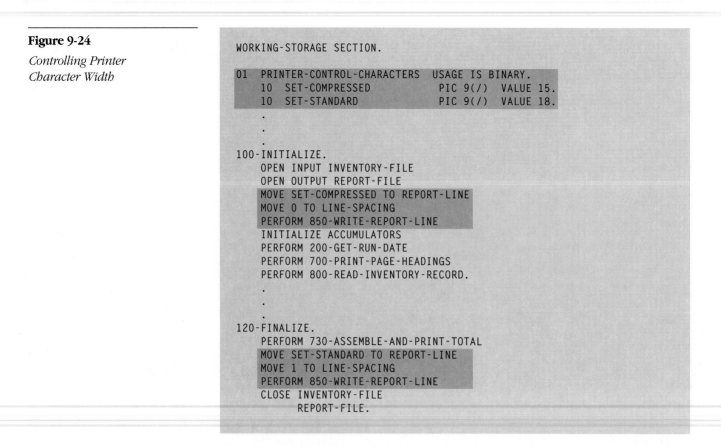

```
WORKING-STORAGE SECTION.

01  PRINTER-CONTROL-CHARACTERS   USAGE IS BINARY.
    10  SET-COMPRESSED                PIC 9(/)  VALUE 15.
    10  SET-STANDARD                  PIC 9(/)  VALUE 18.
     .
     .
     .
100-INITIALIZE.
    OPEN INPUT INVENTORY-FILE
    OPEN OUTPUT REPORT-FILE
    MOVE SET-COMPRESSED TO REPORT-LINE
    MOVE 0 TO LINE-SPACING
    PERFORM 850-WRITE-REPORT-LINE
    INITIALIZE ACCUMULATORS
    PERFORM 200-GET-RUN-DATE
    PERFORM 700-PRINT-PAGE-HEADINGS
    PERFORM 800-READ-INVENTORY-RECORD.
     .
     .
     .
120-FINALIZE.
    PERFORM 730-ASSEMBLE-AND-PRINT-TOTAL
    MOVE SET-STANDARD TO REPORT-LINE
    MOVE 1 TO LINE-SPACING
    PERFORM 850-WRITE-REPORT-LINE
    CLOSE INVENTORY-FILE
          REPORT-FILE.
```

■ In the 120 module, printing the SET-STANDARD data item returns the printer to standard printing. Notice that 1 is moved to LINE-SPACING. The reason for this is that if you display the printed output on the screen, the control code will overlay the first positions of the output line. However, this will be no problem if the output is printed.

Chapter Summary

General

A great deal of emphasis has been placed on printing output in a readable form and with a pleasing, easy-to-read appearance. It might seem that these "frills" are not necessary and are a waste of time and money. In reality, these methods more than pay for themselves in the clarity that they bring to the printed report. The preparation of well-designed, well-balanced, and easy-to-read printed output is one of the hallmarks of the good programmer. This chapter discussed several tools and techniques to improve the quality of the printed report.

Reports can include three types of output lines:

Heading—report heading lines that describe the report and column heading lines that identify the columns of output.

Detail—a line that contains data from a single record.

Summary—a line that contains summarized data from two or more detail records.

Line spacing is more easily controlled by using a data item for line spacing indication, as opposed to using a literal. Prior to printing, a value representing the line desired spacing is moved into the data item.

Each output record description is defined in the WORKING-STORAGE SECTION. Prior to writing, the desired record is moved to the output record defined in the FD.

The current date is obtained from the computer with the ACCEPT/DATE statement (see the following COBOL statement summary).

An accumulator is a data item used to total the values of some field. For instance, in RET-VAL3, the calculated retail-value field from each record is totalled. In using an accumulator, you must:

1. Define it as a numeric field in the WORKING-STORAGE SECTION

2. Initialize it with a VALUE clause in the DATA DIVISION or with a MOVE statement in the PROCEDURE DIVISION

3. Add the appropriate field to it as each record is processed

The INITIALIZE statement is used to initialize one or more fields to zero or spaces—see the description in the following COBOL statement summary.

The PAGE clause of the WRITE statement causes the printer to position the paper to the top of the next page—see the description in the following COBOL statement summary.

COBOL Language Elements

The COBOL statements you have studied in this chapter are

ACCEPT/DATE   Allows the program to access the date or time from the computer system.

$$\text{ACCEPT identifier } \underline{\text{FROM}} \begin{Bmatrix} \underline{\text{DATE}} \\ \underline{\text{DATE}} \\ \underline{\text{TIME}} \end{Bmatrix}$$

INITIALIZE   Sets selected types of data items to predetermined values. The extent of the form used in this book sets numeric data items to 0 and nonnumeric data items to spaces.

$\underline{\text{INITIALIZE}}$ identifier

WRITE   The WRITE statement sends the designated output record to the output device. If the output device is a printer, line spacing is controlled by the AFTER/BEFORE ADVANCING clause. The AFTER/BEFORE can also be used with the PAGE, which causes the paper to be positioned at the top of a new page.

$$\underline{\text{WRITE}} \text{ record-name} \left[\left[\begin{Bmatrix} \underline{\text{AFTER}} \\ \underline{\text{BEFORE}} \end{Bmatrix} \text{ ADVANCING} \right] \begin{Bmatrix} \begin{Bmatrix} \text{identifier} \\ \text{integer} \\ \underline{\text{PAGE}} \end{Bmatrix} \begin{bmatrix} \text{LINE} \\ \text{LINES} \end{bmatrix} \end{Bmatrix} \right]$$

Programming Conventions

To define headings in the WORKING-STORAGE SECTION, do not use continuation lines for literals. Break the heading line into two or more parts. For column headings, define the description for each column as a separate field. Include a field width sufficient to span to the next column.

As a convention, use two separate write modules—one to position to a new page prior to printing and the other for all other printing. Use consecutive module numbers for these; for instance, 850 and 851.

Do not use the WRITE-FROM option. It is not consistent with the conventions adopted for this book.

In general, when using variable line control, your program should check to ensure that there are sufficient lines remaining in the body *before* printing. An alternative approach is to print, test, and progress to a new page. This can result in printing in the margin with variable line control.

In setting up page control, decide what you need for the top margin and bottom margins, then compute the number of lines in the body. For each WRITE, add the line spacing for that WRITE to the line counter.

Define all output records in the WORKING-STORAGE SECTION; the output area defined in the FD should be defined as a single field with the length of the desired output record.

Error Prevention/ Detection

The most common error encountered with accumulators is the failure to initialize them. Initialize all accumulators in the PROCEDURE DIVISION, rather than using a VALUE clause in the DATA DIVISION. This is good practice and reduces the chances of errors. It is also necessary if an accumulator is to be reinitialized after processing part of the data file.

As you step through the logic of your program, be especially wary to ensure that all accumulators are properly initialized at the appropriate time.

Another common error with accumulators is to define them with insufficient size, thereby resulting in an overflow during execution. If the ADD statement does not include a SIZE ERROR option, the overflow value will be lost without warning.

Always check your sample output against the programming specifications (printer spacing chart) to ensure that the line spacing is correct. Errors here can be minimized by ensuring that prior to each WRITE, the desired line spacing value has been moved into the line spacing data item.

Questions and Exercises

Give a brief description of each of the following terms that were introduced in this chapter.

Key Terminology

accumulators	detail line	report generation
body (of report)	heading line	top margin
bottom margin	page control	variable line spacing

General Questions

1. Determine the number of lines available for detail lines in the body of the form for the following conditions:

> Paper is 8 1/2 inches deep.
> Printing is 8 LPI.
> Top margin is 3/4 inch."
> Bottom margin is 1 inch.
> Headings take up five lines.

2. What are the three types of output lines usually found on reports?

3. Defining report lines in the WORKING-STORAGE SECTION instead of the FILE-SECTION uses an additional clause. What is it and is there a reason for doing this?

4. The ACCEPT statement in COBOL returns the computer date to a program. Can this statement return anything else? Describe what is returned in all cases.

5. Accumulators are commonly used in COBOL programs. What four steps must be accomplished for their effective use?

6. What is the difference between using PAGE or LINE-SPACING?

Question Relating to the Example Programs

1. In all report generation programs prior to this chapter, the output line has been initialized by a statement such as

```
MOVE SPACES TO REPORT-LINE
```

being executed prior to moving data fields into the output line area. If you inspect RET-VAL2 (Figure 9-7), you will see that this MOVE is not used. Explain why it is not needed.

2. The program RET-VAL3 (Figure 9-17) has been modified to add a module to print a total line. During modifications, the programmer decides to revise it as follows. In each case described, explain what will happen to the program when it is run.

   a. On line 87, the programmer does not see a need for VALUE SPACES adjacent to 01 DETAIL-LINE and removes it.

   b. The programmer spots the PERFORM for 700-PRINT-PAGE-HEADINGS on line 121 and decides it is in the wrong location. This is moved to line 133 instead.

   c. The programmer inserts the code to increment the accumulators (lines 130–132) after line 170.

3. RET-VAL4 (Figure 9-23) is modified for page control. This time, the programmer makes some new discoveries. The changes are as follows. Describe what happens to the program as it executes.

   a. The programmer decides there is no need to read in the 100-INITIALIZE module since the 110 module does it also. Line 128 is deleted.

   b. The 200-GET-RUN-DATE module is shown all alone. The programmer feels this is not necessary. Lines 149–152 are inserted after line 154. Then lines 148–152 are deleted.

   c. The programmer modifies the program correctly for page control. What is your opinion of this programmer's work?

4. Before the RET-VAL4 program (Figure 9-23) is run, it is important to position the printer paper so that the print element is at the physical page line at which the first heading line is to be printed. Thus, the printer will be ready to go when output is forthcoming. However, the first execution of the WRITE is from the 100 module (PERFORM 700... at line 127), which in turn causes the 851 module to be executed (PERFORM 851... at line 158). Thus, the printer skips (needlessly) to a new page before beginning to print the report. Modify the 700 module so that the printer does not advance to a new page for page 1. (However, it should advance for all pages after page 1.)

Writing Program Statements

1. You have been asked to prepare an employee report that lists each employee number and name, the hours worked, the pay rate, and the bonus increment. For each employee, gross pay is to be calculated and printed. In addition, there needs to be a final total for the gross pay column and a record count. The EXAMPLE-RECORD that follows describes your input records.

Field	Field Positions	Format
Employee number	1–5	
Name	6-27	
Hours worked	31–33	$nn_\wedge n$
Pay rate	34–37	$nn_\wedge nn$
Bonus increment	38–40	$_\wedge nnn$
Accumulated vacation	41–42	nn

Write the File Description and record description.

2. Create appropriate report headings for this employee report and write the WORKING-STORAGE SECTION entries.

3. Design the output detail line and total line. Write the WORKING-STORAGE SECTION entries that are needed to produce each.

4. Write the WORKING-STORAGE SECTION and PROCEDURE DIVISION statements necessary to produce the final total for the gross pay column and a record count.

Programming Assignments

Programming assignments in this and following chapters use data files. For the record description of all files used in the assignments, you must use Appendix A.

9-1 Employee Payroll Register

The payroll clerk of Programming Assignment 6-2 is not very happy with a report that does not contain descriptive headings and a total summary. That report must be brought up to par.

Output Requirements:
A printed report with the following output and format.

```
            0         1         2         3         4         5         6         7         8
   1234567890123456789012345678901234567890123456789012345678901234567890123456789012345 6
 1 Z9/99/99                    DONUT  MANUFACTURING  COMPANY                          Page  ZZ
 2                             EMPLOYEE  PAYROLL  SUMMARY
 3
 4
 5                                         Gross        YTD         YTD           YTD
 6 Soc  Sec  Num   Employee  Name          Pay        Earnings    Withholding      FICA
 7
 8 XXX-XX-XXXX  X-----------------------X  Z,ZZZ.99   ZZZ,ZZZ.99   ZZ,ZZZ.99     Z,ZZZ.99
 9
10 XXX-XX-XXXX  X-----------------------X  Z,ZZZ.99   Z-Z,ZZZ.99   ZZ,ZZZ.99     Z,ZZZ.99
11
12
13                                  TOTALS  ZZ,ZZZ,ZZZ.99  Z,ZZZ,ZZZ.99  ZZZ,ZZZ.99
```

File name: EMPLOYEE.DL
Record description: See Appendix A

Processing Requirements:
For page headings (see the printer spacing chart):
1. On the first heading line, print the date, the company name, and the page number.

For each record in the file:
2. Accumulate totals for the following fields:
   Year-to-date earnings
   Year-to-date income tax withholding
   Year-to-date FICA withholding
3. Print a line as illustrated in the printer spacing chart.

Summary line:
4. Print the totals for the accumulated fields.

9-2 Courses Below Minimum Enrollment

The class enrollment report of Programming Assignment 8-1 serves the needs of the administration but it is lacking headings and report totals.

Output Requirements:
A printed report with the following output and format.

```
            0         1         2         3         4         5         6         7         8
   1234567890123456789012345678901234567890123456789012345678901234567890123456789012345 6
 1 Z9/99/99          COMPUTER  INSTITUTE  OF  TECHNOLOGY               Page  ZZ
 2                   LOW  ENROLLMENT  REPORT
 3
 4 Cutoff  percentage  of  minimum  enrollment:  ZZ9
 5
 6 Class                        Course  Section  Minimum  Actual
 7 Code      Course  Name       Number  Number   Enroll.  Enroll.  Percentage
 8
 9 XXXX   X------------------X  XXX      XX      ZZ9      ZZ9      ZZ9.9
10
11 XXXX   X------------------X  XXX      XX      ZZ9      ZZ9      ZZ9.9
12
13
14 ZZ9  Classes  under  cutoff         TOTALS    Z,ZZ9    Z,ZZ9
```

Input Description:
    File name: ENROLL01.DL
    Record description: See Appendix A

Processing Requirements:
1. Accept from the keyboard a value for the Cutoff percentage. The range can be from 25 to 100 percent.
2. Convert the Cutoff percentage to a fractional value by dividing it by 100.

For page headings (see the printer spacing chart):
3. On the first heading line print the date, the institution name, and the page number.
4. Print the Cutoff percentage (the value accepted from the keyboard).

For each record in the file:
5. Calculate the Enrollment cutoff as
    Cutoff percentage × Minimum permissible enrollment
6. If the Actual enrollment is less than the Cutoff percentage,
    a. Count the record and accumulate the totals for the minimum and actual enrollments.
    b. Print a line as illustrated in the printer spacing chart.

Summary line:
7. Print the record count and the minimum and actual enrollment totals.

Program run: Make a program run using a Cutoff percentage of 80%.

9-3 Student Scholarship Report With Headings

The registrar of Programming Assignment 8-2 is pleased with the scholarship listing but would like descriptive headings and some summaries.

Output Requirements:
    A printed report with the following output and format.

Input Description:
    File name: STUDENTS.DL
    Record description: See Appendix A

Processing Requirements:

For page headings (see the printer spacing chart):

1. On the first heading line, print the date, the institution name, and the page number.

For each record in the file:

2. Calculate the Cumulative GPA as:

$$= \frac{\text{Cumulative points}}{\text{Cumulative units}}$$

3. If the Cumulative GPA is less than 2.5, skip this record; otherwise, continue to the next step.
4. Increment the appropriate record counter (Freshman, Sophomore, ...).
5. Edit each field as designated in the preceding Output Format description.
6. In place of the Class-standing code, print the appropriate word as follows:
   1   FRESHMAN
   2   SOPHOMORE
   3   JUNIOR
   4   SENIOR
   5   GRADUATE
7. Print one double-spaced line for each record that qualifies.

Summary line:

8. Sum the individual counters to obtain the total students processed.
9. Print the totals according to the printer spacing chart.

9-4 Soft Drink Sales Analysis Report

The manager of a soft drinks distributorship likes the report from Programming Assignment 7-1, but needs descriptive headings so that he can see at a glance what each column of numbers mean. Also, he would like to have a report summary.

Output Requirements:

A printed report with the following output.

1. One (or more) report heading lines; the first line must include the date, a company name, and the page number.
2. One or more column headings.
3. Detail lines with the format described in Programming Assignment 7-1 (it may be necessary to insert more space between columns in order to accommodate the totals).
4. A total line that includes column totals for the following:
   Monthly sales of Cola
   Monthly sales of Diet
   Monthly sales of Energy
   Total monthly sales (dollars)

You must do all format planning. Prepare a printer spacing chart in the process.

Input Description:

File name: DRINKS01.DL

Record description: See Appendix A

Processing Requirements:

For page headings (see your printer spacing chart):

1. On the first heading line, print the date, the company name, and the page number.

For each record in the file:

2. For each drink, calculate the percent of target as:

$$= \frac{\text{Monthly sales for drink}}{\text{Monthly target sales for drink}} \times 100$$

The percent must include three digits to the left of the decimal and one to the right; for instance, 125.6.

3. Round off each percentage calculation.

4. Calculate the Total monthly sales (dollars) for the three drinks. Be certain to make your result field large enough to hold the maximum possible value.

5. Print the detail line according to your printer spacing chart.

6. Accumulate values for the four designated fields.

Summary line:

7. Print the totals according to your printer spacing chart.

9-5 Registered Voters Detail Report

The For-Everything Political Action Committee is in the process of building a file of registered voters. One of the reports they want to generate from this file is a list of voters making in excess of 25,000 per year, identified by their party affiliation and marital status.

Output Requirements:

A printed report with the following output.

1. One (or more) report heading lines; the first line must include the date, the organization name, and the page number.

2. One or more column headings.

3. The detail line must include the following fields.

    Voter's name
    City
    State
    Annual income
    Party of registration—print: REPUBLICAN
                                     DEMOCRAT
                                     INDEPENDENT
    Marital status—print: YES
                                     NO

4. Total lines that include the following:

    Total number of voters processed
    Number of Republicans
    Number of Democrats
    Number of Independents
    Number of married voters
    Number of unmarried voters

You must do all format planning. Prepare a printer spacing chart in the process.

Input Description:

File name: VOTERS.DL
Record description: See Appendix A

Processing Requirements:

For page headings (see your printer spacing chart):

1. On the first heading line, print the date, the organization name, and the page number.

For each record in the file:

2. If the annual income field is not greater than 25,000, ignore this record; otherwise, continue to the next step.
3. Increment the appropriate counter for party of registration.
4. Increment the appropriate counter for marital status.
5. Print the detail line according to your printer spacing chart.

Summary line:

6. Print the totals according to your printer spacing chart.

Improving Softcopy Output and Keyboard Input

Chapter Objectives

Chapter 9's topics—designing clear, easy-to-read printed reports—is important. With the wide availability of CRTs (cathode ray tubes) on mainframe computers and the personal nature of the personal computer, designing clear, easy-to-read displays is equally important. This is commonly called *screen design*, the topic of this chapter. Three sample programs are used as the focal points of screen input and output. From them, you will learn about the following topics:

- Planning and laying out the format of a screen display
- The ACCEPT statement, together with its variety of options, that allows for low-volume data entry from the keyboard
- The DISPLAY statement, together with its variety of options, that allows for low-volume display of output at the terminal
- The SCREEN SECTION that provides for definition of screen layouts in the DATA DIVISION
- Versions of the ACCEPT and DISPLAY statements to be used with SCREEN SECTION
- Opening an existing file and adding records to it

When using the report generation programs of preceding chapters, you could understand how they functioned by studying the sample output. However, for interactive programs, you really need to run them to fully appreciate what they do and how it is done. Thus, before studying each of the examples in this chapter, you should run it and experiment with the various options. Then the explanations in the text will have more meaning. However, remember that the S-EXTEND program adds records to the existing SOFTWAR2.DL file. Be certain to use a copy of the original so that you will not destroy your only copy.

Full Screen Record Display

Some Screen Features of RM/COBOL-85

Although the 1985 Standard includes no provisions for screen input and display beyond the simple ACCEPT and DISPLAY, most versions of COBOL (including RM/COBOL-85) provide additional features. In RM/COBOL-85, a large number of options can be used with the DISPLAY and ACCEPT statements. In Chapter 4, you learned three of them for use with the ACCEPT: TAB, NO BEEP, and PROMPT. They all influence the manner in which data is input. Other options allow you to change the way that data is displayed on the screen.

Furthermore, in Chapters 4 and 5, each execution of the DISPLAY caused the designated item to be displayed on the next line, starting at the left edge of the screen. Other options of the RM/COBOL-85 ACCEPT and DISPLAY statements allow the positioning of the cursor at any desired point on the screen by designating the row and column. Since monitors commonly used with the personal computers display 25 lines of 80 positions each, RM/COBOL-85 refers to a given position on the screen by its line number (1–25) and column number (1–80).

Using DISPLAY Control Clauses

To illustrate screen positioning control, consider the display shown in Figure 10-1 of the Stock-number field from the inventory file (from the RAN-DISP program of Figure 5-8). This DISPLAY positions the output on the next line of the screen, with the literal beginning in column 1. The value of the data item IR-STOCK-NUMBER is displayed immediately following the literal.

Figure 10-1

Simple DISPLAY and Sample Output

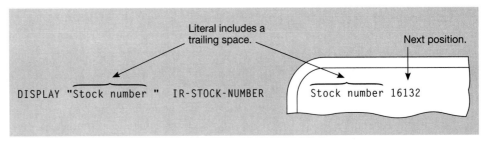

On the other hand, assume that you want the screen display to be as follows:

| | Starting Position | | |
Output	Line	Column	Display
"Stock number"	4	1	Low intensity
IR-STOCK-NUMBER	4	16	Reversed

The DISPLAY statement—together with needed screen control clauses—is shown in Figure 10-2. The clauses used here (plus two others that are similar in nature) are as follows:

1. *Line positioning* (**LINE**): Defines the screen line (numbered 1 through 25) on which the output is to be displayed.

2. *Column positioning* (**POSITION**): Defines the screen column (numbered 1 through 80) at which the output to be displayed is to begin.

3. *Low intensity* (**LOW**): The conventional brightness to which you are accustomed on the screen.

4. *High intensity* (**HIGH**): Information can be displayed with "extra" brightness, which is the default of the DISPLAY verb.

5. *Reverse video* (**REVERSE**): Normal display is light characters on a dark background. With reverse video, the area surrounding the displayed characters is lighted and the characters themselves are dark.

6. *Blinking* (**BLINK**): Causes the displayed characters to blink on and off on the screen.

In general, each item to be displayed must include its own set of control clauses, or else the default values will be used. In this respect, the general form of the DISPLAY can be abbreviated to:

$$\underline{\text{DISPLAY}} \quad \left\{ \begin{Bmatrix} \text{identifier-1} \\ \text{literal-1} \end{Bmatrix} [\text{control-clause-1...}] \right\}...$$

Notice in Figure 10-2 that the items to be displayed are coded on separate lines. This is necessary because the statement is too long for one line. Furthermore, it is consistent with

Figure 10-2

DISPLAY with Control Options and a Sample Output

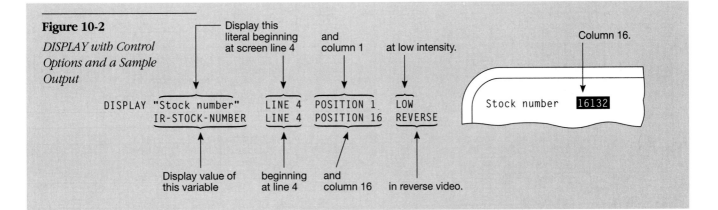

previous guidelines for making programs easy to read and modify. Actually, this can be expanded to include an entire screen display from a single statement, using the form:

```
DISPLAY item-1 control-clause-1
        item-2 control-clause-2
        item-3 control-clause-3
        ...
```

where item-*n* can be an identifier or a literal.

Let's apply these principles to a complete program to display records from a file.

Example Definition— Example 10-1

The RAN-DISP program of Chapter 5 (Figure 5-8) allows a user to enter the stock number of an inventory record, accesses that record from the inventory file, then displays selected fields on the screen. The next example is a refinement of RAN-DISP.

Example 10-1 Displaying Records from an Indexed Inventory File

Problem Description

The owner of UNISOFT wants to inspect selected records from the inventory file. The program must allow the user to enter the stock number of the desired record, access the record, and display it on the screen.

Output Requirements

Output of this program is to be a single-record screen display; the screen format is shown in Figure 10-3.

Input Description

Input file name: SOFTWAR2.DI

Record format:

Field	Positions	Data Type	Format
Stock number	1–5	Alphanumeric	
Software name	6–35	Alphanumeric	
Vendor name	36–55	Alphanumeric	
Copies on hand	56–58	Numeric	*nnn*
Reorder level	59–62	Numeric	*nnn*
Price	62–66		$nnn_\wedge nn$

Key field: Stock number

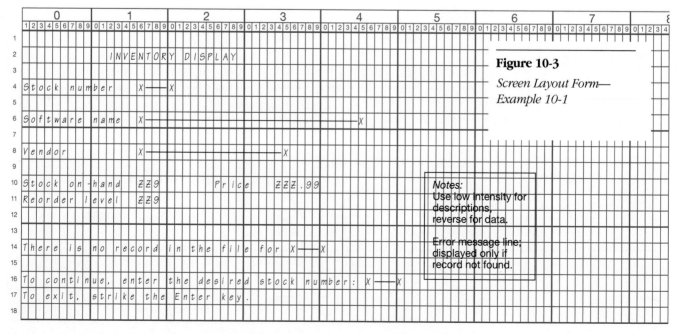

Figure 10-3

Screen Layout Form— Example 10-1

Processing Requirements

This random access display program is to function as follows:

1. Accept the stock number from the keyboard of the desired record.
2. Read the record from disk and display it on the screen, as specified in the screen format of Figure 10-1.
3. If there is no record with the requested stock number, display an error message.
4. Allow the user to terminate processing after each record is displayed.

This program will be basically the same as the RAN-DISP program in Chapter 5 (Figure 5-8). However, it will utilize screen handling features of RM/COBOL-85 that allow for a more elegant display than the limited capabilities used previously. You can see by referring to the screen display format that the display—including the exact positioning and format of output—is precisely defined. Furthermore, this program will reflect the modularization standards introduced in Chapter 8.

Program Solution Documentation— Example 10-1

A complete program solution is shown in Figures 10-4 through 10-7. The structure chart of Figure 10-4 is reasonably straightforward.

The processing requirements of this example state that after a record is displayed, the user is given the option to obtain another record or to terminate processing. A common method used in query programs such as this is to prompt the user as follows:

```
To continue, enter the desired stock number
To exit, strike the Enter key.
```

If the stock number entry is blank, processing can be terminated.

This approach is illustrated in the flowchart of Figure 10-5. You can see both here and in the structure chart of Figure 10-4 that the user is queried from both the 100-Initialize and 110-Display modules. Equivalent pseudocode is shown in Figure 10-6.

Program Solution— Example 10-1

The program structure and logic are clearly evident in program of Figure 10-7 (see page 226). Some points to notice about this program are the following:

000-ACCESS-INVENTORY-FILE. This mainline module differs from those of previous example programs in that the PERFORM 110... and PERFORM 120... statements are executed conditionally. The condition depends upon the initial user response.

Figure 10-4

Structure Chart for Example 10-1

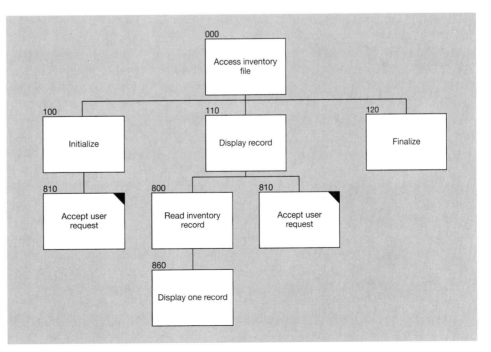

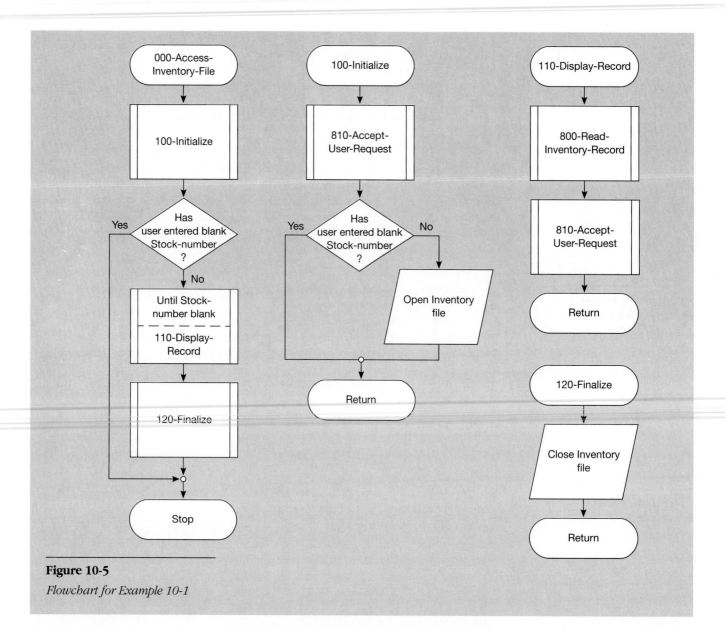

Figure 10-5

Flowchart for Example 10-1

810-ACCEPT-USER-REQUEST. The user is queried for a stock number in the 810 module. Because spaces are moved into IR-STOCK-NUMBER prior to the ACCEPT statement, making no entry (merely striking the Enter key) causes those spaces to remain, thereby providing the exit control.

100-INITIALIZE. The 810 module is executed from the 100 module prior to any other action being taken. If for some reason the user decides not to proceed, he or she can strike the Enter key and terminate processing immediately without further action. This is the result of conditional execution of both the 110 module (which is normally executed repeatedly) and the 120 module. An alternative to this approach is explored in a question at the end of the chapter.

110-DISPLAY-RECORD. This module performs two other modules: one to access the previously requested record and the other to query the user for the next record request.

800-READ-INVENTORY-RECORD. Once the key field value of the desired record has been accepted into the key field IR-STOCK-NUMBER (in the 810 module) the desired record is read in the 800 module. If the record is not found (INVALID KEY), the screen is cleared and an error message is displayed. If the record is found, the 860 module is performed.

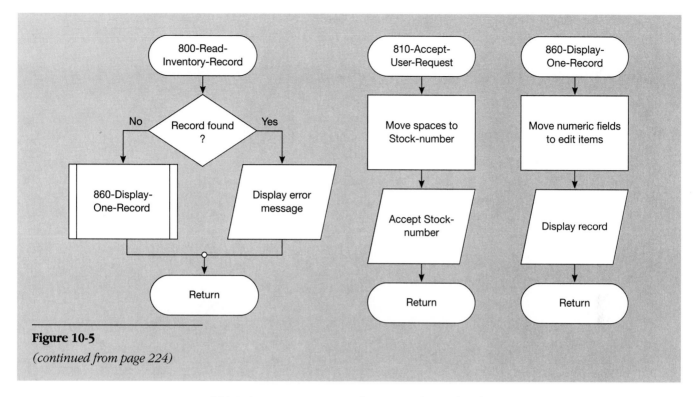

Figure 10-5

(continued from page 224)

860-DISPLAY-1-RECORD. The retrieved record is displayed from this module. Notice that the numeric fields are first moved into numeric-edited data items defined in the WORKING-STORAGE SECTION. These, in turn, are displayed by the single DISPLAY statement that shows the entire screen.

Two sample screens are shown in Figure 10-8 (see page 227) for RAN-DIS2. The first shows the display of an accessed record. The second shows the message resulting from a stock number not in the file (INVALID KEY).

Cursor Positioning and the ERASE

After executing a DISPLAY, the cursor remains positioned following the last character displayed. It is only the next DISPLAY or ACCEPT that causes the cursor to be repositioned to the next line (or elsewhere if LINE and POSITION are used). In Figure 10-9(a), you can see the effect of this; it is not especially appealing or functional.

Figure 10-6

Pseudocode for Example 10-1

```
000-Access-Inventory-File
      Perform 100-Initialize
      If user has entered non-blank Stock-number
            Perform 110-Display-Record until Stock-number blank
            Perform 120-Finalize
      Stop

100-Initialize
      Perform 810-Accept-User-Request
      If user has entered non-blank Stock-number
            Open Inventory-file
```

```
110-Display-Record
      Perform 800-Read-Inventory-Record
      Perform 810-Accept-User-Request

800-Read-Inventory-Record
      If requested record found
            Perform 860-Display-One-Record
      else
            Display error message

810-Accept-User-Request
      Move spaces to Stock-number
      Accept Stock-number

860-Display-One-Record
      Move numeric fields to edit items
      Display the record
```

Figure 10-7

The RAN-DIS2 Program—Example 10-1

```
1        IDENTIFICATION DIVISION.
2        PROGRAM-ID. RAN-DIS2.
3
4        *    Written by J.Olson
5        *    August 14, 1990
6
7        *    This program displays records from the indexed
8        *    inventory file.  Following each record display,
9        *    the user is given the option to display the next
10       *    record or to terminate processing.
11
12       *    Screens are defined in ACCEPT and DISPLAY statements.
13
14       ENVIRONMENT DIVISION.
15       CONFIGURATION SECTION.
16       SOURCE-COMPUTER. IBM-PC.
17
18       INPUT-OUTPUT SECTION.
19       FILE-CONTROL.
20           SELECT INVENTORY-FILE        ASSIGN TO DISK "SOFTWAR2.DI"
21                                        ORGANIZATION IS INDEXED
22                                        ACCESS IS RANDOM
23                                        RECORD KEY IS IR-STOCK-NUMBER.
24
25       DATA DIVISION.
26
27       FILE SECTION.
28
29       FD  INVENTORY-FILE.
30       01  INVENTORY-RECORD.
31           10  IR-STOCK-NUMBER          PIC X(5).
32           10  IR-SOFTWARE-NAME         PIC X(30).
33           10  IR-VENDOR-NAME           PIC X(20).
34           10  IR-QUANT-ON-HAND         PIC 9(3).
35           10  IR-REORDER-LEVEL         PIC 9(3).
36           10  IR-PRICE                 PIC 9(3)V9(2).
37
38       WORKING-STORAGE SECTION.
39
40       01  EDITED-FIELDS.
41           10  QUANT-ON-HAND            PIC ZZ9.
42           10  REORDER-LEVEL            PIC ZZ9.
43           10  PRICE                    PIC ZZZ.99.
44
45       PROCEDURE DIVISION.
46
47       000-ACCESS-INVENTORY-FILE.
48           PERFORM 100-INITIALIZE
49           IF IR-STOCK-NUMBER NOT = SPACES
50               PERFORM 110-DISPLAY-RECORD
51                   UNTIL IR-STOCK-NUMBER = SPACES
52               PERFORM 120-FINALIZE
53           END-IF
54           STOP RUN.
55
56       100-INITIALIZE.
57           DISPLAY  " " ERASE
58           PERFORM 810-ACCEPT-USER-REQUEST
59           IF IR-STOCK-NUMBER NOT = SPACES
60               OPEN INPUT INVENTORY-FILE
61           END-IF.
62
63       110-DISPLAY-RECORD.
64           PERFORM 800-READ-INVENTORY-RECORD
65           PERFORM 810-ACCEPT-USER-REQUEST.
66
67       120-FINALIZE.
68           CLOSE INVENTORY-FILE.
69
70       800-READ-INVENTORY-RECORD.
71           READ INVENTORY-FILE
72             INVALID KEY
73               DISPLAY "There is no record in the file for "
74                                    LINE 14  ERASE
75               DISPLAY IR-STOCK-NUMBER  POSITION 0
76             NOT INVALID KEY
77               PERFORM 860-DISPLAY-1-RECORD
78           END-READ.
79
80
81       810-ACCEPT-USER-REQUEST.
82           MOVE SPACES TO IR-STOCK-NUMBER
83           DISPLAY "To continue, enter the desired stock number:"
84                                    LINE 16
85           DISPLAY "To exit, strike the Enter key."
86                                    LINE 17
87           ACCEPT IR-STOCK-NUMBER  LINE 16   POSITION 46
88               TAB, PROMPT, NO BEEP.
89
90       860-DISPLAY-1-RECORD.
91           MOVE IR-QUANT-ON-HAND TO QUANT-ON-HAND
92           MOVE IR-REORDER-LEVEL TO REORDER-LEVEL
93           MOVE IR-PRICE TO PRICE
94           DISPLAY
95             "INVENTORY DISPLAY"    LINE  2  POSITION 11  LOW  ERASE
96             "Stock number"         LINE  4  POSITION  1  LOW
97             IR-STOCK-NUMBER        LINE  4  POSITION 16  REVERSE
98             "Software name"        LINE  6  POSITION  1  LOW
99             IR-SOFTWARE-NAME       LINE  6  POSITION 16  REVERSE
100            "Vendor"               LINE  8  POSITION  1  LOW
101            IR-VENDOR-NAME         LINE  8  POSITION 16  REVERSE
102            "Stock onhand"         LINE 10  POSITION  1  LOW
103            QUANT-ON-HAND          LINE 10  POSITION 16  REVERSE
104            "Price"                LINE 10  POSITION 26  LOW
105            PRICE                  LINE 10  POSITION 34  REVERSE
106            "Reorder level"        LINE 11  POSITION  1  LOW
107            REORDER-LEVEL          LINE 11  POSITION 16  REVERSE.
```

However, if the next DISPLAY or ACCEPT statement includes the clause POSITION 0, the cursor will *not* be repositioned. You can see the effect of this in Figure 10-9(b).

Notice that a space is included following the question mark of the query so that it does not appear crowded. Upon displaying the message, the cursor is positioned following this space and remains there when the ACCEPT is executed.

The ERASE is used in the DISPLAY of lines 73 and 74 to clear the screen of the preceding record before displaying the error message.

Actually, the ERASE has the following three forms:

ERASE Erases the entire screen

ERASE EOL Erase end of line (clears to the end of the line)

ERASE EOS Erase end of screen (clears to the end of the screen)

Remember from Chapter 4 that with the ERASE clause, the entire screen is first erased, the cursor is positioned at the upper left corner of the screen, and then the balance of the ACCEPT is carried out. If it includes LINE and POSITION, the cursor is positioned accordingly. Then the item is displayed.

Figure 10-8

Screen Displays—
Example 10-1

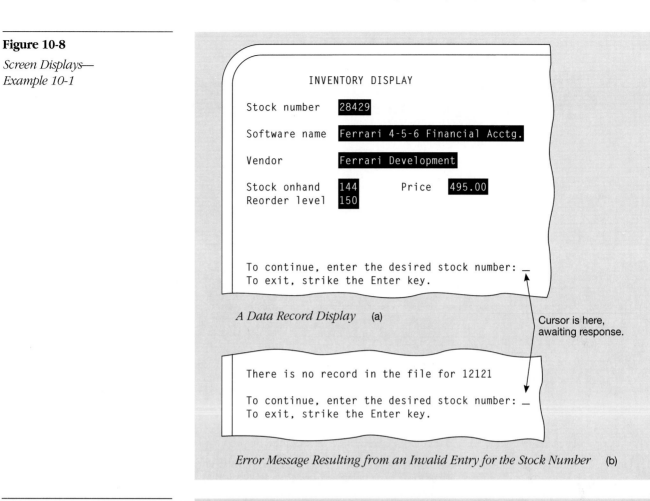

A Data Record Display   (a)

Error Message Resulting from an Invalid Entry for the Stock Number   (b)

Figure 10-9

Cursor Positioning

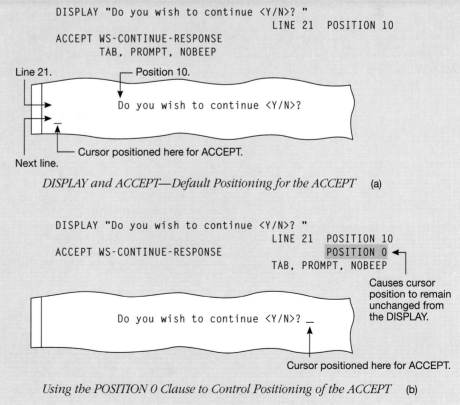

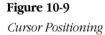

DISPLAY and ACCEPT—Default Positioning for the ACCEPT   (a)

Using the POSITION 0 Clause to Control Positioning of the ACCEPT   (b)

Figure 10-10

The ERASE EOL

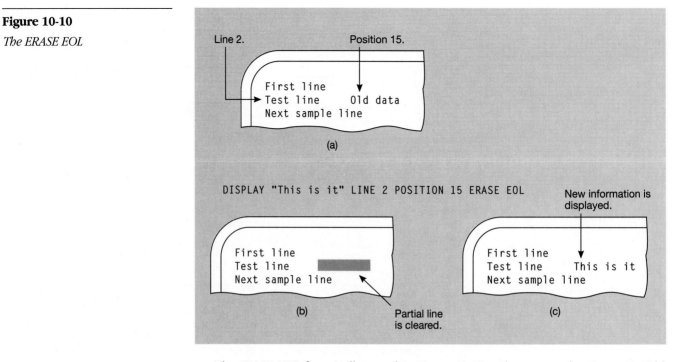

The ERASE EOL form is illustrated in Figure 10-10 with an example. Figure 10-10(a) shows the appropriate portion of the screen prior to execution of the statement. Then the following sequence of events takes place:

1. The cursor is positioned as specified by the LINE and POSITION of the DISPLAY.

2. The screen is cleared from the position of the cursor to the end of the line—see Figure 10-10(b). The cursor is not moved. Note that displayed information preceding the cursor on line 2 and on other lines is not disturbed.

3. The information is displayed—see Figure 10-10(c).

Figure 10-11

The ERASE EOS

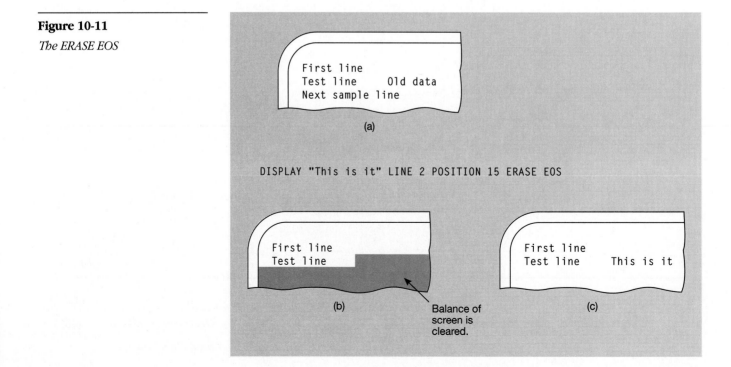

The ERASE EOS form is illustrated in Figure 10-11 with essentially the same example. The following sequence of events takes place:

1. The cursor is positioned as specified by the LINE and POSITION of the DISPLAY.

2. The screen is cleared from the position of the cursor to the end of the screen—see Figure 10-11(b). The cursor is not moved. Note that displayed information preceding the cursor is not disturbed.

3. The information is displayed—see Figure 10-11(c).

The UPDATE Clause of the ACCEPT

The program of Example 10-1 displays data and requires little data entry from the user (only the stock number value). On the other hand, the sole purpose of data entry programs—such as those in Chapter 4—is to accept data entered from the keyboard. For such interaction with the user, it is important that screens and procedures be designed to maximize data entry speed and minimize the possibility of errors. One condition that commonly occurs in data entry applications is repeating values for one or more fields.

To illustrate, consider the programs of Chapter 4 for creating the software file. The 110-ADD-RECORD module from SFCREATE (Figure 4-8) is repeated here as Figure 10-12. As each ACCEPT is executed, the keyboard entry is accepted and moved into the listed data item, thereby replacing the previous value (for instance, see the description for VENDOR-NAME in Figure 10-12). Note that the value of VENDOR-NAME prior to execution of the ACCEPT does not enter into the operation in any way.

Now, assume that the records to be entered are grouped by vendor name—that is, all records for Ferrari Development are grouped together, all for MicroPerimeter, Inc. are grouped together, and so on. With the code of Figure 10-12, the data entry person would need to unnecessarily key the Vendor-name—value even though it might be the same as that of the preceding entry and is still stored in the data item VENDOR-NAME. The UPDATE clause overcomes this problem by offering an existing value as a default. (A *default value* is a value assigned to the data item if nothing else is entered.)

In the modified module of Figure 10-13, the UPDATE clause has been added to the three ACCEPT statements that are likely to contain repeat data values. Now, assume that record 1 has been entered and the Vendor-name was Ferrari Development. As record 2 is entered and the statement ACCEPT VENDOR-NAME... is executed, Ferrari Development would be displayed as the default value, as illustrated in Figure 10-14. Striking the Enter key would leave it unchanged in VENDOR-NAME. If another entry is to be made, it would simply be typed in over the default display.

Figure 10-12

Data Entry from the SFCREATE Program of Chapter 4 (Figure 4-8)

```
110-ADD-RECORD.
    DISPLAY " " ERASE
    DISPLAY "Stock number?"
    ACCEPT STOCK-NUMBER  TAB, NO BEEP, PROMPT
    DISPLAY "Software name?"
    ACCEPT SOFTWARE-NAME TAB, NO BEEP, PROMPT       Keyboard entry is accepted
    DISPLAY "Vendor name?"                           and moved into VENDOR-NAME,
    ACCEPT VENDOR-NAME    TAB, NO BEEP, PROMPT       thereby replacing the previous
    DISPLAY "Quantity on hand?"                      contents.
    ACCEPT QUANT-ON-HAND TAB, NO BEEP, PROMPT
    DISPLAY "Reorder level?"
    ACCEPT REORDER-LEVEL TAB, NO BEEP, PROMPT
    WRITE INVENTORY-RECORD
    DISPLAY "Record written.  Enter 1 to repeat, 0 to end."
    ACCEPT CONTIN.
```

Figure 10-13

*Using the UPDATE Clause to
Repeat the Previously
Entered Value*

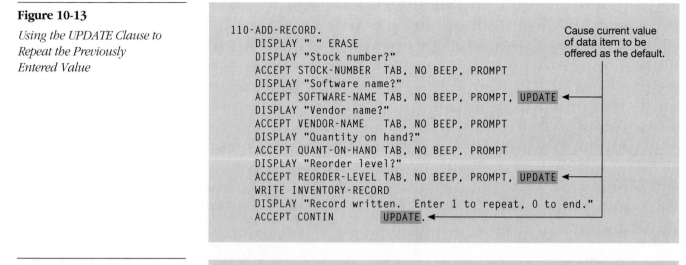

```
110-ADD-RECORD.
    DISPLAY " " ERASE
    DISPLAY "Stock number?"
    ACCEPT STOCK-NUMBER  TAB, NO BEEP, PROMPT
    DISPLAY "Software name?"
    ACCEPT SOFTWARE-NAME TAB, NO BEEP, PROMPT, UPDATE  ◄
    DISPLAY "Vendor name?"
    ACCEPT VENDOR-NAME    TAB, NO BEEP, PROMPT
    DISPLAY "Quantity on hand?"
    ACCEPT QUANT-ON-HAND TAB, NO BEEP, PROMPT
    DISPLAY "Reorder level?"
    ACCEPT REORDER-LEVEL TAB, NO BEEP, PROMPT, UPDATE  ◄
    WRITE INVENTORY-RECORD
    DISPLAY "Record written.  Enter 1 to repeat, 0 to end."
    ACCEPT CONTIN        UPDATE.  ◄
```

Cause current value
of data item to be
offered as the default.

Figure 10-14

*Typical Screen Display Using
the UPDATE Clause*

Vendor name?
Ferrari Development ◄

The cursor is positioned here, awaiting user response.
The previously entered value is offered as the default.
Strike the Enter key to accept it; type over the displayed
value for another value.

Using the SCREEN SECTION for Record Display

One of the characteristics of the COBOL language is that data formatting information is included in the DATA DIVISION, separate from the imperative commands of the PROCEDURE DIVISION. This is convenient for several reasons. One is that it simplifies standardization among programs in a system. Hence, for any program you might write that uses a software file for input, you could simply copy the record description from a program library. You don't have to retype it every time it's needed.

However, the use of the ACCEPT and DISPLAY in the RAN-DIS2 program requires that the formatting information be included as part of the PROCEDURE DIVISION. In general, this is poor practice because it makes the action of importing a standard screen from a program library clumsy. COBOL sorely needs the capability for defining screen formatting within the DATA DIVISION.

Unfortunately, the COBOL-85 Standard does not include screen handling capabilities. However, there is another standard in use, one defined by a consortium of European computer manufacturers (called X/OPEN) as part of their effort to create portability guides. Among other things, this standard defines a SCREEN SECTION for the DATA DIVISION that allows the programmer to remove formatting data for screen I/O from the PROCEDURE DIVISION and place it in the DATA DIVISION where it belongs. RM/COBOL-85 Release 5.0 includes a SCREEN SECTION that conforms to the X/OPEN standard. At first, you may encounter some confusion because a few of the keywords are different from those that you studied for the ACCEPT and DISPLAY (which Ryan-McFarland had used prior to including a SCREEN SECTION). For instance, the screen column with the ACCEPT/DISPLAY is designated by the keyword POSITION. With the X/OPEN SCREEN SECTION, it is designated by the keyword COLUMN. If you keep this in mind, you can minimize the confusion.

Figure 10-15

The RAN-DIS3 Program—
Example 10-1

```
 1      IDENTIFICATION DIVISION.                              61     01  USER-REQUEST-SCREEN.
 2      PROGRAM-ID. RAN-DIS3.                                 62         10  VALUE "To continue, enter the desired stock number: "
 3                                                            63                             LINE 16               HIGHLIGHT.
 4      *   Written by J.Olson                                64         10  PIC X(5)        TO IR-STOCK-NUMBER
 5      *   August 14, 1990                                   65                             LINE PLUS 0  COL PLUS 0.
 6                                                            66         10  VALUE "To exit, strike the Enter key. "
 7      *   This program displays records from the indexed    67                             LINE PLUS 1           HIGHLIGHT.
 8      *   inventory file. Following each record display,    68
 9      *   the user is given the option to display another   69     01  NOT-IN-FILE-SCREEN.
10      *   record or to terminate processing.                70         10  VALUE "There is no record in the file for "
11                                                            71                             LINE 14  BLANK SCREEN  HIGHLIGHT.
12      *   Screens are defined in the SCREEN SECTION.        72         10  PIC X(5)        FROM IR-STOCK-NUMBER
13                                                            73                             LINE PLUS 0  COL        HIGHLIGHT.
14      ENVIRONMENT DIVISION.                                 74
15      CONFIGURATION SECTION.                                75     PROCEDURE DIVISION.
16      SOURCE-COMPUTER. IBM-PC.                              76
17                                                            77     000-ACCESS-INVENTORY-FILE.
18      INPUT-OUTPUT SECTION.                                 78         PERFORM 100-INITIALIZE
19      FILE-CONTROL.                                         79         IF IR-STOCK-NUMBER NOT = SPACES
20          SELECT INVENTORY-FILE      ASSIGN TO DISK "SOFTWAR2.DI"  80         PERFORM 110-DISPLAY-RECORD
21                                     ORGANIZATION IS INDEXED  81             UNTIL IR-STOCK-NUMBER = SPACES
22                                     ACCESS IS RANDOM       82         PERFORM 120-FINALIZE
23                                     RECORD KEY IS IR-STOCK-NUMBER.  83     END-IF
24                                                            84     STOP RUN.
25      DATA DIVISION.                                        85
26                                                            86     100-INITIALIZE.
27      FILE SECTION.                                         87         DISPLAY " " ERASE
28                                                            88         MOVE SPACES TO IR-STOCK-NUMBER
29      FD  INVENTORY-FILE.                                   89         DISPLAY USER-REQUEST-SCREEN
30      01  INVENTORY-RECORD.                                 90         ACCEPT  USER-REQUEST-SCREEN
31          10  IR-STOCK-NUMBER    PIC X(5).                  91         IF IR-STOCK-NUMBER NOT = SPACES
32          10  IR-SOFTWARE-NAME   PIC X(30).                 92             OPEN INPUT INVENTORY-FILE
33          10  IR-VENDOR-NAME     PIC X(20).                 93         END-IF.
34          10  IR-QUANT-ON-HAND   PIC 9(3).                  94
35          10  IR-REORDER-LEVEL   PIC 9(3).                  95     110-DISPLAY-RECORD.
36          10  IR-PRICE           PIC 9(3)V9(2).             96         PERFORM 800-READ-INVENTORY-RECORD
37                                                            97         DISPLAY USER-REQUEST-SCREEN
38      SCREEN SECTION.                                       98         ACCEPT  USER-REQUEST-SCREEN.
39                                                            99
40      01  INVENTORY-RECORD-SCREEN.                         100     120-FINALIZE.
41          10  VALUE "INVENTORY DISPLAY" BLANK SCREEN       101         CLOSE INVENTORY-FILE.
42                              LINE 2     COL 11.           102
43          10  VALUE "Stock number"  LINE PLUS 2  COL 1.   103     800-READ-INVENTORY-RECORD.
44          10  PIC X(5)       FROM IR-STOCK-NUMBER         104         READ INVENTORY-FILE
45                              LINE PLUS 0  COL 16  REVERSE.  105         INVALID KEY
46          10  VALUE "Software name"  LINE PLUS 2  COL 1.  106             DISPLAY NOT-IN-FILE-SCREEN
47          10  PIC X(30)      FROM IR-SOFTWARE-NAME        107         NOT INVALID KEY
48                              LINE PLUS 0  COL 16  REVERSE.  108             DISPLAY INVENTORY-RECORD-SCREEN
49          10  VALUE "Vendor"      LINE PLUS 2  COL 1.     109         END-READ.
50          10  PIC X(20)      FROM IR-VENDOR-NAME          110
51                              LINE PLUS 0  COL 16  REVERSE.
52          10  VALUE "Stock onhand"  LINE PLUS 2  COL 1.
53          10  PIC Z99        FROM IR-QUANT-ON-HAND
54                              LINE PLUS 0  COL 16  REVERSE.
55          10  VALUE "Price"      LINE PLUS 0  COL 26.
56          10  PIC ZZ9.99     FROM IR-PRICE
57                              LINE PLUS 0  COL 34  REVERSE.
58          10  VALUE "Reorder level"  LINE PLUS 1  COL 1.
59          10  PIC ZZ9        FROM IR-REORDER-LEVEL
60                              LINE PLUS 0  COL 16  REVERSE.
```

[handwritten annotations: "screen display" near line 38; "changes background to make box" near lines 59-60]

The Inventory Record Program Using a SCREEN SECTION

The revised display program (RAN-DIS3 using a SCREEN SECTION) for Example 10-1 is shown in Figure 10-15. Although the overall structure appears significantly different, the basic organization and logic are little different than that of RAN-DIS2. There *is* a significant change in the way that screen input and output are handled:

■ A SCREEN SECTION has been added to the DATA DIVISION

■ The 800-ACCEPT-USER-REQUEST and 860-DISPLAY-1-RECORD modules have been deleted from the PROCEDURE DIVISION

■ Most of the code necessary to control the input and output operations has been shifted from the PROCEDURE DIVISION to the DATA DIVISION

The SCREEN SECTION is similar to the WORKING-STORAGE SECTION in that "records" are defined using an 01 entry, followed by 02–49 level entries. There are some similarities in that both include PIC clauses and VALUE clauses. However, as you can see, there are also numerous differences.

For this program, interaction with the user is controlled through the following three screen definitions.

INVENTORY-RECORD-SCREEN: Displays the complete record together with field descriptions. This screen is equivalent to the list of items in the DISPLAY statement of the 860-DISPLAY-1-RECORD module in RAN-DIS2 (Figure 10-7).

USER-REQUEST-SCREEN: Prompts the user to enter a stock number and accepts the entry. This screen is equivalent to the 810-ACCEPT-USER-REQUEST module of RAN-DIS2 (Figure 10-7).

NOT-IN-FILE-SCREEN: Tells the user that there is no record with the requested stock number value. This screen is equivalent to the DISPLAY statements under the INVALID KEY clause in the 800-READ-INVENTORY-RECORD module of RAN-DIS2 (Figure 10-7).

The INVENTORY-RECORD-SCREEN Definition

Consider the first two entries of the INVENTORY-RECORD-SCREEN record—they are repeated in Figure 10-16. Because you know about the DISPLAY from the RAN-DIS2 program, the characteristics of these statements should be reasonably straightforward.

■ Positioning of the literal to be displayed is done by specifying the row and column positions (as with the DISPLAY statements of the RAN-DIS2 program). Notice that the keyword COL is used instead of POSITION (COLUMN is also permissible).

■ No PICTURE clause exists; it is not allowed in a SCREEN SECTION field that includes a VALUE clause.

■ The keywords BLANK SCREEN are used to clear the screen—instead of ERASE used with the DISPLAY.

■ The second entry uses LINE PLUS 2 to designate the line number. This functions exactly as the English suggests: the current LINE value plus 2 more. In this case, the value for LINE is designated as 4 in the preceding entry. Thus, *Stock number* will be displayed on line 6. The advantage of using line positioning relative to the first line is that if you decide to move the entire display down one or two lines, you need not make a change in every LINE entry.

Literals are displayed by items with a VALUE entry. On the other hand, data values are displayed by items that include the data-name from which data is obtained for display. For instance, the description for IR-QUANT-ON-HAND is shown in Figure 10-17.

■ The keyword FROM is followed by the name of the data item to be displayed.

■ The PIC (PICTURE can be used) identifies the format by which the output data is to be displayed. Notice that it can be numeric edited as needed.

■ The relative line positioning LINE PLUS 0 causes this item to be displayed on the same line as the preceding item.

■ The REVERSE functions exactly as with the DISPLAY; it causes the output to be displayed in reversed video.

Figure 10-16

Defining Literal Data to be Displayed from the SCREEN SECTION

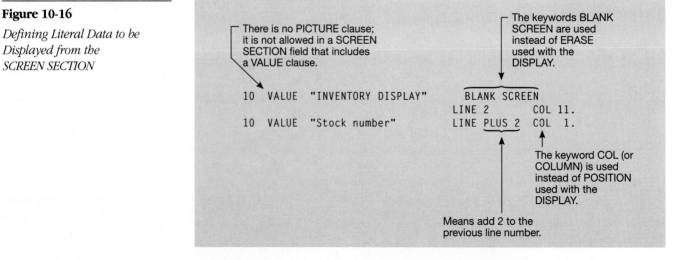

The USER-REQUEST-SCREEN Definition

The next screen definition (USER-REQUEST-SCREEN at lines 62 through 68) is designated to prompt the user and obtain the stock number entry. The latter is done through the entry repeated here in Figure 10-18. Whenever data is accepted from the keyboard through a SCREEN SECTION field, it is stored in a temporary memory area until the entire ACCEPT operation is completed. Then it is transferred from the temporary area to the designated input data item. This explains the components annotated in Figure 10-18.

- The PICTURE (PIC X(5) in this example) defines the temporary work area into which the data is read during keyboard entry.

- The keyword TO indicates that data typed from the keyboard and stored in the temporary work area must be moved to this field (IR-STOCK-NUMBER in this example) defined elsewhere in the DATA DIVISION.

Generalizing the SCREEN SECTION Entries

You can see that the overall form of the SCREEN SECTION is like that of the FILE SECTION and the WORKING-STORAGE SECTION: a 01 entry with subordinate 02-49 entries. The format of the SCREEN SECTION entries is as follows:

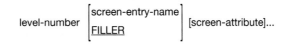

$$\text{level-number} \begin{bmatrix} \text{screen-entry-name} \\ \underline{\text{FILLER}} \end{bmatrix} \text{[screen-attribute]...}$$

Note that the screen-entry-name is optional; in the SCREEN SECTION of the RAN-DIS3 program, only the 01 entry includes a screen-entry-name.

Notice that those entries referred to as control-options with the DISPLAY statements are correspondingly called *screen-attributes* in the SCREEN SECTION. In addition to the LINE, COL, BLANK SCREEN, REVERSE, and HIGHLIGHT screen-attributes, you will learn about a number of others later in this chapter.

Although the PICTURE clause used in this program looks the same as those used in other sections of the DATA DIVISION, it has a significantly different format:

$$\begin{Bmatrix} \underline{\text{PICTURE}} \\ \underline{\text{PIC}} \end{Bmatrix} \text{IS character-string [picture-item]}$$

The element *character-string* is defined in the same way and has the same interpretation as in the other sections of the DATA DIVISION (for instance, XXXX, 99V99, and ZZZ.99).

Figure 10-17

Defining a Data Item to be Displayed from the SCREEN SECTION

Figure 10-18

Defining a Data Item to be Accepted from the Keyboard

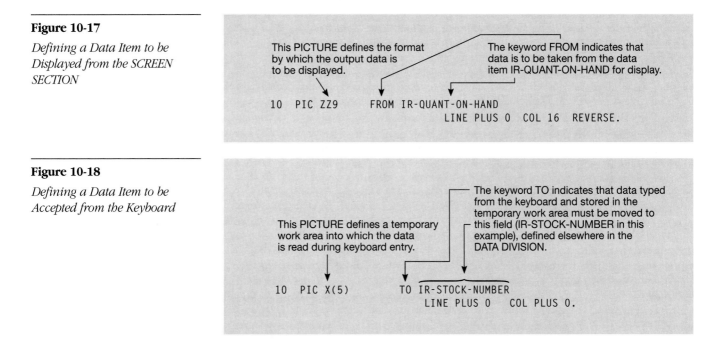

The element *picture-item* may be any of the following:

<u>FROM</u> identifier

<u>FROM</u> nonnumeric literal

<u>TO</u> identifier

<u>USING</u> identifier

As you have already discovered, the FROM marks the screen item as an output item that is active during DISPLAY operations. Similarly, the TO marks the screen item as an input item that is active during ACCEPT operations. You will see how the USING is used in the next example program.

The ACCEPT and DISPLAY Used With the SCREEN SECTION

Do not get the idea that the SCREEN SECTION definitions perform input and output functions—they only *control* the activity with the execution of an ACCEPT or DISPLAY statement. In the RAN-DIS3 program of Figure 10-15, the data record is displayed in the 800 module (line 109) by the statement:

```
DISPLAY INVENTORY-RECORD-SCREEN
```

Each elementary item of the referenced screen record causes the value of a data item or a literal to be displayed as defined.

Where the INVENTORY-RECORD-SCREEN contains only output entries (those to be displayed), the USER-REQUEST-SCREEN contains output entries as well as an input entry—see Figure 10-19. When the DISPLAY is executed, only output entries are affected; they are indicated by the keyword FROM or as literals. Any input entries—as indicated by the keyword TO—are ignored. Similarly, when the ACCEPT is executed, only input entries are affected and output entries are ignored.

Thus, both the DISPLAY and ACCEPT refer to the same screen, as follows (from lines 98 and 99 of the program):

```
DISPLAY USER-REQUEST-SCREEN
ACCEPT USER-REQUEST-SCREEN
```

This is no different from the sequence in RAN-DIS2 in which the prompt is displayed by a DISPLAY and the input is done by an ACCEPT. The difference, which can be confusing, is that both actions are defined in one SCREEN SECTION record.

Figure 10-19

The Effect of Screen Record Entries on the ACCEPT and DISPLAY

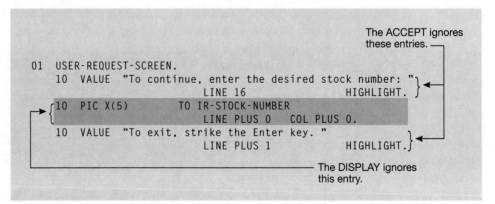

Data Entry—Extending a Sequential File

Data Entry—Extending a Sequential File

Example Definition— Example 10-2

In Chapter 4, you learned how to create a new file and enter data into it through the keyboard. That program was relatively primitive because you were just beginning with COBOL. The next example expands on the data entry programs of Chapter 4 by utilizing SCREEN SECTION capabilities and incorporating some "user friendliness" into the interaction.

Example 10-2 Adding Records to the Software File

Problem Description

Periodically, new records must be added to the software file—existing records are to remain unchanged.

Output Requirements
Name of file to be extended: SOFTWAR2.DL
Record format:

Field	Positions	Data Type	Format
Stock number	1–5	Alphanumeric	
Software name	6–35	Alphanumeric	
Vendor name	36–55	Alphanumeric	
Copies on hand	56–58	Numeric	*nnn*
Reorder level	59–62	Numeric	*nnn*
Price	62–66		*nnn∧nn*

Input Description
Keyboard data entry

Processing Requirements
This data entry program is to function as follows:
1. Display a program description screen and query the user regarding continuing. If the user does not wish to continue, terminate the program.
2. Accept one complete record from the keyboard.
3. Query the user regarding the action to take with the currently displayed set of entries; the options must be
   1 Write the record to the file
   2 Allow the user to make corrections to screen entries
   3 Ignore the screen entries and continue
4. Query the user about continuing. The options must be to either terminate processing or enter another record.

Program Solution Documentation— Example 10-2

Figure 10-13 was used to illustrate how the UPDATE clause for the ACCEPT statement can improve data entry. Perhaps the weakest link in the accurate processing of data is getting it into the computer without error. Well-designed data entry programs and screens can be helpful in speeding up the data entry process and in reducing the probability of entering invalid data. For instance, a good data entry program should, whenever possible, display default values that can be accepted at the tap of the Enter key. Furthermore, the user should be requested to confirm adding a record to a file before the actual writing takes place. In general, data entry programs should be designed so that they are easy to use, guard against erroneous actions wherever possible, and allow the user to recover from his or her mistakes. Programs that possess these qualities are said to be *user friendly*. Some user friendly features are incorporated into this example program.

The solution to Example 10-2 is shown in Figures 10-20 through 10-22. From the logic of the flowchart in Figure 10-20, you can see that the user is queried in the 100 module and is given the choice of continuing or terminating without any data entry. Whether or not execution proceeds in the 000 module depends upon this user response. The overall logic should be relatively routine to you by now. A new feature is found in the 300 module, in which the user is given a choice regarding the action to be taken with the data just entered.

The pseudocode of Figure 10-21 (page 238) illustrates this logic in a different form.

Program Solution— Example 10-2

The complete program is shown in Figure 10-22 (page 239); let's consider some of the features of this program.

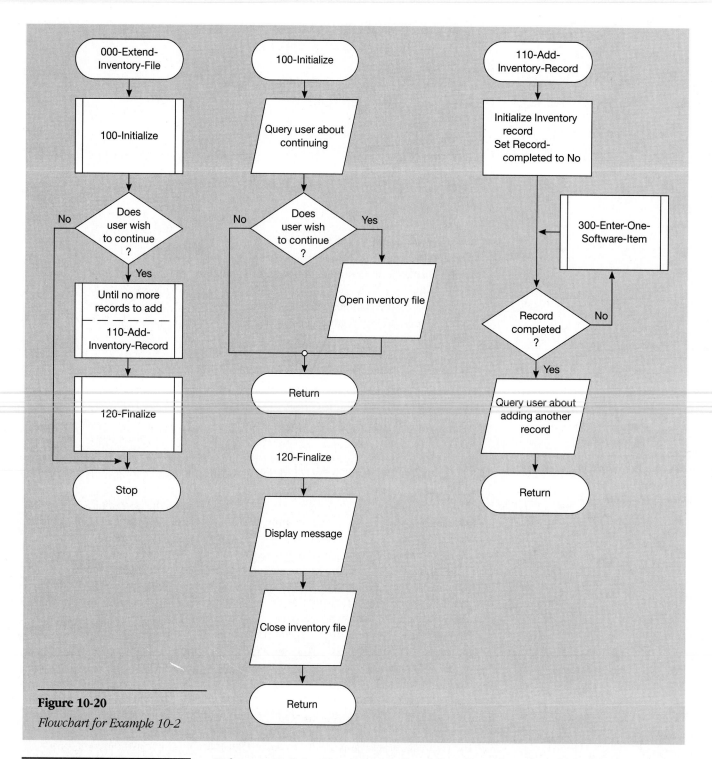

Figure 10-20

Flowchart for Example 10-2

About Opening the File

Before proceeding with screen I-O, let's first consider the way in which the data file must be opened. Because records are to be added to an existing file (SOFTWAR2.DL), a special version of the OPEN statement must be used. That is, the file cannot be opened for OUTPUT because opening for OUTPUT creates a new file; if there is an existing file by that name, it is destroyed. Although opening for INPUT does open an existing file, it only allows input, not output.

This dilemma is resolved in COBOL with the following OPEN EXTEND (refer to line 127 of the program):

```
OPEN EXTEND INVENTORY-FILE
```

Figure 10-20

(continued from page 236)

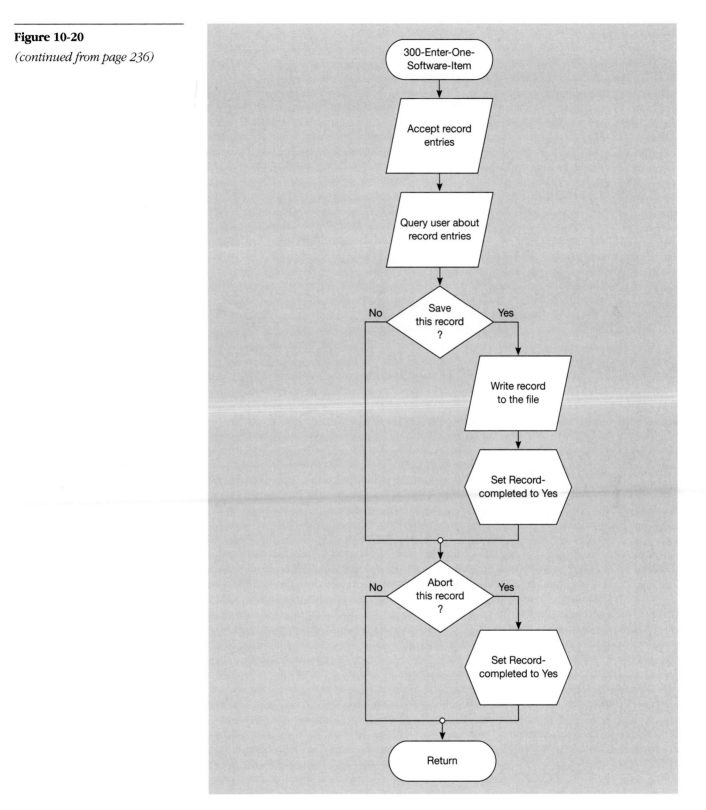

When the EXTEND option is used, the following takes place:

■ The designated file is located on the disk and is opened as with the INPUT option

■ Access to the file is positioned to the end of the file

The file is then ready for output; all records written will be added to the end of the file.

Figure 10-21

Pseudocode for Example 10-2

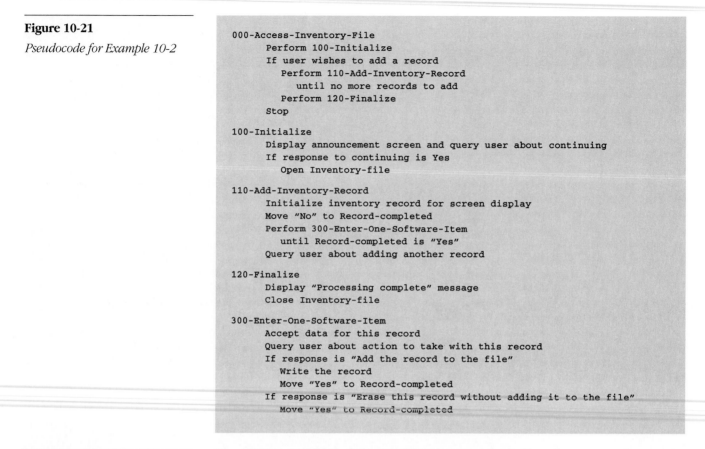

```
000-Access-Inventory-File
     Perform 100-Initialize
     If user wishes to add a record
        Perform 110-Add-Inventory-Record
            until no more records to add
        Perform 120-Finalize
     Stop

100-Initialize
     Display announcement screen and query user about continuing
     If response to continuing is Yes
        Open Inventory-file

110-Add-Inventory-Record
     Initialize inventory record for screen display
     Move "No" to Record-completed
     Perform 300-Enter-One-Software-Item
        until Record-completed is "Yes"
     Query user about adding another record

120-Finalize
     Display "Processing complete" message
     Close Inventory-file

300-Enter-One-Software-Item
     Accept data for this record
     Query user about action to take with this record
     If response is "Add the record to the file"
        Write the record
        Move "Yes" to Record-completed
     If response is "Erase this record without adding it to the file"
        Move "Yes" to Record-completed
```

The USING in the SCREEN SECTION PICTURE

The SCREEN SECTION of the S-EXTEND program includes only one new feature: the USING picture-item option. You see this in each PIC screen attribute of the INVENTORY-RECORD-SCREEN (beginning line 72) and in the ADD-ANOTHER-RECORD (beginning line 52) screen records. For instance, line 76 is

```
    10  PIC X(5)     USING IR-STOCK-NUMBER
```

Whereas the FROM marks the screen item as an output item active during DISPLAY operations and the TO marks the screen item as an input item active during ACCEPT operations, the USING marks the screen item as both input *and* output. That is, if a DISPLAY is executed, the value FROM the named data item (IR-STOCK-NUMBER in this example) is displayed. If an ACCEPT is executed, the data entered from the keyboard is moved TO the named data item (again, IR-STOCK-NUMBER in this example). An advantage of the USING is that it can function to display the current value as a default. This is an important aspect of the S-EXTEND program.

SCREEN SECTION PICTURE Entries

Remember that the PICTURE clause you use for screen entries defines the characteristics of the temporary memory area used for the data element. For instance, at line 76 the element PIC X(5) causes creation of a five-position memory area. If the Stock-number were to be defined as a numeric field, PIC 9(5) would be used—the same as in the FILE SECTION and the WORKING-STORAGE SECTION. However, unlike these sections, when data is defined as numeric in the SCREEN SECTION, the definition *controls the data that can be entered.* That is, because the field is defined as PIC 9, COBOL will allow only digits and spaces to be entered (a sign can be entered if the PICTURE includes sign capabilities). If any other characters are entered, COBOL automatically displays an error message and positions the cursor within the field for reentry of the data. This is in contrast to PIC definitions in the FILE SECTION and data entered into the program via the READ statement, in which no control over the data input is exercised.

```
1        IDENTIFICATION DIVISION.
2        PROGRAM-ID. S-EXTEND.
3
4     *     Written by J.Olson/W.Price
5     *     August 17, 1990
6
7     *     This program adds records to a sequential disk file by
8     *     opening it in the EXTEND mode.  The user is given the option
9     *     to correct fields already entered if a mistake is discovered
10    *     and is provided with a "safety valve" option to abort adding
11    *     the record displayed on the screen.
12
13    *     Screens are defined in the SCREEN SECTION.
14
15       ENVIRONMENT DIVISION.
16       CONFIGURATION SECTION.
17       SOURCE-COMPUTER. IBM-PC.
18
19       INPUT-OUTPUT SECTION.
20       FILE-CONTROL.
21           SELECT INVENTORY-FILE     ASSIGN TO DISK FILE-NAME
22                                      ORGANIZATION IS LINE SEQUENTIAL.
23
24       DATA DIVISION.
25       FILE SECTION.
26
27       FD  INVENTORY-FILE.
28       01  INVENTORY-RECORD.
29           10  IR-STOCK-NUMBER       PIC X(5).
30           10  IR-SOFTWARE-NAME      PIC X(30).
31           10  IR-VENDOR-NAME        PIC X(20).
32           10  IR-QUANT-ON-HAND      PIC 9(3).
33           10  IR-REORDER-LEVEL      PIC 9(3).
34           10  IR-PRICE             PIC 9(3)V9(2).
35
36       WORKING-STORAGE SECTION.
37       01  CONSTANT-VALUES.
38           10  FILE-NAME             PIC X(14) VALUE "SOFTWAR2.DL".
39
40       01  PROGRAMMED-SWITCHES.
41           10  RECORD-COMPLETED     PIC X.
42           10  ADD-ANOTHER-RECORD   PIC X.
43
44       01  OTHER-VARIABLES.
45           10  DESIRED-OPTION       PIC 9.
46           10  WAIT                 PIC X     VALUE SPACE.
47           10  YES-NO               PIC X(3).
48
49       SCREEN SECTION.
50
51
52       01  ADD-ANOTHER-RECORD-SCREEN.
53           10  VALUE
54           "Do you want to add another record <Y/N>? "
55                               LINE 18 COL  1      HIGHLIGHT.
56           10  PIC X   USING ADD-ANOTHER-RECORD
57                               LINE 18  COL PLUS 1 REVERSE AUTO.
58
59       01  INTRODUCTION-SCREEN.
60           05  VALUE "This program allows you to add records to the"
61                     BLANK SCREEN   LINE 6          HIGHLIGHT.
62           05  VALUE  "software inventory file named"
63                               LINE PLUS 1          HIGHLIGHT.
64           05  PIC X(14)     FROM FILE-NAME
65                               LINE PLUS 2 COL 8 HIGHLIGHT.
66           05  VALUE "Do you wish to proceed <Y/N>? "
67                     BELL   LINE PLUS 2        HIGHLIGHT.
68           05  PIC X   USING ADD-ANOTHER-RECORD
69                                           COL PLUS 0
70                                           REVERSE AUTO.
71
```

```
72       01  INVENTORY-RECORD-SCREEN.
73           10  VALUE "ADD INVENTORY RECORD" BLANK SCREEN
74                               LINE  2     COL 11.
75           10  VALUE "Stock number"  LINE PLUS 2 COL 1.
76           10  PIC X(5)   USING IR-STOCK-NUMBER
77                               LINE PLUS 0 COL 16 REVERSE.
78           10  VALUE "Software name"  LINE PLUS 2 COL 1.
79           10  PIC X(30)  USING IR-SOFTWARE-NAME
80                               LINE PLUS 0 COL 16 REVERSE.
81           10  VALUE "Vendor"    LINE PLUS 2 COL 1.
82           10  PIC X(20)  USING IR-VENDOR-NAME
83                               LINE PLUS 0 COL 16 REVERSE.
84           10  VALUE "Stock onhand"   LINE PLUS 2 COL 1.
85           10  PIC ZZ9    USING IR-QUANT-ON-HAND
86                               LINE PLUS 0 COL 16 REVERSE.
87           10  VALUE "Price"    LINE PLUS 0 COL 26.
88           10  PIC ZZZ.99 USING IR-PRICE
89                               LINE PLUS 0 COL 34 REVERSE.
90           10  VALUE "Reorder level"  LINE PLUS 1 COL 1.
91           10  PIC ZZ9    USING IR-REORDER-LEVEL
92                               LINE PLUS 0 COL 16 REVERSE.
93
94       01  SELECT-OPTION-SCREEN.
95           10  VALUE "Options:"    LINE 18 COL 1.
96           10  VALUE
97           " 1   Data is correct.  Add this record to the file."
98                               LINE PLUS 1 COL 1.
99           10  VALUE
100          " 2   Data as shown needs to be corrected."
101                              LINE PLUS 1 COL 1.
102          10  VALUE
103          " 3   Erase the above data; do not add it to the file."
104                              LINE PLUS 1 COL 1.
105          10  VALUE
106          "Please enter 1, 2, or 3 for desired option: "
107                              LINE PLUS 2 COL 1 HIGHLIGHT.
108   *     Get option from keyboard
109          10  PIC X         TO DESIRED-OPTION
110                              LINE 23   COL 45 REVERSE  AUTO.
111
112      PROCEDURE DIVISION.
113      000-EXTEND-INVENTORY-FILE.
114          PERFORM 100-INITIALIZE
115          IF ADD-ANOTHER-RECORD = "Y"
116              PERFORM 110-ADD-INVENTORY-RECORD
117                  UNTIL ADD-ANOTHER-RECORD NOT = "Y"
118              PERFORM 120-FINALIZE
119          END-IF
120          STOP RUN.
121
122      100-INITIALIZE.
123          MOVE "Y" TO ADD-ANOTHER-RECORD
124          DISPLAY INTRODUCTION-SCREEN
125          ACCEPT  INTRODUCTION-SCREEN
126          IF ADD-ANOTHER-RECORD = "Y"
127              OPEN EXTEND INVENTORY-FILE
128          END-IF.
129
130      110-ADD-INVENTORY-RECORD.
131          INITIALIZE INVENTORY-RECORD
132          MOVE "N" TO RECORD-COMPLETED
133          PERFORM 300-ENTER-1-SOFTWARE-ITEM
134              UNTIL RECORD-COMPLETED = "Y"
135          DISPLAY ADD-ANOTHER-RECORD-SCREEN
136          ACCEPT  ADD-ANOTHER-RECORD-SCREEN.
137
138      120-FINALIZE.
139          DISPLAY FILE-NAME               LINE 21
140          DISPLAY " has been extended."   POSITION 0
141          CLOSE INVENTORY-FILE.
142
143      300-ENTER-1-SOFTWARE-ITEM.
144          DISPLAY INVENTORY-RECORD-SCREEN
145          ACCEPT  INVENTORY-RECORD-SCREEN
146          DISPLAY SELECT-OPTION-SCREEN
147          ACCEPT  SELECT-OPTION-SCREEN
148
149          IF DESIRED-OPTION = 1
150              WRITE INVENTORY-RECORD
151              MOVE "Y" TO RECORD-COMPLETED
152              DISPLAY "This record added to the file"
153                          LINE 16   ERASE EOS
154          END-IF
155
156          IF DESIRED-OPTION = 3
157              MOVE "Y" TO RECORD-COMPLETED
158              DISPLAY "This record NOT added to the file"
159                          LINE 16   ERASE EOS
160          END-IF.
```

Figure 10-22

The S-EXTEND Program—
Example 10-2

For the three numeric fields (Stock-on-hand, Reorder-level, and Price), you can see that these PIC definitions are numeric edited. The only advantage to doing this is that the program displays default values according to the PICTURE you have used.

Default Values and the USING

The way in which the USING is utilized to offer a default value is most easily understood by referring to the 100-INITIALIZE module in which the user is queried regarding continuing. In this module, the following takes place:

1. The value "Y" is moved to the programmed switch ADD-ANOTHER-RECORD.

2. The DISPLAY is executed designating the INTRODUCTION-SCREEN; the screen appears as shown in Figure 10-23. The value currently stored in ADD-ANOTHER-RECORD is displayed. Remember, the USING triggers both the ACCEPT and DISPLAY.

3. The user is allowed to enter a value with execution of the ACCEPT statement (line 125). Striking the Enter key accepts the displayed default. Striking any other key enters the character of that key.

Controlling Repeated Record Entry

Initial execution—as well as repetition in this program—is controlled by the programmed switch ADD-ANOTHER-RECORD. Overall actions are as follows:

1. A value of "Y" is moved into the switch at line 123 and the user is queried regarding continuing (Figure 10-23).

2. Execution is permitted through the IF statement at line 115 only if the user response was "Y".

3. The 110 module is performed repeatedly until the switch contains a value other than Y.

4. The last two statements in the 110 module query the user as follows:

```
Do you want to add another record <Y/N>?  Y
```

Striking the Enter key accepts the default value of Y, which is stored in the switch ADD-ANOTHER-RECORD. Another record will be accepted. Typing the letter *N* stores an N in the switch; this will end the record entry loop (at the PERFORM of lines 116 and 117).

User Options for a Record Entered

At lines 133 and 134, data entry is controlled by the statement:
```
PERFORM 300-ENTER-1-SOFTWARE-ITEM
    UNTIL RECORD-COMPLETED = "Y"
```

Notice that prior to executing this statement, the data record INVENTORY-RECORD defined in the FD is initialized (line 131) and a value of "N" is moved to the switch RECORD-COMPLETED (line 132).

Figure 10-23

The Announcement Screen and Query to the User

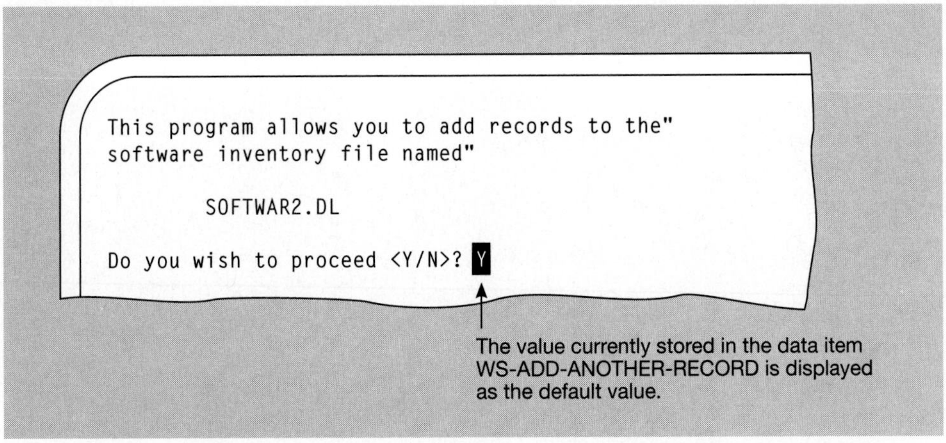

```
This program allows you to add records to the"
software inventory file named"

      SOFTWAR2.DL

Do you wish to proceed <Y/N>?  Y
```

The value currently stored in the data item WS-ADD-ANOTHER-RECORD is displayed as the default value.

In the 300 module, two sets of DISPLAY/ACCEPTs are executed (lines 144 through 147). The first allows the user to enter data for the next record; the second allows the user to respond regarding the disposition of this record. A typical set of screen entries is shown in Figure 10-24. Notice that the user has three options: (1) add the record to the file, (2) correct the displayed data, or (3) discard the displayed data. The following are the actions that must occur for each selection:

Add record	Write the record to the file.
	Move "Y" to the switch RECORD-COMPLETED to indicate that work is completed on this record.
Change record	Do not write the record to the file.
	Do not change the value in the switch. This will cause the 300 module to be executed again, using the previously entered values as defaults. Thus, the values can be edited.
Discard record	Do not write the record to the file.
	Move "Y" to the switch RECORD-COMPLETED to indicate that work is completed on this record.

You can see these actions in the two IF statements (lines 149 and 156). Note that no action need be taken if the user selects the change option (2) because the 300 will be executed again automatically.

Figure 10-24

The User Option Screen

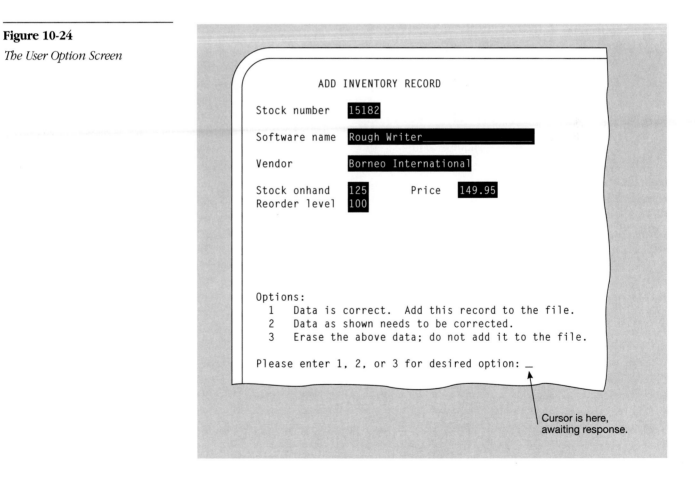

```
              ADD INVENTORY RECORD

Stock number    15182

Software name   Rough Writer_____

Vendor          Borneo International

Stock onhand    125        Price    149.95
Reorder level   100




Options:
    1   Data is correct.  Add this record to the file.
    2   Data as shown needs to be corrected.
    3   Erase the above data; do not add it to the file.

Please enter 1, 2, or 3 for desired option: _
```

Cursor is here, awaiting response.

Screen-Name Entries

In both of this chapter's example SCREEN SECTION programs, you have dealt with only one screen-name entry: the name of the screen record itself defined by the 01. None of the entries subordinate to this 01 included names—they were not necessary for the applications. For instance, the statement

```
ACCEPT INVENTORY-RECORD-SCREEN
```

causes data to be accepted into each elementary item defined in that screen record with a TO or a USING.

In some situations, it is necessary to refer to individual elements of a screen record. For this, you can give those elements individual screen-names. For example, the screen description for INVENTORY-RECORD-SCREEN could have been as shown in Figure 10-25. The value of this form is that you can now refer to individual fields with an ACCEPT. For instance,

```
ACCEPT SCR-STOCK-NUMBER
```

allows data entry into only the IR-STOCK-NUMBER field. The definition of the screen-name causes the temporary memory area associated with this entry to be given the screen-name SCR-STOCK-NUMBER. However, this screen-name can be referred to *only* by an ACCEPT or DISPLAY. For instance, you cannot move data into or out of it with the MOVE statement.

Screen-names for each field are used in Chapter 12, "Data Validation," because each field must be validated as it is entered.

About SCREEN SECTION Organizing

The SCREEN SECTION of the S-EXTEND program has four screen record descriptions—not a large number. If you need to refer to only one of them, finding it is not difficult. However, a large interactive program can have many screen records. While coding or maintaining such a program, finding a desired record can involve searching through two or more pages of them. To avoid this, some organized arrangement is necessary.

Several methods might work. You could define screen records according to the sequence in which they are encountered in the program, but this would provide little assistance in finding a desired one. You could precede each record with a two-digit number and keep them in order by the number (the number would have no meaning

Figure 10-25

Screen-Names on Elementary Screen Items

```
01  INVENTORY-RECORD-SCREEN.
    10   VALUE  "ADD INVENTORY RECORD" BLANK SCREEN
                                       LINE  2  COL  11.
    10   VALUE  "Stock number"         LINE PLUS 2  COL  1.
    10   SCR-STOCK-NUMBER     PIC X(5)
         USING IR-STOCK-NUMBER         LINE PLUS 0  COL 16  REVERSE.
    10   VALUE  "Software name"        LINE PLUS 2  COL  1.
    10   SCR-SOFTWARE-NAME    PIC X(30)
         USING IR-SOFTWARE-NAME        LINE PLUS 0  COL 16  REVERSE.
    10   VALUE  "Vendor"               LINE PLUS 2  COL  1.
    10   SCR-VENDOR-NAME      PIC X(20)
         USING IR-VENDOR-NAME          LINE PLUS 0  COL 16  REVERSE.
    10   VALUE  "Stock onhand"         LINE PLUS 2  COL  1.
    10   SCR-QUANT-ON-HAND    PIC Z99
         USING IR-QUANT-ON-HAND        LINE PLUS 0  COL 16  REVERSE.
    10   VALUE  "Price"               LINE PLUS 0  COL 26.
    10   SCR-PRICE            PIC ZZ9.99
         USING IR-PRICE                LINE PLUS 0  COL 34  REVERSE.
    10   VALUE  "Reorder level"        LINE PLUS 1  COL  1.
    10   SCR-REORDER-LEVEL    PIC ZZ9
         USING IR-REORDER-LEVEL        LINE PLUS 0  COL 16  REVERSE.
```

other than to indicate where to find a given screen record in the SCREEN SECTION). For instance, the four screen records in the S-EXTEND program might be named as follows:

```
01   10-ADD-ANOTHER-RECORD-SCREEN.
01   11-INTRODUCTION-SCREEN.
01   12-INVENTORY-RECORD-SCREEN.
01   13-SELECT-OPTION-SCREEN.
```

Then if you are working on the program and need to look at the screen record for the command

```
DISPLAY 11-INTRODUCTION-SCREEN
```

you could easily find it in the SCREEN SECTION as long as you are careful to keep them in their assigned numeric order.

An alternative is to simply keep them in alphabetic sequence according to the screen-name. At first, this may appear to be clumsy, but it is not because the capabilities of the editor included with RM/CO* (and most other editors and word processors) make it easy to move around within the source program during entry/editing operations. This alphabetic sequencing is used in the S-EXTEND program and is used in the much larger data validation program of Chapter 12.

Screen Design

The editor or word processing program that you use to enter COBOL programs allows you to enter text (the COBOL program) into a file and to change the contents by operating on the screen-displayed information. Not only is it possible to make minor editing changes, but entire blocks of information can be moved from one place in the text to another.

This technique is also the simplest and most convenient way to design a screen. In fact, the commercially available version of RM/COBOL-85 includes such a screen design utility. With it, the programmer can simply lay out all desired field positions on the screen, move them as with a word processor, edit as needed, and then save the information. The utility then converts this information to corresponding COBOL code consisting of DISPLAY and ACCEPT statements—together with screen descriptions—to create the screens exactly as designed. With the absence of such a utility, it is necessary for the programmer to carefully lay out (on paper) the desired screen format and then code the appropriate statements.

Chapter Summary

General

Two forms of the both ACCEPT and DISPLAY statements were described in this chapter: with one or more data-names and with a screen-name.

The ACCEPT-data-name allows for the data entry into one or more fields. The DISPLAY-data-name can display literals and/or data from identifiers.

The SCREEN SECTION provides for the screen layout definition. Its basic structure is like that of the other sections of the DATA DIVISION in that it consists of an 01 entry followed by subordinate entries with level numbers ranging from 02 to 49. Each elementary item can include a level-number, a screen-name, and one or more screen-attributes.

If the screen-name of an ACCEPT or DISPLAY refers to a group item, then all elementary-items subordinate to that group item are active.

COBOL Language Elements

The ACCEPT-data-name and DISPLAY-data-name statements were introduced in Chapter 4. They can include the following clauses:

BLINK	Causes characters in the area of the screen defined by the field (or literal for the DISPLAY) to blink on and off.
ERASE	Clears the entire screen to spaces and positions the cursor at the upper left of the screen before proceeding.
ERASE EOL	Clears from the position of the cursor to the end of the line.
ERASE EOS	Clears from the position of the cursor to the end of the line and all lines that follow.
HIGH	Causes characters in the area of the screen defined by the data item (or literal for the DISPLAY) to be shown in high intensity.
LINE	Identifies the screen line on which the cursor is to be positioned for the associated input or output action.
POSITION	Identifies the screen column on which the cursor is to be positioned for the associated input or output action.
REVERSE	Shows the area of the screen defined by the data item for an ACCEPT or DISPLAY (or literal for the DISPLAY) in reversed video.

The following clauses are usable only with the terminal ACCEPT statement:

NO BEEP	Suppresses the computer sound (a bell) when entry of a field is completed.
PROMPT	Causes underscore characters to be positioned on the screen at positions from which data is to be entered.
TAB	In an ACCEPT statement, requires that the Enter key be struck before the entry is accepted. Otherwise, the entry is accepted automatically when the field is filled.
ACCEPT screen-item	Allows data to be accepted from the keyboard under control of the *screen-item* description in the SCREEN SECTION of the DATA DIVISION.
DISPLAY screen-item	Allows data to be displayed on the screen from literals and data items defined by the *screen-item* description in the SCREEN SECTION of the DATA DIVISION.

The following screen attributes include those described in this chapter and others that you might find useful.

AUTO	*ACCEPT only.* During execution of an ACCEPT, any field with the AUTO attribute is considered complete when sufficient characters have been entered to fill the field. Without the AUTO, the Enter key must always be pressed to signal completion for that field.
BELL	*DISPLAY only.* Rings the BELL when the item is displayed.
BLANK SCREEN	*ACCEPT and DISPLAY.* Clears the entire screen to spaces and positions the cursor at the upper left of the screen before proceeding. Same as ACCEPT-data-name ERASE clause.
BLANK LINE	*ACCEPT and DISPLAY.* Clears from the position of the cursor to the end of the line. Same as ACCEPT-data-name ERASE EOL clause.

BLANK REMAINDER   *ACCEPT and DISPLAY.*

Clears from the position of the cursor to the end of the line and all lines that follow.

Same as ACCEPT-data-name ERASE EOS clause.

BLINK   *ACCEPT and DISPLAY.*

Causes the screen field to blink on and off. Same as ACCEPT-data-name BLINK clause.

COLUMN   *ACCEPT and DISPLAY.*
(or **COL**)

Identifies the screen column on which the cursor is to be positioned for the associated input or output action. Same as ACCEPT-data-name POSITION clause.

COLUMN PLUS *n*   *ACCEPT and DISPLAY.*

The PLUS is an option of the COLUMN. It provides for column positioning relative to the last column position of the cursor. For instance, PLUS 0 causes the cursor to remain at its current column, PLUS 1 causes it to be positioned one column later than the current column, and so on.

FULL   *ACCEPT only.*

Requires that sufficient characters be entered to fill the entire field.

HIGHLIGHT   *ACCEPT and DISPLAY.*

Causes characters in the area of the screen defined by the data item (or literal for the DISPLAY) to be shown in high intensity.

Same as ACCEPT-data-name HIGH clause.

LINE   *ACCEPT and DISPLAY.*

Identifies the screen line on which the cursor is to be positioned for the associated input or output action. Same as ACCEPT-data-name LINE clause.

LINE PLUS *n*   *ACCEPT and DISPLAY.*

The PLUS is an option of the LINE. It provides for line positioning relative to the last line position of the cursor. For instance, PLUS 0 causes the cursor to remain at its current line, PLUS 1 causes it to be positioned one line later than the current line, and so on.

PICTURE   *ACCEPT and DISPLAY.*
(or **PIC**)

Defines the screen format of a screen field. It can be used with any of the following:

> FROM identifier
>
> FROM nonnumeric-literal
>
> TO identifier
>
> USING identifier

The FROM and the USING signify an item that is active during a DISPLAY; the TO and the USING signify an item that is active during an ACCEPT.

REQUIRED   *ACCEPT only.*

Indicates that an entry must be made in the field.

REVERSE   *ACCEPT or DISPLAY.*

Shows the area of the screen defined by the data item for an ACCEPT or DISPLAY (or literal for the DISPLAY) in reversed video.

VALUE   *DISPLAY only.*

Defines a value to be displayed. Cannot be used in a screen description entry containing PICTURE, AUTO, REQUIRED, or FULL.

Programming Conventions

Keep formatting information in the DATA DIVISION by using the ACCEPT and DISPLAY with the SCREEN SECTION (except for occasional brief messages).

Use some convention for organizing screen records in the SCREEN SECTION. Two possibilities are (1) prefix each screen record name with a number for the ordering or (2) arrange them in alphabetic sequence based on the record name.

Error Prevention/ Detection

Plan your screen layout using a layout form.

Use relative line and column positioning. This simplifies moving the entire screen layout.

If data items defined in a screen record are not displayed or accepted as they should be, check the PICTURE. For instance, if in a data entry program you want to accept a value into a data item and you use FROM instead of TO, that data item will be ignored by the ACCEPT statement. Be careful in your use of TO, FROM, and USING.

Questions and Exercises

Give a brief description of each of the following terms that were introduced in this chapter.

Key Terminology

default value	low intensity	screen-attributes
high intensity	reversed video	user friendly

General Questions

1. What is meant by the term *softcopy output?*
2. Which control clauses can be used with the DISPLAY statement in COBOL?
3. When the contents of a field need to be reused, which clause of the ACCEPT statement permits this? Note that the data entry person would not have to key the same field again using this clause.
4. If a programmer decides to use the SCREEN SECTION in RM/COBOL-85, where is this coded and what is included in it?
5. What are "screen-attributes" in the SCREEN SECTION?
6. How are ACCEPT and DISPLAY statements used in a program containing a SCREEN SECTION?

Questions Relating to the Example Programs

1. In the RAN-DIS2 program of Figure 10-7, the WORKING-STORAGE SECTION includes edited field definitions for the numeric items of this record. Then, in the 860 module, data is moved into them immediately prior to displaying. This could be avoided, simply by using numeric-edited PICTUREs for the IR versions of these fields (in lines 34 through 36). Why not do this?
2. Lines 95 through 107 list the items to be displayed and the order in which they are displayed. Would the screen display be different if the order of the items were reversed. That is, if

```
        "INVENTORY DISPLAY"   LINE  2  POSITION 11  LOW  ERASE
```
were last and
```
        REORDER-LEVEL          LINE 11  POSITION 16  REVERSE.
```
were first?

3. In the RAN-DIS2 program, the 000 module appears to be unnecessarily complicated with the inclusion of an IF and a PERFORM-UNTIL, both acting on effectively the same condition. Consider the following alternative:

```
000-ACCESS-INVENTORY-FILE.
    PERFORM 100-INITIALIZE
    PERFORM 110-DISPLAY-RECORD
        UNTIL IR-STOCK-NUMBER = SPACES
    PERFORM 120-FINALIZE
        STOP RUN.
```

With this, the 110 module will not be performed at all if the user entered no Stock-number value (and instead entered spaces) for the first inquiry from the 100 module. What would be the problem with this approach and how could the problem be avoided?

4. What would happen in the RAN-DIS3 program of Figure 10-15 if TO were accidentally used instead of FROM for the INVENTORY-RECORD-SCREEN entries (lines 41–60)?

5. What would happen if FROM were accidentally used instead of TO for the second entry (line 65) of the USER-REQUEST-SCREEN?

6. What would be the effect on the screen display of omitting the BLANK SCREEN from the first entry (line 41) of the INVENTORY-RECORD-SCREEN in the RAN-DIS3 program? Consider all aspects of this omission.

7. The 300 module of the S-EXTEND program (Figure 10-22) provides the user three options after data entry is completed. However, the program only tests and takes action for two of them (value 1 at line 149 and value 3 at line 156). Why is no test and action taken for the user response 2?

8. Lines 153 and 159 include the ERASE EOS clause in the DISPLAY statements of the S-EXTEND program. What would happen if this clause were omitted?

9. Execution of the S-EXTEND program involves output of new records to the SOFTWAR2 file. What is wrong with opening it for output?

10. What would happen in the S-EXTEND program if the statement

```
MOVE "Y" TO RECORD-COMPLETED
```

at line 157 were omitted?

Writing Program Statements

1. Write DISPLAY-data-name statements to do each of the following:
   a. Display the message "The current balance is:"
   b. Clear the screen, then display the message "The current balance is:"" starting in row 4, column 7.
   c. Clear line 9, then display the description "Current balance:" followed by the value in the variable CURRENT-BALANCE. The data is to be in reverse display.
   d. Clear the screen from line 12 down, then display the description "Credit limit" at line 15, column 20, and the value of the field CREDIT-LIMIT at line 16, column 30 blinking.

2. Write ACCEPT-data-name statements to do each of the following:
   a. Accept a keyboard entry into the data-name ITEM-DESCRIPTION beginning row 7, column 6. Include prompt characters.
   b. Accept a keyboard entry into the data-name QUANT-SOLD from the last position of the cursor. Use reverse video.
   c. Accept entries into the data-names UNIT-NUMBER (line 10, column 12) and DESCRIPTION (line 10, column 30). The DESCRIPTION field must be highlighted. Use only one ACCEPT statement.

3. Write elementary-item entries for the SCREEN SECTION to define each of the four DISPLAY actions in Question 1. Assume appropriate PICTUREs for data items.

4. Write elementary-item entries for the SCREEN SECTION to define each of the following:
  a. Clear the screen, display the message "Enter the code:", and then accept an entry into the field FILE-CODE, which is defined with PIC X(5). The message is to begin in row 5, column 20 and the input screen field must immediately follow. Use reverse on the input.
  b. Clear line 15, then display the message "Should this be saved <Y/N>?" Accept as a response into SAVE-SWITCH a single character input. Offer the letter *N* as a default.
  c. Accept a dollar and cent amount (less than $100, but not less than zero) into the field PAYMENT. Offer the original value in PAYMENT as the default. This is a required field. It must have a screen-name of SCR-PAYMENT and be positioned beginning row 5, column 25.

5. Write DISPLAY-data-name statements to do each of the following:
  a. Clear the entire screen and display the message "The employee number requested is:" starting in row 6, column 10.
  b. Clear line 10 and display the description "Employee Number:" followed by the value in the variable EMP-NUMBER. The data is to be high intensity.
  c. Clear the remainder of the screen from line 11 down. Display the description "Employee Name:" at line 13, column 5. The value of the field EMP-NAME is to appear on line 13, column 21 in reverse display.

6. Write elementary item entries for the SCREEN SECTION to define each of the three DISPLAY actions in Exercise 5. Assume appropriate PICTUREs for data items. Use one 01-level entry.

Programming Assignments

10-1 Employee File Information Display

The more capabilities you provide for computer users, the more they want. The payroll clerk of Programming Assignments 6-2 and 9-1 now wants the ability to query the employee file.

Output Requirements:

A full screen display of the following fields:

Field	Required Editing
Social Security number	Insert hyphens; for instance: 123-45-6789
Employee name	
Department code	
Monthly gross pay	Insert decimal point and commas and zero suppress
Year-to-date earnings	Same actions as Gross pay
Year-to-date income tax withholding	Same actions as Gross pay
Year-to-date FICA withholding	Same actions as Gross pay
Tax sheltered annuity code	
Tax sheltered annuity deduction	Insert decimal point zero suppress

Design a balanced, easy-to-read screen layout. Use appropriate titles and descriptions.

Input Description:

Keyboard input: Social Security number of desired employee
Indication to terminate processing
File name: EMPLOYEE.DI
Record description: See Appendix A

Processing Requirements:

This random access display program is to function as follows:
1. Accept the Social Security number of the desired record from the keyboard.
2. Read the record from disk and display it on the screen according to your screen format design.
3. If there is no record with the requested Social Security number, display an error message.
4. Allow the user to terminate processing after each record is displayed.

10-2   Airport Traffic Information Display

The airport manager of Programming Assignment 6-1 would like to display on the screen all the information for any flight.

Output Requirements:

A full-screen display of all fields in the input record. Design a balanced, easy-to-read screen layout. Use appropriate titles and descriptions.

Input Description:

File name: AIRPORT1.DI

Record description: See Appendix A

Processing Requirements:

This random access display program is to function as follows.
1. Accept the flight number for the desired record from the keyboard.
2. Read the record from disk and display it on the screen according to your screen format design.
3. If there is no record with the requested flight number, display an error message.
4. Allow the user to terminate processing after each record is displayed.

10-3   Enrollment Information Display

The dean of instruction at the Computer Institute of Technology would like to be able to inquire into the enrollment file to check the enrollment of classes. He would like the display to draw his attention to the displayed class if it is underenrolled.

Output Requirements:

A full-screen display of all fields in the input record. Design a balanced, easy-to-read screen layout. Use appropriate titles and descriptions. Highlight any display in which the actual enrollment is less than the minimum enrollment.

Input Description:

File name: ENROLL01.DI

Record description: See Appendix A

Processing Requirements:

This random access display program is to function as follows:
1. Accept the class code for the desired record from the keyboard.
2. Read the record from disk and display it on the screen according to your screen format design.
3. If there is no record with the class code, display an error message.
4. If the actual enrollment is less than the minimum permissible enrollment, display the message (blinking)

```
LOW ENROLLMENT
```

next to the actual enrollment field.
5. Allow the user to terminate processing after each record is displayed.

10-4   Display Student Information

The financial aid officer at the Computer Institute of Technology would like to be able to inquire into the student file to check the progress of students receiving financial aid. She would like the display to draw her attention to any student with a GPA for the last semester that exceeds his or her cumulative GPA.

Output Requirements:

A full-screen display of all fields in the input record. Design a balanced, easy-to-read screen layout. Use appropriate titles and descriptions. Highlight any display in which the GPA for the last semester exceeds the cumulative GPA.

Input Description:

File name: STUDENTS.DI

Record description: See Appendix A

Processing Requirements:

This random access display program is to function as follows:

1. Accept the student number for the desired record from the keyboard.
2. Read the record from disk.
3. Calculate the Cumulative GPA as:

$$= \frac{\text{Cumulative points}}{\text{Cumulative units}}$$

4. Display the following on the screen according to your screen format design:
   All fields from the record
   The word Freshman, Sophomore, Junior, Senior, or
      Graduate for the class standing
   The Cumulative GPA
   The following message (blinking) if the GPA last semester exceeds the
      Cumulative GPA:

   Above average semester

5. If there is no record with the student number, display an error message.
6. Allow the user to terminate processing after each record is displayed.

10-5 Display Inventory Status

The owner of Oldies-But-Goodies Record Distributors would like to be able to display the status of his inventory for any selected title. The information he needs is readily available from his recording library.

Output Requirements:

A full-screen display of all fields in the input record. Design a balanced, easy-to-read screen layout. Use appropriate titles and descriptions.

Input Description:

File name: RECORD01.DI

Record description: See Appendix A

Processing Requirements:

This random access display program is to function as follows:

1. Accept the inventory control number for the desired record from the keyboard.
2. Read the record from disk.
3. Calculate the Current quantity on hand as
         Number on hand, beginning of month
      - Number sold this month
      + Number received this month
4. Display the following on the screen according to your screen format design:
      All fields from the record
      The Current quantity on hand
      A message that an order must be placed if
      Current quantity on hand + Number on order
      is less than the Reorder quantity
5. If there is no record with the inventory control number, display an error message.
6. Allow the user to terminate processing after each record is displayed.

11

CONDITIONAL OPERATIONS

Chapter Objectives

In Chapter 8, you learned the basic features of the IF statement; this chapter is a comprehensive study of conditional operations. From it, you will learn about the following topics:

- The three types of tests that can be used in conditional statements:
  1. *Relation:* allows for two quantities to be compared
  2. *Sign:* determines if a number is negative, zero, or positive
  3. *Class:* determines whether data in a variable is numeric or alphabetic

- The IF statement—the COBOL selection structure statement that allows for the conditional execution of a block of statements

- One or more IF statements included within a conditional block of another IF

- Compound test conditions in which the determination involves a given condition *and* another, or a given condition *or* another

- The notion of a programmed switch, whereby the result of an action at one place in a program results in a conditional operation at some later point in the program

- The EVALUATE statement, which provides the tool for executing any of several alternative actions, depending on a tested condition

- Condition names that add a convenient documentation factor in forming test conditions

Review of the IF Statement

The General Form of the IF

In Chapter 8, you learned the basic principles of the IF statement, which has the general format (to the extent that you will use it in this book):

```
IF condition
    imperative-statement-1
[ELSE
    imperative-statement-2]
END-IF
```

This statement allows you to implement the selection structure of structured programming theory. One of the examples you studied in Chapter 8 was

```
IF SENIORITY IS GREATER THAN 20
    MOVE AMOUNT TO AMOUNT-OUT
    WRITE EMPLOYEE
    ADD 1 TO S-COUNT
ELSE
    MOVE LOW-COUNT TO AMOUNT-OUT
    ADD 1 TO L-COUNT
END-IF
```

When this statement is executed, the following takes place:

1. The value stored in the data item SENIORITY is compared to the literal 20. The result will be either true or false. For instance, if SENIORITY contains 25, the condition is true. If it contains 15 (or even 20), it is false.

2. If the resulting conditional test is true, the three statements immediately following the IF are executed; those following the ELSE are ignored.

3. If the resulting conditional test is false, the two statements immediately following the ELSE are executed; those following the IF are ignored.

4. In either case, execution continues to the statement following the END-IF.

In the general form, notice that the ELSE portion is optional. This allows you to implement a limited form of the selection in which an action is taken or omitted, as illustrated by the following example:

```
IF SENIORITY IS GREATER THAN 20
    MOVE AMOUNT TO AMOUNT-OUT
    WRITE EMPLOYEE
    ADD 1 TO S-COUNT
END-IF
```

In this example, if the test condition is true, the three statements between the IF and END-IF are executed; if false, they are not executed.

The General Form of the Relation Condition

The test condition of the preceding examples is called a *relation condition*; it compares two operands to arrive at a truth value of true or false. The general form of the relation condition is

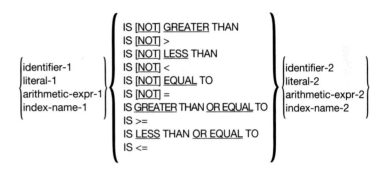

Note: In the preceding general form, the relational characters >, <, and = are required but are not underlined (the standard for indicating required entries). The underlining is omitted here to avoid confusion with other mathematical symbols.

The operand to the left is called the *subject* of the condition; the operand to the right is called the *object* of the condition. You will see a distinction between the two later in this chapter.

The meanings of the relational operators shown in the general form are summarized in the following table:

Relational Operator	Meaning
IS [NOT] GREATER THAN IS [NOT] >	Greater than (optionally, not greater than)
IS [NOT] LESS THAN IS [NOT] <	Less than (optionally, not less than)
IS [NOT] EQUAL TO IS [NOT] =	Equal to (optionally, not equal to)
IS GREATER THAN OR EQUAL TO IS >=	Greater than or equal to
IS LESS THAN OR EQUAL TO IS <=	Less than or equal to

Notice that some of these forms are equivalent; for instance,

```
HOURS-WORKED IS NOT GREATER THAN 40
```

is equivalent to

```
HOURS-WORKED IS LESS THAN OR EQUAL TO 40
```

When writing programs, you should select the form that has the best documentation value for the particular application. Bear in mind that use of the word *NOT* in a condition can be confusing (to the average programmer, although not to the computer).

As you might expect, a comparison in which both operands are numeric is done strictly on the magnitudes of the numbers; the sizes of data items has nothing to do with the test. For instance, 857 (three digits) is greater than 000065 (six digits). Also, a positive value is always greater than any negative value.

Other Condition Tests

Comparing Alphanumeric Quantities

When the operands being compared are nonnumeric, the comparison is done differently. To illustrate, consider the five examples in Figure 11-1, in which the respective field lengths are as indicated by the artwork. The criterion for determining if two fields are equal is that they are identical, position by position. Thus, in (a) these two fields are not equal because the first position of one contains the letter J and that of the other contains a space. In (b) the entries are obviously not equal. In (c) the subject operand is shorter than the object operand. For this comparison, COBOL automatically extends the length of the shorter field, fills those positions with spaces, then makes the comparison using equal length fields. Obviously, these two are not equal. However, in (d) the compared fields are identical, so an equal condition results. The comparison of (e) is not equal because upper-case letters are different from lowercase letters.

If a greater or less determination is to be made, it is based on alphabetic ordering. That is, SMITH is greater than JONES because "A" is the "smallest" uppercase letter and "Z" is the "greatest." However, if fields being compared include both uppercase and lowercase letters and/or digits, then the ordering is determined by the *collating sequence*, the ordering of the characters in the character set. Collating sequence ordering of the upper and lowercase letters and the digits for internal coding used on personal computers is shown on the next page.

Figure 11-1

Object and Subject Fields for Comparison

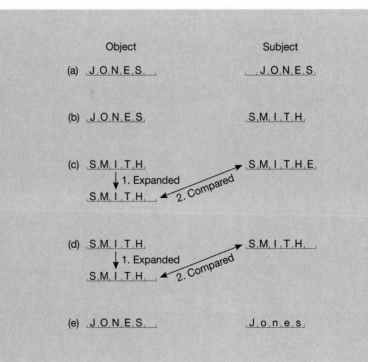

	Collating Sequence
Low	space
	0–9
	A–Z
High	a–z

Thus, in Figure 11-1(a) the subject is larger than the object because the letter *J* is larger than the space. Similarly, in (b) SMITH is larger than JONES, and in (e) Jones is larger than JONES because lowercase "o" is larger than uppercase "O".

Unfortunately, two different character sets are in common use: EBCDIC used by IBM mainframe computers and ASCII used by most other computers, including all personal computers. (The preceding sequence is for ASCII.) In EBCDIC, the sequence is reversed: lowercase letters, uppercase letters, and digits. You will learn more about the collating sequence in Chapter 15, when you study sorting.

Although you can compare a numeric field to a nonnumeric field, you must be careful to recognize that the comparison will take place as if both fields were defined as nonnumeric.

The Sign Test

Two other condition tests may be used in an IF statement: the sign test and the class test. The *sign test* simply determines whether a data item or arithmetic expression is positive (> 0), negative (< 0), or zero (= 0). Its basic form is as follows:

The sign test is not used often because a relational test can achieve the same result. However, it is sometimes useful for its documentation value.

The Class Test

The *class test* allows you to determine whether a data item is numeric, alphabetic, alphabetic uppercase, alphabetic lowercase, or consists of characters of a set of characters you have designated. Its general form is

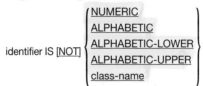

The class of a data item is determined as

■ NUMERIC if the data item contains only digits 0 through 9, with or without an operational sign

■ ALPHABETIC if the data item contains only uppercase letters *A* through *Z*, lowercase letters *a* through *z*, the space character, or any combination of uppercase letters, lowercase letters, and spaces

■ ALPHABETIC-LOWER if the data item contains only lowercase letters *a* through *z*, the space character, or any combination of lowercase letters and spaces

■ ALPHABETIC-UPPER if the data item contains only uppercase letters *A* through *Z*, the space character, or any combination of uppercase letters and spaces

With this capability, you can determine whether the data in the named data item is or is not alphabetic or numeric. A first reaction to this might be, "Does it make any difference whether or not a data value is, for instance, numeric?" The answer is a very positive *yes*. If your program adds two data items, they must be numeric; otherwise, the arithmetic operation becomes meaningless. On some computers, this will cause an error condition, which terminates execution of the program. On others, the program will not crash, but the result will be unpredictable.

The *class-name* category requires that you define a list of characters in the SPECIAL-NAMES paragraph of the CONFIGURATION SECTION of the ENVIRONMENT DIVISION. For instance, the following sequence of code defines two class names, the first representing the upper- and lowercase letter *Y* and the second the digits and the first three letters of the alphabet.

```
ENVIRONMENT DIVISION.
CONFIGURATION SECTION.
SPECIAL-NAMES.
    CLASS YES-RESPONSE IS "yY".
    CLASS VALID-CONTROL-CODE "0123456789ABC".
```

Within a program, the YES-RESPONSE might be used as follows:

```
DISPLAY "Do you want to perform this action <Y/N>?"
ACCEPT USER-RESPONSE
IF USER-RESPONSE IS YES-RESPONSE
    PERFORM 400-PROCESS-SPECIAL-CASE
ENDIF
```

For the second example (VALID-CONTROL-CODE), assume that your program must process a data item named CONTROL-CODE. If CONTROL-CODE contains any characters other than the digits 0 through 9 or the letters A, B, or C, then an error procedure must be performed. The needed IF statement would take the following form:

```
IF CONTROL-CODE IS NOT VALID-CONTROL-CODE
    PERFORM 900-CONTROL-CODE-ERROR
END-IF
```

More About the IF

An IF Statement within Another IF

Chapter 8 covered the point that the block of statements to be executed conditionally under an IF can include other IF statements. This IF within an IF is commonly called a *nested* IF. To illustrate this, consider the following example:

Example 11-1

Perform the following operations if the value of SENIORITY is greater than 20.
1. If E-CODE contains "P" then subtract 10 from AMOUNT and set the value of TEMP to 0.
2. Set AMOUNT-OUT equal to the value in AMOUNT.
3. Write to the EMPLOYEE file.
4. Increase the value of S-COUNT by 1.

At first thought, this might appear confusing. However, writing it in the following form clarifies its meaning:

```
IF SENIORITY is greater than 20
    1.  IF E-CODE is equal to "P"
            Subtract 10 from AMOUNT
            Move zero to TEMP
    2.  Move AMOUNT to AMOUNT-OUT
    3.  Write to the EMPLOYEE file
    4.  Increment S-COUNT by 1
```

As pseudocode, it appears as follows:

```
IF test condition
    IF E-CODE is equal to "P"
        Subtract 10 from AMOUNT
        Move zero to TEMP
    END-IF
    Move AMOUNT to AMOUNT-OUT
    Write to the EMPLOYEE file
    Increment S-COUNT by 1
END-IF
```

Converting this pseudocode to COBOL is a relatively simple task; the resulting code and corresponding logic are shown in Figure 11-2.

At first thought, forms such as this can be very confusing. However, if pseudocode is used to gradually refine the components, the end result is usually achieved with a minimum of pain.

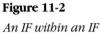

Figure 11-2

An IF within an IF

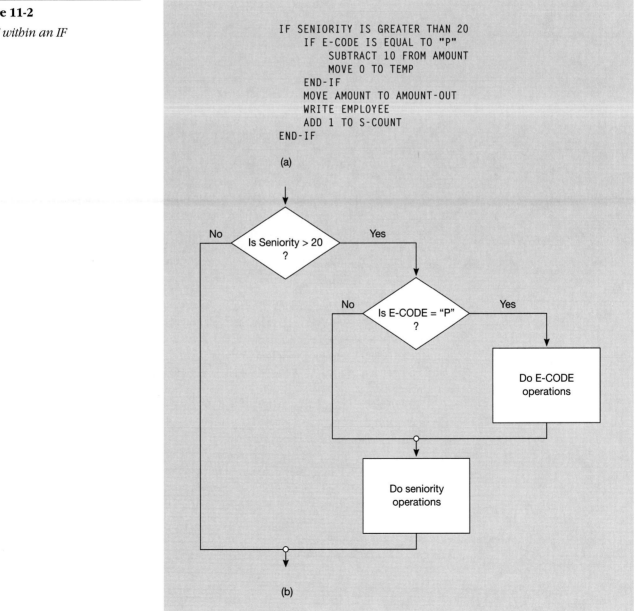

The CONTINUE Statement

As another example, assume that you must check E-CODE for a value of 9. If it is equal to 9, then execution must continue to the next statement, which involves writing an output record and continuing from there. If it does not equal 9, then the routine ERROR-CHECK must be executed before writing. The following statement to carry out this function is fairly simple:

```
IF E-CODE NOT EQUAL TO 9
    PERFORM ERROR-CHECK
END-IF
WRITE OUTPUT-RECORD
```

Occasionally, for the sake of documentation (or for some other reason), the programmer may not wish to use the negation in the relational operation. For this, a special "do nothing" statement named CONTINUE can be employed. The CONTINUE statement is a no-operation statement and can be used anywhere a conditional statement or an imperative statement may be used. It causes execution to continue to the next statement in the sequence. For instance, upon encountering the CONTINUE in the sequence

```
MOVE DETAIL-LINE TO REPORT-LINE
CONTINUE
WRITE REPORT-LINE
```

execution will immediately progress to the WRITE statement as if the CONTINUE were not there. Although of no value in this instance, it can be used in an IF to indicate that no action is to be taken under one of the options. For instance:

```
IF E-CODE = 9
    CONTINUE
ELSE
    PERFORM ERROR-CHECK
END-IF
WRITE OUTPUT-RECORD
```

In this instance, when the test condition is true, execution continues to the next statement (following the END-IF) since CONTINUE does nothing. If the condition is false, the ELSE option is exercised and ERROR-CHECK is performed. The CONTINUE is a convenient device to use when it allows a more exact coding representation of the English description. It is especially useful when the condition consists of two or more tests, a principle described in the next section.

Terminating the IF with a Period

Recall from Chapter 2 that each statement of a paragraph can be designated as an independent sentence by ending the statement with a period. Prior to COBOL-85, the use of periods was especially critical with the IF statement. The scope terminators (for instance, END-IF) provide much more flexibility and are the basis for the standard in this book. The period is used in the PROCEDURE DIVISION only after each paragraph name and after the last statement of each paragraph.

However, you can use a period following *any* statement within a paragraph. In particular, the period can be used to terminate the scope of an IF statement. Using a period for this purpose is shown in Figure 11-3(a); note that COBOL treats the two forms shown here identically.

Before COBOL-85, using the period to terminate an IF consisting of several conditionally executed statements was risky. For instance, consider the example of Figure 11-4(a), in which an extra period has been included accidentally. In spite of the indention, the ADD statement is not part of the IF; it will be executed during each pass through the program, regardless of the value in SENIORITY, as illustrated by the flowchart segment of Figure 11-4(b). In this case, it is the next statement following the IF. If you run the program containing this sequence, the value in the variable S-COUNT would be incorrect. If this variable were changed by other statements—as well as that of Figure 11-4—finding

Figure 11-3

Terminating the IF with a Period

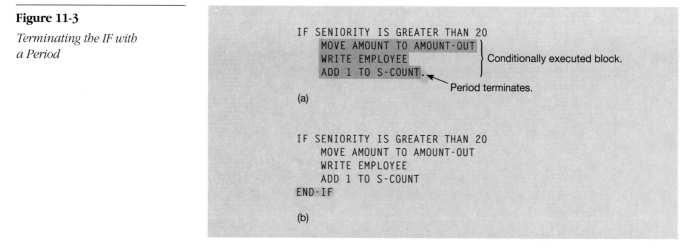

```
IF SENIORITY IS GREATER THAN 20
    MOVE AMOUNT TO AMOUNT-OUT ⎫
    WRITE EMPLOYEE            ⎬ Conditionally executed block.
    ADD 1 TO S-COUNT.         ⎭
                        ← Period terminates.
(a)


IF SENIORITY IS GREATER THAN 20
    MOVE AMOUNT TO AMOUNT-OUT
    WRITE EMPLOYEE
    ADD 1 TO S-COUNT
END-IF

(b)
```

the problem might be very difficult. It is simple errors of this type that are easily overlooked; you "see" what the indention tells you, not what the punctuation tells the compiler.

The same subtle problem potential does not exist when using the END-IF form because the compiler will detect an error. For instance, assume that this sequence has been entered as shown in Figure 11-5. Here the period terminates the IF statement. Then the compiler will see the END-IF and have no IF with which to associate it. An END-IF can only be used in conjunction with an IF.

Figure 11-4

A Difficult-to-Find Error

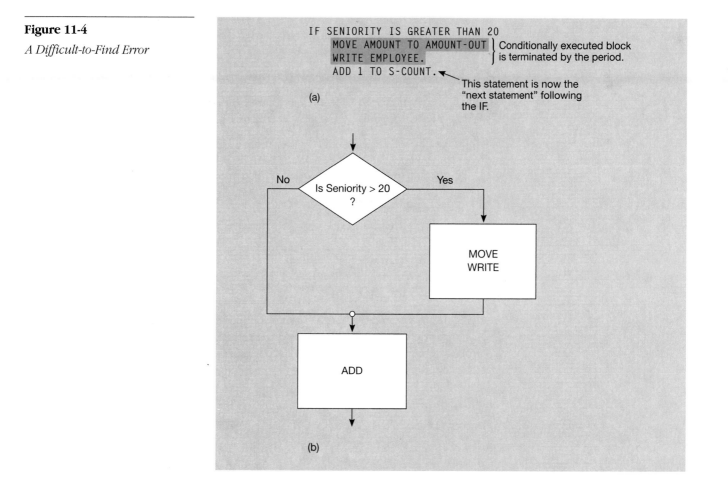

```
IF SENIORITY IS GREATER THAN 20
    MOVE AMOUNT TO AMOUNT-OUT ⎫ Conditionally executed block
    WRITE EMPLOYEE.           ⎬ is terminated by the period.
    ADD 1 TO S-COUNT. ←
                        This statement is now the
(a)                     "next statement" following
                        the IF.
```

(b)

Figure 11-5

An IF That Will Cause a
Compiler-Generated Error

```
IF SENIORITY IS GREATER THAN 20
    MOVE AMOUNT TO AMOUNT-OUT
    WRITE EMPLOYEE.                This is the IF statement.
                                   It is ended by this period.
    ADD 1 TO S-COUNT
END-IF                             This END-IF has no corresponding
                                   IF; therefore, the compiler signals
                                   an error.
```

Another factor to be considered with regard to the period as an IF terminator relates to using an IF statement within another IF or as part of another block structure. That is, the 1985 Standard defines an imperative statement in such a way as to exclude an IF unless it is terminated by an END-IF. In general, the explicit use of the END scope terminator is very clear with regard to its meaning. Examples in this book use it in all instances.

Compound Conditional Statements

Multiple Tests

Condition tests that you have considered have all involved a single condition. In practice, many situations occur in which an action is to be taken based on two or more conditions. To illustrate this concept and a variety of situations in which conditionals are used, let's consider the SFCREATE program of Chapter 4 (Figure 4-8). In this program, the user is queried about continuing by the following pair of statements:

```
DISPLAY "Record written. Enter 1 to repeat, 0 to end."
ACCEPT CONTIN.
```

Repeated execution of the main routine was via the following PERFORM statement:

```
PERFORM 110-ADD-RECORD UNTIL CONTIN = 0
```

Note that if a 0 is entered into CONTIN, execution of the loop will be terminated. Although the instructions to the user indicate a 1 causes repetition, you can see that any value other than 0 serves the purpose. One of the important tasks of any interactive program is to protect the user from his or her own blunders. Hence, it is good practice to verify all user responses. In this case, the program asks for a 0 or a 1, so the response should be checked. This forms the basis for the next example.

Example 11-2

A query routine is required that requests the user to enter a 0 or a 1. If anything else is entered, then an error message must be displayed and the user must be requested to reenter the response.

In this example, if the user response is 0 or 1, then execution should continue. If not, then the query should be repeated—this represents a loop. The pseudocode is

```
Repeat the following until response is 0 or 1
    Display instructions
    Accept response
    If response is other than 0 or 1
        display an error message.
```

Studying this pseudocode, you can see that you have a candidate for an in-line PERFORM. From what you have already seen of this problem, you know that the loop will be controlled by testing the value of CONTIN (the user response). You also know that if the condition is true when the PERFORM is first encountered, the loop will not be executed at all. Hence, the value of CONTIN must contain other than 0 or 1 to force execution of the loop at least once. With this in mind, the first conversion step to COBOL code is as follows.

```
         MOVE 2 TO CONTIN
         PERFORM UNTIL (CONTIN is 0 or 1)
             DISPLAY "Record written. Enter 1 to repeat, 0 to end."
             ACCEPT CONTIN
             IF  (CONTIN is not 0 and it is not 1)
                  DISPLAY "You must enter 0 or 1, try again"
                  DISPLAY " "
             END-IF
         END-PERFORM
```

The Logic of And and Or

The two conditional forms of the preceding code are expanded in a more formal way in Figure 11-6. Even though the English is clumsy, the meaning is quite clear. The portions enclosed within parentheses are called *compound conditionals* and are identical to their COBOL counterparts. In a compound conditional, the tests are joined by the word *and* or the word *or*. In the first example, an *or* is used. Note that the compound condition using an *or* is true if either of its conditions is true. If both are false, then the compound condition is false. Placing this in context of querying the user, this is what you desire. For example, assume that the user has entered the digit 2, in which case the loop should be repeated. Then you have

2 equal 0	false condition
2 equal 1	false condition

Hence, the loop will be performed another time. However, if a 1 is entered you would have

1 equal 0	false condition
1 equal 1	true condition

The compound condition would be true, and the PERFORM would not be executed again.

In the IF example, the condition is a little more confusing because of the *not* operator. However, consider the case of an entry 1 for this example:

1 not equal 0	true condition
1 not equal 1	false condition

Since the *and* requires that both component conditions be true for the compound condition to be true, the compound condition is false in this case. Hence, the error message will not be printed, which is the proper action if either 0 or 1 is entered.

Figure 11-6

Compound Conditional Forms

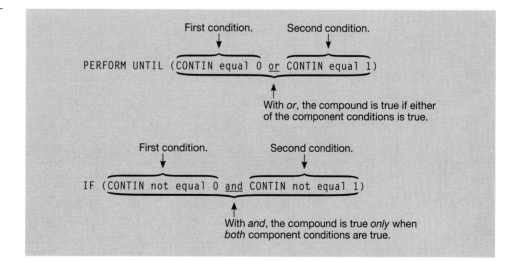

On the other hand, if an invalid entry of 2 has been made, then the error message will be printed because

2 not equal 0	true condition
2 not equal 1	true condition

Here both conditions are true (an invalid entry has been made) and the compound condition is true (the error message will be printed).

The AND and OR COBOL Logical Operators

In COBOL, the AND and OR (together with the NOT) are called *logical operators.* They take the same form and are used in COBOL exactly as shown in Figure 11-6. Thus, the COBOL code to monitor the user response becomes that shown in Figure 11-7. In forming compound conditionals such as this, be sure to use the precise COBOL form and do not be confused with English equivalents. Examples later in this chapter illustrate some abbreviated forms that are similar to the corresponding English forms.

Figure 11-7

Using Logical Operators— Example 11-2

```
MOVE 2 TO CONTIN
PERFORM UNTIL CONTIN = 0 OR CONTIN = 1
   DISPLAY "Record written.  Enter 1 to repeat, 0 to end."
   ACCEPT CONTIN
   IF CONTIN NOT = 0 AND CONTIN NOT = 1
      DISPLAY "You must enter 0 or 1, try again"
      DISPLAY
   END-IF
END-PERFORM
```

Hierarchy of Operations

The compound conditional statement can be further extended by using two or more operators. If several ANDs or several ORs are used to form a conditional, the effect is quite predictable. For example, the following condition is true only if *all* of the component conditions are true:

```
IF AMOUNT > 0 AND CREDIT = "Y" AND BALANCE < LIMIT ...
```

In a similar way, the following example with ORs is true if *any* of the component conditions is true:

```
IF HOLD = "Y" OR CREDIT = "N" OR BALANCE > LIMIT ...
```

These forms are fairly obvious; however, mixing ANDs and ORs is not as simple as it might appear. This is illustrated by the following example:

Example 11-3

A record-of-the-month club has adopted a new policy for rewarding active customers. The 320-CALCULATE-BONUS module is to be executed for those customer orders in which RECORDS-ORDERED is greater than 1 and STAR-CUST equal "Y" or BONUS-PNTS is greater than 10. For all others, the 310-CALCULATE-STANDARD module is to be executed.

Here you encounter the problem that the English statement of the problem is ambiguous. That is, in which of the following two ways should you interpret the statement?

1. (a) RECORDS-ORDERED > 1 and (b) STAR-CUST = "Y"
  or (c) BONUS-PNTS > 10

2. (a) RECORDS-ORDERED > 1
  and (b) STAR-CUST = "Y" or (c) BONUS-PNTS > 10

That these produce different results is clearly evident by using the sample values of Figure 11-8. In the first form, you see that the compound condition is true, but in the second case, it is false. The ambiguity of this problem statement is eliminated with the following restatement:

Example 11-3 Restated

A record-of-the-month club has adopted a new policy for rewarding active customers. The 320-CALCULATE-BONUS module is to be executed for those customer orders in which

      (a) RECORDS-ORDERED > 1

and (b) STAR-CUST = "Y" or (c) BONUS-PNTS > 10

For all others, the 310-CALCULATE-STANDARD module is to be executed.

The ambiguity that we experience in ordinary English does not exist in programming languages such as COBOL. The reason is that a strict set of *hierarchy* rules is utilized to determine the sequence of operations when evaluating conditional tests. When a compound conditional is evaluated, the hierarchy rules require that all AND operators be evaluated before OR operators. Therefore, the conditional

```
RECORDS-ORDERED > 1 AND STAR-CUST = "Y" OR BONUS-PNTS > 10
```

will *not* produce the result desired in Example 11-3 because it will be evaluated as the first form in Figure 11-8. This dilemma is resolved by the use of parentheses, which override the normal sequence. Using parentheses, the correct conditional form is as shown in Figure 11-9. In evaluating this conditional, the compiler will first examine the conditions within the parentheses, then carry out the OR operation. The result will be precisely what is required. When forming compound conditionals involving both ANDs and ORs, you should use parentheses always, even when the hierarchy order provides the desired result without them. If for no other reason, this practice provides better documentation and usually leads to fewer errors.

Figure 11-8

Illustrating an Ambiguity

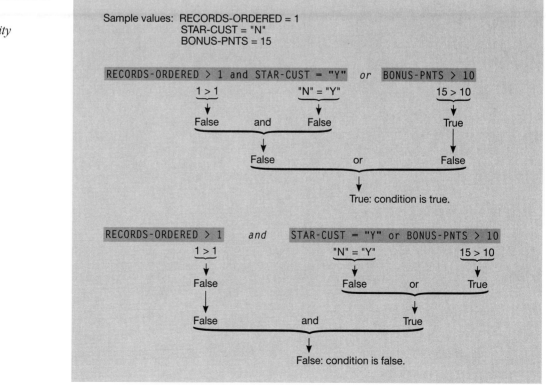

In evaluating the condition test, COBOL examines the statement from left to right a number of times, each time doing one of the steps in the hierarchy. When it has finished the last examination, the statement has been completely evaluated.

1. Expressions within parentheses are evaluated first, according to the hierarchy rules

2. Relation conditions are evaluated

3. NOT conditions are evaluated

4. AND conditions are evaluated

5. OR conditions are evaluated

Implied Subjects and Operators

The Implied Subject

A simple relational expression is made up of three parts: *subject, logical operator,* and *object.* For instance, in the expression

        A > B

these parts are

A subject (part to the left of the operator)
> operator
B object (part to the right of the operator)

The subject of a conditional statement is the data-name, literal, or arithmetic expression that appears to the left of the operator. You can expand this one step further; the condition

        A < B   AND   A > 0

is a compound conditional in which A is the subject of the first relational expression and is also the subject of the second. Since A is the subject of both conditions, an *implied subject* can be used. An implied subject is simply a subject that applies to two or more operators and objects. It can be used *only* with relational tests. The following example illustrates its use.

Figure 11-9

Multiple Conditions in a Test—Example 11-3

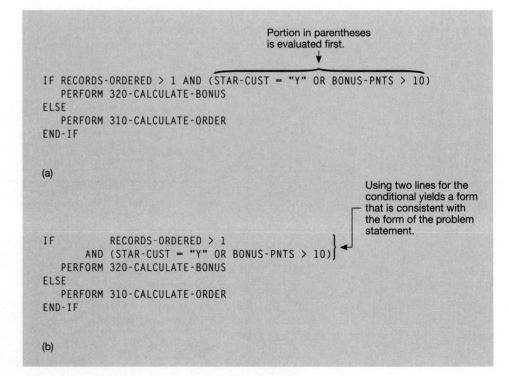

Portion in parentheses is evaluated first.

```
IF RECORDS-ORDERED > 1 AND (STAR-CUST = "Y" OR BONUS-PNTS > 10)
   PERFORM 320-CALCULATE-BONUS
ELSE
   PERFORM 310-CALCULATE-ORDER
END-IF
```

(a)

Using two lines for the conditional yields a form that is consistent with the form of the problem statement.

```
IF          RECORDS-ORDERED > 1
        AND (STAR-CUST = "Y" OR BONUS-PNTS > 10)
   PERFORM 320-CALCULATE-BONUS
ELSE
   PERFORM 310-CALCULATE-ORDER
END-IF
```

(b)

Figure 11-10

Implied Subject

```
IF STOCK-NUMBER > "0150"  AND  STOCK-NUMBER < "8500"
  CONTINUE
ELSE
  PERFORM 900-STOCK-NUMBER ERROR
END-IF

IF STOCK-NUMBER > "0150"  AND  < "8500"
  CONTINUE
ELSE
  PERFORM 900-STOCK-NUMBER ERROR
END-IF

IF STOCK-NUMBER NOT > "0150"  OR  NOT < "8500"
  PERFORM 900-STOCK-NUMBER-ERROR
END-IF
```

Example 11-4

A data file is to be edited for validity; that is, certain data in each record is to be tested to see that it falls within valid limits. One of the tests is that the field called STOCK-NUMBER must be greater than 150 but less than 8500. If STOCK-NUMBER is not within these limits, then perform 900-STOCK-NUMBER-ERROR.

The COBOL statements of Figure 11-10 illustrate three different ways of coding the required test. The first IF uses two relational tests in the conventional way. However, since the subject is STOCK-NUMBER for both tests, the name STOCK-NUMBER does not need to be repeated, as illustrated by the second and third examples. It is the explicit subject for the "> 0150" test and the implicit subject for the "< 8500" test. This is illustrated in Figure 11-11(a).

On the other hand, note that the NOT in the third example statement *cannot* be implied, since it is a part of the logical operator. Its relationship is illustrated in Figure 11-11(b).

This is an excellent example of the problems caused because COBOL is an "almost English" language. In conversation, the statement, "If it is not raining or snowing, I will go to the show tonight," would be understood to mean "If it is not raining and if it is not snowing. . . ." COBOL, however, would apply the "not" only to the operator with which it was associated and would interpret that condition test as "if it is not raining or if it is snowing." Thus, the COBOL form

```
        IF STOCK-NUMBER NOT > "0150" OR < "8500"
```

would be interpreted, "If STOCK-NUMBER is not greater than 0150, or if it is less than 8500," which would not produce the required result.

Figure 11-11

Explicit and Implicit Subjects

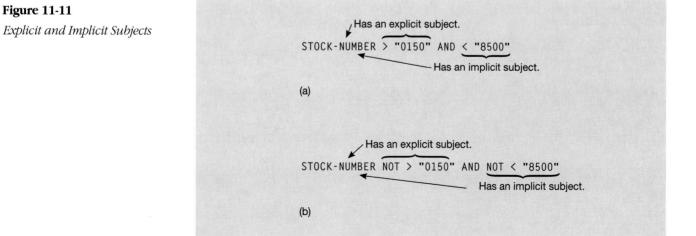

The Implied Operator

Example 11-4 illustrates the use of an implied subject (in which the subject remains the same and the relational operator and the object change). If a situation exists in which both the subject *and* the relational operator remain unchanged and only the object changes, then an implied operator may be used along with the implied subject. The following example illustrates this concept:

Example 11-5
In a billing program, a special 1.5% service charge is to be computed whenever STOCK-NUMBER has a value equal to 0348, 1650, or 4795.

Figure 11-12 includes three example sets of coding that will perform the required function. In both the second and third coding examples, STOCK-NUMBER is the subject for all three tests, so it appears only once: as the explicit subject of the "0348" test and the implicit subject for the "1650" and "4795" tests. The same is true of the relational operator, which is "=" in the second coding example and "NOT =" in the third coding example. The third statement again illustrates NOT as an integral part of the relational operator.

Implied subjects and operators can simplify the coding of many compound conditional statements. However, similar to the compound conditional statement itself, the implied subject and operator should be used with great care when incorporating them into a program.

Figure 11-12

Implied Operators

```
IF STOCK-NUMBER = "0348"
    OR STOCK-NUMBER = "1650"
    OR STOCK-NUMBER = "4795"
   MULTIPLY SALE-AMOUNT BY .015 GIVING SERVICE-CHARGE
END-IF

IF STOCK-NUMBER = "0348" OR "1650" OR "4795"
    MULTIPLY SALE-AMOUNT BY .015 GIVING SERVICE-CHARGE
END-IF

IF STOCK-NUMBER NOT = "0348" AND "1650" AND "4795"
   CONTINUE
ELSE
   MULTIPLY SALE-AMOUNT BY .015 GIVING SERVICE-CHARGE
END-IF
```

The EVALUATE Statement

The Case Structure

The IF statement allows you to implement the structured programming selection structure: the ability to perform either of two actions, depending on whether a given condition is true or false. Remember from Chapter 8 that another type of situation commonly occurs in computing, whereby the result of a test may cause one of several actions being taken—the case structure. To illustrate this, consider the following example:

Example 11-6
The contents of the variable TEST-CODE determine which of the following actions is to be taken in a program:

TEST-CODE	Action
1	PERFORM 320-PROCESS-STANDARD
2	PERFORM 330-PROCESS-COMP
	Increment COMP-COUNTER by 1
3-7	PERFORM 370-CATCH-ALL
	Increment CATCH-COUNTER by 1
	Move zero to CATCH-ACCUM
Any other value	PERFORM 910-PROCESS-CODE-ERROR

Figure 11-13

A Series of Selections

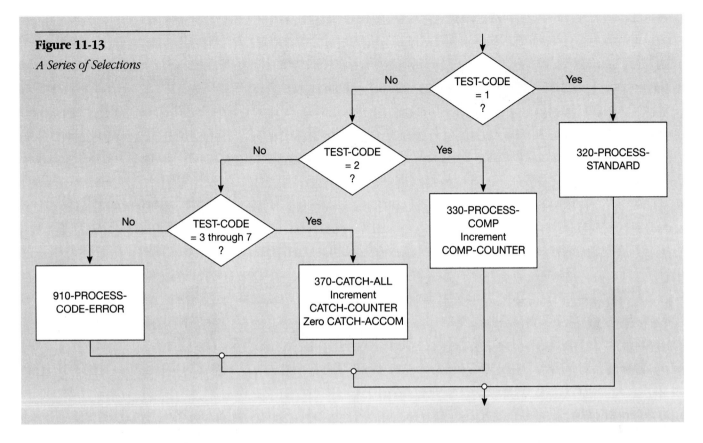

Here you have four different options, rather than two. The logic of this problem is illustrated by the series of selection structures in Figure 11-13. The solution uses a series of IF statements, one within the other, and is shown in Figure 11-14. Note the pairing of IFs and corresponding END-IFs.

Recall from Chapter 8 that the case structure is commonly shown in a flowchart such as Figure 11-15. Although the case can be coded using a series of IF's—as in Figure 11-14—the structure is sufficiently common that most modern languages, including COBOL-85, have special case types of statements to handle this form. In COBOL-85, the statement is EVALUATE.

Figure 11-14

Levels of IF

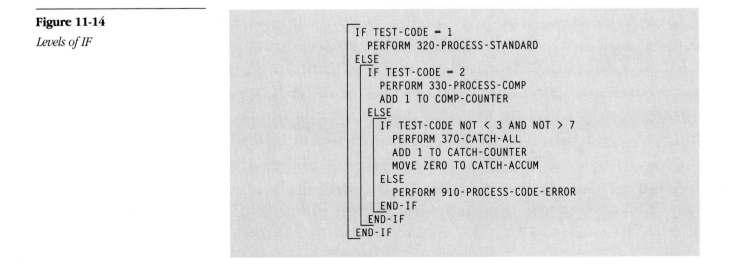

```
IF TEST-CODE = 1
    PERFORM 320-PROCESS-STANDARD
ELSE
    IF TEST-CODE = 2
        PERFORM 330-PROCESS-COMP
        ADD 1 TO COMP-COUNTER
    ELSE
        IF TEST-CODE NOT < 3 AND NOT > 7
            PERFORM 370-CATCH-ALL
            ADD 1 TO CATCH-COUNTER
            MOVE ZERO TO CATCH-ACCUM
        ELSE
            PERFORM 910-PROCESS-CODE-ERROR
        END-IF
    END-IF
END-IF
```

Figure 11-15

The Case Structure

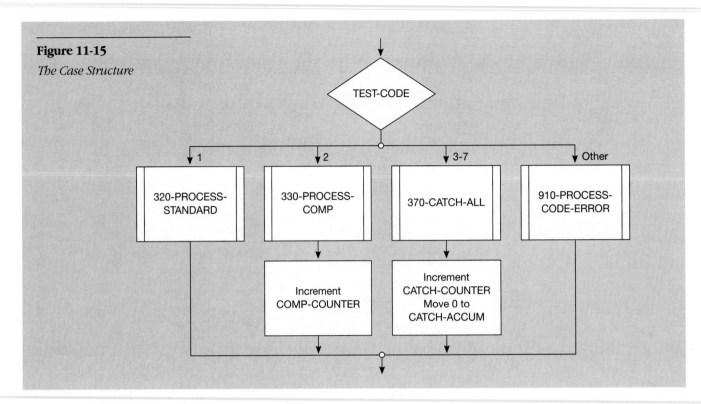

A Basic Form of the EVALUATE Statement

The EVALUATE statement (which was incorporated into COBOL by the 1985 Standard) is one of the most complex forms in COBOL. In the interest of simplicity, its entire general form is not introduced here. It is instead introduced in two "versions," which will make it relatively straightforward to use. The first, shown in Figure 11-16, is almost self-explanatory. The following are important points about this example:

1. The entry immediately following the keyword EVALUATE (TEST-CODE, in this case) is called the *selection subject*. It is the entry against which comparisons that follow will be made.

2. The entry immediately following each keyword WHEN is called the *selection object*. This is the entry to which the selection subject is compared.

Figure 11-16

The EVALUATE Statement

```
                          Selection subject.
                          ⎧‾‾‾‾‾‾‾‾‾⎫
              EVALUATE TEST-CODE

                  WHEN 1  ◄──────────────────────  Selection objects.
                     PERFORM 320-PROCESS-STANDARD

                  WHEN 2  ◄─────────────────────┐
                     PERFORM 330-PROCESS-COMP
                     ADD 1 TO COMP-COUNTER

                  WHEN 3 THROUGH 7  ◄───────────┤
                     PERFORM 370-CATCH-ALL
                     ADD 1 TO CATCH-COUNTER
                     MOVE ZERO TO CATCH-ACCUM

                  WHEN OTHER  ◄─────────────────┘
                     PERFORM 910-PROCESS-CODE-ERROR

              END-EVALUATE
```

3. For evaluation purposes, comparisons are made in exactly the same way as an equal comparison in an IF statement. The first equal condition that occurs causes the corresponding sequence of object statements to be executed. Upon completion of the sequence, control is passed to the END-EVALUATE and execution of the EVALUATE is completed. For instance, if TEST-CODE contains a 2, then 330-PROCESS-COMP will be executed, 1 added to COMP-COUNTER, and control passed to the END-EVALUATE.

4. A range of values may be specified; for instance

   3 THROUGH 7

   means exactly what it says in English—that is, any value in the range 3 through 7 inclusive.

5. If none of the preceding WHENs produces an equal condition, then the OTHER option is executed. This option is not required and can be omitted if no action is to be taken when none of the preceding conditions is satisfied.

The general form of this limited version of the EVALUATE is as follows:

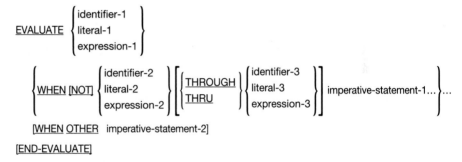

Another Form of the EVALUATE Statement

Situations often arise in programming in which one of several actions is to be taken, but the test conditions for each is quite different from the others. The following example illustrates this.

Example 11-7

Under the terms of a new union contract, the record-of-the-month club of previous examples must pay certain employees special benefits, depending on their age and seniority with the company, as follows:

> If (age 60 or greater) and (seniority 20 or greater)
> perform 410-CALCULATE-SPECIAL-BENEFITS-1
>
> If (age 60 or greater) and (seniority less than 20)
> perform 420-CALCULATE-SPECIAL-BENEFITS-2
>
> If (seniority 20 or greater) and (age less than 60)
> perform 430-CALCULATE-SPECIAL-BENEFITS-3
>
> Otherwise perform 400-CALCULATE-STANDARD-BENEFITS

As with Example 11-6, the English of this statement in Figure 11-17 practically tells you what it does. The following are important points about this example:

1. The selection subject is simply the reserved word TRUE, a logical value. Hence, the selection objects must give logical values of either true or false.

2. Execution of this statement involves evaluating the selection objects (following the WHENs) until one is found with a truth value matching the selection subject (TRUE in this case). When that occurs, the corresponding object statements are executed and control passes to the END-EVALUATE.

3. In the second WHEN, only the AGE is tested for a value equal to or greater than 60. SENIORITY need not be tested. If the AGE criterion is satisfied and the SENIORITY is not less than 20, the first WHEN condition would have been satisfied.

4. If none of the WHEN subjects is true, then the OTHER option is executed.

The general form of this limited version of the EVALUATE statement is as follows:

$$\underline{\text{EVALUATE}} \begin{Bmatrix} \text{TRUE} \\ \text{FALSE} \end{Bmatrix}$$

{<u>WHEN</u> [<u>NOT</u>] logical-expression imperative-statement-1} ...

[<u>WHEN</u> <u>OTHER</u> imperative-statement-2]

[<u>END-EVALUATE</u>]

Figure 11-17

Another Form of the EVALUATE Statement

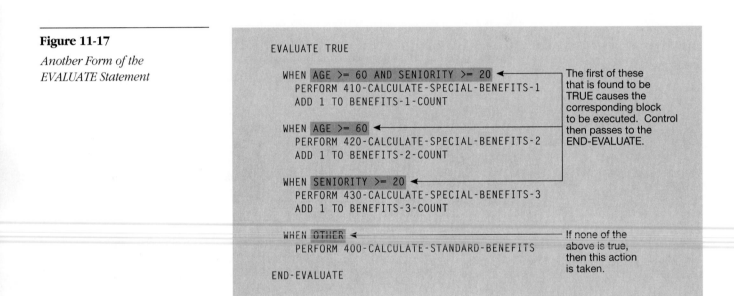

```
EVALUATE TRUE

    WHEN AGE >= 60 AND SENIORITY >= 20        The first of these
        PERFORM 410-CALCULATE-SPECIAL-BENEFITS-1    that is found to be
        ADD 1 TO BENEFITS-1-COUNT                   TRUE causes the
                                                    corresponding block
    WHEN AGE >= 60                              to be executed. Control
        PERFORM 420-CALCULATE-SPECIAL-BENEFITS-2    then passes to the
        ADD 1 TO BENEFITS-2-COUNT                   END-EVALUATE.

    WHEN SENIORITY >= 20
        PERFORM 430-CALCULATE-SPECIAL-BENEFITS-3
        ADD 1 TO BENEFITS-3-COUNT

    WHEN OTHER                                  If none of the
        PERFORM 400-CALCULATE-STANDARD-BENEFITS     above is true,
                                                    then this action
END-EVALUATE                                        is taken.
```

Programmed Switches

The Concept of the Programmed Switch

You have learned how the IF statement can be used to evaluate simple or complex conditions and then to carry out selected operations based on the results of that evaluation. But sometimes the programmer faces a more complicated problem.

Earlier in this book, you learned that a programmed switch is a data item whose value is changed at one point in a program for the purpose of affecting program execution at another point in the program. Often a programmer needs to know whether a particular condition has existed in the past during execution of the program, as opposed to whether it currently exists. In such cases, the program's path must be modified on the basis of whether the particular condition has existed at *any* time during program execution. One characteristic of the programmed switch is that it is set in either of two ways: *on* and *off*. A programmed switch is nothing more than a storage area that can be assigned either of two values by the program in order to indicate whether the desired condition has occurred. (It may be one *or more* characters long.) The programmer *initializes* the switch to one of its two values by using a value clause in the DATA DIVISION entry or by moving the desired initial value into it in the PROCEDURE DIVISION. When the particular condition occurs that the programmer has been looking for, the switch is set by changing it to the other of its two values. Then, at the proper time in the program, the program *tests* the switch with an IF statement. If it still contains its original value, then the particular condition has not occurred during the execution of the program. However, if the switch contains its other value, then the condition has occurred. In either case, the program can be directed to take the desired action based on the contents of the programmed switch. Appropriate lines of code from the SEQ-LIST program (Figure 5-13) are included here as Figure 11-18 to review this concept.

Although the EOF switch has used values of YES and NO, this choice is up to the programmer because any two values will do. Some commonly used switch values are

| YES | Y | ON | 1 | meaning switch is ON |
| NO | N | OFF | 0 | meaning switch is OFF |

Switches are commonly used in two ways. One use is to set its initial value in the VALUE clause and then change it to its new value at some point during execution. This is the EOF technique illustrated in Figure 11-18. The other use involves a switch that is continually changing back and forth during execution of the program.

Examples of Programmed Switches

Examples 11-8 and 11-9 illustrate two uses of the programmed switch. In an effort to allow the programmed switch concept to be illustrated as clearly as possible, only the applicable DATA DIVISION and PROCEDURE DIVISION coding is shown.

Example 11-8

A program is required that will edit a file of records for validity. Each valid record is to be printed, and each invalid record is to be printed with a special error message. If no errors are detected, then the message NO ERRORS DETECTED is to be printed at the conclusion of the program.

Figure 11-19 shows the appropriate coding of the programmed switch. Here the values N (no errors) and Y (yes, there were errors) were selected for ERROR-SWITCH. The switch is initialized to N. It will remain that way throughout the program unless the *record valid test* is false and the ELSE option is executed. Thus, the condition of ERROR-SWITCH at the end of the program indicates whether errors were detected. If errors were detected, the program "remembers" the fact by changing the value of ERROR-SWITCH from N to Y.

Example 11-9

At the end of each month, a bank performs a service charge determination for each of its customers. Input data for each customer consists of transactions arranged in daily batches. If the balance at the end of any day falls below $150.00, then a monthly service charge of $2.00 must be assessed; otherwise, there is no service charge.

Figure 11-18

The EOF Switch

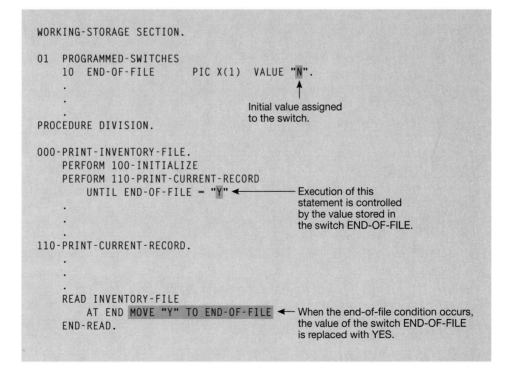

```
WORKING-STORAGE SECTION.

01  PROGRAMMED-SWITCHES
    10  END-OF-FILE      PIC X(1)  VALUE "N".
    .
    .                                          Initial value assigned
    .                                          to the switch.
PROCEDURE DIVISION.

000-PRINT-INVENTORY-FILE.
    PERFORM 100-INITIALIZE
    PERFORM 110-PRINT-CURRENT-RECORD
        UNTIL END-OF-FILE = "Y"  ◄──────── Execution of this
    .                                      statement is controlled
    .                                      by the value stored in
    .                                      the switch END-OF-FILE.
110-PRINT-CURRENT-RECORD.
    .

    .
    READ INVENTORY-FILE
        AT END MOVE "Y" TO END-OF-FILE  ◄── When the end-of-file condition occurs,
    END-READ.                               the value of the switch END-OF-FILE
                                            is replaced with YES.
```

Figure 11-19

A Simple Error Switch—
Example 11-8

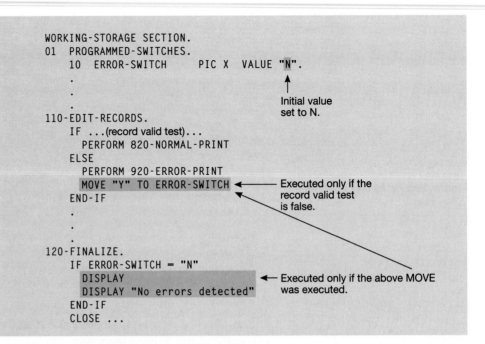

```
WORKING-STORAGE SECTION.
01  PROGRAMMED-SWITCHES.
    10  ERROR-SWITCH    PIC X  VALUE "N".
                                        ↑
                                   Initial value
                                   set to N.
  .
  .
110-EDIT-RECORDS.
    IF ...(record valid test)...
        PERFORM 820-NORMAL-PRINT
    ELSE
        PERFORM 920-ERROR-PRINT
        MOVE "Y" TO ERROR-SWITCH ◄──── Executed only if the
    END-IF                              record valid test
  .                                     is false.
  .
  .
120-FINALIZE.
    IF ERROR-SWITCH = "N"
        DISPLAY
        DISPLAY "No errors detected" ◄── Executed only if the above MOVE
    END-IF                               was executed.
    CLOSE ...
```

The applicable coding is shown in Figure 11-20. In this example, the switch is used to "remember" if a particular condition (BALANCE < 150.00) occurred as the transactions for the customer were being processed. The values selected for the switch are

Value	Implication
0	Balance has dropped below 150.00 at some point
1	Balance has never dropped below 150.00

Figure 11-20

A Programmed Switch—
Example 11-9

```
WORKING-STORAGE SECTION.
01  PROGRAMMED-SWITCHES.
    10  LOW-BALANCE    PIC X  VALUE 1.
  .
  .
  .
300-PROCESS-CUSTOMER.
    PERFORM 350-PROCESS-CUST-TRANSACTIONS UNTIL ...(next customer criterion)...
    PERFORM 500-CALCULATE-CUSTOMER-SUMMARY
  .
  .
  .
350-PROCESS-CUST-TRANSACTIONS.
    PERFORM 400-PROCESS-TRANSACTION
    IF BALANCE < 150
        MOVE 0 TO LOW-BALANCE ◄──── Move 0 to LOW-BALANCE only
    END-IF                          if BALANCE is less than 150.
  .
  .
  .
500-CALCULATE-CUSTOMER-SUMMARY.
    IF LOW-BALANCE = 0
        MOVE 2.00 TO SERVICE-CHARGE ⎫◄── If BALANCE never dropped below 150,
        MOVE 1 TO LOW-BALANCE       ⎬    LOW-BALANCE will still be 1 and this
    ELSE                            ⎭    sequence will not be executed.
        MOVE ZERO TO SERVICE-CHARGE ◄── Set switch back to 1 for
    END-IF                              processing next customer.
```

The switch is required because the program needs to know if the customer's balance went below $150.00 at any time during the month. If it did, LOW-BALANCE = 0 will "remember" the fact, even if the ending balance is well above $150.00.

Since the test is to be made for each customer, the switch must be initialized to 1 at the beginning of each customer's processing. The VALUE clause accomplished this for the first customer; the CUST-SUMMARY routine accomplishes it for all other customers by resetting LOW-BALANCE to 1 if it has been changed to 0.

Condition Names

Level 88 Entries

A good COBOL program has two characteristics: it does what it is supposed to do and it can be understood by anyone who reads it. Clarity can be achieved to a great degree by the use of good data-names, but a problem may arise when the program refers to data that exists in coded form. No one would have much trouble interpreting

```
       IF GENDER-CODE = "F"
   or  IF MARITAL-STATUS = "M"
```

But suppose a color code can have a value of 1, 2, 3, 4, or 5 for the colors red, blue, green, yellow and orange, respectively. If, in trying to debug a program, you encounter

```
   IF COLOR-CODE = 3
```

you cannot tell at a glance the color for which the test is being made. Similarly, if a student record processing program refers to

```
   SCHOLARSHIP-CODE = 3
```

does this indicate a student who is on the Dean's List, one who is average, or one who is failing?

To provide documentation for such condition tests, COBOL permits the assignment of *condition names* to conditions. Thus, instead of coding

```
   IF COLOR = 3
```

the programmer can code

```
   IF GREEN
```

Obviously, this makes the condition test obvious to anyone reading the program. A condition name is assigned the special level number 88 in the DATA DIVISION. It consists of the level number (88), the name assigned by the programmer to the condition, and a VALUE clause that gives the value to be tested.

Examples Using Condition Names

Coding and using condition names are illustrated in the following Examples 11-10 and 11-11.

Example 11-10

A flag manufacturer purchases cloth in three colors: red, white, and blue. The company maintains an inventory file that contains a record for each type and color of cloth. The record contains a one-digit color code recorded with the appropriate value as follows:

1   red
2   white
3   blue

The segment of the DATA DIVISION shown in Figure 11-21 illustrates how the 88-level entry is defined. Here the names RED, WHITE, and BLUE are assigned to the conditions as follows:

Condition Name	Equivalent Condition
RED	COLOR = 1
WHITE	COLOR = 2
BLUE	COLOR = 3

Note that when defining the 88-level entry in the DATA DIVISION, this entry must immediately follow the elementary item to which it is assigned. Then in the PROCEDURE DIVISION, any IF statement testing for color can use the condition name in place of the relational expression. That is, in the examples of Figure 11-22, each pair is equivalent.

An especially convenient feature of the condition names is that COBOL allows the name to be assigned a given value or a range of values. Example 11-11 illustrates a range.

Example 11-11

A college wishes to group its students into the categories shown according to their cumulative GPA (grade point average).

Group	Cumulative GPA
GPA-HONORS	3.50 and up
GPA-GOOD	2.50–3.49
GPA-AVERAGE	2.00–2.49
GPA-PROBATIONARY	Below 2.00

The DATA DIVISION segment of Figure 11-23 defines the condition names corresponding to the required ranges. Any test in the PROCEDURE DIVISION can now use the condition names in place of relational tests, as illustrated by the statement pairs of Figure 11-24. Because GPA-GOOD has been defined in the condition name entry as meaning CUM-GPA > 2.49 AND < 3.50, either coding can be used.

Figure 11-21

Defining Condition Names— Example 11-10

```
01  FABRIC-RECORD.
    10  RECORD-CODE    PIC X(2).
    10  FABRIC-TYPE    PIC X(15).
    10  COLOR          PIC 9.
        88     COLOR-IS-RED     VALUE 1.
        88     COLOR-IS-WHITE   VALUE 2.
        88     COLOR-IS-BLUE    VALUE 3.
    10  DISTRIBUTOR    PIC X(3).
```

These 88-level items relate to the item immediately preceding them (COLOR).

Figure 11-22

Using Condition Names

```
IF COLOR-IS-RED PERFORM R-ROUTINE
IF COLOR = 1 PERFORM R-ROUTINE
```
Equivalent

```
IF COLOR-IS-WHITE PERFORM W-ROUTINE
IF COLOR = 2 PERFORM W-ROUTINE
```
Equivalent

```
IF COLOR-IS-BLUE PERFORM B-ROUTINE
IF COLOR = 3 PERFORM B-ROUTINE
```
Equivalent

In Example 11-10, each condition name was assigned a concrete value. In Example 11-11, each condition name was assigned a range of values by use of the THRU clause. In each example, the condition name (88-level) entries immediately follow the data-names to which they apply and are indented for the sake of clarity. The condition name statement is the only COBOL statement that permits the use of THRU in a VALUE clause, and the only one that permits the use of a VALUE clause in the FILE SECTION.

Condition names can be very useful in cases in which a condition is referenced several times in a program. If the value of the condition changes, the program can be modified by simply changing the 88-level entry. When using condition names, be certain to select meaningful names or else they will have little documentation value. For instance, in a long program, the statement

```
IF GOOD...
```

gives no indication of what is being tested. However, the condition name GPA-GOOD more clearly identifies the test condition as follows:

```
IF GPA-GOOD...
```

As with the other forms of the condition test, condition names should be used where they simplify or clarify the program.

Using the SET Command with Condition Names

The COBOL-85 Standard includes an extension of previous versions that is very convenient to use for conditions that can be either true or false. For instance, the END-OF-FILE variable could assume values of "Y" or "N"; the CONTIN variable could assume values of 0 or 1. Now consider the following data definitions:

```
10  END-OF-FILE-SW   PIC X.
    88  END-OF-FILE  VALUE "Y"  FALSE "N"
```

This effectively sets up the following corresponding relationships.

Contents of EOF-SWITCH	Value of END-OF-FILE
Y	TRUE
N	FALSE

Figure 11-23

Ranges in Condition Names

Figure 11-24

Using Condition Names with Ranges of Values

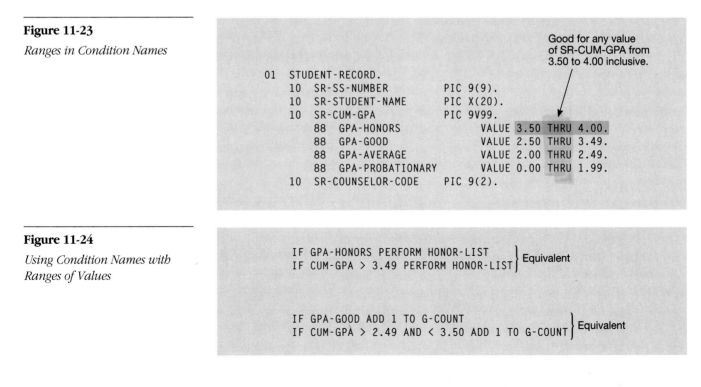

Now instead of coding

```
MOVE "Y" TO END-OF-FILE-SW
```

you can code

```
SET END-OF-FILE TO TRUE
```

These actions are equivalent. With the combination of this form of the condition name and the SET command, code to process until the end of file is reached can be as shown in Figure 11-25(a). For comparison, the equivalent code using the previous method is shown in Figure 11-25(b). This form is convenient and will be used in example programs that follow.

You should be aware that use of the FALSE phrase, although included in the *CODASYL COBOL Journal of Development 1984* and in RM/COBOL-85, is not included in the COBOL-85 Standard.

In using condition names, you will often find that all reference in the program is to the condition name and none is to the data item itself. For instance, in Figure 11-25(a) it is unnecessary to refer to END-OF-FILE-SW because the SET statement and all tests refer to END-OF-FILE. In situations such as this, it is unnecessary to name the data item. That is, the switch could be defined as follows:

```
10                    PIC X.
    88  END-OF-FILE  VALUE "Y"  FALSE "N"
```

Most switches in future programs of this book will be defined in this way.

Figure 11-25

Using the SET Statement

```
01  PROGRAMMED-SWITCHES.
    10  END-OF-FILE-SW      PIC X(1).
        88  END-OF-FILE  VALUE "Y"  FALSE "N".    .
        .
        .
        .
PROCEDURE DIVISION.

000-PRINT-INVENTORY-FILE.
    PERFORM 100-INITIALIZE
    PERFORM 110-PRINT-CURRENT-RECORD
        UNTIL END-OF-FILE      Note: Test refers to
    PERFORM 120-FINALIZE            END-OF-FILE, not
    STOP RUN.                       END-OF-FILE-SW.

100-INITIALIZE.
    OPEN INPUT INVENTORY-FILE
    OPEN OUTPUT REPORT-FILE
    SET END-OF-FILE TO FALSE  ◄── Initialize the switch
    READ INVENTORY-FILE            in the 100 module.
        AT END SET END-OF-FILE TO TRUE
    END-READ.
```

(a)

```
01  PROGRAMMED-SWITCHES.
    10  END-OF-FILE-SW      PIC X(1).
        .
        .
        .
PROCEDURE DIVISION.

000-PRINT-INVENTORY-FILE.
    PERFORM 100-INITIALIZE
    PERFORM 110-PRINT-CURRENT-RECORD
        UNTIL END-OF-FILE-SW = "Y"
    PERFORM 120-FINALIZE
    STOP RUN.

100-INITIALIZE.
    OPEN INPUT INVENTORY-FILE
    OPEN OUTPUT REPORT-FILE
    MOVE "N" TO END-OF-FILE-SW
    READ INVENTORY-FILE
        AT END MOVE "Y" TO END-OF-FILE-SW
    END-READ.
```

(b)

Chapter Summary

General

This chapter's IF statement provides the selection structure of structured programming.

Three types of tests can be used in conditional statements:

1. *Relation:* allows for one or more values to be compared to others
2. *Sign:* determines if a number is negative, zero, or positive
3. *Class:* determines whether data in a variable is numeric or alphabetic

The term *imperative statement* is defined as a PROCEDURE DIVISION statement that
(a) is an unconditional statement and starts with a verb or
(b) is a conditional statement and is terminated by its explicit scope
   terminator

The AND and OR are logical operators that are used to form compound test conditions in which the determination involves a given condition *and* another, or a given condition *or* another.

The hierarchy of actions in determining the truth value of a complex expression is

1. Expressions within parentheses are evaluated first, according to the hierarchy rules
2. Relation conditions are evaluated
3. NOT conditions are evaluated
4. AND conditions are evaluated
5. OR conditions are evaluated

If the same subject is used for two or more relational tests of a compound conditional; for instance

```
A < B AND A > 0
```

then the subject can be implied as follows:

```
A < B AND  > 0
```

If both the same subject and relational operator are used for two or more relational tests of a compound conditional; for instance

```
STOCK-NUMBER  = "0348"
OR STOCK-NUMBER  = "1650"
OR STOCK-NUMBER  = "4795"
```

then the subject and the operator can be implied as follows:

```
STOCK-NUMBER  = "0348" OR "1650" OR "4795"
```

Condition names provide the ability to equate an identifier to represent a particular test condition. For instance, in the example of this chapter, the test condition

```
COLOR = 3
```

was equated to the condition name COLOR-IS-BLUE by use of a level 88 item in the DATA DIVISION. Condition names may be used in many instances to implement programmed switches.

The IF statement provides the selection capability in which either of two actions can be taken. By comparison, the EVALUATE statement provides the case capability, which is the ability to execute any of a number of alternative actions, depending on a tested condition.

A programmed switch is a software device whereby the result of an action at one place in a program can be used to take action at some later point in the program.

COBOL Language Elements

The COBOL statements that you have studied in this chapter are

CONTINUE This is a no-operation statement; when encountered in a program, execution simply continues to the next statement. It is commonly used as an IF option in order to better match the form of a condition to the nature of the application.

EVALUATE Provides for the implementation of the case structure whereby any one of two or more actions is to be taken, depending upon the result of one or more conditions. For simplicity, the EVALUATE is considered in two forms in this chapter; their general formats are as follows:

$$\underline{\text{EVALUATE}} \left\{ \begin{array}{l} \text{identifier-1} \\ \text{literal-1} \\ \text{expression-1} \end{array} \right\}$$

$$\left\{ \underline{\text{WHEN}}\ [\underline{\text{NOT}}] \left\{ \begin{array}{l} \text{identifier-2} \\ \text{literal-2} \\ \text{expression-2} \end{array} \right\} \left[\left\{ \begin{array}{l} \underline{\text{THROUGH}} \\ \underline{\text{THRU}} \end{array} \right\} \left\{ \begin{array}{l} \text{identifier-3} \\ \text{literal-3} \\ \text{expression-3} \end{array} \right\} \right] \text{imperative-statement-1...} \right\}...$$

[WHEN OTHER imperative-statement-2]

[END-EVALUATE]

$$\underline{\text{EVALUATE}} \left\{ \begin{array}{l} \underline{\text{TRUE}} \\ \underline{\text{FALSE}} \end{array} \right\}$$

{WHEN [NOT] logical-expression imperative-statement-1} ...

[WHEN OTHER imperative-statement-2]

[END-EVALUATE]

IF Provides for implementation of the selection structure. Its general form is as follows:

  IF condition
   imperative-statement-1
  [ELSE
   imperative-statement-2]
  END-IF

SET Allows you to change the truth value of condition name from true to false or from false to true.

Other language elements that you have studied in this chapter are

AND Logical operator that allows a condition test in which both of two conditions must be true

OR Logical operator that allows a condition test in which either of two conditions may be true

The *condition* in any conditional statement can be any of three types: relation, sign, or class. Their general forms are

Relation

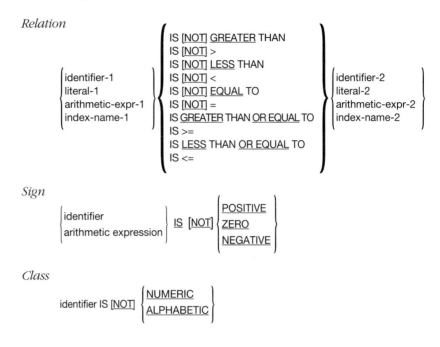

Sign

Class

Programming Conventions

Always terminate an IF with an END-IF; do not use a period. Repeating from an earlier chapter, periods are used only following the paragraph name and after the last statement of a paragraph.

When forming compound relational conditions involving both AND and OR logical operators, always use parentheses to indicate the order in which evaluations are to be made. Do so even if the natural hierarchy does not require them. This makes the condition more readable and easily understood.

To improve readability, write condition expressions in a form that is consistent with the English description of the application. When used this way, the CONTINUE statement can be helpful.

Use indention rules with the EVALUATE statement. Each condition should be indented either two or four spaces; corresponding actions under the conditions should be indented an additional two or four spaces.

When using condition names, make certain that each condition name adequately describes the condition. Documentation value is lost if you must refer back to its definition in the DATA DIVISION whenever you see it in the PROCEDURE DIVISION.

**Error Prevention/
Detection**

When writing nested IF statements, always use indention to indicate each level of IF. If you have several levels, you may wish to indent two spaces rather than four. Check each IF to be certain you have a corresponding END-IF. Sometimes it is helpful to connect each IF with its corresponding END-IF with a line (on the program listing), as illustrated in Figure 11-14.

When checking a condition, step through it using sample values to ensure that it will perform the function you desire—refer to the example of Figure 11-8. Be certain to test all possibilities.

Exercise caution when using implied subjects or operators. Be careful of an English description that may be misleading because it is similar to the proper COBOL form.

Questions and Exercises

Key Terminology

Give a brief description of each of the following terms that were introduced in this chapter.

class condition	implied object	relational operator
collating sequence	implied subject	selection object
compound conditional	logical operator	selection subject
condition name	nested IF	sign condition
hierarchy rules	programmed switch	
imperative statement	relation condition	

General Questions

1. The relational test can involve identifiers or literals. Would it be practical to compare two literals? Explain.

2. Determine whether FIELDX or FIELDY is the greater in each of the following cases:

	FIELDX		FIELDY	
	Contents	PICTURE	Contents	PICTURE
a.	123	9(3)	00106	9(5)
b.	0123	9(4)	00106	9(5)
c.	RALSTON	X(7)	CHARLES	X(7)
d.	JONES	X(5)	JOHNSON	X(7)
e.	JONES	X(5)	JONES	X(7)
f.	Jones	X(5)	Johnson	X(7)

3. What is a "nested" IF? Why would a programmer want to use it?

4. In compound conditionals, the tests are joined by the word "AND" or the word "OR". What is the difference between using each of these words?

5. What type of structure does the EVALUATE statement represent and why is it useful?

6. Why are "programmed switches" beneficial to the programmer?

7. What is the purpose of level 88 entries in a COBOL program?

Questions Relating to the Example Programs

1. What would happen in the program segment of Figure 11-20 if the switch LOW-BALANCE were not reset to 1 in the 500-CALCULATE-CUSTOMER-SUMMARY module?

2. What will result from the first IF statement shown in Figure 11-24 if the VALUE for the 88 GPA-HONORS condition name is 2.50 through 4.00? Assume the other VALUES are as shown.

3. What will happen to the logic of the nested IF statement in Figure 11-14 if the line IF TEST-CODE NOT < 3 AND NOT > 7 is removed?

4. Figure 11-16 is an EVALUATE statement that is equivalent to the IF statement in Figure 11-14. What occurs in either case if the WHEN...PERFORM 910-PROCESS-CODE-ERROR is left out by the programmer?

5. In Figure 11-25, what happens if the programmer codes the AT END phrase of the READ statement to say "SET END-OF-FILE TO FALSE"?

Writing Program Statements

1. Write relational tests for each of the following:
   a. New balance exceeds credit limit
   b. Record type is not zero
   c. Union dues are less than or equal to maximum dues
   d. Number of dependents is four or more
   e. Inventory code is F8117G

2. Write the condition form for each of the following:
   a. AMOUNT-IN is less than 0 (give two types of test for this)
   b. SALARY is not numeric

3. Write COBOL statements to perform each of the following operations, using the basic IF form described in the preceding pages:
   a. If CHECK-VALUE is 9, then display the message "Check value point"
   b. If GPA is equal to or exceeds 3.2, then increase CREDIT-POINTS by 1
   c. Calculate COMMISSION, given SALES, QUOTA, LOW-RATE, and HIGH-RATE as follows:

   if SALES exceed QUOTA
       COMMISSION = 1.2 x SALES x HIGH-RATE + 500
   if SALES does not exceed QUOTA
       COMMISSION = 1.2 x SALES x LOW-RATE + 500

   In both cases, add COMMISSION to TOTAL-AMOUNT and continue processing.

4. For only those employees with a value of "A" for CLASSIFICATION, perform ROUTINE-A if the value of GROSS is equal to or greater than 2,000, or ROUTINE-B if the value of GROSS is less than 2,000.

5. Write a single IF statement for each of the following:
   a. PERFORM PARTIAL-SS if YTD-SS is less than 495.00 and GROSS-PAY is more than 100.00
   b. PERFORM DANGER-ROUTINE if DEBT-AMOUNT is greater than DEBT-CEILING or if CASH-ON-HAND is less than CASH-MINIMUM
   c. PERFORM REORDER-ROUTINE if ON-HAND is less than REORDER-POINT. Also perform REORDER-ROUTINE if CUR-SALES is greater than AVE-SALES and ACTIVITY is 4

6. Use the EVALUATE statement to take the following actions, depending on the value of AMOUNT:
   If AMOUNT < 0 then perform NEG-AMNT-ROUTINE
   If AMOUNT = 0 then perform ZERO-AMNT-ROUTINE
   If AMOUNT > 0 then perform POS-AMNT-ROUTINE

7. In a payroll program, the factor for computing state withholding tax is determined by the following table:

Marital Status	Gross Pay	Factor
M	Less than 900	0.015
M	900 or more	0.021
S	Less than 500	0.019
S	500 or more	0.027

   Write an EVALUATE statement to set the value of WH-FACTOR according to these values in MARITAL-STATUS and GROSS-PAY.

8. Assume that the program in the preceding Exercise 7 contains the data entries
   ```
   02  MARITAL-STATUS  PIC X.
   02  GROSS-PAY       PIC 9(4).
   ```

   Write the condition name statements for these two data entries, using the condition names MARRIED, M-LOW-PAY, and M-HIGH-PAY, and SINGLE, S-LOW-PAY, and S-HIGH-PAY. Then write the solution for Exercise 7 using these condition names.

9. Write *one* IF statement, using implied subjects and (when possible) operators for each of the following:
   a. PERFORM 400-LESS-RTN if AMOUNT is less than either MIN-SALE or SPECIAL-MIN
   b. PERFORM 500-A-RTN if A is equal to B, or if A is equal to C, or if A is greater than D

Programming Assignments

11-1 Airline Load Summary Report

The airport manager (Programming Assignments 6-1 and 10-2) must submit a monthly performance report to the 12-Star Rating Service for all flights into and out of the Anacin airport.

Output Requirements:

A printed report with the following output and format.

```
         0         1         2         3         4         5         6         7         8
   1234567890123456789012345678901234567890123456789012345678901234567890123456789012345678
 1 Z9/99/99                          METROPOLITAN AIRPORT                           Page ZZ
 2                         12-STAR RATING SERVICE REPORT
 3
 4 Flight                   Inbound/   Flight              Load    Passenger   Performance
 5    ID        Date   Time Outbound   Number   Airline   Ratio   Crew Ratio   Rating
 6
 7 XXXXX    XX/XX/XX  Z9:99AM  XXX     XXXX     X-----X   Z.999      Z9        X-----X
 8
 9 XXXXX    XX/XX/XX  Z9:99PM  XXX     XXXX     X-----X   Z.999      Z9        X-----X
10
11
12                              AVERAGES                  Z.999      Z9
13
```

Input Description:

File name: AIRPORT1.DL

Record description: See Appendix A

Processing Requirements:

For page headings (see the printer spacing chart):

1. On the first heading line, print the date, the organization name, and the page number.

For each record in the file with the Airline equal to METRO (ignore all records with other values):

2. Convert the Arrival/departure time from a 24-hour time to AM/PM format.
3. Calculate the Load Ratio by dividing the Actual-number-of passengers-on-flight by the Total-number-of-seats-on-airplane.
4. Calculate the Passenger Crew Ratio by dividing the Actual-number-of passengers-on-flight by the Number-of-crew-members.
5. The report entry Performance Rating is to be printed as follows:

Generalized Performance Score	Performance Rating
Less than -100	POOR
-100 to 0 (inclusive)	MARGINAL
Greater than 0 but less than 500	ACCEPTABLE
Equal to or greater than 500	EXCELLENT

6. Print the detail line according to the printer spacing chart.
7. Increment the appropriate counter for number of flights.
8. Accumulate the Load Ratio and Passenger Crew Ratio values.

Summary line:

9. Calculate the averages for Load Ratio and Passenger Crew Ratio.
10. Print the averages according to the printer spacing chart.

11-2 Employee Pay Register

Undoubtedly the most important component to most employees of any data processing department is the program that prepares paychecks. One of the outputs of a payroll run is a pay register listing all employees for whom checks have been issued, the amount of the check, and other significant information.

Output Requirements:

A printed pay register with the following output fields.

Employee name
Social Security number
Updated year-to-date earnings
Updated year-to-date income tax withholding
Updated year-to-date FICA withholding
Monthly gross pay
Income tax withholding
FICA withholding
Tax sheltered annuity deduction
Net Pay

You must design the output format; prepare a printer spacing chart.

Input Description:

File name: EMPLOYEE.DL
Record description: See Appendix A

Processing Requirements:

For page headings:

1. On the first heading line, print the date, the organization name, and the page number. Include appropriate column headings.

For each record in the file:

2. Calculate the Monthly income tax withholding according to the following table.

Pay Range	Tax Computation
Monthly gross pay is not greater than 200	0
Monthly gross pay (MGP) is between 200 and 1200	(MGP -200) x .20
Monthly gross pay is greater than 1200	200 + (MGP -1200) x .35

3. Calculate the Monthly FICA withholding as follows:
    If the Updated YTD FICA withholding does not exceed 4,000 use 7% of the Monthly gross salary
    If the Updated YTD FICA withholding does exceed 4,000 use the difference between the input YTD Fica withholding and 4,000.
    If the input YTD FICA withholding is equal to 4,000 use 0.
4. Calculate the Updated YTD income tax withholding by adding the Monthly income tax withholding to the YTD income tax withholding.
5. Calculate the Updated YTD FICA withholding by adding the Monthly FICA withholding to the YTD FICA withholding.
6. Calculate the Net pay as
    Monthly gross pay
    - Monthly income tax withholding
    - Monthly FICA withholding
7. Print the detail line according to your printer spacing chart.

8. Accumulate values for Monthly gross pay, Monthly income tax withholding, Monthly FICA withholding, and Net pay.

Summary line:

9. Print a summary line, appropriately titled with the totals for Monthly gross pay, Monthly income tax withholding, Monthly FICA withholding, and Net pay.

11-3 Segment of Order Entry System

Programmer's Paradise is a bookstore specializing in books on programming. To encourage quantity purchases, they have a quantity purchase policy. For instance, if you purchase up to 11 copies of a book, you pay full wholesale price. However, if you purchase 12 or more, you pay discounted wholesale price; if you purchase 100 or more, you pay an even lower discounted wholesale price. One of their data files contains one record for each book in their inventory. Included in the record are three wholesale price fields and the two quantity "price break points."

Output Requirements:

This is a single element of an order processing system. Output will be to both the screen and the printer. Screen output will be the result of interaction with the user. Upon completion of entry for a single item in an order, the screen line must include the following:

Book inventory number (entered by user)
Title
Author
Wholesale price (determined by the quantity ordered)
Quantity (entered by user)
Amount (Wholesale price times Quantity)

The printed line must contain the same data.

Input Description:

File name: BOOKS.DI
Record description: See Appendix A

Processing Requirements for Each Order to be Entered:

For each item to be ordered:

1. Accept the Book inventory number value.
2. Access the requested record; if not found, display an error message and request again.
3. Display the Title, Author, and Wholesale price.
4. Accept the Quantity.
5. Compute the Amount as the Wholesale price times Quantity. Use the wholesale price that corresponds to the quantity. (That is, use Wholesale price, Quantity 1 wholesale price, or Quantity 2 wholesale price.)
6. Accumulate the Amount.

Summary line:

7. After the last entry for each order, display (and print) a line with the total amount.
8. Assume that there will never be more items in an order than will fit on a single screen.
9. Print each order on a separate page.

11-4 Query Voters File for Selected Information

The For-Everything Political Action Committee has found the report of Programming Assignment 9-5 very useful. Now they would like to have interactive capabilities for querying the voters file. They would like to be able to display records for voters meeting designated criteria for Annual income, Party of registration, and Marital status.

Output Requirements:

A screen display with the following output.

Upper portion of the screen:

General description lines

Criteria for record selection

Column headings

Lower portion of the screen (10 lines):

One line for each record selected displaying:

Name

City

State

Annual income

Party of registration

Marital status

Input Description:

File name: VOTERS.DL

Record description: See Appendix A

Processing Requirements:

Record selection criteria:

1. Minimum salary amount; if the user does not wish to designate a minimum, the user simply strikes Enter key (accepted as 0).
2. Maximum salary amount; if the user does not wish to designate a maximum, then user simply strikes Enter key (accepted as 0).
3. Desired Party of registration (reject any entry that is not R, D, or I).
4. Desired Marital status (reject any entry that is not 1 or 2).

For each record in the file that meets the user-entered criteria (salary range, party, and marital status):

5. Display the detail line.
6. Display up to 10 detail lines per screen.
7. After the tenth line, query the user and provide the options to see the next set of 10 records, or to terminate display for this set of criterion.
8. After the last record, give the user the option of entering another set of criterion or terminating the program.

12

DATA VALIDATION

Outline

Chapter Objectives

Since Chapter 4, you have worked with data stored in data files. For each assignment, your programming focus has been on producing a good, well-organized COBOL program that yields correct results. In all cases, your assumption has been that the stored data your program has been processing was accurate—that someone had checked the data thoroughly. Checking data to ensure that it is correct, called *data validation*, is the topic of this chapter. Two broad ways of validating data before it is placed into service in a computer application are

■ Batch validation is the validation of a data file that is already in machine-readable form. The program inspects each record, identifies errors according to a designated set of criterion, and prints a report summarizing the errors.

■ On-line validation is the validation of data on a field-by-field (or record-by-record) basis as it is entered through a keyboard. Errors are identified immediately and the keyboard operator is prompted to correct the entry before proceeding.

The example programs of this chapter (one each of the two types) make full use of the conditional tools that you learned in Chapter 11. From them, you will learn how to make the following types of validity checks:

■ That the components of a field meet certain criterion.

■ That a value exists in a field (the field cannot be empty).

■ That the value entered for a field is one of an approved list of values for that field.

■ That a value entered into a numeric field indeed be numeric.

■ That a numeric entry be within a designated range; for instance, not negative, or between 0 and 100.

■ That the value in an alphanumeric field be left-justified.

■ That allowable values in one field are controlled by the value entered into another field (*field dependence*).

■ That an entry be "reasonable." For instance, a price field might be defined with a PIC 9999V99. However, an entry greater than 1,200.00 might be very unlikely for the application.

Introduction to Data Validation

Since the beginning of automated data processing, much attention has been focused on the accurate conversion of data from a manual form to a machine-readable form. During the era of punched card processing, data was punched into cards by one machine operator and the same data rekeyed by a verification machine operator as a comparison to ensure that the entries were correct. Once in a data processing system (whether on punched cards or in disk storage), incorrect data can be both clumsy and expensive to correct. For instance, consider the customer who pays the full $350 balance on a charge account. If the amount is incorrectly entered as $35, the company will soon have an irate customer on the telephone, complaining about the wrong credit amount and the unjustified service charge. On a larger scale, incorrect data might even halt a production run or cause a program to terminate with an error condition. Finding and correcting data errors before that data is placed in service are obviously high priorities.

The punched card machines formerly used to convert data to a machine-readable form functioned totally independent of the computer. This method of data entry is called *off-line data entry*. Before being placed in service, the data was commonly checked by a data validation program. Commonly, the program printed a list of records with appropriate error identification so that errors could be corrected. This is called *batch validation* because a "batch" of data was accumulated and then checked all at once.

Today, because of the wide use of terminals directly connected to the computer and the flourishing of powerful microcomputers, most data validation is done during data entry. This is called *on-line data entry* because the keyboard and screen are directly connected to the computer and data entry is done under control of a program that monitors the entries. Furthermore, the validation is *on-line validation* because it is done as the data is being entered into the computer. For instance, as each data value is entered, it can be checked to ensure that it meets the criterion set for that field.

Your first reaction might be that all data should be validated on-line and therefore there is no need for batch validation. Although most data validation is done on-line, occasionally situations appear in which data entry is done off-line with only partial validation. Furthermore, the situation sometimes arises in which data is imported (brought in) from another application and must be verified and/or converted before it can be used.

The batch and on-line verification examples of this chapter use almost the same data verification criteria and operate with the software inventory file. The batch example is described first because its logic is simpler than that of the on-line example.

A Batch Data Validation Example

The Validation Criteria

All six fields of the software inventory file are involved in the data validation process: Stock-number, Product-name, Vendor, Quantity-on-hand, Reorder-level, and Price. The following are the validation criteria for each of these fields:

Stock-number

The five-position stock number is to be considered with the format *vvtnn*.

vv   The vendor identification must be one of an allowable set of vendors as identified in the VENDORS.DI file. Each record in this file includes a vendor identification and the vendor name.

t   The type of software (word processing, spreadsheet, and so on) is encoded by a single digit in the third position. The permissible values are 1 through 6 (general software) and 9 (sample software).

nn   A number assigned to a product; it must be numeric.

Product-name

The product name must be present (this field cannot be blank).

The first character must not be blank. This is necessary for sorting since sorting the file on the product name would cause every product with a space for the first character to be positioned at the beginning of the file, regardless of the first letter of the name.

Vendor

Must match the vendor name from the VENDORS.DI file.

Quantity-on-hand

Must be numeric.

Must not be negative (it must be greater than 0).

Any value that is greater than 100 must be identified for a reasonableness check.

Reorder-level

Must be numeric.

Must be between 1 and 100 (inclusive).

Price

Must be numeric.

Must be greater than 0 if the software type is 1 through 6.

Must be 0 if the software type is 9.

Example Definition—
Example 12-1

The following is the example definition for batch validation of a software inventory data file:

Example 12-1 Batch Validation of a Data File

Problem Description

UNISOFT has acquired the inventory of another software distributor. Also included is an inventory file that has been converted to the format of the UNISOFT inventory system. However, the data has not been fully validated, so a program is required to perform this validation (as described previously).

Output Requirements

A report listing only those records with invalid entries. Following each invalid record detail line must be one line describing each error detected in that record. A printer spacing chart is shown in Figure 12-1.

Input Description

Input file name: SOFTWAR2.DLE (the final *E* means *Error*)

Record format: Standard SOFTWAR2.DL format

For vendor number and name verification, the following file is also required.

Input file name: VENDORS.DI (Indexed file containing a list of the allowable vendors)

Record format:

Field	Positions	Data Type
Vendor number	1–2	Alphanumeric
Vendor name	3–22	Alphanumeric

Key field: Vendor number

Processing Requirements

This program is to process each record from the input file SOFTWAR2.DLE as follows:

1. Validate each of the six fields according to the defined validation requirements
2. Any record found in error must be printed on the invalid record report
3. Following each error record on the report must be one error message for each error detected
4. Do not list records that are error free

Sample Output

The program output from the sample software file (stored on the distribution disk as SOFTWAR2.DLE) is shown in Figure 12-2. As you look at this, refer back to the printer spacing chart and the program requirements. As you are studying the program, you may find it helpful to correlate this output with the program description.

Figure 12-1

Printer Spacing Chart—
Example 12-1

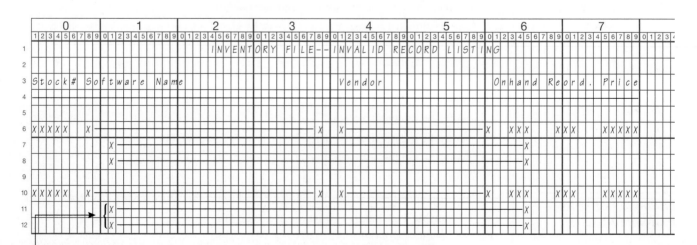

Error message lines
(one or more).

```
                    INVENTORY FILE--INVALID RECORD LISTING

Stock#  Software Name              Vendor              Onhand Reord.  Price

11164   Sluggish Writer           Archaic Software      093    100   04995
          STOCK NUMBER ERROR: THERE IS NO RECORD FOR VENDOR # 11

15589   Travelling Side Punch      Borneo International  1X0    200   0299E
          QUANTITY ON HAND CONTAINS NON-NUMERIC CHARACTERS
          REORDER LEVEL IS ZERO OR GREATER THAN MAXIMUM
          PRICE CONTAINS NON-NUMERIC CHARACTERS

15674   Supercharged Turbo COBOL   Borneo International  120    100   59900
          FIRST POSITION OF SOFTWARE NAME MUST NOT BE BLANK
          QUANTITY ON HAND IS OVER MAXIMUM--IS THIS CORRECT?

28429   Ferrari 4-5-6 Financial Acctg.  Ferrari Development  144  150  49500
          QUANTITY ON HAND IS OVER MAXIMUM--IS THIS CORRECT?
          REORDER LEVEL IS ZERO OR GREATER THAN MAXIMUM

28558   Orchestra II               Ferrarri Development  102    100   00000
          VENDOR NAME SHOULD BE Ferrari Development
          QUANTITY ON HAND IS OVER MAXIMUM--IS THIS CORRECT?
          PRICE IS INCONSISTENT WITH SOFTWARE TYPE

32506   Bottom View                Galactic Bus. Mach.   105    100   09995
          QUANTITY ON HAND IS OVER MAXIMUM--IS THIS CORRECT?

ABCDE   UnderFile, Rev 64          International Soft     095    075   03750
          STOCK NUMBER ERROR: THERE IS NO RECORD FOR VENDOR # AB
          STOCK NUMBER ERROR: SOFTWARE TYPE MUST BE 1-6 OR 9
          STOCK NUMBER ERROR: SOFTWARE NUMBER IS NOT NUMERIC

45991   Word Comet 7               Micro Am              104    100   39900
          QUANTITY ON HAND IS OVER MAXIMUM--IS THIS CORRECT?
          PRICE IS INCONSISTENT WITH SOFTWARE TYPE

49165                              Microhard             143    125   34995
          SOFTWARE NAME MUST BE PRESENT
          QUANTITY ON HAND IS OVER MAXIMUM--IS THIS CORRECT?
          REORDER LEVEL IS ZERO OR GREATER THAN MAXIMUM

53351   QBase 7000                 MicroPerimeter, Inc.  176    150   69500
          QUANTITY ON HAND IS OVER MAXIMUM--IS THIS CORRECT?
          REORDER LEVEL IS ZERO OR GREATER THAN MAXIMUM

60544   Nobodies Disk Utilities    Nobodies, Unlimited   133    100   04950
          QUANTITY ON HAND IS OVER MAXIMUM--IS THIS CORRECT?
```

Figure 12-2

Sample Output—
Example 12-1

**Program Solution—
Example 12-1**

At first glance, the complete program solution in Figures 12-3 through 12-6 (see page 296) can be overwhelming. However, as you view individual components, you will see that they represent a series of successive applications of principles already familiar to you. In the structure chart of Figure 12-3, you can see that many of the blocks are repetitious—there is one set of blocks for each field to be verified. Ignore that repetition and you can see that the chart is similar to others you've encountered.

The first two levels of logic shown in the flowchart of Figure 12-4 and pseudocode of Figure 12-5 are identical to most of the programs you have studied and written. Even the validation modules are relatively basic applications of the IF statement studied in Chapter 11. You should take particular notice of two items.

The first relates to the general way in which errors are handled and a line is printed. Unlike previous programs, the input record cannot be printed immediately after it has been read because it is to be printed only if an error is detected. Furthermore, regardless of the number of errors encountered for a record, the record must be printed only one time—even though two or more error lines will be printed for it. This is to be controlled by a switch as follows:

1. Read the next data record
2. Move its contents to the output line area, but do not print
3. Set the switch Error-found to false
4. Repeat the following for each field:
   If the field is invalid
     If Error-found switch is false
       Write the report line   *(Note: The line output area still contains the input record contents.)*
     Move the appropriate message to the output area
     Write the report line (error message)
     Set the Error-found switch to true

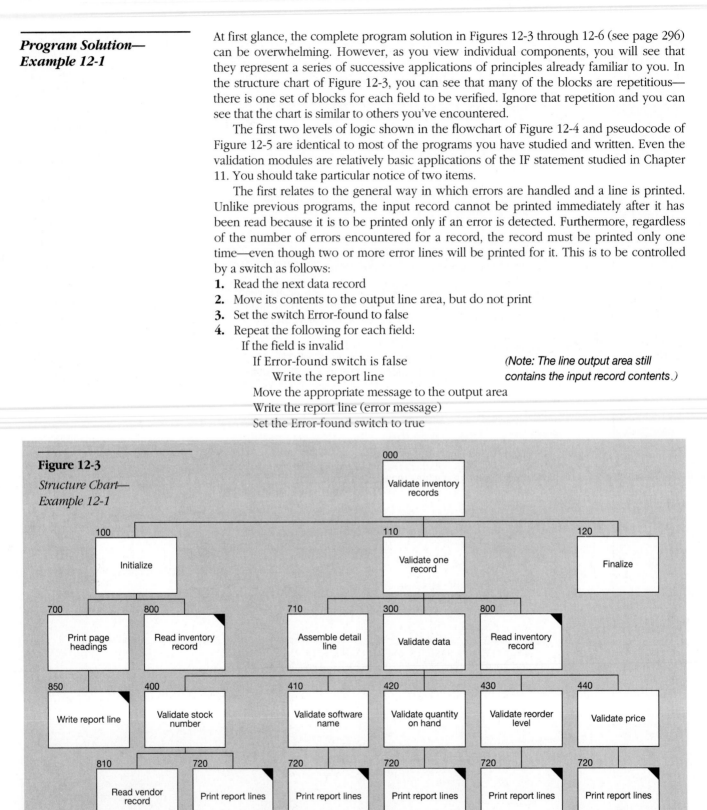

Figure 12-3

*Structure Chart—
Example 12-1*

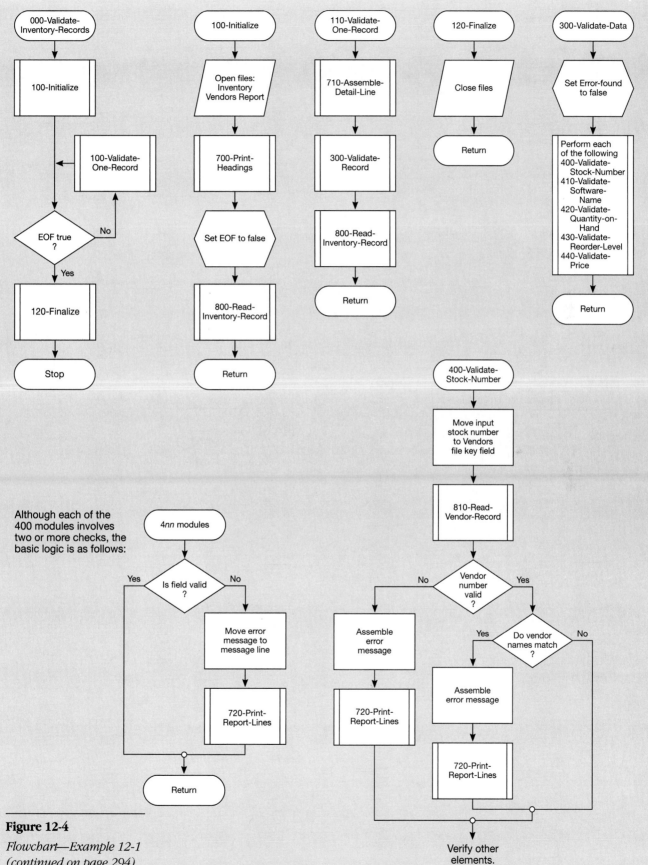

Figure 12-4

Flowchart—Example 12-1
(continued on page 294)

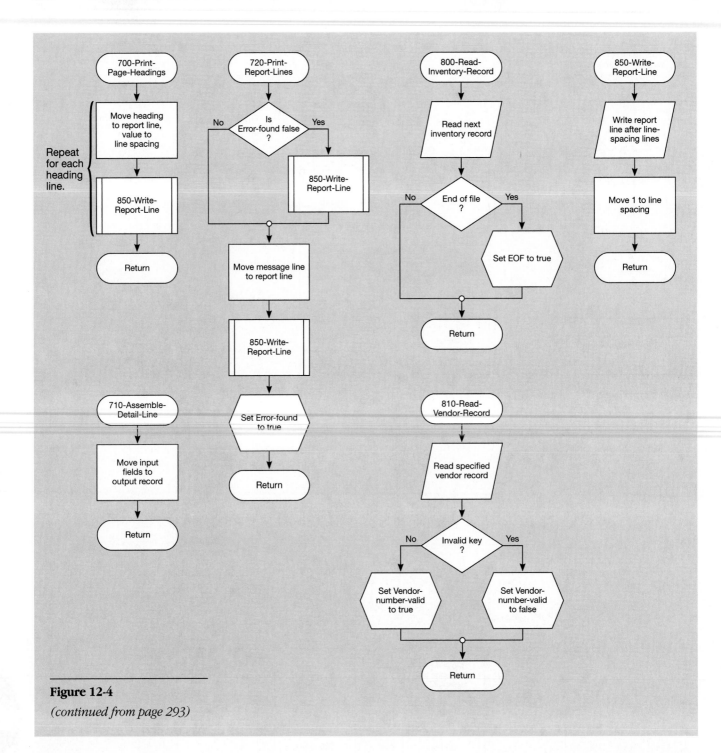

Figure 12-4

(continued from page 293)

Figure 12-5

Pseudocode—Example 12-1

```
000-Access-Inventory-File
      Perform 100-Initialize
      Perform 110-Validate-1-Record until end of file
      Perform 120-Finalize
      Stop

100-Initialize
      Open  Inventory-file
            Vendor-file
            Report-file
      Perform 700-Print-Page-Headings
      Set End-of-file to false
      Perform 800-Read-Inventory-Record

110-Validate-1-Record
      Perform 710-Assemble-Detail-Line
      Perform 300-Validate-Record
      Perform 800-Read-Inventory-Record

300-Validate-Data
      Set Error-found to false
      Perform 400-Validate-Stock-Number
      Perform 410-Validate-Software-Name
      Perform 420-Validate-Quantity-On-Hand
      Perform 430-Validate-Reorder-Level
      Perform 440-Validate-Price

400-Validate-Stock-Number
      Move Input-stock-number to VENDORS key field
      Perform 810-Read-Vendor-Record
      If Vendor-number-valid is false
        Move message to error line
        Perform 720-Print-Report-Lines
      else
        If Input-vendor-name not same as VENDORS file vendor-
name
          Move message to error line
          Perform 720-Print-Report-Lines
      If Software-type not equal 1 through 6 or 9
        Move message to error line
        Perform 720-Print-Report-Lines
      If Software-number is not numeric
        Move message to error line
        Perform 720-Print-Report-Lines

410-Validate-Software-Name
      If Software-name blank
        Move message to error line
        Perform 720-Print-Report-Lines
      else
        If first position of Software-name blank
          Move message to error line
          Perform 720-Print-Report-Lines

420-Validate-Quantity-On-Hand
      If Quantity-on-hand not numeric
        Move message to error line
        Perform 720-Print-Report-Lines
      else
        If Quantity-on-hand greater than maximum
          Move message to error line
          Perform 720-Print-Report-Lines

430-Validate-Reorder-Level
      If Reorder-level not numeric
        Move message to error line
        Perform 720-Print-Report-Lines
      else
        If Reorder-level equal 0 or greater than maximum
          Move message to error line
          Perform 720-Print-Report-Lines

440-Validate-Price
      If Price not numeric
        Move message to error line
        Perform 720-Print-Report-Lines
      else
        If software code = 1-6 and Price not greater than 0
        or software code = 9 and Price not equal 0
          Move message to error line
          Perform 720-Print-Report-Lines

700-Print-Page-Headings
      For each heading line
      Move the page heading to the output area
      Perform 850-Write-Report-Line

710-Assemble-Detail-Line
      Move input fields to output area

720-Print-Report-Lines
      If Error-found is false
        Perform 850-Write-Report-Line
      Move message line to output area
      Perform 850-Write-Report-Line
      Set Error-found to true

800-Read-Inventory-Record
      Read Inventory-record
        at end set End-of-file to true

810-Read-Vendor-Record
      Read vendor record
      If requested record found
        Set Vendor-number-valid to true
      else
        Set Vendor-number-valid to false

850-Write-Report-Line
      Write Report-line after advancing Line-spacing
      Move 1 to Line-spacing
```

Figure 12-6

The Batch Data Validation
Program—Example 12-1

```
  1        IDENTIFICATION DIVISION.
  2        PROGRAM-ID. FILE-VAL.
  3
  4    *    Written by J.Olson/W.Price
  5    *    August 19, 1990
  6
  7    *    This program validates records in the sequential file
  8    *    SOFTWAR2.DL.   The assumption is that the file was created
  9    *    without validating the data.  This program reads every record
 10    *    in the file and checks every field in each record for
 11    *    validity.  Output is a listing containing an error message
 12    *    for every invalid field found.
 13
 14    *    Validation criteria:
 15    *        Stock number (format vvtnn):
 16    *            vv (vendor ID) must be present in VENDORS.DI
 17    *            t (type of software) must be 1-6 or 9
 18    *            nn (number) must be numeric
 19    *        Product name:
 20    *            Must be present
 21    *            First character must not be blank
 22    *        Quantity on hand:
 23    *            Must be numeric and not negative  ( >= 0 )
 24    *            Question if greater than 100
 25    *        Reorder level:
 26    *            Must be numeric
 27    *            Must be 1-100 (inclusive)
 28    *        Price:
 29    *            Must be numeric
 30    *            Must be > 0 if software type is 1-6
 31    *            Must be zero if software type is 9 (demo)
 32
 33        ENVIRONMENT DIVISION.
 34        CONFIGURATION SECTION.
 35        SOURCE-COMPUTER. IBM-PC.
 36
 37        INPUT-OUTPUT SECTION.
 38        FILE-CONTROL.
 39            SELECT INVENTORY-FILE      ASSIGN TO DISK "SOFTWAR2.DLE"
 40                                       ORGANIZATION IS LINE SEQUENTIAL.
 41
 42            SELECT VENDOR-FILE         ASSIGN TO DISK "VENDORS.DI"
 43                                       ORGANIZATION IS INDEXED
 44                                       ACCESS IS RANDOM
 45                                       RECORD KEY IS VR-VENDOR-NUMBER.
 46
 47            SELECT REPORT-FILE         ASSIGN TO PRINTER "PRN-FILE".
 48
 49        DATA DIVISION.
 50
 51        FILE SECTION.
 52
 53        FD  INVENTORY-FILE.
 54        01  INVENTORY-RECORD.
 55            10  IR-STOCK-NUMBER.
 56                20  IR-VENDOR-NUMBER     PIC X(2).
 57                20  IR-SOFTWARE-TYPE     PIC X(1).
 58                    88  REGULAR-SOFTWARE VALUE "1" THRU "6".
 59                    88  SAMPLE-SOFTWARE  VALUE "9".
 60                20  IR-SOFTWARE-NUMBER   PIC X(2).
 61            10  IR-SOFTWARE-NAME.
 62                20  IR-POS-1-OF-NAME     PIC X(1).
 63                20  IR-BALANCE-OF-RECORD PIC X(29).
 64            10  IR-VENDOR-NAME          PIC X(20).
 65            10  IR-QUANT-ON-HAND        PIC 9(3).
 66            10  IR-REORDER-LEVEL        PIC 9(3).
 67            10  IR-PRICE                PIC 9(3)V9(2).
 68            10  IR-PRICE-X REDEFINES IR-PRICE  PIC X(5).
 69
 70        FD  VENDOR-FILE.
 71        01  VENDOR-RECORD.
 72            10  VR-VENDOR-NUMBER            PIC X(2).
 73            10  VR-VENDOR-NAME              PIC X(20).
 74
 75        FD  REPORT-FILE.
 76        01  REPORT-RECORD                   PIC X(78).
 77
 78        WORKING-STORAGE SECTION.
 79
 80        01  REPORT-LINE         VALUE SPACES.
 81            10  RL-STOCK-NUMBER            PIC X(7).
 82            10  RL-SOFTWARE-NAME           PIC X(32).
 83            10  RL-VENDOR-NAME             PIC X(22).
 84            10  RL-QUANT-ON-HAND           PIC X(6).
 85            10  RL-REORDER-LEVEL           PIC X(6).
 86            10  RL-PRICE                   PIC X(5).
 87
 88        01  HEADING-LINE.
 89            10                             PIC X(18)  VALUE SPACES.
 90            10                             PIC X(43)  VALUE
 91                "INVENTORY FILE—INVALID RECORD LISTING".
 92
 93        01  COLUMN-HEADING.
 94            10                  PIC X(7)   VALUE "Stock#".
 95            10                  PIC X(32)  VALUE "Software Name".
 96            10                  PIC X(20)  VALUE "Vendor".
 97            10                  PIC X(7)   VALUE "Onhand".
 98            10                  PIC X(7)   VALUE "Reord.".
 99            10                  PIC X(5)   VALUE "Price".
100
101        01  MESSAGE-LINE.
102            10                             PIC X(10)  VALUE SPACES.
103            10  ML-MESSAGE                 PIC X(65).
104
105        01  PROGRAMMED-SWITCHES.
106            10                             PIC X.
107                88  END-OF-FILE            VALUE "Y"  FALSE "N".
108            10                             PIC X.
109                88  ERROR-FOUND            VALUE "Y"  FALSE "N".
110            10                             PIC X.
111                88  VENDOR-NUMBER-VALID    VALUE "Y"  FALSE "N".
112
113        01  VALIDATION-VALUES.
114            10  MAXIMUM-QUANTITY    PIC 9(3)  VALUE 100.
115
116        01  PRINT-CONTROL-VARIABLES.
117            10  LINE-SPACING       PIC 9.
118
119        01  INVALID-VENDOR-NUMBER-MESSAGE.
120            10                             PIC X(52)  VALUE
121                "STOCK NUMBER ERROR: THERE IS NO RECORD FOR VENDOR # ".
122            10  IV-VENDOR-NUMBER           PIC X(2).
123
124        01  INVALID-VENDOR-NAME-MESSAGE.
125            10                             PIC X(22)  VALUE
126                "VENDOR NAME SHOULD BE ".
127            10  IV-VENDOR-NAME             PIC X(20).
128
129        PROCEDURE DIVISION.
130
131        000-VALIDATE-INVENTORY-RECORDS.
132            PERFORM 100-INITIALIZE
133            PERFORM 110-VALIDATE-1-RECORD
134                UNTIL END-OF-FILE
135            PERFORM 120-FINALIZE
136            STOP RUN.
137
138        100-INITIALIZE.
139            OPEN INPUT  INVENTORY-FILE
140            OPEN INPUT  VENDOR-FILE
141            OPEN OUTPUT REPORT-FILE
142            PERFORM 700-PRINT-PAGE-HEADINGS
143            SET END-OF-FILE TO FALSE
144            PERFORM 800-READ-INVENTORY-RECORD.
145
146        110-VALIDATE-1-RECORD.
147            PERFORM 710-ASSEMBLE-DETAIL-LINE
148            PERFORM 300-VALIDATE-DATA
149            PERFORM 800-READ-INVENTORY-RECORD.
150
151        120-FINALIZE.
152            CLOSE INVENTORY-FILE
153                  VENDOR-FILE
154                  REPORT-FILE.
155
```

Figure 12-6

```
156     300-VALIDATE-DATA.
157         SET ERROR-FOUND TO FALSE
158         PERFORM 400-VALIDATE-STOCK-NUMBER
159         PERFORM 410-VALIDATE-SOFTWARE-NAME
160         PERFORM 420-VALIDATE-QUANTITY-ON-HAND
161         PERFORM 430-VALIDATE-REORDER-LEVEL
162         PERFORM 440-VALIDATE-PRICE.
163
164     400-VALIDATE-STOCK-NUMBER.
165         MOVE IR-VENDOR-NUMBER TO VR-VENDOR-NUMBER
166         PERFORM 810-READ-VENDOR-RECORD
167         IF NOT VENDOR-NUMBER-VALID
168           MOVE IR-VENDOR-NUMBER TO IV-VENDOR-NUMBER
169           MOVE INVALID-VENDOR-NUMBER-MESSAGE TO ML-MESSAGE
170           PERFORM 720-PRINT-REPORT-LINES
171         ELSE
172           IF IR-VENDOR-NAME NOT = VR-VENDOR-NAME
173             MOVE VR-VENDOR-NAME TO IV-VENDOR-NAME
174             MOVE INVALID-VENDOR-NAME-MESSAGE TO ML-MESSAGE
175             PERFORM 720-PRINT-REPORT-LINES
176           END-IF
177         END-IF
178
179         IF IR-SOFTWARE-TYPE IS < "1"
180         OR > "6" AND NOT = "9"
181           MOVE "STOCK NUMBER ERROR: SOFTWARE TYPE MUST BE 1-6 OR 9"
182             TO ML-MESSAGE
183           PERFORM 720-PRINT-REPORT-LINES
184         END-IF
185
186         IF IR-SOFTWARE-NUMBER IS NOT NUMERIC
187           MOVE "STOCK NUMBER ERROR: SOFTWARE NUMBER IS NOT NUMERIC"
188             TO ML-MESSAGE
189           PERFORM 720-PRINT-REPORT-LINES
190         END-IF.
191
192     410-VALIDATE-SOFTWARE-NAME.
193         IF IR-SOFTWARE-NAME = SPACES
194           MOVE "SOFTWARE NAME MUST BE PRESENT" TO ML-MESSAGE
195           PERFORM 720-PRINT-REPORT-LINES
196         ELSE
197           IF IR-POS-1-OF-NAME = SPACE
198             MOVE "FIRST POSITION OF SOFTWARE NAME MUST NOT BE BLANK"
199               TO ML-MESSAGE
200             PERFORM 720-PRINT-REPORT-LINES
201           END-IF
202         END-IF.
203
204     420-VALIDATE-QUANTITY-ON-HAND.
205         IF IR-QUANT-ON-HAND IS NOT NUMERIC
206           MOVE "QUANTITY ON HAND CONTAINS NON-NUMERIC CHARACTERS"
207             TO ML-MESSAGE
208           PERFORM 720-PRINT-REPORT-LINES
209         ELSE
210           IF IR-QUANT-ON-HAND IS > MAXIMUM-QUANTITY
211             MOVE "QUANTITY ON HAND IS OVER MAXIMUM—IS THIS CORRECT?"
212               TO ML-MESSAGE
213             PERFORM 720-PRINT-REPORT-LINES
214           END-IF
215         END-IF.
216
217     430-VALIDATE-REORDER-LEVEL.
218         IF IR-REORDER-LEVEL IS NOT NUMERIC
219           MOVE "REORDER LEVEL CONTAINS NON-NUMERIC CHARACTERS"
220             TO ML-MESSAGE
221           PERFORM 720-PRINT-REPORT-LINES
222         ELSE
223           IF IR-REORDER-LEVEL IS > MAXIMUM-QUANTITY OR = 0
224             MOVE "REORDER LEVEL IS ZERO OR GREATER THAN MAXIMUM"
225               TO ML-MESSAGE
226             PERFORM 720-PRINT-REPORT-LINES
227           END-IF
228         END-IF.
229
230     440-VALIDATE-PRICE.
231         IF IR-PRICE IS NOT NUMERIC
232           MOVE "PRICE CONTAINS NON-NUMERIC CHARACTERS" TO ML-MESSAGE
233           PERFORM 720-PRINT-REPORT-LINES
234         ELSE
235           IF REGULAR-SOFTWARE
236           AND IR-PRICE IS NOT > 0
237           OR SAMPLE-SOFTWARE
238           AND IR-PRICE IS NOT = 0
239             MOVE "PRICE IS INCONSISTENT WITH SOFTWARE TYPE"
240               TO ML-MESSAGE
241             PERFORM 720-PRINT-REPORT-LINES
242           END-IF
243         END-IF.
244
245     700-PRINT-PAGE-HEADINGS.
246         MOVE ZERO TO LINE-SPACING
247         MOVE HEADING-LINE TO REPORT-RECORD
248         PERFORM 850-WRITE-REPORT-LINE
249         MOVE 2 TO LINE-SPACING
250         MOVE COLUMN-HEADING TO REPORT-RECORD
251         PERFORM 850-WRITE-REPORT-LINE
252         MOVE 1 TO LINE-SPACING
253         MOVE ALL "-" TO REPORT-RECORD
254         PERFORM 850-WRITE-REPORT-LINE.
255
256     710-ASSEMBLE-DETAIL-LINE.
257         MOVE IR-STOCK-NUMBER TO RL-STOCK-NUMBER
258         MOVE IR-SOFTWARE-NAME TO RL-SOFTWARE-NAME
259         MOVE IR-VENDOR-NAME TO RL-VENDOR-NAME
260         MOVE IR-QUANT-ON-HAND TO RL-QUANT-ON-HAND
261         MOVE IR-REORDER-LEVEL TO RL-REORDER-LEVEL
262         MOVE IR-PRICE-X TO RL-PRICE
263         MOVE REPORT-LINE TO REPORT-RECORD
264         MOVE 2 TO LINE-SPACING.
265
266     720-PRINT-REPORT-LINES.
267         IF NOT ERROR-FOUND
268           PERFORM 850-WRITE-REPORT-LINE
269         END-IF
270         MOVE MESSAGE-LINE TO REPORT-RECORD
271         PERFORM 850-WRITE-REPORT-LINE
272         SET ERROR-FOUND TO TRUE.
273
274     800-READ-INVENTORY-RECORD.
275         READ INVENTORY-FILE
276           AT END
277             SET END-OF-FILE TO TRUE
278         END-READ.
279
280     810-READ-VENDOR-RECORD.
281         READ VENDOR-FILE
282           INVALID KEY
283             SET VENDOR-NUMBER-VALID TO FALSE
284           NOT INVALID KEY
285             SET VENDOR-NUMBER-VALID TO TRUE
286         END-READ.
287
288     850-WRITE-REPORT-LINE.
289         WRITE REPORT-RECORD
290           AFTER ADVANCING LINE-SPACING LINES.
291         MOVE 1 TO LINE-SPACING.
```

Notice that the data record will be printed only when an error condition is detected and the Error-found switch is still false. Since an error condition action involves changing the switch to true, printing will not occur with the detection of subsequent errors for this record.

The second item to notice is that validation of the Stock-number field includes verifying that the vendor number (first two positions) is that of a valid vendor. The criterion is that the vendor be in the VENDORS.DI file. Since the VENDORS.DI file is indexed and is to be used for random access, it must be defined accordingly. The necessary verification requires the following steps:

1. Move the vendor number from the input record to the VENDORS.DI key field
2. Read the desired vendor from the VENDORS.DI file
3. If there is no record for that vendor number (INVALID KEY)
     Move the appropriate message to the output area
     Write the report line (error message)
     Set the Error-found switch to true
   Else
     If input record Vendor-name not = to Vendor-name from VENDORS.DI
         Move the appropriate message to the output area
         Write the report line (error message)
         Set the Error-found switch to true

The complete program is included in Figure 12-6 (pages 296 and 297). Before proceeding to the logic of the PROCEDURE DIVISION, let's consider some of the elements preceding it.

Data Definition Elements of the Batch Data Validation Program

The Vendor File

In the ENVIRONMENT DIVISION, the vendor file VENDOR.DI is defined as an indexed file with the vendor number as the key field. Referring to its record definition (lines 70–73), you can see that the record includes two fields: the vendor number and corresponding vendor name. For a vendor number portion of a Product-code field (from an inventory record) to be valid, there must be an entry in this vendor file. Once found, the vendor name of the inventory record must match up to the corresponding vendor name from the vendor file.

The Inventory File Record

After numerous encounters in previous chapters, you have become quite familiar with the inventory record. However, a more detailed breakdown is required for this program. The Stock-number field is broken down into its component fields by the entries of Figure 12-7.

Here you see the three-part breakdown as required for the validation operations. Furthermore, condition-names (level 88 items) are included to provide logical names to the software code ranges.

The REDEFINES Clause

When an error record is detected, it must be printed field by field exactly as the data is read in. To accommodate the fact that numeric fields may have other than numeric data, the output line is defined with X PICTUREs for each output item (see lines 84–86). On one hand, moving integer data to an alphanumeric field is valid (for example, IR-QUANT-ON-HAND at line 65 to RL-QUANT-ON-HAND at line 84). However, moving non-integer data to an alphanumeric field is not valid—this would occur if IR-PRICE (line 68) were moved to RL-PRICE (line 86).

Figure 12-7

Stock-Number Subfields

```
10  IR-STOCK-NUMBER.
    20  IR-VENDOR-NUMBER          PIC X(2).
    20  IR-SOFTWARE-TYPE          PIC X(1).
        88  REGULAR-SOFTWARE      VALUE "1" THRU "6".
        88  SAMPLE-SOFTWARE       VALUE "9".
    20  IR-SOFTWARE-NUMBER        PIC X(2).
```

This problem can be avoided by giving a second name and definition to the Price field, using the REDEFINES clause as follows:

```
10   IR-PRICE                        PIC 9(3)V9(2).
10   IR-PRICE-X REDEFINES IR-PRICE   PIC X(5).
```

This clause causes the five positions of memory defined for IR-PRICE as PIC 9(3)V9(2) to be given a second name: IR-PRICE-X defined as PIC X(5). Remember that the data is stored in memory without the decimal point. If the data is referred to as IR-PRICE, it has an assumed decimal point between the third and fourth digits. If that same data is referred to as IR-PRICE-X, it is treated as simply a five-position field and hence can be moved to another alphanumeric data item.

In general, keep in mind four syntactical rules when using the REDEFINES clause:

■ The REDEFINES clause must be coded immediately after the data-name in the data item description entry
■ The redefining entry must immediately follow, at that level number, the area being redefined
■ A field that contains a REDEFINES clause cannot be redefined (however, the redefined entry can have multiple redefinitions)
■ The field with the REDEFINES clause cannot contain a VALUE clause

Remember that a field specified with the REDEFINES clause does not define additional areas of storage or different data. Rather, it permits a different name and/or a different PICTURE clause to be assigned to the same area of memory.

Programmed Switches

This program includes three programmed switches, each assigned a condition name as shown in Figure 12-8.

END-OF-FILE serves the usual purpose: indicating when the EOF file has been encountered upon reading the inventory file. VALIDITY-SWITCH-1, which will be tested using the condition name ERROR-FOUND, is the switch used to control when the invalid detail software record is to be printed. VALIDITY-SWITCH-2, which is tested using the condition name VENDOR-NUMBER-VALID, indicates whether or not the vendor record for the current product number exists in the vendor file.

Logic of the Batch Data Validation Program

The Steps in Validating a Field

You can see that the first two levels of code (the 000 and 100 levels in lines 131–154) are much the same as numerous programs you have encountered. For an understanding of the validation logic, let's trace the flow through the program, beginning with the first statement of the 110 module, repeated here in Figure 12-9. For this exercise, assume that all fields of the next record to be validated are correct—except the Software-name field, which is blank.

1. In the 710 module (lines 256–264), the fields from the inventory record just read are moved to the detail line in the WORKING-STORAGE SECTION and then to the output line area. However, *the record is not printed.*

Figure 12-8

Programmed Switches

```
01   PROGRAMMED-SWITCHES.
     10   END-OF-FILE-SWITCH           PIC X.
          88   END-OF-FILE             VALUE "Y"  FALSE "N".
     10   VALIDITY-SWITCH-1            PIC X.
          88   ERROR-FOUND             VALUE "Y"  FALSE "N".
     10   VALIDITY-SWITCH-2            PIC X.
          88   VENDOR-NUMBER-VALID     VALUE "Y"  FALSE "N".
```

Figure 12-9

The 110 Module

```
110-VALIDATE-1-RECORD.
    PERFORM 710-ASSEMBLE-DETAIL-LINE
    PERFORM 300-VALIDATE-DATA
    PERFORM 800-READ-INVENTORY-RECORD.
```

2. The 300 module is executed and the switch ERROR-FOUND is initialized for this record to false (line 157).

3. For this description, assume that the 400 module has already been executed (no errors found). Figure 12-10 is the 410 module that will be executed next (from the PERFORM at line 192). Since IR-SOFTWARE-NAME of this record contains spaces, an appropriate error message is moved to an error message line in the WORKING-STORAGE SECTION and the 720 module is executed.

4. Figure 12-11 is the 720 module. Since no error has yet been detected (ERROR-FOUND is false), the current contents of the output area (the input record remains there) are printed. The error message is moved to the output area and printed, and the switch ERROR-FOUND is set to true.

5. Because ERROR-FOUND is now true, subsequent errors for this record will cause the printing only of the error message and not of the data record.

Notice in Figure 12-10 that if the test IR-SOFTWARE-NAME = SPACES is false, the ELSE option is executed. In this case, if the first character position is a space, then an equivalent error sequence is carried out.

Each of the test modules functions in much the same way as the 410 module that tests the Software-name field. The exception is the 400 module, which requires access to the vendor file to determine if the vendor number of the current stock number is valid.

Validating the Stock-Number Field

The first fourteen lines of the 400-VALIDATE-STOCK-NUMBER are repeated here in Figure 12-12. When this is executed, the following takes place:

1. The Vendor-number value from the input record is moved to the key field of the vendor file.

2. The 810 module reads this file for the specified record. Referring to lines 282–286, you can see that the switch VENDOR-NUMBER-VALID is set to false if the record is not found in the file (INVALID KEY) and is set to true if the record is found in the file (NOT INVALID KEY).

3. If VENDOR-NUMBER-VALID is false, the error message line is assembled and the 720 module is executed.

4. If VENDOR-NUMBER-VALID is true, the Vendor-name value from the inventory record is compared to the corresponding Vendor-name from the vendor file. If they are not the same, the error is processed.

Figure 12-10

The 410 Module

```
410-VALIDATE-SOFTWARE-NAME.
    IF IR-SOFTWARE-NAME = SPACES
      MOVE "SOFTWARE NAME MUST BE PRESENT" TO ML-MESSAGE
      PERFORM 720-PRINT-REPORT-LINES
    ELSE
    IF IR-POS-1-OF-NAME = SPACE
      MOVE "FIRST POSITION OF SOFTWARE NAME MUST NOT BE BLANK"
        TO ML-MESSAGE
      PERFORM 720-PRINT-REPORT-LINES
    END-IF
    END-IF.
```

Figure 12-11

The 720 Module

```
720-PRINT-REPORT-LINES.
    IF NOT ERROR-FOUND
      PERFORM 850-WRITE-REPORT-LINE
    END-IF
    MOVE MESSAGE-LINE TO REPORT-LINE
    PERFORM 850-WRITE-REPORT-LINE
    SET ERROR-FOUND TO TRUE.
```

Figure 12-12

Partial 400 Modules

```
400-VALIDATE-STOCK-NUMBER.
   MOVE IR-VENDOR-NUMBER TO VR-VENDOR-NUMBER
   PERFORM 810-READ-VENDOR-RECORD
   IF NOT VENDOR-NUMBER-VALID
      MOVE IR-VENDOR-NUMBER TO IV-VENDOR-NUMBER
      MOVE INVALID-VENDOR-NUMBER-MESSAGE TO ML-MESSAGE
      PERFORM 720-PRINT-REPORT-LINES
   ELSE
      IF IR-VENDOR-NAME NOT = VR-VENDOR-NAME
         MOVE VR-VENDOR-NAME TO IV-VENDOR-NAME
         MOVE INVALID-VENDOR-NAME-MESSAGE TO ML-MESSAGE
         PERFORM 720-PRINT-REPORT-LINES
      END-IF
   END-IF
```

Some Final Observations About the FILE-VAL Program

The FILE-VAL program is missing some of the ingredients of a complete data validation/report program. Specifically, report headings have been kept to a minimum, page control has not been implemented, and nothing has been done with the valid records. In a production environment, all of the procedures for producing a good, functional report would be incorporated. In addition, valid records and invalid records would probably be written to separate files. These actions were all omitted from the program in order to focus on the data validation techniques, the topic of this chapter.

An On-Line Data Entry/Validation Example

Example Definition—Example 12-2

Although the batch validation program of Example 12-1 is fairly long, the logic is not overly complex. The actions are straightforward: read a record and identify errors. The program includes no provisions for making corrections. On the other hand, a data entry/validation program must: (1) accept each field, (2) identify any errors, and (3) allow the user to make the appropriate correction or to simply abort that record. The increased logic is significant, as you will learn from the next example.

Example 12-1 Data Entry/Validation

Problem Description

UNISOFT requires a data entry/validation program for the indexed software file. The basic data entry functions are to be those of the S-EXTEND program (Chapter 10, Figure 10-22) for adding records to the sequential version of the software file. Each field is to be validated as it is entered; validation standards are the same as those for the batch file validation application (Example 12-1).

Output Requirements

Name of file for record addition: SOFTWAR2.DI
Record format: Standard SOFTWAR2.DI format

Input Description

Keyboard data entry. The data entry screen is shown in Figure 12-13.
For vendor number verification and name access, the following file is required:
Input file name: VENDORS.DI (Indexed file containing a list of the allowable vendors)

Record format:

Field	Positions	Data Type
Vendor number	1–2	Alphanumeric
Vendor name	3–22	Alphanumeric

Key field: Vendor number

Processing Requirements

This data entry program is to function as follows:

1. Upon entry to the program, provide the user with the option of aborting without data entry.
2. From the keyboard, accept the stock number of the next record to be entered.
3. Execute a random access read to obtain a record from the software inventory file with the keyboard entry stock number.
4. If the read is successful, display an error message that there is already a record in the file for this stock number and abort this entry.
5. Using the vendor number subfield from the stock number, read the vendor record from the vendor file.
6. If the read is not successful, display an error message that there is no vendor for this vendor number and abort this entry.
7. Obtain the vendor field from the vendor file.
8. Accept each of the remaining fields from the keyboard and verify it before progressing to the next field. If the field does not meet the validation requirements, provide the user with the following options:

    Enter another value

    Abort this record

    The user must be able to abort a screen record from any field on the screen without progressing through each field that follows.

9. Query the user regarding the action to take with the currently displayed set of entries. The options must be

    1 Write the record to the file

    2 Allow the user to make corrections to screen entries

    3 Abort these screen entries and continue

10. Terminate processing if the user enters a blank stock number value.

Figure 12-13

Input Screen Format—
Example 12-2

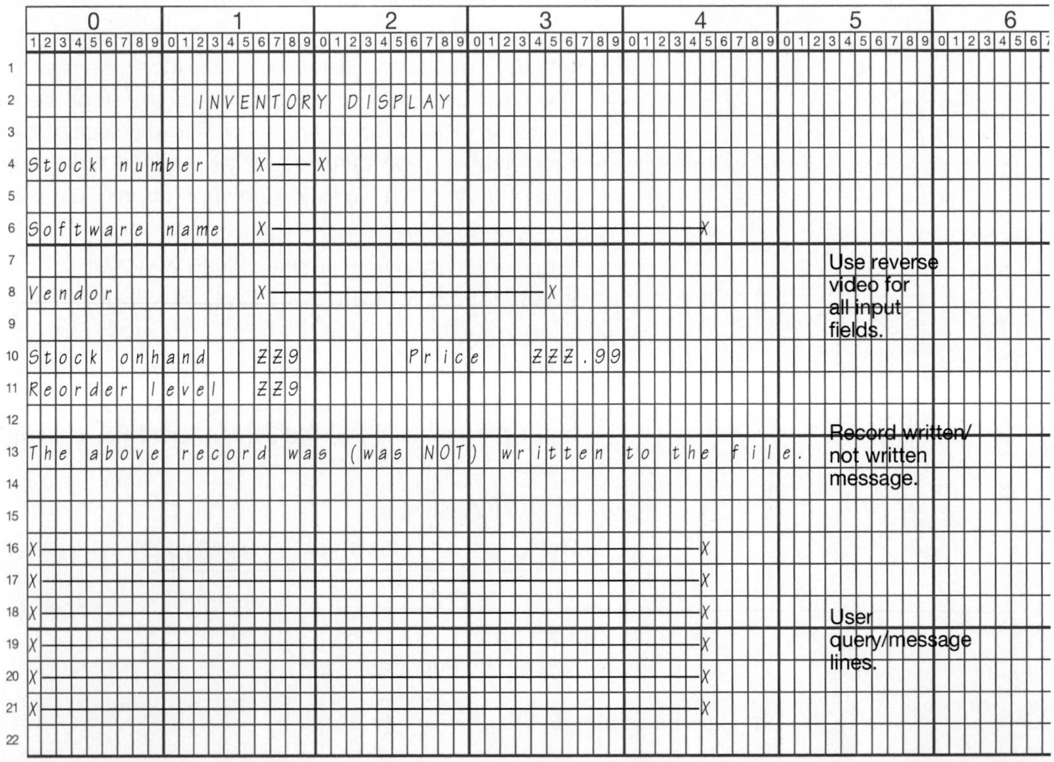

**Program Solution—
Example 12-2**

The complete solution to the data entry/validation example is shown in Figures 12-14 through 12-17 (see page 308). At first glance, the structure chart in Figure 12-14 appears less complex than that of the batch data validation (Figure 12-3). However, if you look closely, you will see that they are much the same. Each shows the validation operations (one for each field to be validated) under the 300 module.

It is the logic of this example that is complex, as illustrated by the flowchart of Figure 12-15 and the pseudocode of Figure 12-16. Some of the advantages of pseudocode over flowcharts are evident from these two figures. First, pseudocode is more concise and considerably less bulky than the flowchart. Second, the pseudocode more closely parallels the logical structure of the program. For instance, the "built-in" logic of the in-line-PERFORM is more evident in pseudocode. To see this, refer to the *Repeat* pseudocode statement in the 300 module. (The text description continues on page 311).

The program solution, KEYB-VAL, is shown in Figure 12-17 (pages 308–310). Before beginning your analysis of this program, you should run it and add a few records to the file (if you have not already done so). When you run it, try all of the options. That is, enter incorrect data and take the different recovery paths. If you do this, you will have a much better feel for the overall program and you will find the logic much easier to understand. For your first run-through, you might follow the sequence described in the next section.

Figure 12-14

*Structure Chart—
Example 12-2*

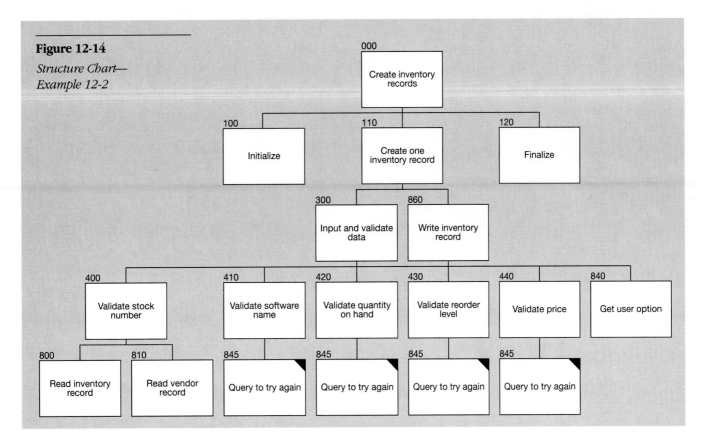

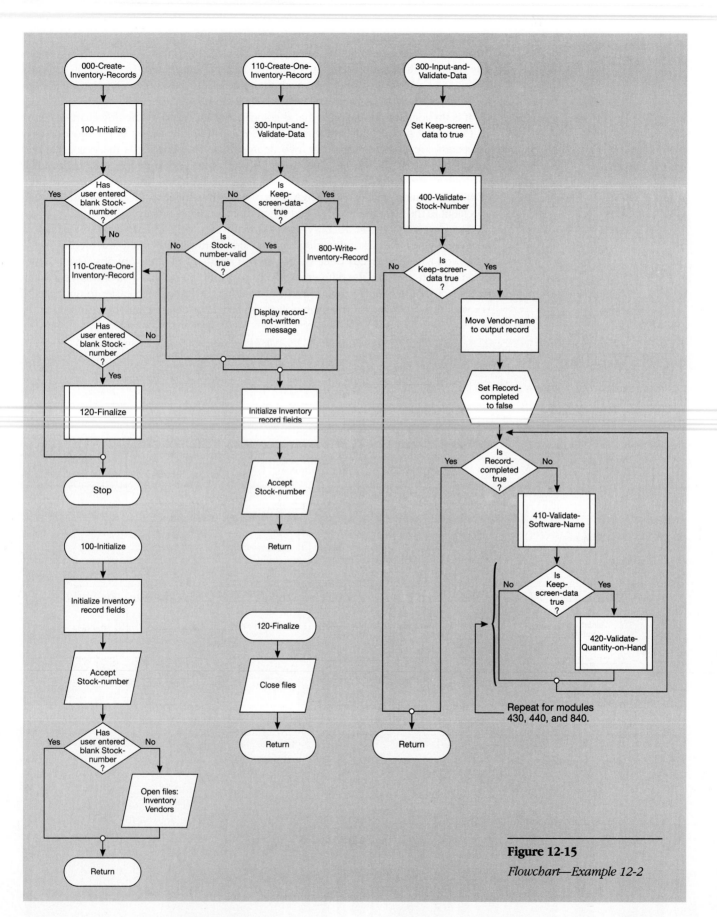

Figure 12-15

Flowchart—Example 12-2

Figure 12-15

(continued on page 306)

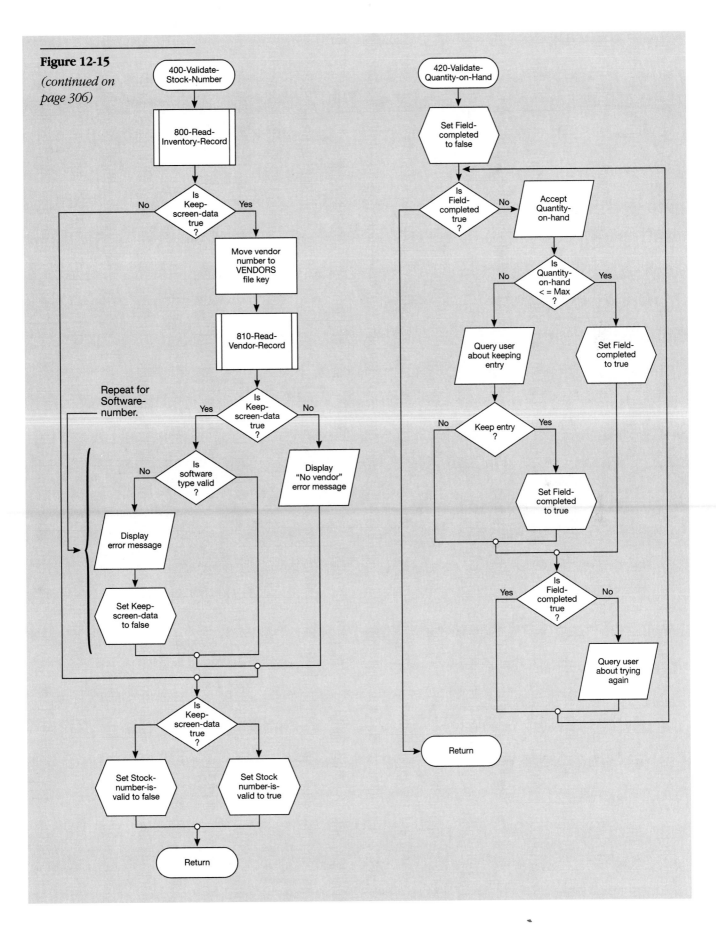

Figure 12-15

(continued from page 305)

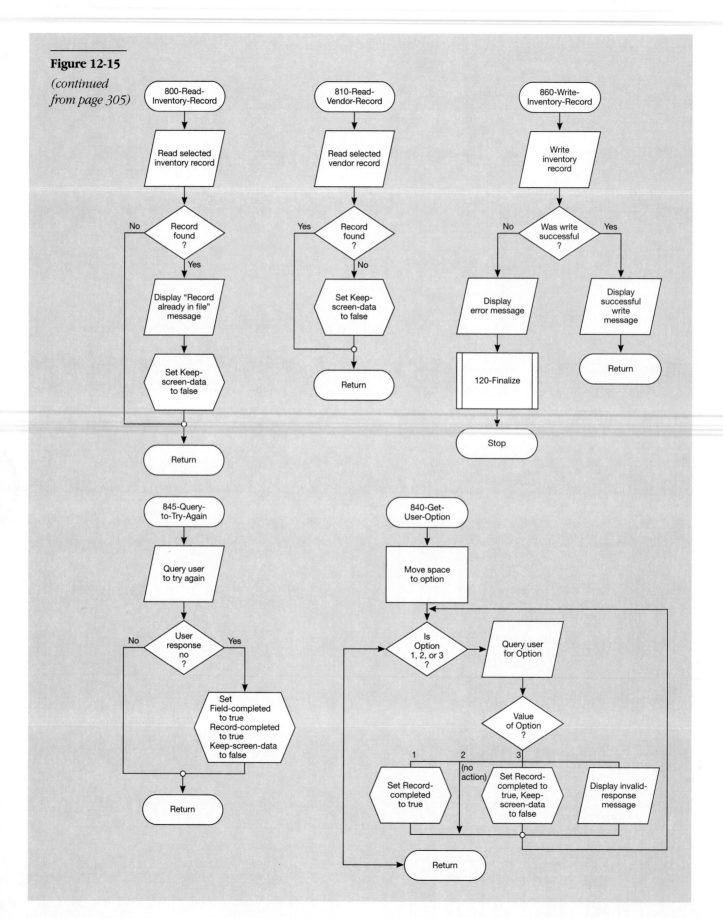

Figure 12-16

*Pseudocode—
Example 12-2*

```
000-Access-Inventory-File
    Perform 100-Initialize
    If user has entered non-blank Stock-number
        Perform 110-Create-1-Inventory-Record
            until Stock-number = spaces
        Perform 120-Finalize
    Stop

100-Initialize
    Initialize Inventory-record fields
    Request Stock-number from user
    If Stock-number not = spaces
        Open Inventory-file
             Vendor-file

110-Validate-1-Record
    Perform 300-Input-And-Validate-Data
    If Keep-screen-data is true
        Perform 860-Write-Inventory-Record
    else
        If Stock-Number-Is-Valid is true
           Display record-not-written message
    Initialize Inventory-record fields
    Request Stock-number from user

120-Finalize
    Close files

300-Input-And-Validate-Data
    Set Keep-screen-data switch to true
    Perform 400-Validate-Stock-Number
    If Keep-screen-data is true
        Move Vendor-name (from Vendors file) to output field
        Set Record-completed switch to false
        Repeat the following until Record-completed is true
            Perform 410-Validate-Software-Name
            If Keep-screen-data is true
               Perform 420-Validate-Quantity-On-Hand
            If Keep-screen-data is true
               Perform 430-Validate-Reorder-Level
            If Keep-screen-data is true
               Perform 440-Validate-Price
            If Keep-screen-data is true
               Perform 840-Get-User-Option

400-Validate-Stock-Number
    Perform 800-Read-Inventory-Record
    If Keep-screen-data is true
        Move input Vendor-number to Vendors file key field
        Perform 810-Read-Vendor-Record
        If Keep-screen-data is false
           Display error message
        else
           If Software-type not equal 1 through 6 or 9
              Display error message
              Set Keep-screen-data to false
           If Software-number is not numeric
              Display error message
              Set Keep-screen-data to false
        If Keep-screen-data is true
           Set Stock-number-is-valid switch to true
        else
           Set Stock-number-is-valid switch to false

410-Validate-Software-Name
    Set Field-completed switch to false
    Repeat until Field-completed is true
        Accept Software-name
        If first position of Software-name blank
           Display error message
           Perform 845-Query-To-Try-Again
        else
           Set Field-completed switch to true

420-Validate-Quantity-On-Hand
    Set Field-completed switch to false
    Repeat until Field-completed is true
        Accept Quantity-on-hand
        If Quantity-on-hand <= maximum
           Set Field-completed switch to true
        else
           Request user to confirm excess value
           If excess value is okay
              Set Field-completed switch to true
        If Field-completed is false
           Perform 845-Query-To-Try-Again

430-Validate-Reorder-Level
    Set Field-completed switch to false
    Repeat until Field-completed is true
        Accept Reorder-level
        If Reorder-level <= maximum and > 0
           Set Field-completed switch to true
        else
           Display error message
        If Field-completed is false
           Perform 845-Query-To-Try-Again

440-Validate-Price
    Set Field-completed switch to false
    Repeat until Field-completed is true
        Accept Price
        Case of
           When software code = 1-6 and Price not greater than 0
              Display error message
           When software code = 9 and Price not equal 0
              Display error message
           When other
              Set Field-completed switch to true
        If Field-completed is false
           Perform 845-Query-To-Try-Again

800-Read-Inventory-Record
    Read Inventory-record
    If requested record found
       Display already-in-file message
       Set Keep-screen-data to false

810-Read-Vendor-Record
    Read vendor record
    If requested record not found
       Set Keep-screen-data to false

840-Get-User-Option
    Move space to Option-selected
    Repeat until Option-selected = 1, 2, or 3
       Query user for option (1, 2, or 3)
       Case of Option-selected
          When 1
             Set Record-completed to true
          When 2
             Continue
          When 3
             Set Record-completed to true
             Set Keep-screen-data to false
          When other
             Display wrong-response error message

845-Query-To-Try-Again
    Query the user about trying again
    If user response is NO
       Set Field-completed to true
       Set Record-completed to true
       Set Keep-screen-data to false

860-Write-Inventory-Record
    Write Inventory-record
    If error on write
       Display write-error message
       Perform 120-Initialize
       Stop
    else
       Display record-written message
```

```
1       IDENTIFICATION DIVISION.
2       PROGRAM-ID. KEYB-VAL.
3
4       *    Written by J.Olson/W.Price
5       *    August 16, 1990
6
7       *    This program adds records to the indexed file SOFTWAR2.DI.
8       *    Each field is validated as it is input.
9       *    A record is not written to the file unless all of its fields
10      *      are valid.
11
12      *    Validation criteria:
13      *        Stock number (format vvtnn):
14      *            Must not already be present in SOFTWAR2.DI
15      *            vv (vendor ID) must be present in VENDORS.DI
16      *            t  (type of software) must be 1-6 or 9
17      *            nn (number) must be numeric
18      *        Product name:
19      *            Must be present
20      *            First character must not be blank
21      *        Quantity on hand:
22      *            Must be numeric and not negative  ( >= 0 )
23      *            Question if greater than 100
24      *        Reorder level:
25      *            Must be numeric
26      *            Must be 1-100 (inclusive)
27      *        Price:
28      *            Must be numeric
29      *            Must be > 0 if software type is 1-6
30      *            Must be zero if software type is 9 (demo)
31
32      ENVIRONMENT DIVISION.
33      CONFIGURATION SECTION.
34      SOURCE-COMPUTER. IBM-PC.
35
36      INPUT-OUTPUT SECTION.
37      FILE-CONTROL.
38          SELECT INVENTORY-FILE       ASSIGN TO DISK "SOFTWAR2.DI"
39                                      ORGANIZATION IS INDEXED
40                                      ACCESS IS RANDOM
41                                      RECORD KEY IS IR-STOCK-NUMBER.
42
43          SELECT VENDOR-FILE          ASSIGN TO DISK "VENDORS.DI"
44                                      ORGANIZATION IS INDEXED
45                                      ACCESS IS RANDOM
46                                      RECORD KEY IS VR-VENDOR-NUMBER.
47
48      DATA DIVISION.
49
50      FILE SECTION.
51
52      FD  INVENTORY-FILE.
53      01  INVENTORY-RECORD.
54          10  IR-STOCK-NUMBER.
55              20  IR-VENDOR-NUMBER        PIC X(2).
56              20  IR-SOFTWARE-TYPE        PIC X(1).
57                  88  REGULAR-SOFTWARE    VALUE "1" THRU "6".
58                  88  SAMPLE-SOFTWARE     VALUE "9".
59              20  IR-SOFTWARE-NUMBER      PIC X(2).
60          10  IR-SOFTWARE-NAME.
61              20  IR-POS-1-OF-NAME        PIC X(1).
62              20  IR-BALANCE-OF-RECORD    PIC X(29).
63          10  IR-VENDOR-NAME          PIC X(20).
64          10  IR-QUANT-ON-HAND        PIC 9(3).
65          10  IR-REORDER-LEVEL        PIC 9(3).
66          10  IR-PRICE                PIC 9(3)V9(2).
67
68      FD  VENDOR-FILE.
69      01  VENDOR-RECORD.
70          10  VR-VENDOR-NUMBER        PIC X(2).
71          10  VR-VENDOR-NAME          PIC X(20).
72
73      WORKING-STORAGE SECTION.
74
75      01  PROGRAMMED-SWITCHES.
76          10                          PIC X.
77              88  KEEP-SCREEN-DATA        VALUE "Y"  FALSE "N".
78          10                          PIC X.
79              88  STOCK-NUMBER-IS-VALID   VALUE "Y"  FALSE "N".
80          10                          PIC X.
81              88  RECORD-COMPLETED        VALUE "Y"  FALSE "N".
82          10                          PIC X.
83              88  FIELD-COMPLETED         VALUE "Y"  FALSE "N".
84
85      01  SIGNAL-FIELDS.
86          10  OPTION-SELECTED         PIC X.
87
88      01  VALIDATION-VALUES.
89          10  MAXIMUM-QUANTITY            PIC 9(3)   VALUE 100.
90
91      SCREEN SECTION.
92
93      01  ALREADY-IN-FILE-SCREEN.
94          10  VALUE  "Stock #"
95                                      LINE 19             HIGHLIGHT.
96          10  PIC X(5)       FROM IR-STOCK-NUMBER
97                                      COL PLUS 1      HIGHLIGHT.
98          10  VALUE  "is already in the file for the following item:"
99                                      COL PLUS 1      HIGHLIGHT.
100         10  PIC X(66)      FROM INVENTORY-RECORD
101                                      LINE PLUS 1     HIGHLIGHT.
102
103     01  CLEAR-MESSAGE-SCREEN.
104         10  VALUE  " "         LINE 16  BLANK REMAINDER.
105
106     01  DISK-ERROR-SCREEN.
107         10  VALUE  "An INVALID KEY condition has occurred while "
108                                      LINE 19             HIGHLIGHT.
109         10  VALUE  "writing the above data to the file."
110                                      LINE PLUS 0    COL PLUS 0   HIGHLIGHT.
111         10  VALUE  "Tap the Enter key to abort this job... "
112                                      LINE PLUS 1    BELL         HIGHLIGHT.
113         10  PIC X               TO OPTION-SELECTED         AUTO
114                                      LINE PLUS 0    COL PLUS 0.
115
116     01  INVALID-NUMBER-SCREEN.
117         10  VALUE "Your Stock number entry was: "
118                                      LINE 19             HIGHLIGHT.
119         10  PIC X(5)       FROM IR-STOCK-NUMBER
120                                      COL PLUS 1      HIGHLIGHT.
121         10  VALUE
122             "The last 2 positions contain non-numeric characters"
123                                      LINE PLUS 2         HIGHLIGHT.
124
125     01  INVALID-PRICE-SCREEN-A.
126         10  VALUE
127             "The price for Type 1-6 software must be greater than zero."
128                                      LINE 19   HIGHLIGHT.
129
130     01  INVALID-PRICE-SCREEN-B.
131         10  VALUE
132             "The price for sample software (Type 9) must be zero."
133                                      LINE 19             HIGHLIGHT.
134
135     01  INVALID-REORDER-LEVEL-SCREEN.
136         10  VALUE
137             "The quantity you entered is either zero or greater than "
138                                      LINE 19             HIGHLIGHT.
139         10  PIC ZZ9.B      FROM MAXIMUM-QUANTITY
140                                      LINE PLUS 0    COL PLUS 0   HIGHLIGHT.
141
142     01  INVALID-TYPE-SCREEN.
143         10  VALUE "Your Stock number entry was: "
144                                      LINE 19             HIGHLIGHT.
145         10  PIC X(5)       FROM IR-STOCK-NUMBER
146                                      COL PLUS 1      HIGHLIGHT.
147         10  VALUE
148             "The third position (software type code) is invalid."
149                                      LINE PLUS 1         HIGHLIGHT.
150
151     01  INVALID-SOFTWARE-NAME-SCREEN.
152         10  VALUE  "The software name must not start with a space."
153                                      LINE 19             HIGHLIGHT.
154
```

Figure 12-17

The KEYB-VAL Program—
Example 12-2

```
155   01  INVENTORY-RECORD-SCREEN.
156       10  VALUE "ADD INVENTORY RECORD"   BLANK SCREEN
157                                    LINE  2      COL 11.
158       10  VALUE "Stock number"      LINE PLUS 2  COL 1.
159       10                            PIC X(5)
160           FROM  IR-STOCK-NUMBER
161               REVERSE              LINE PLUS 0  COL 16.
162       10  VALUE "Software name"     LINE PLUS 2  COL 1.
163       10  SCR-SOFTWARE-NAME    PIC X(30)
164           USING IR-SOFTWARE-NAME
165               REQUIRED  REVERSE    LINE PLUS 0  COL 16.
166       10  VALUE "Vendor"           LINE PLUS 2  COL 1.
167       10                           PIC X(20)
168           FROM  IR-VENDOR-NAME
169               REVERSE              LINE PLUS 0  COL 16.
170       10  VALUE "Stock onhand"     LINE PLUS 2  COL 1.
171       10  SCR-QUANT-ON-HAND  PIC ZZ9
172           USING IR-QUANT-ON-HAND
173               REQUIRED   REVERSE   LINE PLUS 0  COL 16.
174       10  VALUE "Price"            LINE PLUS 0  COL 26.
175       10  SCR-PRICE        PIC ZZ9.99
176           USING IR-PRICE
177               REQUIRED  REVERSE    LINE PLUS 0  COL 34.
178       10  VALUE "Reorder level"    LINE PLUS 1  COL 1.
179       10  SCR-REORDER-LEVEL   PIC ZZ9
180           USING IR-REORDER-LEVEL
181               REQUIRED  REVERSE    LINE PLUS 0  COL 16.
182
183   01  NO-VENDOR-RECORD-SCREEN.
184       10  VALUE "Your Stock number entry was: "
185                         LINE 19               HIGHLIGHT.
186       10  PIC X(5)       FROM IR-STOCK-NUMBER
187                         COL PLUS 1      HIGHLIGHT.
188       10  VALUE  "There is no vendor record for Vendor # "
189                         LINE PLUS 1          HIGHLIGHT.
190       10  PIC X(2)       FROM VR-VENDOR-NUMBER
191                         LINE PLUS 0  COL PLUS 0  HIGHLIGHT.
192
193   01  QUESTION-QUANTITY-SCREEN.
194       10  VALUE "The quantity which you entered is greater than "
195                         LINE 18              HIGHLIGHT.
196       10  PIC ZZ9       FROM MAXIMUM-QUANTITY
197                         LINE PLUS 0  COL PLUS 0  HIGHLIGHT.
198       10  VALUE "Are you sure that this is correct <y/n> ? "
199                         LINE PLUS 1          HIGHLIGHT.
200       10  PIC X         TO OPTION-SELECTED       AUTO
201                         LINE PLUS 0  COL PLUS 0.
202
203   01  RECORD-COMPL-WRONG-OPT-SCREEN.
204       10  VALUE "Invalid option—try again."
205                         LINE 23        BELL    HIGHLIGHT.
206
207   01  RECORD-COMPLETED-MENU-SCREEN.
208       10  VALUE "You have the follow options for this screen:"
209                         LINE 16              HIGHLIGHT.
210       10  VALUE "   1  All data correct.  OK to write new record."
211                         LINE PLUS 2.
212       10  VALUE "   2  A correction needs to be made."
213                         LINE PLUS 1.
214       10  VALUE "   3  CANCEL the data shown above."
215                         LINE PLUS 1.
216       10  VALUE "Please enter your choice from the above menu: "
217                         LINE PLUS 1          HIGHLIGHT.
218       10  PIC X       USING OPTION-SELECTED      AUTO
219                         LINE PLUS 0  COL PLUS 0.
220
221   01  RECORD-NOT-WRITTEN-SCREEN.
222       10  VALUE "The above record was NOT written to the file."
223                         LINE 13              HIGHLIGHT.
224
225   01  RECORD-WRITTEN-SCREEN.
226       10  VALUE "The above record has been written to the file."
227                         LINE 13              HIGHLIGHT.
228
229   01  TRY-AGAIN-SCREEN.
230       10  VALUE "Do you want to try again <y/n>? "
231                         LINE 21              HIGHLIGHT.
232       10  PIC X         TO OPTION-SELECTED       AUTO
233                         LINE PLUS 0  COL PLUS 0.
234
235   01  USER-REQUEST-SCREEN.
236       10  VALUE "To create a new record, enter the stock number:"
237                         LINE 16              HIGHLIGHT.
238       10  VALUE "To exit, strike the Enter key."
239                         LINE PLUS 1          HIGHLIGHT.
240       10  PIC X(5)      TO IR-STOCK-NUMBER
241                         FULL  LINE 16   COL 49.
```

```
242
243   PROCEDURE DIVISION.
244
245   000-CREATE-INVENTORY-RECORDS.
246       PERFORM 100-INITIALIZE
247       IF IR-STOCK-NUMBER NOT = SPACES
248           PERFORM 110-CREATE-1-INVENTORY-RECORD
249               UNTIL IR-STOCK-NUMBER = SPACES
250           PERFORM 120-FINALIZE
251       END-IF
252       STOP RUN.
253
254   100-INITIALIZE.
255       DISPLAY " " ERASE
256       INITIALIZE INVENTORY-RECORD
257       DISPLAY USER-REQUEST-SCREEN
258       ACCEPT  USER-REQUEST-SCREEN
259       DISPLAY CLEAR-MESSAGE-SCREEN
260       IF IR-STOCK-NUMBER NOT = SPACES
261           OPEN I-O INVENTORY-FILE
262           OPEN INPUT VENDOR-FILE
263       END-IF.
264
265   110-CREATE-1-INVENTORY-RECORD.
266       PERFORM 300-INPUT-AND-VALIDATE-DATA
267       IF KEEP-SCREEN-DATA
268           PERFORM 860-WRITE-INVENTORY-RECORD
269       ELSE
270           IF STOCK-NUMBER-IS-VALID
271               DISPLAY RECORD-NOT-WRITTEN-SCREEN
272           END-IF
273       END-IF
274       INITIALIZE INVENTORY-RECORD
275       DISPLAY USER-REQUEST-SCREEN
276       ACCEPT  USER-REQUEST-SCREEN
277       DISPLAY CLEAR-MESSAGE-SCREEN.
278
279   120-FINALIZE.
280       CLOSE INVENTORY-FILE, VENDOR-FILE.
281
282   300-INPUT-AND-VALIDATE-DATA.
283       SET KEEP-SCREEN-DATA TO TRUE
284       PERFORM 400-VALIDATE-STOCK-NUMBER
285       IF KEEP-SCREEN-DATA
286           MOVE VR-VENDOR-NAME TO IR-VENDOR-NAME
287           SET RECORD-COMPLETED TO FALSE
288           PERFORM UNTIL RECORD-COMPLETED
289               DISPLAY INVENTORY-RECORD-SCREEN
290
291   *         Accept and validate Software Name
292               PERFORM 410-VALIDATE-SOFTWARE-NAME
293
294   *         Accept and validate Quantity On Hand
295               IF KEEP-SCREEN-DATA
296                   PERFORM 420-VALIDATE-QUANTITY-ON-HAND
297               END-IF
298
299   *         Accept and validate Reorder Level
300               IF KEEP-SCREEN-DATA
301                   PERFORM 430-VALIDATE-REORDER-LEVEL
302               END-IF
303
304   *         Accept and validate Price
305               IF KEEP-SCREEN-DATA
306                   PERFORM 440-VALIDATE-PRICE
307               END-IF
308
309   *         Data entry completed
310               IF KEEP-SCREEN-DATA
311                   PERFORM 840-GET-USER-OPTION
312               END-IF
313           END-PERFORM
314       END-IF.
315
```

Figure 12-17

(continued on page 310)
(continued on page 310)

```
316   400-VALIDATE-STOCK-NUMBER.
317       PERFORM 800-READ-INVENTORY-RECORD
318
319       IF KEEP-SCREEN-DATA
320           MOVE IR-VENDOR-NUMBER TO VR-VENDOR-NUMBER
321           PERFORM 810-READ-VENDOR-RECORD
322
323           IF NOT KEEP-SCREEN-DATA
324               DISPLAY NO-VENDOR-RECORD-SCREEN
325
326           ELSE
327               IF IR-SOFTWARE-TYPE IS < 1
328               OR > 6 AND NOT = 9
329                   DISPLAY INVALID-TYPE-SCREEN
330                   SET KEEP-SCREEN-DATA TO FALSE
331               END-IF
332
333               IF IR-SOFTWARE-NUMBER IS NOT NUMERIC
334                   DISPLAY INVALID-NUMBER-SCREEN
335                   SET KEEP-SCREEN-DATA TO FALSE
336               END-IF
337           END-IF
338       END-IF
339
340       IF KEEP-SCREEN-DATA
341           SET STOCK-NUMBER-IS-VALID TO TRUE
342       ELSE
343           SET STOCK-NUMBER-IS-VALID TO FALSE
344       END-IF.
345
346   410-VALIDATE-SOFTWARE-NAME.
347       SET FIELD-COMPLETED TO FALSE
348       PERFORM UNTIL FIELD-COMPLETED
349           ACCEPT SCR-SOFTWARE-NAME
350           IF IR-POS-1-OF-NAME NOT = SPACE
351               SET FIELD-COMPLETED TO TRUE
352           ELSE
353               DISPLAY INVALID-SOFTWARE-NAME-SCREEN
354               PERFORM 845-QUERY-TO-TRY-AGAIN
355           END-IF
356       END-PERFORM.
357
358   420-VALIDATE-QUANTITY-ON-HAND.
359       SET FIELD-COMPLETED TO FALSE
360       PERFORM UNTIL FIELD-COMPLETED
361           ACCEPT SCR-QUANT-ON-HAND
362           IF IR-QUANT-ON-HAND IS <= MAXIMUM-QUANTITY
363               SET FIELD-COMPLETED TO TRUE
364           ELSE
365               DISPLAY QUESTION-QUANTITY-SCREEN
366               ACCEPT QUESTION-QUANTITY-SCREEN
367               DISPLAY CLEAR-MESSAGE-SCREEN
368               IF OPTION-SELECTED = "y" OR "Y"
369                   SET FIELD-COMPLETED TO TRUE
370               END-IF
371           END-IF
372           IF NOT FIELD-COMPLETED
373               PERFORM 845-QUERY-TO-TRY-AGAIN
374           END-IF
375       END-PERFORM.
376
377   430-VALIDATE-REORDER-LEVEL.
378       SET FIELD-COMPLETED TO FALSE
379       PERFORM UNTIL FIELD-COMPLETED
380           ACCEPT SCR-REORDER-LEVEL
381           IF IR-REORDER-LEVEL IS <= MAXIMUM-QUANTITY AND > 0
382               SET FIELD-COMPLETED TO TRUE
383           ELSE
384               DISPLAY INVALID-REORDER-LEVEL-SCREEN
385           END-IF
386           IF NOT FIELD-COMPLETED
387               PERFORM 845-QUERY-TO-TRY-AGAIN
388           END-IF
389       END-PERFORM.
390
391   440-VALIDATE-PRICE.
392       SET FIELD-COMPLETED TO FALSE
393       PERFORM UNTIL FIELD-COMPLETED
394           ACCEPT SCR-PRICE
395           EVALUATE TRUE
396               WHEN REGULAR-SOFTWARE
397               AND IR-PRICE IS NOT > 0
398                   DISPLAY INVALID-PRICE-SCREEN-A
399               WHEN SAMPLE-SOFTWARE
400               AND IR-PRICE IS NOT = 0
401                   DISPLAY INVALID-PRICE-SCREEN-B
402               WHEN OTHER
403                   SET FIELD-COMPLETED TO TRUE
404           END-EVALUATE
405           IF NOT FIELD-COMPLETED
406               PERFORM 845-QUERY-TO-TRY-AGAIN
407           END-IF
408       END-PERFORM.
409
410   800-READ-INVENTORY-RECORD.
411       READ INVENTORY-FILE
412           INVALID KEY
413               CONTINUE
414           NOT INVALID KEY
415               DISPLAY ALREADY-IN-FILE-SCREEN
416               SET KEEP-SCREEN-DATA TO FALSE
417       END-READ.
418
419   810-READ-VENDOR-RECORD.
420       READ VENDOR-FILE
421           INVALID KEY
422               SET KEEP-SCREEN-DATA TO FALSE
423       END-READ.
424
425   840-GET-USER-OPTION.
426       MOVE SPACE TO OPTION-SELECTED
427       PERFORM UNTIL OPTION-SELECTED = "1" OR "2" OR "3"
428           DISPLAY RECORD-COMPLETED-MENU-SCREEN
429           ACCEPT  RECORD-COMPLETED-MENU-SCREEN
430           EVALUATE OPTION-SELECTED
431               WHEN 1
432                   SET RECORD-COMPLETED TO TRUE
433               WHEN 2
434                   CONTINUE
435               WHEN 3
436                   SET RECORD-COMPLETED TO TRUE
437                   SET KEEP-SCREEN-DATA TO FALSE
438               WHEN OTHER
439                   DISPLAY RECORD-COMPL-WRONG-OPT-SCREEN
440           END-EVALUATE
441       END-PERFORM
442       DISPLAY CLEAR-MESSAGE-SCREEN.
443
444   845-QUERY-TO-TRY-AGAIN.
445       DISPLAY TRY-AGAIN-SCREEN
446       ACCEPT  TRY-AGAIN-SCREEN
447       IF OPTION-SELECTED = "n" OR "N"
448           SET FIELD-COMPLETED TO TRUE
449           SET RECORD-COMPLETED TO TRUE
450           SET KEEP-SCREEN-DATA TO FALSE
451       END-IF
452       DISPLAY CLEAR-MESSAGE-SCREEN.
453
454   860-WRITE-INVENTORY-RECORD.
455       WRITE INVENTORY-RECORD
456           INVALID KEY
457               DISPLAY DISK-ERROR-SCREEN
458               ACCEPT  DISK-ERROR-SCREEN
459               PERFORM 120-FINALIZE
460               STOP RUN
461           NOT INVALID KEY
462               DISPLAY RECORD-WRITTEN-SCREEN
463       END-WRITE.
```

Figure 12-17

(continued from page 309)

Analysis of the Data Entry/Validation Program

Program Execution

To illustrate the general feel of this program, let's consider the various screens for different data scenarios. The data entry sequence will include the following:

1. Enter an invalid stock number (07ABC)
2. Respond with a valid stock number (07143)
3. Enter the software name with a leading space
4. Abort the record
5. Enter a valid stock number and software name
6. Enter a Stock-on-hand value that exceeds the warning level
7. Enter a Reorder-level that is negative

When the program is first run, the prompt of Figure 12-18(a) is displayed. If you strike the Enter key without typing a stock number, processing will be terminated without proceeding further. If you type the stock number 07ABC, appropriate error messages are displayed as shown in Figure 12-18(b), the stock number entry field is cleared to spaces, and the cursor is awaiting reentry.

Entering the stock number 07143 (valid) causes the data entry screen to be displayed as shown in Figure 12-19. Notice that the vendor name—as well as the stock number—

Figure 12-18

Stock Number Entry

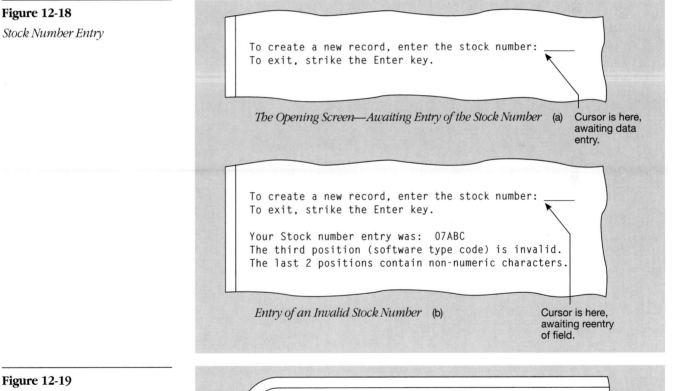

```
To create a new record, enter the stock number: _____
To exit, strike the Enter key.
```

The Opening Screen—Awaiting Entry of the Stock Number   (a)   Cursor is here, awaiting data entry.

```
To create a new record, enter the stock number: _____
To exit, strike the Enter key.

Your Stock number entry was:  07ABC
The third position (software type code) is invalid.
The last 2 positions contain non-numeric characters.
```

Entry of an Invalid Stock Number   (b)   Cursor is here, awaiting reentry of field.

Figure 12-19

A Valid Stock Number and the Vendor Name are Displayed

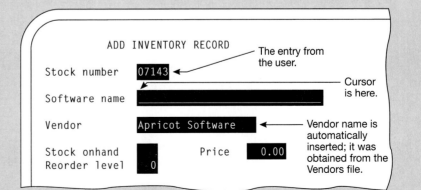

```
            ADD INVENTORY RECORD        The entry from
                                        the user.
Stock number      07143

Software name                                       Cursor
                                                    is here.
Vendor            Apricot Software       Vendor name is
                                         automatically
Stock onhand            Price   0.00     inserted; it was
Reorder level     0                      obtained from the
                                         Vendors file.
```

have been inserted in this screen record. Because the vendor name is obtained from the Vendors file (for the selected vendor number), the vendor name is not a keyboard entry, nor can it be modified from the keyboard.

In Figure 12-20, the software name has been entered, preceded by a space. Remember that one of the validation criteria is that the first position not be a space. Notice that the cursor does not automatically return to the invalid field; you are provided with an option regarding your next action. If you elect not to try again and strike the letter *n,* this screen record will be aborted, as shown by the screen contents of Figure 12-21. Here the cursor is positioned for you to begin entry of another record or to terminate processing. Had you responded with *y* to the query of Figure 12-20, the cursor would have been repositioned to the vendor name field and you would have been able to make the appropriate correction.

Figure 12-20

The Error Message Resulting from a Leading Space in the Software Name

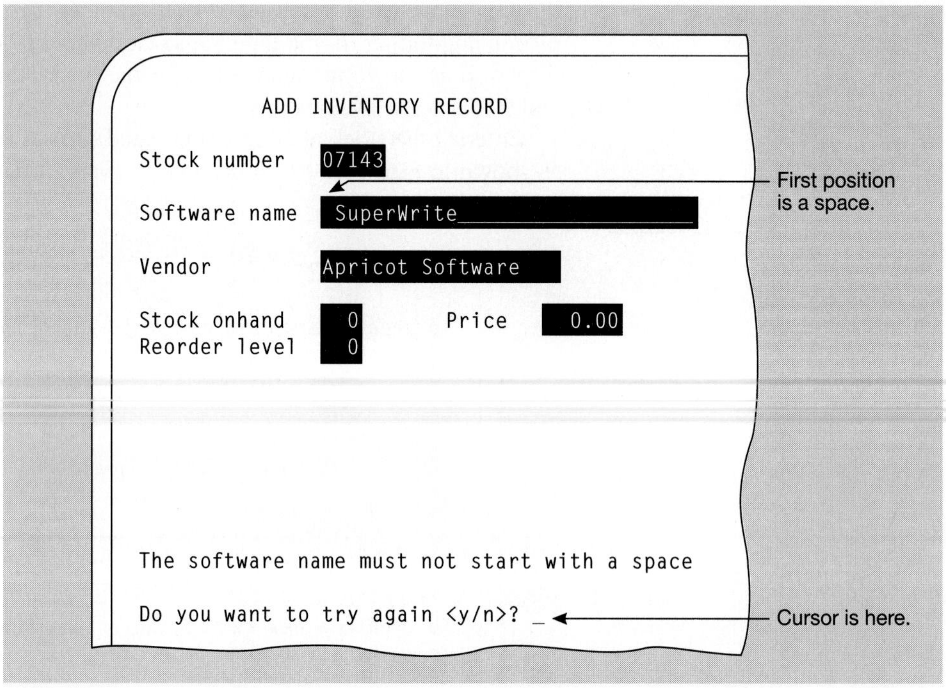

```
                    ADD INVENTORY RECORD

    Stock number    07143
                                                                First position
    Software name    SuperWrite_____                    is a space.

    Vendor           Apricot Software

    Stock onhand     0          Price     0.00
    Reorder level    0




    The software name must not start with a space

    Do you want to try again <y/n>? _                           Cursor is here.
```

Figure 12-21

The Effect of Choosing Not to Correct the Invalid Name

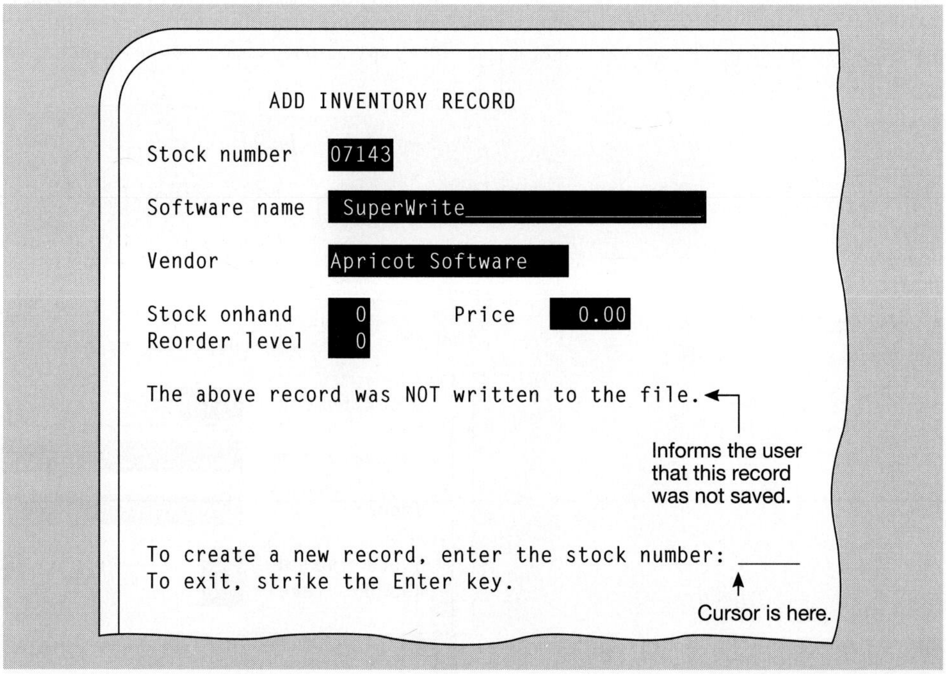

```
                    ADD INVENTORY RECORD

    Stock number    07143

    Software name    SuperWrite_____

    Vendor           Apricot Software

    Stock onhand     0          Price     0.00
    Reorder level    0

    The above record was NOT written to the file.
                                                        Informs the user
                                                        that this record
                                                        was not saved.


    To create a new record, enter the stock number: _____
    To exit, strike the Enter key.
                                                        Cursor is here.
```

Figure 12-22 reflects an invalid entry for the Stock-on-hand field. For this program, the warning value has been defined as 100; this is a reasonableness check. You are simply being warned that this is an unusually large value and, if it is to be retained, you must confirm this. Striking the letter *y* causes the value to be accepted.

Each of the preceding error messages results from program code and the display of a message defined in the SCREEN SECTION. However, in Figure 12-23 is a message displayed automatically by the RM/COBOL-85 system because the data entered does not correspond to the PICTURE definition for the field (it does not include a sign). A similar message would have occurred had nonnumeric data been entered into this field. Unlike the READ statement that does not monitor the data placed into numeric fields, the ACCEPT statement does. It will not allow you to enter data that is not consistent with the PICTURE definition of that field.

As with the S-EXTEND program, when the screen record has been completed, you are provided three options: *1* to save the record, *2* to edit it, and *3* to abort it. If you elect to

Figure 12-22

A Warning Message About a "Large" Entry for the Stock on Hand

Figure 12-23

An Error Automatically Detected by the COBOL System

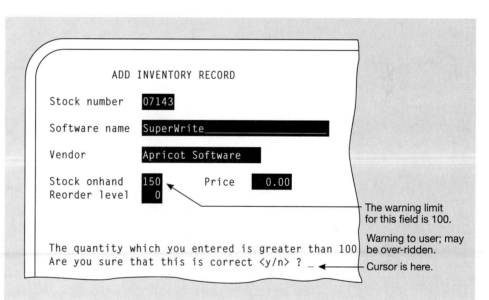

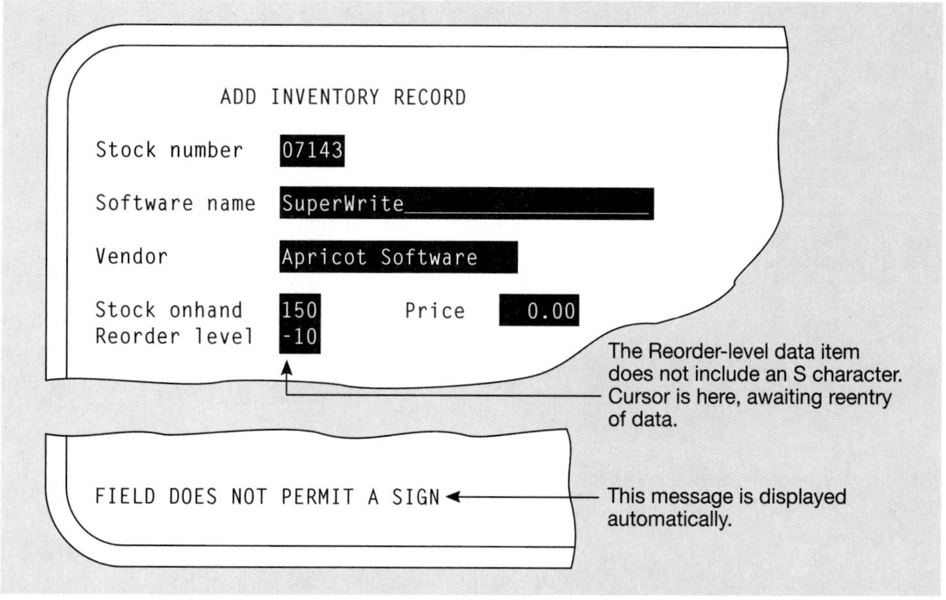

Figure 12-24

Enter a Stock Number or Terminate Data Entry

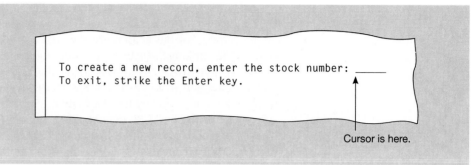

edit, the cursor is positioned at the Software-name field on the screen and you can proceed to change (or leave unchanged) fields as appropriate. When you are finished with the record and save (or abort it), the query of Figure 12-24 is again displayed. You may enter another record or terminate processing.

Programmed Switches

Before looking at the program and its logical structure, you should be aware of the following four programmed switches that it uses (these are their condition names, not their data-names):

> FIELD-COMPLETE
> RECORD-COMPLETED
> KEEP-SCREEN-DATA
> STOCK-NUMBER-IS-VALID

Understanding the purpose of these is critical to understanding how the program functions.

FIELD-COMPLETE. The entry of each field lies within a loop that is controlled by this switch. Prior to accepting each field, this switch is set to false. A valid field entry or a request to abort causes this switch to be set to true, thus exiting the loop.

RECORD-COMPLETED. The entry of a record lies within a loop that is controlled by this switch. Prior to beginning a record, this switch is set to false. A request to save the record or a request to abort it causes this switch to be set to true, thus exiting the loop.

KEEP-SCREEN-DATA. This switch is effectively the abort switch. Prior to beginning a record, this switch is set to true. If during the entry of any field or after the entire record has been entered, the user decides to abort the screen record, the switch is set to false. The screen record is written to the software file only if this switch is true.

STOCK-NUMBER-IS-VALID. The sole purpose of this switch is to determine the message displayed after an otherwise valid record has been completed. If, at the request of the user, the completed record is not to be written, the message reflects this.

The SCREEN SECTION

The variety of screen displays and error messages are defined in the SCREEN SECTION beginning at line 91 (Figure 12-17). To make each name easy to find, they are organized in alphabetic sequence based on the screen-record name. Notice that all messages are defined in the SCREEN SECTION and are displayed with a DISPLAY screen-name statement. Relative screen positioning (for instance, LINE PLUS 2) is used wherever possible to simplify the task of moving display elements in case a change in the screen design is desired.

Overall Program Execution

Overall control, as with all this book's programs, is through the 000 mainline module that repetitively executes a processing module (110). Both the 110 module and the 300 module, which controls field validation, are shown in Figure 12-25. The broad sequence of steps in the 110 module are

1. Accept and verify the keyboard data

2. If the switch KEEP-SCREEN-DATA is true, write the screen record to disk

3. Prepare for the next record

The first action of the 300 module (before beginning data entry) is to initialize the KEEP-SCREEN-DATA switch to true. Then through the 400 module, the stock number is accepted and validated. If it is not valid, KEEP-SCREEN-DATA is set to false. This is done in the 400 module (as well as in each of the other field validation modules if the user elects to abort a record at any point in the data entry sequence). In the 300 module, each data entry/validation module is executed only if KEEP-SCREEN-DATA is true. Thus, if at any field during the data entry the user decides to abort this record, the remainder of the modules are skipped.

Validating the User-Entered Stock Number

Validation of the stock number is the most complex single evaluation. It consists of ensuring the following:

1. That there is not already a record in the software inventory file for this stock number; for this, the inventory file must be read

2. That the vendor number (first two positions of the stock number) are for a vendor in the vendors file; for this, the vendors file must be read

3. That the software type (third position of the stock number) is a digit 1 through 6 or 9

4. That the software number (last two positions of the stock number) are numeric

This validation is done in the 400 module. However, before looking at it, consider the 800 and 810 modules to read the two files (see Figure 12-26). In the 800 module, an attempt is made to read a record from the inventory file with a stock number equal to the newly entered stock number. A successful read means that there is already a record in the file for the stock number, which is an invalid condition. An error message is displayed and KEEP-SCREEN-DATA is set to false.

In the 810 module, the vendors file is read to verify that the stock number includes the vendor number of an existing vendor and to obtain the vendor name. An unsuccessful read means the vendor is not in the file; KEEP-SCREEN-DATA is set to false.

Figure 12-25

The 110 and 300 Modules

```
110-CREATE-1-INVENTORY-RECORD.                 300-INPUT-AND-VALIDATE-DATA.
    PERFORM 300-INPUT-AND-VALIDATE-DATA            SET KEEP-SCREEN-DATA TO TRUE
    IF KEEP-SCREEN-DATA                            PERFORM 400-VALIDATE-STOCK-NUMBER
      PERFORM 860-WRITE-INVENTORY-RECORD           IF KEEP-SCREEN-DATA
    ELSE                                             MOVE VR-VENDOR-NAME TO IR-VENDOR-NAME
      IF STOCK-NUMBER-IS-VALID                       SET RECORD-COMPLETED TO FALSE
        DISPLAY RECORD-NOT-WRITTEN-SCREEN            PERFORM UNTIL RECORD-COMPLETED
      END-IF                                           DISPLAY INVENTORY-RECORD-SCREEN
    END-IF
    INITIALIZE INVENTORY-RECORD             *         Accept and validate Software Name
    DISPLAY USER-REQUEST-SCREEN                       PERFORM 410-VALIDATE-SOFTWARE-NAME
    ACCEPT  USER-REQUEST-SCREEN
    DISPLAY CLEAR-MESSAGE-SCREEN.           *         Accept and validate Quantity On Hand
                                                      IF KEEP-SCREEN-DATA
                                                        PERFORM 420-VALIDATE-QUANTITY-ON-HAND
                                                      END-IF

                                           *         Accept and validate Reorder Level
                                                      IF KEEP-SCREEN-DATA
                                                        PERFORM 430-VALIDATE-REORDER-LEVEL
                                                      END-IF

                                           *         Accept and validate Price
                                                      IF KEEP-SCREEN-DATA
                                                        PERFORM 440-VALIDATE-PRICE
                                                      END-IF

                                           *         Data entry completed
                                                      IF KEEP-SCREEN-DATA
                                                        PERFORM 840-GET-USER-OPTION
                                                      END-IF
                                                    END-PERFORM
                                                END-IF.
```

Figure 12-26

The 800 and 810 Modules

```
800-READ-INVENTORY-RECORD                        810-READ-VENDOR-RECORD.
   READ INVENTORY-FILE                               READ VENDOR-FILE
     INVALID KEY                                        INVALID KEY
       CONTINUE                                            SET KEEP-SCREEN-DATA TO FALSE
     NOT INVALID KEY                                 END-READ.
       DISPLAY ALREADY-IN-FILE-SCREEN
       SET KEEP-SCREEN-DATA TO FALSE
   END-READ.
```

Now consider the 400 module included in Figure 12-27 to accept and validate the stock number. Execution of this module proceeds as follows:

1. The 800 module is performed to ensure that no record already exists in the software file. If none is found, KEEP-SCREEN-DATA will still be true and the sequence following the IF will be executed.

2. The 810 module is performed to check the existence of the vendor in the vendors file. If the vendor is found, KEEP-SCREEN-DATA will still be true.

3. If KEEP-SCREEN-DATA is false, an error message will be displayed (the test condition is NOT KEEP-SCREEN-DATA).

4. If KEEP-SCREEN-DATA is true, the software type will be tested; KEEP-SCREEN-DATA is set to false if the type is not in the allowable range. Similarly, the software number is tested for being numeric.

5. At the end of the sequence, the switch STOCK-NUMBER-IS-VALID is set to true or false, depending upon the value of KEEP-SCREEN-DATA.

The data entry modules 410, 420, 430, and 440 are similar in their structure to the 400 module (although they are less complicated).

Aborting a Record— The 845 Module

Recall from Figures 12-20 and 12-21 that an invalid field produces a query asking if you want to continue. Responding with an *N* aborts the current screen record (regardless of the field with which you are working). This is done in the 845 module, repeated here in Figure 12-28. Notice that the switches FIELD-COMPLETED and RECORD-COMPLETED are both set to true so that no more action will be taken with this field or with this record. However, KEEP-SCREEN-RECORD is set to false, which will cause the record to be aborted.

Figure 12-27

The 400 Module

```
400-VALIDATE-STOCK-NUMBER.
   PERFORM 800-READ-INVENTORY-RECORD

   IF KEEP-SCREEN-DATA
     MOVE IR-VENDOR-NUMBER TO VR-VENDOR-NUMBER
     PERFORM 810-READ-VENDOR-RECORD

     IF NOT KEEP-SCREEN-DATA
       DISPLAY NO-VENDOR-RECORD-SCREEN

     ELSE
       IF IR-SOFTWARE-TYPE IS < 1
       OR > 6 AND NOT = 9
         DISPLAY INVALID-TYPE-SCREEN
         SET KEEP-SCREEN-DATA TO FALSE
       END-IF

       IF IR-SOFTWARE-NUMBER IS NOT NUMERIC
         DISPLAY INVALID-NUMBER-SCREEN
         SET KEEP-SCREEN-DATA TO FALSE
       END-IF
     END-IF
   END-IF

   IF KEEP-SCREEN-DATA
     SET STOCK-NUMBER-IS-VALID TO TRUE
   ELSE
     SET STOCK-NUMBER-IS-VALID TO FALSE
   END-IF.
```

Figure 12-28

The 845 Module

```
845-QUERY-TO-TRY-AGAIN.
    DISPLAY TRY-AGAIN-SCREEN
    ACCEPT  TRY-AGAIN-SCREEN
    IF OPTION-SELECTED = "n" OR "N"
        SET FIELD-COMPLETED TO TRUE
        SET RECORD-COMPLETED TO TRUE
        SET KEEP-SCREEN-DATA TO FALSE
    END-IF
    DISPLAY CLEAR-MESSAGE-SCREEN.
```

Providing the User with an Option—The 840 Module

Referring back to the 300 module (see Figure 12-25), notice that the sequence of data entry/validation for modules 410 through 440 is controlled by the in-line PERFORM:

```
PERFORM UNTIL RECORD-COMPLETED
```

Since RECORD-COMPLETED is initialized to false, it must be changed to true before this loop can be exited.

After the last field is accepted and validated, the 840 module is performed. This module, shown in Figure 12-29, gives the user the option to write (option 1), edit (option 2), or abort (option 3) the record. If the user selects the 2 option (edit), RECORD-COMPLETED remains unchanged and the data entry/validation sequence of the 300 module is repeated. A selection of 1 or 3 causes the switch to be changed to false. Also, the 3 option changes KEEP-SCREEN-DATA to false.

Notice that the query is executed within a loop to ensure that the proper entry is made (the in-line PERFORM). If anything other than 1, 2, or 3 is entered, a message is displayed and the response is requested again.

Program Termination on an Error—The 860 Module

The 860 module (Figure 12-30) writes the validated record to disk, a relatively simple action. Notice that this WRITE includes an INVALID KEY clause. Since the inventory file has been checked to ensure that a record does not already exist for this stock number, there will never be an error resulting from a duplicate key.

The remaining possibility is some type of error relating to the physical writing of the record to disk: a hardware error. In later chapters, you will learn about error recovery procedures. In this program, execution is simply terminated with an error message. You should be aware that terminating execution from within a called module is considered poor structured practice. Modifying the program to terminate with the STOP RUN at line 252 is the subject of an exercise that follows.

Figure 12-29

The 840 Module

```
840-GET-USER-OPTION.
    MOVE SPACE TO OPTION-SELECTED
    PERFORM UNTIL OPTION-SELECTED = "1" OR "2" OR "3"
        DISPLAY RECORD-COMPLETED-MENU-SCREEN
        ACCEPT  RECORD-COMPLETED-MENU-SCREEN
        EVALUATE OPTION-SELECTED
            WHEN 1
                SET RECORD-COMPLETED TO TRUE
            WHEN 2
                CONTINUE
            WHEN 3
                SET RECORD-COMPLETED TO TRUE
                SET KEEP-SCREEN-DATA TO FALSE
            WHEN OTHER
                DISPLAY RECORD-COMPL-WRONG-OPT-SCREEN
        END-EVALUATE
    END-PERFORM
    DISPLAY CLEAR-MESSAGE-SCREEN.
```

Figure 12-30

The 860 Module

```
860-WRITE-INVENTORY-RECORD.
    WRITE INVENTORY-RECORD
      INVALID KEY
        DISPLAY DISK-ERROR-SCREEN
        ACCEPT  DISK-ERROR-SCREEN
        PERFORM 120-FINALIZE
        STOP RUN
      NOT INVALID KEY
        DISPLAY RECORD-WRITTEN-SCREEN
    END-WRITE.
```

Chapter Summary

General

Two broad ways of validating data before it is placed into service in a computer application are

■ Batch validation is the validation of a data file that is already in machine-readable form. A batch validation program inspects each record, identifies errors according to a designated set of criterion, and prints a report summarizing the errors.

■ On-line validation is the validation of data on a field-by-field (or record-by-record) basis as each field is entered through a keyboard. Errors are identified immediately and the keyboard operator is prompted to correct the entry before proceeding.

COBOL Language Elements

Only one new language element was introduced in this chapter.

REDEFINES   This clause—for use in the DATA DIVISION—allows the same memory area to be described with different data description entries.

Questions and Exercises

Key Terminology

Give a brief description of each of the following terms that were introduced in this chapter.

batch validation	off-line data entry
data validation	on-line data entry
field dependence	on-line validation

General Questions

1. Describe each of the data validation methods discussed in this chapter. Is one method preferred over the other?

2. Why is it important to validate data being input into any system?

3. How can numeric fields be described so that checks may be done for non-numeric data?

4. What four syntactical rules must be followed when using the REDEFINES clause?

5. What fields are validated for the software inventory file records? Why are multiple checks made against many of the fields?

6. How does the on-line data validation for the software inventory file records differ from the batch validation?

Questions Relating to the Example Programs

The FILE-VAL program (Figure 12-6).

1. What would be printed for the report if the file processed contained no invalid data?

2. What changes would be necessary if the application needs required that all input records be printed? Those with no errors are to be printed with no message; those with errors are to be printed as in the current program.

3. In the 410 module for validating the software name, would it make any difference if the order of the tests were reversed (that is, if the first IF tested IR-POS-1-OF-NAME for a space and the second IF tested IR-SOFTWARE-NAME for spaces)?

4. What would be the effect of omitting the SET statement from the 720 module (line 272) that sets the ERROR-FOUND switch to true? Consider a record with nonnumeric fields for both the Quantity-on-hand and Reorder-level fields.

The KEYB-VAL program (Figure 12-17).

5. In the FILE-VAL program, all numeric fields are tested to be numeric (for instance, see the 420 module for testing the Quantity-on-hand field, line 205). However, the KEYB-VAL program does not include a numeric test (refer to its 420 module, beginning line 358). Why does it not include the numeric test?

6. In the screen definition for the inventory-record-screen (beginning line 155), all the fields are defined with USING—except IR-STOCK-NUMBER and IR-VENDOR-NAME, which are defined with FROM. Why are these two different from the others?

7. What would happen if TO were used in entries of the inventory-record-screen (beginning line 155), rather than USING?

8. What would occur if the WHEN OTHER option were omitted from the EVALUATE statement in the 840 module (at lines 438 and 439)?

9. The following statements (lines 459 and 460) are to be deleted from the program:

```
PERFORM 120-FINALIZE
STOP RUN
```

Insert needed statements in this module and in the 110 module so that execution will be terminated immediately, but via the 000 module. To do this, you will need to define a switch, initialize it in the 100 module, set it on a disk error, and test it at the appropriate place in the 110 module.

Programming Assignments

12-1 Batch Data Validation of Airport Data

The data processing manager for the Anacin Airport has just received an airport file containing data that has not been verified for validity. Before this data is placed into service, it must be validated. (The airport file was used in Programming Assignments 6-1, 10-2, and 11-1.)

Output Requirements:
　　A report listing only those records with invalid entries. Following each invalid record detail line must be one line describing each error detected in that record. Output must be according to the following printer spacing chart.

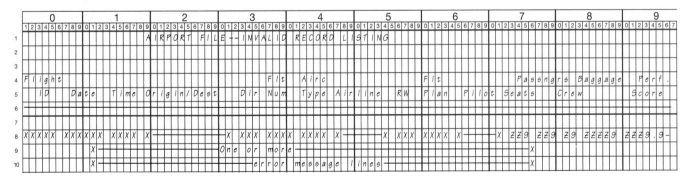

Input Description:
　　File name: AIRPORT1.DLE
　　Record description: Same as AIRPORT1.DL; see Appendix A

Processing Requirements:

This program is to process each record from the input file as follows.

1. Validate the following fields as indicated.

Date of flight	Month between 01 and 12
	Day between 01 and 31
Arrival/depart time	Between 0001 and 2400
Direction	Must be IN or OUT
Runway used be	If last character is not a digit or space, it must be C, L, or R
Total seats	Must be numeric
Number of passengers	Must be numeric
	Must not be > Total seats
Number of crew members	Must be numeric
Baggage weight	Must be numeric
Performance score	Must be numeric

2. Any record found in error must be printed on the invalid record report.
3. Following each error record on the report must be one error message for each error detected.
4. Do not list records that are error free.

12-2 Data Validation During Keyboard Input

One of the first programming assignments in this book is to create and enter data into an airport file (Programming Assignment 4-5). At that point, the objective was simply to get the data into the file (no validation). As a rule, all data must be validated before being entered into a system. This is an expansion of Assignment 4-5 that incorporates data validation.

Output Requirements:

Name of file for record addition: AIRPORT1.DI

Record description: See Appendix A

Input Description:

Keyboard data entry.

Processing requirements:

This data entry program is to function as follows.

1. Upon entry to the program, provide the user with the option of aborting without data entry.
2. Accept from the keyboard the Flight ID of the next record to be entered.
3. Execute a random access read to determine if there is already a record in the file with the keyboard entry Flight ID. If the read is successful, display an error message that there is already a record in the file for this flight and abort this entry.
4. Accept each of the remaining fields from the keyboard and verify it according to the following criteria before progressing to the next field.

Date of flight	Month between 01 and 12
	Day between 01 and 31
Arrival/depart time	Between 0001 and 2400
Direction	Must be IN or OUT
Runway used	If last character is not a digit or space, it must be C, L, or R
Total seats	Must be numeric
Number of passengers	Must be numeric
	Must not be > Total seats
Number of crew members	Must be numeric
Baggage weight	Must be numeric
Performance score	Must be between -500 and 2000.

5. If the field does not meet the validation requirements, provide the user with the following options:

   Enter another value

   Abort this record

   The user must be able to abort a screen record from any field on the screen without progressing through each field that follows.

6. Query the user regarding the action to take with the currently displayed set of entries; the options must be

   1 Write the record to the file

   2 Allow the user to make corrections to screen entries

   3 Abort these screen entries and continue

7. Terminate processing if the user enters a blank Flight ID value.

13

ADVANCED REPORT GENERATION AND GROUP TOTALS

Outline

- **Printing Page Totals**
    Problem Definition
    About Accumulators
    The Program Solution—Example 13-1

- **Group Total Principles**
    Control Groups
    Group Total Logic
    A Group Total Example—Example 13-2
    Control-Break Actions
    Program Planning—Example 13-2
    A Program Solution—Example 13-2

- **Multiple-Level Control-Break Processing**
    Multiple-Level Control Breaks
    Control-Break Logic
    Example Definition—Example 13-3
    A Program Solution—Example 13-3
    About Control-Break Processing

Chapter Objectives

In Chapter 9, you learned how to improve the functionality of reports. One of the techniques you used was accumulating and printing report totals. The value of many reports can be further increased by expanding the summary totals that are printed. For instance, a simple expansion of the RET-VAL4 program could include printing the value of all items on a page, which essentially produces subtotals. Many applications require that a report include subtotals based on grouping of records (for instance, a subtotal of the software retail value for each vendor). However, in order to compute and print subtotals for each vendor, records of the file must be grouped by vendor. Processing of this type is called *control-break processing* because special control methods are used to detect a break in the record sequence to indicate progression from one group to another. This chapter discusses programming control-break processing applications; from it, you will learn about the following topics:

- Accumulating and printing page totals: the totals for selected fields of a report
- The principles of control groups: groups of records of a given type that are grouped together
- Calculation of totals for control groups
- Detecting the end of one control group and the beginning of the next

Printing Page Totals

Problem Definition

The RET-VAL4 program of Chapter 9 prints totals at the end of the report. Totaling and subtotaling are important operations in COBOL programming. Perhaps the simplest type of subtotaling is to print the totals for all details on each page; these totals are commonly called *page totals*. Obviously, the sum of all page totals gives the report totals of the RET-VAL4 program. To illustrate page totals, consider the following variation of RET-VAL4.

Example 13-1 Page Totals

Problem Description

The retail value report program RET-VAL4 must be expanded to include page totals at the bottom of each page. Print report totals at the end of the report.

Output Requirements

The output requirements of this report are identical to those of RET-VAL4, except that each page must include a count of the number of items printed on that page and the total retail value for all items on the page. The format is shown in the printer spacing chart of Figure 13-1.

Input Description

Input file name: SOFTWAR3.DL (Same as that used for RET-VAL4)

Processing Requirements

General processing requirements for this example are the same as those for Example 9-1, except that totals must be accumulated.

As each detail record is read, it must be counted. Each retail value figure (calculated as the Price times the Quantity-on-hand) must be added to an accumulator that totals the retail value.

General processing requirements for this example are the same as those for Example 9-3 (the RET-VAL4 program), except page totals must be printed. That is, processing will be as follows:

For each record:
1. Count the record
2. Calculate the retail value as the Price times the Quantity-on-hand
3. Accumulate the retail value
4. Print the input data and the calculated retail value

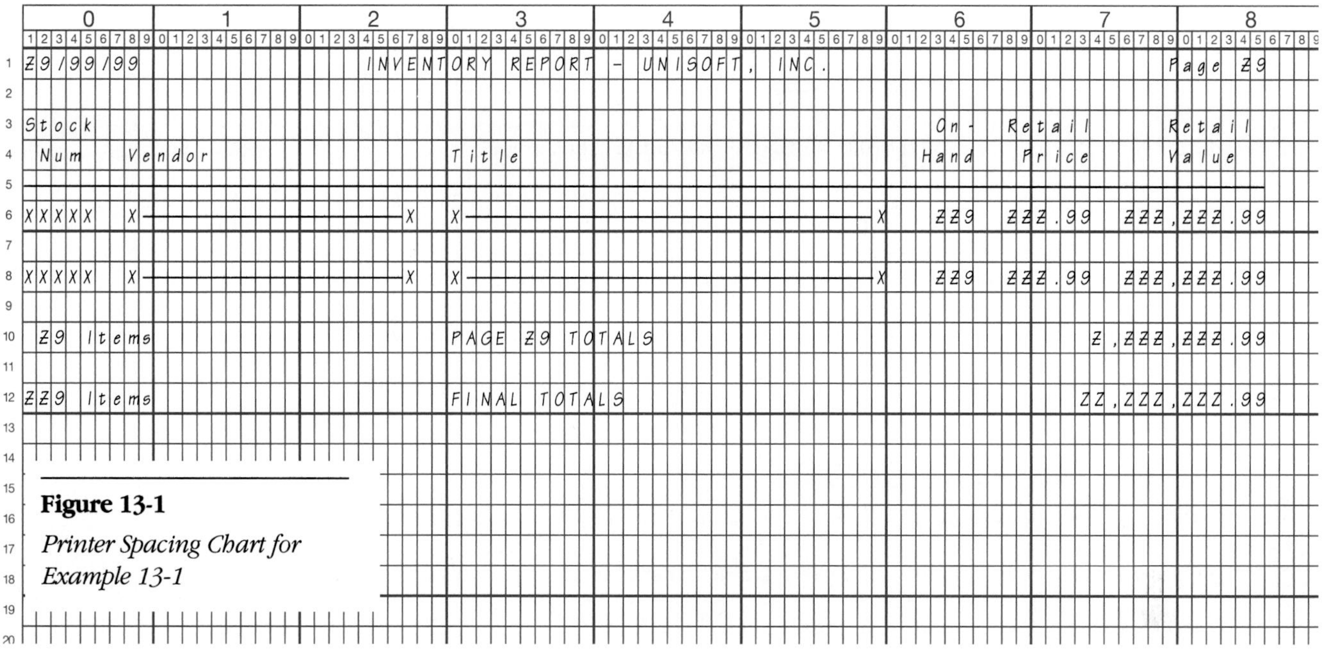

Figure 13-1

Printer Spacing Chart for Example 13-1

At the end of the page:
1. Print the record count and the accumulated retail value for that page
2. Accumulate the page record count and retail value for report totals
3. Progress to a new page and print the page headings

At the end of the report:
1. Print the report record count and accumulated retail value

A portion of a sample report is shown in Figure 13-2.

About Accumulators

The important facet of this example is the use of *accumulators,* a commonly encountered concept in business data processing that you learned about in Chapter 9. Although it has not been evident, an accumulator is always associated with a specific data group. Previous examples have been associated with the group consisting of the entire file. They have been given initial values of zero and then increased by appropriate data values during the program. At completion of processing, they have been printed.

An examination of Example 13-1 reveals that it involves two data groups: the *current page* and the *entire file*. In general, accumulators must always be initialized to zero at the beginning of the data group with which they are associated, and their contents must be output at the conclusion of the data group. Accumulator requirements and characteristics for this example (together with names that will be used in the program) are summarized in Figure 13-3.

The "entire file" data group can be considered to consist of all the "current page" data groups. For this reason, only the lower-level (current page) accumulators are incremented from the detail record. The higher-level (entire file) accumulators are incremented from the page totals, rather than from the detail records. Each grand total is thus a sum of page totals, rather than a sum of detail amounts. This "sum of sums" concept is more efficient for the computer and is considered a better technique in cases where the final total must balance to a predetermined total.

```
   8/24/90              INVENTORY REPORT - UNISOFT, INC.                Page  1

   Stock                                          On-   Retail      Retail
   Num    Vendor              Title               Hand  Price       Value

   07410  Apricot Software    Apricot-tree Accounts Payable   27  349.95     9,448.65

   07414  Apricot Software    Apricot-tree Accts. Receivable  18  349.95     6,299.10

   07427  Apricot Software    Apricot-tree General Ledger     65  349.95    22,746.75
```

```
   28424  Ferrari Development  Ferrari Personal Finance Mgr.  137   87.50    11,987.50

   28429  Ferrari Development  Ferrari 4-5-6 Financial Acctg. 144  495.00    71,280.00

   28558  Ferrari Development  Orchestra II                   102  649.00    66,198.00


   25 Items                    PAGE  1 TOTALS                            451,857.10  ◄── Page totals.
```

```
   8/24/90              INVENTORY REPORT - UNISOFT, INC.                Page  3

   Stock                                          On-   Retail      Retail
   Num    Vendor              Title               Hand  Price       Value

   91655  20th Century Soft.  Potent BASIC Interpreter         97    9.50       921.50

   91659  20th Century Soft.  Potent Interpretive COBOL       143  349.99    50,048.57

   91663  20th Century Soft.  Potent Interpretive Fortran     159  349.99    55,648.41

   91667  20th Century Soft.  Potent Interpretive RPG         102  349.99    35,698.98


    4 Items                    PAGE  3 TOTALS                            142,317.46  ◄── 


   54 Items                    FINAL TOTALS                            1,320,351.11  ◄── Report total.
```

Figure 13-2

Partial Sample Report for Example 13-1

Figure 13-3

Accumulators for Example 13-1

Accumulator Name	Accumulates	Initialized at	Incremented by
PAGE-NUMBER	Report page number	Beginning of program	1 for each page printed
PAGE-RECORD-COUNT	Number of records on this page	Beginning of program and each subsequent page	1 for each record processed
FINAL-RECORD-COUNT	Total number of records processed	Beginning of program	PAGE-RECORD-COUNT at the end of each page
PAGE-TOTAL-VALUE	Total of inventory value on this page	Beginning of program and each subsequent page	Inventory value for each detail record that is printed
FINAL-TOTAL-VALUE	Total of inventory value for all records printed	Beginning of program	PAGE-TOTAL-VALUE at the end of each page

**The Program Solution—
Example 13-1**

This program—together with the next two—illustrate the value of careful design and modularization. You will see that each new need represents a relatively minor change or addition to the previous program.

Consider what will be needed to modify the RET-VAL4 program in Chapter 9 (which includes page control and report totals) to print page totals.

1. Two levels of accumulators will be needed, as described in the preceding section.

2. Whenever a new page is determined to be full, the following must be done:

> Print the page totals
> Add the page totals to the final total accumulators
> Initialize the page totals

3. Prior to printing the final totals (after the end of file is detected), add the page totals to the final total accumulators.

The entire solution to this example is included in Figures 13-4 through 13-7 (see page 332). In the structure chart of Figure 13-4, the added modules are highlighted. Notice that these additions reflect the page needs described previously.

Similarly, in the logic of the flowchart (Figure 13-5) and the pseudocode (Figure 13-6), the added components are highlighted. There are two new modules: 310-Start-New-Page and 730-Print-Page-Totals. You can see that the 730 module does as the name implies: assembles and prints the page total line. The 310 module prepares for a new page by adding the page totals to the final totals, then initializing the page totals. Since page totals must be printed when the current page becomes full *and* after the last record is processed, the 730 and 310 modules are performed from both the 720-Assemble-and-Print-Detail and the 120-Finalize modules. (*The text continues on page 331.*)

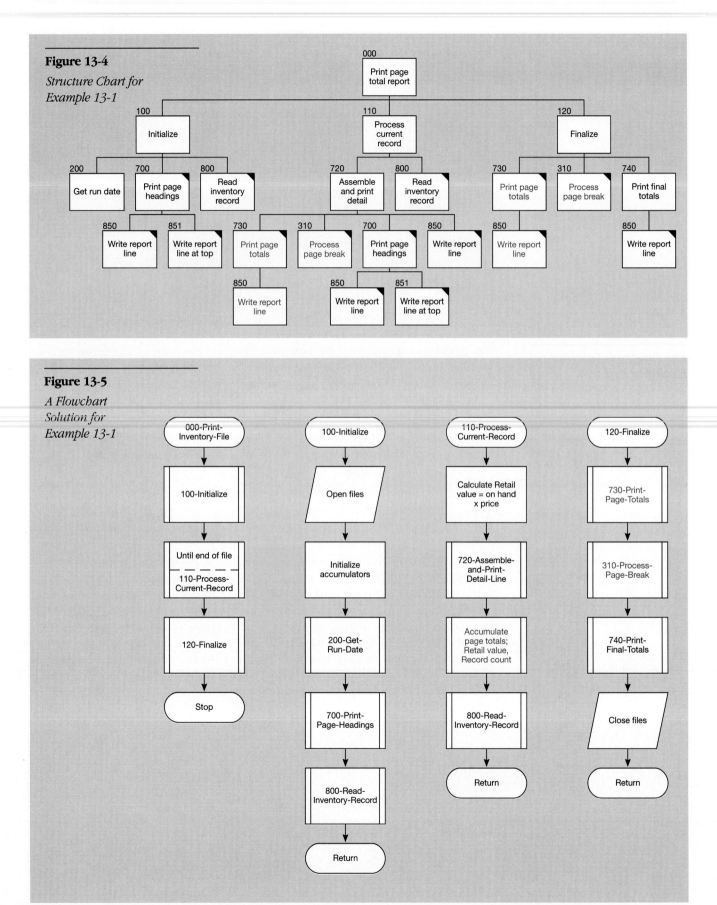

Figure 13-4

*Structure Chart for
Example 13-1*

Figure 13-5

*A Flowchart
Solution for
Example 13-1*

Figure 13-5

(continued on page 330)

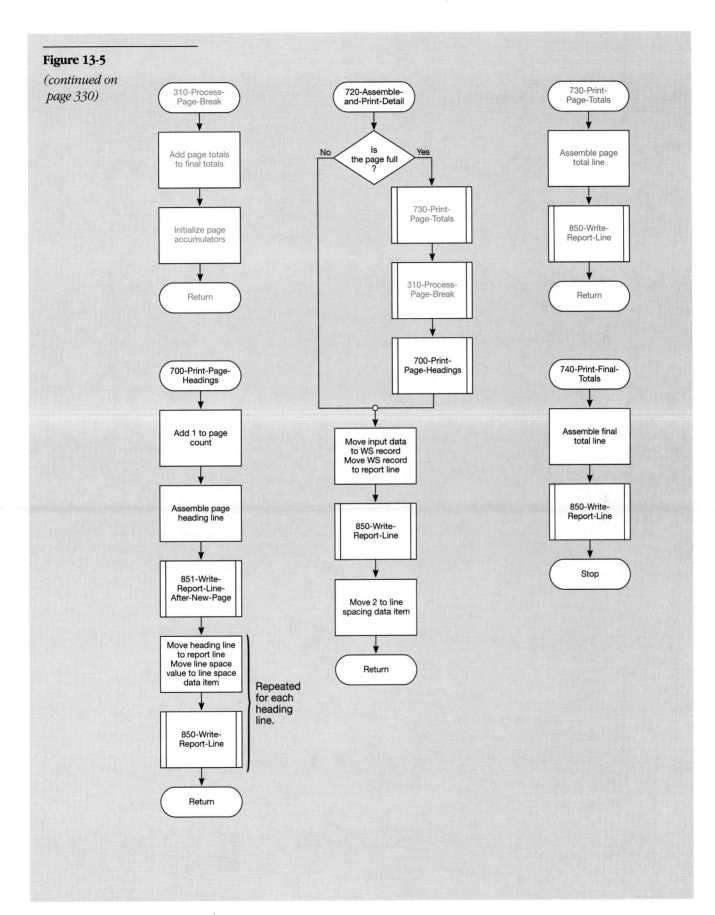

Figure 13-5

(continued from page 329)

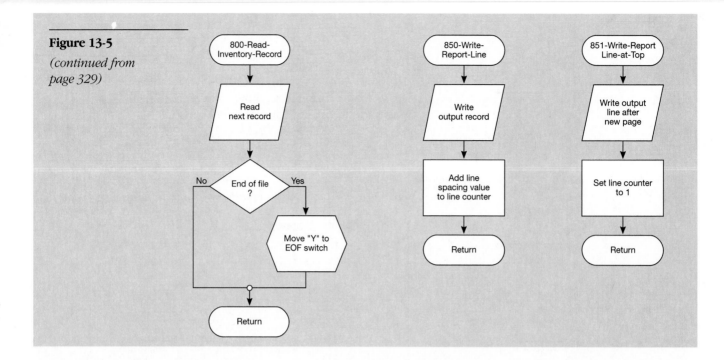

Figure 13-6

A Pseudocode Solution for Example 13-1

```
100-Initialize module
    Open data files
    Initialize accumulators
    Perform 200-Get-Run-Date module
    Perform 700-Print-Page-Headings module
    Perform 800-Read-Inventory-Record module

110-Process-Current-Record module
    Calculate Retail-value equals
           Quantity-on-hand times Price
    Accumulate the Retail-value
    Count this record
    Perform 720-Assemble-and-Print-Detail module
    Perform 800-Read-Inventory-Record module

120-Finalize
    Perform 730-Print-Page-Totals
    Perform 310-Start-New-Page
    Perform 740-Print-Final-Totals
    Close files

200-Get-Run-Date
    Obtain the current date
    Move month, day, and year to heading line

310-Process-Page-Break
    Add page totals to final totals
    Initialize page totals

700-Print-Page-Headings
    Increment the page number
    Move heading (with page number)
         to report output line
    Perform 851-Write-Report-Line-at-Top module
    Repeat the following for each remaining heading line
         Move heading to report output line
         Move line spacing value to line spacing data item
         Perform 850-Write-Report-Line module
```

```
720-Assemble-and-Print-Detail
    If page full
         Perform 730-Print-Page-Totals
         Perform 310-Start-New-Page
         Perform 700-Print-Page-Headings
    Move input data to output detail record
    Move output detail record to report output line
    Perform 850-Write-Report-Line module
    Move 2 to line spacing data item

730-Print-Page-Totals
    Move page totals to detail record
    Move 3 to line spacing data item
    Move output detail record to report output line
    Perform 850-Write-Report-Line module

740-Assemble-and-Write-Final-Totals
    Move final totals to detail record
    Move 3 to line spacing data item
    Move output detail record to report output line
    Perform 850-Write-Report-Line module

800-Read-Inventory-Record
    Read next record
           if EOF move "Y" to EOF switch

850-Write-Report-Line
    Print the output record
    Add Line-spacing value to Lines-used

851-Write-Report-Line-at-Top
    Print the output record after advancing page
    Set the value of Lines-used to 1
```

In the program of Figure 13-7, the added statements (over the RET-VAL4 program) are highlighted. The following are some points that you should note about this program:

■ A WORKING-STORAGE SECTION record is defined that contains the accumulators. All four of these accumulators are set to zero in the 110-INITIALIZE module by the single statement

```
INITIALIZE ACCUMULATORS
```

which designates the record name. When only the page total accumulators must be initialized (line 167 of the 310 module), the level 10 name is designated as follows:

```
INITIALIZE PAGE-TOTAL-ACCUMULATORS
```

■ The new page test from lines 184–189 consists of the following IF:

```
IF LINES-USED-ON-PAGE + LINE-SPACING
   IS GREATER THAN LINES-DESIRED-ON-PAGE
       PERFORM 730-PRINT-PAGE-TOTALS
       PERFORM 310-START-NEW-PAGE
       PERFORM 700-PRINT-PAGE-HEADINGS
END-IF
```

■ The 730 module (starting line 200) prints the page totals. Then the 310 module (starting line 164) adds the page totals to the final totals and initializes the page totals as needed for starting a new page.

■ The 310-START-NEW-PAGE module is performed from the 120-FINALIZE module. This is necessary (even though the name is a misnomer) so that the page totals from the last page will be added to the final totals. Although the page totals are unnecessarily initialized, this causes no problem.

Group Total Principles

Control Groups

Recall from Chapter 12 that the software stock number field (5 positions) consists of three basic parts:

Component	Size (Positions)
Vendor code	2
Software type	1
Item identifier	2

For example, consider the stock number 28429. This number can be interpreted as follows:

28	Vendor code for Ferrari Development
4	General software type (spreadsheet)
29	Item identifier; represents Ferrari 4-5-6 Financial Acctg.

Thus, through the stock number, it is possible to relate a piece of software to its vendor or its general software type. Both of these elements are used to illustrate control groups.

Two very basic principles of business data processing are *control groups* and *group total logic*. To illustrate, consider Figure 13-8(a) on page 334, which shows a group of records selected from the inventory file in random order. As you can see, the records have no meaningful sequence; records for each vendor are scattered throughout the file. To prepare a report in which records for each vendor were grouped together would be quite impractical with a file that gives access to the records only in this sequence.

On the other hand, consider the records when they are arranged in *sequence* by stock number (starting with the lowest number and ending with the highest), as shown in Figure 13-8(b). Because of the nature of the stock number field, the records end up in groups based on the vendor: the first two digits of the stock number field. In this example, the vendor number portion of the stock number is called the *control field*; a group of records with the same control field is called a *control group*. When reading records from the file, a *control break* occurs when the control field value of the newly read record is different from that of the previously read record.

Figure 13-7

A Program Solution
for Example 13-1

```
1        IDENTIFICATION DIVISION.
2
3        PROGRAM-ID. PAGE-TOT.
4
5    *      Written by J.Olson/W.Price
6    *      August 26, 1990
7
8    *      This program prints a total line for each page,
9    *      as well as a final total line.
10
11       ENVIRONMENT DIVISION.
12
13       CONFIGURATION SECTION.
14       SOURCE-COMPUTER. IBM-PC.
15
16       INPUT-OUTPUT SECTION.
17       FILE-CONTROL.
18           SELECT INVENTORY-FILE   ASSIGN TO DISK "SOFTWAR3.DL"
19                                    ORGANIZATION IS LINE SEQUENTIAL.
20           SELECT REPORT-FILE      ASSIGN TO PRINTER "PRN-FILE".
21
22       DATA DIVISION.
23
24       FILE SECTION.
25
26       FD  INVENTORY-FILE.
27       01  INVENTORY-RECORD.
28           10  IR-STOCK-NUMBER     PIC X(5).
29           10  IR-SOFTWARE-NAME    PIC X(30).
30           10  IR-VENDOR-NAME      PIC X(20).
31           10  IR-QUANT-ON-HAND    PIC 9(3).
32           10                      PIC X(3).
33           10  IR-PRICE            PIC 9(3)V9(2).
34
35       FD  REPORT-FILE.
36       01  REPORT-RECORD           PIC X(85).
37
38       WORKING-STORAGE SECTION.
39
40       01  PROGRAMMED-SWITCHES.
41           10  END-OF-FILE         PIC X       VALUE "N".
42
43       01  ARITHMETIC-WORK-AREAS.
44           10  RETAIL-VALUE        PIC 9(6)V9(2).
45
46       01  ACCUMULATORS.
47           10  PAGE-TOTAL-ACCUMULATORS.
48               20  PAGE-TOTAL-VALUE   PIC 9(7)V9(2).
49               20  PAGE-RECORD-COUNT  PIC 9(2).
50           10  FINAL-TOTAL-ACCUMULATORS.
51               20  FINAL-TOTAL-VALUE  PIC 9(8)V9(2).
52               20  FINAL-RECORD-COUNT PIC 9(3).
53
54       01  PRINT-CONTROL-VARIABLES.
55           10  LINE-SPACING        PIC 9.
56           10  LINES-DESIRED-ON-PAGE  PIC 99     VALUE 54.
57           10  LINES-USED-ON-PAGE  PIC 99.
58           10  PAGE-NUMBER         PIC 99      VALUE ZERO.
59
60       01  RUN-DATE.
61           10  RUN-YEAR            PIC 99.
62           10  RUN-MONTH           PIC 99.
63           10  RUN-DAY             PIC 99.
64
65       01  PAGE-HEADING-LINE.
66           10  PH-MONTH            PIC Z9.
67           10                      PIC X       VALUE "/".
68           10  PH-DAY              PIC 99.
69           10                      PIC X       VALUE "/".
70           10  PH-YEAR             PIC 99.
71           10                      PIC X(15)   VALUE SPACES.
72           10                      PIC X(32)   VALUE
73                   "INVENTORY REPORT - UNISOFT, INC.".
74           10                      PIC X(23)   VALUE SPACES.
75           10                      PIC X(5)    VALUE "Page ".
76           10  PH-PAGE-NUMBER      PIC Z9.
77
78       01  COLUMN-HEADING-1.
79           10                      PIC X(62)   VALUE "Stock".
80           10                      PIC X(5)    VALUE "On-".
81           10                      PIC X(11)   VALUE "Retail".
82           10                      PIC X(7)    VALUE "Retail".
83
84       01  COLUMN-HEADING-2.
85           10                      PIC X(7)    VALUE " Num".
86           10                      PIC X(22)   VALUE "Vendor".
87           10                      PIC X(32)   VALUE "Title".
88           10                      PIC X(7)    VALUE "Hand".
89           10                      PIC X(10)   VALUE "Price".
90           10                      PIC X(7)    VALUE "Value".
```

```
91
92       01  DETAIL-LINE                         VALUE SPACES.
93           10  RL-STOCK-NUMBER    PIC X(5).
94           10                     PIC X(2).
95           10  RL-VENDOR-NAME     PIC X(20).
96           10                     PIC X(2).
97           10  RL-SOFTWARE-NAME   PIC X(30).
98           10                     PIC X(3).
99           10  RL-QUANT-ON-HAND   PIC ZZ9.
100          10                     PIC X(2).
101          10  RL-PRICE           PIC ZZZ.99.
102          10                     PIC X(2).
103          10  RL-RETAIL-VALUE    PIC ZZZ,ZZZ.99.
104
105      01  PAGE-TOTAL-LINE.
106          10                     PIC X(1).
107          10  PT-RECORD-COUNT    PIC Z9.
108          10                     PIC X(26)   VALUE " Items".
109          10                     PIC X(5)    VALUE "PAGE ".
110          10  PT-PAGE-NUMBER     PIC Z9.
111          10                     PIC X(37)   VALUE " TOTALS".
112          10  PT-TOTAL-VALUE     PIC Z,ZZZ,ZZZ.99.
113
114      01  FINAL-TOTAL-LINE.
115          10  FT-RECORD-COUNT    PIC ZZ9.
116          10                     PIC X(26)   VALUE " Items".
117          10                     PIC X(43)   VALUE "FINAL TOTALS".
118          10  FT-TOTAL-VALUE     PIC ZZ,ZZZ,ZZZ.99.
119
120      PROCEDURE DIVISION.
121
122      000-PRINT-PAGE-TOTAL-REPORT.
123          PERFORM 100-INITIALIZE
124          PERFORM 110-PROCESS-CURRENT-RECORD
125              UNTIL END-OF-FILE = "Y"
126          PERFORM 120-FINALIZE
127          STOP RUN.
128
129      100-INITIALIZE.
130          OPEN INPUT INVENTORY-FILE
131          OPEN OUTPUT REPORT-FILE
132          INITIALIZE ACCUMULATORS
133          PERFORM 200-GET-RUN-DATE
134          PERFORM 700-PRINT-PAGE-HEADINGS
135          PERFORM 800-READ-INVENTORY-RECORD.
136
137      110-PROCESS-CURRENT-RECORD.
138
139    *  Calculate retail value
140          MOVE IR-PRICE TO RETAIL-VALUE
141          MULTIPLY IR-QUANT-ON-HAND BY RETAIL-VALUE
142
143          PERFORM 720-ASSEMBLE-AND-PRINT-DETAIL
144
145    *  Increment accumulators
146          ADD RETAIL-VALUE TO PAGE-TOTAL-VALUE
147          ADD 1 TO PAGE-RECORD-COUNT
148
149          PERFORM 800-READ-INVENTORY-RECORD.
150
151      120-FINALIZE.
152          PERFORM 730-PRINT-PAGE-TOTALS
153          PERFORM 310-PROCESS-PAGE-BREAK
154          PERFORM 740-PRINT-FINAL-TOTALS
155          CLOSE INVENTORY-FILE
156              REPORT-FILE.
157
158      200-GET-RUN-DATE.
159          ACCEPT RUN-DATE FROM DATE
160          MOVE RUN-MONTH TO PH-MONTH
161          MOVE RUN-DAY   TO PH-DAY
162          MOVE RUN-YEAR  TO PH-YEAR.
163
164      310-PROCESS-PAGE-BREAK.
165          ADD PAGE-RECORD-COUNT TO FINAL-RECORD-COUNT
166          ADD PAGE-TOTAL-VALUE  TO FINAL-TOTAL-VALUE
167          INITIALIZE PAGE-TOTAL-ACCUMULATORS.
168
169      700-PRINT-PAGE-HEADINGS.
170          ADD 1 TO PAGE-NUMBER
171          MOVE PAGE-NUMBER TO PH-PAGE-NUMBER
172          MOVE PAGE-HEADING-LINE TO REPORT-RECORD
173          PERFORM 851-WRITE-REPORT-LINE-AT-TOP
174          MOVE COLUMN-HEADING-1 TO REPORT-RECORD
175          MOVE 2 TO LINE-SPACING
176          PERFORM 850-WRITE-REPORT-LINE
177          MOVE COLUMN-HEADING-2 TO REPORT-RECORD
178          MOVE 1 TO LINE-SPACING
179          PERFORM 850-WRITE-REPORT-LINE
180          MOVE ALL "-" TO REPORT-RECORD
181          PERFORM 850-WRITE-REPORT-LINE.
182
```

Figure 13-7

```
183    720-ASSEMBLE-AND-PRINT-DETAIL.
184        IF LINES-USED-ON-PAGE + LINE-SPACING
185            IS GREATER THAN LINES-DESIRED-ON-PAGE
186            PERFORM 730-PRINT-PAGE-TOTALS
187            PERFORM 310-PROCESS-PAGE-BREAK
188            PERFORM 700-PRINT-PAGE-HEADINGS
189        END-IF
190        MOVE IR-STOCK-NUMBER TO RL-STOCK-NUMBER
191        MOVE IR-SOFTWARE-NAME TO RL-SOFTWARE-NAME
192        MOVE IR-VENDOR-NAME TO RL-VENDOR-NAME
193        MOVE IR-QUANT-ON-HAND TO RL-QUANT-ON-HAND
194        MOVE IR-PRICE TO RL-PRICE
195        MOVE RETAIL-VALUE TO RL-RETAIL-VALUE
196        MOVE DETAIL-LINE TO REPORT-RECORD
197        PERFORM 850-WRITE-REPORT-LINE
198        MOVE 2 TO LINE-SPACING.
199
200    730-PRINT-PAGE-TOTALS.
201        MOVE PAGE-RECORD-COUNT TO PT-RECORD-COUNT
202        MOVE PAGE-TOTAL-VALUE  TO PT-TOTAL-VALUE
203        MOVE PAGE-NUMBER TO PT-PAGE-NUMBER
204        MOVE 3 TO LINE-SPACING
205        MOVE PAGE-TOTAL-LINE TO REPORT-RECORD
206        PERFORM 850-WRITE-REPORT-LINE.


207
208    740-PRINT-FINAL-TOTALS.
209        MOVE FINAL-RECORD-COUNT TO FT-RECORD-COUNT
210        MOVE FINAL-TOTAL-VALUE  TO FT-TOTAL-VALUE
211        MOVE 3 TO LINE-SPACING
212        MOVE FINAL-TOTAL-LINE TO REPORT-RECORD
213        PERFORM 850-WRITE-REPORT-LINE.
214
215    800-READ-INVENTORY-RECORD.
216        READ INVENTORY-FILE
217            AT END MOVE "Y" TO END-OF-FILE
218        END-READ.
219
220    850-WRITE-REPORT-LINE.
221        WRITE REPORT-RECORD
222            AFTER ADVANCING LINE-SPACING LINES
223        ADD LINE-SPACING TO LINES-USED-ON-PAGE.
224
225    851-WRITE-REPORT-LINE-AT-TOP.
226        WRITE REPORT-RECORD
227            AFTER ADVANCING PAGE
228        MOVE 1 TO LINES-USED-ON-PAGE.
```

A control group, then, is a group of records that have an identical control field. The control field is the field in the record that contains the identifier of the control group. This concept is basic to any type of processing that produces an output record from a group of input records. For example, when the telephone company prepares the phone bills each month, it starts out with a file containing a record of each call made and each payment received. This file initially is in no usable sequence. However, when the file is sorted by telephone number, all of the records for each telephone number are brought together, so one bill can be prepared for each customer. A file of records can always be grouped into control groups by sorting the file on the proper control fields.

Group Total Logic

In Example 13-1, you studied the concept of computing page totals for the updated inventory and the inventory value. Page totals were printed at the end of each page and grand totals were printed at the end of the report. In data processing, these page totals are a simple form of what is commonly referred to as *group totals*. That is, they represent the totals for a particular group of records (the group printed on the page). Of course, the records that compose a page group have no logical relationship such as that of the control group in Figure 13-8(b). However, the needs are similar; that is, the computer must read all of the records for the first control group, print the total for that group, read all of the records for the second control group, print the total for that group, and so on. This type of operation is known as a *group total operation*, and the PROCEDURE DIVISION logic to implement it is known as *group total logic.*

What exactly is involved in group total logic? When you look at an illustration such as Figure 13-8(b), the processing of control groups seems quite simple. Since you can see all the records of the file, the end of one group and the beginning of the next is obvious. But the situation is more difficult when processing one record at a time—as with the computer. To illustrate why, give several blank cards to a friend, then follow these instructions:

1. Have your friend write the number "1" on some of the cards and the number "2" on the rest of them.

2. Ask your friend to place the cards in sequence, with all of the 1's first, followed by all of the 2's.

3. Tell your friend to show you the cards one at a time, each time asking, "Is this the last card with the number 1 on it?"

Figure 13-8

Record Sequencing

```
28558   Orchestra II                    Ferrari Development   102 100 64900
32517   Disk Consolidator               Galactic Bus. Mach.  110 100 03995
32506   Bottom View                     Galactic Bus. Mach.  105 100 09995
15564   Speedy Sorter                   Borneo International  102 100 07995
28421   Ferrari Investment Forecaster   Ferrari Development   074 065 19995
15586   Time Manager                    Borneo International  217 200 03995
28417   Ferrari Flexible Payroll        Ferrari Development   038 025 24995
28424   Ferrari Personal Finance Mgr.   Ferrari Development   137 100 08750
15589   Travelling Side Punch           Borneo International  180 200 02995
28429   Ferrari 4-5-6 Financial Acctg.  Ferrari Development   144 150 49500
15514   Disk Manager                    Borneo International  150 100 09995
32563   Resident Sort/Merge             Galactic Bus. Mach.  103 100 05950
15583   Thesaurus                       Borneo International  137 100 05995
32568   Run-Em-All Integrator           Galactic Bus. Mach.  097 100 13050
```

File in Random Sequence   (a)

Grouped by first
two digits.

```
          ┌  15514   Disk Manager            Borneo International 150 100 09995
          │  15564   Speedy Sorter           Borneo International 102 100 07995
Group ──► │  15583   Thesaurus               Borneo International 137 100 05995
          │  15586   Time Manager            Borneo International 217 200 03995
          └  15589   Travelling Side Punch   Borneo International 180 200 02995
          ┌  28417   Ferrari Flexible Payroll        Ferrari Development 038 025 24995
          │  28421   Ferrari Investment Forecaster   Ferrari Development 074 065 19995
Group ──► │  28424   Ferrari Personal Finance Mgr.   Ferrari Development 137 100 08750
          │  28429   Ferrari 4-5-6 Financial Acctg.  Ferrari Development 144 150 49500
          └  28558   Orchestra II                    Ferrari Development 102 100 64900
          ┌  32506   Bottom View             Galactic Bus. Mach. 105 100 09995
          │  32517   Disk Consolidator       Galactic Bus. Mach. 110 100 03995
Group ──► │  32563   Resident Sort/Merge     Galactic Bus. Mach. 103 100 05950
          └  32568   Run-Em-All Integrator   Galactic Bus. Mach. 097 100 13050
```

In sequence based
on Stock-number field.

File in Sequence by Stock Number   (b)

From this activity, you will quickly see that you have absolutely no way of telling when you are looking at the last record in the group. The basic technique used in programming involves remembering the number on the record just read, then reading the next record and comparing the two numbers.

Group total logic involves essentially the same principles; expanding them as appropriate yields the following:

1. Read the next record.

2. Compare the control field on the record just read to the previous control field that has been "saved."

3. If the control fields are equal
      process the detail record
   else
      perform the group total operations
      save the control field of this record
      process the detail record that triggered the group total operation.

Figure 13-9

*Detecting the
End of a
Control Group*

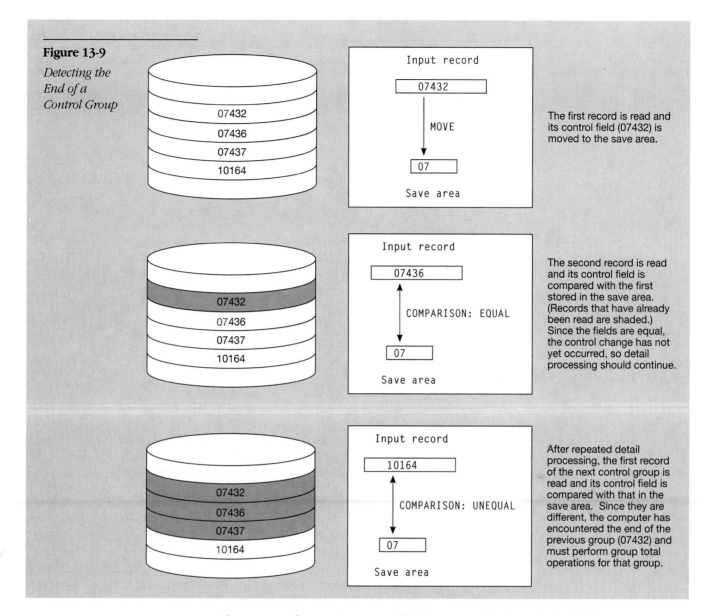

The first record is read and its control field (07432) is moved to the save area.

The second record is read and its control field is compared with the first stored in the save area. (Records that have already been read are shaded.) Since the fields are equal, the control change has not yet occurred, so detail processing should continue.

After repeated detail processing, the first record of the next control group is read and its control field is compared with that in the save area. Since they are different, the computer has encountered the end of the previous group (07432) and must perform group total operations for that group.

The process of saving the control field is accomplished merely by defining an elementary item in the WORKING-STORAGE SECTION and moving the desired field to it. Use of such a *save area* is illustrated and described in Figure 13-9.

*A Group Total Example—
Example 13-2*

Following is the formal definition of this group total application.

Example 13-2 Group Totals

Problem Description

   The page total report program, PAGE-TOT, must be modified to print group totals, using the vendor number as the control field.

Output Requirements

   The output requirements of this report are identical to those of the PAGE-TOT program (Figure 13-7). Group totals are to be printed for each vendor. Page totals are not required. The format is shown in the printer spacing chart of Figure 13-10. A portion of the sample output is shown in Figure 13-11 (page 338).

Input Description

Input file name: SOFTWAR3.DL (the same as that used for PAGE-TOT)

Note: Records of this file are in sequence based on the Product-number field

Processing Requirements

General processing requirements for this example are the same as those for PAGE-TOT for the group total requirement. That is, processing will be as follows:

As each record is read:
1. Check to see if the vendor number is the same as that of the preceding record
2. If it is not:
   a. Print the record count and the accumulated retail value for the preceding vendor
   b. Accumulate the page record count and retail value for report totals
3. Count the record
4. Calculate the retail value as the Price times the Quantity-on-hand
5. Accumulate the retail value
6. Print the input data and the calculated retail value

At the end of the page:
1. Progress to a new page and print the page headings

At the end of the report:
1. Print the totals for the last vendor
2. Print the final report totals

Control-Break Actions

When printing page totals, certain actions must be carried out with each page break:

Print the page headings
Add the page total accumulators to the final total accumulators
Initialize the page total accumulators

In addition to the usual progressing from one page to the next (on page breaks), you know that two other conditions occur that cause part of these break actions to take place: beginning the first page and ending the last page (detecting the end of file triggers this).

For the first page, which you can consider a "pseudo-break," both the printing and initializing must occur; accumulation does not occur because there are no preceding totals. Following detection of the end of file (another "pseudo-break"), only the accumulation action occurs; neither new page headings nor initialization are necessary. These conditions are summarized in the following table, in which *First* refers to the first-record pseudo-break, *Other* refers to regular page breaks, and *Last* refers to the end-of-file pseudo-break.

| | Pseudo-Break | | |
Action	First	Other	Last
Print	X	X	
Accumulate		X	X
Initialize	X	X	

Activities with group-total processing are very similar, except breaks occur as the result of a change in the control field value. Furthermore, the printing to take place as the result of the break is printing of the group totals. In Example 13-2, these will be the vendor totals. Another activity that must happen when a break occurs is the saving of the control field value causing the break. This is necessary so the saved value can be used in comparisons for subsequent checking for the next control break as records continue to be read and processed. As with page breaks, if reading the first record and the end-of-file

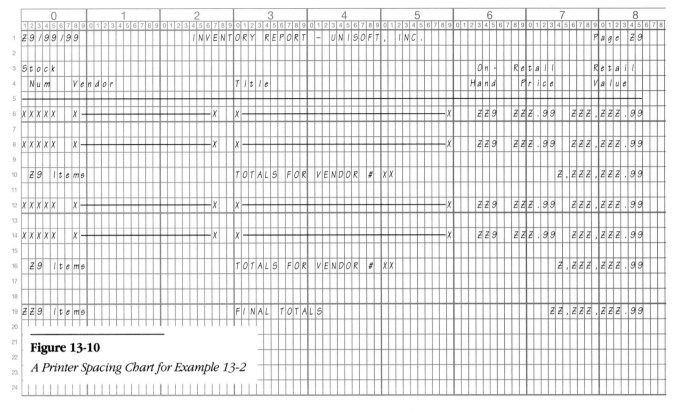

Figure 13-10

A Printer Spacing Chart for Example 13-2

record are considered "pseudo-breaks," then the actions to be taken can be summarized in the following table:

| | Pseudo-Break | | |
Action	First	Other	Last
Print		X	X
Accumulate		X	X
Initialize	X	X	
Save Field	X	X	

Notice that with the first record, there is no group total line to print—nor are there group totals to add to the final totals—an obvious consequence of no records yet having been processed. Similarly, when the end of file is detected, printing and accumulating must occur, but there is no new control field to save and it is needless to initialize accumulators.

Program Planning— Example 13-2

Both the program structure and logic are very similar to those of the page total program. However, because of the differences in the way breaks are detected and handled, there are some important differences. You can see this in the structure chart of Figure 13-12.

Although page control is still required, positioning to a new page has no significance as far as the control-break processing is concerned. Modules of this solution that represent the principal difference from the page-total application are shown in flowchart form in Figure 13-13 (see page 340) and in pseudocode in Figure 13-14.

First
page.

```
8/24/90            INVENTORY REPORT - UNISOFT, INC.                Page  1

Stock                                          On-   Retail      Retail
Num    Vendor            Title                  Hand  Price        Value
_____

07410  Apricot Software  Apricot-tree Accounts Payable    27  349.95   9,448.65
07414  Apricot Software  Apricot-tree Accts. Receivable   18  349.95   6,299.10
07427  Apricot Software  Apricot-tree General Ledger      65  349.95  22,746.75
07432  Apricot Software  Apricot-tree Hourly Payroll      35  349.95  12,248.25
07436  Apricot Software  Apricot-tree Inventory Control   25  349.95   8,748.75
07474  Apricot Software  Apricot-tree Salaried Payroll    34  349.95  11,898.30

  6 Items                 TOTALS FOR VENDOR # 07                    71,389.80  ←


10164  Archaic Software  Sluggish Writer                  93   49.95   4,645.35
10165  Archaic Software  Sluggish Writer, Economy Model   93   49.95   4,645.35
10166  Archaic Software  Sluggish Writer, Power Model     67   99.95   6,696.65
10279  Archaic Software  Ten-Column Spreadsheet, Econ.   105   49.95   5,244.75
10281  Archaic Software  Ten-Column Spreadsheet, Power    48   99.95   4,797.60

  5 Items                 TOTALS FOR VENDOR # 10                    26,029.70  ←
```

Second
page.

```
60541  Nobodies, Unlimited  Nobodies Computer Friday     126   49.50   6,237.00
60544  Nobodies, Unlimited  Nobodies Disk Utilities      133   49.50   6,583.50
60547  Nobodies, Unlimited  Nobodies File Finder          97   49.50   4,801.50
60550  Nobodies, Unlimited  Nobodies Panes                75  129.95   9,746.25

  4 Items                 TOTALS FOR VENDOR # 60                    27,368.25  ←

91651  20th Century Soft.  Potent BASIC Compiler         180  199.50  35,910.00
91653  20th Century Soft.  Potent BASIC Emulator         127  347.50  44,132.50
91655  20th Century Soft.  Potent BASIC Interpreter       97    9.50     921.50
91659  20th Century Soft.  Potent Interpretive COBOL     143  349.99  50,048.57
91663  20th Century Soft.  Potent Interpretive Fortran   159  349.99  55,648.41
91667  20th Century Soft.  Potent Interpretive RPG       102  349.99  35,698.98

  6 Items                 TOTALS FOR VENDOR # 91                   222,359.96  ←


 54 Items                 FINAL TOTALS                           1,320,351.11
```

Group totals. ─────────

Figure 13-11

*Sample Output for
Example 13-2*

Let's look first at the 310-Process-Break module. You can see that the four pseudo-break actions are executed conditionally. For the first record, vendor totals are not printed or added to final totals. For the end-of-file condition, vendor accumulators are not added to final totals and the vendor number is not saved. These are consistent with the preceding action table.

You can see that the 310 module is performed first from the 100-Initialize module; the First-record switch is set to true prior to its execution, then changed to false after its execution. The 310 module is also performed from the 110-Process-Current-Record module when a control break occurs, and from the 120-Finalize module.

A Program Solution—Example 13-2

A complete control-break program is shown in Figure 13-15 (pages 342 and 343). Referring to the highlighted areas, you can see the following:

- The sub-field IR-VENDOR-NUMBER is defined under the stock number to provide access to the vendor number (line 29).

- A save area is defined to hold the vendor number of the most recently read record (lines 51 and 52).

- A first-switch is defined (lines 45 and 46) to handle processing of the first record—the pseudo-break.

- The VENDOR-TOTAL-LINE is defined in lines 113 through 121; it replaces PAGE-TOTAL-LINE of the page-total program.

- In the 100-INITIALIZE module, the 310-PROCESS-BREAK module is performed. The switch FIRST-RECORD is set to true prior to performing 310 and reset to false after returning.

- The following IF statement (from lines 163–165) detects the control break and conditionally performs the 310 module:

```
IF IR-VENDOR-NUMBER NOT = WS-VENDOR-NUMBER
   PERFORM 310-PROCESS-BREAK
END-IF
```

- In the 310 module (beginning line 179), execution of the four functions that print totals, add to final accumulators, initialize vendor totals, and save vendor number are controlled by two IF statements. They represent the implementation of the actions described earlier.

Figure 13-12

Structure Chart for Example 13-2

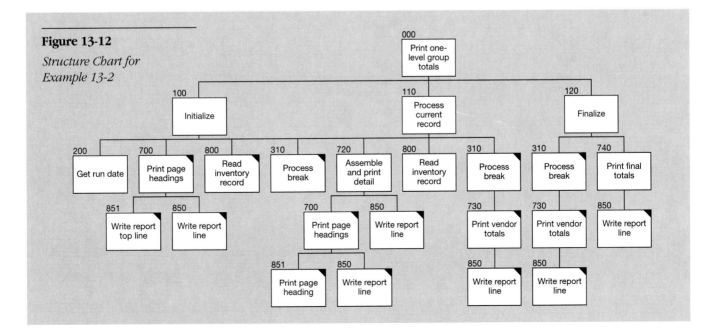

Figure 13-13

*Partial Flowchart
for Example 13-2*

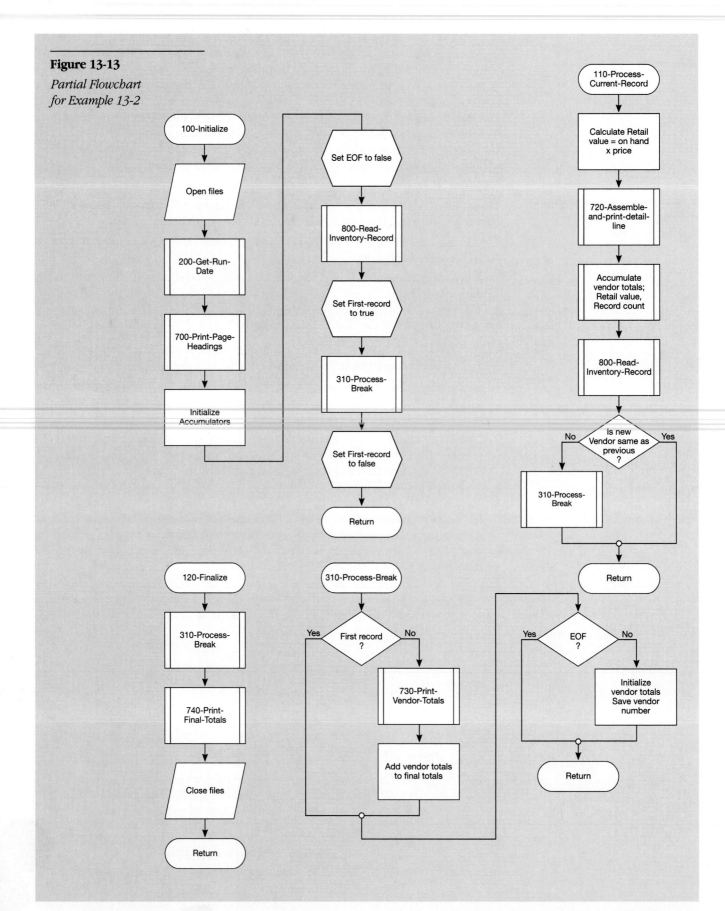

Figure 13-14

*Partial Pseudocode
Solution for Example 13-2*

```
100-Initialize
    Open data files
    Perform 200-Get-Run-Date
    Perform 700-Print-Page-Headings
    Initialize all accumulators
    Set EOF switch to false
    Perform 800-Read-Inventory-Record
    Set First-record switch to true
    Perform 310-Process-Break
    Set First-record switch to false

110-Process-Current-Record
    Calculate Retail-value equals
        Quantity-on-hand times Price
    Accumulate the Retail-value
    Count this record
    Perform 720-Assemble-and-Print-Detail
    Perform 800-Read-Inventory-Record
    If new vendor is different than previous vendor
        Perform 310-Process-Break

120-Finalize
    Perform 310-Process-Break
    Perform 740-Print-Final-Totals
        Close files

310-Process-Break
    If not First-record
        Perform 730-Print-Vendor-Totals
        Add vendor totals to final total
    If not EOF
        Initialized vendor totals
        Save new vendor number
```

Multiple-Level Control-Break Processing

Multiple-Level Control Breaks

The preceding example is a relatively basic control break application. Because it is based on a single control group, the report (Figure 13-11) is sometimes referred to as a *single-level control-break report*. In many instances, two or more levels are required. For instance, consider the output of a salesperson report that the sales manager of UNISOFT might require.

Detail listing of sales from the sales file
A summary of the sales for each salesperson
A summary of the sales for each sales office
A final summary of total sales

This is a *two-level control-break report* because output is controlled by two control fields and group totals are printed based on two control groups. Here the first control level is for the salesperson group; the second level is the sales office group. For this two-level application, totals are accumulated as follows:

1. Salesperson totals are accumulated from each input record

2. Sales office totals are accumulated from each salespersons totals

3. Final totals are accumulated from sales office totals

You might correctly anticipate that the records within the file must be grouped according to both of these fields. Figure 13-16 (page 344) illustrates how the records must be grouped first on the most inclusive field; in this case, the sales office. This is called the *major field*; totals calculated on the major control field are sometimes called *major totals*. Within each major group, records are further grouped on the "lesser" field, called the *minor field*; totals calculated on the minor control field are sometimes called *minor totals*.

The needs of the manager could be extended even further; for instance, to three levels:

Detail listing of sales from the sales file
A summary of each software type sold by each salesperson
A summary of the sales for each salesperson
A summary of the sales for each sales office
A final summary of total sales

Figure 13-15

A Program Solution for Example 13-2

```
  1        IDENTIFICATION DIVISION.
  2
  3        PROGRAM-ID. GRP-TOT1.
  4
  5    *    Written by J.Olson/W.Price
  6    *    August 23, 1990
  7
  8    *    This program prints a total line for each vendor,
  9    *    as well as a final total line.
 10
 11        ENVIRONMENT DIVISION.
 12
 13        CONFIGURATION SECTION.
 14        SOURCE-COMPUTER. IBM-PC.
 15
 16        INPUT-OUTPUT SECTION.
 17        FILE-CONTROL.
 18            SELECT INVENTORY-FILE   ASSIGN TO DISK "SOFTWAR3.DL"
 19                                    ORGANIZATION IS LINE SEQUENTIAL.
 20            SELECT REPORT-FILE      ASSIGN TO PRINTER "PRN-FILE".
 21
 22        DATA DIVISION.
 23
 24        FILE SECTION.
 25
 26        FD  INVENTORY-FILE.
 27        01  INVENTORY-RECORD.
 28            10  IR-STOCK-NUMBER.
 29                20  IR-VENDOR-NUMBER     PIC X(2).
 30                20                      PIC X(3).
 31            10  IR-SOFTWARE-NAME        PIC X(30).
 32            10  IR-VENDOR-NAME          PIC X(20).
 33            10  IR-QUANT-ON-HAND        PIC 9(3).
 34            10                          PIC X(3).
 35            10  IR-PRICE                PIC 9(3)V9(2).
 36
 37        FD  REPORT-FILE.
 38        01  REPORT-RECORD               PIC X(85).
 39
 40        WORKING-STORAGE SECTION.
 41
 42        01  PROGRAMMED-SWITCHES.
 43            10                          PIC X.
 44                88  END-OF-FILE         VALUE "Y" FALSE "N".
 45            10                          PIC X.
 46                88  FIRST-RECORD        VALUE "Y" FALSE "N".
 47
 48        01  ARITHMETIC-WORK-AREAS.
 49            10  RETAIL-VALUE            PIC 9(6)V9(2).
 50
 51        01  SAVE-AREAS.
 52            10  VENDOR-NUMBER           PIC X(2).
 53
 54        01  ACCUMULATORS.
 55            10  VENDOR-TOTAL-ACCUMULATORS.
 56                20  VENDOR-TOTAL-VALUE   PIC 9(7)V9(2).
 57                20  VENDOR-RECORD-COUNT  PIC 9(2).
 58            10  FINAL-TOTAL-ACCUMULATORS.
 59                20  FINAL-TOTAL-VALUE    PIC 9(8)V9(2).
 60                20  FINAL-RECORD-COUNT   PIC 9(3).
 61
 62        01  PRINT-CONTROL-VARIABLES.
 63            10  LINE-SPACING            PIC 9.
 64            10  LINES-DESIRED-ON-PAGE   PIC 99       VALUE 54.
 65            10  LINES-USED-ON-PAGE      PIC 99.
 66            10  PAGE-NUMBER             PIC 99       VALUE ZERO.
 67
 68        01  RUN-DATE.
 69            10  RUN-YEAR                PIC 99.
 70            10  RUN-MONTH               PIC 99.
 71            10  RUN-DAY                 PIC 99.
 72
 73        01  PAGE-HEADING-LINE.
 74            10  PH-MONTH                PIC Z9.
 75            10                          PIC X        VALUE "/".
 76            10  PH-DAY                  PIC 99.
 77            10                          PIC X        VALUE "/".
 78            10  PH-YEAR                 PIC 99.
 79            10                          PIC X(15)    VALUE SPACES.
 80            10                          PIC X(32)    VALUE
 81                       "INVENTORY REPORT - UNISOFT, INC.".
 82            10                          PIC X(23)    VALUE SPACES.
 83            10                          PIC X(5)     VALUE "Page ".
 84            10  PH-PAGE-NUMBER          PIC Z9.
 85
 86        01  COLUMN-HEADING-1.
 87            10                          PIC X(62)    VALUE "Stock".
 88            10                          PIC X(5)     VALUE "On-".
 89            10                          PIC X(11)    VALUE "Retail".
 90            10                          PIC X(7)     VALUE "Retail".
 91
 92        01  COLUMN-HEADING-2.
 93            10                          PIC X(7)     VALUE " Num".
 94            10                          PIC X(22)    VALUE "Vendor".
 95            10                          PIC X(32)    VALUE "Title".
 96            10                          PIC X(7)     VALUE "Hand".
 97            10                          PIC X(10)    VALUE "Price".
 98            10                          PIC X(7)     VALUE "Value".
 99
100        01  DETAIL-LINE                 VALUE SPACES.
101            10  RL-STOCK-NUMBER         PIC X(5).
102            10                          PIC X(2).
103            10  RL-VENDOR-NAME          PIC X(20).
104            10                          PIC X(2).
105            10  RL-SOFTWARE-NAME        PIC X(30).
106            10                          PIC X(3).
107            10  RL-QUANT-ON-HAND        PIC ZZ9.
108            10                          PIC X(2).
109            10  RL-PRICE                PIC ZZZ.99.
110            10                          PIC X(2).
111            10  RL-RETAIL-VALUE         PIC ZZZ,ZZZ.99.
112
113        01  VENDOR-TOTAL-LINE.
114            10                          PIC X(1).
115            10  VT-RECORD-COUNT         PIC Z9.
116            10                          PIC X(26)    VALUE " Items".
117            10                          PIC X(20)    VALUE
118                       "TOTALS FOR VENDOR # ".
119            10  VT-VENDOR-NUMBER        PIC X(2).
120            10                          PIC X(22)    VALUE SPACES.
121            10  VT-TOTAL-VALUE          PIC Z,ZZZ,ZZZ.99.
122
123        01  FINAL-TOTAL-LINE.
124            10  FT-RECORD-COUNT         PIC ZZ9.
125            10                          PIC X(26)    VALUE " Items".
126            10                          PIC X(43)    VALUE "FINAL TOTALS".
127            10  FT-TOTAL-VALUE          PIC ZZ,ZZZ,ZZZ.99.
```

Figure 13-15

```
128
129          PROCEDURE DIVISION.
130
131          000-PRINT-1-LEVEL-GROUP-TOTALS.
132              PERFORM 100-INITIALIZE
133              PERFORM 110-PROCESS-CURRENT-RECORD
134                  UNTIL END-OF-FILE
135              PERFORM 120-FINALIZE
136              STOP RUN.
137
138          100-INITIALIZE.
139              OPEN INPUT INVENTORY-FILE
140              OPEN OUTPUT REPORT-FILE
141              PERFORM 200-GET-RUN-DATE
142              PERFORM 700-PRINT-PAGE-HEADINGS
143              INITIALIZE ACCUMULATORS
144              SET END-OF-FILE TO FALSE
145              PERFORM 800-READ-INVENTORY-RECORD
146              SET FIRST-RECORD TO TRUE
147              PERFORM 310-PROCESS-BREAK
148              SET FIRST-RECORD TO FALSE.
149
150          110-PROCESS-CURRENT-RECORD.
151
152      *   Calculate retail value
153              MOVE IR-PRICE TO RETAIL-VALUE
154              MULTIPLY IR-QUANT-ON-HAND BY RETAIL-VALUE
155
156              PERFORM 720-ASSEMBLE-AND-PRINT-DETAIL
157
158      *   Increment accumulators
159              ADD RETAIL-VALUE TO VENDOR-TOTAL-VALUE
160              ADD 1 TO VENDOR-RECORD-COUNT
161
162              PERFORM 800-READ-INVENTORY-RECORD
163              IF IR-VENDOR-NUMBER NOT = VENDOR-NUMBER
164                  PERFORM 310-PROCESS-BREAK
165              END-IF.
166
167          120-FINALIZE.
168              PERFORM 310-PROCESS-BREAK
169              PERFORM 740-PRINT-FINAL-TOTALS
170              CLOSE INVENTORY-FILE
171                    REPORT-FILE.
172
173          200-GET-RUN-DATE.
174              ACCEPT RUN-DATE FROM DATE
175              MOVE RUN-MONTH TO PH-MONTH
176              MOVE RUN-DAY   TO PH-DAY
177              MOVE RUN-YEAR  TO PH-YEAR.
178
179          310-PROCESS-BREAK.
180              IF NOT FIRST-RECORD
181                  PERFORM 730-PRINT-VENDOR-TOTALS
182                  ADD VENDOR-RECORD-COUNT TO FINAL-RECORD-COUNT
183                  ADD VENDOR-TOTAL-VALUE  TO FINAL-TOTAL-VALUE
184              END-IF
185              IF NOT END-OF-FILE
186                  INITIALIZE VENDOR-TOTAL-ACCUMULATORS
187                  MOVE IR-VENDOR-NUMBER TO VENDOR-NUMBER
188              END-IF.
189
190          700-PRINT-PAGE-HEADINGS.
191              ADD 1 TO PAGE-NUMBER
192              MOVE PAGE-NUMBER TO PH-PAGE-NUMBER
193              MOVE PAGE-HEADING-LINE TO REPORT-RECORD
194              PERFORM 851-WRITE-REPORT-LINE-AT-TOP
195              MOVE COLUMN-HEADING-1 TO REPORT-RECORD
196              MOVE 2 TO LINE-SPACING
197              PERFORM 850-WRITE-REPORT-LINE
198              MOVE COLUMN-HEADING-2 TO REPORT-RECORD
199              MOVE 1 TO LINE-SPACING
200              PERFORM 850-WRITE-REPORT-LINE
201              MOVE ALL "-" TO REPORT-RECORD
202              PERFORM 850-WRITE-REPORT-LINE.
203
204          720-ASSEMBLE-AND-PRINT-DETAIL.
205              IF LINES-USED-ON-PAGE + LINE-SPACING
206                  IS GREATER THAN LINES-DESIRED-ON-PAGE
207                      PERFORM 700-PRINT-PAGE-HEADINGS
208              END-IF
209              MOVE IR-STOCK-NUMBER TO RL-STOCK-NUMBER
210              MOVE IR-SOFTWARE-NAME TO RL-SOFTWARE-NAME
211              MOVE IR-VENDOR-NAME TO RL-VENDOR-NAME
212              MOVE IR-QUANT-ON-HAND TO RL-QUANT-ON-HAND
213              MOVE IR-PRICE TO RL-PRICE
214              MOVE RETAIL-VALUE TO RL-RETAIL-VALUE
215              MOVE DETAIL-LINE TO REPORT-RECORD
216              PERFORM 850-WRITE-REPORT-LINE
217              MOVE 1 TO LINE-SPACING.
218
219          730-PRINT-VENDOR-TOTALS.
220              MOVE VENDOR-RECORD-COUNT TO VT-RECORD-COUNT
221              MOVE VENDOR-TOTAL-VALUE  TO VT-TOTAL-VALUE
222              MOVE VENDOR-NUMBER        TO VT-VENDOR-NUMBER
223              MOVE 2 TO LINE-SPACING
224              MOVE VENDOR-TOTAL-LINE TO REPORT-RECORD
225              PERFORM 850-WRITE-REPORT-LINE.
226
227          740-PRINT-FINAL-TOTALS.
228              MOVE FINAL-RECORD-COUNT TO FT-RECORD-COUNT
229              MOVE FINAL-TOTAL-VALUE  TO FT-TOTAL-VALUE
230              MOVE 3 TO LINE-SPACING
231              MOVE FINAL-TOTAL-LINE TO REPORT-RECORD
232              PERFORM 850-WRITE-REPORT-LINE.
233
234          800-READ-INVENTORY-RECORD.
235              READ INVENTORY-FILE
236                  AT END SET END-OF-FILE TO TRUE
237              END-READ.
238
239          850-WRITE-REPORT-LINE.
240              WRITE REPORT-RECORD
241                  AFTER ADVANCING LINE-SPACING LINES
242              ADD LINE-SPACING TO LINES-USED-ON-PAGE.
243
244          851-WRITE-REPORT-LINE-AT-TOP.
245              WRITE REPORT-RECORD
246                  AFTER ADVANCING PAGE
247              MOVE 1 TO LINES-USED-ON-PAGE.
```

Figure 13-16

*Record Grouping for a
Two-Level Control-Break
Application*

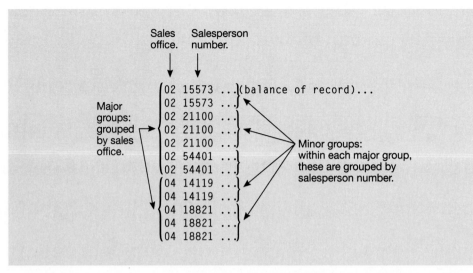

You now have three levels of control fields to handle: major, *intermediate*, and minor. Figure 13-17 illustrates how the records must be grouped first on the major field (in this case, the sales office), then on the intermediate field (the salesperson number), and finally within each salesperson group (on the software type).

By inspecting this sample sequence of data records, you can get an idea of control break logic. That is, control breaks trigger events as follows:

A Break on This Field...	...Requires This Action
Major field	Process minor group totals
	Process intermediate group totals
	Process major group totals
Intermediate field	Process minor group totals
	Process intermediate group totals
Minor field	Process minor group totals

The sequence in which control break actions and testing are carried out is critical. For instance, you cannot look only at the minor field to determine if a minor field control break has occurred. To see this, look at records five and six of Figure 13-17. Even though the minor field does not change (software type 4), the intermediate field does. As a result, this is considered a minor field control break because the records are in two different intermediate groups.

Control-Break Logic

You are already familiar with the single-level control-break logic illustrated by the flowchart segment shown in Figure 13-18 for the GRP-TOT1 program. As you know, if the vendor number of the record just read is different than that of the preceding record, a control break has occurred and control-break processing must occur.

In Figure 13-19, two-level control-break logic is illustrated. Notice that the major field is tested first. If a control break has occurred, the minor total processing is performed, followed by the major total processing. However, if a major control break has not occurred, a test must be made to determine if a minor break has occurred. If so, minor total processing must be performed.

Figure 13-20 shows three-level control-break logic; it is simply more of the same. Tests are made at major, intermediate, then minor levels. If a break is detected, control-break processing occurs for that level and subordinate levels.

**Example Definition—
Example 13-3**

The following is the formal definition of this group total application:

Example 13-3 Two-Level Group Totals
Problem Description

The group total program of Example 13-2 (GRP-TOT1) must be modified to produce a two-level group total report. The major control field is the vendor number and the minor field is the software type.

Output Requirements

The output requirements of this report are the same as those of GRP-TOT1, except that two levels are required. Major totals must be printed for each vendor and minor totals printed for each software type. The report format is shown in the printer spacing chart of Figure 13-21 (see page 348). A portion of sample output is shown in Figure 13-22.

Figure 13-17

Record Grouping for a Three-Level Control-Break Application

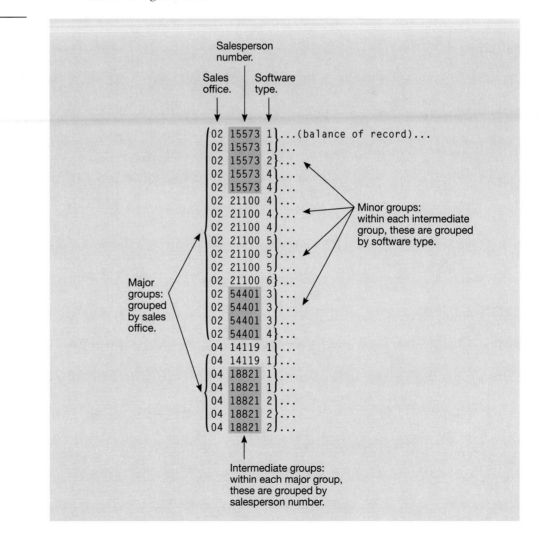

Figure 13-18

*Single-Level
Control-Break Logic*

Figure 13-19

*Two-Level
Control-Break Logic*

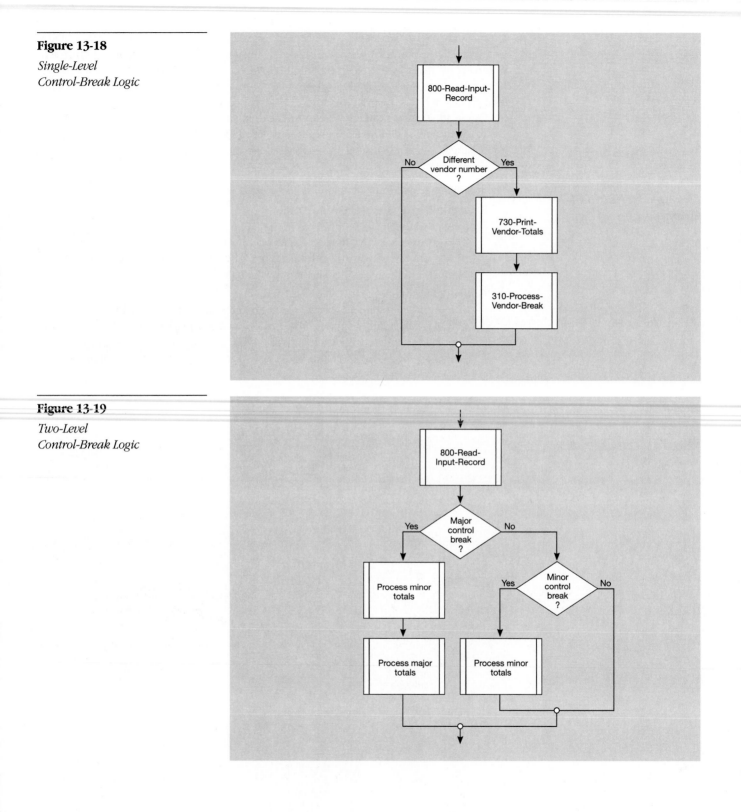

Figure 13-20

Three-Level
Control-Break Logic

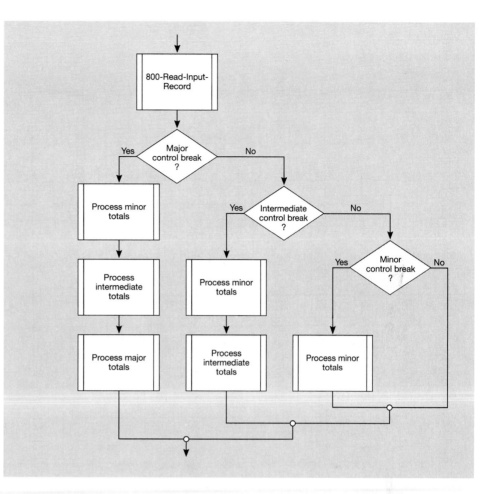

Input Description

Input file name: SOFTWAR3.DL (the same as that used for GRP-TOT1)

Note: Records of this file are in sequence based on the Product-number field and within Product-number on Software-type

Processing Requirements

General processing requirements for this example are the same as those for PAGE-TOT for the group total requirement. That is, processing will be as follows:

As each record is read:

1. Check for control breaks and take appropriate action, as illustrated by the flowchart segment of Figure 13-19
2. Count the record
3. Calculate the retail value as the Price times the Quantity-on-hand
4. Accumulate the retail value
5. Print the input data and the calculated retail value

At the end of the page:

1. Progress to a new page and print the page headings

At the end of the report:

1. Print the totals for the last software type
2. Print the totals for the last vendor
3. Print the final report totals

Figure 13-21

A Printer Spacing Chart for Example 13-3

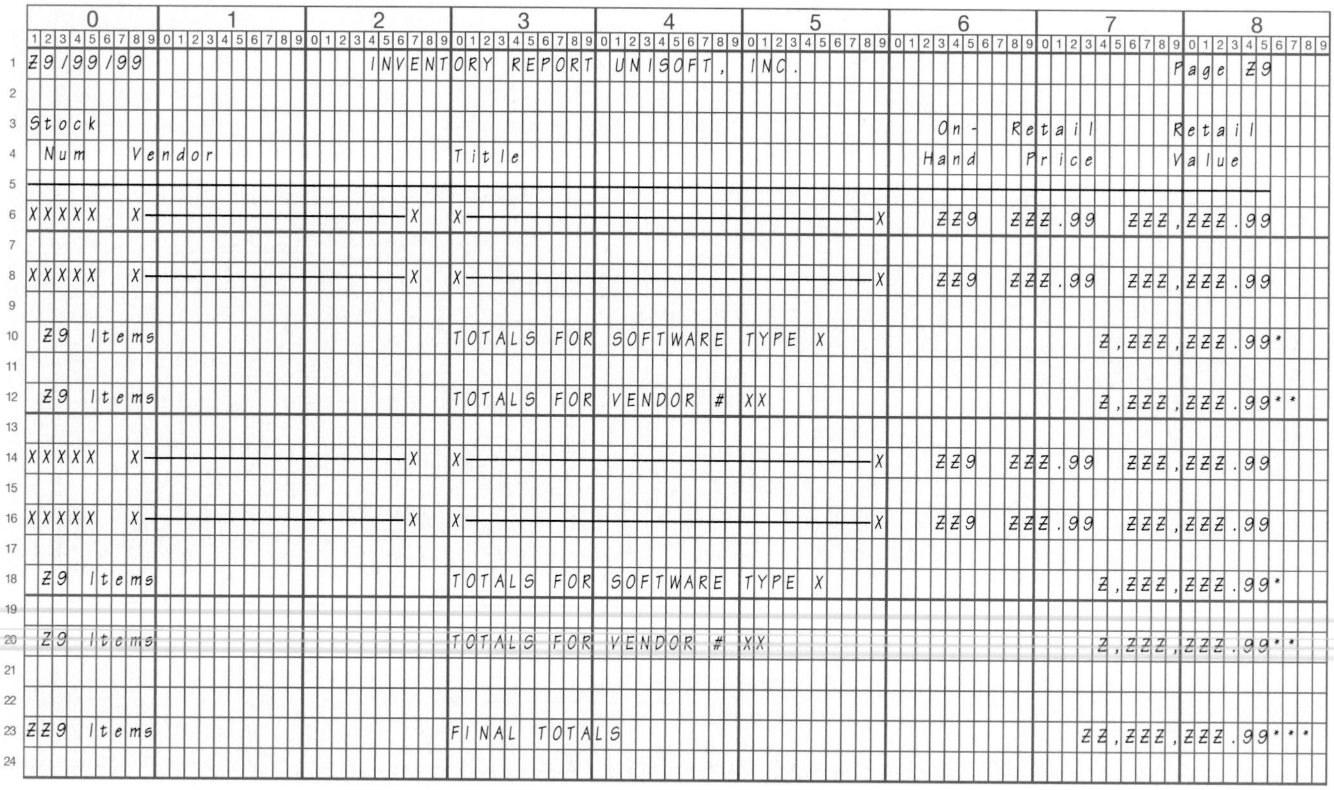

```
    0         1         2         3         4         5         6         7         8
1234567890123456789012345678901234567890123456789012345678901234567890123456789012345678901234567890
Z9/99/99                    INVENTORY  REPORT  UNISOFT,  INC.                              Page  Z9

Stock                                                          On-    Retail      Retail
Num    Vendor                      Title                       Hand   Price       Value

XXXXX  X---------------------X X----------------------------X  ZZ9    ZZZ.99   ZZZ,ZZZ.99

XXXXX  X---------------------X X----------------------------X  ZZ9    ZZZ.99   ZZZ,ZZZ.99

 Z9  Items                    TOTALS  FOR  SOFTWARE  TYPE  X                   Z,ZZZ,ZZZ.99*

 Z9  Items                    TOTALS  FOR  VENDOR  #  XX                       Z,ZZZ,ZZZ.99**

XXXXX  X---------------------X X----------------------------X  ZZ9    ZZZ.99   ZZZ,ZZZ.99

XXXXX  X---------------------X X----------------------------X  ZZ9    ZZZ.99   ZZZ,ZZZ.99

 Z9  Items                    TOTALS  FOR  SOFTWARE  TYPE  X                   Z,ZZZ,ZZZ.99*

 Z9  Items                    TOTALS  FOR  VENDOR  #  XX                       Z,ZZZ,ZZZ.99**

ZZ9  Items                    FINAL  TOTALS                                   ZZ,ZZZ,ZZZ.99***
```

Referring to the single-level control-break program of Example 13-2, notice that the group total lines stand out clearly from the detail lines. You can see the group total lines at a glance. This report presents its output in a concise, easy-to-read form. On the other hand, with multiple-level reports, the various total lines can easily run together and often are not easily spotted without looking carefully. One technique that is commonly used to make them stand out is to print asterisks following the total line—with one asterisk indicating the lowest control group, two representing the next higher, and so on. You can see these on both the printer spacing chart (Figure 13-21) and the sample output (Figure 13-22).

A Program Solution—Example 13-3

In the program solution of Figure 13-23, you can see that the additions required to GRP-TOT1 are relatively minor. The DATA DIVISION requires the following changes (highlighted in the program listing):

- The stock number field breakdown is expanded to include the software type (line 30)
- The report line length has been increased from 85 to 87 in order to handle the asterisks for total lines (line 39)
- A save area has been inserted for the software type (line 54)
- A set of accumulators (minor total) have been defined for the type totals (lines 57-59)
- A new output record has been defined for the type totals (lines 118-127)
- Lines 127, 138, and 145 include a FILLER containing asterisks that indicates a total line

(The text continues on page 352.)

Figure 13-22

*Sample Output
for Example 13-3*

```
  8/26/90              INVENTORY REPORT - UNISOFT, INC.               Page  1

Stock                                                        On-   Retail     Retail
Num     Vendor               Title                           Hand  Price      Value

07410   Apricot Software     Apricot-tree Accounts Payable    27   349.95     9,448.65
07414   Apricot Software     Apricot-tree Accts. Receivable   18   349.95     6,299.10
07427   Apricot Software     Apricot-tree General Ledger      65   349.95    22,746.75
07432   Apricot Software     Apricot-tree Hourly Payroll      35   349.95    12,248.25
07436   Apricot Software     Apricot-tree Inventory Control   25   349.95     8,748.75
07474   Apricot Software     Apricot-tree Salaried Payroll    34   349.95    11,898.30

  6 Items                    TOTALS FOR SOFTWARE TYPE 4                      71,389.80*

  6 Items                    TOTALS FOR VENDOR # 07                         71,389.80**

10164   Archaic Software     Sluggish Writer                  93    49.95     4,645.35
10165   Archaic Software     Sluggish Writer, Economy Model   93    49.95     4,645.35
10166   Archaic Software     Sluggish Writer, Power Model     67    99.95     6,696.65

  3 Items                    TOTALS FOR SOFTWARE TYPE 1                      15,987.35*

10279   Archaic Software     Ten-Column Spreadsheet, Econ.   105    49.95     5,244.75
10281   Archaic Software     Ten-Column Spreadsheet, Power    48    99.95     4,797.60

  2 Items                    TOTALS FOR SOFTWARE TYPE 2                      10,042.35*

  5 Items                    TOTALS FOR VENDOR # 10                         26,029.70**
```

```
  8/26/90              INVENTORY REPORT - UNISOFT, INC.               Page  3

Stock                                                        On-   Retail     Retail
Num     Vendor               Title                           Hand  Price      Value

53355   MicroPerimeter, Inc. QBase 7000                      176   695.00   122,320.00

  5 Items                    TOTALS FOR SOFTWARE TYPE 3                     343,857.00*

53635   MicroPerimeter, Inc. MicroPer C Interpreter           83   249.50    20,708.50

  1 Items                    TOTALS FOR SOFTWARE TYPE 6                      20,708.50*

  6 Items                    TOTALS FOR VENDOR # 53                        364,565.50**

60541   Nobodies, Unlimited  Nobodies Computer Friday        126    49.50     6,237.00
60544   Nobodies, Unlimited  Nobodies Disk Utilities         133    49.50     6,583.50
60547   Nobodies, Unlimited  Nobodies File Finder             97    49.50     4,801.50
60550   Nobodies, Unlimited  Nobodies Panes                   75   129.95     9,746.25

  4 Items                    TOTALS FOR SOFTWARE TYPE 5                      27,368.25*

  4 Items                    TOTALS FOR VENDOR # 60                         27,368.25**

91651   20th Century Soft.   Potent BASIC Compiler           180   199.50    35,910.00
91653   20th Century Soft.   Potent BASIC Emulator           127   347.50    44,132.50
91655   20th Century Soft.   Potent BASIC Interpreter         97     9.50       921.50
91659   20th Century Soft.   Potent Interpretive COBOL       143   349.99    50,048.57
91663   20th Century Soft.   Potent Interpretive Fortran     159   349.99    55,648.41
91667   20th Century Soft.   Potent Interpretive RPG         102   349.99    35,698.98

  6 Items                    TOTALS FOR SOFTWARE TYPE 6                     222,359.96*

  6 Items                    TOTALS FOR VENDOR # 91                        222,359.96**

 54 Items                    FINAL TOTALS                              1,320,351.11***
```

Figure 13-23

A Program Solution for Example 13-3

```
  1        IDENTIFICATION DIVISION.
  2
  3        PROGRAM-ID. GRP-TOT2.
  4
  5    *      Written by J.Olson/W.Price
  6    *      August 24, 1990
  7
  8    *      This program prints a total line for each vendor,
  9    *      as well as a final total line.
 10
 11       ENVIRONMENT DIVISION.
 12
 13       CONFIGURATION SECTION.
 14       SOURCE-COMPUTER. IBM-PC.
 15
 16       INPUT-OUTPUT SECTION.
 17       FILE-CONTROL.
 18           SELECT INVENTORY-FILE   ASSIGN TO DISK "SOFTWAR3.DL"
 19                                   ORGANIZATION IS LINE SEQUENTIAL.
 20           SELECT REPORT-FILE      ASSIGN TO PRINTER "PRN-FILE".
 21
 22       DATA DIVISION.
 23
 24       FILE SECTION.
 25
 26       FD  INVENTORY-FILE.
 27       01  INVENTORY-RECORD.
 28           10  IR-STOCK-NUMBER.
 29               20  IR-VENDOR-NUMBER    PIC X(2).
 30               20  IR-SOFTWARE-TYPE    PIC X(1).
 31               20                      PIC X(2).
 32           10  IR-SOFTWARE-NAME        PIC X(30).
 33           10  IR-VENDOR-NAME          PIC X(20).
 34           10  IR-QUANT-ON-HAND        PIC 9(3).
 35           10                          PIC X(3).
 36           10  IR-PRICE                PIC 9(3)V9(2).
 37
 38       FD  REPORT-FILE.
 39       01  REPORT-RECORD               PIC X(87).
 40
 41       WORKING-STORAGE SECTION.
 42
 43       01  PROGRAMMED-SWITCHES.
 44           10                          PIC X.
 45               88  END-OF-FILE         VALUE "Y" FALSE "N".
 46           10                          PIC X.
 47               88  FIRST-RECORD        VALUE "Y" FALSE "N".
 48
 49       01  ARITHMETIC-WORK-AREAS.
 50           10  RETAIL-VALUE            PIC 9(6)V9(2).
 51
 52       01  SAVE-AREAS.
 53           10  VENDOR-NUMBER           PIC X(2).
 54           10  SOFTWARE-TYPE           PIC X.
 55
 56       01  ACCUMULATORS.
 57           10  TYPE-TOTAL-ACCUMULATORS.
 58               20  TYPE-TOTAL-VALUE    PIC 9(7)V9(2).
 59               20  TYPE-RECORD-COUNT   PIC 9(2).
 60           10  VENDOR-TOTAL-ACCUMULATORS.
 61               20  VENDOR-TOTAL-VALUE  PIC 9(7)V9(2).
 62               20  VENDOR-RECORD-COUNT PIC 9(2).
 63           10  FINAL-TOTAL-ACCUMULATORS.
 64               20  FINAL-TOTAL-VALUE   PIC 9(8)V9(2).
 65               20  FINAL-RECORD-COUNT  PIC 9(3).
 66
 67       01  PRINT-CONTROL-VARIABLES.
 68           10  LINE-SPACING            PIC 9.
 69           10  LINES-DESIRED-ON-PAGE   PIC 99        VALUE 54.
 70           10  LINES-USED-ON-PAGE      PIC 99.
 71           10  PAGE-NUMBER             PIC 99        VALUE ZERO.
 72

 73       01  RUN-DATE.
 74           10  RUN-YEAR                PIC 99.
 75           10  RUN-MONTH               PIC 99.
 76           10  RUN-DAY                 PIC 99.
 77
 78       01  PAGE-HEADING-LINE.
 79           10  PH-MONTH                PIC Z9.
 80           10                          PIC X         VALUE "/".
 81           10  PH-DAY                  PIC 99.
 82           10                          PIC X         VALUE "/".
 83           10  PH-YEAR                 PIC 99.
 84           10                          PIC X(15)     VALUE SPACES.
 85           10                          PIC X(32)     VALUE
 86               "INVENTORY REPORT - UNISOFT, INC.".
 87           10                          PIC X(23)     VALUE SPACES.
 88           10                          PIC X(5)      VALUE "Page ".
 89           10  PH-PAGE-NUMBER          PIC Z9.
 90
 91       01  COLUMN-HEADING-1.
 92           10                          PIC X(62)     VALUE "Stock".
 93           10                          PIC X(5)      VALUE "On-".
 94           10                          PIC X(11)     VALUE "Retail".
 95           10                          PIC X(7)      VALUE "Retail".
 96
 97       01  COLUMN-HEADING-2.
 98           10                          PIC X(7)      VALUE " Num".
 99           10                          PIC X(22)     VALUE "Vendor".
100           10                          PIC X(32)     VALUE "Title".
101           10                          PIC X(7)      VALUE "Hand".
102           10                          PIC X(10)     VALUE "Price".
103           10                          PIC X(7)      VALUE "Value".
104
105       01  DETAIL-LINE                 VALUE SPACES.
106           10  RL-STOCK-NUMBER         PIC X(5).
107           10                          PIC X(2).
108           10  RL-VENDOR-NAME          PIC X(20).
109           10                          PIC X(2).
110           10  RL-SOFTWARE-NAME        PIC X(30).
111           10                          PIC X(3).
112           10  RL-QUANT-ON-HAND        PIC ZZ9.
113           10                          PIC X(2).
114           10  RL-PRICE                PIC ZZZ.99.
115           10                          PIC X(2).
116           10  RL-RETAIL-VALUE         PIC ZZZ,ZZZ.99.
117
118       01  TYPE-TOTAL-LINE.
119           10                          PIC X(1).
120           10  TT-RECORD-COUNT         PIC Z9.
121           10                          PIC X(26)     VALUE " Items".
122           10                          PIC X(25)     VALUE
123               "TOTALS FOR SOFTWARE TYPE ".
124           10  TT-SOFTWARE-TYPE        PIC X(1).
125           10                          PIC X(18)     VALUE SPACES.
126           10  TT-TOTAL-VALUE          PIC Z,ZZZ,ZZZ.99.
127           10                          PIC X(1)      VALUE "*".
128
129       01  VENDOR-TOTAL-LINE.
130           10                          PIC X(1).
131           10  VT-RECORD-COUNT         PIC Z9.
132           10                          PIC X(26)     VALUE " Items".
133           10                          PIC X(20)     VALUE
134               "TOTALS FOR VENDOR # ".
135           10  VT-VENDOR-NUMBER        PIC X(2).
136           10                          PIC X(22)     VALUE SPACES.
137           10  VT-TOTAL-VALUE          PIC Z,ZZZ,ZZZ.99.
138           10                          PIC X(2)      VALUE "**".
139
140       01  FINAL-TOTAL-LINE.
141           10  FT-RECORD-COUNT         PIC ZZ9.
142           10                          PIC X(26)     VALUE " Items".
143           10                          PIC X(43)     VALUE "FINAL TOTALS".
144           10  FT-TOTAL-VALUE          PIC ZZ,ZZZ,ZZZ.99.
145           10                          PIC X(3)      VALUE "***".
146
```

Figure 13-23

```
147    PROCEDURE DIVISION.
148
149    000-PRINT-1-LEVEL-GROUP-TOTALS.
150        PERFORM 100-INITIALIZE
151        PERFORM 110-PROCESS-CURRENT-RECORD
152            UNTIL END-OF-FILE
153        PERFORM 120-FINALIZE
154        STOP RUN.
155
156    100-INITIALIZE.
157        OPEN INPUT INVENTORY-FILE
158        OPEN OUTPUT REPORT-FILE
159        PERFORM 200-GET-RUN-DATE
160        PERFORM 700-PRINT-PAGE-HEADINGS
161        INITIALIZE ACCUMULATORS
162        SET END-OF-FILE TO FALSE
163        PERFORM 800-READ-INVENTORY-RECORD
164        SET FIRST-RECORD TO TRUE
165        PERFORM 300-PROCESS-TYPE-BREAK
166        PERFORM 310-PROCESS-VENDOR-BREAK
167        SET FIRST-RECORD TO FALSE.
168
169    110-PROCESS-CURRENT-RECORD.
170
171    * Calculate retail value
172        MOVE IR-PRICE TO RETAIL-VALUE
173        MULTIPLY IR-QUANT-ON-HAND BY RETAIL-VALUE
174
175        PERFORM 720-ASSEMBLE-AND-PRINT-DETAIL
176
177    * Increment accumulators
178        ADD RETAIL-VALUE TO TYPE-TOTAL-VALUE
179        ADD 1 TO TYPE-RECORD-COUNT
180
181        PERFORM 800-READ-INVENTORY-RECORD
182
183        IF IR-VENDOR-NUMBER NOT = VENDOR-NUMBER
184            PERFORM 300-PROCESS-TYPE-BREAK
185            PERFORM 310-PROCESS-VENDOR-BREAK
186        ELSE
187            IF IR-SOFTWARE-TYPE NOT EQUAL SOFTWARE-TYPE
188                PERFORM 300-PROCESS-TYPE-BREAK
189            END-IF
190        END-IF.
191
192    120-FINALIZE.
193        PERFORM 300-PROCESS-TYPE-BREAK
194        PERFORM 310-PROCESS-VENDOR-BREAK
195        PERFORM 740-PRINT-FINAL-TOTALS
196        CLOSE INVENTORY-FILE
197            REPORT-FILE.
198
199    200-GET-RUN-DATE.
200        ACCEPT RUN-DATE FROM DATE
201        MOVE RUN-MONTH TO PH-MONTH
202        MOVE RUN-DAY   TO PH-DAY
203        MOVE RUN-YEAR  TO PH-YEAR.
204
205    300-PROCESS-TYPE-BREAK.
206        IF NOT FIRST-RECORD
207            PERFORM 725-PRINT-TYPE-TOTALS
208            ADD TYPE-RECORD-COUNT TO VENDOR-RECORD-COUNT
209            ADD TYPE-TOTAL-VALUE  TO VENDOR-TOTAL-VALUE
210        END-IF
211        IF NOT END-OF-FILE
212            INITIALIZE TYPE-TOTAL-ACCUMULATORS
213            MOVE IR-SOFTWARE-TYPE TO SOFTWARE-TYPE
214        END-IF.
215
216    310-PROCESS-VENDOR-BREAK.
217        IF NOT FIRST-RECORD
218            PERFORM 730-PRINT-VENDOR-TOTALS
219            ADD VENDOR-RECORD-COUNT TO FINAL-RECORD-COUNT
220            ADD VENDOR-TOTAL-VALUE  TO FINAL-TOTAL-VALUE
221        END-IF
222        IF NOT END-OF-FILE
223            INITIALIZE VENDOR-TOTAL-ACCUMULATORS
224            MOVE IR-VENDOR-NUMBER TO VENDOR-NUMBER
225        END-IF.
226
227    700-PRINT-PAGE-HEADINGS.
228        ADD 1 TO PAGE-NUMBER
229        MOVE PAGE-NUMBER TO PH-PAGE-NUMBER
230        MOVE PAGE-HEADING-LINE TO REPORT-RECORD
231        PERFORM 851-WRITE-REPORT-LINE-AT-TOP
232        MOVE COLUMN-HEADING-1 TO REPORT-RECORD
233        MOVE 2 TO LINE-SPACING
234        PERFORM 850-WRITE-REPORT-LINE
235        MOVE COLUMN-HEADING-2 TO REPORT-RECORD
236        MOVE 1 TO LINE-SPACING
237        PERFORM 850-WRITE-REPORT-LINE
238        MOVE ALL "-" TO REPORT-RECORD
239        PERFORM 850-WRITE-REPORT-LINE.
240
241    720-ASSEMBLE-AND-PRINT-DETAIL.
242        IF LINES-USED-ON-PAGE + LINE-SPACING
243            IS GREATER THAN LINES-DESIRED-ON-PAGE
244                PERFORM 700-PRINT-PAGE-HEADINGS
245        END-IF
246        MOVE IR-STOCK-NUMBER TO RL-STOCK-NUMBER
247        MOVE IR-SOFTWARE-NAME TO RL-SOFTWARE-NAME
248        MOVE IR-VENDOR-NAME TO RL-VENDOR-NAME
249        MOVE IR-QUANT-ON-HAND TO RL-QUANT-ON-HAND
250        MOVE IR-PRICE TO RL-PRICE
251        MOVE RETAIL-VALUE TO RL-RETAIL-VALUE
252        MOVE DETAIL-LINE TO REPORT-RECORD
253        PERFORM 850-WRITE-REPORT-LINE
254        MOVE 1 TO LINE-SPACING.
255
256    725-PRINT-TYPE-TOTALS.
257        MOVE TYPE-RECORD-COUNT TO TT-RECORD-COUNT
258        MOVE TYPE-TOTAL-VALUE  TO TT-TOTAL-VALUE
259        MOVE SOFTWARE-TYPE     TO TT-SOFTWARE-TYPE
260        MOVE 2 TO LINE-SPACING
261        MOVE TYPE-TOTAL-LINE TO REPORT-RECORD
262        PERFORM 850-WRITE-REPORT-LINE.
263
264    730-PRINT-VENDOR-TOTALS.
265        MOVE VENDOR-RECORD-COUNT TO VT-RECORD-COUNT
266        MOVE VENDOR-TOTAL-VALUE  TO VT-TOTAL-VALUE
267        MOVE VENDOR-NUMBER       TO VT-VENDOR-NUMBER
268        MOVE 2 TO LINE-SPACING
269        MOVE VENDOR-TOTAL-LINE TO REPORT-RECORD
270        PERFORM 850-WRITE-REPORT-LINE.
271
272    740-PRINT-FINAL-TOTALS.
273        MOVE FINAL-RECORD-COUNT TO FT-RECORD-COUNT
274        MOVE FINAL-TOTAL-VALUE  TO FT-TOTAL-VALUE
275        MOVE 3 TO LINE-SPACING
276        MOVE FINAL-TOTAL-LINE TO REPORT-RECORD
277        PERFORM 850-WRITE-REPORT-LINE.
278
279    800-READ-INVENTORY-RECORD.
280        READ INVENTORY-FILE
281            AT END SET END-OF-FILE TO TRUE
282        END-READ.
283
284    850-WRITE-REPORT-LINE.
285        WRITE REPORT-RECORD
286            AFTER ADVANCING LINE-SPACING LINES
287        ADD LINE-SPACING TO LINES-USED-ON-PAGE.
288
289    851-WRITE-REPORT-LINE-AT-TOP.
290        WRITE REPORT-RECORD
291            AFTER ADVANCING PAGE
292        MOVE 1 TO LINES-USED-ON-PAGE.
```

The PROCEDURE DIVISION includes several additions. Note the following:

- For detail processing, accumulations are made to the lowest level accumulators (the type accumulators) at lines 178 and 179.

- A 300 module (starting line 205) and a 725 module (starting line 256) have been added for software type group processing. These parallel the 310 and 730 modules for vendor group processing.

- After a record is read, a test is made to determine whether or not a vendor break has occurred (line 183). If so, the type break is first processed, then the vendor break.

- If a vendor break (major control break) has *not* occurred, a test is made to determine if a type break has occurred (minor control break). If so, the type break is processed.

- In the 120-FINALIZE module (beginning line 192), the minor break is processed, the major break is processed, and the final totals are printed.

About Control-Break Processing

Students are commonly confused by multiple levels of control-break processing—which is understandable because it can be a confusing topic. However, if approached in an organized way using good modular construction, multiple levels are little more difficult to handle than single levels.

Files that you will work with in writing your own control-break programs are already in the proper sequence. Frequently, the order of the records in a file are not in the needed order to produce a desired report. Putting the records of a file into a required sequence is called *sorting* and is the topic of Chapter 15.

Sorting a File

Perhaps you have wondered what you would do in the group total processing of Examples 15-2 and 15-3 if the records in the SOFTWAR3 file were not already in the proper sequence. The answer is that you would sort the file. Although Chapter 15 is devoted entirely to sorting, you need to know a little about the SORT verb in order to sort files for your programming assignments of this chapter. Using the SORT verb, you designate the following:

1. The field or fields on which you want the file sequenced

2. The name of the input file

3. The name the SORT verb should use for a temporary work file that it will need in rearranging the records

4. The name you want the SORT verb to use for the newly created file in which the records are in your requested sequence

A complete program to sort the SOFTWAR3.DL file into a sequence on the Stock number field is shown in Figure 13-24. Notice that the PROCEDURE DIVISION consists of only two statements: SORT and STOP RUN. Annotations included with this program describe most of its features. Other points you must be aware of in sorting files for the programming assignments of this chapter are as follows:

1. The input file (INVENTORY-FILE) and the sort work file (SORT-FILE) both include complete record descriptions. Technically, you need identify only the fields on which sorting is to be done. Other areas of the record can be defined as FILLER.

2. The output record is designated as FILLER—no reference to the individual fields is needed.

3. The ASCENDING clause specifies ascending sequence (smallest to largest) and identifies the field on which the sorting is to be performed.

4. If sorting is required on two or more fields, then both must be specified in the

Figure 13-24

Demonstrating Simple Sorting

```
1        IDENTIFICATION DIVISION.
2
3        PROGRAM-ID.  SORT-INV.
4
5        *     Written by W.Price  12/12/90
6
7        *     A simple SORT program.
8
9        ENVIRONMENT DIVISION.
10
11       CONFIGURATION SECTION.
12       SOURCE-COMPUTER.   IBM-PC.
13
14       INPUT-OUTPUT SECTION.
15       FILE-CONTROL.
16           SELECT INVENTORY-FILE         ASSIGN TO DISK, "SOFTWAR3.DL",  ◄────── This is the original file.
17                                         ORGANIZATION IS LINE SEQUENTIAL.
18                                                                                 This is a file that the SORT
19           SELECT SORT-FILE              ASSIGN TO DISK, "SOFTWORK.TMP". ◄────── verb will create as a temporary
20                                                                                 work file.
21           SELECT SORTED-INVENTORY-FILE ASSIGN TO DISK,  "SOFTWAR3.DLS", ◄───── This will be the new file in
22                                         ORGANIZATION IS LINE SEQUENTIAL.        sorted sequence.
23
24       DATA DIVISION.
25
26       FILE SECTION.
27
28       FD   INVENTORY-FILE.
29       01   INVENTORY-RECORD.
30            10   IR-STOCK-NUMBER        PIC X(5).
31            10   IR-SOFTWARE-NAME       PIC X(30).
32            10   IR-VENDOR-NAME         PIC X(20).
33            10   IR-QUANT-ON-HAND       PIC 9(3).
34            10   IR-REORDER-LEVEL       PIC X(3).
35            10   IR-PRICE               PIC 9(3)V9(2).
36
37       SD   SORT-FILE. ◄──────────────────────────────── Note that the sort work file is
38       01   SORT-RECORD.                                  defined with an SD, not an FD.
39            10   SR-STOCK-NUMBER        PIC X(5).
40            10   SR-SOFTWARE-NAME       PIC X(30).
41            10   SR-VENDOR-NAME         PIC X(20).          Make the record description the
42            10   SR-QUANT-ON-HAND       PIC 9(3).           same as the input file.
43            10   SR-REORDER-LEVEL       PIC X(3).
44            10   SR-PRICE               PIC 9(3)V9(2).
45
46       FD   SORTED-INVENTORY-FILE.
47       01   SORTED-INVENTORY-RECORD      PIC X(66).  ◄────── Individual fields need not be defined
48                                                             in the new sorted file.
49       PROCEDURE DIVISION.
50       000-SORT-INVENTORY-FILE.
51           SORT SORT-FILE ◄──────────────────────────── Designate the sort work file in the SORT statement.
52             ON ASCENDING KEY SR-SOFTWARE-NAME ◄──────── Field on which sorting is to take place.
53             USING INVENTORY-FILE ◄──────────────────── The original (input) file.
54             GIVING SORTED-INVENTORY-FILE ◄───────────── The new sorted file.
55           STOP RUN.
```

ASCENDING clause. This was not a problem in Example 13-3 because the major field (vendor number) and minor field (software type) were both part of the stock number. However, had they been separate fields (and not adjacent to one another), the ASCENDING clause would need to specify both of them as follows:

```
ON ASCENDING KEY SR-VENDOR-NUMBER, SR-SOFTWARE-TYPE
```

Notice that the major field is designated first and the minor field last.

This gives you enough information about the SORT verb to use it in sorting the files for the programming assignments of this chapter. For each input DL file you sort, use the extension DLS for the sorted output file. Then it will be easy for you to keep track of the files. You will use the DLS file in your group total program.

Chapter Summary
General

Group total programs require that input records be in sequence, based on the control field(s). For multi-level control-break programs, the records must be in order first on the major field, then on control fields of decreasing significance.

A control break occurs whenever the value of the current-record control field is different from that of the preceding record. Technically, a control break also occurs when the first record is read and when the end-of-file is read.

With multiple-level control-break programs, a break at one control level automatically represents a break at lower levels.

As each record in a multiple-level control-break program is read, the major control field must be tested first, followed by successively lower significant control fields.

Error Prevention/Detection

Processing logic of multiple-level control-break programs can easily become confusing. Treat multiple levels as simple expansions of single levels, as illustrated by the examples in this chapter. Remember that a high-level break requires that processing be done for each lower control break as well. As each lower level total is printed, add the contents of the accumulators to the next higher level accumulators *before* initializing to zero. Otherwise, the contents will be lost.

It is easy to design logic that causes a false indication of a control break as a result of reading the first record, and thereby prints meaningless totals before the first detail record is even processed. Guard against this.

Poorly designed program logic can cause trouble when the end-of-file is encountered. That is, under this condition make certain that the control-break actions are executed and that low-level totals are properly added to higher levels and that all levels of group totals are printed.

Questions and Exercises
Key Terminology

Give a brief description of each of the following terms that were introduced in this chapter.

accumulator	group total logic	single-level control-break report
control break	intermediate field	report
control field	major field	two-level control-break report
control group	minor field	report
group total	page total	

General Questions

1. Name the two conditions that indicate it is time to start a new page. Also name the two conditions that indicate it is time to print page totals.
2. Fill in the blanks:
   To arrange the records in a file by control _____, it is necessary to sort them on the proper control _____.

3. A department store maintains a file of all sales records made during the previous month. Each record contains information about one sale, including the customer number, the salesperson number, the inventory number for the item sold, the date of sale, and the amount of sale. Name the field in the record that would be the control field for each of the following reports:
   a. Sales volume report for each salesperson
   b. Sales listing by day
   c. Total quantity of each item sold during the month
   d. Customer billing

4. Before a program can be run using group total logic, how must the records of the input file be arranged?

5. The end of a control group is indicated by a change in the control group number. What other condition indicates the end of a control group?

6. What purpose do accumulators serve in a control-break program?

7. What does it mean when a report needs to contain multiple-level control breaks?

Questions Relating to the Example Programs

1. In the PAGE-TOT program of Figure 13-7, what would be the consequence of making the INITIALIZE the first statement in the 310 module?

2. Referring to the GRP-TOT1 program of Figure 13-15, describe the errors in the output report if the 310 module were not performed from the 120-FINALIZE module.

3. Describe the problems that would occur if the IF statement were removed from the 310 module of the GRP-TOT1 program and all the statements were executed unconditionally.

4. In the GRP-TOT2 program (Figure 13-23), describe what would happen if the PERFORM 800-READ-INVENTORY-RECORD statement (line 163) was inserted after line 149 instead.

5. Describe what would happen in the GRP-TOT2 program if lines 193 and 194 were removed from the 120-FINALIZE module.

6. If the PERFORM 850-WRITE-REPORT-LINE statement (line 253) in the 720 module is inadvertently commented out, what would print on the report in the GRP-TOT2 program?

7. If the perform statement for the read in the 110 module is moved from line 181 to after line 190, what effect would this have on the output from the GRP-TOT2 program?

Programming Assignments

13-1 Instructor Load Summary Report

The dean of instruction at the Computer Institute of Technology needs a summary report from the enrollment file. So that the dean can assess the developing load for each instructor during class registration week, a summary report is needed that gives the current number of student contacts for each instructor.

Output Requirements:
   A single-level group total report with the output and format shown in the printer spacing chart on the following page. Note that the Instructor name is printed only on the first line for that instructor.

```
        0           1           2           3           4           5           6           7           8
  1234567890123456789012345678901234567890123456789012345678901234567890123456789012345678901234567890
1 Z9/99/99                  COMPUTER INSTITUTE OF TECHNOLOGY                              Page ZZ
2                           INSTRUCTOR LOAD REPORT
3
4                 Class  Course  Section                           Min       Max       Act
5 Instructor      Code   Number  Number   Course                   Enr       Enr       Enr
6 ═══════════════════════════════════════════════════════════════════════════════════════════
7 X─────────────X XXXX   XXX     XX    X─────────────────────X     ZZ9       ZZ9       ZZ9
8                 XXXX   XXX     XX    X─────────────────────X     ZZ9       ZZ9       ZZ9
9
10   Z9 Courses                           Total for this instructor         Z,ZZ9*
11
12 X─────────────X XXXX   XXX     XX    X─────────────────────X     ZZ9       ZZ9       ZZ9
13                 XXXX   XXX     XX    X─────────────────────X     ZZ9       ZZ9       ZZ9
14   Z9 Courses
15                                        Total for this instructor         Z,ZZ9*
16
17 ZZ9 Courses
18                                        Total for all instructors        ZZZ,ZZ9**
```

Input Description:
    File name: ENROLL01.DL
      This file must be sorted on Instructor name
    Record description: See Appendix A

Processing Requirements:
    As each enrollment record is read:
1. Check to see if the Instructor name is the same as that of the preceding record.
2. If it is not:
    a. Print the number of courses and student enrollment for the preceding instructor.
    b. Accumulate the record count and student count for report totals.
3. Count the grade record and accumulate the number of students (student enrollment).
4. Print the detail line according to the printer spacing chart. Note that the instructor name is printed on only the first line for that instructor.

    At the end of the page:
5. Progress to a new page and print the page headings.

    At the end of the report:
6. Print the totals for the last instructor.
7. Print the final report totals.

13-2 Student Grade Summary

In most institutions, the grade reporting process operates on data from two sources: a student master file and a scholarship file. The student master contains fixed data about the student plus the number of accumulated units and points. The scholarship file contains one record for each course taken by each student; stored data includes the course units and grade received. Grade processing involves updating the student master data from data stored in the scholarship file. Although this assignment does not require updating the student master, it does require access to the records of that file in order to produce a group total report based on the scholarship file.

Output Requirements:

A single-level group total report with the following output and format. Note that the student number and name are printed only on the first line for that student.

```
        0         1         2         3         4         5         6         7        8
1234567890123456789012345678901234567890123456789012345678901234567890123456789012345678901234
 1 Z9/99/99                STUDENT  GRADE  SUMMARY                              Page  ZZ
 2
 3               Student                      Course               Units      Points
 4 Number        Last  Name      First Name   Code      Units   Grade   Earned    Earned
 5
 6 XXX-XX-XXXX   X---------X  X--------X   XXXXXX    ZZ.9      X     ZZ.9      ZZ.9
 7                                         XXXXXX    ZZ.9      X     ZZ.9      ZZ.9
 8
 9                                         TOTALS              ZZ.9      ZZ.9*
10
11 XXX-XX-XXXX   X---------X  X--------X   XXXXXX    ZZ.9      X     ZZ.9      ZZ.9
12                                         XXXXXX    ZZ.9      X     ZZ.9      ZZ.9
13
14                                         TOTALS              ZZ.9      ZZ.9*
15
16
17                                  FINAL TOTALS     ZZ.9      ZZ.9**
18
19
```

Input Description:

File name: GRADES.DL

This file must be sorted on Student number

For access to student name: STUDENTS.DI

Record descriptions: See Appendix A

Processing Requirements:

As each grade record is read:

1. Check to see if the Student number is the same as that of the preceding record.
2. If it is not:
   a. Print the accumulated units and points for the preceding student.
   b. Accumulate the units and points for report totals.
   c. Using the Student number from the grade record, access the student's record from the student file.
3. Determine the units earned from the grade as follows:

Grade	Earned Units
A, B, C, or D	Equal to input Course units
F or W	0

4. Calculate the points earned for this grade record, as the Earned units times Grade points. Grade points are determined as follows:

Grade	Grade Points
A	4
B	3
C	2
D	1

5. Accumulate the earned units and points.
6. Print the detail line according to the printer spacing chart. Note that the student number and name are printed on only the first line for that student.

At the end of the page:

7. Progress to a new page and print the page headings.

At the end of the report:

8. Print the totals for the last student.
9. Print the final report totals.

13-3 Voter Average Incomes

The For-Everything Political Action Committee (of Programming Assignments 9-5 and 11-4) would like a report listing average annual income for records in the voters file. To provide the type of information in which they are interested they want a two-level group total report with control breaks on Marital status and Party of registration.

Output Requirements:

A two-level group total report with the following output and format.

```
         0         1         2         3         4         5         6         7         8
    1234567890123456789012345678901234567890123456789012345678901234567890123456789012345678
 1  Z9/99/99                    VOTER INCOME SUMMARY                        Page  ZZ
 2
 3  Married  Party        Name                        City         State    Income
 4
 5  XXX      X----------X X----------------------X X X----------X XX   ZZ,ZZ9
 6  XXX      X----------X X----------------------X X X----------X XX   ZZ,ZZ9
 7
 8  XXX      X----------X                          PARTY TOTAL          Z,ZZZ,ZZ9*
 9
10  XXX      X----------X X----------------------X X X----------X XX   ZZ,ZZ9
11  XXX      X----------X X----------------------X X X----------X XX   ZZ,ZZ9
12
13  XXX      X----------X                          PARTY TOTAL          Z,ZZZ,ZZ9*
14
15  XXX                         MARITAL GROUP TOTAL                    ZZ,ZZZ,ZZ9**
16
17
18                              REPORT TOTAL                           ZZ,ZZZ,ZZ9***
19
20
21
```

The entry in the *Married* column must be YES (Marital status is 1) or NO (marital status is 2). The entry under *Party* must be REPUBLICAN, DEMOCRAT, or INDEPENDENT.

Input Description:

File name: VOTERS.DL

This file must be sorted on two fields—Marital status (major field) and Party of registration (minor field).

Record description: See Appendix A

Processing Requirements for Each Order to be Entered:

The group totals are to be printed for

A count of the number of records processed

The average annual income for each group

As each grade record is read:

1. Check for a control break on the major field (Marital status).
2. If there is a major field control-break, perform major control-break processing.

The group totals are to be printed for

    A count of the number of records processed

    The average annual income for each group

Each average is to be based on total accumulated income divided by the number of records in the group.

3. Check for a control break on the minor field (Party of registration).
4. If there is a minor field control break, perform minor control-break processing.
5. Print the detail line according to the printer spacing chart.

At the end of the page:

6. Progress to a new page and print the page headings.

At the end of the report:

7. Print the totals for the minor and major groups.
8. Print the final report totals.

13-4 Airline Load Summary With Group Totals

Programming Assignment 11-1 requires the calculation of aircraft passenger load factor and passenger/crew factor. Services evalution agencies want a report with group totals based on inbound and outbound service on a daily basis.

Output Requirements:

    A two-level group total report with the following output and format.

```
         0         1         2         3         4         5         6         7        8
  1234567890123456789012345678901234567890123456789012345678901234567890123456789012345
 1 Z9/99/99                    METROPOLITAN AIRPORT              Page ZZ
 2                             DAILY SERVICE SUMMARY
 3
 4 Inbound/                    Flight              Load    Passenger
 5 Outbound      Date          Number   Airline    Ratio   Crew Ratio
 6
 7  XXX    MM/DD/YY   Z9:99AM   XXXX      X-------X  Z.999       Z9
 8  XXX    MM/DD/YY   Z9:99PM   XXXX      X-------X  Z.999       Z9
 9
10  XXX    MM/DD/YY          DAILY AVERAGES         Z.999       Z9
11
12  XXX    MM/DD/YY   Z9:99AM   XXXX      X-------X  Z.999       Z9
13  XXX    MM/DD/YY   Z9:99PM   XXXX      X-------X  Z.999       Z9
14
15  XXX    MM/DD/YY          DAILY AVERAGES         Z.999       Z9*
16
17                    XXXBOUND AVERAGES             Z.999       Z9**
18
19
20                    REPORT AVERAGES               Z.999       Z9***
21
```

The entry in the *Inbound/Outbound* column must be IN or OUT. The entry under *Date* must be in month/day/year format.

Input Description:

    File name: AIRPORT1.DL

        This file must be sorted on three fields—Inbound/Outbound (major), Date (intermediate), and Time (minor).

    Record description: See Appendix A

Processing Requirements for Each Order to be Entered:

The group totals are to be printed for

A count of the number of records processed

The average Load ratio and Passenger/crew ratio for each group

As each grade record is read:

1. Check for a control break on the major field (Direction).
2. If there is a major field control break, perform major control-break processing. The group totals are to be printed for

    A count of the number of records processed

    The average Load ratio and Passenger/crew ratio for each group

3. Check for a control break on the intermediate field (Date).
4. If there is a minor field control break, perform minor control-break processing.
5. Calculate the Load Ratio for this record by dividing the Actual-number-of passengers-on-flight by the Total-number-of-seats-on-airplane.
6. Calculate the Passenger Crew Ratio for this record by dividing the Actual-number-of passengers-on-flight by the Number-of-crew-members.
7. Print the detail line according to the printer spacing chart.

At the end of the page:

8. Progress to a new page and print the page headings.

At the end of the report:

9. Print the totals for the minor and major groups.
10. Print the final report totals.

14

SUBSCRIPTING AND TABLES

Chapter Objectives

As you have seen, a computer can work only with data stored in its memory. In normal operations, space in memory is allocated for only one record from each file. This means that it is impossible for the computer to "see" the entire data file as a whole, and normally there is no reason to do so. Sometimes, however, it is desirable to store an entire set of data in the computer's memory so that the computer can quickly access any element of that data when processing a second data set. The type of data organization that permits the programmer to store an entire set of data in memory is called a *table*. From this chapter, you will learn the following concepts of table processing:

■ The PERFORM/VARYING statement, which simplifies table access

■ How to define subscripted variables with the OCCURS clause and how to use them in the program

■ How to create a table in memory

■ How to load data into a table

■ General table-processing principles, including actions to take on error conditions

■ The SEARCH command, which provides powerful capabilities for accessing the data in a table

■ How to use tables consisting of two columns

■ How to use two-dimensional tables

The PERFORM Statement

Before starting on COBOL subscripting and tables, you should analyze a specific form of the PERFORM statement because it is useful in working with tables. As you know, the PERFORM/UNTIL gives you the ability to repeatedly execute a sequence of statements or a module until a designated condition occurs. Through program control, you can set up a loop with a counter to execute until a given condition occurs or until a loop has been executed a predetermined number of times. To simplify programming, COBOL includes the PERFORM/VARYING statement that automatically handles counting within a loop.

Calculating Compound Interest—Example 14-1

As a simple illustration of the PERFORM/VARYING and how it works, let's consider an example of computing compound interest.

Example 14-1 Calculating Compound Interest

Problem Description

The accumulated amount (A) resulting from a principal (P) compounded at an interest rate (i) for a number of years (n) is calculated by the formula:

$$A = P(1 + i/100)_n$$

For $1.00 invested at 8%, this formula becomes:

$$A = 1.08_n$$

This program should compute and display compound interest until the amount A exceeds a value of 2.

Output Requirements

Display on the screen a table of number of years and accumulated amount. For instance, the first three table lines would be

Years	Amount
1	1.08
2	1.17
3	1.26

**Program Solution—
Example 14-1**

The logic of this program is relatively basic and is illustrated by the flowchart and pseudocode of Figure 14-1. Essential elements of this logic that will be related to the PERFORM/VARYING are

- A data item is used as a counter. It is
  - given an initial value prior to entering the loop
  - incremented with each execution of the loop

- A condition test is made to control continued execution of the loop

In the program of Figure 14-2, which uses the familiar PERFORM/UNTIL, statements that carry out the three basic elements of this loop are highlighted. Prior to entering the loop, the control data item YEARS is given an initial value of 1. The last statement in the loop increases it by 1. The test is carried out following the UNTIL.

These three items are all incorporated into the equivalent form by using PERFORM/VARYING in Figure 14-3. Notice that this form of the PERFORM identifies:

1. The data item to be incremented (VARYING YEARS).

2. The value to which it is to be initialized (FROM 1)

3. The increment to be added each time the loop is executed (BY 1)

4. The test condition to control repetition of the loop (UNTIL AMOUNT >2)

Figure 14-1

*Program Logic for
Example 14-1*

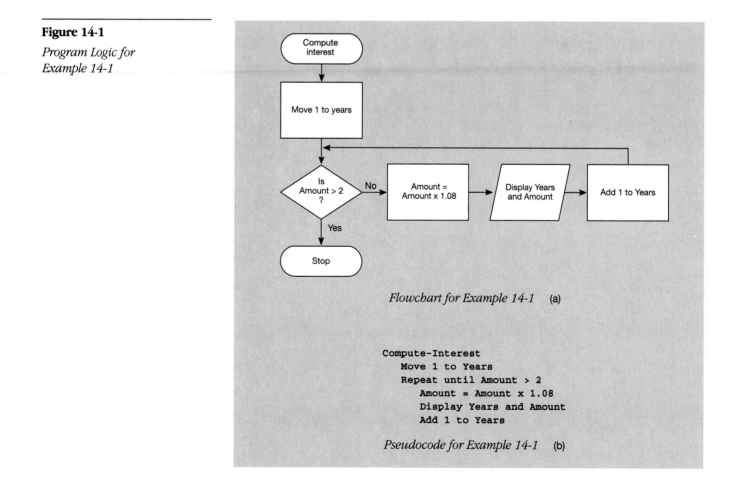

Flowchart for Example 14-1   (a)

```
Compute-Interest
    Move 1 to Years
    Repeat until Amount > 2
        Amount = Amount x 1.08
        Display Years and Amount
        Add 1 to Years
```

Pseudocode for Example 14-1   (b)

Figure 14-2

*Program Solution for
Example 14-1*

```
1       IDENTIFICATION DIVISION.
2       PROGRAM-ID. INTEREST.
3
4       DATA DIVISION.
5       WORKING-STORAGE SECTION.
6       01  WORK-FIELDS.
7           10  YEARS           PIC 99.
8           10  AMOUNT          PIC 9V99  VALUE 1.
9           10  WAIT            PIC X.
10      01  DISPLAY-FIELDS.
11          10                  PIC X(2).
12          10  DF-YEARS        PIC Z9.
13          10                  PIC X(5)  VALUE SPACES.
14          10  DF-AMOUNT       PIC 9.99.
15
16      PROCEDURE DIVISION.
17
18      COMPUTE-INTEREST.
19          DISPLAY "Years   Amount"   ERASE
20
21          MOVE 1 TO YEARS
22          PERFORM UNTIL AMOUNT > 2
23            MULTIPLY 1.08 BY AMOUNT ROUNDED
24            MOVE YEARS TO DF-YEARS
25            MOVE AMOUNT TO DF-AMOUNT
26            DISPLAY DISPLAY-FIELDS
27            ADD 1 TO YEARS
28          END-PERFORM
29
30          DISPLAY "Table complete--strike Enter to terminate"
31                  LINE 24
32          ACCEPT WAIT   POSITION 0
33          STOP RUN.
```

Figure 14-3

*The PERFORM/VARYING
Statement*

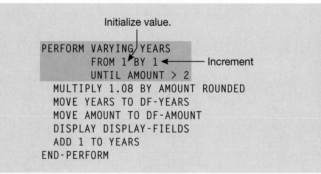

Although this example uses an in-line PERFORM, the VARYING option can be used in-line or out-of-line. The two limited general forms of the statement are

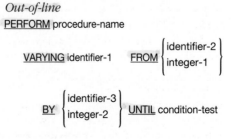

Out-of-line
PERFORM procedure-name

VARYING identifier-1   FROM { identifier-2 / integer-1 }

BY { identifier-3 / integer-2 } UNTIL condition-test

In-line

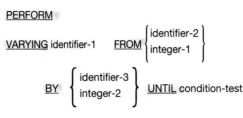

<u>PERFORM</u>

<u>VARYING</u> identifier-1   <u>FROM</u> $\begin{Bmatrix} \text{identifier-2} \\ \text{integer-1} \end{Bmatrix}$

<u>BY</u> $\begin{Bmatrix} \text{identifier-3} \\ \text{integer-2} \end{Bmatrix}$ <u>UNTIL</u> condition-test

imperative-statement

<u>END-PERFORM</u>

You can see that the starting value (FROM) and increment (BY) can both be either fixed values or data-names that can be given values during execution of the program. As you will learn later in this chapter, COBOL includes special indexing capabilities for the PERFORM/VARYING.

<table>
<tr><td>**The TIMES Option of the PERFORM**</td><td>The PERFORM/TIMES is one other form of the PERFORM statement. Although it has no special functions specifically for subscripting, it is presented here solely for the sake of completeness. The PERFORM/TIMES allows you to designate a loop that is to be executed a specific number of times. For instance, if within a program you needed to execute the module 400-CALCULATE-LIMITS exactly 20 times, you could use the following PERFORM/TIMES statement:</td></tr>
</table>

```
PERFORM 400-CALCULATE-LIMITS 20 TIMES
```

This statement is fairly straightforward. Its general forms are as follows:

Out-of-line

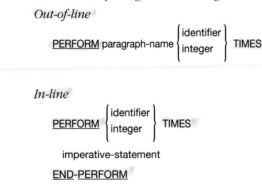

<u>PERFORM</u> paragraph-name $\begin{Bmatrix} \text{identifier} \\ \text{integer} \end{Bmatrix}$ TIMES

In-line

<u>PERFORM</u> $\begin{Bmatrix} \text{identifier} \\ \text{integer} \end{Bmatrix}$ TIMES

imperative-statement

<u>END-PERFORM</u>

Note that a fixed value can be used (for example, 20 TIMES) as well as a variable quantity (as designated by *identifier*).

Basic Principles of Tables

Subscripting

Assume that you have a programming application in which you must work with 10 different three-digit job codes. Your program is to involve reading the 10 codes into memory and then performing processing operations based on the codes. Within the program, you could easily name them C-1, C-2, C-3 . . . C-10. However, using separate and distinct names creates severe problems in many applications.

On the other hand, you can take a mathematician's approach and use the concept of subscripting (the word *subscript* comes from a Latin word meaning "to write below"). With the standard subscript notation, you might refer to these 10 codes as c_1, c_2, c_3 . . . c_{10}. Now you can refer to the entire set of codes as c and to any individual code by including the appropriate subscript; for example c_7 (which is called "c subseven" or simply "c seven"). To further generalize, you can refer to a code as c_i, in which i is limited to the range of 1 through 10. A variable that includes a subscript, such as c_i in this case, is commonly referred to as a *subscripted variable*.

Subscripting provides such a powerful capability that most computers have special hardware features for implementing the basic notions involved with subscripted quantities. Indeed, most high-level languages include extensive provisions for using subscripting. In algebra, a subscripted variable takes a form such as c_3; in most programming languages, the form is C(3). Because it is impractical to enter a character through a terminal as a subscript in the usual sense, a subscripted quantity consists of a data-name followed by a pair of parentheses enclosing a data item (the subscript). In COBOL, as in most languages, the subscript can be a data-name or a numeric literal. Thus, C(I) is equivalent to c_i and C(3) to c_3; this capability represents a powerful feature of COBOL.

Defining a Table in the WORKING-STORAGE SECTION

For your first consideration of tables, assume that the job codes you must use are fixed and never changing (which is unlikely in the average organization). Defining the 10 subscripted elements in the WORKING-STORAGE SECTION is done with the OCCURS clause shown in Figure 14-4. The elements of JOB-CODE-TABLE are addressable by subscripts; that is

JOB-CODE(1)	is the first element
JOB-CODE(2)	is the second element
JOB-CODE(3)	is the third element
and so on.	

The general format of the OCCURS clause is

OCCURS integer TIMES

Because the OCCURS clause directs the compiler to reserve a fixed number of memory positions for the specified data item, an integer quantity must be used; a data-name is unacceptable. An OCCURS clause can be used on a data item at any level 02–49; it must *not* be used for levels 01, 77 (77 is not used in this book), and 88.

Because each of the elements of the table is to contain different values, using a VALUE clause with the OCCURS is not very practical. (Prior to COBOL-85, a VALUE clause could not be used with an OCCURS.) An easy way to handle this is by using the REDEFINES shown in Figure 14-5. Here you see that the table of values is first defined with a series of

Figure 14-4

The OCCURS Clause

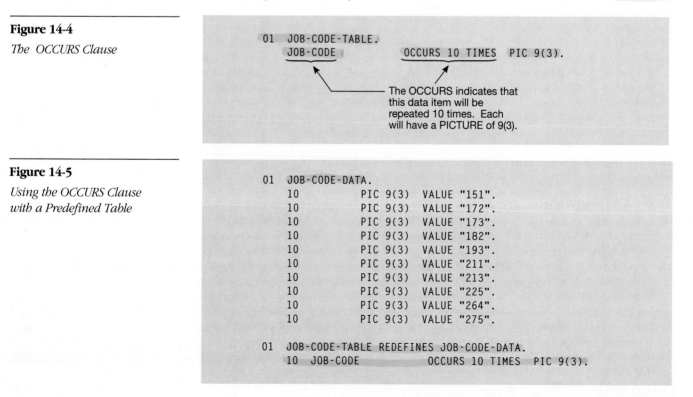

Figure 14-5

Using the OCCURS Clause with a Predefined Table

VALUE clauses. Then a second record is redefined to occupy the same memory area. That record is composed of the 10 subscripted items with the OCCURS. Thus, JOB-CODE-TABLE and JOB-CODE-DATA are allocated the same memory areas. As a result, JOB-CODE(1) will have a value of 151, JOB-CODE(2) will have a value of 172, and so on. FILLER (implied) is used for the succession of values because all references to them will be through the subscripted items. You should be aware that you cannot reverse the order of these two records (you cannot place the table definition first). The reason is that a VALUE clause cannot be used together with a REDEFINES clause or a clause that is subordinate to a REDEFINES.

Searching the Table— Example 14-2

Almost all table applications involve searching the table for a desired entry. For instance, the job-code table could represent jobs that a company considers hazardous and thus required special processing. This is illustrated by the next example.

Example 14-2 Searching the Table

Problem Description

As part of their benefits package, the Universal Software Cultivation Company (USC) wishes to identify all employees with one of the job codes in the job-code table. A module is required to search the table to determine whether or not a given employee job code is in the table.

Module Input

Employee job code from the input record: ER-JOB-CODE

Table Information

Subscripted data-element name: JOB-CODE
Number of elements in table: 10

Module Output

CODE-FOUND   Set to true if input code in table
              Set to false if input code not in table

The flowchart and pseudocode of Figure 14-6 illustrate the logic of this solution; the COBOL code to perform the search operation is shown in Figure 14-7. Note that the condition on termination of the PERFORM is based on two criterion: finding the employee code in the table or reaching the end of the table. The following describes the actions that will take place:

1. The CODE-FOUND switch is set to false before beginning the search. Then the value of the variable JC-SUBSCRIPT is initialized to 1 by the PERFORM statement to begin the loop.

2. Upon detecting a table entry equal to the employee job code, the CODE-FOUND switch is set to true. This condition will terminate the in-line PERFORM and control will be returned to the calling module.

3. If the employee job code is not in the table, the VARYING clause eventually increments beyond the end of the table. (The value in JC-SUBSCRIPT exceeds 10.) This also causes termination of the in-line PERFORM. The CODE-FOUND switch remains false.

The USAGE Clause

COBOL allows you to use the computer without concern about how actions are physically carried out within the computer or how data is stored in memory. It has been pointed out that each data item in the DATA DIVISION causes the compiler to reserve one storage position of memory for each position of the field. (The basic addressable unit of memory in most computers is called a *byte*. It can store one character.) For instance, the following PICs reserve the indicated memory:

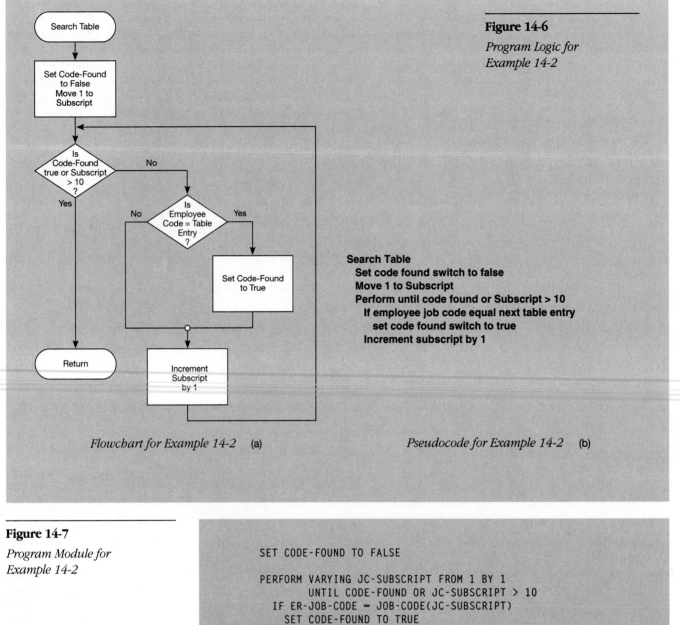

Figure 14-6

Program Logic for Example 14-2

Search Table

Set Code-Found to False
Move 1 to Subscript

Is Code-Found true or Subscript > 10 ?

Is Employee Code = Table Entry ?

Set Code-Found to True

Return

Increment Subscript by 1

Search Table
  Set code found switch to false
  Move 1 to Subscript
  Perform until code found or Subscript > 10
    If employee job code equal next table entry
      set code found switch to true
    Increment subscript by 1

Flowchart for Example 14-2   (a)

Pseudocode for Example 14-2   (b)

Figure 14-7

Program Module for Example 14-2

```
SET CODE-FOUND TO FALSE

PERFORM VARYING JC-SUBSCRIPT FROM 1 BY 1
        UNTIL CODE-FOUND OR JC-SUBSCRIPT > 10
   IF ER-JOB-CODE = JOB-CODE(JC-SUBSCRIPT)
     SET CODE-FOUND TO TRUE
   END-IF
END-PERFORM.
```

PIC XXX	3 bytes
PIC X(34)	34 bytes
PIC 99	2 bytes
PIC 999V99	5 bytes (decimal positioning is understood)

Within the computer, each character of any field is stored using the coding method of that computer (for the IBM PC, it is ASCII—the American Standard Code for Information Interchange). This is termed the DISPLAY format or *usage*. For alphanumeric data, it is the only way of storing data.

However, for numeric data, other methods exist. As a rule, for most COBOL programming (which is file-processing oriented and has limited computation powers), efficiency of arithmetic operations is not an important consideration. But in some instances, it is useful to consider faster arithmetic operations. COBOL allows the programmer to store data in more efficient forms; one of them is *binary*. Quantities that will always be whole numbers (such as subscripts) can be stored internally in a binary form. This form offers two advantages: arithmetic and indexing operations are very fast and memory is used to the fullest. Regarding the latter point, a number in the range of approximately plus or minus two billion can be stored in four bytes.

Whenever a field or group of fields (elementary item or group item) is defined in the DATA DIVISION, it is automatically set as DISPLAY type unless specified otherwise. However, you can override the default value through the USAGE clause, which is incorporated in the following definition of the subscript data item used in the search module of Figure 14-7:

```
10 JC-SUBSCRIPT  USAGE IS BINARY PIC 99.
```

Although the USAGE is used here with an elementary item, it is not so restricted. That is, it can be used with a group item with the effect that the USAGE applies to all items making up the group item. The extent to which USAGE is used in this book is summarized by the following limited general form:

$$\underline{\text{USAGE}}\ \text{IS}\ \left\{\begin{array}{l}\text{BINARY}\\\text{DISPLAY}\\\text{INDEX}\end{array}\right\}$$

Note the following points about this form:

■ The word IS is optional.

■ DISPLAY is the default.

■ INDEX is described later in this chapter.

■ One other USAGE commonly encountered in mainframe COBOL is the COMP-3 (called PACKED-DECIMAL in RM/COBOL-85). This special format—which allows two digits to be stored in one byte—is not used in this book because it is oriented to IBM mainframe computers.

It is important to understand that, with the exception of USAGE INDEX, the internal format has absolutely no effect on the way the PROCEDURE DIVISION is written. The internal format in which the information is stored is handled automatically by the system.

Loading a Table into Memory

Example Definition—Example 14-3

In Example 14-1, the table is assumed to be one that will never change. Some tables do indeed contains values that never change. For instance, a table of the twelve-month names will consist of exactly twelve entries (January, February, and so on) that will always be the same. However, it is very unlikely that the job-code table falls in the fixed-and-never-changing category. In cases such as this, the table is commonly loaded from a file, as illustrated by the next example.

Example 14-3 Loading a Table into Memory

Problem Description

The payroll manager of USC has come to the realization that job codes change and that having a fixed table defined as part of the DATA DIVISION is not practical. The perceived solution is to store the job codes in a separate file, then read the file and load the codes into the table area defined in the program. Since there are currently more than 10 job codes, a decision has been made to provide space for up to 25 job codes.

Output Requirements

A screen display of the table as it is being loaded.

Input Description

Input file name: JOBCODE.TBL

Job codes are stored in the file, one per record, according to the following format. Record format:

Field	Record Positions	Format
Job code	1–3	PIC 9(3)
Not used	4–7	

Processing Requirements

This is not to be a complete program; it is to be the table-loading portion of a processing program.

1. Read each job-code record and store it in the table.
2. Display each job-code entry as it is read and stored.
3. If the number of table entries from the file exceeds 25 (the maximum table size), display an error message and terminate processing.
4. When the table is loaded successfully, store the table entry count in the data item TABLE-SIZE.

Program Planning— Example 14-3

Because there may be as many as 25 job codes, it is necessary to reserve memory for 25 fields with the OCCURS clause. However, there may not be 25 entries to be loaded. In devising a solution for a problem such as this, it is helpful to consider the different possibilities that can occur. In this application, you should look at each of three possibilities: a number of code records less than, equal to, and greater than the maximum allowed. The implications of these are summarized in the table of Figure 14-8. The implication of this table is that the table-loading process can terminate in either of two ways: more than 25 table records have been read (an error condition) or the end of the table file is detected. Thus, the read-move sequence must be repeated until either of these conditions occur.

Figure 14-8

The Implication of Various Numbers of Job-Code Records

Number of Job Code Records	End-of-Data Record	Number of Entries in Table
12	Thirteenth record	12
25	Twenty-sixth record	25
26	Twenty-seventh record	Program cancel

The read-load operation will end with either of the following:

1. The expected case in which the number of job code records is 25 or fewer, and loading will be terminated by a normal end-of-file.

2. The error situation in which the number of records is greater than 25 (indicating that the table data requires more memory space than has been reserved).

The program logic is shown in the flowchart of Figure 14-9 and the pseudocode of Figure 14-10. In the flowchart, just preceding the first decision symbol is a box indicating what takes place with the subscript; this is called a *notation box*. Here it is used in conjunction with the decision symbol at the beginning of the loop to convey the information that the loop involves an item that is automatically incremented by the loop control statement (the PERFORM).

Figure 14-9

Selection Structure for
Example 14-3

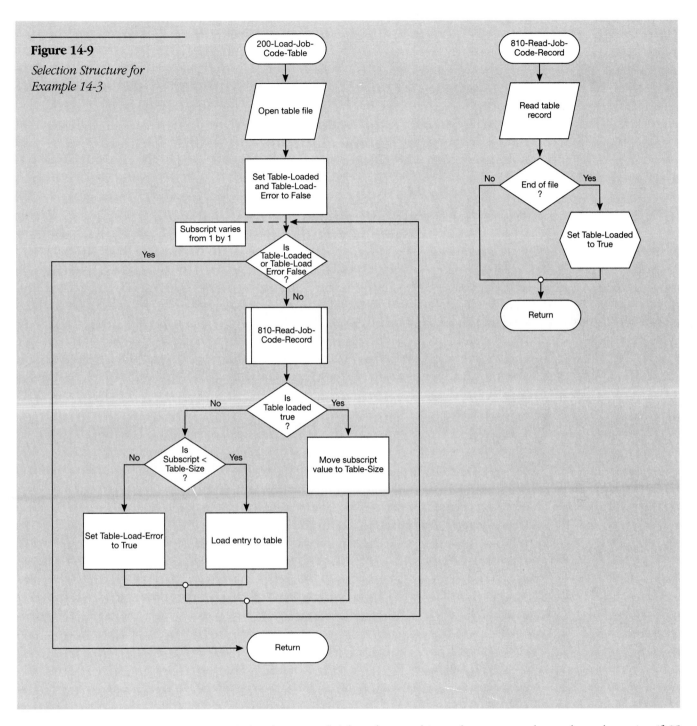

Notice that as each job code record is read, a test must be made to determine if 25 records have already been read. If so, then the job code data set consists of more entries than the maximum allowable number (25 in this case). Consequently, an error message is printed, and processing is terminated.

Program Segment—
Example 14-3

The program segments of Figure 14-11 include coding that reads job code records, increments the subscript, and moves each job code to the table entry specified by the subscript. Processing is terminated when either an end-of-file record is read (indicating the end of the table data), or the subscript equals the maximum allowable number of entries (indicating that the table data requires more memory space than has been reserved for it).

Figure 14-10

*Pseudocode for
Example 14-3*

```
Open the table file
Set the Table-load and Table-loaded-error switches to false
Perform the following sequence
    until Table-loaded is true or Table-loaded-error is true
        Read the next table file record
            at end of file set table-loaded to true
        If Table-loaded is true
            Save the table size
        else
            If the subscript is less than 25
                move input table value into table
            else
                set Table-load-error to true
Close the table file
```

Figure 14-11

*Loading a Table—
Example 14-3*

```
DATA DIVISION.

FILE SECTION.

FD  JOB-CODE-FILE.
01  JOB-CODE-RECORD.
    10  JC-JOB-CODE           PIC 9(3).
    .
    .
    .
WORKING-STORAGE SECTION.

01  TABLE-ACCESS-ITEMS    USAGE BINARY.
    10  JC-SUBSCRIPT          PIC 99  VALUE ZERO.
    10  TABLE-SIZE            PIC 99  VALUE 25.

01  PROGRAMMED-SWITCHES.
    10                        PIC X.
        88  TABLE-LOADED      VALUE "Y"  FALSE "N".
    10                        PIC X.
        88  TABLE-LOAD-ERROR  VALUE "Y"  FALSE "N".
    10                        PIC X.
        88  CODE-FOUND        VALUE "Y"  FALSE "N".

01  OTHER-VARIABLES.
    10  DISPLAY-SUBSCRIPT     PIC Z9.

01  JOB-CODE-TABLE.
    10  JOB-CODE              OCCURS 25 TIMES  PIC 9(3).


PROCEDURE DIVISION.

100-INITIALIZE.
    PERFORM 200-LOAD-JOB-CODE-TABLE
    IF TABLE-LOAD-ERROR
      DISPLAY " "
      DISPLAY "Table size exceeded!!"  REVERSE
      DISPLAY "Processing terminated."
      STOP RUN
    END-IF
    .
    .
    .
```

```
200-LOAD-JOB-CODE-TABLE.
    OPEN INPUT JOB-CODE-FILE
    MOVE ALL "?" TO JOB-CODE-TABLE
    SET TABLE-LOAD-ERROR TO FALSE
    SET TABLE-LOADED TO FALSE
    DISPLAY "Loading Table" ERASE
    DISPLAY "Entry number   Code"

    PERFORM VARYING JC-SUBSCRIPT FROM 1 BY 1
            UNTIL TABLE-LOADED OR TABLE-LOAD-ERROR
        PERFORM 810-READ-JOB-CODE-RECORD
        IF TABLE-LOADED
            COMPUTE TABLE-SIZE = JC-SUBSCRIPT - 1
            DISPLAY " "
            DISPLAY "Table load complete."
        ELSE
            IF JC-SUBSCRIPT NOT > TABLE-SIZE
                MOVE JC-JOB-CODE TO JOB-CODE(JC-SUBSCRIPT)
                MOVE JC-SUBSCRIPT TO DISPLAY-SUBSCRIPT
                DISPLAY "     ", DISPLAY-SUBSCRIPT,
                        "     ", JC-JOB-CODE
            ELSE
                SET TABLE-LOAD-ERROR TO TRUE
            END-IF
        END-IF
    END-PERFORM

    CLOSE JOB-CODE-FILE.
    .
    .
    .
810-READ-JOB-CODE-RECORD.
    READ JOB-CODE-FILE
      AT END
        SET TABLE-LOADED TO TRUE
    END-READ.
```

To keep the user informed about the action taking place during execution of the program, the program displays table-loading information. Note that the item DISPLAY-SUBSCRIPT is defined in order to display the subscript count. JC-SUBSCRIPT has a usage of BINARY and therefore cannot be included in a DISPLAY statement.

One subtle feature that sometimes causes programmers problems is the value of the loop control variable when processing is complete. Referring to the table in Figure 14-8, remember that the successful loading of the program causes the loop to be executed one time more than the number of table records (because the EOF record is read). Consequently, the value of the loop control item JC-SUBSCRIPT will be one greater than the number of table entries. This is reflected by subtracting 1 from JC-SUBSCRIPT value before storing it in TABLE-SIZE.

Subscripts and Tables in Memory

In this program, the variable TABLE-SIZE serves two purposes. While the table is being loaded, TABLE-SIZE specifies the maximum number of entries that the table can contain, so the program uses this value to ensure that the capacity of the table is not exceeded. Once the table-load operation has been completed, the contents of JC-SUBSCRIPT less 1 are moved to TABLE-SIZE, so that TABLE-SIZE now shows the actual, rather than the maximum, size of the table.

Although the OCCURS clause defines the size of the table and causes the compiler to set aside the specified amount of memory for the table, it does not control the table-load operation. To appreciate this, you must recognize that in the object program, the computer knows only where the table begins in memory. Knowing this beginning point and the length of each field, it can easily calculate where any desired entry is. For example, JOB-CODE(3) is simply "two down the line" from the first; similarly, if you refer to JOB-CODE(80), it is "79 down the line." Most implementations of COBOL make no check to determine if the subscript exceeds the number of entries defined in the OCCURS clause.

In the example program, if the number of table entries exceeds the number specified in the OCCURS clause without being detected by the program logic, the table-load operation will continue to build the table in memory, obliterating whatever follows the table in memory. It could be other DATA DIVISION entries or it could be part of the instructions generated by the PROCEDURE DIVISION.

In many applications, the number of entries in a table file will vary from run to run as items are added to or deleted from the table file. Thus, it becomes the responsibility of the programmer to evaluate the situation and determine the maximum number of entries likely to occur. This figure then would be reflected in the VALUE clause for TABLE-SIZE and in the OCCURS clause.

Loading and Processing a Table

Problem Definition— Example 14-4

In the preceding two examples, you have learned how to load a table from data in a file and how to search the table. The next example combines these two actions into a single program.

Example 14-4 Using the Job-Code Table

Problem Description

The USC company wishes to provide special benefits to all of its employees with job codes identified in the job-code file. To provide the special benefits, a program is required that will read the employee file (which contains one record for each employee), perform the special-benefits processing, and print a report listing qualifying employees and their benefits. You need not do the special benefits and report generation portion of this program because it is being done by another programmer and will be merged with your program.

Output Requirements

Output from this program is to be
- A screen display of the table as it is being loaded
- A display of the employee name and job code of each employee, with the job code matching one in the table

The report generation portion of this program is being done by another program.

Input Description

Table file
File name: JOBCODE.TBL (Same as Example 14-3)
Employee file
File name: EMPL-BEN.DL
Record format:

Field	Positions	Data Type
Employee number	1–5	Alphanumeric
Employee job code	6–8	Numeric
Not used	9–34	

Interfacing Modules

The following module to process special benefits will be inserted in the program at a later time:

```
310-PROCESS-SPECIAL-BENEFITS
```

Processing Requirements

1. Load the table per Example 14-3.
2. For each input employee record:
   a. Search the table for the employee's job code
   b. If the job code is in the table, perform the module 310-PROCESS-SPECIAL-BENEFITS
   c. From the 310 module, display the employee name and job code

Program Planning—Example 14-4

You are already familiar with the major elements of this example: loading and searching the table. These components will be brought together as shown by the structure chart of Figure 14-12. Program logic is summarized in the flowchart of Figure 14-13 and the pseudocode of Figure 14-14.

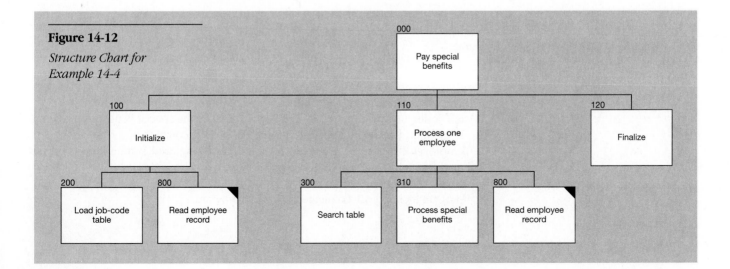

Figure 14-12

Structure Chart for Example 14-4

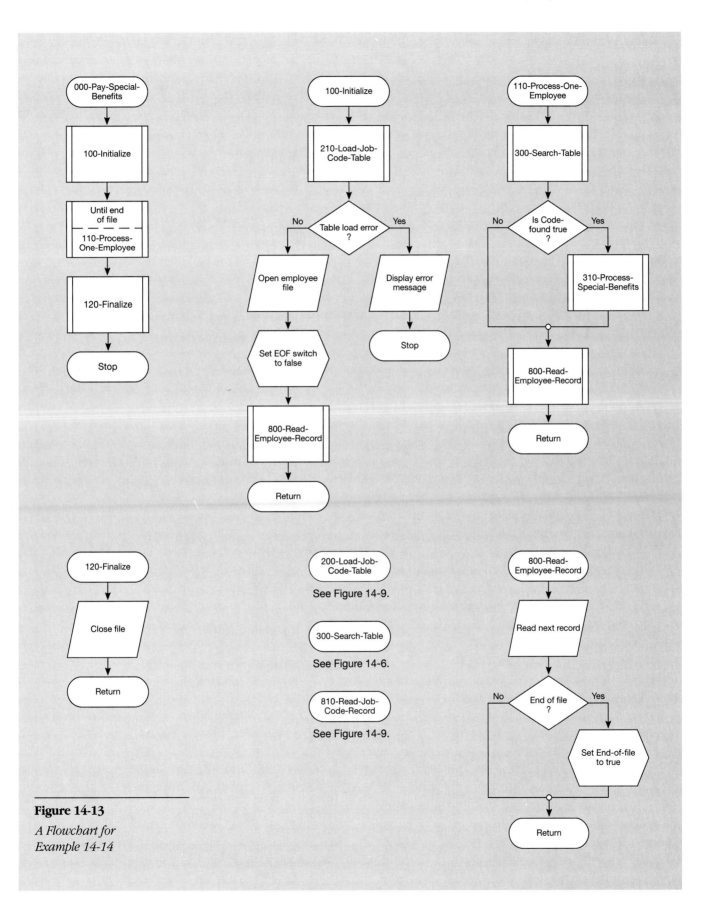

Figure 14-13

*A Flowchart for
Example 14-14*

The sequence of operations for each of these modules is summarized by the following pseudocode.

Figure 14-14

Pseudocode for
Example 14-4

```
100-Initialize
    Perform 200-Load-Job-Code-Table
    If table-load error
        terminate processing
    Open employee file
    Perform 800-Read-Employee-Record

110-Process-1-Employee
    Perform 300-Search-Table on employee job code
    If code found in table
        Perform 310-Process-Special-Benefits
    Perform 800-Read-Employee-Record

120-Finalize
    Close file

200-Load-Job-Code-Table
    Open the table file
    Set the Table-load and Table-loaded-error switches to false
    Perform the following sequence
      until Table-loaded is true or Table-loaded-error is true
        Read the next table file record
            at end of file set table-loaded to true
        If Table-loaded is true
            Save the table size
        else
            If the subscript is less than 25
                move input table value into table
            else
                set Table-load-error to true
    Close the table file

300-Search-Table
    Set code-found switch to false
    Perform until code-found or table size exceeded
        If employee job code equal next table entry
            set code-found switch to true

310-Process-Special-Benefits
    Display employee name and job code

800-Read-Employee-Record
    Read next employee record
        at end of file set End-of-file to true

810-Read-Job-Code-Record
    Read next job-code record
        at end of file set Table-loaded to true
```

Program Solution—
Example 14-4

The program solution shown in Figure 14-15 includes nothing new; it is simply an integration of previously discussed topics. You can see beginning line 76 that the 110 module (1) searches the table for the job code of the previously read employee record, (2) processes that record if the employee's code was found in the table, and (3) reads the next record.

One other significant structured programming concept illustrated by this example is that it can be tested without the special benefits routine. Since the program is complete as

Figure 14-15

Processing a Table—
Example 14-4

```
1        IDENTIFICATION DIVISION.
2        PROGRAM-ID. PAY-BEN1.
3
4    *    Pay special benefits - Table lookup
5
6        ENVIRONMENT DIVISION.
7        CONFIGURATION SECTION.
8        SOURCE-COMPUTER. IBM-PC.
9
10       INPUT-OUTPUT SECTION.
11       FILE-CONTROL.
12           SELECT EMPLOYEE-FILE  ASSIGN TO DISK  "EMPL-BEN.DL"
13                                 ORGANIZATION IS LINE SEQUENTIAL.
14
15           SELECT JOB-CODE-FILE  ASSIGN TO DISK  "JOB-CODE.TBL"
16                                 ORGANIZATION IS LINE SEQUENTIAL.
17
18       DATA DIVISION.
19
20       FILE SECTION.
21
22       FD  EMPLOYEE-FILE.
23       01  EMPLOYEE-RECORD.
24           10  ER-EMPL-NUMBER        PIC X(5).
25           10  ER-EMPL-JOB-CODE      PIC 9(3).
26           10                        PIC X(42).
27
28       FD  JOB-CODE-FILE.
29       01  JOB-CODE-RECORD.
30           10  JC-JOB-CODE           PIC 9(3).
31           10                        PIC X(4).
32
33       WORKING-STORAGE SECTION.
34
35       01  TABLE-ACCESS-ITEMS   USAGE BINARY.
36           10  JC-SUBSCRIPT          PIC 99  VALUE ZERO.
37           10  TABLE-SIZE            PIC 99  VALUE 25.
38
39       01  PROGRAMMED-SWITCHES.
40           10            PIC X.
41               88  END-OF-FILE       VALUE "Y"  FALSE "N".
42           10            PIC X.
43               88  TABLE-LOADED      VALUE "Y"  FALSE "N".
44           10            PIC X.
45               88  TABLE-LOAD-ERROR  VALUE "Y"  FALSE "N".
46           10            PIC X.
47               88  CODE-FOUND        VALUE "Y"  FALSE "N".
48
49       01  OTHER-VARIABLES.
50           10  DISPLAY-SUBSCRIPT     PIC Z9.
51
52       01  JOB-CODE-TABLE.
53           10  JOB-CODE              OCCURS 25 TIMES  PIC 9(3).
54
55       PROCEDURE DIVISION.
56
57       000-PAY-SPECIAL-BENEFITS.
58           PERFORM 100-INITIALIZE
59           PERFORM 110-PROCESS-1-EMPLOYEE
60               UNTIL END-OF-FILE
61           PERFORM 120-FINALIZE
62           STOP RUN.
63
64       100-INITIALIZE.
65           PERFORM 200-LOAD-JOB-CODE-TABLE
66           IF TABLE-LOAD-ERROR
67               DISPLAY " "
68               DISPLAY "Table size exceeded!!"  REVERSE
69               DISPLAY "Processing terminated."
70               STOP RUN
71           END-IF
72           OPEN INPUT  EMPLOYEE-FILE
73           SET END-OF-FILE TO FALSE
74           PERFORM 800-READ-EMPLOYEE-RECORD.
75
76       110-PROCESS-1-EMPLOYEE.
77           PERFORM 300-SEARCH-TABLE
78
79           IF CODE-FOUND
80               PERFORM 310-PROCESS-SPECIAL-BENEFITS
81           END-IF
82
83           PERFORM 800-READ-EMPLOYEE-RECORD.
84
85       120-FINALIZE.
86           DISPLAY " "  BEEP
87           DISPLAY "Special benefits processing has been completed."
88           CLOSE EMPLOYEE-FILE.
89
90       200-LOAD-JOB-CODE-TABLE.
91           OPEN INPUT JOB-CODE-FILE
92           MOVE ALL "?" TO JOB-CODE-TABLE
93           SET TABLE-LOAD-ERROR TO FALSE
94           SET TABLE-LOADED TO FALSE
95           DISPLAY "Loading Table" ERASE
96           DISPLAY "Entry number   Code"
97
98           PERFORM VARYING JC-SUBSCRIPT FROM 1 BY 1
99               UNTIL TABLE-LOADED OR TABLE-LOAD-ERROR
100              PERFORM 810-READ-JOB-CODE-RECORD
101              IF TABLE-LOADED
102                  COMPUTE TABLE-SIZE = JC-SUBSCRIPT - 1
103                  DISPLAY " "
104                  DISPLAY "Table load complete."
105              ELSE
106                  IF JC-SUBSCRIPT NOT > TABLE-SIZE
107                      MOVE JC-JOB-CODE TO JOB-CODE(JC-SUBSCRIPT)
108                      MOVE JC-SUBSCRIPT TO DISPLAY-SUBSCRIPT
109                      DISPLAY "   ", DISPLAY-SUBSCRIPT,
110                          "       ", JC-JOB-CODE
111                  ELSE
112                      SET TABLE-LOAD-ERROR TO TRUE
113                  END-IF
114              END-IF
115          END-PERFORM
116
117          CLOSE JOB-CODE-FILE.
118
119      300-SEARCH-TABLE.
120          SET CODE-FOUND TO FALSE
121
122          PERFORM VARYING JC-SUBSCRIPT FROM 1 BY 1
123              UNTIL CODE-FOUND OR JC-SUBSCRIPT > TABLE-SIZE
124              IF ER-EMPL-JOB-CODE = JOB-CODE(JC-SUBSCRIPT)
125                  SET CODE-FOUND TO TRUE
126              END-IF
127          END-PERFORM.
128
129      310-PROCESS-SPECIAL-BENEFITS.
130          DISPLAY " "
131          DISPLAY "Employee: ", ER-EMPL-NUMBER
132          DISPLAY "Job Code: ", ER-EMPL-JOB-CODE.
133
134      800-READ-EMPLOYEE-RECORD.
135          READ EMPLOYEE-FILE
136              AT END
137                  SET END-OF-FILE TO TRUE
138          END-READ.
139
140      810-READ-JOB-CODE-RECORD.
141          READ JOB-CODE-FILE
142              AT END
143                  SET TABLE-LOADED TO TRUE
144          END-READ.
```

shown, it can be compiled and run. The dummy version of the 310-PROCESS-SPECIAL-BENEFITS routine includes DISPLAY statements so that the programmer can check to ensure that processing and testing is taking place correctly. When this module is completed and tested (together with the report generation code), it can be inserted and the program will be ready for final testing.

Principles of Tables with Two Columns

Arguments and Functions

Examples of the preceding sections serve to illustrate the basic notion of a very simple type of a data table. Now consider a more generalized form of the table, a form with which everyone is familiar. For example, almost everyone has been given an assignment such as "Read Chapter 10." To begin, you scanned the book's table of contents for "Chapter 10," then read across for the page number. Similarly, a clerk in a store will total the sales, then look up the amount in a tax table to find the sales tax due.

Careful consideration of these examples will show that they both have two things in common. First of all, in each case the data is organized into a certain sequence. Secondly, each table contains two types of data: something known and something unknown. When using the table of contents in a book, for example, you know the name (or at least the general nature) of the assigned chapter; what is not known is the page number of the beginning of that chapter. Similarly, when the amount of the purchase is known, the table tells the amount of the tax (which is currently unknown).

These table concepts are formalized by the job-code/pay-rate table in Figure 14-16. Each entry in the table consists of two data values: the *argument*, which you think of as the known quantity, and the *function*, which you think of as the unknown quantity. For example, to find the pay rate for job code 225 (225 would be referred to as the *search argument*), scan the list of arguments to find that entry, then read across to obtain the corresponding function value of 15.10. For a long table, the search is greatly simplified if the list of arguments is in some type of sequence. Let's see how these table principles are implemented in COBOL.

Defining a Table with Arguments and Functions

Earlier in this chapter, you learned how the OCCURS clause is used to define a table. In the example given, the OCCURS was used with an elementary item. However, it may be used on a group item as well; for instance, consider the examples of the job-code table

Figure 14-16

Using a "Two-Column" Table in Memory

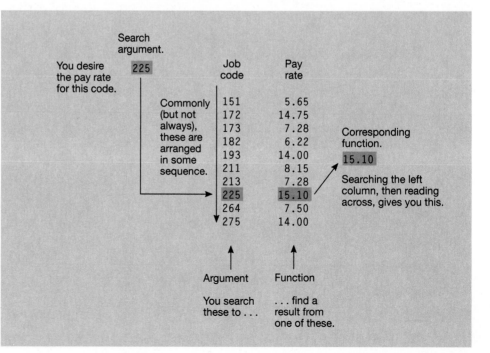

Figure 14-17

The OCCURS Clause

```
01  JOB-CODE-TABLE-1.
    10  JOB-CODE            OCCURS 25 TIMES PIC 999.
    10  PAY-RATE            OCCURS 25 TIMES PIC 99V99.




01  JOB-CODE-TABLE-2.
    10  JOB-CODE-TABLE-ENTRY   OCCURS 25 TIMES.
        20  JOB-CODE               PIC 999.
        20  PAY-RATE               PIC 99V99.
```

with pay rates shown in Figure 14-17. In the first case, you see that you effectively have two tables: one consisting of the job codes, and the other of the pay rates. In the second, you have one table in which each entry has two parts. In other words, the elementary items composing a group item are subscripted according to the definition of the group item.

Here is what will happen during the compilation for each of these two cases.

JOB-CODE-TABLE-1

1. Memory is reserved for 25 occurrences of JOB-CODE with each item requiring 3 positions: total memory reserved is 25 × 3 = 75 bytes.

2. Immediately following, memory is reserved for 25 occurrences of PAY-RATE with each item requiring 4 positions: total memory reserved is 25 × 4 = 100 bytes.

3. The two entries will require a total of 75 + 100 = 175 bytes.

JOB-CODE-TABLE-2

1. Memory is reserved for 25 occurrences of JOB-CODE-TABLE-ENTRY, which consists of JOB-CODE (3 positions) and PAY-RATE (4 positions): total memory reserved is 25 × 7= 175 bytes.

Figure 14-18 illustrates how the memory areas for the two cases are reserved. Even though the actual memory arrangements are different, it makes no difference to you when writing PROCEDURE DIVISION code.

Figure 14-18

Tables in Memory

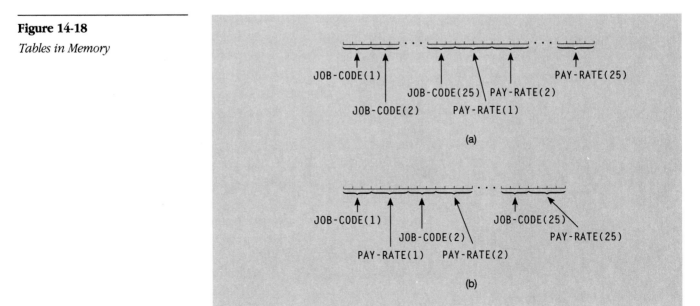

For instance, statements such as

```
MOVE JOB-CODE(TEST-VALUE) TO HOLD-AREA
MOVE PAY-RATE(3) TO PAY-RATE-CHECK
```

will work exactly the same for both WORKING-STORAGE SECTION definitions.

Some added flexibility is provided by the definition of JOB-CODE-TABLE-2 in which the OCCURS is associated with the group item. For instance, consider the following MOVE statement operating on the definition of JOB-CODE-TABLE-2:

```
10  HOLD-ENTRY.
    20  HOLD-JOB-CODE PIC 999.
    20  HOLD-PAY-RATE PIC 99V99.
    .
    .
    .

MOVE JOB-CODE-TABLE-ENTRY(6) TO HOLD-ENTRY
```

Here *both* JOB-CODE(6) and PAY-RATE(6) will be moved in a group move.

<table>
<tr><td>

*Finding the Pay Rate
Given the Job Code—
Example 14-5*

</td><td>

In Example 14-4, a single list table is searched to determine if the search argument is contained in the table. No corresponding function is to be accessed. Let's consider an expansion of this searching concept.

</td></tr>
</table>

Example 14-5 Accessing the Pay Rate from the Job-Code Table

Problem Description

The management of USC has decided that the special benefits provided for selected job codes are to depend on the employee's pay rate. Pay rate is set according to job code, and the rates are stored together with the code in the job code file.

Output Requirements

Output from this program is to be

- A screen display of the table as it is being loaded
- A display of the employee name, job code, and pay rate of each employee with a job code matching one in the table

The report generation portion of this program is being done by another program.

Input Description

Table file
File name: JOBCODE.TBL
Record format:

Field	Positions	Format
Job code	1–3	
Pay rate	4–7	$nn_\wedge nn$

Employee file
File name: EMPL-BEN.DL (Same as Example 14-4)

Interfacing Modules

The following module to process special benefits will be inserted in the program at a later time.

```
300-PROCESS-SPECIAL-BENEFITS
```

Processing Requirements

Processing requirements are identical to those of Example 14-4, except that the pay rate must be accessed from the job-code table and moved to the data item PAY-RATE for access by the 310-PROCESS-SPECIAL-BENEFITS module.

The modularization of this program makes this modification very simple; the following changes are required:

1. Change appropriate portions of the DATA DIVISION to reflect the new table form
2. Expand the table load to handle the second table column
3. Add the needed statement to move the desired pay rate into the work variable desired by the 310 module

The modified program is shown in Figure 14-19; changes to the PAY-BEN1 program are highlighted. Note that loading each table record requires that two fields, the argument and the corresponding function, be moved into the table in memory. Also, the searching operation uses JC-SUBSCRIPT as a pointer, as in PAY-BEN1 program. However, when an equal compare occurs (as illustrated in Figure 14-16), the value in JC-SUBSCRIPT is pointing to the equal argument *and* the corresponding function. The required function (pay rate) is moved to the work area.

Further consideration of this program is left to the exercises at the end of this chapter.

COBOL Table Handling Using the SEARCH Statement

Table processing is such a common type of operation in business programming that COBOL includes special statements to simplify such operations. This is called the COBOL *table-handling feature*. Table-handling statements not only simplify the programmer's task, but they also produce more efficient object code than the detailed operations they replace.

A Program Using the SEARCH Feature

Figure 14-20 shows segments of the PAY-BEN3 program that include changes to the PAY-BEN2 program for using the SEARCH. The table-load module (200) is almost the same as that of PAY-BEN2. However, the 300-SEARCH-TABLE module has been replaced with another, using the table search features. A comparison of the shaded areas in this program with the corresponding program of Figure 14-19 shows both similarities and differences. All of the basic pieces are still there. The table must still be defined in the DATA DIVISION, then loaded and used in the PROCEDURE DIVISION. But beyond that there are significant differences. They fall into three basic areas: the use of the OCCURS DEPENDING ON clause, the use of an *index*, and the use of the SEARCH statement.

The OCCURS DEPENDING ON Clause

The OCCURS clause, when used with the COBOL table-handling feature, includes additional entries, as illustrated in Figure 14-21. Let's consider each component of this example.

1. OCCURS 1 TO 25 TIMES. As with the simple OCCURS, it is necessary to define the amount of memory to be reserved by the compiler (space for 25 entries, in this case). It is important to recognize that the amount of memory allocated is not variable, as the clause might imply, but that the number of entries that will be loaded during execution will be variable, yet will not exceed 25.

2. DEPENDING ON TABLE-SIZE. This defines TABLE-SIZE as the program data-name that will contain the number of entries actually loaded into the table. It corresponds in usage to the TABLE-SIZE entry used in the PAY-BEN2 program.

3. INDEXED BY JOB-INDEX. COBOL provides two methods by which table data can be referenced: by subscript or by *index*. An index differs from a subscript in two ways. The first is that the programmer does not have to define the index as a data field; the COBOL compiler creates the index field and gives it the name assigned by the programmer in the INDEXED BY clause. The second difference is one of technique and relates to the method used by the computer to locate table entries in memory.

To illustrate the second difference, assume that you are interested in the third entry of JOB-CODE-TABLE, which you would refer to as JOB-CODE-TABLE-ENTRY(3). Because the computer only knows the location of the beginning of the table, it must perform a calculation using the length of each entry (a simple multiplication). This concept is

Figure 14-19

*Two-Column Table
Processing—Example 14-4*

```
1        IDENTIFICATION DIVISION.
2        PROGRAM-ID. PAY-BEN2.
3
4    *     Pay special benefits - Pay Rate lookup
5
6        ENVIRONMENT DIVISION.
7        CONFIGURATION SECTION.
8        SOURCE-COMPUTER. IBM-PC.
9
10       INPUT-OUTPUT SECTION.
11       FILE-CONTROL.
12           SELECT EMPLOYEE-FILE  ASSIGN TO DISK  "EMPL-BEN.DL"
13                                 ORGANIZATION IS LINE SEQUENTIAL.
14
15           SELECT JOB-CODE-FILE  ASSIGN TO DISK  "JOB-CODE.TBL"
16                                 ORGANIZATION IS LINE SEQUENTIAL.
17       DATA DIVISION.
18
19       FILE SECTION.
20
21       FD  EMPLOYEE-FILE.
22       01  EMPLOYEE-RECORD.
23           10  ER-EMPL-NUMBER      PIC X(5).
24           10  ER-EMPL-JOB-CODE    PIC 9(3).
25           10                      PIC X(42).
26
27       FD  JOB-CODE-FILE.
28       01  JOB-CODE-RECORD.
29           10  JC-JOB-CODE         PIC 9(3).
30           10  JC-PAY-RATE         PIC 9(2)V9(2).
31
32       WORKING-STORAGE SECTION.
33
34       01  TABLE-ACCESS-ITEMS   USAGE BINARY.
35           10  JC-SUBSCRIPT        PIC 99  VALUE ZERO.
36           10  TABLE-SIZE          PIC 99  VALUE 25.
37
38       01  PROGRAMMED-SWITCHES.
39           10  EOF-SWITCH          PIC X.
40               88  END-OF-FILE     VALUE "Y"  FALSE "N".
41           10  TABLE-LOADED        PIC X.
42               88  TABLE-LOADED    VALUE "Y"  FALSE "N".
43           10  TABLE-LOAD-ERROR    PIC X.
44               88  TABLE-LOAD-ERROR  VALUE "Y"  FALSE "N".
45           10  SEARCH-STATUS       PIC X.
46               88  CODE-FOUND      VALUE "Y"  FALSE "N".
47
48       01  OTHER-VARIABLES.
49           10  DISPLAY-SUBSCRIPT   PIC Z9.
50           10  PAY-RATE            PIC ZZ.99.
51
52       01  JOB-CODE-TABLE.
53           10  JOB-CODE-TABLE-ENTRY   OCCURS 25 TIMES.
54               20  JOB-CODE        PIC 999.
55               20  PAY-RATE        PIC 99V99.
56
57       PROCEDURE DIVISION.
58
59       000-PAY-SPECIAL-BENEFITS.
60           PERFORM 100-INITIALIZE
61           PERFORM 110-PROCESS-1-EMPLOYEE
62               UNTIL END-OF-FILE
63           PERFORM 120-FINALIZE
64           STOP RUN.
65
66       100-INITIALIZE.
67           PERFORM 200-LOAD-JOB-CODE-TABLE
68           IF TABLE-LOAD-ERROR
69               DISPLAY " "
70               DISPLAY "Table size exceeded!!"  REVERSE
71               DISPLAY "Processing terminated."
72               STOP RUN
73           END-IF
74           OPEN INPUT  EMPLOYEE-FILE
75           SET END-OF-FILE TO FALSE
76           PERFORM 800-READ-EMPLOYEE-RECORD.
77
78       110-PROCESS-1-EMPLOYEE.
79           PERFORM 300-SEARCH-TABLE
80
81           IF CODE-FOUND
82               PERFORM 310-PROCESS-SPECIAL-BENEFITS
83           END-IF
84
85           PERFORM 800-READ-EMPLOYEE-RECORD.
86
87       120-FINALIZE.
88           DISPLAY " "  BEEP
89           DISPLAY "Special benefits processing has been completed."
90           CLOSE EMPLOYEE-FILE.
91
92       200-LOAD-JOB-CODE-TABLE.
93           OPEN INPUT JOB-CODE-FILE
94           MOVE ALL "?" TO JOB-CODE-TABLE
95           SET TABLE-LOAD-ERROR TO FALSE
96           SET TABLE-LOADED TO FALSE
97           DISPLAY "Loading Table" ERASE
98           DISPLAY "Entry number    Code"
99
100          PERFORM VARYING JC-SUBSCRIPT FROM 1 BY 1
101              UNTIL TABLE-LOADED OR TABLE-LOAD-ERROR
102              PERFORM 810-READ-JOB-CODE-RECORD
103              IF TABLE-LOADED
104                  COMPUTE TABLE-SIZE = JC-SUBSCRIPT - 1
105                  DISPLAY " "
106                  DISPLAY "Table load complete."
107              ELSE
108                  IF JC-SUBSCRIPT NOT > TABLE-SIZE
109                      MOVE JC-JOB-CODE TO JOB-CODE(JC-SUBSCRIPT)
110                      MOVE JC-PAY-RATE TO PAY-RATE(JC-SUBSCRIPT)
111                      MOVE JC-SUBSCRIPT TO DISPLAY-SUBSCRIPT
112                      DISPLAY "      ", DISPLAY-SUBSCRIPT,
113                              "      ", JC-JOB-CODE
114                  ELSE
115                      SET TABLE-LOAD-ERROR TO TRUE
116                  END-IF
117              END-IF
118          END-PERFORM
119
120          CLOSE JOB-CODE-FILE.
121
122      300-SEARCH-TABLE.
123          SET CODE-FOUND TO FALSE
124
125          PERFORM VARYING JC-SUBSCRIPT FROM 1 BY 1
126              UNTIL CODE-FOUND OR JC-SUBSCRIPT > TABLE-SIZE
127              IF ER-EMPL-JOB-CODE = JOB-CODE(JC-SUBSCRIPT)
128                  MOVE PAY-RATE(JC-SUBSCRIPT) TO PAY-RATE
129                  SET CODE-FOUND TO TRUE
130              END-IF
131          END-PERFORM.
132
133      310-PROCESS-SPECIAL-BENEFITS.
134          DISPLAY " "
135          DISPLAY "Employee: ", ER-EMPL-NUMBER
136          DISPLAY "Job Code: ", ER-EMPL-JOB-CODE
137          DISPLAY "Pay Rate: ", PAY-RATE.
138
139      800-READ-EMPLOYEE-RECORD.
140          READ EMPLOYEE-FILE
141              AT END
142                  SET END-OF-FILE TO TRUE
143          END-READ.
144
145      810-READ-JOB-CODE-RECORD.
146          READ JOB-CODE-FILE
147              AT END
148                  SET TABLE-LOADED TO TRUE
149          END-READ.
```

Figure 14-20

The COBOL Table-Handling Feature—Example 14-5

```
  1        IDENTIFICATION DIVISION.
  2        PROGRAM-ID. PAY-BEN3.
  3
  4     *    Pay special benefits - Pay Rate lookup using the SEARCH statement.
  .          .
  .          .
  .          .
 51        01  JOB-CODE-TABLE.
 52            10  JOB-CODE-TABLE-ENTRY     OCCURS 1 TO 25 TIMES
 53                                         DEPENDING ON TABLE-SIZE
 54                                         INDEXED BY JOB-INDEX.
 55                20  JOB-CODE             PIC 999.
 56                20  PAY-RATE            PIC 99V99.
  .          .
  .          .
  .          .
 93        200-LOAD-JOB-CODE-TABLE.
 94            OPEN INPUT JOB-CODE-FILE
 95            MOVE ALL "?" TO JOB-CODE-TABLE
 96            SET TABLE-LOAD-ERROR TO FALSE
 97            SET TABLE-LOADED TO FALSE
 98            DISPLAY "Loading Table" ERASE
 99            DISPLAY "Entry number   Code"
100            SET JOB-INDEX TO 1
101

102            PERFORM VARYING ENTRY-COUNTER FROM 1 BY 1
103                UNTIL TABLE-LOADED OR TABLE-LOAD-ERROR
104                PERFORM 810-READ-JOB-CODE-RECORD
105                IF TABLE-LOADED
106                    COMPUTE TABLE-SIZE = ENTRY-COUNTER - 1
107                    DISPLAY " "
108                    DISPLAY "Table load complete."
109                ELSE
110                    IF ENTRY-COUNTER NOT > TABLE-SIZE
111                        MOVE JC-JOB-CODE TO JOB-CODE(JOB-INDEX)
112                        MOVE JC-PAY-RATE TO PAY-RATE(JOB-INDEX)
113                        SET JOB-INDEX UP BY 1
114                        DISPLAY "      ", ENTRY-COUNTER,
115                                "       ", JC-JOB-CODE
116                    ELSE
117                        SET TABLE-LOAD-ERROR TO TRUE
118                    END-IF
119                END-IF
120            END-PERFORM
121
122            CLOSE JOB-CODE-FILE.
123
124        300-SEARCH-TABLE.
125            SET JOB-INDEX TO 1
126
127            SEARCH JOB-CODE-TABLE-ENTRY
128                AT END
129                    SET CODE-FOUND TO FALSE
130                WHEN ER-EMPL-JOB-CODE = JOB-CODE(JOB-INDEX)
131                    MOVE PAY-RATE(JOB-INDEX) TO PAY-RATE
132                    SET CODE-FOUND TO TRUE
133            END-SEARCH.
134
135        310-PROCESS-SPECIAL-BENEFITS.
136            DISPLAY " "
137            DISPLAY "Employee: ", ER-EMPL-NUMBER
138            DISPLAY "Job Code: ", ER-EMPL-JOB-CODE
139            DISPLAY "Pay Rate: ", PAY-RATE.
```

Figure 14-21

The OCCURS DEPENDING ON Clause

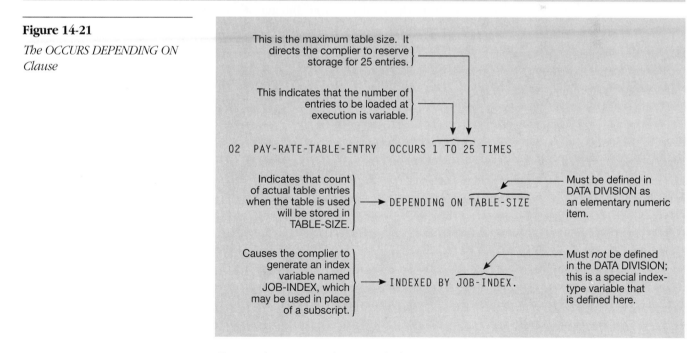

illustrated in Figure 14-22, in which you can see that JOB-CODE-TABLE-ENTRY(3) is 14 bytes away from the beginning of the table. This is called the *displacement* and is the number used in the index to reference the entries in the table. Thus, subscript values of 1, 2, 3, 4, and so on correspond to index values of 0, 7, 14, 21, and so on. Because the index contains the actual displacement value, internal computations performed by the computer for subscripting are eliminated, resulting in faster program execution.

Figure 14-22

A Table in Memory

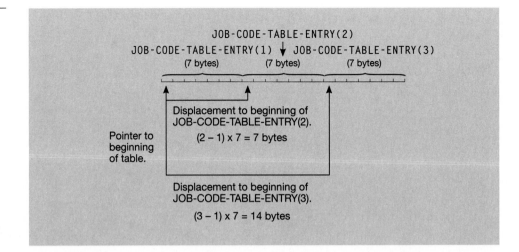

The SET Statement

If you compare the table load module (200) in Figures 14-19 and 14-20, you see relatively minor differences in the two. The most significant difference relates to the use of JOB-INDEX rather than JC-SUBSCRIPT as the subscript in referring to elements of the table. Because JOB-INDEX is defined in the OCCURS as being the index, it will require displacement values rather than consecutive integers.

It is important to understand that index values may be used only where COBOL syntax explicitly allows. For instance, an index value cannot be used as an operand in either a MOVE or an ADD statement. Both the initializing and incrementing of index values are done with the SET statement; for instance, the statement

```
SET JOB-INDEX TO 1
```

places a value of 1 in JOB-INDEX, because the index value (displacement) of the first entry is always 0. Similarly, if an integer other than 1 were used in the SET, the corresponding displacement would be generated and stored in JOB-INDEX.

For the purpose of incrementing the index, the statement

```
SET JOB-INDEX UP BY 1
```

increases the value of JOB-INDEX to point at the next entry by adding the table entry size (in this example, 7) to the existing value. Thus, if JOB-INDEX had a value of 14, execution of this statement would cause it to be increased by 7 to 21.

The SEARCH Statement

It is interesting to compare the table search routines from PAY-BEN2 and PAY-BEN3, which are repeated here in Figure 14-23. Here you see the identical functions carried out by two different statements. In a nutshell, the SEARCH statement says to search the table (PAY-RATE-TABLE), entry by entry, until one of two things happens: the condition in the

Figure 14-23

The SEARCH Statement

```
300-SEARCH-TABLE.
    SET CODE-FOUND TO FALSE

    PERFORM VARYING JC-SUBSCRIPT FROM 1 BY 1
            UNTIL CODE-FOUND OR JC-SUBSCRIPT > WS-TABLE-SIZE
        IF ER-EMPL-JOB-CODE = JOB-CODE(JC-SUBSCRIPT)
        MOVE PAY-RATE(JC-SUBSCRIPT) TO WS-PAY-RATE
        SET CODE-FOUND TO TRUE
        END-IF
    END-PERFORM
```

```
300-SEARCH-TABLE.
    SET JOB-INDEX TO 1

    SEARCH WS-JOB-CODE-TABLE-ENTRY
        AT END
            SET CODE-FOUND TO FALSE
        WHEN ER-EMPL-JOB-CODE = JOB-CODE(JOB-INDEX)
            MOVE PAY-RATE(JOB-INDEX) TO WS-PAY-RATE
            SET CODE-FOUND TO TRUE
    END-SEARCH.
```

WHEN clause is satisfied or the end of the table is reached. If the condition in the WHEN clause is satisfied, the action specified in the WHEN clause is taken. If the search argument is not found in the table, the action specified in the AT END clause is taken. In either case, the program then goes on to the sentence following the END-SEARCH. To provide complete flexibility, the SEARCH statement permits the use of CONTINUE in place of an imperative statement. Note that the data-name specified in the SEARCH clause is the name of the data item that contains the OCCURS and INDEXED BY clauses.

The most noteworthy thing about the SEARCH statement is its total lack of concern with the index. In the equivalent table lookup operation, the subscript (JC-SUBSCRIPT) had to be defined with a PICTURE in the DATA DIVISION and had to be incremented and compared to the number of entries in the PROCEDURE DIVISION. In the SEARCH statement, the programmer is responsible only for initializing the index prior to using the SEARCH and for stating what is to be done at the successful or unsuccessful end of the table lookup operation. The SEARCH statement, by referring to the DEPENDING ON and INDEXED BY clauses associated with the table entry, takes care of all incrementing and testing.

The SEARCH ALL Statement

The SEARCH statement executes a sequential search (also known as a serial or linear search) of a table; that is, it starts where the index points, and continues, item by item, from there. If the arguments in the table are in no particular sequence, this is the only way that the table can be searched. If, however, the arguments in the table are in sequence (ascending or descending), it is more efficient to use the SEARCH ALL statement. SEARCH ALL executes a *nonserial search* by applying a search algorithm that uses the sequential arrangement of the arguments to find the desired item much more quickly.

The SEARCH ALL statement differs from the SEARCH statement in the following ways:

1. The sequence of the table arguments is specified by the KEY clause, which is a part of the OCCURS clause. Its format is

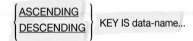

(*Note:* The KEY clause does not put the records into sequence; that is the responsibility of the programmer.)

2. The initial setting of the index is ignored; the SEARCH ALL algorithm determines where it will start searching in the table.

3. Only one WHEN statement may be used, and it can only specify an equal condition or a condition name having a single value. However, the WHEN may test for two or more equalities if they are connected by AND. (The compound OR condition is not permitted.)

To illustrate the SEARCH ALL, the PAY-BEN3 program of Figure 14-20 has been modified to use the SEARCH ALL; appropriate segments of the PAY-BEN4 program are included in Figure 14-24. You should pay particular attention to the following features (which are highlighted):

1. The ASCENDING KEY clause specifies that the entries in the table will be in ascending sequence by the field JOB-CODE.

2. As each table entry is read from the table file, a check is made to ensure that it is larger than the preceding one (lines 112 through 116). The data item JOB-CODE is used for this sequence check. As each pair of table values is loaded into the table (lines 119 and 120), the job-code value for the current entry is moved to JOB-CODE (line 124) in preparation for the next one to be read.

3. The table is initially filled with 9's (line 97), so that any unloaded table slots will be

Figure 14-24

Using the SEARCH ALL

```
1       IDENTIFICATION DIVISION.
2       PROGRAM-ID. PAY-BEN4.
3
4    *     Pay special benefits - Pay Rate lookup using SEARCH ALL.
5
.          .
.          .
.          .
32      WORKING-STORAGE SECTION.
.          .
.          .
.          .
47      01  OTHER-VARIABLES.
48          10  ENTRY-COUNTER        PIC 99.
49          10  PAY-RATE             PIC ZZ.99.
50          10  JOB-CODE             PIC 999     VALUE ZERO.
51
52      01  JOB-CODE-TABLE.
53          10  JOB-CODE-TABLE-ENTRY    OCCURS 1 TO 25 TIMES
54                                      DEPENDING ON TABLE-SIZE
55                                      ASCENDING KEY IS JOB-CODE
56                                      INDEXED BY JOB-INDEX.
57              20  JOB-CODE            PIC 999.
58              20  PAY-RATE            PIC 99V99.
59
```

```
95      200-LOAD-JOB-CODE-TABLE.
96          OPEN INPUT JOB-CODE-FILE
97          MOVE ALL "9" TO JOB-CODE-TABLE
98          SET TABLE-LOAD-ERROR TO FALSE
99          SET TABLE-LOADED TO FALSE
100         DISPLAY "Loading Table" ERASE
101         DISPLAY "Entry number   Code"
102         SET JOB-INDEX TO 1
103
104         PERFORM VARYING ENTRY-COUNTER FROM 1 BY 1
105             UNTIL TABLE-LOADED OR TABLE-LOAD-ERROR
106             PERFORM 810-READ-JOB-CODE-RECORD
107         IF TABLE-LOADED
108             COMPUTE TABLE-SIZE = ENTRY-COUNTER - 1
109             DISPLAY " "
110             DISPLAY "Table load complete."
111         ELSE
112             IF JC-JOB-CODE NOT > JOB-CODE
113                 DISPLAY " "
114                 DISPLAY "Job code ", JC-JOB-CODE,
115                     " is out of sequence."
116                 SET TABLE-LOAD-ERROR TO TRUE
117             ELSE
118                 IF ENTRY-COUNTER NOT > TABLE-SIZE
119                     MOVE JC-JOB-CODE TO JOB-CODE(JOB-INDEX)
120                     MOVE JC-PAY-RATE TO PAY-RATE(JOB-INDEX)
121                     SET JOB-INDEX UP BY 1
122                     DISPLAY "      ", ENTRY-COUNTER,
123                         "      ", JC-JOB-CODE
124                     MOVE JC-JOB-CODE TO JOB-CODE
125                 ELSE
126                     DISPLAY " "
127                     DISPLAY "Table size exceeded.  ",
128                         JC-JOB-CODE, " cannot be loaded."
129                     SET TABLE-LOAD-ERROR TO TRUE
130                 END-IF
131             END-IF
132         END-IF
133         END-PERFORM
134
135         CLOSE JOB-CODE-FILE.
136
137     300-SEARCH-TABLE.
138         SEARCH ALL JOB-CODE-TABLE-ENTRY
139             AT END
140                 SET CODE-FOUND TO FALSE
141             WHEN JOB-CODE(JOB-INDEX) = ER-EMPL-JOB-CODE
142                 MOVE PAY-RATE(JOB-INDEX) TO PAY-RATE
143                 SET CODE-FOUND TO TRUE
144         END-SEARCH.
            .
            .
            .
```

greater than the highest loaded job code. If PIC X(3) had been specified for the job code, then the table would have been initialized to VALUE HIGH-VALUES.

4. The SEARCH ALL statement is not preceded by a SET statement, because it is not necessary to initialize the index.

5. The WHEN clause with the SEARCH ALL has a rather unique requirement. That is, in the relational condition, the subscripted item must be on the left. Therefore,

```
WHEN JOB-CODE(JOB-INDEX) = ER-EMPL-JOB-CODE
```

is valid but

```
WHEN ER-EMPL-JOB-CODE = JOB-CODE(JOB-INDEX)
```

is not valid and will give a compiler error.

The savings in execution time that result with large tables from the use of the SEARCH ALL will usually justify the extra programming effort to ensure that the arguments are in the proper sequence.

Using the SEARCH Statement to Create a Table

Example Definition— Example 14-6

All of the examples so far have shown tables that were loaded with table data at the beginning of a program and then referred to by the program as it processed the data file. It is also possible (and often useful) to have the program create a table while it is processing the data file, as is illustrated in the following example.

Example 14-6 Building a Table with the SEARCH Statement
Problem Description
The local office of the telephone company maintains a file of long-distance calls made by customers in the area. The input record includes both the caller's number and the called number. The research manager wishes to know the total number of message units of calls made to each area code.

Output Requirements
Screen display of each area code called and the total number of message units to that area.

Input Description
File name: LD-CALLS.DL
Record format:

Record Position	Description
1–6	Date of call
7–13	Caller's phone number (*xxx-xxxx*)
14–23	Destination phone number (*xxx/xxx-xxxx*)
24–26	Number of message units

Processing Requirements
1. For each input record:
   a. Search the table to determine if the area code is already in the table.
   b. If the area code is not in the table, insert it and the message units.
   c. If the area code is in the table, add the message units to the total message units for that area code entry.
2. When the last input record is processed, display the area codes and their message unit totals.

Program Planning— Example 14-6

This example will require a table consisting of two entries: the area code and the corresponding total message units to that area code. The table processing is somewhat unique in that as each input record is read, either of two conditions can exist (assuming no errors):

■ The area code is one that is not already in the table, in which case the code—together with the message unit value—will need to be added to the table.

■ The area code is one that is already in the table, in which case the message unit value will need to be added to the value currently stored for that area code.

In order to focus on table-processing principles, the output needs of this example have been kept to a minimum of simply displaying the area codes and their accumulated message unit totals on the screen.

Program documentation is included in Figures 14-25 through 14-27 (page 390). In the 200 module to load the table, you can see the logic involved in handling the different conditions.

Figure 14-25

Structure Chart for Example 14-6

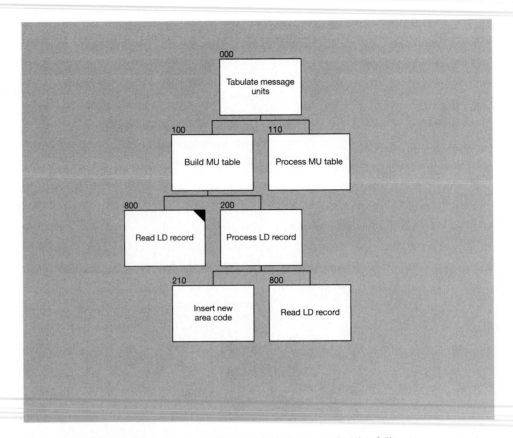

Program Solution— Example 14-6

The complete program is shown in Figure 14-28 (page 391). The following commentary pertains to this coding:

1. The area-code table is defined by the OCCURS clause in line 42. It is variable in size because processing will probably not require all 122 entries.

2. The table size (NEW-ENTRY-POINTER) is initialized at zero at line 38 to show that there are initially zero entries in the table. This item is included in the DEPENDING ON clause (line 43).

3. Before each new entry is added to the table, the data item NEW-ENTRY-POINTER is incremented (line 92) so that it points to the next open position in the table (the position following the last entry previously inserted into the table).

4. When a long-distance record is processed, the area-code table is searched for a matching area code.
   a. If a matching area code is found by the first WHEN clause, the message units from the input record are added to the corresponding message-unit accumulator.
   b. If no matching area code is found in the table (AT END), the index AREA-NDX is compared to the current entry count MAXIMUM-ENTRIES. If the index is greater, a message is displayed. Otherwise, a new entry is inserted into the table.

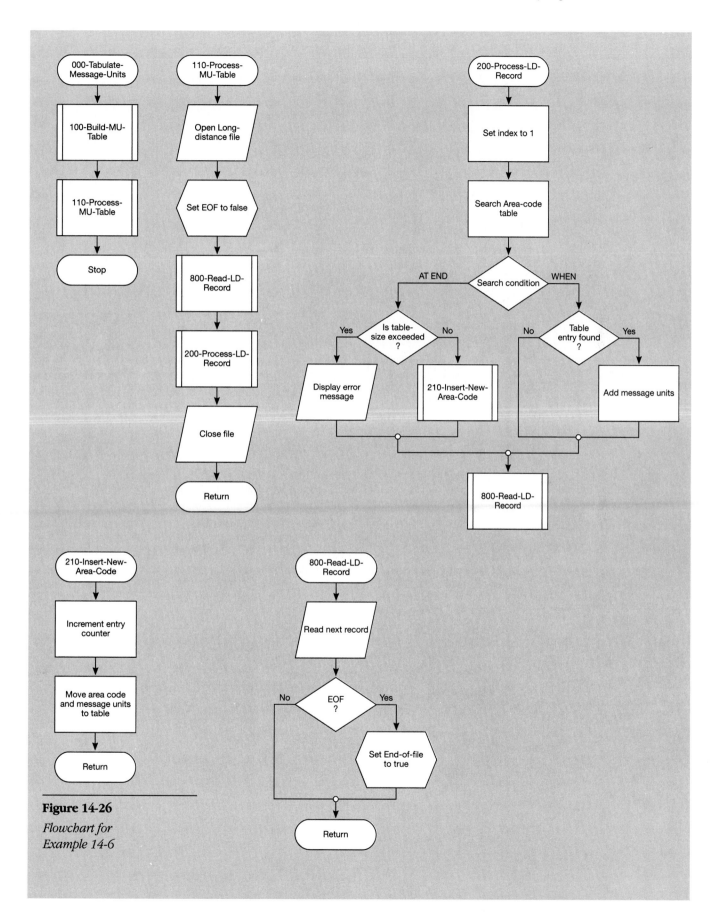

Figure 14-26

*Flowchart for
Example 14-6*

Figure 14-27

*Pseudocode for
Example 14-6*

```
000-Tabulate-Message-Units
    Perform 100-Build-MU-Table
    Perform 110-Process-MU-Table
    Stop run
100-Build-MU-Table
    Open long-distance file
    Set EOF switch to false
    Perform 800-Read-LD-Record
    Perform 200-Process-LD-Record until EOF
    Close LD file
110-Process-MU-Table
    Perform varying index by 1 from 1
        Display Area-code and
                Area-code-message-units
```

```
200-Process-LD-Record
    Set index to 1
    Search area-code table
      AT END
        If table size exceeded
            Display message
        else
            Perform 210-Insert-New-Area-Code
      WHEN table entry found
        Add message units of input record to
            table message units for this area code
    Perform 800-Read-LD-Record
210-Insert-New-Area-Code
    Add 1 to table-entry counter
    Move input area code and message units to
        table
800-Read-LD-Record
    Read next record
        at end set EOF to true
```

Multiple-Level Tables

Wall Paneling in a Table

Assume that you work for a company that manufactures six different styles of wall paneling, with prices as shown in Figure 14-29. Using the principles of preceding sections, you could define a table memory area, consisting only of functions, using the following OCCURS clause:

```
01  PANEL-PRICE-TABLE.
    10 PANEL-PRICE OCCURS 6 TIMES PIC 99V99.
```

If you assume that the search argument (named STYLE) contains a code of 1 for style Mundane, 2 for style Modern, and so on, then you can use the search argument as a subscript. For instance, an inquiry for a price might be handled as in Figure 14-30. Since the value of STYLE must be between 1 and 6, a check is made using procedures with which you are familiar. Note that in using this table, you need not perform a search. Since the style number corresponds to the subscript value, you can access the value directly. This technique is sometimes called *direct table lookup.*

A Two-Level Table

Assume that your employer responds to market demand and decides to offer four types of finishes for each of the six styles. Thus, the inventory includes 24 style-finish combinations, each with its own retail price. The pricing information can be summarized in a *two-level* (or *two-dimensional*) *table* such as that in Figure 14-31.

COBOL includes the capability for handling two-level (two-dimensional) tables such as these through multiple levels of the OCCURS clause. For instance, the following will define required memory area for this functions-only table:

```
01 PANEL-PRICE-TABLE.
    10 PANEL-FINISH OCCURS 4 TIMES.
        20 PANEL-PRICE OCCURS 6 TIMES PIC 99V99.
```

In essence, this says

1. There are four PANEL-FINISH fields

2. Each is composed of six PANEL-PRICE fields

Figure 14-28

*Using the SEARCH
Statement to Build a
Table—Example 14-6*

```
 1      IDENTIFICATION DIVISION.
 2      PROGRAM-ID.    LD-CALLS.
 3
 4    * This program uses the SEARCH statement to build a table from
 5    * a file of long-distance calls.  The table is used to determine
 6    * the number of message units for long-distance calls made to
 7    * each area code.
 8
 9      ENVIRONMENT DIVISION.
10      CONFIGURATION SECTION.
11      SOURCE-COMPUTER.   IBM-PC.
12
13      INPUT-OUTPUT SECTION.
14      FILE-CONTROL.
15          SELECT LONG-DISTANCE-FILE   ASSIGN TO DISK  "LD-CALLS.DL"
16                                      ORGANIZATION IS LINE SEQUENTIAL.
17
18      DATA DIVISION.
19
20      FILE SECTION.
21
22      FD  LONG-DISTANCE-FILE.
23      01  LONG-DISTANCE-RECORD.
24          10  LD-DATE              PIC X(6).
25          10  LD-CALLERS-NUMBER    PIC X(7).
26          10  LD-DESTINATION.
27              20  LD-CALLED-AREA   PIC X(3).
28              20  LD-CALLED-NUMBER PIC X(7).
29          10  LD-MESSAGE-UNITS     PIC 9(3).
30
31      WORKING-STORAGE SECTION.
32
33      01  PROGRAMMED-SWITCHES.
34          10                       PIC X.
35              88  END-OF-FILE      VALUE "Y"  FALSE "N".
36
37      01  TABLE-VARIABLES.
38          10  NEW-ENTRY-POINTER    PIC 9(3)  BINARY   VALUE ZERO.
39          10  MAXIMUM-ENTRIES      PIC 9(3)  BINARY   VALUE 122.
40
41      01  AREA-CODE-TABLE.
42          10  AREA-CODE-DATA       OCCURS 1 TO 122 TIMES
43                                   DEPENDING ON NEW-ENTRY-POINTER
44                                   INDEXED BY AREA-NDX.
45              20  AREA-CODE        PIC X(3).
46              20  AREA-MESSAGE-UNITS PIC 9(5).
47
48      01  DISPLAY-VARIABLES.
49          10  AREA-MESSAGE-UNITS   PIC ZZZZ9.
50
51      PROCEDURE DIVISION.
52
53      000-TABULATE-MESSAGE-UNITS.
54          PERFORM 100-BUILD-M-U-TABLE.
55          PERFORM 110-PROCESS-M-U-TABLE.
56          STOP RUN.
57
58      100-BUILD-M-U-TABLE.
59          OPEN INPUT LONG-DISTANCE-FILE
60          SET END-OF-FILE TO FALSE
61          PERFORM 800-READ-LD-RECORD
62          PERFORM 200-PROCESS-LD-RECORD UNTIL END-OF-FILE
63          CLOSE LONG-DISTANCE-FILE.
64
65      110-PROCESS-M-U-TABLE.
66          DISPLAY "Area  Message" LINE 5 ERASE
67          DISPLAY "code  Units "
68          PERFORM VARYING AREA-NDX FROM 1 BY 1
69              UNTIL AREA-NDX > NEW-ENTRY-POINTER
70          MOVE AREA-MESSAGE-UNITS(AREA-NDX)
71              TO AREA-MESSAGE-UNITS
72          DISPLAY AREA-CODE(AREA-NDX), "  ",
73              AREA-MESSAGE-UNITS
74          END-PERFORM.
75
76      200-PROCESS-LD-RECORD.
77          SET AREA-NDX TO 1.
78          SEARCH AREA-CODE-DATA
79          AT END
80              IF AREA-NDX > MAXIMUM-ENTRIES
81                  DISPLAY "No room in table for ", LONG-DISTANCE-RECORD
82              ELSE
83                  PERFORM 210-INSERT-NEW-AREA-CODE
84              END-IF
85          WHEN LD-CALLED-AREA = AREA-CODE(AREA-NDX)
86              ADD LD-MESSAGE-UNITS
87              TO AREA-MESSAGE-UNITS(AREA-NDX)
88          END-SEARCH.
89          PERFORM 800-READ-LD-RECORD.
90
91      210-INSERT-NEW-AREA-CODE.
92          ADD 1 TO NEW-ENTRY-POINTER
93          MOVE LD-CALLED-AREA TO AREA-CODE(AREA-NDX)
94          MOVE LD-MESSAGE-UNITS TO AREA-MESSAGE-UNITS(AREA-NDX).
95
96      800-READ-LD-RECORD.
97          READ LONG-DISTANCE-FILE
98          AT END
99              SET END-OF-FILE TO TRUE
100         END-READ.
```

Figure 14-29

Wall Panel Price List

			Style		
Mundane	**Modern**	**Cave**	**Ultima**	**Decorator**	**Colonial**
23.75	26.12	19.95	42.25	31.00	28.22

Figure 14-30

Direct Table Lookup

```
MOVE 0 TO STYLE
PERFORM UNTIL STYLE = ZERO
  DISPLAY "Which style number do you want (0 if finished)? "
  ACCEPT STYLE  POSITION 0
  IF STYLE < 0 OR > 6
    DISPLAY "Style number must be 1-6 (or 0)"  BEEP
  ELSE
    MOVE PANEL-PRICE(STYLE) TO DISPLAY-PRICE
    DISPLAY "The price is: ", DISPLAY-PRICE
  END-IF
END-PERFORM
```

Figure 14-31

Wall Panel Price Chart

Finish	Style					
	Mundane	Modern	Cave	Ultima	Decorator	Colonial
None	23.75	26.12	19.95	42.25	31.00	28.22
Standard	28.15	30.50	25.38	46.35	36.15	33.21
Heavy duty	29.38	31.22	27.05	47.50	37.28	34.07
All-weather	31.50	34.73	28.65	49.83	39.75	36.12

Thus, you have a total of 24 fields, which satisfies the needs of Figure 14-31. It is important to recognize the distinction between the PANEL-FINISH field and the PANEL-PRICE field. You see that there are four occurrences of PANEL-FINISH that consist of six component prices (Figure 14-32 illustrates this for the standard finish). If you refer to, for example, PANEL-FINISH(2), you are addressing the price list for all six styles of the standard finish panels. Needless to say, you would not be likely to require the entire collection of six prices at one time.

Directly Accessing a Two-Level Table

To access the next level down, PANEL-PRICE, you must use *two* subscripts. The first is to designate the PANEL-FINISH element (can range from 1 to 4) and the second to designate the PANEL-PRICE element (can range from 1 to 6) within that PANEL-FINISH group. Thus, you refer to any required table entry by using two subscripts, as shown in Figure 14-33. Remember that the first subscript refers to the first OCCURS and the second subscript to the second OCCURS.

To practice using a table of this type, assume that you need to allow the entry of the desired style and finish from the keyboard. The keyed entries are to be verified as follows:

Finish must be from 1 to 4.

Style must be from 1 to 6.

Figure 14-32

One "Row" of the Table in Memory

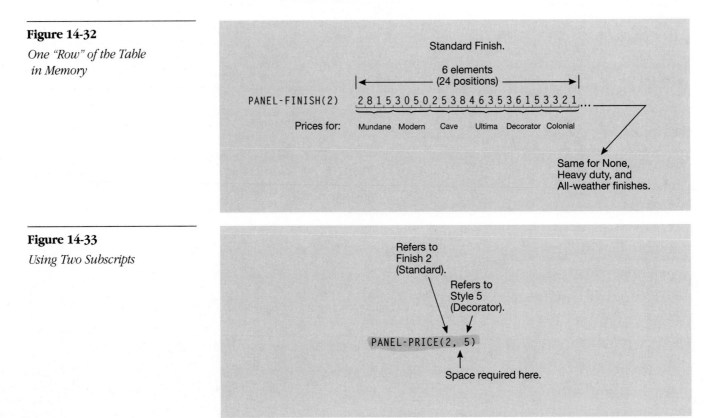

Figure 14-33

Using Two Subscripts

Figure 14-34

Direct Lookup of a Two-Level Table

```
01  PANEL-PRICE-TABLE.
    10  PANEL-FINISH OCCURS 4 TIMES.
        20  PANEL-PRICE OCCURS 6 TIMES, PIC 99V99.

01  OTHER-VARIABLES.
    10  PANEL-PRICE-DISPLAY   PIC ZZ.99.
    10  FINISH                PIC 9.
        88  DONE         VALUE 0.
        88  FINISH-OKAY  VALUE 1 THRU 4.
    10  STYLE                 PIC 9.
        88  STYLE-OKAY   VALUE 1 THRU 6.
    .
    .
    .
```

```
MOVE 1 TO FINISH
PERFORM UNTIL DONE
    DISPLAY "Which Finish number do you want (0 if finished)? "
    ACCEPT FINISH POSITION 0
    IF FINISH-OKAY
       MOVE 0 TO STYLE
       PERFORM UNTIL STYLE-OKAY
          DISPLAY "Which Style number do you want? "
          ACCEPT STYLE POSITION 0
          IF STYLE-OKAY
             MOVE PANEL-PRICE(FINISH,STYLE) TO PANEL-PRICE-DISPLAY
             DISPLAY "The price is: ", PANEL-PRICE-DISPLAY
          ELSE
             DISPLAY "Style number must be between 1 and 6"
          END-IF
       END-PERFORM
    ELSE
       IF NOT DONE
          DISPLAY "Finish number cannot be negative or greater than 4"
       END-IF
    END-IF
END-PERFORM
```

The corresponding price from the table must be displayed on the screen. Assume that the table is already loaded into memory.

In this case, the input codes themselves can be used as subscripts, thus giving "direct access" to the desired table entry. The code segments of Figure 14-34 consist mainly of checking to ensure that the input data is valid. Note that level 88 entries are used to improve the self-documentation features of this code.

Using the SEARCH on a Two-Level Table— Example 14-7

For the programmer, access to the table by having the user enter style and finish numbers that correspond to the subscript values (as in Figure 14-34) is quite convenient. This is a case in which the finish and style numbers are selected for the convenience of the programmer. However, in an actual environment, this is not usually the case (nor should it be). Such decisions are normally made according to some policy of the company. For instance, the marketing department might decide that a series classification has more zip in its sound. Hence, they may offer four finish series: the 100 series might be their low grade and the 680 series their high grade. Catchy-sounding numbers in between could be used for other finishes. Then reference would always be to the series number, obviously not suited to direct lookup. The next example gives an insight as to how this type of situation might be handled.

Example 14-7 Searching a Two-Level Table

Problem Description

Your company has decided to use the three-position codes for panel finish and style shown in Figure 14-35. A program is needed that will prompt the user for the finish and style codes, then display the price.

Output Requirements

The screen display illustrated by the sample screen of Figure 14-36.

Figure 14-35

Finish and Style Codes

Finish	Code	Style	Code
None	NON	Mundane	MUN
Standard	STD	Modern	MOD
Heavy duty	H-D	Cave	CAV
All-weather	A-W	Ultima	ULT
		Decorator	DEC
		Colonial	COL

Figure 14-36

Sample Screen Display—
Example 14-7

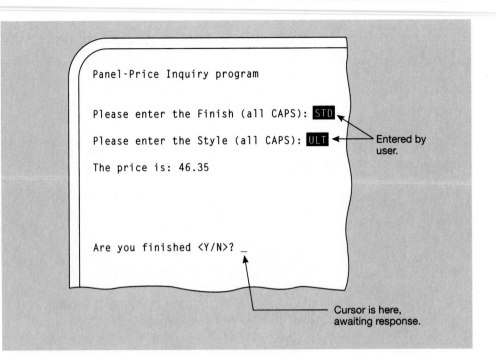

Input Description

Table file

File name: PANEL-PR.TBL

Record format:

Each record contains the data for one complete finish, as shown in Figure 14-37.

Processing Requirements

This program is to read the table file into a two-level table, then allow the user to inquire using the foregoing codes.

1. Load the table
2. Repeat until the user requests to terminate
   a. Accept the finish and style; prompt user if either is not in the table
   b. Search the table for the requested finish/style entry
   c. Display the price from the table
   d. Query the user about continuing

For a problem of this type, there is usually more than one way of setting up the table in memory. The method used here was selected primarily to illustrate searching a multiple-level table.

Figure 14-37

Table File for Example 14-7

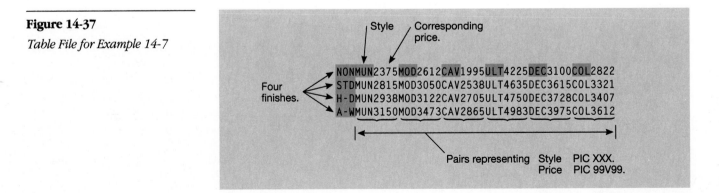

Figure 14-38

Table Definition for Example 14-7

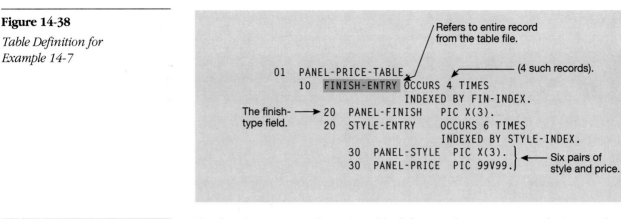

Program Planning—Example 14-7

The first thing to consider is the table definition shown in Figure 14-38. Note that each of the four FINISH-ENTRY elements corresponds to one entire record. It consists of

1. A 3-position finish code

2. A group of 6-style entries, which in turn consist of

     A 3-position panel code

     The price (4 positions)

The following example elements should give some insight to the meaning of these components.

FINISH-ENTRY(1)	Refers to the entire record for the first finish (in Figure 14-37, this is the entire first line)
PANEL-FINISH(1)	Refers to the first finish code (NON)
PANEL-FINISH(2)	Refers to the second finish code (STD)
STYLE-ENTRY(2, 4)	Refers to the style/price for the second finish code, fourth style (ULT4635)
PANEL-STYLE(2, 4)	Refers to the style for the second finish code, fourth style (ULT)
PANEL-PRICE(2, 4)	Refers to the price for the second finish code, fourth style (4635)

Searching this table will require two SEARCH statements, one within the other. The first search will be to find the finish. The second search will be to find the style within that finish type. The logic of this segment of the solution is illustrated in Figure 14-39.

Program Solution—Example 14-7

The complete program is shown in Figure 14-40; execution of the SEARCH (starting line 71) proceeds as follows:

1. The first search is on the finish code. Upon execution of the first SEARCH (line 71), if the AT END condition occurs, the entry is not in the table, and an error message is given. Execution exits the SEARCH.

2. If the finish code is found, execution proceeds to the DISPLAY and ACCEPT, where the user is asked for the style.

3. The second search is on the style. Upon execution of the second SEARCH (line 80), if the AT END condition occurs, the entry is not in the table, and an error message is given. Execution exits the SEARCH.

4. WHEN the requested table entry is found, the desired price is displayed.

Figure 14-39

Logic of Search for
Example 14-7

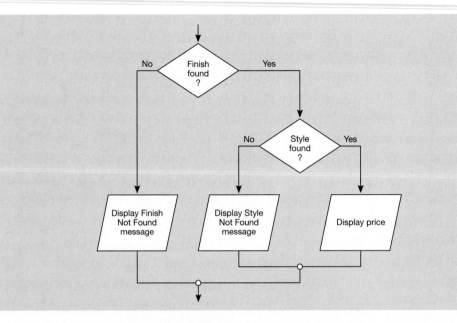

Figure 14-40

A Two-Level Table Search—
Example 14-7

```
1       IDENTIFICATION DIVISION.
2       PROGRAM-ID. PANEL-PR.
3
4    *     This program determines the price of wood paneling by using
5    *     the SEARCH statement to search a two-level table.
6
7       ENVIRONMENT DIVISION.
8       CONFIGURATION SECTION.
9       SOURCE-COMPUTER. IBM-PC.
10
11      INPUT-OUTPUT SECTION.
12      FILE-CONTROL.
13          SELECT PANEL-TABLE-FILE ASSIGN TO DISK  "PANEL-PR.TBL"
14                          ORGANIZATION IS LINE SEQUENTIAL.
15
16      DATA DIVISION.
17      FILE SECTION.
18
19      FD  PANEL-TABLE-FILE.
20      01  PANEL-TABLE-RECORD    PIC X(45).
21
22      WORKING-STORAGE SECTION.
23
24      01  PROGRAMMED-SWITCHES.
25          10  COMPLETED-SW     PIC X.
26              88  COMPLETED    VALUE "Y"  FALSE "N".
27
28      01  OTHER-VARIABLES.
29          10  ENTRY-COUNTER    PIC 99  VALUE ZERO.
30          10  FINISH           PIC XXX.
31          10  STYLE            PIC XXX.
32          10  DISPLAY-PRICE    PIC ZZ.99.
33
34      01  PANEL-PRICE-TABLE.
35          10  FINISH-ENTRY     OCCURS 4 TIMES
36                               INDEXED BY FIN-INDEX.
37              20  PANEL-FINISH PIC X(3).
38              20  STYLE-ENTRY  OCCURS 6 TIMES
39                               INDEXED BY STYLE-INDEX.
40                  30  PANEL-STYLE   PIC X(3).
41                  30  PANEL-PRICE   PIC 99V99.
42
43      PROCEDURE DIVISION.
44
45      DISPLAY-PANEL-PRICES.
46          PERFORM 100-INITIALIZE
47          PERFORM 110-INQUIRE UNTIL COMPLETED
48          PERFORM 120-FINALIZE
49          STOP RUN.
50
51      100-INITIALIZE.
52          OPEN INPUT PANEL-TABLE-FILE
53          DISPLAY "Loading table"  ERASE
54          PERFORM VARYING ENTRY-COUNTER FROM 1 BY 1
55                          UNTIL ENTRY-COUNTER > 4
56              PERFORM 800-READ-PANEL-TABLE-RECORD
57              MOVE PANEL-TABLE-RECORD
58                  TO FINISH-ENTRY(ENTRY-COUNTER)
59          END-PERFORM
60          CLOSE PANEL-TABLE-FILE
61
62          DISPLAY "Panel-Price Inquiry program"
63                  LINE 1 POSITION 10  ERASE
64          SET COMPLETED TO FALSE.
65
66      110-INQUIRE.
67          DISPLAY "Please enter the Finish (all CAPS): "
68                  LINE 4, POSITION 10 ERASE EOS
69          ACCEPT FINISH  POSITION 0  NO BEEP REVERSE PROMPT
70          SET FIN-INDEX TO 1
71          SEARCH FINISH-ENTRY
72              AT END
73              DISPLAY "There is no finish type " LINE 12 POSITION 10
74                      FINISH POSITION 0  REVERSE  BEEP
75          WHEN FINISH = PANEL-FINISH(FIN-INDEX)
76              DISPLAY "Please enter the Style (all CAPS): "
77                      LINE 6, POSITION 10
78              ACCEPT STYLE POSITION 0  NO BEEP REVERSE PROMPT
79              SET STYLE-INDEX TO 1
80              SEARCH STYLE-ENTRY
81                  AT END
82                  DISPLAY "There is no Style type " LINE 12 POSITION 10
83                          STYLE POSITION 0  REVERSE  BEEP
84              WHEN STYLE =
85                  PANEL-STYLE(FIN-INDEX, STYLE-INDEX)
86                  MOVE PANEL-PRICE(FIN-INDEX, STYLE-INDEX)
87                      TO DISPLAY-PRICE
88                  DISPLAY "The price is: " LINE 8 POSITION 10
89                          DISPLAY-PRICE POSITION 0 REVERSE
90              END-SEARCH
91          END-SEARCH
92
93          DISPLAY "Are you finished <Y/N>? " LINE 14 POSITION 10
94          ACCEPT COMPLETED-SW  POSITION 0  PROMPT.
95
96      120-FINALIZE.
97          DISPLAY " "  BEEP
98          DISPLAY "Processing complete.".
99
100     800-READ-PANEL-TABLE-RECORD.
101         READ PANEL-TABLE-FILE
102             AT END
103             DISPLAY "Not enough records in table file."
104             DISPLAY "Processing terminated."
105             STOP RUN
106         END-READ.
```

Chapter Summary

General

The subscripting feature of COBOL provides the programmer with a powerful tool for manipulation of tabular data. With the OCCURS clause, the programmer can define an entire array of data items, all with a common name. Access to an individual item is through the use of subscripting. For instance, if the item RATE has been defined to consist of 20 elements, then the twelfth would be referred to as RATE (12).

A table to be used by a program can be fixed in nature and hence its values can be defined by VALUE clauses in the DATA DIVISION. For a table in which the values frequently change, it is more practical to define the table area in the DATA DIVISION, but to load the values from a file during execution of the program.

Searching a table for a desired entry is such a common operation that COBOL includes the SEARCH statement. This statement causes a table to be searched, entry by entry, until either of two things happens: the condition in the WHEN clause is satisfied, or the end of the table is reached. If the search argument is not found in the table, the action specified in the AT END clause is taken.

COBOL Language Elements

The COBOL statements that you have studied in this chapter are

PERFORM/TIMES   The TIMES option of the PERFORM provides for the automatic execution of a module a selected number of times.

Out-of-line

PERFORM paragraph-name $\begin{Bmatrix} \text{identifier} \\ \text{integer} \end{Bmatrix}$ TIMES

In-line

PERFORM $\begin{Bmatrix} \text{identifier} \\ \text{integer} \end{Bmatrix}$ TIMES

imperative-statement
END-PERFORM

PERFORM/VARYING   The VARYING option of the PERFORM provides for repeated execution of a module as controlled by a specified condition. Incrementing of one or more identifiers or indexes is automatically carried out.

Out-of-line

PERFORM procedure-name

VARYING identifier-1 FROM $\begin{Bmatrix} \text{identifier-2} \\ \text{integer-1} \end{Bmatrix}$

BY $\begin{Bmatrix} \text{identifier-3} \\ \text{integer-2} \end{Bmatrix}$ UNTIL condition-test

In-line

PERFORM

VARYING identifier-1 FROM $\begin{Bmatrix} \text{identifier-2} \\ \text{integer-1} \end{Bmatrix}$

BY $\begin{Bmatrix} \text{identifier-3} \\ \text{integer-2} \end{Bmatrix}$ UNTIL condition-test

imperative-statement
END-PERFORM

SEARCH   The SEARCH statement is used to search a table for a table element that satisfies a specified condition.

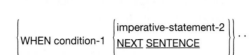

[AT END imperative-statement-1]

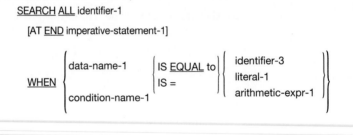

[END-SEARCH]

SEARCH ALL   The SEARCH ALL statement is used to search a sequenced table for a table element that satisfies a specified condition.

SEARCH ALL identifier-1

[AT END imperative-statement-1]

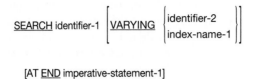

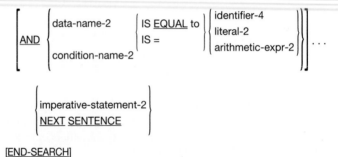

[END-SEARCH]

Other language elements that you have studied in this chapter are

OCCURS   The OCCURS clause provides for the definition of repeated data items.

OCCURS integer-2 TIMES

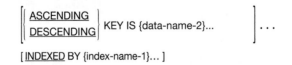

[INDEXED BY {index-name-1}...]

OCCURS integer-1 TO integer-2 TIMES DEPENDING ON data-name-1

$$\left[\begin{Bmatrix} \underline{\text{ASCENDING}} \\ \underline{\text{DESCENDING}} \end{Bmatrix} \text{KEY IS } \{\text{data-name-2}\}... \right] ...$$

[INDEXED BY {index-name-1}...]

USAGE The USAGE clause specifies the internal memory format of data items defined in the DATA DIVISION.

$$\underline{\text{USAGE}} \text{ IS } \begin{Bmatrix} \underline{\text{BINARY}} \\ \underline{\text{DISPLAY}} \\ \underline{\text{INDEX}} \end{Bmatrix}$$

Error Prevention/Detection

When loading a table from a file, remember that the record counter will count the EOF record. It must be decremented by 1 if its value is to be used to designate the table size.

If a table search fails for entries that you know are in the table, check the table to certain that it is properly loaded.

When loading a table from a file, always display the table and other appropriate data so that you can be certain it is entered properly.

In searching a two-dimensional array, be certain to include both subscripts in their correct order.

Questions and Exercises

Key Terminology

Give a brief description of each of the following terms that were introduced in this chapter.

argument   search argument
byte   subscript
direct table lookup   subscripted variable
displacement   table
function   two-level table
index

General Questions

1. What is the consequence of defining a table in memory as consisting of 100 fields (OCCURS 100 TIMES) and using only 75 of them in the program?

2. In prior chapters, the PERFORM/UNTIL has been used. Which two variations are introduced in this chapter?

3. What purpose does the OCCURS clause serve?

4. What is the difference between an "argument" and a "junction" in a table? How is the "junction" obtained?

5. How does an "index" differ from a "subscript"?

6. When a SEARCH statement is used in table lookups instead of PERFORM/VARYING, which two clauses must be used to control the search?

7. A programmer is asked to code a two-level table in a program. How is each level in the table defined in memory and accessed by the program?

Questions Relating to the Example Programs

1. In the job-code table of Figure 14-5, could JOB-CODE-TABLE have been coded first, followed by JOB-CODE-DATA? If so, show what changes would be necessary. If not, why not?

2. If you were to prepare a test employee file to thoroughly test and prove the table load and search in the PAY-BEN1 program (Figure 14-15), what employee number values would you include in the file?

3. In 200-LOAD-JOB-CODE-TABLE of PAY-BEN2 (Figure 14-19), would it be possible to move both the argument (JC-JOB-CODE) and the function (JC-PAY-RATE) with one MOVE statement? If so, how would it be coded?

4. In the PAY-BEN2 (Figure 14-19) program, the pay rate is moved to the work area PAY-RATE for use in the 300 module. Remember that the 300 module shown in Figure 14-19 is a dummy module; the full version is to be written by another programmer. Assume that the 300 routine contains the statement:

```
COMPUTE GROSS-PAY ROUNDED = HOURS-WORKED * PAY-RATE
```

Would it be possible to eliminate the PAY-RATE field and have the COMPUTE statement obtain the pay rate directly from the table? If so, how?

5. In the PAY-BEN2 program (Figure 14-19), the data item JC-SUBSCRIPT is used as a subscript to load the table (lines 109 and 110); it is incremented automatically by the PERFORM/VARYING (line 100). In PAY-BEN3 (Figure 14-20), the index JOB-INDEX is used for subscripting; it is incremented within the PERFORM loop with a SET statement. Thus, there appears to be no need to include ENTRY-COUNTER. Why not make the following changes?

    Lines 102 and 103 become:

    ```
    PERFORM UNTIL TABLE-LOADED OR TABLE-LOAD-ERROR
    ```

    Replace line 106 with:

    ```
    MOVE TABLE-INDEX TO TABLE-SIZE
    ```

6. The PAY-BEN4 program (Figure 14-24) contains two switches: TABLE-LOAD-ERROR and TABLE-LOADED. What would happen in this program if the programmer set both of these to TRUE on lines 98 and 99?

7. The PANEL-PR program (Figure 14-40) contains a two-level table. The programmer decides to code another 20-level number line as follows:

    ```
    20  PRICE-ENTRY  OCCURS 6 TIMES
                    INDEXED BY PRICE-INDEX.
    ```

    It is inserted after line 40. How does this change the table?

Writing Program Statements

1. Using the PERFORM/VARYING, write an in-line PERFORM to calculate the powers of 2 for odd values of n. Display the number and the corresponding powers of 2. Terminate when n exceeds 29 or when power exceeds 750,000.

2. Define a fixed table that contains the names of the days of the week, beginning with Sunday. The table name must be WEEK-DAY-TABLE and the subscripted data-name must be WEEK-DAY.

3. In the PAY-BEN2 program (Figure 14-19), if an input job code is not in the table, the entire table will be searched before the not-in-table exit occurs. Assume that the table data is loaded with the job codes in ascending sequence. How could the table search operation be modified to determine that an employee job code was not in the table without always searching the entire table? Write the additional coding to accomplish this (refer to the PERFORM at line 125).

4. Assume that the table for the PANEL-PR program (Figure 14-40) must be loaded from the file TABLE.FLE, with each record containing one entry as follows:

Field	Record Positions	Defined in FD as
Style code (1–6)	1	STYLE PIC 9
Finish code (1–4)	2	FINISH PIC 99
Price	3–6	PRICE PIC 99V99

The following assumptions can be made about this file:
1. All codes are within the allowable ranges.
2. Th.ere is one record for each finish and style;
   thus, there are exactly 24 records.

Write the simplest possible set of PROCEDURE DIVISION statements to load the table.

5. Define a fixed table that contains the number and name of each month, beginning with January. In addition, the Julian day for the beginning and ending day of each month are to be included. For example, January starts with 01 and ends with 031; February starts with 032 and ends with 059 (assume Februrary has 28 days). The table name is to be MONTH-TABLE and the field names are MONTH-NBR, MONTH-NAME, MONTH-BEG-DAY, and MONTH-END-DAY. Set up an index for accessing the table entries.

6. Assuming that the value in MONTH-NBR-IN is to be used as a search argument against the table in Exercise 5, how would you code a SEARCH statement in the PROCEDURE DIVISION to obtain all three junctions in the table?

Programming Assignments

Programming assignments in this and following chapters use data files. For the record description of all files used in the assignments, you must use Appendix A.

14-1 Student List With Majors

The dean of students at the Computer Institute of Technology wants a list of students with their majors. The major must be obtain from a table based on the major field code in the student file. (*Note:* This assignment is a variation of Assignment 9-3.)

Output Requirements:
A printed report with the following output and format.

Input Description:
> File name: STUDENTS.DL
> Record description: See Appendix A
> Major table:

Code	Major
ACT	Accounting
ANT	Anthropology
EDU	Education
BIO	Biology
BUS	Business Admin
CHE	Chemistry
CIS	Computer Info Sys
CRI	Criminal Justice
ECO	Economics
ENG	English
FIN	Finance
FOR	Forestry
GEO	Geology
HIS	History
HOR	Horticulture
MAR	Marketing
MAT	Mathematics
MUS	Music
PHI	Philosophy
PED	Physical Education
PHY	Physics
POL	Political Science
PSY	Psychology
SOC	Sociology
UND	Undeclared

Processing Requirements for Each Order to be Entered:
> For each input record:
> 1. Look up the Major description, using the Major code from the input record.
> 2. If the Major code is found, insert the Major description in the output line; otherwise, insert INVALID CODE.
> 3. Print the report line.

14-2 Employee List With Tax-Sheltered Annuities

The payroll manager of Donut Manufacturing needs a report listing the tax-sheltered annuity company for each employee and the number of employees selecting each annuity company. The names of the TSA companies are contained in a table of codes and names.

Output Requirements:
> A printed report with the output and format shown in the printer chart on the next page.

```
         0         1         2         3         4         5         6         7         8
1234567890123456789012345678901234567890123456789012345678901234567890123456789012345

Z9/99/99                    DONUT MANUFACTURING COMPANY                        Page ZZ
                         TAX-SHELTERED ANNUITY SUMMARY

                                                        Tax-Sheltered Annuity
                                        Gross
Soc Sec Num   Employee Name             Pay        Deduction     Company

XXX-XX-XXXX X————————————————X Z,ZZZ.99    ZZZ.99   X————————————————X
XXX-XX-XXXX X————————————————X Z,ZZZ.99    ZZZ.99   X————————————————X


TAX-SHELTERED ANNUITY
COMPANY COUNT

Company              Count

X————————X           Z9
X————————X           Z9
```

Note that this report consists of two parts. The first part is a detailed line-per-record printout of the file (including the TSA company name from the table lookup). The second part, which is to begin on a new page, is a summary of the number of employees enrolled in the program of each TSA company.

Input Description:

File name: EMPLOYEE.DL

Record description: See Appendix A

Code	Company Name
AA	All-American Investments
AF	Aloha Funds
AX	Ayxa
BO	Boise Fund
DR	Dravel Fund
FM	Fresno Mutual
HF	High-Flyers Mutual
HL	Hotline Investments
LF	Low-Flyers Investment
LS	Lincoln High Flyers
OE	Orient Express Fund
OR	Orinda Mutual
S2	So-Shall Securities II
SF	Soyanora Funds
SS	Safe and Sound
SS	So-Shall Securities
TB	Tres Bien
TI	Titanic Conservative
UI	USA Tomorrow Investments
UP	Unprudent Investments
WI	Winnemucca General

Processing Requirements for Each Order to be Entered:
> For each input record:
> 1. Look up the Company name, using the Tax-sheltered annuity code from the input record.
> 2. If the annuity code is found, insert the company name description in the output line; otherwise, insert INVALID CODE.
> 3. Count the occurrence for this company.
> 4. Print the report line.
>
> Table definition suggestion: In defining the TSA company table, include three columns: the code, the name, and a numeric element to be used for tallying.

14-3 Voters and Party Affiliation

The way in which the VOTERS file is being used by the For-Everything Political Action Committee has changed in that the Party-of-registration field no longer necessarily represents a political party. To provide flexibility, this field (which indicates some type of group affiliation) is stored on disk as a table so that it can be accessed by any program processing the file.

Output Requirements:
> A printed report with the following output.
>
> Name
> City
> State
> Annual income
> Group affiliation
>
> The report must include appropriate heading lines with page numbering. Group affiliation is to be obtained from a table by using the Party of registration code field from the input record. Detail lines are to be double-spaced.

Input Description:
> File name: VOTERS.DL
> Table file name: GROUPS.DLT
> Record descriptions: See Appendix A

Processing Requirements for Each Order to be Entered:
> 1. Read and load the groups table from the file.
>
> For each input record:
> 2. Look up the Group name, using the Party of registration code from the input record.
> 3. If the Party of registration code is found, insert the Group name in the output line; otherwise, insert INVALID CODE.
> 4. Print the report line.

14-4 Summarizing Enrollment Statistics

The dean of instruction at the Computer Institute of Technology would like a statistical summary of enrollment. He wants a program that, for each class, will calculate Actual enrollment as a percentage of Minimum permissible enrollment. These results must be tabulated as illustrated by the following example:

00-04	3
05-09	6
10-14	7
.	.
.	.
.	.
95-99	47
100	77

This example indicates that there are 3 classes with enrollments in the 0 to 4% range, 6 in the 5% to 9% range, and so on. Also, there are 77 classes with Actual enrollments that are 100% or more of the Minimum permissible enrollment.

Output Requirements:
A screen display of the tabulation. Include appropriate descriptions.

Input Description:
File name: ENROLL01.DL
Record description: See Appendix A

Processing Requirements:
For each input record:
1. Calculate the percent enrollment as:

$$= \frac{\text{Actual enrollment}}{\text{Minimum permissible enrollment}} \times 100$$

Round the result to the nearest whole number.
2. Tally the appropriate accumulator

After the last record is read:
3. Display the table of counts

Programming Tip:
Your counters can be set up as an array (for instance, ENROLL-TALLY). Then ENROLL-TALLY(1) will be the counter for the 0-4 range, ENROLL-TALLY(2) will be the counter for the 5-9 range, and so on. With some ingenuity, you can calculate the needed subscript. Consider the following:

Range 0-4 $\qquad \dfrac{0}{5} = 0 \qquad \dfrac{4}{5} = 0$

Range 5-9 $\qquad \dfrac{5}{5} = 1 \qquad \dfrac{9}{5} = 1$

Range 10-14 $\qquad \dfrac{10}{5} = 2 \qquad \dfrac{14}{5} = 2$

You can see that the result of integer division gives a quotient that is one less that the desired subscript value.

15

SORTING IN COBOL

Outline

- **The Concept of Sorting**
  Introduction
  Sorting by Computer

- **COBOL Sort Feature**
  Coding the Sort Feature—Example 15-1
  A Simple Sort Program—Example 15-1
  The ENVIRONMENT DIVISION
  The DATA DIVISION
  PROCEDURE DIVISION Coding

- **Sort Sequence and Sort Keys**
  Sort Sequence
  The Collating Sequence
  Sort Keys

- **Using an Input Procedure with the Sort**
  About Input Procedures
  Example Definition—Example 15-2
  Program Solution—Example 15-2
  The RECORD CONTAINS Clause
  The SORT Statement
  The Input Procedure

- **Using an Output Procedure with the Sort**
  About Output Procedures
  Example Definition—Example 15-3
  Program Solution—Example 15-3

- **Restrictions on the Sort Prior to COBOL-85**
  Using Sections in the PROCEDURE DIVISION
  A Pre-1985 Sort Program

- **Sorting Data in Memory**
  A Simple Sort Algorithm
  A Program to Sort the Area-Code Table

Chapter Objectives

As you recall, Examples 13-2 and 13-3 illustrate group total processing. To perform the group total operations, the data file must be in order by the stock number. This chapter illustrates the COBOL sort feature for sorting files. From this chapter, you will learn about the following topics:

■ Basic principles of and the need for sorting

■ The concepts of character coding and the collating sequence, whereby characters of the character set are ranked relative to one another

■ The SORT verb, which allows you to make a copy of a file with the records in sequence based on one or more key fields

■ How to sort information in a table

The Concept of Sorting

Introduction

The concept of sequence, or order, is so familiar that it is easy to overlook it completely. We assume that data will naturally be in order—the phone book by last name, the calendar by date within week within month, the team roster in the football program by player number, the class schedule by section within course within department, and so on.

COBOL allows you to use indexed files so that you can access a file through the index as if the data file itself were in sequence on the key field. Because of the versatility of indexed files, the indexed file organization is widely used. However, in certain applications, the added overhead is undesirable or an indexed file simply is not practical, so the sequential organization is used. For most applications, though, it is important that records of the file be in some type of sequence. You saw this need in Chapter 13, where the records of the file were in sequence based on the stock number so that group totals could be calculated by vendor. Situations commonly occur in which a sequential file must be in placed in a particular order for one type of processing, but in another order for a different type of processing.

To illustrate, assume that a career counselor works with students from several high schools. For each student, a 5 × 7" information card is maintained with the student's name, high school code, and other information. For the sake of convenience in quickly finding the card of a given student, the counselor keeps the cards in alphabetical order, as shown in Figure 15-1(a). Periodically, the counselor prepares a report summarizing the results of each school's students. To work from the file of Figure 15-1(a) would be very clumsy because the cards are not grouped by high school. However, if the cards are rearranged so that they are in sequence by high school code, as shown in Figure 15-1(b), the task is much easier. The process of rearranging the cards into another sequence is called *sorting*; it is one of the most basic operations in data processing.

In addition to sequencing, the sorting operation *groups* data. Once the data items are in sequence, then naturally all identical items are grouped together. The set of cards in Figure 15-1(b) contains two cards for high school 087, two cards for high school 125, and two cards for high school 749. These cards are separated from each other when the file is in alphabetical sequence. However, when the file has been sorted into sequence by high school code, cards with the same number are grouped, or placed together, in the file. This concept is not new to you since it is precisely the principle around which group total concepts revolve.

As a further illustration, consider the case of a computer repair technician who has 20 different clients. A typical day might involve three hours of working for one client, two for another and five for a third. To keep track of the amount of time spent for each client, the technician fills out a work form with the client number and amount of time worked that day for the client. At the end of each day, the forms are placed in a file. By the end of the month, the file would appear as in Figure 15-2(a), where you notice that the work forms for any given client are spread throughout the file. When it comes time to prepare bills for each client, this file is not convenient to use. The cards are in ascending order by date

Figure 15-1

File Sequences

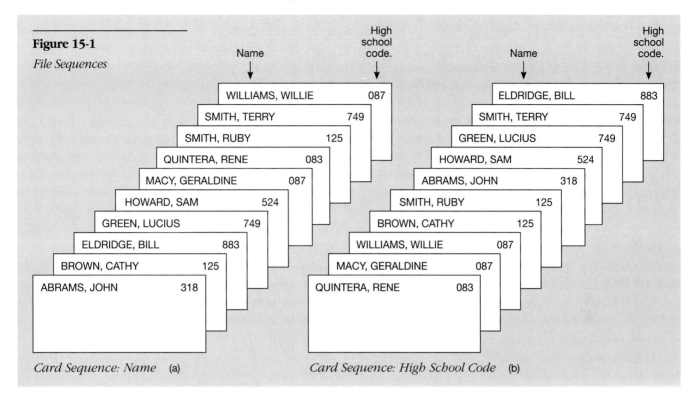

Card Sequence: Name (a)

Card Sequence: High School Code (b)

worked, which is not a meaningful sequence for customer billing. However, observe the result shown in Figure 15-2(b) when the file has been sorted by client number. In this example, sorting the records on client number places them in a meaningful sequence for processing. The sequence is meaningful because

1. The records are grouped so that all of each client's forms are together and can be processed together

2. The records are in sequence so that they can be combined with a file of customer master records in the same sequence when preparing the customer bills

Figure 15-2

Sorting with Grouping

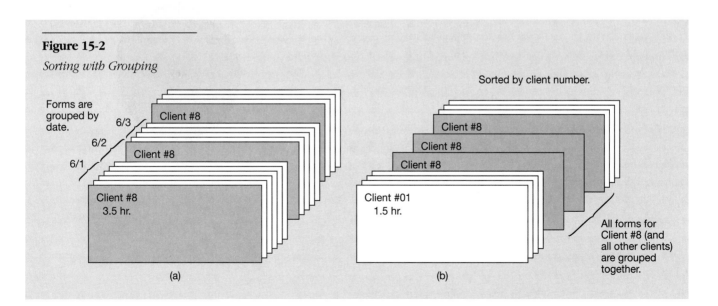

(a)

(b)

Operations of this type are so common in data processing that most computer systems include a generalized, simple-to-use sort routine as a part of the system software. Most of them can be used to sort data into any desired sequence. In addition, COBOL compilers allow the sort program to be used as a part of a COBOL program. This is known as the *COBOL Sort Feature*, and its use is discussed in this chapter.

Sorting by Computer

When cards of the counselor or the technician are sorted, they are actually rearranged into the new sequence; once in the new sequence, they are obviously not in the old sequence. You see this in Figure 15-1(a), where the cards have been placed in student name sequence. To prepare the high school summary report, the counselor must resort the cards into the high school code sequence. However, once the sort has been completed, the cards are no longer in sequence by student name. To put them back in sequence by student name would require another time-consuming sort, and so on. However, if the file is computerized and stored on disk, you have far more flexibility. Then the records of the original file can be copied and sorted into another file.

"Normal" processing to which you have become accustomed has one input file and one output file, as illustrated in Figure 15-3(a). On the other hand, sorting with the COBOL sort feature involves three files: an input file, an output file and a special *sort work file* (or simply the *sort file*), as illustrated in Figure 15-3(b). With the sort file, the sorting operation is done in three steps, or phases, as shown in Figure 15-4. When the sorting operation is completed, the input file is still in its original sequence. The output file contains a copy of every record in the input file, but the records are arranged in the desired sequence. The computer accomplishes the sorting operation quickly and accurately by using the sort file for intermediate storage of the data to be sorted.

Figure 15-3

Simple Processing Versus Sorting

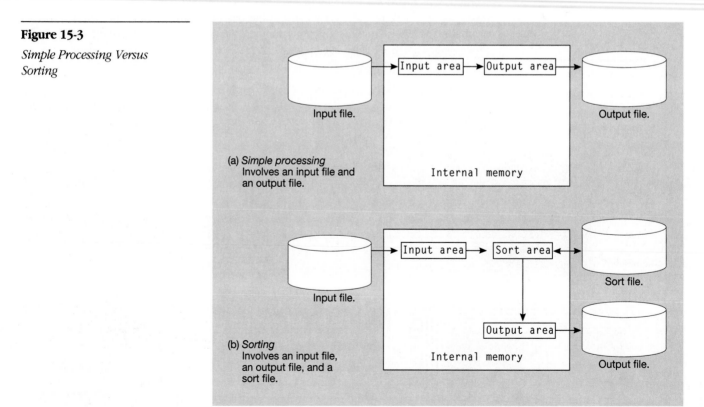

Input file.   Input area → Output area   Output file.

(a) *Simple processing*
Involves an input file and an output file.

Internal memory

Input file.   Input area → Sort area   Sort file.

Output area   Output file.

(b) *Sorting*
Involves an input file, an output file, and a sort file.

Internal memory

Figure 15-4

The Three Phases of Sorting

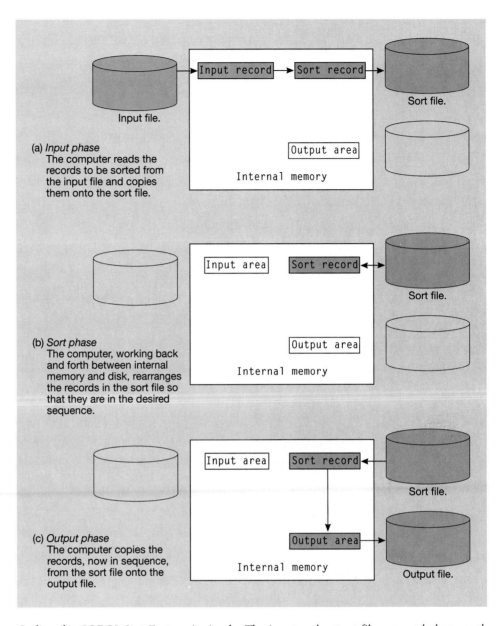

(a) *Input phase*
The computer reads the records to be sorted from the input file and copies them onto the sort file.

(b) *Sort phase*
The computer, working back and forth between internal memory and disk, rearranges the records in the sort file so that they are in the desired sequence.

(c) *Output phase*
The computer copies the records, now in sequence, from the sort file onto the output file.

COBOL Sort Feature

Coding the Sort Feature—Example 15-1

Coding the COBOL Sort Feature is simple. The input and output files are coded as usual; the only additional coding is for the sort file and the sort statement itself. For an example of COBOL sort coding, let's go back to the software inventory file.

Example 15-1 Sorting the Inventory File

Problem Description

The software inventory file SOFTWAR3.DL, which contains one record for each inventory item, is stored in sequence based on the Stock-number. A particular report to be run requires that this file be in sequence on the Software-name field.

Output Requirements

Output file name: SOFTWAR3.DLS
Record format: Same as the input file
Other: Must be in sequence based on the Software-name field

Input Description
Input file name: SOFTWAR3.DL
Record format:

Field	Positions
Not used*	1–5
Software name	6–35
Not used*	36–66

Note: The data in these columns is not used in this application, but the positions must be accounted for in both the input and output record descriptions.

Processing Requirements
Create a new software file that is in sequence based on the Software-name field.

A Simple Sort Program— Example 15-1

If you stopped and thought for a moment about writing a program to sort records of a file, it would become apparent that the logic of such a program would be rather complicated. With this in mind, the program of Figure 15-5 using the COBOL sort feature is astonishingly simple. The coding of each division is described in the following paragraphs.

The ENVIRONMENT DIVISION

As you have learned from the preceding descriptions of sorting (refer to Figure 15-4), the program involves three files: an input file, a sort file, and an output file. Because each file in a program requires a SELECT, the ENVIRONMENT DIVISION of Figure 15-5 includes three SELECTs. As with any other file, the SELECT for the temporary sort file specifies the internal name by which the file is to be referenced in the program and the DOS file name.

```
SELECT SORT-FILE ASSIGN TO DISK, "SORTWORK.TMP".
```

In this SELECT from Figure 15-5, the name SORT-FILE was used for the sort file because it is short and yet descriptive. However, any valid name could have been used. The name of the temporary work file that will be created is SORTWORK.TMP. The name SORTWORK is used because it is descriptive; the extension TMP reminds you that the file is temporary.

The DATA DIVISION

Referring to the DATA DIVISION of Figure 15-5, you see that there is the necessary *File Description* (FD) for each of the input and output files. The equivalent form for the sort file is called the *Sort-File Description* (SD). Coding rules are the same for the SD as for the FD.

Just as each FD must be followed by one or more data-record descriptions (01), so must each SD be followed by one or more sort-record descriptions (01). Depending on circumstances (which will be discussed later), the sort-record description may be the same as the input and/or output descriptions, or it may be different from either or both of them. Because the program in Figure 15-5 is to produce an output file with a record format identical to that of the input file, no field specifications are necessary. Hence, for both of these, the 01 is defined with a PIC X(66), the size of the record itself. However, the sort-record description is a different matter. It must specify the field on which the data is to be sorted. This field is called the *sort key* and it must be defined in the sort-record description. In this example, the records are to be sorted on vendor name, which occupies 30 positions, beginning with position 6. The sort-record description, which is repeated below, defines this field and gives it a name so that the field can be referenced in the PROCEDURE DIVISION.

```
01  SORT-RECORD.
    10                          PIC X(5).
    10  SR-SOFTWARE-NAME        PIC X(30).
    10                          PIC X(31).
```

Figure 15-5

A Sorting Program—
Example 15-1

```
1        IDENTIFICATION DIVISION.
2
3        PROGRAM-ID.  S-SORT.
4
5     *     Written by J.Olson  7/10/86
6     *     Modified by W.Price 8/31/90
7
8     *     A simple SORT program with USING and GIVING to
9     *     sort the SOFTWARE file on the Software-Name field.
10
11       ENVIRONMENT DIVISION.
12
13       CONFIGURATION SECTION.
14       SOURCE-COMPUTER.  IBM-PC.
15
16       INPUT-OUTPUT SECTION.
17       FILE-CONTROL.
18           SELECT INVENTORY-FILE          ASSIGN TO DISK, "SOFTWAR3.DL",
19                                           ORGANIZATION IS LINE SEQUENTIAL.
20           SELECT SORT-FILE               ASSIGN TO DISK, "SORTWORK.TMP".
21           SELECT SORTED-INVENTORY-FILE ASSIGN TO DISK, "SOFTWAR3.DLS",
22                                           ORGANIZATION IS LINE SEQUENTIAL.
23
24       DATA DIVISION.
25
26       FILE SECTION.
27
28       FD  INVENTORY-FILE.
29       01  INVENTORY-RECORD          PIC X(66).
30
31       SD  SORT-FILE.
32       01  SORT-RECORD.
33           10                        PIC X(5).
34           10  SR-SOFTWARE-NAME      PIC X(30).
35           10                        PIC X(31).
36
37       FD  SORTED-INVENTORY-FILE.
38       01  SORTED-INVENTORY-RECORD   PIC X(66).
39
40       PROCEDURE DIVISION.
41       000-SORT-INVEN-SOFTWARE-NAME.
42           SORT SORT-FILE
43               ON ASCENDING KEY SR-SOFTWARE-NAME
44               USING INVENTORY-FILE
45               GIVING SORTED-INVENTORY-FILE
46           STOP RUN.
```

PROCEDURE DIVISION Coding

The sort file, which was defined in the ENVIRONMENT DIVISION and described in the DATA DIVISION, is used in the PROCEDURE DIVISION. Interestingly, the PROCEDURE DIVISION of this program consists of only two statements: SORT and STOP RUN. The SORT statement shown in Figure 15-6 provides four items of information:

1. The name of the sort file, identified by:

    SORT SORT-FILE

2. The name of the field on which the records are to be sorted, identified by:

    ON ASCENDING KEY SR-SOFTWARE-NAME

3. The name of the input data file, identified by:

    USING INVENTORY-FILE

4. The name of the output data file, identified by:

    GIVING SORTED-INVENTORY-FILE

Figure 15-6

The Sort Statement

```
SORT SORT-FILE ◄─────────────────── Name of the sort file.
                                     The key field upon which
ON ASCENDING KEY SR-SOFTWARE-NAME ◄── sorting is to be done
                                     (defined in the sort file).
USING INVENTORY-FILE ◄───────────── The input file.

GIVING SORTED-INVENTORY-FILE ◄────── The output file.
```

Glance at the PROCEDURE DIVISION of Figure 15-5; you do not see much more than the SORT statement itself. There are no statements such as OPEN, CLOSE, READ, MOVE, and so on. The SORT statement causes *all* of these operations to occur. In this example, the SORT does the following:

1. Opens INVENTORY-FILE and SORT-FILE

2. Reads the records from INVENTORY-FILE and copies them into SORT-FILE

3. Closes INVENTORY-FILE

4. Rearranges the records in SORT-FILE so that they are in ascending sequence by the field called SR-SOFTWARE-NAME

5. Opens SORTED-INVENTORY-FILE

6. Copies the sorted records from SORT-FILE to SORTED-INVENTORY-FILE

7. Closes SORTED-INVENTORY-FILE and SORT-FILE

This is indeed a powerful statement.

Sort Sequence and Sort Keys

Sort Sequence

From your earlier studies, you know that an ascending sequence is one in which items are arranged from the smallest through the largest. For instance, the first of the following ascending sequences is numeric and the second is alphabetic:

251, 289, 292, 311, 322, 323,...

ALBERTS, ALLEN, BAKER, BASS, BENDER,...

But how is it that you know one field is larger than another, especially if you are dealing with alphabetic rather than numeric quantities? The mathematician's answer would involve the concept of ordered sets. A set is simply a collection of things; if the set is ordered, these things have a predetermined relationship to one another. The two most common examples of ordered sets are the alphabet—where A precedes and Z follows all other elements of the set—and the digits, which have the sequencing 0 through 9.

In these terms, an ascending sequence is an arrangement of quantities in which the smallest is first and the largest is last, according to the rules of the particular ordered set involved. Although the ascending-sequence concept is most commonly encountered, it is sometimes helpful and necessary to place data in a *descending* sequence—one that begins with the largest value and ends with the smallest. In both of the following examples, the data is more meaningful because it is in descending sequence based on the second column:

Honor Roll		**The Nation's Hot Spots**	
Jones, John	4.0	Phoenix	104
Sanchez, Maria	4.0	Tucson	103
Baily, Rhonda	3.8	Albuquerque	101
Jones, Sam	3.7	New Orleans	101
Adams, Jim	3.5	Des Moines	100

The COBOL sort feature can sort data into either ascending or descending sequence. The programmer simply specifies ON ASCENDING KEY or ON DESCENDING KEY in the SORT statement, and the data will be sorted into the specified sequence.

The Collating Sequence

A question seldom arises about sequence when working with a single ordered set, such as the alphabet or the digits. But what happens when you combine two sets? Do letters come before digits, or digits before letters? Is a blank space higher or lower than a letter? And where do the special characters, such as dashes, slashes, commas, and periods come in Surprisingly enough, there is no one answer to these questions for all computer models; the answers vary according to the computer being considered.

The basic unit of storage in the internal memories of most modern computers is the *8-bit byte.* (The word *bit* is a contraction of *b*inary *d*igit, which can assume either a value of 0 or 1.) When each computer is first designed, a decision is made regarding which configuration of bits will be used to represent each of the characters in the character set. Two major codes are in use today: ASCII (American Standard Code for Information Interchange), and EBCDIC (Extended Binary Coded Decimal Interchange Code). ASCII is used in virtually all personal computers, including the IBM PC. EBCDIC is used on IBM full-scale computers. Unfortunately, the codes are entirely different. For instance, in ASCII, the codes for the letters A and F and the digit 5 have equivalent decimal values of 65, 70, and 53. In EBCDIC, the equivalent decimal values for the codes of the same characters are 193, 198, and 245. These equivalent decimal values determine the relative ranking of each character; they represent the *collating sequence* for the character set.

Referring to the preceding example values, you can see that in ASCII the digits have a lower ranking than the letters, but in EBCDIC the opposite is true. In fact, the collating sequence for these two codes rank the space, letters, and digits as follows:

ASCII   Space, 0-9, A-Z a-z
EBCDIC   Space, a-z, A-Z, 0-9

To illustrate the problem relating to sorting, consider the following set of data when sorted using the ASCII collating sequence (for instance, on the IBM PC):

Unsorted Data	Sorted in Ascending Sequence
DiMarco	DiMarco
Dimsdale III	Dimsdale
Dimsdale	Dimsdale 3rd
Dimsdale 3rd	Dimsdale III

However, if the same data is sorted using the EBCDIC collating sequence (for instance, on an IBM mainframe computer), the result would be

Unsorted Data	Sorted in Ascending Sequence
DiMarco	Dimsdale
Dimsdale III	Dimsdale III
Dimsdale	Dimsdale 3rd
Dimsdale 3rd	DiMarco

This example illustrates to a certain extent the difference between collating sequences in different computers, but it does not include special characters that differ even more. Thus, although the COBOL language may be standard, collating sequences are not. This is a factor to consider if a particular installation does some processing on a PC and other processing on a mainframe.

Sort Keys

Up to this point, the discussion has centered on a file being sorted on one control field. In many instances, it is desirable to sort on several fields (such as name within department number, or city code within county code within state code). The COBOL sort feature provides this necessary flexibility by permitting multiple sort key fields to be specified. If more than one key field is to be used, the most significant one is listed first, followed by the next most significant, and so on, ending with the least significant field. In the example "city code within county code within state code," the records are to be arranged primarily by state code. Within each state code, they are to be in sequence by county code, and within each county code they are to be in sequence by city code. In this case, the SORT statement might appear as follows:

```
SORT  SORT-FILE
    ON ASCENDING KEY STATE-CODE, COUNTY-CODE, CITY-CODE
    USING INPUT-FILE
    GIVING OUTPUT-FILE
```

Because the words ON and KEY are optional, this statement can also be written as

```
SORT  SORT-FILE
    ASCENDING STATE-CODE, COUNTY-CODE, CITY-CODE
    USING INPUT-FILE
    GIVING OUTPUT-FILE
```

In both cases, you see that the most significant field (STATE-CODE) is listed first, and the least significant field (CITY-CODE) is listed last.

You have already learned that the SORT statement can sort data into either ascending or descending sequence. The COBOL Sort Feature permits the ascending and descending specifications to be applied to *each individual* sort key field if desired. The words ASCENDING or DESCENDING apply to all of the key fields following until another ASCENDING or DESCENDING is encountered. Each of the examples in Figure 15-7 involves printing a list of students, as required by a college. Included is a description of the needed sequencing, an example sequence, and the KEY clause that would be required in the SORT statement. Note that in Examples 3 and 4, the optional words ON and KEY are omitted.

With these examples in mind, the logical question is, "How many key fields can be handled by SORT?" The answer is that the number of sort key fields and the total number of characters that they may contain will vary from compiler to compiler, but the capacity is usually more than sufficient. For example, the RM/COBOL-85 sort permits a maximum of 12 sort key fields and 256 bytes of key field information.

Using an Input Procedure with the Sort

About Input Procedures

When the SORT statement executes the input phase, it causes the computer to read the records to be sorted from the input file, one record at a time, and copy them into the sort file. No processing of any kind is done to the records as they are transferred from the input file to the sort file. However, it is often desirable to do some type of processing during the input phase, such as editing for validity so that invalid records can be rejected and only the valid ones sorted, or reformatting the records so that the sort record contains only the necessary data for the job to be done. The SORT statement permits such processing by allowing the programmer to replace the USING clause in the SORT statement with the name of an input procedure that is to be performed. The following is an example of the SORT statement that includes the use of an input procedure:

```
SORT SORT-FILE
    ON ASCENDING KEY CUSTOMER-NUMBER
    INPUT PROCEDURE IS INPUT-EDIT
    GIVING PRINT-FILE.
```

In preceding examples, which include the USING clause, the SORT statement automatically opens, reads, copies, and closes the input file. When an input procedure is used, these functions become the programmer's responsibility. Thus, these operations must be done by the input procedure. In the preceding example, it is INPUT-EDIT, which is simply the name of a paragraph containing the statements to be executed. That is, during execution of the SORT, the specified procedure will be executed as if a PERFORM statement were used.

Figure 15-7

Multiple-Level Sorting

1. Desired sequencing: Records are to be arranged within the high-school-of-graduation code.

```
001 CENTRAL HIGH
  ADAMS, CHARLES
    .
    .
002 SUNNYSIDE HIGH
  ABRAMS, JANE
  AVRO, JOHN
  BAKER, THOMAS
  BAUM, MARTHA
  BLACK, SUSAN
    .
    .
003 JUNIPER HIGH
  ADLER, MORTON
    .
    .
```

Use the following KEY clause:

```
ON ASCENDING KEY HIGH-SCHOOL-CODE, STUDENT-NAME
```

2. Records are to be arranged by cumulative grade point average (GPA) in descending sequence. Within GPA, names are to be in alphabetic order.

```
4.0 GPA
  BAKER, THOMAS
  CHARLES, ANNETTE
  FRANKLIN, JOHN
  KNOWLAND, BETTY
3.9 GPA
  ANDERSON, ANNE
    .
    .
```

Use the following KEY clause:

```
ON DESCENDING KEY CUM-GPA
    ASCENDING KEY  STUDENT-NAME
```

3. The sequencing of Example 2 is to be modified to list all females first, followed by all males. The sex code in the student record is

         F   Female
         M   Male

```
4.0 GPA
  CHARLES, ANNETTE   F
  KNOWLAND, BETTY    F
3.9 GPA
    .
    .
2.0 GPA
    .
    .
4.0 GPA
  BAKER, THOMAS      M
  FRANKLIN, JOHN     M
    .
    .
```

Use the following KEY clause:

```
ASCENDING   SEX-CODE
DESCENDING  CUM-GPA
ASCENDING   STUDENT-NAME
```

4. The sequencing of Example 2 is to be modified to list all females first, followed by all males. The gender code in the student record is

         1   Female
         2   Male

```
4.0 GPA
  CHARLES, ANNETTE   2
  KNOWLAND, BETTY    2
3.9 GPA
    .
    .
2.0 GPA
    .
    .
4.0 GPA
  BAKER, THOMAS      1
  FRANKLIN, JOHN     1
    .
    .
```

Use the following KEY clause:

```
DESCENDING SEX-CODE
           CUM-GPA
ASCENDING  STUDENT-NAME
```

Figure 15-8

Linkage Concepts with the SORT

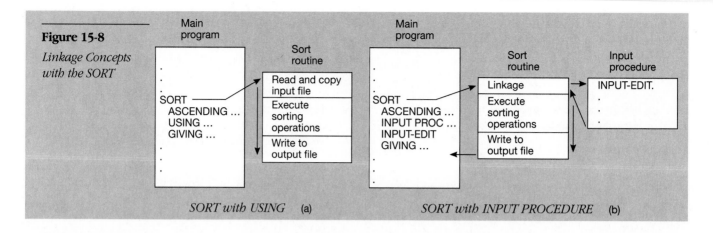

SORT with USING (a)   SORT with INPUT PROCEDURE (b)

Example Definition—Example 15-2

The sequence that takes place when executing a SORT statement is illustrated in Figure 15-8. As you can see, the SORT effectively executes a PERFORM input procedure, thus establishing the standard linkage for "going and returning." This means that the programmer must ensure that the program reaches the physical end of the input procedure, rather than ending somewhere in the middle of it. (This may seem obvious, but it is an easy mistake to make, and care must be taken to avoid it.) Use of an input procedure in a program is illustrated by Example 15-2.

Example 15-2 Using an Input Procedure

Problem Description

Each transaction record of a petroleum company is recorded into one record; the collection of these records is stored in the billing file. This file includes records of two types: sales records and payment records. The file must be sorted by customer number and record type.

Output Requirements

Output file name: BILLFILE.DL

Record format:

Field	Positions	Format
Record type	1	
Customer number	2–11	
Date of payment	12–16	$nnn_\wedge nn$

Input Description

Input file name: BILLING.DL

Record format:

Sales record—Record type = "S"

Field	Positions	Format
Record type	1	
Dealer identification	2–6	
Customer number	7–16	
Date of sale	17–22	
Product code	23–25	
Quantity sold	26–28	$nn_\wedge n$
Amount of sale	29–33	$nn_\wedge nn$

Payment record—Record type = "P"

Field	Positions	Format
Record type	1	
Customer number	2–11	
Date of payment	12–17	
Amount of payment	18–22	$nnn_\wedge nn$

Processing Requirements

1. The output file must be in sequence by customer number and within each customer number. Within each customer group, the sales records must be first and the payment records next.
2. Each record in the output file will be 16 positions long and will consist of
     Record identification
     Customer number
     Amount of transaction
3. Any record with a record identification other than "S" or "P" should be ignored.

Program Solution— Example 15-2

The input procedure for this example will represent most of the program structure and logic. Similar to previous programs in this book, it will involve relatively simple read-process-write actions. Hence, the input procedure will include the following actions:

1. Open the billing file (the input file) and read the first record

2. Process each record:
     move input fields to sort record area
     release (write) the sort record to the sort file
     read the next record

3. Close the billing file

The input procedure for the example involves two operations commonly encountered by the programmer. The first is editing for validity—that is, rejecting records with an invalid type code. The second is reformatting—or extracting data from two different input formats to create a sort record with a completely different format. The actions of this portion of the procedure will be

     Evaluate record type of input record
     When "S" move sales data to sort record
          release (write) sort record to sort work file
     When "P" move payment information to sort record
          release (write) sort record to sort work file
     When other display invalid record

The complete program is shown in Figure 15-9. Items of interest about this program are

■ Definition of the input record using the RECORD CONTAINS clause

■ The SORT statement

■ Interfacing between the SORT statement and the input procedure

■ The RELEASE statement

The RECORD CONTAINS Clause

The input file for this example includes a feature that you have not encountered until now: it contains records with two different formats and record lengths. The record length of the sales record is 30 and that of the payment record is 22. For this, entries in the DATA DIVISION must provide the compiler with two pieces of information: the sizes of the records and their formats. The FD of BILLING-FILE identifies the lengths with the RECORD CONTAINS clause in this way:

```
FD BILLING-FILE    RECORD CONTAINS 22 TO 33 CHARACTERS.
```

Figure 15-9

*A Sample Program for
Example 15-2*

```
1      IDENTIFICATION DIVISION.                                        55      PROCEDURE DIVISION.
2                                                                      56
3      PROGRAM-ID.  I-SORT.                                            57      000-SORT-BILLING-FILE.
4                                                                      58          SORT SORT-FILE
5      *   A sort program with an Input Procedure and a GIVING.        59              ON ASCENDING   KEY SR-CUSTOMER-NUMBER
6                                                                      60                 DESCENDING KEY SR-RECORD-TYPE
7      *    Written by J.Olson  7/10/86                                61              INPUT PROCEDURE IS SIP-000-REFORMAT-INPUT
8      *    Modified by W.Price 8/31/90                                62              GIVING BILL-FILE
9                                                                      63          STOP RUN.
10     ENVIRONMENT DIVISION.                                           64
11                                                                     65      * Sort Input Procedure (SIP)
12     CONFIGURATION SECTION.                                          66
13     SOURCE-COMPUTER.  IBM-PC.                                       67      SIP-000-REFORMAT-INPUT.
14                                                                     68          PERFORM SIP-100-INITIALIZE.
15     INPUT-OUTPUT SECTION.                                           69          PERFORM SIP-110-PROCESS-1-RECORD
16     FILE-CONTROL.                                                   70              UNTIL END-OF-BILLING-FILE
17         SELECT BILLING-FILE    ASSIGN TO DISK, "BILLING.DL",        71          PERFORM SIP-120-FINALIZE.
18                                ORGANIZATION IS LINE SEQUENTIAL.     72
19         SELECT SORT-FILE       ASSIGN TO DISK, "SORTWORK.TMP".      73      SIP-100-INITITALIZE.
20         SELECT BILL-FILE       ASSIGN TO DISK, "BILLFILE.DL",       74          OPEN INPUT BILLING-FILE
21                                ORGANIZATION IS LINE SEQUENTIAL.     75          SET END-OF-BILLING-FILE TO FALSE
22                                                                     76          PERFORM SIP-800-READ-BILLING-RECORD.
23     DATA DIVISION.                                                  77
24                                                                     78      SIP-110-PROCESS-1-RECORD.
25     FILE SECTION.                                                   79          EVALUATE SA-RECORD-TYPE
26                                                                     80              WHEN "S"
27     FD  BILLING-FILE           RECORD CONTAINS 22 TO 30 CHARACTERS. 81                  PERFORM SIP-720-ASSEMBLE-RELEASE-SALE
28     01  SALES-RECORD.                                               82              WHEN "P"
29         10  SA-RECORD-TYPE        PIC X(1).                         83                  PERFORM SIP-730-ASSEMBLE-RELEASE-PAY
30         10  SA-DEALER-ID          PIC X(5).                         84              WHEN OTHER
31         10  SA-CUSTOMER-NUMBER    PIC X(10).                        85                  DISPLAY "Invalid Record: ", SALES-RECORD
32         10  SA-DATE-OF-SALE       PIC X(6).                         86          END-EVALUATE
33         10  SA-QUANTITY-SOLD      PIC 99V9.                         87          PERFORM SIP-800-READ-BILLING-RECORD.
34         10  SA-MONEY-AMOUNT       PIC 9(3)V99.                      88
35     01  PAYMENT-RECORD.                                             89      SIP-120-FINALIZE.
36         10  PA-RECORD-TYPE        PIC X(1).                         90          CLOSE BILLING-FILE
37         10  PA-CUSTOMER-NUMBER    PIC X(10).                        91          DISPLAY "End of Input Procedure"
38         10  PA-DATE-OF-PAYMENT    PIC X(6).                         92          DISPLAY SPACES.
39         10  PA-MONEY-AMOUNT       PIC 9(3)V99.                      93
40                                                                     94      SIP-720-ASSEMBLE-RELEASE-SALE.
41     SD  SORT-FILE.                                                  95          MOVE SA-RECORD-TYPE     TO SR-RECORD-TYPE
42     01  SORT-RECORD.                                                96          MOVE SA-CUSTOMER-NUMBER TO SR-CUSTOMER-NUMBER
43         10  SR-RECORD-TYPE        PIC X(1).                         97          MOVE SA-MONEY-AMOUNT    TO SR-MONEY-AMOUNT
44         10  SR-CUSTOMER-NUMBER    PIC X(10).                        98          PERFORM SIP-850-RELEASE-TO-SORT-RECORD.
45         10  SR-MONEY-AMOUNT       PIC 9(3)V99.                      99
46                                                                     100     SIP-730-ASSEMBLE-RELEASE-PAY.
47     FD  BILL-FILE.                                                  101         MOVE PA-RECORD-TYPE     TO SR-RECORD-TYPE
48     01  BILL-RECORD            PIC X(16).                           102         MOVE PA-CUSTOMER-NUMBER TO SR-CUSTOMER-NUMBER
49                                                                     103         MOVE PA-MONEY-AMOUNT    TO SR-MONEY-AMOUNT
50     WORKING-STORAGE SECTION.                                        104         PERFORM SIP-850-RELEASE-TO-SORT-RECORD.
51     01  PROGRAMMED-SWITCHES.                                        105
52         10                     PIC X.                              106     SIP-800-READ-BILLING-RECORD.
53             88  END-OF-BILLING-FILE VALUE "Y" FALSE "N".           107         READ BILLING-FILE
54                                                                     108             AT END SET END-OF-BILLING-FILE TO TRUE
                                                                       109         END-READ.
                                                                       110
                                                                       111     SIP-850-RELEASE-TO-SORT-RECORD.
                                                                       112         RELEASE SORT-RECORD.
```

Following the FD are two record descriptions, one for the sales record and the other for the payment record. Note that these do *not* cause two input areas to be created; they simply provide two different means to refer to the data in the input area. When two records are defined under an FD, the second (and succeeding ones) can be considered as implicit redefinitions of the input area. Because the record type is in the first position for each of these records, referring to SA-RECORD-TYPE (defined under SALE-RECORD) is exactly the same as referring to PA-RECORD-TYPE (defined under PAYMENT-RECORD).

The SORT Statement

Following is the SORT statement from this program:

```
SORT SORT-FILE
    ON ASCENDING KEY SR-CUSTOMER-NUMBER
        DESCENDING KEY SR-RECORD-TYPE
    INPUT PROCEDURE IS SIP-000-REFORMAT-INPUT
    GIVING BILL-FILE
STOP RUN.
```

You can see that the sort sequence first identifies the major field SR-CUSTOMER-NUMBER for ascending sequence. Because the sales records (type "S") are to precede the payment records (type "P"), the minor sort field SR-RECORD-TYPE is designated for descending sequence (this way, "S" precedes "P").

In place of the USING to designate the input file to the sort (as in Example 15-1), the INPUT PROCEDURE clause designates the procedure that will make the input file data available to the sort.

The Input Procedure

When the SORT statement with an input procedure is executed, control is transferred to that procedure exactly as if it were executed from a PERFORM. In this case, control is transferred to the module named SIP-000-REFORMAT-INPUT. When execution of this module is completed, control is returned to the SORT statement.

Notice that the sequence of code beginning with this module (line 67) has all the features of a complete program. In order to explicitly identify it as a sort input procedure, each paragraph-name is prefixed with SIP- (indicating Sort Input Procedure). Other than that, paragraph-naming conventions are followed. That is, it has a controlling module numbered 000 and first-level modules numbered 100, 110, and 120. It also has 700 and 800 modules.

Only two features of this overall procedure distinguish it as being related to a SORT statement. First is the absence of a STOP RUN at the end of the SIP-000 module. Remember, this module is the "mainline" module of the input procedure (not the overall program). When its execution is completed, control returns to the SORT statement.

The second is the RELEASE statement in the SIP-850 module. Outputting records to the sort file is done with the RELEASE statement instead of the WRITE statement. The RELEASE is a special statement that is used only in an input procedure and only to write records onto a sort file. It works exactly like the WRITE, except that it has no INVALID KEY clause.

You should beware of one other thing when using an input procedure. The input procedure must *only* be executed by the SORT. Execution should never be transferred in by a PERFORM, nor should the procedure fall in the normal program sequence. For one thing, the RELEASE statement has no meaning unless it is under the control of the SORT statement. For another, amazing things can happen when a program executes in line a routine that was intended to be performed.

Using an Output Procedure with the Sort

About Output Procedures

In the previous section, you saw how an input procedure can be used to process records during the input phase of the sort. From this, it might be inferred that the same thing could be done for the output phase; this is indeed the case. If an output procedure is desired, then the GIVING clause must be replaced with

OUTPUT PROCEDURE IS procedure-name.

This causes the SORT statement to perform the output procedure as the output phase. Coding requirements for the output procedure are similar to those for the input procedure. It must do all the things that the output phase would have done: open the output file, input the sorted records from the sort file, write the desired records on the output file, and close the output file at the completion of the output procedure. Any operations (except sort) that are valid in a "normal" COBOL program are valid in an output procedure. As with an input procedure, the output procedure must be executed by the SORT statement; the program must not PERFORM it or execute it in line.

**Example Definition—
Example 15-3**

For an illustration of an output procedure, let's look at Example 15-3.

Example 15-3 Using an Output Procedure

Problem Description

The petroleum company of Example 15-2 requires a brief detail listing of only the sales records from the billing file. The records are to be sorted on customer number. A summary line is to be included, giving the total sales.

Output Requirements

The output is to be a printed report that includes a summary line of total sales. A printer spacing chart is shown in Figure 15-10.

Input Description

Input file name: BILLING.DL (Same as Example 15-2)

Processing Requirements

1. The report must be in sequence by customer number.
2. For the report, process record type "S" only. Print the customer number and sales amount.
3. At the end of the report, print the total sales.

Although this example could use an input procedure (to select the records for sorting) as well as an output procedure, only an output procedure is used in the sample program. Inclusion of an input procedure is left as an exercise for the end of the chapter.

Figure 15-10

Printer Spacing Chart for Example 15-3

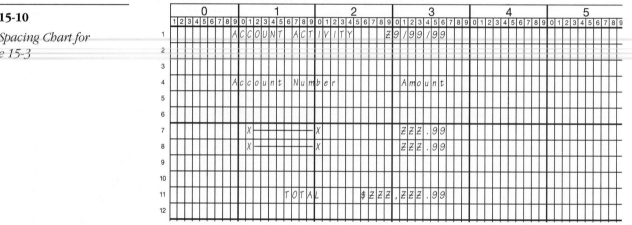

**Program Solution—
Example 15-3**

The output procedure is a fairly simple report generation program. Both its structure and logic are almost identical to those of the RET-VAL2 program in Chapter 9 (see Figures 9-4 through 9-6). The primary difference is that a test is required to determine if a record is to be processed (payment records must be ignored).

The use of an output procedure for performing this task is illustrated in Figure 15-11. The following commentary relates to this program:

1. The SORT automatically reads the input records from BILLING-FILE, sorts them, and places the sorted result in SORT-FILE. The record-name used is SORT-RECORD, which includes a record definition matching the input format. The three fields explicitly defined in SORT-RECORD are required because the sort work file will be processed to create the report.

2. In the sort record "read" module (SOP-800), the records are read from SORT-FILE by the RETURN statement. The RETURN is equivalent to the READ statement, except that it can be used only when reading records from the sort file in an output procedure.

3. Because the sort file is sequential, the last record in the file is an end-of-file record. Therefore, the RETURN statement must include an AT END clause that specifies the operations to be carried out when the end-of-file record is encountered.

Figure 15-11

*Using an Output
Procedure—Example 15-3*

```
 1      IDENTIFICATION DIVISION.
 2
 3      PROGRAM-ID.    O-SORT.
 4
 5      *    A Sort program with USING and an Output Procedure.
 6
 7      *    Written by J.Olson  7/10/86
 8      *    Modified by W.Price 8/31/90
 9
10      ENVIRONMENT DIVISION.
11
12      CONFIGURATION SECTION.
13      SOURCE-COMPUTER. IBM-PC.
14
15      INPUT-OUTPUT SECTION.
16      FILE-CONTROL.
17          SELECT BILLING-FILE      ASSIGN TO DISK, "BILLING.DL",
18                                   ORGANIZATION IS LINE SEQUENTIAL.
19          SELECT SORT-FILE         ASSIGN TO DISK, "SORTWORK.TMP".
20          SELECT REPORT-FILE       ASSIGN TO PRINTER, "PRN-FILE".
21
22      DATA DIVISION.
23
24      FILE SECTION.
25
26      FD  BILLING-FILE       RECORD CONTAINS 22 TO 30 CHARACTERS.
27      01  SALES-RECORD           PIC X(30).
28
29      SD  SORT-FILE.
30      01  SORT-RECORD.
31          10  SR-RECORD-TYPE     PIC X(1).
32          10                     PIC X(5).
33          10  SR-CUSTOMER-NUMBER PIC X(10).
34          10                     PIC X(12).
35          10  SR-MONEY-AMOUNT    PIC 9(3)V9(2).
36
37      FD  REPORT-FILE.
38      01  REPORT-RECORD          PIC X(36).
39
40      WORKING-STORAGE SECTION.
41
42      01  PROGRAMMED-SWITCHES.
43          10                     PIC X.
44              88  END-OF-FILE    VALUE "Y"  FALSE "N".
45
46      01  ACCUMULATORS.
47          10  SALES-TOTAL        PIC 9(6)V99  VALUE ZERO.
48
49      01  PRINT-CONTROL-VARIABLES.
50          10  LINE-SPACING       PIC 9.
51
52      01  RUN-DATE.
53          10  YEAR               PIC 99.
54          10  MONTH              PIC 99.
55          10  WS-DAY             PIC 99.
56
57      01  PAGE-HEADING-LINE.
58          10                     PIC X(8).
59          10                     PIC X(16)    VALUE
60                                              "ACCOUNT ACTIVITY".
61          10                     PIC X(4)     VALUE SPACES.
62          10  PH-MONTH           PIC Z9.
63          10                     PIC X        VALUE "/".
64          10  PH-DAY             PIC 99.
65          10                     PIC X        VALUE "/".
66          10  PH-YEAR            PIC 99.
67
68      01  COLUMN-HEADING-LINE.
69          10                     PIC X(8)     VALUE SPACES.
70          10                     PIC X(22)    VALUE
71                                              "Account Number".
72          10                     PIC X(6)     VALUE "Amount".
73
74      01  SALES-LISTING-RECORD.
75          02                     PIC X(10).
76          02  SL-CUSTOMER-NUMBER PIC X(10).
77          02                     PIC X(10).
78          02  SL-MONEY-AMOUNT    PIC ZZZ.99.
79
80      01  TOTAL-LINE.
81          10                     PIC X(15)    VALUE SPACES.
82          10                     PIC X(10)    VALUE "TOTAL".
83          10  TL-SALES-TOTAL     PIC $$$$,$$9.99.
84
85      PROCEDURE DIVISION.
86
87      000-SORT-SALES-ON-CUST-NUMBER.
88          SORT SORT-FILE
89              ON ASCENDING KEY SR-CUSTOMER-NUMBER
90              USING BILLING-FILE
91              OUTPUT PROCEDURE IS SOP-000-PRINT-SALES-LISTING
92          STOP RUN.
93
94      *Sort Output Procedure (SOP)
95
96      SOP-000-PRINT-SALES-LISTING.
97          PERFORM SOP-100-INITIALIZE
98          PERFORM SOP-110-PROCESS-CURRENT-RECORD
99              UNTIL END-OF-FILE
100         PERFORM SOP-120-FINALIZE.
101
102     SOP-100-INITIALIZE.
103         OPEN OUTPUT REPORT-FILE
104         SET END-OF-FILE TO FALSE
105         PERFORM SOP-200-GET-RUN-DATE
106         PERFORM SOP-700-PRINT-PAGE-HEADINGS
107         PERFORM SOP-800-RETURN-SORT-RECORD.
108
109     SOP-110-PROCESS-CURRENT-RECORD.
110         IF SR-RECORD-TYPE = "S"
111             ADD SR-MONEY-AMOUNT TO SALES-TOTAL
112             PERFORM SOP-710-ASSEMBLE-PRINT-DETAIL
113         END-IF
114         PERFORM SOP-800-RETURN-SORT-RECORD.
115
116     SOP-120-FINALIZE.
117         PERFORM SOP-720-ASSEMBLE-PRINT-TOTAL
118         CLOSE REPORT-FILE.
119
120     SOP-200-GET-RUN-DATE.
121         ACCEPT RUN-DATE FROM DATE
122         MOVE MONTH TO PH-MONTH
123         MOVE WS-DAY  TO PH-DAY
124         MOVE YEAR  TO PH-YEAR.
125
126     SOP-700-PRINT-PAGE-HEADINGS.
127         MOVE PAGE-HEADING-LINE TO REPORT-RECORD
128         MOVE ZERO TO LINE-SPACING
129         PERFORM SOP-850-WRITE-REPORT-LINE
130         MOVE COLUMN-HEADING-LINE TO REPORT-RECORD
131         MOVE 2 TO LINE-SPACING
132         PERFORM SOP-850-WRITE-REPORT-LINE.
133
134     SOP-710-ASSEMBLE-PRINT-DETAIL.
135         MOVE SR-CUSTOMER-NUMBER TO SL-CUSTOMER-NUMBER
136         MOVE SR-MONEY-AMOUNT TO SL-MONEY-AMOUNT
137         MOVE SALES-LISTING-RECORD TO REPORT-RECORD
138         PERFORM SOP-850-WRITE-REPORT-LINE
139         MOVE 1 TO LINE-SPACING.
140
141     SOP-720-ASSEMBLE-PRINT-TOTAL.
142         MOVE SALES-TOTAL TO TL-SALES-TOTAL
143         MOVE TOTAL-LINE TO REPORT-RECORD
144         MOVE 3 TO LINE-SPACING
145         PERFORM SOP-850-WRITE-REPORT-LINE.
146
147     SOP-800-RETURN-SORT-RECORD.
148         RETURN SORT-FILE
149             AT END SET END-OF-FILE TO TRUE
150         END-RETURN.
151
152     SOP-850-WRITE-REPORT-LINE.
153         WRITE REPORT-RECORD
154             AFTER ADVANCING LINE-SPACING LINES.
```

For ease of use, the output requirements have been kept simple, but it should be clearly understood that the output procedure could have been as complicated as desired— with single- or multiple-level group totals, extensive page headings, detail or group printing, and so on. Just as there are no limitations on what can be done in an input procedure, so there are no limitations on what can be done in an output procedure.

In general, the overall examples used in this chapter have deliberately been made simple so that the coding did not obscure the point being illustrated. In each case, the main program consisted of only the SORT and STOP RUN. From these examples, you might infer that a program that sorts can do nothing else, and that a SORT statement cannot contain both input and output procedures. Neither of these inferences is correct. Because the input procedure and output procedure have no effect on each other, the SORT statement may contain either, neither, or both.

By the same reasoning, the SORT statement has no effect on the rest of the program. It is simply another statement like READ, ADD, or MOVE. As such, it can appear anywhere in a program (except in an input or output procedure), and a program can contain as many SORT statements as required. The only limitation is the amount of memory available for the program.

As you have seen, the COBOL Sort Feature permits the programmer to sort records into any desired sequence, with complete flexibility in the handling of input and output data. It permits the accomplishment of one of the key data processing functions— sorting—with a minimum of programmer effort. It greatly simplifies the programmer's task of writing programs that produce the desired results.

Restrictions on the Sort Prior to COBOL-85

Using Sections in the PROCEDURE DIVISION

As you are aware, the emphasis in this book is on using COBOL of the 1985 Standard. Many of the techniques of this book rely heavily on COBOL-85 features. For instance, some logic is more easily and better programmed with the in-line PERFORM and the EVALUATE statements than without them. However, if you were to use an earlier compiler without them, you could still write the program using equivalent forms you already know. For instance, the out-of-line PERFORM can always be used in place of the in-line PERFORM (although not as conveniently in some cases) and nested IF statements can be used in place of the EVALUATE. Unavailability of the scope terminators would be a real nuisance.

But the SORT statement presents a different problem: procedures cannot be used as illustrated by the preceding example programs. That is, the procedure name identified in the SORT statement must be the name of a section. You are already familiar with sections from the DATA DIVISION, which consists of the FILE SECTION and the WORKING-STORAGE SECTION. Similarly, in the PROCEDURE DIVISION, two or more paragraphs can be grouped together and defined as a section, as illustrated in Figure 15-12. If a program with this section included the statement

```
PERFORM 2000-FIELD-CALCULATION
```

then control would be transferred to that point in the program. Because it is a section, every paragraph comprising that section would be executed before control was returned. In the same way that the end of a paragraph is signalled by the name of the next paragraph, the end of a section is indicated by the section name of the next section.

The requirement of pre-1985 COBOL that the sort procedure name be a section name is, in itself, no problem. The difficulty arises from the fact that execution of a sort procedure must remain within that procedure. That is, control cannot be transferred to a module outside the procedure. This introduces the need for two additional statements: GO TO and EXIT.

Figure 15-12

Sections in the
PROCEDURE DIVISION

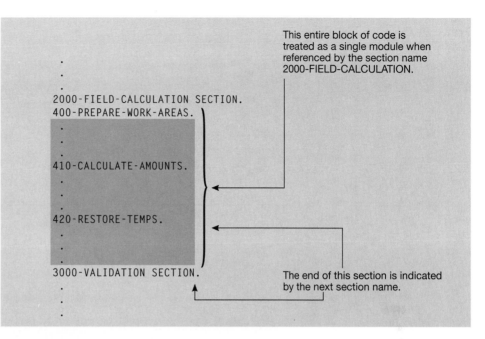

```
          .
          .
          .
   2000-FIELD-CALCULATION SECTION.
   400-PREPARE-WORK-AREAS.
          .
          .
          .
   410-CALCULATE-AMOUNTS.
          .
          .
          .
   420-RESTORE-TEMPS.
          .
          .
          .
   3000-VALIDATION SECTION.
          .
          .
          .
```

This entire block of code is
treated as a single module when
referenced by the section name
2000-FIELD-CALCULATION.

The end of this section is indicated
by the next section name.

A Pre-1985 Sort Program

The PROCEDURE DIVISION for the I-SORT program of Example 15-2 has been rewritten to pre-1985 COBOL standards in Figure 15-13 (the name of this program is I-SORT2). The following commentary describes this program:

■ The program consists of two sections: 0000-MAIN-PROGRAM and 1000-SORT-INPUT-PROCEDURE.

■ The section name is identified as the input procedure in the SORT statement (line 63).

■ The 1000-SORT-INPUT-PROCEDURE section includes all the paragraphs that are executed as part of the input procedure. Thus, execution never goes outside of the named input procedure (a limitation of pre-1985 COBOL).

■ After the last statement of the SIP-000 paragraph is executed, control must be returned to the SORT statement. To avoid execution continuing to the SIP-100 module, a GO TO statement is included that transfers control to a dummy paragraph.

The GO TO allows you to transfer control from one point in a program to another in much the same way as the PERFORM. However, the difference is that the GO TO include no provisions for returning to the paragraph from which the transfer is made. Once control is transferred to a paragraph with a GO TO, execution continues from that point on. The overuse of this statement is considered to be *the* taboo of structured programming. (In fact, most structured programming languages do not even include a GO TO type of statement.) However, there are a few occasions in which it is quite useful, such as recovering from error conditions with input/output activities. An example later in this book uses it.

Since the GO TO must refer to a paragraph-name, an additional paragraph has been added to the I-SORT program at the end of the 1000 section. This paragraph does nothing except provide a point of reference for the GO TO statement. The reserved word EXIT provides a null statement (similar to the CONTINUE of COBOL-85) for a dummy paragraph—one that contains no other statements. When EXIT is used, it must be the only statement in the paragraph and must be followed by a period.

Figure 15-13

PROCEDURE DIVISION of
Pre-1985 Sort Program with
an Input Procedure

```
55      PROCEDURE DIVISION.
56
57      0000-MAIN-PROGRAM SECTION.
58
59      000-SORT-BILLING-FILE.
60         SORT SORT-FILE
61            ON ASCENDING  KEY SR-CUSTOMER-NUMBER
62               DESCENDING KEY SR-RECORD-TYPE
63            INPUT PROCEDURE IS 1000-SORT-INPUT-PROCEDURE
64            GIVING BILL-FILE
65         STOP RUN.
66
67      1000-SORT-INPUT-PROCEDURE SECTION.
68
69      * Sort Input Procedure (SIP)
70
71      SIP-000-REFORMAT-INPUT.
72         PERFORM SIP-100-INITIALIZE.
73         PERFORM SIP-110-PROCESS-1-RECORD
74            UNTIL END-OF-BILLING-FILE
75         PERFORM SIP-120-FINALIZE
76         GO TO SIP-999-PROCEDURE-EXIT.
77
78      SIP-100-INITIALIZE.
79         OPEN INPUT BILLING-FILE
80         SET END-OF-BILLING-FILE TO FALSE
81         PERFORM SIP-800-READ-BILLING-RECORD.
82
83      SIP-110-PROCESS-1-RECORD.
84         EVALUATE SA-RECORD-TYPE
85            WHEN "S"
86               PERFORM SIP-720-ASSEMBLE-RELEASE-SALE
87            WHEN "P"
88               PERFORM SIP-730-ASSEMBLE-RELEASE-PAY
89            WHEN OTHER
90               DISPLAY "Invalid Record: ", SALES-RECORD
91         END-EVALUATE
92         PERFORM SIP-800-READ-BILLING-RECORD.
93
94      SIP-120-FINALIZE.
95         CLOSE BILLING-FILE
96         DISPLAY "End of Input Procedure"
97         DISPLAY SPACES.
98
99      SIP-720-ASSEMBLE-RELEASE-SALE.
100        MOVE SA-RECORD-TYPE     TO SR-RECORD-TYPE
101        MOVE SA-CUSTOMER-NUMBER TO SR-CUSTOMER-NUMBER
102        MOVE SA-MONEY-AMOUNT    TO SR-MONEY-AMOUNT
103        PERFORM SIP-850-RELEASE-TO-SORT-RECORD.
104
105     SIP-730-ASSEMBLE-RELEASE-PAY.
106        MOVE PA-RECORD-TYPE     TO SR-RECORD-TYPE
107        MOVE PA-CUSTOMER-NUMBER TO SR-CUSTOMER-NUMBER
108        MOVE PA-MONEY-AMOUNT    TO SR-MONEY-AMOUNT
109        PERFORM SIP-850-RELEASE-TO-SORT-RECORD.
110
111     SIP-800-READ-BILLING-RECORD.
112        READ BILLING-FILE
113           AT END SET END-OF-BILLING-FILE TO TRUE
114        END-READ.
115
116     SIP-850-RELEASE-TO-SORT-RECORD.
117        RELEASE SORT-RECORD.
118
119     SIP-999-PROCEDURE-EXIT.
120        EXIT.
```

Section

Section

Sorting Data in Memory

A Simple Sort Algorithm

You have seen how the COBOL SORT statement sorts files of records into any desired sequence. However, the SORT statement can be used only for data files that are external to the computer's memory. If a set of data (such as a table) that resides entirely within the memory must be sorted, then the programmer must write the necessary program statements to accomplish this.

Many sorting algorithms have been developed by computer scientists and computer programmers over the years. As a general rule, the complexity of these algorithms increases with their efficiency. Hence, any algorithm that is easy to understand is quite inefficient; and the principles of an algorithm that is very efficient are quite difficult to grasp. One of the most basic of the sorting algorithms involves the following steps to sort the elements of a table:

1. Find the largest item in the table; put it at the end of the table

2. Find the next-largest item in the table; put it second from the end of the table

3. Find the third-largest item; put it third from the end of the table

4. Continue this procedure until the entire table is in sequence

With a table in the computer, this algorithm involves switching the contents of table elements. For instance, consider a five-entry table in which the largest value is stored in table element 2. Hence, the contents of element 2 must be moved to element 5. However, to avoid losing the current contents of element 5, you would simply exchange the contents of elements 2 and 5. This must be done in a multi-step process using a temporary memory area, as illustrated in Figure 15-14.

After completion of this first interchange, the table entries may not be in order, but at least the largest one will be last (it will be in sequence). Now the next-to-largest element can be located and moved to the next-to-last position of the table, and so on until the entire table is in sequence. This process is illustrated in Figure 15-15. Notice that after the first execution, you can see that the next search for the "next largest" element need not go to the end of the table because the last element is properly positioned. Progressing step-by-step, you see that only the unshaded area of Figure 15-15 need be searched on each successive step.

These considerations allow you to restate the algorithm in a form that will be used in the program. If you assume that TABLE-SIZE contains the number of elements in the table and that SORT-TABLE-SIZE reflects the portion of the table that remains unsorted, then you have the following:

> Move TABLE-SIZE to SORT-TABLE-SIZE
> Repeat the following procedure until SORT-TABLE-SIZE = 1:
>   Find the largest item in the table up to the SORT-TABLE-SIZE element
>   Exchange the contents of this element and that at SORT-TABLE-SIZE
>   Reduce SORT-TABLE-SIZE by 1.

Figure 15-14

Interchanging Two Table Elements

	TEMP	(1)	(2)	(3)	(4)	(5)
Original table contents		13	72	11	8	19
MOVE (2) to TEMP	72	13	72	11	8	19
MOVE (5) to (2)	72	13	19	11	8	19
MOVE TEMP to (5)	72	13	19	11	8	72

Figure 15-15

Sorting by Interchanging Elements

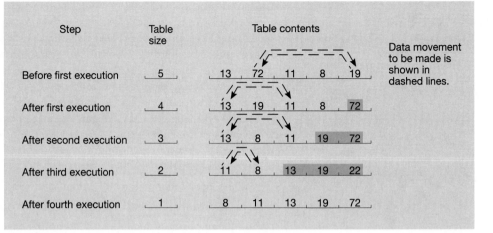

Step	Table size	Table contents
Before first execution	5	13 72 11 8 19
After first execution	4	13 19 11 8 72
After second execution	3	13 8 11 19 72
After third execution	2	11 8 13 19 22
After fourth execution	1	8 11 13 19 72

Data movement to be made is shown in dashed lines.

Referring to the example of Figure 15-15, the first two iterations would involve the following sequence of events:

1. Move 5 to SORT-TABLE-SIZE
2. Search elements 1-5 for the largest value: 72 at element 2
3. Exchange the values of elements 2 and 5 (contents of SORT-TABLE-SIZE)
4. Subtract 1 from SORT-TABLE-SIZE, giving 4
5. Search elements 1-4 for the largest value: 19 at element 2
6. Exchange the values of elements 2 and 4 (contents of SORT-TABLE-SIZE)
7. Subtract 1 from SORT-TABLE-SIZE, giving 3

A Program to Sort the Area-Code Table

The LD-CALLS program (Example 14-6 of Chapter 14) involves building a table containing telephone area codes and corresponding numbers of message units. The program of Figure 15-16 shows how this table could be built and then sorted, using the sort algorithm described previously. This particular program has no end-purpose other than to demonstrate memory sorting. The table-loading portion of the program is taken directly from the LD-CALLS program. Program output is a display of the unsorted table prior to sorting and a display of the table after sorting.

1. The program requires two indexes for table access. The first, AREA-NDX, is used as the index to be incremented during the search of the table. The second, LARGEST-AREA, is used as a pointer to "remember" the location of the largest area code in the table during each search pass.

2. The variable SORT-TABLE-SIZE is used to specify the size of the table to be sorted.

3. The statement (line 77)

```
PERFORM 300-FIND-LARGEST-AREA-CODE
```

corresponds to the "Repeat" sentence in the table sort algorithm.

4. The paragraph 300-FIND-LARGEST-AREA-CODE causes the following actions to take place:
   a. To begin the process, it treats the first area code in the table as the largest one by setting LARGEST-AREA to 1.
   b. It compares each succeeding area code in the table to the largest one found in this search (whose index is stored in LARGEST-AREA). If a new larger area code is found, LARGEST-AREA is set to its location.
   c. It interchanges the largest and last items in the active portion of the table (unless the largest is already the last).

Figure 15-16

Sorting a Table Using a
Simple Table Sort
Algorithm

```
1        IDENTIFICATION DIVISION.                                          69     110-SORT-M-U-TABLE.
2                                                                          70         DISPLAY " "
3        PROGRAM-ID.    MEM-SORT.                                          71         DISPLAY "Area Code Table before sorting: "
4                                                                          72         PERFORM VARYING AREA-NDX FROM 1 BY 1
5    *    Sorting a table in memory.                                       73             UNTIL AREA-NDX > AREA-CODE-TABLE-SIZE
6                                                                          74             DISPLAY AREA-CODE(AREA-NDX), "  "
7    *    Written by J.Olson  1/20/86                                      75                 AREA-MESSAGE-UNITS(AREA-NDX)
8    *    Revised by W.Price  9/1/90                                       76         END-PERFORM
9                                                                          77         PERFORM 300-FIND-LARGEST-AREA-CODE
10       ENVIRONMENT DIVISION.                                             78            VARYING SORT-TABLE-SIZE
11                                                                         79                FROM AREA-CODE-TABLE-SIZE BY -1
12       CONFIGURATION SECTION.                                            80                UNTIL SORT-TABLE-SIZE = 1
13       SOURCE-COMPUTER.  IBM-PC.                                         81
14                                                                         82         DISPLAY " "
15       INPUT-OUTPUT SECTION.                                             83         DISPLAY "Area Code Table after sorting: "
16       FILE-CONTROL.                                                     84         PERFORM VARYING AREA-NDX FROM 1 BY 1
17           SELECT LONG-DISTANCE-FILE   ASSIGN TO DISK, "LD-CALLS.DL",    85             UNTIL AREA-NDX > AREA-CODE-TABLE-SIZE
18                                       ORGANIZATION IS LINE SEQUENTIAL.  86             DISPLAY AREA-CODE(AREA-NDX), "  "
19                                                                         87                 AREA-MESSAGE-UNITS(AREA-NDX)
20       DATA DIVISION.                                                    88         END-PERFORM
21                                                                         89         DISPLAY " ".
22       FILE SECTION.                                                     90
23                                                                         91     200-PROCESS-LD-RECORD.
24       FD  LONG-DISTANCE-FILE.                                           92         SET AREA-NDX TO 1
25       01  LONG-DISTANCE-RECORD.                                         93         SEARCH AREA-CODE-DATA
26           10  LD-DATE          PIC X(6).                                94             AT END
27           10  LD-CALLERS-NUMBER  PIC X(7).                              95             IF AREA-NDX > MAXIMUM-ENTRIES
28           10  LD-DESTINATION.                                           96                 DISPLAY "No room in table for ", LONG-DISTANCE-RECORD
29               20  LD-CALLED-AREA    PIC X(3).                           97             ELSE
30               20  LD-CALLED-NUMBER  PIC X(7).                           98                 PERFORM 210-INSERT-NEW-AREA-CODE
31           10  LD-MESSAGE-UNITS  PIC 9(3).                               99             END-IF
32                                                                        100             WHEN LD-CALLED-AREA = AREA-CODE(AREA-NDX)
33       WORKING-STORAGE SECTION.                                         101             ADD LD-MESSAGE-UNITS
34                                                                        102                 TO AREA-MESSAGE-UNITS(AREA-NDX)
35       01  PROGRAMMED-SWITCHES.                                         103         END-SEARCH.
36           10                  PIC X.                                   104         PERFORM 800-READ-LD-RECORD.
37               88  END-OF-FILE  VALUE "Y"  FALSE "N".                   105
38                                                                        106     210-INSERT-NEW-AREA-CODE.
39       01  TABLE-VARIABLES.                                             107         ADD 1 TO NEW-ENTRY-POINTER
40           10  NEW-ENTRY-POINTER  PIC 9(3)  BINARY  VALUE ZERO.         108         MOVE LD-CALLED-AREA TO AREA-CODE(AREA-NDX)
41           10  MAXIMUM-ENTRIES    PIC 9(3)  BINARY  VALUE 122.          109         MOVE LD-MESSAGE-UNITS TO AREA-MESSAGE-UNITS(AREA-NDX).
42           10  AREA-CODE-TABLE-SIZE  PIC 9(3)  BINARY.                  110
43           10  SORT-TABLE-SIZE    PIC 9(3)  BINARY.                     111     300-FIND-LARGEST-AREA-CODE.
44           10  HOLD-AREA          PIC X(8).                             112         SET LARGEST-AREA TO 1
45                                                                        113         PERFORM VARYING AREA-NDX FROM 2 BY 1
46       01  AREA-CODE-TABLE.                                             114             UNTIL AREA-NDX > SORT-TABLE-SIZE
47           10  AREA-CODE-DATA     OCCURS 1 TO 122 TIMES                 115         IF AREA-CODE(AREA-NDX) > AREA-CODE(LARGEST-AREA)
48                                  DEPENDING ON NEW-ENTRY-POINTER        116             SET LARGEST-AREA TO AREA-NDX
49                                  INDEXED BY AREA-NDX LARGEST-AREA.     117         END-IF
50               20  AREA-CODE           PIC X(3).                        118         END-PERFORM
51               20  AREA-MESSAGE-UNITS  PIC 9(5).                        119         SET AREA-NDX DOWN BY 1
52                                                                        120         IF AREA-NDX NOT = LARGEST-AREA
53       PROCEDURE DIVISION.                                              121           MOVE AREA-CODE-DATA(LARGEST-AREA) TO HOLD-AREA
54                                                                        122           MOVE AREA-CODE-DATA(AREA-NDX)
55       000-BUILD-AND-SORT-TABLE.                                        123             TO AREA-CODE-DATA(LARGEST-AREA)
56           PERFORM 100-BUILD-M-U-TABLE                                  124           MOVE HOLD-AREA TO AREA-CODE-DATA(AREA-NDX)
57           PERFORM 110-SORT-M-U-TABLE                                   125         END-IF.
58           STOP RUN.                                                    126
59                                                                        127     800-READ-LD-RECORD.
60       100-BUILD-M-U-TABLE.                                             128         READ LONG-DISTANCE-FILE
61           OPEN INPUT LONG-DISTANCE-FILE                                129             AT END
62           SET END-OF-FILE TO FALSE                                     130                 SET END-OF-FILE TO TRUE
63           PERFORM 800-READ-LD-RECORD                                   131         END-READ.
64           PERFORM 200-PROCESS-LD-RECORD
65               UNTIL END-OF-FILE
66           MOVE NEW-ENTRY-POINTER TO AREA-CODE-TABLE-SIZE
67           CLOSE LONG-DISTANCE-FILE.
68
```

5. The interchanging of two areas in memory requires a third area (called HOLD-AREA in this example), where one of the items can be held until a vacancy has been created for it. Note that the hold area must be large enough to hold the entire table entry—both argument and function.

Chapter Summary

General

Sorting files is one of the cornerstones of data processing. The COBOL SORT statement provides the programmer a powerful tool for sorting. This statement requires the following four pieces of information:

1. The name of the input data file (the file to be sorted) or the name of an input procedure that will supply the data file

2. The name of the sort file that is to be used as a work file during the sorting process

3. The name of the field or fields on which the records are to be sorted, and whether the result is to be in ascending or descending sequence

4. The name of the output data file (the file that will contain the sorted file) or the name of an output procedure

The sorting operation consists of three phases:

1. *Input*: Records are copied from the input file to the sort work file

2. *Sort*: Records in the sort work file are sorted into the desired sequence

3. *Output*: Records are copied from the sort work file to the output file

When used without input or output procedures, all opening and closing of files, copying of records from one file to another are done automatically by the SORT statement action.

If an input procedure is specified, then the entire input phase is left to the programmer to be defined in the input procedure.

If an output procedure is specified, then the entire output phase is left to the programmer to be defined in the output procedure.

The sort work file is *never* opened or closed by the programmer; this is done automatically by the sort procedure.

COBOL Language Elements

The COBOL statements that you have studied in this chapter are

EXIT   Provides a reference point in a PROCEDURE DIVISION section. Must be the only statement in a paragraph.

EXIT

GO TO   Causes control to be transferred from one part of the program to another.

GO TO [procedure-name]

RELEASE   Transfers (writes) a record to a sort file during a sort operation. May be used only in a sort input procedure.

RELEASE record-name

RETURN   Transfers (reads) a record from a sort file during a sort operation. May be used only in a sort output procedure.

RETURN sort-file-name

SORT   The SORT statement creates a sort file by executing an input procedure or by transferring records from another file, sorts the records in the sort file on the specified keys, and makes the sort file records available to an output file or an output procedure.

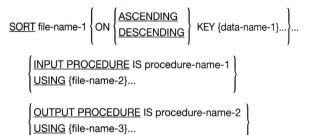

Other language elements that you have studied in this chapter are

RECORD   Specifies the size of data records. In this book, used only to designate a record size range for a file that has records of different lengths.

RECORD CONTAINS integer-1 [TO integer-2] CHARACTERS

SD   Identifies the beginning of the sort file description in the DATA DIVISION (analogous to the FD).

SD file-name

      [RECORD CONTAINS integer-1 [TO integer-2] CHARACTERS

      {record-description-entry} ...

Error Prevention/ Detection

When laying out your program logic, be certain that it does not allow execution to fall through into a sort input or output procedure.

Sort input and output procedures must only be executed from the sort statement. They must never be executed by a PERFORM.

Remember to use the RELEASE in a sort input procedure to write the record to the sort file. Do not use a WRITE statement.

Remember to use the RETURN in a sort output procedure to read the record from the sort file. Do not use a READ statement.

Questions and Exercises

Give a brief description of each of the following terms that were introduced in this chapter.

Key Terminology

COBOL Sort Feature

collating sequence

descending sequence

sort

sort key

General Questions

1. What are the two requirements for arranging data in a file?
2. Name the two effects that sorting has on data in a file.
3. List the three steps in the COBOL sort procedure.

4. Study the following diagram of a sorting operation, then fill in the blanks of the following statements:
   a. In the input phase, records are copied from the file named _____ onto the file named _____.
   b. In the sort phase, the records in the file named _____ are sorted according to the field named _____.
   c. In the output phase, the records in the file named _____ are copied onto the file named _____.

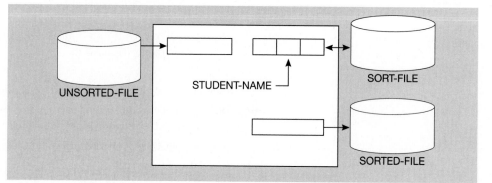

5. List the four items of information in the COBOL SORT statement.

6. Place the following data items in ascending sequence according to the collating sequence of the IBM mainframe and PC. (The lowercase letter b with a slash through it, ƀ, represents a space.)

      R17   BQ9   Mƀ3   BƀX   RL4   B3Y   3AL

7. A COBOL SORT statement can use a(n)_____ instead of an input file or a(n)_____ instead of an output file.

8. _____ sequence arranges fields sorted in order from smallest to largest. _____ sequence arranges fields from largest to smallest.

9. Can entries that reside in tables in memory be sorted with the SORT statement?

Questions Relating to the Example Programs

1. State whether or not each of the following operations could validly be included in the input procedure of the I-SORT program (Figure 15-9). If the operation would not be valid, give the reason.
   a. Count the number of sales records and payment records
   b. Accumulate the total of the sales and payment amounts
   c. Test the customer number and amount fields for nonnumeric characters
   d. Output a listing of the valid records on the printer
   e. Use the WRITE statement to write the sort records onto the sort file

2. State what would have happened if the STOP RUN statement in the I-SORT program were accidentally omitted.

3. In the MEM-SORT program, Figure 15-16, it would have been simpler to code the interchanging of the largest and last items in the table as follows:

```
MOVE AREA-CODE-DATA(LARGEST-AREA) TO AREA-CODE-DATA(AREA-NDX)
MOVE AREA-CODE-DATA(AREA-NDX) TO AREA-CODE-DATA(LARGEST-AREA)
```

Why was this not done?

4. The O-SORT program selects only those records from the sort file that are sales records (have a type code of "S"); the test is made in line 110 of the program in Figure 15-11. This selection could better have been made in an input procedure producing a sort file with only sales records. What modifications would be required to accomplish this?

5. In the I-SORT program, Figure 15-9, what would happen if the programmer forgot to code line 104 in the PROCEDURE DIVISION?

6. The PERFORM/VARYING statement on lines 77–80 in the MEM-SORT program, Figure 15-16, is unusual. It varies SORT-TABLE-SIZE from AREA-CODE-TABLE-SIZE by -1. Why does it do this?

Writing Program Statements

1. Assume that a sort-record description includes the fields PRODUCT-CODE, DATE-OF-SALE, and AMOUNT-OF-SALE. Write the key clause to arrange the records by date of sale within each product code.

2. Using the field names of the preceding exercise, write the KEY clause to arrange the records by amount of sale within each product code. In each case, the highest amount of sale is to be listed first and the lowest last.

3. Write the sort record-description entry for the FILE SECTION for the fields in Exercise 1. Assume that PRODUCT-CODE is in positions 31-35, DATE-OF-SALE is in positions 45-50, and AMOUNT-OF-SALE is in positions 70-77. The record is 80 positions long.

4. As a new programmer for a company, you are asked to take an existing report program and change it to include an internal sort. What could you code to accomplish this without changing much of the existing program?

5. Assuming that the report program in Exercise 4 is to sort students into descending order by OVERALL-GPA and ascending order by STUDENT-NAME, how would you code the sort record-description entry? STUDENT-NAME is in positions 20-35 of each record and OVERALL-GPA is in positions 78-80. The records are 100 positions long.

6. Write the sort statement that could be used in conjunction with Exercises 4 and 5.

Programming Assignments

15-1 List of Books Grouped by Programming Language in Author Sequence

The manager of Programmer's Paradise Bookstore needs a quick-reference listing of books handled by the bookstore.

Output Requirements:
    A printed report with the following output.
        Programming language
        Author
        Title
        Book inventory number

    The listing is to be grouped by programming language and, within each programming language group, must be in sequence by author. At the end of the report, print the count of the number of records processed.

Input Description:
    File name: BOOKS.DL
    Record description: See Appendix A

Processing Requirements:

Initial processing:

1. On the first heading line print the date, the organization name, and the page number. Include appropriate column headings.
2. Sort the file on the indicated fields.

For each record:

3. In the output procedure, count each record.
4. Print the detail line as specified in Output Requirements.

Summary line:

5. Print a summary line, appropriately titled with the number of records processed.

15-2 Outgoing Airline Flights in Destination Sequence

The manager of the Anacin Airport needs a quick reference display of outgoing flights for any selected day. A user must be able to enter the date and receive a listing in sequence based on the aircraft destination.

Output Requirements:

A screen display that includes the following output.
Destination
Flight number
Time of flight
Airline

Input Description:

File name: AIRPORT1.DL
Record description: See Appendix A

Processing Requirements:

1. Accept from the user the date for which flights are to be selected from the input file.
2. In the input procedure, select flights for the day indicated.
3. Sort the file on the indicated field.
4. In the output procedure, display each record.
5. Assume that the number of records to be listed will not exceed the number of lines available on the screen.
6. Allow the user to request a listing for another day.

15-3 Student Scholars Grouped by Class Standing

The dean of students at the Computer Institute of Technology would like a report of scholars (students with a cumulative GPA of 3.0 or greater). The report is to be in ascending sequence by class standing and descending sequence by GPA.

Output Requirements:

A printed report with the following output.
Student name (last name and first name)
Class standing (the word FRESHMAN, SOPHOMORE,...)
Major code
Cumulative GPA

Input Description:

File name: STUDENTS.DL
Record description: See Appendix A

Processing Requirements:

Input procedure:

1. Select records with a cumulative GPA equal to or greater than 3.0

Sort:

2. Sort the file on the indicated fields.

Output procedure:

3. On the first heading line print the date, the institution name, and the page number. Include appropriate column headings.
4. Print each detail line.

15-4 Employee List in Sequence by Tax-Sheltered Annuity

The benefits director of Donut Manufacturing wants a list of employees grouped by the tax-sheltered annuity designated by the employee. The sequencing of the TSA companies is to be based on the company name, not the abbreviation included in the file. (For the correspondence between abbreviation and name, see the table included with Programming Assignment 14-2.)

Output Requirements:

A printed report with the following output.

Tax-sheltered annuity company name
Social Security number
Employee name
Tax-sheltered annuity deduction

Input Description:

File name: EMPLOYEE.DL
Record description: See Appendix A

Processing Requirements:

Input procedure:

1. For each employee record, build a sort work record that includes a tax-sheltered annuity company name.
    a. Read the next input record.
    b. Using the Tax-sheltered annuity code, look up the TSA company name in a table.

Sort:

2. Sort the file on the indicated fields.

Output procedure:

3. On the first heading line print the date, the institution name, and the page number. Include appropriate column headings.
4. Print each detail line single space. Leave a blank line between each group of companies.

Manipulation of Character String Data

Outline

- **Reference Modification**

- **The INSPECT Statement**
  Searching a Character STRING
  The TALLYING Option of the INSPECT
  The REPLACING Option of the INSPECT
  The TALLYING and REPLACING Options Together

- **The STRING Statement**
  Basic Principles of Combining Character Strings
  Basic Principles of the STRING Statement
  Other Options of the STRING Statement

- **The UNSTRING Statement**
  Basic Principles of the UNSTRING Statement
  Additional Features of the UNSTRING Statement

- **A Typical Character String Manipulation Application**
  Fixed Format and Delimited Files
  Problem Definition
  About Reading Variable-Length Records
  Program Planning—Example 16-5
  A Program Solution—Example 16-5

Chapter Objectives

Until now, you have done little with alphanumeric fields other than to move them from one place to another. When necessary, you have worked with an entire field or with components. For example, a group item of 20 positions might be broken down into three elementary items of 6, 9, and 5 positions, each a fixed length. There are many instances in which the operations to be performed are other than the simple move, and the subfields to be operated on do not have fixed formats. This brings us to the topic of *string manipulation*. In COBOL, you have used the term *alphanumeric data* to describe data that may consist of letters, digits, and special characters (defined by the X PICTURE). In the computing field in general, such data are commonly called *character string data* or simply *string data*. Operations on string data that you will study include:

- Searching a character string for a desired substring. A *substring* is, as the name implies, part of a string field.

- Counting the number of times that a selected substring occurs in a string. For example, the one-character substring hyphen (-) occurs in a Social Security number twice.

- Replacing a selected substring with another; for instance, changing all spaces to asterisks.

- Combining two or more strings into a single string.

- Splitting a string into two or more component parts according to specific criterion for determining the end of each substring.

Reference Modification

In COBOL applications, the programmer commonly encounters the need to work with fields that consist of subfields. The software product code used by UNISOFT in the earlier chapters is a good example. Remember from Chapter 13 that this five-position field consists of three parts:

First two positions	Vendor number
Third position	Software type
Last two positions	Software number

In the program GRP-TOT2 (Figure 13-23), this field is defined as:

```
10 IR-STOCK-NUMBER.
   20 IR-VENDOR-NUMBER      PIC X(2).
   20 IR-SOFTWARE-TYPE      PIC X(1).
   20                       PIC X(2).
```

Here IR-STOCK-NUMBER gives access to the full five-position field. On the other hand, IR-VENDOR-NUMBER gives access to the vendor number (the first two positions) and IR-SOFTWARE-TYPE gives access to the software type (the third position). This is very simple to handle. If you wanted access to the software number (the last two positions), you need to insert data-name.

It is important to recognize that the key to doing this is that the stock number has a *fixed format*. This means that every stock number has exactly the same format as every other stock number:

Two-position vendor number
One-position software type
Two-position software number

For fields with fixed formats, COBOL provides another way of gaining access to a portion of a field; it is called *reference modification*. Reference modification allows you to designate a starting position and the number of characters desired from a field (the field must be in DISPLAY format). For example, consider the two forms shown in Figure 16-1. The first is the IF statement that tests for a control break in the GRP-TOT2 program. The second uses reference modification to specify the subfield required from the full

IR-STOCK-NUMBER field. Using reference modification to obtain a subfield from a field, the starting point can be at any point in the field and the length can be as desired. If the length is omitted, the subfield begins with the starting point and goes to the end of the field. For instance,

```
IR-STOCK-NUMBER(4)
```

would yield the last two positions of IR-STOCK-NUMBER. Note that COBOL will not confuse this as a subscripted data item because it is not defined with an OCCURS.

In cases such as the stock number, where each subfield has its predefined positions, you will find that it is best to break the field down into subfields in the DATA DIVISION rather than use reference modification. However, in some situations you may not know ahead of time exactly where each subfield is located within a field. For instance, assume that you need a subfield from the field WAREHOUSE-CODE. The beginning position of the subfield is sorted in the data item SUB-CODE-START and the number of characters in the data item SUB-CODE-LEN. Although you could not designate this subfield in the DATA DIVISION, you could make it available in the PROCEDURE DIVISION using the following form of reference modification.

```
WAREHOUSE-CODE(SUB-CODE-START:SUB-CODE-LEN)
```

The INSPECT Statement

Searching a Character STRING

Although most multicomponent fields have fixed formats, sometimes there is no such structure. To illustrate, consider the following example.

Example 16-1 Inspecting Individual Positions of a Field

Problem Description

A control code field that must be processed within a program is broken down into component parts, with each part separated from the next by the hyphen character. The following are some sample control codes:

A24-1156-Q-1399
B6-119489-C-00800-5-SD
C127-216-X-556-9

Note that the format is not predictable: the codes do not necessarily contain the same number of parts and the lengths of the parts are not fixed. At least one component will always be in every code field.

Output Requirements

A count stored in the field FIELD-COUNT of the number of components in the code field.

Input Description

The control field value in the data item RT-CODE-FIELD.

Processing Requirements

Count the number of hyphens in the field; the number of code components will be 1 greater than the number of hyphens.

Figure 16-1

Reference Modification

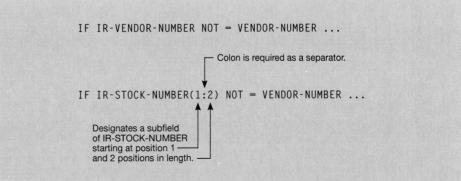

One glance at the sample control codes is enough to indicate that a simple definition—such as that for the stock number—will not be adequate. Whereas the stock number is broken into parts of fixed length, the parts of this code are separated by the hyphen character. A character that is used to separate two parts of a field is commonly called a *delimiter*, since it implies the limit of a given field. Hence, the substrings of this code are *delimited* by the hyphen character.

At first, the example requirement to count the number of code components might appear to be impossible with the COBOL principles you have studied. However, it is not. You can use subscripting to give access to individual character positions, as shown in the segment of code in Figure 16-2. Although this is somewhat clumsy for such a simple task, it does the job.

On the other hand, the COBOL INSPECT statement is designed specifically for operations such as this. This statement can be used to perform either or both of the following functions on a designated character string:

1. TALLYING Option   Count (tally) the number of occurrences of a specified character string.

2. REPLACING Option   Replace occurrences of a specified character string with another.

The TALLYING Option of the INSPECT

The INSPECT statement is illustrated in Figure 16-3, where it is used to perform the identical counting function as the corresponding code sequence of Figure 16-2. Note that all of the actions of Figure 16-2's sequence are carried out by different components of the INSPECT.

■ The field to be inspected (RT-CODE-FIELD) is identified, following the word INSPECT.

■ The counter (FIELD-COUNT) is identified, following the word TALLYING. Notice that it is initialized prior to the INSPECT.

■ The element for which the field RT-CODE-FIELD is being inspected (the hyphen) is enclosed in quotes and follows the words FOR ALL.

Before considering the general form of this statement, consider the additional INSPECT examples of Figure 16-4; these each operate on the data field:

```
AAAACQ/GHRSQ/&ABC/&SAMPLE
```

In these examples, notice the variety.

■ Search/tallying can be for a single character or for several—also called a *substring* (a portion of a character string). Compare Example 1, in which the search string consists of the single character A, and Example 2, in which the search string consists of the two characters /&.

Figure 16-2

Searching a Field

```
          20  RT-CODE-FIELD   PIC X(30).
          20  RT-CODE-POSITION PIC X
                 REDEFINES RT-CODE-FIELD  OCCURS 30 TIMES.
          .
          .
          .
      10  ACCUMULATORS.
          20  FIELD-COUNT     PIC 99.
          20  FIELD-PNTR      PIC 99.
          .
          .
          .
          MOVE 0 TO FIELD-PNTR
          MOVE 1 TO FIELD-COUNT
          PERFORM 30 TIMES
            ADD 1 TO FIELD-PNTR
            IF RT-CODE-POSITION(FIELD-PNTR) = "-"
              ADD 1 TO FIELD-COUNT
            END-IF
          END-PERFORM
```

Figure 16-3

A Simpler Form of the INSPECT Statement

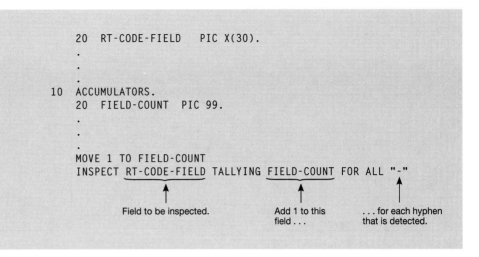

■ Restrictions can be placed on the search. For instance, search/tallying can terminate upon finding a designated substring (Examples 3 and 4) or it can begin only upon finding a designated substring (Example 5).

■ It can be used to count the number of characters preceding or following a designated substring (Examples 6 and 7).

Figure 16-4

INSPECT-TALLYING Examples

> *Note:* Some of the example statements given are too long to fit on one COBOL line. They are shown here on a single line to illustrate their nature. In a source program, they would be split into two or more lines.
>
> Operating on: AAAACQ/GHRSQ/&ABC/&SAMPLE
>
> Required to initialize counter: MOVE 0 TO COUNTER
>
> 1. INSPECT SAMPLE-FIELD TALLYING COUNTER FOR ALL "A"
>
>   The total number of times the letter A occurs:
>   6 occurrences; that is, COUNTER = 6.
>
> 2. INSPECT SAMPLE-FIELD TALLYING COUNTER FOR ALL "/&"
>
>   The number of times that the two-character combination /& occurs:
>   2 occurrences; that is, COUNTER = 2.
>
> 3. INSPECT SAMPLE-FIELD TALLYING COUNTER FOR LEADING "A"
>
>   The number of leading A's (the number of times that the letter A occurs before any other character occurs):
>   4 occurrences; that is, COUNTER = 4.
>
> 4. INSPECT SAMPLE-FIELD TALLYING COUNTER FOR ALL "A" BEFORE INITIAL "/"
>
>   The number of A's that occur before the first slash character is encountered:
>   4 occurrences; that is, COUNTER = 4.
>
> 5. INSPECT SAMPLE-FIELD TALLYING COUNTER FOR ALL "A" AFTER INITIAL "/"
>
>   The number of A's that occur after the first slash character is encountered:
>   2 occurrences; that is, COUNTER = 2.
>
> 6. INSPECT SAMPLE-FIELD TALLYING COUNTER FOR CHARACTERS BEFORE INITIAL "/"
>
>   The number of characters before the first slash character is encountered:
>   6 characters; that is, COUNTER = 6.
>
> 7. INSPECT SAMPLE-FIELD TALLYING COUNTER FOR CHARACTERS AFTER INITIAL "/"
>
>   The number of characters after the first slash character is encountered:
>   18 characters; that is, COUNTER = 18.

This is indeed a versatile statement. Following is the general form of the INSPECT-TALLYING.

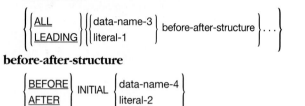

tally-structure

CHARACTERS before-after-structure

$$\left\{ \left\{ \begin{matrix} \underline{ALL} \\ \underline{LEADING} \end{matrix} \right\} \left\{ \begin{matrix} \text{data-name-3} \\ \text{literal-1} \end{matrix} \right\} \text{before-after-structure} \right\} \ldots$$

before-after-structure

$$\left\{ \begin{matrix} \underline{BEFORE} \\ \underline{AFTER} \end{matrix} \right\} \text{INITIAL} \left\{ \begin{matrix} \text{data-name-4} \\ \text{literal-2} \end{matrix} \right\}$$

This statement will

1. Select the portion of data-name-1 that is to be inspected, as specified by the tally-structure.

2. INSPECT each group of positions in the selected portion, moving from left to right. Each time a group of characters is found that satisfies the tally-structure, data-name-2 is incremented by 1.

Since inspection is done on a byte-by-byte basis, data-name-1 should specify an item that is DISPLAY usage. Data-name-2 must be a numeric item, since it is used as an accumulator. INSPECT does not initialize this accumulator; it is the programmer's responsibility to do so (note that FIELD-COUNT is initialized to 1 in Figure 16-3 and COUNTER to 0 in Figure 16-4).

The tally-structure components' meanings (as illustrated by the examples in Figure 16-4) are as follows:

CHARACTERS means that every byte of the specified portion of data-name-1 is to be counted. Examples 6 and 7 of Figure 16-4 illustrate this.

ALL means that every substring of data-name-1 that is equal to the value of data-name-3 or literal-1 is to be counted. Examples 1 and 2 of Figure 16-4 illustrate this.

LEADING means that the counting will go on only until a substring not equal to data-name-3 or literal-1 is found. Example 3 of Figure 16-4 illustrates this. Note that had the search been for the letter *Q*, for example, the search would have been terminated immediately, and the counter not incremented at all.

Note that a figurative constant (for example, SPACE) can be used in place of literal-1. However, the figurative constant is treated as a single character.

The *before-after-structure* components' meanings (as illustrated by the examples in Figure 16-4) are

BEFORE means that tallying is done until a substring equal to the value of data-name-4 or literal-2 is detected. Examples 4 and 6 of Figure 16-4 illustrate this.

AFTER means that tallying must not begin until a substring equal to the value of data-name-4 or literal-2 is detected. Examples 5 and 7 of Figure 16-4 illustrate this.

As you can see, the word INITIAL is not required, but it helps to remind the programmer of exactly how the statement is to function (see Examples 4 through 7).

The REPLACING Option of the INSPECT

The general form and the ways in which operations are carried out with the REPLACING option are very similar to those of the TALLYING. To illustrate, operations corresponding to those of Figure 16-4 are carried out for the REPLACING option in Figure 16-5. In each of these examples, a substring within a character string is *replaced* by another string *of equal length*. Although the search and replace can operate on substrings of one or more bytes, the replacing quantity must be the same length as the replaced quantity. The overall effect is that the length of the character string being operated on does not change. If the lengths are not the same, a compiler error is generated. The general form for the REPLACING option of INSPECT is as follows:

<u>INSPECT</u> data-name-1 <u>REPLACING</u> replace-structure

replace-structure

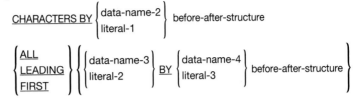

before-after-structure

This structure is identical to that described for the TALLYING.

Figure 16-5

*INSPECT-REPLACING
Examples*

```
1.   INSPECT SAMPLE-FIELD REPLACING ALL "A" BY "*"

        Before    AAAACQ/GHRSQ/&ABC/&SAMPLE
        After     ****CQ/GHRSQ/&*BC/&S*MPLE

2.   INSPECT SAMPLE-FIELD REPLACING ALL "AA" BY "**"

        Before    AAAACQ/GHRSQ/&ABC/&SAMPLE
        After     ****CQ/GHRSQ/&ABC/&SAMPLE

3.   INSPECT SAMPLE-FIELD REPLACING ALL "/&" BY "**"

        Before    AAAACQ/GHRSQ/&ABC/&SAMPLE
        After     AAAACQ/GHRSQ**ABC**SAMPLE

4.   INSPECT SAMPLE-FIELD REPLACING LEADING "A" BY "*"

        Before    AAAACQ/GHRSQ/&ABC/&SAMPLE
        After     ****CQ/GHRSQ/&ABC/&SAMPLE

5.   INSPECT SAMPLE-FIELD REPLACING FIRST "/&" BY "**"

        Before    AAAACQ/GHRSQ/&ABC/&SAMPLE
        After     AAAACQ/GHRSQ**ABC/&SAMPLE

6.   INSPECT SAMPLE-FIELD REPLACING ALL "A" BY "*" BEFORE INITIAL "/"

        Before    AAAACQ/GHRSQ/&ABC/&SAMPLE
        After     ****CQ/GHRSQ/&ABC/&SAMPLE

7.   INSPECT SAMPLE-FIELD REPLACING ALL "A" BY "*" AFTER INITIAL "/"

        Before    AAAACQ/GHRSQ/&ABC/&SAMPLE
        After     AAAACQ/GHRSQ/&*BC/*SAMPLE

8.   INSPECT SAMPLE-FIELD REPLACING CHARACTERS BY "*" BEFORE INITIAL "/"

        Before    AAAACQ/GHRSQ/&ABC/&SAMPLE
        After     ******/GHRSQ/&ABC/&SAMPLE

9.   INSPECT SAMPLE-FIELD REPLACING CHARACTERS BY "*" AFTER INITIAL "/"

        Before    AAAACQ/GHRSQ/&ABC/&SAMPLE
        After     AAAACQ/*****************
```

This INSPECT/REPLACING statement will

1. Select the portion of data-name-1 that is to be searched, as specified by the replace-structure.

2. INSPECT each group of positions in the selected portion, moving from left to right. Each time a substring is found that satisfies the replace-structure, it is replaced by the designated string.

The replace-structure components' meanings (as illustrated by the examples of Figure 16-5) are as follows:

CHARACTERS means that every byte is to be replaced by the value of data-name-2 or literal-1. Note that these must be single character operands.

ALL means that every substring of data-name-1 that is identical to the value of data-name-3 or literal-2 is to be replaced with the value of data-name-4 or literal-3.

LEADING means that the replacement will go on only until a substring not equal to data-name-3 or literal-2 is found. Example 4 of Figure 16-5 illustrates this. Note that had the search been for the letter Q, the search would have been terminated immediately, and no replacements would have been made.

FIRST means that only the first occurrence of data-name-3 or literal-2 will be replaced.

The TALLYING and REPLACING Options Together

The INSPECT statement permits the TALLYING and the REPLACING options to be used in one INSPECT statement. When this is done, the criteria for the TALLYING and REPLACING clauses do not have to be the same; however, the TALLYING clause must appear first. This general form is

```
INSPECT data-name-1 TALLYING data-name-2 FOR tally-structure
        REPLACING replace-structure
```

The STRING Statement

Basic Principles of Combining Character Strings

One of the most common operations to perform when manipulating character string data is to combine two or more strings into one. (This is called *concatenation* of string data, although the term is not commonly used in COBOL.) To illustrate, let's consider the following example, which illustrates a variety of principles.

Example 16-2 Combining Character String Fields

Problem Description

A program includes three separate fields: MDAY, MONTH, and YEAR. The needs of a report require that the information in these fields be combined into the single field FULL-DATE.

Output Requirements

The month, day, and year combined into the single field FULL-DATE defined as:

```
10 FULL-DATE PIC X(18).
```

Typical output would be:

```
May 30, 1934
```

Input Description

Three individual fields are defined as follows:

```
10 MONTH PIC X(3).
10 YEAR PIC X(4).
10 MDAY PIC X(2).
```

This basic principle is illustrated in Figure 16-6(a). The task then is to string these fields and appropriate literals together as illustrated in Figure 16-6(b). This is done with the STRING statement.

Figure 16-6

Combining Several Character Strings into a Single String

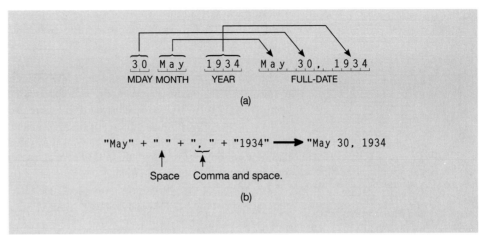

Basic Principles of the STRING Statement

The STRING statement copies the specified sending field(s) into the designated receiving field. The receiving field must be a DISPLAY field. Use of the STRING to build the required date field is illustrated in Figure 16-7. The following are important points illustrated by this example:

1. The sending fields are copied into the receiving field one after the other, in the order they are listed in the statement. Notice that the data flow is similar to that of the MOVE:

    MOVE (*sending field*) TO (*receiving field*)

    Hence, you can think of the STRING statement as somewhat of a "super move."

2. The sending fields can consist of data-names, literals, or figurative constants. As with the INSPECT, if a figurative constant is used, it is treated as a 1-position field. In this example, a single space is inserted in place of SPACE.

3. The operation stops when it has copied all of the sending fields. Notice that the remainder of the receiving field is unchanged. Usually when an operation such as this is to be carried out, the first action is to move spaces into the receiving field to ensure that garbage does not remain if the entire receiving field is not required to hold the data. (Note that in this example, the asterisks are included in the original field only to illustrate what occurs.)

The term DELIMITED BY SIZE means that the delimiter (the signal that the end of the sending field has been reached) is the field size itself. That is, every character from each of the sending fields is to be copied into the receiving field.

However, this might not always give the desired result. For example, let's assume that the month name is obtained from a table of the months in which nine positions are

Figure 16-7

A Simple Form of the STRING

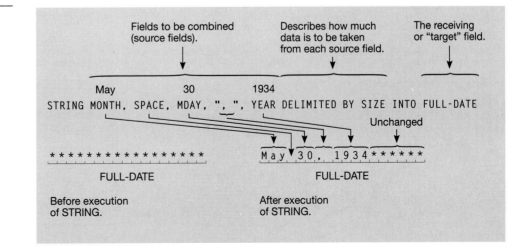

provided for each month (this takes care of September, the month with the most letters). Then if MONTH had been defined as PIC X(9), the results of executing the foregoing statement would be as shown in Figure 16-8. Needless to say, this leaves something to be desired.

In this case, the delimiter for the field MONTH should be a space, rather than the size of the field. This means that as soon as a space is encountered in MONTH, the copying from MONTH is to stop, as is illustrated in Figure 16-9. Note that the delimiter (space) is *not* copied, so SPACE must still be specified as a sending field to separate the month and the day. Furthermore, this example shows that different delimiters can be specified for different sending fields. Each DELIMITED BY clause applies to all preceding sending fields that do not already have a delimiter.

The forms of the preceding examples can be represented by the following limited general form of the STRING statement:

$$\underline{\text{STRING}} \left\{ \left\{ \begin{array}{l} \text{identifier-1} \\ \text{literal-1} \end{array} \right\} \dots \underline{\text{DELIMITED}} \text{ BY} \left\{ \begin{array}{l} \text{identifier-2} \\ \text{literal-2} \\ \underline{\text{SIZE}} \end{array} \right\} \right\} \dots$$

$\underline{\text{INTO}}$ identifier-3

The following example illustrates this form:

```
STRING FLD-A, FLD-B, FLD-C DELIMITED BY SPACE
       FLD-M DELIMITED BY "-"
       FLD-X, FLD-Y, FLD-Z DELIMITED BY SIZE
       INTO FULL-FIELD
```

In this example, the first three fields—FLD-A, FLD-B, and FLD-C—will be delimited by a space character. The single field FLD-M will be delimited by a hyphen. All characters of the last three fields—FLD-X, FLD-Y, and FLD-Z—will be moved because they are delimited by their sizes.

Other Options of the STRING Statement

So far, all examples have started at the beginning of the receiving field. In some cases, it is desirable to copy the sending fields into the receiving at some point other than the beginning. To illustrate this and the use of the STRING and INSPECT together, consider the following example.

Example 16-3 Combining Fields

Problem Description

The control field described in Example 16-1 (length of 30, with each component part separated from the next by the hyphen character) is to be modified as follows:

1. Blank out all subfields after the first. For instance, the field

C127-216-X-556-9

would become

C127-

Figure 16-8

Excess Spaces

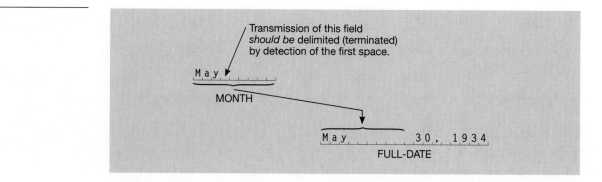

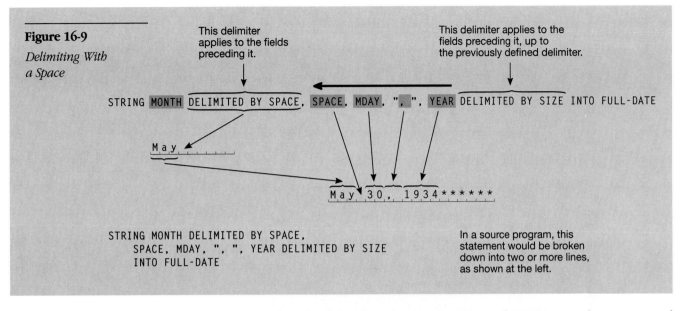

Figure 16-9

Delimiting With a Space

2. Three other fields, named PART-1, PART-2, and PART-3, are to be concatenated (appended), separated by hyphens, onto this field.

3. Store the length of the resulting code field in the variable CODE-FIELD-LEN.

Output Requirements

A modified code field as described.

Input Description

The 30-position code field of Example 16-1.

The sequence of statements to do this is shown with explanations in Figure 16-10. Notice the sequence of these operations.

1. The unwanted portion of CODE-FIELD is replaced by spaces.

2. The position of the first space is determined; this represents the position at which the new code field components are to be added.

3. The new components are added, using the STRING statement with a POINTER phrase. The pointer (CODE-FIELD-LEN) is a field that contains an integer value, which the STRING statement uses as a specification of where to start copying into the receiving field.

Obviously, STRING cannot do the impossible. That is, if the pointer field contains an integer less than 1 or greater than the size of the receiving field, an error situation occurs and no data is copied. Also, STRING cannot make the receiving field larger than defined in the DATA DIVISION. As soon as the receiving field has been filled, the STRING operation stops. This would occur in the example of Figure 16-10 if all three of the component fields were full. Typical results are shown in Figure 16-11.

If truncation of the excess characters—as in Figure 16-11—is acceptable, then the STRING statement of Figure 16-10 will do the job. However, if some action must be taken whenever this overflow possibility occurs, then the OVERFLOW phrase should be included in the STRING statement, as follows:

```
STRING PART-1,"-", PART-2, "-", PART-3
   DELIMITED BY SPACE
   INTO CODE-FIELD
   POINTER CODE-FIELD-LEN
   ON OVERFLOW
     PERFORM 900-CODE-OVERFLOW
END-STRING
```

Figure 16-10

Using the POINTER Phrase

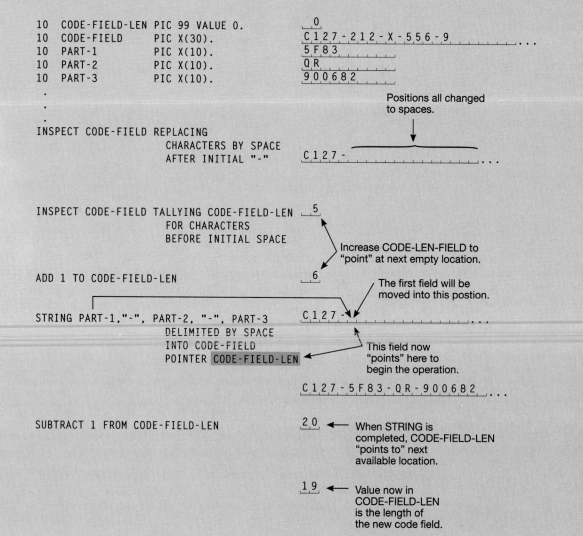

Figure 16-11

Overflowing the Target Field

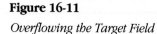

With this form, the STRING statement will put as much data as it can into the receiving field. If the receiving field becomes full before the sending fields are exhausted, as illustrated in Figure 16-11, then the OVERFLOW option will be executed. In this example, the routine 900-CODE-OVERFLOW will be executed. As with the error condition on all such statements, the error sequence can consist of a single—or many—statements. The complete format of the STRING statement is

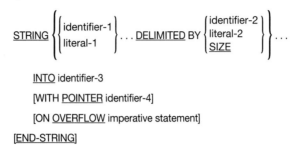

STRING
$\left\{ \left\{ \begin{matrix} \text{identifier-1} \\ \text{literal-1} \end{matrix} \right\} \dots \underline{\text{DELIMITED}} \text{ BY} \left\{ \begin{matrix} \text{identifier-2} \\ \text{literal-2} \\ \underline{\text{SIZE}} \end{matrix} \right\} \right\} \dots$

    INTO identifier-3

    [WITH POINTER identifier-4]

    [ON OVERFLOW imperative statement]

[END-STRING]

The UNSTRING Statement

Basic Principles of the UNSTRING Statement

The UNSTRING statement is the opposite of the STRING statement: it breaks a string down by copying pieces of it into one or more receiving fields. To illustrate this, consider the following example.

Example 16-4 Separating a Field into Subfields

Problem Description
    The control field described in Example 16-1 (length of 30, with each component part separated from the next by the hyphen character) is to be broken down into its individual components. Assume that no more than five parts will be required.

Output Requirements
    Component code subfields stored in the 10-position fields PART-1, PART-2, PART-3, PART-4, and PART-5.

Input Description
    CODE-FIELD (30 positions) as described in Example 16-1.

An UNSTRING statement, together with illustrations of how it works, is shown in Figure 16-12. Notice the following features of this example:

1. The characters in CODE-FIELD, beginning at the left, are copied into the first receiving field (PART-1). The copying continues until a delimiter, the hyphen following C127, is encountered. Note that the delimiter is *not* copied.

2. Copying continues into the second receiving field (PART-2), starting with the character following the delimiter and continuing until the next delimiter is found. When CODE-FIELD is exhausted, execution of the statement terminates.

3. The effect on each receiving field is as though a MOVE had been executed: the remainder of the receiving field is blanked.

4. In this example, five receiving fields are specified. However, with the hyphen as a delimiter, CODE-FIELD contains only four subfields. Therefore, the last receiving field, PART-5, is left undisturbed.

5. The sending field CODE-FIELD remains unchanged.

Let's consider another example, this one the reverse operation of Example 16-2, in which the full date was built from its month, day, and year components. In Figure 16-13, you see a slight problem; that is, the comma has been moved together with the day. If you look closely, you can see the problem: one delimiter is a single space, but the other is the two-character comma and space. Often in UNSTRING operations, the sending field will contain more than one type of delimiter. UNSTRING permits specification of multiple delimiters by the OR option. The word OR has the same meaning in UNSTRING that it has

Figure 16-12

The UNSTRING Statement—
Example 16-4

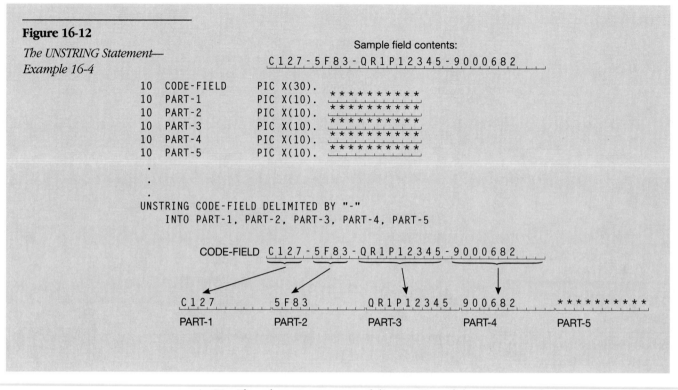

in IF: either character acts as a delimiter. Use of the OR to rectify the problem of Figure 16-13 is illustrated in the statement of Figure 16-14.

A general form representation of the UNSTRING statement to the extent you have considered it so far is as follows:

UNSTRING identifier-1 DELIMITED BY $\begin{Bmatrix} \text{identifier-2} \\ \text{literal-1} \end{Bmatrix}$ $\begin{bmatrix} \underline{\text{OR}} \begin{Bmatrix} \text{identifier-3} \\ \text{literal-1} \end{Bmatrix} \end{bmatrix}$ ...

INTO identifier-4 ...

Additional Features of the UNSTRING Statement

Sometimes strange things happen that really are not strange at all if you understand what is going on. For instance, Figure 16-15 shows the final result from executing the Figure 16-13 UNSTRING. Note that in this example, the month and day are separated by *two* spaces. During execution, the following takes place:

1. Characters are copied one at a time from FULL-DATE into MONTH. After the first space (the delimiter) is encountered, copying to MONTH is terminated.

2. Execution continues; characters are to be transmitted from the position following the delimiter into the second field MDAY.

Figure 16-13

Picking Up an Unwanted
Character

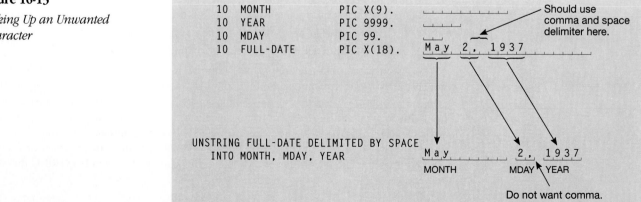

Figure 16-14

Using the OR in the UNSTRING

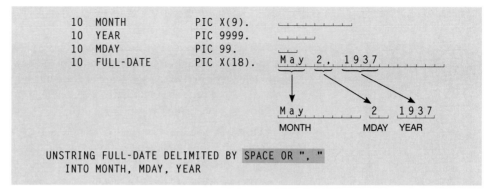

```
        10   MONTH          PIC X(9).
        10   YEAR           PIC 9999.
        10   MDAY           PIC 99.
        10   FULL-DATE      PIC X(18).      May 2, 1937
```

```
                                          May            2  1937
                                         MONTH         MDAY YEAR
```

```
        UNSTRING FULL-DATE DELIMITED BY SPACE OR ", "
            INTO MONTH, MDAY, YEAR
```

3. The next character in MONTH is *another* delimiter (space). Hence, the computer has delimited the second field. However, since it consists of no characters, it is termed a *null field*. When copied to the MDAY receiving field, it consists of nothing but the spaces normally used to fill a receiving field that is longer than the data transmitted.

4. The "third" field transmitted is the day field, which is placed in YEAR.

5. Since there are no more receiving fields, execution of the statement is terminated and the year is not copied from FULL-DATE.

If multiple occurrences of a delimiter are to be considered as just one delimiter (as in this example), the ALL option must be used as follows:

```
        UNSTRING FULL-DATE DELIMITED BY ALL SPACE OR ", "
            INTO MONTH, MDAY, YEAR
```

With this form, 1 or 100 spaces can separate component fields, and they will still be treated as one. The ALL may be used with any delimiter, whether it is a single character or many; it is not limited to use with the space (as in this example). Also, the ALL applies only to the delimiter immediately following it. For example, in the preceding case, the ALL applies only to the SPACE delimiter, not the comma/space combination.

The ALL option—together with other features—is shown in the following complete general form of the UNSTRING statement:

UNSTRING identifier-1

DELIMITED BY $\begin{Bmatrix} \text{identifier-2} \\ \text{literal-1} \end{Bmatrix}$ $\begin{bmatrix} \text{OR [ALL]} \begin{Bmatrix} \text{identifier-3} \\ \text{literal-1} \end{Bmatrix} \end{bmatrix}$ . . .

INTO identifier-4 [DELIMITER IN identifier-5] [COUNT IN identifier-6] . . .

[WITH POINTER identifier-7]

[TALLYING IN identifier-8]

[ON OVERFLOW imperative-statement-1]

[NOT ON OVERFLOW imperative-statement-2]

[END-UNSTRING]

Figure 16-15

Getting a Null String

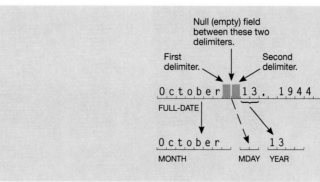

Here you see a number of options that are not illustrated by preceding examples. Their functions are as follows:

DELIMITER IN causes the delimiting character(s) to be moved into the variable specified as identifier-5. If the termination of data movement is the result of reaching the end of the sending field (identifier-1), then identifier-5 is filled with spaces. The program can then test the value in this variable if it is necessary to know how the action was terminated.

COUNT IN specifies how many characters in the sending field were examined in completing the unstring operation. This includes data copied *and* delimiters that you examined.

POINTER names the field containing the number of the position in the sending field where copying is to start. If no pointer is specified, copying begins from the leftmost position. As with STRING, a pointer that is less than 1 or greater than the sending field length terminates the operation. Unlike STRING, UNSTRING *changes* the pointer value by copying the final pointer value into the pointer field.

TALLYING names the accumulator to which is added the number of fields found in the sending field. This accumulator must be initialized by the programmer.

OVERFLOW specifies the action to be taken if the receiving fields are not large enough or numerous enough to accommodate the sending field.

Figure 16-16 gives some additional examples of what can be done by first using the UNSTRING on a field, and then using the STRING to reorganize the components.

Figure 16-16

Using the UNSTRING, Then Using the STRING

```
Typical Input Data              Typical Output Form

Smith John P                    John P Smith
Smith Mary Jones                Mary Jones Smith
Summerfield Adolphus N          Adolphus N Summerfield
Travers Thomas P                Thomas P Travers
O_Donnell Maureen S             Maureen S O_Donnell
Johnson_Jr. Richard X           Richard X Johnson_Jr.
Ng Wilberforce A                Wilberforce A Ng
Breckes-Smythe Algernon P.      Algernon P. Breckes-Smythe
```

A Typical Character String Manipulation Application

Fixed Format and Delimited Files

Many times, the programmer is faced with the task of adapting something to do a task for which it was never intended. This might be expanding a program, using a data file from some other application, or any number of other tasks (most of which are unpleasant). A typical task is using data from another programming system. For example, a person programming with a database management system might want to use files created by a COBOL program, or a BASIC programmer might need to use COBOL files. Even if the data stored is the same, the appearance of the files on disk would likely be quite different. This is because of differences in the methods used by each system for storing information about the file, such as the record length, indexes if any, and so on. Fortunately, some "standard" forms can be used to convert a data file from one programming system to another. To illustrate, consider a name and address file with records consisting of the following fields:

Field	Length
Last name	12
First name	12
Street address	25
City	12
State	2
Zip code	5

Figure 16-17

Data Records

```
Lukenbill   Christopher 138 South Garden Street   Boise        ID83705
```

A Fixed-Length ASCII Record   (a)

```
"Lukenbill","Christopher","138 South Garden Street","Boise","83705"
```

A Delimited Record   (b)

In line sequential format (which you have been using in this book), a typical record would appear as shown in Figure 16-17(a). As you know, each record of this file would consist of 68 positions and would have exactly the same format. One of the characteristics of line sequential files is that each record is terminated by a special end-of-line character. However, fields within the record are not so delimited; one field immediately follows the other. Although you have no indication of where one field ends and the other begins, the formatting data of the DATA DIVISION explicitly defines each field.

With this format, you could create a file that could be read and processed by, for example, a BASIC program exactly as if it had been created by BASIC. This is called a *fixed-format ASCII* file and is a common format used with the IBM-PC. Files created with editors are ASCII files, but they differ from the address file in that records need not all be of the same length. Most software systems have the capability for generating a copy of a file in the fixed-length ASCII form.

Another file format that is commonly encountered with the PC is the *delimited* file. With a delimited file, each field within the record is enclosed in quotes and separated from the others by a comma. In delimited form, the name-address record is as shown in Figure 16-17(b). Generally, records in a delimited file have different lengths (although the records usually contain the same number of fields). Since delimiters are included, there simply is no need to pad a field such as

> Jones

so that it will be the same length as

> Lukenbill

Problem Definition

With this background, let's consider what is involved in converting a file from one form to another.

Example 16-5 File Conversion

Problem Description

A mailing address file has been received from a company that uses dBASE IV. Although dBASE IV is capable of writing files in the fixed-length format, the one sent is delimited. There is no time to wait. A program is required that will convert from a delimited file to a fixed-length record file for the COBOL mailing system.

Output Requirements

Output file name: ADDR.DL

Record format:

Field	Positions
Last name	1–20
First name	21–40
Street address	41–70
City	71–90
State	91–92
Zip	93–97

Output error file name: ADDR.ERR

Record length: 120

Record format: Unformatted (copy of input record)

Input Description
Input file name: ADDR.DLM
Record length: 120
Record format: Delimited with following fields

Field	Contents	Sample Data
1	Name	Johnson, Alice
2	Street address	120 Pine, Apt.#2
3	City/state/Zip	Portland, Oregon 97201

Special notes:
The data has been validated to the extent that the following rules apply:

1. In the name field, the sequence is always last name, then the first name. They are separated by a comma, followed by a space.
2. In the city/state/Zip field, the city is always followed by a comma and space. The state name is separated from the Zip code by two spaces.
3. No record will consist of fewer than 20 bytes or more than 120 bytes.

Processing Requirements

1. Records are to be tested for validity.
   a. Any record that does not include the three field groups defined is considered invalid
   b. Only the records for five following western states are considered valid; all others are invalid:
      California
      Idaho
      Nevada
      Oregon
      Washington

2. Each state name must be converted to its two-letter abbreviation
3. All valid records are to be written to the file ADDR.DL
4. All invalid records are to be written to the file ADDR.ERR

About Reading Variable-Length Records

Example 15-2 uses a billing file that can contain two types of records: one with a record length of 22 and the other with a record length of 30. For this, the RECORD CONTAINS clause was used and two record descriptions were defined, one for each of the two record formats. The input record for Example 16-5 differs in that there is no fixed format: an input record can have any length, ranging from 20 to 120. In this situation, the FD must include the RECORD VARYING clause, which is illustrated in Figure 16-18.

1. A RECORD VARYING clause, which specifies the size range of the record, must be included in the FD. In this example, records as short as 20 characters and as long as 120 characters may be read.

2. The defined record length of the record must be equal to the maximum size specified in the FD or a compiler error will occur.

Figure 16-18

The FD for a Variable-Length Record Line Sequential File

```
FD  DELIM-FILE            LABEL RECORDS ARE STANDARD,
                          RECORD VARYING 20 TO 120
                          DEPENDING ON REC-LENGTH.
01  DELIMITED-RECORD      PIC X(120).
    .
    .
    .
01  WORK-AREAS.
    10  REC-LENGTH        PIC 999.
```

Record can contain anywhere from 20 to 120 bytes.

Defined record must have same length as maximum in FD.

Special variable into which the record length is placed when a record is read. Must be defined in the program.

3. Whenever a record is read, the system provides a count of the number of bytes in that record and stores it in the variable declared by the DEPENDING ON clause (REC-LENGTH in this example). This must be a numeric data item defined in the WORKING-STORAGE SECTION.

Program Planning—Example 16-5

The first thing to do is to take a careful look at the data; a typical record is shown in Figure 16-19(a). Studying this record, you might consider delimiting on the basis of the quotation mark, as illustrated in Figure 16-19(b). This would give five fields, with two of them containing a single comma; they could be discarded. However, often a single record can be misleading; you must carefully examine data in the file (and try to imagine all the remote possibilities). For example, assume that one of the records has the following for an address:

> 4301 "O" Street

This would obviously cause a problem if the quote mark were used as a delimiter. This type of occurrence is a common problem when performing conversions on character string data, since there tends to be relatively little control over the nature of some types of data fields.

Another approach to this problem is to use the quote/comma/quote sequence to delimit, as shown in Figure 16-19(c). The difficulty here is that the last field is delimited with only a quote. A solution to this is to insert a comma/quote after this last field before commencing the processing, as shown in Figure 16-19(d). Thus, each of the three major field groups would be delimited by the quote/comma/quote sequence. Using this approach, the operational steps in separating these fields would be as follows:

INSPECT the input record and check for two quote/comma/quote groups. Insert the trailing comma/quote.

UNSTRING into name, street address and city/state/Zip using the quote/comma/quote as the delimiter.

UNSTRING the name into the last name and first name using the comma/space as the delimiter

UNSTRING the city/state/Zip into city, state, and Zip using the comma/space or space/space as the delimiter.

Convert the state name to its two-letter abbreviation.

Figure 16-19

A Typical Data Record—Example 16-5

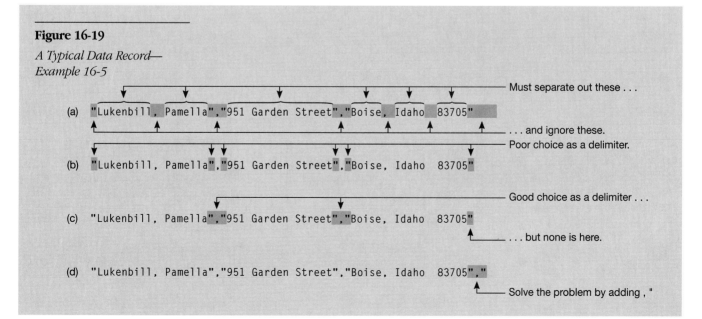

Notice that delimiters are used that are appropriate to the field or subfield requiring further breakdown.

This technique is incorporated into the program solution that is documented in Figure 16-20 (structure chart), Figure 16-21 (flowchart), and Figure 16-22 (pseudocode). As you can see, both the structure and logic are relatively straightforward.

A Program Solution—Example 16-5

A sample program is shown in Figure 16-23 (on page 459). The program itself brings together a number of techniques from this chapter and from Chapter 14 (on tables). The 110 module performs the overall record-handling operations, and the 200 module performs the field extraction operations. Important points about this program are as follows.

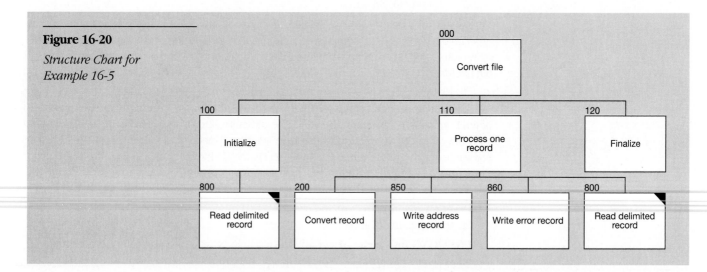

Figure 16-20

Structure Chart for Example 16-5

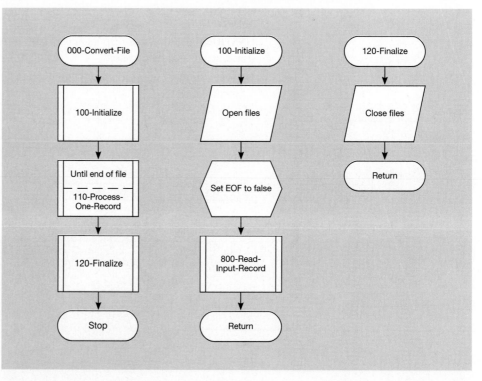

Figure 16-21

A Flowchart for Example 16-5

Figure 16-21

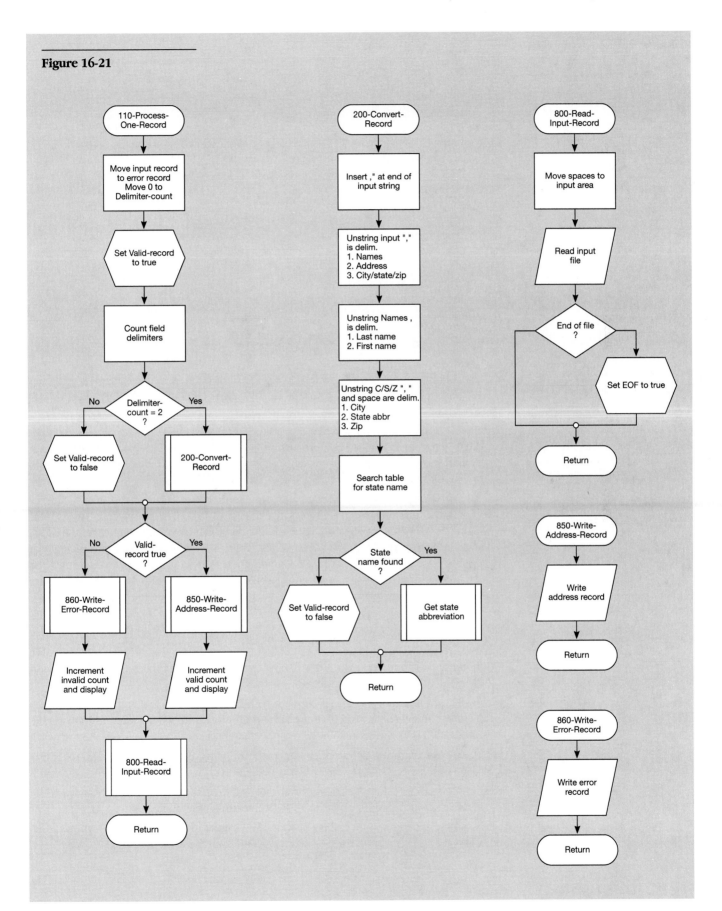

Figure 16-22

Pseudocode for Example 16-5

```
000-Convert-File                              200-Convert-Record
    Perform 100-Initialize                        Insert comma/quote at end of input string
    Perform 110-Process-1-record                  UNSTRING into name, street address
        until End-of-file                                 and city/state/Zip.
                                                      using the quote/comma/quote as the delimiter
100-Initialize                                    UNSTRING the name into the last name
    Open files                                            and first name
    Set EOF to false                                  using the comma/space as the delimiter
    Perform 800-Read-Input-Record                 UNSTRING the city/state/Zip into city, state
                                                          and Zip
110-Process-1-Record                                  using the comma/space or space/space
    Move input record to error record area                as the delimiter
    Move 0 to Delimiter-count                      SEARCH table for state name
    Set Valid-record to true                      If state name found
    Count field delimiters in input record           Move state abbreviation to output area
    If Delimeter-count = 2                         else
      Perform 200-Convert-Record                      Set Valid-record to false
    else
      Set Valid-record to false               800-Read-Input-Record
    If Valid-record                               Move spaces to input area
      Perform 850-Write-Address-Record            Read Address file
      Increment Valid-record count                    at end set EOF to true
      Display status
    else                                      850-Write-Address-Record
      Perform 860-Write-Error-Record              Write Address-record
      Increment Invalid-record count
      Display status                          860-Write-Error-Record
    Perform 800-Read-Input-Record                 Write Error-record

120-Finalize
    Close files
    Display termination message
```

1. The 120-byte input record DELIMITED-RECORD is defined in two parts: a 1-byte filler (to omit the leading quote) and the 119-byte field DELIMITED-RECORD-ELEMENTS, which consists of 119 elements to provide access to any position of the record.

2. When the record is read, it is first moved to ERROR-RECORD. This is necessary to save the original record before any processing because the trailing delimiter is added prior to field separation. If any error is detected, the original record must be written without any modification.

3. With the INSPECT-TALLYING statement, the number of quote/comma/quote delimiters is counted and the result is stored in DELIM-COUNT. If it is not equal to 2, then VALID-RECORD is set to false. Since the delimiter includes a double quote, the literal is defined with single quotes. With RM/COBOL, it is possible to use either single or double quotes to define a literal. If a single quote is used to begin the literal, then the compiler searches for the next single quote to end it. Everything inside the single quotes, including any double quotes, is treated as part of the literal.

4. If DELIM-COUNT is equal to 2, the 200 convert module is executed. This module separates all fields.

5. If the record is valid, the converted version is written to the fixed-format file; if invalid, the original is written to the error file. Note that counters of the number of valid and invalid records are also incremented.

6. In the 200 module, the actual conversion takes place. The first step is to insert the trailing comma/quote. Note that the subscripting uses the value stored in the variable REC-LENGTH. A question at the end of the chapter relates to the value in this variable.

7. The fields are broken out of the records by using three consecutive UNSTRING statements, as described in the earlier pseudocode.

8. A table search is done to convert the state name to its two-letter abbreviation. If the name is not in the table, the VALID-RECORD switch is set to false.

A sample set of data file listings is shown in Figure 16-24. Here you see the original delimited file, the converted fixed-length record file, and the error file.

Figure 16-23

*Data Conversion—
Example 16-5*

```
 1     IDENTIFICATION DIVISION.
 2
 3     PROGRAM-ID. FILE-CVT.
 4
 5   *   Written by W.Price  8/1/86
 6   *   Modified by W.Price  9/2/90
 7
 8     ENVIRONMENT DIVISION.
 9     CONFIGURATION SECTION.
10     SOURCE-COMPUTER. IBM-PC.
11
12     INPUT-OUTPUT SECTION.
13     FILE-CONTROL.
14        SELECT DELIM-FILE     ASSIGN TO DISK, "ADDR.DLM",
15                              ORGANIZATION IS LINE SEQUENTIAL.
16        SELECT ADDRESS-FILE   ASSIGN TO DISK, "ADDR.DL"
17                              ORGANIZATION IS LINE SEQUENTIAL.
18        SELECT ERROR-FILE     ASSIGN TO DISK, "ADDR.ERR"
19                              ORGANIZATION IS LINE SEQUENTIAL.
20
21     DATA DIVISION.
22
23     FILE SECTION.
24
25     FD  DELIM-FILE     RECORD VARYING 20 TO 120
26                        DEPENDING ON REC-LENGTH.
27     01  DELIMITED-RECORD.
28         10           PIC X.
29         10  DELIMITED-RECORD-ELEMENTS.
30             20  DL-CHARA  OCCURS 119 TIMES   PIC X.
31
32     FD  ADDRESS-FILE.
33     01  ADDRESS-RECORD.
34         10  AR-LAST-NAME  PIC X(20).
35         10  AR-FIRST-NAME PIC X(20).
36         10  AR-STREET     PIC X(30).
37         10  AR-CITY       PIC X(20).
38         10  AR-STATE      PIC X(2).
39         10  AR-ZIP        PIC X(5).
40
41     FD  ERROR-FILE.
42     01  ERROR-RECORD   PIC X(120).
43
44     WORKING-STORAGE SECTION.
45
46     01  PROGRAMMED-SWITCHES.
47         10                    PIC X.
48             88  END-OF-FILE   VALUE "Y"  FALSE "N".
49         10                    PIC X.
50             88  VALID-RECORD  VALUE "Y"  FALSE "N".
51
52     01  WORK-AREAS.
53         10  REC-LENGTH       PIC 999.
54         10  BOTH-NAMES       PIC X(31).
55         10  CITY-STATE-ZIP   PIC X(35).
56         10  STATE-WORK       PIC X(10).
57         10  DELIM-COUNT      PIC 9.
58         10  VALID-REC-COUNT  PIC 999 VALUE 0.
59         10  INVALID-REC-COUNT PIC 999 VALUE 0.
60
61   * Table definition
62     01  TABLE-SIZE.
63         10  STATE-TABLE-SIZE   PIC 9  VALUE 5.
64
65     01  STATE-NAME-LIST.
66         10        PIC X(12)  VALUE "WashingtonWA".
67         10        PIC X(12)  VALUE "Oregon    OR".
68         10        PIC X(12)  VALUE "CaliforniaCA".
69         10        PIC X(12)  VALUE "Idaho     ID".
70         10        PIC X(12)  VALUE "Nevada    NV".
71
72     01  STATE-NAME-TABLE REDEFINES STATE-NAME-LIST.
73         10  STATE-ENTRY OCCURS 5 TIMES
74                         INDEXED BY STATE-INDEX.
75             20  STATE-NAME    PIC X(10).
76             20  STATE-ABBREV  PIC XX.
77
78     SCREEN SECTION.
79
80     01  MONITOR-ACTION-SCREEN.
81         10  VALUE "Valid records written: "  BLANK SCREEN
82                                               LINE 4.
83         10  PIC ZZ9  FROM VALID-REC-COUNT  LINE PLUS 0
84                                            COL PLUS 0.
85         10  VALUE "Invalid records written: " LINE 6.
86         10  PIC ZZ9  FROM INVALID-REC-COUNT LINE PLUS 0
87                                             COL PLUS 0.
88         10  VALUE "Invalid records written:"  LINE 6.
89
90     PROCEDURE DIVISION.
91
92     000-CONVERT-FILE.
93         PERFORM 100-INITIALIZE
94         PERFORM 110-PROCESS-1-RECORD
95             UNTIL END-OF-FILE
96         PERFORM 120-FINALIZE
97         STOP RUN.
98
99     100-INITIALIZE.
100        OPEN INPUT DELIM-FILE
101        OPEN OUTPUT ADDRESS-FILE
102                ERROR-FILE
103        SET END-OF-FILE TO FALSE
104        PERFORM 800-READ-DELIMITED-RECORD.
105
106    110-PROCESS-1-RECORD.
107        SET VALID-RECORD TO TRUE
108        MOVE ZERO TO DELIM-COUNT
109        MOVE DELIMITED-RECORD TO ERROR-RECORD
110
111        INSPECT DELIMITED-RECORD
112            TALLYING DELIM-COUNT FOR ALL '","'
113
114        IF DELIM-COUNT = 2
115          PERFORM 200-CONVERT-RECORD
116        ELSE
117          SET VALID-RECORD TO FALSE
118        END-IF
119
120        IF VALID-RECORD
121          PERFORM 850-WRITE-ADDRESS-RECORD
122          ADD 1 TO VALID-REC-COUNT
123          DISPLAY MONITOR-ACTION-SCREEN
124        ELSE
125          PERFORM 860-WRITE-ERROR-RECORD
126          ADD 1 TO INVALID-REC-COUNT
127          DISPLAY MONITOR-ACTION-SCREEN
128        END-IF
129
130        PERFORM 800-READ-DELIMITED-RECORD.
131
132    120-FINALIZE.
133        DISPLAY "Conversion complete." LINE 8 POSITION 1
134        CLOSE DELIM-FILE
135              ADDRESS-FILE
136              ERROR-FILE.
137
138    200-CONVERT-RECORD.
139        MOVE ',' TO DL-CHARA(REC-LENGTH)
140        MOVE '"' TO DL-CHARA(REC-LENGTH + 1)
141
142        UNSTRING DELIMITED-RECORD-ELEMENTS DELIMITED BY '","'
143            INTO BOTH-NAMES, AR-STREET, CITY-STATE-ZIP
144
145        UNSTRING BOTH-NAMES DELIMITED BY ", "
146            INTO AR-LAST-NAME, AR-FIRST-NAME
147
148        UNSTRING CITY-STATE-ZIP DELIMITED BY ", " OR " "
149            INTO AR-CITY, STATE-WORK, AR-ZIP
150
151        SET STATE-INDEX TO 1
152
153        SEARCH STATE-ENTRY
154          AT END
155            SET VALID-RECORD TO FALSE
156          WHEN STATE-WORK = STATE-NAME(STATE-INDEX)
157            MOVE STATE-ABBREV(STATE-INDEX) TO AR-STATE
158        END-SEARCH.
159
160    800-READ-DELIMITED-RECORD.
161        MOVE SPACES TO DELIMITED-RECORD
162        READ DELIM-FILE
163            AT END SET END-OF-FILE TO TRUE
164        END-READ.
165
166    850-WRITE-ADDRESS-RECORD.
167        WRITE ADDRESS-RECORD.
168
169    860-WRITE-ERROR-RECORD.
170        WRITE ERROR-RECORD.
```

Figure 16-24

Sample File Listings for Example 16-5

```
"Baldwin, Scott ","105 Ramona St.","El Cerrito, California  94611"
"Stram, H","1355 B Street","Kansas City, Missouri  64117"
"Davidson, Henrietta","6836 175th N.W.","Seattle, Washington  98177"
"Cook, John","125 A Stre
"Lukenbill, Pamella","951 Garden Street","Boise, Idaho  83705"
"Harcourt, Amy","12500 Central Campus Way","Eugene, Oregon  97401"
```

The Delimited File   (a)

```
Baldwin      Scott       105 Ramona St.               El Cerrito   CA94611
Davidson     Henrietta   6836 175th N.W.              Seattle      WA98177
Lukenbill    Pamella     951 Garden Street            Boise        ID83705
Harcourt     Amy         12500 Central Campus Way     Eugene       OR97401
```

The Converted Fixed-Length Record File   (b)

```
"Stram, H","1355 B Street","Kansas City, Missouri  64117"
"Cook, John","125 A Stre
```

The Error File   (c)

The final point relates to a very practical consideration. That is, if the file to be converted is very large, the process would take more than a few seconds. You would know that activity is taking place by observing the disk drive light, but you would have no idea of how much progress is being made. For programs such as this, it is good practice to display something on the screen to let the computer user know how processing is progressing. To this end, the screen is cleared and messages are displayed regarding the number of records written to each file (refer to lines 123 and 127 and the SCREEN SECTION beginning line 78). Then as each record is written, the screen count is updated. The final screen display from processing the six-record file is shown in Figure 16-25.

Figure 16-25

Screen Display for Example 16-5

```
Valid records written:    4

Invalid records written:    2


Conversion complete
```

Chapter Summary

General

This chapter presents methods for manipulating character string data. You learned how to search for a desired substring, replace a substring with another, combine two or more strings into a single string, and break a string into two or more strings. The basis for these operations is two powerful statements: INSPECT and STRING.

COBOL Language Elements

The COBOL statements that you have studied in this chapter are

INSPECT

TALLYING option	Provides the ability to count the occurrence of a character or group of characters. Counting can be for • The entire string • Leading occurrences of the substring • Preceding the occurrence of another substring • Following the occurrence of another substring

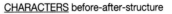

INSPECT data-name-1 TALLYING data-name-2 FOR tally-structure

tally-structure

CHARACTERS before-after-structure

$$\left\{ \left\{ \begin{array}{l} \underline{ALL} \\ \underline{LEADING} \end{array} \right\} \left\{ \begin{array}{l} \text{data-name-3} \\ \text{literal-1} \end{array} \right\} \text{before-after-structure} \right\} \ldots$$

before-after-structure

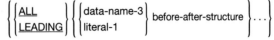

$$\left\{ \begin{array}{l} \underline{BEFORE} \\ \underline{AFTER} \end{array} \right\} \text{INITIAL} \left\{ \begin{array}{l} \text{data-name-4} \\ \text{literal-2} \end{array} \right\}$$

REPLACING option	Provides the ability to replace a substring with another string of equal length. Substring replacement can be for • All occurrences in the string being operated upon • Only leading occurrences of the substring • Only the first occurrence of the substring

INSPECT data-name-1 REPLACING replace-structure

replace-structure

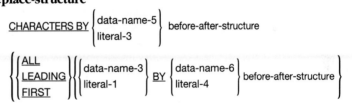

$$\text{CHARACTERS BY} \left\{ \begin{array}{l} \text{data-name-5} \\ \text{literal-3} \end{array} \right\} \text{before-after-structure}$$

$$\left\{ \left\{ \begin{array}{l} \underline{ALL} \\ \underline{LEADING} \\ \underline{FIRST} \end{array} \right\} \left\{ \begin{array}{l} \text{data-name-3} \\ \text{literal-1} \end{array} \right\} \underline{BY} \left\{ \begin{array}{l} \text{data-name-6} \\ \text{literal-4} \end{array} \right\} \text{before-after-structure} \right\}$$

before-after-structure

This structure is identical to that described for the TALLYING.
Both the REPLACING and TALLYING can be used in a single INSPECT.

INSPECT data-name-1   TALLYING data-name-2 FOR tally-structure
                              REPLACING replace-structure

STRING	Provides the ability to combine (concatenate) two or more strings into a single resulting field. The component strings may be combined in their entirety (DELIMITED BY SIZE) or up to a certain point in the string (DELIMITED BY substring specified in the statement).

$$\text{STRING} \left\{ \left\{ \begin{array}{l} \text{identifier-1} \\ \text{literal-1} \end{array} \right\} \ldots \underline{DELIMITED} \text{ BY} \left\{ \begin{array}{l} \text{identifier-2} \\ \text{literal-2} \\ \underline{SIZE} \end{array} \right\} \right\} \ldots$$

INTO identifier-3

[WITH POINTER identifier-2]

[ON OVERFLOW imperative statement]

[END-STRING]

UNSTRING   Provides the ability to break down a field into two or more fields. Criterion to distinguish the end of each field is indicated by one or more delimiters specified in the statement.

UNSTRING identifier-1

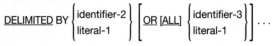

     INTO identifier-4 [DELIMITER IN identifier-5] [COUNT IN identifier-6] . . .

     [WITH POINTER identifier-7]

     [TALLYING IN identifier-8]

     [ON OVERFLOW imperative-statement]

     [NOT ON OVERFLOW imperative-statement-2]

UNSTRING identifier-1 [END-UNSTRING]

Other language elements that you have studied in this chapter are

RECORD VARYING   This FD clause specifies the range of character positions in a variable length record.

      RECORD IS VARYING IN SIZE [[FROM integer-1] [TO integer-2] CHARACTERS]

Reference modification   Allows the programmer to designate a subfield within a field in the PROCEDURE DIVISION.

      data-name (left-most-character-position: [length])

Error Prevention/ Detection

For most applications in which access is required to components of a fixed-field record, define them as subfields in the DATA DIVISION; this provides better documentation than using reference modification.

Before setting up an UNSTRING or INSPECT statement, always inspect the data with care to ensure that unexpected delimiting situations do not exist.

Questions and Exercises

Key Terminology

character string data	fixed format	string manipulation
concatenation	null field	substring
delimited file	reference modification	
delimiter	string data	

General Questions

1. What is meant when a field has a "fixed format"?
2. Any character that is used to separate two parts of a field is known as a _____?
3. INSPECT/TALLYING permits a programmer to do what?
4. If a programmer wants to substitute one or more specified characters with other characters, how can this be accomplished?
5. What are the three components of the INSPECT statement's tally-structure and how are they defined?
6. The INSPECT statement's replace-structure has one additional component that the tally-structure does not have. What is it and how is it used?
7. The STRING statement can be used to assemble individual fields and appropriate literals together into one field. What statement can be used to separate one field into individual subfields?

Questions Relating to the Example Programs

1. Referring to the program segment of Figure 16-10, assume that the first hyphen that terminates the original field is not to be included in the output field. What change would be required in the statement sequence?

2. In the FILE-CVT program (Figure 16-23), the leading quote in the delimited record is omitted by operating on the data item DELIMITED-RECORD-ELEMENTS with the UNSTRING. Modify the first UNSTRING in the 200 routine (line 142) to operate on the full record DELIMITED-RECORD, yet still leave the first single quote behind.

3. In the FILE-CVT program (Figure 16-23), the value in the variable REC-LENGTH is used to insert a trailing comma at the end of the field (see line 139). Since the value in REC-LENGTH contains the length of the record, it appears that the element DL-CHARA(REC-LENGTH) is the last position of the record, not the first unused one. However, this is not the case. Why not?

4. Lines 145 through 148 in the FILE-CVT program (Figure 16-23) use intermediate work areas called BOTH-NAMES and CITY-STATE-ZIP. Why is this being done?

5. What would happen during execution of the FILE-CVT program (Figure 16-23) if the programmer left out the INSPECT/TALLYING statement, lines 111-112?

Writing Program Statements

1. Operating on the character string in TEST-FIELD, write an INSPECT statement to perform each of the following counts:
   a. The total number of hyphens (-).
   b. The number of hyphens after the first occurrence of the letter Z.
   c. The total number of double hyphens (--).

2. Write the INSPECT statements for each of the following cases:
   a. Count the number of Z's in ITEM-A. In addition, replace every X before the first Y with a 0 (zero), and replace every space with an asterisk (*).
   b. Assume the following DATA DIVISION coding:

   ```
   05 ITEM-B            PIC ZZ,ZZZ.9.
   05 FRACTION-SWITCH   PIC 9.
   ```

   Store a value of 0 in FRACTION-SWITCH if ITEM-B is fractional; store a value of 1 if ITEM-B is not fractional. (*Note:* If the digit to the right of the decimal is not zero, the number is fractional.)
   c. Count the number of times each vowel A, E, I, O, and U appears in ITEM-C.

3. Assume that an input record definition includes the following fields:

   ```
   05 FLD-A             PIC X(5).
   05 FLD-B             PIC X(10).
   05 FLD-C             PIC X(4).
   ```

   Use the STRING statement to combine the contents of these three fields into:

   ```
   FLD-X                PIC X(19)
   ```

   FLD-A an.d FLD-C contain any characters, including spaces, and are to be copied in their entirety. FLD-B will contain one or more letters, and the remainder of the field will be blank. Only the letters in FLD-B are to be copied into FLD-X. (*Note:* Be sure that no residual data remains in FLD-X from the previous record.)

4. Use the INSPECT, UNSTRING, and STRING statements to "de-edit" FLD-E into DOLLARS and CENTS, assuming the following definitions:

   ```
   10 FLD-E             PIC $ZZZ.99
   10 DOLLARS           PIC 999.
   10 CENTS             PIC 99.
   ```

5. Use the INSPECT statement to tally each dollar sign, pound sign, and asterisk in a field called NAME-FIELD. If any of the three counts (DOL-COUNT, LB-COUNT, or AST-COUNT) is greater than zero, replace the contents as follows. The dollar sign and asterisk are to become a space and the pound sign is to become a comma.

6. Assuming that the NAME-FIELD in Exercise 5 now contains a blank in the first position followed by last name, comma, and first name, UNSTRING this to create two separate fields. Redefine NAME-FIELD to start with the correct position.

```
10 NAME-FIELD       PIC X(25).
```

Programming Assignments

16-1 Combine First and Last Names

The dean of student services at the Computer Institute of Technology feels that it would be useful if each student had a name tag during the first week of classes.

Output Requirements:
    A printed name tag with the following output.
        Student name (first name, one space, and last name)
        Class standing (Freshman, Sophomore, . . .)
        Major (description, not code)

Input Description:
    File name: STUDENTS.DL
    Record description: See Appendix A

Processing Requirements:
    For each student (record):
1. Convert the separate fields First name and Last name to a single field with one space separating the two names.
2. Print the name.
3. From the input Class standing code use the word Freshman, Sophomore, . . . (see the record definition) for the next output line line.
4. Print the second output line.
5. From a table of majors (see Programming Assignment 14-1), obtain the major description using the input Major code.
6. Print the third output line.
7. Print three blank lines.

16-2 Reading Level Analysis

Individuals who study the writing styles of authors perform many types of analyses to determine characteristics of each style. One of the most commonly used methods is to count the number of letters in each word of a manuscript and tabulate the results. For this application, the words are to be tabulated as follows:

    Short   Words with 3 letters or fewer
    Mid   Words with 4-7 letters
    Long   Words with more than 7 letters

With the high speed of a computer, this is an ideal computer application.

Output Requirements:
    A screen display listing the word count for each manuscript:

```
MANUSCRIPT aaaa CONTAINS xxx SHORT WORDS
                         yyy MID WORDS
                         zzz LONG WORDS
```

Input Description:
    File name: MANU.DL
    Record description: See Appendix A

Processing Requirements:
    For each manuscript, repeat the following for each record:
1. Read a record.
2. Scan the record, counting the length of each word encountered.

When a new manuscript number is encountered:
3. Display the count and continue to the next manuscript.

16-3 Elements of Word Processing

Word processing involves the computerized handling of text information. One of the important functions of a word processor is to make certain that each printed line conforms to the paper width and margin requirements of the given document. This problem involves rearranging lines of text data stored in a file to fit a standard page. For instance, assume that the first four records in the file are

> High, scattered clouds marked the weather. The best
> way to
> describe my thoughts
> was "Thank goodness the rain has stopped."

This text is to be printed with a maximum line width of 50 characters. Thus, after "rearranging," the above four lines would be printed as follows.

> High, scattered clouds marked the weather. The
> best way to describe my thoughts was "Thank
> goodness the rain has stopped."

Output Requirements:
> Printed text with an output line width of 50 characters.

Input Description:
> File name: MANU.DL
> Record description: See Appendix A
> *Note:* The first four positions contain the manuscript number. Ignore these columns for this assignment.

Processing Requirements:
1. Read each input record.
2. Extract the "next" word from the input record and move it to the output area. Repeat until the remaining space on the output line is not sufficient to hold the next word.
3. Print the output line.
4. You can assume that a "word" is any substring delimited by a space. (Assume that there is only one space between sentences.) In this respect, *"Thank,* including the open quote, would be treated as a word. If a line is empty (no characters in it beyond column 4), treat it as a blank line and leave a blank line in the printed output.

PROGRAM MANAGEMENT

Chapter Objectives

The principle of program modularization is one of the cornerstones of this book. The PERFORM has provided you with the basis for creating your programs as sets of relatively independent modules, each of which is executed (performed) from a higher level module. This has resulted in programs that are, among other things, easy to write, maintain, and modify—critical traits in a business programming environment. However, in the general business environment, there are other needs. For instance, most programs are much larger than those you have been writing and are written by two or more programmers (or even programming teams) working on separate portions of the program. Also, it is very common for particular sections of code to be the same in two or more programs. For instance, any program using the job-code/pay-rate table of Chapter 14 would require the table load modules. It is through that example (the PAY-BEN4 program) that different techniques are examined for separating the table load operation from the main program. The three techniques that you will learn in this chapter are

- The COPY statement, which allows source code to be stored as separate files and inserted into the program during the compiling operation

- The CALL statement, which allows one program to cause a second to be loaded into memory, whereby control is switched between the programs

- Nested programs, wherein a program fully contains one or more subordinate programs

Introduction to Managing Large Programs

About Data and Data Descriptions

When writing programs to process data, you deal with two major entities: the data to be processed and the programs to process that data. You learned very early in this book that the data file contains data only; it does not contain information about the data. For instance, look at Figure 17-1 and you see one of the records from the software file in which numeric fields run into one another. Without additional information, you have no idea where one field ends and the next begins, nor do you know anything about the data types. By now, you know that this information is contained in the DATA DIVISION of any program processing this file. The relationship between a COBOL program and the data file it processes is illustrated in Figure 17-2. In a broad sense, this is contrary to structured principles. The data—along with information describing the data—should be together.

Think of the application in which a file is used by 50 different programs and some new fields must be added. The data description (DATA DIVISION) must be modified in each of the 50 programs and the programs recompiled. A partial solution to this dilemma is to store the record description as a separate file and copy it into the program whenever the program is to be compiled. This serves two useful functions. First, the entire record

Figure 17-1

A Data Record without Formatting Information

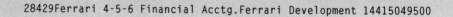

```
28429Ferrari 4-5-6 Financial Acctg.Ferrari Development 14415049500
```

Figure 17-2

Relationship between a COBOL Program and a Data File

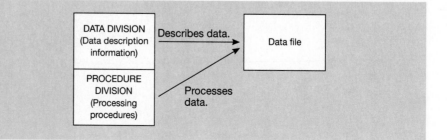

description need not be keyed in for each program, thereby saving time and reducing the possibility of keying errors. Second, it allows each program to function from a single master description that can be updated as changes are made to the data file.

COBOL provides the capability for the automatic inclusion of separately stored code (anywhere in the program, not just the DATA DIVISION) by the compiler during the compile operation. This is done with the COPY statement.

Before proceeding to the COPY statement, it is worthwhile to reflect on the nature of COBOL and traditional programming languages, as illustrated in Figure 17-2. Inclusion of data description data in the processing program is a simple result of the evolution of the data processing and dates back to the punched card days, when each record of a file was punched in a card. Necessarily, programs to process the data needed to include data about the data (individual field positions, their types, and decimal positioning for numeric quantities). When computers first began to be used in business, punched card processing techniques were adapted to computers and the magnetic tape storage medium. Thus, programming languages that were developed reflected the need to keep the data description data with the processing programs, rather than the data files.

However, with the development of random access storage devices such as the magnetic disk, it became practical to store data about the data together with the data file, as illustrated in Figure 17-3. In fact, that is one of the characteristics of database management systems (DBMS). With a DBMS, what you know as the DATA DIVISION of a COBOL program is essentially part of the data file. This vastly simplifies the maintenance of data stored in the file and also simplifies programming, since it makes the processing procedures independent of the data file structure.

Figure 17-3

Storing Data Description Data with the Data: A Characteristic of a Database Management System

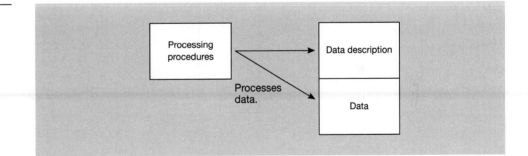

The PAY-BEN4 Program— The Illustration Program

The PAY-BEN series of programs in Chapter 14 illustrate tables. In these programs, a job-code/pay-rate is read from a file into a table for processing. Although the learning focus was on the table-loading process, the primary point of the program was to perform processing on the employee file, using the table during processing. Loading the table was merely a preliminary action necessary before beginning "real" processing activities.

You can probably imagine that in a business environment, there would likely be more than one program using the table and therefore, each would need to load it as part of the initializing procedure. The section of PROCEDURE DIVISION code—together with the table description entries for the PAY-BEN4 program—will be "extracted" from the program to illustrate the COPY and CALL statements and nested programs. These sections of code are highlighted in Figure 17-4.

Figure 17-4

The PAY-BEN4 Program and Code to be Extracted

```
1        IDENTIFICATION DIVISION.
2        PROGRAM-ID. PAY-BEN4.
3
4    *    Pay special benefits - Pay Rate lookup using SEARCH ALL.
5    *    Written by J.Olson 10/1/86
6
7        ENVIRONMENT DIVISION.
8        CONFIGURATION SECTION.
9        SOURCE-COMPUTER. IBM-PC.
10
11       INPUT-OUTPUT SECTION.
12       FILE-CONTROL.
13           SELECT EMPLOYEE-FILE  ASSIGN TO DISK  "EMPL-BEN.DL"
14                                 ORGANIZATION IS LINE SEQUENTIAL.
15
16           SELECT JOB-CODE-FILE  ASSIGN TO DISK  "JOB-CODE.TBL"
17                                 ORGANIZATION IS LINE SEQUENTIAL.
18       DATA DIVISION.
19
20       FILE SECTION.
21
22       FD  EMPLOYEE-FILE.
23       01  EMPLOYEE-RECORD.
24           10  ER-EMPL-NUMBER       PIC X(5).
25           10  ER-EMPL-JOB-CODE     PIC 9(3).
26           10                       PIC X(42).
27
28       FD  JOB-CODE-FILE.
29       01  JOB-CODE-RECORD.
30           10  JC-JOB-CODE          PIC 9(3).
31           10  JC-PAY-RATE          PIC 9(2)V9(2).
32
33       WORKING-STORAGE SECTION.
34
35       01  TABLE-ACCESS-ITEMS    USAGE BINARY.
36           10  TABLE-SIZE           PIC 99  VALUE 25.
37
38       01  PROGRAMMED-SWITCHES.
39           10                       PIC X.
40               88  END-OF-FILE      VALUE "Y"   FALSE "N".
41           10                       PIC X.
42               88  TABLE-LOADED     VALUE "Y"   FALSE "N".
43           10                       PIC X.
44               88  TABLE-LOAD-ERROR VALUE "Y"   FALSE "N".
45           10                       PIC X.
46               88  CODE-FOUND       VALUE "Y"   FALSE "N".
47
48       01  OTHER-VARIABLES.
49           10  ENTRY-COUNTER        PIC 99.
50           10  PAY-RATE-DISPLAY     PIC ZZ.99.
51           10  PREVIOUS-JOB-CODE    PIC 999   VALUE ZERO.
52
53       01  JOB-CODE-TABLE.
54           10  JOB-CODE-TABLE-ENTRY OCCURS 1 TO 25 TIMES
55                                    DEPENDING ON TABLE-SIZE
56                                    ASCENDING KEY IS JOB-CODE
57                                    INDEXED BY JOB-INDEX.
58               20  JOB-CODE         PIC 999.
59               20  PAY-RATE         PIC 99V99.
60
61       PROCEDURE DIVISION.
62
63       000-PAY-SPECIAL-BENEFITS.
64           PERFORM 100-INITIALIZE
65           PERFORM 110-PROCESS-1-EMPLOYEE
66               UNTIL END-OF-FILE
67           PERFORM 120-FINALIZE
68           STOP RUN.
69
70       100-INITIALIZE.
71           PERFORM 200-LOAD-JOB-CODE-TABLE
72           IF TABLE-LOAD-ERROR
73               DISPLAY " "
74               DISPLAY "Table size exceeded!!"  REVERSE
75               DISPLAY "Processing terminated."
76               STOP RUN
77           END-IF
78           OPEN INPUT  EMPLOYEE-FILE
79           SET END-OF-FILE TO FALSE
80           PERFORM 800-READ-EMPLOYEE-RECORD.
81
82       110-PROCESS-1-EMPLOYEE.
83           PERFORM 300-SEARCH-TABLE
84
85           IF CODE-FOUND
86               PERFORM 310-PROCESS-SPECIAL-BENEFITS
87           END-IF
88
89           PERFORM 800-READ-EMPLOYEE-RECORD.
90
91       120-FINALIZE.
92           DISPLAY " "  BEEP
93           DISPLAY "Special benefits processing has been completed."
94           CLOSE EMPLOYEE-FILE.
95
96       200-LOAD-JOB-CODE-TABLE.
97           OPEN INPUT JOB-CODE-FILE
98           MOVE ALL "9" TO JOB-CODE-TABLE
99           SET TABLE-LOAD-ERROR TO FALSE
100          SET TABLE-LOADED TO FALSE
101          DISPLAY "Loading Table" ERASE
102          DISPLAY "Entry number    Code"
103          SET JOB-INDEX TO 1
104
105          PERFORM VARYING ENTRY-COUNTER FROM 1 BY 1
106              UNTIL TABLE-LOADED OR TABLE-LOAD-ERROR
107          PERFORM 810-READ-JOB-CODE-RECORD
108          IF TABLE-LOADED
109              COMPUTE TABLE-SIZE = ENTRY-COUNTER - 1
110              DISPLAY " "
111              DISPLAY "Table load complete."
112          ELSE
113              IF JC-JOB-CODE NOT > PREVIOUS-JOB-CODE
114                  DISPLAY " "
115                  DISPLAY "Job code ", JC-JOB-CODE,
116                      " is out of sequence."
117                  SET TABLE-LOAD-ERROR TO TRUE
118              ELSE
119                  IF ENTRY-COUNTER NOT > TABLE-SIZE
120                      MOVE JC-JOB-CODE TO JOB-CODE(JOB-INDEX)
121                      MOVE JC-PAY-RATE TO PAY-RATE(JOB-INDEX)
122                      SET JOB-INDEX UP BY 1
123                      DISPLAY "    ", ENTRY-COUNTER,
124                          "     ", JC-JOB-CODE
125                      MOVE JC-JOB-CODE TO PREVIOUS-JOB-CODE
126                  ELSE
127                      DISPLAY " "
128                      DISPLAY "Table size exceeded. ",
129                          JC-JOB-CODE, " cannot be loaded."
130                      SET TABLE-LOAD-ERROR TO TRUE
131                  END-IF
132              END-IF
133          END-IF
134          END-PERFORM
135
136          CLOSE JOB-CODE-FILE.
137
138      300-SEARCH-TABLE.
139          SEARCH ALL JOB-CODE-TABLE-ENTRY
140          AT END
141              SET CODE-FOUND TO FALSE
142          WHEN JOB-CODE(JOB-INDEX) = ER-EMPL-JOB-CODE
143              MOVE PAY-RATE(JOB-INDEX) TO PAY-RATE-DISPLAY
144              SET CODE-FOUND TO TRUE
145          END-SEARCH.
146
147      310-PROCESS-SPECIAL-BENEFITS.
148          DISPLAY " "
149          DISPLAY "Employee: ", ER-EMPL-NUMBER
150          DISPLAY "Job Code: ", ER-EMPL-JOB-CODE
151          DISPLAY "Pay Rate: ", PAY-RATE-DISPLAY.
152
153      800-READ-EMPLOYEE-RECORD.
154          READ EMPLOYEE-FILE
155          AT END
156              SET END-OF-FILE TO TRUE
157          END-READ.
158
159      810-READ-JOB-CODE-RECORD.
160          READ JOB-CODE-FILE
161          AT END
162              SET TABLE-LOADED TO TRUE
163          END-READ.
```

Extract from this program.

Extract from this program.

Copying Source Components into a Program

Using the COPY Statement—Example 17-1

Although the COPY statement by no means provides database capabilities to COBOL, it does provide the ability to prepare standardized code for use in multiple programs. The key to its use in an application system is to designate sections of code that are to be standardized and to store them as individual source code files.

Example 17-1

The PAY-BEN4 program is to be modified by extracting two sections of code for storage to a source library as follows:

LOAD-JC.DTA The table definition together with data items required during table loading

LOAD-JC.PRO The PROCEDURE DIVISION code to load the table (modules 300 and 810)

In their places, appropriate COPY statements must be inserted.

In the revised program named PAY-BEN5 of Figure 17-5, the COPY statements are highlighted. You can see that the COPY statement identifies the source code file to be

Figure 17-5

Using the COPY Statement—Example 17-1

```
1      IDENTIFICATION DIVISION.
2      PROGRAM-ID. PAY-BEN5.
3
4    *    Pay special benefits - Pay Rate lookup using SEARCH ALL.
5    *    Written by J.Olson 10/1/86
6    *    Modified by W.Price 9/6/90 to incorporate
7    *       using the COPY for the table load component
8
9      ENVIRONMENT DIVISION.
10     CONFIGURATION SECTION.
11     SOURCE-COMPUTER. IBM-PC.
12
13     INPUT-OUTPUT SECTION.
14     FILE-CONTROL.
15         SELECT EMPLOYEE-FILE  ASSIGN TO DISK  "EMPL-BEN.DL"
16                               ORGANIZATION IS LINE SEQUENTIAL.
17
18         SELECT JOB-CODE-FILE  ASSIGN TO DISK  "JOB-CODE.TBL"
19                               ORGANIZATION IS LINE SEQUENTIAL.
20     DATA DIVISION.
21
22     FILE SECTION.
23
24     FD  EMPLOYEE-FILE.
25     01  EMPLOYEE-RECORD.
26         10  ER-EMPL-NUMBER     PIC X(5).
27         10  ER-EMPL-JOB-CODE   PIC 9(3).
28         10  FILLER             PIC X(42).
29
30     FD  JOB-CODE-FILE.
31     01  JOB-CODE-RECORD.
32         10  JC-JOB-CODE        PIC 9(3).
33         10  JC-PAY-RATE        PIC 9(2)V9(2).
34
35     WORKING-STORAGE SECTION.
36
37     01  PROGRAMMED-SWITCHES.
38         10                     PIC X.
39             88  END-OF-FILE    VALUE "Y"  FALSE "N".
40         10                     PIC X.
41             88  CODE-FOUND     VALUE "Y"  FALSE "N".
42
43     01  OTHER-VARIABLES.
44         10  PAY-RATE-DISPLAY   PIC ZZ.99.
45         10  PREVIOUS-JOB-CODE  PIC 999   VALUE ZERO.
46
47    * Copy the table-load data items
48      COPY LOAD-JC.DTA.
49
50     PROCEDURE DIVISION.
51
52     000-PAY-SPECIAL-BENEFITS.
53         PERFORM 100-INITIALIZE
54         PERFORM 110-PROCESS-1-EMPLOYEE
55             UNTIL END-OF-FILE
56         PERFORM 120-FINALIZE
57         STOP RUN.
58
59     100-INITIALIZE.
60         PERFORM 200-LOAD-JOB-CODE-TABLE
61         IF TABLE-LOAD-ERROR
62             DISPLAY " "
63             DISPLAY "Table size exceeded!!"  REVERSE
64             DISPLAY "Processing terminated."
65             STOP RUN
66         END-IF
67         OPEN INPUT  EMPLOYEE-FILE
68         SET END-OF-FILE TO FALSE
69         PERFORM 800-READ-EMPLOYEE-RECORD.
70
71     110-PROCESS-1-EMPLOYEE.
72         PERFORM 300-SEARCH-TABLE
73
74         IF CODE-FOUND
75             PERFORM 310-PROCESS-SPECIAL-BENEFITS
76         END-IF
77
78         PERFORM 800-READ-EMPLOYEE-RECORD.
79
80     120-FINALIZE.
81         DISPLAY " "  BEEP
82         DISPLAY "Special benefits processing has been completed."
83         CLOSE EMPLOYEE-FILE.
84
85    * Copy the table-load procedure
86      COPY LOAD-JC.PRO.
87
88     300-SEARCH-TABLE.
89         SEARCH ALL JOB-CODE-TABLE-ENTRY
90             AT END
91                 SET CODE-FOUND TO FALSE
92             WHEN JOB-CODE(JOB-INDEX) = ER-EMPL-JOB-CODE
93                 MOVE PAY-RATE(JOB-INDEX) TO PAY-RATE-DISPLAY
94                 SET CODE-FOUND TO TRUE
95         END-SEARCH.
96
97     310-PROCESS-SPECIAL-BENEFITS.
98         DISPLAY " "
99         DISPLAY "Employee: ", ER-EMPL-NUMBER
100        DISPLAY "Job Code: ", ER-EMPL-JOB-CODE
101        DISPLAY "Pay Rate: ", PAY-RATE-DISPLAY.
102
103    800-READ-EMPLOYEE-RECORD.
104        READ EMPLOYEE-FILE
105            AT END
106                SET END-OF-FILE TO TRUE
107        END-READ.
```

inserted by its file name. For instance,

```
COPY LOAD-JC.DTA
```

designates the file LOAD-JC.DTA. A listing of this file is shown in Figure 17-6(a). A listing of LOAD-JC.PRO is shown in Figure 17-6(b). Remember, these are two completely independent files stored on the disk. The following commentary describes the nature of the COPY as used here:

1. The source-code modules LOAD-JC.DTA and LOAD-JC.PRO are not complete programs and cannot be compiled by themselves. They are only meaningful as part of the PAY-BEN5 program.

2. During compilation, as each COPY statement is encountered, the compiler finds the corresponding source code file and inserts it following the COPY statement. This is done in memory during the compilation process. *The original source program is not changed.*

3. The compiled program will be complete in that it will be the result of the original source program plus the copied statements.

Figure 17-6

Loading a Table

```
* Table/table-access items
* LOAD-JC.DTA
  01  TABLE-ACCESS-ITEMS   USAGE BINARY.
      10  TABLE-SIZE            PIC 99.

  01  PROGRAMMED-SWITCHES.
      10                        PIC X.
          88  TABLE-LOADED      VALUE "Y"  FALSE "N".
      10                        PIC X.
          88  TABLE-LOAD-ERROR  VALUE "Y"  FALSE "N".

  01  OTHER-VARIABLES.
      10  ENTRY-COUNTER         PIC 99.

  01  JOB-CODE-TABLE.
      10  JOB-CODE-TABLE-ENTRY OCCURS 1 TO 25 TIMES
                           DEPENDING ON TABLE-SIZE
                           ASCENDING KEY IS JOB-CODE
                           INDEXED BY JOB-INDEX.
          20  JOB-CODE          PIC 999.
          20  PAY-RATE          PIC 99V99.
```

The Data-Definition Source Code—LOAD-JC.DTA   (a)

```
* Load Job-code/Pay-rate table
* Extracted from PAY-BEN4.CBL
*  by W.Price 9/6/90

200-LOAD-JOB-CODE-TABLE.
    OPEN INPUT JOB-CODE-FILE
    MOVE ALL "9" TO JOB-CODE-TABLE
    SET TABLE-LOAD-ERROR TO FALSE
    SET TABLE-LOADED TO FALSE
    DISPLAY "Loading Table" ERASE
    DISPLAY "Entry number   Code"
    SET JOB-INDEX TO 1

    PERFORM VARYING ENTRY-COUNTER FROM 1 BY 1
            UNTIL TABLE-LOADED OR TABLE-LOAD-ERROR
        PERFORM 810-READ-JOB-CODE-RECORD
        IF TABLE-LOADED
            COMPUTE TABLE-SIZE = ENTRY-COUNTER - 1
            DISPLAY " "
            DISPLAY "Table load complete."
        ELSE
            IF JC-JOB-CODE NOT > PREVIOUS-JOB-CODE
                DISPLAY " "
                DISPLAY "Job code ", JC-JOB-CODE,
                        " is out of sequence."
                SET TABLE-LOAD-ERROR TO TRUE
            ELSE
                IF ENTRY-COUNTER NOT > TABLE-SIZE
                    MOVE JC-JOB-CODE TO JOB-CODE(JOB-INDEX)
                    MOVE JC-PAY-RATE TO PAY-RATE(JOB-INDEX)
                    SET JOB-INDEX UP BY 1
                    DISPLAY "      ", ENTRY-COUNTER,
                            "        ", JC-JOB-CODE
                    MOVE JC-JOB-CODE TO PREVIOUS-JOB-CODE
                ELSE
                    DISPLAY " "
                    DISPLAY "Table size exceeded.  ",
                            JC-JOB-CODE, " cannot be loaded."
                    SET TABLE-LOAD-ERROR TO TRUE
                END-IF
            END-IF
        END-IF
    END-PERFORM

    CLOSE JOB-CODE-FILE.

810-READ-JOB-CODE-RECORD.
    READ JOB-CODE-FILE
        AT END
            SET TABLE-LOADED TO TRUE
    END-READ.
```

The Table-Load Procedure Source Code—LOAD-JC.PRO   (b)

4. The post-compile listing (PAY-BEN5.LST in this case) will include the inserted statements. Figure 17-7 shows some segments of this listing. Notice that the copied statements are clearly identified by +1+ to the left of the statement.

General Format of the COPY Statement

As used in the program of Figure 17-5, LOAD-JC.DTA and LOAD-JC.PRO must be stored on the same diskette or in the same subdirectory as the PAY-BEN5 program. In actual practice, source code segments that are copied into programs are cataloged in *source code libraries*, where they are separate from the programs that use them. The modules stored in the source libraries can be made available to programmers (for use in their programs), as dictated by needs of the individual application. To accommodate this, the COPY statement allows you to designate the name of the library in which the required source module is stored; the following limited general form shows this:

$$\underline{\text{COPY}} \text{ text-name} \left[\left\{ \begin{array}{c} \underline{\text{OF}} \\ \underline{\text{IN}} \end{array} \right\} \text{ library-name} \right]$$

Figure 17-7

Copied Source Code as It Appears in the Post-Compile Listing

Indicates copied code.

```
1              IDENTIFICATION DIVISION.                    71              PROCEDURE DIVISION.
2              PROGRAM-ID. PAY-BEN5.                         .
3                                                            .
4           *    Pay special benefits - Pay Rate lookup using SEARCH ALL.
5           *    Written by J.Olson 10/1/86                101  000104    120-FINALIZE.
6           *    Modified by W.Price 9/6/90 to incorporate  102  000107       DISPLAY " " BEEP
7           *      using the COPY for the table load component 103 000113    DISPLAY "Special benefits processing has been completed."
8                                                          104  000119       CLOSE EMPLOYEE-FILE.
 .             .                                           105
 .             .                                           106           * Copy the table-load procedure
 .             .                                           107               COPY LOAD-JC.PRO.
43          01  OTHER-VARIABLES.                           108  +1+       * Load Job-code/Pay-rate table
44             10  PAY-RATE-DISPLAY      PIC ZZ.99.        109  +1+       * Extracted from PAY-BEN4.CBL
45             10  PREVIOUS-JOB-CODE     PIC 999   VALUE ZERO. 110 +1+    *  by W.Price 9/6/90
46                                                         111  +1+
47          * Copy the table-load data items              112  000128+1+  200-LOAD-JOB-CODE-TABLE.
48              COPY LOAD-JC.DTA.                          113  000131+1+     OPEN INPUT JOB-CODE-FILE
49   +1+    * Table/table-access items                    114  000138+1+     MOVE ALL "9" TO JOB-CODE-TABLE
50   +1+    * LOAD-JC.DTA                                  115  000146+1+     SET TABLE-LOAD-ERROR TO FALSE
51   +1+    01  TABLE-ACCESS-ITEMS    USAGE BINARY.        116  000152+1+     SET TABLE-LOADED TO FALSE
52   +1+       10  TABLE-SIZE          PIC 99  VALUE 25.   117  000158+1+     DISPLAY "Loading Table" ERASE
53   +1+                                                   118  000165+1+     DISPLAY "Entry number   Code"
54   +1+    01  PROGRAMMED-SWITCHES.                       119  000171+1+     SET JOB-INDEX TO 1
55   +1+       10                       PIC X.              .               .
56   +1+          88  TABLE-LOADED      VALUE "Y"  FALSE "N".  .            .
57   +1+       10                       PIC X.              .               .
58   +1+          88  TABLE-LOAD-ERROR  VALUE "Y"  FALSE "N". 154 000384+1+ 810-READ-JOB-CODE-RECORD.
59   +1+                                                   155  000387+1+     READ JOB-CODE-FILE
60   +1+    01  OTHER-VARIABLES.                           156  +1+          AT END
61   +1+       10  ENTRY-COUNTER        PIC 99.            157  +1+             SET TABLE-LOADED TO TRUE
62   +1+                                                   158  +1+          END-READ.
63   +1+    01  JOB-CODE-TABLE.                            159
64   +1+       10  JOB-CODE-TABLE-ENTRY OCCURS 1 TO 25 TIMES  160 000404    300-SEARCH-TABLE.
65   +1+                               DEPENDING ON TABLE-SIZE 161 000407   SEARCH ALL JOB-CODE-TABLE-ENTRY
66   +1+                               ASCENDING KEY IS JOB-CODE 162         AT END
67   +1+                               INDEXED BY JOB-INDEX.  163             SET CODE-FOUND TO FALSE
68   +1+          20  JOB-CODE         PIC 999.            164           WHEN JOB-CODE(JOB-INDEX) = ER-EMPL-JOB-CODE
69   +1+          20  PAY-RATE         PIC 99V99.          165             MOVE PAY-RATE(JOB-INDEX) TO PAY-RATE-DISPLAY
70                                                         166             SET CODE-FOUND TO TRUE
                                                           167           END-SEARCH.
                                                           168
                                                           169  000455    310-PROCESS-SPECIAL-BENEFITS.
                                                           170  000458       DISPLAY " "
                                                           171  000464       DISPLAY "Employee: ", ER-EMPL-NUMBER
```

Copied program segments.

Copied program segments.

The implication to the MS-DOS user is that source modules can be stored in a different subdirectory than the program that uses them. However, since the compiler will not search the entire disk, the COPY statement must identify the subdirectory in which the source module is stored. For instance, assume that UNISOFT has their payroll application stored on the D disk drive as follows:

Programs   In the PAY-PROG subdirectory
(thus identified as D:\PAY-PROG)

Source library   In the SRCE-LIB subdirectory
(thus identified as D:\SRCE-LIB)

If PAY-BEN5 is being compiled from the PAY-PROG subdirectory, the copy statements must be:

```
COPY LOAD-JC.DTA OF D:\SRCE-LIB
COPY LOAD-JC.PRO OF D:\SRCE-LIB
```

Replacing Elements of the Copied Source Code

In general, the programmer who plans to use code from source code library must write his or her program as if the code were physically included in the program. This means that data-names used in the copying program must conform to those of the copied source module. However, some latitude is possible because the COPY statement does allow changes to be made during the copying operation. For instance, assume that you had written the PAY-BEN5 program and that all of your table references were

```
TABLE-JOB-CODE instead of JOB-CODE
TABLE-PAY-RATE instead of PAY-RATE
```

Thus your program refers to, for instance, TABLE-JOB-CODE(JOB-INDEX) rather than JOB-CODE(JOB-INDEX), as specified in the OCCURS clause. To accommodate this, you can use the form shown in Figure 17-8(a). The REPLACING clause identifies each change to be made; you can see the results in Figure 17-8(b). Needless to say, if you use this

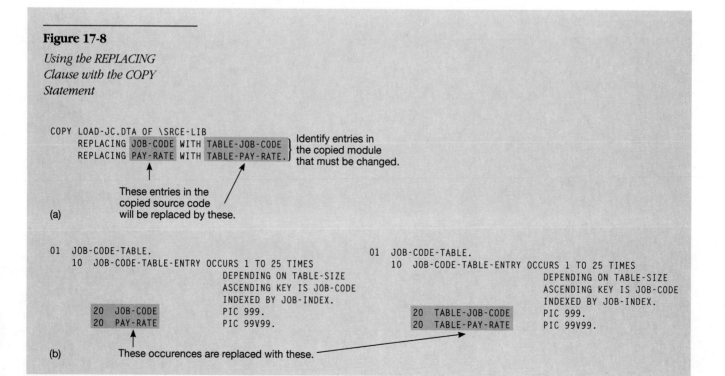

Figure 17-8

Using the REPLACING Clause with the COPY Statement

```
COPY LOAD-JC.DTA OF \SRCE-LIB
    REPLACING JOB-CODE WITH TABLE-JOB-CODE
    REPLACING PAY-RATE WITH TABLE-PAY-RATE.
```
Identify entries in the copied module that must be changed.

These entries in the copied source code will be replaced by these.

(a)

```
01  JOB-CODE-TABLE.                              01  JOB-CODE-TABLE.
    10  JOB-CODE-TABLE-ENTRY OCCURS 1 TO 25 TIMES    10  JOB-CODE-TABLE-ENTRY OCCURS 1 TO 25 TIMES
                    DEPENDING ON TABLE-SIZE                      DEPENDING ON TABLE-SIZE
                    ASCENDING KEY IS JOB-CODE                    ASCENDING KEY IS JOB-CODE
                    INDEXED BY JOB-INDEX.                        INDEXED BY JOB-INDEX.
        20  JOB-CODE    PIC 999.                          20  TABLE-JOB-CODE    PIC 999.
        20  PAY-RATE    PIC 99V99.                         20  TABLE-PAY-RATE    PIC 99V99.
```

(b)   These occurences are replaced with these.

REPLACING clause for LOAD-JC.DTA, you must also use it for LOAD-JC.PRO.

Any entry of the copied source code can be changed, including reserved words (except another COPY statement). The full general form of the COPY is

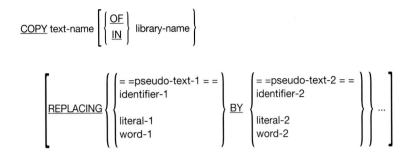

Here *word* is any reserved word except COPY, *literal* is any alphanumeric or numeric literal, and *identifier* is any programmer-defined name. *Pseudo-text* is defined as any sequence of text words, comment lines, or the separator space in a source program. If the text to be replaced contains one or more spaces, the compiler will sense an error. For instance, in the following COMPUTE statement

```
COMPUTE HOLD-VALUE = TEMP-VALUE * FACTOR
```

assume that you need to replace

```
TEMP-VALUE * FACTOR with HI-LIMIT - CORRECTION
```

If the REPLACING clause is written as

```
REPLACING TEMP-VALUE * FACTOR BY TEMP-VALUE * FACTOR
```

the compiler will expect the word BY upon detecting the space following TEMP-VALUE because the space delimits the entity to be replaced. Pseudo-text can be isolated in situations such as this by enclosing it in two consecutive = characters (these are called *pseudo-text delimiters*). Actually, they serve much the same purpose as quotes around a literal. Thus, the previous REPLACING clause becomes

```
REPLACING ==TEMP-VALUE * FACTOR== BY ==HI-LIMIT - CORRECTION==
```

Calling a Separate Program from Another Program

Data Definition Considerations with Multiple Modules

Including in a source library commonly used code that can be copied into programs as needed saves coding and debugging time and promotes standardization. However, one potential problem in using this technique for procedures relates to the use and definition of data items. To illustrate, assume that you work for a mortgage company and that you must write a procedure to calculate monthly payments for loans. Notice that your procedure will have output: the monthly payment amount. It will also have input: the loan amount, the interest rate, and the loan period necessary to perform the calculations. This concept is illustrated in Figure 17-9. In writing the procedure, you are concerned with the input, output, and details of what goes on inside the procedure. However, other programmers that wish to use the procedure are interested only in the output and the input required to produce that output. They think of the procedure as the traditional electronic "black box" that somehow does what is supposed to do.

If you view this in terms of procedures that are copied into a program, the implication is that data items required by the procedure must be defined in the program's DATA DIVISION. In the case of the monthly-payment example, data items would need to be

Figure 17-9

Input To and Output From an Independent Procedure

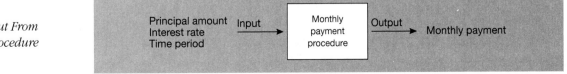

defined for the principal amount, interest rate, and time period (input quantities) and for the monthly payment (output quantity).

In the case of the table-load procedure for the PAY-BEN5 program, the table and table-processing data items are defined by a separate source module (LOAD-JC.DTA). Let's examine the four simple data items included in the LOAD-JC.DTA source component—Figure 17-6(a).

Data Item (or Condition Name)	Input or Output	Explanation
TABLE-SIZE	Both	This provides input to the procedure in that it has an initial value of 25. It is required by the MOVE statement that moves 9's to the table before loading. When the procedure is completed, it contains the number of entries placed in the able.
TABLE-LOAD-ERROR	Output	Although this is not a data item (it is a condition name), it gives access to the memory area allocated for a load-error indication. It is set to true or false, then is tested after the table-load operation is completed (see line 72, Figure 17-4).
TABLE-LOADED	Neither	Another condition name, this is used solely within the table-load procedure to control file read/table-load loop.
ENTRY-COUNTER	Neither	This data item is also used only within the procedure.

Notice that there are not simply two categories of data items that you must utilize (input and output), but three. The third consists of data items used within the procedure as work items that have no relationship to anything outside the procedure. If you plan to incorporate the table-load procedure into a program, then in your program you must be careful to

■ Use the names assigned to the table within the procedure when you are accessing the table

■ Avoid using data-names in your program that are the same as those defined for the procedure

Both of these tend to make the programming clumsy, especially having to avoid duplicating names that are used for work items in the procedure.

Separating the PAY-BEN4 Program into Two Independent Modules

Let's examine the PAY-BEN4 program even more closely in order to make the pay-benefits program and the table-load module as independent from one another as is possible. In Figure 17-10, those entries relating to the table load action are shown highlighted. Those that are associated with input to or output from the load procedure are shaded with dark blue. Those that are not associated with either input or output (but are required for operations within the procedure) are shaded in medium blue. This includes the table file and its descriptions. You can see that the table-load procedure requires elements from three of the four divisions. Interestingly, it could be a program by itself.

Example 17-2

The PAY-BEN4 program is to be split into two separate programs as follows:

JOB-LOAD   Load the job-code/pay-rate table from the table file.

PAY-BEN6   Process employee benefits. This program will need to "call" the JOB-LOAD program to load the job-code/pay-rate table.

Figure 17-10

*Program Elements Relating
to the Table-Load
Procedure*

```
 1      IDENTIFICATION DIVISION.
 2      PROGRAM-ID. PAY-BEN4.
 3
 4    *    Pay special benefits - Pay Rate lookup using SEARCH ALL.
 5    *    Written by J.Olson 10/1/86
 6
 7      ENVIRONMENT DIVISION.
 8      CONFIGURATION SECTION.
 9      SOURCE-COMPUTER. IBM-PC.
10
11      INPUT-OUTPUT SECTION.
12      FILE-CONTROL.
13          SELECT EMPLOYEE-FILE  ASSIGN TO DISK  "EMPL-BEN.DL"
14                                ORGANIZATION IS LINE SEQUENTIAL.
15
16          SELECT JOB-CODE-FILE  ASSIGN TO DISK  "JOB-CODE.TBL"
17                                ORGANIZATION IS LINE SEQUENTIAL.
18      DATA DIVISION.
19
20      FILE SECTION.
21
22      FD  EMPLOYEE-FILE.
23      01  EMPLOYEE-RECORD.
24          10  ER-EMPL-NUMBER      PIC X(5).
25          10  ER-EMPL-JOB-CODE    PIC 9(3).
26          10                      PIC X(42).
27
28      FD  JOB-CODE-FILE.
29      01  JOB-CODE-RECORD.
30          10  JC-JOB-CODE         PIC 9(3).
31          10  JC-PAY-RATE         PIC 9(2)V9(2).
32
```

```
33      WORKING-STORAGE SECTION.
34
35      01  TABLE-ACCESS-ITEMS   USAGE BINARY.
36          10  TABLE-SIZE             PIC 99   VALUE 25.
37
38      01  PROGRAMMED-SWITCHES.
39          10                         PIC X.
40              88  END-OF-FILE        VALUE "Y"   FALSE "N".
41          10                         PIC X.
42              88  TABLE-LOADED       VALUE "Y"   FALSE "N".
43          10                         PIC X.
44              88  TABLE-LOAD-ERROR   VALUE "Y"   FALSE "N".
45          10                         PIC X.
46              88  CODE-FOUND         VALUE "Y"   FALSE "N".
47
48      01  OTHER-VARIABLES.
49          10  ENTRY-COUNTER          PIC 99.
50          10  PAY-RATE-DISPLAY       PIC ZZ.99.
51          10  PREVIOUS-JOB-CODE      PIC 999    VALUE ZERO.
52
53      01  JOB-CODE-TABLE.
54          10  JOB-CODE-TABLE-ENTRY OCCURS 1 TO 25 TIMES
55                                   DEPENDING ON TABLE-SIZE
56                                   ASCENDING KEY IS JOB-CODE
57                                   INDEXED BY JOB-INDEX.
58              20  JOB-CODE           PIC 999.
59              20  PAY-RATE           PIC 99V99.
```

As they are independent programs, each must be compiled. Once compiled, the execution scenario will be as follows:

1. You enter the run command, causing the PAY-BEN6 program to be loaded from disk into memory, as illustrated in Figure 17-11(a). Execution of the program begins.

2. The PAY-BEN6 programs "calls" the JOB-LOAD program, causing it to be loaded into memory, as illustrated in Figure 17-11(b). As you can see, both programs now reside in memory.

3. Control of the computer is passed to JOB-LOAD, which then proceeds to load the table.

4. Upon completion of the table load, execution is returned to the "calling program," PAY-BEN6, and employee processing proceeds.

Actually, the action is somewhat like a "super-perform" in that control is transferred to another segment of the overall program and then returned when complete. However, unlike the PERFORM statement, the module to which control is passed is an entirely separate program, a *subprogram*. Most programming languages, including machine language programs, include special capabilities for linking programs and subprograms. This requires the following three entities, commonly called *subprogram linkage:*

1. The name (or location) of the subprogram

2. The ability to return to the calling program from the subprogram when its execution has been completed

3. Communication between the two components of the input to the subprogram and output from it

With the PERFORM statement (which passes control to a paragraph within a single program), the linkage is achieved as follows:

Figure 17-11

Using Subprograms

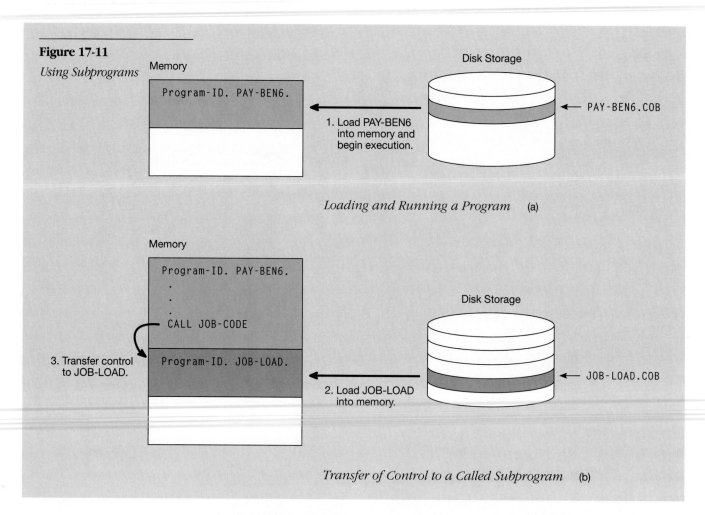

Loading and Running a Program   (a)

Transfer of Control to a Called Subprogram   (b)

- The PERFORM includes the paragraph name of the paragraph to be executed.

- Return from the performed paragraph occurs automatically after the last statement in the paragraph is executed.

- Because the performed paragraph is part of the same program as the PERFORM statement, all data items defined in the program are completely accessible to any performed paragraph. Any data item that is accessible to every part of a program is said to be *global*. Later in this chapter, you will see cases of data that are not global.

Calling and Called Programs—Example 17-2

PAY-BEN6 for processing the employee benefits is shown in Figure 17-12; the JOB-LOAD program that it calls to load the table is shown in Figure 17-13 (page 480). Note that each is complete in that it includes all four divisions. Two COBOL statements needed to implement the simple form of program linking are highlighted in these programs:

1. The CALL statement causes a designated program to be loaded from disk and execution transferred to that program

2. The EXIT PROGRAM statement causes execution of the current program to be terminated and execution returned to the program that called the current program

Although in running the PAY-BEN6 program, you would need to call the JOB-LOAD program only one time, in many situations a subprogram might be called numerous times. For instance, the main employee benefits program might call, for processing of each employee, a separate subprogram for tax-sheltered annuity calculations.

In this respect, after a subprogram is called (loaded and executed) and control is returned to the calling program, the called subprogram remains undisturbed in memory. If the subprogram is called a second time, the program state will remain unchanged from when control was previously returned to the calling program. For instance, any changes

Figure 17-12

*The PAY-BEN6 Program—
Example 17-2*

```
1        IDENTIFICATION DIVISION.
2        PROGRAM-ID. PAY-BEN6.
3
4    *      Pay special benefits - Pay Rate lookup using SEARCH ALL.
5    *      Written by J.Olson 10/1/86
6    *      Modified by W.Price 9/6/90 to incorporate
7    *        using the CALL for the table load component
8
9        ENVIRONMENT DIVISION.
10       CONFIGURATION SECTION.
11       SOURCE-COMPUTER. IBM-PC.
12
13       INPUT-OUTPUT SECTION.
14       FILE-CONTROL.
15           SELECT EMPLOYEE-FILE  ASSIGN TO DISK  "EMPL-BEN.DL"
16                            ORGANIZATION IS LINE SEQUENTIAL.
17       DATA DIVISION.
18
19       FILE SECTION.
20
21       FD  EMPLOYEE-FILE.
22       01  EMPLOYEE-RECORD.
23           10  ER-EMPL-NUMBER      PIC X(5).
24           10  ER-EMPL-JOB-CODE    PIC 9(3).
25           10  FILLER              PIC X(42).
26
27       WORKING-STORAGE SECTION.
28
29       01  PROGRAMMED-SWITCHES.
30           10                      PIC X.
31               88  END-OF-FILE     VALUE "Y"  FALSE "N".
32           10                      PIC X.
33               88  CODE-FOUND      VALUE "Y"  FALSE "N".
34
35       01  OTHER-VARIABLES.
36           10  PAY-RATE-DISPLAY    PIC ZZ.99.
37
38       01  LINKAGE-ITEMS.
39
40           10  TABLE-ACCESS-ITEMS   USAGE BINARY.
41               20  TABLE-SIZE          PIC 99.
42
43           10  PROGRAMMED-SWITCHES.
44               20                      PIC X.
45                   88  TABLE-LOAD-ERROR  VALUE "Y"  FALSE "N".
46
47           10  JOB-CODE-TABLE.
48               20  JOB-CODE-TABLE-ENTRY OCCURS 1 TO 25 TIMES
49                                  DEPENDING ON TABLE-SIZE
50                                  ASCENDING KEY IS JOB-CODE
51                                  INDEXED BY JOB-INDEX.
52                   30  JOB-CODE       PIC 999.
53                   30  PAY-RATE       PIC 99V99.
54
```

```
55       PROCEDURE DIVISION.
56
57       000-PAY-SPECIAL-BENEFITS.
58           PERFORM 100-INITIALIZE
59           PERFORM 110-PROCESS-1-EMPLOYEE
60               UNTIL END-OF-FILE
61           PERFORM 120-FINALIZE
62           STOP RUN.
63
64       100-INITIALIZE.
65           CALL "JOB-LOAD" USING LINKAGE-ITEMS.
66           IF TABLE-LOAD-ERROR
67               DISPLAY " "
68               DISPLAY "Table size exceeded!!"   REVERSE
69               DISPLAY "Processing terminated."
70               STOP RUN
71           END-IF
72           OPEN INPUT  EMPLOYEE-FILE
73           SET END-OF-FILE TO FALSE
74           PERFORM 800-READ-EMPLOYEE-RECORD.
75
76       110-PROCESS-1-EMPLOYEE.
77           PERFORM 300-SEARCH-TABLE
78
79           IF CODE-FOUND
80               PERFORM 310-PROCESS-SPECIAL-BENEFITS
81           ELSE
82               DISPLAY ER-EMPL-JOB-CODE
83           END-IF
84
85           PERFORM 800-READ-EMPLOYEE-RECORD.
86
87       120-FINALIZE.
88           DISPLAY " "  BEEP
89           DISPLAY "Special benefits processing has been completed."
90           CLOSE EMPLOYEE-FILE.
91
92       300-SEARCH-TABLE.
93           SEARCH ALL JOB-CODE-TABLE-ENTRY
94               AT END
95                   SET CODE-FOUND TO FALSE
96               WHEN JOB-CODE(JOB-INDEX) = ER-EMPL-JOB-CODE
97                   MOVE PAY-RATE(JOB-INDEX) TO PAY-RATE-DISPLAY
98                   SET CODE-FOUND TO TRUE
99           END-SEARCH.
100
101      310-PROCESS-SPECIAL-BENEFITS.
102          DISPLAY " "
103          DISPLAY "Employee: ", ER-EMPL-NUMBER
104          DISPLAY "Job Code: ", ER-EMPL-JOB-CODE
105          DISPLAY "Pay Rate: ", PAY-RATE-DISPLAY.
106
107      800-READ-EMPLOYEE-RECORD.
108          READ EMPLOYEE-FILE
109              AT END
110                  SET END-OF-FILE TO TRUE
111          END-READ.
```

Loads and runs the JOB-LOAD program. *(annotation pointing to line 65)*

When control is returned, it will go to the next statement. *(annotation pointing to line 66)*

that have been made to the values of data items will remain, files that were opened and not closed will still be open, and so on. This has significant implications regarding the use of data items in a called program. That is, if switches or accumulators are to have certain initial values when program execution begins, then *these values must be set in the* PROCEDURE DIVISION. If the initial values from the VALUE clause of the DATA DIVISION are assumed, they will be dependable only the first time that the called program is entered. However, the CANCEL statement, described later, provides the means for ensuring that a subprogram is in its initial state each time it is called.

Figure 17-13

The JOB-LOAD Subprogram—
Example 17-2

```
1        IDENTIFICATION DIVISION.
2        PROGRAM-ID. JOB-LOAD.
3
4    *    Load job-code/pay-rate table.
5    *    Extracted from PAY-BEN4.CBL
6    *       by W.Price 9/6/90
7
8        ENVIRONMENT DIVISION.
9        CONFIGURATION SECTION.
10       SOURCE-COMPUTER. IBM-PC.
11
12       INPUT-OUTPUT SECTION.
13       FILE-CONTROL.
14           SELECT JOB-CODE-FILE  ASSIGN TO DISK  "JOB-CODE.TBL"
15                                 ORGANIZATION IS LINE SEQUENTIAL.
16       DATA DIVISION.
17
18       FILE SECTION.
19
20       FD  JOB-CODE-FILE.
21       01  JOB-CODE-RECORD.
22           10  JC-JOB-CODE          PIC 9(3).
23           10  JC-PAY-RATE          PIC 9(2)V9(2).
24
25       WORKING-STORAGE SECTION.
26
27       01  PROGRAMMED-SWITCHES.
28           10                       PIC X.
29               88  TABLE-LOADED     VALUE "Y"  FALSE "N".
30
31       01  OTHER-VARIABLES.
32           10  ENTRY-COUNTER        PIC 99.
33           10  PREVIOUS-JOB-CODE    PIC 999     VALUE ZERO.
34           10  MAXIMUM-SIZE-OF-TABLE PIC 99     VALUE 25.
35
36       LINKAGE SECTION.
37
38       01  LINKAGE-DATA-ITEMS.
39           10  TABLE-ACCESS-ITEMS   USAGE BINARY.
40               20  SIZE-OF-TABLE        PIC 99.
41
42           10  PROGRAMMED-SWITCHES.
43               20                   PIC X.
44                   88  LOAD-ERROR   VALUE "Y"  FALSE "N".
45
46           10  JOB-CODE-PAY-RATE-TABLE.
47               20  JC-PR-TABLE-ENTRY OCCURS 1 TO 25 TIMES
48                                     DEPENDING ON SIZE-OF-TABLE
49                                     ASCENDING KEY IS JOB-CODE-ENTRY
50                                     INDEXED BY JC-PR-INDEX.
51                   30  JOB-CODE-ENTRY      PIC 999.
52                   30  PAY-RATE-ENTRY      PIC 99V99.
53
```

```
54       PROCEDURE DIVISION USING LINKAGE-DATA-ITEMS.
55
56       000-LOAD-JOB-CODE-TABLE.
57           PERFORM 100-INITIALIZE
58           PERFORM 110-LOAD-JOB-CODE-TABLE
59               VARYING ENTRY-COUNTER FROM 1 BY 1
60               UNTIL TABLE-LOADED OR LOAD-ERROR
61           PERFORM 120-FINALIZE
62           EXIT PROGRAM.
63
64       100-INITIALIZE.
65           OPEN INPUT JOB-CODE-FILE
66           MOVE MAXIMUM-SIZE-OF-TABLE TO SIZE-OF-TABLE
67           MOVE ALL "9" TO JOB-CODE-PAY-RATE-TABLE
68           SET LOAD-ERROR TO FALSE
69           SET TABLE-LOADED TO FALSE
70           DISPLAY "Loading Table" ERASE
71           DISPLAY "Entry number    Code"
72           SET JC-PR-INDEX TO 1.
73
74       110-LOAD-JOB-CODE-TABLE.
75           PERFORM 810-READ-JOB-CODE-RECORD
76           IF TABLE-LOADED
77               COMPUTE SIZE-OF-TABLE = ENTRY-COUNTER - 1
78               DISPLAY " " 79          DISPLAY "Table load complete."
80           ELSE
81               IF JC-JOB-CODE NOT > PREVIOUS-JOB-CODE
82                   DISPLAY " "
83                   DISPLAY "Job code ", JC-JOB-CODE,
84                       " is out of sequence."
85                   SET LOAD-ERROR TO TRUE
86               ELSE
87                   IF ENTRY-COUNTER NOT > MAXIMUM-SIZE-OF-TABLE
88                       MOVE JC-JOB-CODE TO JOB-CODE-ENTRY(JC-PR-INDEX)
89                       MOVE JC-PAY-RATE TO PAY-RATE-ENTRY(JC-PR-INDEX)
90                       SET JC-PR-INDEX UP BY 1
91                       DISPLAY "     ", ENTRY-COUNTER,
92                               "     ", JC-JOB-CODE
93                       MOVE JC-JOB-CODE TO PREVIOUS-JOB-CODE
94                   ELSE
95                       DISPLAY " "
96                       DISPLAY "Table size exceeded.  ",
97                           JC-JOB-CODE, " cannot be loaded."
98                       SET LOAD-ERROR TO TRUE
99                   END-IF
100              END-IF
101          END-IF.
102
103      120-FINALIZE.
104          CLOSE JOB-CODE-FILE.
105
106      810-READ-JOB-CODE-RECORD.
107          READ JOB-CODE-FILE
108          AT END
109              SET TABLE-LOADED TO TRUE
110          END-READ.
```

This statement causes control to be returned to the statement of the calling program that follows the call.

Passing Data between Programs

Although the actions of passing control that we see with the CALL and PERFORM are similar, there is one important difference. That is, performed modules are all part of a single program in which field definitions of the DATA DIVISION are available to all modules of the program. The CALL involves separate programs, each with its own DATA DIVISION; fields in the DATA DIVISION of one program are not available to the other. Thus, any data from one program that is to be used by the other must explicitly be passed. For this, COBOL includes a special LINKAGE SECTION in the DATA DIVISION that allows fields to be defined that are to contain data for interprogram communication. In COBOL, the following program components are needed to accomplish this.

The calling program

A USING clause in the CALL statement that lists the names of the data items whose values are to be made available to the called subprogram. These items must be defined in the FILE SECTION or WORKING-STORAGE SECTION.

The called subprogram

A list of data-names whose values will be obtained from the calling program. These must be defined in the LINKAGE SECTION of the DATA DIVISION.

A USING clause in the PROCEDURE DIVISION header that lists the names of the data items whose values are to be obtained from the the calling program. This clause must correspond in form to that of the calling program.

These principles are illustrated in the program segments shown in Figure 17-14. Following are the important features of this example:

1. A single 01 data item is passed from the calling program to the called subprogram. This is the data item LINKAGE-ITEMS. Notice that it consists of all the individual data items necessary to pass information between the program and subprogram. Within the calling program, they are defined and used as any other variables. Values will be stored in these variables by action within the calling program prior to execution of the CALL.

2. The USING clause of the CALL statement lists the name of the data item whose values are to be passed to the called subprogram. In this example, there is only one listed data item, LINKAGE ITEMS. A limitless number of data items can be listed in the CALL.

Figure 17-14

Program Linkage Statements

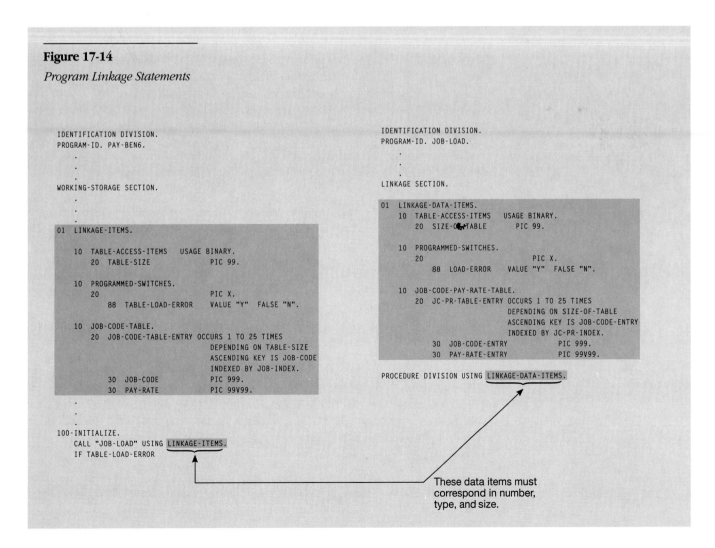

3. The called subprogram includes a LINKAGE SECTION, which defines the data item. It must correspond to the data item of the calling program whose values are being passed. Note that the components of this data item must be identical in their pictures (but not necessarily their names) to those of the calling program. In general, when writing a LINKAGE SECTION in a program, you have the same restrictions as when writing a WORKING-STORAGE SECTION.

4. The PROCEDURE DIVISION header of the called subprogram contains a USING clause that corresponds to that of the calling program. Notice that the names of the data item (or data items) may be different since they must be consistent with name usage in the individual programs. If two or more data items are listed following the USING, then the correspondence between data items is based on position. That is, the first listed data item in the calling program corresponds to the first listed data item of the called program, and so on. The names may be different or the same since these are two separate programs and are compiled separately.

5. The data items comprising the LINKAGE SECTION of the called subprogram can be operated upon in the called subprogram just as any other data items. However, a change in any of them will change the value of the corresponding data item of the calling program. (For instance, if SIZE-OF-TABLE in the called subprogram is changed, the corresponding data item in the called program, TABLE-SIZE, is also changed.)

You may have noticed that most of the data item names of JOB-LOAD have been changed so that they are slightly different from their counterparts in PAY-BEN6. This was done to illustrate the point that the names need not be the same. Remember, the programs are completely separate from one another and are compiled separately. Item 5 of the preceding commentary scratches the surface of how this aspect of inter-program communication works. The reason that changing a value of a linkage data item in the called subprogram causes the corresponding data item of the calling program to change relates to the way in which data is made available to the called program from the calling program. When the subprogram is compiled, the compiler does *not* reserve memory space for entries of the LINKAGE SECTION. However, it does make provisions so that the called subprogram will be able to be told where the data is to be found. When the CALL is executed, the calling program passes the *memory addresses* of the variables listed in the USING. Then the calling program actually operates on data areas in the called program.

The CANCEL Statement

As mentioned earlier, a called program remains in memory even after control has been returned to the calling program. In many cases this is desirable, but in some it is not. You might not want the subprogram to remain in two circumstances.

First, the program needs might be such that with each execution of the subprogram, it must be in its initial state (that is, all data items at their initial values). However, remember that if the subprogram is called again after it has once been exited, the state of the subprogram will be the same as it was when exited.

Second, if you have a large application with numerous subprograms, they might exceed the memory capacity of the computer. In most programs that call many subprograms, some of them are used only one time and are no longer needed. Furthermore, it is rare that all of the subprograms need to be in memory at the same time.

The solution to both of these situations is to direct the system to remove one or more subprograms from memory. This is done with the CANCEL statement. To remove, for example, the subprogram JOB-LOAD from memory, would require the following statement in the calling program:

```
CANCEL "JOB-LOAD"
```

The memory occupied by this program will then be made available for other use. If the needs of the PAY-BEN6 program were such that the subprogram were called again later in the program, it will be reloaded into memory and run from its initial state.

Called Subprograms Calling Other Subprograms

The Educational version of RM/COBOL-85 does not allow a called subprogram to call another subprogram. However, the commercially available version does allow one subprogram to call another from any level. For instance, assume that special actions are required by JOB-LOAD after opening the table file, but prior to beginning the table load process. If desired, these actions could be coded as a separate subprogram (for instance, FILE-CHK) called by JOB-LOAD. Thus, you would have:

PAY-BEN6 would call JOB-LOAD
JOB-LOAD would call FILE-CHK

Again, this second-level call capability is not available with the Educational version of RM/COBOL-85.

Object Libraries

JOB-LOAD is an example of a subprogram that would likely be used by many of the programs in the UNISOFT data processing department. In most data processing installations, numerous functions such as this are common to many programs. To minimize redundant programming, common functions are programmed as subprograms, compiled, and stored in an *object library*—a library specifically for compiled subprograms. Then whenever a programmer is working on an application that requires a cataloged subprogram, it can easily be made available.

Nested Programs

Characteristics of Nested Programs

The third major topic of this chapter is nested programs. In a nutshell, a *nested program* is a complete program that is contained within another program—as illustrated in Figure 17-15. On the surface, the nested program may appear to be similar to the called subprogram (or to using source code from a library with the COPY command), but it is not. Although subprograms allow a program to be divided into separate, independent modules of code, the primary function of subprograms is to make common functions in a pre-programmed, compiled form available to the programmer. On the other hand, program nesting provides COBOL with the basic tools to implement modular programming principles to an extent impossible using previously described techniques.

To illustrate, assume that an inventory control system has been designed for UNISOFT and that the primary processing program has been broken into four components, each assigned to a programming team. During the design phase of the program, the input to and output from each component was carefully defined. Each programming team knows exactly which file formats it will be using and the names of data items required to interface to the other components. Thus, each group can write its component independent of the other groups. However, a problem exists regarding data-names. Each group will create numerous data items for use within its component. Thus, some convention must be established for selecting names so that names used in one program component are not accidentally selected by another team. You can appreciate this from your knowledge of PAY-BEN5, in which the table-loading function is copied from a source library. The programmer who uses the table load source code must be careful to avoid using data-names already used in the copied code. Remember, the names selected are global, meaning that they are available throughout the program.

On the other hand, in a separately compiled subprogram, no such problem, exists because data-names defined in the subprogram are said to be *local data-names* since they are meaningful only within the subprogram and not within the program that calls the subprogram. In this sense, you have *independence of data* between the program and the called subprograms. There is simply no way that the subprogram can accidentally cause a conflict with data-names selected in the calling program or change values of data items— except those explicitly identified in the linkage.

Two COBOL language elements that you will need in studying the nested program of this chapter are (1) the END PROGRAM statement and (2) the IS GLOBAL clause.

The END PROGRAM Statement

Figure 17-15 shows the two programs, one nested within the other, terminated by corresponding END PROGRAM statements. The END PROGRAM statement does exactly as the English indicates: tells the compiler that it has reached the end of the named program. Its general form is

<u>END PROGRAM</u> program-name.

Notice the similarity of this nested program to nested IF statements in which PROGRAM-ID corresponds to IF and END PROGRAM corresponds to END-IF. Technically speaking, PAY-BEN7 includes its own code plus the nested program JOB-CODE—everything up to the corresponding END PROGRAM statement. However, the end of the PAY-BEN7 PROCEDURE DIVISION code is signalled by the PROGRAM-ID of the nested program. Thus, you will never see code of a program split by a nested program.

Although the illustration of Figure 17-15 shows one program nested within another (one level of nesting), programs can be nested to any desired level. For instance, assume that PAY-BEN7 required two programs—JOB-LOAD and ADJ-RATE—and that JOB-LOAD itself required the programs FILE-CHK and TBLE-MOD. This means two levels of nesting and is illustrated in Figure 17-16. Notice that JOB-LOAD, which itself contains two nested programs, is at the same nesting level (within PAY-BEN7) as ADJ-RATE.

Figure 17-15

A Nested Program

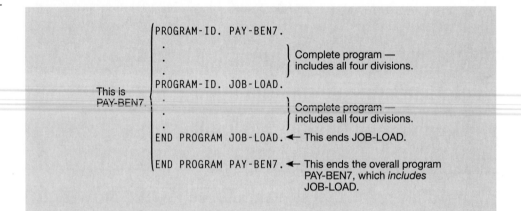

The IS GLOBAL Clause

The significant feature of the nested program capability is that it provides data independence among components of a single program. That is, data items defined within one of the programs are local to that program and have nothing to do with other programs; thus, they are protected from accidental corruption by the other programs. In the context of Figure 17-15, this means that names defined in JOB-LOAD (including file names, record names, data-names, and procedure names) have no meaning outside of the JOB-LOAD program that is nested in PAY-BEN7. Similarly, names used in PAY-BEN7 are not available to JOB-LOAD *unless specifically indicated* by an IS GLOBAL clause. In this respect, it is as if the two programs were compiled independently of one another.

As you have learned, communicating data between a program and a called subprogram is done through the LINKAGE section and the USING clause. Exactly the same technique is used in communicating between a program and its nested programs. However, a program containing nested programs can use another technique for making data "visible" to its nested programs: global declaration. Any data item declared as global becomes available to any program included within the program containing the global declaration. To illustrate, consider two examples in the context of Figure 17-16.

■ If the data item SAVE-TABLE is declared global in PAY-BEN7, then it is available to all the nested programs (JOB-LOAD, FILE-CHK, TBLE-MOD, and ADJ-RATE).

■ If the data item HOLD-RATE is declared global in JOB-LOAD, it is available only within JOB-LOAD and its nested programs—TBLE-MOD and ADJ-RATE. It is not available in ADJ-RATE nor is it available in PAY-BEN7 itself.

Figure 17-16

Two-Level Nesting

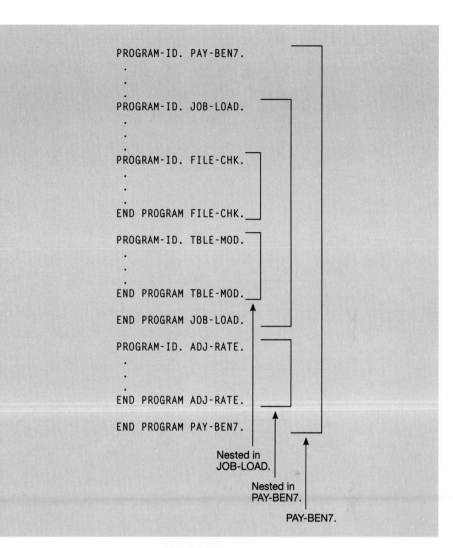

You must be aware that the IS GLOBAL clause can be used only with a data item defined as a level 01; *it cannot be used at any lower level.* However, all data items subordinate to the 01 declared as global are themselves global. You will see how this is handled in the next example program.

The JOB-LOAD Program as a Nested Program—Example 17-3

Example 17-3

The PAY-BEN4 program is to be split into two separate programs as follows:

PAY-BEN7 Process employee benefits.

JOB-LOAD Load the job-code/pay-rate table from the table file. This program is to be nested in PAY-BEN7.

The program solution for this example is shown in Figure 17-17. Actually, most of this program's points have already been described. As you study this program, notice the following:

1. Data items defined in the DATA DIVISION of PAY-BEN7 (starting line 40) are those needed by JOB-LOAD. They are defined under the 01 entry GLOBAL-ITEMS, which is declared as global; remember, all subordinate items to an 01 entry declared as global are themselves global. Thus, they are available to the nested program JOB-LOAD, as well as to PAY-BEN7.

Figure 17-17

A Nested Program—
Example 17-3

```
 1        IDENTIFICATION DIVISION.
 2        PROGRAM-ID. PAY-BEN7.
 3
 4    *    Pay special benefits - Pay Rate lookup using SEARCH ALL.
 5    *    Written by J.Olson 10/3/86o incorporate
 7    *       a nested program for the table load component
 8
 9        ENVIRONMENT DIVISION.
10
11        CONFIGURATION SECTION.
12        SOURCE-COMPUTER. IBM-PC.
13
14        INPUT-OUTPUT SECTION.
15
16        FILE-CONTROL.
17            SELECT EMPLOYEE-FILE  ASSIGN TO DISK  "EMPL-BEN.DL"
18                               ORGANIZATION IS LINE SEQUENTIAL.
19        DATA DIVISION.
20
21        FILE SECTION.
22
23        FD  EMPLOYEE-FILE.
24        01  EMPLOYEE-RECORD.
25            10  ER-EMPL-NUMBER      PIC X(5).
26            10  ER-EMPL-JOB-CODE    PIC 9(3).
27            10  FILLER             PIC X(42).
28
29        WORKING-STORAGE SECTION.
30
31        01  PROGRAMMED-SWITCHES.
32            10                     PIC X.
33                88  END-OF-FILE    VALUE "Y" FALSE "N".
34            10                     PIC X.
35                88  CODE-FOUND     VALUE "Y" FALSE "N".
36
37        01  OTHER-VARIABLES.
38            10  PAY-RATE-DISPLAY   PIC ZZ.99.
39
40        01  GLOBAL-ITEMS  IS GLOBAL.
41
42            10  TABLE-ACCESS-ITEMS    USAGE BINARY.
43                20  TABLE-SIZE        PIC 99.
44
45            10  PROGRAMMED-SWITCHES.
46                20                    PIC X.
47                    88  TABLE-LOAD-ERROR  VALUE "Y" FALSE "N".
48
49            10  JOB-CODE-TABLE.
50                20  JOB-CODE-TABLE-ENTRY OCCURS 1 TO 25 TIMES
51                                     DEPENDING ON TABLE-SIZE
52                                     ASCENDING KEY IS JOB-CODE
53                                     INDEXED BY JOB-INDEX.
54                    30  JOB-CODE     PIC 999.
55                    30  PAY-RATE     PIC 99V99.
56
57        PROCEDURE DIVISION.
58
59        000-PAY-SPECIAL-BENEFITS.
60            PERFORM 100-INITIALIZE
61            PERFORM 110-PROCESS-1-EMPLOYEE
62                UNTIL END-OF-FILE
63            PERFORM 120-FINALIZE
64            STOP RUN.
65
66        100-INITIALIZE.
67            CALL "JOB-LOAD".
68            IF TABLE-LOAD-ERROR
69                DISPLAY " "
70                DISPLAY "Table size exceeded!!"  REVERSE
71                DISPLAY "Processing terminated."
72                STOP RUN
73            END-IF
74            OPEN INPUT  EMPLOYEE-FILE
75            SET END-OF-FILE TO FALSE
76            PERFORM 800-READ-EMPLOYEE-RECORD.
77
78        110-PROCESS-1-EMPLOYEE.
79            PERFORM 300-SEARCH-TABLE
80
81            IF CODE-FOUND
82                PERFORM 310-PROCESS-SPECIAL-BENEFITS
83            ELSE
84                DISPLAY ER-EMPL-JOB-CODE
85            END-IF
86
87            PERFORM 800-READ-EMPLOYEE-RECORD.
88
89        120-FINALIZE.
90            DISPLAY " " BEEP
91            DISPLAY "Special benefits processing has been completed."
92            CLOSE EMPLOYEE-FILE.
93
94        300-SEARCH-TABLE.
95            SEARCH ALL JOB-CODE-TABLE-ENTRY
96                AT END
97                    SET CODE-FOUND TO FALSE
98                WHEN JOB-CODE(JOB-INDEX) = ER-EMPL-JOB-CODE
99                    MOVE PAY-RATE(JOB-INDEX) TO PAY-RATE-DISPLAY
100                   SET CODE-FOUND TO TRUE
101           END-SEARCH.
102
103       310-PROCESS-SPECIAL-BENEFITS.
104           DISPLAY " "
105           DISPLAY "Employee: ", ER-EMPL-NUMBER
106           DISPLAY "Job Code: ", ER-EMPL-JOB-CODE
107           DISPLAY "Pay Rate: ", PAY-RATE-DISPLAY.
108
109       800-READ-EMPLOYEE-RECORD.
110           READ EMPLOYEE-FILE
111               AT END
112                   SET END-OF-FILE TO TRUE
113           END-READ.
114
```

2. There is no corresponding set of data item definitions in JOB-LOAD (see lines 129 through 147) since the needed data items are available from PAY-BEN7.

3. During execution, control is transferred to the nested program JOB-LOAD using the CALL statement (see line 67); this is the same CALL used to transfer control to a subprogram.

4. During execution, control is returned from the nested program to the calling program by the EXIT PROGRAM statement (see line 158); this is the same EXIT PROGRAM used to return control from a subprogram.

Figure 17-17

```
115     ******TABLE-LOAD PROGRAM******            160     100-INITIALIZE.
116     IDENTIFICATION DIVISION.                  161         OPEN INPUT JOB-CODE-FILE
117                                               162         MOVE MAXIMUM-TABLE-SIZE TO TABLE-SIZE
118     PROGRAM-ID. JOB-LOAD.                     163         MOVE ALL "9" TO JOB-CODE-TABLE
119                                               164         SET TABLE-LOAD-ERROR TO FALSE
120     *    Load job-code/pay-rate table.        165         SET TABLE-LOADED TO FALSE
121                                               166         DISPLAY "Loading Table" ERASE
122     ENVIRONMENT DIVISION.                     167         DISPLAY "Entry number    Code"
123                                               168         SET JOB-INDEX TO 1.
124     INPUT-OUTPUT SECTION.                     169
125                                               170     110-LOAD-JOB-CODE-TABLE.
126     FILE-CONTROL.                             171         PERFORM 810-READ-JOB-CODE-RECORD
127         SELECT JOB-CODE-FILE  ASSIGN TO DISK  "JOB-CODE.TBL"   172         IF TABLE-LOADED
128                           ORGANIZATION IS LINE SEQUENTIAL.     173             COMPUTE TABLE-SIZE = ENTRY-COUNTER - 1
129     DATA DIVISION.                            174             DISPLAY " "
130                                               175             DISPLAY "Table load complete."
131     FILE SECTION.                             176         ELSE
132                                               177             IF JC-JOB-CODE NOT > PREVIOUS-JOB-CODE
133     FD  JOB-CODE-FILE.                        178                 DISPLAY " "
134     01  JOB-CODE-RECORD.                      179                 DISPLAY "Job code ", JC-JOB-CODE,
135         10  JC-JOB-CODE        PIC 9(3).      180                     " is out of sequence."
136         10  JC-PAY-RATE        PIC 9(2)V9(2). 181                 SET TABLE-LOAD-ERROR TO TRUE
137                                               182             ELSE
138     WORKING-STORAGE SECTION.                  183                 IF ENTRY-COUNTER NOT > MAXIMUM-TABLE-SIZE
139                                               184                     MOVE JC-JOB-CODE TO JOB-CODE(JOB-INDEX)
140     01  PROGRAMMED-SWITCHES.                  185                     MOVE JC-PAY-RATE TO PAY-RATE(JOB-INDEX)
141         10                     PIC X.         186                     SET JOB-INDEX UP BY 1
142             88  TABLE-LOADED   VALUE "Y"  FALSE "N".   187                     DISPLAY "    ", ENTRY-COUNTER,
143                                               188                         "    ", JC-JOB-CODE
144     01  OTHER-VARIABLES.                      189                     MOVE JC-JOB-CODE TO PREVIOUS-JOB-CODE
145         10  ENTRY-COUNTER      PIC 99.        190                 ELSE
146         10  PREVIOUS-JOB-CODE  PIC 999   VALUE ZERO.    191                     DISPLAY " "
147         10  MAXIMUM-TABLE-SIZE PIC 99    VALUE 25.      192                     DISPLAY "Table size exceeded. ",
148                                               193                         JC-JOB-CODE, " cannot be loaded."
149                                               194                     SET TABLE-LOAD-ERROR TO TRUE
150     PROCEDURE DIVISION.                       195                 END-IF
151                                               196             END-IF
152     000-LOAD-JOB-CODE-TABLE.                  197         END-IF.
153         PERFORM 100-INITIALIZE                198
154         PERFORM 110-LOAD-JOB-CODE-TABLE       199     120-FINALIZE.
155             VARYING ENTRY-COUNTER FROM 1 BY 1 200         CLOSE JOB-CODE-FILE.
156             UNTIL TABLE-LOADED OR TABLE-LOAD-ERROR   201
157         PERFORM 120-FINALIZE                  202     810-READ-JOB-CODE-RECORD.
158         EXIT PROGRAM.                         203         READ JOB-CODE-FILE
159                                               204             AT END
                                                  205                 SET TABLE-LOADED TO TRUE
                                                  206         END-READ.
                                                  207
                                                  208     END PROGRAM JOB-LOAD.
                                                  209
                                                  210     END PROGRAM PAY-BEN7.
```

One final note of caution regarding global data-names: If a data-name used for a global data item is then used to define a data item in a nested program, that data-name becomes local to the nested program. For instance, consider Figure 17-18, in which the program JOB-LOAD is nested in PAY-BEN7, and the programs FILE-CHK and TBLE-MOD are nested in JOB-LOAD. In PAY-BEN7, the data item ERROR-FLAG is global because it is defined under GLOBAL-DATA, which is declared global. That two-position numeric item is available to all nested programs except FILE-CHK (medium blue shading) because the name is redefined within the nested program FILE-CHK. The one-position alphanumeric version of ERROR-FLAG is local to FILE-CHK and therefore available to FILE-CHK.

Figure 17-18

*A Local Definition Overriding
a Global Declaration*

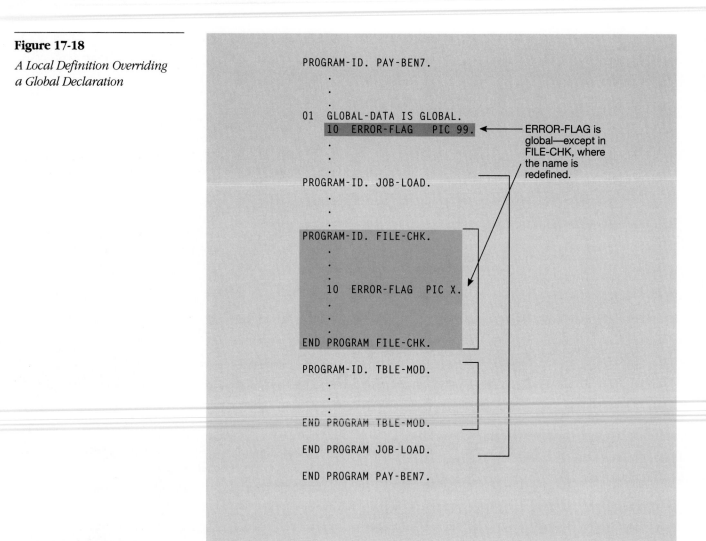

```
PROGRAM-ID. PAY-BEN7.
     .
     .
     .
01  GLOBAL-DATA IS GLOBAL.
    10  ERROR-FLAG   PIC 99.  ◄────── ERROR-FLAG is
     .                                 global—except in
     .                                 FILE-CHK, where
     .                                 the name is
PROGRAM-ID. JOB-LOAD.                  redefined.
     .
     .
     .
PROGRAM-ID. FILE-CHK.
     .
     .
     .
    10   ERROR-FLAG   PIC X.
     .
     .
     .
END PROGRAM FILE-CHK.

PROGRAM-ID. TBLE-MOD.
     .
     .
END PROGRAM TBLE-MOD.

END PROGRAM JOB-LOAD.

END PROGRAM PAY-BEN7.
```

Chapter Summary

General

From this chapter, you have learned the following three techniques for managing programs:

■ The COPY statement, which allows source code to be stored standardized and in source statement libraries. When needed in a program, the COPY causes a designated source code module to be inserted into the program during the compiling operation. Code can be inserted into any division of the program.

■ Subprograms that allow you to program common operations, compile them, and store them as separate code in an object library. A subprogram is incorporated into a program with the CALL statement.

■ Data is passed between a program and a called subprogram through the LINKAGE SECTION of the subprogram and the USING clause of the CALL statement.

■ One or more programs can be fully contained within another program. This is called program nesting. Nesting provides the means to isolate program functions and data in separate programs.

COBOL Language Elements

The COBOL statements that you have studied in this chapter are

CALL
The CALL statement causes control to be transferred from one object program to another. Its general format (to the extent used in this book) is

$$\underline{CALL} \quad \begin{Bmatrix} \text{identifier-1} \\ \text{literal-1} \end{Bmatrix} \quad [\text{USING \{identifier-2\}...}]$$

CANCEL
The CANCEL statement ensures that the next time the referenced program is called, it will be in its initial state.

$$\underline{CANCEL} \quad \begin{Bmatrix} \text{identifier-1} \\ \text{literal-1} \end{Bmatrix} ...$$

COPY
The COPY statement provides the means to copy text from a source statement library into a source program.

$$\underline{COPY} \text{ text-name} \left[\begin{Bmatrix} \underline{OF} \\ \underline{IN} \end{Bmatrix} \text{ library-name} \right]$$

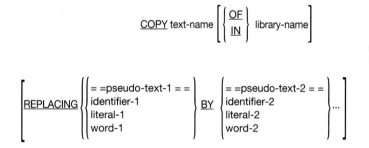

EXIT PROGRAM
The EXIT PROGRAM statement marks the logical end of a called program.

$$\underline{EXIT\ PROGRAM}$$

Other language elements that you have studied in this chapter are

LINKAGE SECTION
The LINKAGE SECTION provides the means for communication between a program and a called subprogram or a nested program. Its structure is identical to that of the WORKING-STORAGE SECTION. Its general format (to the extent used in this book) is

$$\underline{LINKAGE}\ \underline{SECTION.}$$
  record-description-entry

USING phrase
The USING phrase of the PROCEDURE DIVISION header identifies the names used by a subprogram or a nested program for any data items passed to it by a calling program.

$$\underline{PROCEDURE\ DIVISION}\ [\underline{USING}\ \{\text{data-name-1}\}...]$$

Programming Conventions

Standardize record descriptions and save them in a source statement library. Any program using a particular file should include a COPY statement to copy the record description into the programming. This promotes standardization and reduces the possibility of errors.

Often used routines and procedures should be set up as independent subprograms, compiled, and stored in an object library. This reduces redundant effort.

Whenever possible in preparing a subprogram, group the linkage data items into a single record. Then the USING can designate that record name.

For a very large program, break the program down into major independent components and program them as nested components of a controlling program. This provides data independence otherwise not available in COBOL.

Error Prevention/Detection

When using the COPY statement, always check data definitions of the copied code carefully before writing your program in order to avoid duplicating names of the copied code.

If a subprogram does not appear to be returning data to the calling program correctly, check to ensure that the formats of the LINKAGE SECTION and the data definition in the calling program are identical. For instance, accidentally switching two fields might not cause a compiler error, but it will give incorrect results.

If a result is not returned to a global data item in a called program from a nested program, check to ensure that the linkage data item used in the nested program was not accidentally defined in the nested program.

Questions and Exercises

Give a brief description of each of the following terms that were introduced in this chapter.

Key Terminology

called program	local	source code library
calling program	object library	subprogram
global	pseudo-text	subprogram linkage

General Questions

1. Why is the COPY statement useful to programmers?
2. Where is the COBOL code stored when COPY statements are used in programs?
3. When one program calls another, the "called" program is referred to as a(n)_____ .
4. How does issuing a CALL for a program differ from using a PERFORM statement?
5. The "calling program" must contain several important COBOL language elements. What are they?
6. In a "called program," there must be some matching or special COBOL language elements. What are they?
7. What is a "nested" program? What two methods can be used for communicating data between a program and one of its nested programs?

Questions Relating to the Example Programs

1. A programmer inserted the COPY LOAD-JC.DTA statement immediately following the DATA DIVISION header at line 20 of the PAY-BEN5 program (Figure 17-5). Would this make any difference during either compiling or execution? Explain your answer.
2. A programmer inserted the COPY LOAD-JC.PRO statement immediately preceding the 100-INITIALIZE paragraph at line 59 of the PAY-BEN5 program (Figure 17-5). Would this make any difference during either compiling or execution? Explain your answer.
3. In the PAY-BEN6 program (Figure 17-12), a programmer reversed the first two entries under LINKAGE-ITEMS and wrote the code as shown at the top of the next page. Will this create a problem? Explain your answer.

```
01  LINKAGE-ITEMS.

    10  PROGRAMMED-SWITCHES.
        20                              PIC X.
            88 TABLE-LOAD-ERROR    VALUE "Y" FALSE "N".

    10  TABLE-ACCESS-ITEMS USAGE BINARY.
        20 TABLE-SIZE                  PIC 99.

    10  JOB-CODE-TABLE.
        20  JOB-CODE-TABLE-ENTRY OCCURS 1 TO 25 TIMES
                                    DEPENDING ON TABLE-SIZE
                                    ASCENDING KEY IS JOB-CODE
                                    INDEXED BY JOB-INDEX.
            30 JOB-CODE                PIC 999.
            30 PAY-RATE                PIC 99V99.
```

4. Line 146 of the JOB-LOAD nested program (Figure 17-17) defines the data item PREVIOUS-JOB-CODE for use within JOB-LOAD. Assume that in writing the employee benefit program, a programmer needed a job-code work area and defined it as PREVIOUS-JOB-CODE under OTHER-VARIABLES (line 37). Explain whether or not this will cause a problem because of duplicate names within the program.

5. In the JOB-LOAD program (Figure 17-13), the programmer decides the table is safer being coded in the WORKING-STORAGE SECTION. Lines 46–52 are moved to line 35. Will this make a difference to any program that calls the JOB-LOAD program?

6. The PAY-BEN7 program (Figure 17-17) calls the JOB-LOAD program, which is nested within this figure. The programmer decides that the CALL and error test statements, lines 67–73, really belong after line 78. This puts it first in the 110-PROCESS-1-EMPLOYEE module. Will this program compile? Does this change have any effect on the program's execution?

Writing Program Statements

1. A student registration system at a university has a need to use a table containing major codes and descriptions in several of their programs. You are to code an 01-level record description that will be saved in SRCE-LIB. The record layout is as follows.

Field	Field Positions	Format
Record Code	1-2	MD
Major Code	3-6	
Major Description	7-31	

Write a COPY statement that can be used to copy this record description into the FILE SECTION of any program.

2. Assuming that the major description records are to be loaded into a table, write another section of code describing this table. There are 100 possible entries in the table and the code is to be saved in SRCE-LIB. Refer to Exercise 1 for the record description. Record code does not need to be included in the table, but major codes must be in ascending sequence. Write a COPY statement that can be used to copy the table into the WORKING-STORAGE SECTION of any program. You may want to consider retrieval also.

3. Write PROCEDURE DIVISION code to load the major description records into a table that can be used in any program The maximum number of table entries in 100 and each record read must contain MD in positions 1-2 in order to be valid. In addition, major codes must be in ascending sequence. Write the COPY statement used to insert this code in any program. The code itself is to be saved in the REG-PROG subdirectory or program library. The code from Exercises 1 and 2 is to be used here.

4. Write PROCEDURE DIVISION code to search the major description table that can be used in any program. The search routine must provide for an entry not being found. This code is to be saved in the REG-PROG subdirectory or program library. Write a COPY statement used to insert this code in any program. Completing Exercise 2 would be helpful for doing this exercise.

5. Create a subprogram that can be "called" from any program to load the major description table. This may be accomplished using the answers from Exercises 1–3 or simply using the record description and table load requirements from Exercises 1–3.

6. Create a subprogram that can be "called" from any program to search the major description table. This may be accomplished by using the answers from Exercises 2 and 4 or by following the requirements stated in each of these exercises.

Programming Assignments

As you have undoubtedly observed by now, the variety of programming assignments are based on a relative small number of applications. In particular, the student file, the enrollment file, the employee file, and the airport file have been used in nearly every chapter. If you have written programs for two or more assignments operating on one of the files, you have essentially built a small application system. The assignments of this chapter involve bringing the programs together under the umbrella of a menu control system. You may include as many or as few of the programs for a single system.

17-1 Menu Control for Access to Student System

Applicable Programming Assignments:

    8-2
    9-3
    10-4   (Uses the indexed file STUDENTS.DI)
    13-2   (Requires a sorted version of STUDENTS.DL)
    14-1
    15-3
    16-1

System Requirements:

1. Select either of the two techniques: separately compiled programs or nested programs.
2. If you select nested programs, you may declare the input file in the calling program. However, recognize that 10-4 and 13-2 use different input files. Also, remember that the maximum number of lines in a program cannot exceed 1,000 for the Educational version of the compiler.
3. Provide appropriate menu control for access to the included programs.

17-2 Menu Control for Access to Airport System

Applicable Programming Assignments:

    10-2   (Uses the indexed file AIRPORT1.DI)
    11-1
    12-1
    12-2
    13-4   (Requires a sorted version of AIRPORT1.DL)
    15-2

System Requirements:

1. Select either of the two techniques: separately compiled programs or nested programs.
2. If you select nested programs, you may declare the input file in the calling program. However, recognize that 10-2 and 13-4 use different input files. Also, remember that that maximum number of lines in a program cannot exceed 1,000 for the Educational version of the compiler.
3. Provide appropriate menu control for access to the included programs.

17-3 Menu Control for Access to Employee System

Applicable Programming Assignments:
- 9-1
- 10-1 (Uses the indexed file EMPLOYEE.DI)
- 11-2
- 14-2
- 15-4

System Requirements:
1. Select either of the two techniques: separately compiled programs or nested programs.
2. If you select nested programs, you may declare the input file in the calling program. However, recognize that 10-1 uses a different input file. Also, remember that the maximum number of lines in a program cannot exceed 1,000 for the Educational version of the compiler.
3. Provide appropriate menu control for access to the included programs.

17-4 Menu Control for Access to Enrollment System

Applicable Programming Assignments:
- 8-1
- 9-2
- 10-3 (Uses the indexed file ENROLL01.DI)
- 13-1 (Requires a sorted version of ENROLL01.DL)
- 14-4

System Requirements:
1. Select either of the two techniques: separately compiled programs or nested programs.
2. If you select nested programs, you may declare the input file in the calling program. However, recognize that 10-3 and 13-1 use different input files. Also, remember that the maximum number of lines in a program cannot exceed 1,000 for the Educational version of the compiler.
3. Provide appropriate menu control for access to the included programs.

18

ADVANCED FILE MANAGEMENT CAPABILITIES OF COBOL

Chapter Objectives

Throughout this book, you have worked with data files, both sequential and indexed. However, the input-output operations that you have performed represent a relatively small subset of the file processing capabilities available to the COBOL programmer. The purpose of this chapter is to introduce most of the input-output features so that you can apply them in the next three chapters, which focus on file processing. From this chapter, you will learn about the following topics:

■ Relative file organization (the third of the three COBOL file organizations)—an alternate to indexed organization for random access. With this organization, records are identified by their relative positioning within the file.

■ The REWRITE statement, which replaces the record (on disk) just read. The typical processing sequence is to read a record, make changes to it, and rewrite it.

■ The DELETE statement, which allows you to remove a record from an indexed or relative file.

■ Dynamic access to a file, which allows a file to be processed both randomly and sequentially in the same program.

■ Defining and using two or more keys for a file.

■ The START statement, which allows positioning within a file in order to begin sequential processing at some point other than the beginning of the file.

■ The multi-user environment, in which two or more programs concurrently access the same file.

■ Programmer-written error recovery routines and the COBOL provision for implementing them (declaratives, I-O status, and the USE statement).

Review of File Processing

In Chapter 4, you learned the distinction between file organization and file access. Since then, you have used files with both sequential organization and indexed organization. A sequential file gives you access to the records of the file only in the order in which the records were written to the file (sequentially). On the other hand, an indexed file gives you access to records in whatever sequence you desire (randomly); it also gives you sequential access to the records in the sequence defined by the key field. The SELECT statement defines both the file organization and file access; Figure 18-1 summarizes forms that you have used.

Figure 18-1

The SELECT Statement

```
SELECT INVENTORY-FILE    ASSIGN TO DISK "SOFTWAR2.DL"
                         ORGANIZATION IS LINE SEQUENTIAL.
```
Organization is LINE SEQUENTIAL; therefore, the type of access is not specified—it can only be sequential.

```
SELECT INVENTORY-FILE    ASSIGN TO DISK "SOFTWAR2.DI"
                         ORGANIZATION IS INDEXED
                         ACCESS IS RANDOM
                         RECORD KEY IS IR-STOCK-NUMBER.
```
Organization is INDEXED; therefore, the key field must be specified (regardless of the access method). Access is specified RANDOM.

```
SELECT INVENTORY-FILE    ASSIGN TO DISK "SOFTWAR2.DI"
                         ORGANIZATION IS INDEXED
                         ACCESS IS SEQUENTIAL
                         RECORD KEY IS IR-STOCK-NUMBER.
```
Organization is INDEXED; therefore, the key field must be specified (regardless of the access method). Access is specified SEQUENTIAL.

Remember that for an indexed file accessed randomly, a value must be moved to the key field of the record to identify the record to be read. On the other hand, accessing an indexed file sequentially is done in exactly the same way as accessing a sequential file. That is, the READ statement gives the next record based on the key field sequence. Also, the AT END clause is used in exactly the same way as with a sequential file READ.

Although these capabilities have allowed you to program a wide variety of applications, numerous other input-output capabilities are available to the COBOL programmer. Let's begin with the relative file organization, the second of two organizations that allow both sequential and random access.

Relative File Organization

Basic Principles

Whereas indexed file organization uses an index to provide access to records in a file, *relative organization* provides access to records by the relative position that they occupy in the file. This is almost identical in concept to the tables that you studied in Chapter 14. For example, in Figure 18-2, space is reserved for 12 month/day entries in a table. Recall from your study of tables that the table definition simply defines space in memory without putting anything into it. During execution of the program, appropriate entries are made. It is important that values may be placed in the table in whatever order is deemed appropriate. If for some reason entries were not made for the months of March and April, the structure of the table would not be affected. There would still be 12 "slots," but two of them would be empty.

In a sense, a relative file is simply a disk-oriented table. The "slots" of the file, like the entries of a table, are numbered beginning with 1 and progressing to 2, 3, and so on. The file can be accessed sequentially by reading the records one after the other, or it can be accessed randomly by specifying the slot, or *relative record number*, of the desired record, much as you specify the subscript of the desired element of an array.

Records in a Relative File

A relative file can best be used when the record key value is the same as the position in the file (its relative record number) or can be adjusted by simple arithmetic. For instance, assume that a company assigns each employee a number beginning with 1001 and progresses by 1 for each employee. Then 1001 would be the first record in the file, 1002 the second, and so on. Note that the record number can be obtained by subtracting 1000 from the employee number. This is illustrated in Figure 18-3, which shows the first three records of such an employee file. To obtain the record of, for instance, employee 1003 would require the following actions:

Figure 18-2

A Table in Memory

Figure 18-3

Records of a Relative File

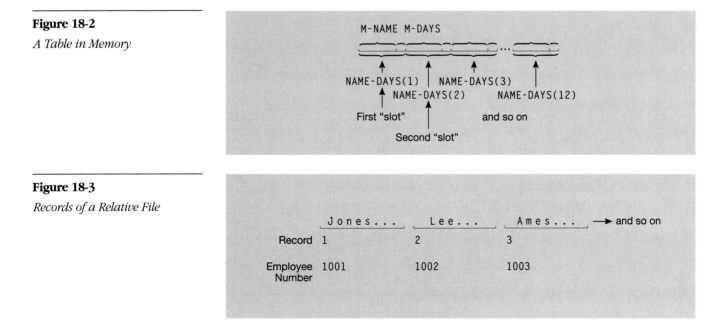

1. Subtract 1000 from 1003 giving 3. This is the relative record number of the desired employee.

2. Access relative record 3 of the file.

Notice that there is no key field in the sense of a key field for an indexed file. In fact, you can see that the record itself does not contain the employee number; such an entity is simply not needed for accessing a record. However, this introduces the potential for a serious error: positioning a record in the wrong record position, thereby implicitly giving it an incorrect key value.

For instance, assume that somehow the data for employee 1003 were accidentally stored in record position 4, as shown in Figure 18-4. If a program required the record for employee 1004, the accessing procedure would cause relative record 4 to be read. The record for Ames (employee 1003) that is misplaced would be read and there would be no way of knowing that the wrong record has been accessed. To avoid such a problem, it is a good idea to include the record key as part of the record, as shown in Figure 18-5. Then whenever a record is read, a comparison can be made to ensure that it is the right one. In this case, the key value stored in the record (1003) is different from the implied employee number (4 plus 1000).

One characteristic of sequential and indexed files is that each record added to a file is physically positioned immediately following the previously added record. Thus, if you have built a file consisting of 500 records each 100 bytes in length, the data in your file will require 50,000 bytes on disk. On the other hand, the relative file organization preserves the "relativeness" of the file by placing each record where it belongs, relative to the other records. For example, assume that you are building the employee file and the first two records you enter are those for employees 1001 and 1004. In Figure 18-6, records for employees 1001 and 1004 (relative records 1 and 4) have been written into their relative locations. Relative records positions 2 and 3 remain empty. This is in contrast to a sequential or indexed file, where record 1004 would immediately follow the previously written 1001. Thus, a relative file will have "gaps" in it if the key values are not consecutive numbers. This represents no problem unless there are many large gaps that consume more storage than is acceptable.

Figure 18-4

An Incorrectly Positioned Record in a Relative File

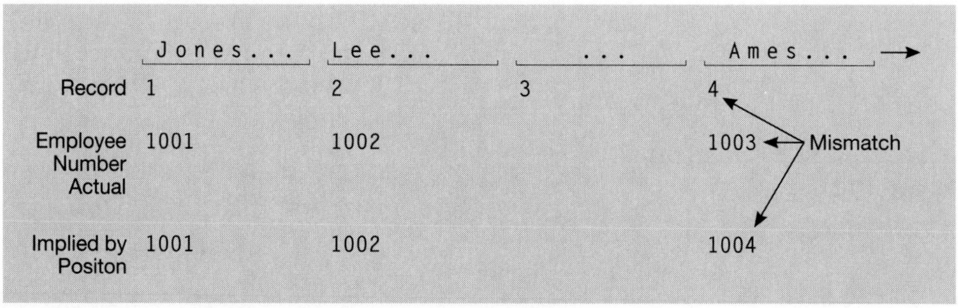

Figure 18-5

Including a Key Field Value in the Relative File Record to Serve as a Check

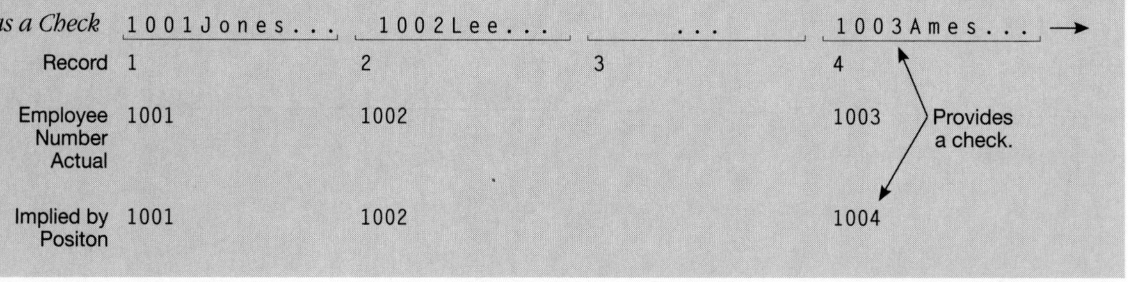

Figure 18-6

Unused Records Positions in a Relative File

```
                           1001Jones...         empty              empty        1004Dodd...→
                    Record 1              2                  3                   4
                 Employee  1001                                                 1004
                   Number
```

Unlike the in-memory table, the size of the relative file is not specified when the file is first created. In that respect, a file consists of "nothing" until records are written to it. If the example employee file were created, the single record for employee 1001 written, and the file then closed, the file would occupy space for only one record. However, if record 500 were written (and none of the others), the space would be reserved for the preceding 499. This is much like an empty table defined by the OCCURS.

The advantage of the relative organization over indexed structure is that there is less overhead, both in processing and disk storage space (if the record key values are consecutive—without gaps). However, it cannot be used in many situations; for instance, with a key field that is alphanumeric or with preassigned numbers such as the Social Security number, where the gaps would be uncontrollably large.

The Relative Key Concept

When accessing a table, you use a subscript or index to specify which item in the table is desired. When accessing a relative file randomly, you tell COBOL which record you want; for example, record 12 or record 153. This is called the *relative key*. The relative key must be an unsigned integer field that *is not defined in the record definition* of the file. A specific record in the relative file is accessed by moving the number of the desired record to the relative key field before executing the input-output statement (READ, WRITE, and so on). This is similar to randomly accessing a record from an indexed file by moving the record key value of the desired record to the record key field before executing the input-output statement. However, the important difference between the two is that the specified field of the relative file is defined in the WORKING-STORAGE SECTION, whereas that of the indexed file is the actual field of the record. You will see this is the next example program.

Accessing Records From a Relative File—Example Definition

The following example illustrates an application that is well suited to the use of a relative file.

Example 18-1

Problem Description

The management of UNISOFT has decided to perform statistical analyses of sales on a state-by-state basis. Eventually, these analyses will include all 50 states. However, initially slightly less than half of the states are to be included in the study. Two consecutive years of data are maintained for studies. The "current" year of the study is considered to be the most recently completed year; the "previous" year is the year preceding the current year. Data for the states is to be stored in a relative file. One of the required programs must allow a user to enter the state number of a desired state and then display the contents of that record.

Output Requirements

Each requested record is to be displayed according to the screen layout shown in Figure 18-7. Suitable error messages are to be displayed directly above the user query line.

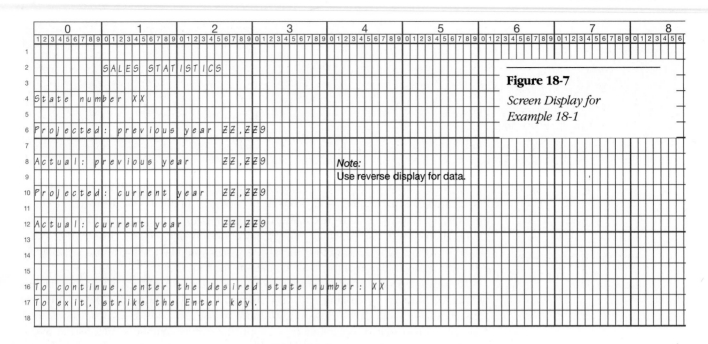

Figure 18-7

Screen Display for Example 18-1

Note:
Use reverse display for data.

Input Description
Input file name: NATSALES.DR
File type: Relative
Record format:

Field	Positions	Data Type	Format
State number	1–2	Numeric	Unsigned whole number
Previous year:			
Projected sales	3–7	Numeric	Unsigned whole number
Actual sales	8–12	Numeric	Unsigned whole number
Current year:			
Projected sales	13–17	Numeric	Unsigned whole number
Actual sales	18–22	Numeric	Unsigned whole number

Key field: State number

Processing Requirements
This program is to function as follows:
1. Accept the state number of the desired record from the keyboard.
2. Read the record from disk and display it on the screen as specified in the screen format of Figure 18-7.
3. If there is no record with the requested state number, display an error message.
4. If the state number stored in the record is different from the relative record number used to access the record, display an error message.
5. Allow the user to terminate processing after each record is displayed.

Accessing Records From a Relative File—Program Solution

The structure and logic of this program solution are virtually identical to those of the RAN-DIS3 program from Chapter 10. The completed program for this example is shown in Figure 18-8; notice the following about the SELECT statement:

1. The organization is defined as relative by the clause:

```
ORGANIZATION IS RELATIVE
```

2. Access to the file is defined as random by the clause:

```
ACCESS IS RANDOM
```

Figure 18-8

Random Processing a Relative File—Example 18-1

```
1      IDENTIFICATION DIVISION.
2
3      PROGRAM-ID.  REL-DIS.
4
5    *   Written by J.Olson   10/26/86
6    *   Modified by W.Price  10/13/90
7
8    *   On a record-by-record basis, this program displays
9    *   requested records from a sales file that has
10   *   relative file organization.
11
12     ENVIRONMENT DIVISION.
13
14     CONFIGURATION SECTION.
15     SOURCE-COMPUTER.  IBM-PC.
16
17     INPUT-OUTPUT SECTION.
18     FILE-CONTROL.
19         SELECT NATIONAL-SALES-FILE   ASSIGN TO DISK, "NATSALES.DR"
20                                      ORGANIZATION IS RELATIVE
21                                      ACCESS IS RANDOM
22                                      RELATIVE KEY IS DESIRED-RECORD.
23
24     DATA DIVISION.
25
26     FILE SECTION.
27
28     FD  NATIONAL-SALES-FILE.
29     01  NATIONAL-SALES-RECORD.
30         10  NS-STATE-NUMBER         PIC 9(2).
31         10  NS-PROJECTED-PREV-YEAR  PIC 9(5).
32         10  NS-ACTUAL-PREV-YEAR     PIC 9(5).
33         10  NS-PROJECTED-CURR-YEAR  PIC 9(5).
34         10  NS-ACTUAL-CURR-YEAR     PIC 9(5).
35
36     WORKING-STORAGE SECTION.
37
38     01  WORK-VARIABLES.
39         10  DESIRED-RECORD          PIC 9(2).
40         10  PROCESSING-OPTION       PIC X.
41
42     SCREEN SECTION.
43
44     01  SALES-RECORD-SCREEN.
45         10  VALUE "SALES STATISTICS" BLANK SCREEN
46                                      LINE 2     COL 11.
47         10  VALUE "State number"   LINE PLUS 2  COL  1.
48         10  PIC XX         FROM NS-STATE-NUMBER
49                                      LINE PLUS 0 COL 16 REVERSE.
50         10  VALUE "Projected: previous year " LINE PLUS 2  COL  1.
51         10  PIC ZZ,ZZ9     FROM NS-PROJECTED-PREV-YEAR
52                                      LINE PLUS 0  COL PLUS 0 REVERSE.
53         10  VALUE "Actual: previous year   " LINE PLUS 2  COL  1.
54         10  PIC ZZ,ZZ9     FROM NS-ACTUAL-PREV-YEAR
55                                      LINE PLUS 0  COL PLUS 0 REVERSE.
56         10  VALUE "Projected: current year " LINE PLUS 2  COL  1.
57         10  PIC ZZ,ZZ9     FROM NS-PROJECTED-CURR-YEAR
58                                      LINE PLUS 0  COL PLUS 0 REVERSE.
59         10  VALUE "Actual: current year    " LINE PLUS 2  COL  1.
60         10  PIC ZZ,ZZ9     FROM NS-ACTUAL-CURR-YEAR
61                                      LINE PLUS 0  COL PLUS 0 REVERSE.
62
63     01  USER-REQUEST-SCREEN.
64         . 10  VALUE "To continue, enter the desired state number: "
65                                      LINE 16               HIGHLIGHT.
66         10  PIC XX          TO DESIRED-RECORD
67                                      LINE PLUS 0  COL PLUS 0 FULL.
68         10  VALUE "To exit, strike the Enter key. "
69                                      LINE PLUS 1           HIGHLIGHT.
70
71     01  NOT-IN-FILE-SCREEN.
72         10  VALUE "There is no record in the file for "
73                                      LINE 14 BLANK SCREEN  HIGHLIGHT.
74         10  PIC X(5)        FROM DESIRED-RECORD
75                                      LINE PLUS 0   COL     HIGHLIGHT.
76
77     01  KEY-FIELD-MISMATCH-SCREEN.
78         10  VALUE "Error in data file. State "
79                                      LINE 13   BLANK SCREEN  HIGHLIGHT.
80         10  PIC XX          FROM NS-STATE-NUMBER
81                                      LINE PLUS 0   COL PLUS 0 HIGHLIGHT.
82         10  VALUE "occupies space for state "
83                                      LINE PLUS 1 HIGHLIGHT.
84         10  PIC XX          FROM DESIRED-RECORD
85                                      LINE PLUS 0   COL PLUS 0 HIGHLIGHT.
86
87     PROCEDURE DIVISION.
88
89     000-DISPLAY-RECORDS.
90         PERFORM 100-INITIALIZE
91         IF DESIRED-RECORD NOT = ZERO
92             PERFORM 110-PROCESS-1-REQUEST
93                 UNTIL DESIRED-RECORD = ZERO
94             PERFORM 120-FINALIZE
95         END-IF
96         STOP RUN.
97
98     100-INITIALIZE.
99         DISPLAY " " ERASE
100        DISPLAY USER-REQUEST-SCREEN
101        ACCEPT  USER-REQUEST-SCREEN
102        IF DESIRED-RECORD NOT = ZERO
103            OPEN INPUT NATIONAL-SALES-FILE
104        END-IF.
105
106    110-PROCESS-1-REQUEST.
107        PERFORM 800-READ-SALES-RECORD
108        DISPLAY USER-REQUEST-SCREEN
109        ACCEPT  USER-REQUEST-SCREEN.
110
111    120-FINALIZE.
112        CLOSE NATIONAL-SALES-FILE.
113
114    800-READ-SALES-RECORD.
115        READ NATIONAL-SALES-FILE
116            INVALID KEY
117                DISPLAY NOT-IN-FILE-SCREEN
118            NOT INVALID KEY
119                IF NS-STATE-NUMBER NOT = DESIRED-RECORD
120                    DISPLAY KEY-FIELD-MISMATCH-SCREEN
121                ELSE
122                    DISPLAY SALES-RECORD-SCREEN
123                END-IF
124        END-READ.
```

3. The data item that will contain the relative record number of the desired record is defined by the clause:

```
RELATIVE KEY IS DESIRED-RECORD
```

Note that DESIRED-RECORD is defined as a separate field in the WORKING-STORAGE SECTION. For a relative file, this key must be an unsigned integer.

Regarding the designated key (DESIRED-RECORD), do not become confused with indexed file and assume that it must be the key within the record (NS-STATE-NUMBER, in this case). Remember that the key field within the record is not required in a relative file because the record number is determined solely by the relative position of the record in the file. You may see NS-STATE-NUMBER as a key field and treat it accordingly within your program, but COBOL sees it simply as another field. Hence, it can be defined as either numeric or alphanumeric.

In the PROCEDURE DIVISION of this program, you can see that the data item DESIRED-RECORD is used as the relative key field, as the data item to query the user, and as the loop control data item. The user is queried by the ACCEPT at lines 101 (for first entry into the loop) and 109 (for subsequent passes through the loop). An entry of 0 (caused by striking the Enter key without typing a number) causes program termination. Entering a number other than 0 causes the record to be read at line 115, with one of the following results:

1. If the requested record is not in the file, the INVALID KEY clause is executed and an appropriate message is displayed.

2. If the requested record is found, the program checks to ensure that the state code stored in the record corresponds to the relative record number. If not, an error message is displayed. This represents good insurance against accidentally loading the wrong record or improperly changing the record contents.

3. If the record is found, it is displayed.

Sequential Processing of Relative Files

From Chapter 5, you know that indexed files can be processed either sequentially or randomly. Recall that a program to process an indexed file sequentially is identical to a corresponding program to process a sequential file—with the exception of the SELECT. For instance, a program to print a sequential listing of the indexed file SOFTWAR3.DI would include the following SELECT:

```
SELECT INVENTORY-FILE    ASSIGN TO DISK, "SOFTWAR2.DI"
                         ORGANIZATION IS INDEXED
                         ACCESS IS SEQUENTIAL
                         RECORD KEY IS IR-STOCK-NUMBER.
```

Similarly, a relative file can be accessed either sequentially or randomly. For instance, if you wished to print a sequential listing of the sales statistic file (of Example 18-1), you would use the following SELECT:

```
SELECT NATIONAL-SALES-FILE    ASSIGN TO DISK, "NATSALES.DR"
                              ORGANIZATION IS RELATIVE
                              ACCESS IS SEQUENTIAL.
```

No indication of a relative key is required because the file is to be processed sequentially. (However, if the START statement—described later in this chapter—is to be used, the relative key must be specified.) If you were to inspect the PROCEDURE DIVISION of the program, you would be unable to tell that the file being processed is a relative file. The READ statement would include an AT END option just as if a sequential file were being processed. The fact that some record positions might be empty is no problem since COBOL skips them. For instance, in Figure 18-6 where relative record positions 2 and 3 are empty, the first record read would be relative record 1 and the second read would be relative record 4, the next record stored in this file.

Changing and Deleting Records

Changing the Contents of a Field in a Record—Example 18-2

In programs to this point, you have either opened a file for input and read from the file, or opened it for output and written to it. You have had no examples in which both input and output were performed on the same file. One of the features of most business data processing applications is that data stored on disk is commonly read from the disk file, modified, and then written back to disk, thus replacing the original. In order to do this, you need two COBOL capabilities:

■ A form of the OPEN statement that allows you to designate that both input and output will be performed on the file—the I-O phrase

■ An output statement that directs COBOL to replace the existing record on disk with the current copy in memory—the REWRITE statement

The next example of a partial program illustrates the REWRITE statement.

Example 18-2
> For certain records of the inventory file, the reorder-level field must be changed to zero. In the program that does the processing, the key field value of the record to be processed is stored in the data item DESIRED-STOCK-NUMBER.

The REWRITE Statement—Example 18-2

In the pertinent sections of code shown in Figure 18-9, you can see that the key word I-O is used in the OPEN statement. This means that the file is to be opened for both input and output, thus allowing records to be read from and written to the file. During execution, records are processed from the 300 module as follows:

Figure 18-9

Performing Both Input and Output Operations on a File

```
FILE-CONTROL.
    SELECT INVENTORY-FILE    ASSIGN TO DISK "SOFTWAR2.DI"
                             ORGANIZATION IS INDEXED
                             ACCESS IS RANDOM
                             RECORD KEY IS IR-STOCK-NUMBER.
    .
    .
    .
100-INITIALIZE.
    OPEN I-O INVENTORY-FILE
        ↑──────────────── Indicates that both input
    .                      and output operations are to
    .                      be performed with this file.
    .
300-PROCESS-SELECTED-RECORD.
    PERFORM 800-READ-INVENTORY-RECORD
    IF INVENTORY-RECORD-FOUND
        MOVE ZERO TO IR-REORDER-LEVEL
        PERFORM 860-REWRITE-UPDATED-RECORD
    END-IF
    .
    .
    .
800-READ-INVENTORY-RECORD.
    MOVE DESIRED-STOCK-NUMBER TO IR-STOCK-NUMBER
    READ INVENTORY-FILE
      INVALID KEY
        SET INVENTORY-RECORD-FOUND TO FALSE
      NOT INVALID KEY
        SET INVENTORY-RECORD-FOUND TO TRUE
    END-READ.

860-REWRITE-UPDATED-RECORD.
    REWRITE INVENTORY-RECORD
      INVALID KEY
        DISPLAY "Invalid key while rewriting", INVENTORY-RECORD
        DISPLAY "Aborting update program."
        STOP RUN
    END-REWRITE.
```

1. In the 800 module, the stock number of the desired record is moved to the inventory record key field. The read is executed. If the record is found, the INVENTORY-RECORD-FOUND switch is set to true; otherwise, it is set to false.

2. In the 300 module, the switch is tested to determine if a record was successfully read. If true, the reorder-level field is set to zero and the 860 module is executed.

3. In the 860 module, the REWRITE statement causes COBOL to write the current record to disk, according to the value in the key field IR-STOCK-NUMBER. Since this value was not changed during the processing, the record in the inventory record area replaces the original copy on disk. Because the record was just read from disk, an INVALID KEY condition represents some type of system error and not a program logic error, so processing is terminated. You will learn about other ways of handling this condition later in this chapter.

This action of replacing an existing record with an updated version of the record is called *updating in place*. It is done with the REWRITE statement, which has the following partial general format (you can see that its format is identical to that of the WRITE):

> REWRITE record-name
>
>   [INVALID KEY imperative-statement-1]
>
>   [NOT INVALID KEY imperative-statement-2]
>
> [END-REWRITE]

The INVALID KEY clause is indicated as optional in this general form. However, it is required unless a USE procedure has been specified for the file; the USE procedure is described later in this chapter.

Although this example uses an indexed file, the descriptions are equally applicable to relative files. That is, records of a relative file can be updated in place in the same way as illustrated here.

Updating in place is not limited to random access files; it can also be done with sequentially organized files. For instance, any record in the inventory file as defined by the following SELECT can be updated:

```
SELECT INVENTORY-FILE   ASSIGN TO DISK "SOFTWAR2.DL"
                        ORGANIZATION IS SEQUENTIAL.
```

A REWRITE can be used after a successful READ for that file to replace a record of a sequential file. Since no key is associated with accessing a sequential file, the REWRITE includes no additional clauses; its partial general form is

> REWRITE record-name

The DELETE Statement

With indexed and relative files, it is also possible to delete records from a file using the DELETE statement, which has the following general format:

> DELETE file-name RECORD
>
>   [INVALID KEY imperative-statement-1]
>
>   [NOT INVALID KEY imperative-statement-2]
>
> [END-DELETE]

If the access mode of a file is designated as SEQUENTIAL in the SELECT, then the INVALID KEY and NOT INVALID KEY phrases cannot be used. Other restrictions and rules of the DELETE are

- The file must be open in the I-O mode.

- If file access is designated as SEQUENTIAL (in the SELECT), then the last input or output operation on that file must have been a successfully executed READ. The record deleted is the one just read.

- For a file in random or dynamic access mode, the record deleted is that record identified by the contents of the designated key data item.
- The INVALID KEY clause functions in the same way as with the READ; if no record corresponds to the key data item contents, the INVALID KEY action is executed.

Dynamac File Access

Accessing a File Both Randomly and Sequentially— Example 18-3

The preceding examples showed you that the ACCESS clause of the SELECT indicates to COBOL that an indexed or relative file is to be accessed *either* sequentially *or* randomly during the execution of a program. For instance, in a program containing the preceding SELECT in which INVENTORY-FILE includes ACCESS IS SEQUENTIAL, you could perform only sequential access; you could not also perform random access. This is reasonable because, in a given program, you normally want to access the file either sequentially *or* randomly. However, consider an application in which processing will be as follows:

1. Access a particular record as a starting point—a random access
2. Accesss one or more records following the previously accessed record—a sequential access

Such a dual accessing capability is called *dynamic access* and is illustrated by the next example.

Example 18-3

Processing the national sales statistics file is to begin at a designated record within the file and proceed sequentially to the end of the file. In the program that does the processing, the key field value of the first record to be processed is stored in the data item DESIRED-RECORD.

The ACCESS IS DYNAMIC Clause

In the program segment of Figure 18-10, you can see that the SELECT contains the clause:

```
ACCESS IS DYNAMIC
```

With this clause, it is possible to use both sequential access and random access I-O statements for a given file. In this program segment, the relative key value of the first record to be processed is available in the data item BEGINNING-RECORD. You can see that the 800 module performs the random access read. Subsequent records are read sequentially in the 810 module, in which the NEXT RECORD phrase tells COBOL that a sequential read is to take place. In other words, when file access is DYNAMIC, a READ with the NEXT RECORD phrase causes sequential access; a READ without the NEXT RECORD phrase causes random access.

The NEXT RECORD phrase gives the ability to read the next sequential record after the positioning within the file via a random operation. In some cases, it is convenient to be able to read a previous record—that is, to read the file in reverse. Although not included in the COBOL-85 Standard, most versions of COBOL (including RM/COBOL-85) provide for this. The general form of the read then becomes as follows:

```
READ file-name [ NEXT / PREVIOUS ] RECORD

   [AT END imperative-statement-1]
   [NOT AT END imperative-statement-2]
   [END-READ]
```

Although this example uses a relative file, exactly the same operation is possible with an indexed file.

Figure 18-10

Performing Both Sequential and Random Access of a File

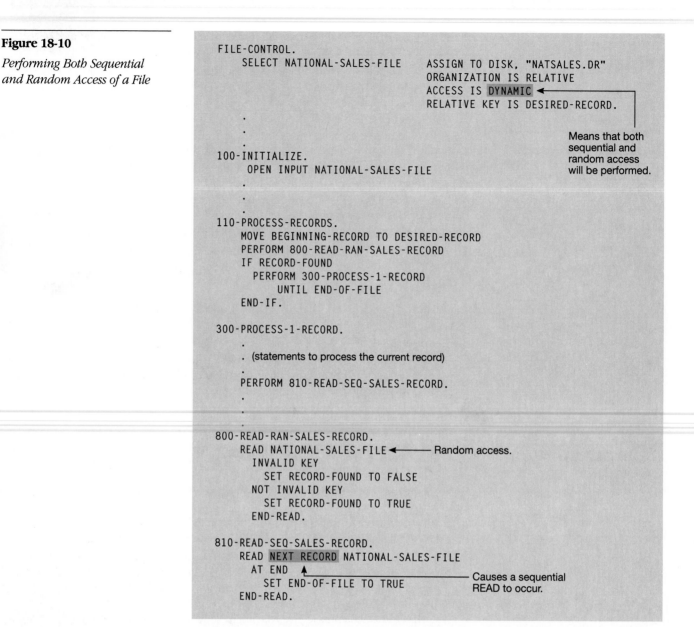

```
FILE-CONTROL.
    SELECT NATIONAL-SALES-FILE    ASSIGN TO DISK, "NATSALES.DR"
                                  ORGANIZATION IS RELATIVE
                                  ACCESS IS DYNAMIC  ◄─────
                                  RELATIVE KEY IS DESIRED-RECORD.
    .
    .                                          Means that both
    .                                          sequential and
100-INITIALIZE.                                random access
    OPEN INPUT NATIONAL-SALES-FILE             will be performed.
    .
    .
    .
110-PROCESS-RECORDS.
    MOVE BEGINNING-RECORD TO DESIRED-RECORD
    PERFORM 800-READ-RAN-SALES-RECORD
    IF RECORD-FOUND
       PERFORM 300-PROCESS-1-RECORD
          UNTIL END-OF-FILE
    END-IF.

300-PROCESS-1-RECORD.
    .
    . (statements to process the current record)
    .
    PERFORM 810-READ-SEQ-SALES-RECORD.
    .
    .
    .
800-READ-RAN-SALES-RECORD.
    READ NATIONAL-SALES-FILE ◄──── Random access.
       INVALID KEY
          SET RECORD-FOUND TO FALSE
       NOT INVALID KEY
          SET RECORD-FOUND TO TRUE
    END-READ.

810-READ-SEQ-SALES-RECORD.
    READ NEXT RECORD NATIONAL-SALES-FILE
       AT END  ▲
          SET END-OF-FILE TO TRUE          Causes a sequential
    END-READ.                              READ to occur.
```

Alternate Keys for Indexed Files

The Need for More Than One Key

Indexing a file provides direct access to the file for random processing and an ordering of the records in the file for sequential accessing based on the key field. For instance, the product number key of the inventory file allows you to access any desired record by its product number and to print a summary report of records in the file in product number sequence. However, what if you need access to the file via another field; for instance, the product name? That is, for a particular application, you must access records by entering the product name; for another, you require a report printed in sequence by product name. For this, another key is needed: one on the product name field.

The preceding is typical of processing needs; many indexed file applications require two or more key fields. For instance, a payroll application might require that records from the employee file be accessible by the employee number and employee name. A sales application to process invoices (sales to customers) might require primary access to invoice file records by the invoice number. However, it might also be necessary to have access to records by the number of the salesperson making the sale.

Each of these three applications requires an indexed file with two key fields. COBOL provides for this by allowing you to define a prime key and one or more alternate keys.

The *prime key* is the key whose contents uniquely identify the record. An *alternate key* is a key, other than the prime key, whose contents identify a record *but not necessarily uniquely.* For instance, the invoice file will contain one invoice record for each sale. Each invoice will have its own invoice number; no two invoice numbers will be the same. Thus, the invoice number uniquely identifies a particular invoice record. Every invoice will also contain a salesperson number. However, many records in the file can contain the same salesperson number since each salesperson will make one or more sales. Thus, you cannot identify a particular record by referring to the salesperson number key of that record because its value is not unique (other records contain the same value).

The next example combines using an alternate key with dynamic processing of a file.

Example 18-4

An invoice file has been created with two keys: the prime key is the invoice number and the alternate key is the salesperson number. Records are to be processed in salesperson groups for selected salespeople. The number of the salesperson will be available in the data item DESIRED-SALESPERSON.

Processing Using an Alternate Index— Example 18-4

Appropriate program segments to illustrate using an alternate key are shown in Figure 18-11. Its execution sequence is

1. The starting salesperson number is moved to the key field IR-SALESPERSON.

2. The 800 module is executed, which reads the designated record. If it does not exist, the switch ANOTHER-RECORD-TO-PROCESS is set to false; otherwise, it is set to true.

3. If the desired record was found, the 300 module to process the record is performed.

4. The last statement of the 300 module performs the 810 module, which reads the next sequential record. The switch ANOTHER-RECORD-TO-PROCESS is set to false if either the end of file is encountered or the newly read record is for a different salesperson.

The three highlighted items in Figure 18-11 are new syntax elements introduced by this example. In the SELECT, you see the clause:

```
ALTERNATE RECORD KEY IS IR-SALESPERSON
                  WITH DUPLICATES.
```

As its English suggests, this clause defines the field of the record that is the alternate key. The phrase WITH DUPLICATES is optional and is required only if a file is to contain multiple records with the same key value. Be aware that you cannot arbitrarily designate any field of an existing file as an alternate key. All alternate keys to be used for processing must have been defined as such when the file was originally created.

If a random access is to be performed with a file in which multiple keys are defined, then the key to be used for the access must be designated. You see this in the following portion of the READ from the 800 module:

```
READ NATIONAL-SALES-FILE
    KEY IS IR-SALESPERSON
```

The KEY IS clause is followed by the name of the alternate key field by which data is to be accessed. If it is omitted, COBOL defaults to the prime key.

In the 810 module, access is sequential because of the NEXT RECORD phrase. However, the key field to be used for record sequencing is not specified. Whenever a sequential access follows a dynamic access, sequential accessing is automatically based on the same key field used for the random access. Thus, the 810 module will access records in the salesperson sequence and not the invoice-number sequence (which is based on the prime key).

The general formats for the READ are included in the summary at the end of this chapter.

Figure 18-11

Using an Alternate Key—
Example 18-4

```
FILE-CONTROL.
    SELECT INVOICE-FILE  ASSIGN TO DISK, "INVOICE.DI"
                         ORGANIZATION IS INDEXED
                         ACCESS IS DYNAMIC
                         RECORD KEY IS IR-INVOICE-NUMBER
                         ALTERNATE RECORD KEY IS IR-SALESPERSON
                                             WITH DUPLICATES.
    .
    .
    .
FD  INVOICE-FILE.
01  INVOICE-RECORD.
    10  IR-INVOICE-NUMBER    PIC 9(6).
    10  IR-INVOICE-DATE      PIC 9(6).
    10  IR-SALESPERSON       PIC X(4).
    .
    .
    .
100-INITIALIZE.
    OPEN INPUT INVOICE-FILE
    .
    .
    .
110-PROCESS-RECORDS.
    .
    . (statements to get next random access salesperson number)
    .
    MOVE DESIRED-SALESPERSON TO IR-SALESPERSON
    PERFORM 800-READ-RAN-INVOICE-RECORD
    PERFORM 300-PROCESS-1-RECORD
        UNTIL NOT ANOTHER-RECORD-TO-PROCESS.

300-PROCESS-1-RECORD.
    .
    . (statements to process the current record)
    .
    PERFORM 810-READ-SEQ-INVOICE-RECORD.
    .
    .
    .
800-READ-RAN-INVOICE-RECORD.
    READ NATIONAL-SALES-FILE
        KEY IS IR-SALESPERSON  ◄──────────────── Designates which key
        INVALID KEY                               is to be used for
            SET ANOTHER-RECORD-TO-PROCESS TO FALSE   the random access.
        NOT INVALID KEY
            SET ANOTHER-RECORD-TO-PROCESS TO TRUE
    END-READ.

810-READ-SEQ-INVOICE-RECORD.
    READ NEXT RECORD NATIONAL-SALES-FILE
      AT END
          SET ANOTHER-RECORD-TO-PROCESS TO FALSE
      NOT AT END
          IF DESIRED-SALESPERSON NOT = IR-SALESPERSON
              SET ANOTHER-RECORD-TO-PROCESS TO FALSE
          END-IF
    END-READ.
```

Designating a Starting Position Within a File

The START Statement

In two of the preceding examples, you learned how you can randomly access a record and then sequentially process preceding or following records (using dynamic access). Another statement (which is more versatile) allows you to position within a relative or indexed file for subsequent sequential retrieval of records. Before looking at the general form, consider the examples shown in Figure 18-12 using the inventory file. Notice that the access is designated as sequential (it could be dynamic, but not random). Also, prior to each START statement, assume that the MOVE statement has been executed, moving the stock-number value 32506 to the record key field IR-STOCK-NUMBER. Execution of these statements causes the following to happen:

1. The first statement positions within the file to the record with a key field value that is equal to 32506. Thus, the next execution of a READ statement will read that record. If the designated record does not exist, an invalid key condition occurs. As you will see in the general format, the INVALID KEY clause is used with the START statement.

2. The second statement does exactly the same thing as the first one. If the KEY phrase is omitted, then the "equal to" condition is assumed.

3. The third statement positions at the first record with a key field value greater than 32506.

4. If a record with the key field value 32506 exists, the fourth statement positions at that record, the same as in the first example. However, if there is no record in the file with that key field value, it positions at the first record with a key field value greater than 32506.

5. The fifth statement positions at the record with the largest key field value that is less than 32506.

Although these examples are based on an indexed file with sequential access, the principles illustrated by these examples are equally applicable to both indexed and relative files in sequential or dynamic access. (As you will see, there is more versatility for indexed files.) The general format of the START statement is shown on the following page.

Figure 18-12

Example START Statements

```
SELECT INVENTORY-FILE    ASSIGN TO DISK, "SOFTWAR2.DI"
                         ORGANIZATION IS INDEXED
                         ACCESS IS SEQUENTIAL
                         RECORD KEY IS IR-STOCK-NUMBER.

(a)


         MOVE "32506" TO IR-STOCK-NUMBER
   1.    START INVENTORY-FILE KEY IS EQUAL TO IR-STOCK-NUMBER
   2.    START INVENTORY-FILE
   3.    START INVENTORY-FILE KEY IS GREATER THAN IR-STOCK-NUMBER
   4.    START INVENTORY-FILE
               KEY IS GREATER THAN OR EQUAL TO IR-STOCK-NUMBER
   5.    START INVENTORY-FILE KEY IS LESS THAN IR-STOCK-NUMBER

(b)
```

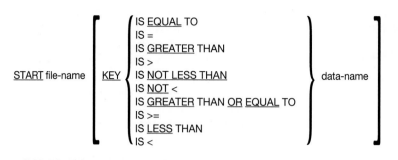

[INVALID KEY imperative-statement-1

[NOT INVALID KEY imperative-statement-2

[END-START]

Execution of the START statement causes positioning within the file according to the contents of the designated key, thus affecting the READ statement that follows. For relative files, the *data-name* entry must be the relative key, as declared in the SELECT clause. For indexed files, it can be the prime key or any alternate key. It can also be any part of a key field that begins with the first character of that field. For instance, in the group total program of Figure 13-23, you saw that the stock-number field was broken down into its components as follows. (Note that the group total programs processed a sequential file, but the field breakdown is equally applicable to the indexed version.)

```
01  INVENTORY-RECORD.
    10  IR-STOCK-NUMBER.
        20  IR-VENDOR-NUMBER PIC X(2).
        20  IR-SOFTWARE-TYPE PIC X(1).
        20                   PIC X(2).
```

.If you had an application in which processing was to begin with vendor number 20 (or the first number following 20), you could use the following START statement:

```
MOVE "20" TO IR-VENDOR-NUMBER
START INVENTORY-FILE KEY IS >= IR-VENDOR-NUMBER
```

Notice that the vendor-number subfield of the stock-number field—the key field—begins in the leftmost position of the key field, a requirement for using a subfield of a key. You could not use, for instance, IR-SOFTWARE-TYPE in the START statement.

File Sharing and Record Locking

All of this book's example programs and programming assignments are based on the assumption that you are operating in an environment in which your program is the only action at a given time. That is, when you run a program to process a data file, your program is the only program processing the file at that time. This is called a *single-user environment*. This is indeed the case with a stand-alone personal computer. However, it is not necessarily the case where computers are connected together in a network and all have the same access to data files stored on a central disk, as illustrated in Figure 18-13. This is called a *multi-user environment* and is commonly encountered in business applications in which wide access is needed to data stored in the organization's files.

For instance, consider the order processing system of the UNISOFT company, in which orders are continually being entered through many computers using the same set of files. In particular, as each order is entered, the inventory file must be updated to reflect the quantity sold of each software item. (Note that the next three chapters focus on file processing, including updating as described here.)

Figure 18-13

Sharing a File

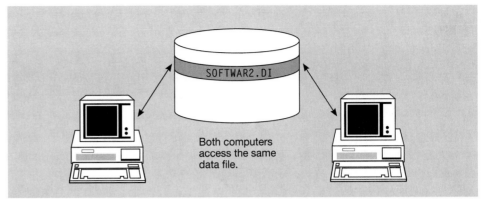

No problem exists if two or more users concurrently read data from a file; the system simply locates the desired record and transmits a copy to the requesting computer. However, if two or more users intend to update the same record of a file at the same time, a conflict can occur. To illustrate, consider the UNISOFT order processing system in which as each order is entered, the inventory file is updated by subtracting the quantity sold from the record's quantity-on-hand field and then rewriting the record. Assume that two orders are being entered (from two computers) and that both orders include software item 07427 (one for 4 copies and the other for 1). A typical sequence of events is shown in Figure 18-14. Here you see that a copy of the record is read from disk into both computers. In computer 1, the quantity 4 is subtracted from the quantity on hand, giving an updated value of 79 (time frame 3). This record is rewritten to the file (time frame 4). Concurrently, in computer 2, the quantity 1 is being subtracted from the original quantity on hand (83, which is now obsolete). In the last time frame, computer 2 rewrites its copy of the record, thus destroying the update from computer 1.

Obviously, the prevention of such interference between concurrent users is critical to a multi-user environment. The Ryan-McFarland multi-user runtime support system includes a feature called *record locking*, which prevents occurrences such as that illustrated in Figure 18-14. In the Ryan-McFarland multi-user environment, a READ statement that references a file that is open in the I-O mode causes the record read to be locked on behalf of the user that executed the READ. This action is automatic. Any record that is *locked* cannot be modified or locked by another user.

Consider this in the context of Figure 18-14, where both users have opened the inventory file in I-O mode (because updating is required). Reading record 07427 by user 1 in time frame 1 causes the runtime system to place a lock on that record. From time frame

Figure 18-14

Concurrent Processing of a Record by Two Users

Time Frame	Record Copy, User (Computer) 1		Data File Record		Record Copy, User (Computer) 2	
			Stock Number	Quantity on Hand		
0			07427 . . . 83			
1	Read record	07427 . . . 83				
2					07427 . . . 83	Read record
3	Change on-hand amount	07427 . . . 79				
4	Write record back to disk	07427 . . . 79	→	07427 . . . 79	07427 . . . 82	Change on-hand amount
5			07427 . . . 82	←	07427 . . . 82	Write record back to disk

1 through time frame 4, user 2 cannot read that same record because reading it would also cause a lock to be placed on the record. When user 1 rewrites the record, its lock is released and the record becomes available to user 2. Actually, the lock is released when any other input-output statement is executed for that file by user 1.

Unless special provisions are made (the topic of the next section), whenever a program attempts to access a locked record for an I-O operation, the runtime system automatically waits until the lock is deleted before allowing the program to proceed.

Exception Handling During Input and Output Operations

Handling Common Exception Conditions

During the execution of any input or output operation, unusual conditions may occur that prevent normal completion of the operation. For instance, in reading a sequential file, the read might encounter the end of file, thereby not allowing the normal read operation to occur. In writing to an indexed file, the record to be written might contain a key field value that is identical to that of a record already in the file, thereby preventing the record from being written. In a multi-user environment, access to a record by one user might require record locking of a record already locked by another user. Any such condition that prevents normal operation is called an *exception condition*.

In your programs, you have provided for two types of exception conditions with the optional phrases AT END and INVALID KEY. For instance, in reading a sequential file, you use

```
READ INVENTORY-FILE
    AT END
        ...
```

If the exception condition exists in which execution has progressed to the end of the file, the statements following AT END are executed. Similarly, to write a record to an indexed file, you use

```
WRITE INVENTORY-RECORD
    INVALID KEY
        ...
```

I-O Status

If there is already a record with the key field value of the record being written, an exception condition exists, which is handled by executing the statements following the INVALID KEY.

The use of an optional phrase in the input or output statement is one of three methods by which exception conditions are communicated to your program. The other two are the I-O status and exception declaratives.

If by this time you have not had a program terminate with an error message, you are an exceptional programmer. For instance, it is easy to forget to make available to a program a data file required by the program. If you tried to run the group total program GRP-TOT1 without the needed data file SOFTWAR3.DL, you would get a message such as:

```
COBOL I/O error 35 on INVENTORY-FILE file   C:\PROGS\SOFTWAR3.DL
```

This message tells you the name assigned to the file within the program (INVENTORY-FILE) and the DOS name and location of the file. It also displays the error number 35. This two-digit number is called the *I-O status* and is one of many such numbers defined by the COBOL-85 Standard to indicate the condition resulting from an input or output operation. You will find a list of these status codes with appropriate descriptions in Appendix H under Input-Output Errors. However, when the I-O status is only two digits, RM/COBOL-85 provides an additional two digits; for instance, *04,06*. Here the *04* is the COBOL standard code and the *06* is a further breakdown implemented in RM/COBOL-85.

The COBOL-85 Standard defines the following six categories of the I-O status as characterized by the first digit of the code.

First Digit (Class)	Condition
0	*Successful completion.* The input-output statement was executed successfully and no exception conditions occurred.
1	*At end condition.* A sequential READ was not executed successfully because of an at end condition. These exceptions are detected by the AT END phrase in the READ statement.
2	*Invalid key* (not meaningful for sequential files). The input-output statement was not executed successfully because of an invalid key condition. These exceptions are detected by the INVALID KEY phrase in the READ or WRITE statement.
3	*Permanent error.* The input-output statement was not executed successfully because of an error that precludes further processing of the file. The problem could be a disk full or a hardware error condition.
4	*Logic error.* The input-output statement was not executed successfully because an improper sequence of input-output statements was performed on the file (for instance, attempting to close a file that has not been open) or because of a violation of a user-defined limit.
9	*Implementor-defined.* The input-output statement was not executed successfully because of some other type of error. These are conditions defined by the supplier of the COBOL compiler (Ryan-McFarland in this case). Appendix H includes an extensive list of them.

All of the I-O status exception conditions (1, 2, 3, 4, and 9) will cause immediate termination of the program if provisions are not included in the program for their handling. For instance, if you omit the AT END from a READ statement and the end of file is read (a class 1 exception), the program will be terminated. The same is true for omitting the INVALID KEY from a random input-output operation and encountering a class 2 exception.

The last three categories—status values 3, 4, and 9—are termed *critical error conditions* and require special provisions to avoid immediate termination of a program. In many instances, you do not want the program to terminate immediately. To illustrate, consider a program that functions as follows:

1. A series of changes is to be made to the inventory file from data in another file. (You will see two examples of this in the next chapter.)

2. A table file is opened early in the program to obtain some data and then closed before proceeding to make the changes.

3. After processing part of the inventory file, an unusual combination of conditions occurs, causing a sequence of steps that was not recognized during program testing.

4. The resulting sequence of operations causes the module that closed the table file to be executed again (erroneously).

If special provisions were not made, the program would be terminated by the system because attempting to close a file that is not open is a class 4 (logic error) condition. As a result, you could find yourself with no idea of how far the program had progressed in making changes within the file. The solution is for the system to pass control to a programmer-written error procedure that evaluates the error and take actions to "clean up" before terminating, or to continue processing if the error can be identified as not critical to continued processing. This capability is available through declarative procedures in the PROCEDURE DIVISION and the USE statement.

Declarative Procedures and the USE Statement

For exception/error recovery, COBOL includes *declaratives*, a set of one or more special purpose sections inserted at the beginning of the PROCEDURE DIVISION. These sections contain statements defining the actions to take when exceptions occur. Recall from Chapter 15 (Figure 15-12) that a section in the PROCEDURE DIVISION is a level above a paragraph in that it allows two or more paragraphs to be treated as a unit. A section is identified by the section name, followed by the word SECTION.

To illustrate using declaratives for exception/error recovery, consider the segment of code shown in Figure 18-15. In this program, two files are to be processed: SOFTWAR2.DI and SOFT-LOG.DI. Three basic elements are illustrated by this example:

■ The FILE STATUS data item

■ The USE statement

■ The structure of the DECLARATIVES

Figure 18-15

Declaratives and the USE Statement

```
    SELECT INVENTORY-FILE    ASSIGN TO DISK "SOFTWAR2.DI"
                             ORGANIZATION IS INDEXED
                             ACCESS IS RANDOM
                             RECORD KEY IS IR-STOCK-NUMBER
                             FILE STATUS IS INVENTORY-FILE-STATUS.

        SELECT LOG-FILE      ASSIGN TO DISK "SOFT-LOG.DI"
                             ORGANIZATION IS INDEXED
                             ACCESS IS RANDOM
                             RECORD KEY IS LR-SEQUENCE-NUMBER
                             FILE STATUS IS LOG-FILE-STATUS.
            .
            .
            .
    01  OTHER-VARIABLES.
        10  INVENTORY-FILE-STATUS    PIC XX.
        10  LOG-FILE-STATUS          PIC XX.
            .
            .
            .
    PROCEDURE DIVISION.

    DECLARATIVES.

    INVENTORY-ERROR SECTION.    ◀──────────────── Section header (required).

        USE AFTER ERROR PROCEDURE ON INVENTORY-FILE.

    990-INVENTORY-FILE-ERROR.   ◀──────────────── Paragraph header
        .                                          (not required).
        . (statements to process this exception)
        .
    LOG-ERROR SECTION.

        USE AFTER ERROR PROCEDURE ON LOG-FILE.

    995-LOG-FILE-ERROR.

        . (statements to process this exception)
        .
    END DECLARATIVES.

    MAIN-PROGRAM SECTION.

    000-UPDATE-INVENTORY-FILE.
        .
        .
        .
```

The FILE STATUS clause in the SELECT designates a data item to which the I-O status will be stored following an input or output operation. This data item must be two characters in size and must be defined in the WORKING-STORAGE SECTION.

In this example, possible errors that may occur are distinguished by the file for which they occur. Consider the statement:

```
USE AFTER ERROR PROCEDURE ON INVENTORY-FILE.
```

This identifies the sequence of code that follows it as that code to be executed if any error condition occurs during an input-output operation with INVENTORY-FILE. For instance, consider a logic error (class 4) in which an OPEN is executed and the file SOFTWAR2.DI is already open. The following takes place:

1. The I-O status code is stored in the file status data item INVENTORY-FILE-STATUS.

2. Control is transferred to the statement following the USE for this file as if accomplished with a PERFORM.

3. The statements in this declarative section are executed. These statements could either terminate execution of the program or allow for continuing processing.

Assume that the following sequence of statements are the last statements of the error sequence:

```
DISPLAY "*** Attempt to close SOFTWAR2.DI when already closed."
DISPLAY "Do you wish to continue <Y/N>? "
ACCEPT USER-RESPONSE
IF USER-RESPONSE NOT = "Y"
   STOP RUN
END-IF.
```

Here the user is queried (presumably after appropriate tests have been made of the I-O status) and is given the option to terminate execution of the program or to continue. Obviously, a response other than Y to the query causes the STOP RUN to be executed and the program terminated. If the program is not terminated, control is automatically returned (after execution of the last statement in the error procedure) to the statement following the OPEN that caused the error. That is, control is returned as if the error procedure were executed by a PERFORM statement.

It is the function of DECLARATIVES and END DECLARATIVES entries to set these error procedures apart from the main program. This portion of the program must immediately follow the PROCEDURE DIVISION header and thus precede the code of the main program. Within the declaratives, each declarative procedure must be preceded by a section header which is, in turn, followed by a USE statement identifying the condition under which the procedure is to be executed. (As you will see, an error procedure need not be restricted to a single file.) Error recovery statements follow the USE. Notice in Figure 18-15 that the recovery procedure can consist of paragraphs of statements if the recovery action is complex. However, the syntax does not *require* use of paragraphs. Use of section headers in the declarative forces the need for sections throughout the program. Thus, the first paragraph of the program (000) is preceded by a section header; the entire program can be this single section.

In the example of Figure 18-15, the USE statements define declarative procedures on the basis of files. That is, there is one procedure for any error occurring with INVENTORY-FILE and another for LOG-FILE. This is one possibility; the other is on the basis of the open mode. For instance, a procedure can be defined for any file open in an INPUT mode. This is illustrated by the following partial general format of the USE statement:

$$
\underline{\text{USE AFTER}} \text{ STANDARD } \underline{\text{ERROR PROCEDURE}} \text{ ON }
\left\{
\begin{array}{l}
\{\text{file-name-1}\}... \\
\underline{\text{INPUT}} \\
\underline{\text{OUTPUT}} \\
\underline{\text{I-O}} \\
\underline{\text{EXTEND}}
\end{array}
\right\}
$$

Assume that the program from which the Figure 18-15 statements are taken contains the statement

```
READ INVENTORY-FILE
```

without an INVALID KEY phrase. What do you think will happen if the product number of the record to be read (the record key) does not exist in the file? (This is an invalid key error.) The answer is that control will be transferred to the declarative error procedure for this file. On the other hand, assume that the READ statement is written as

```
READ INVENTORY-FILE
   INVALID KEY
      ...
```

In this case, the INVALID KEY phrase takes precedence and execution is as if the USE did not exist. This applies to the AT END phrase as well.

In some programs, error recovery is a major factor and requires extensive code. The exact way in which each type of error (as determined by examining the I-O status) is handled depends upon the nature of the application and the standards of the installation using the program. This description of declarative procedures is presented solely as a brief introduction and merely introduces you to tools available for error handling.

Chapter Summary

General

Relative file structure is the third of the three file structures available to the COBOL programmer. This structure is similar to that of a table in which the table subscript corresponds to the relative record number. Relative files are practical when the logical key reference consists of consecutive (or near consecutive) numbers.

A file can be opened in any of four modes: input, output, I-O, and extend.

Three input-output statements can be used with sequential files: READ, WRITE, and REWRITE. The permissible uses of each are summarized in the table of Figure 18-16.

The file access mode is defined in the SELECT. For relative and indexed files, it can be sequential, random, or dynamic. Five input-output statements can be used with relative and indexed files: READ, WRITE, REWRITE, START, and DELETE. The permissible uses of each are summarized in the table of Figure 18-17.

COBOL Language Elements

The COBOL statements that you have studied in this chapter are

DELETE file-name RECORD

    [INVALID KEY imperative-statement-1]

    [NOT INVALID KEY imperative-statement-2]

[END-DELETE]

OPEN
$\left\{\begin{array}{l} \text{INPUT \{file-name-1\}...} \\ \text{OUTPUT \{file-name-2\}...} \\ \text{I-O \{file-name-3\}...} \\ \text{EXTEND \{file-name-4\}...} \end{array}\right\}$ ...

Figure 18-16

Permissible Input-Output Actions— Sequential Files

Statement	Open Mode			
	Input	Output	I-O	Extend
READ	X		X	
WRITE		X		X
REWRITE			X	

Figure 18-17

Permissible Input-Output Actions—Indexed and Relative Files

File Access Mode	Statement	Open Mode			
		Input	Output	I-O	Extend
Sequential	READ	X		X	
	WRITE		X		X
	REWRITE			X	
	START	X		X	
	DELETE			X	
Random	READ	X		X	
	WRITE		X	X	
	REWRITE			X	
	START				
	DELETE			X	
Dynamic	READ	X		X	
	WRTE		X	X	
	REWRITE			X	
	START	X		X	
	DELETE			X	

Sequential read—Relative I-O

READ file-name $\begin{bmatrix} \underline{NEXT} \\ \underline{PREVIOUS} \end{bmatrix}$ RECORD

[AT <u>END</u> imperative-statement-1]

[<u>NOT</u> AT <u>END</u> imperative-statement-2]

[<u>END-READ</u>]

Random read—Relative I-O

<u>READ</u> file-name RECORD

    [<u>INVALID</u> KEY imperative-statement-1]

    [<u>NOT</u> <u>INVALID</u> KEY imperative-statement-2]

[<u>END-READ</u>]

Sequential read—Indexed I-O

<u>READ</u> file-name $\begin{bmatrix} \underline{NEXT} \\ \underline{PREVIOUS} \end{bmatrix}$ RECORD

    [AT <u>END</u> imperative-statement-1]

    [<u>NOT</u> AT <u>END</u> imperative-statement-2]

[<u>END-READ</u>]

Random read—Indexed I-O

READ file-name RECORD
  [KEY IS data-name]
  [INVALID KEY imperative-statement-1]
  [NOT INVALID KEY imperative-statement-2]
[END-READ]

REWRITE record-name
  [INVALID KEY imperative-statement-1]
  [NOT INVALID KEY imperative-statement-2]
[END-REWRITE]

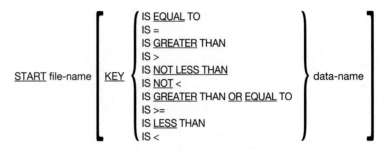

[INVALID KEY imperative-statement-1

[NOT INVALID KEY imperative-statement-2

[END-START]

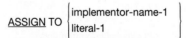

Other language elements that you have studied in this chapter are

Indexed I-O

SELECT file-name

[ORGANIZATION IS] INDEXED

ACCESS MODE IS { SEQUENTIAL / RANDOM / DYNAMIC }

RECORD KEY IS data-name-1

[ALTERNATE RECORD KEY IS data-name-2 [WITH DUPLICATES]] ...

[FILE STATUS IS data-name-3] .

Relative I-O

SELECT file-name

ASSIGN TO $\begin{Bmatrix} \text{implementor-name-1} \\ \text{literal-1} \end{Bmatrix}$

[ORGANIZATION IS] RELATIVE

$\left[\text{ACCESS MODE IS} \begin{Bmatrix} \text{SEQUENTIAL } [\underline{\text{RELATIVE}} \text{ KEY IS data-name-1}] \\ \underline{\text{RANDOM}} \\ \underline{\text{DYNAMIC}} \quad \underline{\text{RELATIVE}} \text{ KEY IS data-name-1} \end{Bmatrix} \right]$

[FILE STATUS IS data-name-2] .

Questions and Exercises

Key Terminology

Give a brief description of each of the following terms that were introduced in this chapter.

alternate key	multi-user environment	relative record number
declaratives	prime key	single-user environment
dynamic access	record locking	update in place
exception condition	relative file organization	
I-O status	relative key	

General Questions

1. Which statement in COBOL gives a programmer the ability to define the file organization and file access?

2. How does a file with relative organization identify each record and how are the records assembled within it?

3. In order to change records on either an indexed or relative file, two COBOL capabilities are required. What are they?

4. When eliminating records from either an indexed or relative file, the_____statement must be used.

5. It is possible to use both sequential and random access at the same time. In order to do this with an indexed or relative file, what type of access must be specified and how does the READ statement change?

6. What is the difference between a "prime" key and an "alternate" key? Give an example.

7. The START statement in COBOL offers a great deal of versatility in processing relative or indexed files. How does it do this?

8. Exception conditions that occur during indexed or relative file processing are designated by_____codes. The programmer can use_____at the beginning of the PROCEDURE DIVISION to define actions to take when exceptions occur.

Questions Relating to the Example Programs

1. When the NATSALES.DR file (Figure 18-8) was created, the relative key was defined as two characters in length. In the program, the two-position data item DESIRED-RECORD is defined as the relative key. Assume that this data item (and the corresponding entries in the SCREEN SECTION) had been defined as four positions instead of two. What do you think would happen if a request were made for record 0003? For record 0156? Do not scour the chapter for the answer because it is not explicitly there; you should be able to reason it out.

2. The NATSALES.DR file (Figure 18-8) has the fields NS-STATE-NUMBER and DESIRED-RECORD both defined as PIC 9(2). What would happen if both were changed to PIC X(2)? What would happen if one (but not the other) was changed to PIC X(2)?

3. Assuming that the REL-DIS program is as described in Figure 18-8, what would happen if the user entered 00 as the first DESIRED-RECORD?

4. In Figure 18-11, what would happen if the line that reads "IF DESIRED-SALESPERSON NOT = IR-SALESPERSON" is inadvertently left out by the programmer?

Writing Program Statements

1. In the REL-DIS program (Figure 18-8), there is no provision for telling the user when the program has ended. Create a new screen to do this that will be displayed anytime zero is entered as the DESIRED-RECORD. Where should the DISPLAY statement for the screen be inserted into the program?

2. Write SELECT and OPEN statements for each of the following. The file is STUDENTS.DR and is relative organization.
   a. The file needs to be updated on-line by a user at a terminal for adds, changes, and deletes. The relative key is STUDENT-ID, PIC 9(5).
   b. The file is to be used to obtain individual student information in the registrar's office. The registrar wants to look up students by STUDENT-ID. Since students come and go all the time, the registrar would like the ability to start at a certain place and process sequentially afterwards. The concept of moving forward or backward in the file is particularly appealing.

3. An indexed file has been set up to handle sales for retail stores within various cities of each state. The prime key consists of a 2-position state code (numeric), the city name (15 positions), and a 3-position store code (numeric). The file is STORESLS.DI. The marketing department wants to create selective reports using all or portions of the prime key. In addition, they want to randomly pick a starting point for processing and sequentially process for groups of like records.
   a. Write a SELECT statement.
   b. Write the FD with the record key description.
   c. Write an OPEN statement for the file.
   d. Write a START statement. Describe how this could be done to handle all combinations requested.

Programming Assignments

Note: This chapter includes only one programming assignment. The principal programming assignment focus of concepts covered here is in the three file processing chapters that follow.

18-1 Dual Direct Access to the Student File

Direct access to the student file is the student number (Social Security number). However, consider the clerk who needs information from the file regarding student Alice Kirkham—the clerk has only the student name, not the number. With an indexed file that includes multiple keys, file access is much more versatile. That is, if the name is an alternate key, then records can be accessed either by the student number or name.

> *Output Requirements:*
> A display of the following data for the selected student.
> Student number
> Student name
> Major
> Cumulative units
> Cumulative GPA

Input Description:

    Keyboard entry: Student number or student name

    File name: STUDENTS.DL

    Record description: See Appendix A

    See the processing requirements.

Processing Requirements:

    Access to the file is required by student name or student number. Thus, the indexed student file must include the student number as the primary key and the student last name as an alternate key.

    File creation program:

1. Read each record from the sequential file STUDENTS.DL.
2. Write the record to the indexed file STUDENTS.DIA defined with index fields as required by this application.

    Inquiry program:

1. Give the user the option of querying by student number or student last name.
2. Accept the appropriate key field value.
3. Access the requested record.
4. If the record is found, display it on the screen.
5. If the request was via the student name, ask the user if this is the correct record.
6. If not, access the next sequential record. If the last name is the same as the request, display it and ask the user if this is the correct record.
7. Repeat this process of accessing and displaying the next record until the user finds the desired record or the record read has a different name.
8. If the desired record is not found, display a message.
9. Allow the user to repeat the process.

FILE PROCESSING AND MAINTENANCE—BATCH

Chapter Objectives

Chapter 18 introduced you to a wide variety of file operations. The purpose of this chapter and the next two is to apply these principal file processing and maintenance applications. In this chapter, you will study the following three example programs involving batch operations with the software inventory file.

■ Batch master-transaction processing with sequential files. Each record of a transaction file contains information regarding additions to or deletions from the sequential software inventory file. The two files (both are sorted on the stock-number field) are processed sequentially and an updated software inventory file is created.

■ Batch master-transaction processing with an indexed master file. The indexed software inventory file is updated from transaction records. Records of the indexed inventory file are accessed and updated (in place) randomly as transaction records are read.

■ Batch maintenance operations with indexed software inventory file.

Principles of Master-Transaction Processing

What Is Master-Transaction Processing?

One of the "bread-and-butter" operations of business data processing applications oriented around magnetic tape processing is bringing data stored in a master file up-to-date as a result of transactions. This is commonly called *master-transaction processing* because data in a master file is brought up-to-date from data stored in a transaction file. A *master file* is one containing data that is relatively permanent; for example, each record of the software inventory file includes the product number, product description, and so on for a given software item. However, it also includes data that changes: the current quantity on hand. By contrast, a *transaction file* is one containing data that is relatively transient; for example, each record of a software transaction file for a given processing period would contain the quantity sold or received for a single transaction during that period. Master-transaction processing then involves updating the data in each record of a master file from data in a transaction file and writing the updated record to a new version of the master. This concept is illustrated in Figure 19-1.

Master-transaction processing in this figure is sequential in nature and hence requires that both files be in sequence by a common key field (the product number in this example). It is also referred to as *batch updating* because transaction records are accumulated over a period of time (it may be as little as one day) and run in batches. With the wide use of magnetic disk and random access capabilities, this type of sequential master-transaction processing is much less common than it once was. However, the application illustrates programming techniques that are useful to the COBOL programmer. For an insight to some of the problems involved in matching records from two different files, let's consider a variety of record sequences.

Figure 19-1

Master-Transaction Processing

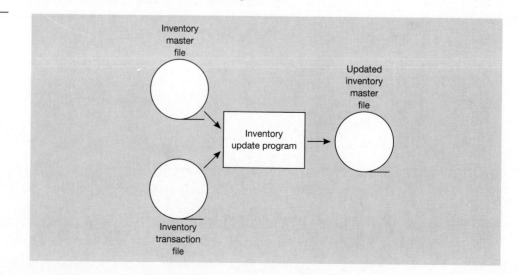

Figure 19-2

Matching Transaction Records with a Corresponding Master

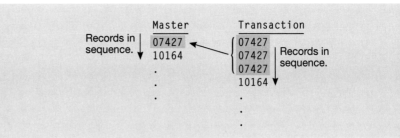

Matching Records From Two Files

In the first record sequence illustrated by Figure 19-2, the next master record to be read has a key field (product number) value of 07427. Three records in the transaction file correspond to it. Execution would proceed as follows:

1. Read the master record (key field 07427).

2. Read the first transaction record; since its key field is 07427 (equal to that of the master), accumulate the transaction amount for updating the master.

3. Read the next transaction record; since its key field is 07427, accumulate the transaction amount for updating the master.

4. Read the next transaction record; since its key field is 07427, accumulate the transaction amount for updating the master.

5. Read the next transaction record; since its key field is 10164, processing for master record 07427 is completed, so write the master record to the new master file.

6. Read the next master record. Since its key field (10164) matches that of the previously read transaction record, repeat the cycle for this master record.

In a nutshell, you can see that processing involves reading a master, then reading and processing the corresponding transactions, a relatively basic operation. However, two conditions make the programming a little tricky. First, there may be master records for which no transactions have occurred during the processing period; that is, unmatched masters. These masters must be written to the new master file with no change. This is a normal condition. Second, the transaction file might contain one or more transaction records with a key field that does not have a corresponding record in the master file. Such an unmatched transaction record represents an error condition.

Let's consider how execution would progress for the unmatched master record of Figure 19-3. Assume that the 15674 transaction record has been read and that the new master for 10164 has been written. Execution would proceed as follows:

1. Read the next master record (15589).

2. Compare the current master record key field value (15589) to the current transaction record key field value (15674). The transaction record value is higher, which indicates that there is no transaction record for this master record. Thus, the master record is written to the new master file without change.

3. Read the next master record. Since its key field (15674) matches that of the current transaction record, repeat the master-transaction cycle for this master record.

Figure 19-3

An Unmatched Master Record

	Master	Transaction	
	10164	10164	
Unmatched master record →	15589	10164	
(it has no corresponding	15674	10164	
transactions).	.	15674	← If there were a transaction
	.	.	record for master 15589,
	.	.	it would be here.
	.	.	

Figure 19-4

An Unmatched Transaction Record—Represents an Error Condition

```
                                        Master      Transaction
                                        10164       10164
            If there were a master ───► 15589       10164
            record for transaction                  10164
            13674, it would be here.    .            13674  ◄─── Unmatched transaction
                                        .            15589        record (it has no
                                        .            .            corresponding master).
                                                     .
                                                     .
```

For the second exception condition, an unmatched transaction, consider the record sequence of Figure 19-4. Assume that the 13674 transaction record has been read and that the new master for 10164 has been written. Execution would proceed as follows:

1. Read the next master record (15589).

2. Compare the current master record key field value (15589) to the current transaction record key field value (13674). The transaction record value is lower, which indicates that there is no master record for this transaction record. Print the unmatched transaction record with an appropriate error message.

3. Read the next transaction record. Since its key field (15589) matches that of the current master record, repeat the master-transaction cycle for this master record.

Notice that in each of the preceding scenarios, the assumption was made that the records were properly sorted and that none was out of sequence.

Since two files are being read, both must be checked for the EOF condition. Detection of the EOF for *either* file signals the end of the normal master-transaction processing activities. In all previous examples, detection of the EOF meant the end of the file processing. However, for master-transaction processing, more needs to be done. The specific actions depend upon whichever of the following data conditions exist:

■ The EOF has been detected for the transaction file and there are no more master records

■ The EOF has been detected for the transaction file and there are one or more master records remaining

■ The EOF has been detected for the master file and there are one or more transaction records remaining

First, consider how execution would terminate when the transaction file EOF is detected and no more master records remain, as illustrated in Figure 19-5. Assume that the third 91655 transaction record has been read and processed. Then reading the next transaction record—EOF in this case—would signal that processing for master record 91655 is completed and it must be written to the new master file. Since there are no more records to be processed, the master-transaction update is complete.

However, processing cannot simply end after the last record is updated—as suggested in the example of Figure 19-5—because the master file might contain additional unmatched records, as illustrated in Figure 19-6. Thus, the execution sequence should be as follows—assuming that the third 91655 transaction record has been read and processed:

1. Read the next transaction record—the EOF in this case.

Figure 19-5

Final Master-Transaction Set

```
                          Master      Transaction
                          91655       91655
                          EOF         91655
                                      91655
                                      EOF  ◄─── Reading this EOF record
                                                triggers the final
                                                processing actions.
```

Figure 19-6

An Unmatched Master at the End of the File

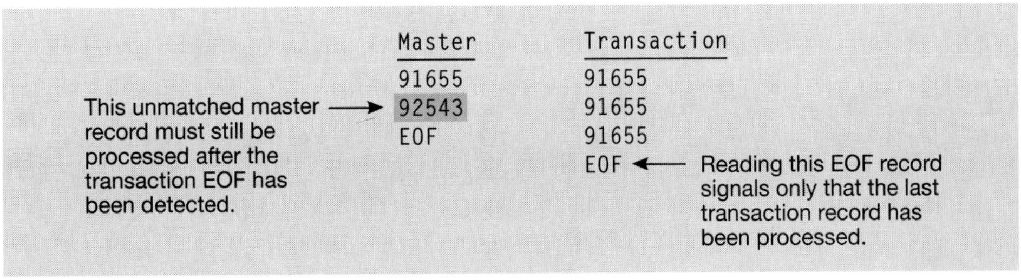

2. Processing for master record 91655 is completed, so write the master record to the new master file.

3. In a "finish-the-other-file" routine, complete processing of the master file by reading records and writing to the new master until the master file EOF is detected.

If there are no unmatched master records at the end of the master file, then the EOF record would be read immediately in the "finish-the-other-file" routine and processing would be terminated.

The other case to consider is one or more unmatched transaction records at the end of the file, as illustrated in Figure 19-7. In this case, assume that the third 91655 transaction record has just been read and processed. Execution would proceed as follows:

1. Read the next transaction record—the 92543 in this case.

2. Processing for master record 91655 is completed, so write the master record to the new master file.

3. Read the next master record. Since this is the EOF, master-transaction processing is completed. The current transaction record and all that follow it must be printed to an error log.

Figure 19-7

Unmatched Transactions at the End of the File—Represent an Error Condition

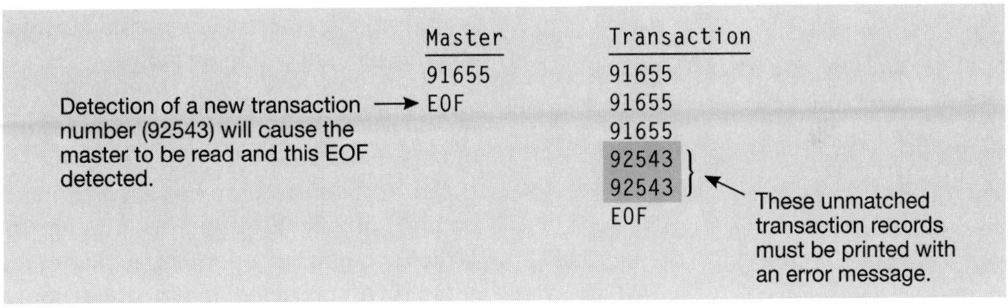

With the preceding background to batch updating a sequential file, let's consider how this would be done in the context of the UNISOFT company.

Batch Updating a Sequentially Organized File

Example Definition— Example 19-1

Example 19-1 Batch Updating a Sequential File

Problem Description

The UNISOFT inventory system includes batch updating of the sequentially organized inventory file. For each transaction during the day, a record is entered into a daily transaction file. There are four types of transactions: receipts from manufacturers, returns from customers, inventory adjustments, and sales to customers. At the end of each day, the master file is updated from the transaction file.

Output Requirements

Output file name: SOFTWAR2.DLU

Record format: Same as the input file SOFTWAR2.DL

Printed error report: This report must include one line for each of the following detected errors.

Unmatched detail record

Detail record with an invalid transaction type code

Updated master quantity-on-hand field that is negative

Input Description

Input master file name: SOFTWAR2.DL

Record format:

Field	Positions	Data Type	Format
Stock number	1–5	Alphanumeric	
Not used	6–55		
Quantity on hand	56–58	Numeric	S999
Not used	59–66		

Record sequence: Sorted by Stock number

Input transaction file name: SWTRANS.DL

Record format:

Field	Positions	Data Type	Format/Description
Document number	1–6	Alphanumeric	
Stock number	7–11	Alphanumeric	
Transaction type	12	Alphanumeric	1 - Receipt
			2 - Return
			3 - Adjustment
			4 - Sale
Quantity	13–16	Numeric	S999 with trailing separate sign

Record sequence: Sorted by Stock number

Processing Requirements

This program is to function as follows:

1. Read each master record and its corresponding transaction records.
2. As each transaction record is read for a given master record, accumulate the transaction quantity. For receipt, return, and adjustment record (types 1, 2, and 3), add the transaction quantity to an accumulator. For sale records (type 4), subtract the transaction quantity.
3. After the last transaction record for a given master is processed, add the accumulated transaction quantity to the master quantity-on-hand field and write the master record to the new master file.
4. If the updated master quantity-on-hand field is negative, write the stock number, quantity, and an error message to the error report.
5. Write each unmatched master record to the new master file without change.
6. Write each unmatched transaction record with an appropriate error message to the error report.
7. Write each transaction record with an invalid transaction-type value to the error report.
8. If the EOF is detected in the transaction file, complete processing of the current master record, then copy all remaining unmatched master records to the new master file.
9. If, during normal processing, the EOF is detected in the master file, there is at least one unmatched transaction record. It and any that follow must be written to the error report.
10. As each error line is written, count it. At the end of the report, print a summary line with this error count.

Notice that the quantity-on-hand field of the inventory record is a signed, three-digit field and that the sign is embedded. In all of the previous programs, this field was treated as unsigned because a negative quantity would be meaningless. However, such an assumption is dangerous because erroneous data in a transaction file could produce a negative quantity-on-hand value, an obvious error. If this field is unsigned, the minus sign will be discarded. By retaining the sign, an appropriate warning can be given.

Where the quantity-on-hand field of the inventory file uses an embedded sign, the quantity field of the transaction record uses a separate sign. That is, it is a signed, three-digit field with a separate sign following the number. As a result, this field—together with its sign—occupies four positions in the input record.

Normally, the quantity field of the transaction record will be positive. You can see in the processing requirements that, for instance, the receipts are added to the quantity accumulator and the sales are subtracted. However, adjustment transaction records (code 3) can represent additions to or deletions from the inventory quantity. Consequently, these will be coded as either positive or negative.

Program Structure and Logic—Example 19-1

In the structure chart of Figure 19-8, you can see the elements necessary for merging the data from two input files. The 100-Initialize module consists of the same components as many of the previous report generation examples. The significant difference is that the first record is read from each of the two input files. Notice that the 110-Process-current-record module includes components that you would expect from preceding descriptions of the master-transaction operations. As you might expect, both the master and transaction files are read from this module.

In contrast to other examples, this example includes an additional second-level module: 120-Finish-Other-File. It is necessary because unmatched masters or detail records may exist at the end of either file. As you can see, this module requires access to most of the same components required by the 110 module.

The logic of this solution is shown in the flowchart of Figure 19-9 and the pseudocode of Figure 19-10 (see page 534). Several points are worth noting:

- The first record from the master file (the inventory file) and the first record from the transaction file are read in the 100 module.

- From the 000 module, the 110 module is repeatedly performed until an EOF condition has occurred for either the inventory file or the transaction file.

- The 110 module to process the current record is much like that of other example programs you have studied: processing is carried out, then the next record is read. However, this module differs in that the processing depends upon the comparison between the key field values of the two records (master and transaction).

  - If they are equal, the transaction record "belongs to" the master record and is processed accordingly (module 300). Then the next transaction record is read (module 810).

  - If the transaction key field value is larger, this transaction record belongs to the next master. Processing for the current master is completed (310 module) and the next master is read (800 module). Then the next transaction record is read.

  - Otherwise (that is, if the transaction key field is smaller), an error condition is processed (320 module) and the next transaction record is read (810 module).

- In the 300 module, the transaction quantity is added to an accumulator for transaction types 1, 2, or 3, and subtracted for a value of 4.

- In the 310 module, the transaction sum is added to the master record quantity on hand, thus updating the inventory record. An error message is printed (720 module) if the resulting quantity on hand is negative.

- Repeated execution of the 110 module is terminated with detection of an EOF for either file. The 120 module then processes any remaining (unmatched) records in the "other" file.

  - If the EOF occurred for the inventory (master) file—No-more-inventory-records is true—then the remaining unmatched transactions must be processed as error records (the 320 and 810 modules).

  - If the EOF occurred for the transaction file—No-more-transaction-records is true—then the remaining unmatched masters must written to the new master file (the 310 and 800 modules).

Figure 19-8

Structure Chart—
Example 19-1

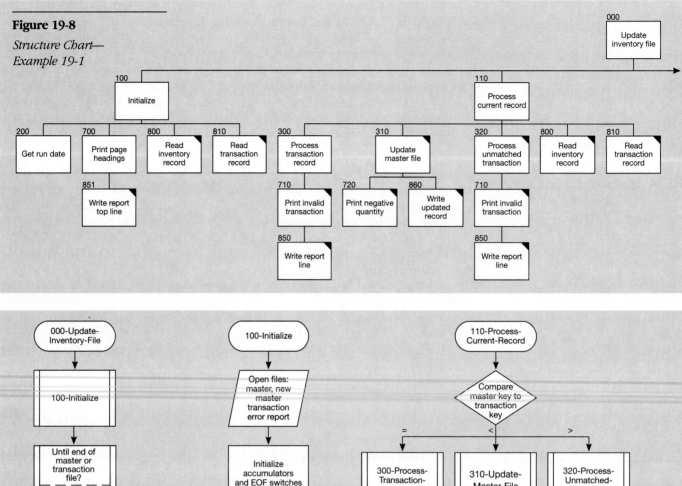

Figure 19-9

Flowchart Solution—
Example 19-1

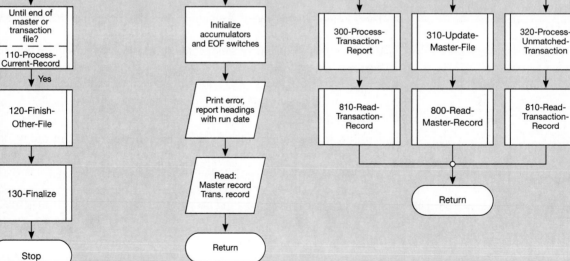

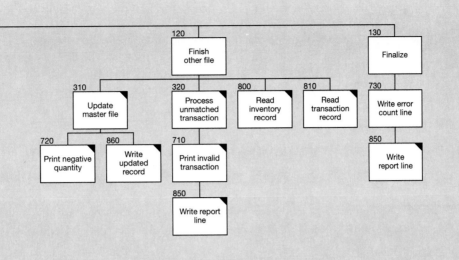

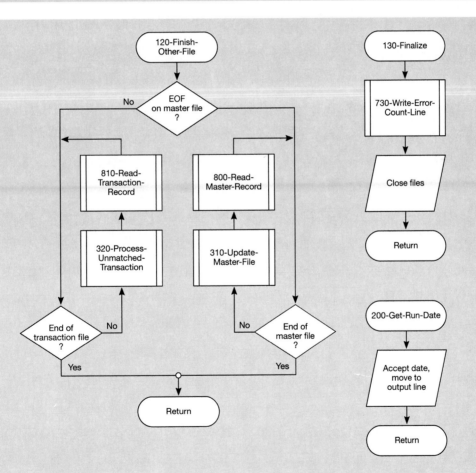

***Program Solution—
Example 19-1***

If you understand the program logic of Figures 19-9 or 19-10, then the completed program of Figure 19-11 (pages 535 and 536) should be reasonably straightforward. In the DATA DIVISION, you see four FDs, one for each of the four files. In the WORKING-STORAGE SECTION, each of the report lines is described as an 01. The data item TRANSACTION-SUM serves as the transaction accumulator for groups of transaction records.

In the PROCEDURE DIVISION, you can see that the EVALUATE statements in the 110, 120, and 300 modules provide excellent documentation regarding the exact conditions under which each action is taken. For instance, in the 120 module, the EVALUATE options

```
WHEN NO-MORE-INVENTORY-RECORDS
```
and
```
WHEN NO-MORE-TRANSACTION-RECORDS
```

clearly describe the condition under which either option is taken.

***Sample Output—
Example 19-1***

Figure 19-12 (see page 537) is the input software inventory file and Figure 19-13 is the input transaction file. As you can see in Figure 19-13, every other column of the transaction file is highlighted so that you can distinguish individual fields. Five records that will produce error conditions are also highlighted.

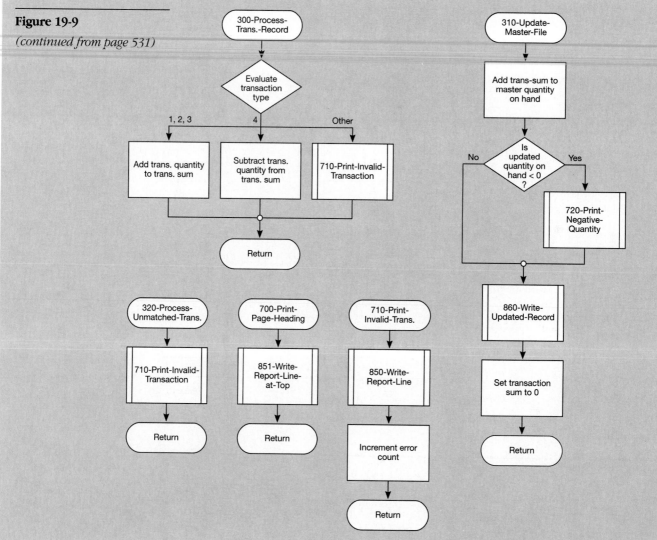

Figure 19-9

(continued from page 531)

Figure 19-14 (see page 538) is the updated inventory file. You might notice that the rightmost digit of each quantity-on-hand field is a letter or the brace { character. The reason is that RM/COBOL-85 automatically encodes a sign in any field that is defined as signed. Remember from Chapter 6 that embedding the sign in the rightmost digit of a number changes the internal coding of that digit to a letter. The correspondence is as follows.

Digit	Encoded as		Digit	Encoded as
+1	A		-1	J
+2	B		-2	R
.	.		.	.
.	.		.	.
.	.		.	.
+9	I		-9	R
+0	{		-0	}

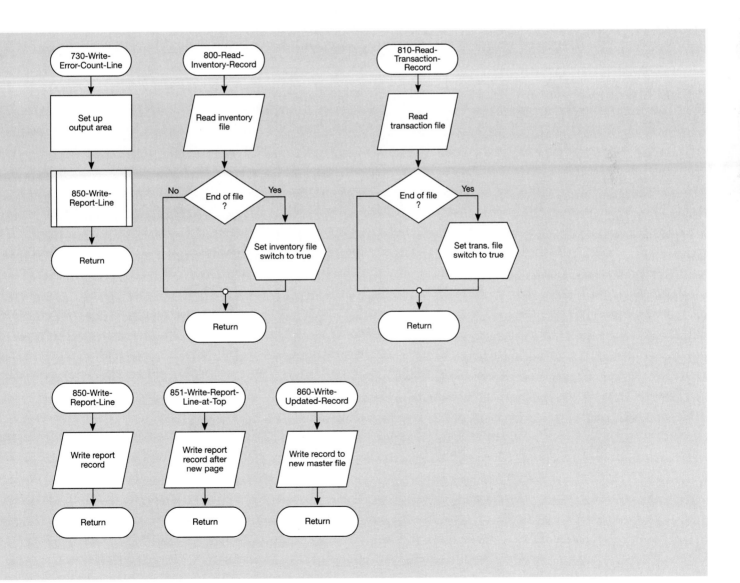

Figure 19-10

Pseudocode Solution—
Example 19-1

```
000-Update-Inventory-File
    Perform 100-Initialize
    Perform 110-Process-Current-Record
        until No-more-inventory-records
            or No-more-transaction-records
    Perform 120-Finish-other-file
    Perform 130-Finalize

100-Initialize
    Open input Inventory and Transaction files
    Open output Report file and Updated inventory file
    Initialize accumulators
    Get run date
    Print headings
    Set No-more-inventory-records and
        No-more-transaction-records to false
    Read first Inventory and Transaction records

110-Process-Current-Record
    EVALUATE
        When Inventory-record-stock-number = Transaction-stock-number
            Perform 300-Process-Transaction-Record
            Perform 810-Read-Transaction-Record
        When Inventory-record-stock-number < Transaction-stock-number
            Perform 310-Update-Master-File
            Perform 800-Read-Inventory-Record
        When other
            Perform 320-Process-Unmatched-Transaction
            Perform 810-Read-Transaction-Record

120-Finish-Other-File
    When No-more-inventory-records
        Perform until No-more-transaction-records
            Perform 320-Process-Unmatched-Transaction
            Perform 810-Read-Transaction-Record
    When No-more-transaction-records
        Perform until No-more-transaction-records
            Perform 310-Update-Master-File
            Perform 800-Read-Inventory-Record

130-Finalize
    Perform 730-Write-Error-Count-Line
    Close files

200-Get-Run-Date
    Accept date from system and move to output area

300-Process-Transaction-Record
    EVALUATE Transaction-type
        When 1 through 3
            Add Transaction-quantity to Transaction-sum
        When 4
            Subtract Transaction-quantity from Transaction-sum
        When other
            Perform 710-Print-Invalid-Transaction
```

```
310-Update-Master-File
    Update quantity on hand
    If updated quantity on hand is less than zero
        Perform 720-Print-Negative-Quantity
    Perform 860-Write-Updated-Record
    Set transaction sum to 0

320-Process-Unmatched-Transaction
    Move error message to output area
    Perform 710-Print-Invalid-Transaction

700-Print-Page-Headings
    Move page heading to output line
    Perform 851-Write-Report-Line-at-Top

710-Print-Invalid-Transaction
    Move transaction record and error message to output area
    Perform 850-Write-Report-Line
    Increment error count

720-Print-Negative-Quantity
    Move stock number and quantity on hand to output area
    Perform 850-Write-Report-Line
    Increment error count

730-Write-Error-Count-Line
    Move error count to output area
    Perform 850-Write-Report-Line

800-Read-Inventory-Record
    Read Inventory-File
        at end set No-more-inventory-records to true

810-Read-Transaction-Record
    Read Transaction-File
        at end set No-more-transaction-records to true

850-Write-Report-Line
    Write Report line after advancing line-spacing lines

851-Write-Report-Line-at-Top
    Write Report line after advancing page

860-Write-Updated-Record
    Write Updated-inventory-record
```

Figure 19-11

Batch Update of a Sequential File—Example 19-1
(continued on page 536)

```
1       IDENTIFICATION DIVISION.
2
3       PROGRAM-ID. BTP-SEQ.
4
5       *    Written by J.Olson
6       *    Sept. 3, 1990
7
8       *    This program does Batch Transaction Processing to a
9       *    Sequential master file.  A new master file is created,
10      *    in which the Quantity-On-Hand field has been updated by
11      *    the contents of the Transaction file: Receipts, Returns,
12      *    Adjustments, and Sales.
13
14      ENVIRONMENT DIVISION.
15
16      CONFIGURATION SECTION.
17      SOURCE-COMPUTER. IBM-PC.
18
19      INPUT-OUTPUT SECTION.
20      FILE-CONTROL.
21          SELECT INVENTORY-FILE   ASSIGN TO DISK "SOFTWAR2.DL"
22                                  ORGANIZATION IS LINE SEQUENTIAL.
23          SELECT UPDATED-INVENTORY-FILE
24                                  ASSIGN TO DISK "SOFTWAR2.DLU"
25                                  ORGANIZATION IS LINE SEQUENTIAL.
26          SELECT TRANSACTION-FILE ASSIGN TO DISK "SWTRANS.DL"
27                                  ORGANIZATION IS LINE SEQUENTIAL.
28          SELECT REPORT-FILE      ASSIGN TO PRINTER "PRN-FILE".
29
30      DATA DIVISION.
31
32      FILE SECTION.
33
34      FD  INVENTORY-FILE.
35      01  INVENTORY-RECORD.
36          10  IR-STOCK-NUMBER        PIC X(5).
37          10                         PIC X(50).
38          10  IR-QUANT-ON-HAND       PIC S9(3).
39          10                         PIC X(8).
40
41      FD  UPDATED-INVENTORY-FILE.
42      01  UPDATED-INVENTORY-RECORD.
43          10  UI-STOCK-NUMBER        PIC X(5).
44          10                         PIC X(50).
45          10  UI-QUANT-ON-HAND       PIC S9(3).
46          10                         PIC X(8).
47
48      FD  TRANSACTION-FILE.
49      01  TRANSACTION-RECORD.
50          10  TR-DOCUMENT-NUMBER     PIC X(6).
51          10  TR-STOCK-NUMBER        PIC X(5).
52          10  TR-TRANSACTION-TYPE    PIC X(1).
53          10  TR-TRANSACTION-QUANTITY PIC S9(3)
54                                     SIGN IS TRAILING SEPARATE.
55

56      FD  REPORT-FILE.
57      01  REPORT-LINE                PIC X(75).
58
59      WORKING-STORAGE SECTION.
60
61      01  PROGRAM-SWITCHES.
62          10                         PIC X.
63              88  NO-MORE-INVENTORY-RECORDS   VALUE "Y"  FALSE "N".
64          10                         PIC X.
65              88  NO-MORE-TRANSACTION-RECORDS VALUE "Y"  FALSE "N".
66
67      01  ACCUMULATORS.
68          10  ERROR-COUNT            PIC 9(3).
69          10  TRANSACTION-SUM        PIC S9(3).
70
71      01  OTHER-VARIABLES.
72          10  LINE-SPACING           PIC 9.
73
74      01  REPORT-DATE.
75          10  REPORT-YEAR            PIC 99.
76          10  REPORT-MONTH           PIC 99.
77          10  REPORT-DAY             PIC 99.
78
79      01  PAGE-HEADING-LINE.
80          10  PH-MONTH               PIC Z9.
81          10                         PIC X       VALUE "/".
82          10  PH-DAY                 PIC 99.
83          10                         PIC X       VALUE "/".
84          10  PH-YEAR                PIC 99.
85          10                         PIC X(10)   VALUE SPACES.
86          10                         PIC X(33)   VALUE
87                  "TRANSACTION PROCESSING ERROR LIST".
88
89      01  TRANSACTION-ERROR-LINE     VALUE SPACES.
90          10  TE-TRANSACTION-RECORD  PIC X(16).
91          10                         PIC X(2).
92          10  TE-ERROR-MESSAGE       PIC X(57).
93
94      01  NEGATIVE-QUANTITY-ON-HAND-LINE.
95          10                         PIC X(38)   VALUE
96                  "Negative Quantity On Hand for Stock # ".
97          10  NQ-STOCK-NUMBER        PIC X(5).
98          10                         PIC X(2)    VALUE ": ".
99          10  NQ-QUANT-ON-HAND       PIC --9.
100
101     01  FINAL-TOTAL-LINE.
102         10  FT-ERROR-COUNT         PIC ZZ9.
103         10                         PIC X(29)   VALUE
104             " error messages were written.".
105
```

As a check, consider the first record of the inventory file and its transactions (product number 07427).

Transaction:			
First record	Type 1 (receipt)	Quantity	50
Second record	Type 4 (sale)	Quantity	1
Total transactions (First record - Second record)			49

Master:	
Quantity on hand	65
Updated quantity on hand (Quantity on hand + Total transactions)	114

Figure 19-11

(continued from page 535)

```
106        PROCEDURE DIVISION.
107
108        000-UPDATE-INVENTORY-FILE.
109            PERFORM 100-INITIALIZE
110            PERFORM 110-PROCESS-CURRENT-RECORD
111                UNTIL NO-MORE-INVENTORY-RECORDS
112                   OR NO-MORE-TRANSACTION-RECORDS
113            PERFORM 120-FINISH-OTHER-FILE
114            PERFORM 130-FINALIZE
115            STOP RUN.
116
117        100-INITIALIZE.
118            OPEN INPUT  INVENTORY-FILE
119            OPEN INPUT  TRANSACTION-FILE
120            OPEN OUTPUT UPDATED-INVENTORY-FILE
121            OPEN OUTPUT REPORT-FILE
122            INITIALIZE ACCUMULATORS
123            PERFORM 200-GET-RUN-DATE
124            PERFORM 700-PRINT-PAGE-HEADINGS
125            SET NO-MORE-INVENTORY-RECORDS TO FALSE
126            SET NO-MORE-TRANSACTION-RECORDS TO FALSE
127            PERFORM 800-READ-INVENTORY-RECORD
128            PERFORM 810-READ-TRANSACTION-RECORD.
129
130        110-PROCESS-CURRENT-RECORD.
131            EVALUATE TRUE
132                WHEN IR-STOCK-NUMBER = TR-STOCK-NUMBER
133                    PERFORM 300-PROCESS-TRANSACTION-RECORD
134                    PERFORM 810-READ-TRANSACTION-RECORD
135                WHEN IR-STOCK-NUMBER < TR-STOCK-NUMBER
136                    PERFORM 310-UPDATE-MASTER-FILE
137                    PERFORM 800-READ-INVENTORY-RECORD
138                WHEN OTHER
139                    PERFORM 320-PROCESS-UNMATCHED-TRANS
140                    PERFORM 810-READ-TRANSACTION-RECORD
141            END-EVALUATE.
142
143        120-FINISH-OTHER-FILE.
144            EVALUATE TRUE
145                WHEN NO-MORE-INVENTORY-RECORDS
146                    PERFORM UNTIL NO-MORE-TRANSACTION-RECORDS
147                        PERFORM 320-PROCESS-UNMATCHED-TRANS
148                        PERFORM 810-READ-TRANSACTION-RECORD
149                    END-PERFORM
150                WHEN NO-MORE-TRANSACTION-RECORDS
151                    PERFORM UNTIL NO-MORE-INVENTORY-RECORDS
152                        PERFORM 310-UPDATE-MASTER-FILE
153                        PERFORM 800-READ-INVENTORY-RECORD
154                    END-PERFORM
155            END-EVALUATE.
156
157        130-FINALIZE.
158            PERFORM 730-WRITE-ERROR-COUNT-LINE
159            CLOSE UPDATED-INVENTORY-FILE
160                  INVENTORY-FILE
161                  TRANSACTION-FILE
162                  REPORT-FILE.
163
164        200-GET-RUN-DATE.
165            ACCEPT REPORT-DATE FROM DATE
166            MOVE REPORT-MONTH TO PH-MONTH
167            MOVE REPORT-DAY   TO PH-DAY
168            MOVE REPORT-YEAR  TO PH-YEAR.
169
170        300-PROCESS-TRANSACTION-RECORD.
171            EVALUATE TR-TRANSACTION-TYPE
172                WHEN "1" THRU "3"
173                    ADD TR-TRANSACTION-QUANTITY TO TRANSACTION-SUM
174                WHEN "4"
175                    SUBTRACT TR-TRANSACTION-QUANTITY
176                        FROM TRANSACTION-SUM
177                WHEN OTHER
178                    MOVE "Transaction Type Code is invalid"
179                        TO TE-ERROR-MESSAGE
180                    PERFORM 710-PRINT-INVALID-TRANSACTION
181            END-EVALUATE.
182
183        310-UPDATE-MASTER-FILE.
184            MOVE INVENTORY-RECORD TO UPDATED-INVENTORY-RECORD
185            ADD TRANSACTION-SUM TO UI-QUANT-ON-HAND
186            IF UI-QUANT-ON-HAND IS NEGATIVE
187                PERFORM 720-PRINT-NEGATIVE-QUANTITY
188            END-IF
189            PERFORM 860-WRITE-UPDATED-RECORD
190            MOVE ZEROES TO TRANSACTION-SUM.
191
192        320-PROCESS-UNMATCHED-TRANS.
193            MOVE "No Inventory Record for this Stock Number"
194                TO TE-ERROR-MESSAGE
195            PERFORM 710-PRINT-INVALID-TRANSACTION.
196
197        700-PRINT-PAGE-HEADINGS.
198            MOVE PAGE-HEADING-LINE TO REPORT-LINE
199            PERFORM 851-WRITE-REPORT-LINE-AT-TOP
200            MOVE 2 TO LINE-SPACING.
201
202        710-PRINT-INVALID-TRANSACTION.
203            MOVE TRANSACTION-RECORD TO TE-TRANSACTION-RECORD
204            MOVE TRANSACTION-ERROR-LINE TO REPORT-LINE
205            PERFORM 850-WRITE-REPORT-LINE
206            ADD 1 TO ERROR-COUNT.
207
208        720-PRINT-NEGATIVE-QUANTITY.
209            MOVE UI-STOCK-NUMBER TO NQ-STOCK-NUMBER
210            MOVE UI-QUANT-ON-HAND TO NQ-QUANT-ON-HAND
211            MOVE NEGATIVE-QUANTITY-ON-HAND-LINE TO REPORT-LINE
212            PERFORM 850-WRITE-REPORT-LINE
213            ADD 1 TO ERROR-COUNT.
214
215        730-WRITE-ERROR-COUNT-LINE.
216            MOVE ERROR-COUNT TO FT-ERROR-COUNT
217            MOVE FINAL-TOTAL-LINE TO REPORT-LINE
218            MOVE 3 TO LINE-SPACING
219            PERFORM 850-WRITE-REPORT-LINE.
220
221        800-READ-INVENTORY-RECORD.
222            READ INVENTORY-FILE
223                AT END SET NO-MORE-INVENTORY-RECORDS TO TRUE
224            END-READ.
225
226        810-READ-TRANSACTION-RECORD.
227            READ TRANSACTION-FILE
228                AT END SET NO-MORE-TRANSACTION-RECORDS TO TRUE
229            END-READ.
230
231        850-WRITE-REPORT-LINE.
232            WRITE REPORT-LINE
233                AFTER ADVANCING LINE-SPACING LINES.
234
235        851-WRITE-REPORT-LINE-AT-TOP.
236            WRITE REPORT-LINE
237                AFTER ADVANCING PAGE.
238
239        860-WRITE-UPDATED-RECORD.
240            WRITE UPDATED-INVENTORY-RECORD.
```

Figure 19-12

The SOFTWAR2.DL Data File— Input for Example 19-1

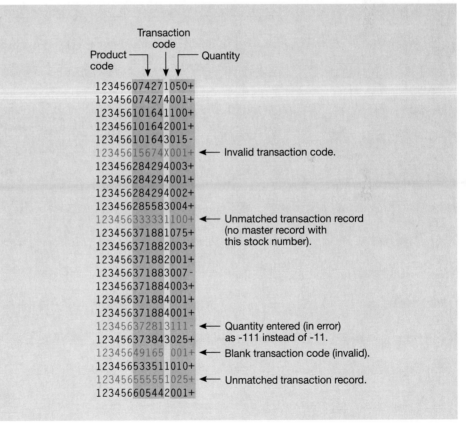

Quantity-on-hand field (to be updated).

```
07427Apricot-tree General Ledger   Apricot Software      06506534995
10164Sluggish Writer               Archaic Software      09310004995
15589Travelling Side Punch         Borneo International   18020002995
15674Supercharged Turbo COBOL      Borneo International   12010059900
28429Ferrari 4-5-6 Financial Acctg.Ferrari Development    14415049500
28558Orchestra II                  Ferrari Development    10210064900
32506Bottom View                   Galactic Bus. Mach.    10510009995
37188UnderWord, Rev 128            International Soft      09007503750
37281UnderCalc, Rev 256            International Soft      08007503750
37384UnderFile, Rev 64             International Soft      09507503750
45191Word Comet 7                  Micro Am               10410039900
49165Sentence                      Microhard              14312534995
53351QBase 7000                    MicroPerimeter, Inc.   17615069500
60544Nobodies Disk Utilities       Nobodies, Unlimited    13310004950
91655Potent BASIC Interpreter      20th Century Soft.     09710000950
```

Figure 19-13

The SWTRANS.DL Transaction File— Input for Example 19-1

```
                    Transaction
                       code
          Product      │   ┌── Quantity
           code   ┌────┤   │
                  │    │   │
           123456074271050+
           123456074274001+
           123456101641100+
           123456101642001+
           123456101643015-
           12345615674X001+   ◄── Invalid transaction code.
           123456284294003+
           123456284294001+
           123456284294002+
           123456285583004+
           123456333331100+   ◄── Unmatched transaction record
                                   (no master record with
                                   this stock number).
           123456371881075+
           123456371882003+
           123456371882001+
           123456371883007-
           123456371884003+
           123456371884001+
           123456371884001+
           123456372813111-   ◄── Quantity entered (in error)
                                   as -111 instead of -11.
           123456373843025+
           12345649165 001+   ◄── Blank transaction code (invalid).
           123456533511010+
           123456555551025+   ◄── Unmatched transaction record.
           123456605442001+
```

In Figure 19-14, you can see that the updated value is 11D. Refer to the preceding signed number table and you'll discover that D is the code for +4.

The error report for this run is shown in Figure 19-15. Notice that adjustment transaction entry erroneously keyed as -111 instead of -11 (for product number 37281) produced a negative Quantity-on-hand value. You can also see this in the file listing of Figure 19-14 (the ninth record) as a value 03J, where J represents -1.

Figure 19-14

*The SOFTWAR2.DLU Updated
Data File—Output from
Example 19-1*

Updated quantity-
on-hand field.

```
07427Apricot-tree General Ledger   Apricot Software      11D06534995
10164Sluggish Writer               Archaic Software      17I10004995
15589Travelling Side Punch         Borneo International   18{20002995
15674Supercharged Turbo COBOL      Borneo International   12{10059900
28429Ferrari 4-5-6 Financial Acctg.Ferrari Development    13H15049500
28558Orchestra II                  Ferrari Development    10F10064900
32506Bottom View                   Galactic Bus. Mach.    10E10009995
37188UnderWord, Rev 128            International Soft      15G07503750
37281UnderCalc, Rev 256            International Soft      03J07503750
37384UnderFile, Rev 64             International Soft      12{07503750
45191Word Comet 7                  Micro Am               10D10039900
49165Sentence                      Microhard              14C12534995
53351QBase 7000                    MicroPerimeter, Inc.   18F15069500
60544Nobodies Disk Utilities       Nobodies, Unlimited    13D10004950
91655Potent BASIC Interpreter      20th Century Soft.     09G10000950
```

Figure 19-15

*Error Report—Output from
Example 19-1*

```
10/03/90            TRANSACTION PROCESSING ERROR LIST

12345615674X001+  Transaction Type Code is invalid

123456333331100+  No Inventory Record for this Stock Number

Negative Quantity On Hand for Stock # 37281:   -31

12345649165 001+  Transaction Type Code is invalid

123456555551025+  No Inventory Record for this Stock Number


5 error messages were written.
```

Figure 19-16

*Master-Transaction
Processing—Two Cycles*

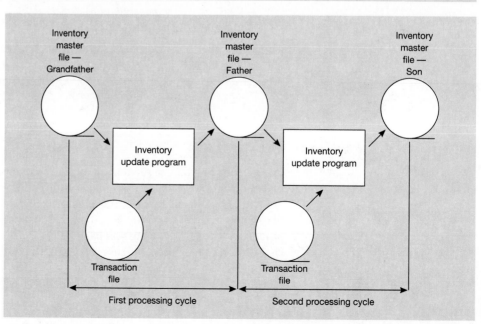

More About Traditional Master-Transaction Processing

In this example, you examined the master-transaction process and program from the point-of-view of a single transaction period. As mentioned early in these descriptions, the master-transaction update process is run periodically, as often as daily. The new master file created from an update serves as the input master for the next processing cycle, as illustrated in Figure 19-16. Here you can see the most recently updated master and the two outdated master files from previous update operations. These are commonly called the *son*, *father*, and *grandfather* files. Saving the father (and sometimes the grandfather) together with transaction files produces a good backup environment. For instance, if it is discovered that the current master file (the son) has been corrupted by an error-riddled transaction file during the last processing cycle, a new master can be created from a corrected transaction file and the father file.

Batch Updating an Indexed File

Example Definition— Example 19-2

In today's world of high-capacity disk drives, most applications take advantage of random accessing capabilities and use file organizations that allow for direct accessing of data. This provides broad versatility for all processing activities. However, even with a random organization, some applications are still amenable to batch transaction processing. Example 19-2 illustrates batch updating of an indexed file.

Example 19-2 Batch Updating an Indexed File

Problem Description

The UNISOFT company uses indexed organization for their software inventory file. Transactions are accumulated during the day and the master file is updated in place each night.

Output Report Requirements

Printed error report: This report (which is the same as the error report from Example 19-1) must include one line for each of the following detected errors.
Unmatched detail record
Detail record with an invalid transaction type code
Updated master quantity-on-hand field that is negative

Master Input/Output Description

Processing is to be done in place. That is, a master record is read, updated, then rewritten to its original position in the file.
File name: SOFTWAR2.DI
Record format:

Field	Positions	Data Type	Format/Description
Stock number	1–5	Alphanumeric	
Not used	6–55		
Quantity on hand	56–58	Numeric	S999
Not used	59–66		

Key field: Stock number

Transaction Input Description

Note that this is the same file as used in Example 19-1.
Input transaction file name: SWTRANS.DL
Record format:

Field	Positions	Data Type	Format/Description
Document number	1–6	Alphanumeric	
Stock number	7–11	Alphanumeric	
Transaction type	12	Alphanumeric	1 - Receipt
			2 - Return
			3 - Adjustment
			4 - Sale
Quantity	13–16	Numeric	S999 with trailing separate sign

Record sequence: Sorted by Stock number

Processing Requirements

This program is to function as follows:

1. Commence processing by reading the first transaction record and the master record with the same Stock-number value.
2. As transaction records are read for the current master record, update the quantity-on-hand field. For receipt, return, and adjustment records (types 1, 2, and 3), add the transaction quantity to the quantity-on-hand field. For sale records (type 4), subtract the transaction quantity.
3. When a transaction record is read with a stock number different from that of the preceding (and that of the current master), rewrite the master record. Then read the master record for the newly read transaction record.
4. If the updated master quantity-on-hand field is negative, write the stock number, quantity, and an error message to the error report.
5. Write each unmatched master record to the new master file without change.
6. Write each transaction record for which there is not a corresponding master to the error report. Include an appropriate error message.
7. Write each transaction record with an invalid transaction-type value to the error report.
8. When the transaction EOF is detected, rewrite the last master record.
9. As each error line is written, count it. At the end of the report, print a summary line with this error count.

Program Solution—
Example 19-2

Although the core of the programming logic of Example 19-1 (batch updating a sequential file) is significantly different from that of Example 19-2 (batch updating an indexed file), the overall program structure and logic are very similar. The programs differ in three significant respects, all related to random accessing of the master record.

1. The processing loop is repeated until the end of the transaction file is detected. There is no EOF test for the master file because it is not accessed sequentially.

2. Each time a transaction record is read with a key field value (stock number) different from the preceding, the current master must be rewritten. Also, the master corresponding to the new transaction record must be read.

3. When the transaction EOF occurs, no further record processing is necessary. However, if there is an unwritten updated master, it must be rewritten.

These logic differences are illustrated in the partial flowchart and pseudocode solutions of Figures 19-17 and 19-18. As each record is read, its product number is compared to that of the preceding transaction record. A new product number requires two actions:

■ The current master record must be rewritten (unless the previous transaction record had been an unmatched transaction, as indicated by the Master-not-found switch). This is done in the 860 module; notice that an invalid key condition means a write error so the program is terminated.

■ The inventory record corresponding to the newly read transaction record must be read (800 module). An invalid key means the record was not found, so the Master-not-found switch is set to false.

The complete BTP-NDX (batch transaction processing—indexed file) program is shown in Figure 19-19. The code elements that are different from those of BTP-SEQ are highlighted. Notice that the 310 module differs only in that the transaction quantities are added directly to the inventory record Quantity-on-hand field rather than to a separate accumulator. This was done to illustrate an alternate approach and is not dictated by the nature of the indexed file application.

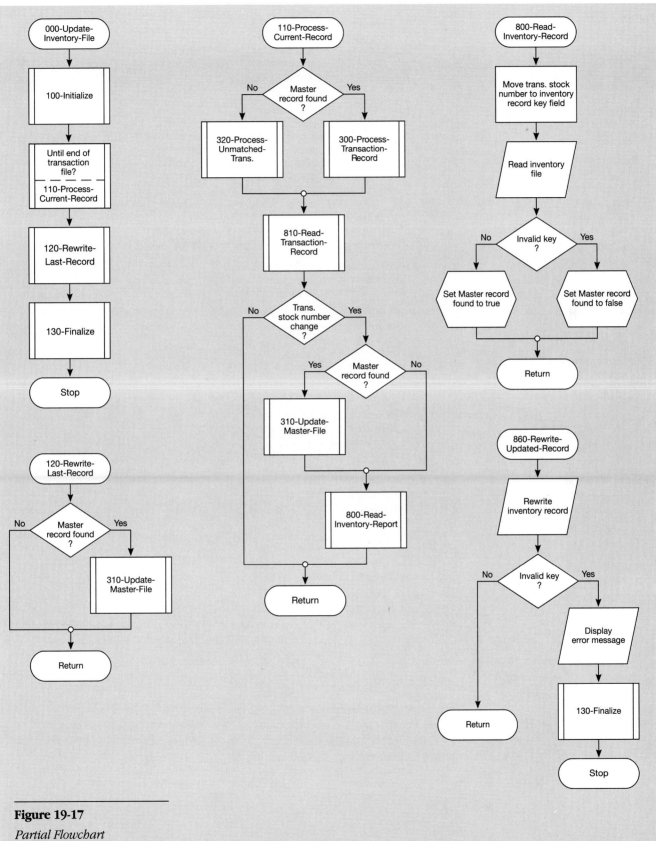

Figure 19-17

*Partial Flowchart
Solution—Example 19-2*

Figure 19-18

*Partial Pseudocode
Solution—Example 19-2*

```
000-Update-Inventory-File
   Perform 100-Initialize
   Perform 110-Process-Current-Record
      until No-more-transaction-records
   Perform 120-Rewrite-last-record
   Perform 130-Finalize

110-Process-Current-Record
   If Master-record-found is true
      Perform 300-Process-Transaction-Record
   else
      Perform 320-Process-Unmatched-Transaction
   Perform 810-Read-Transaction-Record
   If Product number of new transaction record equal
         Product number of previous transaction record
      If Master-record-found is true
         Perform 310-Update-Master-File
      Perform 800-Read-Inventory-Record

120-Rewrite-Last-Record
   If Master-record-found is true
      Perform 310-Update-Master-File

800-Read-Inventory-Record
   Move transaction Stock number to inventory record key field
   Read Inventory-File
   If invalid key
      Set Master-record-found to false
   else
      Set Master-record-found to true

860-Rewrite-Updated-Record
   Rewrite Updated-inventory-record
   If invalid key
      Display error message
      Perform 130-Finalize
   Stop
```

The REWRITE statement is used in this program in the 860 module, which is repeated here.

```
860-REWRITE-UPDATED-RECORD.
    REWRITE INVENTORY-RECORD
      INVALID KEY
         DISPLAY "Invalid key while rewriting", INVENTORY-RECORD
         DISPLAY "Aborting update program."
         PERFORM 130-FINALIZE
         STOP RUN
    END-REWRITE.
```

You can see that execution of the program is terminated if the INVALID KEY condition occurs. In this case, an attempt is made to rewrite the record previously read so the INVALID KEY condition should not occur. If it does, a serious system problem has occurred and processing must be terminated.

Figure 19-19

*Batch Transaction Processing of an
Indexed File—Example 19-2*
(continued on page 544)

```
1       IDENTIFICATION DIVISION.
2
3       PROGRAM-ID. BTP-NDX.
4
5    *     Written by J.Olson
6    *     Sept. 21, 1990
7
8    *     This program does Batch Transaction Processing by updating
9    *     an Indexed inventory file. In this file, the Quantity-On-
10   *     Hand field is updated by the contents of the Transaction
11   *     file: Receipts, Returns, Adjustments, and Sales. Since
12   *     the records in the transaction file are in sequence by
13   *     stock number, the inventory record is not rewritten until
14   *     all transaction records for that stock number have been
15   *     processed.
16
17      ENVIRONMENT DIVISION.
18
19      CONFIGURATION SECTION.
20      SOURCE-COMPUTER. IBM-PC.
21
22      INPUT-OUTPUT SECTION.
23      FILE-CONTROL.
24          SELECT INVENTORY-FILE  ASSIGN TO DISK "SOFTWAR2.DI"
25                                 ORGANIZATION IS INDEXED
26                                 ACCESS IS RANDOM
27                                 RECORD KEY IS IR-STOCK-NUMBER.
28          SELECT TRANSACTION-FILE ASSIGN TO DISK "SWTRANS.DL"
29                                 ORGANIZATION IS LINE SEQUENTIAL.
30          SELECT REPORT-FILE     ASSIGN TO PRINTER "PRN-FILE".
31
32      DATA DIVISION.
33
34      FILE SECTION.
35
36      FD  INVENTORY-FILE.
37      01  INVENTORY-RECORD.
38          10  IR-STOCK-NUMBER       PIC X(5).
39          10                        PIC X(50).
40          10  IR-QUANT-ON-HAND      PIC S9(3).
41          10                        PIC X(8).
42
43      FD  TRANSACTION-FILE.
44      01  TRANSACTION-RECORD.
45          10  TR-DOCUMENT-NUMBER    PIC X(6).
46          10  TR-STOCK-NUMBER       PIC X(5).
47          10  TR-TRANSACTION-TYPE   PIC X(1).
48          10  TR-TRANSACTION-QUANTITY PIC S9(3)
49                                    SIGN IS TRAILING SEPARATE.
50
51      FD  REPORT-FILE.
52      01  REPORT-LINE               PIC X(75).
53
54      WORKING-STORAGE SECTION.
55
56      01  PROGRAM-SWITCHES.
57          10                        PIC X.
58            88  NO-MORE-TRANSACTION-RECORDS  VALUE "Y"  FALSE "N".
59          10                        PIC X.
60            88  MASTER-RECORD-FOUND         VALUE "Y"  FALSE "N".
61
62      01  ACCUMULATORS.
63          10  ERROR-COUNT           PIC 9(3).
64
65      01  OTHER-VARIABLES.
66          10  LINE-SPACING          PIC 9.
67
68      01  RUN-DATE.
69          10  RUN-YEAR              PIC 99.
70          10  RUN-MONTH             PIC 99.
71          10  RUN-DAY               PIC 99.
72
73      01  PAGE-HEADING-LINE.
74          10  PH-MONTH              PIC Z9.
75          10                        PIC X     VALUE "/".
76          10  PH-DAY                PIC 99.
77          10                        PIC X     VALUE "/".
78          10  PH-YEAR               PIC 99.
79          10                        PIC X(10) VALUE SPACES.
80          10                        PIC X(33) VALUE
81                  "TRANSACTION PROCESSING ERROR LIST".
82
83      01  TRANSACTION-ERROR-LINE    VALUE SPACES.
84          10  TE-TRANSACTION-RECORD PIC X(16).
85          10                        PIC X(2).
86          10  TE-ERROR-MESSAGE      PIC X(57).
87
88      01  NEGATIVE-QUANTITY-ON-HAND-LINE.
89          10                        PIC X(38)  VALUE
90                  "Negative Quantity On Hand for Stock # ".
91          10  NQ-STOCK-NUMBER       PIC X(5).
92          10                        PIC X(2)   VALUE ": ".
93          10  NQ-QUANT-ON-HAND      PIC ---9.
94
95      01  FINAL-TOTAL-LINE.
96          10  FT-ERROR-COUNT        PIC ZZ9.
97          10                        PIC X(29)  VALUE
98                  " error messages were written.".
99
```

Batch Maintenance of an Indexed File

Common Maintenance Operations

Remember from earlier descriptions in this chapter that a master file is one containing data that is relatively permanent; for example, each record of the software inventory file includes the product number, product description, and so on for a given software item. However, it also includes the current quantity on hand, data that changes as the result of transactions such as sales and receipts of product items. The two preceding examples illustrate transaction processing that updates this field—it changes data in the file. In addition to transaction processing program(s), an inventory system would include one or more programs to make other changes to the file. These are called *maintenance operations* and provide the user with the ability to perform activities such as adding and deleting records and changing data stored in fields that do not normally change. For instance, the wrong vendor name might be entered for a software product and require changing.

Figure 19-19

(continued from page 543)

```
100    PROCEDURE DIVISION.
101
102    000-UPDATE-INVENTORY-FILE.
103        PERFORM 100-INITIALIZE
104        PERFORM 110-PROCESS-CURRENT-RECORD
105            UNTIL NO-MORE-TRANSACTION-RECORDS
106        PERFORM 120-REWRITE-LAST-RECORD
107        PERFORM 130-FINALIZE
108        STOP RUN.
109
110    100-INITIALIZE.
111        OPEN I-O    INVENTORY-FILE
112        OPEN INPUT  TRANSACTION-FILE
113        OPEN OUTPUT REPORT-FILE
114        INITIALIZE ERROR-COUNT
115        PERFORM 200-GET-RUN-DATE
116        PERFORM 700-PRINT-PAGE-HEADINGS
117        SET NO-MORE-TRANSACTION-RECORDS TO FALSE
118        PERFORM 810-READ-TRANSACTION-RECORD
119        PERFORM 800-READ-INVENTORY-RECORD.
120
121    110-PROCESS-CURRENT-RECORD.
122        IF MASTER-RECORD-FOUND
123            PERFORM 300-PROCESS-TRANSACTION-RECORD
124        ELSE
125            PERFORM 320-PROCESS-UNMATCHED-TRANS
126        END-IF
127
128        PERFORM 810-READ-TRANSACTION-RECORD
129
130        IF TR-STOCK-NUMBER NOT = IR-STOCK-NUMBER
131            IF MASTER-RECORD-FOUND
132                PERFORM 310-UPDATE-MASTER-FILE
133            END-IF
134            PERFORM 800-READ-INVENTORY-RECORD
135        END-IF.
136
137    120-REWRITE-LAST-RECORD.
138        IF MASTER-RECORD-FOUND
139            PERFORM 310-UPDATE-MASTER-FILE
140        END-IF.
141
142    130-FINALIZE.
143        PERFORM 730-WRITE-ERROR-COUNT-LINE
144        CLOSE INVENTORY-FILE
145              TRANSACTION-FILE
146              REPORT-FILE.
147
148    200-GET-RUN-DATE.
149        ACCEPT RUN-DATE FROM DATE
150        MOVE RUN-MONTH TO PH-MONTH
151        MOVE RUN-DAY   TO PH-DAY
152        MOVE RUN-YEAR  TO PH-YEAR.
153
154    300-PROCESS-TRANSACTION-RECORD.
155        EVALUATE TR-TRANSACTION-TYPE
156            WHEN "1" THRU "3"
157            ADD TR-TRANSACTION-QUANTITY TO IR-QUANT-ON-HAND
158            WHEN "4"
159            SUBTRACT TR-TRANSACTION-QUANTITY
160                FROM IR-QUANT-ON-HAND
161            WHEN OTHER
162            MOVE "Transaction Type Code is invalid"
163                TO TE-ERROR-MESSAGE
164            PERFORM 710-PRINT-INVALID-TRANSACTION
165        END-EVALUATE.
166
167    310-UPDATE-MASTER-FILE.
168        IF IR-QUANT-ON-HAND IS NEGATIVE
169            PERFORM 720-PRINT-NEGATIVE-QUANTITY
170        END-IF
171        PERFORM 860-REWRITE-UPDATED-RECORD.
172
173    320-PROCESS-UNMATCHED-TRANS.
174        MOVE "No Inventory Record for this Stock Number"
175            TO TE-ERROR-MESSAGE
176        PERFORM 710-PRINT-INVALID-TRANSACTION.
177
178    700-PRINT-PAGE-HEADINGS.
179        MOVE PAGE-HEADING-LINE TO REPORT-LINE
180        PERFORM 851-WRITE-REPORT-LINE-AT-TOP
181        MOVE 2 TO LINE-SPACING.
182
183    710-PRINT-INVALID-TRANSACTION.
184        MOVE TRANSACTION-RECORD TO TE-TRANSACTION-RECORD
185        MOVE TRANSACTION-ERROR-LINE TO REPORT-LINE
186        PERFORM 850-WRITE-REPORT-LINE
187        ADD 1 TO ERROR-COUNT.
188
189    720-PRINT-NEGATIVE-QUANTITY.
190        MOVE IR-STOCK-NUMBER TO NQ-STOCK-NUMBER
191        MOVE IR-QUANT-ON-HAND TO NQ-QUANT-ON-HAND
192        MOVE NEGATIVE-QUANTITY-ON-HAND-LINE TO REPORT-LINE
193        PERFORM 850-WRITE-REPORT-LINE
194        ADD 1 TO ERROR-COUNT.
195
196    730-WRITE-ERROR-COUNT-LINE.
197        MOVE ERROR-COUNT TO FT-ERROR-COUNT
198        MOVE FINAL-TOTAL-LINE TO REPORT-LINE
199        MOVE 3 TO LINE-SPACING
200        PERFORM 850-WRITE-REPORT-LINE.
201
202    800-READ-INVENTORY-RECORD.
203        MOVE TR-STOCK-NUMBER TO IR-STOCK-NUMBER
204        READ INVENTORY-FILE
205            INVALID KEY
206                SET MASTER-RECORD-FOUND TO FALSE
207            NOT INVALID KEY
208                SET MASTER-RECORD-FOUND TO TRUE
209        END-READ.
210
211    810-READ-TRANSACTION-RECORD.
212        READ TRANSACTION-FILE
213            AT END SET NO-MORE-TRANSACTION-RECORDS TO TRUE
214        END-READ.
215
216    850-WRITE-REPORT-LINE.
217        WRITE REPORT-LINE
218            AFTER ADVANCING LINE-SPACING LINES.
219
220    851-WRITE-REPORT-LINE-AT-TOP.
221        WRITE REPORT-LINE
222            AFTER ADVANCING PAGE.
223
224    860-REWRITE-UPDATED-RECORD.
225        REWRITE INVENTORY-RECORD
226            INVALID KEY
227                DISPLAY "Invalid key while rewriting", INVENTORY-RECORD
228                DISPLAY "Aborting update program."
229                PERFORM 130-FINALIZE
230                STOP RUN
231        END-REWRITE.
```

To illustrate file maintenance, the following example involves performing batch maintenance operations on the inventory file:

Example 19-3 Batch Maintenance on the Inventory File

Problem Description

The UNISOFT company requires a batch processing program to allow the following maintenance operations to be performed on the inventory file:

- Add a new record to the file

- Delete an existing record from the file

- Change any field in the record except the Product-number and Quantity-on-hand

Output Report Requirements

Printed error report: This report must include one line for each of the following detected errors.

> Invalid maintenance activity requested
> Stock number already in file for record to be added
> Inventory record not found for record to be modified
> Invalid data in input maintenance record
> Attempt to change the Quantity-on-hand field

Master Input/Output Description

Processing is to be done in place. That is, a master record is read, updated, then rewritten to its original position in the file.

File name: SOFTWAR2.DI

Record format:

Field	Positions	Data Type	Format
Stock number	1–5	Alphanumeric	
Software name	6–35	Alphanumeric	
Vendor name	36–55	Alphanumeric	
Quantity on hand	56–58	Numeric	S999
Reorder level	59–61	Numeric	999
Price	62–66	Numeric	999V99

Key field: Stock number

Transaction Input Description

Note that this is the same file as used in Example 19-1.

Input transaction file name: SWTRANS.DL

Record format:

Field	Positions	Data Type	Format/Description
Maintenance type	1	Alphanumeric	A - Add record
			C - Change record
			D - Delete record
Stock number	2–6	Alphanumeric	
Software name	7–36	Alphanumeric	
Vendor name	37–56	Alphanumeric	
Quantity on hand	57–59	Numeric	S999
Reorder level	60–62	Numeric	999
Price	63–67	Numeric	999V99

Record sequence: Not sorted

Processing Requirements

As each maintenance record is read, the program is to function as follows:

1. Verify that it is a valid maintenance record (Maintenance type is A, C, or D). If not, write an error message and continue to the next record.
2. For a type A maintenance (a record to be added to the inventory file):
    a. Validate the record:
        1. Ensure that there is not a record in the master file with the same Product-number (key) field value.
        2. Check that all fields contain entries (that none is empty).
        3. Check that all numeric fields contain numeric data.
    b. If the record passes the validity checks, write a new inventory record using the data from the maintenance record.
3. For a type C maintenance (an inventory record is to be changed by data in the maintenance record):
    a. Read the inventory record with the Product-number field value corresponding to that of the maintenance record. If the record does not exist, print an error message and proceed to the next maintenance record.
    b. If the inventory record is found:
        1. Move non-blank fields of the maintenance record to the inventory record area.
        2. If the Quantity-on-hand field of the maintenance record is not blank, print an error message. This record must not be processed because the Quantity-on-hand field cannot be changed by the maintenance program.
        3. If any non-blank numeric fields do not contain numeric data, print an error message. This record must not be processed.
    c. If no errors are detected, rewrite the inventory record.
4. For a type D maintenance (a record to be deleted from the inventory file):
    a. Read the inventory record with the Product-number field value corresponding to that of the maintenance record. If the record does not exist, print an error message and proceed to the next maintenance record.
    b. If the record exists, delete it from the inventory file.
5. As each maintenance record error is detected and printed, increment an error counter.
6. After the last maintenance record is processed, print a summary line indicating the number of errors detected.

**Sample Data—
Example 19-3**

Before looking at program logic, let's consider the results of a test run using the sample data file of Figure 19-20. As you can see, this file includes 13 maintenance records: four adds, six changes, two deletes, and one record with an invalid maintenance type code. Fields that will make a record invalid for its maintenance type are highlighted. The following is a description of each of these records:

1. For an add record, all fields must contain data. This record is invalid because the Quantity-on-hand field does not contain data. Also, the Price field is not numeric.
2. This is a valid record that will be added to the file.
3. The Vendor-name field is blank—invalid for an add.
4. The Stock-number value (32506) is the stock number of a record that is currently in the file; therefore, this record cannot be added.
5. A valid change record—changes the software name only.
6. A valid change record—changes the vendor name, reorder level, and price.
7. The Quantity-on-hand field cannot be changed from the maintenance program; therefore, this record is not valid.
8. The Reorder-level value for this change is entered as 1OO, but the *digits* "00" have been erroneously recorded as the *letters* "OO," thus giving an invalid numeric field.

Figure 19-20

Test Maintenance File

9. The Price field entry includes a letter in the rightmost position. Since this field is unsigned, the letter will produce a nonnumeric error.

10. A change is requested for a record that does not exist.

11. A delete is requested for a record that does not exist.

12. A valid delete record—the record with a product code of 53351 is to be deleted (this record does exist in the inventory file).

13. The letter *B* is an invalid maintenance code.

Figure 19-21 is a listing of the original inventory file; impending changes are highlighted. Figure 19-22 is a listing after the program has been run and the maintenance file of Figure 19-20 has been processed. Record changes and the addition and deletion are highlighted and annotated.

The printed error listing resulting from this run is shown as Figure 19-23. Notice that each record in error includes an appropriate error message. As you can see, since the first maintenance record contains two errors, it is printed twice—each time with an appropriate error message.

Figure 19-21

The SOFTWAR2.DI Data File before the Maintenance Run

Figure 19-22

*The SOFTWAR2.DI Data File
after the Maintenance Run*

```
07427Apricot-tree General Ledger   Apricot Software     06506534995
10164Sluggish Writer               Archaic Software     09310004995
15589Travelling Side Punch         Borneo International18020002995
15674Supercharged Turbo COBOL      Borneo International12010059900
15683Supercharged Ada              Borneo International00005078995  ← Record added.
28429Ferrari 4-5-6 Financial Acctg.Ferrari Development 14415049500
28558Orchestra II++                 Ferrari Development 10210064900  ← Software name changed.
32506Bottom View                    Galactic Bus. Mach. 10510009995
37188UnderWord, Rev 128             International  Soft 09007503750
37281UnderCalc, Rev 256             International  Soft 08007503750
37384UnderFile, Rev 64              International  Soft 09507503750      Vendor name,
45191Word Comet 7                   Micro USA           10412534998  ← reorder level,
49165Sentence                       Microhard           14312534995    and price changed.
60544Nobodies Disk Utilities        Nobodies, Unlimited 13310004950
91655Potent BASIC Interpreter       20th Century Soft.  09710000950      Record deleted.
```

Figure 19-23

*The Error Report from the
Test Maintenance Run*

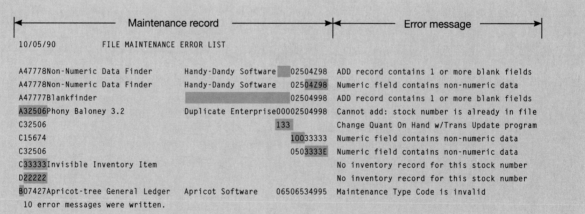

```
|←────────── Maintenance record ──────────→|←────── Error message ──────→|

10/05/90        FILE MAINTENANCE ERROR LIST

A47778Non-Numeric Data Finder   Handy-Dandy Software   02504Z98  ADD record contains 1 or more blank fields
A47778Non-Numeric Data Finder   Handy-Dandy Software   02504Z98  Numeric field contains non-numeric data
A47777Blankfinder                                      02504998  ADD record contains 1 or more blank fields
A32506Phony Baloney 3.2          Duplicate Enterprise00002504998  Cannot add: stock number is already in file
C32506                                            133           Change Quant On Hand w/Trans Update program
C15674                                           10033333        Numeric field contains non-numeric data
C32506                                           0503333E        Numeric field contains non-numeric data
C33333Invisible Inventory Item                            No inventory record for this stock number
D22222                                                    No inventory record for this stock number
B07427Apricot-tree General Ledger  Apricot Software   06506534995  Maintenance Type Code is invalid
     10 error messages were written.
```

**Program Solution—
Example 19-3**

This program requires three distinct operations on the inventory file: new records must be added to the file, existing records must be changed (in place), and existing records must be deleted. Because new records are added and existing records are changed, the program requires extensive data validation. That is, each field from the maintenance record to be incorporated into the inventory file must be validated. Because of these broad needs, the program structure is rather significant, as shown in the structure chart of Figure 19-24. You can see that the main portion of the structure falls beneath the 300-Process-Maintenance-Record module. It consists of three primary components: processing each of the three activities (add, change, and delete).

Figure 19-25 is a partial set of flowcharts displaying the basic logic of the three maintenance activities. You can see that adding a new record (310 module) and changing an existing one (module 320) are controlled by the switch Valid-maintenance-record. This switch is set to true in the 810 module (read the next maintenance record). It is set to false in 740 module, which prints each error message. The record is written (310 module) or rewritten (320 module) only if this switch is still true. A complete pseudocode solution is included in Figure 19-26 (see page 553).

Figure 19-24

Structure Chart—
Example 19-3

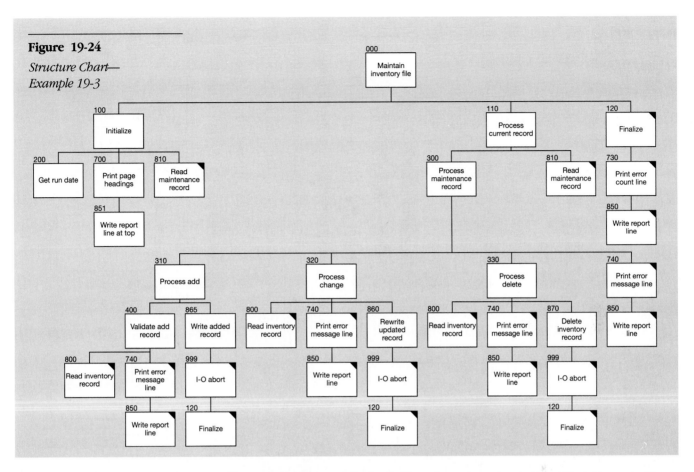

The complete program for batch file maintenance of an indexed file is shown in Figure 19-27 (see pages 554 and 555). After studying the program structure and logic and the sample output, you should find the program to be reasonably straightforward.

The Batch File Maintenance Program— DATA DIVISION Features

The code that you see in the BFM-NDX program's DATA DIVISION is relatively basic at this point in your studies. You should notice that the three numeric fields of the input maintenance record are defined as numeric, then redefined as alphanumeric. Remember, the program requires that they be tested for blanks and, if non-blank, as valid numeric fields.

This program uses three program switches. NO-MORE-MAINTENANCE-RECORDS is the EOF switch for sequentially reading the input maintenance file. VALID-MAINTENANCE-RECORD is used during validation of the input maintenance record. MASTER-RECORD-FOUND is used to indicate whether or not a random read of the inventory file has been successful.

All error messages are defined in a separate record (beginning line 104); you will see these items moved to the output line in the PROCEDURE DIVISION.

The Batch File Maintenance Program— PROCEDURE DIVISION Features

At the first two modular levels (lines 120–145), you can see that the code is that of "standard" sequential processing of a file (the maintenance file). The 110 module processes the current maintenance record, then reads the next. The 300 module (called by 110) evaluates the maintenance record type (add, change, or delete) and performs the appropriate module (310, 320, 330, or 340). However, before considering these, let's focus our attention on the variety of two read modules of this program.

810-READ-MAINTENANCE-RECORD. This module is the sequential read for accessing the next maintenance record. Notice that after the record is read, VALID-MAINTENANCE-RECORD is set to true.

Figure 19-25

Partial Flowchart Solution—
Example 19-3

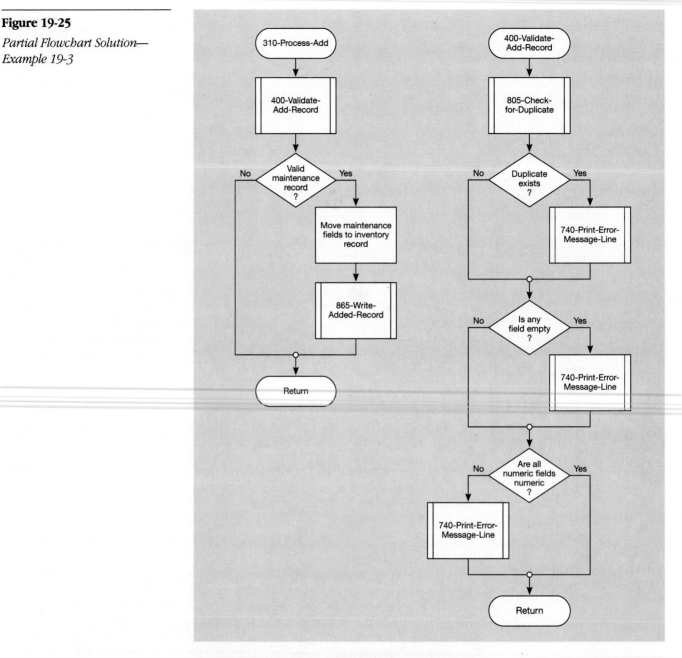

800-READ-INVENTORY-RECORD. For each maintenance record to be processed, the inventory file must be read. Access is random, using the record key value obtained from the maintenance record (line 269). INVALID KEY means that there is no record for the key field (product number) value, so MASTER-RECORD-FOUND is set to false; otherwise, it is set to true.

Returning to the 300 module, you can see that it simply serves as a springboard to the appropriate maintenance module (or error module). Let's consider these next.

310-PROCESS-ADD and 400-VALIDATE-ADD-RECORD. Since the add maintenance function adds a new record to the inventory file, the first action must be to validate the data in the maintenance record. Validation in the 400 module consists of:

■ Ensuring that there is not a record in the inventory file with the same stock number as that of the record to be added. If the read (lines 226/268) is successful, the record exists. This represents an error condition and the 740 error message module is executed (lines 227–230).

Figure 19-25

(continued on page 552)

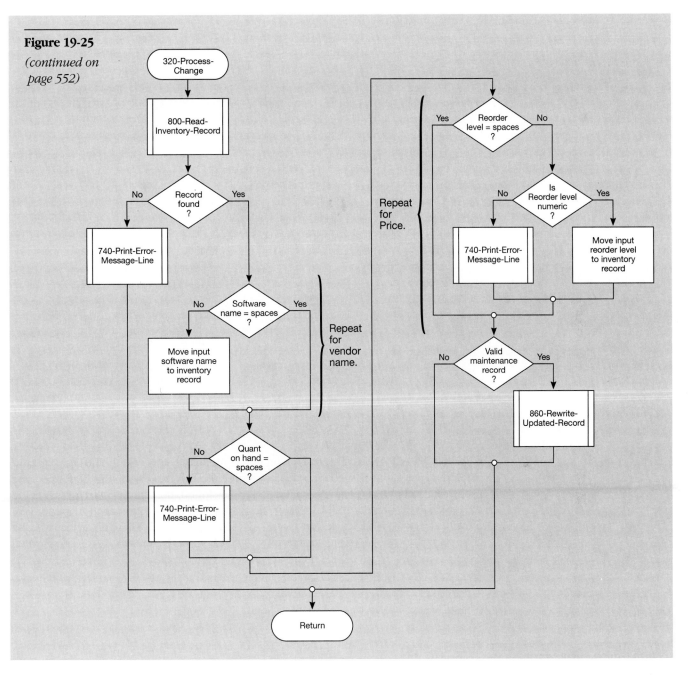

- Ensuring that all fields contain nonblank values (field existence). This is done in lines 231–239. Notice that the redefined alphanumeric versions of the numeric fields are referenced. If any blank fields are detected, the 740 module is performed.
- Ensuring that all numeric fields are indeed numeric. This is done in lines 240–248. In order to avoid having an empty numeric field treated both as a blank field and as a nonnumeric entry, a compound test is used.

After printing the record and an appropriate error message, VALID-MAINTENANCE-RECORD is set to false (line 266 in the 740 module). After execution returns to the 310 module from the 400 module, this switch is tested to determine if the record should be written to the file. If so, the 865 module is performed (line 175) and the record written.

Figure 19-25

(continued from page 551)

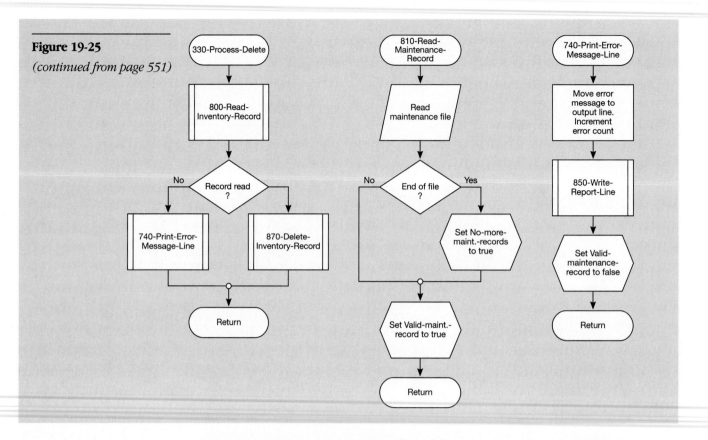

Use of the GO TO statement in the 865 module is the topic of discussion later.

320-PROCESS-CHANGE. The first action in this module is to access the inventory record to be changed. If the desired record is not found, the 740 error module is performed and processing within this module is completed. If it is found, non-empty fields are moved to the inventory record after validation. Invalid fields cause the 740 module to be performed. As with the add maintenance function, VALID-MAINTENANCE-RECORD (which will be false if any error was detected) determines whether or not the changed record is rewritten (lines 211–213).

330-PROCESS-DELETE. Of the three maintenance modules, this is obviously the simplest. A read is executed to obtain the record to be deleted. If the record is found, it is deleted; otherwise, the 740 error module is performed.

Aborting a Program

You should pay particular attention to one other feature of this program. It is the way in which INVALID KEY action is handled for the WRITE, REWRITE, and DELETE statements (lines 219–316). For convenient reference, the 860 module is repeated here.

```
860-REWRITE-UPDATED-RECORD.
    REWRITE INVENTORY-RECORD
      INVALID KEY
        DISPLAY "Invalid key while rewriting"
        GO TO 999-I-O-ABORT
    END-REWRITE.
```

Recall from the BTP-NDX program that any error (INVALID KEY) occurring on the REWRITE statement requires that program execution be terminated. This is equally true for the DELETE statement (line 306) because it has already been determined that the record exists, and the WRITE statement because it has already been determined that there is not already a record in the file. Technically, the BTP-NDX program violates one of the

Figure 19-26

Pseudocode Solution—
Example 19-3

```
000-Maintain-Inventory-File
   Perform 100-Initialize
   Perform 110-Process-Current-Record
      until No-more-maintenance-records
   Perform 120-Finalize

100-Initialize
   Open input I/O Inventory file
   Open Maintenance file
   Open output Report file
   Initialize error-count
   Perform 200-Get-Run-Date
   Perform 700-Print-Page-Headings
   Set No-more-maintenance-records to false
   Read first Maintenance record

110-Process-Current-Record
   Perform 300-Process-Maintenance-Record
   Perform 810-Read-Maintenance-Record

120-Finalize
   Perform 730-Write-Error-Count-Line
   Close files

200-Get-Run-Date
   Accept date from system and move to output area

300-Process-Maintenance-Record
   EVALUATE Maintenance-type
      When A
         Perform 310-Process-Add
      When C
         Perform 320-Process-Change
      When D
         Perform 330-Process-Delete
      When other
         Perform 740-Print-Error-Message-Line

310-Process-Add
   Perform 400-Validate-Add-Record
   If Valid-maintenance-record is true
      Move maintenance-record fields to inventory record
      Perform 865-Write-Added-Record

320-Process-Change
   Perform 800-Read-Inventory-Record
   If master (inventory) record not found
      Perform 740-Print-Error-Message-Line
   else
      If change-software-name field not spaces
      Move change-software-name to inventory record
      If change-software-vendor field not spaces
      Move change-software-vendor to inventory record
      If change-quant-on-hand not spaces
         Perform 740-Print-Error-Message-Line
      If change-reorder-level not spaces
         If change-reorder-level is numeric
           move change-reorder-level to inventory record
         else
           Perform 740-Print-Error-Message-Line
      If change-price not spaces
         If change-price is numeric
         move change-price to inventory record
         else
           Perform 740-Print-Error-Message-Line
      If Valid-maintenance-record switch is true
      Perform 860-Rewrite-Updated-Record

330-Process-Delete
   Perform 800-Read-Inventory-Record
   If master (inventory) record found
      Perform 870-Delete-Inventory-Record
   else
      Perform 740-Print-Error-Message-Line
```

```
400-Validate-Add-Record
   Perform 800-Read-Inventory-Record
   If duplicate inventory record exists
      Perform 740-Print-Error-Message-Line
   If any maintenance-record field is blank
      Perform 740-Print-Error-Message-Line
   If any non-blank maintenance-record numeric field
         is not numeric
      Perform 740-Print-Error-Message-Line

700-Print-Page-Headings
   Move page heading to output line
   Perform 851-Write-Report-Line-at-Top

730-Print-Error-Count-Line
   Move error count to output area
   Perform 850-Write-Report-Line

740-Print-Error-Message-Line
   Move maintenance record and error message to output area
   Perform 850-Write-Report-Line
   Increment error count
   Set Valid-maintenance-record switch to false

800-Read-Inventory-Record
   Move maintenance-stock number to inventory key field
   Read Inventory-File
      invalid key
         Set Master-record-found switch to false
      valid key
         Set Master-record-found switch to true

805-Check-for-Duplicate
   Move maintenance-stock number to inventory key field
   Read Inventory-File
      Invalid key
         Set Master-record-found switch to true
      Valid key
         Set Master-record-found switch to false

810-Read-Maintenance-Record
   Read Maintenance-File
      at end set No-more-maintenance-records to true
   Set Valid-maintenance-record switch to true

850-Write-Report-Line
   Write Report line after advancing line-spacing lines

851-Write-Report-Line-at-Top
   Write Report line after advancing page

860-Rewrite-Updated-Record
   Rewrite Inventory-record
      Invalid key
         Display error message
         Go to 999-I-O-Abort

865-Write-Added-Record
   Write Inventory-record
      Invalid key
         Display error message
         Go to 999-I-O-Abort

870-Delete-Inventory-Record
   Delete Inventory-File
      Invalid key
         Display error message
         Go to 999-I-O-Abort

999-I-O-Abort
   Display maintenance record
   Perform 120-Finalize
   Stop
```

Figure 19-27

Batch Maintenance of an
Indexed File—Example 19-3

```
1        IDENTIFICATION DIVISION.
2
3        PROGRAM-ID. BFM-NDX.
4
5    *      Written by J.Olson/W.Price
6    *      October 5, 1990
7
8    *      This program does Batch File Maintenance on an indexed
9    *      inventory file.  File Maintenance operations include
10   *      adding new records to the file, deleting records from
11   *      the file, and changing data fields on existing records.
12
13   *      Since there will normally be only one maintenance record
14   *      for each stock number, the inventory file is updated from
15   *      each maintenance record.  This means that the maintenance
16   *      records do not have to be in any sequence.
17
18       ENVIRONMENT DIVISION.
19
20       CONFIGURATION SECTION.
21       SOURCE-COMPUTER. IBM-PC.
22
23       INPUT-OUTPUT SECTION.
24       FILE-CONTROL.
25           SELECT INVENTORY-FILE    ASSIGN TO DISK "SOFTWAR2.DI"
26                                    ORGANIZATION IS INDEXED
27                                    ACCESS IS RANDOM
28                                    RECORD KEY IS IR-STOCK-NUMBER.
29           SELECT MAINTENANCE-FILE ASSIGN TO DISK "SWMAINT.DL"
30                                    ORGANIZATION IS LINE SEQUENTIAL.
31           SELECT REPORT-FILE       ASSIGN TO PRINTER "PRN-FILE".
32
33       DATA DIVISION.
34
35       FILE SECTION.
36
37       FD  INVENTORY-FILE.
38       01  INVENTORY-RECORD.
39           10  IR-STOCK-NUMBER      PIC X(5).
40           10  IR-SOFTWARE-NAME     PIC X(30).
41           10  IR-VENDOR-NAME       PIC X(20).
42           10  IR-QUANT-ON-HAND     PIC S9(3).
43           10  IR-REORDER-LEVEL     PIC 9(3).
44           10  IR-PRICE             PIC 9(3)V9(2).
45
46       FD  MAINTENANCE-FILE.
47       01  MAINTENANCE-RECORD.
48           10  MR-MAINTENANCE-TYPE  PIC X(1).
49           10  MR-STOCK-NUMBER      PIC X(5).
50           10  MR-SOFTWARE-NAME     PIC X(30).
51           10  MR-VENDOR-NAME       PIC X(20).
52           10  MR-QUANT-ON-HAND     PIC S9(3).
53           10  MR-QUANT-ON-HAND-X REDEFINES MR-QUANT-ON-HAND  PIC X(3).
54           10  MR-REORDER-LEVEL     PIC 9(3).
55           10  MR-REORDER-LEVEL-X REDEFINES MR-REORDER-LEVEL  PIC X(3).
56           10  MR-PRICE             PIC 9(3)V9(2).
57           10  MR-PRICE-X REDEFINES MR-PRICE                  PIC X(5).
58
59       FD  REPORT-FILE.
60       01  REPORT-LINE              PIC X(112).
61
62       WORKING-STORAGE SECTION.
63
64       01  PROGRAM-SWITCHES.
65           10                                  PIC X.
66               88  NO-MORE-MAINTENANCE-RECORDS VALUE "Y"  FALSE "N".
67           10                                  PIC X.
68               88  VALID-MAINTENANCE-RECORD       VALUE "Y"  FALSE "N".
69           10                                  PIC X.
70               88  MASTER-RECORD-FOUND         VALUE "Y"  FALSE "N".
71
72       01  ACCUMULATORS.
73           10  ERROR-COUNT             PIC 9(3).
74
75       01  OTHER-VARIABLES.
76           10  LINE-SPACING            PIC 9.
77           10  WS-STOCK-NUMBER         PIC X(5).
78
79       01  PAGE-HEADING-LINE.
80           10  PH-MONTH                PIC Z9.
81           10                          PIC X       VALUE "/".
82           10  PH-DAY                  PIC 99.
83           10                          PIC X       VALUE "/".
84           10  PH-YEAR                 PIC 99.
85           10                          PIC X(10)   VALUE SPACES.
86           10                          PIC X(27)   VALUE
87                        "FILE MAINTENANCE ERROR LIST".
88
89       01  MAINTENANCE-ERROR-LINE      VALUE SPACES.
90           10  ME-MAINTENANCE-RECORD       PIC X(67).
91           10                             PIC X(2).
92           10  ME-ERROR-MESSAGE           PIC X(43).
93
94       01  FINAL-TOTAL-LINE.
95           10  FT-ERROR-COUNT             PIC ZZ9.
96           10                             PIC X(29)   VALUE
97                    " error messages were written.".
98
99       01  RUN-DATE.
100          10  RUN-YEAR                    PIC 99.
101          10  RUN-MONTH                   PIC 99.
102          10  RUN-DAY                     PIC 99.
103
104      01  ERROR-MESSAGES.
105          10  INVALID-MAINTENANCE-CODE-MSG    PIC X(43)
106                  VALUE "Maintenance Type Code is invalid".
107          10  INVALID-MAINTENANCE-RECORD-MSG  PIC X(43)
108                  VALUE "Cannot add: stock number is already in file".
109          10  MASTER-RECORD-NOT-FOUND-MSG     PIC X(43)
110                  VALUE "No inventory record for this stock number".
111          10  BLANK-FIELDS-MSG                PIC X(43)
112                  VALUE "ADD record contains 1 or more blank fields".
113          10  NON-NUMERIC-FIELDS-MSG          PIC X(43)
114                  VALUE "Numeric field contains non-numeric data".
115          10  NO-CHANGE-QUANT-ON-HAND-MSG     PIC X(43)
116                  VALUE "Change Quant On Hand w/Trans Update program".
117
118      PROCEDURE DIVISION.
119
120      000-MAINTAIN-INVENTORY-FILE.
121          PERFORM 100-INITIALIZE
122          PERFORM 110-PROCESS-CURRENT-RECORD
123              UNTIL NO-MORE-MAINTENANCE-RECORDS
124          PERFORM 120-FINALIZE
125          STOP RUN.
126
127      100-INITIALIZE.
128          OPEN I-O    INVENTORY-FILE
129          OPEN INPUT  MAINTENANCE-FILE
130          OPEN OUTPUT REPORT-FILE
131          INITIALIZE ERROR-COUNT
132          PERFORM 200-GET-RUN-DATE
133          PERFORM 700-PRINT-PAGE-HEADINGS
134          SET NO-MORE-MAINTENANCE-RECORDS TO FALSE
135          PERFORM 810-READ-MAINTENANCE-RECORD.
136
137      110-PROCESS-CURRENT-RECORD.
138          PERFORM 300-PROCESS-MAINTENANCE-RECORD
139          PERFORM 810-READ-MAINTENANCE-RECORD.
140
141      120-FINALIZE.
142          PERFORM 730-PRINT-ERROR-COUNT-LINE
143          CLOSE INVENTORY-FILE
144              MAINTENANCE-FILE
145              REPORT-FILE.
146
147      200-GET-RUN-DATE.
148          ACCEPT RUN-DATE FROM DATE
149          MOVE RUN-MONTH TO PH-MONTH
150          MOVE RUN-DAY   TO PH-DAY
151          MOVE RUN-YEAR  TO PH-YEAR.
152
153      300-PROCESS-MAINTENANCE-RECORD.
154          EVALUATE MR-MAINTENANCE-TYPE
155              WHEN "A"
156                  PERFORM 310-PROCESS-ADD
157              WHEN "C"
158                  PERFORM 320-PROCESS-CHANGE
159              WHEN "D"
160                  PERFORM 330-PROCESS-DELETE
161              WHEN OTHER
162                  MOVE INVALID-MAINTENANCE-CODE-MSG TO ME-ERROR-MESSAGE
163                  PERFORM 740-PRINT-ERROR-MESSAGE-LINE
164          END-EVALUATE.
165
166      310-PROCESS-ADD.
167          PERFORM 400-VALIDATE-ADD-RECORD
168          IF VALID-MAINTENANCE-RECORD
169              MOVE MR-STOCK-NUMBER   TO IR-STOCK-NUMBER
170              MOVE MR-SOFTWARE-NAME  TO IR-SOFTWARE-NAME
171              MOVE MR-VENDOR-NAME    TO IR-VENDOR-NAME
172              MOVE MR-QUANT-ON-HAND TO IR-QUANT-ON-HAND
173              MOVE MR-REORDER-LEVEL TO IR-REORDER-LEVEL
174              MOVE MR-PRICE         TO IR-PRICE
175              PERFORM 865-WRITE-ADDED-RECORD
176          END-IF.
177
```

Figure 19-27

```
178    320-PROCESS-CHANGE.
179        PERFORM 800-READ-INVENTORY-RECORD
180        IF NOT MASTER-RECORD-FOUND
181            MOVE MASTER-RECORD-NOT-FOUND-MSG TO ME-ERROR-MESSAGE
182            PERFORM 740-PRINT-ERROR-MESSAGE-LINE
183        ELSE
184    *       Stock Number is the record key and cannot be changed.
185            IF MR-SOFTWARE-NAME NOT = SPACES
186                MOVE MR-SOFTWARE-NAME TO IR-SOFTWARE-NAME
187            END-IF
188            IF MR-VENDOR-NAME NOT = SPACES
189                MOVE MR-VENDOR-NAME TO IR-VENDOR-NAME
190            END-IF
191            IF MR-QUANT-ON-HAND-X NOT = SPACES
192                MOVE NO-CHANGE-QUANT-ON-HAND-MSG TO ME-ERROR-MESSAGE
193                PERFORM 740-PRINT-ERROR-MESSAGE-LINE
194            END-IF
195            IF MR-REORDER-LEVEL-X NOT = SPACES
196                IF MR-REORDER-LEVEL IS NUMERIC
197                    MOVE MR-REORDER-LEVEL TO IR-REORDER-LEVEL
198                ELSE
199                    MOVE NON-NUMERIC-FIELDS-MSG TO ME-ERROR-MESSAGE
200                    PERFORM 740-PRINT-ERROR-MESSAGE-LINE
201                END-IF
202            END-IF
203            IF MR-PRICE-X NOT = SPACES
204                IF MR-PRICE IS NUMERIC
205                    MOVE MR-PRICE TO IR-PRICE
206                ELSE
207                    MOVE NON-NUMERIC-FIELDS-MSG TO ME-ERROR-MESSAGE
208                    PERFORM 740-PRINT-ERROR-MESSAGE-LINE
209                END-IF
210            END-IF
211            IF VALID-MAINTENANCE-RECORD
212                PERFORM 860-REWRITE-UPDATED-RECORD
213            END-IF
214        END-IF.
215
216    330-PROCESS-DELETE.
217        PERFORM 800-READ-INVENTORY-RECORD
218        IF MASTER-RECORD-FOUND
219            PERFORM 870-DELETE-INVENTORY-RECORD
220        ELSE
221            MOVE MASTER-RECORD-NOT-FOUND-MSG TO ME-ERROR-MESSAGE
222            PERFORM 740-PRINT-ERROR-MESSAGE-LINE
223        END-IF.
224
225    400-VALIDATE-ADD-RECORD.
226        PERFORM 800-READ-INVENTORY-RECORD
227        IF MASTER-RECORD-FOUND
228            MOVE INVALID-MAINTENANCE-RECORD-MSG TO ME-ERROR-MESSAGE
229            PERFORM 740-PRINT-ERROR-MESSAGE-LINE
230        END-IF
231        IF    MR-STOCK-NUMBER   = SPACES
232        OR MR-SOFTWARE-NAME   = SPACES
233        OR MR-VENDOR-NAME     = SPACES
234        OR MR-QUANT-ON-HAND-X = SPACES
235        OR MR-REORDER-LEVEL-X = SPACES
236        OR MR-PRICE-X         = SPACES
237            MOVE BLANK-FIELDS-MSG TO ME-ERROR-MESSAGE
238            PERFORM 740-PRINT-ERROR-MESSAGE-LINE
239        END-IF
240        IF   (MR-QUANT-ON-HAND  IS NOT NUMERIC
241               AND MR-QUANT-ON-HAND-X NOT = SPACES)
242        OR (MR-REORDER-LEVEL  IS NOT NUMERIC
243               AND MR-REORDER-LEVEL-X NOT = SPACES)
244        OR (MR-PRICE          IS NOT NUMERIC
245               AND MR-PRICE-X        NOT = SPACES)
246            MOVE NON-NUMERIC-FIELDS-MSG TO ME-ERROR-MESSAGE
247            PERFORM 740-PRINT-ERROR-MESSAGE-LINE
248        END-IF.
249
250    700-PRINT-PAGE-HEADINGS.
251        MOVE PAGE-HEADING-LINE TO REPORT-LINE
252        PERFORM 851-WRITE-REPORT-LINE-AT-TOP
253        MOVE 2 TO LINE-SPACING.
254
255    730-PRINT-ERROR-COUNT-LINE.
256        MOVE ERROR-COUNT TO FT-ERROR-COUNT
257        MOVE FINAL-TOTAL-LINE TO REPORT-LINE
258        MOVE 3 TO LINE-SPACING
259        PERFORM 850-WRITE-REPORT-LINE.
260
261    740-PRINT-ERROR-MESSAGE-LINE.
262        MOVE MAINTENANCE-RECORD TO ME-MAINTENANCE-RECORD
263        MOVE MAINTENANCE-ERROR-LINE TO REPORT-LINE
264        PERFORM 850-WRITE-REPORT-LINE
265        ADD 1 TO ERROR-COUNT
266        SET VALID-MAINTENANCE-RECORD TO FALSE.
267
268    800-READ-INVENTORY-RECORD.
269        MOVE MR-STOCK-NUMBER TO IR-STOCK-NUMBER
270        READ INVENTORY-FILE
271            INVALID KEY
272                SET MASTER-RECORD-FOUND TO FALSE
273            NOT INVALID KEY
274                SET MASTER-RECORD-FOUND TO TRUE
275        END-READ.
276
277    810-READ-MAINTENANCE-RECORD.
278        READ MAINTENANCE-FILE
279            AT END SET NO-MORE-MAINTENANCE-RECORDS TO TRUE
280        END-READ
281        SET VALID-MAINTENANCE-RECORD TO TRUE.
282
283    850-WRITE-REPORT-LINE.
284        WRITE REPORT-LINE
285            AFTER ADVANCING LINE-SPACING LINES.
286
287    851-WRITE-REPORT-LINE-AT-TOP.
288        WRITE REPORT-LINE
289            AFTER ADVANCING PAGE.
290
291    860-REWRITE-UPDATED-RECORD.
292        REWRITE INVENTORY-RECORD
293            INVALID KEY
294                DISPLAY "Invalid key while rewriting"
295                GO TO 999-I-O-ABORT
296        END-REWRITE.
297
298    865-WRITE-ADDED-RECORD.
299        WRITE INVENTORY-RECORD
300            INVALID KEY
301                DISPLAY "Invalid key while writing"
302                GO TO 999-I-O-ABORT
303        END-WRITE.
304
305    870-DELETE-INVENTORY-RECORD.
306        DELETE INVENTORY-FILE
307            INVALID KEY
308                DISPLAY "Invalid key while deleting"
309                GO TO 999-I-O-ABORT
310        END-DELETE.
311
312    999-I-O-ABORT.
313        DISPLAY INVENTORY-RECORD
314        DISPLAY "Aborting maintenance program."
315        PERFORM 120-FINALIZE
316        STOP RUN.
```

fundamental rules of structured programming by having program termination in two different places (the 120 module and within an I-O module). However, to conform to this aspect of structured programming is not practical with COBOL in this case.

In the BFM-NDX program, the problem is compounded because there are three modules in which the program can be terminated: 860, 865, and 870. Rather than "sprinkling" STOP RUN statements in different modules, a special module numbered 999 is included to accommodate an aborted run. Notice in the three modules that transfer control to it, the GO TO statement is used, rather than the PERFORM. Recall that this statement transfers control in the same way as the PERFORM, except that no return is possible. Since processing is terminated in the 999 module, it would be misleading (although not incorrect) to transfer control with a PERFORM.

An alternative to the error termination procedures of this program would be using declaratives and the USE statement. To do so would involve the following changes:

1. A declaratives section would be inserted following the PROCEDURE DIVISION header

2. The statement following USE statement would be required to identify the file for error handling:

```
USE AFTER ERROR PROCEDURE ON INVENTORY-FILE.
```

3. The existing 999 module would be inserted following the USE statement

4. The INVALID KEY phrases in the input-output statements of modules 860, 865, and 870 would be deleted

5. The I-O status code would need to be interrogated in order to determine the exact nature of the error message to be printed (see the error message displays of modules 860, 865, and 870)

The last item would require detailed testing for the variety of codes and would be clumsy. For the purpose of this program, the error termination technique used in BFM-NDX is relatively simple and quite adequate to do the job.

Chapter Summary

This chapter has concentrated on batch processing applications, using the inventory file as the basis for illustration. You have learned about batch file updating and batch file maintenance via three examples:

1. Traditional magnetic tape-oriented master-detail sequential processing involves the updating of data in a master file from transaction data in a transaction file. Because of the sequential nature of magnetic tape, both files must be sorted on a common key field. For the BTP-SEQ (batch transaction processing—sequential) program, the product number was the common key. The processing cycle involves reading the next sequential record from one of the files, then reading the next sequential record from the other and looking for a match of the key field values. The quantity-on-hand field of the master is updated by data from the transaction records. An updated master file is created by writing each master record to a new file. Any transaction record that does not have a corresponding master record represents an error condition and is written to an error report.

2. With high-capacity disk drives in wide use, master files in almost all applications have random accessing capabilities. The second example program was BTP-NDX (batch transaction processing—indexed); it utilizes random access of the master. This program differs from BTP-SEQ in two important respects:

   - Repeated processing is controlled by sequentially reading the transaction file. For each transaction record with a new product number, the corresponding master record is read (using random access).

   - The updated master record is rewritten to disk and thus replaces the original copy.

3. In addition to master-transaction processing, maintenance operations must be performed on the master file periodically. This includes the operations of adding new records, changing field contents in existing records, and deleting existing records. This is illustrated by the BFM-NDX (batch file maintenance—indexed) program. With the addition of new records and entering new values into fields of existing records, extensive data validation is done.

Questions and Exercises

Key Terminology

Give a brief description of each of the following terms that were introduced in this chapter.

batch updating
maintenance operations
master file
master-transaction processing
transaction file

General Questions

1. Master-transaction processing is very common among business applications. What are the two input files used and what type of data does each contain?

2. When sequential master-transaction processing or "batch updating" is being done, what must be determined before the program can end? Why is this important?

3. What is the difference between batch updating a sequential master file and an indexed master file?

4. When indexed master-transaction processing is being done, what indicates that updating is finished?

5. What is the difference between reading and writing when sequential versus indexed batch updating is to be accomplished?

6. Why is it necessary to abort a batch update program that is using an indexed master file? How could this be done?

Questions Relating to the Example Programs

1. In the BTP-SEQ program, an EVALUATE statement is used to take the appropriate action. Replace this EVALUATE with an IF statement.

2. The BTP-NDX (batch update of the indexed file), requires that the transaction file be in sequence by the Stock-number field. Would the program function properly (that is, would all master records be correctly updated) if the transaction file were not in sequence by the stock number? Explain your answer and describe any implications of the non-sequenced transaction file.

3. In the BTP-NDX program, what would occur if the REWRITE statement in the 860 module were replaced with a WRITE statement?

4. The BFM-NDX program does not allow the stock number to be changed. What would occur in the program if an IF sequence for stock number (such as that in lines 185–187 for the software name) were inserted at line 184?

5. What changes would be necessary to the 320 module in order to avoid the problem of the preceding Question 4 and to allow a stock number change?

Programming Assignments

19-1 Batch Transaction Updating With Sequential Files

At the end of each term, the data processing department at the Computer Institute of Technology must update student records based on the "transactions" of the completed term. This involves incorporating the data from the enrollment file into the student master file.

Output Requirements:

A printed report with the following output and format.

```
                              GRADE REPORT

Student Number    XXX-XX-XXXX      Name X--------X  X--------X

XXX-XX-XXXX   X--------X  X--------X  ZZZ.9  ZZZ.9   Z.99

Course  Code      Description           Units      Grade    Points

        XXXX    X---------------X       ZZ.9        X        ZZ.9
        XXXX    X---------------X       ZZ.9        X        ZZ.9

Current  semester       GPA  ZZ.9      ZZZ.9                 ZZZ.9

         Cumulative     GPA  ZZ.9      ZZZ.9                 ZZZ.9
```

Note that the output comes from three sources:

Student record: Student name

Grade record: Course data (code, description,...)

Calculated: New cumulative units and grade points

Input Description:

File names: STUDENTS.DL and GRADES.DL

Record descriptions: See Appendix A

Note: Both of these files must be sorted on the student number field.

Processing Requirements:

Sort requirements:

1. Write a program to sort the Students file on the student number field. Write only the first six records to the output file. This will keep your Students file small and avoid the problem of many pages of output.

2. Write a program to sort the Grades file on the student number field.

Grade processing:

1. Read and match each student master record and its corresponding grade records.

2. Print the first line of the grade report (student name and number).

3. Determine the units earned from the grade as follows:

Grade	Earned units
A, B, C, or D	Equal to input Course units
F or W	0

4. Calculate the points earned for this grade record as the Earned units times Grade points, where Grade points are determined as follows.

Grade	Grade Points
A	4
B	3
C	2
D	1

5. Print each detail line (from the grade file) as the records are read and processed.

6. Add the calculated units and points for the current grade record to the cumulative current units and points.

7. When the grade record is detected for the next student:
   a. Write the current semester summary line.
   b. Write the cumulative line.
   c. In the student record, update the "last semester" fields by replacing them with the newly calculated current semester values. Also, update the cumulative fields.
   d. REWRITE the student student record. (*Note:* Example 19-1 creates a new file; this program will update the existing file.)
8. Skip to a new page for each grade report.
9. Write a copy of each unmatched grade record to an error file.

19-2 Batch Transaction Updating With an Indexed File

The requirements of this assignment are identical to those of Assignment 19-1, except that a direct access file is used for access to the student data.

Output Requirements:

See the Output Requirements for Assignment 19-1.

Input Description:

File names: STUDENTS.DI and GRADES.DL
Record descriptions: See Appendix A
Note: The Grades file must be sorted on the student number field..

Processing Requirements:

Sort requirements:

1. Write a program to sort the Grades file on the student number field.

Grade processing:

1. Read the next sequential grade record.
2. If the grade record is for the next student:
   a. Write the current semester summary line.
   b. Write the cumulative line.
   c. In the student record, update the "last semester" fields by replacing them with the newly calculated current semester values. Also, update the cumulative fields.
   d. REWRITE the student record.
   e. Read the student record (direct access) corresponding to the new student number of the grade record. If no student record is found, write the grade record to an error file.
   f. Print the first line of the grade report (student name and number).
3. Determine the units earned from the grade as follows:

Grade	Earned units
A, B, C, or D	Equal to input Course units
F or W	0

4. Calculate the points earned for this grade record as the Earned units times Grade points, where Grade points are determined as follows.

Grade	Grade Points
A	4
B	3
C	2
D	1

5. Print each detail line (from the grade file) as the records are read and processed.
6. Add the calculated units and points for the current grade record to the cumulative current units and points.
7. Skip to a new page for each grade report.

FILE PROCESSING AND MAINTENANCE—INTERACTIVE

Chapter Objectives

In Chapter 19, you learned about updating a master file from data stored in a transaction file (batch processing). Two broad types of processing were described in the context of the inventory file: transaction and maintenance. These same two processing types are illustrated in this chapter, using interactive processing via the following two examples:

- The quantity-on-hand field of the indexed software inventory file is updated from data entered through the keyboard. The program allows for four categories of entries: receipts of goods, returns, inventory adjustments, and sales. Updating is done in place.

- The standard maintenance operations with indexed software inventory file of record entry, modification, and deletion are done through the keyboard. One of the features of this program is the inclusion of security measures that control access to the program and provide a history of changes.

A primary focus of these two examples is controlling the input from the user with suitable recovery capabilities for incorrect entries by the user.

About Batch and Interactive File Updating

Batch transaction and maintenance processing as illustrated in Chapter 19 is still encountered in many types of processing systems. However, for most applications, it is simply better to perform these operations interactively with instant updating of files. The inventory file is a classic example. Consider the UNISOFT customer who calls with the immediate need for 50 copies of a particular software product. Are they in stock? With a batch transaction processing system, you only know the quantity on hand as of the last processing run; you do not know what has occurred since then. In other words, you cannot be certain that the desired 50 copies are indeed in stock.

On the other hand, with *on-line processing*, the user interacts with the computer, and data in the master file is updated while the transaction is being entered into the computer. As a rule, interactive updating programs are more complex than batch updating programs. You have already seen this in Chapter 12, in which both batch and interactive data validation are described. With batch processing, the program must identify any errors existing in the input record, then reject that record. With interactive processing, the program must identify those same errors. However, as each error is detected, the user must be informed and given remedial action to take. As a result, the interactive data validation program of Chapter 12 is more than 50% larger than its batch counterpart. As you will see in studying this chapter's two examples, the actual processing functions of interactive file updating are much the same as those of batch updating. However, the interaction with the user adds considerable complexity to the programs.

Interactive Transaction Processing

Example Definition— Example 20-1

This first example is an interactive parallel to Example 19-2, batch updating of an indexed file. In an actual business environment, the functions illustrated by this example would likely be elements of other components of the system. For example, subtracting the quantity sold from the quantity-on-hand field of the inventory file would most likely be done in an order processing program. (You will see this in the order processing example of Chapter 21.) To an extent, this interactive transaction updating example is somewhat contrived; however, it illustrates well the types of actions required when updating interactively.

Example 20-1 Interactive Transaction Updating an Indexed File

Problem Description

The UNISOFT inventory system requires interactive updating of the indexed inventory file. Each transaction is entered into the system and the quantity-on-handfield of the file is updated (in place). There are four types of transactions: receipts from manufacturers, returns from customers, inventory adjustments, and sales to customers.

Input/Output Description

Processing is to be done in place. That is, an inventory record is read, updated, then rewritten to its original position in the file.

File name: SOFTWAR2.DI

Record format:

Field	Positions	Data Type	Format
Stock number	1–5	Alphanumeric	
Not used	6–55		
Quantity on hand	56–58	Numeric	S999
Not used	59–66		

Key field: Stock number

Transaction Input Data

The following input from the keyboard is to update the quantity-on-hand field.

Receipts from manufacturers—add to quantity on hand

Returns from customers—add to quantity on hand

Inventory adjustments—add to quantity on hand

Sales to customers—subtract from quantity on hand

Processing Requirements

This program is to function as follows:

1. Request from the user the product number of the inventory record to be updated.
2. Access the record from the file and display it on the screen. If there is no record in the file, display an error message.
3. Query the user for type of transaction (receipt, return, adjustment, or sale).
4. Accept the transaction quantity.
5. Compute the updated quantity on hand by adding the transaction if receipt, return, or adjustment and subtracting if sale.
6. If the resulting quantity is negative, warn the user. Provide the user with the ability to abort this entry.
7. Rewrite the updated inventory record (unless aborted due to negative value).

Trial Runs with the Interactive Transaction Updating Program

If you think back to Chapter 13's coverage of group totals, you will recall that sample reports were presented before the discussion of the program solution. Looking at the output first and examining what was required was helpful in placing the needs of the program in a meaningful context before proceeding to the solution. This notion of getting a "feel" for the output is every bit as valuable with an interactive program such as Example 20-1. To that end, this section describes a sequence of file update activities that you should perform with the inventory file; it involves processing the indicated records as follows.

Product Number	Quantity on Hand	Action
37188		Not the desired record; no action.
37281	80	A Receipt transaction will be entered, but will be aborted without updating the file.
53351	176	This record will be updated by a Receipt transaction (quantity of 30).
15589	180	This record will be updated by a Return transaction (quantity of 5).
37281	80	This record will be updated by a Sale transaction (quantity of 10).
10164	93	This record will be updated by an Adjustment transaction (quantity of -10).

The sequence of steps you take will include making incorrect entries so that you will see the variety of provisions that the programmer must consider in writing an interactive program. After you complete the session at your computer, you will better understand the needs of this program.

The first step is to copy the program ITP-NDX.CBL and the software file SOFTWAR2.DI from the data/program diskette that accompanies this book onto a work diskette or your hard disk. Then compile and run the program. When run, the program will greet you with an introduction screen and ask if you wish to continue. Respond with Y (for Yes) and the following will appear on your screen.

```
90/10/27              UPDATE QUANTITY ON HAND              8:27
~~~~~~~~~~~~~~~~~~~~~~~~~~~~~~~~~~~~~~~~~~~~~~~~~~~~~~~~~~~~~~~~~~
Enter the stock number to be updated (strike the Enter key
to terminate): _____
```

Test the program as follows.
Access record 37188 and abort data entry (wrong record)

1. Enter the stock number 37188. The partial record for this stock number—together with a query—will be displayed as follows.

```
Stock number: 37188    Software name: UnderWord, Rev 128
                       Current Quantity On Hand:  90
Correct record <y/n>? _
```

2. Assume that this is not the record you desire, so type N (Not the correct record). You do not need to strike the Enter key.

Access record 37281, enter a Receipt transaction, and abort the transaction

3. Enter the stock number 37281. The partial record for this stock number will be displayed as follows.

```
Stock number: 37281    Software name: UnderCalc, Rev 256

                       Current Quantity On Hand:  80
```

4. Type Y (Yes, this is the correct record).

5. You will be presented with the following list of transaction type options.

```
Transaction Types:  1  Receipt
                    2  Return
                    3  Adjustment
                    4  Sale
```

Type the digit 1 (transaction type is a Receipt).

6. In response to the request for the quantity, type 25 and strike the Enter key.

7. You will be presented with the following list of options.

```
Options:  1  Updated quantity is correct.
          2  Data is not correct; retry.
          3  Cancel this transaction.
```

Type the digit 2, indicating that the data you have entered is not correct.

8. You will be returned to the Transaction Type selection (shown in the preceding Step 5). Type the digit 1 (transaction type is a Receipt).

9. In response to the request for the quantity, type 30 and strike the Enter key.

10. In response to the option request (see Step 7), type 4, an invalid entry. The following error message will be displayed at the bottom of the screen.

```
       THAT RESPONSE IS INVALID! Strike the Enter key to try again... _
```

11. After striking Enter, type 3 (for Option 3) to cancel this transaction. This aborts any change for this record and displays the request for the stock number of the next record to be processed.

12. To confirm that the quantity on hand has not been changed, type the stock number of the record just aborted—37281. You will see that the quantity on hand is still its original value 80. Type N to abort any further activity with this record.

Access record 53351 and enter a Receipt transaction

13. Enter the stock number 53351. The partial record for this stock number will be displayed as follows.

```
Stock number: 53351      Software name: QBase 7000
                         Current Quantity On Hand: 176
```

Type Y to indicate that this is the desired record.

14. In response to the transaction type request (see Step 5), type 5, which is an invalid entry. The error message of Step 10 will be displayed at the bottom of the screen.

15. After striking Enter, type 1 (Transaction type 1) for a receipt. In response to the request for transaction quantity, type 30 and then strike the Enter key. The updated quantity 206 and the Option list (see Step 7) will be displayed.

16. Type 1 (for Option 1), indicating that the quantity is correct. This causes the record to be rewritten and the screen to display the request for the next stock number.

17. To confirm that the record was actually updated, enter the stock number 53351. The displayed quantity on hand should be 206 (or else you have done something wrong in your entry sequence). Strike N to abort further action with this record.

Attempt to access record 15588; it does not exist

18. Enter the stock number 15588. The following error message will be displayed at the bottom of the screen.

```
There is no inventory record for Stock # 15588
When you are ready to continue, strike the Enter key...
```

Strike the Enter key.

Access record 15589 and enter a Return transaction

19. Enter the stock number 15589. The partial record for this stock number will be displayed as follows.

```
Stock number: 15589    Software name: Travelling Side Punch
                       Current Quantity On Hand: 180
```

Type Y to indicate that this is the desired record.

20. For the Transaction type, type 2 (for a Return).

21. For the quantity, type -5 (negative 5, an error) and strike the Enter key. The following error message will be displayed at the bottom of the screen.

```
Negative quantities are valid only for Adjustments!
   Strike the Enter key to try again...
```

22. Strike the Enter key and you will be requested to reenter the transaction quantity. Type 5 and strike the Enter key. The updated quantity on hand will be displayed as 185.

23. Type 1 for Option 1 (Updated quantity is correct). The record will be rewritten and you will be requested to enter the next stock number.

Access record 37281 and enter a Sale transaction

24. Enter the stock number 37281. The partial record for this stock number will be displayed as follows.

```
Stock number: 37281    Software name: UnderCalc, Rev 256
                       Current Quantity On Hand:  80
```

Type Y to indicate that this is the desired record.

25. For the Transaction type, type 4 (for a Sale). For the quantity, type 100 and strike the Enter key. The following error message will be displayed at the bottom of the screen.

```
This transaction makes the quantity on hand NEGATIVE!
Enter Y to confirm the negative quantity on hand, or enter N to
try again... _
```

Type N to abort this entry.

26. You will be prompted to reenter the transaction quantity; type 10 and strike the Enter key.

27. Type 1 for Option 1 (Updated quantity is correct). The record will be rewritten and you will be requested to enter the next stock number.

Access record 10164 and enter an Adjustment transaction

28. Enter the stock number 10164. The partial record for this stock number will be displayed as follows.

```
Stock number: 10164    Software name: Sluggish Writer
                       Current Quantity On Hand:  93
```

Type Y to indicate that this is the desired record.

29. For the Transaction type, type 3 (for an Adjustment). For the quantity, type -10 and strike the Enter key. Remember, an Adjustment can be either positive or negative. Notice that the updated quantity on hand is 83.

30. Type 1 for Option 1 (Updated quantity is correct). The record will be rewritten and you will be requested to enter the next stock number.

31. Strike the Enter key without typing anything and processing will be terminated.

The preceding sequence of steps should give you a good idea of the program actions. You might wish to experiment some more. Note that if you had written this program, you would perform all of the preceding actions *and more* as part of the program testing in order to exercise every possible component of the program before placing it into service.

Program Structure and Logic—Example 20-1

The basic action of this example is relatively simple: accept a product number from the user, access the record, accept a transaction quantity from the user, calculate the new quantity on hand, and rewrite the record. The structure chart of Figure 20-1 reflects this simplicity in the form of a relatively few number of modules and a limited structure.

However, the logic of the example is considerably more complex because of interaction with the user. That is, each entry from the user must be checked and action taken for incorrect entries. The program logic for this solution is shown in the flowchart of Figure 20-2 and the pseudocode of Figure 20-3 (page 572).

Inspecting the logic of the 400 module gives you an idea of the extent to which checks must be performed. That is:

1. If the user-entered transaction quantity is negative and the transaction type is not 3 (an adjustment), an error action must be taken.

2. If the transaction type is 1, 2, or 3, the transaction quantity must be added to the quantity on hand; otherwise, it must be subtracted.

3. If the new quantity on hand is negative, the user must be queried.

4. A switch must be set according to the response of the user regarding handling a negative new quantity on hand.

The 110, 300, and 410 modules include similar conditional actions. You probably recognize much of this logic from running the program.

Notice in the flowchart and pseudocode that the 300 module uses post-tests. That is, the test for repetition of the PERFORM-UNTIL statements are executed at the end of the module, rather than at the beginning.

Figure 20-1

Structure Chart for Example 20-1

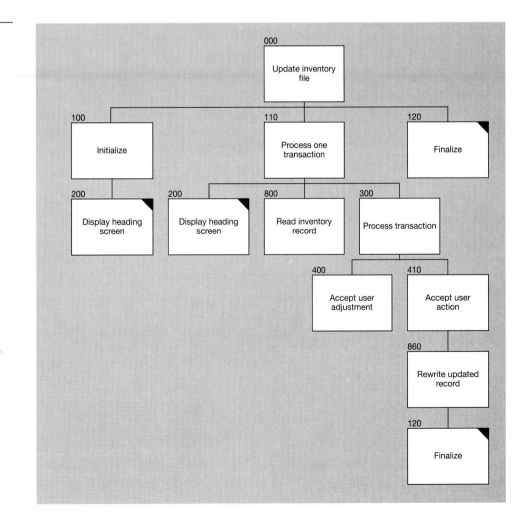

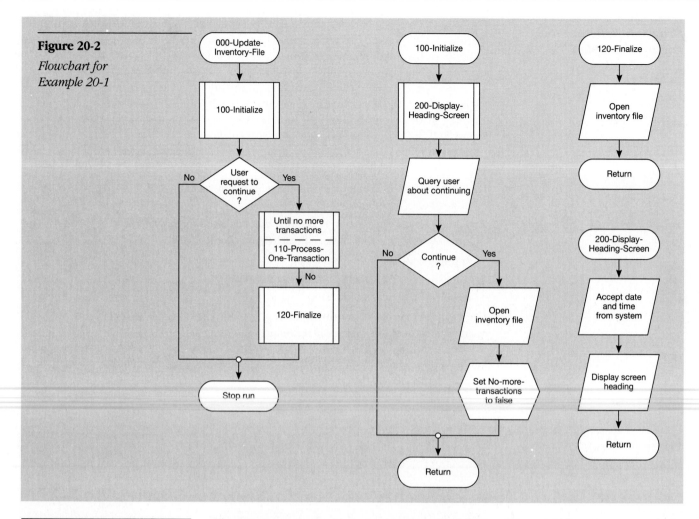

Figure 20-2

Flowchart for Example 20-1

Program Solution—Example 20-1

The program solution is shown in Figure 20-4 (pages 573 and 574). Consistent with the extensive logic of this program, you see the following programmed switches defined (beginning at line 40):

NO-MORE-TRANSACTIONS This switch (initially true) provides repeated execution of record processing. It is set to false in the 100 module if the user wishes to continue. Repetition occurs only if it is false. During repeated execution of the 110 module, it is set to true if the user does not enter a product number (line 212).

MASTER-RECORD-FOUND This switch is set (in the 800 module) to true if the requested record is found (NOT INVALID KEY) and to false if the requested record is not found. It is tested at line 215.

QUANTITY-IS-VALID This switch indicates whether or not the input transaction quantity is valid. Two conditions can produce an invalid transaction quantity: (1) a negative entry for other than an Adjustment transaction (type 3) and (2) a quantity that results in a negative new quantity on hand. This switch is set in the 400 module and controls repeated execution of the module (from the 300 module from line 259).

TYPE-IS-VALID This switch is used to ensure that the user enters an acceptable transaction type (1, 2, 3, or 4). It controls repeatedly requesting the transaction type from the user until a correct type is entered (beginning at line 246 of the 300 module). (Descriptions of the switches are continued on page 572.)

Figure 20-2

(continued on page 570)

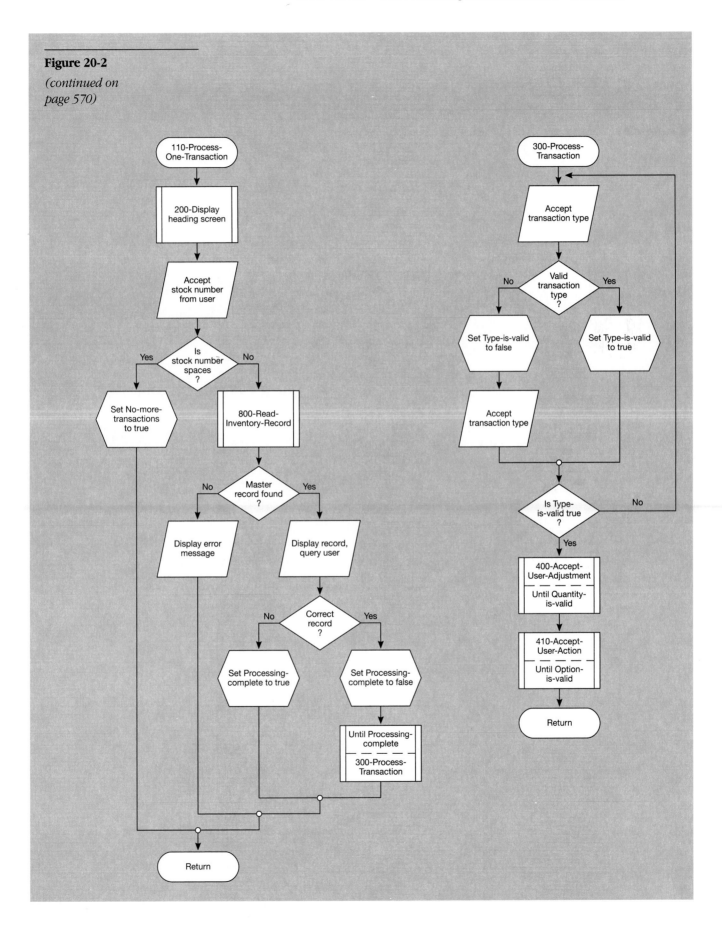

Figure 20-2

(continued from page 569)

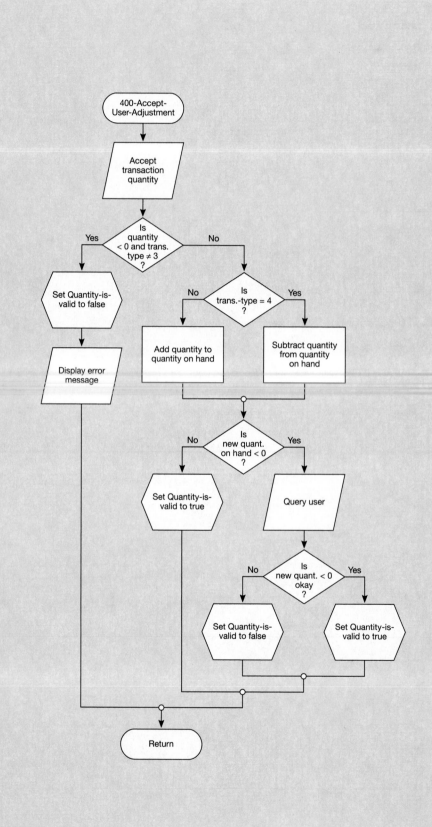

Figure 20-2

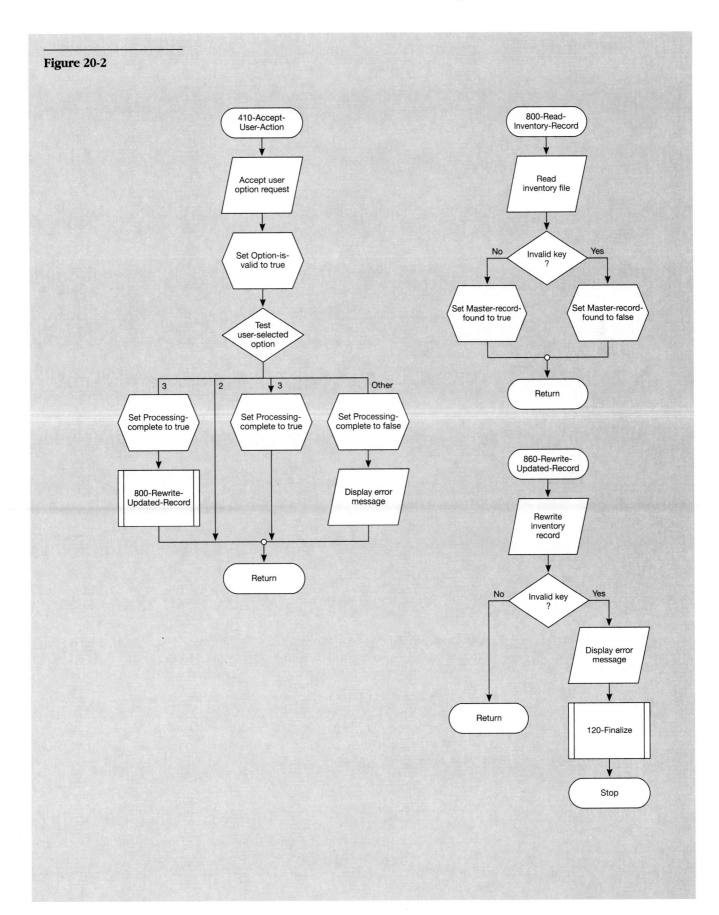

Figure 20-3

Pseudocode for Example 20-1

```
000-Update-Inventory-File
    Perform 100-Initialize
    If user requests to continue
        Perform 110-Process-One-Transaction
            until No-more-transactions
        Perform 120-Finalize

100-Initialize
    Perform 200-Display-Heading-Screen
    Query user about continuing
    If user requests to continue
        Open inventory file for I-O
        Set No-more-transactions switch to false

110-Process-One-Transaction
    Perform 200-Display-Heading-Screen
    Accept Stock-number from user
    If Stock-number contains spaces
        Set No-more-transactions switch to true
    else
        Perform 800-Read-Inventory-Record
        If master record found
            Ask user if this is correct record
            If correct record
                Set Processing-complete switch to false
                Perform 300-Process-Transaction
                    until Processing-complete is true
            else
                Set Processing-complete switch to true
        else
            Display record not found message

120-Finalize
    Close inventory file

200-Get-Run-Date
    Obtain the current date and time
    Move date and time to display header
    Display heading screen

300-Process-Transaction
    Perform with test after until Type-is-valid switch is true
        Accept transaction type from user
        If transaction type 1, 2, 3, or 4
            Set Type-is-valid switch to true
        else
            Set Type-is-valid switch to false
            Display error message
    Perform 400-Accept-User-Adjustment with test after
        until Quantity-is-valid switch is true
    Perform 410-Accept-User-Action with test after
        until Option-is-valid switch is true
```

```
400-Accept-User-Adjustment
    Accept adjustment quantity from user
    If adjustment quantity is negative and is not 3
        Set Quantity-is-valid switch to false
        Display error message
    else
        Evaluate Transaction-type
            When 1, 2, or 3
                Add adjustment quantity to quantity on hand
            When 4
                Subtract adjustment quantity from quantity on hand
        If updated quantity on hand is not negative
            Set Quantity-is-valid switch to true
        else
            Query user: negative quantity okay?
            If negative quantity okay
                Set Quantity-is-valid switch to true
            else
                Set Quantity-is-valid switch to false

410-Accept-User-Action
    Accept user option (for current update)
    Set Option-is-valid switch to true
    Evaluate requested option
        when 1
            Move updated quantity on hand to record
            Perform 860-Rewrite-Updated-Record
            Set Processing-completed switch to true
        when 2
            Continue
        when 3
            Set Processing-completed switch to false
        when other
            Set Option-is-valid switch to false
            Display error message

800-Read-Inventory-Record
    Read Inventory-File
    invalid key
        Set Master-record-found to false
    not invalid key
        Set Master-record-found to true

860-Rewrite-Updated-Record
    Rewrite Inventory-record
    invalid key
        Display error message
        Perform 120-Finalize
        Stop run
```

OPTION-IS-VALID This switch is similar to TYPE-IS-VALID in that it ensures that the user enters an acceptable option (1, 2, or 3) designating the action to be taken with the currently displayed record. It controls execution of the PERFORM at line 261.

PROCESSING-COMPLETE After a transaction quantity is entered, the user is given the option of rewriting the record, making a change, or aborting changes to the record through repeated execution of the 300 module from the 110 module (line 221). A value of true (set at line 301 or 305) for this switch indicates that processing for this record is completed.

By inspecting the modules of the PROCEDURE DIVISION, you can see that the code is a straightforward application of the logic illustrated by the flowchart and pseudocode. In the 300 module, you see that the in-line and two out-of-line PERFORM statements include the WITH TEST AFTER phrase. Remember that with this phrase, the PERFORM sequence or module is executed and then the test is made to determine if it should be executed again. That is, the test is made at the end of the sequence execution.

Figure 20-4

The ITP-NDX Program—Example 20-1
(continued on page 574)

(continued on page 574)

```cobol
1        IDENTIFICATION DIVISION.
2
3        PROGRAM-ID. ITP-NDX.
4
5    *    Written by J.Olson
6    *    Oct. 6, 1990
7
8    *    This program does Interactive Transaction Processing by
9    *    updating an Indexed inventory file.  Transactions are
10   *    processed in random order, and the inventory record is
11   *    rewritten after each transaction.
12
13       ENVIRONMENT DIVISION.
14
15       CONFIGURATION SECTION.
16       SOURCE-COMPUTER. IBM-PC.
17
18       INPUT-OUTPUT SECTION.
19       FILE-CONTROL.
20           SELECT INVENTORY-FILE    ASSIGN TO DISK "SOFTWAR2.DI"
21                                    ORGANIZATION IS INDEXED
22                                    ACCESS IS RANDOM
23                                    RECORD KEY IS IR-STOCK-NUMBER.
24
25       DATA DIVISION.
26
27       FILE SECTION.
28
29       FD  INVENTORY-FILE.
30       01  INVENTORY-RECORD.
31           10  IR-STOCK-NUMBER       PIC X(5).
32           10  IR-SOFTWARE-NAME      PIC X(30).
33           10  IR-VENDOR-NAME        PIC X(20).
34           10  IR-QUANT-ON-HAND      PIC S9(3).
35           10  IR-REORDER-LEVEL      PIC 9(3).
36           10  IR-PRICE              PIC 9(3)V9(2).
37
38       WORKING-STORAGE SECTION.
39
40       01  PROGRAM-SWITCHES.
41           10                        PIC X.
42               88  NO-MORE-TRANSACTIONS   VALUE "Y"  FALSE "N".
43           10                        PIC X.
44               88  MASTER-RECORD-FOUND    VALUE "Y"  FALSE "N".
45           10                        PIC X.
46               88  QUANTITY-IS-VALID      VALUE "Y"  FALSE "N".
47           10                        PIC X.
48               88  TYPE-IS-VALID          VALUE "Y"  FALSE "N".
49           10                        PIC X.
50               88  OPTION-IS-VALID        VALUE "Y"  FALSE "N".
51           10                        PIC X.
52               88  PROCESSING-COMPLETED   VALUE "Y"  FALSE "N".
53
54       01  ARITHMETIC-FIELDS.
55           10  ADJUSTMENT-QUANT      PIC S9(3).
56           10  NEW-QUANT-ON-HAND     PIC S9(3).
57
58       01  SCREEN-DATA-FIELDS.
59           10  RAW-DATE-TIME-FIELDS.
60               20  RAW-DATE.
61                   30  RAW-YEAR         PIC X(2).
62                   30  RAW-MONTH-DAY    PIC X(4).
63               20  RAW-TIME.
64                   30  RAW-HOUR         PIC 99.
65                   30  RAW-MINUTE       PIC 99.
66           10  EDITED-DATE-TIME-FIELDS.
67               20  ED-DATE.
68                   30  ED-MONTH-DAY     PIC XX/XX/.
69                   30  ED-YEAR          PIC XX.
70               20  ED-TIME.
71                   30  ED-HOUR          PIC Z9.
72                   30  FILLER           PIC X       VALUE ":".
73                   30  ED-MINUTE        PIC 99.
74           10  HDG-UNDERLINE          PIC X(79)    VALUE ALL "~".
75           10  RESPONSE               PIC X.
76           10  TRANSACTION-TYPE       PIC X.
77           10  OPTION                 PIC X.
78
79       SCREEN SECTION.
80
81       01  HEADING-SCREEN.
82           10  PIC X(8)  FROM ED-DATE      LINE 2 COL  1
83                                           BLANK SCREEN.
84           10  PIC X(5)  FROM ED-TIME      LINE 2 COL 75.
85           10  VALUE "UPDATE QUANTITY ON HAND"
86                                           LINE 2  COL 30.
87           10  PIC X(79) FROM HDG-UNDERLINE LINE 3 COL  1.
88
89       01  INTRODUCTION-SCREEN.
90           10  VALUE  "This program allows you to update the"
91                             LINE 9     COL 23             HIGHLIGHT.
92           10  VALUE  "Quantity-On-Hand field in the software"
93                             LINE PLUS 1    COL 23         HIGHLIGHT.
94           10  VALUE  "inventory file."
95                             LINE PLUS 1    COL 23         HIGHLIGHT.
96           10  VALUE  "Are you ready to proceed <y/n>? "
97                             LINE PLUS 2    COL 23  BELL   HIGHLIGHT.
98           10  PIC X(1)   TO RESPONSE    COL PLUS 0        AUTO.
99
100      01  STOCK-NUMBER-SCREEN.
101          10  VALUE "Enter the stock number to be updated "
102                                        LINE 6      COL 1.
103          10  VALUE "(strike the Enter key to terminate): "
104                                        COL PLUS 0.
105          10  PIC X(5)   TO IR-STOCK-NUMBER.
106
107      01  RECORD-READ-SCREEN.
108          10  VALUE "Stock number: "        LINE 8     COL 1
109                  BLANK REMAINDER.
110          10  PIC X(5)   FROM IR-STOCK-NUMBER REVERSE    COL PLUS 0.
111          10  VALUE "Software name: "                     COL 25.
112          10  PIC X(30)  FROM IR-SOFTWARE-NAME REVERSE   COL PLUS 0.
113          10  VALUE "Current Quantity On Hand:   " LINE PLUS 2 COL 40.
114          10  PIC ZZ9-   FROM IR-QUANT-ON-HAND REVERSE   COL PLUS 0.
115          10  VALUE "Correct record <y/n>? "
116                             LINE PLUS 2    COL 1         HIGHLIGHT.
117          10  PIC X(1)   TO RESPONSE    COL PLUS 0        AUTO.
118
119      01  SELECT-TRANSACTION-TYPE-SCREEN.
120          10  VALUE "Transaction Types:"       LINE 11     COL 1
121                  BLANK REMAINDER.
122          10  VALUE "1  Receipt"                           COL 20.
123          10  VALUE "2  Return"              LINE PLUS 1 COL 20.
124          10  VALUE "3  Adjustment"          LINE PLUS 1 COL 20.
125          10  VALUE "4  Sale"                LINE PLUS 1 COL 20.
126          10  VALUE "Enter Transaction Type: "  LINE PLUS 2 COL 1.
127          10  PIC X TO TRANSACTION-TYPE    AUTO REVERSE  COL PLUS 0.
128
129      01  GET-QUANTITY-SCREEN.
130          10  VALUE " "    BLANK REMAINDER    LINE 23     COL 1.
131          10  VALUE "Enter Transaction Quantity: "  LINE 12   COL 40.
132          10  PIC S9(3)   TO ADJUSTMENT-QUANT    REVERSE COL PLUS 0.
133
134      01  SELECT-OPTION-SCREEN.
135          10  VALUE "Updated Quantity On Hand:   " LINE 14    COL 40.
136          10  PIC ZZ9-   FROM NEW-QUANT-ON-HAND REVERSE COL PLUS 0.
137          10  VALUE "Options:"                 LINE PLUS 4 COL 31.
138          10  VALUE "1  Updated quantity is correct."      COL 41.
139          10  VALUE "2  Data is not correct; retry."
140                                           LINE PLUS 1 COL 41.
141          10  VALUE "3  Cancel this transaction."
142                                           LINE PLUS 1 COL 41.
143          10  VALUE "Please enter desired option: "
144                  HIGHLIGHT   BLANK REMAINDER LINE PLUS 2 COL 31.
145          10  PIC X(1)   TO OPTION         AUTO REVERSE  COL PLUS 0.
146
147      01  INVALID-QUANTITY-SCREEN.
148          10  VALUE
149              "Negative quantities are valid only for Adjustments!"
150                  HIGHLIGHT        BELL    LINE 23    COL 10.
151          10  VALUE
152              "Strike the Enter key to try again... "
153                  HIGHLIGHT               LINE 24    COL 12.
154          10  PIC X(1)   TO RESPONSE              COL PLUS 0.
155
156      01  NEGATIVE-QUANTITY-SCREEN.
157          10  VALUE
158              "This transaction makes the quantity on hand NEGATIVE!"
159                  HIGHLIGHT        BELL    LINE 23    COL 10.
160          10  VALUE
161              "Enter Y to confirm the negative quantity on hand, "
162                  HIGHLIGHT               LINE 24    COL 1.
163          10  VALUE "or enter N to try again... "
164                  HIGHLIGHT                          COL PLUS 0.
165          10  PIC X(1)   TO RESPONSE   AUTO REVERSE COL PLUS 0.
166
167      01  RECORD-NOT-FOUND-SCREEN.
168          10  VALUE "There is no inventory record for Stock # "
169                  HIGHLIGHT        BELL    LINE 18    COL 12.
170          10  PIC X(5)    FROM IR-STOCK-NUMBER
171                  HIGHLIGHT                          COL PLUS 0.
172          10  VALUE
173              "When you are ready to continue, strike the Enter key..."
174                                       LINE PLUS 3 COL 12.
175          10  PIC X(1)   TO RESPONSE
176                                                    COL PLUS 0.
177
178      01  INVALID-RESPONSE-SCREEN.
179          10  VALUE "THAT RESPONSE IS INVALID! "
180                  HIGHLIGHT        BELL    LINE 24    COL 1.
181          10  VALUE "Strike the Enter key to try again... "
182                                                    COL PLUS 0.
183          10  PIC X(1)   TO RESPONSE
184                                                    COL PLUS 0.
185
```

Figure 20-4

(continued from page 573)

```
186    PROCEDURE DIVISION.
187
188    000-UPDATE-INVENTORY-FILE.
189        PERFORM 100-INITIALIZE
190        IF RESPONSE = "y" OR "Y"
191            PERFORM 110-PROCESS-ONE-TRANSACTION
192                UNTIL NO-MORE-TRANSACTIONS
193            PERFORM 120-FINALIZE
194        END-IF
195        STOP RUN.
196
197    100-INITIALIZE.
198        PERFORM 200-DISPLAY-HEADING-SCREEN
199        DISPLAY INTRODUCTION-SCREEN
200        ACCEPT  INTRODUCTION-SCREEN
201        IF RESPONSE = "y" OR "Y"
202            SET NO-MORE-TRANSACTIONS TO FALSE
203            OPEN I-O  INVENTORY-FILE
204        END-IF.
205
206    110-PROCESS-ONE-TRANSACTION.
207        MOVE SPACES TO IR-STOCK-NUMBER
208        PERFORM 200-DISPLAY-HEADING-SCREEN
209        DISPLAY STOCK-NUMBER-SCREEN
210        ACCEPT  STOCK-NUMBER-SCREEN
211        IF IR-STOCK-NUMBER = SPACES
212            SET NO-MORE-TRANSACTIONS TO TRUE
213        ELSE
214            PERFORM 800-READ-INVENTORY-RECORD
215            IF MASTER-RECORD-FOUND
216                DISPLAY RECORD-READ-SCREEN
217                ACCEPT RECORD-READ-SCREEN
218                IF RESPONSE = "y" OR "Y"
219                    MOVE ZEROES TO ADJUSTMENT-QUANT
220                    SET PROCESSING-COMPLETED TO FALSE
221                    PERFORM 300-PROCESS-TRANSACTION
222                        UNTIL PROCESSING-COMPLETED
223                ELSE
224                    SET PROCESSING-COMPLETED TO TRUE
225                END-IF
226            ELSE
227                DISPLAY RECORD-NOT-FOUND-SCREEN
228                ACCEPT  RECORD-NOT-FOUND-SCREEN
229            END-IF
230        END-IF.
231
232    120-FINALIZE.
233        CLOSE INVENTORY-FILE.
234
235    200-DISPLAY-HEADING-SCREEN.
236        ACCEPT RAW-DATE FROM DATE
237        ACCEPT RAW-TIME FROM TIME
238        MOVE RAW-MONTH-DAY TO ED-MONTH-DAY
239        MOVE RAW-YEAR TO ED-YEAR
240        MOVE RAW-HOUR TO ED-HOUR
241        MOVE RAW-MINUTE TO ED-MINUTE
242        DISPLAY HEADING-SCREEN.
243
244    300-PROCESS-TRANSACTION.
245
246        PERFORM WITH TEST AFTER UNTIL TYPE-IS-VALID
247            DISPLAY SELECT-TRANSACTION-TYPE-SCREEN
248            ACCEPT  SELECT-TRANSACTION-TYPE-SCREEN
249            IF TRANSACTION-TYPE IS >= "1" AND <= "4"
250                SET TYPE-IS-VALID TO TRUE
251            ELSE
252                SET TYPE-IS-VALID TO FALSE
253                DISPLAY INVALID-RESPONSE-SCREEN
254                ACCEPT  INVALID-RESPONSE-SCREEN
255            END-IF
256        END-PERFORM
257
258        PERFORM 400-ACCEPT-USER-ADJUSTMENT WITH TEST AFTER
259                UNTIL QUANTITY-IS-VALID
260
261        PERFORM 410-ACCEPT-USER-ACTION WITH TEST AFTER
262                UNTIL OPTION-IS-VALID.
263
264    400-ACCEPT-USER-ADJUSTMENT.
265        DISPLAY GET-QUANTITY-SCREEN
266        ACCEPT  GET-QUANTITY-SCREEN
267        IF ADJUSTMENT-QUANT IS NEGATIVE
268        AND TRANSACTION-TYPE NOT = "3"
269            SET QUANTITY-IS-VALID TO FALSE
270            DISPLAY INVALID-QUANTITY-SCREEN
271            ACCEPT  INVALID-QUANTITY-SCREEN
272        ELSE
273            MOVE IR-QUANT-ON-HAND TO NEW-QUANT-ON-HAND
274            EVALUATE TRANSACTION-TYPE
275                WHEN "1" THRU "3"
276                    ADD ADJUSTMENT-QUANT TO NEW-QUANT-ON-HAND
277                WHEN "4"
278                    SUBTRACT ADJUSTMENT-QUANT FROM NEW-QUANT-ON-HAND
279            END-EVALUATE
280            IF NEW-QUANT-ON-HAND IS NOT NEGATIVE
281                SET QUANTITY-IS-VALID TO TRUE
282            ELSE
283                DISPLAY NEGATIVE-QUANTITY-SCREEN
284                ACCEPT  NEGATIVE-QUANTITY-SCREEN
285                IF RESPONSE = "y" OR "Y"
286                    SET QUANTITY-IS-VALID TO TRUE
287                ELSE
288                    SET QUANTITY-IS-VALID TO FALSE
289                END-IF
290            END-IF
291        END-IF.
292
293    410-ACCEPT-USER-ACTION.
294        DISPLAY SELECT-OPTION-SCREEN
295        ACCEPT  SELECT-OPTION-SCREEN
296        SET OPTION-IS-VALID TO TRUE
297        EVALUATE OPTION
298            WHEN "1"
299                MOVE NEW-QUANT-ON-HAND TO IR-QUANT-ON-HAND
300                PERFORM 860-REWRITE-UPDATED-RECORD
301                SET PROCESSING-COMPLETED TO TRUE
302            WHEN "2"
303                CONTINUE
304            WHEN "3"
305                SET PROCESSING-COMPLETED TO TRUE
306            WHEN OTHER
307                SET OPTION-IS-VALID TO FALSE
308                DISPLAY INVALID-RESPONSE-SCREEN
309                ACCEPT  INVALID-RESPONSE-SCREEN
310        END-EVALUATE.
311
312    800-READ-INVENTORY-RECORD.
313        READ INVENTORY-FILE
314            INVALID KEY
315                SET MASTER-RECORD-FOUND TO FALSE
316            NOT INVALID KEY
317                SET MASTER-RECORD-FOUND TO TRUE
318        END-READ.
319
320    860-REWRITE-UPDATED-RECORD.
321        REWRITE INVENTORY-RECORD
322            INVALID KEY
323                DISPLAY "Invalid key while rewriting", INVENTORY-RECORD
324                DISPLAY "Aborting update program."
325                PERFORM 120-FINALIZE
326                STOP RUN
327        END-REWRITE.
```

Interactive File Maintenance

*Example Definition—
Example 20-2*

The second example of this chapter illustrates interactive file maintenance. It corresponds to the batch file maintenance of Example 19-3.

Example 20-2 Interactive Maintenance of an Indexed File

Problem Description

The UNISOFT company requires an interactive maintenance program to allow the following operations on the inventory file:

- Display a requested record from the file
- Change any field in the record except the Product-number and Quantity on-hand
- Add a new record to the file
- Delete an existing record from the file

Master Input/Output Description

Processing is to be done in place. That is, a master record is read, updated, then rewritten to its original position in the file.

File name: SOFTWAR2.DI

Record format:

Field	Positions	Data Type	Format
Stock number	1–5	Alphanumeric	
Software name	6–35	Alphanumeric	
Vendor name	36–55	Alphanumeric	
Quantity on hand	56–58	Numeric	S999
Reorder level	59–61	Numeric	999
Price	62–66	Numeric	999V99

Key field: Stock number

Activity Log—Output File

For each change made to the file, one or more records are to be written to a log file.

File name: SOFT-LOG.DI

Record format:

Field	Positions	Data Type	Format
Sequence number	1–4	Numeric	Whole number
Record identifier			
Date	5–10	Numeric	Year/month/day
Person code	11–15	Alphanumeric	
Activity type	16	Alphanumeric	A - Add record
			C - Change record
			D - Delete record
Stock number	17–21	Alphanumeric	
Software name	22–51	Alphanumeric	
Vendor name	52–71	Alphanumeric	
Quantity on hand	72–74	Numeric	S999
Reorder level	75–77	Numeric	999
Price	78–82	Numeric	999V99

Note. Positions 17–82 contain the inventory record.

Input Data

Access to the program is to be restricted to approved users, as defined by a user table. Initial program input is the user number.

The user is to be allowed to request from the keyboard the type of maintenance operation to perform: record display, addition, change, or deletion. All program input is to be through the keyboard.

Processing Requirements

1. Accept user identification code. If the user-entered code does not correspond to one of the table entries, abort the program.
2. Query the user for the maintenance operation to be performed.
   The operation is to display a record.
   a. Accept the product number of the desired record.
   b. Access the record.
   c. If record found, display it; otherwise, display an error message.
   The operation is to edit a record.
   a. Accept the product number of the desired record.
   b. Access the record.
   c. If record found, display it; otherwise, display an error message.
   d. If record found, accept changes for any field except the stock number and the quantity on hand.
   e. Rewrite the corrected record if requested.
   f. If the inventory record was rewritten, write the original to the log file.
   g. If the inventory record was rewritten, write the updated record to the log file.

   The operation is to add a record.
   a. Accept the product number of the desired record to be added.
   b. Ensure that there is not already a record with this stock number. If so, display an error message.
   c. If no other record with this stock number, accept input for all fields.
   d. Write the new record if requested.
   e. If the inventory record was written, write a copy to the log file.

   The operation is to delete a record.
   a. Accept the product number of the desired record.
   b. Access the record.
   c. If record found, display it; otherwise, display an error message.
   d. If record found, request from the user confirmation to delete the record.
   e. If delete confirmed, delete the record.
   f. If the record was deleted, write a copy to the log file.

3. Display an appropriate error message and terminate processing on any unexpected disk operation.

Security Measures for Safeguarding Data

In Chapter 12, "Data Validation," you learned about some of the measures taken to ensure that data entered into a system is correct. Safeguarding the data files of a organization from corruption (intentional or accidental) is also an important element in most data processing environments. The file activities of a given program determine the extent and nature of the safeguards. For instance, some programs are no threat to the integrity of a file. The program that only displays records of the inventory file and does not perform updates can hardly harm the file. However, most programs that provide users with the capability to change data in files have some level of controls and safeguards to make certain that valuable data is not destroyed or corrupted. On one extreme is a program to enter orders for product; for each item purchased, the order entry program will update the quantity-on-hand field of the inventory file. In this instance, the inventory file is not updated directly by the user; it is done as an auxiliary operation of the order entry activity.

At the other extreme, a file maintenance program "bares" the file to whatever changes the user desires. As a result, access to the maintenance program is often restricted to certain qualified individuals. For example, UNISOFT might employ numerous salespeople who have access to the order entry system (which ultimately updates the inventory file), but only one or two people who are responsible for file maintenance and therefore have access to the file maintenance program. Another method of maintaining control over the integrity of files is to maintain a separate file of all changes to the file. You will see when Example 20-2 operates on the inventory file that for each record added or deleted, a record is written to a log file; for each record changed, two records are written to the log file. Thus, the log file provides a history of changes; it is commonly called an *audit trail*.

Trial Runs with the Interactive Maintenance Program

As with the program of Example 20-1, it will be helpful to you in studying the file maintenance program to have actually run the program and performed maintenance activities. To that end, this section describes a sequence of activities that you should perform with the inventory file. You will display a record, edit a record, add a new record, and delete a record.

For this exercise, you will need to copy the following files from the data/program diskette that accompanied this book onto a work diskette or your hard disk.

RF-MAINT.CBL	The maintenance program
CREA-LOG.CBL	Program to create a new log file
LIST-LOG.CBL	Program to display the log file on the screen
SOFTWAR2.DI	The indexed version of the data file

When ready, do the following:

1. Compile each of the three programs.
2. Run the CREA-LOG program to create a new log file. This is necessary before running the maintenance program.

You can now begin your test sequence.

1. Run the RF-MAINT program; the program will greet you with the following screen.

```
        This is Inventory Maintenance.

    To run you must enter your five-digit
    authorization code.

    Please enter your code: _____
```

2. This is protection to restrict user access to the program. Type 55555 and strike Enter. The program will be terminated immediately because 55555 is not an authorized code.
3. Run the RF-MAINT program again; this time, type an authorization code of 12345 and strike the Enter key.
4. You will be presented with the following main menu.

```
    I N V E N T O R Y   M A I N T.  M E N U

    Please enter the number for the desired option:

        1   Display existing inventory records
        2   Edit fields of existing records
        3   Add new inventory records
        4   Delete records from the inventory file
        5   Exit from this menu

    Option desired: _
```

5. Type the digit 6 (an invalid entry); you will receive an error message.

6. Type the digit 1 (Display a record); you will see the following display.

```
This program allows you to inspect records from
the software inventory file named SOFTWAR2.DI


To continue, enter the desired stock number: _____
To exit, strike the Enter key.
```

7. Type the stock number 11111 and strike the Enter key. Since there is no record with this stock number, an error message will be displayed.

8. Type the stock number 07427 and strike the Enter key. The record for Apricot-tree General Ledger will be displayed.

9. In response to the request for the next stock number, simply strike Enter to return to the main menu.

10. Type 2 for the Edit option.

11. In response to the request for the stock number of the record to be edited, type 07427 and strike Enter. This gives the following record display.

```
            EDIT AN INVENTORY RECORD

Stock number    07427

Software name   Apricot-tree General Ledger

Vendor          Apricot Software

Stock onhand    65        Price   349.95
Reorder level   65
```

12. Make the following changes:

Software name:	Apricot-tree	to	Plum-tree
Vendor:	Apricot Software	to	Plum Software

Notice that the Stock-number and Stock onhand fields are not highlighted and cannot be changed through the maintenance program.

13. Repeatedly strike the Enter key to progress through the other fields. After the last field, the following will be displayed.

```
Options:
    1  Editing is correct. Write this to the file.
    2  Data as shown needs to be corrected.
    3  Abort editing of this record.

Please enter 1, 2, or 3 for desired option: _
```

14. These are exactly the same options that you used in Example 20-1. Type 1 to update this record.

15. In response to the request for the next product number, strike the Enter key to return to the main menu.

16. Type 3 (Add a record option). This gives the following prompt.

```
This program allows you to add records to the
software inventory file named SOFTWAR2.DI

To add another record, enter the stock number: _____
To exit, strike the Enter key.
```

17. For the product number of the record to be added, enter 67890. You will be presented with the following screen.

```
            ADD INVENTORY RECORD

   Stock number   67890

   Software name   ▓▓▓▓▓▓▓▓▓▓▓▓▓▓▓▓▓▓▓▓▓▓▓

   Vendor          ▓▓▓▓▓▓▓▓▓▓▓▓▓▓▓▓▓▓▓▓▓▓▓

   Stock onhand   0       Price   .00
   Reorder level  0
```

18. Make the following entries for this new record:

Software name	Wolfbase
Vendor	Wolf Software
Stock onhand	0
Reorder level	100
Price	149.95

In making these entries, you can move back to preceding fields with the Up arrow key. Notice that you cannot move to the product number.

19. When you enter the last field and strike Enter, you are given the option menu for your desired action. Strike 1 to write this record to disk.

20. In response to the request for the next stock number, strike the Enter key to return to the main menu.

21. Type 4 (Delete a record); you will be presented with the following screen.

```
This program allows you to DELETE records from
the software inventory file named SOFTWAR2.DI

     Please note that once you delete a record,
     it is IMPOSSIBLE to get it back.

To continue, enter the desired stock number: _____
To exit, strike the Enter key.
```

22. Type the stock number 32506 and strike the Enter key. The record for Bottom View will be displayed, accompanied by the following prompt.

```
Are you certain that you want to delete this record? N
```

Notice that the default response is N (for No). In order to delete this record, you must enter Y (for Yes). Strike Y.

23. Strike Enter in response to the request for the next stock number to return to the main menu.

24. Type 1 (Display a record). Enter the stock number 32506 (the record just deleted). You should see an error message indicating that there is no record for this stock number (you just deleted it).

25. Strike the Enter key to return to the menu.

26. Type 5 to terminate processing.

For more orientation to the program, try running it again. This time, use the authorization code 17901. Write down the changes that you make to the file so that you will be able to confirm what you have done by looking at the log file.

The Maintenance Log File

When you ran the program CREA-LOG prior to RF-MAINT, a new log file was created. This file, named SOFT-LOG.DI, is an indexed file; its record includes fields identifying the action taken and a copy of the record. For each record added or deleted, a copy of that record is included in the file. For each record changed (edited), two records are written: one containing the original version of the inventory record and the other containing the updated version. You can see this in the printed listing of the log file in Figure 20-5. Note the following:

■ The key field occupies the first four positions of the record (it is shaded in this figure). Numbers are assigned sequentially, beginning with 0001.

■ The first record in the file is called a *header record*. Positions 5–8 of this record contain the key field value of the last record written to the file. As you will see when you study the program, this value is used to determine the key field value to be assigned to the next log record that will be written.

■ The second field is the date that the changes were made to the file. (Obviously, the date in your log file will be different.)

■ The third field is the user authorization code that was entered to gain access to the program.

■ The fourth field is the transaction code: A means the record was added, C means a record was changed, and D means a record was deleted.

■ The balance of the record is a copy of the inventory record.

■ For each change to an inventory record, two log records are written: one containing the original inventory record (line 1) and the other containing the updated inventory record (line 2).

■ Inspecting the third line, you see a transaction code of A. This is the record you added for Wolfbase. Similarly, the last line contains a transaction code D. This is the record you deleted.

Because the log file is an indexed file, it is clumsy to inspect. To make it easier to check your log file, run the LIST-LOG program, one of the three you compiled before beginning this exercise. The first five records displayed on the screen will contain the same header record and inventory records as Figure 20-5 (if you followed all of the steps). If you made additional changes, they will also be included. Notice that the authorization code will be different, corresponding to your entry when running the program for the second time.

The RF-MAINT Program— Example 20-2

Program Overview

The four actions of this program—display a record, add a new record, edit a record, and delete a record—are all actions that you have studied in previous chapters.

■ The RAN-DIS3 program of Chapter 10 allows you to request a record for display (access is via the product number).

■ The S-EXTEND program of Chapter 10 allows you to add records to the sequential version of the inventory file. Minimal changes are necessary to convert this program to process an indexed file.

Figure 20-5

*A Sample
Maintenance
Log File*

Header record.

```
00010005
0002901030 12345 C 07427 Apricot-tree General Ledger     Apricot Software       06506534995 ①
0003901030 12345 C 07427 Plum-tree General Ledger        Plum Software          06506534995 ②
0004901030 12345 A 67890 Wolfbase                        Wolf Software          00010014995 ③
0005901030 12345 D 32506 Bottom View                     Galactic Bus. Mach.    10510009995 ④
```

Key   Date   Inventory record.
field.
         Authorization   Transaction code.
         code of user.   A-Addition   1 and 2: Edited record.
                               C-Change   3: Added record.
                               D-Deletion   4: Deleted record.

- The S-EXTEND program includes the provision to edit the record just entered. The edit-record component of this example combines accessing an existing record (as in RAN-DIS3) and editing it (as in S-EXTEND).

- Deletion of a record simply requires that the record be accessed (as done in RAN-DIS3) and deleted as requested by the user.

There are two ways of designing this application. One approach is to incorporate all four of the functions into a single program in which the primary processing module presents the user with a menu of options, then performs the appropriate section of code.

On the other hand, the four functions required by this application are relatively independent of one another and are amenable to using separate programs that are called from a controlling program. Recall from Chapter 17 that this can be done in either of two ways: (1) separately compiled programs where one calls another and (2) nested programs in which one or more programs are included within another. Example 20-2 is programmed using nested programs, as illustrated by the code outline of Figure 20-6.

As you will see in studying the program, the display and delete programs are similar and relatively simple. The add and edit programs are also similar, but more complicated.

Because of the large size of the overall program (more than 900 lines), it will be considered in parts: first the calling/menu program and then the nested edit programs. Significant features of the calling/menu program component (included here in Figure 20-7) are

1. The global definitions within this program component of files and records used by the nested programs

2. The record definition of the log file

3. Controlled access to the program

**Global Definitions within
the DATA DIVISION**

This program requires the use of two files: SOFTWAR2.DI and SOFT-LOG.DI. They are identified in the SELECTs at lines 29 and 33; their record formats are correspondingly defined under the FDs at lines 45 and 54. Because both of these files are used by all of the nested programs, they are defined with the clause

```
IS GLOBAL
```

thereby making the file names, record names, and all subordinate field names available to all programs nested within RF-MAINT.

In addition, a group of data items in the WORKING-STORAGE SECTION are defined as GLOBAL (line 78). These are also names that will be available to the nested programs.

The Log File

You have learned that as each maintenance operation is performed on the inventory record, one or more copies of that record are written to the log file. This file includes two types of records: a header record and transaction records (refer to Figure 20-5). The format of the transaction record is repeated here (from the earlier example definition).

Field	Positions	Data Type	Format
Sequence number	1–4	Numeric	Whole number
Record identifier			
Date	5–10	Numeric	Year/month/day
Person code	11–15	Alphanumeric	
Activity type	16	Alphanumeric	
Inventory record	17–82		

If you inspect the program record definition (lines 56–70), you will see the correspondence.

Because of the way in which this file will be processed by other programs, it must be indexed. Unlike the software file, there may be more than one record in this file for a given product number. Since the primary key of an indexed file must be unique, the product number cannot be used as the key field. For this reason, the sequence-number field was created, thereby providing a field that is not duplicated in any two records and thus can be used as the primary key.

For reporting and inquiry into the log file (not part of this program), access is required to the log file via the product-number field. Thus, the product number is designated as an alternate key. With the possibility of two or more records having the same product number, it is necessary to include the WITH DUPLICATES clause in the SELECT for this file. You can see the designation of keys in the SELECT, beginning at line 33 of Figure 20-7.

Figure 20-6

The Program/Nested Program Structure of the RF-MAINT Program

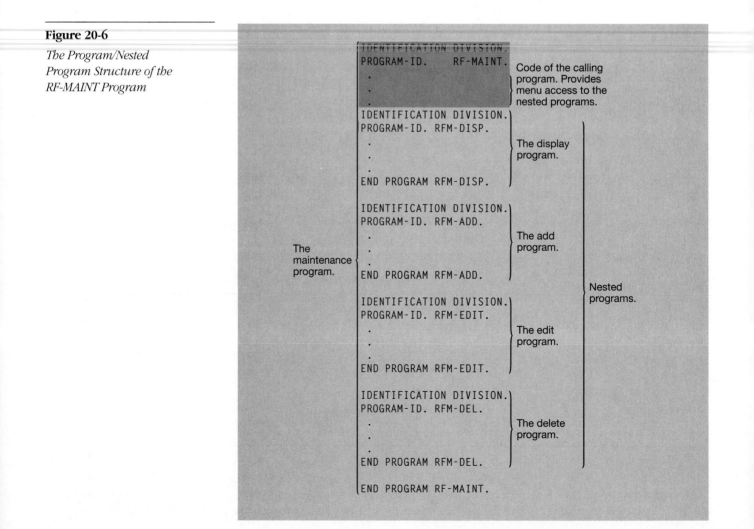

Figure 20-7

The Calling/Menu Program—Example 20-2
(continued on page 584)

(continued on page 584)

```
1        IDENTIFICATION DIVISION.                              76      WORKING-STORAGE SECTION.
2                                                              77
3        PROGRAM-ID.    RF-MAINT.                              78      01  GLOBAL-FIELDS IS GLOBAL.
4                                                              79          10  LOG-IDENTIFIER.
5     *    Written by W.Price                                  80              20  ACTIVITY-DATE.
6     *    October 12, 1990                                    81                  30  ACTIVITY-YEAR      PIC 9(2).
7                                                              82                  30  ACTIVITY-MONTH     PIC 9(2).
8     *    RF-MAINT is the file maintenance program for the    83                  30  ACTIVITY-DAY       PIC 9(2).
9     *    inventory file; it consists of the following elements 84              20  PERSON-AUTH-CODE      PIC X(5).
10    *      Main program                                      85              20  ACTIVITY-TYPE         PIC X.
11    *        RF-MAINT: Primary control and menu              86          10  LAST-LOG-RECORD           PIC 9(4).
12    *      Nested programs                                   87          10  HOLD-INVENTORY-RECORD     PIC X(66).
13    *        RFM-DISP: Display a requested record            88          10                            PIC X.
14    *        RFM-EDIT: Modify fields of an existing record   89              88  FATAL-IO-ERROR        VALUE "Y"    FALSE "N".
15    *        RFM-ADD:  Add a new record                      90
16    *        RFM-DEL:  Delete an existing record             91      01  AUTHORIZATION-CODE-ENTRIES.
17                                                             92          10              PIC X(5)    VALUE "12345".
18    *    Access to this program is provided through a user code. 93        10              PIC X(5)    VALUE "17901".
19    *    Each activity (record change, addition, deletion) is 94          10              PIC X(5)    VALUE "11801".
20    *    written to the log file SOFT-LOG.DI.                95          10              PIC X(5)    VALUE "32831".
21                                                             96          10              PIC X(5)    VALUE "98765".
22        ENVIRONMENT DIVISION.                                97      01  AUTHORIZATION-CODE-TABLE
23                                                             98              REDEFINES AUTHORIZATION-CODE-ENTRIES.
24        CONFIGURATION SECTION.                               99          10  AUTHORIZATION-CODE    PIC X(5)
25        SOURCE-COMPUTER.  IBM-PC.                            100                               OCCURS 5 TIMES
26                                                             101                               INDEXED BY CODE-INDEX.
27        INPUT-OUTPUT SECTION.                                102
28        FILE-CONTROL.                                        103     01  PROGRAMMED-SWITCHES.
29            SELECT INVENTORY-FILE    ASSIGN TO DISK "SOFTWAR2.DI" 104        10                        PIC X.
30                                     ORGANIZATION IS INDEXED 105            88  ABORT-PROGRAM         VALUE "Y" FALSE "N".
31                                     ACCESS IS RANDOM        106
32                                     RECORD KEY IS IR-STOCK-NUMBER. 107 01  OTHER-VARIABLES.
33            SELECT LOG-FILE          ASSIGN TO DISK "SOFT-LOG.DI" 108        10  OPTION                PIC X.
34                                     ORGANIZATION IS INDEXED 109            88  DISPLAY-REC           VALUE "1".
35                                     ACCESS IS RANDOM        110            88  UPDATE-REC            VALUE "2".
36                                     RECORD KEY IS LR-SEQUENCE-NUMBER 111        88  ADD-REC           VALUE "3".
37                                     ALTERNATE RECORD KEY    112            88  DELETE-REC            VALUE "4".
38                                         IS LR-STOCK-NUMBER  113            88  FINISHED              VALUE "5".
39                                         WITH DUPLICATES.    114
40                                                             115     SCREEN SECTION.
41        DATA DIVISION.                                       116
42                                                             117     01  ANNOUNCE-SCREEN.
43        FILE SECTION.                                        118         10  VALUE "This is Inventory Maintenance."
44                                                             119                 BLANK SCREEN
45        FD  INVENTORY-FILE IS GLOBAL.                        120                 LINE 2      COL 5.
46        01  INVENTORY-RECORD.                                121         10  VALUE "To run you must enter your five-digit"
47            10  IR-STOCK-NUMBER      PIC X(5).               122                 LINE PLUS 3  COL 2.
48            10  IR-SOFTWARE-NAME     PIC X(30).              123         10  VALUE "authorization code."
49            10  IR-VENDOR-NAME       PIC X(20).              124                 LINE PLUS 1  COL 2.
50            10  IR-QUANT-ON-HAND     PIC 9(3).               125         10  VALUE "Please enter your code: "
51            10  IR-REORDER-LEVEL     PIC 9(3).               126                 LINE PLUS 2  COL 2.
52            10  IR-PRICE             PIC 9(3)V9(2).          127         10  PIC X(5)     TO PERSON-AUTH-CODE
53                                                             128                 LINE PLUS 0  COL PLUS 0
54        FD  LOG-FILE IS GLOBAL.                              129                 REVERSE .
55        01  LOG-RECORD.                                      130
56            10  LR-SEQUENCE-NUMBER   PIC X(4).               131     01  MENU-SCREEN.
57            10  LR-LOG-IDENTIFIER.                           132         10  VALUE "I N V E N T O R Y   M A I N T.   M E N U"
58                20  LR-ACTIVITY-DATE.                        133                 BLANK SCREEN
59                    30  LR-ACTIVITY-YEAR   PIC 9(2).         134                 LINE 2      COL 5.
60                    30  LR-ACTIVITY-MONTH  PIC 9(2).         135         10  VALUE "Please enter the number for the desired option:"
61                    30  LR-ACTIVITY-DAY    PIC 9(2).         136                 LINE PLUS 3  COL 2.
62                20  LR-PERSON-AUTH-CODE    PIC X(5).         137         10  VALUE "  1   Display existing inventory records"
63                20  LR-ACTIVITY-TYPE       PIC X.            138                 LINE PLUS 2  COL 2.
64            10  LR-INVENTORY-RECORD.                         139         10  VALUE "  2   Edit fields of existing records"
65                20  LR-STOCK-NUMBER        PIC X(5).         140                 LINE PLUS 2  COL 2.
66                20  LR-SOFTWARE-NAME       PIC X(30).        141         10  VALUE "  3   Add new inventory records"
67                20  LR-VENDOR-NAME         PIC X(20).        142                 LINE PLUS 2  COL 2.
68                20  LR-QUANT-ON-HAND       PIC S9(3).        143         10  VALUE "  4   Delete records from the inventory file"
69                20  LR-REORDER-LEVEL       PIC 9(3).         144                 LINE PLUS 2  COL 2.
70                20  LR-PRICE               PIC 9(3)V9(2).    145         10  VALUE "  5   Exit from this menu"
71        01  LOG-HEADER-RECORD.                               146                 LINE PLUS 2  COL 2.
72            10  LH-SEQUENCE-NUMBER   PIC X(4).               147         10  VALUE "Option desired: "
73            10  LH-LAST-SEQUENCE-NUM PIC 9(4).               148                 LINE PLUS 2  COL 2.
74            10  LH-REST-OF-LOG-RECORD PIC X(74).             149         10  PIC X     TO OPTION
75                                                             150                 LINE PLUS 0  COL PLUS 0
                                                               151                 REVERSE  AUTO.
```

Figure 20-7

(continued from page 583)

```
152                                                     199   110-INITIALIZE.
153     01  INVALID-RESPONSE-SCREEN.                    200       OPEN I-O INVENTORY-FILE
154         10  VALUE                                   201       OPEN I-O LOG-FILE
155             "Please enter a valid option: 1, 2, 3, 4, or 5!"  202       SET FATAL-IO-ERROR TO FALSE
156                     LINE 19   COL 2.                203       ACCEPT ACTIVITY-DATE FROM DATE.
157         10  VALUE "To try again, strike the Enter key..."     204
158                     LINE PLUS 2  COL 2.             205   120-EVALUATE-USER-REQUEST.
159         10  PIC X    TO OPTION                      206       DISPLAY MENU-SCREEN
160                     LINE PLUS 0  COL PLUS 0         207       ACCEPT MENU-SCREEN
161                     AUTO.                           208       EVALUATE TRUE
162                                                     209         WHEN DISPLAY-REC
163     01  ERROR-TERMINATION-SCREEN-1.                 210           CALL "RFM-DISP"
164         10  VALUE "Note the above error; then strike Enter "   211         WHEN UPDATE-REC
165             HIGHLIGHT     BELL       LINE 20      COL 1.  212           CALL "RFM-EDIT"
166         10  VALUE "to terminate the Order Entry program.  "    213         WHEN ADD-REC
167                             LINE PLUS 1   COL 1.   214           CALL "RFM-ADD"
168         10  PIC X     TO OPTION       COL PLUS 0.  215         WHEN DELETE-REC
169                                                     216           CALL "RFM-DEL"
170     01  ERROR-TERMINATION-SCREEN-2.                 217         WHEN FINISHED
171         10  VALUE "Abnormal termination of Order Entry program."  218           CONTINUE
172             BLINK        BELL       LINE 23      COL 1.  219         WHEN OTHER
173                                                     220           DISPLAY INVALID-RESPONSE-SCREEN
174     PROCEDURE DIVISION.                             221           ACCEPT INVALID-RESPONSE-SCREEN
175                                                     222       END-EVALUATE
176     000-QUERY-USER-FOR-MAINT.                       223       IF FATAL-IO-ERROR
177         PERFORM 100-CLEAR-THE-USER                  224         GO TO 900-TERMINATE-ON-ERROR
178         IF ABORT-PROGRAM                            225       END-IF.
179             DISPLAY "ACCESS DENIED"                 226
180             STOP RUN                                227   130-FINALIZE.
181         END-IF                                      228       CLOSE INVENTORY-FILE
182         PERFORM 110-INITIALIZE                      229             LOG-FILE.
183         PERFORM 120-EVALUATE-USER-REQUEST           230
184             UNTIL FINISHED                          231   900-TERMINATE-ON-ERROR.
185         PERFORM 130-FINALIZE                        232       DISPLAY ERROR-TERMINATION-SCREEN-1
186         STOP RUN.                                   233       ACCEPT  ERROR-TERMINATION-SCREEN-1
187                                                     234       DISPLAY ERROR-TERMINATION-SCREEN-2
188     100-CLEAR-THE-USER.                             235       STOP RUN.
189         DISPLAY ANNOUNCE-SCREEN
190         ACCEPT ANNOUNCE-SCREEN
191         SET CODE-INDEX TO 1
192         SEARCH AUTHORIZATION-CODE
193           AT END
194             SET ABORT-PROGRAM TO TRUE
195           WHEN AUTHORIZATION-CODE (CODE-INDEX) = PERSON-AUTH-CODE
196             SET ABORT-PROGRAM TO FALSE
197         END-SEARCH.
198
```

The sole function of this file's header record is to provide program control over the assignment of a sequence number to each new log file record. In Figure 20-5, you can see that positions 5–8 of the header record contains 0005. This is the last assigned sequence number. When you study the edit program later in this chapter, you will see how this information is used by the program.

Because the log file includes two different types of records, the FD includes two record definitions (01). In Figure 20-7, you can see that the header record format is defined, beginning at line 71.

The PROCEDURE DIVISION

By now, you probably see the overall structure and logic of this part of the program (lines 174–235) as relatively simple. It includes the controlling module 000 and four first level modules. The 100 module provides controlled access to the program and is described in the next section. The 110-INITIALIZE module opens both files for I-O, thereby providing opened files for all access by the nested programs. This module also accesses the date from the system into the global data item ACTIVITY-DATE, thereby making it available to the nested programs.

The 120 module displays the menu, accepts the user response, and passes control to the appropriate nested program. Recall from running the program that you enter a selection of 1 to display a record, 2 to edit a record, and so on. (See the menu screen, beginning at line 131.) These single-digit options are related to condition names in lines 109–113.

When control is returned to the calling program from any of the called programs, the switch FATAL-IO-ERROR is tested (see line 223). If it is true, an unexpected disk error has occurred in the called program and processing must be terminated. You can see that a GO TO is used in place of a PERFORM. The GO TO is meaningful here because there is no return from the 900 module—processing is terminated at line 235.

Controlling Access to the Maintenance Program

Recall when you ran the program that you were requested to enter an authorization code. An invalid entry caused the program to abort; you can see the program code causing this in lines 178–180. Actual access control consists of two elements: a list of valid authorization codes and statements to determine if the user entered value is in the list. For the sake of simplicity, the list of valid codes is included as a WORKING-STORAGE SECTION defined table (see lines 92–96). In an actual application, this list would likely be stored in a separate file with a special set of programs for adding new codes, deleting existing codes, and performing other operations.

The authorization code is entered by the user via the ANNOUNCE-SCREEN (beginning line 117) into the data item PERSON-AUTH-CODE. The table is then searched by the SEARCH statement:

```
SEARCH AUTHORIZATION-CODE
   AT END
      SET ABORT-PROGRAM TO TRUE
   WHEN AUTHORIZATION-CODE (CODE-INDEX) = PERSON-AUTH-CODE
      SET ABORT-PROGRAM TO FALSE
END-SEARCH.
```

When the value in PERSON-AUTH-CODE is matched to an entry in the table, the switch ABORT-PROGRAM is set to false. If the end of the table is encountered, meaning that no such entry exists in the table, ABORT-PROGRAM is set to true. The latter action causes the program to abort via line 180. (If you need to refresh your memory regarding the SEARCH statement, refer to Chapter 14.)

The EDIT Program—Example 20-2

Program Structure and Logic—The Edit Program

The purpose of the edit program is to allow the user to make changes to all fields of the inventory record except the stock number and quantity on hand. Changing the stock number is not allowed because it is the primary key. Changing the quantity on hand is done through the transaction processing program of Example 20-1. Whenever a change is made to an inventory record, two records are written to the log file: the first contains the original version of the record and the second contains the updated version.

However, selecting a record for editing does not automatically mean that the record will be changed and rewritten. You should recall from running RF-MAINT that when you finish editing a record, you are given the option of rewriting the modified record or aborting the changes you have made. If you abort, then the record is not rewritten and there is no need to write to the log file. You will see this in the program.

Figure 20-8 is the structure chart for this program. The program logic is illustrated in the flowchart of Figure 20-9 and the pseudocode of Figure 20-10 (page 589).

After some of the programs you have seen, the structure and logic of this program is not overly complex. In fact, the logic is much simpler than the logic of the ITP-NDX program of Example 20-1.

Figure 20-8

*Structure Chart for
Example 20-2*

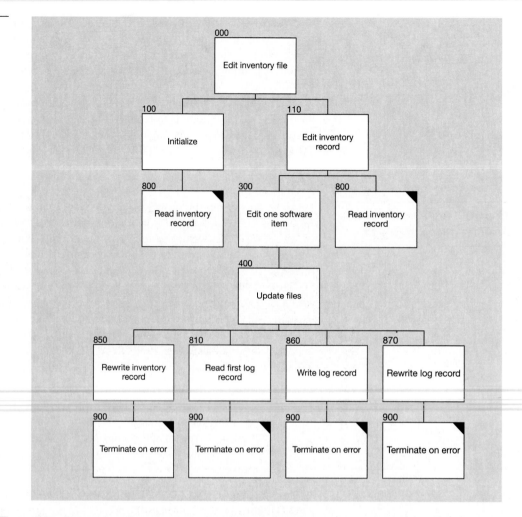

***Program Solution—
The Edit Program***

The edit program from RF-MAINT is shown in Figure 20-11 (page 590). The first item to notice is that it includes no ENVIRONMENT DIVISION or FILE SECTION (DATA DIVISION entry). These are not necessary because all required information regarding the files to be processed is defined as global in the calling program. The DATA DIVISION includes a small WORKING-STORAGE SECTION defining elements required by this program and not defined globally in the calling program. In addition, the DATA DIVISION includes a SCREEN SECTION defining the input and output screens used within the program. When you study the other nested programs, you will find that some of the screens defined for this program are the same as those defined in the other programs. Do not conclude that the common screens should be defined globally in the calling program. The IS GLOBAL clause *cannot be used* in the SCREEN SECTION.

For an insight to the rationale of the edit program logic, recall the sequence of actions when you ran the preceding exercises. Upon acknowledging the displayed record to be the one you want:

1. Proceed field by field through the record, making changes as appropriate. You may make changes to all the fields *or to none of them*. After the last field, you are presented with the option menu.

2. If your changes are correct and you want to save the record, you select the 1 option (write the updated record). The record will be rewritten to the file. If, for any reason, you decide against making these changes, you select the 3 option (abort these edits). The record will not be rewritten to the file.

Figure 20-9

Flowchart for Example 20-2
(continued on page 588)

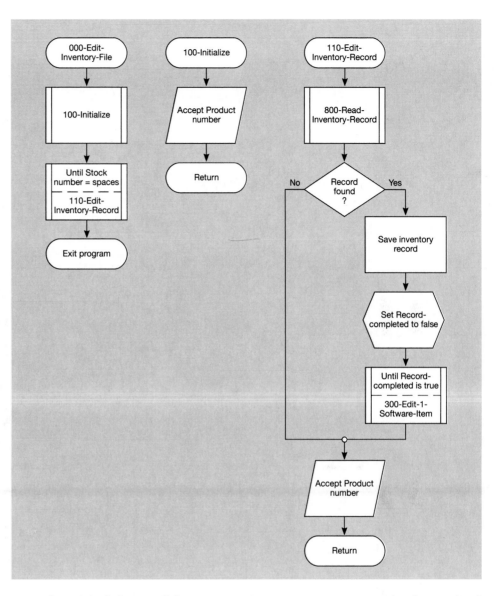

In the original design of this program, it was necessary to consider the needs of the following four combinations of user actions taken with a record that has been accessed for editing.

User Action	Program Action
Changes made, request write record	Rewrite record, write log records
Changes made, request abort editing	Do not rewrite or write
No changes made, request abort editing	Do not rewrite or write
No changes made, request write record	Do not rewrite or write

The last combination, in which a user makes no changes but requests that the record be rewritten, introduces a complication in the program logic. At first, you might conclude that there is no harm in rewriting the record because it will not change the inventory file contents. However, remember that "before" and "after" copies of the record are written to the log file for an edit record update. If the rewritten inventory record is unchanged, the two log records will be identical, a potentially confusing situation to anyone examining the log files. To avoid this, a copy of the newly read inventory record is moved (line 438) to

Figure 20-9

(continued from page 587)

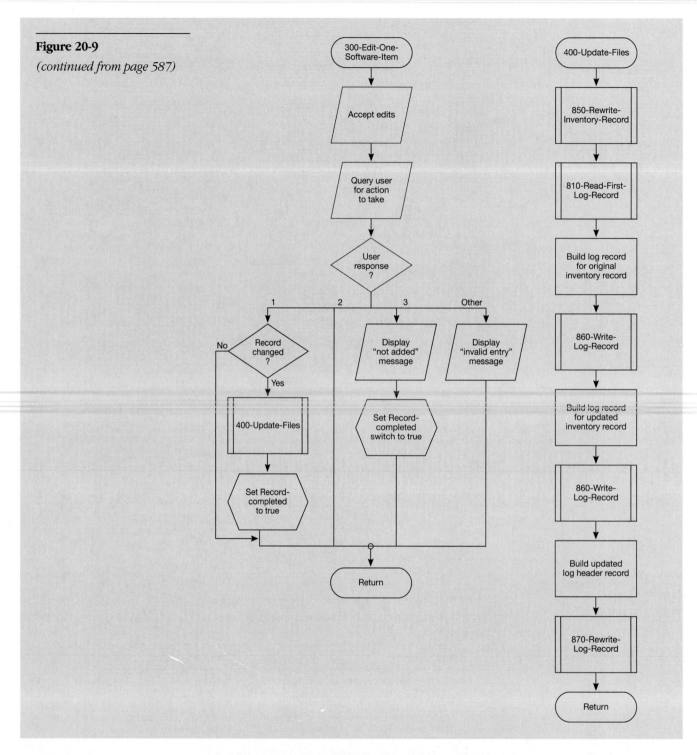

the data item HOLD-INVENTORY-RECORD, which is defined in the calling program as a global. This copy of the original serves two purposes.

First, it is used in the IF statement at line 453. At this point, the copy of the record stored in INVENTORY-RECORD has been subjected to editing (it may or may not have been changed). When the user requests the 1 option (write the record), the two copies of the record are compared by:

```
IF INVENTORY-RECORD NOT = HOLD-INVENTORY-RECORD
```

If they are different, the 400 module is executed.

Figure 20-9

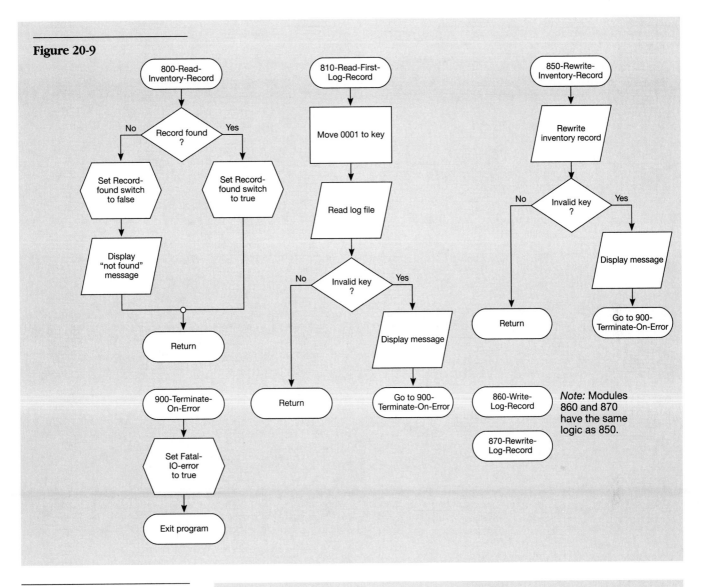

Figure 20-10

Pseudocode for Example 20-2

```
000-Edit-Inventory-File
    Perform 100-Initialize
    Perform 110-Edit-Inventory-Record
        until Stock number contains spaces
    Exit program

100-Initialize
    Accept user entry for product number

110-Edit-Inventory-Record
    Perform 800-Read-Inventory-Record
    If record found
        Save inventory record
        Set record-completed switch to false
        Perform 300-Edit-1-Software-Item
            until record-completed switch is true
    Accept user entry for next product number

300-Edit-1-Software-Item
    Accept edits to the inventory record
    Query user for action to take
    EVALUATE user option selection
        when 1
            If the record has been changed
                Perform 400-Update-Files
            Set record-completed switch to true
        when 2
            No action
        when 3
            Set record-completed switch to true
        when other
            Display error message
```

```
400-Update-Files
    Perform 850-Rewrite-Inventory-Record
    Perform 810-Read-First-Log-Record
    Build log record for original inventory record
    Perform 860-Write-Log-Record
    Build log record for edited inventory record
    Perform 860-Write-Log-Record
    Build updated log file header record
    Perform 870-Rewrite-Log-Record

800-Read-Inventory-Record
    Read inventory file
    If record not found
        Set record-found switch to false
        Display error message
    else
        Set record-found switch to true

850-Rewrite-Inventory-Record
    Move 0001 to log file key
    Read log file
        Invalid key
            Display error message
            Go to 900-Terminate-On-Error

860-Write-Log-Record
    Write log record
        Invalid key
            Display error message
            Go to 900-Terminate-On-Error
```

Figure 20-11

The RFM-EDIT PRogram—
Example 20-2

```
331        IDENTIFICATION DIVISION.
332
333        PROGRAM-ID. RFM-EDIT.
334
335    *    Written by W.Price
336    *    October 15, 1990
337
338    *    This program allows the user to interactively edit fields
339    *    of the indexed inventory file. However, editing of the
340    *    product number (the key field) and the quantity on hand
341    *    (changed only through transactions) is not allowed.
342
343    *    The input data file and record are defined in the
344    *    calling program as globals.
345
346        DATA DIVISION.
347
348        WORKING-STORAGE SECTION.
349
350        01  PROGRAMMED-SWITCHES.
351            10                       PIC X.
352                88  RECORD-COMPLETED     VALUE "Y" FALSE "N".
353            10                       PIC X.
354                88  RECORD-FOUND     VALUE "Y" FALSE "N".
355
356        01  OTHER-VARIABLES.
357            10  DESIRED-OPTION        PIC X.
358
359        SCREEN SECTION.
360
361        01  INTRODUCTION-SCREEN.
362            10  VALUE "This program allows you to edit records of the"
363                    BLANK SCREEN    LINE 6              HIGHLIGHT.
364            10  VALUE  "software inventory file named SOFTWAR2.DI"
365                                    LINE PLUS 1    HIGHLIGHT.
366
367        01  USER-REQUEST-SCREEN.
368            10  VALUE  "To edit a record, enter the stock number: "
369                                    LINE 16                HIGHLIGHT.
370            10  PIC X(5)      TO IR-STOCK-NUMBER
371                                    LINE PLUS 0   COL PLUS 0.
372            10  VALUE  "To exit, strike the Enter key. "
373                                    LINE PLUS 1            HIGHLIGHT.
374
375        01  NOT-IN-FILE-SCREEN.
376            10  VALUE  "There is no record in the file for "
377                                    LINE 14  BLANK SCREEN  HIGHLIGHT.
378            10  PIC X(5)      FROM IR-STOCK-NUMBER
379                                    LINE PLUS 0   COL      HIGHLIGHT.
380
381        01  SELECT-OPTION-SCREEN.
382            10  VALUE  "Options:"    LINE 18  COL 1.
383            10  VALUE
384            "  1   Editing is correct. Write this to the file."
385                                    LINE PLUS 1  COL 1.
386            10  VALUE
387            "  2   Data as shown needs to be corrected."
388                                    LINE PLUS 1  COL 1.
389            10  VALUE
390            "  3   Abort editing of this record."
391                                    LINE PLUS 1  COL 1.
392            10  VALUE
393            "Please enter 1, 2, or 3 for desired option: "
394                                    LINE PLUS 2  COL 1  HIGHLIGHT.
395    *    Get option from keyboard
396            10  PIC X         TO DESIRED-OPTION
397                                    LINE 23   COL 45  REVERSE  AUTO.
398
399        01  INVENTORY-RECORD-SCREEN.
400            10  VALUE "EDIT AN INVENTORY RECORD" BLANK SCREEN
401                                    LINE 2       COL 11.
402            10  VALUE "Stock number"  LINE PLUS 2  COL 1.
403            10  PIC X(5)   FROM  IR-STOCK-NUMBER
404                                    LINE PLUS 0  COL 16.
405            10  VALUE "Software name"  LINE PLUS 2  COL 1.
406            10  PIC X(30)   USING IR-SOFTWARE-NAME
407                                    LINE PLUS 0  COL 16  REVERSE.
408            10  VALUE "Vendor"   LINE PLUS 2  COL 1.
409            10  PIC X(20)   USING IR-VENDOR-NAME
410                                    LINE PLUS 0  COL 16  REVERSE.
411            10  VALUE "Stock onhand"  LINE PLUS 2  COL 1.
412            10  PIC ZZ9   FROM IR-QUANT-ON-HAND
413                                    LINE PLUS 0  COL 16.
414            10  VALUE "Price"   LINE PLUS 2  COL 26.
415            10  PIC ZZZ.99  USING IR-PRICE
416                                    LINE PLUS 0  COL 34  REVERSE.
417            10  VALUE "Reorder level"  LINE PLUS 1  COL 1.
418            10  PIC ZZ9   USING IR-REORDER-LEVEL
419                                    LINE PLUS 0  COL 16  REVERSE.
420
```

```
421        PROCEDURE DIVISION.
422
423        000-EDIT-INVENTORY-FILE.
424            PERFORM 100-INITIALIZE
425            PERFORM 110-EDIT-INVENTORY-RECORD
426                UNTIL IR-STOCK-NUMBER = SPACES
427            EXIT PROGRAM.
428
429        100-INITIALIZE.
430            MOVE SPACES TO IR-STOCK-NUMBER
431            DISPLAY INTRODUCTION-SCREEN
432            DISPLAY USER-REQUEST-SCREEN
433            ACCEPT  USER-REQUEST-SCREEN.
434
435        110-EDIT-INVENTORY-RECORD.
436            PERFORM 800-READ-INVENTORY-RECORD
437            IF RECORD-FOUND
438                MOVE INVENTORY-RECORD TO HOLD-INVENTORY-RECORD
439                SET RECORD-COMPLETED TO FALSE
440                PERFORM 300-EDIT-1-SOFTWARE-ITEM
441                    UNTIL RECORD-COMPLETED
442            END-IF
443            DISPLAY USER-REQUEST-SCREEN
444            ACCEPT  USER-REQUEST-SCREEN.
445
446        300-EDIT-1-SOFTWARE-ITEM.
447            DISPLAY INVENTORY-RECORD-SCREEN
448            ACCEPT  INVENTORY-RECORD-SCREEN
449            DISPLAY SELECT-OPTION-SCREEN
450            ACCEPT  SELECT-OPTION-SCREEN
451            EVALUATE DESIRED-OPTION
452                WHEN "1"
453                    IF INVENTORY-RECORD NOT = HOLD-INVENTORY-RECORD
454                        PERFORM 400-UPDATE-FILES
455                    END-IF
456                    SET RECORD-COMPLETED TO TRUE
457                WHEN "2"
458                    CONTINUE
459                WHEN "3"
460                    DISPLAY "This record NOT added to the file"
461                                LINE 16    ERASE EOS
462                    SET RECORD-COMPLETED TO TRUE
463                WHEN OTHER
464                    DISPLAY "Invalid entry—try again"
465                                LINE 16    ERASE EOS
466            END-EVALUATE.
467
468        400-UPDATE-FILES.
469            PERFORM 850-REWRITE-INVENTORY-RECORD
470            PERFORM 810-READ-FIRST-LOG-RECORD
471            MOVE LH-LAST-SEQUENCE-NUM TO LAST-LOG-RECORD
472            ADD 1 TO LAST-LOG-RECORD
473            MOVE LAST-LOG-RECORD TO LR-SEQUENCE-NUMBER
474            MOVE "C" TO ACTIVITY-TYPE
475            MOVE LOG-IDENTIFIER TO LR-LOG-IDENTIFIER
476            MOVE HOLD-INVENTORY-RECORD TO LR-INVENTORY-RECORD
477            PERFORM 860-WRITE-LOG-RECORD
478            MOVE INVENTORY-RECORD TO LR-INVENTORY-RECORD
479            ADD 1 TO LAST-LOG-RECORD
480            MOVE LAST-LOG-RECORD TO LR-SEQUENCE-NUMBER
481            PERFORM 860-WRITE-LOG-RECORD
482            MOVE "0001" TO LH-SEQUENCE-NUMBER
483            MOVE LAST-LOG-RECORD TO LH-LAST-SEQUENCE-NUM
484            MOVE SPACES TO LH-REST-OF-LOG-RECORD
485            PERFORM 870-REWRITE-LOG-RECORD
486            DISPLAY "This record added to the file"
487                        LINE 16    ERASE EOS.
488
489        800-READ-INVENTORY-RECORD.
490            READ INVENTORY-FILE
491                INVALID KEY
492                    SET RECORD-FOUND TO FALSE
493                    DISPLAY NOT-IN-FILE-SCREEN
494                NOT INVALID KEY
495                    SET RECORD-FOUND TO TRUE
496            END-READ.
497
498        810-READ-FIRST-LOG-RECORD.
499            MOVE "0001" TO LR-SEQUENCE-NUMBER
500            READ LOG-FILE
501                INVALID KEY
502                    DISPLAY "Error reading log header record "
503                    GO TO 900-TERMINATE-ON-ERROR
504            END-READ.
505
506        850-REWRITE-INVENTORY-RECORD.
507            REWRITE INVENTORY-RECORD
508                INVALID KEY
509                    DISPLAY "Error rewriting inventory record ",
510                    IR-STOCK-NUMBER
511                    GO TO 900-TERMINATE-ON-ERROR
512            END-REWRITE.
513
514        860-WRITE-LOG-RECORD.
515            WRITE LOG-RECORD
516                INVALID KEY
517                    DISPLAY "Error writing log record ",
518                    LR-SEQUENCE-NUMBER
519                    GO TO 900-TERMINATE-ON-ERROR
520            END-WRITE.
521
522        870-REWRITE-LOG-RECORD.
523            REWRITE LOG-RECORD
524                INVALID KEY
525                    DISPLAY "Error rewriting log header"
526                    GO TO 900-TERMINATE-ON-ERROR
527            END-REWRITE.
528
529        900-TERMINATE-ON-ERROR.
530            SET FATAL-IO-ERROR TO TRUE
531            EXIT PROGRAM.
532
533        END PROGRAM RFM-EDIT.
534
```

In the 400 module, the inventory record is rewritten and the two log records are prepared and written. The former task is simple and involves only one statement. The latter task is more complex because the log records must be built using data from the log header record. The sequence of steps is

1. Access the log header record to obtain the sequence number of the last record in the file (LH-LAST-SEQENCE-NUMBER).

2. Increment the sequence number by 1.

3. Move the sequence number and the activity type (C for Change) to the WORKING-STORAGE SECTION log identifier area. This is defined globally in the WORKING-STORAGE SECTION of the calling program (beginning line 79 of Figure 20-7). Note that the date and person code are already stored in this area from initialization actions of calling program (see lines 190 and 127 for the person code and line 203 for the date).

4. Move the WORKING-STORAGE SECTION log identifier and the original copy of the inventory record (stored in HOLD-INVENTORY-RECORD) to the log file output record area.

5. Write the log record.

6. Repeat Steps 2 through 5 for the edited copy of the inventory record (in INVENTORY-RECORD).

7. Set up the log record output area in preparation for rewriting the log header record. Data item references to the alternate record area are defined in lines 72–74.

8. Rewrite the log header record.

One other item that you should notice is the error handling for unexpected errors. If you look at the 810, 850, 860, and 870 modules, you will see that a message is displayed and a GO TO 900 is executed. In the 900 module, the switch FATAL-IO-ERROR is set to true and control is returned to the calling program, at which point execution will be terminated. Refer to line 223 and the 900 module in the calling program (Figure 20-7).

Other Maintenance Programs

The remaining three nested programs are shown on pages 592–595 in Figure 20-12 (the display program RFM-DISP), Figure 20-13 (the add program RFM-ADD), and Figure 20-14 (the delete program RFM-DEL). You can see that the display program RFM-DISP is essentially the RAN-DIS3 program of Chapter 10.

The add program, RFM-ADD, is an adaptation of the S-EXTEND program of Chapter 10. Notice also that it uses many of the same components as the edit program. One feature unique to this program is that the stock number entered by the user must be checked to ensure that a record for that stock number does *not* exist in the file. Consequently, after the user enters the stock number, the inventory file is read for that stock number (refer to the 310 module beginning at line 669 of Figure 20-13).

The delete program, RFM-DEL, was actually created from a copy of the add program. That is, using the RM/CO* editor, cutting and pasting a copy of the add program resulted in over 75% of the needed code for the delete program.

Figure 20-12

The RFM-DISP Program—
Example 20-2

```
237        IDENTIFICATION DIVISION.
238
239        PROGRAM-ID. RFM-DISP.
240
241    *      Adapted by W.Price
242    *      October 12, 1990
243    *      from the program RAN-DIS3
244    *                      Written by J.Olson
245    *                      August 14, 1990
246
247    *      This program is to be used as a nested program under
248    *      the general file maintenance program RF-MAINT.
249    *      It displays records from the indexed inventory file.
250    *      After each record display, the user is given the option
251    *      to display another record or to terminate.
252
253    *      The input data file and record are defined in the
254    *      calling program as globals.
255
256        DATA DIVISION.
257
258        SCREEN SECTION.
259
260        01  INTRODUCTION-SCREEN.
261            10  VALUE "This program allows you to inspect records from "
262                     BLANK SCREEN    LINE  6            HIGHLIGHT.
263            10  VALUE  "the software inventory file named SOFTWAR2.DI"
264                              LINE PLUS 1      HIGHLIGHT.
265
266        01  INVENTORY-RECORD-SCREEN.
267            10  VALUE  "INVENTORY DISPLAY" BLANK SCREEN
268                              LINE  2      COL 11.
269            10  VALUE  "Stock number"  LINE PLUS 2  COL  1.
270            10  PIC X(5)      FROM IR-STOCK-NUMBER
271                              LINE PLUS 0  COL 16  REVERSE.
272            10  VALUE  "Software name"  LINE PLUS 2  COL  1.
273            10  PIC X(30)      FROM IR-SOFTWARE-NAME
274                              LINE PLUS 0  COL 16  REVERSE.
275            10  VALUE  "Vendor"      LINE PLUS 2  COL  1.
276            10  PIC X(20)      FROM IR-VENDOR-NAME
277                              LINE PLUS 0  COL 16  REVERSE.
278            10  VALUE  "Stock onhand"  LINE PLUS 2  COL  1.
279            10  PIC Z99      FROM IR-QUANT-ON-HAND
280                              LINE PLUS 0  COL 16  REVERSE.
281            10  VALUE  "Price"        LINE PLUS 0  COL 26.
282            10  PIC ZZ9.99    FROM IR-PRICE
283                              LINE PLUS 0  COL 34  REVERSE.
284            10  VALUE  "Reorder level"  LINE PLUS 1  COL  1.
285            10  PIC ZZ9      FROM IR-REORDER-LEVEL
286                              LINE PLUS 0  COL 16  REVERSE.
287
288        01  USER-REQUEST-SCREEN.
289            10  VALUE  "To continue, enter the desired stock number: "
290                              LINE 16            HIGHLIGHT.
291            10  PIC X(5)      TO IR-STOCK-NUMBER
292                              LINE PLUS 0    COL PLUS 0.
293            10  VALUE  "To exit, strike the Enter key. "
294                              LINE PLUS 1      HIGHLIGHT.
295
296        01  NOT-IN-FILE-SCREEN.
297            10  VALUE  "There is no record in the file for "
298                     LINE 14  BLANK SCREEN  HIGHLIGHT.
299            10  PIC X(5)      FROM IR-STOCK-NUMBER
300                              LINE PLUS 0    COL      HIGHLIGHT.
301
302        PROCEDURE DIVISION.
303
304        000-ACCESS-INVENTORY-FILE.
305            PERFORM 100-INITIALIZE
306            PERFORM 110-DISPLAY-RECORD
307                UNTIL IR-STOCK-NUMBER = SPACES
308            EXIT PROGRAM.
309
310        100-INITIALIZE.
311            MOVE SPACES TO IR-STOCK-NUMBER
312            DISPLAY INTRODUCTION-SCREEN
313            DISPLAY USER-REQUEST-SCREEN
314            ACCEPT  USER-REQUEST-SCREEN.
315
316        110-DISPLAY-RECORD.
317            PERFORM 800-READ-INVENTORY-RECORD
318            DISPLAY USER-REQUEST-SCREEN
319            ACCEPT  USER-REQUEST-SCREEN.
320
321        800-READ-INVENTORY-RECORD.
322            READ INVENTORY-FILE
323            INVALID KEY
324                DISPLAY NOT-IN-FILE-SCREEN
325            NOT INVALID KEY
326                DISPLAY INVENTORY-RECORD-SCREEN
327            END-READ.
328
329        END PROGRAM RFM-DISP.
330
```

Figure 20-13

The RFM-ADD Program—
Example 20-2

```
535        IDENTIFICATION DIVISION.
536
537        PROGRAM-ID. RFM-ADD.
538
539    *      Adapted by W.Price
540    *      October 13, 1990
541    *      from the program S-EXTEND
542    *                      Written by J.Olson/W.Price
543    *                      August 17, 1990
544
545    *      This program allows the user to interactively add records
546    *      to the indexed inventory file.
547
548    *      The input data file and record are defined in the
549    *      calling program as globals.
550
551        DATA DIVISION.
552
553        WORKING-STORAGE SECTION.
554
555        01  PROGRAMMED-SWITCHES.
556            10                      PIC X.
557                88  RECORD-COMPLETED    VALUE "Y" FALSE "N".
558            10                      PIC X.
559                88  NON-DUPLICATE-KEY    VALUE "Y" FALSE "N".
560
561        01  OTHER-VARIABLES.
562            10  DESIRED-OPTION      PIC X.
563            10  LAST-LOG-RECORD      PIC 9(4).
564            10  STOCK-NUMBER        PIC X(5).
565
566        SCREEN SECTION.
567
568        01  INTRODUCTION-SCREEN.
569            10  VALUE "This program allows you to add records to the"
570                     BLANK SCREEN  LINE  6      HIGHLIGHT.
571            10  VALUE "software inventory file named SOFTWAR2.DI"
572                              LINE PLUS 1      HIGHLIGHT.
573
574        01  USER-REQUEST-SCREEN.
575            10  VALUE "To add another record, enter the stock number: "
576                              LINE 16            HIGHLIGHT.
577            10  PIC X(5)      TO STOCK-NUMBER
578                              LINE PLUS 0    COL PLUS 0.
579            10  VALUE "To exit, strike the Enter key. "
580                              LINE PLUS 1      HIGHLIGHT.
581
582        01  SELECT-OPTION-SCREEN.
583            10  VALUE  "Options:"      LINE 18  COL 1.
584            10  VALUE
585            "  1  Data is correct. Add this record to the file."
586                              LINE PLUS 1  COL  1.
587            10  VALUE
588            "  2  Data as shown needs to be corrected."
589                              LINE PLUS 1  COL  1.
590            10  VALUE
591            "  3  Erase the above data; do not add it to the file."
592                              LINE PLUS 1  COL  1.
593            10  VALUE
594            "Please enter 1, 2, or 3 for desired option: "
595                              LINE PLUS 2  COL  1  HIGHLIGHT.
596            10  PIC X        TO DESIRED-OPTION
597                              LINE 23    COL 45  REVERSE  AUTO.
598
```

Figure 20-13

The RFM-ADD Program—Example 20-2

```
599    01  ALREADY-IN-FILE-SCREEN.
600        10  VALUE  "There is already a record in the file for "
601                                 LINE 14  BLANK SCREEN  HIGHLIGHT.
602        10  PIC X(5)        FROM   STOCK-NUMBER
603                                 LINE PLUS 0  COL        HIGHLIGHT.
604
605    01  INVENTORY-RECORD-SCREEN.
606        10  VALUE  "ADD INVENTORY RECORD" BLANK SCREEN
607                                 LINE  2     COL 11.
608        10  VALUE  "Stock number"  LINE PLUS 2  COL 1.
609        10  PIC X(5)    FROM  STOCK-NUMBER
610                                 LINE PLUS 0  COL 16.
611        10  VALUE  "Software name" LINE PLUS 2  COL 1.
612        10  PIC X(30)   USING IR-SOFTWARE-NAME
613                                 LINE PLUS 0  COL 16  REVERSE.
614        10  VALUE  "Vendor"       LINE PLUS 2  COL 1.
615        10  PIC X(20)   USING IR-VENDOR-NAME
616                                 LINE PLUS 0  COL 16  REVERSE.
617        10  VALUE  "Stock onhand" LINE PLUS 2  COL 1.
618        10  PIC ZZ9    USING IR-QUANT-ON-HAND
619                                 LINE PLUS 0  COL 16  REVERSE.
620        10  VALUE  "Price"        LINE PLUS 0  COL 26.
621        10  PIC ZZZ.99  USING IR-PRICE
622                                 LINE PLUS 0  COL 34  REVERSE.
623        10  VALUE  "Reorder level" LINE PLUS 1  COL 1.
624        10  PIC ZZ9    USING IR-REORDER-LEVEL
625                                 LINE PLUS 0  COL 16  REVERSE.
626
627    PROCEDURE DIVISION.
628
629    000-EXTEND-INVENTORY-FILE.
630        PERFORM 100-INITIALIZE
631        PERFORM 110-ADD-INVENTORY-RECORD
632            UNTIL STOCK-NUMBER = SPACES
633        EXIT PROGRAM.
634
635    100-INITIALIZE.
636        DISPLAY INTRODUCTION-SCREEN
637        MOVE "START" TO STOCK-NUMBER
638        PERFORM 310-GET-AND-CHECK-NEW-NUMBER.
639
640    110-ADD-INVENTORY-RECORD.
641        INITIALIZE INVENTORY-RECORD
642        MOVE STOCK-NUMBER TO IR-STOCK-NUMBER
643        SET RECORD-COMPLETED TO FALSE
644        PERFORM 300-ENTER-1-SOFTWARE-ITEM
645            UNTIL RECORD-COMPLETED
646        PERFORM 310-GET-AND-CHECK-NEW-NUMBER.
647
648    300-ENTER-1-SOFTWARE-ITEM.
649        DISPLAY INVENTORY-RECORD-SCREEN
650        ACCEPT  INVENTORY-RECORD-SCREEN
651        DISPLAY SELECT-OPTION-SCREEN
652        ACCEPT  SELECT-OPTION-SCREEN
653
654        EVALUATE DESIRED-OPTION
655            WHEN "1"
656                PERFORM 400-UPDATE-FILES
657                SET RECORD-COMPLETED TO TRUE
658            WHEN "2"
659                CONTINUE
660            WHEN "3"
661                SET RECORD-COMPLETED TO TRUE
662                DISPLAY "This record NOT added to the file"
663                                 LINE 16    ERASE EOS
664            WHEN OTHER
665                DISPLAY "Invalid entry—try again"
666                                 LINE 16    ERASE EOS
667        END-EVALUATE.
668
669    310-GET-AND-CHECK-NEW-NUMBER.
670        SET NON-DUPLICATE-KEY TO FALSE
671        PERFORM UNTIL NON-DUPLICATE-KEY
672               OR STOCK-NUMBER = SPACES
673            DISPLAY USER-REQUEST-SCREEN
674            ACCEPT  USER-REQUEST-SCREEN
675            MOVE STOCK-NUMBER TO IR-STOCK-NUMBER
676            PERFORM 800-READ-INVENTORY-RECORD
677        END-PERFORM.
678
679    400-UPDATE-FILES.
680        PERFORM 850-WRITE-NEW-INVENTORY-RECORD
681        SET RECORD-COMPLETED TO TRUE
682        MOVE INVENTORY-RECORD TO HOLD-INVENTORY-RECORD
683        PERFORM 810-READ-FIRST-LOG-RECORD
684        MOVE LH-LAST-SEQUENCE-NUM TO LAST-LOG-RECORD
685        ADD 1 TO LAST-LOG-RECORD
686        MOVE LAST-LOG-RECORD TO LR-SEQUENCE-NUMBER
687        MOVE "A" TO ACTIVITY-TYPE
688        MOVE LOG-IDENTIFIER TO LR-LOG-IDENTIFIER
689        MOVE HOLD-INVENTORY-RECORD TO LR-INVENTORY-RECORD
690        PERFORM 860-WRITE-LOG-RECORD
691        MOVE "0001" TO LH-SEQUENCE-NUMBER
692        MOVE LAST-LOG-RECORD TO LH-LAST-SEQUENCE-NUM
693        MOVE SPACES TO LH-REST-OF-LOG-RECORD
694        PERFORM 870-REWRITE-LOG-RECORD
695        DISPLAY "This record added to the file"
696                                 LINE 16    ERASE EOS.
697
698    800-READ-INVENTORY-RECORD.
699        READ INVENTORY-FILE
700            INVALID KEY
701                SET NON-DUPLICATE-KEY TO TRUE
702            NOT INVALID KEY
703                DISPLAY ALREADY-IN-FILE-SCREEN
704        END-READ.
705
706    810-READ-FIRST-LOG-RECORD.
707        MOVE "0001" TO LR-SEQUENCE-NUMBER
708        READ LOG-FILE
709            INVALID KEY
710                DISPLAY "Error reading log header record"
711                GO TO 900-TERMINATE-ON-ERROR
712        END-READ.
713
714    850-WRITE-NEW-INVENTORY-RECORD.
715        WRITE INVENTORY-RECORD
716            INVALID KEY
717                DISPLAY "Error writing inventory record",
718                    IR-STOCK-NUMBER
719                GO TO 900-TERMINATE-ON-ERROR
720        END-WRITE.
721
722    860-WRITE-LOG-RECORD.
723        WRITE LOG-RECORD
724            INVALID KEY
725                DISPLAY "Error writing log record",
726                    LR-SEQUENCE-NUMBER
727                GO TO 900-TERMINATE-ON-ERROR
728        END-WRITE.
729
730    870-REWRITE-LOG-RECORD.
731        REWRITE LOG-RECORD
732            INVALID KEY
733                DISPLAY "Error rewriting log header"
734                GO TO 900-TERMINATE-ON-ERROR
735        END-REWRITE.
736
737    900-TERMINATE-ON-ERROR.
738        SET FATAL-10-ERROR TO TRUE
739        EXIT PROGRAM
740
741    END PROGRAM RFM-ADD.
742
```

Figure 20-14

The RFM-DEL Program—Example 20-2

```
743     IDENTIFICATION DIVISION.
744
745     PROGRAM-ID. RFM-DEL.
746   *    Deleting records from an indexed file.
747
748   *    Written by W.Price
749   *    October 15, 1990
750
751   *    This program allows the user to delete selected records
752   *    from the indexed inventory file.
753
754   *    The input data file and record are defined in the
755   *    calling program as globals.
756
757     DATA DIVISION.
758
759     WORKING-STORAGE SECTION.
760
761     01  PROGRAMMED-SWITCHES.
762         10                         PIC X.
763             88  RECORD-FOUND    VALUE "Y" FALSE "N".
764         10  OK-TO-DELETE-SW     PIC X.
765
766     01  OTHER-VARIABLES.
767         02  DUMMY               PIC X.
768
769     SCREEN SECTION.
770
771     01  INTRODUCTION-SCREEN.
772         10  VALUE "This program allows you to DELETE records from "
773                 BLANK SCREEN    LINE 6              HIGHLIGHT.
774         10  VALUE  "the software inventory file named SOFTWAR2.DI"
775                                 LINE PLUS 1         HIGHLIGHT.
776         10  VALUE "Please note that once you delete a record, "
777                         LINE PLUS 2 COL 8 HIGHLIGHT.
778         10  VALUE "it is IMPOSSIBLE to get it back."
779                         LINE PLUS 2 COL 8 HIGHLIGHT.
780
781     01  USER-REQUEST-SCREEN.
782         10  VALUE "To continue, enter the desired stock number: "
783                         LINE 16              HIGHLIGHT.
784         10  PIC X(5)     TO IR-STOCK-NUMBER
785                         LINE PLUS 0    COL PLUS 0.
786         10  VALUE "To exit, strike the Enter key. "
787                         LINE PLUS 1          HIGHLIGHT.
788
789     01  NOT-IN-FILE-SCREEN.
790         10  VALUE "There is no record in the file for "
791                         LINE 14  BLANK SCREEN HIGHLIGHT.
792         10  PIC X(5)     FROM IR-STOCK-NUMBER
793                         LINE PLUS 0   COL      HIGHLIGHT.
794
795     01  DELETE-RECORD-SCREEN.
796         10  VALUE
797             "Are you certain that you want to delete this record?"
798                     LINE 14 BLANK REMAINDER HIGHLIGHT.
799         10  PIC X       USING OK-TO-DELETE-SW
800                     LINE PLUS 0   COL AUTO HIGHLIGHT.
801
802     01  INVENTORY-RECORD-SCREEN.
803         10  VALUE  "INVENTORY DISPLAY" BLANK SCREEN
804                             LINE 2       COL 11  REVERSE.
805         10  VALUE  "Stock number"  LINE PLUS 2 COL 1.
806         10  PIC X(5)      FROM IR-STOCK-NUMBER
807                             LINE PLUS 0  COL 16.
808         10  VALUE  "Software name"  LINE PLUS 2 COL 1.
809         10  PIC X(30)     FROM IR-SOFTWARE-NAME
810                             LINE PLUS 0  COL 16 REVERSE.
811         10  VALUE  "Vendor"     LINE PLUS 2 COL 1.
812         10  PIC X(20)     FROM IR-VENDOR-NAME
813                             LINE PLUS 0  COL 16 REVERSE.
814         10  VALUE  "Stock onhand"  LINE PLUS 2 COL 1.
815         10  PIC Z99       FROM IR-QUANT-ON-HAND
816                             LINE PLUS 0  COL 16 REVERSE.
817         10  VALUE  "Price"     LINE PLUS 0  COL 26.
818         10  PIC ZZ9.99    FROM IR-PRICE
819                             LINE PLUS 0  COL 34 REVERSE.
820         10  VALUE  "Reorder level"  LINE PLUS 1 COL 1.
821         10  PIC ZZ9       FROM IR-REORDER-LEVEL
822                             LINE PLUS 0  COL 16 REVERSE.
823
824     PROCEDURE DIVISION.
825
826     000-DELETE-RECORD.
827         PERFORM 100-INITIALIZE
828         PERFORM 110-DELETE-RECORD
829             UNTIL IR-STOCK-NUMBER = SPACES
830         EXIT PROGRAM.
831
832     100-INITIALIZE.
833         MOVE SPACES TO IR-STOCK-NUMBER
834         DISPLAY INTRODUCTION-SCREEN
835         DISPLAY USER-REQUEST-SCREEN
836         ACCEPT  USER-REQUEST-SCREEN.
837
838     110-DELETE-RECORD.
839         PERFORM 800-READ-INVENTORY-RECORD
840         IF RECORD-FOUND
841             MOVE "N" TO OK-TO-DELETE-SW
842             DISPLAY DELETE-RECORD-SCREEN
843             ACCEPT DELETE-RECORD-SCREEN
844             IF OK-TO-DELETE-SW = "y" OR "Y"
845                 MOVE INVENTORY-RECORD TO HOLD-INVENTORY-RECORD
846                 DELETE INVENTORY-FILE
847                 PERFORM 810-READ-FIRST-LOG-RECORD
848                 MOVE LH-LAST-SEQUENCE-NUM TO LAST-LOG-RECORD
849                 ADD 1 TO LAST-LOG-RECORD
850                 MOVE LAST-LOG-RECORD TO LR-SEQUENCE-NUMBER
851                 MOVE "D" TO ACTIVITY-TYPE
852                 MOVE LOG-IDENTIFIER TO LR-LOG-IDENTIFIER
853                 MOVE HOLD-INVENTORY-RECORD TO LR-INVENTORY-RECORD
854                 PERFORM 860-WRITE-LOG-RECORD
855                 MOVE "0001" TO LH-SEQUENCE-NUMBER
856                 MOVE LAST-LOG-RECORD TO LH-LAST-SEQUENCE-NUM
857                 MOVE SPACES TO LH-REST-OF-LOG-RECORD
858                 PERFORM 870-REWRITE-LOG-RECORD
859             END-IF
860         END-IF
861         DISPLAY USER-REQUEST-SCREEN
862         ACCEPT  USER-REQUEST-SCREEN.
863
864     800-READ-INVENTORY-RECORD.
865         READ INVENTORY-FILE
866             INVALID KEY
867                 DISPLAY NOT-IN-FILE-SCREEN
868                 SET RECORD-FOUND TO FALSE
869             NOT INVALID KEY
870                 DISPLAY INVENTORY-RECORD-SCREEN
871                 SET RECORD-FOUND TO TRUE
872         END-READ.
873
874     810-READ-FIRST-LOG-RECORD.
875         MOVE "0001" TO LR-SEQUENCE-NUMBER
876         READ LOG-FILE
877             INVALID KEY
878                 DISPLAY "Error reading log header record "
879                 GO TO 900-TERMINATE-ON-ERROR
880         END-READ.
881
882     860-WRITE-LOG-RECORD.
883         WRITE LOG-RECORD
884             INVALID KEY
885                 DISPLAY "Error writing log record ",
886                     LR-SEQUENCE-NUMBER
887                 GO TO 900-TERMINATE-ON-ERROR
888         END-WRITE.
889
890     870-REWRITE-LOG-RECORD.
891         REWRITE LOG-RECORD
892             INVALID KEY
893                 DISPLAY "Error rewriting log header"
894                 GO TO 900-TERMINATE-ON-ERROR
895         END-REWRITE.
896
897     900-TERMINATE-ON-ERROR.
898         SET FATAL-IO-ERROR TO TRUE
899         EXIT PROGRAM.
900
901     END PROGRAM RFM-DEL.
902
903     END PROGRAM RF-MAINT.
```

Chapter Summary

Like Chapter 19, this chapter introduced no new COBOL syntax, but rather applied most of the COBOL principles you learned from preceding chapters. You have learned about interactive file processing via two examples:

■ Interactive transaction processing, as illustrated by the ITP-NDX program, provides the means for maintaining accurate, up-to-the-minute data. As each transaction takes place, it is entered into the system and the data updated. This is in contrast to batch transactions, in which the data are accurate only as of the last batch processing cycle. As you will learn in the next chapter, transaction updating is commonly performed as an activity of other processing (that is, updating the quantity on hand is done by an order entry program).

■ File maintenance processing is illustrated by the RF-MAINT program. In any organization, only selected individuals have access to maintenance programs. Thus, access is commonly limited as a security measure. RF-MAINT requires a user authorization code to gain entry to the program. In order to provide an audit trail of activities, this program writes one or more records to a transaction log file. Processing the log file is the topic of one of the programming assignments of this chapter.

Questions and Exercises

Give a brief description of each of the following terms that were introduced in this chapter.

Key Terminology

audit trail
header record
on-line processing

General Questions

1. In general terms, what is the difference between batch and "on-line" transaction and maintenance processing?

2. What makes "on-line" processing unique and more difficult to program?

3. In this chapter, the WITH TEST AFTER phrase is used in conjunction with the PERFORM statement. What is the purpose for this?

4. What is a "log file" and why is it important?

5. When an on-line application has required functions that are relatively independent of one another and amenable to using separate programs, two different programming techniques can be used. What are they?

6. The maintenance program of this chapter uses two different record descriptions for the log file. How does the programmer know which to refer to when processing the file?

Questions Relating to the Example Programs

1. In the 300 module of the ITP-NDX program (Figure 20-4), what would happen if the WITH TEST AFTER phrase were omitted from the PERFORM at line 246?

2. What change to the program would eliminate the problem introduced by the deletion proposed in Question 1?

3. The purpose of the 410 module is to accept and verify the action to be taken with the current record (1—rewrite, 2—make changes, and 3—abort). This is done by the EVALUATE statement of lines 297–310. If option 2 is selected, no action is required, so the CONTINUE statement is used. Since no action is required for option 2, why not simply remove the WHEN "2" phrase (lines 302–303)?

4. Regarding the maintenance program of Example 20-2, based on what you know about the log file and its contents, what do you think it contains when it is first created? (When you ran the exercise sequence, you generated this file by running CREA-LOG.)

5. The calling program of RF-MAINT defines the one-character data item OPTION at line 108 (see Figure 20-7). Similarly, the RFM-ADD program defines the one-character data item DESIRED-OPTION at line 562 (see Figure 20-13). Had the latter been given the name OPTION instead of DESIRED-OPTION, would there have been a conflict of names within RF-MAINT because OPTION would be defined in two different places? Justify your answer.

6. What would occur in the add program RFM-ADD (Figure 20-13), given the following conditions?
   a. The NON-DUPLICATE-KEY test were omitted from the UNTIL condition of the PERFORM (line 671).
   b. The PERFORM at line 676 were omitted.
   c. The product number of the record entered by the user for addition to the file already existed in the file.

7. Upon detecting an unexpected input or output error, the RF-MAINT program displays an error message and then terminates. Depending upon where in the program this occurs, various files can be corrupted, requiring repair. Describe the potential inconsistencies that would result in the edit program for an error occurring in each of the modules 810, 850, 860, and 870. Base your description on the 400 module of the edit program (Figure 20-11).

Programming Assignments

20-1 Accessing the Log File

The log file of Example 20-2 represents a history of changes to the inventory file. Whenever data in the inventory file appear suspicious, one action is to check the log file to determine what activities, if any, have occurred. For instance, assume that you are running a program and you attempt to access record 07427, but you get an error message indicating it is not in the file. This is strange because you used it last week. By inspecting the log file, you can determine when and by whom it was deleted. A needed component of the inventory control system would be a program that gives you access to the log file.

Output Requirements:

   Printed report: Records (as designated) of the log file. Separate each field by one space. Include appropriate headings.

   Screen display: All log records for a designated product number. Display the product number and then on subsequent lines, each record (exclude the product number) for that product item. Realize that a record may have several entries. For instance, a given record may have an add entry, one or more pairs of change entries, and a delete entry. Assume that there will not be so many entries that the display scrolls off the screen.

Input Description:

   File name: SOFT-LOG.DIA
   A different name has been selected for log file for this assignment so that it will not conflict with any log file that you create in exercising the program.

   Record format: The same as that of SOFT-LOG.DI—see Example 20-2 (page 575).

Processing Specifications:

   1. A single program is to provide the user with the option of obtaining a printed report or accessing log records interactively.

   2. The user must be able to request that the printed report be printed with records in sequence by the sequence number or by the product number (the alternate key).

   3. The user must be able to select records as follows:
      ▪ All log records in the file
      ▪ All records since a user-specified date
      ▪ Records written between user-specified beginning and ending dates

4. For interactive display, the user must be queried for the stock number of the log records to be displayed. Only log records for that product must be displayed.

5. After a display, the user must be allowed to request the display for another product number.

20-2 Interactive File Maintenance

A variety of assignments in preceding chapters have used the Student file. As any application system, maintenance capabilities are required. This assignment addresses these needs. The assignment is modularized so that you can do one or more of the maintenance functions.

Student File Processing:

The following maintenance activities are required for the Student file:

Delete a record

Add a record

Change data in a record

Deletion implications for Grades file:

If a student record is deleted (from the Students file), records for that student must be deleted from the Grades file.

Activity log output file:

For each addition or deletion, write a record to the Activity log file; for each change to a record, write both the original and the changed version.

Input Description:

File names: STUDENTS.DI and GRADES.DL

Record description: See Appendix A

Processing Requirements:

You may elect to code one, two, or three of the listed maintenance functions. Your project can consist of a menu-controlled system or you can code programs each run independently of the others. In all cases where you code a particular operation, you program must:

For record deletion:

1. Write a copy of the deleted record to the activity log file.
2. Delete the corresponding grade records from the Grades file. For this you have two options. First, you can simply read the Grades file sequentially and write a new one omitting the records to be deleted. (The DELETE statement cannot be used with sequential files.) This would be a clumsy and inefficient process, especially if several records are to be deleted. The alternate is to write a program to copy the file GRADES.DL into an indexed file. The problem with this method is that the current version of GRADES does not have a field with unique contents to serve as the primary key. (You would want Student number to be an alternate key because of duplicates.) The solution to this problem is to add a sequence number to the record and give the records consecutive sequence numbers.

For record addition:

3. Write a copy of the added record to the activity log file.
4. Validate input fields as you deem appropriate.

For record changes:

5. Write a copy of the original record to the activity log file.
6. Write a copy of the record as changed to the activity log file.
7. Do not allow the student number to be changed because it is the key field.

21

DISK PROCESSING APPLICATIONS

Outline

Chapter Objectives

With the completion of the last three chapters, you should feel reasonably confident in your ability to write file processing applications. From these chapters, you have learned a wide variety of file processing techniques. However, each example has, in itself, represented a relatively narrow application area and the principal focus has been on processing a single file (for instance, entering transactions into the inventory file).

This chapter is devoted to an order processing case study that is typical of the processing activities at any sales-oriented company such as UNISOFT. The portion of the order processing system described in this chapter consists of two processing components: entering orders and printing invoices.

In this chapter, you will see how many of the file processing principles you have studied in previous chapters are integrated into a whole to form a processing system. You will see how the output of one component of a system (order entry) creates input for another component of a system (invoice preparation). Whereas the primary focus in previous file processing examples has been on using one or two files (exclusive of the printer file), this example requires four files, each contributing essential data to the eventual output.

No new COBOL principles are introduced by this case study; it simply brings together a wide variety of techniques encountered in business programming.

A Business Programming Application

Order Processing

The entire focus of this chapter is on an order processing application example. As an introduction to order processing, assume that a UNISOFT customer has just received software that she has ordered. Enclosed in the package is a copy of an invoice as shown in Figure 21-1. (An invoice is an itemized statement of merchandise shipped to a purchaser.) Notice that the invoice includes her name, address, and data regarding each product item that she has ordered. For each item ordered, there is one line on the invoice; these are commonly called *line items*.

As an illustration of how order information is entered into the computer and stored, let's consider the actions that took place when the customer placed her telephone order. Assume that Richardson (the customer) is a regular UNISOFT customer.

1. The salesperson enters customer number 12555, Richardson's customer number. The computer must access her record from the customer file and display needed data.

2. The salesperson enters product number 53351. The computer must access and display product information for QBase 7000.

3. The salesperson enters 2 for a quantity of 2. The computer must calculate the amount as the unit price times the quantity.

4. The process must be repeated for product number 28558.

5. When the order entry process is completed, the order entry screen into which the salesperson has made the entries would typically appear as shown in Figure 21-2.

You can see that access to at least two files is necessary in order to obtain required information for entry of the order: the customer file and the inventory (product) file.

The order entry process also involves output. That is, some type of invoice file must exist that includes one record for each order. Consider the basic fields that must comprise the record of an invoice file.

1. A key field that uniquely identifies each order. For this example, each order is given a unique invoice number (key field) that is generated from data stored in one of the files.

2. The customer number of the customer placing the order.

3. The stock number and quantity of each item of the order.

Figure 21-1

A Sample Invoice

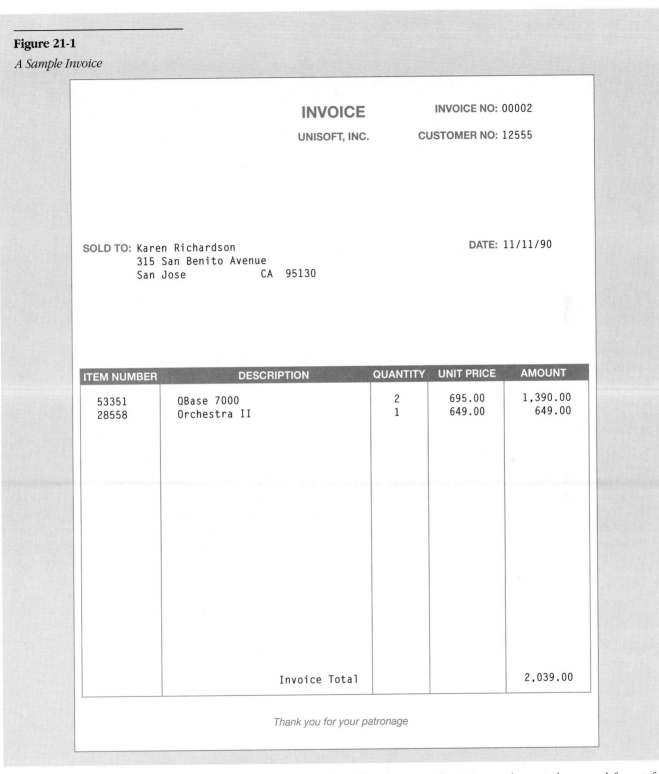

When designing the data files for an application, you lay out the record format for each file by listing each field to be stored and its space requirement. Consider the needed inventory file necessary for the data displayed in Figure 21-2. The invoice record must include at least the invoice number and the customer number. It must also include data for *each* item ordered. The question arises: "How many items will each order include?" The answer is that there is no set number. For instance, some customers might order only one item; another customer might order several. In other words, the number of items ordered will vary from invoice to invoice.

Figure 21-2

Order Entry Screen

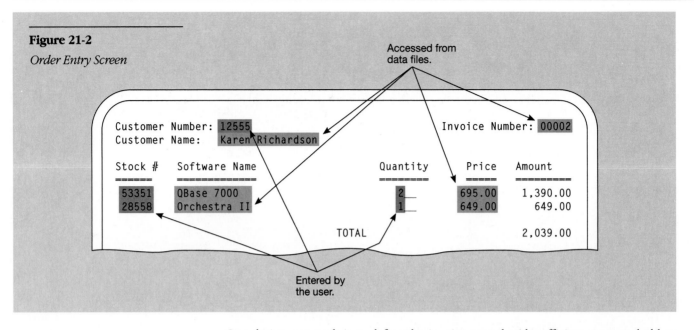

One design approach is to define the invoice record with sufficient space to hold an arbitrarily determined maximum number of items (for instance, 20). Such a record is illustrated schematically in Figure 21-3. There are a number of disadvantages to this approach*, the primary one being that processing the file tends to be clumsy.

Another design approach is to separate the data into two related files: an invoice master file and an invoice line-item file. For each invoice, there is one record in the invoice file; for each line item of an invoice, there is one record in the line-item file. This technique, illustrated in Figure 21-4, actually forms the basis for the relational database model. It is the technique used in this chapter's example.

The Need to Separate Order Entry and Invoice Preparation

One of the important ground rules in the design of this system is that entering order information into the computer and printing invoices must be two completely independent operations. By contrast, if you compare the sample invoice of Figure 21-1 and the interactive screen display of Figure 21-2, you will see that it would be a simple matter to print the invoice as the order is being entered. This might appear to be a good approach on the surface, but it has many drawbacks in practice. For instance, what if the printer is temporarily out of service and you must continue entering orders? What do you do if the printer ribbon jumps off the track and is noticed only after several invoices have been processed but nothing is printed? Obviously, a means is needed to print invoices as an activity independent of order entry.

---

* At first, you might conclude that this method would be very wasteful of disk storage space, especially if most orders are for only a few items. For instance, if there is a provision for 20 items, an order for one item would occupy one set of item fields and would leave the record's remaining 19 empty. However, data compression techniques that utilize special encoding techniques to reduce the amount of storage required by data are now in common use. For instance, a string of blank characters might be reduced to a one- or two-byte binary code. The Ryan-McFarland compiler uses data compression techniques for indexed files. You can see this by displaying an indexed file with the DOS TYPE command.

Figure 21-3

*An Invoice Record Layout
That Includes Space for
Multiple Item Entries*

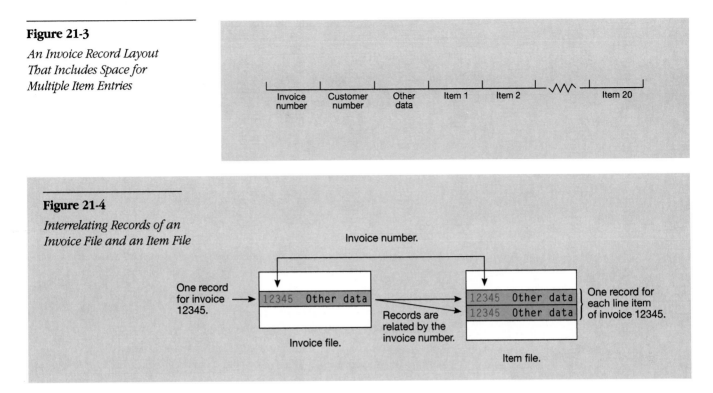

Figure 21-4

*Interrelating Records of an
Invoice File and an Item File*

***Order Entry Definition—
Example 21-1***

The following is the example definition for the order entry component of this system; the definition of the invoice preparation segment is deferred until later in the chapter.

Example 21-1 Order Entry

Problem Description

An order processing system is required for UNISOFT that will allow the salespeople to enter orders interactively. As each order is entered, customer data is to be accessed from a customer master file and product information for each item is to be accessed from the inventory file. The customer file and inventory file are to be updated, reflecting activity of the order. Order information is to be written to invoice files for later preparation of invoices. The order processing system is to consist of two components: order entry and invoice preparation.

Output Requirements

There is no printed output from the order entry component; all output is to files.
Customer file: CUSTOMER.DI
    Update customer balance (amount owed by the customer).

Inventory file: SOFTWAR2.DI
    Update quantity on hand for each product item sold.

Invoice master file: INVOICE.MAS
    Organization is relative
    Relative key: Invoice number

Contains one record for each invoice. The invoice number is the relative record number. Invoice numbers are assigned, beginning with the number 00002. The record includes the following fields.

Positions	Field	Format
Header record (relative record 1)		
1–5	Last used invoice number	
6–30	Unused	
Subsequent records		
1–5	Invoice number—key field (corresponds to relative record number)	
6–10	Customer number for this sale	
11–16	Date of invoice	*yymmdd*
17–23	Total billed amount of invoice	99999V99
24–30	Amount paid on this invoice	99999V99

Invoice transaction (line item) file: INVOICE.TRA
    Organization is indexed
    Key field: Invoice number + line number

Contains one record for each item ordered of each invoice. The key field is composed of the invoice number followed by a two-digit number, which is the line number of that entry on the invoice. The record includes the following data.

Positions	Field	Format
1–5	Invoice number	
6–7	Line number of this invoice entry	
8–12	Customer number	
13–17	Stock number of item purchased	
18–47	Description of item purchased	
48–50	Quantity purchased of this item	
51–55	Item price	999V99
56–62	Amount (quantity purchased times price)	99999V99

Input Specifications
    Inventory file: SOFTWAR2.DI

Customer master file: CUSTOMER.DI
    Organization is indexed
    Key field: Customer number

The customer file consists of one record for each customer with the following data.

Positions	Field	Format
1–5	Customer number (key field)	
6–35	Name	
36–65	Street address	
66–85	City	
86–87	State	
88–96	Zip code	
97–104	Balance owed on account	S999999V99

Processing Requirements

The order entry program is to function as follows.

1. Accept the customer number of the customer placing the order.
2. Access the customer record from the customer file.
3. Repeat the following for each ordered item.
   a. Accept the product number of the item ordered.
   b. Access the product record from the inventory file.
   c. Accept the quantity for the entered product.
   d. If the quantity on hand is sufficient for this order, calculate:
      Amount = quantity times price
   e. If the quantity on hand is insufficient for this order, display an error message and do not accept this line entry.
      Note: This check is not done in the example program that you will be studying. Its implementation is left as a programming assignment described at the end of the chapter.
   f. Subtract the quantity ordered from the inventory record quantity-on-hand field and rewrite the record.
   g. Accumulate the amount for the ordered item.
4. Add the accumulated amount to the customer-balance field of the customer record and rewrite the record.
5. Write an invoice record to the invoice file for this order.
6. Update the invoice file header record to contain the invoice number of the last invoice in the file.
7. Write one record to the invoice transaction (line-item) file for each line item of the order.

Some Design Considerations Regarding the Invoice Files

About the Invoice Number

In any order processing system, it is critical that the invoice number be unique. From the programming aspect, this need is obvious: the prime key of a random file (indexed or relative) must be unique. From the practical aspect, real chaos could result if the orders for several customers had the same invoice number. One way of ensuring uniqueness is to use computer assignment of the invoice number, the approach used in this application.

To that end, the first record of the invoice master file is a header record containing the next available invoice number. Creation of a new invoice record includes the following steps:

1. Access the header record (from the invoice master file)
2. Increment the last-invoice-number value from the header record as the invoice number for the new invoice record
3. Build and write the new invoice master record
4. Rewrite the header record

You are familiar with this concept from Chapter 20; the transaction log file uses a header record to control assignment of a transaction number to each transaction record.

About the Invoice Files

The preparation of invoices (and other activities associated with an order/invoice system) requires random access to data stored in the invoice files. Thus, both the master and transaction files must have a random organization. Because invoice numbers are consecutively assigned beginning with 00002, the relative file organization is used.* That is,

---

* Although this is a reasonable choice for order processing and invoice preparation, it will prove unsatisfactory for other processing needs. These needs, plus the necessary modifications to the invoice file structure and to the programs, are the basis for programming assignments at the end of this chapter.

the relative record position and the invoice number are identical. Because the relative record position corresponds to the invoice number, the invoice number is not required as a field in the record itself. However, consistent with good practice (to allow verification), the invoice number is included as a separate field in the record.

The invoice transaction file presents a different problem in that it can contain more than one record for a single invoice master record. Yet it must include the invoice number in its key to establish the "linkage" between the invoice master and transaction files. This is done, and uniqueness of the key field preserved, by adding a line number suffix to the invoice number. That is, the first two fields of the INVOICE.TRA are defined as follows.

Positions	Field
1–5	Invoice number
6–7	Line number of this invoice entry

The combination of these two fields, which is unique, serves as the key field for the file. As you will see in the program, the invoice-number component provides the desired random access for processing transaction records together with their corresponding invoice record.

The order entry program must allow the user to enter one or more orders during a session. Upon completion of the entry of an order, the order entry screen must appear as shown in Figure 21-2. This screen illustrates the following features of the order entry program.

1. The customer number is entered by the user and the remaining customer information is filled in from the customer file by the program.

2. For each transaction line, the stock number of the desired item is entered by the user and the description and price are filled in from the file.

3. The desired quantity for the item is entered; then, the extended price is calculated as the quantity times the unit price.

Trial Runs

As with the example programs of Chapter 20, making some trial runs in which you enter orders and prepare invoices will provide you with an insight to some of the needs of these programs. To that end, the distribution disk contains the following program files that you will need:

ORD-MENU.CBL	The "front-end" menu program
ORD-ENT.CBL	The order entry program
ORD-INVO.CBL	The invoice preparation program
CREAINVO.CBL	A program to create new invoice master and transaction files (INVOICE.MAS and INVOICE.TRA)

Each of these four programs must be compiled. Then, prior to beginning, you must run the program CREAINVO to create the required invoice files.

In addition, you will need the following two data files that are also stored on the distribution disk. (If you did the sample runs in Chapter 20, do not use the copy of SOFTWAR2.DI used in those runs because it will have been changed.)

SOFTWAR2.DI	The inventory file used in Chapter 20
CUSTOMER.DI	The indexed customer file; it contains records for the following customers:

12345	21911
12555	24001
20000	25541
20001	

After you have copied the needed files, compiled the programs, and run CREAINVO to generate new invoice files, you may run the ORD-MENU program. You will be presented with the following menu:

```
     ORDER ENTRY / INVOICE PROCESSING

       Please enter the number for the desired option:

          1   Enter orders
          2   Prepare invoices
          3   Exit from this menu

       Option desired: ___
```

Order Entry

For this trial run, you will be entering orders for three customers: 12555, 12345, and 20000. You will also be selecting incorrect entries to demonstrate checking features of the program.

1. Type the digit 4 for your menu selection; you will receive a message to enter a valid option selection.

2. Type the digit 1 (order entry). After the announcement screen, strike Enter to continue. You will be presented with the following:

```
Enter customer number _____
```

3. Type the customer number 99999 (there is no such customer) and strike Enter; you will receive an error message and be prompted to reenter the customer number.

4. Enter the customer number 12555. The screen will display the following:

```
Customer Number: 12555                          Invoice Number: 00002
Customer Name:    Karen Richardson


Stock #  Software Name                Quantity    Price   Amount
======   =============                ========    =====   ======

  ____
```

5. Enter the stock number 99999 (there is no such stock number in the software file). You will receive an error message and be prompted to reenter the stock number.

6. Enter the stock number 53351. The screen display will include:

```
Stock #  Software Name                Quantity     Price   Amount
======   =============                ========     =====   ==========

 53351   QBase 7000                      ____     695.00

  ____
```

7. Enter the quantity 2. The screen display will include:

```
Stock #  Software Name                Quantity     Price   Amount
======   =============                ========     =====   ==========

 53351   QBase 7000                      2__      695.00   1,390.00

  ____
```

8. For the next item, enter the stock number 28558, then enter a quantity of 1. The screen display will include the second line item and the cursor will be awaiting entry of the third stock number.

9. This completes the order, so strike the Enter key without typing a stock number.

10. You will be requested to enter a customer number (for the next order). Enter the number 20000 (for Harvey Mitchell).

11. Enter the stock number 45191 (for Word Comet 7) and a quantity of 1.

12. For the second line item, strike the Enter key without entering a stock number to terminate entry for this order as it is complete.

13. For the third order, enter the customer number 12345 (for Zeno Universal Products).

14. Enter the stock number 10164 (for Sluggish Writer) and a quantity of 3.

15. For the second line item, strike the Enter key without entering a stock number to terminate entry for this order as it is complete.

16. Strike the Enter key without entering a customer number to terminate order entry. You will be returned to the main menu. Do not strike 3 to exit the program because you will go on to invoice preparation, as described in the next section.

This completes the order entry trial run. You now have records for three invoices: 00002, 00003, and 00004.

Invoice Preparation

The trial run for invoice preparation includes two parts: preparation of invoices for records just entered and preparation of selected invoices.

1. Select the Prepare-invoices option of the menu by typing 2.

2. Since you have just completed entering orders, you will be queried with the following:

```
Do you wish to run invoices for the orders just entered? <Y/N> _
```

Respond by striking Y.

3. A one-line message will be displayed as each invoice is being prepared. After the last one, you will be prompted to strike Enter to return to the menu. Strike the Enter key.

This completes the first part of the trial run. The invoices will be stored in the file PRN-FILE. You may terminate the program (option 3) and inspect them either with the DOS TYPE command or through RM/CO*. Note that the file includes three invoices, one for each order entered during the preceding order entry session.

For the next part of this trial run, you will enter some erroneous ranges to observe the error responses. Then you will print the invoices for 00003 and 00004. If you terminated processing to inspect the output file, run ORD-MENU again.

1. From the main menu, select option 2 and you will be presented with the following screen:

```
You may print a group of invoices with
consecutive invoice numbers by entering the
beginning and ending numbers. If you must print
only one invoice, enter the same number for the
beginning and ending entries.

Beginning invoice number? _____

Ending invoice number? _____
```

2. For the beginning invoice number, enter 00001. Note that this is the relative record number of the header record; the first invoice is numbered 00002.

3. For the ending invoice number, enter 00006. Note that this is larger than the invoice number of the last order entered (00004). You will receive the following error messages:

```
Beginning number less than 00002.
Ending number larger than last in file.

Do you wish reenter the numbers? <Y/N> _
```

4. If you respond with N (for No), control will be returned to the main menu. Type Y so that you can reenter.

5. Enter 00003 and 00002 for the beginning and ending invoice numbers; notice that the beginning number is less than the ending number. An appropriate error message will be displayed. Type Y so that you can reenter the numbers.

6. This time, enter the correct values: 00003 and 00004 for the beginning and ending invoice numbers.

7. The invoices will be prepared and control will be returned to the main menu.

8. Terminate processing by selecting the 3 option.

A newly created copy of the file PRN-FILE will contain invoices for 00003 and 00004. As before, you may inspect them either with the DOS TYPE command or through RM/CO*.

Menu Control of the Order Entry System

The Relationship Between Programs

As you are aware from compiling programs of the order entry system, the system consists of three programs:

ORD-MENU	The menu program, which provides access to the other two programs. It is a relatively short one.
ORD-ENT	The order entry program.
ORD-INVO	The invoice preparation program.

Actually, the two programs are almost completely independent of one another. The only need for "communication" between them is for the entry program to tell the invoicing program the invoice numbers of the orders that have just been entered. The relationship between these two programs and the menu program is illustrated in Figure 21-5. Thus, not only does the menu program provide access to the entry and invoicing programs, but it also provides the means for communicating the data from the entry program to the invoice program.

Figure 21-5

Relationship Between the Menu and Two Called Programs

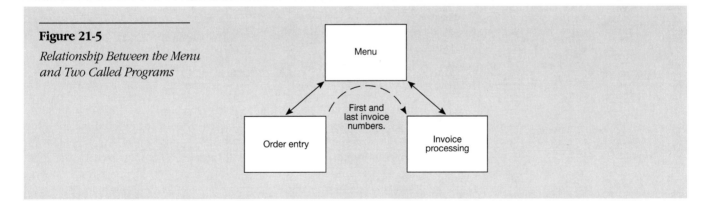

The Menu Program

The menu program, shown in Figure 21-6, is by far the simplest of the three programs. You should recognize most of its components from your trial run. Menu selection is controlled through the programmed switch OPTION (the input data item at line 47 of the menu screen).

The CALL statements at lines 79 and 81 both include the following phrase for the purpose of communicating parameters:

```
USING ORDER-PROCESSING-PARAMETERS
```

The data item ORDER-PROCESSING-PARAMETERS is an 01 defined beginning line 28 and includes four elementary items. The first and last invoice numbers of orders entered during an order entry session are passed via BEGINNING-INVOICE-NUMBER and ENDING-

Figure 21-6

The Menu Program—
Example 21-1

```
1      IDENTIFICATION DIVISION.                          48
2                                                        49   01  INVALID-OPTION-SCREEN.
3      PROGRAM-ID.    ORD-MENU.                          50       10  VALUE "Please enter a valid option: 1, 2, or 3!"
4                                                        51            HIGHLIGHT   BELL              LINE 22       COL  2.
5    *    Written by W.Price  10-29-86                   52       10  VALUE "To try again, strike the Enter key... "
6    *    Modified by J.Olson/W.Price 11-2-90            53                                         LINE PLUS 2  COL  2.
7                                                        54       10  PIC X     TO OPTION          REVERSE      COL PLUS 0.
8    *    Menu program for Order Entry/Invoice Preparation. 55
9                                                        56   01  ERROR-TERMINATION-SCREEN-1.
10   *    This program controls access to the            57       10  VALUE "Note the above error; then strike Enter "
11   *    Order Entry / Invoice Processing system.       58            HIGHLIGHT   BELL              LINE 20       COL  1.
12                                                       59       10  VALUE "to terminate the Order Entry program.  "
13     ENVIRONMENT DIVISION.                             60                                         LINE PLUS 1  COL  1.
14                                                       61       10  PIC X      TO OPTION                       COL PLUS 0.
15     CONFIGURATION SECTION.                            62
16     SOURCE-COMPUTER.  IBM-PC.                         63   01  ERROR-TERMINATION-SCREEN-2.
17                                                       64       10  VALUE "Abnormal termination of Order Entry program."
18     DATA DIVISION.                                    65            BLINK       BELL              LINE 23       COL  1.
19                                                       66
20     WORKING-STORAGE SECTION.                          67   PROCEDURE DIVISION.
21                                                       68
22   01  PROGRAMMED-SWITCHES.                            69   000-EXECUTE-MENU.
23       10  OPTION              PIC X     VALUE SPACE.  70       SET FATAL-IO-ERROR TO FALSE
24           88  ENTER-ORDERS        VALUE "1".          71       SET NO-NEW-INVOICES TO TRUE
25           88  RUN-INVOICES        VALUE "2".          72
26           88  FINISHED            VALUE "3".          73       PERFORM UNTIL FINISHED
27                                                       74           MOVE SPACE TO OPTION
28   01  ORDER-PROCESSING-PARAMETERS.                    75           DISPLAY MENU-SCREEN
29       10  BEGINNING-INVOICE-NUMBER PIC 9(5).          76           ACCEPT  MENU-SCREEN
30       10  ENDING-INVOICE-NUMBER   PIC 9(5).           77           EVALUATE TRUE
31       10                          PIC X.              78               WHEN ENTER-ORDERS
32           88  NO-NEW-INVOICES    VALUE "Y"  FALSE "N". 79                   CALL "ORD-ENT" USING ORDER-PROCESSING-PARAMETERS
33       10                          PIC X.              80               WHEN RUN-INVOICES
34           88  FATAL-IO-ERROR     VALUE "Y"  FALSE "N". 81                   CALL "ORD-INVO" USING ORDER-PROCESSING-PARAMETERS
35                                                       82               WHEN FINISHED
36     SCREEN SECTION.                                   83                   CONTINUE
37                                                       84               WHEN OTHER
38   01  MENU-SCREEN.                                    85                   DISPLAY INVALID-OPTION-SCREEN
39       10  VALUE "ORDER ENTRY / INVOICE PROCESSING"    86                   ACCEPT  INVALID-OPTION-SCREEN
40            BLANK SCREEN               LINE  2   COL 5. 87           END-EVALUATE
41       10  VALUE "Please enter the number for the desired option:" 88           IF FATAL-IO-ERROR
42                                       LINE  5   COL 2. 89               GO TO 900-TERMINATE-ON-ERROR
43       10  VALUE "  1   Enter orders"    LINE PLUS 2 COL 2. 90          END-IF
44       10  VALUE "  2   Prepare invoices" LINE PLUS 2 COL 2. 91       END-PERFORM
45       10  VALUE "  3   Exit from this menu" LINE PLUS 2 COL 2. 92
46       10  VALUE "Option desired: "    LINE PLUS 2 COL 2. 93       STOP RUN.
47       10  PIC X    TO OPTION    AUTO REVERSE  COL PLUS 0. 94
                                                         95   900-TERMINATE-ON-ERROR.
                                                         96       DISPLAY ERROR-TERMINATION-SCREEN-1
                                                         97       ACCEPT  ERROR-TERMINATION-SCREEN-1
                                                         98       DISPLAY ERROR-TERMINATION-SCREEN-2
                                                         99       STOP RUN.
```

INVOICE-NUMBER. The first condition name NO-NEW-INVOICES (at line 32) is initialized by the menu program to true. It is changed to false if orders are entered via the order entry program. The invoicing program tests this switch.

The second condition name FATAL-IO-ERROR (at line 34) is initialized by the menu program to false. If any unexpected error condition occurs during a read or write operation, this switch is set to true and control returned to the menu program. A true test at line 88 causes a branch to the 900 module and termination of the program.

The Order Entry Program

Some Initial Program Planning

As you know by now, before you begin to design and program a solution to a problem, you should first define exactly what you want from the program. Then you begin an iterative process of defining the program structure and the general logic of the solution. Before looking at the detailed structure chart and logic solutions, consider the broad actions involved in processing an order.

Read the desired customer record
Get the next invoice number from the invoice master header
Process each transaction as entered by the user
Create a new Inventory master record
Update the last invoice number field in the invoice master header

Next, consider what is to be done for each of these overall actions.

> Read the desired customer record
> > Accept customer number from keyboard
> > Read customer record from customer master file
> > > if customer not found, ask for another customer number
>
> Get the last invoice number from the invoice master header
> > Read record 1 from invoice master file for last invoice number
> > > if error on read, terminate processing
> > If this is the first order entered for this run
> > > save the invoice number for invoice printing
>
> Process each transaction as entered by the user
> > Accept stock number from user
> > Read record from inventory file
> > > if record not found, ask for another stock number
> > Accept quantity from user
> > Build and write invoice transaction record
> > Update quantity on hand and rewrite inventory record
>
> Create new invoice master record
> > Write invoice master record
> > > if error on write, terminate processing
>
> Update next invoice number of inventory master file
> > Increment invoice number by 1
> > Rewrite record 1 of invoice master file
> > > if error on rewrite, terminate processing

You should study the preceding carefully because it serves as the basis for laying out both the structure and the logic of the program.

Program Structure and Logic—Order Entry

The preceding broad outline of the order entry program needs suggests a logical organization of program components, as illustrated by the structure chart of Figure 21-7. The logic of the program solution is illustrated by the flowcharts of Figure 21-8 (pages 613-615) and the pseudocode of Figure 21-9 (page 617). You should notice several points here.

To enter an order, the user must enter a customer number and a product number for each item to be purchased. For both of these, there are three possibilities regarding the value entered by the user:

Entered Value	Required Action
Blank	Terminate this phase of the program
Found in file	Continue processing
Not found in file	Alert user and accept another value

Let's consider the logic of how this is handled for the customer number. In the 300 module (refer to the flowchart or the pseudocode), the entry is accepted within a test-after loop (this is indicated in the flowchart by the decision symbol positioned at the end of the loop). The following takes place:

1. The customer number is accepted.

2. The customer number is tested.
   a. If it contains spaces (meaning that no more orders are to be entered), the loop control condition is satisfied and control is returned to the preceding module.
   b. If it does *not* contain spaces (it contains a customer number), the 800 module is performed.
      1. In the 800 module, the customer number is read.
      2. If the requested record is found, the customer-record-found switch is set to true; if it is not found, the switch is set to false.

Figure 21-7

Structure Chart for Order Entry—Example 21-1

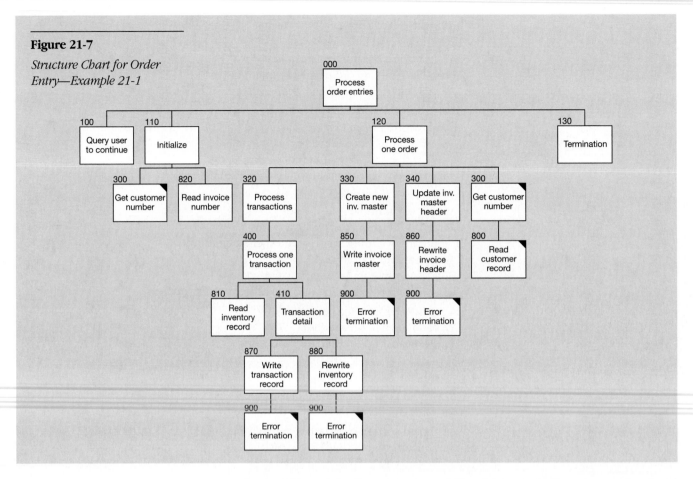

c. In the 300 module, if customer-record-found is true, the loop is completed and control returned to the preceding module; otherwise, the loop is repeated.

Handling orders is treated similarly, except that for each order, one or more items may be preserved. By inspecting modules 400 and 810, you can see that this logic is only a slight expansion of that required for processing the customer number. The rest of the logic of this program is relatively straightforward.

The Program Solution— Order Entry

The programmed solution is shown in Figure 21-10 (page 618). First, let's consider the program switches used in this program.

OK-TO-CONTINUE This switch provides the user with the ability to abort order entry following the initial announcement screen. Its value is controlled through INSTRUCTION-SCREEN (accessed from line 222), in which the user response is stored in the data item CONTINUE-OR-RETURN. It is tested in the 000 module at line 212.

CUSTOMER-RECORD-READ This switch controls the repeated execution of the accept loop in the event that the requested customer is not in the file. It is set to either true of false by the READ of the 800 module and it controls repeated execution of the PERFORM at lines 252–254.

INVENTORY-RECORD-READ This switch indicates whether or not a successful read was executed for a requested software item. It is set in the 810 module to either true or false; a true value causes execution of the 410 module (from line 296) to process one transaction.

Figure 21-8

Flowchart Solution for Order Entry—
Example 21-1
(continued on page 614)

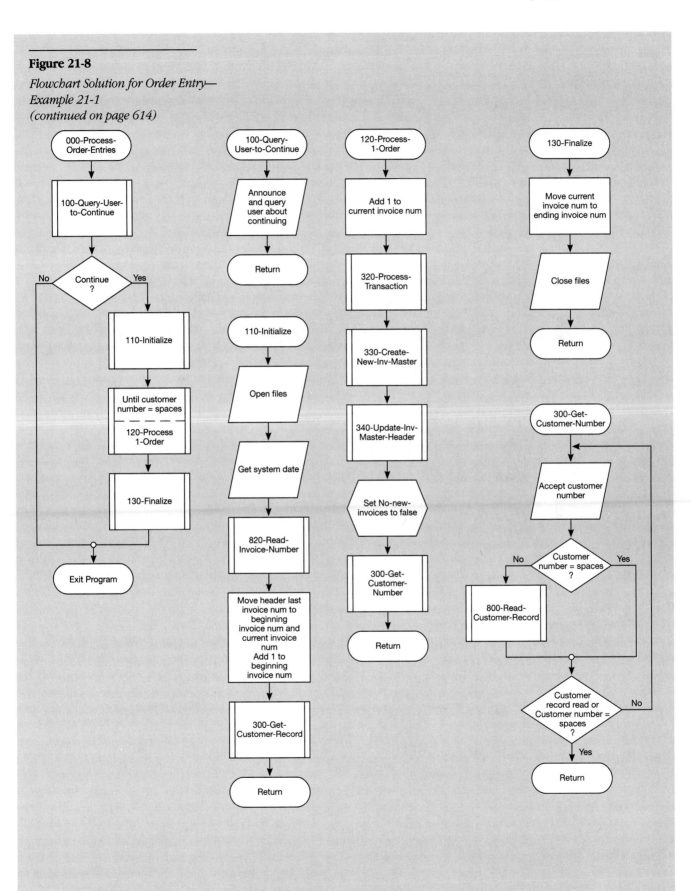

Figure 21-8

(continued from page 613)

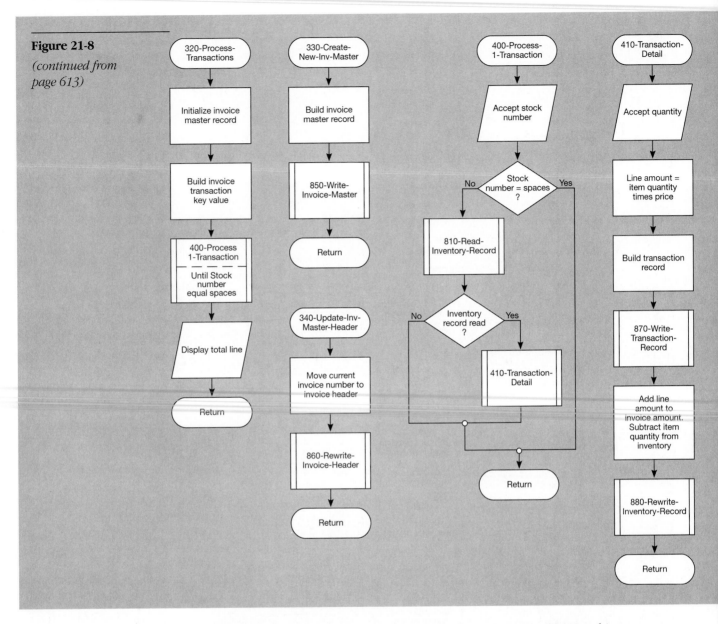

NO-NEW-INVOICES This switch is defined in the LINKAGE SECTION and is common to both the order entry program and the invoice preparation program. It is initialized to true in the menu program (prior to calling of the order entry program). If one or more orders are entered, it is set to false after the entry of an order has been completed (line 241). If invoice preparation is selected immediately after order entry, this switch will remain false and is tested by the invoice preparation program.

FATAL-IO-ERROR This switch is also defined in the LINKAGE SECTION. It is initialized to false in the menu program and set to true when an unexpected input or output error occurs (see line 378).

To begin an order entry session, the program must access the invoice file header record for the last assigned invoice number. This action is accomplished in the 110 module, where the 820 module is performed at line 230. This header value is moved to the data item CURRENT-INVOICE-NUMBER, which is used for invoice number assignment during the run. It is incremented by 1 prior to beginning each order entry (line 237).

You know that the order entry program must return the beginning and ending invoice numbers to the menu program for this order entry run. The beginning invoice number is stored in the linkage data item BEGINNING-INVOICE-NUMBER and incremented by 1 at lines 231–233 in the initialization module. The number of the last processed invoice is

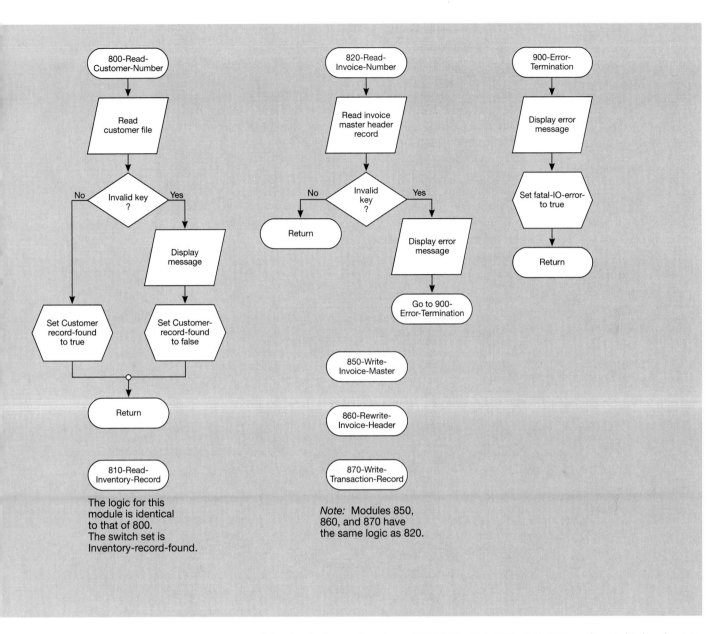

The logic for this module is identical to that of 800. The switch set is Inventory-record-found.

Note: Modules 850, 860, and 870 have the same logic as 820.

stored in the linkage data item ENDING-INVOICE-NUMBER at line 245 (in the 130 module) prior to returning control to the menu program.

You should pay special attention to one other feature of this program: the way in which the record key for the invoice transaction record is built. Referring to the record definition in Figure 21-10, notice that the key field TRANS-RECORD-KEY is defined as follows:

```
01  TRANSACTION-RECORD.
    10  TR-RECORD-KEY.
        20  TR-INVOICE-NUMBER        PIC 9(5).
        20  TR-INVOICE-NUMBER-SUFFIX PIC 9(2).
```

The invoice number is obtained from the invoice master header and will be different for each order. The suffix is a sequential number assigned to each item in an order (each line in the order). Thus, with an order for three different items, this suffix will be 01, 02, and 03 for the respective items. For instance, if the invoice number for this order is 00067, then the key field values for each of these transaction lines will be 0006701, 0006702, and 0006703. Unless the file structure has become corrupt, the transaction record written to the invoice transaction file should never result in an invalid key.

Protecting Files from Corruption

One of the most significant differences between the average textbook program and one in the business world relates to error-handling procedures. Any interactive program—whether it is written in COBOL, FORTRAN, a database language, or whatever—will include a very large percentage of code devoted to handling errors. The preceding discussions approached most of the invalid key situations from the point of view that they simply should not happen. If one of them does, the file is corrupt and processing terminated; processing cannot be continued until someone repairs the file. For some of these errors, this may be extreme.

But, on the other hand, how could such an error possibly occur? If the program is completely debugged, then these values are carefully controlled by the program and should never be in error. There is one very simple way that this can occur: a power failure. For instance, assume that a user is in the process of entering an order (invoice number 00053), has entered the following two items, and is about to enter the third.

Stock Number	Quantity Ordered
45191	6
53355	4

At this point, what has taken place? The answer is that the following files have been changed to reflect this entry.

1. **Invoice transaction file:** The records with the key field values 0005301 and 0005302 have been added.

2. **Inventory file:** The record for stock number 45191 has had its on-hand amount decreased by 6 and that for 53355 decreased by 4.

Note that the invoice master header record remains at 00052 (the last invoice number used), and the new invoice master record has not been written since these operations take place only when the order is completed.

Now assume that a power failure occurs and the computer goes dead. When the computer is restarted and numbers entered, the following sequence of events will occur:

1. The first order entered will use the invoice number 00053, one greater than the "last" invoice number stored in the invoice master header.

2. The customer number will be accepted.

3. The first order item will be accepted and will be assigned a key field value of 0005301.

4. Upon attempting to write this transaction record, processing will be terminated because that record is already in the file. It was entered before the power failure.

How can programs be written to protect against consequences such as this? One approach is to include a variety of error recovery procedures that allow the user to "back out" garbage in the file based on a clearly defined set of procedures. This is usually very difficult. Another is to write all transactions to temporary files. After each order is completed or after the entire run, then the master files are updated from the temporary files and the temporary files are initialized. This file-to-file batch update procedure is very fast, and hence the "window of vulnerability" is much shorter than if it is done during a long interactive session.

Figure 21-9

Pseudocode Solution for Order Entry—
Example 21-1

```
000-Process-Order-Entries
    Perform 100-Query-User-to-Continue
    If okay to continue
        Perform 110-Initialize
        Perform 120-Process-1-Order
            until customer number contains spaces
        Perform 130-Finalize

100-Query-User-to-Continue
    Announce and query user about continuing

110-Initialize
    Open files
    Accept date from system
    Perform 820-Read-Invoice-Number
    Move header last invoice number to beginning
        invoice number and current invoice number
    Add 1 to beginning invoice number
    Perform 300-Get-Customer-Number

120-Process-1-Order
    Add 1 to current invoice number
    Perform 320-Process-Transactions
    Perform 330-Create-New-Inv-Master
    Perform 340-Update-Inv-Master-Header
    Set no-new-invoices switch to false
    Perform 300-Get-Customer-Number

130-Finalize
    Move current invoice number to ending invoice number
    Close files

300-Get-Customer-Number
    Perform with test after
            until customer number not spaces
            or customer number read
        Accept customer number from user
        If customer number not spaces
            Perform 800-Read-Customer-Number

320-Process-Transactions
    Initialize invoice master record
    Build invoice transaction key field value
    Perform 400-Process-1-Transaction
        with test after
        until stock number contains spaces
    Display total line

330-Create-New-Inv-Master
    Build invoice master output record
    Perform 850-Write-Invoice-Master

340-Update-Inv-Master-Header
    Move current-invoice-number to invoice header
    Move 1 to invoice relative key
    Perform 860-Rewrite-Invoice-Header

400-Process-1-Transaction
    Move spaces to stock number
    Accept stock number from user
    If stock number not spaces
        Perform 810-Read-Inventory-Record
        If inventory record read
            Perform 410-Transaction-Detail
```

```
410-Transaction-Detail
    Accept item quantity from user
    Calculate line amount = item quantity times price
    Display line amount
    Increment invoice number suffix by 1
    Build invoice transaction record
    Perform 870-Write-Transaction-Record
    Add line amount to invoice amount
    Subtract item quantity from inventory quantity
    Perform 880-Rewrite-Inventory-Record

800-Read-Customer-Number
    Read Customer-file
        Invalid key
            Display error message
            Set customer-record-found switch to false
        Not invalid key
            Set customer-record-found switch to true

810-Read-Inventory-Record
    Read Inventory-file
        Invalid key
            Display error message
            Set inventory-record-read switch to false
        Not invalid key
            Set inventory-record-read switch to true

820-Read-Invoice-Number
    Move 1 to invoice relative key
    Read Invoice-master
        Invalid key
            Display error message
            Go to 900-Terminate-on-Error

850-Write-Invoice-Master
    Write Invoice-master-record
        Invalid key
            Display error message
            Go to 900-Terminate-on-Error

860-Rewrite-Invoice-Header
    Rewrite Next-invoice-number-record
        Invalid key
            Display error message
            Go to 900-Terminate-on-Error

870-Write-Transaction-Record
    Write Transaction-record
        Invalid key
            Display error message
            Go to 900-Terminate-on-Error

880-Rewrite-Inventory-Record
    Rewrite Inventory-record
        Invalid key
            Display error message
            Go to 900-Terminate-on-Error

900-Terminate-on-Error
    Set fatal-IO-switch to true
    Exit program
```

Figure 21-10

The Order Entry Program—
Example 21-1

```
1       IDENTIFICATION DIVISION.
2
3       PROGRAM-ID.    ORD-ENT.
4
5    *    Written by W.Price  10-16-86
6    *    Modified by J.Olson/W.Price 10-22-90
7    *    Order entry program.
8
9    *    This program allows the user to enter orders.
10   *    Customer data is accessed from the customer file
11   *    Product data is accessed from the inventory file
12   *      The inventory quantity-on-hand field is updated
13   *      for each product sold
14   *    Each order creates records in the invoice master file and
15   *    the invoice transaction file as follows:
16   *      One record in the invoice master master for each order.
17   *      One record in the invoice transaction for each record
18   *        of an order.
19
20      ENVIRONMENT DIVISION.
21
22      CONFIGURATION SECTION.
23      SOURCE-COMPUTER. IBM-PC.
24
25      INPUT-OUTPUT SECTION.
26      FILE-CONTROL.
27          SELECT INVENTORY-FILE      ASSIGN TO DISK, "SOFTWAR2.DI"
28                                     ORGANIZATION IS INDEXED
29                                     ACCESS MODE IS RANDOM
30                                     RECORD KEY IV-STOCK-NUMBER.
31
32          SELECT CUSTOMER-FILE       ASSIGN TO DISK, "CUSTOMER.DI"
33                                     ORGANIZATION IS INDEXED
34                                     ACCESS MODE IS RANDOM
35                                     RECORD KEY IS CR-CUSTOMER-NUMBER.
36
37          SELECT INVOICE-MASTER-FILE ASSIGN TO DISK, "INVOICE.MAS"
38                                     ORGANIZATION IS RELATIVE
39                                     ACCESS IS RANDOM
40                                     RELATIVE KEY IS INVOICE-REL-KEY.
41
42          SELECT TRANSACTION-FILE    ASSIGN TO DISK, "INVOICE.TRA"
43                                     ORGANIZATION IS INDEXED
44                                     ACCESS MODE IS RANDOM
45                                     RECORD KEY IS TR-RECORD-KEY.
46
47      DATA DIVISION.
48
49      FILE SECTION.
50
51      FD  INVENTORY-FILE.
52      01  INVENTORY-RECORD.
53          10  IV-STOCK-NUMBER        PIC X(5).
54          10  IV-SOFTWARE-NAME       PIC X(30).
55          10  IV-VENDOR-NAME         PIC X(20).
56          10  IV-QUANT-ON-HAND       PIC S9(3).
57          10  IV-REORDER-LEVEL       PIC 9(3).
58          10  IV-PRICE               PIC 9(3)V9(2).
59
60      FD  CUSTOMER-FILE.
61      01  CUSTOMER-RECORD.
62          10  CR-CUSTOMER-NUMBER     PIC X(5).
63          10  CR-CUSTOMER-NAME       PIC X(30).
64          10  CR-CUSTOMER-ADDRESS    PIC X(30).
65          10  CR-CUSTOMER-CITY       PIC X(20).
66          10  CR-CUSTOMER-STATE      PIC X(2).
67          10  CR-CUSTOMER-ZIP        PIC X(9).
68          10  CR-CUSTOMER-BALANCE    PIC S9(6)V99.
69
70      FD  INVOICE-MASTER-FILE.
71      01  INVOICE-MASTER-RECORD.
72          10  IM-INVOICE-NUMBER      PIC 9(5).
73          10  IM-CUSTOMER-NUMBER     PIC X(5).
74          10  IM-INVOICE-DATE        PIC X(6).
75          10  IM-INVOICE-AMOUNT      PIC 9(5)V99.
76          10  IM-AMT-PAID            PIC 9(5)V99.
77      01  LAST-INVOICE-NUMBER-RECORD.
78          10  IM-LAST-INVOICE-NUMBER PIC 9(5).
79          10  REST-OF-INVOICE-MASTER PIC X(25).
80
81      FD  TRANSACTION-FILE.
82      01  TRANSACTION-RECORD.
83          10  TR-RECORD-KEY.
84              20  TR-INVOICE-NUMBER        PIC 9(5).
85              20  TR-INVOICE-NUMBER-SUFFIX PIC 9(2).
86          10  TR-STOCK-NUMBER        PIC X(5).
87          10  TR-SOFTWARE-NAME       PIC X(30).
88          10  TR-QUANTITY            PIC 9(3).
89          10  TR-PRICE               PIC 9(3)V99.
90          10  TR-LINE-AMOUNT         PIC 9(5)V99.
91
92      WORKING-STORAGE SECTION.
93
94      01  PROGRAMMED-SWITCHES.
95          10                         PIC X.
96              88  INVENTORY-RECORD-READ  VALUE "Y"   FALSE "N".
97          10                         PIC X.
98              88  CUSTOMER-RECORD-READ   VALUE "Y"   FALSE "N".
99          10  CONTINUE-OR-RETURN     PIC X.
100             88  OK-TO-CONTINUE         VALUE SPACE.
101
102     01  KEY-FIELD-VARIABLES.
103         10  INVOICE-REL-KEY        PIC 9(5).
104         10  CURRENT-INVOICE-NUMBER PIC 9(5).
105
106     01  OTHER-VARIABLES.
107         10  TODAYS-DATE            PIC X(6).
108         10  RESPONSE               PIC X.
109         10  LINE-NUMBER            PIC 99.
110
111     LINKAGE SECTION.
112
113     01  ORDER-PROCESSING-PARAMETERS.
114         10  BEGINNING-INVOICE-NUMBER  PIC 9(5).
115         10  ENDING-INVOICE-NUMBER     PIC 9(5).
116         10                            PIC X.
117             88  NO-NEW-INVOICES          VALUE "Y"   FALSE "N".
118         10                            PIC X.
119             88  FATAL-IO-ERROR           VALUE "Y"   FALSE "N".
120
121     SCREEN SECTION.
122
123     01  INSTRUCTION-SCREEN.
124         10  VALUE "  ********************************"
125                        BLANK SCREEN         LINE  1      COL 1.
126         10  VALUE "      *   ORDER  ENTRY  PROGRAM   *"
127                                             LINE PLUS 1  COL 1.
128         10  VALUE "  ********************************"
129                                             LINE PLUS 1  COL 1.
130         10  VALUE "This program permits the entry of software orders"
131                                             LINE PLUS 2  COL 1.
132         10  VALUE "which have already been filled.  The program "
133                                             LINE PLUS 1  COL 1.
134         10  VALUE "first requests the entry of the customer number,"
135                                             LINE PLUS 1  COL 1.
136         10  VALUE "finds the customer record."
137                                             LINE PLUS 1  COL 1.
138         10  VALUE "When the customer number has been entered, the "
139                                             LINE PLUS 2  COL 1.
140         10  VALUE "program requests the item number and quantity for"
141                                             LINE PLUS 1  COL 1.
142         10  VALUE "each item ordered.  When all items for a customer"
143                                             LINE PLUS 1  COL 1.
144         10  VALUE "have been entered, strike the Return key to com-"
145                                             LINE PLUS 1  COL 1.
146         10  VALUE "plete the processing of that customer."
147                                             LINE PLUS 1  COL 1.
148         10  VALUE "When all customers have been processed, strike "
149                                             LINE PLUS 2  COL 1.
150         10  VALUE "the Return key to terminate the program."
151                                             LINE PLUS 1  COL 1.
152         10  VALUE "To enter orders, simply strike the Return key."
153                                             LINE PLUS 2  COL 1.
154         10  VALUE "If you do not wish to enter orders at this time,"
155                                             LINE PLUS 1  COL 1.
156         10  VALUE "strike the M key to return to the menu.  "
157                                             LINE PLUS 1  COL 1.
158         10 PIC X  TO CONTINUE-OR-RETURN      AUTO     COL PLUS 0.
159
160     01  PRESENT-ENTRY-SCREEN.
161         10  VALUE "Customer Number: "
162                        BLANK SCREEN         LINE  2      COL 1.
163         10  PIC X(5) FROM CR-CUSTOMER-NUMBER          COL PLUS 0.
164         10  VALUE "Invoice Number: "   LINE PLUS 0  COL 54.
165         10  PIC X(5) FROM CURRENT-INVOICE-NUMBER      COL PLUS 0.
166         10  VALUE "Customer Name:   "  LINE PLUS 1  COL 1.
167         10  PIC X(30) FROM CR-CUSTOMER-NAME           COL PLUS 0.
168         10  VALUE "Stock #   Software Name"  LINE PLUS 2  COL 1.
169         10  VALUE "Quantity     Price   Amount"            COL 44.
170         10  VALUE "-----   --------------"  LINE PLUS 1  COL 1.
171         10  VALUE "--------     -----   ------"            COL 44.
172
173     01  GET-CUSTOMER-NUMBER-SCREEN.
174         10  VALUE "Enter customer number: "
175                        BLANK SCREEN         LINE  5      COL 1.
176         10  PIC X(5)    TO CR-CUSTOMER-NUMBER          COL PLUS 0.
177
178     01  GET-STOCK-NUMBER-SCREEN.
179         10  PIC X(5) USING IV-STOCK-NUMBER
180                        FULL BLANK REMAINDER LINE LINE-NUMBER COL 2.
181
```

```
182    01  DETAIL-LINE-SCREEN-1.
183        10  PIC X(5)    FROM IV-STOCK-NUMBER LINE LINE-NUMBER COL  2.
184        10  PIC X(30)   FROM IV-SOFTWARE-NAME LINE LINE-NUMBER COL 11.
185        10  PIC 999     TO TR-QUANTITY       LINE LINE-NUMBER COL 47.
186        10  PIC ZZZ.99 FROM IV-PRICE         LINE LINE-NUMBER COL 57.
187
188    01  DETAIL-LINE-SCREEN-2.
189        10  PIC ZZ9       FROM TR-QUANTITY LINE LINE-NUMBER COL 47.
190        10  PIC ZZ,ZZZ.99  FROM TR-LINE-AMOUNT
191                                          LINE LINE-NUMBER COL 66.
192
193    01  TOTAL-LINE-SCREEN.
194        10  VALUE "TOTAL"            LINE LINE-NUMBER COL 37.
195        10  PIC ZZ,ZZZ.99  FROM IM-INVOICE-AMOUNT
196                                          LINE LINE-NUMBER COL 66.
197
198    01  NO-CUSTOMER-RECORD-SCREEN.
199        10  VALUE "No customer record for "
200                                  LINE 18      COL  1.
201        10  PIC X(5)  FROM CR-CUSTOMER-NUMBER    COL PLUS 0.
202
203    01  INSPECTION-HALT-SCREEN.
204        10  VALUE "When ready to continue, strike the Enter key... "
205                                  LINE 20    COL  1.
206        10  PIC X      TO RESPONSE            COL PLUS 0.
207
208    PROCEDURE DIVISION USING ORDER-PROCESSING-PARAMETERS.
209
210    000-PROCESS-ORDER-ENTRIES.
211        PERFORM 100-QUERY-USER-TO-CONTINUE
212        IF OK-TO-CONTINUE
213            PERFORM 110-INITIALIZE
214            PERFORM 120-PROCESS-1-ORDER
215                UNTIL CR-CUSTOMER-NUMBER = SPACES
216            PERFORM 130-FINALIZE
217        END-IF
218        EXIT PROGRAM.
219
220    100-QUERY-USER-TO-CONTINUE.
221        DISPLAY INSTRUCTION-SCREEN
222        ACCEPT  INSTRUCTION-SCREEN.
223
224    110-INITIALIZE.
225        OPEN I-O  INVENTORY-FILE
226                  INVOICE-MASTER-FILE
227                  TRANSACTION-FILE
228        OPEN INPUT  CUSTOMER-FILE
229        ACCEPT TODAYS-DATE FROM DATE
230        PERFORM 820-READ-INVOICE-NUMBER
231        MOVE IM-LAST-INVOICE-NUMBER TO CURRENT-INVOICE-NUMBER
232                                    BEGINNING-INVOICE-NUMBER
233        ADD 1 TO BEGINNING-INVOICE-NUMBER
234        PERFORM 300-GET-CUSTOMER-NUMBER.
235
236    120-PROCESS-1-ORDER.
237        ADD 1 TO CURRENT-INVOICE-NUMBER
238        PERFORM 320-PROCESS-TRANSACTIONS
239        PERFORM 330-CREATE-NEW-INV-MASTER
240        PERFORM 340-UPDATE-INV-MASTER-HEADER
241        SET NO-NEW-INVOICES TO FALSE
242        PERFORM 300-GET-CUSTOMER-NUMBER.
243
244    130-FINALIZE.
245        MOVE CURRENT-INVOICE-NUMBER TO ENDING-INVOICE-NUMBER
246        CLOSE CUSTOMER-FILE
247              INVENTORY-FILE
248              INVOICE-MASTER-FILE
249              TRANSACTION-FILE.
250
251    300-GET-CUSTOMER-NUMBER.
252        PERFORM WITH TEST AFTER
253            UNTIL CUSTOMER-RECORD-READ
254            OR CR-CUSTOMER-NUMBER = SPACES
255        MOVE SPACES TO CR-CUSTOMER-NUMBER
256        DISPLAY GET-CUSTOMER-NUMBER-SCREEN
257        ACCEPT  GET-CUSTOMER-NUMBER-SCREEN
258        IF CR-CUSTOMER-NUMBER NOT = SPACES
259            PERFORM 800-READ-CUSTOMER-RECORD
260        END-IF
261        END-PERFORM.
262
263    320-PROCESS-TRANSACTIONS.
264        INITIALIZE INVOICE-MASTER-RECORD
265        DISPLAY PRESENT-ENTRY-SCREEN
266        MOVE CURRENT-INVOICE-NUMBER TO TR-INVOICE-NUMBER
267        MOVE ZEROES TO TR-INVOICE-NUMBER-SUFFIX
268        MOVE 7 TO LINE-NUMBER
269        PERFORM 400-PROCESS-1-TRANSACTION WITH TEST AFTER
270            UNTIL IV-STOCK-NUMBER = SPACES
271        ADD 1 TO LINE-NUMBER
272        DISPLAY TOTAL-LINE-SCREEN
273        DISPLAY INSPECTION-HALT-SCREEN
274        ACCEPT  INSPECTION-HALT-SCREEN.
275
276    330-CREATE-NEW-INV-MASTER.
277        MOVE CURRENT-INVOICE-NUMBER TO IM-INVOICE-NUMBER
278        MOVE CR-CUSTOMER-NUMBER TO IM-CUSTOMER-NUMBER
279        MOVE TODAYS-DATE TO IM-INVOICE-DATE
280        MOVE CURRENT-INVOICE-NUMBER TO INVOICE-REL-KEY
281        PERFORM 850-WRITE-INVOICE-MASTER.
```

```
282
283    340-UPDATE-INV-MASTER-HEADER.
284        MOVE CURRENT-INVOICE-NUMBER TO IM-LAST-INVOICE-NUMBER
285        MOVE ALL "*" TO REST-OF-INVOICE-MASTER
286        MOVE 1 TO INVOICE-REL-KEY
287        PERFORM 860-REWRITE-INVOICE-HEADER.
288
289    400-PROCESS-1-TRANSACTION.
290        MOVE SPACES TO IV-STOCK-NUMBER
291        DISPLAY GET-STOCK-NUMBER-SCREEN
292        ACCEPT GET-STOCK-NUMBER-SCREEN
293        IF IV-STOCK-NUMBER NOT = SPACES
294            PERFORM 810-READ-INVENTORY-RECORD
295            IF INVENTORY-RECORD-READ
296                PERFORM 410-TRANSACTION-DETAIL
297                ADD 1 TO LINE-NUMBER
298            END-IF
299        END-IF.
300
301    410-TRANSACTION-DETAIL.
302        DISPLAY DETAIL-LINE-SCREEN-1
303        ACCEPT DETAIL-LINE-SCREEN-1
304        MULTIPLY TR-QUANTITY BY IV-PRICE GIVING TR-LINE-AMOUNT
305        DISPLAY DETAIL-LINE-SCREEN-2
306        ADD 1 TO TR-INVOICE-NUMBER-SUFFIX
307        MOVE IV-STOCK-NUMBER TO TR-STOCK-NUMBER
308        MOVE IV-SOFTWARE-NAME TO TR-SOFTWARE-NAME
309        MOVE IV-PRICE TO TR-PRICE
310        PERFORM 870-WRITE-TRANSACTION-RECORD
311        ADD TR-LINE-AMOUNT TO IM-INVOICE-AMOUNT
312        SUBTRACT TR-QUANTITY FROM IV-QUANT-ON-HAND
313        PERFORM 880-REWRITE-INVENTORY-RECORD.
314
315    800-READ-CUSTOMER-RECORD.
316        READ CUSTOMER-FILE
317            INVALID KEY
318                DISPLAY NO-CUSTOMER-RECORD-SCREEN
319                DISPLAY INSPECTION-HALT-SCREEN
320                ACCEPT  INSPECTION-HALT-SCREEN
321                SET CUSTOMER-RECORD-READ TO FALSE
322            NOT INVALID KEY
323                SET CUSTOMER-RECORD-READ TO TRUE
324        END-READ.
325
326    810-READ-INVENTORY-RECORD.
327        READ INVENTORY-FILE
328            INVALID KEY
329                DISPLAY " " BEEP
330                DISPLAY "No record for Stock # ", IV-STOCK-NUMBER
331                DISPLAY INSPECTION-HALT-SCREEN
332                ACCEPT INSPECTION-HALT-SCREEN
333                SET INVENTORY-RECORD-READ TO FALSE
334            NOT INVALID KEY
335                SET INVENTORY-RECORD-READ TO TRUE
336        END-READ.
337
338    820-READ-INVOICE-NUMBER.
339        MOVE 1 TO INVOICE-REL-KEY
340        READ INVOICE-MASTER-FILE
341            INVALID KEY
342                DISPLAY "Invoice header record not found."
343                GO TO 900-TERMINATE-ON-ERROR
344        END-READ.
345
346    850-WRITE-INVOICE-MASTER.
347        WRITE INVOICE-MASTER-RECORD
348            INVALID KEY
349                DISPLAY "Error on writing invoice record for ",
350                INVOICE-REL-KEY
351                GO TO 900-TERMINATE-ON-ERROR
352        END-WRITE.
353
354    860-REWRITE-INVOICE-HEADER.
355        REWRITE LAST-INVOICE-NUMBER-RECORD
356            INVALID KEY
357                DISPLAY "Error on rewriting invoice header"
358                GO TO 900-TERMINATE-ON-ERROR
359        END-REWRITE.
360
361    870-WRITE-TRANSACTION-RECORD.
362        WRITE TRANSACTION-RECORD
363            INVALID KEY
364                DISPLAY "Invalid key while writing transaction record:"
365                DISPLAY TRANSACTION-RECORD
366                GO TO 900-TERMINATE-ON-ERROR
367        END-WRITE.
368
369    880-REWRITE-INVENTORY-RECORD.
370        REWRITE INVENTORY-RECORD
371            INVALID KEY
372                DISPLAY "Error on rewriting inventory record ",
373                IV-STOCK-NUMBER
374                GO TO 900-TERMINATE-ON-ERROR
375        END-REWRITE.
376
377    900-TERMINATE-ON-ERROR.
378        SET FATAL-IO-ERROR TO TRUE
379        EXIT PROGRAM.
```

The Invoice Generation Program

Invoice Preparation Definition—Order Entry

The second component of the order entry system is to prepare invoices from orders previously entered.

Problem Description

Invoices are generated from data stored in the invoice files. If the invoice preparation immediately follows order entry, those orders just entered must be printed. Otherwise, the user must be allowed to select a range of invoice numbers identifying those invoices to be printed.

Output Requirements

Printed Invoice: For the output format, see Figure 21-11.

Figure 21-11

Sample Invoice with Line Numbers

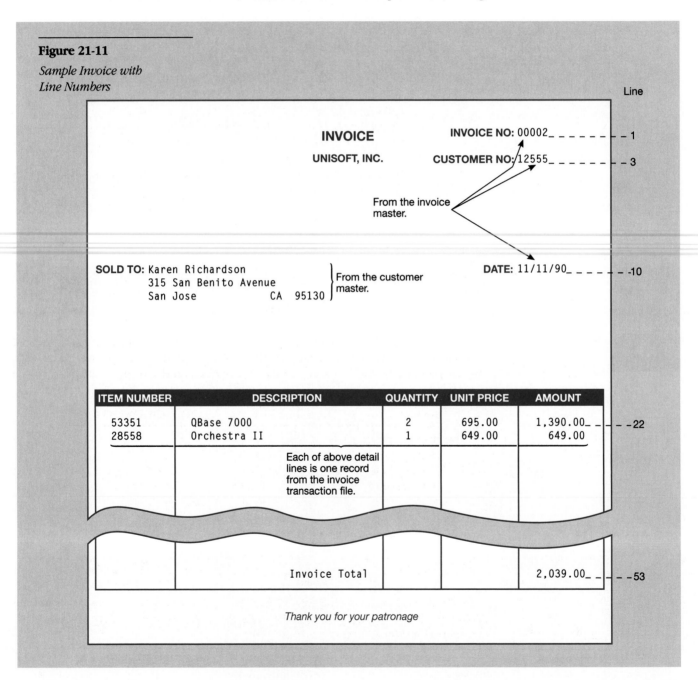

Input Specifications

Customer master file:	CUSTOMER.DI
Invoice master file:	INVOICE.MAS
Invoice transaction (line item) file:	INVOICE.TRA

For the record format definitions, see the corresponding descriptions for the Order Entry segment of this application at the beginning of this chapter.

Processing Requirements

The invoice preparation program is to function as follows:

1. If this program is entered immediately after order entry, then print invoices for those orders entered during that session.
2. Otherwise, ask the user to designate the beginning and ending invoice numbers of the invoices to be printed. Check to ensure that the requested beginning invoice number is not less than 00002 and that the ending invoice number is not larger than the number of the last invoice in the file.
3. For each invoice master record in the requested invoice number range:
   a. Read the invoice master record.
   b. Using the customer number value from the invoice master, read the customer record corresponding to this invoice record.
   c. Print the upper portion of the invoice.
   d. Read each invoice transaction (line item) record corresponding to this invoice master and print a detail line.
   e. After the last invoice transaction record for this invoice is processed, print the invoice total line.

Output Format of the Preprinted Invoice Form

Even though the layout requirements of report programs of earlier chapters were very precise, minor errors in positioning were usually not very noticeable. However, using preprinted forms (such as the sample invoice of Figure 21-11) requires fields to be positioned properly. For instance, if transaction line printing were started two lines early (see Figure 21-11), the first transaction would be printed over the preprinted column heading. Line numbers shown to the right of the sample form are based on the assumption that the invoice form will be positioned initially in the printer so that the invoice number line is at the printer top-of-form position. Paper positioning within the program will be controlled with AFTER ADVANCING, as follows:

Output	Line	AFTER ADVANCING Value
Invoice number	1	PAGE
Customer number	3	2
Customer name; invoice date	10	7
Customer address	11	1
Customer city	12	1
First transaction line	22	10
Second transaction line and so on	23	1
Total line	53	32 minus (number of transaction lines printed)

The implication regarding the total line is that a counter of the number of detail lines printed will need to be maintained in order to establish the number of lines to be advanced for the total line.

Some Preliminary Program Planning—Invoice Preparation

Recall from the order entry portion of the program that the only customer data included in the invoice files is the customer number stored in the invoice master. Thus, preparation of an invoice requires that the customer file be used to obtain the customer name and address for printing on the invoice. This means that data to prepare invoices will come from three files:

Invoice master
Invoice transaction
Customer

Overall, the action of preparing an invoice is relatively simple (especially when compared to some of the examples you have studied). The general steps are

Get Invoice Master
  Move next invoice number to key field
  Read record from invoice master file
Get Customer Record
  Move customer number (from invoice master) to key field
  Read record from customer file
Print Invoice Heading
  Set up and print the top invoice lines
Print Transactions
  Read first transaction record
  Repeat the following until no transaction records
    for this invoice
  Write transaction line
  Read next transaction record
Print Total Line
  Assemble and print the invoice total line

Notice that the first transaction record of an invoice will be accessed randomly. Subsequent records will be accessed sequentially.

Program Structure and Logic—Invoice Preparation

The preceding broad outline of the invoice program needs suggests a logical organization of program components, as illustrated by the structure chart of Figure 21-12. The logic of the program solution is illustrated by the flowcharts of Figure 21-13 (pages 623-625) and the pseudocode of Figure 21-14 (page 626). *(The text continues on page 626.)*

Figure 21-12

Structure Chart for Invoice Preparation—Example 21-1

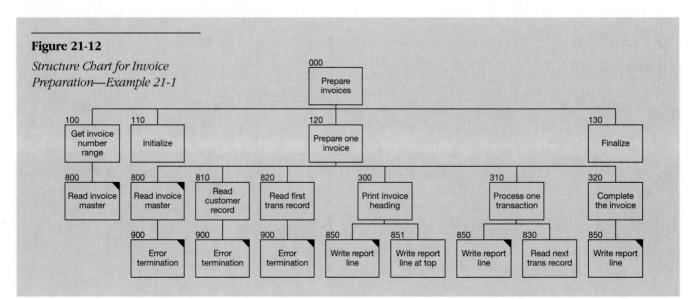

Figure 21-13

Flowchart Solution for Invoice Preparation—Example 21-1 (continued on page 624)

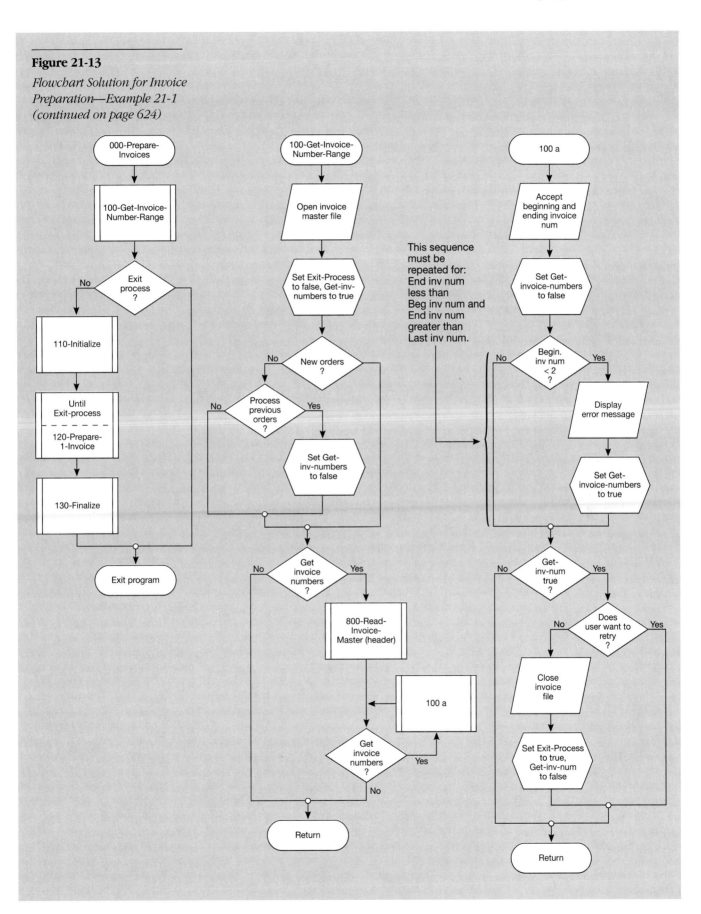

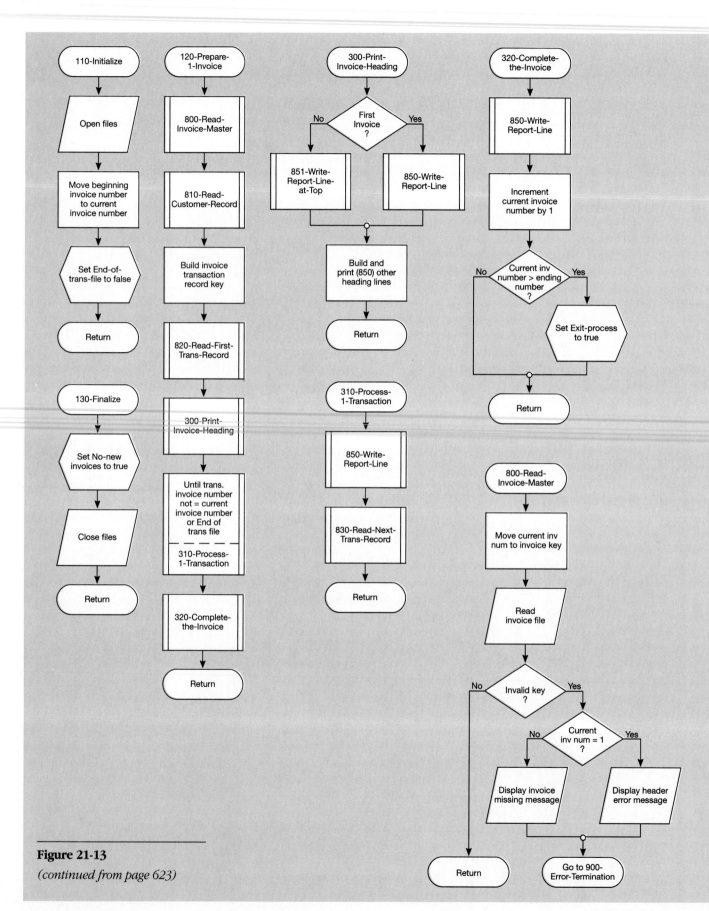

Figure 21-13

(continued from page 623)

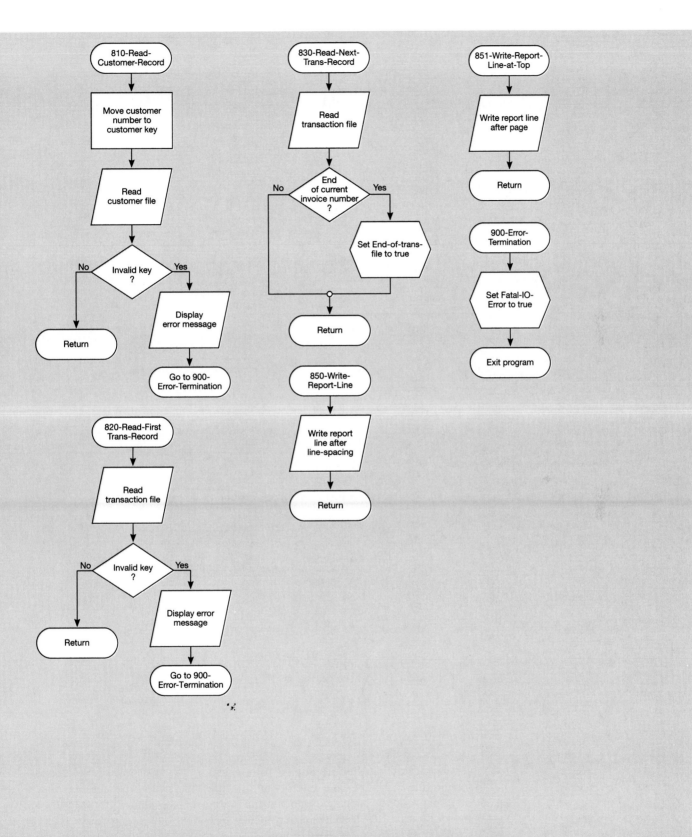

Figure 21-14

*Pseudocode Solution for
Invoice Preparation—
Example 21-1*

```
000-Prepare-Invoices
    Perform 100-Get-Invoice-Number-Range
    If Exit-process switch false
        Perform 110-Initialize
        Perform 120-Prepare-1-Invoice
            until Exit-process
        Perform 130-Finalize
    Exit program

100-Get-Invoice-Number-Range
    Open invoice master file
    Set Exit-process switch to false
    Set Get-invoice-numbers to true
    If not No-new-invoices
        Query user about processing previously entered orders
        If response is yes
            Set Get-invoice-numbers to false
    If Get-invoice-numbers is true
        Move 1 to invoice master key
        Perform 800-Read-Invoice-Master
        Perform until Get-invoice-numbers is false
            Accept beginning and ending invoice numbers
            Set Get-invoice-numbers to false
            If beginning invoice number < 2
                Display error message
                Set Get-invoice-numbers to true
            If ending invoice number > header last invoice number
                Display error message
                Set Get-invoice-numbers to true
            If ending invoice number < beginning invoice number
                Display error message
                Set Get-invoice-numbers to true
            If Get-invoice-numbers is true
                Query user about retrying
                If not retry
                    Close invoice master file
                    Set Exit-process switch to true
                    Set Get-invoice-numbers to false

110-Initialize
    Open files
    Move beginning invoice number to current invoice number
    Set End-of-trans-file switch to false

120-Prepare-1-Invoice
    Perform 800-Read-Invoice-Master
    Perform 810-Read-Customer-Record
    Build invoice transaction record key
    Perform 820-Read-First-Trans-Record
    Perform 300-Print-Invoice-Heading
    Perform 310-Process-1-Transaction
        until transaction invoice number not = current invoice number
            or End-of-transaction-file is true
    Perform 320-Complete-the-Invoice
```

```
130-Finalize
    Set No-new-invoices switch to true
    Close files

300-Print-Invoice-Heading
    Move invoice number to heading line
    If first invoice
        Perform 850-Write-Report-Line
    else
        Perform 851-Write-Report-Line-at-Top
    Build and print remaining heading lines

310-Process-1-Transaction
    Build detail line
    Perform 850-Write-Report-Line
    Decrement line counter
    Perform 830-Read-Next-Trans-Record

320-Complete-the-Invoice
    Build total line
    Perform 850-Write-Report-Line
    Increment current invoice number by 1
    If current invoice number > ending invoice number
        Set Exit-process switch to true

800-Read-Invoice-Master
    Move current invoice number to invoice relative key
    Read invoice master file
        Invalid key
            If current-invoice-number = 1
                Display header record error message
            else
                Display invoice record error message
            Go to 900-Terminate-on-Error

810-Read-Customer-Record
    Move invoice customer number to customer file key
    Read customer file
        Invalid key
            Display error message
            Go to 900-Terminate-on-Error

820-Read-First-Trans-Record
    Read transaction file
        Invalid key
            Display error message
            Go to 900-Terminate-on-Error

830-Read-Next-Trans-Record
    Read transaction file
        at end
            Set End-of-transaction-file switch to true

850-Write-Report-Line
    Write report line
        after advancing line-spacing lines

851-Write-Report-Line-at-Top
    Write report line
        after advancing page

900-Terminate-on-Error
    Set Fatal-IO-switch to true
    Exit program
```

One way of viewing this program is to consider it as consisting of two broad components: one involving user interaction and the other, batch processing. User interaction is required to obtain the beginning and starting invoice numbers for the run. As is commonly the case, the user interaction (which comprises only one module: 100) is more complicated than any other part of the program. Referring to the logic of the flowchart or the pseudocode, you can see that the first test is to determine if orders have just been entered (new orders). If so, the user is queried about preparing those invoices; if the response is positive, nothing more is to be done in this module. Otherwise, the user must be queried for the beginning and ending invoice numbers for the run. Three checks must be made on the entries:

1. The beginning number must not be less than 00002

2. The ending number must not be greater than the last invoice number in the file (from the invoice header)

3. The ending number must not be less than the beginning number

Program Solution— Invoice Preparation

The complete invoice preparation program is shown in Figure 21-15. As with the order entry program, let's begin by considering the programmed switches used in the program.

NO-NEW-INVOICES: This switch is defined in the LINKAGE SECTION and is common to both the order entry program and the invoice preparation program. It is initialized to true in the menu program (prior to calling of the order entry program). It is set to false after the entry of an order has been completed. If invoice preparation is selected immediately after order entry, this switch will remain false. It is tested in the 100 module (line 214). If false, meaning that there are new orders, the user is given the option of printing these orders or entering a range of invoice numbers.

GET-INVOICE-NUMBERS: This switch is used extensively in the 100 module. It is initialized to true at line 213. If the user elects to prepare invoices for newly entered records, it is changed to false at line 218. The scope of the IF in which it is tested (at line 221) encompasses the remainder of the module. A false value causes control to be returned to the calling module and invoices to be prepared for the newly entered orders. Once execution of the IF sequence is begun, the switch is then used to control repetition of the in-line PERFORM starting at line 224. It is set to false early in the loop (line 227) and changed back to true for any invalid invoice number range (lines 231, 235, and 239). It is also set to false if the user decides not to continue after an invalid invoice number range message (line 246).

EXIT-PROCESS: Entry into the program—as well as repetition of the main processing loop—are controlled by this switch. If, upon receiving an invalid invoice number range message from the 100 module, the user decides not to continue, this switch is set to true (at line 247). When control is returned to the main module, it is tested at line 202. A true condition causes an immediate exit to the menu program; a false condition causes program execution to continue. Repetition of the 120 module is controlled by this switch at line 205. It is set to true in the 320 module (line 339) after the last invoice has been completed.

END-OF-TRANS-FILE: Two conditions can signal the last invoice transaction record for a given invoice: detecting a transaction record with a different invoice number or encountering the end of the file. The purpose of this switch is to signal the end of the invoice transaction file. It is set to false at line 258 in the 110 module and to true at line 376 when an EOF is detected during a read. It controls repeated execution of the 310 module (see lines 268–270).

FATAL-IO-ERROR: This switch is defined in the LINKAGE SECTION. It is initialized to false in the menu program and set to true when an unexpected input or output error occurs (see line 388).

Excluding the 100 module to get the invoice number range, the PROCEDURE DIVISION of this program is relatively small. In studying it, you might pay particular attention to the following:

■ During execution, the data item CURRENT-INVOICE-NUMBER contains the invoice number of the invoice currently being processed. It is initialized to BEGINNING-INVOICE-NUMBER (in the 110 module, line 257) and is incremented to the next invoice number with the completion of an invoice (line 337). When it exceeds ENDING-INVOICE-NUMBER, the switch EXIT-PROCESS is set to true at line 339.

Figure 21-15

The Invoice Preparation Program—Example 21-1

```
1          IDENTIFICATION DIVISION.
2
3          PROGRAM-ID.    ORD-INVO.
4
5     *    Written by W.Price  10-25-86
6     *    Modified by J.Olson/W.Price 10-27-90
7
8     *    Invoice preparation program.
9
10    *    This program prints invoices from orders entered via the
11    *    order entry component of this system.
12    *    If the program is entered immediately after orders have
13    *    been entered, those newly entered orders will be printed.
14    *    Otherwise, the user is asked for a range of invoices to
15    *    be printed (by invoice number).
16
17         ENVIRONMENT DIVISION.
18
19         CONFIGURATION SECTION.
20         SOURCE-COMPUTER. IBM-PC.
21
22         INPUT-OUTPUT SECTION.
23         FILE-CONTROL.
24             SELECT CUSTOMER-FILE       ASSIGN TO DISK  "CUSTOMER.DI"
25                                        ORGANIZATION IS INDEXED
26                                        ACCESS MODE IS RANDOM
27                                        RECORD KEY IS CR-CUSTOMER-NUMBER.
28
29             SELECT INVOICE-MASTER-FILE ASSIGN TO DISK  "INVOICE.MAS"
30                                        ORGANIZATION IS RELATIVE
31                                        ACCESS IS RANDOM
32                                        RELATIVE KEY IS INVOICE-REL-KEY.
33
34             SELECT TRANSACTION-FILE    ASSIGN TO DISK  "INVOICE.TRA"
35                                        ORGANIZATION IS INDEXED
36                                        ACCESS MODE IS DYNAMIC
37                                        RECORD KEY IS TR-RECORD-KEY.
38
39             SELECT REPORT-FILE         ASSIGN TO PRINTER "PRN-FILE".
40
41
42         DATA DIVISION.
43
44         FILE SECTION.
45
46         FD  CUSTOMER-FILE.
47         01  CUSTOMER-RECORD.
48             10  CR-CUSTOMER-NUMBER      PIC X(5).
49             10  CR-CUSTOMER-NAME        PIC X(30).
50             10  CR-CUSTOMER-ADDRESS     PIC X(30).
51             10  CR-CUSTOMER-CITY        PIC X(20).
52             10  CR-CUSTOMER-STATE       PIC X(2).
53             10  CR-CUSTOMER-ZIP         PIC X(9).
54             10  CR-CUSTOMER-BALANCE     PIC S9(6)V99.
55
56         FD  INVOICE-MASTER-FILE.
57         01  INVOICE-MASTER-RECORD.
58             10  IM-INVOICE-NUMBER       PIC 9(5).
59             10  IM-CUSTOMER-NUMBER      PIC X(5).
60             10  IM-INVOICE-DATE.
61                 20  IM-INVOICE-YEAR     PIC 9(2).
62                 20  IM-INVOICE-MONTH    PIC 9(2).
63                 20  IM-INVOICE-DAY      PIC 9(2).
64             10  IM-INVOICE-AMOUNT       PIC 9(5)V99.
65             10  IM-AMT-PAID             PIC 9(5)V99.
66         01  LAST-INVOICE-NUMBER-RECORD.
67             10  IM-LAST-INVOICE-NUMBER  PIC 9(5).
68             10  FILLER                  PIC X(25).
69
70         FD  TRANSACTION-FILE.
71         01  TRANSACTION-RECORD.
72             10  TR-RECORD-KEY.
73                 20  TR-INVOICE-NUMBER       PIC 9(5).
74                 20  TR-INVOICE-NUMBER-SUFFIX PIC 9(2).
75             10  TR-STOCK-NUMBER         PIC X(5).
76             10  TR-SOFTWARE-NAME        PIC X(30).
77             10  TR-QUANT                PIC 9(3).
78             10  TR-PRICE                PIC 9(3)V99.
79             10  TR-AMOUNT               PIC 9(5)V99.
80
81         FD  REPORT-FILE.
82         01  REPORT-LINE                 PIC X(80).
83
84         WORKING-STORAGE SECTION.
85
86         01  PROGRAMMED-SWITCHES.
87             10                          PIC X.
88                 88  END-OF-TRANS-FILE   VALUE "Y"    FALSE "N".
89             10                          PIC X.
90                 88  EXIT-PROCESS        VALUE "Y"    FALSE "N".
91             10                          PIC X.
92                 88  GET-INVOICE-NUMBERS VALUE "Y"    FALSE "N".
93
94         01  PRINT-CONTROL-VARIABLES.
95             10  LINE-SPACING            PIC 99.
96             10  LINES-TO-TOTAL          PIC 99.
97             10  LINES-TO-TOTAL-LIMIT    PIC 99      VALUE 32.
98
99         01  INVOICE-NUMBER-WORK-FIELDS.
100            10  INVOICE-REL-KEY         PIC 9(5).
101            10  CURRENT-INVOICE-NUMBER  PIC 9(5).
102
103        01  OTHER-VARIABLES.
104            10  TODAYS-DATE             PIC X(6).
105            10  USER-RESPONSE           PIC X.
106
107        01  INVOICE-NUMBER-LINE.
108            10                          PIC X(64)  VALUE SPACES.
109            10  HEADING-INVOICE-NUMBER  PIC 9(5).
110
111        01  CUSTOMER-NUMBER-LINE.
112            10                          PIC X(64)  VALUE SPACES.
113            10  HEADING-CUSTOMER-NUMBER PIC X(5).
114
115        01  CUSTOMER-NAME-LINE.
116            10                          PIC X(9)   VALUE SPACES.
117            10  HEADING-CUSTOMER-NAME   PIC X(30).
118            10                          PIC X(25)  VALUE SPACES.
119            10  HEADING-MONTH           PIC Z9.
120            10                          PIC X      VALUE "/".
121            10  HEADING-DAY             PIC Z9.
122            10                          PIC X      VALUE "/".
123            10  HEADING-YEAR            PIC 99.
124
125        01  CUSTOMER-ADDRESS-LINE.
126            10                          PIC X(9)   VALUE SPACES.
127            10  HEADING-ADDRESS         PIC X(30).
128
129        01  CUSTOMER-CITY-LINE.
130            10                          PIC X(9)   VALUE SPACES.
131            10  HEADING-CITY            PIC X(20).
132            10  HEADING-STATE           PIC X(2).
133            10                          PIC X(2)   VALUE SPACES.
134            10  HEADING-ZIP             PIC X(9).
135
136        01  DETAIL-LINE  VALUE SPACES.
137            10                          PIC X(4).
138            10  DETAIL-STOCK-NUMBER     PIC X(5).
139            10                          PIC X(5).
140            10  DETAIL-SOFTWARE-NAME    PIC X(30).
141            10                          PIC X(9).
142            10  DETAIL-QUANT            PIC ZZ9.
143            10                          PIC X(4).
144            10  DETAIL-PRICE            PIC ZZZ.99.
145            10                          PIC X(4).
146            10  DETAIL-AMOUNT           PIC ZZ,ZZZ.99.
147
148        01  INVOICE-TOTAL-LINE.
149            10                          PIC X(36)   VALUE SPACES.
150            10                          PIC X(13)   VALUE "Invoice Total".
151            10                          PIC X(21).
152            10  INVOICE-TOTAL-OUT       PIC ZZ,ZZZ.99.
153
154        LINKAGE SECTION.
155
156        01  ORDER-PROCESSING-PARAMETERS.
157            10  BEGINNING-INVOICE-NUMBER PIC 9(5).
158            10  ENDING-INVOICE-NUMBER    PIC 9(5).
159            10                           PIC X.
160                88  NO-NEW-INVOICES      VALUE "Y"    FALSE "N".
161            10                           PIC X.
162                88  FATAL-IO-ERROR       VALUE "Y"    FALSE "N".
163
164        SCREEN SECTION.
165
166
167        01  GET-INVOICE-NUMBERS-SCREEN.
168            10  VALUE "You may print a group of invoices with "
169                           BLANK SCREEN  LINE 6         COL 5.
170            10  VALUE "consecutive invoice numbers by entering the "
171                                         LINE PLUS 1 COL 5.
172            10  VALUE "beginning and ending numbers. If you must print"
173                                         LINE PLUS 1 COL 5.
174            10  VALUE "only one invoice, enter the same number for the"
175                                         LINE PLUS 1 COL 5.
176            10  VALUE "beginning and ending entries."
177                                         LINE PLUS 1 COL 5.
178            10  VALUE "Beginning invoice number? "
179                                         LINE PLUS 2 COL 5.
180            10  PIC 9(5)    TO BEGINNING-INVOICE-NUMBER
181                    FULL  REQUIRED REVERSE  LINE PLUS 0 COL PLUS 0.
182            10  VALUE "Ending invoice number? "
183                                         LINE PLUS 2 COL 5.
184            10  PIC 9(5)    TO ENDING-INVOICE-NUMBER
185                    FULL     REVERSE   LINE PLUS 0 COL PLUS 0.
186
187        01  INVOICE-OPTION-SCREEN.
188            10  VALUE "Do you wish to run invoices for the orders "
189                           BLANK SCREEN   LINE 6        COL 5.
190            10  VALUE "just entered? <Y/N> "          COL PLUS 0.
191            10  PIC X    TO USER-RESPONSE     AUTO  COL PLUS 0.
192
193        01  USER-RETRY-SCREEN.
194            10  VALUE "Do you wish reenter the numbers? <Y/N> "
195                                         LINE 20       COL 5.
196            10  PIC X    TO USER-RESPONSE     AUTO  COL PLUS 0.
```

```
197
198     PROCEDURE DIVISION USING ORDER-PROCESSING-PARAMETERS.
199
200     000-PREPARE-INVOICES.
201         PERFORM 100-GET-INVOICE-NUMBER-RANGE
202         IF NOT EXIT-PROCESS
203             PERFORM 110-INITIALIZE
204             PERFORM 120-PREPARE-1-INVOICE
205                 UNTIL EXIT-PROCESS
206             PERFORM 130-FINALIZE
207         END-IF
208         EXIT PROGRAM.
209
210     100-GET-INVOICE-NUMBER-RANGE.
211         OPEN INPUT INVOICE-MASTER-FILE
212         SET EXIT-PROCESS TO FALSE
213         SET GET-INVOICE-NUMBERS TO TRUE
214         IF NOT NO-NEW-INVOICES
215             DISPLAY INVOICE-OPTION-SCREEN
216             ACCEPT  INVOICE-OPTION-SCREEN
217             IF USER-RESPONSE = "Y" OR "y"
218                 SET GET-INVOICE-NUMBERS TO FALSE
219             END-IF
220         END-IF
221         IF GET-INVOICE-NUMBERS
222             MOVE 1 TO CURRENT-INVOICE-NUMBER
223             PERFORM 800-READ-INVOICE-MASTER
224             PERFORM UNTIL NOT GET-INVOICE-NUMBERS
225                 DISPLAY GET-INVOICE-NUMBERS-SCREEN
226                 ACCEPT GET-INVOICE-NUMBERS-SCREEN
227                 SET GET-INVOICE-NUMBERS TO FALSE
228                 DISPLAY " "
229                 IF BEGINNING-INVOICE-NUMBER < 2
230                     DISPLAY "   Beginning number less than 00002."
231                     SET GET-INVOICE-NUMBERS TO TRUE
232                 END-IF
233                 IF ENDING-INVOICE-NUMBER > IM-LAST-INVOICE-NUMBER
234                     DISPLAY "  Ending number larger than last in file."
235                     SET GET-INVOICE-NUMBERS TO TRUE
236                 END-IF
237                 IF ENDING-INVOICE-NUMBER < BEGINNING-INVOICE-NUMBER
238                     DISPLAY "   Ending number less than beginning."
239                     SET GET-INVOICE-NUMBERS TO TRUE
240                 END-IF
241                 IF GET-INVOICE-NUMBERS
242                     DISPLAY USER-RETRY-SCREEN
243                     ACCEPT USER-RETRY-SCREEN
244                     IF USER-RESPONSE NOT = "Y" AND NOT = "y"
245                         CLOSE INVOICE-MASTER-FILE
246                         SET GET-INVOICE-NUMBERS TO FALSE
247                         SET EXIT-PROCESS TO TRUE
248                     END-IF
249                 END-IF
250             END-PERFORM
251         END-IF.
252
253     110-INITIALIZE.
254         OPEN INPUT  CUSTOMER-FILE
255                     TRANSACTION-FILE
256         OPEN OUTPUT REPORT-FILE
257         MOVE BEGINNING-INVOICE-NUMBER TO CURRENT-INVOICE-NUMBER
258         SET END-OF-TRANS-FILE TO FALSE
259         DISPLAY " " ERASE.
260
261     120-PREPARE-1-INVOICE.
262         PERFORM 800-READ-INVOICE-MASTER
263         PERFORM 810-READ-CUSTOMER-RECORD
264         MOVE CURRENT-INVOICE-NUMBER TO TR-INVOICE-NUMBER
265         MOVE 01 TO TR-INVOICE-NUMBER-SUFFIX
266         PERFORM 820-READ-FIRST-TRANS-RECORD
267         PERFORM 300-PRINT-INVOICE-HEADING
268         PERFORM 310-PROCESS-1-TRANSACTION
269             UNTIL TR-INVOICE-NUMBER NOT = CURRENT-INVOICE-NUMBER
270             OR END-OF-TRANS-FILE
271         PERFORM 320-COMPLETE-THE-INVOICE.
272
273     130-FINALIZE.
274         DISPLAY " "
275         DISPLAY "Strike Enter to return to menu"
276         ACCEPT USER-RESPONSE
277         SET NO-NEW-INVOICES TO TRUE
278         CLOSE CUSTOMER-FILE
279               TRANSACTION-FILE
280               INVOICE-MASTER-FILE
281               REPORT-FILE.
282
283     300-PRINT-INVOICE-HEADING.
284         DISPLAY "Now preparing Invoice # ", CURRENT-INVOICE-NUMBER,
285             " for ", CR-CUSTOMER-NAME
286         MOVE CURRENT-INVOICE-NUMBER TO HEADING-INVOICE-NUMBER
287         MOVE INVOICE-NUMBER-LINE TO REPORT-LINE
288         IF CURRENT-INVOICE-NUMBER = BEGINNING-INVOICE-NUMBER
289             MOVE 0 TO LINE-SPACING
290             PERFORM 850-WRITE-REPORT-LINE
291         ELSE
292             PERFORM 851-WRITE-REPORT-LINE-AT-TOP
293         END-IF
294         MOVE CR-CUSTOMER-NUMBER TO HEADING-CUSTOMER-NUMBER
295         MOVE 2 TO LINE-SPACING
296         MOVE CUSTOMER-NUMBER-LINE TO REPORT-LINE
297         PERFORM 850-WRITE-REPORT-LINE
298         MOVE CR-CUSTOMER-NAME TO HEADING-CUSTOMER-NAME
299         MOVE IM-INVOICE-MONTH TO HEADING-MONTH
300         MOVE IM-INVOICE-DAY TO HEADING-DAY
301         MOVE IM-INVOICE-YEAR TO HEADING-YEAR
302         MOVE 7 TO LINE-SPACING
303         MOVE CUSTOMER-NAME-LINE TO REPORT-LINE
304         PERFORM 850-WRITE-REPORT-LINE
305         MOVE CR-CUSTOMER-ADDRESS TO HEADING-ADDRESS
306         MOVE 1 TO LINE-SPACING
307         MOVE CUSTOMER-ADDRESS-LINE TO REPORT-LINE
308         PERFORM 850-WRITE-REPORT-LINE
309         MOVE CR-CUSTOMER-CITY TO HEADING-CITY
310         MOVE CR-CUSTOMER-STATE TO HEADING-STATE
311         MOVE CR-CUSTOMER-ZIP TO HEADING-ZIP
312         MOVE CUSTOMER-CITY-LINE TO REPORT-LINE
313         PERFORM 850-WRITE-REPORT-LINE
314         MOVE 9 TO LINE-SPACING
315         MOVE SPACES TO REPORT-LINE
316         PERFORM 850-WRITE-REPORT-LINE
317         MOVE 1 TO LINE-SPACING
318         MOVE LINES-TO-TOTAL-LIMIT TO LINES-TO-TOTAL.
319
320     310-PROCESS-1-TRANSACTION.
321         MOVE TR-STOCK-NUMBER TO DETAIL-STOCK-NUMBER
322         MOVE TR-SOFTWARE-NAME TO DETAIL-SOFTWARE-NAME
323         MOVE TR-QUANT TO DETAIL-QUANT
324         MOVE TR-PRICE TO DETAIL-PRICE
325         MOVE TR-AMOUNT TO DETAIL-AMOUNT
326         MOVE DETAIL-LINE TO REPORT-LINE
327         PERFORM 850-WRITE-REPORT-LINE
328         SUBTRACT 1 FROM LINES-TO-TOTAL
329         PERFORM 830-READ-NEXT-TRANS-RECORD.
330
331     320-COMPLETE-THE-INVOICE.
332         MOVE IM-INVOICE-AMOUNT TO INVOICE-TOTAL-OUT
333         MOVE INVOICE-TOTAL-LINE TO REPORT-LINE
334         MOVE LINES-TO-TOTAL TO LINE-SPACING
335         PERFORM 850-WRITE-REPORT-LINE
336     *   Increment the invoice number for the next invoice
337         ADD 1 TO CURRENT-INVOICE-NUMBER
338         IF CURRENT-INVOICE-NUMBER > ENDING-INVOICE-NUMBER
339             SET EXIT-PROCESS TO TRUE
340         END-IF.
341
342     800-READ-INVOICE-MASTER.
343         MOVE CURRENT-INVOICE-NUMBER TO INVOICE-REL-KEY
344         READ INVOICE-MASTER-FILE
345             INVALID KEY
346                 IF CURRENT-INVOICE-NUMBER = 1
347                     DISPLAY "Header record not found in invoice master"
348                 ELSE
349                     DISPLAY "No master record found for Invoice # ",
350                         CURRENT-INVOICE-NUMBER
351                 END-IF
352                 GO TO 900-TERMINATE-ON-ERROR
353         END-READ.
354
355     810-READ-CUSTOMER-RECORD.
356         MOVE IM-CUSTOMER-NUMBER TO CR-CUSTOMER-NUMBER
357         READ CUSTOMER-FILE
358             INVALID KEY
359                 DISPLAY "No record for Customer" CR-CUSTOMER-NUMBER
360                 DISPLAY
361                     "while processing Invoice # " CURRENT-INVOICE-NUMBER
362                 GO TO 900-TERMINATE-ON-ERROR
363         END-READ.
364
365     820-READ-FIRST-TRANS-RECORD.
366         READ TRANSACTION-FILE
367             INVALID KEY
368                 DISPLAY "No transaction record found for Invoice # ",
369                     CURRENT-INVOICE-NUMBER
370                 GO TO 900-TERMINATE-ON-ERROR
371         END-READ.
372
373     830-READ-NEXT-TRANS-RECORD.
374         READ TRANSACTION-FILE NEXT RECORD
375             AT END
376                 SET END-OF-TRANS-FILE TO TRUE
377         END-READ.
378
379     850-WRITE-REPORT-LINE.
380         WRITE REPORT-LINE
381             AFTER ADVANCING LINE-SPACING LINES.
382
383     851-WRITE-REPORT-LINE-AT-TOP.
384         WRITE REPORT-LINE
385             AFTER ADVANCING PAGE.
386
387     900-TERMINATE-ON-ERROR.
388         SET FATAL-IO-ERROR TO TRUE
389         EXIT PROGRAM.
```

- The relative key for the invoice master file is INVOICE-REL-KEY. Prior to the READ statement in the 800 module, the value in CURRENT-INVOICE-NUMBER is moved into this key (line 343).

- After an invoice master is read (beginning the 120 module), the key field value for the first invoice transaction record is constructed by moving the invoice number to TR-INVOICE-NUMBER and 01 (the first line-item number) to TR-INVOICE-NUMBER-SUFFIX. These two subfields comprise TR-RECORD-KEY, the key field for this file (see lines 72–74). The first inventory transaction record is read, using this key field value for random access.

- Subsequent invoice transaction records are read sequentially by the 830 module (via the PERFORM at line 329). Notice that since the invoice transaction file is read both randomly and sequentially, its access mode is designated as DYNAMIC at line 36.

- The printing of the 300 module is reasonably straightforward. One point that might be confusing relates to the IF sequence in lines 288–293. For the first invoice, the printing is performed without carriage positioning, since it is assumed that the invoice was properly positioned before execution was begun. However, for subsequent invoices, the printer is positioned to a new page.

- Another item relating to printing is the method used to control eventual skipping to the total line. That is, the data item LINES-TO-TOTAL-LIMIT contains the value 32 (see line 97), the line count between the line preceding the first detail line and the total line. This value is moved to LINES-TO-TOTAL (at line 318) after the last top-of-invoice line is printed. As each detail line is printed, it is decremented by 1 (line 328). After the last detail line is printed, its value represents the number of lines on the preprinted form between the current line and the total line position.

This completes the study of the order entry/invoice processing system. In programming assignments at the end of this chapter, you will add more components to this system.

Chapter Summary

As indicated in the preview, this chapter utilizes principles you have used earlier and brings together a wide variety of techniques encountered in business programming. You have seen how the activities of two basic elements of an order processing system are integrated and accessed via a controlling component (the menu program). Not only does the menu program provide access to each of the two system components, but it acts as a vehicle for passing data between the two programs. In the programming assignments that follow, you will expand this system further by adding one or more components.

Questions and Exercises

General Questions

1. The order processing case study in this chapter is concerned with both order and invoice data. Both the order and the invoice have identifying numbers and a customer number that are constant. What is considered to be the variable data and what are the file design approaches discussed?

2. Since order entry and invoice preparation are discussed as two independent operations, do they both need to use on-line processing?

3. The menu, order entry, and invoice preparation programs in this chapter do not use a log file to keep a history of transactions. Why don't they do this?

4. Why is it important to pass parameters between programs in the order processing case study?

5. How can programs be written to guard against updating problems that result from power failure?

6. When printing the invoices on a preprinted form, the invoice preparation program specifications assume that the first invoice is properly positioned in the printer. From your knowledge of programming techniques, could this be done another way?

Questions Relating to the Example Programs

1. There is a flaw in ORD-ENT that will be evident for an order with a large number of line items (for instance, 20). Identify the problem and describe how it could be remedied. If you do not see the problem, it may help to make some trial entries.

2. As the records for the files of the order entry system are currently defined, what is the limiting factor on the number of items that can be included in a single order?

3. The text describes a potential error situation that can occur from a power failure while entering an order. That is, upon restarting, the next order to be entered produces an invalid key error because there is already a record in the invoice transaction file with the key value of the record to be written. If the sequence of operations in the program is set up properly, this invoice number will not be used again when the program is rerun and the order being entered at the time of failure can be reentered. What changes would be necessary in the program to do this?

4. The preceding Exercise 3 avoids one problem that would result from a power failure. What other problem(s) would have to be resolved?

5. An order includes three line items. How many records will be read in processing this record? Identify them.

6. Referring to Figure 21-11, you can see that the customer number is printed on line 3 of the invoice and the customer name and date on line 10. Thus, a value of 7 is moved to LINE-SPACING (Figure 21-15, line 302) before printing the name and date line. The city-state is positioned at line 12 and the first detail line at line 22, a difference of 10. However, a value of 9 is moved to LINE-SPACING at program line 314. Why is 9 used instead of 10?

7. In Figure 21-15, what would be the consequence of deleting the IF and its conditionally executed statements in lines 241–248?

Programming Assignments

When the order entry/invoice processing system was first prepared for UNISOFT, the system designer was assured by the accounting department manager that this system was an interim solution to processing needs. It needed to support only the two functions of order entry and invoice preparation and would not be expanded. The long-range plan was to acquire a complete accounting system from a company specializing in accounting software. Now, however, the UNISOFT management has decided to expand the current system to handle customer billing. Unfortunately, some of the design decisions made in the limited context will require changes to the existing programs and the file structure of the invoice master file. The following program assignments provide for improving the current order entry program and expanding the system to provide for processing of payments and billing customers.

21-1　*Note:* The additional system components of Assignments 21-3 and 21-4 require that the modification of this assignment be made.
The invoice master file format must be modified as follows.
a. Organization from relative to indexed
b. Prime key remains the invoice number, but designate the customer number as the alternate key
Change the SELECT entry in both the order entry and invoice processing programs to reflect this change.
Modify the order entry program to move the letter C into the current-indicator field of the invoice master record as each record is created. This code indicates that the invoice record is current.

21-2   *Note:* The additional system components of Assignments 21-3 and 21-4 do *not* require that the modification of this assignment be made.

In the existing ORD-ENT program, there is no safeguard to ensure that an order is not placed for more units of an item than are currently in inventory. This can be checked because one of the fields of the inventory file is the quantity on hand. Make the necessary modifications to this program to prohibit the user from entering an order if insufficient product is on hand to fill that order. There are several methods of approaching this. One good solution is to make your modification in the 400 module as follows:

a.   Move the statements that accept the quantity ordered from the 410 module to the 400 module.

b.   After the inventory record is read (in the 400 module), compare the quantity ordered to the quantity on hand. If the quantity ordered is the larger amount, then display an error message.

c.   With a little ingenuity, repeating the request for the current line can be controlled through the statement that performs the 400 module.

21-3 Payment Processing

One of the essential activities of UNISOFT is collecting money due from customers. As each payment is received from a customer, a record is created in the payment file, the amount is deducted from the balance field in the customer file, and the amount paid is applied to one or more invoice master records. Regarding updating the invoice master, consider a typical example in which the file contains the following four records for a customer:

Invoice Number	Invoice Amount	Amount Paid
00037	245.95	245.95
00049	182.50	
00063	212.00	
00089	722.49	

If this customer submitted a 300.00 payment, 182.50 would be applied to invoice 00049 and the balance, 117.50, would be applied to invoice 00063 with the following result:

Invoice Number	Invoice Amount	Amount Paid
00037	245.95	245.95
00049	182.50	182.50
00063	212.00	117.50
00089	722.49	

Output Requirements:

There is no printed output from this program; all output is to system files.

Customer file: CUSTOMER.DI
    Action: Update the customer balance field
Invoice file: INVOICE.MA2
    Organization is indexed
    Key field: Invoice number
    Alternate key: Customer number
    Record format: Same as INVOICE.MAS
    Action: Update the amount paid field
Payment file: PAYMENT.DI
    Organization is indexed
    Key field: Payment number
    Alternate key: Customer number
    Record format: See Appendix A
    Action: Insert a new record for each payment

Input Description:
   Customer file: CUSTOMER.DI
   Invoice file: INVOICE.MA2

Processing Specifications:
   For each payment received record, the program must:
   1. Accept the payment data from the terminal.
   2. Insert a record into the payment file. To do so, access the header record to obtain the last payment number used (required to generate the key field value). Update the header record.
   3. Get the first invoice master record for this customer.
   4. If in this invoice master the amount-paid field is equal to the invoice-amount field, get subsequent records for this customer until one is encountered in which the amount-paid field is less than the invoice-amount field.
   5. If the payment amount is greater than the remaining amount on the invoice, set the amount-paid field equal to the invoice-amount field; decrease the remaining payment amount accordingly.
   6. If a payment amount remains, repeat the process for subsequent invoice records for this customer.
   7. If after processing the last invoice record for this customer, a payment amount still remains, ignore it because it will be handled by the customer billing program.

21-4 Customer Billing

At the end of each month, UNISOFT prepares customer bills listing all transactions for that month. This program requires that data from the customer, invoice master, and payment files be merged. If a customer has no transactions and no balance due, then no bill is to be created.

Output Requirements:
   Printed output: One bill must be printed for each customer with activity during the month or with an outstanding balance. The bill is to be printed on a preprinted customer statement form as shown in Figure 21-16. This sample is full size so that you can measure to determine the positioning of each field.
   Customer file: CUSTOMER.DI
   Action: Update the customer balance field

Input Description:
   Customer file: CUSTOMER.DI
   Invoice file: INVOICE.MA2
   Payment file: PAYMENT.DI

Figure 21-16

Sample Customer Bill

UNISOFT, INCORPORATED
STATEMENT

STATEMENT DATE	CUSTOMER NO.
06/01/91	31153

Granger County Ranch Supply
P.O. Box 27
Winona   WY 82775

PLEASE RETURN THIS PORTION
WITH YOUR PAYMENT   AMOUNT ENCLOSED _____

- -

DATE	INVOICE NO.	DESCRIPTION	AMOUNT	BALANCE
		Opening balance		863.25
05/07/91		Payment received	700.00	
05/19/91		Payment received	160.00	
05/15/91	01012		322.50	
05/16/91	01033		68.95	
05/27/91	01315		212.49	
		Balance due		607.19

Processing Specifications:

1. Prepare a bill for each customer having (1) a customer-balance field not equal to zero or (2) one or more payments or purchases during the processing period.
2. The processing cycle is monthly (based on the calendar month). The test data file included on the disk is designed for month 06. In your program, you may either request that the month number be entered or code month 06 directly.
3. Print the statement date, customer number, and customer name and address on the upper portion of the form. Since the trial data file is set up for month 06, you may use 06/01/91 for the statement date.
4. For each payment received during the current month:
   a. Print one line on the customer statement
   b. Subtract the amount from the customer-balance field (in the customer record)
5. For each invoice processed during the current month:
   a. Print one line on the customer statement
   b. Add the amount to the customer-balance field (in the customer record)
6. For the summary line, print:
   a. "Balance due" and the amount if the customer-balance field is positive
   b. "Account is current" if the customer-balance field is zero
   c. "Customer credit" and the amount followed by the letters CR if the customer-balance field is negative

21-5 Student Enrollment

Enrollment of students into classes at the Computer Institute of Technology is done via computer terminals. When a student is enrolled in a class, considerable file activity takes place.

The Enrollment Activity:

When a student is enrolled in a class, the student's record is first accessed from the Student file to ensure that the student is currently registered. Then, for each course desired by the student, the following occurs.

1. The record for the requested class is read from the Enroll file.
2. If the Actual enrollment is less than the Maximum permissible enrollment, the student is enrolled.
3. The Actual enrollment field of the Enroll file is increased by 1.
4. The updated record is written back to the Enroll file.
5. A new record for the Grades file is built for this student, using data from the Enroll file.
6. The new record is written to the Grades file.

Input Description:

File name: ENROLL01.DI, STUDENTS.DI, and GRADES.DL

Record description: See Appendix A

Other Needs:

If you have done Assignments 19-2 and 20-2, you have many of the components of a college enrollment/grade processing system. There are two components that are clearly missing.

At some time between the completion of grade processing (the topic of the Chapter 19 assignments) and class enrollment, the Grades file must be initialized. A common process is to store the current copy to magnetic tape and create a new one. This option creates a new Grades file. However, there must be tight security associated with this action because you would not want the Grades file to be destroyed accidentally.

At the end of the semester, grades from instructors must be entered into the Grades file records. This is a relatively simple operation.

A

DATA RECORD FORMATS FOR PROGRAMMING ASSIGNMENT FILES

This appendix includes the record format for each file used in programming assignments of this book. Notice that most of the files exist in two forms: sequential and indexed. The file extension tells you the type of file; that is:

DL   Data file, Line sequential
DI   Data file, Indexed

In some cases, a third letter is used to indicate its usage; for instance:

DLT Data file, Line sequential, Table

AIRPORT1.DL or
AIRPORT1.DI
(Airport File)

Positions	Field Description	Format/Comments
1-5	Flight ID	Key field for indexed file
6-11	Date of flight	Year-Month-Day *(yymmdd)*
12-15	Arrival/departure time	Twenty-four-hour clock Hours-Minutes *(hhmm)*
16-28	Origin/destination	
29-31	Direction	Value: IN or OUT
32-35	Flight number	
36-39	Airplane type	
40-47	Airline	
49-51	Runway used	
54-57	Flight plan ID	
59-65	Pilot's last name	
66-68	Total number of seats on airplane	Whole number
69-71	Actual number of passengers on flight	Whole number
72-73	Number of crew members	Whole number
74-78	Baggage weight (kg)	Whole number
79-84	Generalized performance score	*nnnn*$_\wedge$*ns**

* Note that this field is signed and that the sign is encoded as a separate, trailing character. This sign position will contain a space or a + indicating that the number is positive or a - indicating that the number is negative.

**BOOKS.DL or
BOOKS.DI
(Book Inventory File)**

Positions	Field Description	Format/Comments
1-10	Book inventory number	Key field for indexed file
11-28	Title	AN
29-43	Author	AN
44-49	Programming language	AN
50	Profit code	Value: 1, 2, or 3
51-54	Number of copies on hand	Whole number
55-58	Number of copies on order	Whole number
59-62	Reorder level	Whole number
63-66	Reorder quantity	Whole number
67-71	Primary vendor (vendor ID)	AN
72-75	Retail price	$nn_\wedge nn$
76-79	Basic wholesale price	$nn_\wedge nn$
80-83	Quantity 1 wholesale price	$nn_\wedge nn$
84-86	Minimum purchase quantity for Quantity 1 wholesale price	Whole number
87-90	Quantity 2 wholesale price	$nn_\wedge nn$
91-93	Minimum purchase quantity for Quantity 2 wholesale price	Whole number

DRINKS01.DL or
DRINKS01.DI
(Soft Drinks File)

Positions	Field Description	Format/Comments
1-5	Customer account number	Key field for indexed file
6-30	Customer name	
31-40	Customer telephone number	
	Monthly sales (number of cases)	
41-43	Cola	Whole number
44-46	Diet drinks	Whole number
47-49	Energy supplement drinks	Whole number
	Monthly sales target (number of cases)	
50-52	Cola	Whole number
53-55	Diet drinks	Whole number
56-58	Energy supplement drinks	Whole number
	Monthly sales (dollar amount)	
59-64	Cola	$nnnn_\wedge nn$
65-70	Diet drinks	$nnnn_\wedge nn$
71-76	Energy supplement drinks	$nnnn_\wedge nn$

EMPLOYEE.DL or
EMPLOYEE.DI
(Employee File)

Positions	Field Description	Format/Comments
1-9	Social Security number	Key field for indexed file
10-33	Employee name	
34	Bonus code	
35-38	Department code	
39-44	Monthly gross pay	Dollars and cents
45-52	Year-to-date earnings	Dollars and cents
53-59	Year-to-date income tax withholding	Dollars and cents
60-65	Year-to-date FICA withholding	Dollars and cents
66-67	Tax sheltered annuity code	
68-72	Tax sheltered annuity deduction	Dollars and cents

ENROLL01.DL or ENROLL01.DI (Enrollment File)

Positions	Field Description	Format/Comments
1-4	Class Code	Key field for indexed file
5-7	Actual enrollment	Whole number
8-29	Course name	
30-43	Instructor name	
44-46	Course number	
47-48	Section number	Whole number
49-51	Course units	$nn_\wedge n$
52-54	Maximum permissible enrollment	Whole number
55-57	Minimum permissible enrollment	Whole number

GRADES.DL (Student Grade File)

Positions	Field Description	Format/Comments
1-9	Student number	
10-13	Class code	
16-37	Course description	
38-40	Course units	$nn_\wedge n$
41	Grade	

GROUPS.DLT (Group Affiliation Table)

Positions	Field Description
1	Affiliation code
2-16	Affiliation group

MANU.DL (Manuscript Text File)

Positions	Field Description
1-4	Manuscript number
5-	Text

- Record length varies from 4 to 126
- Each record will contain at least a manuscript number
- Punctuation marks that may be encountered are the comma, period, colon, and question mark

**PAYMENT.DI
(Payments File)**

Positions	Field	Format
Header record (record 1)		
1-5	Last used payment number	
6-30	Unused	
Subsequent records		
1-5	Payment number—key field	Key field
6-10	Customer number for this payment	
11-16	Date entered	*yymmdd*
17-23	Total amount of payment	*99999V99*

**RECORD01.DL or
RECORD01.DI
(Recordings File)**

Positions	Field Description	Format/Comments
1-10	Inventory control number	Key field for indexed file
11-35	Title of recording	
36-60	Artist or group	
61-66	Medium	Value: CASSET or CD
67-70	Number on hand, beginning of month	Whole number
71-74	Number sold this month	Whole number
75-78	Number received this month	Whole number
79-82	Number currently on order	Whole number
83-86	Reorder Quantity	Whole number

STUDENTS.DL or
STUDENTS.DI
(Students File)

Positions	Field Description	Format/Comments
1-9	Student number (Social Security number)	Key field for indexed file
10-20	Student first name	
21-32	Student last name	
33	Class standing	1 - Freshman 2 - Sophomore 3 - Junior 4 - Senior 5 - Graduate
34	Gender	F - Female M - Male
35-37	Major	
38-41	Cumulative units	$nnn_\wedge n$
42-45	Cumulative points	$nnn_\wedge n$
46-48	Units last semester	$nn_\wedge n$
49-51	GPA last semester	$n_\wedge nn$

VOTERS.DL or
VOTERS.DI
(Voters File)

Positions	Field Description	Format/Comments
1-20	Name	
21-40	Street address	
41-53	City	
54-55	State	
56-64	Zip code	
65-69	Annual income	Dollars
70	Party of registration (for Assignments 9-5 and 11-4 only)	R - Republican D - Democratic I - Independent
71	Party of registration (for Assignment 14-3 only)	
72	Marital status	1 - Married 2 - Not married

DISK PREPARATION/ SYSTEM SETUP

This appendix provides you with the information you need to prepare your system for using this book's software. It tells you how to:

1. Set up your computer system and copy needed files from the Distribution Disks included with this book

2. Prepare your computer for a work session using the Ryan-McFarland COBOL software

3. Copy example programs from the Distribution Disk so that you can run the programs and inspect the results

Outline

- **Introduction**
  Special Note
  What You Have Received
  Configuration Options
  Other Configurations

- **Option 1: Hard Disk Operation—No Diskettes**
  Loading the Files to Disk
  Setting Up to Run

- **Option 2: Hard Disk Operation—Programs on Diskette**
  Loading the Compiler Onto the Hard Disk
  Loading the Data Files Onto a Diskette
  Setting Up to Run

- **Options 3 and 4: 5 1/4" Diskette-Based System**
  Loading the Distribution Files Onto Diskettes
  Setting Up to Run
  Obtaining Data Files

- **Options 5 and 6: High-Capacity Diskette-Based System**
  Loading the Distribution Files Onto Diskettes
  Setting Up to Run

- **Using Example Programs**

Introduction

Special Note

In the manual for most software that you purchase, you will find a notice telling you to check the disk for documentation about the latest changes or additions to the software. The documentation file is commonly called READ.ME, README, or something similar. It describes changes or additions to the software that have been made since the software manual was printed. If any changes are made to the disk procedures after this book's printing, they will be included as a special file named READ.ME on Distribution Disk #1. You can display the file on the screen by typing the DOS command:

```
TYPE READ.ME
```

If there have been no changes, the file will not exist.

What You Have Received

Your *Modern COBOL* package includes either two 3 1/2" diskettes labelled *Distribution Disk #1* and *Distribution Disk #2*, or three 5 1/4" (360KB) diskettes labelled *Distribution Disk #1*, *Distribution Disk #2*, and *Distribution Disk #3*. These contain the following files for using the RM/COBOL system on a personal computer.

1. Ryan-McFarland software:
   - The RM/COBOL-85 compiler and run-time system
   - The RM/CO* system
2. Programs used as examples in the textbook
3. Data files for all programming assignments in the textbook
4. DOS batch control files for automatic disk preparation

The way in which you use the COBOL system included with this book depends upon the configuration of the computer hardware that you will be using. That is, your computer may be diskette-oriented, using either 5 1/4" 360KB diskettes or 3 1/2" diskettes. On the other hand, you may be working with a computer that includes a hard disk. The following sections describe a number of typical situations and the loading procedures needed to prepare your system for daily use. In these descriptions, the term *Distribution Disk* refers to the diskettes included with the *Modern COBOL* package. *Do not use these for daily operations.* Follow the appropriate set of instructions for preparing the diskettes that you will use in writing your programs. For this, you will need 1 or 2 diskettes, depending on your computer configuration. (If you are operating on your own hard disk computer, you will not need any diskettes.)

Configuration Options

The following instructions are for setups in several modes. You should select the one that is appropriate to your equipment and needs.

■ *Hard disk computer*

Option 1 All files (the Ryan-McFarland software and the programs that you create) will be stored on the hard disk. You would probably use this if you have your own hard disk computer.

Option 2 The Ryan-McFarland software files stored on hard disk and program/data files stored on diskette—one diskette required. You would use this if you are using a hard-disk computer in a computer lab where the compiler and editor files are stored on the hard disk (or on a network file server) and you keep your programs on your own diskette.

■ *Non-hard disk computer (5 1/4", 360KB diskettes)*

Option 3 You plan to use the RM/CO* system provided with the Ryan-McFarland software—two diskettes required.

Option 4 You do not plan to use the RM/CO* system provided with the Ryan-McFarland software—two diskettes required.

■ *Non-hard disk computer (diskette capacity 720KB or more)*

Option 5 You plan to use the RM/CO* system provided with the Ryan-McFarland software—two diskettes required.

Option 6 You do not plan to use the RM/CO* system provided with the Ryan-McFarland software—two diskettes required.

Other Configurations

If you elect to use some other configuration that better suits your needs, then you will have to create whatever subdirectories you require and load individual programs from the Distribution Diskettes. The Ryan-McFarland files stored on one (or more) of the Distribution Diskettes are as follows.

The compiler includes the files:

    RMCOBOL.EXE
    RMCOBOL.OVY

The run-time system includes the file:

    RUNCOBOL.EXE

RM/CO* includes the files:

    RMCOSTAR.EXE
    RMCOSTAR.HLP

The compiler and run-time system files are required; the COSTAR files are needed only if you intend to use the RM/CO* system (highly recommended).

Option 1: Hard Disk Operation— No Diskettes

Loading the Files to Disk

For this option, all files (the compiler and the programs that you create) will be stored on the hard disk. If you are not using your own computer, then you probably should not use this option.

The control instructions to prepare your computer will create two subdirectories:

RM   for the RM-COBOL system files

RM-PRGS   into which the data files for all the assignments of the book will be placed. This will serve as the subdirectory in which you will create your COBOL programs.

Carry out the following steps to prepare your computer:

1. Switch to the A> prompt by typing

        A:

2. Insert Distribution Disk #1 into drive A.
3. Type the following command and strike the Enter key:

        OPTION-1

4. Follow the instructions displayed on the screen. When you are finished, the system will be ready to use.

Setting Up to Run

To create, edit, compile, and run your programs, you will work from the subdirectory RM-PRGS. In order to use the Ryan-McFarland software, you must tell DOS where it is located. You do this with the PATH command. For instance, assuming that the subdirectory RM is on drive C, you must enter the following command:

        PATH C:\RM

If you place this command in your AUTOEXEC.BAT startup file, the path will be set automatically when you start the computer and you need not enter it each time you use the computer.

Once the path is set, you must change to the RM-PRGS subdirectory, using the following command:

        CD \RM-PRGS

Option 2: Hard Disk Operation— Programs on Diskette

Loading the Files to Disk

If you are one of many persons using a shared computer (or a network), you will probably not perform this action. The lab director or someone else has probably already done it.) If not, carry out the following steps to prepare the computer:

1. Switch to the A> prompt by typing

        A:

2. Insert Distribution Disk #1 into drive A.

3. Type the following command and strike the Enter key:

    OPTION-2

4. Follow the instructions displayed on the screen. When you are finished, the system will be ready to use.

Loading the Data Files Onto a Diskette

If you are using a shared hard disk computer and must keep your programs on a diskette, then you should have a set of the data files for your assignments on that diskette. For this, carry out the following procedure:

1. Bring the computer up and format a diskette (do *not* format a Distribution Disk). If you want to be able to start the computer from this disk, format it as a system disk or else follow the instructions for your installation. Label it *Programs/Data*.

2. Make certain the computer is at the A> prompt by typing

    A:

3. Insert Distribution Disk #2 into drive A.

4. Type the following command and strike the Enter key:

    COPYDATA

5. Follow the instructions displayed on the screen. When copying takes place, you will see a list of files being copied. When you are finished, the diskette will be ready to use.

Setting Up to Run

To create, edit, compile, and run your programs, you will work from your diskette. In order to use the Ryan-McFarland software, you must tell DOS where it is located. You do this with the PATH command. For instance, assuming the subdirectory RM is on drive C, you must enter the following command:

    PATH C:\RM

If this command is placed in the AUTOEXEC.BAT startup file, the path will be set automatically when the computer is started. Determine the procedures used in your lab before acting on this.

To use the Ryan-McFarland software, insert your Programs/Data diskette into drive A, set the DOS prompt to A by typing

    A:

and then proceed.

Options 3 and 4
5 1/4" Diskette-Based System

Loading the Distribution Files Onto Diskettes

Whether or not you plan to use RM/CO*, you will require two 360KB diskettes. The diskette preparation procedure is

1. Bring the computer up and format two diskettes (do *not* format a Distribution Disk). Label these diskettes as follows:

    RM Software
    Data/RM Software-2

2. Make certain the computer is at the A> prompt by typing

    A:

3. Insert Distribution Disk #1 into drive A.

4. Type one of the following commands and strike the Enter key:

   OPTION-3   (You intend to use RM/CO*)

   OPTION-4   (You do not intend to use RM/CO*)

5. Follow the instructions displayed on the screen. When copying takes place, you will see a list of files being copied. When you are finished, the system will be ready to use.

Setting Up to Run

These two configurations stretch diskette capacity the most because a large amount of software is stored on two diskettes that also require space for your programs. To use your two-diskette-based system, proceed as follows:

1. Insert the Data/RM Software-2 disk in drive A
2. Insert the RM Software disk in drive B
3. Make certain that you are at the A prompt by typing

   A:

4. Enter the DOS command:

   PATH B:

5. Proceed with your activity (enter, compile, or run a program)

Step 4 of the preceding instructions is required because part of the software will be located on one diskette and part on the other. Therefore, you must provide DOS with some help in finding files that it needs.

Obtaining Data Files

Because of the limited space on the Data/RM Software-2 diskette, data files that you will need for your programs (beginning in Chapter 5) are not copied from the Distribution Diskettes. For every programming assignment you receive that processes a file, you will need to copy that file from the appropriate Distribution Disk to your Data/RM Software-2 diskette. To illustrate, assume that your next assignment requires the data file AIRPORT1.DL.

1. Insert your Data/RM Software-2 diskette into drive A

2. Insert Distribution Disk #2 into drive B

3. From the DOS prompt, type the following command:

   COPY B:AIRPORT1.DL A:

Options 5 and 6: High-Capacity Diskette-Based System

Loading the Distribution Files Onto Diskettes

1. Bring the computer up and format two diskettes (do *not* format the Distribution Disk). Label these diskettes as follows:

   RM Software
   Program/Data

2. Make certain the computer is at the A> prompt by typing

   A:

3. Insert Distribution Disk #1 into drive A.

4. Type one of the following commands and strike the Enter key:

   OPTION-5   (You intend to use RM/CO*)

   OPTION-6   (You do not intend to use RM/CO*)

5. Follow the instructions displayed on the screen. When copying takes place, you will see a list of files being copied. When you are finished, the system will be ready to use.

Setting Up to Run

To use your two-diskette-based system, proceed as follows:

1. Insert the Program/Data disk in drive A
2. Insert the RM Software disk in drive B
3. Make certain that you are at the A prompt by typing

    ```
    A:
    ```

4. Enter the DOS command:

    ```
    PATH B:
    ```

5. Proceed with your activity (enter, compile, or run a program)

Using Example Programs

All of the example programs in the textbook—together with the necessary data files—are included on Distribution Disk #3 (5 1/4" disk) and Distribution Disk #2 (3 1/2" disk). Thus, you can compile and run them or experiment by making changes that you wish to investigate. You will find it especially helpful in studying the interactive programs to first run them and get a feel for how each program works before making any changes.

Because there are many (more than 40) example programs and because they occupy a substantial amount of disk space, the preceding disk preparation operations did not copy any of them to your disk. If you have your own computer, you may want to create a separate subdirectory and copy all of them into that subdirectory.

Otherwise, whenever you want to use an example program, you will need to copy it to your program disk or subdirectory as follows:

1a. If using a hard disk, make certain that you are in the subdirectory into which you want the program copied (use the appropriate CD command for this).

1b. If working with diskettes, make drive A the default drive, then insert the disk on which you keep your programs into drive A.

2. Insert Distribution Disk #3 (5 1/4" disk) and Distribution Disk #2 (3 1/2" disk) into drive B.

3. Enter the appropriate COPY command(s). For instance, if you want to try the SEQ-LIST program (Chapter 5), you will need to copy the program SEQ-LIST.CBL and its data file, SOFTWARE.DL, with the following commands:

    ```
    COPY B:SEQ-LIST.CBL
    COPY B:SOFTWARE.DL
    ```

USING RM/COSTAR (RM/CO*)

A Basic Programming Sequence

Operating from the DOS Prompt

Using this book, you will be writing computer programs to perform functions defined in the programming assignment sections at the end of chapters. From Chapter 1, you know that the overall problem-solving aspect of programming consists of the following five steps: map out the solution, write the program, enter the program into the computer, compile the program, and run the program. Errors in the use of the COBOL language, which will be detected by the compiler, must be corrected and the program recompiled before you can run it.

When using RM/COBOL-85 you can operate in two basic ways: directly from the Disk Operating System (DOS), or through RM/CO*. To give you an idea of the difference between these two environments, assume that you have written a program to print a list of customers for your employer from data in disk storage. Unknown to you, your program contains errors (that will be detected by the compiler). Of course, the existence of errors means that you will need to correct them and recompile the program. Following is a description of the sequence of steps you would follow in operating from the DOS environment; after that is description of the corresponding sequence of steps using RM/CO*.

DOS—Phase 1

Activity: Enter the program into the computer

End result: The source program stored on disk

1. From DOS, run your word processor.
2. Enter the program.
3. Save the completed program to disk.
4. Exit the word processor, thus returning to DOS.

Phase 2

Activity: Compile the program and print a post-compile listing

End result: Post-compile listing with error messages

5. From DOS, run the compiler.
6. Print the post-compile listing. You can do this from DOS or from your word processor (in order to control the appearance of the printed output).

Phase 3

Activity: Make corrections to the source program

End result: A corrected source program

7. From DOS, run your word processor.
8. Load your program.
9. Using the post-compile listing as a reference, correct each error in the source program.
10. Save the corrected program to disk.
11. Exit the word processor, thus returning to DOS.

Phase 4

Activity: Compile the program

End result: The object program ready to run

12. From DOS, run the compiler. When the compilation is completed, control is automatically returned to DOS.

Phase 5

Activity: Run the program

End result: The program report stored on disk as a file

13. From DOS, run the program. When the run is completed, control is automatically returned to DOS.

Phase 6

Activity: Inspect the program output stored on disk

End result: A display on the screen of the finished report

14. From DOS, use the TYPE command to display the program output. Alternately, run your word processor and load the program output for more convenient browsing.

With this approach, your interface with the computer is the operating system DOS. Each of the pieces of software you use is invoked by entering its multi-letter name, along with any command-line words or codes that are required. The compiler and the word processor are each completely self-contained and have no communication with each other.

Operating under RM/CO*

How does RM/CO* change this? RM/CO* (pronounced Are-Emm-CoStar) is described by Ryan McFarland as "… an interactive, menu-driven environment, within which you can write, edit, compile, run and debug RM/COBOL-85 programs." It is the type of environment that is sometimes referred to as "a programmer's workbench," as opposed to a "normal" or "typical" programming environment. Rather than jumping back and forth between DOS and independent software units, you are always functioning under the controlled, COBOL-oriented environment of the menu-driven RM/CO*. For instance, in Figure C-1, you see the main menu of RM/CO*. By merely typing the appropriate letter, you can enter or edit, compile, or run your program. As an illustration, consider the preceding scenario when operating under RM/CO*.

1. To start RM/CO* from the DOS prompt, type the following and strike the Enter key:

```
RMCOSTAR
```

2. Invoke the RM/CO* editor by striking the letter E.

3. Type in your program.

4. Exit the editor, thus returning to the menu of Figure C-1. The program is saved automatically to disk.

5. Check the program for errors by striking the letter S to invoke Syntax-Check. When the check is complete, RM/CO* displays a count of the number of errors detected.

6. Invoke the editor by striking the letter E (for Enter Member). The listing resulting from the syntax check, *which includes the error messages,* is displayed on the screen with the cursor at the first line that is in error.

7. Correct each error in the program while working with the error listing.

8. Exit the editor, thus returning to the RM/CO* menu.

9. Compile the program by striking the letter C (for Compile).

10. Run the compiled program by striking the letter R (for Run).

Figure C-1

The RM/CO Main Menu*

```
┌──────────────────── Project Commands ────────────────────┐
│                                                           │
│  A dd Member    O ptions      U pdate          │ S yntax-Check │
│  D rop Member   Q uit Project V iew Status/File │ C ompile      │
│  Enter  Member                X ecute OS Command │ R un          │
│                                                           │
└───────────────────────────────────────────────────────────┘
```

11. When the run is complete, you can view the program output on the screen by striking the letter V (for View Status/File).

Notice with RM/CO* that basically the same steps are required, but their execution is considerably simplified. The fact that all of the activities are managed by RM/CO* makes it possible for you, the programmer, to move freely between phases of the overall process with a minimum of effort and confusion.

Using RM/CO*

RM/CO* Projects

One of the features of RM/CO* is its facility that allows you to organize groups of related files into *projects*. For instance, as a student you might set up one project for each semester. Each project would identify the COBOL source files for that semester's work. It also designates the output files (from program runs) and even the input data files. In an advanced applications course, you might set up a separate project for each application. For instance, Chapter 21 is a study of a three-program order entry system; assignments at the end of the chapter require additional programs. You might identify these programs and the data files used by the programs as members of an order processing project, as shown in the project display of Figure C-2. The first three files listed are COBOL source files and the last four are data files required by these programs. The source files *must* be included in the project if you wish to have access to them through RM/CO* (to edit, compile, and run). However, the data files *need not be identified* as part of the project in order for the programs to have access to them. Program access is a function of COBOL and has nothing to do with RM/CO*. The only reason they are designated as members in this example is so that the programmer working on the project can tell at a glance which files are used by the project.

Notice in the preceding descriptions that a project is said to "identify" files that belong to the project. Do not get the idea that RM/CO* sets up a separate entity analogous to a DOS subdirectory. It does not. For each project, RM/CO* creates a project file (the extension is CPJ for COBOL Project) containing the names of all files associated with the project. For instance, assume that you have created the COBOL program file JOB-LIST.CBL through RM/CO* from within the project ASSGNMTS. The file name JOB-LIST.CBL is written to the ASSGNMTS project file, thereby making this program file a member of ASSGNMTS. If, from DOS, you deleted JOB-LIST.CBL from your disk, the name would still remain in the project file—even though the file no longer exists. Only when you attempt to access the file under RM/CO* would you receive a message that there is no such file. It is even possible to identify a file as being a member of two or more projects. However, if you do this, remember that identifying a file as belonging to a second project does not create another copy of your file; both projects "point to" the same file.

For your convenience, the diskettes included with this book contain a project file with the project EXAMPLES. (You are familiar with EXAMPLES if you ran the ADDER demonstration of Chapter 1.) EXAMPLES is intended for use with the example programs described in the text. It already identifies three COBOL program files: ADDER.CBL,

Figure C-2

Typical "Members" of an Order Processing Project.

| ORDER: 7 Members | | | | Comp | | | 11/26 09:13 |

#	Member Name	U	Last Edit: Lines	C	Last Comp: Err Wng	Options
1	ORD-MENU.CBL		98			
2	ORD-ENT.CBL		379			
3	ORD-INVO.CBL		389			
4	SOFTWAR2.DI		Program files			
5	CUSTOMER.DI					
6	INVOICE.MAS					
7	INVOICE.TRA		Data files			

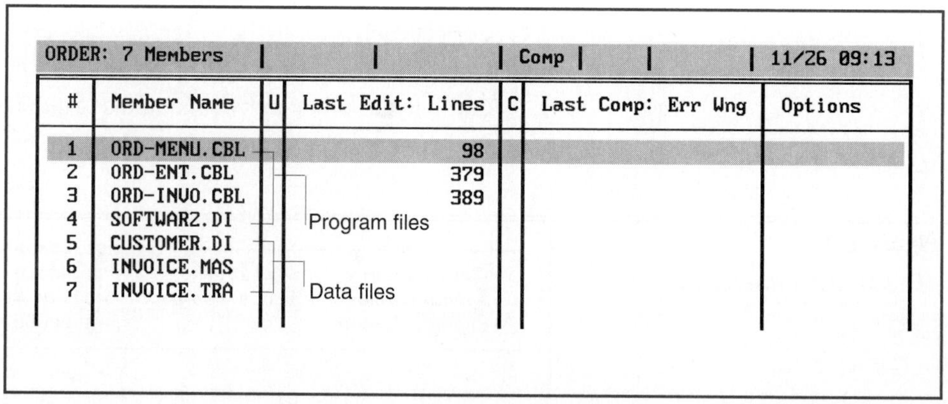

DIAGMSG1.CBL, and DEBUG-X. You will work with DIAGMSG1 later in this chapter and DEBUG-X in Appendix D. As you study example programs in the text, you may find it useful to run some of them, especially those that are interactive. For each that you use, you may designate it as a member of EXAMPLES, load it to your disk, and process it through RM/CO*.

You should create another project that you can use when preparing your programming assignments. You will learn how to create projects later in this appendix.

Descriptions that follow explain how to use various components of RM/CO*. Your learning will be simplified if you first read the material, then sit down at a computer and perform the actions described. You can easily delete projects and project members that you create when you finish your practice session.

Starting RM/CO*

If you have not already configured your diskettes or hard disk for running RM/CO*, you should do so before proceeding here (refer to Appendix B). If you have completed that task, then each time you wish to use RM/CO*, you need only follow the necessary steps to activate the RM/CO* environment (described in Appendix B), then type the following command from the DOS prompt and strike the Enter key:

```
RMCOSTAR
```

When the announcement screen is displayed, strike the Enter key. If you are using the EXAMPLES project included with the distribution diskettes, your screen will appear as shown in Figure C-3. If you have not copied the EXAMPLES project file to your system, your screen will be the same as that in Figure C-3, except that a project will not be listed. Also, the function list at the bottom of the screen will not include the Enter Project option.

From Figure C-3, you can select either of the three functions: Enter Project, Make a New Project, or Quit. As indicated by the message at the bottom of the screen, you select the desired option by striking the highlighted key. For instance, to terminate RM/CO* (Quit), strike the letter Q—you need not strike Enter. To create a new project, strike N. To enter a project, thereby giving you access to the files identified by that project, strike the Enter key (you could also enter the project by striking E). If you have more than one project listed on the screen, move the highlight with the down arrow key to the project in which you wish to work prior to entering.

Notice the highlighting in this menu. The entire word "Enter" is highlighted, but only the "N" in "New" and the "Q" in "Quit" are highlighted. In any RM/CO* menu, if an entire word is highlighted, that option can be selected by simply striking the Enter key (it is the default option).

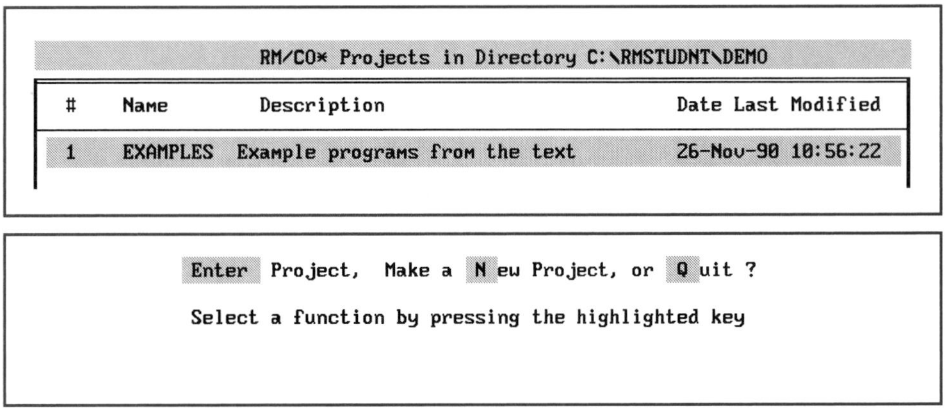

Figure C-3

The Project Screen (from the Project on the Distribution Diskettes).

RM/CO* Projects in Directory C:\RMSTUDNT\DEMO

#	Name	Description	Date Last Modified
1	EXAMPLES	Example programs from the text	26-Nov-90 10:56:22

Enter Project,   Make a New Project, or Quit ?

Select a function by pressing the highlighted key

Getting Help

RM/CO* includes a special Help facility that allows you to obtain information about any aspect of RM/CO* as you are working with the system by simply striking the F1 function key. From the screen of Figure C-3, try it by striking F1. You will be presented with a short description of the Project Directory menu that you have been viewing and, at the bottom of the screen, the following prompt:

`PgUp` = Previous Screen   `ESC` = Exit   `PgDn` = Next Screen

Strike the PgDn and you will get the next screen of Help; in this case, it describes each of the menu options you were viewing. You can progress up and down through the Help screens as you wish. When finished, strike the Escape key to exit Help.

Creating a New Project

If you want to add another project (or create your first one), strike N from the screen of Figure C-3. The bottom of the screen will appear as shown in Figure C-4; you must enter the name of the project. Rules for a project name are the same as for a file name: 8 characters maximum, no spaces except at the end, and some special characters, such as the hyphen, may be used. After entering the name, strike the Enter key.

Next, you will be requested to enter a description (40 characters maximum) of the project. This description is displayed with the project screen whenever you enter RM/CO*. For instance, you can see that the description in Figure C-3 is *Example programs from the text*; its purpose is to identify the nature of the project for you.

Starting RM/CO*

Each program that you want to process through RM/CO* must be identified as a member of a project. Assume that you are ready to enter your Programming Assignment number 7, using the file name ASSGN-7.CBL. Furthermore, the input data file is named DATA-7.DL and the name of the file you will be using for the output report is REPORT.7 (refer to the boxed text on page 657 for a discussion of file names). To designate these files as members of the project, you must do the following.

1. From the screen of Figure C-3, make certain the project you desire is highlighted (if you have only one project, as in Figure C-3, it will automatically be highlighted). Enter the project by striking the Enter key. You will be presented the Project Commands menu shown in Figure C-5. If this is a new project to which you have not yet assigned any members, only the Add, Quit, View, and Xecute functions will be highlighted.

2. You wish to add a project member, so strike A. You will be requested to type the name of the file.

3. To enter the name of the COBOL file, type ASSGN-7.CBL and strike the Enter key. (*Note*: If you do not include the extension, RM/CO* assumes it to be CBL and thereby a COBOL program.)

4. If this file does not exist on disk, RM/CO* will notify you and ask if you wish to create it. If you respond with the letter Y, RM/CO* will create a file on disk with the name ASSGN-7.CBL. The file will be empty—that is, it will contain no program statements or other code. However, it will be available to you when you wish to enter the program. Normally, you will respond with Y to create the file. If you are stepping

Figure C-4

Screen to Designate the Project Name

```
        Type a name for the new Project (up to 8 letters/numbers)

              (Press  Enter  when done,  Esc  to cancel)

    Project Name (1-8 Characters):
```

Figure C-5

The Project Commands Menu

```
┌─────────────────────────── Project Commands ───────────────────────────┐
│  A dd Member      O ptions       U pdate            │  S yntax-Check      │
│  D rop Member     Q uit Project  V iew Status/File  │  C ompile           │
│  Enter  Member                   X ecute OS Command │  R un               │
└─────────────────────────────────────────────────────────────────────────┘
       Select a function by pressing the highlighted key
```

through this sequence simply as practice, you do not want the file created, so strike N. If you respond with N, the file will not be created and the name will not be added to the member list. Type Y (and strike Enter).

If you wish to designate the input and output file names as members of the project (not required), then you must enter them. In addition to serving as documentation regarding the project, RM/CO* allows you to view files that belong to the project. For instance, if the output report file is designated as a member, you can view it any time you wish—even while making corrections to your program. You will learn how to view a file later in this appendix. To designate the output file for this assignment, you would repeat the preceding Steps 1 through 4 with the file name REPORT.7. Note that this will create an empty file, but you need not be concerned because execution of your program will cause the program output file to replace it.

There is limited value in declaring the input file as a member of a project; actually, the authors did not do so in preparing example programs for this book. However, if you desire to do this, then repeat the preceding Steps 1 through 4 with the file name of your data file.

Do not be afraid to add some additional members if you wish to experiment further because they are easy to delete. As you enter each member, notice that the member name is inserted in the list of members immediately following the entry that is highlighted. For instance, assume that you have several members listed in a project and the highlight is positioned on the second member. When you strike A (for Add Member), a blank line will be inserted following the second entry and the other entries will be moved down. If the highlight is positioned on the last entry, the new entry is placed at the end.

If any of the files you intend to designate as a member does not include an file extension in the name, you must include the terminating period or RM/CO* will assume that the extension is CBL. For instance, if you must designate the file PRN-FILE (no extension), you must enter it as "PRN-FILE."—including the period.

File Names

The discussion of printed output files does not begin until Chapter 5—see the program SEQ-LIST, Figure 5-13. In that program and all others in the text, the file name used for printer output is PRN-FILE. When using RM/CO*, you may find it convenient to use a different output report file name for each program. For instance, in the preceding example, ASSGN-7.CBL is the file name of the program and REPORT.7 is the file name of the output report for Assignment 7. (REPORT.7 is the DOS file name that is designated in the SELECT clause of the ENVIRONMENT DIVISION.) Use of the digit 7 clearly ties these two together. Another option would be to use ASSGN-7.RPT for the output report—the same name as the program, but a different extension. However, this can be dangerous. If you accidentally used an extension of CBL instead of the RPT in the SELECT, execution of the program would cause the program to be erased from disk and replaced with the program output. Using a name of an entirely different form will help avoid this problem.

When you are finished, look at the names you have entered. If any of them needs to be changed, use the arrow keys to highlight the member to be changed, then select the Drop option (to drop that member) by striking D. Then you can Add the member back by using the correct name. If you have entered these practice file names as members of the EXAMPLES project, you should delete now. When you are finished working with RM/CO*, you should also delete these files from your disk.

Getting Help—
Project Commands Menu

From the Project Commands menu of Figure C-5 you have two levels of Help available to you. If you strike F1, a set of general description screens of the project commands will be displayed. If you want information about a specific command, strike command letter (for instance, for the Drop command, strike D), then strike F1. After you have terminated the Help, strike the Escape to avoid executing the Drop command (unless you want to execute it).

Entering a COBOL
Source Program

One of the components of RM/CO* is the Editor, which is essentially a specialized word processor for entering and editing COBOL programs. With the Editor, you can either type in a new program or you can edit (make changes to) an existing program. When editing, you have access to two types of displays: the *source display,* which shows only the lines of the COBOL program you have entered, and the *listing display,* which gives you access to the post-compile listing form (Figure 2-19 in Chapter 2 is a post-compile listing). In this section, you will learn the basic elements of entering a program and making simple changes. In later sections of this appendix, you will learn more about editing and working with the listing display.

There are two parts to the Editor. *Edit commands* allow you to perform actions such as undo edit changes made during a session, find the next error in a listing display, and switch to full-screen edit mode. The Edit Commands menu is shown in Figure C-6. *Edit functions,* accessible from the full-screen edit mode, allow you to enter and edit programs. The Edit Function menu is shown in Figure C-7.

Because you enter text from the keyboard in the full-screen edit mode, RM/CO* must use something besides single-letter codes to designate which action to take. To distinguish between a function (such as Delete in Figure C-7) and the letter D to be entered as the first letter of DATA DIVISION, RM/CO* requires you to use a combination of the Alt key and the function letter. For instance, to use the Delete function, you must hold down the Alt key and strike the letter D; then you can release the Alt key. This two-key action is commonly referred to as Alt-D.

Figure C-6

The Edit Commands Menu

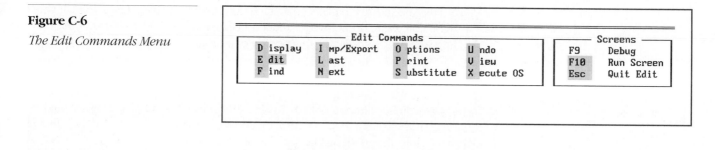

Figure C-7

The Edit Functions Menu

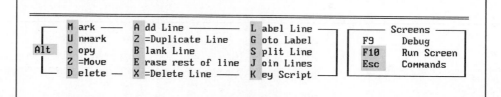

Any time after you have identified a file name as a member of a project, you may use the Editor to enter and edit that file. Let's consider an example using the ADDER program of Chapter 1 as the basis. For this, you will need to add another member to your project. Based on the assumption that you are using the EXAMPLES project and that it contains the ADDER demonstration program, the following example will use the file name ADDER2.

1. If you are not in a project, enter the EXAMPLES project by highlighting EXAMPLES and striking the Enter key (or letter E) from the screen of Figure C-3.

2. Strike A for Add Member from the menu of Figure C-5. Add the file ADDER2 to this project. When you are notified that the file does not exist, respond with Y to create it.

3. Make certain that the ADDER2 line is highlighted and strike the Enter or E from the menu of Figure C-5 for Enter Member. The lower portion of your screen will appear as shown in Figure C-6.

4. To get into the full-screen edit mode, strike E (for Edit); the menu at the bottom will be replaced with the list of edit functions of Figure C-7. The upper portion of the screen will be as shown in Figure C-8; the first line is called the *status line*—it provides information you will use. Since this is an empty file, the screen shows only the "Top-of-File" and "Bottom-of-File" prompts with nothing in between.

5. To begin entering the program, execute the Add Line function with an Alt-A (hold down the Alt key and, while holding it down, strike the letter A). This causes the following to happen:

   a. The editor is placed in the Input mode (the word INPUT appears in the status line at the top of the screen).

   b. A line is opened up between the Top and Bottom message lines on the screen.

   c. The cursor is positioned at column 8 (the beginning of Area A), awaiting data entry.

   d. The current row and column numbers are shown at the righthand end of the status line. The column number is 08. The row number, which should be 02 on your screen, designates the number of the edit-screen row, rather than the program line. The "Top-of-Line" prompt, which will *not* be included in your program file, is Line 01.

6. Type the line:

   ```
   PROCEDURE DIVISION.
   ```

   and strike the Enter key. (*Note:* Programs do not begin with PROCEDURE DIVISION. However, enter it as above so that you can change it.)

7. Make the line-by-line entries shown in Figure C-9—do not strike the Enter key after typing the last line. Try to make your entries as shown here (including errors). If yours is slightly different, do not worry about it because you will learn some of the basic editing features by correcting this portion of a program.

Figure C-8

Empty Screen Awaiting Program Entry

```
EXAMPLES: ADDER2.CBL  | SOURCE |    |    |    |    |    | 07:12
**** Top of File ****
**** End of File ****
```

Making Minor Corrections to a Program

A number of changes that must be made to the program lines of Figure C-9:

■ Change PROCEDURE DIVISION to IDENTIFICATION DIVISION
■ Insert a hyphen between PROGRAM and ID
■ Insert a blank line preceding DATA DIVISION
■ Delete the letter S from DATA DIVISIONS
■ Delete the second occurrence of FIRST-NUM

To move the cursor around the edit screen, use the Up, Down, Left, and Right arrow keys. Strike the Up key once and you will notice that INPUT is deleted from the status line—moving the cursor from the current line automatically takes you from input mode to edit mode. To make the needed corrections, do the following:

1. *Change PROCEDURE to IDENTIFICATION:* Move the cursor to the letter P and begin typing the word IDENTIFICATION. Notice that each letter you type replaces the one at the cursor position; this is called *overtyping.* When you get to the end of PROCE-DURE, you will have typed IDENTIFIC. Strike the Insert key on your keyboard. Notice that the word INSERT is displayed on the status line. You are now in insert mode; continue typing (ATION) and you will see that each letter is inserted, with the remainder of the line being moved to the right.

2. *Insert the hyphen between PROGRAM and ID:* Move the cursor so that it is positioned at the space between these two words. The editor is still in the insert mode (from the preceding operation). You want to overtype the blank, so strike the Insert key and you will see that the word INSERT is removed from the status line. (The Insert key is called *a toggle* because repeatedly striking it activates and deactivates the insert mode.) Type the needed hyphen.

3. *Insert a blank line preceding DATA DIVISION:* The Add Line function causes the Editor to insert a blank line immediately following the line on which the cursor is positioned. Since the cursor is currently on the line that the blank line is to follow, enter an Alt-A and the desired blank line will be inserted.

4. *Delete the letter S from DATA DIVISIONS:* Move the cursor down and to the right so that it is positioned on the letter S in DIVISIONS. Strike the Delete key and the S will be deleted. You can also delete characters by positioning the cursor to the right of the character to be deleted and striking the Backspace key.

5. *Delete the second occurrence of FIRST-NUM:* You could delete the second occurrence of FIRST-NUM (line 8) one character at a time by moving the cursor to the first position of the line (column 12) and holding down the Delete key. However, this would leave a blank line. The Delete Line function gets rid of the line on which the cursor is positioned and closes up the empty line. To do this, move the cursor to line 8, then enter an Alt-X.

These illustrate a minimum set of edit functions that is adequate for you to enter all of your programs. Summarizing, they are

Figure C-9

Partial Program with Errors

```
EXAMPLES: ADDER2.CBL  | SOURCE |    | CAPS |    |    | INPUT | 09,40
**** Top of File ****
             PROCEDURE DIVISION.
             PROGRAM ID. ADDER2.
             DATA DIVISIONS.
             01 WORK-FIELDS.
                 10  FIRST-NUM      PIC 999.
                 10  SECOND-NUM     PIC 999.
                 10  FIRST-NUM      PIC 999.
                 10  TOTAL          PIC 9999.
**** End of File ****
```

- *Up, Down, Left, Right:* Move the cursor up, down, left, and right
- *Insert:* Toggle between overtype and insert modes
- *Delete:* Delete the character at the position of the cursor
- *Backspace:* Delete the character to the left of the cursor
- *Alt-A:* Insert a blank line following the line on which the cursor is positioned and switch to input mode
- *Alt-X:* Delete the line on which the cursor is positioned

As you will see in a later section, the other functions shown in the menu of Figure C-7 are relatively easy to use and make editing programs much simpler.

You can now back out of edit by striking the Escape key. If you are in the full-screen edit mode (you have the menu of Figure C-7), you can return directly to the Project Commands menu (Figure C-5) by striking the F3 function key. If instead you strike the Escape key, you will return to the Edit Commands mode (Figure C-6); striking the Escape again returns you to the Project Commands mode.

Getting Help—Edit Commands and Functions

You can receive help from the Edit Commands menu in the same way that you do from the Project Commands menu. That is, from the Edit Commands menu, strike the F1 key for general information or the letter of the desired command followed by F1 for descriptions of individual commands.

From the Edit Function menu, you have only one level of Help. That is, the F1 key puts you into a large Help text that describes all of the edit functions.

About Deleting Files

As you have seen, whenever you enter a new member into a project, RM/CO* gives you the option to create a new file on disk if the named file does not exist. As a result of the preceding exercise, the file ADDER2.CBL resides on your disk. You should both remove ADDER2.CBL from the project and delete the file from the disk. To remove it from the project, move the highlight to the ADDER2.CBL line and select the Drop Member command from the Project Manager menu of Figure C-1. Although this removes the file from the project, it does not delete it from disk. If you want to delete it (and a companion change file to be described later) from disk, you must use the DOS DELETE command.

Correcting and Running Programs

Syntax Checking

As a program is being compiled, the compiler checks each statement for syntax errors—errors in the use of the language. The post-compile listing includes an indication of these errors so that you can correct them. Because the compiler must write the compiled file to disk, you should first run the syntax checker to check for errors. Since the syntax checker does not create a compiled program, it is much faster than the compiler. To illustrate syntax checking and making necessary corrections, the distribution disk (and the EXAMPLES project) includes the program file DIAGMSG1.CBL, which is used as an example in Chapter 2.

1. If you are not in the EXAMPLES project, enter it. Your display should include three members: ADDER.CBL, DIAGMSG1.CBL, and DEBUG-X.CBL. Highlight the DIAGMSG1.CBL line.

2. Select the Syntax-Check command (see Figure C-1) by striking S. The following message will be displayed on the screen:

   `Syntax-check  Changed  Files, O ne File, or A ll Files ?`

3. You want only the highlighted file checked, so strike O for One File.

4. When the syntax check is completed, the bottom two lines of your screen will be:

```
Compilation Complete: 1 Program, 2 Errors, 0 Warnings.
1 File Syntax-Checked: Total of 2 Errors, 0 Warnings issued (Press [ESC])
```

Strike the Escape key to get the Project Commands menu.

You now have available a program listing that includes identification of errors (the same as the post-compile listing described in Chapter 2). These detected errors, whether detected by the syntax checker or the compiler, can be corrected as described in the next section.

Correcting Syntax-Checker/ Compiler-Detected Errors

You may now proceed to correct the errors detected by the syntax checker. In making corrections, you will be performing three basic operations on the lines of code in the program: changing existing lines, inserting new lines, and deleting existing lines. You know how to do each of these from the previous description of editing. From the Project Commands menu (Figure C-5), proceed as follows:

1. The DIAGMSG1.CBL project entry should still be highlighted; if it is not, move the highlight accordingly.

2. Enter this member by striking E (Enter Member). Your screen will appear as shown in Figure C-10. Here you can see that the compiler diagnostics are included, just as in the example of Chapter 2. Also, notice that the file you are viewing is identified as the listing file by the word LISTING on the status line.

3. The first error is identified at line 0005 (the hyphen is missing from WORKING STORAGE). To begin editing, select the Edit command by striking E. Then move the cursor to the space between WORKING and STORAGE and overtype with the hyphen.

4. Move the cursor to the next line and you will see your edited line become two, as follows:

```
          WORKING-STORAGESECTION.
0005 ───── WORKING-STORAGE-SECTION. ──────────────────
```

The first line is the corrected version and the second, which is ruled out, is the original. Because in the original version of the statement, all blanks are replaced with a line (to indicate that it has been replaced), this example is confusing. That is, the hyphen in

Figure C-10

Listing Display of the DIAGMSG1 Program

```
┌──────────────────────────────────────────────────────────────────────────┐
│ ▓EXAMPLES: DIAGMSG1.CBL▓│▓LISTING▓│      │      │      │      │ 01,01 │
│ **** Top of File ****                                                      │
│ 0001          IDENTIFICATION DIVISION.                                     │
│ 0002          PROGRAM-ID. DIAGMSG1.                                        │
│ 0003                                                                       │
│ 0004          DATA DIVISION.                                               │
│ 0005          WORKING STORAGE SECTION.                                     │
│                  $                                                         │
│ *****  1) E 138: DATA DIVISION SYNTAX (SCAN SUPPRESSED)*E*E*E*E*E*E*E*E*E*E │
│ 0006          01  WORK-FIELDS.                                             │
│                  $                                                         │
│ *****  1) I   5: SCAN RESUME *I*I*I*I*I*I*I*I*I*I*I*I*I*I*I*I*I*I*I*I*I*I*I  │
│ 0007              10  FIRST-NUM    PICTURE 999.                            │
│ 0008              10  SECOND-NUM   PICTURE 999.                            │
│ 0009              10  TOTAL        PICTURE 9999.                           │
│ 0010              10  CONTIN       PICTURE 9 VALUE 1.                      │
│ 0011                                                                       │
│ 0012          PROCEDURE DIVISION.                                          │
│                                                                            │
│ ┌──────────────── Edit Commands ──────────────┐  ┌──── Screens ────┐      │
│ │ D isplay   I mp/Export   O ptions   U ndo    │  │ F9    Debug     │      │
│ │ E dit      L ast         P rint     V iew    │  │ F10   Run Screen│      │
│ │ F ind      N ext         S ubstitute X ecute OS│ │ Esc   Quit Edit │     │
│ └──────────────────────────────────────────────┘  └─────────────────┘     │
└──────────────────────────────────────────────────────────────────────────┘
```

the corrected statement and the ruling inserted in the corrected line look the same.

5. Sometimes viewing the listing file while making corrections becomes confusing, especially when you have numerous corrected statements. You can toggle to the source file by striking the F7 function key. Try it and you will see that the error messages and the ruled-out line are deleted. Then strike it again to return to the listing file.

6. To get to the next error, you can either repeatedly strike the PageDown key until you find it in the listing or use an edit command to find it for you. For the latter you should first use the Down arrow key to progress below the diagnostic line SCAN RESUMED (the Editor will see this as the next error message). Then return to the Edit Commands screen of Figure C-6 by striking the Escape key and select the Next command by striking N.

7. You will receive a prompt regarding the next diagnostic or program; strike the Enter key for the next diagnostic (the default). The editor will locate the next error and your screen display will be as shown in Figure C-11.

8. An undefined identifier message means that the data item CONT was not correctly defined in the DATA DIVISION. If you need to check the DATA DIVISION, simply page up to the appropriate spot. You will see that the name is CONTIN, not CONT. Then return to the error either by paging down or by using the Next command. Position the cursor following the letter T in CONT and type IN.

9. Move the cursor to another line and you will see the original line ruled out and replaced with a corrected line, as follows:

```
           ACCEPT CONTIN
0029 ——— ACCEPT-CONT ————————————————
```

This completes the task of correcting the syntax errors of the program DIAGMSG1. If you have used another compiler language, you may find this experience of making changes to the listing file (rather than the original source file) rather disturbing. However, in RM/CO*, the changes are actually made to a *change file,* which is then applied to the source file the next time the program is syntax-checked or compiled. This process is explained in greater detail in a later section of this appendix.

Comments About Basic Editing

In correcting the syntax-detected errors of this program, you have done the following:

1. Locate the first error. If it is not on the screen, use the Next command (from the Edit Commands menu of Figure C-6).

2. Make the correction.

3. Find the next error. If you need to use the Next command, move the cursor with the Down arrow key so that it is past the SCAN RESUME diagnostic line. Strike the Escape key to return to the Edit Command menu and type N for Next.

4. Repeat Steps (3) and (4) until all errors that caused diagnostic messages have been

Figure C-11

The Next Error in the DIAGMSG1 Program

```
 EXAMPLES: DIAGMSG1.CBL | LISTING |     |     |     |     |   | 07,08
 0025                ADD SECOND-NUM TO TOTAL
 0026                DISPLAY "The sum is ", TOTAL
 0027                DISPLAY " "
 0028                DISPLAY "Enter 1 to repeat, 0 to end"
 0029                ACCEPT CONT
                          $
 *****   1) E 263: IDENTIFIER UNDEFINED (SCAN SUPPRESSED)*E*E*E*E*E*E*E*E*E*E*E
 0030                END-PERFORM
                          $
 *****   1) I   5: SCAN RESUME *I*I*I*I*I*I*I*I*I*I*I*I*I*I*I*I*I*I*I*I*I*I*I*I
```

corrected. Then strike the Escape key twice (or the F3 key) to return to the Project Commands menu and repeat the Syntax-Check.

The preceding examples only illustrate a few ways of moving around in your program. The summary of commands later in this chapter describe others. In particular, you should pay particular attention to the Find command.

Perhaps you have noticed that if you are in the Edit Commands mode and you move the cursor off the current line, you are automatically switched to the Edit Function mode (the menu of Figure C-7). Do not be concerned; the Editor is designed to work this way.

Another item you should notice is that the Editor "remembers" where you were editing when you quit editing. The next time you edit (for instance, after another syntax check) the Editor will enter the listing file at the point from which it exited the last editing operation. For instance, if the previous editing operation exited the editor at line 200, then the listing file will be reentered at line 200.

Operating from the DOS Prompt

Beginning in Chapter 5, your programs will prepare printed output. The recommended technique for printed output is to write it to a file so that you can view it on the screen and have it available to print when necessary. This is especially convenient when running under RM/CO* because you can view the output at any time, even while editing a program. To illustrate, assume the following:

■ You have run the Chapter 5 program SEQ-LIST, which sends the printed output to the file PRN-FILE.

■ The file PRN-FILE has been designated as a member of the project in which you are working.

■ After checking the output, you see that columns of output are not positioned exactly and you determine the changes that are necessary to the program to correct this error.

■ You begin editing the program and realize that the changes you intended to make are not correct. You want to view the output file again.

From the Edit Commands menu, select the View command by striking V. You will be asked the name of the file that you want to view. Type the name PRN-FILE (the name of the output file you want) and strike the Enter key. Your program will be replaced on the screen with the contents of PRN-FILE. You can move up or down in the file with the arrow keys and PageUp/PageDown keys. You can also use the Find command (displayed at the bottom of the screen) to locate any combination of text. This command is described in a later section of this chapter. When you are finished, strike the Escape key and your program will be returned to the screen, ready for you to continue editing.

Compiling and Running a Program

From the demonstration of Chapter 1, you are already familiar with compiling and running programs. Before a program can be run, it must be compiled. The result of the compile is an object module (file) stored on disk with the same name as your program but with an extension of COB. For instance, if you compile ADDER, your disk will contain ADDER.CBL (your source program) and ADDER.COB (the resulting object module or program). This is, in effect, a translation of the source program into machine language. The two actions of compiling and running operate with your files as follows:

Compile: Read the source program
Generate an object program

Run: Execute the object program to process your data

Notice that the source program is not involved when a program is run.

Perhaps you have already noticed that RM/CO* gives you an indication of whether or not a source program must be compiled. For instance, in Figure C-12, notice in the column marked C that DIAGMSG1 has an asterisk, but ADDER does not. RM/CO* places an asterisk in this column whenever you make a change to a program and must recompile it. Note that this indicator *does not* prevent you from running if you have previously compiled a program because the COB file of that compile will still be present. However, the results of execution will not reflect the most recent change of the program until you recompile. This means that *each time you make a change to a source program, you must compile it before running it again.*

In addition to an indication of the need to compile a program, you can see from the annotations in Figure C-12, that this screen conveys considerable information regarding the status of a program.

If you wish to compile and run the program DIAGMSG1 (that you corrected in the preceding sections), return to the Project Commands menu (Figure C-5). Make certain that the DIAGMSG1.CBL entry is highlighted, then strike C for Compile. To the query that follows, strike O to compile the one program. After compilation is complete, strike the Escape to return to the menu.

Running the program and the corresponding Run command are relatively straightforward. For instance, to run the ADDER program you would

1. Make certain you are at the Project Commands level (Figure C-5).

2. Highlight the program you want to run (ADDER.CBL in this case).

3. Strike R (for Run).

4. Strike R again (to run the specified program).

5. The Educational Version of RM/COBOL-85 automatically comes up in the debug mode (debug is described in Appendix D). Usually you will not be using debug, so you type E (and strike Enter) to Exit debug. Your program will then be run.

Figure C-12

Information about the Members of a Project

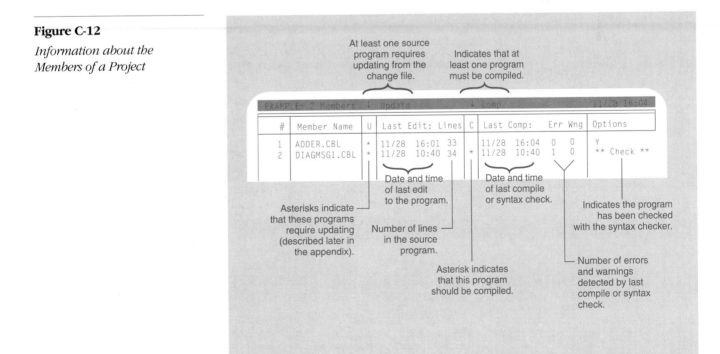

Obtaining a Printed Copy of the Post-Compile Listing

In most instances, when working under RM/CO*, you will not need a printed copy of the post-compile listing. However, if for some reason you do, you can get one in two ways, both through the Options command of the Project Commands menu (Figure C-5). Striking O produces a list of options on the screen. If you strike the PageDown key, you will see that there are three screens of options. One such option is shown as

```
          Option                      File    Proj
   L   Produce Disk Listing            —>      No
```

This option directs the compiler to create a separate file (during compilation) with an extension LST containing the post-compile listing. For instance, if you designate this option and compile the program ASSGMNT7, your output will be two files: ASSGMNT7.COB and ASSGMNT7.LST (the post-compile listing).

Notice that there are two columns: File and Proj. You can designate that a listing file be created for a single file or for all files in the project. A No entry means that a post-compile file will not be created. The arrow under File means that the entry is the same as that of the project (No in this example). To change to Yes, you must first move the highlight to this option, then strike the F key for File or the P key for Project. After you compile, the resulting listing file can be printed from DOS, as described later in this appendix.

If you desire, you can have the compiler send the listing directly to the printer as compilation is taking place. For this, you would move the highlight to the following option:

```
   P   Print Compilation Listing   —>      No
```

Then change the appropriate option to Yes.

Viewing an Output File

Assume that you have just run the program for Assignment 7, and that you have used the name REPORT.7 for the output report file. After the run is completed, you can view the report using any of two project commands. From the Project Commands menu (Figure C-5), you would

1. Select the View Status/File command by striking V.
2. In response to the Status/File query, strike F to view the file.
3. In response to the request for the name of the file to be viewed, type the name REPORT.7 and strike the Enter key. The file will be displayed.

It is significant that to view a file through this command, the file *need not* be designated as a member of the project. That is, the View command allows you to view the contents of a file whether it is inside or outside the project. However, if the file is a member of the project, you can view the Status (see Step 2 in the preceding list). The status screen will tell you how many lines are in the file and the date and time it was created.

If the file is a member of the project, you can also view it through the Enter Member command. That is, highlight the file name on the screen and strike E. The file contents will be displayed in the full-screen edit mode.

For reports in which you are using page control (skip to a new page when the current one is full), you will see a confusing display in some cases. That is, to signal a new page, your program sends a special page code (that the printer will recognize) to the output file. Unfortunately, RM/CO* does not recognize this code as such, thereby confusing the output display at the last line of any given page and the first line of the next page (commonly page headings).

Note that you have limited capability for viewing input data files using these techniques. That is, RM/CO* will only access ASCII text files—files that consist only of printable characters and do not contain special binary codes. Program files, output report files, and line sequential data files are all text files and can thus be viewed. Random access file (indexed and relative) are not text files and therefore cannot be viewed through RM/CO*.

Printing Files

From the Edit Commands menu (Figure C-6), you can use the Print command to print copies of your source program, a line sequential data file, or any output file that does not include page control. However, you should not use it for any report that includes page control or for a post-compile listing (an LST file) because the Print command will page format, thus interfering with page formatting embedded in the file. The simplest way to print these is through DOS. For instance, to print the listing file ASSGNMT7.LST, you would use the following DOS command:

```
TYPE ASSGNMT7.LST>PRN
```

You do not need to exit RM/CO* and get back to DOS in order to execute this command. You can execute DOS commands from within RM/CO* through Xecute OS Command of the Project Commands menu (Figure C-5). That is, strike X, enter your DOS command (for instance, the preceding TYPE command), and strike the Enter key. The command will be carried out and control will be returned to the Project Commands menu.

The Change File and Quitting an RM/CO* Work Session

One of the great advantages of the RM/CO* environment is that it permits you to make corrections to either the source file (input to the compiler) or the listing file (output from the compiler). RM/CO* accomplishes this by using another file, called the *change file,* which functions as follows:

■ Changes made from the keyboard through the Editor are posted to the change file rather than to the source file. If you are using a floppy disk-based computer, you will probably encounter situations when you are editing in which the computer stops accepting keyboard entries and begins disk operations. This means that the Editor is updating the change file for accumulated changes that it has stored in memory.

■ Output from the compiler (diagnostic messages, statistics, and so on.) is written to the change file, rather than to a listing file.

■ When you edit the source file, the RM/CO* Editor shows you the *original* source file updated by those lines in the change file that apply to the source file. The source file that you view through the Editor reflects all changes made to date; this concept is illustrated in Figure C-13. If you were to exit from RM/CO* and list the source file, you would find that no changes had been made to it. All of the changes are recorded in the change file.

Figure C-13

How RM/CO* Displays a conceptual Program

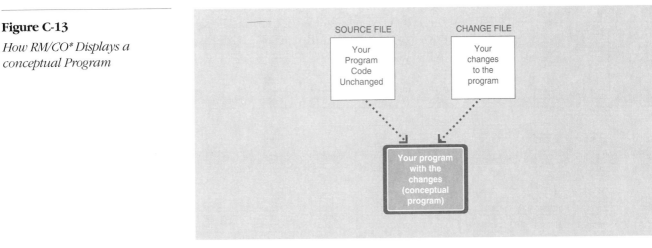

■ When you edit the listing file, the RM/CO* Editor shows you the *original source* file updated by those lines in the change file that apply to the listing file. This means that the listing file is a "conceptual" file; it doesn't exist at all, except as a function of RM/CO*.

■ If you need a copy of all or part of the listing file (for example, to hand in to an instructor), the Print option in the Edit Command menu will print the conceptual listing file with the current time and date.

What this means is that program changes can be made using the most convenient medium. If diagnostics are being corrected, then the changes can be made to the listing file where the exact diagnostic message can be seen. If, on the other hand, corrections to program logic are being made and the diagnostic messages serve only as meaningless clutter that just gets in the way, a single keystroke (F7) changes to the source listing, where the file is seen in its most current form and only the current lines are shown.

Technically, RM/CO* can function continuously, operating from the conceptual program formed from your original source program and your changes in the change file. However, it is a good idea to have the changes copied into the source file periodically— to *update* the source file. If you are operating with a hard disk, you may wish to designate the Automatic Update feature for the program you are currently using. To do this, select the Options command (from the Project Commands menu). Locate the option entitled Automatic Update and change it from No to Yes. Then every time you exit the Editor, your file will be updated. You can do this with a floppy-based system as well, but you will find that getting out of the Editor is slowed considerably.

If you do not wish to use automatic updating, then a good procedure is to select the Update command from the Project Commands menu before terminating your RM/CO* session. From Update, you can designate One file, Changed files, or All files. Usually, Changed files is appropriate. Thus, the sequence of terminating (from the Project Commands menu) will be

1. Select the Update command and update appropriately
2. Select the Quit Project command
3. After exiting the project, select the Quit command to quit RM/CO*

Since updating writes all changes from the change file to the source file, information stored in the change file is duplicate information. Actually, you could delete the change file from disk after any update operation. However, it is a good idea to retain it while you are continuing to work on the program because RM/CO* uses it to tell you when the last update occurred. However, after you have completed a programming assignment (finished program), you may wish to delete the change file simply to conserve disk space. This will be especially important if you do not have a hard disk. The change file has the same name as the source program, but its extension is C00.

Additional Editing Operations

This section contains a brief description of some of the most useful editing operations. Additional information on these and other operations can be obtained by accessing the Help screen for the feature desired.

The material in this section is grouped by subject, rather than by the edit mode (Command or Function) that contains the subject operation. All of the following discussions assume that the user is in the proper mode; that is, that the menu containing the desired operation is shown at the bottom of the screen. Movement between the Command and Function menus is achieved as follows:

- To move from the Edit Commands menu to the Edit Functions menu, strike either the E key or the Enter key

- To move from the Edit Functions menu to the Edit Commands menu, strike the Escape key

- Note that each menu specifies how to get to the other one

The Undo Command

Every programmer has had (or will have) the experience, after a keystroke is made, of saying, "Oh no!" To alleviate this situation, the RM/CO* Editor provides the Undo command.

Two levels of "undoing" are provided: Last Operation and Entire Session. To undo the results of the last edit operation, select Undo from the Edit Commands menu and strike the Enter key. Note that only the last operation done can be Undone. If any other editing operation has been done after the unfortunate one, it is impossible to Undo it.

On some occasions, the results of an editing session are so disastrous that you may wish the session had never been started. The results of the entire session can be undone by selecting the Undo option from the Command menu and striking the A key to specify Undo All.

Block Operations

It is often useful to do something with an entire block of code. For example, if two record descriptions are very similar, it is easier to enter the first one, make a copy of it, and then make the required changes to the copy than it is to key in the entire second description. If a paragraph needs to be moved to a different location in the PROCEDURE DIVISION, it is easier to move the existing paragraph to its new location than it is to retype the entire paragraph. And if a block of code needs to be deleted, it is easier to delete it as a block than it is to delete it line by line.

Block operations require two (or three) steps:

1. Mark the block of code to be operated on.
2. Do the necessary operation (Move, Copy, Delete) with the marked block.
3. If necessary, unmark the block.

Note that Block operations are done in the Edit Functions mode.

To mark a block:

1. Move the cursor to the first line of the block.
2. Enter Alt-M to mark the line. The marked line is highlighted.
3. If the block to be marked contains more than one line, move the cursor to the last line of the block and use Alt-M again to mark the end of the block. The entire block will be highlighted.

If the block is to be moved or copied:

1. Move the cursor to the new location (the place where the new block is to go).

2. Alt-C (Copy) will copy the marked block to the cursor location. The block remains marked so that it can be copied to an additional location if desired.

Alt-Z (Move) will move the marked block to the cursor location. It is deleted from its original (marked) location.

If the block is to be deleted:

Alt-D will delete the marked block. Note that the cursor must be within the marked block before it can be deleted.

If the block is to be unmarked:

Alt-U will unmark a block. Two situations commonly arise in which you need to do this: after a Move operation, or simply because the current marking is no longer appropriate.

Line Operations

Block operations are intended to deal with blocks, or sets, of lines. The RM/CO* Editor also provides operations for dealing with single lines. Each of the operations described next is performed on the "current line"—the line on which the cursor is positioned.

Delete the current line:

Alt-X deletes the current line.

Blank the entire current line:

Alt-B blanks all data on the current line, thereby providing a blank line for the insertion of replacement text.

Erase the last part of the current line:

Alt-E blanks the portion of the current line from the cursor to the end of the line.

Duplicate the current line:

Alt-2 creates a duplicate of the line on which the cursor is currently positioned. When making corrections to a line, it is often helpful to be able to see the original. Using Alt-2 to create a duplicate line allows you to make changes to the duplicate while still keeping the original line visible. When the correction is completed, the original line can be deleted.

Split a line:

Alt-S splits the current line at the position of the cursor, thereby forming two lines. The "cursor character" becomes the first character on the new line.

Join two lines:

Alt-J operates on the line on which the cursor is positioned and the next line by making them one (the next line is appended to the end of the current line). The cursor must be at the end of the current line when executing this function.

Labelling a Line

Consider the following scenario. You are making a correction to a line in the PROCEDURE DIVISION, but you want to check the definition of a data item in the DATA DIVISION before making the change. Thus, you might search toward the top for the data item and when finished return to the statement in the PROCEDURE DIVISION. The Editor simplifies the task of returning by allowing you to mark the spot with a temporary label and then returning via the label. The sequence of steps (assuming that you are at the PROCEDURE DIVISION statement) would be

1. From the full-screen Editor, enter Alt-L (the Label function). The Editor will respond with the prompt:

   ```
   Press Label key:
   ```

2. You can type any single letter or digit as your label. For example, if the statement you are working on is a subtract, you might find it easier to remember if you label it S. (It makes no difference if you use uppercase or lowercase—S is treated the same as s.)

3. Move to the item of interest in the DATA DIVISION.

4. When you are ready to return to the subtract in the PROCEDURE DIVISION, use the Goto Label function by typing Alt-G. The following query will be displayed:

   ```
   Press Label key:
   ```

   The label to which you want to return is S, so strike the S key. The cursor will be positioned at the beginning of the statement to which you had assigned this label.

The Find Command

Assume that you are editing a very large program and you need to make a correction to one of the statements in the 330-CALCULATE-DEDUCTIONS paragraph. To find the paragraph, you could simply strike the PageDown key repeatedly until you reached this paragraph. However, with a large program, this would be a slow operation. An alternative would be using the Find command; upon striking the letter F, you would be presented with the following prompt:

```
Enter the Target to FIND...
```

In response, you would type the string of characters you want to find (the paragraph name in this case), enclosed within quotes as follows:

```
"330-CALCULATE-DEDUCTIONS."
```

The Editor would then search for this sequence of characters and, upon finding it, position the cursor on the line containing this sequence. Be aware that it will stop at the *first* occurrence. Thus, if the 200 module includes the statement

```
PERFORM 330-CALCULATE-DEDUCTIONS.
```

execution would stop at this point and another Find would need to be executed. In general, the Find command allows you to search a file from the cursor position either toward the end of the file or the beginning of the file for a specified target. The target can be a string of characters (as in the preceding example), a line number, the top or end of the file, a line label, or a relative line displacement. The following examples illustrate the Find; notice the effect of the + and - in these examples.

+   specifies an increase in the current line number (a move toward the end of the file).

−   specifies a decrease in the current line number (a move toward the top of the file).

Find Target	Search Actions
*	Move the cursor to the end of the file.
-*	Move the cursor to the top of the file (the first line).
"T-CODE"	Search toward the end of the file for the string of characters *T-CODE*. When found, the cursor is positioned on that line. If it is not found, a not-found message is displayed and the cursor position is unchanged.
"T-CODE"	Exactly the same as the preceding example, except that the search is toward the *beginning* of the file.
153	Move the cursor to line 153 in the file. Since line numbers are assigned by the compiler, this method cannot be used until the file has been Syntax-Checked or Compiled.
-35	Move the cursor 35 lines toward the beginning of the file (reduces the current line number by 35).
+72	Move the cursor 72 lines toward the end of the file (increases the current line number by 72). Including the + sign in optional.
.S	Move the cursor to the line labelled S (lines are labelled with the Label Line function). The period preceding the label tells the Editor that this is a label.

In the preceding examples, to find the string of characters T-CODE, the string is enclosed in quotes; these serve to designate the string of characters and are commonly called *delimiters*. Although quotes were used in these examples, any non-numeric character (except + or -) that does not appear in the string being searched for can be used. In other words

```
"T-CODE"
/T-CODE/
!T-CODE!
```

are equivalent. If the first occurrence of the string is not the one desired, strike the F and Enter keys to find the next occurrence. If it is necessary to make the Find "case sensitive" (that is, to detect "PUT" but ignore "put"), the Option command can be used to specify this.

The Substitute Command

Assume that you have a large program in which you defined the input record item CK-SUM in the DATA DIVISION, but used the name CA-SUM throughout the PROCEDURE DIVISION, and you must change all occurrences of CA-SUM to CK-SUM. The RM/CO* Editor simplifies this task with the Substitute command, which combines the searching capabilities of the Find with the ability to replace the designated character string. Upon striking the letter S (for Substitute), you could enter the following:

```
/CK-SUM/CA-SUM/**
```

The components of this Substitute command are

CK-SUM   The current character string that is to be replaced.

CA-SUM   The new character string that will replace the current.

**   Indicates that searching is to begin at the present position of the cursor (the first asterisk indicates this) and that all occurrences of the current string are to be replaced with the new string (the second asterisk indicates this).

Note that in this example, all substitutions will be made automatically— a potentially dangerous situation. For instance, assume that your program contained the data items BLOCK-SUM and CK-SUM-LIMIT. These would be changed to BLOCA-SUM and CA-SUM-LIMIT. Also, your program might include the data item CK-SUM (another field), as well as CA-SUM, so you would need to change only part of the occurrences in the PROCEDURE DIVISION. By including the code P at the end of the command; that is,

```
/CK-SUM/CA-SUM/**P
```

you will force the editor to stop at each occurrence and display the following prompt:

```
Change this instance of the String? N
```

If you strike the Enter key, no change occurs (No is the default). If you overtype with the letter Y and strike Enter, the replacement occurs. In either case, the search proceeds. You can terminate the search at any point with a Ctrl-Break.

In this example, the character / is the delimiter. Rules for delimiters are the same as for the Find command. All three delimiters as illustrated in the example are required. Although the current string and new string in this example are the same length, this is not a requirement. If you want to get rid of the occurrences of the current string, then the substitution can be a null string (two delimiters with no intervening space).

Summary of Edit Operations

Edit Commands

Display	Select source or listing display mode
Edit	Descend to the full-screen edit level
Find	Find a string, statement label, or line
Imp/Export	Import a block from, or export it to, an external file
Last	Locate the previous diagnostic or program unit in the file
Next	Locate the next diagnostic or program unit in the file
Options	Select Compiler or RM/CO* environment options
Print	Print all or part of the file
Substitute	Perform string replacement
Undo	Undo last edit operation or all edits from this session
View	View current file status, another file, or edit macros
Xecute OS	Execute Operating System command(s)

Full-Screen Editing—
Cursor/Window
Motion Keys

In the following summaries, Left, Right, Up, and Down refer to the respective arrow keys.

Left	Moves the cursor one character to the left
Right	Moves the cursor one character to the right
Up	Moves the cursor up one line
Down	Moves the cursor down one line
Home	Moves the cursor to position 8 or 1 of the current line, based on the file type
End	Moves the cursor to end of the current line
Ctrl-PgDn	Moves the cursor to the bottom line of the screen
Ctrl-PgUp	Moves the cursor to the top line of the screen
Ctrl-Left	Moves the cursor to the beginning of the word to the left
Ctrl-Right	Moves the cursor to the beginning of the word to the right (RM/CO* considers any string of nonblank characters a word)
PgDn	Displays the next page
PgUp	Displays the previous page
Ctrl-Home	Displays the first page
Ctrl-End	Displays the last page
Alt-F	Scrolls the window down one line
Alt-V	Scrolls the window up one line

Full-Screen Editing—
Editing Keys

Enter (non-Input mode)	Moves the cursor to column 1 of the next line for files that are not RM/COBOL-85 source or copy files and to column 8 of the next line for RM/COBOL-85 source and copy files.
Enter (Input mode)	Inserts a new line below that on which the cursor was positioned. The cursor is then positioned at column 1 or 8 of the new line. Alt-A starts input mode.
Ins	Toggles Insert mode on and off. In Insert mode, new characters entered are inserted: they normally overlay the current contents of the line. You will see INSERT in the 6th field of the Status Line.
Del	Deletes the character under which the cursor is positioned.
Caps Lock	Toggles Caps Lock mode on and off. In Caps Lock mode, alphabetic characters you type are entered in uppercase. In this mode, hold down Shift to enter lowercase letters. When on, you'll see CAPS in the 4th field of the Status Line.
Num Lock	Toggles Num Lock mode on and off. In Num Lock mode, the cursor control keys on the numeric keypad are not active. To move the cursor, hold down the Shift key and press a cursor motion key on the keypad. When on, you'll see NUMS in the 5th field of the Status Line.

Default Function Key Definitions

RM/CO* has built in these macro definitions for the function keys; those marked by an asterisk (below) apply anywhere in RM/CO*. The rest are only usable within the editor.

F1	*(Alt-H)*	* Displays a context-sensitive HELP panel
F2	*(Alt-A)*	Add a line (and enter INPUT mode) within the editor
F3	*(Esc Esc)*	Leave the Editor
F5	*(Alt-B)*	* Blank the cursor line
F6	*(Alt-E)*	* Blank from the cursor position to the end of the line
F7	*(Esc D T)*	Toggle between Source and Listing Displays
F8	*(Esc U L)*	Perform an UNDO LAST Edit Command
F9	*(Alt-W)*	* Jump between the Debug and the Editor windows
F10	*(Alt-R)*	* Show the Run Screen

Using RM/COBOL-85 Debug

D

Sometimes even carefully planned programs do not work and attempts to find the errors (bugs) lead only to frustration. This appendix describes an aid for debugging programs (locating errors); it is called *Debug* and it allows you to interact with the program during its execution. Be aware that the availability of a debugging tool does not mean that you should spend less time carefully planning and checking your programs. With the proper design and checking, most program bugs should be eliminated before the program is even run. However, when errors do creep in and prove difficult to locate, a good debugging aid is valuable. It is in this context that the RM/COBOL-85 Debug facility must be considered. Using Debug, you can make the program:

1. Stop at a specified statement

2. Display values currently stored in program data items

3. Modify values of program data items

4. Step through the program one statement at a time

5. Resume normal program execution

Outline

- **Debug Sample**
  - Example Program Definition
  - A Program Solution

- **RM/COBOL Debug**
  - Invoking Debug Commands
  - Using the Step Command to Trace Program Execution
  - The Quit Command

- **Finding the Program Bug Using Debug**
  - Inspecting the Values of Program Variables
  - The Display Command
  - The Breakpoint and Resume Commands
  - Switching Between Debug and the Editor Under RM/CO*

- **Other Debug Commands**
  - More About the Step Command
  - More About the Breakpoint Command
  - The Clear Command
  - The Address Stop Command
  - The Trap Command
  - The Modify Command
  - The Condition Code
  - About Using Debug

Debug Sample

Example Program Definition

To illustrate using the RM/COBOL-85 Interactive Debug feature, consider the following example problem.

Debug Example

A credit card company maintains a file consisting of one record for each customer. The input record includes the following information:

Record Positions	Field
1–6	Customer number
7–30	Customer name
31	First billing code digit
32	Second billing code digit
51–55	Balance due (dollars and cents)

For each record, it will be necessary to calculate a field named TEST-CODE as follows:

TEST-CODE = First billing code digit
+ second billing code digit

The service charge rate depends upon the value of TEST-CODE as follows:

TEST-CODE	Rate (%)
1	0.75
2	1.00
3–7	1.50

The monthly service charge is to be calculated as the balance due times the service charge percentage. For example, a TEST-CODE value of 4 and a balance of $351.45 would be calculated as

Service charge = 351.45 x 0.015

If the value of TEST-CODE is not between 1 and 7, then no calculation is to be made. For each record with a TEST-CODE value between 1 and 7, print the following fields:

Customer number
Customer name
Balance due
Total due (balance plus service charge)

A Program Solution

A program solution to this example is shown in Figure D-1. With the exception of the condition placed on processing by the value of TEST-CODE (and its subsequent testing), this is a relatively simple example. If you have not yet covered Chapter 11 ("Conditional Operations"), you will not recognize the EVALUATE statement. Do not be concerned; the statement operates exactly as the English suggests. That is:

WHEN TEST-CODE is 1, multiply CR-BALANCE by 1.0075
WHEN TEST-CODE is 2, multiply CR-BALANCE by 1.01
WHEN TEST-CODE is 3, 4, 5, 6, or 7 multiply CR-BALANCE by 1.015
WHEN TEST-CODE is anything else, move N to PROCESS-RECORD

Notice that the record will be processed and printed (lines 81–86) only if the value of PROCESS-RECORD is Y. This switch is set to Y at the beginning of the 110 module (line 67) and changed to N only if the value of TEST-CODE is not between 1 and 7 (line 77). If you have reached Chapter 8, you will notice that the input and output operations are not included as separate modules. The form here is used to simplify investigating Debug.

Figure D-1

*A Program for the Debug
Example*

```
 1      IDENTIFICATION DIVISION.
 2      PROGRAM-ID. DEBUG-X.
 3
 4      ENVIRONMENT DIVISION.
 5
 6      CONFIGURATION SECTION.
 7      SOURCE-COMPUTER. IBM-PC.
 8
 9      INPUT-OUTPUT SECTION.
10
11      FILE-CONTROL.
12          SELECT CREDIT-FILE  ASSIGN TO DISK, "DEBUG-X.DL"
13                              ORGANIZATION IS LINE SEQUENTIAL.
14          SELECT REPORT-FILE  ASSIGN TO PRINTER "REPORT.X".
15
16      DATA DIVISION.
17
18      FILE SECTION.
19
20      FD  CREDIT-FILE.
21      01  CREDIT-RECORD.
22          10  CR-CUSTNUM   PIC X(6).
23          10  CR-CUSTNAME  PIC X(24).
24          10  CR-FIRST-CODE  PIC 9(1).
25          10  CR-SECOND-CODE PIC 9(1).
26          10             PIC X(18).
27          10  CR-BALANCE   PIC 999V99.
28
29      FD  REPORT-FILE.
30      01  REPORT-LINE.
31          10  RL-CUSTNUM   PIC X(6).
32          10             PIC X(3).
33          10  RL-CUSTNAME  PIC X(24).
34          10             PIC X(3).
35          10  RL-BALANCE   PIC ZZ9.99.
36          10             PIC X(3).
37          10  RL-TOTAL     PIC ZZ9.99.
38
39      WORKING-STORAGE SECTION.
40
41      01  OTHER-VARIABLES.
42          10  TEST-CODE   PIC 9.
43          10  TOTAL-W     PIC 999V99.
44      01  PROGRAMMED-SWITCHES.
45          10  END-OF-FILE    PIC X.
46          10  PROCESS-RECORD PIC X.
47
48      PROCEDURE DIVISION.
49
50      000-PROCESS-BILLINGS.
51          PERFORM 100-INITIALIZE
52          PERFORM 110-PROCESS-1-RECORD
53              UNTIL END-OF-FILE = "Y"
54          PERFORM 120-FINALIZE
55          STOP RUN.
56
57      100-INITIALIZE.
58          OPEN INPUT CREDIT-FILE
59          OPEN OUTPUT REPORT-FILE
60          MOVE "N" TO END-OF-FILE
61          READ CREDIT-FILE
62            AT END
63              MOVE "Y" TO END-OF-FILE
64          END-READ.
65
66      110-PROCESS-1-RECORD.
67          MOVE "Y" TO PROCESS-RECORD
68          ADD CR-FIRST-CODE CR-SECOND-CODE GIVING TEST-CODE
69          EVALUATE TEST-CODE
70            WHEN 1
71              MULTIPLY CR-BALANCE BY 1.0075 GIVING TOTAL-W
72            WHEN 2
73              MULTIPLY CR-BALANCE BY 1.01 GIVING TOTAL-W
74            WHEN 3 THROUGH 7
75              MULTIPLY CR-BALANCE BY 1.015 GIVING TOTAL-W
76            WHEN OTHER
77              MOVE "N" TO PROCESS-RECORD
78          END-EVALUATE
79
80          IF PROCESS-RECORD = "Y"
81            MOVE SPACES TO REPORT-LINE
82            MOVE CR-CUSTNUM TO RL-CUSTNUM
83            MOVE CR-CUSTNAME TO RL-CUSTNAME
84            MOVE CR-BALANCE TO RL-BALANCE
85            MOVE TOTAL-W TO RL-TOTAL
86            WRITE REPORT-LINE
87          END-IF
88
89          READ CREDIT-FILE
90            AT END
91              MOVE "Y" TO END-OF-FILE
92          END-READ.
93
94      120-FINALIZE.
95          CLOSE CREDIT-FILE
96              REPORT-FILE.
```

The data file DEBUG-X.DL, which is shown in Figure D-2, is used in this appendix to illustrate the Debug feature. If you inspect this listing, you will see that three records (those shaded) have values outside the allowable range. Hence, these records should not be printed when the program is run.

Figure D-3 is the result of running the program with this data. Upon comparing the input of Figure D-2 to the output of Figure D-3, notice that two of the records with the value of TEST-CODE greater than 7 were not printed. However, the record for Janice Olson, which has a value of 14, did print. Let's see how you might use the Debug feature to find the error in the program.

RM/COBOL Debug

The sections that follow describe using Debug in the context of the program DEBUG-X. You will find these descriptions more meaningful if you read the material first, then use your computer to work through the sequences. To do this, you will need to copy the following two files from the appropriate distribution disk to your own disk: DEBUG-X.CBL and DEBUG-X.DL.

Invoking Debug Commands

Whenever you have run a program (from RM/CO* or from DOS using the RUNCOBOL command), the computer displays a prompt similar to that shown in Figure D-4. This is a Debug prompt that tells you that execution is under control of the Debug facility. Furthermore, this particular prompt says that control has been halted *prior to* executing statement 50 of program DEBUG-X. Referring to the program of Figure D-1, you see that statement 50 is the first line of the PROCEDURE DIVISION. As you know, striking the letter *E* followed by the Enter key causes the program to execute. Actually, the *End* command— code *E*—releases control of the program from Debug and allows it to run uninterrupted. End is one of 12 Debug commands.

Where the End command causes program execution to take place without the involvement of Debug, other commands allow you to control execution without making any changes to the program. For instance, the Step command causes the Debug to allow execution of only the next statement. Hence, if you responded to the Debug prompt for Figure D-4 with a *Step* command—code *S*—Debug would respond with a second prompt line, as shown in Figure D-5(a). This tells you that execution has progressed to (but not

Figure D-2

Sample Data File (DEBUG-X.DL) for Debug Example

	First billing code digit.	Second billing code digit.
138761Hamilton Jones	10	38565
110374Christie Lukenbill	27	10035
490186Harland B. Johnson	06	62287
922541Janice Olson	77	35000
853720Erika Price	23	05675
883774Alecia Burnett	11	12550
765230Megan Howarth	44	14498
133286James Q. Funston	10	75587
852049Hubert Long	21	50000
703723A. B. Jacobson	11	50500

2+7=9
7+7=14 } These three TEST-CODE values exceed the
4+4=8   maximum allowed values. The corresponding shaded records above should not be printed.

Figure D-3

Program output for debug example

138761	Hamilton Jones	385.65	388.54
490186	Harland B. Johnson	622.87	632.21
922541	Janice Olson	350.00	353.50
853720	Erika Price	56.75	57.60
883774	Alecia Burnett	125.50	126.75
133286	James Q. Funston	755.87	761.53
852049	Hubert Long	500.00	507.50
703723	A. B. Jacobson	505.00	510.05

Erroneous Output

yet executed) statement 51. If you were to enter two more S commands, you would see the display of Figure D-5(b). Relating this to the program of Figure D-1, you can clearly see the sequence of execution. Statement 51 is a PERFORM and causes program execution to jump to statement 57, the first statement of the 100 module.

Using the Step Command to Trace Program Execution

One of many ways to use Debug when conditional execution of statements is involved is to step through the offending portion of the program and observe the sequence in which various statements of the program are executed. Although that is not the most efficient way to debug this program, it will give you a feel for following the execution sequence of the statements in the program. But first, you must have some idea of what you are seeking. Appropriate portions of the first four input records of the data file are shown in Figure D-6. Execution for these four data records should proceed as follows:

First record—TEST-CODE is 1

The EVALUATE statement will execute the MULTIPLY at line 71; the conditional sequence in lines 81–86 will be executed.

Second record—TEST-CODE is 9

The EVALUATE statement will execute the MOVE at line 77 (the value of TEST-CODE is "other" than any of the listed values); consequently, the conditional sequence in lines 81–86 will *not* be executed.

Second record—TEST-CODE is 6

The EVALUATE statement will execute the MULTIPLY at line 75; the conditional sequence in lines 81–86 will be executed.

Second record—TEST-CODE is 14

The EVALUATE statement will execute the MOVE at line 77; consequently, the conditional sequence in lines 81–86 will not be executed.

Figure D-4

The Debug prompt

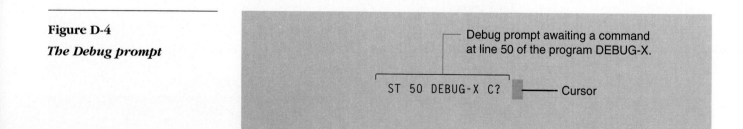

Debug prompt awaiting a command at line 50 of the program DEBUG-X.

ST 50 DEBUG-X C?   ——— Cursor

Figure D-5

The Step Command

The Step command
steps to the next statement.

```
ST 50 DEBUG-X C? S           ST 50 DEBUG-X C? S
ST 51 DEBUG-X C?             ST 51 DEBUG-X C? S
                             ST 57 DEBUG-X C? S
                             ST 58 DEBUG-X C?

     (a)                          (b)
```

Successive execution of the Step command is shown in Figure D-7. (Note that after the letter *S* is entered as the first command, it is only necessary to strike the Enter key and the Step command is repeated.) For the first record, you can clearly see the sequence of statement execution:

1. The value for TEST-CODE is calculated at line 68 (1 + 0 gives 1).

2. Line 69 is the EVALUATE that evaluates TEST-CODE.

3. The value 1 for TEST-CODE causes the alternative at line 71 to be executed (as predicted in the preceding consideration of this first record).

4. This completes the EVALUATE statement, so execution continues to statement 80, the IF statement.

5. Since PROCESS-RECORD is true, statements 81 through 86 are executed as predicted.

Progressing to the second record, the value for TEST-CODE becomes 9 (2 + 7); this will cause a difference sequence of statement execution):

1. Execution progresses from line 69 (the EVALUATE) to the OTHER option at line 77.

2. At line 77, PROCESS-RECORD to be set to false.

3. At line 80, the IF condition is false, so the conditional sequence is not executed.

4. Execution proceeds to line 89.

The third record is processed in the same way as the first, except that the EVALUATE alternative is line 75.

Figure D-6

Portions of the First Four Input Records

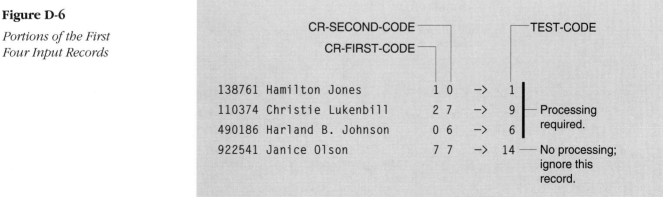

```
                    CR-SECOND-CODE               TEST-CODE
                       CR-FIRST-CODE

138761 Hamilton Jones            1 0    ->    1
110374 Christie Lukenbill        2 7    ->    9    Processing
490186 Harland B. Johnson        0 6    ->    6    required.
922541 Janice Olson              7 7    ->   14    No processing;
                                                   ignore this
                                                   record.
```

Figure D-7

Repeated Execution of the Step Command

```
        ST  50  DEBUG-X  C?  S ────── Step command entered by
        ST  51  DEBUG-X  C?           programmer.
        ST  57  DEBUG-X  C?
        ST  58  DEBUG-X  C?
        ST  59  DEBUG-X  C?
        ST  60  DEBUG-X  C?
        ST  61  DEBUG-X  C?
        ST  52  DEBUG-X  C?
First data record.
        ST  66  DEBUG-X  C?
        ST  67  DEBUG-X  C?
        ST  68  DEBUG-X  C? ────── Execution of this (line 68) should
        ST  69  DEBUG-X  C?         yield TEST-CODE=1.
        ST  71  DEBUG-X  C? ────── EVALUATE alternative when
        ST  80  DEBUG-X  C?         TEST-CODE=1.
        ST  81  DEBUG-X  C?
        ST  82  DEBUG-X  C?
        ST  83  DEBUG-X  C? ────── Executed because PROCESS-RECORD
        ST  84  DEBUG-X  C?         contains Y.
        ST  85  DEBUG-X  C?
        ST  86  DEBUG-X  C?
        ST  89  DEBUG-X  C? ────── Read next record.
Second data record.
        ST  66  DEBUG-X  C?
        ST  67  DEBUG-X  C?
        ST  68  DEBUG-X  C? ────── Yields TEST-CODE=9.
        ST  69  DEBUG-X  C?
        ST  77  DEBUG-X  C? ────── EVALUATE alternative moves N to
        ST  80  DEBUG-X  C?         PROCESS-RECORD.
        ST  89  DEBUG-X  C?
Third data record.                  IF here skips statement sequence 81–86.
        ST  66  DEBUG-X  C?
        ST  67  DEBUG-X  C?
        ST  68  DEBUG-X  C? ────── Yields TEST-CODE=6.
        ST  69  DEBUG-X  C?
        ST  75  DEBUG-X  C? ────── EVALUATE Alternative when TEST-CODE=6.
        ST  80  DEBUG-X  C?
        ST  81  DEBUG-X  C?
        ST  82  DEBUG-X  C?
        ST  83  DEBUG-X  C?
        ST  84  DEBUG-X  C?
        ST  85  DEBUG-X  C?
        ST  86  DEBUG-X  C?
        ST  89  DEBUG-X  C?
Fourth data record.
        ST  66  DEBUG-X  C?
        ST  67  DEBUG-X  C?
        ST  68  DEBUG-X  C? ────── Should yield TEST-CODE=14.
        ST  69  DEBUG-X  C?
        ST  75  DEBUG-X  C? ────── Should not be at line 75; should be at line 77.
        ST  80  DEBUG-X  C?
        ST  81  DEBUG-X  C?
        ST  82  DEBUG-X  C?
        ST  83  DEBUG-X  C?
        ST  84  DEBUG-X  C?
        ST  85  DEBUG-X  C?
        ST  86  DEBUG-X  C?
        ST  89  DEBUG-X  C?
```

The fourth record represents the problem. Because the value for TEST-CODE is 14 (7 + 7), the sequence should be identical to that of the second record; that is, statements 68, 77, 80, and 89. However, you see that statement 72 of the EVALUATE is executed, implying that the program is treating TEST-CODE as if it were between 3 and 7.

If you are running from DOS, the entire screen will be used in displaying the commands. If you are running from RM/CO*, only a small window of several lines will be allocated for the commands. The remainder of the screen will be used to display the source program. As you step through the program under RM/CO*, the statement at which execution is halted will be highlighted. This is obviously a huge advantage because you need not refer to line numbers and a separated program listing to determine where you are at any given time.

The Quit Command

If, in the sequence of Figure D-7, you had spotted the error in the program, you would most likely terminate processing in order to make the appropriate correction. This is done with the Quit command--code Q. That is, simply enter the letter Q, and strike the Enter key. Control will be returned to DOS or RM/CO*.

Finding the Program Bug Using Debug

Inspecting the Values of Program Variables

After the stepping sequence of Figure D-7, you know that the apparent TEST-CODE value 14 is not handled properly. In this case, it would be convenient to be able to verify the values in TEST-CODE and in FIRST-CODE and SECOND-CODE. Debug allows you to display values stored in any data item defined in the program. Obviously, to do this, Debug must know the location in memory of each data item, information not normally available after the program is compiled. To accommodate this need, the compiler can be directed to include in the object program file a complete table of all data-names and index names used in a program, together with their memory locations. The RM/CO* options are defined to produce this symbol table automatically. However, if you are operating from DOS, you must include the Y option with the RMCOBOL command to produce a symbol table, since the default is no table. Thus, your command to compile DEBUG-X would be:

```
RMCOBOL DEBUG-X Y
```

If you also want a post-compile listing, you can include both the L and Y options as follows:

```
RMCOBOL DEBUG-X Y L
```

The Display Command

At any Debug stop in a program, you can show the value stored in any data item using the *Display* command—code *D*. For instance, assume that you had stepped through the program to the fourth record (the sequence shown in Figure D-7) and that Debug is displaying the prompt:

```
ST 69 DEBUG-X C?
```

If you respond with

```
D TEST-CODE
```

Debug will display the value currently stored in the data item TEST-CODE. Notice that the command consists of two components separated by a space: the command letter *D* and the name of the data item to be displayed. If the data item you want is subscripted, include the subscript value in the same way you would within the program itself.

The Breakpoint and Resume Commands

With the Display command at your disposal, you could indeed step through the program as in Figure D-7 and, upon reaching the fourth record, display the contents of TEST-CODE. However, stepping statement by statement is a slow process and would be especially cumbersome if the program were 960 lines in length rather than only 96. For this, you need the ability to allow the program to proceed normally, but to stop at a selected statement. This is done by designating the statement as a *breakpoint*. In this program, it would be convenient to inspect the value of TEST-CODE after each execution of the ADD statement of line 68. Thus, you could set a breakpoint at line 69 with the *Breakpoint* command—code *B*—as follows:

```
B 69
```

After a breakpoint halt, you can enter any other command you need—such as the Display. To resume execution, use the *Resume* command—code *R*. Execution will continue until the breakpoint at line 69 is encountered again.

Use of the Breakpoint, Display, and Resume commands to isolate the problem in this program is shown in Figure D-8. The following commentary describes what you see here; each of the screen lines is numbered for convenience reference.

1. The breakpoint is set (defined) at line 1.
2. The Breakpoint command only sets the breakpoint. The Resume command (line 2) is required to direct Debug to resume execution of the program.
3. At line 3, Debug identifies that a breakpoint stop has occurred at line 69 of the program (BP 69). To display the contents of TEST-CODE, enter the Display command as shown.
4. The display (line 4) includes three items: the memory address of the data item relative to the beginning of the program (128), the data type (NSU means numeric, unsigned), and the value stored in the data item (1). Your primary concern will normally be the value. In this case, the value of TEST-CODE is 1, which is correct—refer to Figure D-6.
5. Successive stops at the breakpoint and displays (lines 5 through 10) show that for data records two and three, the values of TEST-CODE are also valid.

Figure D-8

Displaying the Contents of a Data Item

```
 1.  ST 50 DEBUG-X C? B 69            Set the breakpoint.
 2.  50 DEBUG-X C? R                  Resume.
 3.  BP 69 DEBUG-X C? D TEST-CODE     Display the contents of
 4.  128 NSU 1                        TEST-CODE.
 5.  69 DEBUG-X C? R
 6.  BP 69 DEBUG-X C? D TEST-CODE     This is the value of
 7.  128 NSU 9                        TEST-CODE.
 8.  69 DEBUG-X C? R
 9.  BP 69 DEBUG-X C? D TEST-CODE
10.  128 NSU 6
11.  69 DEBUG-X C? R
12.  BP 69 DEBUG-X C? D TEST-CODE
13.  128 NSU 4
14.  BP 69 DEBUG-X C? D CR-FIRST-CODE
15.  38 NSU 77
16.  BP 69 DEBUG-X C? D CR-SECOND-CODE
17.  39 NSU 7
18.  69 DEBUG-X C?
```

6. However, line 13 yields a surprise: the value for TEST-CODE is 4 rather than 14.

7. In an attempt to understand what is taking place, the Display commands of lines 14 and 16 request the values of FIRST-CODE and SECOND-CODE, respectively. You can see that they are both 7, correct according to the input record.

If you have not already found the error in the program, then consider what you are seeing: 7 + 7 equals 4, which means that the first digit has been lost. The reason for the discrepancy lies in the definition of TEST-CODE with a length of 1 (line 42 of the program). When the addition is performed in line 68 and the result moved to TEST-CODE, the leading digit (1) is discarded and the stored result is 4. Changing the definition of TEST-CODE from PIC 9 to PIC 99 will correct this bug. If you are running under RM/CO*, you can switch from Debug directly to the Editor to make the change.

Switching Between Debug and the Editor Under RM/CO*

If you are using RM/CO* and you stepped through the preceding debug sequences, you are aware of the convenience of having RM/CO* highlight the statement at which execution is halted. Another convenience is that you can make changes to the source program at any time during the debugging session. For instance, assume that you have just completed the sequence of Figure D-8 and that you want to check the definition of TEST-CODE in the DATA DIVISION. You can temporarily suspend program execution and switch to the Edit mode by striking the F9 function key (a message to that effect appears at the bottom of the screen). Do so and you will see the standard Edit menu from which you can use the PageUp key to find TEST-CODE. Go ahead and change it—the change will be made to the change file as if you had been working from the Editor all along. You can return to Debug by striking the F9 key from the Editor and resume debugging operations. However, recognize that changes you have made will not affect execution of the program because the changes were made to the source program (via the change file), not to the object program that is currently being executed under Debug. In this case, there would be little value in proceeding under Debug.

Other Debug Commands

More About the Step Command

You have used the Step command to proceed from one statement to the next. In progressing to the fourth record, a lot of stepping was required (see Figure D-7). A minor variation of the Step allows you to step by paragraph. That is, if you enter SP as the command, the program executes as before, but only stops each time a new paragraph is encountered. When the desired paragraph is reached, then the Step (single statement) can be used to observe sequencing within that paragraph.

More About the Breakpoint Command

In the DEBUG-X example, the error occurred in the fourth pass through the processing loop, so you simply resumed after each breakpoint stop. However, if you needed to inspect values after the 40th loop, the method used in Figure D-8 would have been slow and inconvenient. This process can be speeded up if you know how many times you want the breakpoint statement to execute before halting. For instance, to halt immediately prior to the 40th execution, you would use the command:

```
B 69,,40
```

Here the 40 indicates halt just before executing statement 69 for the 40th time. Two commas are required in order to tell Debug that an operand (in which you have no interest) is being omitted.

After the breakpoint halt occurs, you can continue processing as usual with the Resume command. After the first breakpoint halt, execution will halt as if the 40 were not included in the original Breakpoint command.

The Clear Command

Do not conclude from the preceding that breakpoints are permanent for a debug session. On the contrary, you can set one or more breakpoints, clear them, and set others as you progress. For instance, assume that you use

```
B 69
```

to set the breakpoint in DEBUG-X. After encountering that breakpoint several times during the session, you want the program to run to completion without further halts. To do this, use the *Clear* command—code *C*—as follows

```
C 69
```

to clear the breakpoint at line 69. Then use the Resume command to resume execution of the program.

The Address Stop Command

The *Address Stop* command—code *A*—sets a breakpoint in the same way as the Breakpoint command. The difference in the two is that the address stop breakpoint is cleared after the first time the breakpoint is encountered. For instance, assume that you entered the command:

```
A 69,,4
```

Execution will immediately proceed; you do not need the Resume command. As with the preceding Breakpoint command, execution halts upon encountering statement 69 for the fourth time. However, execution of the Resume command after the stop causes this breakpoint to be cleared and execution to continue as if the breakpoint were never set.

The Trap Command

Sometimes in the debugging process, it is useful to know when the value of a particular data item changes. To this end, the *Trap* command—code *T*—causes execution to halt whenever a designated data item changes in value. For instance, Figure D-9 illustrates using a Trap command in the DEBUG-X program. As you can see, after setting the trap break, the Resume must be given. When the trap point is encountered, the new value of the specified variable is displayed, and execution halts and awaits the next command. In this example, you see a series of values as execution is repeatedly resumed.

Figure D-9

The Trap Command

```
ST 50 DEBUG-X C? T TEST-CODE
50 DEBUG-X C? R
TEST-CODE
128 NSU   1
DT 69 DEBUG-X C? R
TEST-CODE
128 NSU   9
DT 69 DEBUG-X C? R
TEST-CODE
128 NSU   6
DT 69 DEBUG-X C? R
TEST-CODE
128 NSU   4
DT 69 DEBUG-X C?
```

The Modify Command

Sometimes you will find it useful to change the value of one or more data items during execution under Debug. You can do this with the *Modify* command—code *M*. To illustrate, assume that you have not yet found the bug in DEBUG-X and that you decide to modify the value in the data item TEST-CODE; you might proceed as shown in Figure D-10. Notice that the Modify command uses three operands: the data item to be modified, the data type, and the new value. In this case, the data type (NSU) was obtained from the preceding line resulting from the Display statement.

The Condition Code

In reviewing the preceding examples, you see that the first two characters of the Debug prompt line are uppercase letters; for example, ST and BP. These letters tell you the condition under which program execution has been halted. The five condition codes are as follows:

BP Breakpoint

DT Data trap (Trap command)

ER A runtime error has occurred

SR The program has executed a STOP RUN statement

ST The Step command has been executed

About Using Debug

The Debug tool is a valuable one, but it is not designed to eliminate thinking. Whenever you encounter a bug in a program, study the logic of your program and the data it is processing. If you cannot find the error, then map out some idea of what you wish to accomplish with Debug. Do not immediately jump to Debug without thinking your problem through. A "jump-in-and-try" attempt will usually waste more time than it saves you.

Figure D-10

The Modify Command

```
ST 50 DEBUG-X C? B 69,,4
50 DEBUG-X C? R
BP 69 DEBUG-X C? D TEST-CODE                    Display TEST-CODE.
128 NSU  4
69 DEBUG-X C? M TEST-CODE,NSU,14                Modify TEST-CODE, data type
69 DEBUG-X C? D TEST-CODE                        NSU, by replacing its current
128 NSU  4                                       value with a new value, 14.
69 DEBUG-X C? M TEST-CODE,NSU,9
69 DEBUG-X C? D TEST-CODE
128 NSU  9
69 DEBUG-X C?
```

COBOL
RESERVED WORDS

ACCEPT	BLANK	**r** COMPUTATIONAL-4	DE
ACCESS	**r** BLINK	**r** COMPUTATIONAL-6	**r** DEBUGGING
ADD	BLOCK	COMPUTE	DEBUG-CONTENTS
ADVANCING	BOTTOM	**r** COMP-1	DEBUG-ITEM
AFTER	BY	**r** COMP-3	DEBUG-LINE
ALL		**r** COMP-4	DEBUG-NAME
ALPHABET	CALL	**r** COMP-6	DEBUG-SUB-1
ALPHABETIC	CANCEL	CONFIGURATION	DEBUG-SUB-2
ALPHABETIC-LOWER	CD	CONTAINS	DEBUG-SUB-3
ALPHABETIC-UPPER	CF	CONTENT	DEBUGGING
ALPHANUMERIC	CH	CONTINUE	DECIMAL-POINT
ALPHANUMERIC-EDITED	CHARACTER	CONTROL	DECLARATIVES
ALSO	CHARACTERS	CONTROLS	DELETE
ALTER	CLASS	**r** CONVERT	DELIMITED
ALTERNATE	CLOCK-UNITS	CONVERTING	DELIMITER
AND	CLOSE	COPY	DEPENDING
ANY	COBOL	CORR	DESCENDING
ARE	CODE	CORRESPONDING	DESTINATION
AREA	CODE-SET	COUNT	DETAIL
AREAS	COLLATING	CURRENCY	DISABLE
ASCENDING	COLUMN	**r** CURSOR	DISPLAY
ASSIGN	COMMA		DIVIDE
AT	COMMON	DATA	DIVISION
AUTHOR	COMMUNICATION	DATE	DOWN
	COMP	DATE-COMPILED	DUPLICATES
r BEEP	COMPUTATIONAL	DATE-WRITTEN	DYNAMIC
BEFORE	**r** COMPUTATIONAL-1	DAY	
BINARY	**r** COMPUTATIONAL-3	DAY-OF-WEEK	

Notation: **r** = RM/COBOL-85 reserved word

r ECHO	FOOTING	LINAGE-COUNTER	PICTURE
EGI	FOR	LINE	PLUS
ELSE	FROM	LINES	POINTER
EMI		LINE-COUNTER	POSITION
ENABLE	GENERATE	LINKAGE	POSITIVE
END	GIVING	LOCK	PRINTING
r END-ACCEPT	GLOBAL	**r** LOW	PROCEDURE
END-ADD	GO	LOW-VALUE	PROCEDURES
END-CALL	**r** GOBACK	LOW-VALUES	PROCEED
END-COMPUTE	GREATER		PROGRAM
END-DELETE	GROUP	MEMORY	PROGRAM-ID
END-DIVIDE		MERGE	**r** PROMPT
END-EVALUATE	HEADING	MESSAGE	PURGE
END-IF	**r** HIGH	MODE	
END-MULTIPLY	HIGH-VALUE	MODULES	QUEUE
END-OF-PAGE	HIGH-VALUES	MOVE	QUOTE
END-PERFORM		MULTIPLE	QUOTES
END-READ	**r** ID	MULTIPLY	
END-RECEIVE	IDENTIFICATION		RANDOM
END-RETURN	IF	NATIVE	RD
END-REWRITE	IN	NEGATIVE	READ
END-SEARCH	INDEX	NEXT	RECEIVE
END-START	INDEXED	NO	RECORD
END-STRING	INDICATE	NOT	RECORDS
END-SUBTRACT	INITIAL	NUMBER	REDEFINES
END-UNSTRING	INITIALIZE	NUMERIC	REEL
END-WRITE	INITIATE	NUMERIC-EDITED	REFERENCE
ENTER	INPUT		REFERENCES
ENVIRONMENT	INPUT-OUTPUT	OBJECT-COMPUTER	RELATIVE
r EOF	INSPECT	OCCURS	RELEASE
r EOL	INSTALLATION	OF	REMAINDER
EOP	INTO	OFF	**r** REMARKS
r EOS	INVALID	OMITTED	REMOVAL
EQUAL	IS	ON	RENAMES
r ERASE	I-O	OPEN	REPLACE
ERROR	I-O-CONTROL	OPTIONAL	REPLACING
ESI		OR	REPORT
EVALUATE	JUST	ORDER	REPORTING
EVERY	JUSTIFIED	ORGANIZATION	REPORTS
EXCEPTION		OTHER	RERUN
EXIT	KEY	OUTPUT	RESERVE
EXTEND		OVERFLOW	RESET
EXTERNAL	LABEL		RETURN
	LAST	PACKED-DECIMAL	**r** RETURN-CODE
FALSE	LEADING	PADDING	**r** REVERSE
FD	LEFT	PAGE	REVERSED
FILE	LENGTH	PAGE-COUNTER	REWIND
FILE-CONTROL	LESS	PERFORM	REWRITE
FILLER	LIMIT	PF	RF
FINAL	LIMITS	PH	RH
FIRST	LINAGE	PIC	RIGHT

Notation: **r** = RM/COBOL-85 reserved word

ROUNDED	**r**	TAB		ZERO
RUN		TABLE		ZEROES
		TALLYING		ZEROS
SAME		TAPE		
SD		TERMINAL	**r**	.
SEARCH		TERMINATE	**r**	,
SECTION		TEST	**r**	;
SECURITY		TEXT	**r**	(
SEGMENT		THAN	**r**	"
SEGMENT-LIMIT		THEN	**r**	'
SELECT		THROUGH		+
SEND		THRU		-
SENTENCE		TIME		*
SEPARATE		TIMES		/
SEQUENCE		TO		**
SEQUENTIAL		TOP		=
SET		TRAILING		>
SIGN		TRUE		<
SIZE		TYPE		>=
SORT				<=
SORT-MERGE		UNIT	**r**	:
SOURCE	**r**	UNLOCK		
SOURCE-COMPUTER		UNSTRING		
SPACE		UNTIL		
SPACES		UP		
SPECIAL-NAMES	**r**	UPDATE		
STANDARD		UPON		
STANDARD-1		USAGE		
STANDARD-2		USE		
START		USING		
STATUS				
STOP		VALUE		
STRING		VALUES		
SUBTRACT		VARYING		
SUB-QUEUE-1				
SUB-QUEUE-2		WHEN		
SUB-QUEUE-3		WITH		
SUM		WORDS		
SUPPRESS		WORKING-STORAGE		
SYMBOLIC		WRITE		
SYNC				
SYNCHRONIZED				

Notation: **r** = RM/COBOL-85 reserved word

Complete COBOL-85 Language Formats

This appendix contains the composite language formats skeleton of the American National Standard COBOL (1985). It completely displays all COBOL-85 language formats.

General Format for IDENTIFICATION DIVISION

```
IDENTIFICATION DIVISION.

PROGRAM-ID. program-name [IS { COMMON
                               INITIAL } PROGRAM] .

[AUTHOR.       [comment-entry]  ...]

[INSTALLATION.    [comment-entry]  ...]

[DATE-WRITTEN.     [comment-entry]  ...]

[DATE-COMPLETED.     [comment-entry]  ...]

[SECURITY.    [comment-entry]  ...]
```

General Format for ENVIRONMENT DIVISION

```
[ENVIRONMENT DIVISION.

[CONFIGURATION SECTION.

[SOURCE-COMPUTER.    [computer-name [WITH DEBUGGING MODE.]]

[OBJECT-COMPUTER.    [computer-name

        ┌                        ⎧ WORDS      ⎫ ┐
        │ MEMORY SIZE integer-1  ⎨ CHARACTERS ⎬ │
        └                        ⎩ MODULES    ⎭ ┘

    [PROGRAM COLLATING SEQUENCE IS alphabet-name-1]

    [SEGMENT-LIMIT IS segment-number].]]

[SPECIAL-NAMES. [[implementor-name-1

    ┌                                                                          ┐
    │ IS mnemonic-name-1 [ON STATUS IS condition-name-1 [OFF STATUS IS condition-name-2]] │
    │                                                                          │
    │ IS mnemonic-name-2 [OFF STATUS IS condition-name-2  [ON STATUS is condition-name-1]] │  ...
    ⎨                                                                          ⎬
    │ ON STATUS IS condition-name-1 [OFF STATUS IS condition-name-2]            │
    │                                                                          │
    └ OFF STATUS IS condition-name-2 [ON STATUS IS condition-name-1]            ┘

    [ALPHABET alphabet-name-1 IS

        ⎧ STANDARD-1                                      ⎫
        │ STANDARD-2                                      │
        │ NATIVE                                          │
        ⎨ implementor-name-2                              ⎬  ...
        │          ⎧ ⎧ THROUGH ⎫ literal-2  ⎫             │
        │ literal-1⎨ ⎨ THRU    ⎬           ⎬ ...          │
        ⎩          ⎩ {ALSO literal-3} ...  ⎭              ⎭
```

```
[SYMBOLIC CHARACTERS {{ {symbolic-character-1} ... { IS  } {integer-1}...}...
                                                   { ARE }
            [IN alphabet-name-2] }] ...

[CLASS class-name IS {literal-4 [{ THROUGH } literal-5 ]} ... ] ...
                                 { THRU    }

[CURRENCY SIGN IS literal-6]

[DECIMAL-POINT IS COMMA].]]]

[INPUT-OUTPUT SECTION.

 FILE-CONTROL.

   {file-control-entry} ...

{I-O-CONTROL.
```

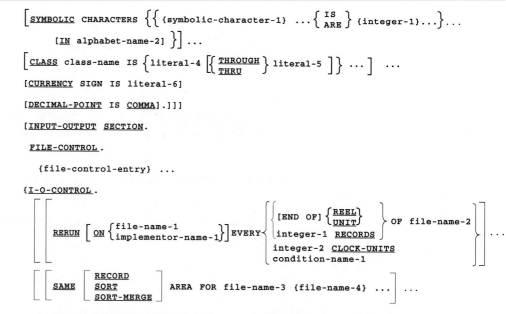

```
    [MULTIPLE FILE TAPE CONTAINS {file-name-5 [POSITION integer-3]} ... ] ... .]
```

General Format for FILE-CONTROL Entry

Sequential File:

```
SELECT [OPTIONAL] file-name-1

    ASSIGN TO { implementor-name-1 } ...
              { literal-1          }

    [ RESERVE integer-1 [ AREA  ] ]
                        [ AREAS ]

    [[ORGANIZATION IS] SEQUENTIAL]

    [ PADDING CHARACTER IS { data-name-1 } ]
                          { literal-2   }

    [ RECORD DELIMITER IS { STANDARD-1           } ]
                          { implementor-name-2   }

    [ACCESS MODE IS SEQUENTIAL]

    [FILE STATUS IS data-name-2].
```

Relative File:

```
SELECT [OPTIONAL] file-name-1

    ASSIGN TO { implementor-name-1 } ...
              { literal-1          }

    [ RESERVE integer-1 [ AREA  ] ]
                        [ AREAS ]

    [ORGANIZATION IS] RELATIVE

    [                    { SEQUENTIAL [RELATIVE KEY IS data-name-1] } ]
    [ ACCESS MODE IS     { { RANDOM  }                             } ]
    [                    { { DYNAMIC } RELATIVE KEY IS data-name-1  } ]

    [FILE STATUS IS data-name-2].
```

Indexed File:

```
SELECT [OPTIONAL] file-name-1

    ASSIGN TO ⎰implementor-name-1⎱ ...
            ⎱literal-1          ⎰

    [RESERVE integer-1 ⎡AREA ⎤]
                       ⎣AREAS⎦

    [ORGANIZATION IS] INDEXED

    ⎡                    ⎧SEQUENTIAL⎫⎤
    ⎢ACCESS MODE IS      ⎨RANDOM    ⎬⎥
    ⎣                    ⎩DYNAMIC   ⎭⎦

    RECORD KEY IS data-name-1

    [ALTERNATE RECORD KEY IS data-name-2 [WITH DUPLICATES]] ...

    [FILE STATUS IS data-name-3].
```

Sort or Merge File:

```
SELECT file-name-1 ASSIGN TO⎰implementor-name-1⎱ ... .
                            ⎱literal-1          ⎰
```

Report File:

```
SELECT [OPTIONAL] file-name-1
    ASSIGN TO ⎰implementor-name-1⎱ ...
            ⎱literal-1          ⎰

    [RESERVE integer-1⎡AREA ⎤]
                      ⎣AREAS⎦

    [[ORGANIZATION IS] SEQUENTIAL]]

    ⎡PADDING CHARACTER IS ⎰data-name-1⎱⎤
    ⎣                     ⎱literal-2  ⎰⎦

    ⎡RECORD DELIMITER IS ⎰STANDARD-1          ⎱⎤
    ⎣                    ⎱implementor-name-2  ⎰⎦

    [ACCESS MODE IS SEQUENTIAL]

    [FILE STATUS IS data-name-2].
```

General Format for DATA DIVISION

```
[DATA DIVISION.

[FILE SECTION.

⎡ file-description-entry {record-description-entry} ...          ⎤
⎢ sort-merge-file-description-entry {record-description-entry} ... ⎥ ...
⎣ report-file-description-entry                                  ⎦

[WORKING-STORAGE SECTION.

⎡ 77-level-description-entry ⎤ ...]
⎣ record-description-entry   ⎦

[LINKAGE SECTION.

⎡ 77-level-description-entry ⎤ ...]
⎣ record-description-entry   ⎦
```

[COMMUNICATION SECTION.

[communication-description-entry [record-description-entry] ...] ...]

[REPORT SECTION.

[report-description-entry {report-group-description-entry} ...] ...]]

General Format for File Description Entry

Sequential File:

FD file-name-1

    [IS EXTERNAL]

    [IS GLOBAL]

$$\left[\text{BLOCK CONTAINS } [\text{integer-1 TO}] \text{ integer-2} \begin{Bmatrix} \text{RECORDS} \\ \text{CHARACTERS} \end{Bmatrix} \right]$$

$$\left[\text{RECORD} \begin{Bmatrix} \text{CONTAINS integer-3 CHARACTERS} \\ \text{IS VARYING IN SIZE [[FROM integer-4] [TO integer-5] CHARACTERS]} \\ \quad [\text{DEPENDING ON data-name-1}] \\ \text{CONTAINS integer-6 TO integer-7 CHARACTERS} \end{Bmatrix} \right]$$

$$\left[\text{LABEL} \begin{Bmatrix} \text{RECORD IS} \\ \text{RECORDS ARE} \end{Bmatrix} \begin{Bmatrix} \text{STANDARD} \\ \text{OMITTED} \end{Bmatrix} \right]$$

$$\left[\text{VALUE OF} \begin{Bmatrix} \text{implementor-name-1 IS} \begin{Bmatrix} \text{data-name-2} \\ \text{literal-1} \end{Bmatrix} \end{Bmatrix} \cdots \right]$$

$$\left[\text{DATA} \begin{Bmatrix} \text{RECORD IS} \\ \text{RECORDS ARE} \end{Bmatrix} \{\text{data-name-3}\} \cdots \right]$$

$$\left[\text{LINAGE IS} \begin{Bmatrix} \text{data-name-4} \\ \text{integer-8} \end{Bmatrix} \text{LINES} \left[\text{WITH FOOTING AT} \begin{Bmatrix} \text{data-name-5} \\ \text{integer-9} \end{Bmatrix} \right] \right.$$

$$\left. \left[\text{LINES AT TOP} \begin{Bmatrix} \text{data-name-6} \\ \text{integer-10} \end{Bmatrix} \right] \left[\text{LINES AT BOTTOM} \begin{Bmatrix} \text{data-name-7} \\ \text{integer-11} \end{Bmatrix} \right] \right]$$

[CODE-SET IS alphabet-name-1].

Relative File:

FD file-name-1

    [IS EXTERNAL]

    [IS GLOBAL]

$$\left[\text{BLOCK CONTAINS } [\text{integer-1 TO}] \text{ integer-2} \begin{Bmatrix} \text{RECORDS} \\ \text{CHARACTERS} \end{Bmatrix} \right]$$

$$\left[\text{RECORD} \begin{Bmatrix} \text{CONTAINS integer-3 CHARACTERS} \\ \text{IS VARYING IN SIZE [[FROM integer-4] [TO integer-5] CHARACTERS]} \\ \quad [\text{DEPENDING ON data-name-1}] \\ \text{CONTAINS integer-6 TO integer-7 CHARACTERS} \end{Bmatrix} \right]$$

$$\left[\text{LABEL} \begin{Bmatrix} \text{RECORD IS} \\ \text{RECORDS ARE} \end{Bmatrix} \begin{Bmatrix} \text{STANDARD} \\ \text{OMITTED} \end{Bmatrix} \right]$$

$$\left[\text{VALUE OF} \begin{Bmatrix} \text{implementor-name-1 IS} \begin{Bmatrix} \text{data-name-2} \\ \text{literal-1} \end{Bmatrix} \end{Bmatrix} \cdots \right]$$

$$\left[\text{DATA} \begin{Bmatrix} \text{RECORD IS} \\ \text{RECORDS ARE} \end{Bmatrix} \{\text{data-name-3}\} \cdots \right] .$$

Indexed File:

```
FD file-name-1

    [IS EXTERNAL]

    [IS GLOBAL]

    [ BLOCK CONTAINS  [integer-1 TO]  integer-2 { RECORDS    } ]
                                                { CHARACTERS }

    [                 ┌ CONTAINS integer-3 CHARACTERS                              ┐ ]
    [                 │ IS VARYING IN SIZE [[FROM integer-4] [TO integer-5] CHARACTERS]│ ]
    [        RECORD  <      [DEPENDING ON data-name-1]                             > ]
    [                 └ CONTAINS integer-6 TO integer-7 CHARACTERS                 ┘ ]

    [ LABEL { RECORD IS   } { STANDARD } ]
    [       { RECORDS ARE }  { OMITTED  } ]

    [ VALUE OF { implementor-name-1 IS { data-name-2 } } ... ]
    [                                  { literal-1    }     ]

    [ DATA { RECORD IS   } {data-name-3} ... ]  .
    [      { RECORDS ARE }                    ]
```

Sort-Merge File:

```
SD file-name-1
    [                 ┌ CONTAINS integer-1 CHARACTERS                              ┐ ]
    [                 │ IS VARYING IN SIZE [[FROM integer-2] [TO integer-3] CHARACTERS]│ ]
    [        RECORD  <      [DEPENDING ON data-name-1]                             > ]
    [                 └ CONTAINS integer-4 TO integer-5 CHARACTERS                 ┘ ]

    [ DATA { RECORD IS   } {data-name-2} ... ]  .
    [      { RECORDS ARE }                    ]
```

Report File:

```
FD file-name-1

    [IS EXTERNAL]

    [IS GLOBAL]

    [ BLOCK CONTAINS [integer-1 TO] integer-2 { RECORDS    } ]
                                              { CHARACTERS }

    [ RECORD { CONTAINS integer-3 CHARACTERS              } ]
    [        { CONTAINS integer-4 TO integer-5 CHARACTERS } ]

    [ LABEL { RECORD IS   } { STANDARD } ]
    [       { RECORDS ARE }  { OMITTED  } ]

    [ VALUE OF { implementor-name-1 IS { data-name-1 } } ... ]
    [                                  { literal-1   }     ]

    [CODE-SET IS alphabet-name-1]

    { REPORT IS   } {report-name-1} ... .
    { REPORTS ARE }
```

General Format for Data Description Entry

Format 1:

```
level-number [ data-name-1 ]
             [ FILLER      ]

    [REDEFINES data-name-2]

    [IS EXTERNAL]

    [IS GLOBAL]

    [ { PICTURE } IS character-string ]
    [ { PIC     }                     ]
```

```
        ┌                      ┌                 ┐ ┐
        │                      │ BINARY          │ │
        │                      │ COMPUTATIONAL   │ │
        │ [USAGE IS]           │ COMP            │ │
        │                      │ DISPLAY         │ │
        │                      │ INDEX           │ │
        │                      │ PACKED-DECIMAL  │ │
        └                      └                 ┘ ┘

        ┌                  ┌ LEADING  ┐                        ┐
        │ [SIGN IS]        │ TRAILING │ [SEPARATE CHARACTER]   │
        └                  └          ┘                        ┘

        ┌                                                               ┐
        │ OCCURS integer-2 TIMES                                        │
        │                                                               │
        │      ┌ ┌ ASCENDING  ┐              ┐                          │
        │      │ │ DESCENDING │ KEY IS {data-name-3} ... │ ...          │
        │      └ └            ┘              ┘                          │
        │                                                               │
        │         [INDEXED BY {index-name-1} ... ]                      │
        │                                                               │
        │ OCCURS integer-1 TO integer-2 TIMES DEPENDING ON data-name-4  │
        │                                                               │
        │      ┌ ┌ ASCENDING  ┐              ┐                          │
        │      │ │ DESCENDING │ KEY IS   {data-name-3} ... │ ...        │
        │      └ └            ┘              ┘                          │
        │                                                               │
        │         [INDEXED BY {index-name-1} ... ]                      │
        └                                                               ┘

        ┌ ┌ SYNCHRONIZED ┐   ┌ LEFT  ┐ ┐
        │ │ SYNC         │   │ RIGHT │ │
        └ └              ┘   └       ┘ ┘

        ┌ ┌ JUSTIFIED ┐        ┐
        │ │ JUST      │ RIGHT  │
        └ └           ┘        ┘

        [BLANK WHEN ZERO]

        [VALUE IS literal-1].
```

Format 2:

```
66 data-name-1 RENAMES data-name-2 ┌ ┌ THROUGH ┐ data-name-3 ┐ .
                                   │ │ THRU    │             │
                                   └ └         ┘             ┘
```

Format 3:

```
88 condition-name-1 ┌ VALUE IS   ┐ ┌ literal-1 ┌ ┌ THROUGH ┐ literal-2 ┐ ┐ ... .
                    │ VALUES ARE │ │           │ │ THRU    │           │ │
                    └            ┘ └           └ └         ┘           ┘ ┘
```

General Format for Communication Description Entry

Format 1:

```
CD cd-name-1
                      ┌ [[SYMBOLIC QUEUE IS data-name-1]          ┐
                      │                                           │
                      │  [SYMBOLIC SUB-QUEUE-1 IS data-name-2]    │
                      │                                           │
                      │  [SYMBOLIC SUB-QUEUE-2 IS data-name-3]    │
                      │                                           │
                      │  [SYMBOLIC SUB-QUEUE-3 IS data-name-4]    │
                      │                                           │
                      │  [MESSAGE DATE IS data-name-5]            │
                      │                                           │
                      │  [MESSAGE TIME IS data-name-6]            │
                      │                                           │
                      │  [SYMBOLIC SOURCE IS data-name-7]         │
  FOR [INITIAL] INPUT │  [TEXT LENGTH IS data-name-8]             │
                      │                                           │
                      │  [END KEY IS data-name-9]                 │
                      │                                           │
                      │  [STATUS KEY IS data-name-10]             │
                      │                                           │
                      │  [MESSAGE COUNT IS data-name-11]]         │
                      │                                           │
                      │  [data-name-1, data-name-2, data-name-3,  │
                      │                                           │
                      │     data-name-4, data-name-5, data-name-6,│
                      │                                           │
                      │     data-name-7, data-name-8, data-name-9,│
                      │                                           │
                      │     data-name-10, data-name-11]           │
                      └                                           ┘
```

Format 2:

```
CD cd-name-1 FOR OUTPUT

    [DESTINATION COUNT IS data-name-1]

    [TEXT LENGTH IS data-name-2]

    [STATUS KEY IS data-name-3]

    [DESTINATION TABLE OCCURS integer-1 TIMES

        [INDEXED BY {index-name-1} ... ]]

    [ERROR KEY IS data-name-4]

    [SYMBOLIC DESTINATION IS data-name-5].
```

Format 3:

```
CD cd-name-1

                              ┌                                        ┐
                              │  [[MESSAGE DATE IS data-name-1]         │
                              │                                        │
                              │    [MESSAGE TIME IS data-name-2]        │
                              │                                        │
                              │    [SYMBOLIC TERMINAL IS data-name-3]   │
                              │                                        │
       FOR [INITIAL] I-O      │    [TEXT LENGTH IS data-name-4]         │
                              │                                        │
                              │    [END KEY IS data-name-5]             │
                              │                                        │
                              │    [STATUS KEY IS data-name-6]]         │
                              │  [data-name-1, data-name-2, data-name-3,│
                              │     data-name-4, data-name-5, data-name-6]│
                              └                                        ┘
```

```
RD report-name-1

    [IS GLOBAL]

    [CODE literal-1]

    [{ CONTROL IS  } { {data-name-1}  ...      }]
    [{ CONTROLS ARE} { FINAL [data-name-1]  ...}]

    ⎡PAGE ⎡LIMIT IS ⎤ integer-1 ⎡LINE ⎤ [HEADING integer-2]
    ⎣     ⎣LIMITS ARE⎦          ⎣LINES⎦

        [FIRST DETAIL integer-1] [LAST DETAIL integer-4]

        [FOOTING integer-5].
```

General Format for Report Group Description Entry

Format 1:

```
01 [data-name-1]

    ⎡LINE NUMBER IS { integer-1 ON NEXT PAGE] }⎤
    ⎣               { PLUS integer-2            }⎦

    ⎡                { integer-3    } ⎤
    ⎢NEXT GROUP IS   { PLUS integer-4} ⎥
    ⎣                { NEXT PAGE     } ⎦
```

$$\text{\underline{TYPE} IS} \begin{Bmatrix} \begin{Bmatrix} \underline{\text{REPORT}} \ \underline{\text{HEADING}} \\ \underline{\text{RH}} \end{Bmatrix} \\ \begin{Bmatrix} \underline{\text{PAGE}} \ \underline{\text{HEADING}} \\ \underline{\text{PH}} \end{Bmatrix} \\ \begin{Bmatrix} \underline{\text{CONTROL}} \ \underline{\text{HEADING}} \\ \underline{\text{CH}} \end{Bmatrix} \begin{Bmatrix} \text{data-name-2} \\ \underline{\text{FINAL}} \end{Bmatrix} \\ \begin{Bmatrix} \underline{\text{DETAIL}} \\ \underline{\text{DE}} \end{Bmatrix} \\ \begin{Bmatrix} \underline{\text{CONTROL}} \ \underline{\text{FOOTING}} \\ \underline{\text{CF}} \end{Bmatrix} \begin{Bmatrix} \text{data-name-3} \\ \underline{\text{FINAL}} \end{Bmatrix} \\ \begin{Bmatrix} \underline{\text{PAGE}} \ \underline{\text{FOOTING}} \\ \underline{\text{PF}} \end{Bmatrix} \\ \begin{Bmatrix} \underline{\text{REPORT}} \ \underline{\text{FOOTING}} \\ \underline{\text{RF}} \end{Bmatrix} \end{Bmatrix}$$

[[USAGE IS] DISPLAY].

Format 2:

```
level-number [data-name-1]
```

$$\left[\underline{\text{LINE}} \text{ NUMBER IS} \begin{Bmatrix} \text{integer-1 [ON } \underline{\text{NEXT}} \ \underline{\text{PAGE}}] \\ \underline{\text{PLUS}} \text{ integer-2} \end{Bmatrix} \right]$$

[[USAGE IS] DISPLAY].

Format 3:

```
level-number [data-name-1]
```

$$\begin{Bmatrix} \underline{\text{PICTURE}} \\ \underline{\text{PIC}} \end{Bmatrix} \text{IS character-string}$$

[[USAGE IS] DISPLAY]

$$\left[[\underline{\text{SIGN}} \text{ IS}] \begin{Bmatrix} \underline{\text{LEADING}} \\ \underline{\text{TRAILING}} \end{Bmatrix} \underline{\text{SEPARATE}} \text{ CHARACTER} \right]$$

$$\left[\begin{Bmatrix} \underline{\text{JUSTIFIED}} \\ \underline{\text{JUST}} \end{Bmatrix} \text{RIGHT} \right]$$

[BLANK WHEN ZERO]

$$\left[\underline{\text{LINE}} \text{ NUMBER IS} \begin{Bmatrix} \text{integer-1 \quad [ON } \underline{\text{NEXT}} \ \underline{\text{PAGE}}] \\ \underline{\text{PLUS}} \text{ integer-2} \end{Bmatrix} \right]$$

[COLUMN NUMBER IS integer-3]

$$\begin{Bmatrix} \underline{\text{SOURCE}} \text{ IS identifier-1} \\ \underline{\text{VALUE}} \text{ IS literal-1} \\ \{\underline{\text{SUM}} \text{ \{identifier-2\} ... [}\underline{\text{UPON}} \text{ \{data-name-2\}...]\} ...} \\ \left[\underline{\text{RESET}} \text{ ON} \begin{Bmatrix} \text{data-name-3} \\ \underline{\text{FINAL}} \end{Bmatrix} \right] \end{Bmatrix}$$

[GROUP INDICATE].

General Format for PROCEDURE DIVISION

Format 1:

[PROCEDURE DIVISION [USING {data-name-1}...].

[DECLARATIVES.

{section-name SECTION [segment-number].

    USE statement.

```
[paragraph-name.

    [sentence] ... ] ... } ...

END DECLARATIVES.]

{section-name SECTION [segment-number].

[paragraph-name.

    [sentence] ... ]... }... ]
```

Format 2:

```
[PROCEDURE DIVISION [USING {data-name-1} ... ].

{paragraph-name.

    [sentence] ... }... ]
```

General Format for COBOL Verbs

The general formats of input/output verbs differ from those of other verbs in that their format depends upon the type of file being processed. For instance, CLOSE for a sequential file has a different general format than CLOSE for an indexed file. To indicate these differences, the following letters are included to the left of the verb.

I Indexed   **R** Relative   **S** Sequential   **W** Report Writer

```
ACCEPT identifier-1   [FROM mnemonic-name-1]

                            ⎧ DATE        ⎫
                            ⎪ DAY         ⎪
ACCEPT identifier-2 FROM    ⎨ DAY-OF-WEEK ⎬
                            ⎩ TIME        ⎭

ACCEPT cd-name-1 MESSAGE COUNT

ADD ⎧ identifier-1 ⎫ ... TO {identifier-2 [ROUNDED]} ...
    ⎩ literal-1    ⎭

    [ON SIZE ERROR imperative-statement-1]

    [NOT ON SIZE ERROR imperative-statement-2]

    [END-ADD]

ADD ⎧ identifier-1 ⎫ ... TO ⎧ identifier-2 ⎫
    ⎩ literal-1    ⎭         ⎩ literal-2    ⎭

    GIVING {identifier-3 [ROUNDED]} ...

    [ON SIZE ERROR imperative-statement-1]

    [NOT ON SIZE ERROR imperative-statement-2]

    [END-ADD]

ADD ⎧ CORRESPONDING ⎫ identifier-1  TO identifier-2 [ROUNDED]
    ⎩ CORR          ⎭
    [ON SIZE ERROR imperative-statement-1]

    [NOT ON SIZE ERROR imperative-statement-2]

    [END-ADD]

ALTER {procedure-name-1 TO  {PROCEED TO} procedure-name-2} ...

CALL ⎧ identifier-1 ⎫ [ USING ⎧ [BY REFERENCE] {identifier-2}... ⎫... ]
     ⎩ literal-1    ⎭         ⎩ BY CONTENT {IDENTIFIER-2}...       ⎭
     [ON OVERFLOW imperative-statement-1]

     [END-CALL]

CALL ⎧ identifier-1 ⎫ [ USING ... ⎧ [BY REFERENCE] {identifier-2}... ⎫... ]
     ⎩ literal-1    ⎭             ⎩ BY CONTENT {Identifier-2}...      ⎭

     [ON EXCEPTION imperative-statement-1]

     [NOT ON EXCEPTION imperative-statement-2]

     [END-CALL]
```

```
     CANCEL   { identifier-1 } ...
              { literal-1    }

SW   CLOSE    ⎧               ⎡ { REEL } [FOR REMOVAL]       ⎤ ⎫
              ⎨ file-name-1   ⎢ { UNIT }                     ⎥ ⎬ ...
              ⎩               ⎢ WITH   { NO REWIND }         ⎥ ⎭
                             ⎣        { LOCK      }          ⎦

RI   CLOSE {file-name-1 {WITH LOCK}} ...


     COMPUTE {identifier-1 [ROUNDED]} ... = arithmetic-expression-1

        [ON SIZE ERROR imperative-statement-1]

        [NOT ON SIZE ERROR imperative-statement-2]

        [END-COMPUTE]

     CONTINUE

     DELETE file-name-1 RECORD

        [INVALID KEY imperative-statement-1]

        [NOT INVALID KEY imperative-statement-2]

        [END-DELETE]

     DISABLE  ⎧ INPUT [TERMINAL] ⎫                ⎡          { identifier-1 } ⎤
              ⎨ I-O TERMINAL     ⎬ cd-name-1      ⎢ WITH KEY { literal-1    } ⎥
              ⎩ OUTPUT           ⎭                ⎣                           ⎦

     DISPLAY { identifier-1 } ... [UPON mnemonic-name-1 [WITH NO ADVANCING]
             { literal-1    }

     DIVIDE { identifier-1 } INTO {identifier-2 [ROUNDED]} ...
            { literal-1    }
        [ON SIZE ERROR imperative-statement-1]

        [NOT ON SIZE ERROR imperative-statement-2]

        [END-DIVIDE]

     DIVIDE { identifier-1 } INTO { identifier-2 }
            { literal-1    }      { literal-2    }
        GIVING {identifier-3 [ROUNDED]} ...

        [ON SIZE ERROR imperative-statement-1]

        [NOT ON SIZE ERROR imperative-statement-2]

        [END-DIVIDE]

     DIVIDE { identifier-1 } BY { identifier-2 }
            { literal-1    }    { literal-2    }
        GIVING {identifier-3 [ROUNDED]} ...

        [ON SIZE ERROR imperative-statement-1]

        [NOT ON SIZE ERROR imperative-statement-2]

        [END-DIVIDE]

     DIVIDE { identifier-1 } INTO { identifier-2 } GIVING identifier-3 [ROUNDED]
            { literal-1    }      { literal-2    }

        REMAINDER identifier-4

        [ON SIZE ERROR imperative-statement-1]

        [NOT ON SIZE ERROR imperative-statement-2]

        [END-DIVIDE]

     DIVIDE { identifier-1 } BY { identifier-2 } GIVING identifier-3 [ROUNDED]
            { literal-1    }    { literal-2    }
        REMAINDER identifier-4
```

[ON <u>SIZE</u> <u>ERROR</u> imperative-statement-1]

[<u>NOT</u> ON <u>SIZE</u> <u>ERROR</u> imperative-statement-2]

[<u>END-DIVIDE</u>]

<u>ENABLE</u> $\left\{\begin{array}{l} \underline{\text{INPUT}} \ [\underline{\text{TERMINAL}}] \\ \underline{\text{I-O}} \ \underline{\text{TERMINAL}} \\ \underline{\text{OUTPUT}} \end{array}\right\}$ cd-name-1 $\left[\text{WITH} \ \underline{\text{KEY}} \left\{\begin{array}{l} \text{identifier-1} \\ \text{literal-1} \end{array}\right\}\right]$

<u>ENTER</u> language-name-1   [routine-name-1].

<u>EVALUATE</u> $\left\{\begin{array}{l} \text{identifier-1} \\ \text{literal-1} \\ \text{expression-1} \\ \underline{\text{TRUE}} \\ \underline{\text{FALSE}} \end{array}\right\}$ $\left[\underline{\text{ALSO}} \left\{\begin{array}{l} \text{identifier-2} \\ \text{literal-2} \\ \text{expression-2} \\ \underline{\text{TRUE}} \\ \underline{\text{FALSE}} \end{array}\right\}\right]$ ...

{{<u>WHEN</u>

$\left\{\begin{array}{l} \underline{\text{ANY}} \\ \text{condition-1} \\ \underline{\text{TRUE}} \\ \underline{\text{FALSE}} \\ [\underline{\text{NOT}}] \left\{\begin{array}{l}\text{identifier-3}\\\text{literal-3}\\\text{arithmetic-expression-1}\end{array}\right\} \left[\left\{\begin{array}{l}\underline{\text{THROUGH}}\\\underline{\text{THRU}}\end{array}\right\}\left\{\begin{array}{l}\text{identifier-4}\\\text{literal-4}\\\text{arithmetic-expression-2}\end{array}\right\}\right]\end{array}\right\}$

[<u>ALSO</u>

$\left\{\begin{array}{l} \underline{\text{ANY}} \\ \text{condition-2} \\ \underline{\text{TRUE}} \\ \underline{\text{FALSE}} \\ [\underline{\text{NOT}}] \left\{\begin{array}{l}\text{identifier-5}\\\text{literal-5}\\\text{arithmetic-expression-3}\end{array}\right\} \left[\left\{\begin{array}{l}\underline{\text{THROUGH}}\\\underline{\text{THRU}}\end{array}\right\}\left\{\begin{array}{l}\text{identifier-6}\\\text{literal-6}\\\text{arithmetic-expression-4}\end{array}\right\}\right]\end{array}\right\}$ ... }} ...

imperative-statement-1} ...

[<u>WHEN</u> <u>OTHER</u> imperative-statement-2]

[<u>END-EVALUATE</u>]

<u>EXIT</u>

<u>EXIT</u> <u>PROGRAM</u>

<u>GENERATE</u> $\left\{\begin{array}{l} \text{data-name-1} \\ \text{report-name-1} \end{array}\right\}$

<u>GO</u> TO [procedure-name-1]

<u>GO</u> TO [procedure-name-1] ...   <u>DEPENDING</u> ON identifier-1

<u>IF</u> condition-1 THEN $\left\{\begin{array}{l} \{\text{statement-1}\} \ ... \\ \underline{\text{NEXT}} \ \underline{\text{SENTENCE}} \end{array}\right\}$ $\left\{\begin{array}{l} \underline{\text{ELSE}} \ \{\text{statement-2}\} \ ... \ [\ \underline{\text{END-IF}}\ ] \\ \underline{\text{ELSE}} \ \underline{\text{NEXT}} \ \underline{\text{SENTENCE}} \\ \underline{\text{END-IF}} \end{array}\right\}$

<u>INITIALIZE</u> {identifier-1} ...

$\left[\underline{\text{REPLACING}} \left\{\left\{\begin{array}{l} \underline{\text{ALPHABETIC}} \\ \underline{\text{ALPHANUMERIC}} \\ \underline{\text{NUMERIC}} \\ \underline{\text{APHANUMERIC-EDITED}} \\ \underline{\text{NUMERIC-EDITED}} \end{array}\right\} \text{DATA} \ \underline{\text{BY}} \left\{\begin{array}{l}\text{identifier-2}\\\text{literal-1}\end{array}\right\}\right\} ...\right]$

<u>INITIATE</u> {report-name-1} ...

<u>INSPECT</u> identifier-1 <u>TALLYING</u>

$\left\{\text{identifier-2} \ \underline{\text{FOR}} \left\{\begin{array}{l} \underline{\text{CHARACTERS}} \left[\left\{\begin{array}{l}\underline{\text{BEFORE}}\\\underline{\text{AFTER}}\end{array}\right\} \text{INITIAL} \left\{\begin{array}{l}\text{identifier-4}\\\text{literal-2}\end{array}\right\}\right] ... \\ \left\{\begin{array}{l}\underline{\text{ALL}}\\\underline{\text{LEADING}}\end{array}\right\} \left\{\left\{\begin{array}{l}\text{identifier-3}\\\text{literal-1}\end{array}\right\} \left[\left\{\begin{array}{l}\underline{\text{BEFORE}}\\\underline{\text{AFTER}}\end{array}\right\} \text{INITIAL} \left\{\begin{array}{l}\text{identifier-4}\\\text{literal-2}\end{array}\right\}\right]\right\} ... \end{array}\right\} ... \right\} ...$

<u>INSPECT</u> identifier-1 <u>REPLACING</u>

$\left\{\begin{array}{l} \underline{\text{CHARACTERS}} \ \underline{\text{BY}} \left\{\begin{array}{l}\text{identifier-5}\\\text{literal-3}\end{array}\right\} \left[\left\{\begin{array}{l}\underline{\text{BEFORE}}\\\underline{\text{AFTER}}\end{array}\right\} \text{INITIAL} \left\{\begin{array}{l}\text{identifier-4}\\\text{literal-2}\end{array}\right\}\right] ... \\ \left\{\begin{array}{l}\underline{\text{ALL}}\\\underline{\text{LEADING}}\\\underline{\text{FIRST}}\end{array}\right\} \left\{\left\{\begin{array}{l}\text{identifier-3}\\\text{literal-1}\end{array}\right\} \underline{\text{BY}} \left\{\begin{array}{l}\text{identifier-5}\\\text{literal-3}\end{array}\right\} \left[\left\{\begin{array}{l}\underline{\text{BEFORE}}\\\underline{\text{AFTER}}\end{array}\right\} \text{INITIAL} \left\{\begin{array}{l}\text{identifier-4}\\\text{literal-2}\end{array}\right\}\right]\right\} ... \end{array}\right\} ...$

```
INSPECT identifier-1 TALLYING

            ⎧                   ⎧                  ⎧ BEFORE ⎫          ⎧ identifier-4 ⎫          ⎫ ⎫
            ⎪                   ⎪ CHARACTERS [[    { AFTER  } INITIAL  { literal-2    } ] ...    ⎪ ⎪
            ⎨ identifier-2 FOR  ⎨                                                               ⎬ ⎬ ...
            ⎪                   ⎪ ⎧ ALL     ⎫ ⎧ identifier-3 ⎫ ⎡⎧ BEFORE ⎫        ⎧ identifier-4 ⎫⎤ ⎫
            ⎩                   ⎩ ⎩ LEADING ⎭ ⎩ literal-1    ⎭ ⎣⎩ AFTER  ⎭ INITIAL ⎩ literal-2    ⎭⎦...⎭ ...


                REPLACING

    ⎧ CHARACTERS BY ⎧ identifier-5 ⎫  ⎡⎧ BEFORE ⎫ INITIAL  ⎧ identifier-4 ⎫⎤ ...                            ⎫
    ⎪               ⎩ literal-3    ⎭  ⎣⎩ AFTER  ⎭          ⎩ literal-2    ⎭⎦                                 ⎪
    ⎨                                                                                                       ⎬ ...
    ⎪ ⎡ ALL     ⎤ ⎧⎧ identifier-3 ⎫ BY ⎧ identifier-5 ⎫ ⎡⎧ BEFORE ⎫ INITIAL ⎧ identifier-4 ⎫⎤  ⎫           ⎪
    ⎩ ⎢ LEADING ⎥ ⎨⎩ literal-1    ⎭    ⎩ literal-3    ⎭ ⎣⎩ AFTER  ⎭         ⎩ literal-1    ⎭⎦...⎬ ...       ⎭
      ⎣ FIRST   ⎦ ⎩                                                                           ⎭

INSPECT identifier-1 CONVERTING ⎧ identifier-6 ⎫ TO ⎧ identifier-7 ⎫
                                ⎩ literal-4    ⎭    ⎩ literal-5    ⎭

    ⎡⎧ BEFORE ⎫ INITIAL ⎧ identifier-4 ⎫⎤ ...
    ⎣⎩ AFTER  ⎭         ⎩ literal-2    ⎭⎦

MERGE file-name-1 ⎧ ON ⎧ ASCENDING  ⎫ KEY {data-name-1} ... ⎫ ...
                  ⎩    ⎩ DESCENDING ⎭                        ⎭

    [COLLATING SEQUENCE IS alphabet-name-1]

    USING file-name-2 {file-name-3} ...

    ⎧ OUTPUT PROCEDURE IS procedure-name-1 ⎡⎧ THROUGH ⎫ procedure-name-2⎤ ⎫
    ⎨                                      ⎣⎩ THRU    ⎭                 ⎦ ⎬
    ⎩ GIVING {file-name-4} ...                                          ⎭

MOVE ⎧ identifier-1 ⎫ TO {identifier-2} ...
     ⎩ literal-1    ⎭

MOVE ⎧ CORRESPONDING ⎫ identifier-1 TO identifier-2
     ⎩ CORR          ⎭

MULTIPLY ⎧ identifier-1 ⎫ BY {identifier-2 [ROUNDED]} ...
         ⎩ literal-1    ⎭

    [ON SIZE ERROR imperative-statement-1]

    [NOT ON SIZE ERROR imperative-statement-2]

    [END-MULTIPLY]

MULTIPLY ⎧ identifier-1 ⎫ BY ⎧ identifier-2 ⎫
         ⎩ literal-1    ⎭    ⎩ literal-2    ⎭

    GIVING {identifier-3 [ROUNDED]} ...

    [ON SIZE ERROR imperative-statement-1]

    [NOT ON SIZE ERROR imperative-statement-2]

    [END-MULTIPLY]

       ⎧ INPUT ⎧ file-name-1 ⎡ REVERSED      ⎤⎫ ...                 ⎫
       ⎪       ⎩            ⎣ WITH NO REWIND ⎦⎭                     ⎪
S OPEN ⎨ OUTPUT {file-name-2} [WITH NO REWIND]} ...                ⎬ ...
       ⎪ I-O {file-name-3} ...                                     ⎪
       ⎩ EXTEND {file-name-4} ...                                  ⎭

        ⎧ INPUT {file-name-1} ...  ⎫
        ⎪ OUTPUT {file-name-2} ... ⎪
RI OPEN ⎨ I-O {file-name-3} ...    ⎬ ...
        ⎩ EXTEND {file-name-4} ... ⎭

       ⎧ OUTPUT {file-name-1 [WITH NO REWIND]} ... ⎫ ...
W OPEN ⎨                                           ⎬
       ⎩ EXTEND {file-name-2} ...                  ⎭

PERFORM ⎡ procedure-name-1 ⎡⎧ THROUGH ⎫ procedure-name-2⎤⎤
        ⎣                  ⎣⎩ THRU    ⎭                 ⎦⎦

    [imperative-statement-1 END-PERFORM]
```

$$\underline{\text{PERFORM}} \left[\text{procedure-name-1} \left[\left\{\begin{array}{l}\underline{\text{THROUGH}}\\ \underline{\text{THRU}}\end{array}\right\} \text{procedure-name-2}\right]\right]$$

$$\left\{\begin{array}{l}\text{identifier-1}\\ \text{integer-1}\end{array}\right\} \underline{\text{TIMES}} \ [\text{imperative-statement-1} \ \underline{\text{END-PERFORM}}]$$

$$\underline{\text{PERFORM}} \left[\text{procedure-name-1} \left[\left\{\begin{array}{l}\underline{\text{THROUGH}}\\ \underline{\text{THRU}}\end{array}\right\} \text{procedure-name-2}\right]\right]$$

$$\left[\text{WITH} \ \underline{\text{TEST}} \left\{\begin{array}{l}\underline{\text{BEFORE}}\\ \underline{\text{AFTER}}\end{array}\right\}\right] \underline{\text{UNTIL}} \ \text{condition-1}$$

[imperative-statement-1 END-PERFORM]

$$\underline{\text{PERFORM}} \left[\text{procedure-name-1} \left[\left\{\begin{array}{l}\underline{\text{THROUGH}}\\ \underline{\text{THRU}}\end{array}\right\} \text{procedure-name-2}\right]\right]$$

$$\left[\text{WITH} \ \underline{\text{TEST}} \left\{\begin{array}{l}\underline{\text{BEFORE}}\\ \underline{\text{AFTER}}\end{array}\right\}\right]$$

$$\underline{\text{VARYING}} \left\{\begin{array}{l}\text{identifier-2}\\ \text{index-name-1}\end{array}\right\} \underline{\text{FROM}} \left\{\begin{array}{l}\text{identifier-3}\\ \text{index-name-2}\\ \text{literal-1}\end{array}\right\}$$

$$\underline{\text{BY}} \left\{\begin{array}{l}\text{identifier-4}\\ \text{literal-2}\end{array}\right\} \underline{\text{UNTIL}} \ \text{condition-1}$$

$$\left[\underline{\text{AFTER}} \left\{\begin{array}{l}\text{identifier-5}\\ \text{literal-3}\end{array}\right\} \underline{\text{FROM}} \left\{\begin{array}{l}\text{identifier-6}\\ \text{index-name-4}\\ \text{literal-3}\end{array}\right\}\right.$$

$$\left.\underline{\text{BY}} \left\{\begin{array}{l}\text{identifier-7}\\ \text{literal-4}\end{array}\right\} \underline{\text{UNTIL}} \ \text{condition-2}\right] \ ...$$

[imperative-statement-1 END-PERFORM]

$\underline{\text{PURGE}}$ cd-name-1

SRI $\underline{\text{READ}}$ file-name-1 [$\underline{\text{NEXT}}$] RECORD [$\underline{\text{INTO}}$ identifier-1]

    [AT $\underline{\text{END}}$ imperative-statement-1]

    [$\underline{\text{NOT}}$ AT $\underline{\text{END}}$ imperative-statement-2]

    [$\underline{\text{END-READ}}$]

R $\underline{\text{READ}}$ file-name-1 RECORD [$\underline{\text{INTO}}$ identifier-1]

    [$\underline{\text{INVALID}}$ KEY imperative-statement-3]

    [$\underline{\text{NOT}}$ $\underline{\text{INVALID}}$ KEY imperative-statement-4]

    [$\underline{\text{END-READ}}$]

I $\underline{\text{READ}}$ file-name-1 RECORD [$\underline{\text{INTO}}$ identifier-1]

    [$\underline{\text{KEY}}$ IS data-name-1]

    [$\underline{\text{INVALID}}$ KEY imperative-statement-3]

    [$\underline{\text{NOT}}$ $\underline{\text{INVALID}}$ KEY imperative-statement-4]

    [$\underline{\text{END-READ}}$]

$\underline{\text{RECEIVE}}$ cd-name-1

    [$\underline{\text{NO}}$ $\underline{\text{DATA}}$ imperative-statement-1]

    [WITH $\underline{\text{DATA}}$ imperative-statement-2]

$$[\underline{\text{END-RECEIVE}}] \left\{\begin{array}{l}\underline{\text{MESSAGE}}\\ \underline{\text{SEGMENT}}\end{array}\right\} \underline{\text{INTO}} \ \text{identifier-1}$$

$\underline{\text{RELEASE}}$ record-name-1 [$\underline{\text{FROM}}$ identifier-1]

$\underline{\text{RETURN}}$ file-name-1 RECORD [$\underline{\text{INTO}}$ identifier-1]

    AT $\underline{\text{END}}$ imperative-statement-1

[$\underline{\text{NOT}}$ AT $\underline{\text{END}}$ imperative-statement-2]

    [$\underline{\text{END-RETURN}}$]

```
 S   REWRITE record-name-1 [FROM identifier-1]

 RI  REWRITE record-name-1 [FROM identifier-1]

        [INVALID KEY imperative-statement-1]

        [NOT INVALID KEY imperative-statement-2]

        [END-REWRITE]


    SEARCH identifier-1  [ VARYING { identifier-2  } ]
                                   { index-name-1  }

        [AT END imperative-statement-1]

        { WHEN condition-1 { imperative-statement-2 } } ...
        {                  { NEXT SENTENCE           } }

        [END-SEARCH]


    SEARCH ALL identifier-1  [AT END imperative-statement-1]

        WHEN { data-name-1 { IS EQUAL TO } { identifier-3            } }
             {             { IS =         } { literal-1              } }
             {                             { arithmetic-expression-1 } }
             { condition-name-1                                        }

             [ AND { data-name-2 { IS EQUAL TO } { identifier-4            } } ] ...
             [     {             { IS =         } { literal-2              } } ]
             [     {                             { arithmetic-expression-2 } } ]
             [     { condition-name-2                                        } ]

        { imperative-statement-2 }
        { NEXT SENTENCE          }

        [END-SEARCH]


    SEND cd-name-1 FROM identifier-1


    SEND cd-name-1 [FROM identifier-1] { WITH identifier-2 }
                                       { WITH ESI          }
                                       { WITH EMI          }
                                       { WITH EGI          }


        [ { BEFORE } ADVANCING { { identifier-3 } [ LINE  ] } ]
        [ { AFTER  }           { { integer-1    } [ LINES ] } ]
        [                      {                            } ]
        [                      { { mnemonic-name-1 }        } ]
        [                      { PAGE                       } ]

        [REPLACING LINE]
    SET { index-name-1 } ...  TO { index-name-2 }
        { identifier-1  }         { identifier-2 }
                                  { integer-1    }

    SET {index-name-3} ... { UP BY   } { identifier-3 }
                           { DOWN BY  } { integer-2    }

    SET { {mnemonic-name-1} ... TO { ON  } } ...
                                   { OFF }

    SET {condition-name-1} ... TO TRUE


    SORT file-name-1 { ON { ASCENDING  } KEY {data-name-1} ... } ...
                     {      { DESCENDING }                     }
        [WITH DUPLICATES IN ORDER]

        [COLLATING SEQUENCE IS alphabet-name-1]
```

$$
\left\{
\begin{array}{l}
\underline{INPUT} \ \underline{PROCEDURE} \ \text{IS procedure-name-1} \left[\left\{ \begin{array}{l} \underline{THROUGH} \\ \underline{THRU} \end{array} \right\} \text{procedure-name-2} \right] \\
\underline{USING} \ \{\text{file-name-2}\} \ \dots
\end{array}
\right\}
$$

$$
\left\{
\begin{array}{l}
\underline{OUTPUT} \ \underline{PROCEDURE} \ \text{IS procedure-name-3} \left\{ \begin{array}{l} \underline{THROUGH} \\ \underline{THRU} \end{array} \right\} \text{procedure-name-4} \\
\underline{GIVING} \ \{\text{file-name-3}\} \ \dots
\end{array}
\right\}
$$

$$
\underline{START} \ \text{file-name-1} \left[\underline{KEY} \left\{ \begin{array}{l} \text{IS } \underline{EQUAL} \text{ TO} \\ \text{IS } = \\ \text{IS } \underline{GREATER} \text{ THAN} \\ \text{IS } > \\ \text{IS } \underline{NOT} \ \underline{LESS} \text{ THAN} \\ \text{IS } \underline{NOT} < \\ \text{IS } \underline{GREATER} \text{ THAN OR } \underline{EQUAL} \\ \text{IS } >= \end{array} \right\} \text{data-name-1} \right]
$$

[$\underline{INVALID}$ KEY imperative-statement-1]

[$\underline{NOT}$ $\underline{INVALID}$ KEY imperative-statement-2]

[$\underline{END\text{-}START}$]

$$
\underline{STOP} \left\{ \begin{array}{l} \underline{RUN} \\ \text{literal1-1} \end{array} \right\}
$$

$$
\underline{STRING} \left\{ \left\{ \begin{array}{l} \text{identifier-1} \\ \text{literal-1} \end{array} \right\} \dots \ \underline{DELIMITED} \text{ BY} \left\{ \begin{array}{l} \text{identifier-2} \\ \text{literal-2} \\ \underline{SIZE} \end{array} \right\} \right\} \dots
$$

$\underline{INTO}$ identifier-3

[WITH $\underline{POINTER}$ identifier-4]

[ON $\underline{OVERFLOW}$ imperative-statement-1]

[$\underline{NOT}$ ON $\underline{OVERFLOW}$ imperative-statement-2]

[$\underline{END\text{-}STRING}$]

$$
\underline{SUBTRACT} \left\{ \begin{array}{l} \text{identifier-1} \\ \text{literal-1} \end{array} \right\} \dots \ \underline{FROM} \ \{\text{identifier-3} \ [\underline{ROUNDED}]\} \ \dots
$$

[ON $\underline{SIZE}$ $\underline{ERROR}$ imperative-statement-1]

[$\underline{NOT}$ ON $\underline{SIZE}$ $\underline{ERROR}$ imperative-statement-2]

[$\underline{END\text{-}SUBTRACT}$]

$$
\underline{SUBTRACT} \left\{ \begin{array}{l} \text{identifier-1} \\ \text{literal-1} \end{array} \right\} \dots \ \underline{FROM} \left\{ \begin{array}{l} \text{identifier-2} \\ \text{literal-2} \end{array} \right\}
$$

$\underline{GIVING}$ {identifier-3 [$\underline{ROUNDED}$]} ...

[ON $\underline{SIZE}$ $\underline{ERROR}$ imperative-statement-1]

[$\underline{NOT}$ ON $\underline{SIZE}$ $\underline{ERROR}$ imperative-statement-2]

[$\underline{END\text{-}SUBTRACT}$]

$$
\underline{SUBTRACT} \left\{ \begin{array}{l} \underline{CORRESPONDING} \\ \underline{CORR} \end{array} \right\} \text{identifier-1} \ \underline{FROM} \text{ identifier-2 } [\underline{ROUNDED}]
$$

[ON $\underline{SIZE}$ $\underline{ERROR}$ imperative-statement-1]

[$\underline{NOT}$ ON $\underline{SIZE}$ $\underline{ERROR}$ imperative-statement-2]

[$\underline{END\text{-}SUBTRACT}$]

$\underline{SUPPRESS}$ PRINTING

$\underline{TERMINATE}$ {report-name-1} ...

UNSTRING identifier-1

$$\left[\underline{\text{DELIMITED}} \text{ BY } [\underline{\text{ALL}}] \left\{ \begin{array}{l} \text{identifier-2} \\ \text{literal-1} \end{array} \right\} \left[\underline{\text{OR}} [\underline{\text{ALL}}] \left\{ \begin{array}{l} \text{identifier-3} \\ \text{literal-2} \end{array} \right\} \right] \ldots \right]$$

$\underline{\text{INTO}}$ [identifier-4 [$\underline{\text{DELIMITER}}$ IN identifier-5] [$\underline{\text{COUNT}}$ IN identifier-6]} ...

[WITH $\underline{\text{POINTER}}$ identifier-7]

[$\underline{\text{TALLYING}}$ IN identifier-8]

[ON $\underline{\text{OVERFLOW}}$ imperative-statement-1]

[$\underline{\text{NOT}}$ ON $\underline{\text{OVERFLOW}}$ imperative-statement-2]

[$\underline{\text{END-UNSTRING}}$]

SRI $\underline{\text{USE}}$ [$\underline{\text{GLOBAL}}$] $\underline{\text{AFTER}}$ STANDARD $\left\{ \begin{array}{l} \underline{\text{EXCEPTION}} \\ \underline{\text{ERROR}} \end{array} \right\}$ $\underline{\text{PROCEDURE}}$ ON $\left\{ \begin{array}{l} \text{\{file-name-1\} } \ldots \\ \underline{\text{INPUT}} \\ \underline{\text{OUTPUT}} \\ \underline{\text{I-O}} \\ \underline{\text{EXTEND}} \end{array} \right\}$

W $\underline{\text{USE}}$ $\underline{\text{AFTER}}$ STANDARD $\left\{ \begin{array}{l} \underline{\text{EXCEPTION}} \\ \underline{\text{ERROR}} \end{array} \right\}$ $\underline{\text{PROCEDURE}}$ ON $\left\{ \begin{array}{l} \text{\{file-name-1\} } \ldots \\ \underline{\text{OUTPUT}} \\ \underline{\text{EXTEND}} \end{array} \right\}$

$\underline{\text{USE}}$ [$\underline{\text{GLOBAL}}$] $\underline{\text{BEFORE}}$ $\underline{\text{REPORTING}}$ identifier-1

$\underline{\text{USE}}$ FOR $\underline{\text{DEBUGGING}}$ $\underline{\text{ON}}$ $\left\{ \begin{array}{l} \text{cd-name-1} \\ [\underline{\text{ALL}} \text{ REFERENCES OF}] \text{ identifier-1} \\ \text{file-name-1} \\ \text{procedure-name-1} \\ \underline{\text{ALL}} \underline{\text{PROCEDURES}} \end{array} \right\} \ldots$

S $\underline{\text{WRITE}}$ record-name-1 [$\underline{\text{FROM}}$ identifier-1]

$$\left[\left\{ \begin{array}{l} \underline{\text{BEFORE}} \\ \underline{\text{AFTER}} \end{array} \right\} \text{ADVANCING} \left\{ \begin{array}{l} \left\{ \begin{array}{l} \text{identifier-2} \\ \text{integer-1} \end{array} \right\} \left[\begin{array}{l} \text{LINE} \\ \text{LINES} \end{array} \right] \\ \left\{ \begin{array}{l} \text{mnemonic-name-1} \\ \underline{\text{PAGE}} \end{array} \right\} \end{array} \right\} \right]$$

$\left[\text{AT } \left\{ \begin{array}{l} \underline{\text{END-OF-PAGE}} \\ \underline{\text{EOP}} \end{array} \right\} \text{imperative-statement-1} \right]$

$\left[\underline{\text{NOT}} \text{ AT } \left\{ \begin{array}{l} \underline{\text{END-OF-PAGE}} \\ \underline{\text{EOP}} \end{array} \right\} \text{imperative-statement-2} \right]$

[$\underline{\text{END-WRITE}}$]

RI $\underline{\text{WRITE}}$ record-name-1 [$\underline{\text{FROM}}$ identifier-1]

[$\underline{\text{INVALID}}$ KEY imperative-statement-1]

[$\underline{\text{NOT}}$ $\underline{\text{INVALID}}$ KEY imperative-statement-2]

[$\underline{\text{END-WRITE}}$]

General Format for Copy and Replace Statements

$\underline{\text{COPY}}$ text-name-1 $\left[\left\{ \begin{array}{l} \underline{\text{OF}} \\ \underline{\text{IN}} \end{array} \right\} \text{library-name-1} \right]$

$$\left[\underline{\text{REPLACING}} \left\{ \left\{ \begin{array}{l} \text{==pseudo-text-1==} \\ \text{identifier-1} \\ \text{literal-1} \\ \text{word-1} \end{array} \right\} \underline{\text{BY}} \left\{ \begin{array}{l} \text{==pseudo-text-2==} \\ \text{identifier-2} \\ \text{literal-2} \\ \text{word-2} \end{array} \right\} \right\} \ldots \right]$$

$\underline{\text{REPLACE}}$ {==pseudo-text-1== $\underline{\text{BY}}$ ==pseudo-text-2==} ...

$\underline{\text{REPLACE}}$ $\underline{\text{OFF}}$

General Format for Conditions

Relation Condition:

```
            ⎧                          ⎫   ⎧ IS [NOT] GREATER THAN          ⎫   ⎧                        ⎫
            ⎪ identifier-1             ⎪   ⎪ IS [NOT] >                     ⎪   ⎪ identifier-2           ⎪
            ⎨ literal-1               ⎬   ⎪ IS [NOT] LESS THAN             ⎪   ⎨ literal-2              ⎬
            ⎪ arithmetic-expression-1 ⎪   ⎨ IS [NOT] <                     ⎬   ⎪ arithmetic-expression-2⎪
            ⎩ index-name-1            ⎭   ⎪ IS [NOT] EQUAL TO              ⎪   ⎩ index-name-2           ⎭
                                          ⎪ IS [NOT] =                     ⎪
                                          ⎪ IS GREATER THAN OR EQUAL TO    ⎪
                                          ⎪ IS >=                          ⎪
                                          ⎪ IS LESS THAN OR EQUAL TO       ⎪
                                          ⎩ IS <=                          ⎭
```

Class Condition:

```
                              ⎧ NUMERIC          ⎫
                              ⎪ ALPHABETIC       ⎪
    identifier-1 IS [NOT]  ⎨ ALPHABETIC-LOWER ⎬
                              ⎪ ALPHABETIC-UPPER ⎪
                              ⎩ class-name-1     ⎭
```

Condition-Name Condition:

```
condition-name-1
```

Switch-Status Condition:

```
condition-name-1
```

Sign Condition:

```
                                          ⎧ POSITIVE ⎫
arithmetic-expression-1 IS [NOT]  ⎨ NEGATIVE ⎬
                                          ⎩ ZERO     ⎭
```

Negated Condition:

```
NOT condition-1
```

Combined Condition:

```
                ⎧ ⎧ AND ⎫             ⎫
condition-1  ⎨ ⎨ OR  ⎬ condition-2 ⎬ ...
                ⎩ ⎩     ⎭             ⎭
```

Abbreviated Combined Relation Condition:

```
                     ⎧ ⎧ AND ⎫                                      ⎫
relation-condition ⎨ ⎨ OR  ⎬ [NOT] [relational-operator] object ⎬ ...
                     ⎩ ⎩     ⎭                                      ⎭
```

Qualification

Format 1:

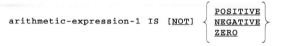

```
⎧ data-name-1      ⎫ ⎧ ⎧ ⎧ IN ⎫           ⎫       ⎡ ⎧ IN ⎫ ⎧ file-name-1 ⎫ ⎤ ⎫
⎨ condition-name-1 ⎬ ⎨ ⎨ ⎨ OF ⎬ data-name-2 ⎬ ... ⎢ ⎨ OF ⎬ ⎨ cd-name-1   ⎬ ⎥ ⎬
⎩                  ⎭ ⎪ ⎩ ⎩    ⎭           ⎭       ⎣ ⎩    ⎭ ⎩             ⎭ ⎦ ⎪
                     ⎪ ⎧ IN ⎫ ⎧ file-name-1 ⎫      IN                       ⎪
                     ⎩ ⎨ OF ⎬ ⎨ cd-name-1   ⎬      OF                       ⎭
                       ⎩    ⎭ ⎩             ⎭
```

Format 2:

```
                       ⎧ IN ⎫
paragraph-name-1  ⎨ OF ⎬   section-name-1
                       ⎩    ⎭
```

Format 3:

```
text-name-1  { IN }  library-name-1
             { OF }
```

Format 4:

```
LINAGE-COUNTER  { IN }  file-name-2
                { OF }
```

Format 5:

```
{ PAGE-COUNTER }  { IN }  report-name-1
{ LINE-COUNTER }  { OF }
```

Format 6:

```
              ⎧ { IN } data-name-4 [ { IN } report-name-2 ] ⎫
              ⎪ { OF }            [ { OF }               ] ⎪
data-name-3  ⎨                                             ⎬
              ⎪ { IN } report-name-2                        ⎪
              ⎩ { OF }                                      ⎭
```

Miscellaneous Formats

Subscripting:

```
{ condition-name-1 }  ( ⎧ integer-1                        ⎫ ... )
{ data-name-1      }    ⎨ data-name-2  [{±} integer-2]     ⎬
                        ⎩ index-name-1 [{±} integer-3]     ⎭
```

Reference Modification:

```
data-name-1 (leftmost-character-position: [length])
```

Identifier:

```
                  [ { IN }             ]       { IN }  ⎧ cd-name-1     ⎫
data-name-1       [ { OF } data-name-2 ] ...   { OF }  ⎨ file-name-1   ⎬
                                                       ⎩ report-name-1 ⎭

   [({subscript} ... )] [(leftmost-character-position: [length])]
```

G

RM/COBOL-85
ERROR MESSAGES

This appendix lists the informational, warning, and error messages that may be generated during compilation. These classes of messages are defined as follows:

1. **I** indicates an information-only record

2. **W** indicates a warning

3. **E** indicates a severe error

Informational Messages

I 1 Indicates the data-name of the particular data record referred to by the previous summary error message. The compiler adds the data-name to the message.

I 2: Provides error threading facilities by pointing to the line location of errors generated during compilation. The compiler adds the line number in which the last error occurred to the message.

I 3: Indicates the approximate line number of the first occurrence of the summary error message printed just prior to this message. The compiler adds the line number to the message.

I 4: Indicates the data-name of the particular record key referred to by the previous summary error message. The compiler adds the data-name to the message.

I 5: Scanning was suppressed at the previous error and resumes at the indicated point in the source program.

I 6: This message is printed following any error messages that cause the compiler to suspend source scanning. Only the text of the message is printed.

I 7: Indicates the data-name for the particular table key referenced by the previous summary message. The compiler adds the data-name to the message.

I 8: The alphabet-name is defined with a literal phrase that lists a duplicate character. The referenced alphabet-name follows this message.

I 9: An alphabet-name has one or more duplicate characters defined. The first or only character that is duplicated follows this message.

Warning Messages

Warning messages are generated when an error occurs during compilation that does not interrupt compilation and that will not prevent program execution.

W 18: More than one character was given for a literal in the ALPHABET clause. It is assumed that each of the characters of the literal was meant to be listed individually in the order given in the source program.

W 19: Level number 01 or 77 is found in Area B. These level numbers should be in Area A, and are treated as if they appeared in Area A.

W 20: A record description entry following an input CD entry implicitly redefines the record area and must be 87 characters in length. A record description entry following an input I-O entry implicitly redefines the record area and must be 33 characters in length. Record entries for output may vary in length, depending on the DESTINATION TABLE OCCURS clause. However, all record entries within a single output CD entry must be the same length.

W 21: Not all eleven data-names for Option 2 of the communication description entry for input have been listed. Data entries will be used in the order listed.

W 22: A COPY or REPLACE statement is missing its closing period. A closing period is assumed.

W 23: The literal specified in the CURRENCY SIGN clause is longer than one character in length. Only the first character will be used.

W 24: The indicated DATA DIVISION division header, section header, paragraph header, or level indicator is not in the required order for a COBOL source program. Scanning continues without regard to proper order.

W 25: A character type operand (INSPECT...CHARACTERS or ACCEPT...PROMPT) specifies more than one character. For ACCEPT...PROMPT, only the first character will be used. For INSPECT...CHARACTERS, the entire operand will be used.

W 26: A procedure-name referenced in the declaratives is not defined in the declaratives. Standard COBOL does not allow references from the declaratives to the imperatives. If later defined, the procedure-name reference will be allowed by RM/COBOL-85 and will execute correctly.

W 27: When Format 2 of the OCCURS clause is used, it is expected that the DEPENDING ON phrase will also be included in the clause.

W 28: The indicated ENVIRONMENT DIVISION division header, section header, or paragraph header is not in the required order for a COBOL source program. Scanning continues without regard to proper order.

W 29: The DATA RECORD/RECORDS clause in the file description entry (FD) for the indicated file lists a data-name that is not defined as a level 01 record-name of the file.

W 30: The data-name or literal specified in the PADDING clause should be one character in length. Only the first character of the specified operand is used.

W 31: The file label data item of the indicated file-name is not defined in the WORKING-STORAGE SECTION as required by the standard. There is no effect on the object program.

W 32: The record key data-name references a data item that is defined as variable in length.

W 33: The record size of the indicated file-name is not appropriate for the context. In a SORT or MERGE statement, the maximum record size of a USING file is greater than the maximum record size of the sort-merge file or the maximum record size of the sort-merge file is greater than the maximum record size of the GIVING file. Records will be truncated during the sort or merge operation if the actual record length is greater than the maximum record length of the sort-merge or GIVING file.

W 34: The numeric data item in the DEPENDING ON phrase of the RECORD clause in the file description entry for the indicated file-name is defined with a sign.

W 35: The relative key declared for the indicated file-name is a signed numeric integer. The standard requires an unsigned numeric integer. The program may be executed, but negative values, if they occur, may cause undesired results.

W 36: The file status data item declared for the indicated file-name is defined in the FILE SECTION of the DATA DIVISION. The standard rules against this situation. The program will execute, but unpredictable results may occur if, for example, the file status data item is defined within the record area associated with the file.

W 37: The indicated data description clause is invalid because a containing group has a VALUE IS clause.

W 38: The imperative sequence contains a GOBACK, GO TO or STOP RUN statement that is not the last statement in the sequence. A GOBACK, GO TO or STOP RUN statement must be followed by a period separator or, if contained within another statement, a scope terminator of the containing statement.

W 39: The nonblank character in the indicator area (column 7) is not an * (comment), / (new page comment), - (continuation), or D (debug line). The character is treated as a blank.

W 40: The integer indicated requires more than 16 bits to represent its value. RM/COBOL-85 is limited to 16-bit words for the representation of some integer values. The low-order 16 bits are used.

W 41: The VALUE OF and LABEL RECORDS OMITTED clauses are specified for the same file. There is no effect on the object program.

W 42: The literal specified in the MEMORY clause of the OBJECT-COMPUTER paragraph is not defined as an elementary unsigned numeric data item. There is no effect on the object program.

W 43: The literal specified in the MEMORY clause of the OBJECT-COMPUTER paragraph is not an integer. There is no effect on the object program.

W 44: A period space separator is repeated where only one period space separator is allowed. The unneeded separator is ignored by the compiler.

W 45: An imperative statement is required at the indicated source location, but a scope terminator was specified instead. The compiler assumes a CONTINUE statement was intended.

W 46: An option phrase is specified more than once or the default option has been specified in violation of syntactic rules. The indicated or later occurrence is ignored.

W 47: The EXIT paragraph of the performed procedure(s) is in a fixed segment (segment number less than 50) and the PERFORM statement is in an independent segment. Only sections or paragraphs wholly contained in the fixed segment or wholly contained in the same independent segment should be used.

W 48: A procedure referenced as the exit of a PERFORM statement contains an unconditional GOBACK, GO TO or STOP RUN statement as its last statement. Therefore, the procedure cannot reach its exit so as to return control to the controlling PERFORM statement.

W 49: A procedure-name is required in Area A because of a preceding section header or unconditional transfer of control (EXIT, GOBACK, GO TO or STOP RUN statement).

W 50: A procedure-name contains a decimal point. The decimal point character is ignored.

W 51: The ASSIGN TO phrase does not specify a known device-type. One of the mass storage device-types (RANDOM, DISC or DISK) is assumed.

W 52: A literal and user-defined word have no separator between them.

W 53: A comma or semicolon character occurs in the source program without a following space. The comma or semicolon is treated as if the space were present.

W 54: A sort-merge file is declared with file control clauses that are not allowed. The clauses are ignored unless they specify illegal options (for example, nonsequential organization).

W 55: The ASCENDING or DESCENDING key comparison is omitted or misspelled. If simply omitted, ASCENDING will be assumed. If misspelled, a syntax error will also occur.

W 56: Nonstandard phrases are specified in the INPUT or OUTPUT procedure declaration of a SORT or MERGE statement.

W 57: A user-defined word is longer than 30 characters in length. The entire word is used.

W 58: A multiple USE declarative exists for the indicated file-name and OPEN mode. When multiple USE declaratives are declared, the last one declared is in effect for the object program, except that a USE declarative for a file-name will take precedence over a USE declarative for an OPEN mode.

W 59: The numeric literal specified in the VALUE clause for a numeric data item is incorrect for initialization of the data item as described by its PICTURE character string, but is within the range of values allowed by the data item. Truncation of nonzero low-order digits was required; or, for a BINARY, COMP-1 or COMP-4 usage data item, more digits were specified than allowed by the PICTURE character-string, but the value can still be expressed within the number of bytes allocated for the data item.

W 60: A verb was found in Area A of the source program. The verb is treated as if it occurred in Area B.

W 61: A clause appears in Area A of a source record. The clause is treated as if it appeared in Area B.

W 62: A hexadecimal literal is not delimited by a matched pair of single or double quotation marks. The compiler assumes that the single or double quotation mark found, even though it does not match the beginning quotation mark, was intended as the terminating delimiter for the hexadecimal literal.

W 63: The indicated ACCEPT or DISPLAY option is invalid for the operand being accepted or displayed. For example, the CONVERT option requires a numeric or edited operand. The option is ignored.

W 64: One or more of the ACCEPT/DISPLAY options are invalid for nondisplay (computational) numeric operands. For DISPLAY of a nondisplay data item, the CONVERT phrase is required and is assumed. For ACCEPT of a nondisplay data item, the ECHO phrase is invalid and ignored unless the UPDATE phrase is also present.

W 65: An integer with the value zero is not allowed in the indicated context. The program may or may not execute correctly. For example, if an index-name is set to the value zero, it will contain an invalid value, but a subsequent SET...UP BY 1 statement will cause the index-name to contain a valid value for the first occurrence.

W 66: The reserved word NOT should not be used with the relational operators >= and <= or with their spelled-out equivalents. Such cases are treated as > and < , respectively.

W 67: A RECORD DELIMITER clause has been specified for a file whose records are not variable length.

W 68: A character has been specified more than once in a CLASS clause.

W 69: The indicated language element is not defined in the standard COBOL language. It is an extension to the standard language defined and supported by Ryan-McFarland.

W 70: The indicated language element is defined in the standard COBOL language, but at a level above the requested level.

W 71: The indicated language element is defined in the standard COBOL language, but has been designated for deletion from the standard language in a future revision.

W 72: The two characters of a pseudo-text delimiter should be contiguous within the same source record. They are treated as if they were contiguous.

W 73: The two operands of a BY phrase in a REPLACE statement should be pseudo-text operands. Operands that are not written as pseudo-text operands are treated by the compiler like the non pseudo-text operands of a REPLACING phrase in a COPY statement.

W 74: The indicated statement can never be executed because it is immediately preceded by another statement that transfers control unconditionally.

W 75: The data-name listed in the ASSIGN clause for the indicated file-name is a variable length data item (that is, a group which contains a data item described with the OCCURS DEPENDING ON clause). The maximum length of the group will be used to resolve the external-file-name for the file.

W 76: The indicated word is not recognized as a valid unit-name known to this implementation. An unspecified device type is assumed. The unspecified device type is changed to mass storage if any clause (for example, ORGANIZATION IS INDEXED) or statement (for example, OPEN I-O) referencing the file so requires. Otherwise, the file may reside on either mass storage or nonmass storage media.

W 77: The indicated syntax is not allowed in a program nested within another program. Clauses that typically affect the remainder of the program are ignored. Declarations of mnemonic-names, alphabet-names, symbolic-characters and class-names are accepted and used for the remainder of the compilation of the separately compiled program that contains the nested program, including programs not nested within the program that was diagnosed with this warning. If nested programs were not desired, use the Z Compile Command Option or the correct configuration to set the object version level to 1 or 2. This causes the compiler to assume that—even in the absence of END PROGRAM headers—the source file contains a sequence of source programs, rather than nested source programs.

W 79: A nested program specifies the same program-name as another program within the separately compiled program containing that nested program. When source programs are nested, a particular program-name may only occur once in the PROGRAM-ID paragraph of any program contained in the separately compiled program.

W 549: A screen-name specified as an operand in an ACCEPT statement has no subordinate elementary fields that specify a TO or USING attribute.

W 633: An attribute is specified in a screen description entry that conflicts with the specification of the VALUE clause in the same screen description entry. A BLANK WHEN ZERO, JUSTIFIED, AUTO, FULL, REQUIRED, or SECURE clause may not be specified in a screen description clause that also specified a VALUE clause.

Error Messages

Error messages are generated if the error detected during compilation may cause the program to fail during execution.

E 80: Use of the "ALL" form of a figurative constant is illegal in the indicated context.

E 81: The integer used in the ALPHABET clause of the SPECIAL-NAMES paragraph must represent an ordinal position in the native character set. The number of characters in the native character set is 256.

E 82: A character has been specified more than once in the ALPHABET clause that is referenced in the COLLATING SEQUENCE clause in the File-Control entry or the COLLATING SEQUENCE phrase of the SORT and MERGE statements. Informational messages 8 and 9, appearing at the end of the program listing, show the alphabet-name and character duplicated.

E 83: The indicated user-defined word has already been defined for some other purpose and cannot be used to define a class-name.

E 84: The context suggests that a class-name is intended at the indicated position, but the specified user-defined word is undefined.

E 85: The indicated user-defined word has already been defined for some other purpose and cannot be used to define an alphabet-name.

E 86: The context requires an alphabet-name, but the indicated user-defined word is not an alphabet-name.

E 87: The indicated context requires an alphabet-name, but the given user-defined word is undefined.

E 88: An unrecognized type is given in the ALPHABET clause of the SPECIAL-NAMES paragraph. Valid alphabet types are STANDARD-1, EBCDIC, NATIVE, or a literal phrase.

E 89: An ALTER statement in the nondeclaratives region is invalid because the procedure-name of the procedure to be altered, the paragraph containing the alterable GO TO statement, references a declarative procedure.

E 90: An ALTER statement is invalid because the procedure-name of the procedure to be altered, the paragraph containing the alterable GO TO statement, references a procedure defined in an independent segment that has a different segment number than the segment containing the ALTER statement.

E 91: An ALTER statement is invalid because the procedure-name of the procedure to be altered, the paragraph containing the alterable GO TO statement, does not reference a paragraph containing only a single Format 1 GO TO statement.

E 92: An ALTER statement is invalid because the procedure-name of the procedure to be altered, the paragraph containing the alterable GO TO statement, references two or more procedures. Qualification of the paragraph-name by its section-name is required to yield a unique reference.

E 93: An ALTER statement is invalid because the procedure-name of the procedure to be altered, the paragraph containing the alterable GO TO statement, references a procedure that is undefined. The procedure-name may be incorrectly qualified.

E 94: A GO TO statement with the procedure-name omitted is not referenced by an ALTER statement and can never be executed.

E 95: A nonnumeric literal is continued, but does not have an opening quotation mark on the continuation line.

E 96: The context requires a nonnumeric literal.

E 97: A nonnumeric literal greater than 2047 characters in length is specified by the source program.

E 98: A nonnumeric literal is not continued and does not have a closing quotation mark.

E 99: Context requires an entry in Area A at the indicated point in the source program.

E 100: The syntax of the arithmetic expression is incorrect. That is, expression is not a permissible combination of variables, numeric literals, arithmetic operators and parentheses.

E 101: The ASSIGN clause is required for each file-name specified in a SELECT clause.

E 102: The AT END clause is required in a RETURN statement.

E 103: The BLANK WHEN ZERO clause is specified in a data description entry in conflict with other clauses specified in the same entry.

E 104: A clause in the communication description entry has been specified more than once.

E 105: The INITIAL clause of the communication description entry may not be used in a program that specifies the USING phrase in the PROCEDURE DIVISION header.

E 106: A duplicate communication description entry with the INITIAL clause has been specified in the source program. Only one CD FOR INITIAL INPUT is allowed in a program.

E 107: The indicated item is incorrect syntax in the context of Format 1 of the communication description entry in the source program.

E 108: The indicated item is incorrect syntax in the context of Format 3 of the communication description entry in the source program.

E 109: The indicated item is incorrect syntax in the context of Format 2 of the communication description entry in the source program.

E 110: A cd-name has previously been defined and cannot be used again.

E 111: An INPUT or I-O cd-name must be referenced in the context of the statement as given in the source program. An INPUT cd-name is required with ACCEPT MESSAGE COUNT, ENABLE INPUT and DISABLE INPUT statements. An INPUT or I-O cd-name is required with RECEIVE statements.

E 112: An OUTPUT or I-O cd-name must be referenced in the context of the statement as given in the source program. An OUTPUT cd-name is required with ENABLE OUTPUT and DISABLE OUTPUT statements. An OUTPUT or I-O cd-name is required with SEND statements.

E 113: The context does not allow a cd-name reference.

E 114: There is an error in the communication description entry associated with the indicated cd-name.

E 115: The cd-name referenced in a SEND, RECEIVE, ACCEPT ENABLE or DISABLE statement is not defined. A communication description entry is required in the context of the statement indicated in the source program.

E 116: The maximum CD record size has been exceeded. Only the first 65,280 characters will be used.

E 117: INPUT, OUTPUT or I-O type is required in the communication description entry.

E 118: The indicated mnemonic-name must be identified with a channel-name. Channel-names are defined in the SPECIAL-NAMES paragraph of the ENVIRONMENT DIVISION.

E 119: The specified class condition conflicts with the data type of the item being tested.

E 120: A code-set was previously defined in the SELECT statement for the indicated file and does not match the code-set in the file description entry.

E 121: A file that is defined with a CODE-SET clause must have a SIGN SEPARATE clause in all signed numeric data descriptions in the file's record description.

E 122: A file that is defined with a CODE-SET clause must not have any of the numeric data items in the record defined with a USAGE IS clause except USAGE IS DISPLAY.

E 123: More than one PROGRAM COLLATING SEQUENCE clause has been specified.

E 124: The COLLATING SEQUENCE clause may be specified for indexed organized files only.

E 125:- The composite size of the operands specified in the indicated statement is greater than the maximum number of digits allowed. The total integer positions plus the total fractional positions must not exceed 18.

E 126: The condition-name indicated is associated with a conditional variable that has been marked invalid by the compiler because of an error in its description.

E 127: The condition-name indicated has already been defined and cannot be redefined.

E 128: The context does not allow a condition-name, but the identifier indicated is that of a condition-name.

E 129: A condition-name referenced in a SEARCH ALL statement must have a single value associated with it.

E 130: The value literal specified for a condition-name has a type that conflicts with the type of the associated conditional variable.

E 131: The syntax of a conditional expression is incorrect. The syntax given in the source is not that of a relation, class, sign, condition-name or switch-status condition. This syntax error may be caused by failure to follow the separator rules of COBOL, which require spaces around the special characters used in relation conditions.

E 132: The syntax of the COPY statement indicated is incorrect. The COPY statement is embedded within another COPY statement or the maximum copy nesting level of five has been exceeded.

E 133: The text-name and, optionally, library-name specified in a COPY statement indicated COPY text that could not be accessed. The file could not be opened, possibly because the nesting level of five open copy files has been exceeded or because the copy text contains a COPY statement that copies itself.

E 134: The context requires an identifier of a group data item that satisfies the rules for CORRESPONDING. The identifier indicated is either not a group or is a group with no subordinate named data items (for example, a group defined by RENAMES).

E 135: The two groups referenced in an ADD CORRESPONDING or SUBTRACT CORRESPONDING statement have no corresponding numeric items. These statements require at least one pair of corresponding numeric items.

E 136: The literal specified in the CURRENCY SIGN clause specifies a character that is not allowed for the currency symbol.

E 137: The indicated data item is incorrect syntax in the context of the data description entry as given in the source program.

E 138: The indicated character-string or separator is incorrect syntax in the context of the DATA DIVISION as given in the source program.

E 139: The context requires a reference to a data item or literal, but the indicated character-string or separator does not reference data.

E 140: The indicated identifier references a data item or condition-name defined in the LINKAGE SECTION of the DATA DIVISION, but its data-name or the data-name of its conditional variable is not listed in the USING phrase of the PROCEDURE DIVISION header, nor is the data item or condition-name defined subordinate to a data-name listed in the USING phrase of the PROCEDURE DIVISION header. Thus, the identifier references a data item that would not be addressable by the program at object time.

E 141: The indicated data description clause is repeated for the same subject.

E 142: The indicated user-defined word is already defined for a purpose that conflicts with its use as a data-name.

E 143: The indicated data item has a size greater than 65,280 characters. Such items may be referenced only in a MOVE statement or in the USING phrase of a CALL statement.

E 144: The VALUE IS clause cannot be used to describe data defined within the current section of the DATA DIVISION. Within the COMMUNICATION SECTION, the VALUE IS clause may be used only with the first 01 level record description following a CD entry.

E 145: The context requires an alphanumeric data item.

E 146: The indicated identifier does not reference an elementary data item as required by the context in which it appears. The identifier references a group data item and group data items are disallowed in this context.

E 147: The context requires a data item with DISPLAY usage.

E 148: The JUSTIFIED clause cannot be used in the data description entry of the data-name as used in the indicated context.

E 149: The context requires a numeric integer data item.

E 150: The context requires a numeric or a numeric-edited data item.

E 151: The context requires a numeric data item; a numeric-edited data item is not allowed.

E 152: The literal type specified in the VALUE literal for a data description entry conflicts with the data type of the item as described by other clauses.

E 153: An END header was found while scanning the declaratives portion of the PROCEDURE DIVISION, but it was not the END DECLARATIVES header.

E 154: A GO TO or ALTER statement in the imperatives illegally references a procedure-name defined in the declaratives.

E 155: The declaratives must begin with a section definition.

E 156: A segment-number greater than 49 is given in the declaratives. Independent segments are not allowed in the declaratives. The last valid segment-number is used instead.

E 157: The indicated verb is not allowed in the declaratives portion of the PROCEDURE DIVISION.

E 158: The previous data description entry defined an elementary data item, but the indicated level-number is not less than or equal to the level-number of the previous entry.

E 159: The indicated item is incorrect syntax in the context of the ENVIRONMENT DIVISION as given in the source program.

E 160: The condition specified is not an equal relation. In a SEARCH ALL statement, only a condition-name or an equal relation is allowed.

E 161: A condition-name cannot be set to false unless the WHEN SET TO FALSE phrase is used when defining the condition-name in the DATA DIVISION.

E 162: The indicated character-string or separator is incorrect syntax in the context of the file description entry as given in the source program.

E 163: The data-name of the LINES AT BOTTOM phrase of the LINAGE clause for the indicated file does not reference an elementary unsigned numeric data item.

E 164: The data-name referenced in the LINES AT BOTTOM phrase of the LINAGE clause for the indicated file has an error in its data description.

E 165: The data-name referenced in the LINES AT BOTTOM phrase of the LINAGE clause for the indicated file is not a valid data item described in the DATA DIVISION.

E 166: The data-name referenced in the LINES AT BOTTOM phrase of the LINAGE clause for the indicated file cannot be defined with an OCCURS clause.

E 167: The data-name referenced in the LINES AT BOTTOM phrase of the LINAGE clause for the indicated file is defined more than once and is not adequately qualified.

E 168: The data-name in the LINES AT BOTTOM phrase of the LINAGE clause for the indicated file has not been defined. An elementary unsigned numeric data entry in the DATA DIVISION is required.

E 169: The data-name in the LINES AT BOTTOM phrase of the LINAGE clause for the indicated file has been defined in the LINKAGE SECTION. The data-name is not listed in the PROCEDURE DIVISION USING phrase, nor is it defined subordinate to such a data-name. The data-name should be included as a USING parameter or defined outside the LINKAGE SECTION.

E 170: A file with a CODE-SET clause specifies an alphabet-name that has a character used more than once. A file opened for any mode other than INPUT cannot reference an alphabet-name that has a character listed more than once.

E 171: A file control clause is repeated for the same file.

E 172: The indicated character-string or separator is incorrect syntax in the context of the file description entry as given in the source program.

E 173: The file description for the indicated file-name is either missing or invalid. No record area is defined for the file.

E 174: The device associated with the file-name does not allow the indicated function.

E 175: The data type of the data item declared for the external-file-name of the indicated file-name is not alphanumeric.

E 176: The data-name declared for the external-file-name of the indicated file-name references a data item that has been marked invalid by the compiler because of an error in its description.

E 177: The data-name declared for the external-file-name of the indicated file-name does not reference a data item.

E 178: The data-name declared for the external-file-name of the indicated file-name references a data item that is described with the OCCURS clause or is subordinate to an item described with the OCCURS clause.

E 179: The data-name declared for the external-file-name of the indicated file-name references two or more data items; the qualification is ambiguous.

E 180: The data-name declared for the external-file-name of the indicated file-name is undefined.

E 181: The data-name declared for the external-file-name references a data item defined in the LINKAGE SECTION, but is not listed in the PROCEDURE DIVISION USING phrase.

E 182: The data-name of the FOOTING phrase of the LINAGE clause for the indicated file does not reference an elementary unsigned numeric data item.

E 183: The data-name referenced in the FOOTING phrase of the LINAGE clause for the indicated file has an error in its data description.

E 184: The data-name referenced in the FOOTING phrase of the LINAGE clause for the indicated file is not a valid data item described in the DATA DIVISION.

E 185: The data-name referenced in the FOOTING phrase of the LINAGE clause for the indicated file cannot be defined with an OCCURS clause.

E 186: The data-name referenced in the FOOTING phrase of the LINAGE clause for the indicated file is defined more than once and is not adequately qualified.

E 187: The data-name in the FOOTING phrase of the LINAGE clause for the indicated file has not been defined. An elementary unsigned numeric data entry in the DATA DIVISION is required.

E 188: The data-name in the FOOTING phrase of the LINAGE clause for the indicated file has been defined in the LINKAGE SECTION. The data-name is not listed in the PROCEDURE DIVISION USING phrase, nor is it defined subordinate to such a data-name. The data-name should be included as a USING parameter or defined outside the LINKAGE SEC-TION.

E 189: The LABEL RECORDS clause specifies an unrecognized label descriptor. The label must be described as STANDARD or OMITTED.

E 190: The data-name declared in the VALUE OF clause for the indicated file-name references a data item that has been marked invalid by the compiler because of an error in its description.

E 191: The data-name declared in the VALUE OF clause for the indicated file-name references a nondata item.

E 192: The data-name declared in the VALUE OF clause for the indicated file-name references a data item that is described with the OCCURS clause or is subordinate to an item described with the OCCURS clause.

E 193: The data-name declared in the VALUE OF clause for the indicated file-name references two or more data items; the qualification is ambiguous.

E 194: The data-name declared in the VALUE OF clause for the indicated file-name is undefined.

E 195: The data-name in the VALUE OF clause of the file description entry is defined in the LINKAGE SEC-TION but is not listed in the PROCEDURE DIVISION USING phrase, and is not defined subordinate to such a data-name. The data-name should be included as a USING parameter or defined outside the LINKAGE SECTION.

E 196: The data-name in the LINAGE clause does not reference an elementary unsigned numeric data item.

E 197: The data-name referenced in the LINAGE IS clause for the indicated file has an error in its data description.

E 198: The data-name referenced in the LINAGE IS clause for the indicated file is not a valid data item described in the DATA DIVISION.

E 199: The data-name referenced in the LINAGE IS clause for the indicated file cannot be defined with an OCCURS clause.

E 200: The data-name referenced in the LINAGE IS clause for the indicated file is defined more than once and is not adequately qualified.

E 201: The data-name referenced in the LINAGE IS clause has not been defined. An elementary unsigned numeric data entry in the DATA DIVISION is required.

E 202: The data-name referenced in the LINAGE IS clause has been defined in the LINKAGE SECTION. The data-name is not listed in the PROCEDURE DIVI-SION USING phrase, and is not defined subordinate to such a data-name. The data-name should be included as a USING parameter or defined outside the LINKAGE SECTION.

E 203: The indicated file-name has already been defined in an FD or SD entry.

E 204: The indicated file description clause is repeated for the same file.

E 205: The indicated user-defined word is already defined for some other purpose and cannot be defined as a file-name.

E 206: The context does not allow a file-name reference.

E 207: The indicated file-name has been marked invalid by the compiler because of an error in its description.

E 208: The context requires a file-name.

E 209: The indicated file-name is not defined. This includes qualification errors such as an attempt to qualify a file-name.

E 210: The data-name declared for a record key of the indicated file-name references a data item that extends outside the minimum record size for the file. All record keys must be totally contained within the minimum record size.

E 211: The data-name declared for a record key of the indicated file-name references a data item that is not defined in a record associated with the file-name. All record keys must be defined within a record associated with the file.

E 212: The data-name declared for a record key of the indicated file-name references a data item that has the same leftmost character offset as another record key of file-name. No two keys may share the same leftmost character position.

E 213: The data-name declared for a record key of the indicated file-name references a data item with a length of more than 255 characters.

E 214: The data-name declared as a record key of the indicated file-name references a data item that does not have an allowed data type. A record key data item must be category alphanumeric or an unsigned numeric data item with DISPLAY usage.

E 215: The data-name declared for a record key of the indicated file-name references a data item that has been marked invalid by the compiler because of an error in its description.

E 216: The data-name declared for a record key of the indicated file-name references a nondata item.

E 217: The data-name declared for a record key of the indicated file-name references a data item that is described with the OCCURS clause or is subordinate to an item described with the OCCURS clause. Record keys may not be table items.

E 218: The data-name declared for a record key of the indicated file-name references two or more data items; the qualification is ambiguous.

E 219: The data-name declared for a record key of the indicated file-name is undefined.

E 220: The data-name used in the VARYING DEPENDING ON phrase of the RECORD clause has been defined in an unallowed section. It must be defined in the WORKING-STORAGE SECTION or the LINKAGE SECTION.

E 221: The data-name used in the VARYING DEPENDING ON phrase of the RECORD clause has not been defined to be large enough to hold the number that represents the maximum number of characters needed for the record. The data item description should be changed so that it can contain the value of the maximum record size for the file.

E 222: The data-name referenced in the VARYING DEPENDING ON phrase of the RECORD clause must be defined as an elementary unsigned integer.

E 223: The declaration of the file record size in the RECORD clause does not match the size described by the record description entry or entries given. This includes specification of the RECORD IS VARYING format when only fixed-length records are described.

E 224: There is an error in the data description of the data-name used in the VARYING DEPENDING ON phrase of the RECORD clause.

E 225: The data-name referenced in the VARYING DEPENDING ON phrase of the RECORD clause is not defined as an elementary numeric data item.

E 226: The data-name referenced in the VARYING DEPENDING ON phrase of the RECORD clause cannot be defined with an OCCURS clause or be subordinate to an OCCURS clause.

E 227: The data-name referenced in the VARYING DEPENDING ON phrase of the RECORD clause is defined more than once and is not adequately qualified.

E 228: The data-name referenced in the VARYING DEPENDING ON phrase of the RECORD clause has not been defined.

E 229: The data-name referenced in the VARYING DEPENDING ON phrase of the RECORD clause for the indicated file-name is defined in the LINKAGE SECTION. The data-name is not listed in the PROCEDURE DIVISION USING phrase, nor is it defined subordinate to such a data-name. The data-name should be included as a USING parameter or defined outside the LINKAGE SECTION.

E 230: The maximum file record size allowed is 65,280 characters.

E 231: The data-name declared for the relative key of the indicated file-name references a data item defined in a record associated with file-name.

E 232: The data-name declared for the relative key of the indicated file-name references a data item that is not a numeric integer.

E 233: The data-name declared for the relative key of the indicated file-name references a data item that has been marked invalid by the compiler because of an error in its description.

E 234: The data-name declared for the relative key of the indicated file-name references a nondata item.

E 235: The data-name declared for the relative key of the indicated file-name references a data item that is described with the OCCURS clause or is subordinate to an item described with the OCCURS clause.

E 236: The data-name declared for the relative key of the indicated file-name references two or more data items; the qualification is ambiguous.

E 237: The data-name declared for the relative key of the indicated file-name is undefined.

E 238: The data-name declared for the relative key of the indicated file-name references a linkage data item that is not subordinate to an item in the PROCEDURE DIVISION header USING phrase.

E 239: The data-name declared for the file status data item of the indicated file-name references a data item that is not two characters in length.

E 240: The data-name declared for the file status data item of the indicated file-name references a data item that is not of the category alphanumeric.

E 241: The data-name declared for the file status data item of the indicated file-name references a data item that has been marked invalid by the compiler because of an error in its description.

E 242: The data-name declared for the file status data item of the indicated file-name references a nondata item.

E 243: The data-name declared for the file status data item of the indicated file-name references a data item that is described with the OCCURS clause or is subordinate to an item described with the OCCURS clause. The file status data item may not be a table item.

E 244: The data-name declared for the file status data item of the indicated file-name references two or more data items; the qualification is ambiguous.

E 245: The data-name declared for the file status data item of the indicated file-name references an undefined data item.

E 246: The data-name declared for the file status data item of the indicated file-name references a linkage data item that is not subordinate to an item in the PROCEDURE DIVISION header USING phrase.

E 247: The data-name referenced in the LINES AT TOP phrase of the LINAGE clause for the indicated file does not reference an elementary unsigned numeric data item.

E 248: The data-name referenced in the LINES AT TOP phrase of the LINAGE clause for the indicated file has an error in its data description.

E 249: The data-name referenced in the LINES AT TOP phrase of the LINAGE clause for the indicated file is not a valid data item described in the DATA DIVISION.

E 250: The data-name referenced in the LINES AT TOP phrase of the LINAGE clause for the indicated file cannot be defined with an OCCURS clause.

E 251: The data-name referenced in the LINES AT TOP phrase of the LINAGE clause for the indicated file is defined more than once and is not adequately qualified.

E 252: The data-name in the LINES AT TOP phrase of the LINAGE clause for the indicated file has not been defined. An elementary unsigned numeric data entry in the DATA DIVISION is required.

E 253: The data-name in the LINES AT TOP phrase of the LINAGE clause for the indicated file has been defined in the LINKAGE SECTION. The data-name is not listed in the PROCEDURE DIVISION USING phrase, nor is it defined subordinate to such a data-name. The data-name should be included as a USING parameter or defined outside the LINKAGE SECTION.

E 254: The previous data description entry did not define an elementary data item, but the indicated level-number is less than or equal to the level-number of the previous data description entry.

E 255: The description of an operand that appears in the USING list of the PROCEDURE DIVISION header may not include a REDEFINES clause.

E 256: The USAGE clause indicated contradicts the USAGE clause for the group to which the subject item belongs.

E 257: The VALUE clause indicated is given for a data item that belongs to a group for which a VALUE clause was also specified.

E 258: The indicated character within a hexadecimal literal is not a valid hexadecimal digit. The allowable characters are: 0 through 9, A through F, and a through f.

E 259: The indicated character-string or separator is incorrect syntax in the context of the IDENTIFICATION DIVISION, as given in the source program.

E 260: The indicated identifier references an item that was marked invalid by the compiler because of an error in its description.

E 261: The identifier references two or more items; the qualification is ambiguous.

E 262: The context requires an identifier instead of a literal.

E 263: The identifier is undefined. This includes qualification errors such as incorrect qualifiers.

E 264: The procedure-name illegally refers to a different independent segment.

E 265: The associated conditional variable is an index data item.

E 266: The context does not allow an index data item.

E 267: The context does not allow index-names or index data items.

E 268: The index-name is already defined and cannot be redefined.

E 269: The context does not allow index-names.

E 270: An index-name cannot be used with a table for which it was not defined unless there is an exact match in the number of character positions in both tables.

E 271: The second integer is less than the first integer in the pair of integers indicated.

E 272: The context requires an integer.

E 273: The context requires an unsigned integer.

E 274: The indicated integer has a value too large for the context in which it was used. The maximum integer value in such contexts is 65,535.

E 275: The context requires a nonzero integer.

E 276: The indicated character-string or separator is incorrect syntax in the context of the I-O-CONTROL paragraph as given in the source program.

E 277: The context requires a file-name that references an I-O file; that is, a file-name of a sequential, relative, or indexed organization file not defined as a sort-merge file.

E 278: The context requires a record-name associated with an I-O file; that is, a sequential, relative, or indexed organization file record-name not defined as a sort-merge record.

E 279: The JUSTIFIED clause is given in the data description entry in conflict with other data description clauses specified for the same subject.

E 280: The indicated data-name is not associated with the sort-merge file referenced in this statement. That is, the data-name is not defined as a record of the file, nor is it defined subordinate to a record of the file. Thus, the data-name does not reference data that can be used as a key for the SORT or MERGE operation.

E 281: The indicated sort-merge key data-name is described with the OCCURS clause or is defined subordinate to an item described with the OCCURS clause. That is, the data-name references a table data item and thus cannot be used as a key for the SORT or MERGE operation.

E 282: The indicated sort-merge key data-name references a group that contains a data item described with Format 2 of the OCCURS clause. That is, the data-name references a variable-length data item and thus cannot be used as a key for the SORT or MERGE operation.

E 283: The level-number indicated is not a valid level number. Valid levelnumbers are 01 through 49, 66, 77, and 88.

E 284: A level-number 77 data description entry did not describe an elementary data item. A PICTURE clause or a USAGE IS INDEX clause is required in level number 77 data description entries.

E 285: The indicated item is not a level-number 88 conditional variable condition-name. The format of the SET statement used requires a conditional variable condition-name.

E 286: The ADVANCING mnemonic-name phrase of the WRITE statement cannot be used for a file that is described with a LINAGE clause.

E 287: The ADVANCING TO LINE and END OF PAGE phrases of the WRITE statement are allowed only when the file is described with the LINAGE clause.

E 288: A data-name in the PROCEDURE DIVISION USING header phrase does not reference a data item described with level number 01 or 77.

E 289: A data-name in the PROCEDURE DIVISION USING header phrase does not reference a data item defined in the LINKAGE SECTION of the program.

E 290: An entry in the LINKAGE SECTION of the DATA DIVISION is neither a record description entry (level-number 01) nor a 77-level description entry (level-number 77).

E 291: The context requires a literal.

E 292: There is a syntax error in the MEMORY clause of the OBJECT-COMPUTER paragraph. A memory size type was incorrect or omitted. The allowable types are WORDS, CHARACTERS, or MODULES.

E 293: A file-name is repeated within a MERGE statement.

E 294: Two or more USING files are required for a MERGE statement, but only one is given.

E 295: The mnemonic-name is already defined and cannot be redefined.

E 296: The MOVE statement is invalid because it attempts to move an alphanumeric edited or alphabetic data item to a numeric-edited or numeric data item.

E 297: The MOVE statement is invalid because it attempts to move a noninteger numeric data item to a nonnumeric data item.

E 298: The MOVE statement is invalid because it attempts to move a numeric-edited data item to an alphabetic data item.

E 299: The MOVE statement is invalid because it attempts to move a numeric data item to an alphabetic data item.

E 300: The indicated literal has zero length. For a numeric literal, this means no digit positions are defined. For a nonnumeric literal, this means that there are no characters enclosed in the quotation marks. This error may also result from the presence of an extraneous plus sign, minus sign, or period in the source text.

E 301: The indicated numeric literal defines more than 18 digit positions.

E 302: The indicated level-number is invalid because it is less than or equal to the level-number of an item described with the OCCURS...DEPENDING clause and is not the beginning of a new record description entry.

E 303: The OCCURS...DEPENDING clause is specified subordinate to a data item described with the OCCURS clause.

E 304: The OCCURS...DEPENDING clause is specified for a data item that is described with the REDEFINES clause or is subordinate to an item described with the REDEFINES clause.

E 305: The OCCURS clause is specified for a data item with a level number of 01 or 77.

E 306: The left pseudo-text operand in a BY phrase must not be empty.

E 307: The open mode type specified is unrecognized. The valid open mode types are EXTEND, INPUT, I-O, and OUTPUT.

E 308: The combination of operands specified is invalid because of their data types and the context.

E 309: The indicated integer cannot be negative in the context of the flagged source statement.

E 310: A paragraph and a section must not be given the same name.

E 311: The specified paragraph is defined more than once within the specified section.

E 312: A PERFORM statement is invalid because either the entry or exit procedure-name references a procedure in a declaratives section and the other references a procedure not in the same declaratives section.

E 313: A PERFORM statement in an independent segment is invalid because the entry procedure-name references a procedure in a different independent segment.

E 314: A PERFORM statement is invalid because the entry procedure-name is ambiguous. Qualification is required to yield a unique reference.

E 315: A PERFORM statement is invalid because the entry procedure-name is undefined. This includes qualification errors such as a qualified section-name.

E 316: A PERFORM statement is invalid because its exit procedure-name references a procedure in a different independent segment than the segment containing the entry procedure.

E 317: A PERFORM statement is invalid because the exit procedure-name is ambiguous. Qualification is required to yield a unique reference.

E 318: A PERFORM statement is invalid because the exit procedure-name is undefined. This includes qualification errors such as a qualified section-name.

E 319: The context requires a period space separator at the indicated point in the source program.

E 320: The BLANK WHEN ZERO clause is used to describe a data item that specifies asterisk zero suppression or a sign(s) in its PICTURE character-string.

E 321: The indicated character in the PICTURE character-string is not a valid PICTURE character.

E 322: The PICTURE clause is used to describe an index data item (USAGE IS INDEX).

E 323: The PICTURE character string contains a "C" not followed by "R."

E 324: The number of character positions described by the PICTURE character string for a single data item cannot exceed 65,280 character positions.

E 325: The PICTURE character string contains a "D" not followed by "B."

E 326: The nearest preceding pseudo-text delimiter was an opening pseudo-text delimiter for which no closing pseudo-text delimiter has been found.

E 327: A character must not appear more than once in a CONVERTING literal.

E 328: The PICTURE character string contains a fixed insertion currency symbol that is not the leftmost character in the character string.

E 329: The PICTURE character string contains a fixed insertion sign character that is not the leftmost or rightmost character in the character string.

E 330: The PICTURE character string contains illegal combinations of scaling characters (P, decimal-point, V) such that the decimal point position is defined in more than one place.

E 331: The PICTURE character string was nonnumeric until the indicated character was found, which is invalid for a nonnumeric PICTURE character string.

E 332: The PICTURE character string defines a numeric or numeric-edited data item with more than 18 digit positions.

E 333: The indicated character in a numeric or numeric-edited PICTURE character string violates the precedence rules.

E 334: The PICTURE character string defines a numeric or numeric-edited data item without any digit positions.

E 335: The PICTURE character string defines digit positions both to the left and right of P characters.

E 336: The indicated character in the PICTURE character string is repeated when it must occur as a single character.

E 337: The indicated character in the PICTURE character string is not allowed in a signed numeric data item (that is, a character string starting with S).

E 338: The PICTURE character string describes a data item that conflicts with the USAGE declared for the data item (for example, nonnumeric picture with COMP usage).

E 339: The nondeclarative portion of the PROCEDURE DIVISION must be sectioned when declaratives are defined.

E 340: The indicated procedure reference is ambiguous and requires qualification to yield a unique procedure reference.

E 341: The indicated Format 1 GO TO statement does not occur in a single statement paragraph (alterable paragraph) and therefore must be followed by a procedure-name. This error may indicate that the procedure-name specified is a reserved word.

E 342: The indicated procedure reference is not defined. This includes qualification errors such as a qualified section-name.

E 343: The alphabet-name referenced in the PROGRAM COLLATING SEQUENCE clause specifies a duplicate character.

E 344: The program defined data in excess of 4 gigabytes.

E 345: The program required object instructions—generated for PROCEDURE DIVISION statements —that were in excess of 16 megabytes for a single segment. Approximately 10 bytes are generated per source statement.

E 346: The program-name specified in the END PROGRAM header does not match the program-name specified in the PROGRAM-ID paragraph of the IDENTIFICATION DIVISION.

E 347: Use of a data item described with the scaling position character P in its PICTURE characterstring is not allowed in the context of the indicated statement in the source program.

E 348: A section-name is qualified in the source program. Section-names must be unique in the set of procedure-names for a given source program and cannot be qualified.

E 349: The context does not allow a file defined with RANDOM access mode. The indicated file-name must be described with SEQUENTIAL or DYNAMIC access mode.

E 350: The context requires a file assigned to a mass-storage unit-name, which is RANDOM, DISK, or DISC.

E 351: The KEY phrase is illegal on the READ statement because the file has sequential access or the NEXT phrase is specified for the same READ statement.

E 352: The level-number of a record entry is not 01.

E 353: The context requires a record entry description at the indicated point in the source program.

E 354: More than 255 record keys are defined for a file.

E 355: The RECORD KEY clause is given for a file that is not indexed organization.

E 356: Context requires a data-name that is a record key of the associated file-name or, for a START statement, a data-name that references a data item whose leftmost character position is the same as the leftmost character position of a record key of the associated file-name.

E 357: An indexed organization file must be described with the RECORD KEY clause; a prime record key is required.

E 358: The REDEFINES clause may not be used in level number 01 entries of the FILE SECTION, LINKAGE SECTION or COMMUNICATION SECTION.

E 359: The data-name referenced in a REDEFINES clause is invalid because it is not that of the last allocated data item, nor the data-name of the last redefinition at the same level.

E 360: The data item to be redefined cannot be described in an OCCURS clause.

E 361: The indicated data-name defines an area of storage larger than the area it is redefining and is not described with level-number 01.

E 362: The VALUE clause is used to describe a data item that is also described with the REDEFINES clause or that is subordinate to a data item described with the REDEFINES clause.

E 363: A data item that is variable length as a result of Format 2 of the OCCURS clause cannot be redefined.

E 364: The relation indicated must reference data items with DISPLAY usage because a numeric data item is being compared to a nonnumeric data item.

E 365: The numeric data item in the indicated relation must be an integer data item because it is being compared to a nonnumeric data item.

E 366: The context does not allow the indicated relation.

E 367: The conditional expression is syntactically incorrect because a conditional expression was found where an arithmetic expression, nonnumeric data item or nonnumeric literal was required as the object of a preceding relation operator.

E 368: The context requires a relation operator.

E 369: The conditional expression is syntactically incorrect because a relation condition with no subject was specified and the relation is not a valid abbreviated relation condition.

E 370: The RELATIVE KEY phrase is specified for a file that does not have relative organization.

E 371: A relative organization file with random or dynamic access must be described with the RELATIVE KEY phrase. Also, if a relative file is referenced by a START statement, the RELATIVE KEY phrase must be specified for that file.

E 372: The object data-name of a RENAMES clause is described with level number 01, 66, or 77.

E 373: The object data-name of a RENAMES clause is described with the OCCURS clause or is subordinate to a data item described with the OCCURS clause.

E 374: The beginning of the area described by data-name-3 begins to the left of the area described by data-name-2 in a RENAMES data-name-2 THRU data-name-3 clause.

E 375: The end of the area described by data-name-3 is not to the right of the area described by data-name-2 in a RENAMES data-name-2 THRU data-name-3 clause.

E 376: The object data-name of a RENAMES clause is described such that it is variable length as defined in the OCCURS clause.

E 377: A RERUN statement has been repeated for the same file.

E 378: An ON phrase is needed in the RERUN clause when either an END OF REEL or END OF UNIT phrase is used and the file-name associated with the END OF REEL or END OF UNIT is not an output file, or when the condition-name format of the RERUN clause is used.

E 379: The ON phrase with the rerun-name option must be specified if either the RECORDS or CLOCK-UNITS phrase is used.

E 380: The indicated item is incorrect syntax in the context of the RERUN clause of the I-O-CONTROL paragraph as used in the source program.

E 381: The integer given in the RESERVE AREAS clause specifies that more than 255 input-output areas be reserved.

E 382: The indicated computer-name is a reserved word; a user-defined word must be given for the computer-name.

E 383: The indicated text-name is a reserved word; a user-defined word must be given for the text-name.

E 384: Context requires a user-defined word at the indicated position in the source program, but a reserved word was found.

E 385: The PICTURE character string contains a repeat count that is not properly terminated with a right parenthesis. The right parenthesis is missing, possibly because it is within the identification area (columns 73-80) of the source record or because text follows the integer specifying the count.

E 386: The indicated file-name appears more than once in a SAME AREA clause.

E 387: The indicated file-name appears in a SAME AREA clause with another file-name that appears in a SAME RECORD AREA clause. The indicated file-name does not appear in the SAME RECORD AREA clause.

E 388: The indicated file-name appears in a SAME AREA clause with another file-name that appears in a SAME SORT AREA clause. The indicated file-name does not appear in the SAME SORT AREA clause.

E 389: The indicated file-name references a sort-merge file and is therefore illegal in a SAME AREA clause.

E 390: The indicated file-name appears more than once in a SAME RECORD AREA clause.

E 391: The indicated file-name is a sort-merge file that appears more than once in a SAME SORT AREA clause.

E 392: The indicated SAME SORT AREA clause does not contain a sort-merge file-name.

E 393: The indicated item is incorrect syntax in the context of the sort-merge file description entry as used in the source program.

E 394: A section definition is illegal because the PROCEDURE DIVISION did not begin with a section. The section definition is accepted.

E 395: The indicated user-defined word is already defined as a section-name or a paragraph-name and therefore cannot be defined as a new section-name.

E 396: Context requires a section-name. A paragraph-name may not be used as a qualifier.

E 397: The SEGMENT-LIMIT clause has been defined more than once.

E 398: The segment-number in the SEGMENT-LIMIT clause must be within the range of 1-49.

E 399: The indicated segment-number is larger than the limit of 127. The last valid segment-number is used instead.

E 400: The context requires a sequential access file. A sequential organization file must be described implicitly or explicitly as having sequential access.

E 401: The context does not allow a sequential organization file.

E 402: The context requires a sequential organization file.

E 403: The SIGN clause is given in conflict with other data description entries.

E 404: The SIGN clause specifies an unrecognized type. The valid types are LEADING and TRAILING.

E 405: The context requires a file-name that references a sort-merge file.

E 406: The context requires a record-name associated with a sort-merge file.

E 407: The file-name following an SD level-indicator must reference a sequential organization file.

E 408: The clauses in the SPECIAL-NAMES paragraph are not listed in the order shown in the paragraph skeleton. The required order is switch-name, ALPHABET, SYMBOLIC CHARACTERS, CLASS, CURRENCY SIGN, and DECIMAL-POINT. Clauses not needed may be omitted.

E 409: The indicated character string or separator is incorrect syntax in the context of the SPECIAL-NAMES paragraph.

E 410: The context does not allow a special-name such as a mnemonic-name or alphabet-name as given.

E 411: The data-name given in the START statement relation for an indexed organization file does not reference a data item that is subordinate to its associated record key.

E 412: The data-name given in the START statement relation for an indexed organization file does not reference a data item with an allowed data type. The data item must be described as category alphanumeric or as an unsigned numeric data item with DISPLAY usage.

E 413: The data-name given in the START statement relation for a relative organization file is not the relative key data-name.

E 414: The indicated statement is incorrect syntax in the context of PROCEDURE DIVISION verbs as given in the source program.

E 415: The context does not allow a subscripted reference. The data item to be referenced at this point must not be described with the OCCURS clause or be subordinate to an item described with the OCCURS clause.

E 416: A data-name specified as a subscript is described with the OCCURS clause or is subordinate to a data item described with the OCCURS clause.

E 417: The syntax of the subscripting for the identifier is incorrect. Either too many subscripts are specified or the right parenthesis is missing, possibly because it is in the identification area (columns 73-80).

E 418: The indicated data-name must be subscripted to provide a unique reference.

E 419: Too few subscripts were specified for the identifier. The data-name portion of the identifier references a table element which, in order to specify a unique reference, requires more subscripts than were specified.

E 420: The indicated literal subscript is greater than the maximum number of table elements that are defined in the OCCURS clause for the referenced table. A relative subscript literal is limited to one less than the number of elements.

E 421: The indicated context requires a switch condition-name, but a user word for some other entity was specified, such as a data-name, file-name or alphabet-name.

E 422: The indicated context requires a switch condition-name, but an undefined user word was specified.

E 423: The indicated mnemonic-name is not associated with an external switch as required by the context in which it appears. SWITCH-1 through SWITCH-8 or the synonyms UPSI-0 through UPSI-7 may be specified in the SPECIAL-NAMES paragraph to associate a mnemonic-name with an external switch.

E 424: Two ON STATUS or OFF STATUS condition-names are defined in the same SPECIAL-NAMES clause for a switch implementor-name. The language syntax requires an ON/OFF or OFF/ON pair or a single ON or OFF status declaration.

E 425: At least one ON or OFF STATUS condition-name must be associated with a switch-name.

E 426: A user-defined word must begin with a letter or digit.

E 427: A data-name must contain at least one letter character.

E 428: The integer specified in the SYMBOLIC CHARACTERS clause of the SPECIAL-NAMES paragraph represents the ordinal position of the character in the native character set or of the character set in the referenced alphabet-name. Valid integer values for the native character set are 1 through 256. Valid integer values for an alphabet-name are dependent on the number of characters included in the description.

E 429: The user-defined word in the indicated SYMBOLIC CHARACTERS clause has been previously defined and cannot be used again.

E 430: A symbolic-character name is required following the indicated figurative constant ALL.

E 431: The indicated name following the figurative constant ALL is presumed to be a user-defined symbolic name, but is not defined in a SYMBOLIC CHARACTERS clause.

E 432: The SYNCHRONIZED clause was specified in conflict with other data description clauses specified in the same entry.

E 433: An index was not defined for a data item with an OCCURS clause in a multidimensional table. When referencing a table in a SEARCH statement, an index must be defined for each data item with an OCCURS clause.

E 434: The data-name for the DEPENDING ON phrase of the OCCURS clause cannot be in the variable-length portion of the table. This may occur with implicit redefinition of the table item.

E 435: The data-name specified in the DEPENDING ON phrase of the OCCURS clause for the indicated table does not reference a data item described as a numeric integer.

E 436: The data-name specified in the DEPENDING ON phrase of the OCCURS clause for the indicated table references a data item that was marked as invalid by the compiler because of an error in its description.

E 437: The data-name specified in the DEPENDING ON phrase of the OCCURS clause for the indicated table references a nondata item.

E 438: The data-name specified in the DEPENDING ON phrase of the OCCURS clause for the indicated table references a data item described with the OCCURS clause or that is subordinate to a data item described with the OCCURS clause.

E 439: The data-name specified in the DEPENDING ON phrase of the OCCURS clause for the indicated table references two or more data items; the qualification is ambiguous.

E 440: The data-name specified in the DEPENDING ON phrase of the OCCURS clause for the indicated table is undefined.

E 441: The data-name for the DEPENDING ON phrase of the OCCURS clause is defined in the LINKAGE SECTION. The data-name is not listed in the PROCEDURE DIVISION USING phrase, nor is it defined subordinate to such a data-name. The data-name should be included as a USING parameter or defined outside the LINKAGE SECTION.

E 442: The maximum table element size has been exceeded. Up to 65,280 characters may be defined.

E 443: Too many AND phrases in the SEARCH ALL statement have been declared for the specified table.

E 444: The indicated table key data-name is not associated with the data entry containing the OCCURS clause or is not subordinate to the entry containing the OCCURS clause.

E 445: The data items to be compared in the SEARCH ALL statement are not given in the same order as they appear in the OCCURS clause of the referenced table, or an item that is not a key of the table has been listed.

E 446: The data-name in the KEY IS phrase of the OCCURS clause has an error in its data description.

E 447: The data-name referenced in the KEY IS phrase of the OCCURS clause is not a valid data item described in the DATA DIVISION.

E 448: The data-name referenced in the KEY IS phrase of the OCCURS clause is defined such that it requires a different number of subscripts than the table defined by the OCCURS clause.

E 449: The data-name referenced in the KEY IS phrase of the OCCURS clause is defined more than once and is not adequately qualified.

E 450: The data-name referenced in the KEY IS phrase of the OCCURS clause has not been defined.

E 451: The indicated identifier in the SEARCH or SEARCH ALL statement does not reference a table. The data item to be searched must be defined with an OCCURS clause.

E 452: The table referenced in the SEARCH or SEARCH ALL statement does not contain an INDEXED BY phrase in the OCCURS clause.

E 453: The table referenced in the SEARCH ALL statement does not have a KEY IS phrase.

E 454: In the COPY statement, a reserved word was used to specify the library-name.

E 455: An illegal character was found in the library-name of the COPY statement.

E 456: The text-name in a COPY statement contains an illegal character.

E 457: The indicated literal must be specified as an unsigned integer.

E 458: An unrecognized usage type is given. The valid usage types are BINARY, COMP, COMPUTATIONAL, COMPUTATIONAL-1, COMPUTATIONAL-3, COMPUTATIONAL-4, COMPUTATIONAL-6, COMP-1, COMP-3, COMP-4, COMP-6, DISPLAY, INDEX, and PACKED-DECIMAL.

E 459: The maximum number of operands in the USING phrase of the PROCEDURE DIVISION header has been exceeded. No more than 255 data-names may be specified.

E 460: A data-name appears more than once in the USING phrase of the PROCEDURE DIVISION header.

E 461: The VALUE clause is specified in conflict with other data description clauses specified in the same entry.

E 462: The numeric literal specified in the VALUE clause for a numeric data item is incorrect for initialization of the data item as described by its PICTURE character-string because truncation of nonzero high-order digits was required.

E 463: The nonnumeric literal specified in the VALUE clause for a nonnumeric data item contains too many characters for initialization of the data item. Characters were truncated from the low-order (rightmost) end of the literal value.

E 464: The fixed-size portion of a group that has a variable-length table subordinate to it cannot be defined to be larger than 65,280 character positions.

E 465: The context requires a verb at the indicated position in the source program.

E 466: An entry in the WORKING-STORAGE SECTION of the DATA DIVISION is neither a record description entry (level number 01) nor a 77-level description entry (level number 77).

E 467: The indicated reference to a table key data-name or condition-name is not subscripted with the first or only index-name of the table referenced by the SEARCH ALL statement. Since only the first index-name of the table will be varied by the execution of the SEARCH ALL statement, the desired results cannot be obtained unless the subscripting is changed to include the first index-name of the table.

E 468: The indicated character-string or separator is syntactically incorrect in the context of the paragraph in which it is specified.

E 469: The indicated scope terminator does not match a previously unmatched verb. For example, an ELSE is specified that is not paired with a previously un-paired IF. This error frequently occurs as a result of previous errors that caused the verb with which the scope terminator was meant to be paired to be either ignored by the compiler or already implicitly terminated by another scope terminator.

E 470: The indicated data description entry must include a data-name since it is a record of a file described with either or both the GLOBAL and EXTERNAL clauses. FILLER or omissions of the data-name are not allowed in level number 01 record description entries for these files.

E 471: The indicated subscripting is prohibited in the context in which it occurs. Although the item referenced is a table element and normally requires subscripting, the subscripting is prohibited in this context.

E 472: The indicated PROCEDURE DIVISION paragraph has caused the generation of more than 32,512 bytes of object code. The paragraph must be divided into two or more paragraphs by insertion of paragraph-names in the source program.

E 473: The indicated sentence has caused the generation of more than 32,512 bytes of object code. The sentence must be divided into two or more sentences by insertion of the period space separator or by replacing a portion of the sentence with a PERFORM statement that references a paragraph or section containing the replaced statements.

E 474: The DELIMITER IN and COUNT IN phrases are not allowed when the DELIMITED BY phrase is not specified in an UNSTRING statement.

E 475: The indicated name does not reference a mnemonic-name defined in the SPECIAL-NAMES paragraph as being associated with a unit-name (for example, CONSOLE). The context requires a mnemonic-name associated with a unit-name: the mnemonic-name in the indicated context may not be associated with a switch-name or with a channel-name.

E 476: The indicated identifier references an edited data item in a context that does not allow edited data items.

E 477: Two or more files referenced in a MERGE statement are listed in the same MULTIPLE FILE TAPE clause in the I-O-CONTROL paragraph.

E 478: Two or more files referenced in a MERGE statement are listed in the same SAME AREA or SAME RECORD AREA clause in the I-O-CONTROL paragraph.

E 479: A data-name listed in a KEY phrase of a SORT or MERGE statement references a data item that is not totally contained within the minimum record length of the sort-merge file.

E 480: The minimum record length of a USING file is less than the minimum record length of a sort-merge file with variable-length records or the minimum record length of the sort-merge file is less than the minimum record length of a GIVING file with variable-length records.

E 481: The PADDING CHARACTER clause may be specified only for sequential files.

E 482: The RECORD DELIMITER clause may be specified only for sequential files.

E 483: The context suggests that a class-name is intended at the indicated position, but the specified identifier is not a class-name.

E 484: There is an error in the declaration of the specified class-name.

E 485: An I-O cd-name must be referenced in the context of the statement as given in the source program. An I-O cd-name is required with the DISABLE I-O and ENABLE I-O statements.

E 486: The data-name declared in the PADDING CHARACTER clause for the indicated file-name must refer to a data item of category alphanumeric.

E 487: The data-name declared in the PADDING CHARACTER clause for the indicated file-name references a data item which has been marked invalid by the compiler because of an error in its description.

E 488: The data-name declared in the PADDING CHARACTER clause for the indicated file-name references a nondata item.

E 489: The data-name declared in the PADDING CHARACTER clause for the indicated file-name references a data item that is described with the OCCURS clause or is subordinate to an item described with the OCCURS clause. The padding character data item may not be a table item.

E 490: The data-name declared in the PADDING CHARACTER clause for the indicated file-name references two or more data items; the qualification is ambiguous.

E 491: The data-name declared in the PADDING CHARACTER clause for the indicated file-name references an undefined data item.

E 492: The data-name declared in the PADDING CHARAC-TER clause for the indicated file-name references a linkage data item that is not subordinate to an item in the PROCEDURE DIVISION header USING phrase.

E 493: When a selection object is specified by a condition or by the words TRUE or FALSE, the corresponding selection subject must also be a condition or either of the words TRUE or FALSE; it may not be an identifier, a literal or an arithmetic expression. When a selection object is an identifier, literal, or arithmetic expression, the corresponding selection subject must also be an identifier, literal, or arithmetic expression.

E 494: The two operands connected by a THROUGH phrase must be of the same class: numeric, alphanumeric or alphabetic.

E 495: The REPLACING phrase of an INITIALIZE statement specifies the same category more than once.

E 496: A primary operand of the INITIALIZE statement must not have been defined with a RENAMES clause.

E 497: A primary operand of an INITIALIZE statement must not have been defined with an OCCURS clause having a DEPENDING ON phrase, nor may it have an item so described subordinate to itself.

E 498: The context does not allow the use of a negative numeric literal.

E 499: The context does not allow the use of a reference modification specification.

E 500: The value of the indicated numeric literal is too large for its use in a reference modification specification. The offset and length values may not exceed the length of the data item being reference modified. If both the offset and length are specified as literals, their sum less 1 may not exceed the length of the data item being reference modified.

E 501: The indicated language feature is incompatible with the requested runtime support revision level.

E 502: A colon separator is required following the left operand of a reference modification specification.

E 504: The indicated clause may not be specified in the current data description entry since either the description does not specify a data-name (that is, is implicitly or explicitly FILLER) or the data-name is the same as another data-name described with the same clause.

E 505: The indicated clause clashes with the level-number of the data description entry in which it is specified. An EXTERNAL or GLOBAL clause may not be specified in a data description entry if the level-number is other than 01. An EXTERNAL clause may be specified in the FILE SECTION only in a file description (FD) entry. An OCCURS clause may be specified in a data description entry only when the level-number is 02 through 49.

E 506: The indicated clause may not be specified in a file description entry for a file that is listed in any Multiple FILE TAPE clause in the I-O-CONTROL paragraph.

E 507: The indicated clause may not be specified for the current file description entry or record description entry for a file since the file is listed in the SAME clause in the I-O-CONTROL paragraph. For the EXTERNAL clause, the file may not be listed in any SAME AREA, SAME RECORD AREA, or SAME SORT AREA clause. For the GLOBAL clause, the file may not be listed in any SAME RECORD AREA clause.

E 508: The indicated clause may not be specified in the current section of the DATA DIVISION.

E 509: The EXTERNAL clause is specified with the REDE-FINES clause. These clauses are mutually exclusive within a single data description entry.

E 510: The EXTERNAL clause is specified with the VALUE clause or the VALUE clause is specified in a data description entry subordinate to the EXTERNAL clause. Data items with the external attribute must not be described with the VALUE clause.

E 511: The indicated syntax is allowed only within a nested program, and the current program is not contained within another program.

E 512: The AT keyword in a Format 5 ACCEPT statement or a Format 3 DISPLAY statement is not followed by LINE, COLUMN, or COL.

E 513: The relation between the current level number and the preceding level number implies that the preceding item is a group, but the preceding item description includes attributes allowed only at the elementary level.

E 519: The data name specified in the COLUMN clause of the indicated SCREEN SECTION data item is defined in the LINKAGE SECTION. The data-name is not listed in the PROCEDURE DIVISION USING phrase, nor is it defined subordinate to such a data-name.

E 520: A SCREEN SECTION attribute has been specified more than once.

E 526: The data-name specified in the LINE clause of the indicated SCREEN SECTION data item is defined in the LINKAGE SECTION. The data-name is not listed in the PROCEDURE DIVISION USING phrase, nor is it defined subordinate to such a data-name.

E 527: If the first primary operand of a DISPLAY statement is a screen-name, all subsequent primary operands of that DISPLAY statement must also be screen-names.

E 533: The data-name specified as a subscript in the description of the indicated SCREEN SECTION data item is defined in the LINKAGE SECTION. The data-name is not listed in the PROCEDURE DIVISION USING phrase, nor is it defined subordinate to such a data-name.

E 534: In the SCREEN SECTION, the PICTURE character string in a PICTURE clause must be followed by a TO, FROM, or USING phrase.

E 535: In the SCREEN SECTION, an item description cannot contain both a PICTURE and a VALUE clause.

E 541: The data-name specified as a source item (FROM or USING) in the description of the indicated SCREEN SECTION data item is defined in the LINKAGE SECTION. The data-name is not listed in the PROCEDURE DIVISION USING phrase, nor is it defined subordinate to such a data-name.

E 547: The data-name specified as a target item (TO or USING) in the description of the indicated SCREEN SECTION data-item is defined in the LINKAGE SECTION. The data-name is not listed in the PROCEDURE DIVISION USING phrase, nor is it defined subordinate to such a data-name.

E 548: An entry in the SCREEN SECTION of the DATA DIVISION is neither a record description entry (level number 01) nor a 77-level description entry (level number 77).

E 669: The context requires a specific reserved word or one of a specific set of words. The required word or one of the set of words is given in quotation marks following the message text.

RUNTIME MESSAGES

This appendix presents the messages that can be generated during program execution: this includes those generated following normal termination, as well as those generated when an error occurs. There are ten types of messages, as highlighted in the following paragraphs.

Data Reference, Input-Output, Procedure, Sort-Merge, Configuration, Initialization, and *Message Control* errors have error numbers along with the error messages (detailed below) to help pinpoint the error being diagnosed.

A *Traceback* traces back through one or more calling programs when an error occurs within a called subprogram; the traceback traces the path from the statement causing the error through all subroutines currently active in the run unit.

An *Internal* error indicates that an inconsistency not normally caused by a flaw in the source program has been detected. The numbers within the error message are needed by your RM/COBOL-85 representative should an internal error occur.

An *Operator Requested Termination* error occurs when the operator terminates execution by pressing the CTRL and BREAK keys.

Error Message Format

The different types of messages use the same general format:

**COBOL [type] error [code] at line [number] in [prog-id]
compiled [date] [time]**

- *Type* is one of the following types of messages:

    data reference

    procedure

    input-output

    internal

    raceback

    operator requested termination

    sort-merge

    message control

    configuration

    initialization

- *Code* is the first two digits of the error numbers listed in this section.

- *Number* identifies a particular line in the PROCEDURE DIVISION of the source program. It is the line in which the statement being referred to starts, and it can be looked up in the leftmost column (labeled LINE) of the source listing produced by the compiler. If a question mark appears in this position, the following prog-id field refers to a machine language subprogram or indicates that a valid line number has not been established following an Interactive Debug Resume (R) Command.

- *Prog-id* identifies the program interrupted in order to produce this message. It has the following format:

    program-name (pathname.ext)

- *Program-name* is taken from the PROGRAM-ID paragraph of the source program.

- *Pathname.ext* is the fully qualified DOS pathname of the object library in which the object program resides.

- *Date and time* are the date and time the program was compiled; they correspond exactly to the date and time printed on the program listing.

NOTES

1. Traceback and Operator Requested Termination messages do not include the "error [code]" portion of this message.

2. The format of Configuration and Initialization errors do not precisely conform to the format shown previously. See "Configuration Errors" on page of this appendix.

Data Reference Errors

Data reference errors include invalid data types, improper data definitions, improper data values, and illegal subscripting.

101 There is a reference to a LINKAGE SECTION data item for which no corresponding operand exists for one of the following reasons:

    a. There are more data items specified in the PROCEDURE DIVISION header than are specified in the USING phrase of the CALL statement in the calling program.

    b. The PROCEDURE DIVISION header in the first (or main) program in the run unit specifies more than one data item.

102 There is a range error on a variable-length group reference.

103 An identifier or literal referenced in an INSPECT CONVERTING statement is illegal for one of the following reasons:

    a. The source translation template (identifier-6 or literal-4) contains multiple occurrences of the same value.

    b. The source translation template (identifier-6 or literal-4) does not have the same length as the destination translation template (identifier-7 or literal-5).

    c. The destination translation template (literal-5) is figurative and its length is not one.

104 A reference to a data item is illegal for one of the following reasons:

    a. The computed composite subscript value for a subscripted reference has a value that is negative, zero, or exceeds the maximum value for the referenced item.

    b. There is a reference to a LINKAGE SECTION data item whose description specifies more characters than are present in the corresponding operand in the USING phrase of the CALL statement.

    c. There is a reference to a LINKAGE SECTION data item in the first (or main) program in the run unit whose description specifies more characters than are supplied by the A Runtime Command Option.

105 A subscript calculation overflowed or underflowed.

106 An index-name value indicates more than 65,535 occurrences.

107 A reference modification is illegal for one of the following reasons:

    a. A reference modification offset value is less than or equal to zero, or is greater than the length of the data item being reference modified.

    b. A reference modification length value is less than or equal to zero or is greater than the remaining length of the data item being reference modified after application of the offset value.

Procedure Errors

Procedure errors include improper program structure or invalid calls.

201 A CANCEL statement has attempted to cancel a program that is still active; that is, a program that has called, directly or indirectly, the program attempting the cancel.

202 The program-name on a CALL statement has a value that is equal to spaces.

203 The program-name on the Runtime Command or CALL statement does not match any of the PROGRAM-ID names in any library, but does match a valid RM/COBOL-85 library object file name. The call-by-file name technique is valid only for single-program object files.

204 The program-name on the Runtime Command or CALL statement does not match any of the PROGRAM-ID names in any library and does not match a valid RM/COBOL-85 object file name or machine language (.EXE) file. Note that an object program with a higher object version number than the runtime version number is not considered a valid program. (For more information, refer to the *RM/COBOL—85 Installation and User's Guide.*)

205 A CALL statement has attempted to call a program that is still active; that is, a program that has called, directly or indirectly, the program attempting the call in error.

206 The called program is not RM/COBOL-85 or valid nonCOBOL.

207 There is not enough memory to load the program from the Runtime Command or the CALL statement, or to build the in-memory library structures indicated in the Runtime Command, or to reserve memory for the accept and display buffers. This may be caused by memory fragmentation resulting from the dynamics of CALL and CANCEL operations and file I-O, or it may mean the requested program is too large for the available memory. (For more information, refer to the *RM/COBOL—85 Installation and User's Guide.*)

208 The ALTER statement has an undefined section or paragraph-name.

209 The "GO TO." statement was not altered before execution of the statement was attempted.

210 The PERFORM statement attempts to perform an undefined section or paragraph.

211 An "E" level compilation error has been encountered.

213 The RM/COBOL-85 object library file specified in the Runtime Command cannot be found.

214 The RM/COBOL-85 object library file specified in the Runtime Command does not contain a valid object program.

215 A PERFORM statement in an independent segment has performed a section or paragraph in a fixed segment that performed a section or paragraph in a different independent segment.

216 An external item with the same name and type (data record, file connector or index name) as an existing external in the run unity has a different description than the existing external.

For an external data record, the length of the record is different.

For an index-name, the span of the table item associated with the index name is different, or the index-name is associated with a different external record. For a file connector, any of the file control clauses, file description clauses or record description lengths are different. For a relative organization external file connector, this error is caused if the new external does not reference the same external data item for the relative key as is referenced by the existing external file connector.

218 There is not enough memory to allocate the data structures necessary to support an external item declared in the program currently being loaded.

219 There is not enough memory to allocate the data structures necessary to support entry into USE GLOBAL procedure following the occurrence of an I-O error for which the USE GLOBAL procedure is applicable. The program will be terminated as if no applicable USE procedure were found.

Input/Output Errors

Input/output errors include all errors that can occur during file access. The format is

**COBOL I-O error [number] on [COBOL-filename]
file
[external-file-name]**

The list presented below shows the values that can appear as numbers in the I-O error messages, and a description of each error. The list is presented in numerical order. The I-O error number has the form:

mm[,nn]

- *mm* is a two-digit decimal number indicating the general class of error that occurred. It is also the value stored into the file status data item if such an item has been specified for the associated file. Thus, this value is available to the program.

- *nn* is a two-digit code that provides more specific information on the nature of the error.

00   The operation was successful.

02   The operation was successful and a duplicate key was detected.

04, 05   The record read from the file is shorter than the minimum record length.

04, 06   The record read from the file is longer than the record area.

05   The OPEN operation was successful and the option file was not present. If the open mode is I-O or EXTEND, the file has been created.

07   The operation was successful. If the operation was a CLOSE statement with a NO REWIND, REEL, UNIT or FOR REMOVAL clause, or if the operation was an OPEN statement with the NO REWIND clause, the referenced file is not on a unit/reel medium.

10   An attempt was made to read past the end of file.

14   A sequential READ statement was attempted for a relative file and the number of significant digits in the relative record number is larger than the size of the relative key data item.

21   Invalid prime key sequence.

22   The new record value attempts to duplicate an indexed file key that prohibits duplicates, or a relative record number that already exists.

23   The specified record does not exist.

24   There is insufficient disk space for the operation.

24, 01   A sequential WRITE statement was attempted for a relative file and the number of significant digits in

the relative record number is larger than the size of the relative key data item.

30, nn   I-O error *nn* occurred, where *nn* may depend on the device or machine on which the file resides. In general, this is the decimal error number from a DOS function call. See the DOS Reference Manual for detailed information on these errors.

On DOS 2.*n* systems, displayed error codes 19-31 correspond to INT 24H error codes 0-12.

A PROCEDURE DIVISION statement that explicitly or implicitly causes an overlay to be loaded may receive this error if the RM/COBOL-85 object file cannot be read when the statement is executed.

34   There is insufficient disk space for the operation.

35   The file is not available because the external file name could not be found. The DOS path or file may not exist or the name may be misspelled. Specifying a pathname or file name that is not a valid DOS name or that is longer than DOS allows also results in this error.

37, 01   The file must be mass storage. The unit-name specified for the file was DISC, DISK, or RANDOM, but the external file name identifies a non-disk or file.

37, 07   The open operation is invalid on a read-only file. An open mode of OUTPUT, EXTEND, or I-O was attempted on a read-only file.

38   The file name could not be opened because it was previously closed WITH LOCK.

39, 01   The file organization specified for the file name does not match the actual file organization of the external file.

39, 02   The minimum record length specified in the RECORD CONTAINS clause or implied by the record descriptions of the file name does not match the actual minimum record length of the external file.

39, 03   The maximum record length specified in the RECORD CONTAINS clause or implied by the record descriptions of the file name does not match the actual maximum record length of the external file.

39, 04   The minimum block length specified in the BLOCK CONTAINS clause for the file name does not match the actual minimum block size of the external file.

39, 05   The maximum block length specified in the BLOCK CONTAINS clause for the file name does not match the actual maximum block size of the external file.

39, 06   The record delimiting technique, LINE or BINARY SEQUENTIAL, specified for the file name does not match the actual record delimiting technique of the external file. (1985 mode)

39, 07 The CODE-SET specified for the file name does not match the actual character code of the external file.

39, 08 The COLLATING SEQUENCE specified for the indexed file does not match the actual collating sequence of the external file.

39, 09 The record type attribute, fixed or variable, specified in the RECORD CONTAINS clause or implied by the record descriptions of the file name does not match the record type attribute of the external file.

39, 30 through **39, 3E**
Mismatched key duplicates allowed flag for keys 0 through 14. The key duplicates allowed flag specified for the indicated key does not match the corresponding key duplicates allowed flag of the external file. The prime record key is 0; alternate record keys are numbered in ascending order of key offset, starting with 1.

39, 3F Mismatched key duplicates allowed flag for key 15 or greater. The key duplicates allowed flag specified for an alternate record key 15 through 254 does not match the corresponding key duplicates allowed flag of the external file.

39, 40 through **39, 4E**
Mismatched key offset for keys 0 through 14. The offset from the start of the record area to the start of the key area for the indicated key does not match the corresponding key offset of the external file. The prime record key is 0; alternate record keys are numbered in ascending order of key offset, starting with 1.

39, 4F Mismatched key offset for key 15 or greater. The offset from the start of the record area to the start of the key area for an alternate key 15 through 254 does not match the corresponding key offset of the external file.

39, 50 through **39, 5E**
Mismatched key length for keys 0 through 14. The length of the key area for the indicated key does not match the corresponding key length of the external file. The prime record key is key 0; alternate record keys are numbered in ascending order of key offset, starting with 1.

39, 5F Mismatched key length for key 15 or greater. The length of the key area for an alternate key 15 through 254 does not match the corresponding key offset of the external file.

This error will also occur if the number of keys specified does not match the actual number of keys in the external file.

41, 01 A duplicate open was rejected by a system that does not allow the external file to be opened twice.

41, 02 A duplicate open was rejected by a system that does not allow the physical file to be opened twice.

42 A CLOSE operation was attempted on an unopened file.

43 A DELETE or REWRITE operation was attempted on a file declared to be ACCESS MODE SEQUENTIAL, and the last operation on the file was not a successful READ operation.

44, 03 The length of the record area specified in the WRITE, REWRITE, or RELEASE statement is less than the minimum record length of the file.

44, 04 The length of the record area specified in the WRITE, REWRITE, or RELEASE statement is greater than the maximum record length of the file.

44, 07 A REWRITE statement attempted to change the length of a record in a sequential organization file.

46 No file position is currently defined. A READ or READ NEXT operation was attempted, but the last READ, READ NEXT, or START operation was unsuccessful or returned an at end condition.

47, 01 The requested operation conflicts with the open mode of the file. A START or READ operation is attempted on a file that is not open in the INPUT or I-O mode.

47, 02 A READ or START operation was attempted on an unopened file.

48, 01 The requested operation conflicts with the open mode of the file. A WRITE operation is attempted on a file that is not open in the OUTPUT or EXTEND mode.

48, 02 A WRITE operation was attempted on an unopened file.

49, 01 The requested operation conflicts with the open mode of the file. A DELETE or REWRITE operation is attempted on a file that is not open in the I-O mode.

49, 02 A DELETE or REWRITE operation was attempted on an unopened file.

90, 03 The requested operation conflicts with the media type. A READ or OPEN INPUT operation was attempted on a file with a unit-name of OUTPUT, PRINT or PRINTER. A WRITE, OPEN OUTPUT, or EXTEND operation was attempted on a file with a unit-name of CARD-READER or INPUT. A DELETE, REWRITE, START, or OPEN I-O operation was attempted on a file with a unit-name other than DISC, DISK, or RANDOM.

90, 04 The requested operation conflicts with the defined organization. A DELETE or START operation was attempted on an ORGANIZATION SEQUENTIAL file.

90, 05 A file truncate operation conflicts with other users. An OPEN OUTPUT operation was attempted on an external file name that is already open.

93, 02 An open was rejected because file lock conflicts with another user. An OPEN WITH LOCK was attempted on a file that is already open, or an OPEN without lock was attempted and the file is already open WITH LOCK.

93, 04 The file could not be opened because another file in the same SAME AREA clause is currently open.

93, 05 The file could not be opened because another file in the same MULTIPLE FILE TAPE clause is already open.

94, 21 The file organization specified is invalid or unsupported, or the requested open operation is illegal on the specified organization.

94, 22 The minimum record length is invalid. The minimum record length specified in the RECORD CONTAINS clause for the file name exceeds the maximum record length.

94, 24 The minimum block size is invalid. The minimum block size specified in the BLOCK CONTAINS clause of the file name exceeds the maximum block size.

94, 25 The maximum block size is invalid. The maximum block size specified in the BLOCK CONTAINS clause of the file name is too large.

94, 26 The record delimiter is invalid. A record delimiting technique other than LINE or BINARY was specified.

94, 27 The code-set specified is invalid or unsupported.

94, 28 The COLLATING SEQUENCE specified for an indexed file is invalid or unsupported.

94, 29 The record type attribute, fixed or variable, specified for the file name is unsupported.

94, 3F Invalid or mismatched key duplicates allowed flag for key 15 or greater. The key duplicates allowed flag specified for an alternate record key 15 through 254.

94, 40 through **94, 4E**
Invalid or mismatched key offset for keys 0 through 14. The offset from the start of the record area to the start of the key area for the indicated key is invalid. The prime record key is 0; alternate record keys are numbered in ascending order of key offset, starting with 1.

Error 94, 40 will also occur if more than 254 alternate record keys are specified.

94, 4F Invalid or mismatched key offset for key 15 or greater. The offset from the start of the record area to the start of the key area for an alternate key 15 through 254 is invalid

94, 50 through **94, 5E**
Invalid or mismatched key length for keys 0 through 14. The length of the key area for the indicated key is invalid. The prime record key is key 0; alternate record keys are numbered in ascending order of key offset, starting with 1.

94, 5F Invalid or mismatched key length for key 15 or greater. The length of the key area for an alternate key 15 through 254.

94, 60 Insufficient memory to open file. The amount of memory required to open a file can be reduced by specifying a smaller maximum block size in the BLOCK CONTAINS clause, or by reducing the number of blocking buffers requested in the RESERVE AREAS clause of the file. More memory can be made available for opening this file by closing other files, reducing the memory requirements of other files, or by canceling inactive programs.

94, 61 There is insufficient disk space to create a file.

94, 62 There are invalid linage parameters. One or more linage parameters could be negative or greater than 32,767, either LINAGE or FOOTING equals zero, or FOOTING is greater than LINAGE.

97, 01 One or more characters in the record are illegal in a line sequential file.

97, 02 One or more characters could not be translated from the native character set to the external code-set.

97, 05 The record read from the file is shorter than the minimum record length.

97, 06 The record read from the file is longer than the record area.

97, 08 LINAGE parameter values error. One or more LINAGE parameters are negative or greater than 32,767, LINAGE equals zero, FOOTING equals zero, or FOOTING is greater than LINAGE.

97, 09 The LINAGE TO LINE value is outside page body.

98, *nn* Invalid file structure or file integrity questionable.

In response to an OPEN statement, this usually indicates that a power failure caused the indexed file not to be closed when it was last opened for modification, and the index structures must be rebuilt. In response to a statement other than OPEN, it indicates an inconsistency in the file structure that may be resolved by rebuilding the index structure.

In response to a sequential or relative file I-O statement, this usually indicates that the wrong type of sequential access is being attempted or there is some other organization mismatch. This may also indicate an inconsistency resulting from an error when the file was written.

99 The record is locked by another user.

Sort-Merge Errors

Sort-merge errors include errors processing a SORT or MERGE statement.

301 There was insufficient memory available to initiate a sort or merge process.

302 Fewer than three intermediate files were available to begin a SORT statement. The sort procedure cannot begin unless it is able to create at least three intermediate files.

303 A record read from a MERGE file or SORT USING file was not long enough to include all the keys.

304 Too many out-of-sequence records were passed to the sort process. Use the B Runtime Command Option to increase the memory available to sort; or divide the records to be sorted into several files, sort the several files, and merge the resulting files.

305 A SORT or MERGE statement was attempted while a sort or merge process was already active.

306 A RELEASE or RETURN statement was attempted and no sort or merge was active.

307 A RELEASE or RETURN statement was attempted for a sort or merge description other than the one currently being sorted or merged.

308 A RELEASE statement was attempted in an OUTPUT PROCEDURE, or a RETURN statement was attempted in an INPUT PROCEDURE.

309 A RETURN statement was attempted in an OUTPUT PROCEDURE after the at end condition was returned on the sort or merge file.

310 An application I-O statement was attempted on a file currently opened as a sort or merge USING or GIVING file.

INDEX